By blending themes developed by other economists and by adding his own contributions, Alfred Marshall became the father of modern microeconomics (the detailed study of how individual goods are produced and priced).

Marshall was born in 1842 in Clapham, then a green suburb of London. His father, a cashier in the Bank of England, was a man of tyrannical disposition who wrote a book called *Man's Rights and Woman's Duties*. As a good Victorian, he exercised strong parental control: He overworked his son, insisted that he prepare himself for the Ministry, and even made him promise not to play chess—"a waste of time." This childhood repression may have left lasting scars: For the rest of his life, Marshall remained fearful of idleness, hypercritical of his own writing, and nervous about his health almost to the point of hypochondria.

Young Marshall did eventually rebel against the father, rejecting the Oxford scholarship he had won to study classics and theology and turning to mathematics instead. This was important to him later in economics: He used diagrams to illustrate economic theory (for which, it is said, some students have never forgiven him). So pervasive was his influence that his simple geometric slip (involving the reversal of the price and quantity axes in his diagrams) is regularly followed by economists to the present day. Marshall eventually became a professor at Cambridge, where he reigned over the British economics profession for almost 25 years until his retirement in 1908. He was everyone's idea of a professor—white hair, white mustache, and bright eyes.

Although a man of overflowing ideas, Marshall—like Adam Smith—was in no hurry to rush into print. Just as Smith had burnt his unfinished writing, Marshall threw much of his into the wastebasket. He kept back printed proofs of one book for 15 years before allowing it to be published. Such long delays meant that many of the ideas he had developed and taught years before had become common knowledge

Alfred Marshall (1842–1924)

by the time they reached the printed page. (Indeed, this makes it difficult for historians to sort out exactly what he discovered and what he did not.)

Marshall's masterpiece was his *Principles of Economics*, first published in 1890. One of his concerns was the problem of poverty: "The study of the causes of poverty is the study of the causes of the degradation of a large part of mankind."

The many dimensions of Marshall's genius are perhaps best summarized by this tribute:

> The master-economist must possess a rare combination of gifts. He must be mathematician, historian, statesman, philosopher. . . . He must be purposeful and disinterested . . . ; as aloof and incorruptible as an artist; yet sometimes as near the earth as a politician.

This tribute was written by Marshall's most illustrious student, John Maynard Keynes, who himself achieved such fame that he is described on the inside of the back cover.

ECONOMICS

ECONOMICS

Paul Wonnacott

Professor of Economics
University of Maryland

Ronald Wonnacott

Professor of Economics
University of Western Ontario

McGraw-Hill Book Company

New York   St. Louis   San Francisco   Auckland   Bogotá   Düsseldorf
Johannesburg   London   Madrid   Mexico   Montreal   New Delhi
Panama   Paris   São Paulo   Singapore   Sydney   Tokyo   Toronto

Library of Congress Cataloging in Publication Data

Wonnacott, Paul.
    Economics.

    Includes index.
    1. Economics.   I.   Wonnacott, Ronald J., joint author.   II.   Title.
HB171.5.W76   330   78-11067
ISBN 0-07-071571-8

ECONOMICS

234567890   VHVH   7832109

This book was set in Caledonia by Black Dot, Inc. The editors were Bonnie E. Lieberman, Michael Elia, and J. W. Maisel; the designer was Merrill Haber; the production supervisor was John F. Harte. The photo editor was Inge King. The part-opening illustrations were done by Danmark & Michaels, Inc./Larry Johnson; all other drawings were done by J & R Services, Inc. The cover illustrations were done by Danmark & Michaels, Inc./John Martucci.
Von Hoffmann Press, Inc., was printer and binder.

Photo Credits

Gilles Peress/Magnum, 8
Randy Matusow, 13
Monkmeyer, 34
United Press International, 110
Kenneth Murray/Nancy Palmer Agency
(wheat harvest), 130
Erich Hartmann/Magnum (dough), 130
Hugh Rogers/Monkmeyer (bakery), 131
Randy Matusow, (loaf of bread), 131
H. Armstrong Roberts, 298
Joe Munroe/Photo Researchers, 388
Andrew Sacks/Editorial Photocolor Archives, 418
H. Armstrong Roberts, 423
Kenneth Karp, 490
United Press International, 498
Wide World Photos, 511
Joe Munroe/Photo Researchers, Inc., 515

Allen Green/Nancy Palmer Agency, 533
United Press International, 608
Webb AgPhotos, 620
Catherine Noren/Photo Researchers, 642
Werner H. Müller/Peter Arnold, 650
Max & Kit Hunn/Photo Researchers, 652
Allan Price/Photo Researchers, 663
Don Morgan/Photo Researchers, 686

United Press International (Back left endpaper)
Library of Congress (Front left endpaper)
National Portrait Gallery, London
(Back right endpaper)
Historical Pictures Service, Chicago
(Front right endpaper)

To Donna and Eloise

Contents

MICROECONOMICS

PART FOUR/MICROECONOMICS: IS OUR OUTPUT PRODUCED EFFICIENTLY?

Preface

Economics is like the music of Mozart. On one level, it holds great simplicity: Its basic ideas can be quickly grasped by those who first encounter it. On the other hand, below the surface there are fascinating subtleties that remain a challenge even to those who spend a lifetime in its study. We therefore hold out this promise. In this introductory study, you will learn a great deal about how the economy works—the simple principles governing economic life that must be recognized by those in government and business who make policy decisions. At the same time, we can also guarantee that you won't be able to master it all. You should be left with an appreciation of the difficult and challenging problems of economics that remain unsolved.

Perhaps some day you will contribute to their solution.

HOW TO USE THIS BOOK

We have tried to design this book to make the basic propositions of economics as easy as possible to grasp. Key steps in the argument and essential definitions are emphasized with a red shaded background. These highlights should be studied carefully during the first reading, and during later review. (A glossary is provided at the back of the book, containing a list of definitions of terms used in this book plus other common economics terms that you may encounter in class or in readings.) The basic arguments of each chapter are summarized in the Key Points at the end of the chapter, and the new concepts of the chapter are also listed.

When you read a chapter for the first time, don't worry about what is in the boxes. This material is optional; it is set aside from the text to keep the main argument as simple and straightforward as possible. (Several types of material are presented in the boxes. Some boxes provide levity or color—for example, Henry Manne's parable of government regulation of the parking lot business on p. 498, and Kurt Vonnegut's tale on p. 676 of the Handicapper-General whose aim is to ensure that people will not only start out equal but also finish that way. Other boxes present detailed theoretical explanations, that are not needed to grasp the main argument.) If you want to glance at the boxes that are fun and easy to read, fine; but don't worry about those that contain more difficult material. Also skip starred (*) sections of the text, along with the footnotes and appendices; these also tend to be more difficult. Come back to them later, as a way of expanding your knowledge and understanding, but only after you have mastered the basic ideas. And listen to your instructor, who will tell you which of the boxes and starred sections are most important for your course.

Economics is not a spectator sport. You can't learn just from observation; you must work at it. When you have finished reading a chapter, work on the problems listed at the end; they are designed to reinforce your understanding of important concepts. Because each chapter builds on preceding ones, and because the solution to some of the problems depends on those that come before, remember this important student's rule: Don't fall behind in a problem-solving course. To assist you in this objective, we recommend Peter Howitt's *Study Guide*, which is designed specially to assist you in working through each chapter; it should be available in your bookstore.

TO THE INSTRUCTOR

In adding one more volume to an already heavily populated field, authors of any new introductory economics text have a substantial responsibility to provide something new. We make no claim to revolutionary innovations. But we do believe that there is room for improvement in the presentation of elementary economics.

In particular, we have aimed at three major objectives. The first two grew out of questions that arose in our teaching—and out of our uneasiness regarding the answers.

For macroeconomics, the question was this. After studying introductory economics, are students able to understand public controversies over such topics as the level of government spending and taxation, the desirability of wage and price controls, and monetary policy? Are we training our students to understand the front page of the newspapers? For many years, the introductory course was aimed at teaching students how policy should be run; that is, at providing a cookbook of "right" answers. While many books express more doubts and qualifications than was the case a decade ago, we have altered the focus of the course even more substantially by building up to the five unsolved, controversial questions dealt with in the chapters of Part 3: Is fiscal policy or monetary policy the key to aggregate demand? How can inflation and unemployment exist at the same time? Why is the economy unstable? To what extent should we attempt to fine-tune the economy? Should exchange rates be fixed or flexible? While there are no simple, indisputably "correct" answers to these questions, we believe that the major issues can be presented clearly to beginning economics students, thereby providing them with an understanding of important, recurring public debates over macroeconomic policy.

For microeconomics, the disturbing question was this. After macroeconomics, is microeconomics a letdown? Too often, we fear that the answer has been yes. We were particularly concerned by the responses when we conducted an informal poll regarding the age-old question of whether macro or micro should be studied first. A common reply was that macro should come first, because it is needed to whet the appetites of beginning students. Even more disconcerting was the response from some universities that teach micro first (including one of the nation's most distinguished): Students should be made to take micro first as a ticket for entry into the more rewarding macro course; if they are given the option, few will take micro. Although universities are not prosecuted under the antitrust laws, we are nevertheless appalled at this "full-line forcing" of what some regard as the bitter microeconomic pill.

The problem with microeconomics, it seems to us, is that it tends to become just one thing after another—a guided tour through the economist's workshop, introducing students to as many polished pieces of analytic machinery as possible for later use in more advanced courses. But most students do not continue in economics. For them, there is little point in mastering analytic techniques for their own sake, when the time could be spent discussing interesting policy issues instead. Even for those who do continue in economics, we doubt that it is useful to invest so heavily in analytic techniques. True, this gives students some headstart in their later courses; but it also increases the risk that they will be bored by repetition. Therefore, we have followed a simple rule: If a concept is not necessary to analyze a policy issue, we don't introduce it.

Microeconomics can, in our view, be made more interesting (and acute indigestion can be avoided) by organizing the course around two continuing themes: *efficiency* and *equity*. Initially, our major focus is on efficiency, with the emphasis on marginal (rather than total or average) curves, and on consumers' and producers' surpluses. For efficiency, equating marginal cost and marginal benefit is the key; hence the emphasis on the marginal concept. And the study of marginal curves leads naturally to consumers' and producers' surpluses, which are building blocks for the study of income distribution. In emphasizing marginal concepts, we have tried to give students an appreciation of what allocative efficiency means: Why it is highly desirable to produce the goods that consumers demand. But we have also tried to show why it is not the last word. In particular, we have discovered that elementary students can fairly easily be shown what many in the past discovered only in graduate school: There is a different efficient solution for each income distribution; hence a solution that is efficient is not necessarily best.

Thus, the study of efficiency leads naturally to the study of the second major microeconomic objective, equity. In recent years, this topic has increased in importance: As our income has grown, we have been redistributing an increasing slice of it. In Part 4 in our discussion of product markets (where the major focus is on efficiency), we also explicitly consider how a policy change will affect income distribution. Similarly, in our discussion in Part 5 of factor markets (where the major focus tends to be on income distribution), we also emphasize how a policy change will affect efficiency.

In our treatment of macroeconomics, we have also tried to keep the theoretical discussion cleanly focused on a few main themes. This has meant leaving out some common tools and steps, particularly those that tend to be roadblocks. And it has meant putting in other steps or concepts which are needed to tie the argument together.

For example, our presentation of the basic Keynesian theory of income determination is leaner in some respects, and more detailed in others, than the standard textbook treatment. Specifically, many books introduce Keynesian economics with a discussion of saving and investment (and sometimes Say's law). Although this approach accurately reflects Keynes' concerns in attacking "classical economics," it has several pedagogical shortcomings. Most important, it constitutes a roadblock. Saving and investment (and Say's law) tend to be mysterious to the beginning student, and to turn the weaker students off. [There are equally grave problems for the better students. Not only do they wonder how classical economists could have been so wrong—a question which naturally arises when a critic's (Keynes') arguments are used to explain classical theories—but they are also sometimes puzzled by the lack of coherence in classical thought. Indeed, the very best may correctly wonder whether Say's law is not inconsistent with the quantity theory. In order to avoid these problems, we emphasize the more sensible part of classical economics, namely, the quantity theory, and exile Keynes' favorite target—Say's law—to an appendix.]

Rather than start with saving and investment, we introduce Keynesian economics with a discussion of aggregate demand and its determinants. Aggregate demand for the nation's total product follows naturally from the concept of demand for an individual product, which students have already studied in Chapter 4. Later, after the consumption function has been introduced and its close ties with its twin (the saving function) explained, equilibrium at the point of equality between intended investment and saving can be mastered as a single additional step.

Other potential roadblocks that have been omitted, downplayed, or set aside in optional boxes include liquidity preference and the IS and LM curves. Liquidity preference is not needed to explain the effect of monetary policy on interest rates; discussion of the effect of open-market operations on the supply and demand for bonds will do (p. 221). Liquidity preference was, of course, featured in Keynes' theory; he used it to explain why expansive monetary policy might not work during a depressed period of very low interest rates. But that was a special case. While it was important in the 1930s, it is much less important in the modern world of high interest rates. It is therefore put in a box (p. 246) explaining the special problems of the depression. IS and LM curves have been omitted because they are difficult, and because many of the propositions derived from them can be deduced more directly and more easily in some other way.

On the other hand, some material not commonly found in introductory texts has been added to throw light on the main themes or to allow the argument to proceed in smaller, more easily understood steps. For example, the effect of proportional taxes on consumption has been explained (p. 175) as a way of bridging the gap between a lump-sum tax and automatic stabilizers.

These, then, are our three main objectives: To provide an understanding of vexing current policy issues in the macro chapters; to provide coherence and interest to the micro chapters by focusing on the major themes of efficiency and equity; and to make the exposition proceed in small, orderly steps.

OTHER POINTS OF INTEREST

Finally, we draw your attention to a number of ways in which our treatment differs from that of many competing books.

• Because of our emphasis on major themes and problems, our discussion of international economics is organized differently than that in most books. The gains from trade and the effects of protection fit into the topic of efficiency, and therefore are included in Part 4 (Chapters 25 and 26). But the question of exchange rate arrangements is related to such policy issues as inflation and unemployment, and to such theoretical concepts as the quantity theory of money. It is therefore included with other macroeconomic topics in Part 3 (Chapter 16). By keeping international topics close to related domestic topics, we hope to counteract the neglect of international economics in many introductory courses.

Similarly, our treatment of other important topics—like agriculture, urban problems, or the oil price increase—is not confined to one chapter. Instead, each of these topics reappears. For example, the oil price increase is discussed first in our macroeconomic discussion of the price level (Chapter 13), and again in microeconomics (Chapters 22 and 30), where we consider its effect on efficiency and the distribution of income. Nor is there a separate chapter on growth; instead it is a recurring theme throughout the book.

● In emphasizing efficiency and the gains from specialization, we have given greater attention to economies of scale than is frequently the case. Indeed, in Chapters 3 and 25, economies of scale are given billing almost equal to comparative advantage.

● Students are introduced to the important idea of dynamic efficiency. Any concrete analysis of dynamic efficiency has traditionally been regarded as too difficult for an elementary course. Initially we sympathized with this view, until we discovered that most elementary students can indeed handle a problem like the most efficient pattern of resource use over time. (See optional Box 30-3.)

● Should indifference curves be included in an elementary book? We are very much of two minds. On the one hand, we don't see great value in the indifference curve demonstration that a demand curve typically slopes downward and to the right. (Every analysis must start somewhere, and we find a downward-sloping demand curve a more appealing starting point than indifference curves in an introductory course.) But we recognize that our view is not shared by all; consequently we include indifference curves in the Appendix to Chapter 18 to

show the standard results. But more important—in an application not typically attempted in books at this level—we use indifference curves (in an Appendix to Chapter 20) to demonstrate the efficiency of perfect competition. (But we also illustrate this important result more simply in the text itself, using only supply and demand curves.)

● We show how conflicts exist not only between policy objectives (such as equity and efficiency) but also between groups of people in the economy. To illustrate: Under standard assumptions the theory of comparative advantage shows how opening foreign trade can bring an efficiency gain. A nation's real income can increase as a consequence. But in this book we go one step further to emphasize how opening trade will also redistribute income. Low-cost imports benefit consumers, but also damage competing domestic producers. In this case, the interests of these producers and consumers are in conflict. In analyzing such microeconomic issues we constantly ask, "Who benefits, and who gets hurt?" We find that it is very easy for students to identify gainers and losers: Any policy that changes a price will benefit some group and damage another. When students develop this feel for who gains and who loses, they can then appreciate the irony of complaints about agricultural price supports that come from business executives who benefit from protective tariffs that prop up the prices of the goods *they* produce. And students who have learned about the gains from trade will not be shaken when some business executives or labor leaders attack foreign imports. Instead they will recognize this to be the normal reaction of a group that is being damaged by imports, rather than a convincing case against what they learned in introductory economics. Moreover, this identification of different groups (and the different degrees of political power exercised by each) helps the student naturally to answer one of the basic questions raised by the theory of public choice: Why is there a difference between what the government *should* do, and what it *does* do?

• Other topics on which we have placed more-than-usual emphasis include externalities (Chapters 23 and 24), the difficulty of policymaking when inflation and unemployment coexist (Chapter 13), and financial instability (Chapters 6 and 14). The gold standard is discussed in some detail because students show a surprising and continuing interest in it. And it can be used to explain and illustrate some of the sources of financial instability in United States history. Furthermore, in a era of high rates of inflation and dollar instability on the foreign exchanges, it is important to explain why a return to the gold standard does not represent a simple solution.

ALTERNATIVE COURSE DESIGNS

As already noted, some of the boxes in the text are used to introduce material that may be too difficult for some students, but highly enlightening for good ones. (See, for example, Box 20-2 on Pareto efficiency and Box 21-1 on the theory of the second best.) We hope that these boxes, along with similarly designed footnotes and appendices, will give you flexibility in pitching this course at the level you wish. Moreover, if you have a particularly good class, you can take them even further with the material provided in the *Instructors' Manual*—which you may reproduce as you wish for class distribution. (Regardless of the level of your class, we recommend that you assign Peter Howitt's *Study Guide.*)

In a further attempt to design the book with maximum flexibility, we have brought all the macro chapters together into Parts 2 and 3, and all the micro chapters together into Parts 4 and 5. The majority who teach macro first can use the chapters in order. Those who wish to cover micro first can cover Parts 1, 4, 5, 2, and 3 in that order.

For instructors teaching a one-semester course, there are two paperback options: *An Introduction to Macroeconomics* and *An Introduction to Microeconomics.* Those who wish to cover both macro and micro quickly in one semester should drop most boxes and appendices, and then use: Chapters 1 to 11, 17 to 19, and Chapter 20 up to p. 445; Chapter 21 to p. 470, Chapter 22, Chapter 23 to p. 511, Chapters 24, 25, 27, 28, and Chapter 29 to p. 638, Chapter 30 to p. 657, Chapter 31, Chapter 32 to p. 692, and Chapter 33 to p. 708.

WE WISH TO THANK . . .

It is impossible for authors to develop an introductory text without accumulating enormous intellectual debts along the way. For their thoughtful criticisms and suggestions, we should like to thank Professors Elisabeth Allison, Charles Brown, Michael Butler, David Conklin, Dudley Dillard, Mark Frankena, Peter Howitt, Sol Kaufler, Kathleen Langley, Allen F. Larsen, Paul Meyer, Lars Osberg, John Palmer, Martin Perline, Hugh Peters, Jonas Prager, Allen R. Sanderson, Marvin Snowbarger, William Tabel, Tom Wonnacott, Donald Yankovic—and, especially David Laidler.

At an early stage, extremely helpful assistance was provided by those who taught this book in an unpolished preliminary form: Professors Lloyd C. Atkinson of American University, Heidemarie C. Sherman and Allen R. Thompson of the University of New Hampshire, and Frank D. Tinari of Seton Hall University. To them—and to the hundreds of students in their classes—we express our deepest thanks.

Paul Wonnacott
Ronald Wonnacott

Part One
BASIC ECONOMIC CONCEPTS

chapter 1
Economic Problems and Economic Goals

Economy is the art of making the most out of life.
George Bernard Shaw

Several years ago, a Japanese mass-circulation newspaper, the *Mainichi*, conducted a survey of 4,000 people, asking them what they thought of first when they heard the word *takai* (high). Twelve percent responded, "Mount Fuji." The overwhelming majority—88 percent—said: "Prices." In the United States, in early 1973 when the Watergate scandal was dominating newspapers and TV news, the magazine *U.S. News and World Report* conducted a poll to determine the main concerns of the public. Its report: "Almost to a man—or woman—those people questioned replied that their number one worry is the rapid rise of the cost of living." The lives of all of us are affected by the problem of inflation. And, with the rare exception of the individual who inherits great wealth, much of our time is of necessity spent in the struggle to make a living.

Economics is the study of how people make their living, how they acquire the food, shelter, clothing, and other material necessities and comforts of this world. It is a study of the problems they encounter, and of the ways in which these problems can be reduced.

Under this broad definition, economics addresses a multitude of specific questions. To list but a few:

• How are goods produced and exchanged?

• How do we choose which goods to produce?

• What jobs are available? What do they pay? What skills are needed to get a good job?

3

- Does it pay to go to college?
- Why is it so hard to get a job at some times, and so easy at other times?
- Why are taxes so high?
- Why did we produce so much more in 1978 than our parents produced in 1948?

Economics is a study of success, and it is a study of failure.

ECONOMIC PROGRESS . . .

From the vantage point of our comfortable homes of the late twentieth century, it is easy for us to forget how many people, through history, have been losers in the struggle to make a living. Unvarnished economic history is the story of deprivation, of 80-hour weeks, of child labor—and of star-vation. But also, it is the story of the slow climb of civilization toward the goal of relative affluence, where the general public as well as the fortunate few can have a degree of material well-being and leisure.

One of the most notable features of the United States economy has been its growth. Although there have been interruptions and setbacks, economic progress has been remarkable. Figure 1-1 shows one of the standard measures of success—the increase in total production per person.[1] The average American now produces about 80 percent more than the average American of 1945, and almost four times as much as the average American at the turn of the century. And the higher output is produced with less effort: The average workweek has declined about 25 percent during this century. Thus, economic progress in the United States has been reflected both in an increase in the

[1]The precise measure of production used is *gross national product*, or GNP for short. This concept will be explained in detail in Chapter 7.

FIGURE 1-1 Production per person and hours worked.

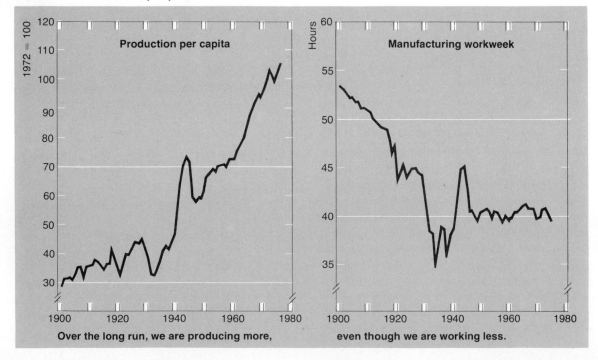

Over the long run, we are producing more, even though we are working less.

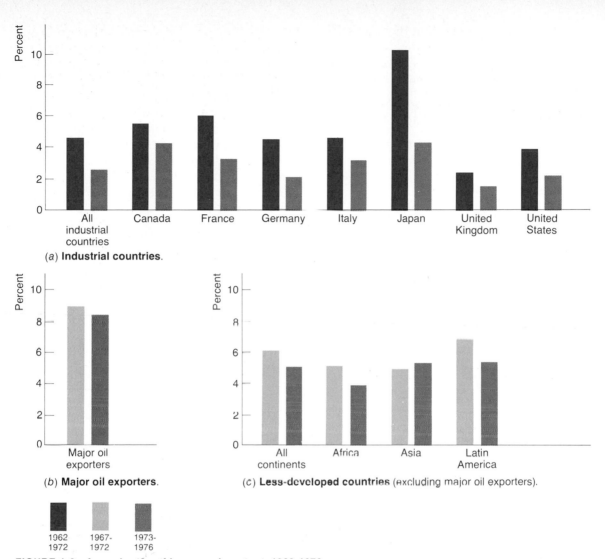

FIGURE 1-2 **Annual rates of increase in output, 1962-1976.**
Rapid rates of growth have occurred in many countries. Growth was particularly fast in
Japan between 1962 and 1972, when output increased by an average annual rate in excess
of 10 percent. Note that for most countries, growth has been much slower since 1973 than
during the previous decade. This slow growth may in part be traced to the disruptions caused by the quadrupling of the price of oil.
SOURCE: International Monetary Fund, *Annual Report, 1977*, pp. 3–7.

goods and services that we produce and
enjoy, and in a greater amount of leisure
time.

A similar tale of success has occurred in
many other countries, as illustrated in Figure 1-2. Between 1962 and 1976, output
grew at an average annual rate of 5.3 percent
in France, 3.9 percent in Germany, 4.2 per-

cent in Italy, and 5.2 percent in Canada. Nor
has growth been confined to the countries of
Europe and North America. Particularly
notable has been the growth of the Japanese
economy. From the ashes of the Second
World War, Japan has emerged as one of the
leading success stories, with output per person that is now greater than that of such

world powers as Britain and the Soviet Union.[2] Other tales of success have come from such diverse countries as Brazil, Italy, Korea, and the Soviet Union.

... AND ECONOMIC PROBLEMS

But successful growth, though widespread, has been neither universal nor automatic. In a number of countries, with India being the biggest and most conspicuous example, the standard of living remains abysmally low. True, even India has enjoyed some growth; over the past two decades, output per person in India has risen by about 1 percent per annum. But progress remains uncertain. The rapid increase in population continuously threatens to outrun the increase in production. The streets of Indian cities, such as Calcutta, are clogged with the homeless and the destitute.

Even in the relatively affluent countries, substantial economic problems remain. For example, we may wonder:

- Why are so many unable to find work, when so much needs to be done?

- Why have prices spiraled upward—to the discomfort of Japanese and United States citizens alike?

- Why are blacks in America so much poorer on average than other citizens?

- Are we really going to run out of oil? What will happen if we do?

- Are we really producing the right things? Should we produce more housing and fewer cars? Or more medical services and fewer sports spectaculars?

- Why is pollution such a problem? And what should be done about it?

ECONOMICS IS A POLICY STUDY

Why? and _What should be done?_ are the two key questions in economics. The ultimate objective of economics is _to develop policies to deal with our problems._ But, before we can formulate policies, we must first make every effort to understand how the economy has worked in the past, and how it works today. Otherwise, well-intentioned policies may go astray and lead to unforeseen and unfortunate consequences.

When economic policies are studied, the center of attention tends to be the policies of the government—policies such as taxation, government spending programs, and the regulation of particular industries, such as electric power and the airlines. But the policies of private businesses are also important. How should they organize production in order to produce their goods at the lowest possible cost? What prices should a business charge? When should a supermarket increase the stocks of goods in its warehouse?

The Controversial Role of Government

For more than two hundred years, economics has been dominated by a controversy over the proper role of government. In what circumstances should the government take an active role? And when is it best for governments to leave decisions to the private participants in the economy? On this topic, the giants of economics have repeatedly met to do battle.

---

[2]Indeed, the very success of the Japanese economy has made that country the subject of good-natured humor. In a recent speech, Prof. Paul McCracken of the University of Michigan—who served as chairman of the President's Council of Economic Advisers from 1969 to 1971—recalled that on his first trip to Japan in the fifties, he had gone to offer the Japanese advice on growth policy. Added McCracken, "I've been trying to remember ever since what we told them."

There are substantial problems in comparing output per person in various countries. However, careful work indicates that Japan passed Britain about 1970. See Irving B. Kravis and others, _A System of International Comparisons of Gross Product and Purchasing Power,_ United Nations International Comparison Project: Phase One (Baltimore: Johns Hopkins University Press, 1975), p. 231.

In 1776, Scottish scholar Adam Smith published his pathbreaking book, *An Inquiry into the Nature and Causes of the Wealth of Nations.*[3] Modern economics may be dated from that historic year, which was also notable for the Declaration of Independence. Smith's message was clear. Private markets should be liberated from the tyranny of government control. In pursuit of their private interests, individual producers would make the goods that consumers want. It is not, said Smith, "from the benevolence of the butcher, the brewer, or the baker that we expect our dinner, but from their regard to their own interest." There is an "invisible hand," he wrote, that causes the producer to promote the interests of society. Indeed, "by pursuing his own interest he frequently promotes that of the society more effectually than when he really intends to promote it." In general, said Smith, the government should be cautious in interfering with the operations of the private market. According to Smith, the best policy is laissez faire— leave it alone. Government intervention usually makes things worse. For example, government imposition of a tariff is generally harmful. (A *tariff* or *duty* is a tax on a foreign-produced good as it enters the country.) Even though domestic producers may well benefit from a tariff (because it gives them an advantage over the foreign producer), the country as a whole loses. Specifically, a tariff increases the cost of goods available to consumers, and this cost to consumers outweighs the benefits to producers. Smith's work has been refined and modified during the past 200 years, but many of his laissez faire conclusions have stood up remarkably well. For example, there is still a very strong economic argument against high tariffs on imported goods. In recent decades, one of the principal areas of international cooperation has been the negotiation of lower tariffs.

A century and a half after the appearance of Smith's *Wealth of Nations* (that is, during the Great Depression of the 1930s), John Maynard Keynes wrote his *General Theory of Employment, Interest and Money* (also known, more simply, as the *General Theory*).[4] In this book, Keynes (which rhymes with Danes) attacked the laissez faire tradition of economics. The government, said Keynes, has the duty to put the unemployed back to work. Of the several ways in which this could be done, one stood out in its simplicity. By building public works, such as roads, post offices, and dams, the government could directly provide jobs, and thus provide a cure for the Depression.

With his proposals for a more active government, Keynes drew the ire of many business executives. They feared that as a result of his recommendations, the government would become larger and larger and private enterprise would gradually be pushed out of the picture. But Keynes did not see this result; in his own way, he was fundamentally conservative. By providing jobs, the government could remove the explosive frustrations caused by the mass unemployment of the 1930s, and could make it possible for Western political and economic institutions to survive. And certainly, when compared with Marx, Keynes was very conservative indeed. (For a brief introduction to Marx and his views, see Box 1-1.)[5]

Thus, Smith and Keynes took apparently contradictory positions—Smith arguing for less government, and Keynes for more. It is possible, of course, that each was right: Perhaps the government should do more in some respects, and less in others. Economic

[3]Available in Modern Library edition (New York: Random House, 1937.) Smith's book is commonly referred to as *The Wealth of Nations.*
[4](London: Macmillan, 1936.)
[5]Throughout this book, the boxes present illustrative and supplementary materials. They can be disregarded without losing the main thread of the argument.

BOX 1-1
KARL MARX

The main text refers to two towering economists—Adam Smith and John Maynard Keynes. In the formation of the intellectual heritage of most American economists, Smith and Keynes have indeed played the leading roles. But, if we consider the intellectual heritage of the world as a whole, Karl Marx is probably the most influential economist of all. In the Soviet Union and the People's Republic of China, Marx is more than the source of economic "truth"; he is the Messiah of the state religion.

Many business executives viewed Keynes as a revolutionary because he openly attacked accepted economic opinion and proposed fundamental changes in economic policy. But, by revolutionary standards, Keynes pales beside Marx. No parlor intellectual was Marx. The Marxist call to revolution was shrill and direct: "Workers of the world, unite! You have nothing to lose but your chains."

Why did they have nothing to lose? Because, said Marx, workers are responsible for the production of all goods. Labor is the sole source of value. But workers get only *part* of the fruits of their labor. A large, and in Marx's view, unearned, share goes to the exploiting class of capitalists. (Capitalists are the owners of factories, machinery, and other equipment.) By taking up arms and overthrowing capitalism, workers could end exploitation and obtain their rightful rewards.

On our main topic—the role of government—Marx was strangely ambivalent. The communist revolution would require the ownership of factories and other capital goods to reside somewhere after the elimination of the capitalist class. Ownership by the state—by all the workers as a group—was the obvious solution. And, indeed, this has been the path taken by countries such as the Soviet Union: The revolution has led to state ownership of the means of production. Yet, Marx also believed that the revolution would eventually lead to the "withering away" of the state. There has been no perceptible sign of this withering away in postrevolutionary Marxist societies.

analysis does not lead inevitably either to an activist or a passive position on the part of the government. The economist's rallying cry should not be, "Do something." Rather, it should be, "Think first."

ECONOMIC GOALS

We have already noted that the ultimate goal of economics is to develop better policies to minimize our problems and to maximize the benefits we get from our daily toil. More specifically, there is widespread agreement that we should strive for the following goals:

1. *A high level of employment.* People willing to work should be able to find jobs reasonably quickly. Widespread unemployment is demoralizing, and it represents an economic waste: The society forgoes the goods and services that the unemployed could have produced.

2. *Price stability.* Rapid increases or decreases in the average price level should be avoided.

3. *Efficiency.* When we work, we want to get as much as we reasonably can out of our productive efforts.

4. *An equitable distribution of income.* When many live in affluence, no group of citizens should suffer stark poverty.

5. *Growth.* As Figure 1-1 illustrates, the United States economy has grown substantially during the twentieth century. Continuing growth, which would make possible an even higher standard of living in the future, is generally considered an important objective (although this objective has become much more controversial during the past decade).

The list is far from complete. Not only do we want to produce more, but we want to do so without the degradation of our environment; the *reduction of pollution* is important. *Economic freedom*—the right of people to choose their own occupations, to

enter contracts, and to spend their incomes as they please—is a desirable goal. So, too, is *economic security*—freedom from the fear that chronic illness or other catastrophe will place an individual or a family in a desperate financial situation.

The achievement of our economic goals provides the principal focus of this book. As a background for later chapters, we will now look at the major goals in more detail.

1. A High Level of Employment

The importance of the employment objective was illustrated most clearly during the Great Depression of the 1930s, when the United States (and many other countries) conspicuously failed to achieve it. During the sharp contraction of the economy from 1929 to 1933, total output in the United States fell by 30 percent, and spending for new buildings and equipment decreased by almost 80 percent. As the economy slid downward, more and more workers were thrown out of jobs; by 1933, 25 percent of the labor force was unemployed. (See Figure 1-3.) Long lines of the jobless gathered at factory gates in the hope of work; disappointment was their common fate. Nor was the problem quickly solved. The downward slide into the depths of the Depression went on for a period of 4 years, and the road back to a high level of employment was even longer. It was not until the beginning of the 1940s, when the production of weapons skyrocketed, that many of the unemployed were able to find jobs. There was not a single year during the whole decade 1931–1940 that unemployment averaged less than 14 percent of the labor force.

A *depression* exists when there is a very high rate of unemployment over a long period of time.

Something had clearly gone wrong with the economy—disastrously wrong. Large-scale unemployment involves tremendous

During the Great Depression, the unemployment rate rose to 25 percent as production collapsed. In recent decades, the unemployment rate has been much more moderate, although it did rise to $8\frac{1}{2}$ percent in 1975.

Recessions ◇◇◇ The Great Depression

FIGURE 1-3   Output and unemployment in the United States, 1929-1978.

waste; time lost in involuntary idleness is gone forever. The costs of unemployment go beyond the loss of output; unemployment involves the dashing of hopes. Those unable to find work suffer frustration and a sense of worthlessness, and their skills are lost as they remain idle.

The term *unemployed* is reserved for those who are willing and able to work, but are unable to find jobs. Thus, those of you who are full-time college students are not included among the unemployed: Your immediate task is to get an education, not a job. Similarly, the 70-year-old retiree is not included in the statistics of the unemployed. Nor are those in prisons or mental institutions, since they are not available for jobs.

> A person is *unemployed* if he or she is available and looking for work, but has not found it.

The unemployment rate is calculated as a percentage of the total labor force—the labor force being the sum of those who are actually employed, plus those who are unemployed. (Labor force and employment statistics are tied to the traditional definition of "jobs." Thus, for example, the mother who stays at home to raise her children is neither "in the labor force" nor "employed," although she certainly *works*.)

At the end of the Second World War, the Great Depression was still a fresh memory in people's minds. The public, the politician, and the economist shared a common determination that a repeat of the 1930s could not be permitted. This determination was reflected in the Employment Act of 1946, which stated that:

It is the continuing responsibility of the Federal Government to use all practical means . . . to promote maximum employment, production, and purchasing power.

Since the end of the Second World War, we have been successful in our determination to prevent a repetition of the unemployment of the 1930s. But the postwar period has not been an unbroken story of success. From time to time, there have been downturns in the economy—much more moderate, it is true, than the slide of 1929 to 1933, but downward movements nonetheless. These more moderate declines, or *recessions*, have been accompanied by an increase in the unemployment rate. In 1975, during the worst recession of the past three decades, the unemployment rate averaged 8½ percent. While we have been successful in preventing big depressions, the problem of periodic recessions has not been solved.

> If production declines for two or more consecutive quarters,[6] a *recession* has occurred.

2. Price Stability

To repeat: Unemployment represents sheer waste; society loses the goods which might have been produced by those out of work. The problem with inflation is less obvious. When a price rises, there is both a gainer and a loser. The buyer has to pay more. But there is an equivalent gain to the seller, who gets more. On balance, it is not clear whether the society is better or worse off.

> *Inflation* is defined as an increase in the average level of prices. (*Deflation* is a fall in the average level of prices.)

There is much resentment against inflation, as the Japanese and United States polls cited at the beginning of this chapter so clearly illustrated. But perhaps this resentment simply reflects a peculiarity of human nature. When producers find their goods rising in price, they see the increases as perfectly right, normal, and justified. But when consumers find a rise in the price of the goods they buy, they often view the increase as evidence of the seller's greed. When the price of wheat rises, farmers see themselves at last getting a reasonable return from their toil. When the price of oil increases, the oil companies argue that they are getting no more than the return necessary to finance the search for more oil. When the price of books rises, authors feel that they are getting no more than a "just" return for their creative efforts, and book publishers insist that they are no more than adequately compensated for their tremendous risks. But when the farmer, the oil company, the author, and the book publisher find that the prices of the goods they buy have increased, they believe they have been cheated by inflation. We may all be the victims of an illusion—the illusion that each of us can and should have a rise in the price of what we sell, but that the price of what we buy should remain stable. For the economy as a whole, this is scarcely possible.

This two-sided nature of price increases—a gain to the seller but a loss to the buyer—makes it difficult to evaluate the dangers of inflation. And, indeed, there has been considerable controversy as to whether a low rate of inflation (say, 1 or 2 percent per annum) is dangerous, or whether, on the contrary, it may actually be beneficial to society. Some say that a small rate of inflation contributes to the adjustments that a dynamic society must undergo and makes it easier to maintain a high level of employment. Others argue that high employment cannot be achieved by inflationary policies, or that even minor rates of inflation will tend

[6]A "quarter" is a 3-month period: January to March is the first quarter of the year; April to June the second quarter; and so on.

to accelerate into runaway inflation. This is not a simple argument; we cannot settle it here, but will return to it in later chapters.

But, when inflation gets beyond a moderate rate, everyone agrees that it becomes a menace. It becomes more than a mere transfer from the buyer to the seller; it interferes with the ability to produce. This has most clearly been the situation during very rapid inflations, when economic activity was severely disrupted. *Hyperinflation*—that is, a skyrocketing of prices at annual rates of 100 percent, 1000 percent, or even more—occurred in the South during our Civil War, in Germany during the early 1920s, and in China during its Civil War in the late 1940s. (Hyperinflations most commonly occur during or soon after a military conflict, when government spending shoots upward.) A hyperinflation means that money rapidly loses its ability to buy goods; people are anxious to spend money as quickly as possible while they can still get something for it.

Clearly, hyperinflation of 100 percent or more per year is an extreme example. But lower rates of inflation, amounting to 10 percent or less per year, can also have serious consequences:

1. Inflation hurts people living on fixed incomes and people who have saved fixed amounts of money for their retirement or for a rainy day (future illness or accident). The couple who put aside $1,000 in 1945 for their retirement have suffered a rude shock: In 1978, $1,000 bought no more than $260 bought in 1945. (Recent inflation growth in the United States is illustrated in Figure 1–4.)

2. Inflation can cause wasteful speculation. Inflation works to the advantage of borrowers; for example, those who borrow to buy real estate. (For a numerical illustration, see Box 1-2.) As a consequence, a rising rate of inflation often creates a rush to "get rich quick" by purchasing real estate for later resale. Speculative excesses can result, with real estate prices being pushed to extravagant heights by the influx of buyers. Many of these buyers are attracted, not by any desire to use the property, but rather by the prospect of a quick profit from an inflated resale. A speculative bubble is created. It bursts when there is a slackening of demand.

Thus, the inflation of the early 1970s involved a rapid upward spiral of real estate

FIGURE 1-4 Consumer prices.
Occasionally prices have fallen—for example, during the early 1930s. In recent decades, however, the trend of prices has been clearly upward. In 1974, the United States suffered from "double-digit" inflation—a rise in the average level of prices at a rate in excess of 10 percent per annum.

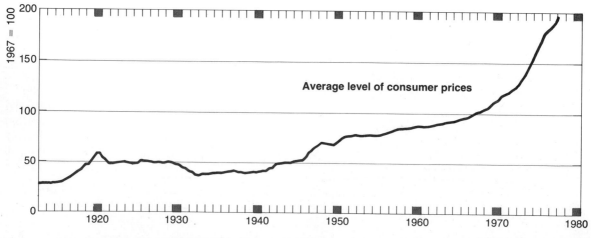

BOX 1-2
PROFITING FROM INFLATION: An Illustration

Inflation hurts both those on fixed incomes and those who have saved for their retirement. But others gain. Consider, for example, the Whitmores, a typical family in a small city. In 1968, they bought their dream house for $30,000, paying $10,000 down and borrowing the rest. In 1978, when their youngest child went off to college, the Whitmores decided to move into something smaller. Their house sold for $60,000. Like almost everything else, it had risen in price.

The Whitmores found that they had a tidy gain. They had quadrupled their original $10,000! (Even though prices had doubled during the 10 years, the $40,000 which they received from the sale was worth much more than their original $10,000. They came out way ahead.)

1968		1978	
Purchase price	$30,000	Selling price	$60,000
Borrowing	20,000	Repayment of loan	20,000
Down payment	$10,000	Net receipt from sale	$40,000

This illustration has skipped over some details. For example, the effect of inflation on interest rates would have to be considered for a more precise calculation. (When inflation is high, so too are the interest rates which homeowners and others have to pay when they borrow.) But the main point is valid: The inflation of the past decade has indeed provided a windfall to the typical homeowner.

prices in Florida, in Ocean City (Maryland), and in other resort areas. Consequently, condominium apartments were substantially overbuilt. The collapse came in the middle of the decade, with many of these buildings standing partially or completely unoccupied. Their construction involved a waste of labor and materials that could have been used to produce other goods.

3. More generally, inflation can cause business mistakes. For good decisions, businesses need an accurate picture of what is going on. When prices are rising rapidly, the picture becomes obscured and out of focus. Decision-makers are cast adrift. (For example, business accounting is done in dollar terms. When there is rapid inflation, some businesses may report profits when, on a more accurate calculation, they might actually be suffering losses. Inflation can temporarily hide problems in the economy.)

Our economy is complex, and it depends on a continuous flow of accurate information. *Prices are an important link in the information chain.* For example, a high price should signal producers that consumers are especially anxious to get more of a particular product. But in a severe inflation, producers find it difficult to know whether this is the message or whether they can raise prices solely because *all* prices are rising. In brief, *a severe inflation obscures the message carried by prices.*

3. Efficiency

Both the unemployment rate and the inflation rate may be very low, but the economy may still be performing poorly. For example, fully employed workers may be engaged in a lot of wasted motion, and the goods being produced may not be those which are most needed. Obviously, this is not a satisfactory state of affairs.

Efficiency is the goal of getting the most out of our productive efforts. Under this broad heading, two types of efficiency can be distinguished: *allocative* efficiency and *technical* efficiency.

To illustrate *technical efficiency,* let us consider two bicycle manufacturers. One uses a large number of workers and many machines to produce 1,000 bicycles. The other uses fewer workers and fewer machines to produce the same number of bicycles. The second manufacturer is not a magician, nor is he a particularly lucky fellow. He is simply a better manager. He is technically efficient, whereas the first manufacturer is technically inefficient. [Technical inefficiency exists when the same output could be produced with fewer machines and fewer workers, working at a reasonable pace. (Technical efficiency does not require a sweatshop.) Technical inefficiency involves wasted motion and sloppy management; better management is the solution.]

Allocative efficiency, on the other hand, involves the production of the best *combination* of goods, using the best combination of inputs. How much bread should we produce, and how much butter? If we produce only bread, we do not achieve the goal of allocative efficiency, because consumers want both bread and butter. Thus, allocative efficiency involves the choice of the right combination of outputs. And it also involves using the right combination of inputs like labor and machines. In producing wheat, should we use many machines and few workers, or few machines and many workers?

4. An Equitable Distribution of Income

Ours is an affluent society. Yet many people remain so poor that they have difficulty in buying the basic necessities of life, such as food, clothing, and shelter. In the midst of plenty, some live in dire need. The moral question must then be faced: Should some have so much, while others have so little?

Put this way, the compelling answer must surely be no. Our sense of justice is offended by extreme differences, and compassion requires that assistance be given to those crushed by illness and to those born and raised in cruel deprivation. There is general agreement that society has a responsibility to help those at the bottom of the economic ladder.

Our sense of equity, or justice, is offended by extreme differences. Thus, most people think of "equity" as a move toward "equality." But not all the way. The two words are far from synonymous. While there is widespread agreement that the least fortunate should be helped, there is no consensus that the objective of society should be an equal income for all. Some are willing to work overtime; it is generally recognized as both just and desirable for them to have a higher income as a consequence. Otherwise, why should they work longer hours? Similarly, it is generally considered "right" for the hardworking to have a larger share of the pie; after all, they have greatly contributed to the production of the pie in the first place. On the other side, some are loafers. If they were automatically given the same income as everyone else, our sense of equity would be offended: They don't deserve an equal share. (And if incomes were guaranteed equal, how many people would work?)

There is no agreement that we should aim toward complete equality of incomes; the "best" division (or distribution) of income is ill-defined. The discussion of income distribution has therefore tended to focus on a relatively narrow question: What is happening to those at the bottom of the ladder? What is happening to the families who live in poverty?

Because of obvious complications, poverty is hard to define in precise dollar terms. For one thing, everyone's needs are not the same. The sickly have the greatest need for medical care; large families have the most compelling need for food and clothing. Those who live in the city, where the costs of food and shelter are high, need more money for basic necessities than do those who live on the farm, where families can grow some of their own food. There is no simple, single measure of the "poverty line,"

below which families may be judged to be poor. Reasonable standards may, however, be established by taking into consideration such obvious complications as the number of individuals in a family. The poverty standards defined by the United States government are shown in Table 1-1.

Over the past two decades, the number of poor families has declined—although not at a steady rate. During the long economic expansion of the 1960s, a particularly large number escaped from poverty. During recessions, on the other hand, people tend to slip back into poverty. Thus, a general increase in production may be one of the most effective ways of fighting poverty. To use a phrase popular during the years when Kennedy was President, "A rising tide lifts all boats." As the general level of incomes throughout the economy rises, the incomes of those at the lower end will also rise.

But an increase in the size of the total pie produced by the economy is only one of the ways of dealing with poverty. Another way is to increase the share of the pie going to people with the lowest incomes. Thus, poverty may be combated by a *redistribution*

TABLE 1-1
Poverty Standards, 1978
(rounded to nearest $100)

Size of family	Poverty standard Nonfarm	Farm
One person	$3,300	$2,800
Two persons	4,200	3,500
Three persons	5,200	4,400
Four persons	6,600	5,600
Five persons	7,800	6,700
Six persons	8,800	7,500
More than six persons	10,800	9,200

According to United States government standards, families were considered poor in 1978 if their incomes fell below these figures. For example, a three-member family was poor if it lived in a city and its income was less than $5,200.
Source: Bureau of the Census. (Data updated by authors.)

of income. For example, the well-to-do may be taxed in order to finance government programs aimed at helping the poor. An important government objective (particularly in the Great Society programs of President Johnson) has been to raise the share of the nation's income going to the poorest families.

During the fifties and sixties, some progress was made toward that goal. Between 1950 and 1960, the share of the poorest 20 percent of families rose from 4.5 to 4.8 percent of the total "pie" of society. By 1969, it had risen to 5.6 percent. Furthermore, between 1950 and 1969, a "rising tide was lifting all boats." Average family income was rising by about 40 percent (even after adjusting for inflation). The "rising tide" and the changing shares combined to raise the incomes of the poorest fifth of the families by more than 70 percent (again, after adjusting for inflation). Thus, the poorest of 1969 were much better off than the poorest of 1950. Nevertheless, they were still very poor by the overall standards of society.

Since 1969, large government expenditures on antipoverty programs have reduced the numbers living in poverty, but the goal of eliminating poverty is still a distant one. Why is this task so difficult? One explanation of why progress has not been more rapid is the unemployment rate, which has been much higher in the 1970s (averaging 7.7 percent between 1975 and 1977) than it was in 1968 and 1969 (3.6 percent). Unemployment adds to the miseries of the poor, and it tends to make incomes less equal. Other possible explanations include the tendency for workers to retire early (at which

time they tend to drop into the low-income group), and the tendency for families to divide into more than one group: Young people move out of the parental home more readily than they used to, old people are less likely to live with their children, and more marriages are splitting up. In other words, families tend to split into several smaller units, some of which have very low incomes. Thus, the general rise in income may have enabled Americans to achieve "the luxury of living apart from their relatives."[7] Another, and disconcerting, possibility is that it may be very difficult to substantially improve the relative position of the poor by major government antipoverty programs.

5. Growth

In an economy with large-scale unemployment, output can be increased by putting the unemployed back to work. But once this is done, there is a limit to the amount that can be produced with the available labor force and the available land, factories, and equipment. To increase output beyond this limit will require either an addition to the available resources (for example, an increase in the number of factories and machines) or an improvement in technology (that is, the invention of new, more productive types of machines or new ways of organizing production). When economists speak of growth, they typically mean an increase in output that results from technological improvement and additional factories, machines, or other resources.

The advantages of growth are obvious. If the economy grows, our incomes will be bigger in the future; we and our children

---

[7]Alice M. Rivlin, "Income Distribution—Can Economists Help?" *American Economic Review*, May 1975, p. 5.

The definition of the family unit makes it difficult to interpret the statistics on income distribution. Yet it is not clear how this problem can be avoided. It makes no sense to look at individuals singly. The 3-month-old baby has zero income, yet it is scarcely poverty-stricken if it lives in the average family. To study poverty, one must look at families—defined somehow.

The measures of poverty are quite sensitive to how the family is defined, and to exactly what is included in income. When the effects of taxation and of "in-kind" transfers (such as food stamps and Medicare benefits) are included in income, then the lowest 20 percent of the population have 7.2 percent of the total income. See Congressional Budget Office, *Poverty Status of Families under Alternative Definitions of Income*, rev. (Washington: Congress of the United States, June 1977), p. 24.

will have higher standards of material comfort. Moreover, as the economy grows, some of the rising production of the economy can be used to benefit the poor. We will be able to provide income to the poorer sections of the population without taking it from the rich. During the early 1960s, growth became a prominent national goal, both because of its economic advantages, and in order to "keep ahead of the Russians."

During the 1970s, doubts began to develop about the importance of growth as an objective of economic policy. While its advantages are obvious, growth comes at a cost. If we are to grow more rapidly, more of our current efforts will have to be directed toward the production of machines, and away from the production of consumption goods. In the future, of course, as the new machines begin operating, they will turn out more consumption goods—more clothing, radios, or canned food. Thus, current policies to stimulate growth will make possible a higher future rate of consumption. But, for the moment, consumption will suffer. Thus, in determining how fast we should grow, we have to balance the advantages of higher *future* consumption against lower *current* consumption. Seen in this light, it is not clear that the faster the rate of growth, the better. Why, for example, should I make do with my beat-up old car, just so my children may at some future date drive in luxurious Cadillacs? The future generations should be considered; but so should the present one.

And, even if we were concerned solely with the welfare of coming generations, it would not be so clear that the more growth, the better. Increasing levels of production use increasing quantities of raw materials. A moderate rate of growth, by making possible a conservation of scarce raw materials, may be in the best interests of future generations.

Furthermore, very rapid rates of growth may harm the environment. If our objective is to produce more and more steel and automobiles, we may pay too little heed to the belching smoke of the steel mills, or to the effect of the automobile on the quality of the air which we breathe. More and more production should not be our unqualified goal. We should weigh the advantages of more production against the costs of that production.

Thus, the growth objective is extremely difficult to pin down in precise terms. A rate of growth of 4 percent per annum is not clearly better than 3 percent. Nevertheless, a healthy rate of economic growth is generally included as one of the major economic objectives.

INTERRELATIONSHIPS AMONG THE GOALS

The achievement of one goal may help in the achievement of others. As we have noted, growth may make it easier to solve the poverty problem. Growth is "a rising tide that raises all boats" and also makes it easier politically to change the *relative* positions of the "boats"; that is, to change the income *shares*. Specifically, additional income may be provided to the poor out of the growth in total income, without reducing the income of those at the top. Thus, social conflicts over the *share* of the pie may be reduced if the *size* of the pie is increasing. Similarly, the poverty problem is easier to solve if the unemployment rate is kept low, so that large numbers of unemployed do not swell the ranks of the poor. When goals are complementary like this (that is, when achieving one helps to achieve the other), economic policymaking is relatively easy. By attacking on a broad front and striving for several goals, we can increase our chances of achieving each.

Unfortunately, however, economic goals are not always complementary; in many cases, they are in conflict. For example, when the unemployment problem is reduced, the inflation problem tends to get worse. There is a good reason for this. Heavy purchasing by the public tends to reduce unemployment and increase inflation. It reduces unemployment because, as the public buys more cars, unemployed workers get jobs again in the auto factories; and when families buy more homes, construction workers find it easier to locate jobs. But, at the same time, heavy purchasing tends to increase inflation because producers are more likely to raise their prices if buyers are clamoring for their products. Such conflicts among goals test the wisdom of policymakers; they feel torn in deciding which objective to pursue.

A PREVIEW

These, then, are the five major objectives of economic policy: *high employment, price stability, efficiency, an equitable distribution of income*, and *growth*.

The first two goals are related to the stability of the economy. If the economy is unstable, moving along like a roller coaster, its performance will be very unsatisfactory. As it heads downhill into recession, large numbers of people will be thrown out of work. And, as it heads upward into a runaway boom, prices will soar as the public scrambles to buy the available goods. The first two goals may therefore be looked on as

two different aspects of a single objective: That of achieving a high-level *equilibrium* in the economy. This will be the major topic in Parts 2 and 3 (Chapters 7 through 16) of this book.

The second E—*efficiency*—will be studied in Part 4 (Chapters 17 through 26). Are we getting the most out of our productive efforts? When does the free market—where buyers and sellers come together without government interference—encourage efficiency? And where the free market does not encourage efficiency, what should be done?

Part 5 (Chapters 27 through 33) deals primarily with the third E—*equity*. If the government takes a laissez faire attitude, how much income will go to workers? To the owners of land? To others? How do labor unions affect the incomes of their members? How can the government improve the lot of the poor?

The final major objective—growth—cuts across a number of other major topics, and thus appears periodically throughout the book. But first, before we get into the meat of policy issues, we must set the stage with some of the basic concepts and tools of economics. To that task we now turn (in Chapters 2 through 6).

Key Points

1. Economics is the study of how people make their living, how they acquire food, shelter, clothing, and other material necessities and comforts. It is a study of the problems they encounter, and of the ways in which these problems can be reduced.

2. During the twentieth century, substantial economic progress has been made in the United States and many other countries. We are producing much more, even though we spend less time at work than did our grandparents.

3. Nevertheless, substantial economic problems remain: Problems such as poverty in the less-developed countries and at home; high rates of unemployment; and inflation.

4. Economics involves the study of how we can deal with our problems, either through private action or through government policies.

5. In the history of economic thought, the role of government has been controversial. Adam Smith in 1776 called for the liberation of markets from the tyranny of government control. By 1936, John Maynard Keynes was appealing to the government to accept its responsibilities and to undertake public works in order to get the economy out of the Depression.

6. Important economic goals include the following:

(*a*) A high-level equilibrium, that is, the achievement of high employment and price stability.

(*b*) Efficiency. Allocative efficiency involves the production of the right combination of goods, using the right combination of inputs. Technical efficiency involves production with the smallest quantity of inputs feasible (while working at a reasonable pace).

(*c*) Equity in the distribution of income.

(*d*) A satisfactory rate of growth.

Key Concepts

economics
laissez faire
depression
recession
unemployment
inflation
hyperinflation
allocative efficiency

technical efficiency
poverty
equal distribution of income
equitable distribution of income
growth
complementary goals
conflicting goals

Problems

1-1 According to Smith's "invisible hand," we are able to obtain meat, not because of the butcher's benevolence, but because of his self-interest. Why is it in the butcher's self-interest to provide us with meat? What does the butcher get in return?

1-2 Suppose another depression occurs like the Depression of the 1930s. How would it affect you? (Thinking about this question provided a major motivation for a generation of economists. They were appalled at the prospect, and determined to play a role in preventing a repeat of the Great Depression.)

1-3 The section on an equitable distribution of income reflects two views regarding the proper approach to poverty:

(*a*) The important thing is to meet the basic needs of the poor; that is, to provide at least a minimum absolute income.

(*b*) The important thing is to reduce inequality; that is, to reduce the gap between the rich and the poor.

These two views are not the same. For example, if there is rapid growth in the economy, objective (*a*) may be accomplished without any progress being made toward (*b*). Which is the more important objective? Why? Do you feel strongly about your choice? Why?

1-4 In Figure 1-1, observe that the downward trend in the length of the workweek ended about 1950. Prior to that date, part of the gains of the average worker came in the form of shorter hours. But, since 1950, practically all the gains have consisted of higher wages and fringe benefits. Why did the workweek level out in 1950?

1-5 Explain how an upswing in purchases by the public will affect (*a*) unemployment and (*b*) inflation. Does this result illustrate economic goals that are complementary, or in conflict?

*1-6 Suppose you correctly anticipate that inflation will rise to a rate of 15 percent per year, and nobody else does.

*An asterisk indicates a more difficult question.

(*a*) How might you make money from your superior insight?

(*b*) As an alternative, assume that most other people also correctly anticipate the 15 percent inflation. Would this change affect your ability to profit from inflation? Explain.

chapter 2
Scarcity: The Economizing Problem

Economize: manage with care or frugality; to be careful in outlay. Webster's Dictionary

In Chapter 1, economics was defined as the study of how people make their living. Such a broad definition was needed to encompass the wide range of issues that economists study—problems such as inflation and depression, and objectives such as efficiency and equity.

The objective of this chapter will be to become more specific, to present a fundamental economic concept: scarcity. Reconsider, for a moment, the broad-brush economic history of the United States in the twentieth century. The average worker now produces about four times as much as the worker at the turn of the century—and does so with less effort, in a shorter workweek. If the average worker can now produce so much, why don't we relax? If, with relatively little effort, we can live as well as, or better than, our grandparents, why should we worry about economic problems at all? Why do we continue to struggle to make a living?

There are two fundamental reasons:

1. Our material *wants* are virtually unlimited or insatiable.

2. Economic *resources* are limited or scarce.

Because of these two basic facts, we cannot have everything we want. We are therefore faced with the necessity of *making choices*.

UNLIMITED WANTS . . .

Consider, first, our wants. If the one-horse shay was good enough for grandpa, why isn't it good enough for us?

Material wants arise for two reasons. First, each of us have basic biological needs: The need for food, the need for shelter, and the need for clothing (particularly in cold climates). But there is also a second reason. Clearly, we are prepared to work more than is required just to meet our minimum needs. We want more than the basic diet of vegetables and water needed to sustain life. We want more than a lean-to shelter which will provide minimal protection from the elements. And we want more than the minimum wardrobe needed to protect us from the cold. In other words, we want the goods and services which can make life more pleasant. Of course, the two basic reasons for material wants cannot be sharply separated. When we sit down to a gourmet meal at a restaurant, we are satisfying our biological need to eat. But we are also doing more. We are savoring exotic foods, in a comfortable and stylish atmosphere. We are getting both the basics and the frills. These frills are sufficiently pleasant that we are willing to work to obtain them.

The range of consumer wants is exceedingly wide. We want *goods*, such as houses, cars, shoes, shirts, and tennis rackets. Similarly, we want *services*: medical care, haircuts, and laundry services. And, when we get what we want, it may whet our appetites for something more. If we own a Chevrolet, perhaps we will want an Oldsmobile next time. Or, after we buy our house, we may wish to replace the carpets and drapes. Furthermore, as new products are introduced, we want them too. We want TV sets, tape recorders, air conditioners, and a host of other products that our great grandparents never even heard of. Even though it is conceivable that, some day, we will say, "Enough," that day seems far away. Our wants show no sign of being completely satisfied.

. . . AND SCARCE RESOURCES

Wants cannot all be satisfied because of the second fundamental fact. While our productive capacity is large, it is not without limit. There are only so many workers in the labor force; and we have only a certain number of machines and factories. In other words, our resources are limited.

Resources are the basic inputs used in the production of goods and services. Therefore, they are also frequently known as *factors of production*. They can be categorized under three main headings: land, labor, and capital.

Economists use the term *land* in a broad sense, to include not only the arable land used by the farmer and the city land used as building lots, but also the other gifts of nature that come with the land. Thus, the minerals which are found under the soil, and the water and sunlight which fall upon the soil, are all part of the land resource.

Labor includes the physical and mental talents of human beings, applied to the production of goods and services. The ditch digger provides labor, and so does the college professor or the physician. (The professor produces educational services, and the doctor produces medical services.)

Capital refers to the buildings, equipment, and other materials used in the productive process. An automobile assembly plant is "capital," and so are the machines in the plant and the steel with which automobiles will be built. In contrast to land, which has been *given* to us by nature, capital has been *produced* at some time in the past. This may have been the distant past; the factory may have been built 15 years ago. Or it may have been the very recent past; the steel may have been manufactured last month. The process of producing and accumulating capital is known as *investment*.

Unlike consumer goods (such as shoes, shirts, or automobiles), capital goods or "investment goods" are not designed to satisfy human wants directly. Rather, they are intended for use in the production of other goods. Capital produced now will satisfy wants only indirectly, and at a later time, when it is used in the production of a consumer good. The production of capital therefore involves the willingness of someone to wait. When a machine is produced, rather, say, than a car, someone is willing to forgo the car now in order to produce the machine and thus be able to produce more cars (or other goods) in the future. Thus, capital formation involves a choice between consumption *now* and more consumption *in the future.*[1]

One final point of terminology should be emphasized. Unless otherwise specified, when economists use the term "capital" they mean *real capital* (buildings, machines) and not financial capital, such as common stocks or money. While an individual might consider 100 shares of General Motors stock as part of his or her "capital," they are not capital in the economic sense. They are not a resource with which goods and services can be produced. Similarly, when economists talk of investment, they generally mean *real investment*—the accumulation of machines and other real capital—and not financial investment (such as the purchase of a government bond).

With unlimited wants and limited resources, we face the fundamental economic problem of *scarcity.* We cannot have everything we want; we must make choices.

SCARCITY AND CHOICE: The Production Possibilities Curve

The problem of scarcity—and the need to make choices—can be illustrated with a *production possibilities curve.* This curve shows what can be produced with the existing quantity of land, labor, and capital at our disposal, and with our existing technology. Although our resources are limited and our capacity to produce is likewise limited, we have an option as to what sorts of goods and services we produce. We may decide to produce fewer cars and more bicycles and aircraft, or less wheat and more corn.

In an economy with thousands of products, the choices before us are complex. In order to reduce the problem to its simplest form, we consider the most basic economy, one in which only two goods (cotton clothing and wheat) can be produced. If we decide to produce more food (wheat), and redirect our efforts in that direction, then we will be able to produce less clothing.

The options open to us are shown in the production possibilities table (Table 2-1) and the corresponding production possibilities curve (Figure 2-1). Consider first an extreme example, where all our resources are directed toward the production of food. In this case, illustrated by option A, we would produce 20 million tons of food. But no clothing would be produced. This clearly does not represent a desirable composition of production; we would be well fed, but would be chilly—and silly—running around with nothing on. But the production possibilities curve is intended to illustrate what is possible; the points on it need not be desirable. And point A is a possibility.

At the other extreme, if we produced nothing but clothing, we could make 5 billion units, as illustrated by point F. Again, this is a possible outcome, but not a desirable one; we would be well dressed as we faced starvation.

The Shape of the Production Possibilities Curve: Increasing Opportunity Costs

More interesting cases, and more reasonable ones, are those in which we produce some of both goods. Consider how the economy might move from point A toward point F. At point A, nothing is produced but food;

---

[1]The preceding paragraphs have presented the traditional division of the factors of production into the categories of land, labor, and capital. While still popular, this traditional division is not universally used by present-day economists. In particular, economists now sometimes talk of "human capital"; that is, education and training which add to the productivity of labor. This human capital has two of the important characteristics of physical capital discussed above. During the training period, waiting is involved; the individual cannot directly produce consumer goods or services while occupied in learning. Second, human capital, like physical capital, can increase the productive capacity of the economy, since a trained worker can produce more than an untrained one.

TABLE 2-1
Production Possibilities

Option	Clothing (billions of yards)	Food (millions of tons)	Units of food that must be given up to produce one more unit of clothing (opportunity cost)
A	0	20	
			1
B	1	19	
			2
C	2	17	
			4
D	3	13	
			5
E	4	8	
			8
F	5	0	

it is grown on all types of arable land throughout the United States. In order to begin to produce clothing, we would plant cotton on the lands which are comparatively best suited for cotton production—those in Alabama and Mississippi. From these lands, we would get a lot of cotton, while giving up just a small amount of food that might have been grown there. This is illustrated as we

move from point *A* to point *B:* only 1 unit of food is given up in order to produce the first unit of clothing.

As we decide to produce more cotton, however, we must move to land which is somewhat less suited to cotton production. Thus, in order to get the second unit of clothing, we must give up 2 units of food: Food production falls from 19 to 17 units as we move from point *B* to point *C*. The *opportunity cost* of the second unit of clothing—what we have to give up in order to get this second unit—is thus greater than the opportunity cost of the first unit.

> The *opportunity cost* of a product is the alternative which must be given up to produce that product. (In this illustration, the opportunity cost of a unit of cotton is the wheat which must be given up when that unit of cotton is produced.)

FIGURE 2-1 The production possibilities curve.
The curve illustrates the options open to society, given its limited resources of land, labor, and capital.

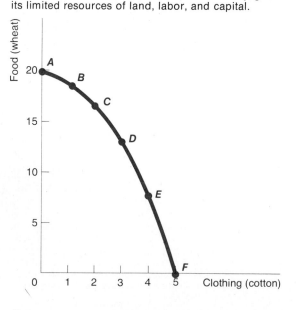

Further increases in the production of clothing come at higher and higher opportunity costs. As we move to the third unit of cloth, we must start planting cotton in the corn belt of Iowa; a lot of food must be given up to produce that third unit of cloth. Finally, as we move from point *E* to point *F*, we are switching all our resources into the production of cotton. This comes at an extremely high opportunity cost in terms of lost output of food. Wheat production is stopped on the farms of North Dakota and Minnesota, which are no good at all for producing cotton. The wheat lands remain idle, and the farmers of North Dakota and Minnesota migrate further south, where they can make only minor contributions to cotton production. Thus, the last unit of clothing (moving from point *E* to *F*) comes at an astronomical cost of 8 units of food.

Thus, the *increasing opportunity cost of cotton is a reflection of the specialized characteristics of our resources.* Our resources are not completely adaptable to alternative uses. The lands of Minnesota and Mississippi are not equally well suited to the production of cotton and wheat. Thus, the opportunity cost of cotton rises as its production is increased. The production possibilities curve is *concave to the origin;* that is, it bows outward, as shown in Figure 2–1.

THE PRODUCTION POSSIBILITIES CURVE IS A "FRONTIER"

The production possibilities curve illustrates what an economy is capable of producing. It shows the maximum possible combined output of the two goods. In practice, actual production can fall short of our capabilities. Obviously, if there is large-scale unemployment, we are wasting some of our labor resources. Such a situation is shown by point *U*, inside the production possibilities curve in Figure 2–2. Beginning at such a point, we could produce more food *and* more clothing (and move to point *D*) by putting our labor force back to work. (With full employment, we alternatively could choose any other point on the production possibilities curve, such as *B, C,* or *E*.)

Thus, while the production possibilities curve represents options open to the society,

FIGURE 2-2 Unemployment and the production possibilities curve.
Point *U* represents a position of large-scale unemployment. If people are put back to work, the economy can be moved to point *D*, with more food *and* more clothing. (Alternatively, the economy can be moved to any other point on the curve, such as *B, C,* or *E*.)

it does not include all conceivable options. Specifically, it does not include options like point *U*, which involve large-scale unemployment and which therefore lie *inside* the curve. Thus, the production possibilities curve traces out a "frontier" of the options open to us. We can pick a point on the frontier if we manage our affairs well and maintain a high level of employment. Or we can end up inside the curve if we mismanage the economy into a depression. But we cannot produce at points (such as *T*) outside the curve with our present quantities of land, labor, and capital, and with our present technology.

GROWTH: The Outward Shift of the Production Possibilities Curve

As time passes, however, a point such as *T* may come within our grasp as our productive capacity increases and the economy grows. There are three main sources of growth:

1. Technological improvement, involving new and better ways of producing goods

2. An increase in the quantity of capital[2]

3. An increase in the labor force

Consider a change in technology. Suppose a new type of fertilizer is discovered that substantially increases the output of our land, whether cotton or wheat is being grown. Then we will be able to produce more wheat and more cotton. The production possibilities curve will shift out to the new curve (PPC$_2$) shown in Figure 2-3.

FIGURE 2-3   Technological improvement.
As a result of the development of a new fertilizer, our productive capabilities increase. (The production possibilities curve moves outward.)

Growth is defined as an outward movement of the production possibilities curve.

GROWTH: The Choice between Consumer Goods and Capital Goods

Alternatively, consider the second source of growth listed above: an increase in the quantity of capital. The capital which we have today is limited. But capital itself can be produced. The quantity of capital in the year 2000 will in large part be determined by how much capital we choose to produce this year and in coming years.

In order to study this choice, we must look at a different production possibilities curve—not one showing food and clothing, but rather, one that shows the choice between the production of *capital goods* (such as machines and factories) and the production of *consumer goods* (such as food, clothing, and TV sets).

In Figure 2-4, two hypothetical economies are compared. Starting in 1980, these two countries face the same initial production possibilities curve (PPC$_{1980}$). The citizens of Extravagania (on the left) believe in living for the moment. They produce mostly consumption goods and very few capital goods (at point *A*). As a result, their capital stock will be not much greater in 2000 than it is today, so their PPC will shift out very little. In contrast, the citizens of Thriftiana (on the right) keep down the production of consumer goods in order to build more capital goods (at point *B*). By the year 2000, their productive capacity will be greatly increased, as shown by the large outward movement of the PPC. Thus, an important question for any country is the choice between consumption now and higher levels of production in the future.

[2]Including "human" capital, which makes an important contribution to growth. Indeed, in his study of the sources of growth in the United States economy, Edward F. Denison found that education was almost as important as physical capital. (According to Denison's estimates, physical capital accounted for growth of 0.50 percent per annum, while education accounted for 0.41 percent.) Edward F. Denison, *Accounting for United States Economic Growth, 1929–1969* (Washington: The Brookings Institution, 1974), p. 127.

(a) **Extravagania.** Most productive capacity is directed toward the satisfaction of current wants (point A). Little investment takes place. The result is slow growth.

(b) **Thriftiana.** Much of current (1980) capacity is used to produce capital goods (point B). The result is rapid growth (that is, a large outward movement of the production possibilities curve by the year 2000).

FIGURE 2-4   Capital formation now helps to determine future productive capacity.

Economic Development: The Problem of Takeoff

For some countries, the question of growth may be approached in a relatively relaxed manner. For the United States, the issue is not a matter of life or death. Even if we consume most of our current output and grow relatively slowly, we will still be relatively comfortable in the year 2000. The same is true for Japan and for the countries of Western Europe. (However, Japan conspicuously has not taken a relaxed approach to the growth question. Japan has been "Thriftiana" *par excellence*, investing a large share of national output and growing very rapidly.)

Some other countries, however, face a much more critical situation. They are so poor that they can scarcely take a relaxed view either of the present or of the future. They face a cruel dilemma (illustrated in Figure 2-5). If they consume all their current output (at point A), then they will remain stuck on the initial production possibilities curve. Their future will be just as bleak as the present.[3] On the other hand, if they want to grow, they will have to produce capital, and this means cutting back on their production of consumer goods. (If they choose the growth strategy and move initially to point B_1, then the production of consumer goods will fall from C_A to C_B.) Since the already low level of consumption is depressed further, more people may starve.

But in the long run, the growth strategy pays off. Because capital is produced at B_1,

---

[3]In this simplified example, it is assumed that only capital can change, and that technology and population remain constant. In the more realistic case, all three major determinants of growth (capital, labor, and technology) may change at the same time. If technology improves, growth may occur even in the absence of investment; the outlook is not as bleak as suggested above. On the other hand, population pressures may make the outlook even worse. As population grows, output must grow if the already low standard of living is not to fall even lower. Thus, just to maintain the present standard, some capital formation may be required.

FIGURE 2-5 "Takeoff" into economic growth.
If point B_1 is initially chosen (on PPC_1), then growth will occur. The economy can move progressively to B_2, B_3, and beyond. The problem is: What short-term miseries will be caused by the initial choice of B_1 rather than A?

productive capacity grows. The production possibilities curve shifts out to PPC_2. Now the nation can pick point B_2, where it consumes as much as it did originally at A, and it also produces capital goods. (Note that B_2 is directly above point A.) The economy has achieved a takeoff. It is now producing capital goods, so its PPC is continuously moving out. Consequently, the nation can produce ever increasing amounts of both consumer and capital goods.

But the long-run process does not solve the painful problem of the present: Should consumption be depressed, at the possible risk of starvation, in order to initiate the growth process? How can the economy take off without the danger of a crack-up halfway down the runway? (The danger may be political as well as economic. If a government chooses point B_1, the population may be unimpressed with promises of a brighter long-run future; they may vote the government out, or rebel.)

One possible solution to this crucial

problem lies with other countries. Richer countries can provide the resources for the early stages of growth, either by granting aid or through private investment. (For example, a Western European tractor manufacturer might build a plant in the developing country.) In this way, economic takeoff might occur without the cruel deprivation required by internally generated capital formation.

AN INTRODUCTION TO ECONOMIC THEORY: The Need to Simplify

The production possibilities curve is the first piece of theoretical equipment which the beginning economics student typically encounters. There will be many more. At this early stage, it is appropriate to address directly a problem which often bothers both the beginning and the advanced student of economics. The production possibilities curve, and many other theoretical concepts that will be introduced in later chapters, represent gross simplifications of the real world. When the PPC is drawn, it is assumed that only two types of goods can be produced—food and clothing, or consumer goods and capital goods. (Diagrams are limited to two alternatives because the printed page has only two dimensions.) Yet obviously, there are thousands of goods produced in the modern economy. This raises a question: With our simple approach, can we say anything of relevance to the real world?

Since we have already used the production possibilities curve, it is not surprising that our answer to this question will be yes. To see why, let us briefly consider the role of theory in economics. Economics is a study of such questions as how consumers behave; why cars are produced in Detroit and steel in Pittsburgh; why prices are sometimes stable and sometimes volatile. To study economics, we must consider *cause* and *effect*.

Theory Necessarily Involves Simplification If we wished to describe the real world in detail, we could go on without end. But a complete description would be useless as a guide to private behavior or public policy; it would be too complex. In a sense, theory is like a map. A road map is necessarily incomplete; in many ways, it is not very accurate, and, indeed, downright wrong. Towns and villages are not round circles. Roads of various qualities do not really come in different colors. If a road map were more realistic, it would be less useful for its intended purpose; if it tried to show every house and every tree, it would be an incomprehensible jumble of detail. A road map is useful precisely because it is a simplification that shows in stark outline the various roads which may be traveled. The objective of economic theory is similarly to draw in stark outline the important relationships among producers and consumers.

A map is useful in part because it involves simplification. When a road map is drawn, with details left out, it gains clarity for its intended purpose as a guide to the auto traveler. But, at the same time, it loses value for other purposes. A road map is a poor guide for airplane pilots. They need a map with the height of mountains clearly marked. A road map is a poor guide for sales managers, who need a map which indicates population density. The way in which a map is constructed depends upon its intended use. Various maps are "true," but they do not represent the "whole truth." An important question for a map user thus becomes: Do I have the best map for my purpose?

The same generalization holds for economic theory. If we wish to study long-run growth, we may use quite different theoretical tools from those we would use to study short-term fluctuations. If we wish to study the consequences of price controls on the housing market, we may use different tools from those we would choose to investigate the economic consequences of a cut in the defense budget. Just as in the case of the map, the "best" theory cannot be identified

unless we know the purposes for which it is to be used.

The purpose of the production possibilities curve is to illustrate the concept of scarcity. If our resources are fully utilized to begin with, and if we decide to produce more of one good, then its production must come at the cost of a lower production of some other good or service. This is a significant point. But the first "if" clause is important. It tells us the assumption behind the production possibilities frontier, and thus it tells us when this theoretical road map is relevant. (When that initial "if" clause is violated—when the economy begins with large-scale unemployment—then quite a different conclusion is correct. The economy *can* produce more consumer goods and more capital goods at the same time.)

For the novice and old hand alike, it is essential to recognize and remember the underlying assumptions of theory. These assumptions are the labels on the theoretical road map. They help to identify the situations in which a theory may safely be used. Thus, they help us to avoid flying our policy airplane into the nearest mountain because we picked the wrong map.

The Distinction between "Positive" and "Normative" Economics

The uses of theory are many, but they may be divided into two main families. *Positive* or *descriptive* economics aims at understanding how the economy works; it is directed toward explaining the way the world is and how various forces can cause it to change. *Normative* economics, on the other hand, deals with the way the world, or some small segment of it, ought to be.

A debate over a positive statement can be settled by an appeal to the facts. For example, the following is a positive statement: "There are millions of barrels of oil in the rocks of Colorado." This statement can be supported or refuted by a geological study. Another positive statement is this: "If 1 ton of dynamite is exploded 100 feet below the surface, 1,000 barrels of oil will be released from the rocks." Again, the facts can settle this point. By experimentation we can find whether this is true.

A *normative* statement is more complex; for example, "We ought to extract oil in large quantities from the Colorado rocks." Facts are relevant here: If there is no oil in the rocks of Colorado (a positive conclusion), then the normative statement that we ought to extract oil must be rejected for the very simple reason that it can't be done. But facts alone will seldom settle a dispute over a normative statement, since it is based on something more—on a view regarding appropriate goals or ethical values. A normative statement involves a value judgment, a judgment about what *ought* to be. It is possible for well-informed individuals of exemplary character to disagree over normative statements, even when they agree completely regarding the facts. For example, they may agree that, in fact, a large quantity of oil is locked in the rocks of Colorado. But they may disagree whether it should be extracted. These differences may develop, perhaps, over the relative importance of a plentiful supply of heating oil as compared with the environmental damage which might accompany the extraction of oil.

In economics, some positive statements may be easily settled by looking at the facts. Among them is: "Steel production last year was 100 million tons," or, "Spending by state and local governments is 10 percent higher this year than last." But, where positive statements involve propositions about causation, they may be quite controversial, because the facts are not easily untangled. Many such controversial statements might

be cited. For example: "If the quantity of money in the economy is increased by 10 percent next year, then inflation will accelerate"; or, "Continuing increases in government spending over the next 10 years will keep the unemployment rate lower than it would be if government spending were constant"; or, "Rent controls have little effect on the number of apartments offered for rent."

In evaluating such statements, economists (and other social scientists) have one major disadvantage compared with natural scientists. In many instances, experiments are difficult or impossible. For obvious reasons, no government will allow economists to try to find the effects of rent control by designing an experiment in which one large city is subjected to rent control while a similar city is not. Nevertheless, economists do have factual evidence to study. By looking at situations where rent controls have been imposed, they may be able to estimate the effects of those controls.

The differences between natural scientists and economists should not be exaggerated. In some instances, economic experiments are possible. Recently, an experiment in New Jersey was undertaken to find whether people would work less if they were provided with a minimum income by the government. (The evidence was that the effects on work were not very great.) Furthermore, while physicists, chemists, and geneticists can carry out experiments, not all natural scientists are in that happy position. To cite one example, astronomers observe; they do not experiment. And, until recent experiments with cloud seeding, meterologists were likewise limited to observation.

Key Points

1. *Scarcity* is a fundamental economic problem. Because wants are virtually unlimited and resources are scarce, we are faced with the need to make choices.

2. The choices open to society are illustrated by the production possibilities curve.

3. Resources are not all uniform; for example, the land of Mississippi has characteristics different from the land of Minnesota. As a consequence, production normally involves increasing opportunity cost. As more cotton is produced, more and more wheat must be given up for each additional unit of cotton. As a result, the production possibilities curve tends to bow outward. (It is concave to the origin.)

4. The production possibilities curve is a frontier, representing the choices open to society if there is full utilization of the available resources of land, labor, and capital. If there is large-scale unemployment, then production occurs at a point within this frontier.

5. The economy can grow and the production possibilities curve can move outward if:
   (a) Technology is improved
   (b) The capital stock grows
   (c) And/or the labor force grows

6. By giving up consumer goods at present, we can produce more capital goods, and thus have a growing economy. The production of capital goods (investment) therefore represents a choice of more future production instead of present consumption.

7. For less developed countries, a choice between present consumption and growth is particularly painful. If they suppress consumption in order to grow more rapidly, people may starve. But growth is essential to raise a low standard of living.

8. Like other theoretical concepts, the production possibilities curve involves simplification. Because the world is so complex, theory cannot reflect the "whole truth." But, like a road map, a theory can be valuable if it is used correctly. In order to determine the appropriate uses of a theory, it is important to identify the assumptions on which the theory was developed.

Key Concepts

scarcity	investment
goods	production possibilities curve
services	increasing opportunity cost
resources	growth
land	takeoff
labor	positive economics
capital	normative economics

Problems

2-1 In Chapter 1, economics was defined as the study of how people make their living, of the problems they encounter, and of the ways in which these problems can be reduced. Frequently, economics is defined differently as the study of "the allocation of scarce resources to satisfy competing human wants." Does either definition cover the study of unemployment? Which definition is broader?

2-2 "Wants aren't insatiable. Nelson Rockefeller's wants have been sated. There is no prospect that he will spend all his money before he dies. His consumption is not limited by his income." Do you agree? Does your answer raise problems for the main theme of this chapter, that wants cannot be sated with the goods and services produced from our limited resources? Why or why not?

2-3 When discussing the sources of growth, technological improvement was illustrated by an improvement in fertilizer, which increases the per-acre production of both wheat and cotton. Suppose that the technological change affects only one of the two products. For example, suppose that a new high-yield strain of wheat is developed. How would this technological improvement affect the production possibilities curve?

2-4 "The more capital goods we produce, the more the United States economy will grow, and the more we and our children will be able to consume in the future. Therefore, the government should encourage capital formation." Do you agree or disagree? Why?

2-5 Does the United States have a moral obligation to aid India with its economic development? Nigeria? Brazil? China?

chapter 3
Specialization, Exchange, and Money

The . . . great achievement of money is that it enables man as producer to concentrate his attention on his own job. . . . The specialization and division of labour . . . would be impossible if every man had to spend a large part of his time and energies in bartering.

D. H. Robertson, *Money*

During the past century, economic progress has been marked by capital accumulation and by a flood of new inventions. First, the mechanical reaper and then the combine were invented to make the harvesting of grain quick and easy. Tractors have been introduced into farming; trucks speed the movement of goods; computers help in the design of products. A long and impressive list could be quickly compiled. The modern worker has not only more tools, but also much better tools than the worker of the nineteenth century.

The new tools have led to a significant increase in the degree of *specialization*. The nineteenth-century artisan produced a wide range of furniture and related wood products from jewelry boxes to caskets. (Indeed, occupations were sometimes combined, with the same individual acting as both carpenter and undertaker.) On the early frontier, the settler was largely self-sufficient; families grew their own food, built their own homes, and often made most of their own clothes. Not so today. Most farms are specialized, producing only one or a few products, such as wheat, corn, or beef. The worker in a modern factory tends a machine designed to produce a single piece of furniture, or perhaps just a single leg of a piece of furniture. The results have not been an unmixed blessing; modern workers are more prone to boredom, and they lack the sense of accomplishment enjoyed by the artisans of old as they saw their creations taking shape. (See Box 3-1.) But the results have undoubtedly contributed to efficiency: By specializing, the modern worker has become very productive.

Thus, the basic reason for specialization is obvious: It is efficient. To use some straightforward examples: It is efficient for the United States to import coffee and to export wheat or business machines to pay

BOX 3-1
67 SECONDS PER CAR

By auto worker Rick King†

I work in the paint department in an enclosed booth. The cars enter and exit through a narrow opening at either end. Our job is to sand the car smooth before it receives its final coat of colored paint.

The booth is hazy with dust from the shift before. The primer coat is lead-based and I wear a surgeon's mask that I bought in San Francisco. Ford provides masks, but they are uncomfortable.

I hold a 10-pound air sander in my right hand and a handful of sandpaper in my left. My responsibility is the right-hand half of the trunk, roof and hood. Since the line speed is usually between 55 and 58 cars per hour, I have to perform my job within 67 seconds.

The work is always physically exhausting, like playing a game of football or soccer. But the real punishment is the inevitability of the line. I have to plan ahead to get a drink of water: five seconds to the fountain, five seconds for the drink, five seconds back into the booth.

The monotony of the line binds us together. Small gaps, usually a few car lengths, happen almost every day. We constantly peer down the line to see if any are coming. The big hope is that a gap won't appear during your break.

I have the least capacity to endure the frustration. One day, hating myself and hating Ford, I smash my $150 sander into a hunk of twisted metal. I look up at my friends. They are amazed. To steal from Ford or to sabotage a car is understandable. But to destroy a tool is simply childish.

Sabotage against the cars themselves is common. The art lies in sabotaging in a way that is not immediately discovered. There is a legendary trim worker whose job is to install six screws. He never puts in more than four.

What makes the assembly line work efficiently is fear, not engineering. The system is based on forcing men and women to produce as much per minute as possible. Once inside the factory, the fear system is immediately apparent. Every problem becomes a crisis, because it threatens to disrupt the smooth flow of the line. Foremen work under the constant threat of being returned to the line. Efficiency experts are forced to hide while doing their inspections. Workers are united in one thing—hating Ford.

If management is harsh, at least it doesn't pretend to help you. But the union does, and some of the worst contempt is reserved for union officials. UAW stands for United Against Workers, a friend tells me. Typically, union officials seem more at home with Labor Relations executives than with workers.

Each worker seemingly stands alone. Some want to work for a few years and then go to school. Most want to last 30 years and retire with a full pension.

---

†Rick King is a California filmmaker who worked at Ford for 7 months in 1974. This passage is excerpted from his article "In the Sanding Booth at Ford," *Washington Monthly,* January 1976, pp. 36–46. By permission.

for this coffee. Coffee could be produced only with difficulty, and at a very high cost, in the United States. Similarly, it is efficient to produce steel in Pittsburgh and corn in Kansas. Kansans presumably could produce their own steel, but the cost would be prohibitively high. Specialization likewise takes place within a locality: Barbers specialize in cutting hair, doctors in treating illnesses, and factory workers in producing goods.

EXCHANGE: The Barter Economy

Specialization implies exchange. The farmer must exchange beef (beyond the family's direct requirements) for furniture, clothing, and other needs.

There are two kinds of exchange: barter, and exchange for money. Under a barter system, with no money involved, one good or service is exchanged directly for another. The farmer specializing in the production of beef may find a hungry barber, and thus get a haircut; or find a hungry tailor, and thus exchange meat for a suit of clothes; or find a hungry doctor, and thus obtain medical treatment. A simple barter transaction is illustrated in Figure 3-1. In a barter economy, there are dozens of such bilateral (two-way) transactions: between the farmer and the tailor; between the farmer and the doctor; between the doctor and the tailor; and so on. It is a testimony to the importance of specialization that, when the monetary system breaks down (as it sometimes does during wartime or political upheaval), people temporarily turn to barter in order to obtain the specialized products and services they desire.

Clearly, barter is inefficient. Farmers can spend half their time producing beef, and the other half searching for someone willing to make the right trade. Barter requires a *coincidence of wants:* The farmer not only must find someone who wants beef, but that someone must also be able to pro-

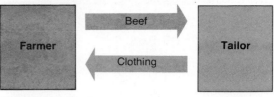

FIGURE 3-1 Barter.
With barter, no money is involved. The farmer directly exchanges beef for clothing.

vide something in exchange that the farmer wants. And, with barter, there is a great problem of *indivisibility* or lumpiness. The farmer may want a suit of clothes, and the tailor may want meat. But the suit of clothes may be worth 100 pounds of beef, yet the tailor need not be *that* hungry, perhaps wishing only 50 pounds. What, then, is the farmer to do? Get only the jacket from this tailor, and set out in search of another hungry tailor in order to obtain a pair of pants? And, if the farmer does so, what are the chances that the pants will match?

EXCHANGE WITH MONEY

With money, exchange can be much more efficient. It is no longer necessary for wants to coincide. In order to get a suit of clothing, the farmer need not find a hungry tailor, but only someone willing to pay money for the beef. The farmer may then take the money and buy the suit of clothes. Thus, money makes possible complex transactions among many parties. Figure 3-2 gives a simple illustration with three parties, but in a monetary economy, transactions may be very complex indeed, involving dozens or hundreds of participants.

Because it breaks the tight bilateral bond between market participants, money also solves the problem of indivisibility. The farmer can sell the whole carcass of beef, and use the proceeds to buy a complete set of clothes. It no longer matters how much beef the tailor wants.

In the simplest barter economy, there is no clear distinction between seller and

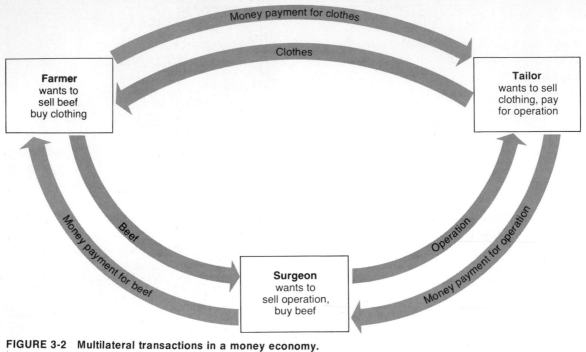

FIGURE 3-2 Multilateral transactions in a money economy.
In a money economy, multilateral transactions among many participants are possible. The farmer gets clothing from the tailor, even though the tailor doesn't want to buy the farmer's beef.

buyer or between producer and consumer. When exchanging beef for clothing, the farmer acts at the same time as both a seller (as the producer of beef) and a buyer (as the consumer of clothing). In a monetary economy, in contrast, a sharp distinction arises between seller and buyer. In the beef market, the farmer is the seller; the hungry tailor is the buyer. The farmer is the producer; the tailor is the consumer.

This distinction between producer (or "business") and consumer (or "household") is illustrated in Figure 3-3. In the top loops, the transactions in consumer goods and services are shown. Beef, clothing, and a host of other products are sold in exchange for money.

In a complex exchange economy, not only are consumer goods bought and sold for money, so are economic resources. In order to be able to buy food and other goods,

households must have money income. They acquire money by providing the labor and other resources which are the inputs of the business sector. These resource transactions are shown in the lower loops of Figure 3-3. For example, labor is provided in exchange for wages and salaries, and the use of land is provided in exchange for rents.

Although Figure 3-3 is becoming complex, it still involves substantial simplifications. There are large government transactions in our economy that have not been included in Figure 3-3. Remember the purpose of simplification discussed in Chapter 2: to show important relationships in sharp outline. Figure 3-3 shows the circular flow of payments; that is, how businesses use the receipts from sales to pay their wages, salaries, and other costs of production, while households use their income receipts from wages, salaries, etc., to buy consumer goods.

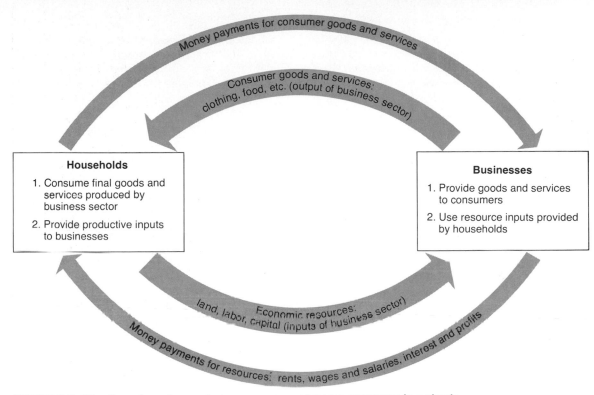

FIGURE 3-3 The flow of goods, services, resources, and money payments in a simple economy.
Monetary payments are shown in the outer loop. These pay for the flow of goods and services and resources shown in the inner loop.

THE MONETARY SYSTEM

Because barter is so inefficient, people turn naturally to the use of money. In most societies, the government becomes deeply involved in the monetary system, issuing paper money and coins. But even if the government does nothing, a monetary system will evolve.

The very powerful tendencies for money to appear, and some of the important characteristics of a good monetary system, may be illustrated by a specific example of an economy that began without money: the prisoner-of-war camp of World War II.[1] Economic relations in such a camp were primitive; the range of goods was very limited. But some things were available: rations supplied by the German captors, and Red Cross parcels which arrived periodically. These parcels contained a variety of items such as canned beef, jam, margarine, cigarettes, and chocolate. Nonsmokers who received cigarettes were obviously eager to trade them for other items. The basis was established for exchange.

At first, trading was rough and ready, with no clear picture of the relative values of the various items. (In one instance, a prisoner started around the camp with only a can of cheese and five cigarettes, and returned with a complete Red Cross parcel. He did so by buying goods where they were cheap,

[1]This illustration is based on R. A. Radford, "The Economic Organization of a P.O.W. Camp," *Economica*, November 1945, pp. 189–201.

and selling them where they were dear.) But as time went by, the prices of various goods tended to become stable, and all prices came to be quoted in terms of cigarettes. For example, a can of cheese was worth seven cigarettes. Not only did cigarettes become the measuring rod for quoting prices, but they were used as the common *medium of exchange*. Goods were bought and sold in exchange for cigarettes, even by nonsmokers. Nonsmokers were willing to accept cigarettes in payment, even though they had no desire to smoke; they knew that they would in turn be able to use the cigarettes to buy chocolate, jam, or other items. In short, cigarettes became the money of the POW camp. This was a natural evolution; there was no government to decree that cigarettes were money, and no authority to enforce that choice. At other times and in other societies, other items have evolved as money: items as diverse as beads, playing cards, porpoise teeth, rice, salt, wampum, and even woodpecker scalps.

Monetary Problems in the POW Camp

Cigarette money made the primitive economy of the prisoner-of-war camp more efficient. But problems occurred, including problems quite similar to those of more advanced money systems. As part of the natural trend toward simplification, distinctions among cigarettes became blurred. Although all cigarettes were not equally desirable to smokers, all were equal as money; in paying for beef or other items, a cigarette was a cigarette. What was the consequence? Smokers held back the desirable brands for their personal use and spent the others. The less desirable cigarettes therefore were the ones used as money; the "good" cigarettes were smoked. This illustrates Gresham's law. This law, first enunciated by Elizabethan financier Sir Thomas Gresham (1519–1579), is popularly and loosely abbreviated: "Bad money drives out good." In this case, "bad" cigarettes drove "good" cigarettes out of circulation as money. (The good cigarettes were smoked instead.)

Gresham's law: If there are two types of money whose values in exchange are equal while their values in another use (like consumption) are different, the more valuable item will be retained for its other use while the less valuable item will continue to circulate as money. Thus, the "bad" (less valuable) money drives the "good" (more valuable) money out of circulation.

The tendency for every cigarette to be treated as equal to every other cigarette caused another monetary problem. As a cigarette was a cigarette, prisoners often pulled out a few strands of tobacco before passing a cigarette along. This corresponds precisely to a problem when gold coins circulate: There is a temptation to chip off bits of gold; that is, to "clip" coins. And the cigarette currency became "debased": Some enterprising prisoners rolled cigarettes from pipe tobacco or broke down cigarettes and re-rolled them, lightening them in the process. Similarly, governments have from time to time given in to the temptation to debase gold coins by melting them down and reissuing them with a smaller gold content. (Private entrepreneurs have had a strong incentive to do the same; however, they have been much discouraged throughout history by severe punishments against counterfeiting.)

But it was not clipping or debasement which led to the greatest monetary problems in the POW camp. As long as there was a balanced inflow of both cigarettes and other goods, the exchange system of the camp worked reasonably well. But, from time to time, the Red Cross issue of 25 or 50 cigarettes per week was interrupted, and as the existing stock of cigarettes was consumed by smokers, cigarettes became more and more scarce. As desperate smokers had to offer more and more to get cigarettes, their value skyrocketed. Other goods now exchanged for only a few cigarettes: A can of beef which previously sold for 20 cigarettes dropped in value to 15, 10, or even fewer cigarettes. In technical terms, there was a

BOX 3-2
WHY CIGARETTES?

In the POW camp, cigarettes emerged as the commonly accepted money. Why cigarettes? Why not canned carrots or beef?

There were two reasons. First, although not everyone wanted cigarettes for his personal use, the market value of cigarettes was high. Thus, cigarettes were chosen over canned carrots because canned carrots were practically worthless. If carrots had been the "money," exchange would have been cumbersome, with prisoners lugging around many cans in order to make exchanges. A good money is one whose value is sufficiently high that the individual may conveniently carry a considerable purchasing power. Thus, in the broader society, it was the precious metals which historically evolved as money—silver, and particularly gold. Lead did not (generally) become money because its value was relatively low, and the use of lead would have been cumbersome. Of course, today our money is even more convenient than the precious metals: A $20, $50, or $100 bill may be carried easily and inconspicuously.

Thus, cigarettes were preferred to canned carrots. But why did cigarettes become money, rather than canned beef? Canned meat, like cigarettes, had a high value. Here, we come to a second important characteristic. A package of cigarettes is easily divisible into subunits—the 20 individual cigarettes. A can of beef, on the other hand, cannot easily be subdivided. If it is opened and cut up, the individual chunks will be messy and will quickly spoil. Moreover, a 2-ounce piece of beef is not easily distinguished from a 3-ounce chunk. The cigarette package, in contrast, can easily be divided into 20 individual cigarettes which are (relatively) long-lasting and easily identified.

Similarly, in the broader society, monies have developed which are easily divisible. Precious metals, for example, are easily divisible into units of any size. And the small units

of gold or silver are durable; indeed, much more durable than the cigarettes of the POW camp. But, in another respect, gold and silver are intrinsically less desirable than cigarettes: As in the case of beef, an ounce of gold is not easily distinguished from an ounce and a half. Thus, governments became involved in the monetary system, dividing quantities of gold into easily identified coins of specific weight and value.

The importance of subdivision also helps to explain the coexistence of gold and silver as money (for example, in the United States in the nineteenth century). Gold is easily divisible—up to a point. Gold coins of $50, $20, or $10 could easily be minted and were relatively convenient. But suppose the government wanted to mint a gold coin worth 25 cents. It would be so tiny that it would be easily lost. While the high value of gold made it an obvious choice for coins of high value, it was very inconvenient for the smaller denominations. Here, silver was the obvious choice: It was less valuable per ounce than gold.

In summary, the evolution of the "cigarette standard" illustrated a number of the characteristics which the item chosen for money should possess: It should be *sufficiently valuable* that a reasonably large purchasing power can be carried conveniently by an individual; it should be *easily divisible;* and it should be *durable*. (Nevertheless, even outside the prisoner-of-war camp, the item which acts as money has not invariably met these qualifications. For example, items used as the means of payment are not always durable. In the nineteenth century, wage earners in the Staffordshire coal mines were paid partly in beer. In his book *Life and Labour in the Nineteenth Century,†* C. R. Fay observed: "This currency was very popular and highly liquid, but it was issued to excess and difficult to store.")

†Cambridge: Cambridge University Press, 1945, p. 197.

deflation of the prices of other goods (measured in terms of cigarette money).

As cigarettes became increasingly scarce and deflationary pressures continued, prisoners tended to revert to barter in exchanging other products. Then, from time to time, thousands of cigarettes would arrive at the camp during a brief period. Prices of other goods soared, and once again the unpredictability of the value of cigarette money caused a partial return to barter exchange. In other words, *the monetary system worked smoothly only so long as a reasonable balance was kept between the quantity of money (cigarettes) and the quantity of other goods.*

Several characteristics of a good monetary system may be drawn out of this story of the "cigarette standard." A smoothly operating monetary system should be made up of money whose value is *uniform.* (Nonuniform money will lead to the operation of Gresham's law, with "bad" money driving out "good" money.) In the United States, the Federal Reserve System and the Treasury Department have the major responsibilities to assure that money is uniform. They are the institutions which issue the currency which circulates as money. It matters not whether the $1 bill I have in my pocket is crisp and new, or whether it is tattered and soiled. The Federal Reserve will replace it with a new bill of equal value when it becomes excessively worn. This means that it represents $1 in value to anyone. This uniformity in the value of each dollar bill obviously adds to the speed and efficiency of exchange (and it means that Gresham's law does not operate in our modern economy). In accepting dollar bills, we need worry only about whether they are genuine; we need not quibble over their exact physical condition.

A second, and critical, responsibility of the monetary authorities is to ensure that there is the proper quantity of money in the system; neither too much nor too little. This will be an important topic of Part 2 of this book.

COMPARATIVE ADVANTAGE: A Reason to Specialize

Money, the development of markets, and (perhaps equally important) the development of a sophisticated transportation and communications system, all make possible a high degree of specialization of production. They make specialization possible and relatively smooth; but they do not provide a reason *why* specialization is advantageous in the first place. This question was raised, and answered at an intuitive level, in earlier pages: Specialization can add to efficiency. It is now time to see *how.*

A good tends to be produced in the place which is best suited for its production: steel near the coal fields of Pennsylvania, corn in Kansas, bananas in Central America, coffee in Brazil, and so on. In technical terms, there is some tendency for a good to be produced in the area that has an *absolute advantage* in its production.

> A country has an *absolute advantage* in the production of a good if it can produce that good with fewer resources (less land, labor, and capital) than other countries.

This same principle applies to specialization among individuals within a city or town. Consider the case of the family doctor and the professional gardener. The doctor is better at dispensing medicine, and the gardener generally is better at gardening, so it is in the interest of each to specialize in the occupation in which he or she has an absolute advantage.

But the truth is often more complicated than this. Suppose a certain doctor is better at gardening than the gardener himself; she's faster and more effective—in short, she has a "greener thumb." She has an absolute advantage in both medicine and gardening. If absolute advantage were the key, she would practice medicine and do her own gardening as well. Does this necessarily happen? The answer: No. Unless this doctor positively enjoys gardening as a recreation, she may well leave the gardening to the professional. Why? Even though the doctor, being an excellent gardener, can do as much gardening in 1 hour (let us say) as the gardener could in 2, she will be better off to stick to medicine and hire the gardener to work on the lawns and shrubbery. In 1 hour's work as a physician, the doctor can give a complete physical examination, for which she charges $50. The gardener's time, in contrast, is worth only $5 per hour. By spending the hour on medicine rather than gardening, the doctor will come out ahead: She will earn $50, and be able to hire the gardener for $10 to put in 2 hours to get the gardening done. The doctor gains $40 by sticking to medicine for that 1 hour.

Similarly, the gardener gains through specialization. Although he has to work 10 hours in order to afford the $50 which will be needed for 1 hour of the doctor's time, the doctor in that single hour can do more for the health of the gardener's family than could the gardener in 20, 100, or even 1,000 hours. Absolute advantage is not necessary for specialization. The doctor has an absolute advantage in both gardening and medicine; the gardener has an absolute disadvantage in both. But the doctor has a *comparative* advantage in medicine; the gardener has a *comparative* advantage in gardening. When the gardener and the doctor stick to their comparative advantage, *both gain from specialization.* (Box 3-3 shows how the doctor gains. The gardener also gains, since he can pay for a competent physical examination for himself or his family by working as a gardener for 10 hours. No matter how much time he is willing to spend, he cannot make a competent examination himself. He can acquire a competent examination only by specialization and exchange.)[2]

British economist David Ricardo enunciated the principle of *comparative advantage* in the early nineteenth century to illustrate how countries gain from international trade. As a consequence, it is customary to consider this principle in detail as part of the study of international economics. But comparative advantage provides a general explanation of the advantages of specialization; it is just as relevant to domestic as to international trade.

Comparative advantage, then, is the first great propellant driving the wheels of commerce (while money acts as the grease, making the machine run with less friction). But there is also a second fundamental reason for specialization.

ECONOMIES OF SCALE: Another Reason to Specialize

Consider two identical small cities, of the same size, with the same amounts of resources. Suppose that the citizens of these cities want both bicycles and lawnmowers, but that neither city has any advantage in the production of either good. Will each city then produce its own, without any trade existing between the two? Probably not. It is likely that one city will specialize in bicycles, and one in lawnmowers. Why?

The answer lies in *economies of scale.* To understand what this term means, first assume that each city does not specialize. Each city directs half its productive resources into the manufacture of bicycles, and half into the manufacture of lawnmowers, thus producing 1,000 bicycles and 1,000 lawnmowers. But if one city specializes and directs all its productive resources toward the manufacture of bicycles, it can acquire specialized machinery and produce 2,500 bicycles. Similarly, if the other city directs all its productive resources toward the production of lawnmowers, it can produce 2,500. Note that each city, by doubling all inputs into the production of a single item, can more than double its output of that item from 1,000 to 2,500 units. There are economies of scale. (When the volume of bicycle output increases, the quantity of inputs required to produce a bicycle falls, and the cost of producing a bicycle likewise falls.) Thus, even though neither city had any fundamental advantage in the production of either product, they can gain by specialization. Before specialization, their combined output was 2,000 bicycles and 2,000 lawnmowers. After specialization, they together make 2,500 bicycles and 2,500 lawnmowers.

[2]The theory of comparative advantage will be studied in more detail in the companion volume in the chapter on international trade. Those who want a formal definition of comparative advantage at this early stage might note that it is based on the concept of opportunity cost introduced in Chapter 2.

If two individuals (or cities, or nations) have different opportunity costs of producing a good or service, then the individual (or city, or nation) with the lower opportunity cost has the *comparative advantage* in that good or service.

In the illustration shown in detail in Box 3-3, the opportunity cost of the doctor producing one complete physical examination is the alternative given up; that is, the gardening she could have done in that hour (planting 20 flowers). The opportunity cost of the gardener producing one competent physical examination has no limit. No matter how many hours he spends and no matter how many flowers he forgoes planting, he cannot produce a competent examination. The doctor's opportunity cost in providing a physical examination is lower than the gardener's; therefore, the doctor has the comparative advantage in the practice of medicine.

> *Economies of scale* exist when a doubling of all inputs more than doubles output.

While Ricardo's theory of comparative advantage dates back to the early nineteenth century, the explanation of economies of scale goes back even further, to Adam Smith's *Wealth of Nations* (1776). In Smith's first chapter, "Of the Division of Labour," there is a famous description of pin-making:[3]

A workman not educated to this business . . . could scarce, perhaps, . . . make one pin in a day, and certainly not twenty. But in the way in which this business is now carried on, not only the whole work is a peculiar trade, but it is divided into a number of branches. . . . One man draws out the wire, another straightens it, a third cuts it, a fourth points it, a fifth grinds it at the top for receiving the head. . . . Ten persons, therefore, could make among them upwards of forty-eight thousand pins in a day. Each person, therefore, . . . might be considered as making four thousand and eight hundred pins in a day.

What is the reason for the gain which comes from the division of pin-making into a number of separate steps? Certainly it is not that some individuals are particularly suited to drawing the wire, while others have a particular gift for straightening it. On the contrary, if two individuals are employed, it matters little which activity each is assigned. Adam Smith's "production line" is efficient because of economies of scale which depend on:

1. The introduction of specialized machinery

2. Specialization of the labor force on that machinery

Modern corporations also derive economies of scale from a major third source:

3. Specialized research and development, which make possible the development of new equipment and technology

In the modern world, economies of scale are very important as an explanation of specialization. They are a major reason why the manufacturers of automobiles, aircraft, and computers are few in number and large in size. It is partly because of economies of scale that the automobile industry is concentrated in the Detroit area, with Michigan shipping cars to other areas in exchange for a host of other products.

But economies of scale explain much more than the trade among the regions, states, and cities *within* a country. They also are an important explanation of trade *between* countries. (See Box 3-4.) For example, economies of scale in the production of large passenger aircraft go on (and costs continue to fall) long after the United States market is met. Thus, there is a major advantage to Boeing—and to the United States—in producing aircraft for the world market. And there are gains to the aircraft buyers, too. For example, Belgians can buy a Boeing 747 for a small fraction of the cost of making a comparable plane themselves.

In this chapter, the advantages of specialization and exchange have been studied. Exchange takes place in markets; how markets operate will be the subject of the next chapter.

[3]Adam Smith, *An Inquiry into the Nature and Causes of the Wealth of Nations* (Modern Library edition, New York: Random House, 1937), pp. 4 and 5.

BOX 3-4
CARS IN CANADA:

How Does a Country with a Small Market Achieve Economies of Scale?

Even the huge United States market is not large enough for some producers, such as aircraft manufacturers, to capture economies of scale fully. But it is large enough for producers of other goods, such as autos. In fact, United States auto manufacturers can offer a wide variety of car models and still produce most of them at the high volume necessary to achieve essentially all economies of scale. Thus, these producers can achieve low cost and at the same time provide a wide range of choice for the consumer.

But the United States economy is unique in this respect, because it is so large. Smaller economies (like Canada's) cannot produce a wide range of models and at the same time achieve the high-volume output necessary to lower costs. Thus, Canada has a choice among three options. It can:

1. Produce a variety of models, each at a small scale and therefore at a high cost, for the domestic Canadian market. This option would present the Canadian car purchaser with the advantage of a choice among various models, but the disadvantage of a high cost per car.

2. Produce a small number of models, each at high volume, for the domestic market. This would provide the advantage of low cost, but the disadvantage of a severely restricted choice of models.

3. Gain both advantages (high-volume, low-cost production and a wide variety of models) by engaging in international trade. Produce only a few models in Canada, at high volume and low cost. Export many of these Canadian-built cars in exchange for a variety of imported models.

Historically, up to the early 1960s, Canadian automotive policy was based on the first choice. But the twin advantages of option 3 are clear, and can come through international trade. In order to gain these advantages, Canada in 1965 entered a special free-trade arrangement with the United States, allowing for tariff-free passage of cars both ways across the border. A similar motivation, that of gaining the advantages both of high-volume, low-cost production and of wide consumer choice, contributed to the decision of Western European countries to establish the European Economic Community, or European Common Market, in the late 1950s. (In a common market, goods are allowed to pass among the members freely, with no tariffs being collected.)

Key Points

1. Specialization contributes to efficiency.

2. Specialization requires exchange. The most primitive form of exchange is barter. This has the disadvantage that it depends on a coincidence of wants.

3. Much more complex exchange, involving many participants, is feasible in an economy with money. Because exchange is so much easier and more efficient with money, money will evolve even in the absence of government action—as happened in the prisoner-of-war camp.

4. If the economy is to operate smoothly, money should be:
   (*a*) Uniform
   (*b*) Issued in moderate quantities (neither too much nor too little, compared with the quantity of goods and services to be bought)
   (*c*) Physically convenient (not bulky or easily lost)
   (*d*) Easily divisible into small denominations

5. There are two major reasons why there are gains from specialization and exchange:
   (*a*) Comparative advantage
   (*b*) Economies of scale

6. An example of comparative advantage is the doctor who is better than the gardener at both medicine and gardening. Even so, she does not do her gardening herself, because she gains by specializing in medicine (her comparative advantage) and hiring the gardener to do the gardening (his comparative advantage).

7. Economies of scale exist if a doubling of all resource inputs leads to an output which is more than doubled.

Key Concepts

specialization	coincidence of wants	Gresham's law	comparative advantage
exchange	indivisibility	debasement of the currency	economies of scale
barter	medium of exchange	absolute advantage	

Problems

3-1 What are the major industries in your home town? Why did those industries locate there?

3-2 Suppose the government taxed all monetary transactions. Would such taxes cause a return to barter or to self-sufficiency? Does the government in fact tax monetary transactions? What are the consequences?

3-3 Suppose that one individual at your college is outstanding, being the best teacher and a superb administrator. If you were the college president, would you ask this individual to teach, or to become the administrative vice-president? Why?

3-4 Draw a production possibilities curve for the doctor mentioned in Box 3-3, putting physical examinations on one axis and flowers planted on the other. (Assume that the doctor is willing to work 40 hours per week.)

*3-5 Draw the production possibilities curve of one of the two identical cities described in the section on economies of scale.

*This is a more difficult problem.

chapter 4
Demand and Supply: The Market Mechanism

Do you know,
Considering the market, there are more
Poems produced than any other thing?
No wonder poets sometimes have to *seem*
So much more business-like than business men.
Their wares are so much harder to get rid of.
Robert Frost, *New Hampshire*

Although some countries are much richer than others, the resources of every economy are limited. Choices must be made. Furthermore, except on Robinson Crusoe's mythical island, every economy involves some degree of specialization. In every economy, therefore, some mechanism is needed to answer the fundamental questions raised by specialization and by the need to make choices:

1. *What* goods and services will be produced? (How do we choose among the various alternatives represented by the production possibilities curve?)
2. *How* will these goods and services be produced? For example, will bicycles be produced by relatively few workers using a great deal of machinery, or by many workers using relatively little capital equipment?

3. *For whom* will the goods and services be produced? Once goods are produced, who will consume them?

The Market and the Government

Basically, there are two mechanisms by which these questions can be answered. First, answers may be provided by Adam Smith's "invisible hand." If people are left alone to make their own transactions, then the butcher, the baker, and the brewer will produce the beef, bread, and beer for our dinner. In other words, answers may be provided by the *private market*.

Second, answers may be provided by the *government*.[1] The government's role may be quite limited, involving simply a modification of the operations of the market. For example, if the government taxes heavy

[1]The market and the government are not the only mechanisms for answering these questions. For example, when a relief organization collects voluntary contributions of clothing or money for distribution to the poor or to the victims of a natural disaster, it is influencing *who* gets the output of society (Question #3). Similarly, within the family, a mechanism other than the market or the government is used to determine how the budget for clothing, etc., is divided among the family members. Nevertheless, the market and the government are the mechanisms on which economists concentrate in answering the three basic questions.

"gas-guzzling" cars, people have an incentive to switch to small cars. Car manufacturers in turn will respond by producing more of the small cars and fewer of the large ones. Without becoming directly involved in the manufacture of automobiles, the government can thus influence *what* goods are produced.

Taxes are not the only way that government may influence what will be produced. For example, Congress may pass laws which require new cars to have safety belts and other specific types of protective equipment. And the government may become directly involved in determining the type of output. Most notably, during wartime the government becomes a direct user of much of the output of the economy in the form of tanks, ships, and aircraft. Finally, the government may own and operate businesses. For example, while much of the electric power in the United States is produced by privately owned utilities, the government-owned Tennessee Valley Authority (TVA) is a large producer of electricity.

Conceivably, an economy might be designed to depend exclusively either on the market or on government to make the three fundamental decisions of *what, how*, and *for whom*. But the real world is one of compromise; in every actual economy, there is some mixture of markets and government decision-making. However, reliance on the market varies substantially among countries. In the United States, most choices are made in the private market. By international standards, the government plays a restricted role, although this role has expanded substantially during the twentieth century.

Toward the other end of the spectrum, the economies of the Soviet Union, the People's Republic of China, and the countries of Eastern Europe rely heavily on government decision-making. As Marxist nations, they particularly object to having the private market determine for whom goods will be produced. They do not permit private individuals to own large amounts of capital. There-

fore, private individuals do not receive large interest and dividend payments with which to buy a considerable fraction of the output of the economy. (In contrast, most capital is privately owned in "capitalist" or "free private enterprise" countries such as the United States.) In a Marxist country where most capital is owned by the state, the government is inevitably involved in detailed decisions as to which products will be produced with this capital. For example, the Soviet Union has a central planning agency which issues directives to the various sectors of the economy to produce target quantities of goods. It would, however, be a mistake to conclude that government planning in the countries of Eastern Europe is a rigid and all-pervasive method of answering the three basic questions. Markets for goods exist in all these countries, and some nations (particularly Yugoslavia) allow many decisions to be made through the market. Thus, these countries too have "mixed" economies, although the mix between market and government decision-making is very different from ours.

A *mixed economy* is one in which the market and the government share the decisions as to what shall be produced, how, and for whom

Because the market is relatively important in the United States, it will be our initial concern. (Later chapters will deal with the economic role of the government in the United States and with the Marxist economic system.) This chapter will explain how the market answers the three basic questions: What will be produced? How? For whom?

THE MARKET MECHANISM

In a market, an item is bought and sold. In most markets, the buyer and the seller come face to face. When you buy a suit of clothes, you talk directly to the salesclerk; when you buy groceries, you physically enter the seller's place of business (the supermarket). But physical proximity is not required to make a market. For example, in a typical stock market transaction, a Georgian puts in a call to his broker to buy 100 shares of IBM common stock. About the same time, a Pennsylvanian calls her broker to sell 100 shares. The transaction takes place on the floor of the New York Stock Exchange, where representatives of the two brokerage houses meet. The buyer and the seller of the stock do not leave their respective homes in Georgia and Pennsylvania.

Some markets are quite simple. For example, a barbershop is a "market," since haircuts are bought and sold there. The transaction is obvious and straightforward; the service of haircutting is produced on the spot. But in other cases, markets are much more complex. Even the simplest everyday activity may be the culmination of a complicated series of market transactions.

As you sat at breakfast this morning drinking your cup of coffee, you were calling on products from distant areas. The coffee itself was probably produced in Brazil. It was made with water that perhaps had been brought to your residence in pipes manufactured in Pennsylvania and purified with chemicals produced in Delaware. The sugar for the coffee may have been produced in Louisiana, and the artificial cream manufactured from soybeans grown in Missouri. Possibly, your coffee was poured into a cup made in New York State, and stirred with a spoon manufactured in Taiwan from Japanese stainless steel which used Canadian nickel in its production. All this was for one little cup of coffee.

In such a complex economy, some mechanism is needed to keep things straight, to bring order out of potential chaos, and to make sure that all the coffee doesn't end up in New York and all the sugar in New Jersey. Markets provide the mechanism for bringing order. In a market, the price performs two important, interrelated functions which help to prevent chaos:

1. The price provides *information*.
2. The price provides *incentives*.

To illustrate, suppose we start from the example of chaos, with all the coffee in New York and all the sugar in New Jersey. Coffee lovers in New Jersey would be desperate and would clamor for coffee even at very high prices. The high price would be a signal, providing *information* to coffee owners that there were eager buyers in New Jersey. And it would provide them with an *incentive* to send coffee to New Jersey. In any market, the price provides the focus for interactions between buyers and sellers.

PERFECT AND IMPERFECT COMPETITION

Some markets are dominated by a few large firms; others have thousands of sellers. The "big three" automobile manufacturers make over 80 percent of the cars sold in the United States, with the remaining 20 percent being divided up among American Motors and a number of foreign firms. Such an industry, which is dominated by a few sellers, is termed an *oligopoly.* (The word "oligopoly" means "a few sellers" just as "oligarchy" means the "rule by a few.") Some markets are even more concentrated. For example, there is just one supplier of telephone services in your area; the telephone company has a *monopoly.* On the other hand, there are thousands of wheat producers.

A *monopoly* exists when there is only *one seller.* An *oligopoly* exists when a *few sellers* dominate a market.

The number of participants in a market has a significant effect on the way in which the price is determined. In the wheat market, there are thousands of buyers and thousands of sellers. The individual farmers know that each of them is producing only a tiny fraction of the total supply of wheat. They know that no one farmer can affect the price of wheat by holding wheat back or by selling. For each one, the price is *given;* the individual farmer's decision is limited to the number of bushels of wheat to be sold. Similarly, the millers realize that they are each buying only a small fraction of the wheat supply. They realize that they cannot, as individuals, affect the price of wheat. Each miller's decision is limited to the number of bushels to be bought at the existing market price. In the wheat market, where *perfect competition* exists, prices are determined by *impersonal market forces.* For the individual seller and the individual buyer, *there is no pricing decision to be made.*

> *Perfect competition* exists when there are many buyers and many sellers, with no single buyer or seller having any influence over the price. (Sometimes, this term is shortened simply to "competition.")

In contrast, individual producers in an oligopolistic or a monopolistic industry know that they have some control over price.

> An *industry* refers to all the producers of a good or service. For example, we may speak of the automobile industry, or the airline industry. (Note that the term "industry" can refer to *any* good or service, whether or not it is manufactured. Thus, we may speak of the "wheat industry.")

For example, during the summer, an automobile firm sets the prices for its new models. That does not mean, of course, that the company can set any price it wants and still be ensured of making a profit. It can offer to sell automobiles at a high price, in which case it will sell only a few cars. Or it can charge a lower price, in which case it will sell more cars. Similarly, the telephone company knows that it is large enough to influence its rates (although its freedom of action is strictly limited by government regulation). On the other side of the market, some buyers may also be large enough to influence price. General Motors is a large enough purchaser of steel to be able to bargain with the steel companies over the price of steel. When individual buyers or sellers can influence price, *imperfect competition* exists.

> *Imperfect competition* exists when any buyer or any seller is able to influence the price. Such a buyer or seller is said to have *market power.*

(Note that the term "competition" is used differently in economics and in business. Don't try to tell someone from Ford that the automobile market isn't very competitive; Ford is very much aware of the competition from General Motors and Chrysler. Yet, according to the economist's definition, the automobile industry is far less competitive than the wheat industry.)

Because price is determined by impersonal forces in a perfectly competitive market, the competitive market is simplest, and will therefore be considered first. The perfectly competitive market should also be given priority attention because competitive markets generally operate more efficiently than imperfect markets. There is no monopolist who may keep production down in order to keep prices up. (Pricing decisions in imperfect markets, and the ways in which imperfect markets can result in inefficiencies, will be major topics in the last third of this book.)

THE PERFECTLY COMPETITIVE MARKET: Demand and Supply

We might as reasonably dispute whether it is the upper or the under blade of a pair of scissors that cuts a piece of paper, as whether the value is governed by utility [demand] or cost of production [supply].

Alfred Marshall, _Principles of Economics_

In a perfectly competitive market, price is determined by *demand* and *supply.*

Demand . . .

Consider, as an example, the market for apples, in which there are many buyers and many sellers, with none having any control over the price. For the buyer, a high price acts as a deterrent; the higher the price, the fewer apples buyers will purchase. Why is this so? As the price of apples rises, consumers will switch to oranges or grapefruit, or they will simply cut down on their total consumption of fruit. Similarly, the lower the price, the more will be bought. A lower price will bring new purchasers into the market, and each purchaser will tend to buy more. The response of buyers to various possible prices is illustrated in the *demand schedule* in Table 4-1.

The information in the demand schedule may alternatively be illustrated with a demand curve; this is done in Figure 4-1.

TABLE 4-1
The Demand Schedule for Apples

	(1) Price *P* ($ per bushel)	(2) Quantity *Q* demanded (thousands of bushels per week)
A	$10	50
B	$ 8	100
C	$ 6	200
D	$ 4	400

Demand is defined as a schedule which shows the various quantities of a good or service which buyers would be willing and able to purchase at various possible prices.

The quantity of the good (in thousands of bushels per week) is shown on the horizontal axis, and the price per bushel is shown on the vertical axis. The first line (*A*) of the demand schedule in Table 4-1 indicates that if the price were $10, consumers would be willing to buy 50,000 bushels of apples per week. This information is given in Figure 4-1 as point *A*, which is plotted at a height of $10, and at 50 units along the horizontal axis. Similarly, points *B*, *C*, and *D* in Figure 4-1 represent the corresponding *B*, *C*, and *D* lines in Table 4-1.

FIGURE 4-1   The demand curve.
At each of the possible prices specified, there is a definite quantity of apples that people would be willing and able to buy. This information is provided in Table 4-1 and is reproduced in this diagram. On the vertical axis, the possible prices are shown. In each case, the quantity of apples that would be bought is measured along the horizontal axis. Since people are more willing to buy at a low price than at a high price, the demand curve slopes downward to the right.

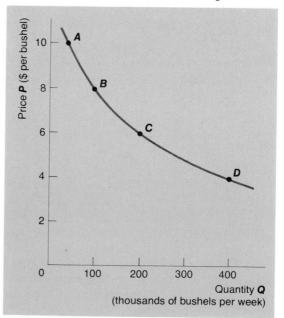

50

TABLE 4-2
The Supply Schedule for Apples

	(1) Price P ($ per bushel)	(2) Quantity Q supplied (thousands of bushels per week)
F	$10	260
G	8	240
H	6	200
J	4	150

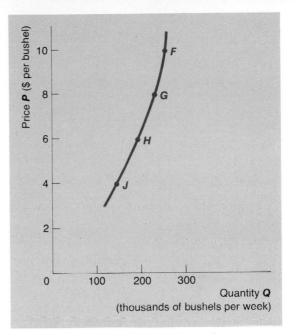

FIGURE 4-2   The supply curve for apples.
For each of the possible prices specified, the supply schedule (Table 4-2) tells how many units the sellers would be willing to sell. This information may alternatively be shown in Figure 4-2, which illustrates how the supply curve slopes upward to the right. At a high price, suppliers will be encouraged to step up production, and offer more apples for sale.

The demand schedule applies to a *specific population* and to a *specific time period*. (Clearly, the number of apples demanded during a month will exceed the number demanded during a week. And the demand by the people of Virginia will be less than the demand in the whole Eastern United States.) In a general discussion of theoretical issues, the population and time framework are not always stated explicitly, but it nevertheless should be understood that a demand curve applies to a specific time and population.

. . . and Supply

While the demand schedule illustrates how buyers behave, the supply schedule illustrates how sellers behave; it shows how much they would be willing to sell at various prices. Needless to say, sellers look at high prices in a different light from that of buyers. Whereas a high price will discourage buyers and cause them to switch to alternative products, a high price will encourage suppliers to produce and sell more of the good. Thus, the higher the price, the higher the quantity supplied. This is shown in Table 4-2, which translates into the upward sloping supply curve illustrated in Figure 4-2. As in the case of the demand curve, the points on the supply curve (F, G, H, and J) are drawn from the information in Table 4-2.

The Equilibrium of Demand and Supply

The demand and supply curves may now be brought together. To use the analogy of turn-of-the-century British economist Alfred Marshall, we may see how the two blades of the scissors jointly determine price. The two curves, for demand and supply, are shown together in Figure 4-3. (See also Table 4-3.)

The market equilibrium will occur at point *E*, where the demand and supply curves intersect. The price will move to $6 per bushel, and the quantity of sales to 200,000 bushels per week.

> An *equilibrium* is a situation where there is no tendency to change. Thus, an equilibrium represents a situation which can persist.

TABLE 4-3
The Equilibrium of Demand and Supply

(1) Price P ($ per bushel)	(2) Quantity Q demanded (thousands of bushels per week)	(3) Quantity Q supplied (thousands of bushels per week)	(4) Surplus (+) or shortage (−) (4) = (3) − (2)	(5) Pressure on price
10	50	260	Surplus +210	▮ Downward
8	100	240	Surplus +140	▼ Downward
6	200	200	0	**Equilibrium**
4	400	150	Shortage −250	▲ Upward

FIGURE 4-3 How demand and supply determine equilibrium price and quantity.
Equilibrium exists at point *E*, where the quantity demanded equals the quantity supplied. At any higher price, the quantity supplied exceeds the quantity demanded. Because of the pressures of unsold stocks, competition among sellers will cause the price to be bid down toward the equilibrium of $6.00. Similarly, at a price less than the $6.00 equilibrium, forces are set in motion to change the price. Because the quantity demanded exceeds the quantity supplied, eager buyers clamor for more apples, and bid the price up toward the equilibrium at $6.00.

To see why *E* represents the equilibrium, consider what will happen if the market price is initially at some other level. Suppose, for example, that the initial price is

$10; that is, it is above the equilibrium price. What will happen? Purchasers will buy only 50,000 bushels (shown by point *A* in Figure 4-3), while sellers will want to sell 260,000 bushels (point *F*). There will be a large *excess supply*, or *surplus*, of 210,000 bush-

> An *excess supply*, or *surplus*, exists when the quantity supplied exceeds the quantity demanded.

els. Some sellers will clearly be disappointed: They will sell much less than they wish at the price of $10. Unsold apples will begin to pile up. In order to get them moving, sellers will begin to accept a lower price. The price will start to come down—to $9, then $8. Still there will be a surplus, or an excess of the quantity supplied over the quantity demanded. (However, the surplus will now be a more modest amount, *BG*). The price will continue to fall. It will not stop falling until it reaches $6, the equilibrium. At this price, buyers purchase 200,000 bushels, which is just the amount the sellers want to sell. Both buyers and sellers will be satisfied with the quantity of their purchases or sales at the existing market price of $6. Therefore there will be no further pressure on the price to change.

Alternatively, suppose that the initial price is $4, below the equilibrium. Eager buyers will be willing to purchase 400,000 bushels (at point *D*), yet producers will be willing to sell only 150,000 bushels (at point

J). There will be an excess demand, or shortage, of 250,000 bushels. As buyers clamor for the limited supplies, the price will be bid upward. The price will continue to rise until it reaches $6, the equilibrium where there is no longer any shortage because the quantity demanded is equal to the quantity supplied. At point *E*, and only at point *E*, will the price be stable.

> An *excess demand*, or *shortage*, exists when the quantity demanded exceeds the quantity supplied.

SHIFTS IN THE DEMAND CURVE WHEN "OTHER THINGS CHANGE"

The quantity of a product which buyers want to purchase depends on the price. As we have seen, the demand curve illustrates this relationship between price and quantity. But the quantity which people want to purchase also depends on other things. For example, if incomes rise, they will want to buy more apples, and more of a whole host of other products, too.

The purpose of a demand curve is to show how the quantity demanded is affected by price, and *by price alone*. When we ask how much people will want to buy at various prices, it is important that our experiment not be disturbed by other factors. In other words, when a demand curve is drawn, *incomes and everything else* (except price) *that can affect the quantity demanded must be held constant*. In an economist's jargon, we make the *ceteris paribus* assumption—that other things remain unchanged. (*Ceteris* is the same Latin word that appears in "et cetera," which literally means "and other things." *Paribus* means "equal" or "unchanged.")

Of course, as time passes, other things do not remain constant. Through time, for example, incomes may rise. When that happens, the quantity of apples demanded at any particular price will increase. The whole demand curve will shift to the right, as

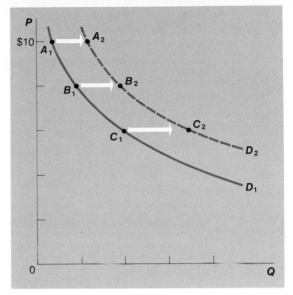

FIGURE 4-4 A change in the demand for apples.
When incomes rise, there will be an increase in the quantity of apples that people will want to buy at any particular price. At a price of $10, for example, the quantity of apples demanded will increase from point *A₁* to *A₂*. At other prices, the increase in incomes will also cause an increase in the quantity demanded. Thus, the whole demand curve shifts to the right, from *D₁* to *D₂*.

illustrated in Figure 4-4. Since economists use the term "demand" to mean the whole demand curve or demand schedule, we may speak of this rightward shift in the curve more simply as an increase in demand.

Demand Shifters

A shift in the demand curve (that is, a change in demand) may be caused by a change in any one of a whole host of "other things." Some of the most important are the following:

1. Income When incomes rise, people are able to consume more. For a typical or *normal* product, the demand curve shifts to the right with rising incomes, as illustrated in Figure 4-4.

There are, however, exceptions. As incomes rise, people may *switch away from* beans and potatoes and eat more steak, which they now can afford. When this happens—when, for example, the increase in income causes a leftward shift of the demand curve for potatoes—the item is an *inferior* good.

2. Prices of Related Goods A rise in the price of one good can cause a shift in the demand curve for another good.

For example, if the price of gasoline spirals upward, people will be less eager to own automobiles. The demand curve for cars will therefore tend to shift to the left as the price of gasoline increases. Such goods—goods used together, so that an increase in the price of one causes a decrease in the demand for the other—are *complementary goods*.

For *substitutes*, exactly the opposite relationship holds. For example, apples and pears are substitutes. If the price of pears were to double, buyers would be encouraged to switch to apples. A rise in the price of pears causes an increase in the demand for apples. So it is with other substitutes, such as tea and coffee, butter and margarine, bus and train tickets, or heating oil and insulating materials.

3. Tastes As time passes, tastes change. Perhaps as a result of increased TV coverage of tennis matches, perhaps as a result of a desire to keep in shape, more people are playing tennis. This trend increases the demand for tennis rackets and other tennis equipment. Tastes, and therefore demand, are quite volatile for some products, particularly fads such as skateboards or rock records.

This list covers some of the most important demand shifters, but it is far from complete. To see how it might be extended, consider the following questions:

1. If the weather changes, how will the change affect the demand for umbrellas? For skiing equipment?

2. If the President wears a hat during his inaugural drive up Pennsylvania Avenue, how might the demand for hats be affected?

3. If cars are expected to be priced $1,000 higher next year, how will the demand for cars this year be affected?

WHAT IS PRODUCED: The Response to a Change in Tastes

At the beginning of this chapter, three basic economic questions were listed. To see how the market mechanism can help to answer the first of these—*What* will be produced?—consider what happens when there is a change in tastes. Suppose, for example, that after watching *Upstairs, Downstairs* and other British programs on TV, Americans develop a desire to drink more tea and less coffee. The change in tastes is illustrated by a rightward shift in the demand curve for tea and a leftward shift for coffee.

As the demand for tea increases, the price is bid up by eager buyers. With a higher price, growers in Sri Lanka (Ceylon) and elsewhere are encouraged to plant more

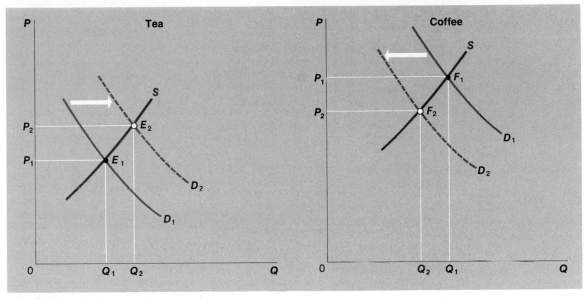

FIGURE 4-5 A change in tastes.
A change in tastes causes the demand for tea to increase and the demand for coffee to decrease. As a result, more tea is bought, at a higher price. Less coffee is bought, and the price of coffee falls.

tea. The equilibrium result, shown as point F_2 in Figure 4-5, involves a higher price and a greater consumption of tea. In the coffee market, the results are the opposite. At the new equilibrium (F_2), the price is lower and a smaller quantity is bought.

Thus, competitive market forces cause producers to "dance to the consumers' tune." In response to a change in consumer tastes, prices change. Tea producers are given an incentive to step up production, and coffee production is discouraged.

SHIFTS IN SUPPLY

But if the market makes producers "dance to the consumers' tune," the opposite is also true. As we shall now show, consumers "dance to the producers' tune," as well. Thus, the market involves a complex interaction, with sellers responding to the desires of buyers, and buyers at the same time responding to the willingness of producers to sell.

The supply curve is similar to the demand curve in one important respect. Its objective is to show how the quantity supplied is affected by price, and by *price alone.* Once again, the *ceteris paribus* assumption is made. When a supply curve is drawn, everything (except price) that can affect the quantity supplied is held constant.

Supply Shifters
As in the case of demand, the "other things" that affect supply can change through time, causing the supply curve to shift. Some of these "other things" are the following:

1. The Cost of Inputs For example, if the price of fertilizer goes up, farmers will be less willing to produce wheat at the previously prevailing price. The supply curve will shift to the left.

2. Technology If there is an improvement in technology, costs of production will fall. With lower costs, producers will be willing to supply more at any particular price. The supply curve will shift to the right. (These first two points illustrate the dependence of the supply curve on the cost of production. The precise relationship between production costs and supply will be considered in detail in Chapter 19.)

3. _Weather_ This is particularly important for agricultural products. For example, a drought will cause a decrease in the supply of wheat (that is, a leftward shift in the supply curve), and a freeze in Florida can cause a reduction in the supply of oranges.

4. _The Prices of Related Goods_ Just as items can be substitutes or complements in consumption, so they can be substitutes or complements in production.

Corn and soybeans are _substitutes_ in production. If the price of corn increases, farmers will be encouraged to switch their lands out of the production of soybeans and into the production of corn. The amount of soybeans they are willing to supply at any given price will decrease; the supply curve for soybeans will shift to the left.

Beef and hides are _complements_, or _joint products_. When more cattle are slaughtered for beef, more hides are produced in the process. An increase in the price of beef will cause an increase in beef production, which will cause a rightward shift of the supply curve of hides.

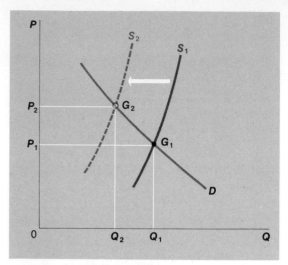

FIGURE 4-6 A shift in supply.
A freeze causes a leftward shift in the supply curve for coffee. The result is a movement of the equilibrium along the demand curve from G_1 to G_2. At the new equilibrium, there is a higher price, and a smaller quantity is sold.

The Response to a Shift in the Supply Curve

To illustrate how "consumers dance to the producers' tune," suppose that there is a frost in Brazil, which wipes out part of the coffee crop. As a result, the quantity of coffee available on the market is reduced. The supply curve shifts to the left, as illustrated in Figure 4-6. With less coffee available, the price is bid upward; the new equilibrium (at G_2) involves a higher price and a smaller quantity.

How will consumers respond to the change in supply? Because of the higher price of coffee, consumers will be discouraged from buying. Some consumers may be relatively indifferent between tea and coffee, and may be persuaded to switch to tea by the high price of coffee. Other consumers may be no longer able to afford coffee; they may retire completely from the market or may buy coffee only for very special occasions. Because of the limited quantity, it is not possible for all those who might like to drink coffee to get it. Anyone who is willing and able to pay the high price will get coffee; those who are unwilling or unable to pay the price will not get it. Thus, the high price acts as a way of allocating the limited supply among buyers. The coffee goes only to buyers who are sufficiently eager to be willing to pay the high price, and sufficiently affluent to be able to afford it.

SHIFTS IN A CURVE AND MOVEMENTS ALONG A CURVE: The Need to Distinguish

Because the term "supply" applies to a supply schedule or a supply curve, a change in supply means a *shift* in the entire curve. Such a shift took place in Figure 4-6 as a result of a freeze in Brazil.

In this figure, observe that the demand curve has not moved. However, as the supply curve shifts and the price consequently changes, there is a movement *along* the demand curve from G_1 to G_2. At the second point, less is bought than at the original point. The quantity of coffee demanded is less at G_2 than at G_1.

The distinction between a shift in a curve and a movement along a curve should be emphasized. As the equilibrium moves from G_1 to G_2:

1. It is correct to say that "supply has decreased." Why? Because the entire supply curve has shifted to the left.

2. It is not correct to say that "demand has decreased." Why? Because the demand curve has not moved.

3. It is, however, correct to say that "the quantity demanded has decreased." Why? Because a smaller quantity is demanded at G_2 than at G_1.

A similar distinction may be made back in Figure 4-5. In the first panel of that diagram, a change in tastes caused an increase in demand; the whole demand curve shifted. This change in the demand curve caused the equilibrium to move along the supply curve. It is incorrect to say that supply changed, since the supply curve did not move. But the quantity supplied did change; it increased as the price rose.

This is more than nit-picking. The distinction between a shift in a curve and a movement along a curve is important in avoiding a classic error. History does not give us diagrams showing demand and supply curves; it (sometimes) does give us quotations on prices and quantities. Suppose that, with a little research, we found that point E_1 in the first panel of Figure 4-5 was observed in 1976 and point E_2 in 1977. If we are not careful, we might jump to the following incorrect conclusion:

The theory of the demand curve tells us that a rise in price should cause a fall in the quantity demanded. In 1977, the price rose, but so did the quantity. Therefore, the facts contradict the theory of demand.

But, of course, the facts do no such thing. The error in logic is this: Between 1976 and 1977, the demand curve *shifted*. As it shifted, equilibrium moved *along* the supply curve. Thus, the two points E_1 and E_2 trace out the supply curve, not the demand curve. Moreover, these two observations are exactly what we would expect as we move along a supply curve. When the price rises, so does the quantity. (Unfortunately, the results are seldom this clear. The reason is that, as time passes, both the demand and supply curves may shift.)[2]

[2]Details: If the demand curve alone shifts to the right, then an increase in the price will be accompanied by an increase in the quantity sold (Figure 4-5). If, on the other hand, the supply curve alone shifts (to the left), then an increase in the price will be accompanied by a decrease in the quantity sold (Figure 4-6). If, finally, both the demand and the supply curves shift, we cannot tell whether an increase in price will be accompanied by an increase or a decrease in the quantity sold.

THE INTERCONNECTED QUESTIONS OF WHAT, HOW, AND FOR WHOM

In the previous pages, we have seen how two tunes are being played. Demand is the tune played by consumers, while supply is the tune played by producers. And we have also noted how each group dances to the tune played by the other.

But if we now want to go beyond the question of *what* will be produced to the other questions *(how? for whom?)*, we must recognize that the world is even more complex. We don't merely have two tunes being played. We have a whole orchestra, with the tune played on any one instrument related to the tunes played on all the others.

The various pieces of the economy are illustrated in Figure 4-7, which adds detail to Figure 3-3 (in Chapter 3). The product markets for wheat, oranges, coffee, etc., are shown in the upper box of the diagram; these are the markets on which we have concentrated thus far. But in the box at the bottom, we see that there are similar markets for factors of production, with their own demands and supplies. For example, to produce wheat, farmers hire workers and rent land. Thus, they create a demand for labor and land in the wheat industry. At the same time, individuals who work on wheat farms supply labor.

In answering the question, *What* will be produced? we began by looking at the top box, where the demand and supply for the various products are shown. If there is a large demand for tea and a small demand for coffee, we may expect much tea to be produced, and little coffee. But eventually we will also have to look at the lower box, which shows the demand and supply for the factors of production. Why is this relevant? Because the demand and supply curves in the upper box are influenced by what happens in the factor markets in the lower box.

As an example, consider what happens when oil is discovered in Alaska. To build the pipeline needed to get the oil out, workers have to be hired. As a consequence, the demand for construction labor in Alaska increases sharply. The wage rate in Alaskan construction shoots up, and workers flock in from the lower 48 states. The spiraling wage payments in Alaska (lower box) have repercussions on the demands for goods in Alaska (upper box). For example, the demands for food and housing in the upper box rise as a result of the increased earnings of construction workers in the lower box. (What happens to the price of a hotel room during the pipeline construction?)

How? and For Whom?

To answer the question, What will be produced? we began by looking at the upper box of Figure 4-7. To answer the questions How? and For Whom? we begin by looking at the lower box.

The prices established in the lower box help to determine *how* goods will be produced. During the Black Death of 1348–1350 and subsequent plagues, an estimated quarter to a third of the Western European population died. As a consequence, labor supply was dramatically reduced and wages rose sharply, by 30 to 40 percent.[3] Because of the scarcity of labor and its high price, wheat producers had an incentive to farm their lands with less labor. Wheat was produced in a different way, with a different combination of labor and land. The market mechanism was the way that the society in those days, as today, conserved its scarce supply of a factor (in this case, labor).

The answer to the question, *For whom* is the nation's output produced? depends on

---

[3]H. Robbins, "A Comparison of the Effects of the Black Death on the Economic Organization of France and England," *Journal of Political Economy*, August 1928, p. 463.

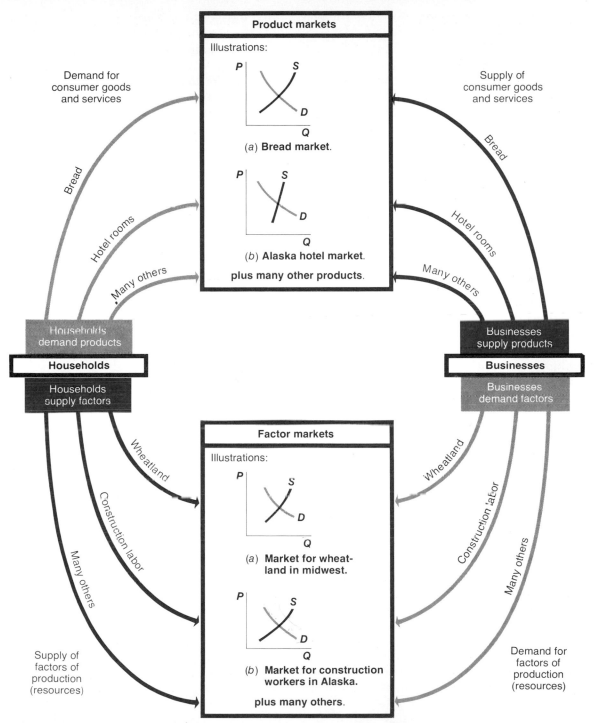

FIGURE 4-7 Markets answer the basic questions of what, how, and for whom.
The product markets (top box) are most important in determining **what** is produced, and the factor markets (lower box) in determining **how** goods are produced, and **for whom**. However, there are many interrelationships among the demand and supply curves in the two boxes. For example, incomes change in response to changing demand and supply conditions in the lower box, and these changing incomes in turn influence the demand for products shown in the upper box.

incomes. In the first instance, it is determined by the interplay of supply and demand in the lower box in Figure 4-7. For example, the supply of doctors is low compared with the demand for doctors; the price of medical "labor" is therefore high. As a consequence, many doctors have high incomes and live in expensive homes. On the other hand, unskilled labor is in large supply, and is therefore cheap. Consequently, the unskilled worker receives a low income. (For further detail on the demand and supply for labor, see Appendix 4-A.)

But, once again, we cannot look at only one box; there are influences from the upper box that must also be taken into account. For example, reconsider the Alaskan pipeline workers. We saw how the increase in demand for labor (in the lower box) drove their wage rate skyward. But that didn't mean that these workers lived like kings. Even though they had very high incomes, the Alaskan economy did not provide a large quantity of housing for them. Because of the tight supply conditions in the Alaskan housing market (upper box), housing prices soared. The construction workers' incomes went into paying these higher prices, rather than into a large increase in the quantity of housing. At least in terms of housing, these workers did not get a much larger share of the nation's output after all.

THE MARKET MECHANISM: A Preliminary Evaluation

There are thousands of markets in the United States, and millions of interconnections among the markets. Changes in market conditions are reflected in changes in prices. As we have seen, prices provide information to market participants; they provide them with incentives to respond to changing conditions; and they bring order out of a potentially chaotic situation—even though there is no individual or government bureaucracy in control.

Strengths of the Market

In some ways, the market works very well. For example:

1. The market gives producers an incentive to produce the goods that the public wants. If people want more tea, the price of tea is bid up, and producers are encouraged to produce more. (In contrast, where a government bureaucracy sets output targets, production may respond exceedingly slowly to changes in consumer tastes.)

2. The market provides an incentive to acquire useful skills. For example, the high fees that doctors charge give students an incentive to undertake the long and expensive training necessary to become a physician.

3. Goods which are particularly scarce sell at high prices. This encourages careful use. When the coffee crop is partially destroyed by bad weather, the price is driven up, and people use coffee sparingly. Those who are relatively indifferent are encouraged to switch to tea. Even those who feel they must have coffee are motivated to conserve. With a high price of coffee, they will be careful not to brew three cups when they intend to use only two.

4. Similarly, the price system encourages producers to conserve on scarce resources. In the pasture lands of Texas, land is plentiful and cheap; it is used to raise cattle. In Japan, in contrast, land is relatively scarce and expensive. Because of its high price, it is used more intensively. Rice is grown rather than livestock.

5. The market involves a high degree of economic freedom. Nobody forces people to do business with specific individuals or firms. People are not directed into specific lines of work by a government official; they are free to choose their own occupations. Moreover, if people save, they are free to use their savings to set themselves up in their own independent business.

6. Decentralized markets provide participants with information on local conditions. For example, if an unusual amount of hay-producing land in a specific county is plowed up to grow corn, then the price of hay in that county will tend to rise. The higher price of hay will signal farmers that they should put some of the land in this county back into hay. No government agency can hope to keep up-to-date and detailed information on the millions of localized markets like this one, each with its own conditions. (Note the amount of information that is relevant, even for this simple decision on whether hay or corn should be planted: the quality of the land, particularly its relative productivity in hay and corn; the number of cattle and horses that eat hay; the cost of fertilizer for hay and for corn; the cost of seed for each; and so on and on.)

In evaluating how well a market works, we should keep in mind the most important question of all: *compared to what?* Even a poor market may work better than the alternatives, particularly those that have been tried in the real world and not simply designed in an ideal theoretical framework. (For an example of some of the problems which arise when the government tries to override the market mechanism, see Box 4-1.) One of the strongest arguments for the market parallels Winston Churchill's case for democracy: It doesn't work very well, but it does work better than the alternatives.

The Market Mechanism: Limitations and Problems

While the market has impressive strengths, it is also the target of substantial criticisms:

1. While the market provides a high degree of freedom for participants in the economy, it may give the weak and the helpless little more than the freedom to starve. In a market, producers do not respond solely to the needs or the eagerness of consumers to have products. Rather, they respond to the desires of consumers which are backed up with cash. Thus, under a system of laissez faire, the pets of the rich may have better meals and better health care than the children of the poor.

2. An unregulated system of private enterprise may be quite unstable, with periods of inflationary boom giving way to sharp recessions. As we shall see in Chapter 11, the economy may be unstable in a number of circumstances; for example, when banks are unregulated (or incompetently regulated).

3. In a system of laissez faire, prices are not always the result of impersonal market forces. As noted earlier, it is only in a *perfectly competitive* market that price is determined by the intersection of a demand and a supply curve. In many markets, one or more participants have the power to influence price. The monopolist or oligopolist may restrict production in order to keep the price high. (For details, see Appendix 4-B.)

4. Activities by private consumers or producers may create side effects, or *externalities*. For example, because nobody owns the air or the rivers, manufacturers have used them freely as garbage dumps, harming those downwind or downstream. The private market provides no incentive to limit such externalities.

> An *externality* is an adverse (or beneficial) side effect of consumption or production, for which no payment is required (or no payment received).

5. In some areas, the market simply won't work. Where there is a military threat, the society cannot provide defense via the market. An individual has no incentive to

BOX 4-1
RENT CONTROL

Next to bombing, rent control seems in many cases to be the most efficient technique so far known for destroying cities, as the housing situation in New York City demonstrates.

Assar Lindbeck

New York City has had considerable experience with rent controls. Even if one wished to quibble with Lindbeck's devastating conclusion, the results cannot be considered encouraging.

The early effects of the imposition of rent controls are illustrated in the left panel of Figure 4-8. The maximum price which can legally be charged is set at P_1, below the free-market price of P_E. As a result, the quantity of housing demanded exceeds the quantity supplied; there is a shortage of AB units. As a consequence, it becomes difficult to find an apartment for rent. When a renter moves out, there is a scramble to get the vacant apartment, and "knowing the right person" becomes a valuable asset. The basic conclusion—that it will be hard to find an apartment if rents are controlled—is important.

But even bigger difficulties show up as time passes. Rent controls reduce the con-struction of new apartment buildings, because they reduce the rental income which owners can hope to receive. Furthermore, if rent ceilings are fixed at low levels, owners may let their buildings go without proper maintenance and repair. When the buildings eventually deteriorate to the point where they can't be rented, owners will abandon them (Lindbeck's bombing effect).

This longer-run effect is shown in the right panel, where the demand curve and the short-run supply (S_S) are copied from the left panel. During the first year of rent control, the quantity of apartments supplied is reduced to A, on the short-run supply curve (S_S). With the rent ceiling continuing at P_1, the effects become more serious as time passes. Because few new buildings are constructed and owners skimp on maintenance and abandon their older buildings, the quantity of apartments declines. After a few years, the number of apartments falls to F, and then to G. Finally it approaches point H on the long-run supply curve. [The long-run supply curve (S_L) shows the ultimate effect of a permanent change in rents.]

This illustrates the difficulties which can be created if rent controls are maintained over a long period. Over the short term, most

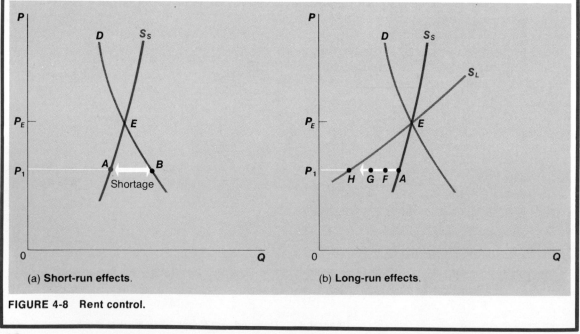

(a) **Short-run effects.**

(b) **Long-run effects.**

FIGURE 4-8 Rent control.

tenants benefit from the control. Observe that tenants pay a lower price, and they get about the same amount of housing at *A* as at the free-market equilibrium *E*. (Nothing much happens to the quantity of apartments supplied in the first year of rent control.) Over the long run, however, it is very doubtful that renters benefit after all. While they still pay a lower price, they have less housing at *H* than at *E*. It is very hard for newcomers to find a place to live. Furthermore, and this does not show up on this diagram: the housing that still can be rented at *H* may be shabby and run-down.

The other effect of rent control is that owners are clearly worse off, because their rental income has fallen. Since both sides lose, a substantial case can be made against long-term rent control.

The problems here are, of course, reasonably obvious, and were recognized in New York City. Several steps were taken to alleviate the situation. First, in order to provide an incentive for new construction, rent control was applied only to existing apartments, and not to apartments constructed after rent control began. Second, in order to give the owners enough income to maintain the buildings properly, provisions were made to raise rents through time. Apartment dwellers are a politically powerful group, however, so a rather interesting formula was devised for the rent increases. The rent on an apartment could be raised by 15 percent, but *only* when there was a change in tenants. Each time the tenants changed, the rent could be increased by another 15 percent.

This regulation in turn led to another complication. The rent on a specific apartment came to depend less on its quality than on the number of times it had changed occupants. This fact obviously made the rent control program harder and harder to defend as being "fair." And, since the rents could be raised only if tenants moved out, owners had an incentive to make life as miserable as possible for them. (Market incentives work. When the government puts a price on making tenants miserable, then owners will make tenants miserable.) Thus, it is not clear that the provision for increases in rents actually contributed to its objective of better maintenance; it may even have made maintenance worse.

The New York experience conveys a strong message. A sensible long-run program of rent control is very difficult to design. It is easier to see the problems than the solutions.

---

buy a rifle for the army, since the benefits go to the society as a whole, not to the individual. Thus, defense is a prime example of a service which can be best provided by the government. The police and the judicial system are others. No matter how well the market works in general, people can't be permitted to "buy" a judge.

6. In a system of laissez faire, businesses may do an admirable job of satisfying consumer demand as expressed in the marketplace. But why should these businesses be given high marks for satisfying wants that they may have created in the first place by advertising? In the words of retired Harvard Prof. John Kenneth Galbraith, "It involves an exercise of imagination to suppose that the taste so expressed originates with the consumer."[4] In this case, the producer (not the consumer) is sovereign. According to Galbraith, the consumer is a puppet, manipulated by producers with the aid of Madison Avenue's bag of advertising tricks. Many of the wants which producers create and then satisfy are trivial: the demands for deodorants, automobile chrome, and junky breakfast foods. Many of the radical Marxist economists of the New Left join Galbraith in this critique of the market.

[4]John Kenneth Galbraith, "Economics as a System of Belief," *American Economic Review*, May 1970, p. 474. See also Galbraith, *The New Industrial State* (Boston: Houghton Mifflin, 1967).

(Without arguing the merits of each and every product, defenders of the market system have a substantial countercase, based in part on the question: Compared with what? If market demands are dismissed, who then is to decide which products are "meritorious" and which are not? Some government official? Should not people be permitted the freedom to make their own mistakes? And how can Galbraith assume that created wants are without merit? After all, we are not born with a taste for art or good music. Our taste for good music is created when we listen to the producer of good music, like the Boston Pops. Should the all-wise government official close down the Boston Pops, on the ground that it satisfies only the want which it has created? Furthermore, Galbraith exaggerates when he argues that business firms can control their sales through advertising, and thus protect themselves from the vagaries of the market. Even after an intense advertising campaign, a product may flop, as the Ford Motor Co. found when it introduced the Edsel some years ago.)

If these six criticisms of the market are taken far enough, they can be made into a case for replacing the market with an alternative system of government direction. Marxist economists lay particular emphasis on the first and last points in their attack on market-oriented economies. But the six criticisms are also often made by those who seek to reform, rather than replace, the market system. The recent economic history of Western Europe, North America, and many other parts of the globe has to a significant extent been written by such reformers. If the market does not provide a living for the weak and the helpless, then its outcome should be modified by private and public assistance programs. If wildcat banking causes economic instability, the government should take responsibility for a stable and sound currency in order to provide a healthy environment for the market system. Where monopolists have excessive market power, they should be broken up or their market power restrained by the government. Where there are externalities, they can be limited by taxation or control programs. In defense, justice, the police, and other areas where the market won't work or will work very poorly, the government can assume responsibility for the provision of goods or services. (With a few notable exceptions, such as limits on cigarette advertising, there has been relatively little response to the sixth criticism. This is in part because of doubts that advertising substantially distorts tastes, and in part because of the intimate relationship between advertising and the press. Because the press is so heavily dependent on advertising, a curtailment of advertising might come at a high cost. It might financially weaken the press, an institution of great importance to a vigorous democracy.)[5]

Although the market is a vital mechanism, it has sufficient weaknesses to provide the government with a major economic role. This role will be the subject of the next chapter.

---

[5]To the New Left (Marxist) critics of the market, the support of the press by advertisers represents no advantage, but rather a disadvantage. The press is beholden to the big-business advertiser, and is not free in this very important respect.

Key Points

1. Every economy has limited resources and involves specialization and exchange. In every economy, a mechanism is needed to answer three fundamental questions:
   - (a) *What* will be produced?
   - (b) *How* will it be produced?
   - (c) *For whom* will it be produced?
2. There are two important mechanisms for answering these questions:
   - (a) The market; that is, the purchase and sale of goods and services by individuals who are free to make their own contracts and transactions.
   - (b) The government, which can influence *what, how*, and *for whom* by taxation and spending policies, by regulation, and by government-owned enterprises.

In the real world, all countries have "mixed" economies; that is, they rely partly on each of the two mechanisms. But the nature of the mix differs among countries. The United States places a relatively heavy reliance on the market. In the U.S.S.R. and other countries of Eastern Europe, broad areas of decision-making are reserved for the government.

3. *Prices* play a key role in markets, providing *information* and *incentives* to buyers and sellers.
4. Markets vary substantially, with some being dominated by one or a few producers, while others have many producers and consumers. A market is *perfectly competitive* if there are many buyers and many sellers, with no single market participant having any influence over the price.
5. In a perfectly competitive market, equilibrium price and quantity are established by the intersection of the demand and supply curves.
6. In drawing both the demand and supply curves, the *ceteris paribus* assumption is made—that "other things" do not change. Everything that can affect the quantity demanded or supplied (with the sole exception of price) is held constant when a demand or supply curve is constructed.
7. If any of these "other things" (such as consumer incomes or the prices of other goods) do change, the demand or supply curve will shift.
8. *What* the economy produces is determined primarily in the market for goods and services (the upper box of Figure 4-7). On the other hand, *how* and *for whom* are determined primarily in the factor markets (the lower box). However, there are numerous interactions among markets. The answer to each of the three questions depends on what happens in both the upper and lower boxes.
9. There is a substantial case to be made for the market, particularly because it encourages producers to make what people demand, and because it encourages the careful use of scarce goods and resources. But the market also has significant weaknesses, which provide the government with an important economic role.

Key Concepts

private market	imperfect competition	shortage	substitutes
central planning	market power	*ceteris paribus*	supply shifter
mixed economy	demand	demand shifter	joint products
monopoly	supply	inferior good	externality
oligopoly	equilibrium	normal or superior good	
perfect competition	surplus	complementary goods	

Problems

4-1 Figure 4-6 illustrates the effect of a Brazilian freeze on the coffee market. How might the resulting change in the price of coffee affect the tea market? Explain with the help of a diagram showing the demand and supply for tea.

4-2 The number of students going to university has declined. What effect do you think this has had on (*a*) tuition; (*b*) teachers' salaries?

4-3 In the subsection "*How?* and *For Whom?*" some of the effects of the discovery of oil in Alaska were considered briefly.

(*a*) Draw a demand and supply diagram illustrating what happened in the market for hotel rooms in Alaska. What happened to the price? To the quantity of hotel rooms?

(*b*) Do the same for the market for clothing in Alaska. Do you conclude that the results were the same in the clothing and hotel markets? Explain.

4-4 The relatively high incomes of doctors give students an incentive to study medicine. Other than the expected income, what are the important things which affect career decisions?

4-5 It is often said that "the market has no ethics. It is impersonal." But individual participants in the market do have ethical values, and these values may be backed up with social pressures. Suppose that in a certain society, it is considered not quite proper to work in a distillery. With the help of demand and supply diagrams, explain how this view will affect:

(*a*) The demand and/or supply of labor in the alcohol industry

(*b*) The demand and supply of capital in the alcohol industry

4-6 Suppose that social sanctions are backed up by law, and that persons caught selling marijuana are given stiff jail sentences. How will this affect the demand and supply of marijuana? The price of marijuana? The quantity sold? The incomes of those selling marijuana?

4-7 In Box 4-1, rent control is discussed. Extend the analysis by describing (*a*) the effects of rent control on the city's tax revenues; (*b*) what will happen if rent control is imposed for 20 years, and then abruptly removed.

*4-8 "Rent control which applies only to structures in existence when the rent control law is passed will not affect new construction." Do you agree or not? Explain.

*4-9 Some writers of the New Left attack both the market system of the United States and the government bureaucracy which has been established in the Soviet Union. Is there any third option? Other than the market and the government, what mechanisms might be used to answer the questions of *what, how*, and *for whom*?

*This question is more difficult.

Appendix 4-A

THE DEMAND AND SUPPLY FOR LABOR: The Malthusian Problem

If we wish to explain *specific* wage rates—for example, the high wage of construction workers in Alaska—we must look at that *specific* labor market. But we may also be interested in the average wage earned by *all* labor in an economy. In that case, we must look at the market for all workers.

This aggregate labor market is quite different from a specific market (like the market for construction workers). First, consider the supply. The supply curve for construction workers in Alaska slopes upward to the right: the higher the wage, the more workers will be attracted from other industries and other states. In contrast, the supply of labor for the United States as a whole is almost vertical (as shown in Figure 4-9). Even if the United States wage rate doubled, there would be little increase in the number of workers offering themselves for employment. The reason is that there are no "other industries" or "other states" from which workers can be attracted (although more workers might come in from other countries).

On the other hand, the demand curve for all United States labor does have the same general shape as the demand for labor in a specific industry. (It slopes downward and to the right.) The higher the wage rate, the fewer jobs will be offered. At a high wage rate, businesses have an incentive to use less labor (and more of other factors) in the production of goods and services. With the demand and supply curves shown, the equilibrium is at *E*.

Now, consider what happens through time. Population increases, and the supply curve for labor therefore shifts to the right. On the demand side as well, a major curve shifter is at work. As time passes, the quantity of capital (machinery and equipment) increases, and this causes the demand for labor to increase. Why? As the quantity of machines and other capital equipment increases, workers have more tools to work with. As a consequence, they can

FIGURE 4-9 The aggregate labor market.
For the labor market as a whole, the supply curve is approximately vertical. A doubling of wage rates will not cause a large increase in the number of people who are willing to work.

FIGURE 4-10 Shifts in the demand and supply of labor.

(a) **Japan.** A high rate of capital formation shifts the demand for labor rapidly to the right. At the same time, population grows very slowly, so that labor supply shifts very little. With labor demand outrunning supply, wages rise rapidly.

(b) **The Malthusian problem.** Countries with rapid population growth and a low rate of capital formation find that labor supply tends to outrun demand, and wages are under downward pressure.

produce more goods; that is, their productivity rises. Therefore, employers are more anxious to hire workers, and are able to pay them a higher wage.

With both the demand and supply curves for labor moving to the right, the net effect on wages depends on the relative strength of the two shifts. Consider the two cases illustrated in Figure 4-10. On the left is Japan, where recent population growth has been very small; the supply of labor has therefore moved only slightly to the right. At the same time, the Japanese have directed a large proportion of their productive capacity into the production of new factories and equipment. As a result of the increase in the quantity of capital, the demand curve for labor has moved rapidly to the right. The net effect has been a large increase in the Japanese wage rate.

In the second panel, the opposite situation is illustrated, namely, a problem which concerns the poorer developing countries. In a number of poor countries, population growth has been very rapid. Improvements in medical services have cut mortality rates while birth rates have remained high. As a result, the supply of labor has shifted rapidly to the right. At the same time, very poor countries have had trouble directing resources into the formation of capital. (Recall from Figure 2-5 that if they divert production away from satisfying their immediate consumption needs, some of the population may starve.) As a consequence, there has been little increase in the capital stock, and the demand curve for labor has shifted out much less rapidly than in a country such as Japan. As a result, wage rates in a number of the poorest countries have risen very little, if at all.

There is a wide variation among the less-developed (or poorer) countries. In some, per capita output has risen rapidly in the past two decades; in others, it has remained relatively stagnant. The least fortunate countries face the Malthusian problem, originally described by the young English clergyman Thomas Malthus in his *Essay on the Principle of Population* (1798). If productive capacity increases slowly while the birth rate is high, the wage rate may be driven down to the subsistence level and remain there.

The Malthusian problem is illustrated in the right-hand panel of Figure 4-10. Productive capacity increases slowly, and therefore the demand for labor shifts out only slowly from D_1 to D_2. With the high birth rate, the supply of labor would have shifted out at a more rapid rate, to S_3, but it has been prevented from doing so by a cruel law of nature. With labor supply S_3, the equilibrium wage rate would be at C, below the subsistence level (W_s). But it never does actually drop this far, because any tendency for it to drop below the subsistence level results in disease, malnutrition, and starvation. These disasters reduce the population to S_2, once more giving an equilibrium (B) with the wage at the subsistence level. During the nineteenth century, this came to be known as the *iron law of wages:* So long as the birth rate provides a natural tendency for population to outstrip any increases in productive capacity, wages will fall toward the subsistence level. Once there, they will remain at this subsistence rate. To escape from this iron trap, either or both of two events must occur. There must be an increase in productive capacity, and therefore in the demand for labor; or there must be a reduction in the birth rate.

This discussion, like other theoretical presentations, has of necessity involved simplifications, and a number of important issues emphasized by Malthus and his contemporaries have been passed over, such as the importance of land and other natural resources. Nevertheless, the main point is a valid and important one: Over the long haul, *the key to an increase in wages is an increase in productivity,* which comes mainly from an increase in the capital stock and improvements in technology.

Appendix 4-B

PRICE IS DETERMINED BY DEMAND AND SUPPLY CURVES ONLY IN A PERFECTLY COMPETITIVE MARKET

To see why it is only in a competitive market that the intersection of the demand and supply curves determines the price, consider the type of question which the supply schedule answers. If the price of apples were (say) $10 per bushel, how many apples would suppliers be willing to sell? This is a question which is relevant in a perfectly competitive market. Individual orchard owners indeed ask themselves how many apples they want to sell at the going market price. They know that they cannot affect that price, so each owner's decision is limited to the number of bushels to be sold.

But that is not the sort of decision a monopolist or oligopolist (like, say, Ford) has to make. It does not take the market price as given. Instead, it quotes a price for its product. (At the beginning of each model year, Ford states what the price of its cars will be.) Because companies like Ford set their own prices (rather than respond to a given market price), there is no supply curve for the auto industry.

On the other side of the market, a similar complication can arise. The demand curve is a meaningful concept only if there are many buyers, with none having any influence over price. In such a case, the demand-schedule question is relevant. If the price is, say, $10 per bushel, how many bushels will buyers be willing to purchase?

But in a market with only one buyer (monopsony) or only a few buyers (oligopsony), the individual buyer *can* influence price. Therefore the question a monopsonist will ask is not, "How many units will I buy at the given market price?" but rather, "What price shall I set?" Thus, for example, the only manufacturer in a small town will have monopsony power in the labor market, and will ask, "What wage rate shall I offer?" In such cases, where a single buyer sets market price rather than taking it as given, there is no demand curve.

The major market forms and the chapters in which they will be studied are outlined in Table 4-4.

TABLE 4-4
Types of Markets

Type	Characteristic	Is demand curve meaningful?	Is supply curve meaningful?	How is price determined	Studied in Chapter(s)
Perfect competition	Many buyers and sellers, with no single market participant affecting price	Yes	Yes	By intersection of demand and supply curves	4, 7–10
Monopoly	One seller, many buyers	Yes	No	By seller	11, 18
Monopsony	One buyer, many sellers	No	Yes	By buyer	18
More complex cases					12, 18

Appendixes 4-A and 4-B
Key Points

10. The wage rate depends on the demand and supply of labor.

11. Increases in the productivity of labor will cause the demand for labor to increase. Increases in the quantity of capital are a principal cause of increases in the productivity of labor.

12. Population growth is the main cause for an increase in the supply of labor.

13. If the demand for labor shifts out faster than the supply of labor, wages will be pulled upward. If the supply shifts out faster than demand, the wage will be depressed. If the tendency for population to increase keeps the wage at a very low level and under downward pressure, the country faces the Malthusian problem.

14. Price is determined by the intersection of the demand and supply curves only in a perfectly competitive market.

Key Concepts

supply of labor in a specific market
supply of labor in the nation as a whole
productivity of labor

Malthusian problem
iron law of wages
monopsony

Problem

4-10 (*a*) Suppose you are the manager of a local drug store. What do you think the supply curve of clerks looks like?

(*b*) What does the supply curve of labor facing General Motors in Michigan look like?

(*c*) What is the supply curve for all labor in the United States like?

(*d*) Explain why the curves in parts *a*, *b*, and *c* have different shapes.

chapter 5
The Economic Role of the Government

As new conditions and problems arise beyond the power of men and women to meet as individuals, it becomes the duty of the Government itself to find new remedies with which to meet them.
Franklin D. Roosevelt

The defects and limitations of the market system, outlined at the end of Chapter 4, provide the government with an important role in the economy. In the words of Abraham Lincoln, a legitimate objective of government is "to do for the people what needs to be done, but which they cannot, by individual effort, do at all, or do so well, for themselves."

Government affects the economy in three major ways: by *spending*, by *taxation*, and by *regulation*. For example, when the government spends for roads or for aircraft, then production is affected; more roads and aircraft are built. The primary function of taxation is to raise revenue for the government; taxes are an unpleasant necessity. But taxes may also be used for secondary purposes; for example, to discourage the production of some goods or to change the distribution of income. Finally, the government can influence economic behavior

through direct regulation. Regulations regarding seat belts and other safety equipment have affected the design of automobiles; safety requirements affect the way in which coal is mined; and government regulations limit the amount of pollution which manufacturers can discharge into the air and water.

In contrast with the private market where people have an option of buying or not, government activities generally involve compulsion. Taxes must be paid; people are not allowed to opt out of the system when the time rolls around for paying income taxes. Similarly, government regulations involve compulsion; car manufacturers are required to install safety equipment. And compulsion sometimes exists even in a government spending program. Young people must go to school (although their parents do have the option of choosing a private school rather than one run by the government).

72

Later sections of this chapter will consider how the government can use expenditures, taxation, and regulations to improve the outcome of the private market. As a preliminary, it is necessary to look at some facts—how the government role has expanded, and what the government is currently doing.

THE GROWTH OF GOVERNMENT EXPENDITURES

During the nineteenth and early twentieth centuries, the government restricted spending to a relatively small range of activities. Government expenditures covered little more than the expenses of the army and navy, a few public works, and the salaries of judges, legislators, and a small body of government officials. Except for wartime periods when spending shot upward to pay for munitions, weapons, and personnel, government spending was small. As late as 1929, all levels of government (federal, state, and local) spent less than $11 billion a year. Of this total, about three-quarters was spent at the state and local levels. Highway maintenance and education were typical government programs. Life was simple. (This does not mean, however, that a rigid policy of laissez faire was followed. Even during the nineteenth century, governments at both the state and local levels participated in some important sectors of the economy. For example, they supported the expanding railroad and canal systems.)

With the Depression of the 1930s, a major increase in government activity began. Distress and unemployment were widespread, and it was increasingly hard to believe that the workings of the private market would lead to the best of all possible worlds. During the decade 1929–1939, federal government spending increased from $3 billion to $9 billion. Part of the increase was specifically aimed at providing jobs through new agencies, such as the Civilian Conser-

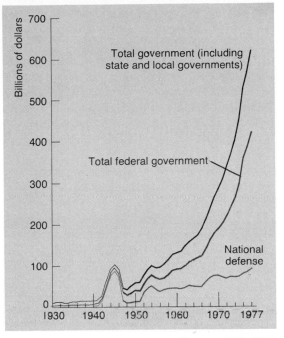

FIGURE 5-1. Government expenditures, 1929–1977. Governments in the United States now spend over 50 times as much money in a year as they did in 1929. Federal government spending has risen particularly rapidly during military conflicts (from 1941 to 1944, 1950 to 1953, and 1965 to 1969). In the past decade, nondefense expenditures by federal, state, and local governments have accounted for the big increases.

vation Corps (CCC). Then, when the United States entered the Second World War in 1941, huge government spending was required to pay for military equipment and for the salaries of military personnel.

With the coming of peace in 1945, the nation demobilized and government spending fell by more than 50 percent. But the decline was only temporary. Over the past three decades, spending at all levels of government has increased rapidly, to total no less than $621 billion in 1977 (Figure 5-1).

Government Expenditures in Perspective

Clearly, government spending has become very large. Indeed, it is hard for the average citizen, accustomed to dealing with a family budget measured in hundreds or thousands of dollars, to comprehend government budgets measured in billions. A billion dollars may be more meaningful if it is reduced to a personal level: A billion dollars represents almost $5 for every man, woman, and child in the United States. Thus, with total budgets approximating $600 billion, our federal, state, and local governments spend an average of $3,000 per person. (The magnitude of a billion dollars may be illustrated in another way. When the government borrows $1 billion at an interest rate of 7 percent per annum, its interest payments amount to $200,000 per *day*.)[1]

The rapid increase in spending has in part been a reflection of the additional responsibilities undertaken by government. During the 1930s, innovations included the social security system, whose principal function is the payment of pensions to retired people. More recently, the government has undertaken programs to provide medical assistance to the needy and to the elderly. Other programs to improve the lot of the needy have also grown rapidly. Furthermore, expenditures for weapons and other military purposes have remained high for the past three decades because of both the increasing complexity (and cost) of armaments and the cold war competition with the Soviet Union.

But the raw data of Figure 5-1 can give a misleading impression of the size of the government in our economy. While the government is spending more and more, so are private individuals and businesses. For both the government and the private sectors, these rising expenditures reflect two major trends: More and more goods and services

are being bought, and at higher and higher prices. We can see government expenditures in better perspective when we look at them, not in dollar terms (as done in Figure 5-1), but rather as a percentage of the total output of the economy.[2]

When we take the latter viewpoint (in Figure 5-2), the increase in government expenditures becomes much less dramatic. Indeed, defense spending, which accounts for a major chunk of the federal government's budget, actually declined from 10 percent of national output in the late 1950s to less than 6 percent by the late 1970s, although there was a bulge during the escalation of the fighting in Vietnam.

Government Purchases versus Transfers

A further complication in measuring the size of the government arises because of the two different categories of government expenditures: (1) government *purchases of goods and services*, and (2) government *transfer payments.*

Government purchases of goods include items such as typewriters, computers, and aircraft. The government purchases services when it hires schoolteachers, police officers, and employees for government departments. When the government purchases such goods and services, *it makes a direct claim on the productive capacity of the nation.* For example, when it spends $600 for a typewriter, then steel, rubber, and labor are used to manufacture the typewriter. Similarly, the purchase of services involves a claim on productive resources. The police officer hired by the government must spend time on the beat, and thus becomes unavailable for work in the private sector.

[1]Hugh Rutledge, in the *Indianapolis News*, has explained a billion this way:
"One billion seconds ago, the first atomic bomb had not been exploded.
"One billion minutes ago, Christ was still on earth.
"One billion hours ago, men were still living in caves.
"Yet, one billion dollars ago (in terms of government spending) was yesterday."

[2]The measure of total output—gross national product (GNP)—is explained in Chapter 7.

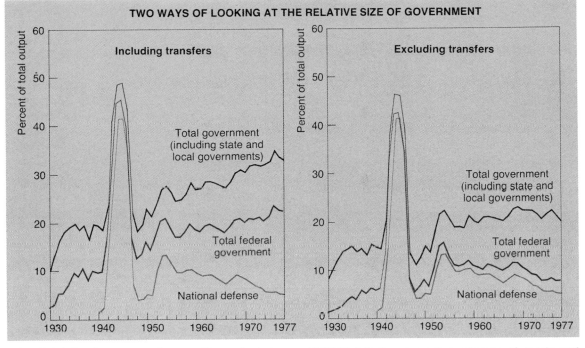

TWO WAYS OF LOOKING AT THE RELATIVE SIZE OF GOVERNMENT

Including transfers

Total government (including state and local governments)

Total federal government

National defense

Excluding transfers

Total government (including state and local governments)

Total federal government

National defense

FIGURE 5-2 Total government expenditures (including transfers).
If we look at what the government takes for itself plus what it takes to redistribute in the form of transfers, then the government has laid claim to a larger and larger share of total output.

FIGURE 5-3 Government purchases of goods and services.
However, government purchases of goods and services have not changed much over the past two decades, as a percentage of total output.

Government *transfer payments*, on the other hand, are payments for which the recipient does not provide any good or service in return. Welfare expenditures and government insurance payments fall into this category. Welfare payments to families with dependent children are transfer payments, and so are social security benefits received by the elderly. In contrast with government purchases, transfer payments represent no direct claim by the government on the productive capacity of the nation. For example, social security benefits paid by the government to retired people do not involve a reallocation of the nation's product away from the private sector toward the government sector. Unlike the typewriter company that manufactures a typewriter and ships it to the government to get the payment of $600, the social security recipient provides neither a good nor a service in return for the benefit. This does not mean, of course, that the social security system is without importance. When the government collects social security taxes[3] from workers and employers and pays benefits to retirees, the pattern of consumer spending is affected. The old have more to spend, and workers have less. As a

[3]Payments into the social security fund are sometimes called contributions, on the ground that individuals acquire a right to pensions and other benefits as a reward for their payments. But it is also correct to label the contributions as taxes, since they are involuntary payments which must be made to the government. (Furthermore, while benefits bear some relation to the "contributions" which an individual has made, they are not closely tied to previous "contributions.")

consequence, producers find themselves faced with greater demands for the things that old people want, and with smaller demands for the products desired by the working population. Social security affects the amount of the nation's product that various individuals can purchase. But the large social security program does not involve a major redirection of the economy toward production for the government.

> A *transfer payment* is a payment by the government to an individual, for which the individual does not provide a good or service in return. Social security benefits, unemployment compensation, and welfare payments are examples of transfers.

As an alternative to total government expenditures (including transfers) which were shown in Figure 5-2, another way of measuring the size of the government is to look only at the expenditures that make a claim on the productive resources of the economy, and that involve a direction of our productive efforts toward the government sector. That is, we may look only at government purchases of goods and services, shown in Figure 5-3. Observe that as a percentage of national output, government purchases of goods and services are approximately what they were two decades ago. Purchases by state and local governments have gone up, but these increases have been approximately matched by the declining percentage for the federal government.

We can thus get two quite different impressions of the government's size, compared with that of the overall economy. If we look only at purchases of goods and services, then the percentage of total output going to the government has been quite stable (Figure 5-3) over the past two decades. If, on the other hand, we include transfers and look at total government expenditures (Figure 5-2), the government's

percentage is increasing. As a percentage, the government is not directly claiming a larger and larger share of the nation's output for itself. But is *is* claiming a larger and larger share, to be *redistributed* in the form of social security, welfare, and other transfer payments.

The main trends of the past two decades, as shown in Figures 5-2 and 5-3, may be summarized. As a percentage of total output:

1. Government purchases of goods and services have been stable. An expansion at the state and local levels has been approximately matched by a decline at the federal level.

2. Government transfers have risen rapidly. (This increase shows up in the contrast between Figure 5-2, which includes transfers, and Figure 5-3, which excludes them.)

3. Defense expenditures have fallen.

INTERNATIONAL COMPARISONS

While the government is a major participant in the United States economy, the governments in Europe assume an even larger role. Table 5-1 shows that the tax burden is rela-

TABLE 5-1
Taxes as a Percentage of Total Output, 1976

Sweden	43	United States	28
Italy	38	Japan	19
United Kingdom	38	India	15
France	36	Philippines	12
West Germany	35		

As a general rule, governments in high-income countries tax and spend more, relative to national output, than do governments in low-income countries. However, the United States and Japan are partial exceptions to this rule: In spite of their high incomes, their governments tax at a lower rate than the governments of Western Europe.

Sources: International Monetary Fund; Organization for Economic Co-operation and Development; United Nations tively heavy in Europe. Sweden heads the list; taxes are high, to pay for the extensive welfare, health care, and other services provided to the public. Also note that, in spite of its free enterprise image, Germany collects almost as large a tax share as does the United Kingdom, France, or Italy; it has a well-developed system of pensions, health care, and other government services. In general, the percentage of income collected in taxes is lower in the poorer countries—15 percent in India and 12 percent in the Philippines. However, there is no rigid relationship between high incomes and high tax collections. In spite of its rapid achievement of a standard of living similar to Western Europe's, Japan has remained a low-tax country, collecting only about half as large a share in taxes as do the Western European countries.

THE BUDGET OF THE FEDERAL GOVERNMENT

Details on federal government expenditures in the United States, and on the taxes that finance these expenditures, are provided in Table 5-2. (This table includes both purchases of goods and services, and transfer payments.) While much of the federal budget continues to be directed toward military expenditures, a larger and larger percentage is going toward the meeting of human needs. Indeed, in 1974, income security (which includes social security benefits, unemployment insurance payments, and some of the federal welfare budget) passed national defense to become the largest single category of expenditure. In addition to income security, federal government expenditures for health have risen particularly rapidly,

TABLE 5-2
The Budget of the Federal Government, 1979
(estimated)

	Billions of dollars	Percentage of total
Budget receipts		
Individual income taxes	$190	43%
Social insurance contributions and taxes	142	32
Corporation income taxes	62	14
All other	46	11
Total budget receipts	$440	100%
Budget outlays		
Income security	$160	32%
Defense	118	24
Health	50	10
Interest on debt	49	10
Education, training, employment, and social services	30	6
Veterans benefits and services	19	4
Transportation	17	3
Natural resources and environment	12	2
All other	45	9
Total budget outlays	$500	100%
Budget deficit (outlays minus receipts)	$ 60	

Source: Council of Economic Advisers, Annual Report, 1978, p. 339.

TABLE 5-3
Federal Income Taxes for a Married Couple with No Dependent Children, 1977

(1) Taxable personal income	(2) Personal income tax	(3) Average tax rate (3) = (2) ÷ (1)	Marginal tax rate (tax on additional income)
Below $ 3,200	$ 0	0.0%	0%
4,000	42	1.1	14
5,000	190	3.8	15
10,000	1,016	10.2	19
20,000	3,304	16.5	28
50,000	14,224	28.4	50
100,000	43,080	43.1	60†
200,000	$108,592	54.3	69†
Above $203,200	—	—	70†

†There is a maximum marginal tax rate of 50 percent on earned income (that is, income from wages, salaries, and professional fees). Rates above 50 percent apply to unearned income from interest, dividends, royalties, etc.

increasing from $13 billion in 1970 to an estimated $50 billion by 1979.

Federal Receipts

On the receipts side, the *personal income tax* is the largest source of federal government revenue. This tax is levied on taxable personal income; that is, on the incomes of individuals and families after the subtraction of exemptions and deductions.[4] For a childless married couple, the personal income tax is levied at the rates shown in Table 5-3.[5]

Observe that the average tax paid rises as a percentage of income as incomes rise (Table 5-3, column 3); the income tax schedule is *progressive*.

Note also the concept of the *marginal tax rate* shown in the last column; this is the rate on *additional* income. For example, in the tax bracket with income between

$19,200 and $23,200, the marginal tax rate is 28 percent. Within this bracket, if income rises by $100 (for example, from $20,000 to $20,100), $28 more must be paid in taxes. It is the higher and higher marginal tax rates which pull up the average tax rate as incomes rise.

If a tax takes a larger percentage of income as income rises, the tax is *progressive*.

If a tax takes a smaller percentage of income as income rises, the tax is *regressive*.

If a tax takes a constant percentage of income, the tax is *proportional*.

While income taxes remain the largest single component of federal government revenues, social insurance taxes (to pay for social security and unemployment insurance) have been rising most rapidly. Social security contributions, or taxes, are paid in order to finance old-age pensions, payments

[4]In order to calculate your taxable income, you may subtract an exemption of $750 for you and for each of your dependents from your gross income. You may also subtract deductions for medical care, charitable contributions, interest payments, and taxes which have been paid to state and local governments, to the extent that these deductions exceed the "zero tax bracket." (For a married couple, the zero tax bracket is the $3,200 shown in the first line of Table 5-3.)

[5]The personal income tax is complicated; a number of details are left out of Table 5-3. For example, under the 1975 tax law, those with incomes of less than $8,000 pay less than shown in the table, and the poorest may receive a payment from the government.

to the families of contributors who die or are disabled, and payments for Medicare (medical benefits for the elderly). In 1978, the tax stood at 12.1 percent of wages and salaries up to a maximum income of $17,700; half the tax is collected from the employer, and half from the employee. Social security taxes have been increased repeatedly in order to finance the rapid increase in social security payouts, which reflect congressional decisions to increase benefits and to tie benefits to the rising cost of living. Legislation passed in 1977 provided for the tax to rise to 13.4 percent by 1983, with the maximum income subject to tax rising to $34,800.

Note that the social security tax is *regressive*. It is collected at a flat percentage on incomes up to a current (1978) limit of $17,700; any additional income is exempt from the tax. Thus, the tax constitutes a higher percentage of the income of an individual making $10,000 per year than of one making $30,000.

Corporate income taxes constitute the third most important source of federal revenue. The tax is collected at a flat rate of 48 percent of all profits above $50,000. (There is a lower rate on the first $50,000.) Minor

amounts of revenues are brought in by other taxes, such as excise taxes (on items such as cigarettes, alcoholic beverages, and gasoline) and customs duties imposed on goods imported into the United States.

The government's revenues have fallen short of its expenditures in most years, including 1978. The government borrows the difference, mostly from corporations (including banks) and from individuals.

STATE AND LOCAL GOVERNMENTS

Education is the biggest expenditure of state and local governments, accounting for 38 percent of the total (Table 5-4). Highways and welfare account for other large chunks of the budgets. (Some welfare programs, such as food stamps for the needy, are paid for entirely by the federal government. Other programs, among them Aid for Families with Dependent Children, AFDC, are partly financed by the federal government and partly by state and local governments.) Other important state and local expenditures include those for police and fire protection, hospitals, and interest on the debt.

On the revenue side, states tax some of

TABLE 5-4
State and Local Government Revenues and Expenditures
(fiscal year 1975–1976)

	Billions of dollars	Percentage of total
Revenues		
Property taxes	$ 57	22
Revenue from federal government	56	22
Sales and gross receipts taxes	55	21
Individual income taxes	25	10
Corporation income taxes	7	3
All other	56	22
Total revenues	$256	100%
Expenditures		
Education	$ 97	38%
Public welfare	32	12
Highways	24	9
All other	104	41
Total expenditures	$257	100%

Source: Council of Economic Advisers, *Annual Report, 1978,* p. 345.

the same items as the federal government. Most states (and some local governments) have personal and corporate income taxes. Note, however, that income taxes provide a much smaller percentage of revenues at the state and local levels than at the federal level. Sales taxes are the largest source of revenues for state governments, and property taxes are the biggest source for local governments.

Revenue Sharing

More than one-fifth of the spending of state and local governments is financed by grants from the federal government. Prior to 1972, virtually all federal government aid to states and localities took the form of "categorical" grants, tied to specific programs such as education or health care. Not only did the money come with strings attached; it also required *matching* state and local funds. In 1972, a new law was passed, providing for *general* revenue sharing—that is, grants from the federal government on a (practically) unrestricted basis. Six billion dollars per year were distributed to the states, with the proviso that two-thirds be passed along to local governments. The size of the grant for each state depended on (1) the state's population, (2) the tax effort of the state and its localities (that is, the height of its taxes), and (3) the state's per capita income. This third provision had the objective of directing funds to the neediest states. The second guideline was the most controversial, since its objective was to encourage state and local governments to spend, rather than to use the federal money to lighten tax burdens. The general revenue-sharing program, introduced on a trial basis in 1972, was extended for another 4 years by 1976 legislation.

Revenue sharing involves grants from the federal government to state and/or local governments. Revenue sharing is said to be *general* when it comes without restrictions on how it may be spent.

Revenue sharing was motivated by the financial squeeze on state and local governments. These governments have had to face some of the most pressing problems; the public has clamored for more and more of the services provided at the state and local levels. But the revenues of state and local governments didn't change much. The federal government got the lion's share of the increases in tax revenues.

Consider, specifically, the major sources of tax revenue at each level of government: for the federal government, this is the personal income tax; for state governments, the sales tax; and for local governments, the property tax. Because of progressive tax rates, economic growth causes federal income tax revenues to rise, not only in absolute terms, but also as a fraction of income. Furthermore, the tax schedule is specified in dollar terms (Table 5-2). Thus, inflation also moves people up into higher tax brackets and increases the percentage of their incomes which must be paid to the federal government. As a machine for extracting money from the public, the income tax is a marvelous invention (or a terrible one, depending on your viewpoint). On the other hand, the sales tax revenues of the states are sticky, rising less rapidly than incomes. Why is this so? As incomes rise, people spend a larger percentage of their incomes on services, which are not taxed, and a smaller fraction on goods, which are taxed. The stickiness of sales tax revenues can be overcome by an increase in the *rate* of taxation, but state governments have understandably been reluctant to raise tax rates. Finally, on the local level, property taxes tended for many years to be quite sticky; local governments were also reluctant to increase tax rates. However, with the rapid escalation of housing prices in recent years, property tax revenues have likewise escalated. But all locations have not benefited equally from rising property values. These values have risen most rapidly in growing, prosperous localities, and they have remained relatively stable (or have even fallen) in declining areas with high unemployment. Yet it is these declining areas that are particularly in need of revenues to finance social services.

Because of the financial problems of states and localities, revenue sharing is expected to be a long-term feature of United States public finance. (Canada and Australia have long had revenue-sharing programs.)

GOVERNMENT REGULATION

The government budget, amounting to hundreds of billions of dollars, has a substantial effect on the types of goods produced and on who gets these goods. But the budget cannot be taken as the sole measure of the government's economic impact. Business behavior is significantly influenced by regulatory programs, even though these programs show up as very small items in the government's budget. (The administrative costs of the major regulatory agencies account for only 2 to 3 percent of the total budget of the federal government.) Indeed, most of the costs of government regulations appear in the budgets of private firms, rather than in the budget of the government itself. For example, it has been estimated that by the early 1980s, regulations of the Environmental Protection Agency (EPA) will require expenditures of $40 billion per year by private firms to control pollution.[6]

During the past century, a series of governmental agencies has been established to limit the most flagrant abuses of private business. In 1887, the Interstate Commerce Commission (ICC) was established to regulate rates and other aspects of railroad transportation between states. The Sherman Act (1890) declared business mergers leading to monopoly to be illegal. Then the Federal Trade Commission (FTC) was established in 1914 in the belief that monopolies should be prevented before the fact, rather than punished after they are established. (Although the FTC's power has been circumscribed by the courts, it still plays a role in limiting business concentration. For example, in 1977, Kennecott divested itself of Peabody Coal to comply with an FTC order which had been upheld by the Supreme Court.) And, since the 1930s, the FTC has had the power to protect the consumer against deceptive advertising practices.

There are many other regulatory agencies. For example, the Food and Drug Administration (FDA) has been charged with determining the effectiveness and safety of drugs before they are permitted on the market. The financial shenanigans of the 1920s (which contributed to the collapse into the Depression) led in 1933 to the establishment of the Securities and Exchange Commission (SEC) to regulate financial markets. For example, the SEC requires corporations to disclose information about their finances. (Joseph Kennedy, the future President's father, was appointed head of the SEC by Franklin Roosevelt.) Banks are extensively regulated by the Federal Reserve System, the Federal Deposit Insurance Corporation, the Comptroller of the Currency, and state regulatory agencies. The Federal Power Commission (FPC), Federal Communications Commission (FCC), Federal Aviation Administration (FAA), and the Civil Aeronautics Board (CAB) regulate power, broadcasting, and aviation. The Equal Employment Opportunity Commission (EEOC) is charged with preventing discrimination in employment.

In recent years, there has been an upswing in regulatory activity, with the addition of (among others) the Environmental

---

[6]Council on Environmental Quality, *Environmental Quality: Seventh Annual Report* (Washington, 1976), p. 145. Allen V. Kneese and Charles L. Schultze put the figure higher: They estimate that by the early 1980s, $60 billion per year will be spent to meet pollution-control laws. Kneese and Schultze, *Pollution, Prices, and Public Policy* (Washington: The Brookings Institution, 1975), p. 76.

Protection Agency (EPA), the Commodity Futures Trading Commission (CFTC), and the Occupational Safety and Health Administration (OSHA).

In many areas, regulation is relatively uncontroversial. For example, few would doubt the desirability of a government agency to certify the airworthiness of aircraft. Similarly, there is widespread support for government regulation aimed at keeping unsafe drugs off the market. (The FDA blocked the introduction of thalidomide, which caused birth defects when used in Europe.) Indeed, each of the regulatory agencies was established to deal with a problem area where the free market had been tried and found wanting.

Problems with Government Regulation

However, doubts have set in after the flurry of regulatory activity of the 1960s and early 1970s. Some of the debate has been quite heated—for example, the controversy over laetrile, which the FDA banned because of lack of evidence of its effectiveness as a treatment for cancer. The opponents asked a pointed question: What right does the government have to deny the terminally ill any treatment that their doctors wish to prescribe? The FDA has also come under criticism for delaying the introduction of drugs of demonstrated effectiveness that seem to be reasonably safe after extensive use in other countries. (No drug, of course, is *perfectly* safe—not even aspirin.) But the harshest criticism has been directed at the newer agencies, particularly the Occupational Safety and Health Administration. OSHA has been charged with harassing businesses and with a lack of perspective. While some industrial occupations remain hazardous, OSHA has left itself open to ridicule by

issuing trivial regulations, including a detailed order on the precise design of ladders and a solemn warning to farmers that they should beware of manure-covered cement floors (they're slippery).

What is needed is a sense of balance. The private market mechanism has substantial defects. Corporations cannot on their own be counted on to pay sufficient attention to safety or to protect the environment from pollution. But government agencies also have defects; they are not run by superhumans capable of solving all our problems. At some point, we should live with the defects of the market. In some cases, the cure may be more costly than the defects themselves.

Following the rapid increase in government activities in recent decades, public opinion surveys indicate a general disenchantment with government regulation. (In a 1977 survey of business economists, 28 percent—up from 8 percent in 1975—ranked excessive government controls as the most important economic problem.) Indeed, the chairman of President Carter's Council of Economic Advisers, Charles L. Schultze, observed:

> There is a growing body of objective evidence that government is not performing its new tasks effectively. . . . Efforts to improve the environment, while far from a failure, are unnecessarily expensive and increasingly bogged down in Rube Goldberg regulations. . . . Even the sympathetic observer finds it hard to recognize many of the regulations [of OSHA] as anything *but* absurdities.[7]

Regulation in the public interest is made particularly difficult because of the political clout of producers. (This fact also

---

[7]Charles L. Schultze, *The Public Use of Private Interest* (Washington: The Brookings Institution, 1977), p. 4.

Concern over the government's ability to deliver on its promises also has been growing in other countries. In Canada, retired senior civil servant Wynne Plumptre concluded that a number of countries (including Canada) "have launched programs which, however worthy individually, collectively outran their financial and administrative competence. The result has been inflation and a proliferation of bureaucratic bungling."

complicates other types of economic policy, including government spending and taxation.) When regulations are being developed, the affected industry makes its views known forcefully. Yet the views of consumers and taxpayers are diffuse and often remain underrepresented. Thus, for example, the regulation of airline fares seems directed more at protecting the airlines than at protecting the traveling public. (This does not mean that business always benefits from regulations. Government regulation contributed to the bankruptcy or near bankruptcy of a number of railroads in the early 1970s. And we have seen in Chapter 4 how rent controls can adversely affect apartment owners.) In an extensive study of regulatory agencies in 1977, the Senate Government Operations Committee concluded that the public is outnumbered and outspent by industry in regulatory proceedings. The committee chairman, Senator Abraham Ribicoff, observed that regulatory hearings "can be likened to the biblical battle of David and Goliath—except that David rarely wins." This conclusion should come as no surprise. For decades, an irreverent definition has circulated in Washington: A sick industry is one which cannot capture control of its regulatory agency.

The predominance of producer influence is not simply the result of a conspiracy of wealth. Rather, it is an intrinsic feature of a highly specialized economy. Each of us has a major, narrow, special interest as a producer; and each of us has a minor interest in a wide range of industries whose goods we consume. We are much more likely to react when our particular industry is affected by government policy; we are much less likely to express our diffused interest as consumers. Narrow producer interests are expressed not only by business, but also by labor. Unions concentrate their attention on events in their particular industry, even though the union members are also consumers, using a wide range of products. (This prevalence of producer influence, it should be reiterated, is primarily a result of modern technology and a high degree of specialization; it is not primarily a result of our particular system. It exists in a wide variety of political-economic systems, including those of Britain, France, Germany, Japan, and the Soviet Union.)

THE ECONOMIC ROLE OF THE GOVERNMENT: What Should the Government Do?

With government budgets reaching hundreds of billions of dollars, and with an extensive list of government regulations, the United States economy is clearly a substantial distance away from a pure market system of laissez faire. What principles and objectives guide the government when it intervenes? In part, government intervention is based on deep social attitudes that are often difficult to explain. Twenty years ago, Americans could look askance at government-financed, "socialized" medicine in Britain, yet at the same time they could consider British education "undemocratic" because of the important role of privately financed elementary and secondary schools. The British, on the other hand, were proud of their educational system, and were puzzled by what they considered a quaint, emotional American objection to public financing of medical care. (During the past two decades, the gap between the two societies has narrowed, with increasing governmental involvement in medicine in the United States and some decline in the relative importance of privately financed education in Britain.)

The government intervenes in the economy for many reasons; it is hard to summarize them all. But we may look at five of the main ones.

1. What the Private Market Can't Do: Pure Public Goods

Consider the largest single item of the federal budget, namely, defense expenditures. For obvious political reasons, defense cannot be left to the private market. The prospect of private armies marching around the country is too painful to contemplate. But there are also economic reasons why defense is a responsibility of the government.

The difference between defense and an average good is the following. If I buy food at the store, I get to eat it; if I buy a movie ticket, I get to see the film; if I buy a car, I get to drive it. In contrast, if I want a larger, better equipped army, my offer to purchase a rifle for the army will not add in any measurable way to my security. My neighbor, and the average person in Alaska, Michigan, or Texas, will benefit as much from the extra rifle as I do. In other words, the benefit from defense expenditures goes broadly to the citizens as a group; it is not directed specifically toward the individual who is willing to pay. Because people are not excluded from the benefits of defense expenditures, whether they actually pay for them or not, defense must be provided collectively, by the government. Defense is one example of a *pure public good.*

A *pure public good* is one with benefits that people cannot be excluded from enjoying, regardless of who pays for the good.

Another example of a pure public good is a lighthouse. Every ship is protected from the rocks, whether its owner has agreed to support the lighthouse or not. People who don't buy a ticket to the theater can be kept out; but those who don't pay for the lighthouse cannot be asked to look the other way. In these circumstances, the market won't work. If people are left to individual action, each has an incentive to hold back in the hope that others will pay for the lighthouse. (While building a lighthouse requires collective action, it may not require government activity. An association of shipowners may build it, although a problem may arise if some owners decide to stay out of the association and become "free riders.")

2. Externalities

The term *externality* is used to designate the effect (good or bad) of an action upon persons or businesses other than those who have undertaken that action. One example of an externality is a pure public good, one where the benefits are open to all regardless of who actually pays for the item. A more ambiguous case occurs where much of the gain goes to the owner of the good, while some peripheral benefits go to others.

The term *externality* applies to external benefits and to external costs.

An *external benefit* is a favorable effect on one or more persons that results from the action of a different person or business.

An *external cost* is an unfavorable effect on one or more persons that results from the action of a different person or business.

There are countless examples of *external benefits.* When individuals are immunized against an infectious disease, they receive a substantial benefit; they are assured that they won't get the disease. But others gain too; they are assured that the inoculated individuals will not catch the disease and pass it along to them. Similarly, families obtain most of the gain resulting from the upkeep of their homes. But neighbors and passersby benefit from more pleasant surroundings when families mow their lawns, shovel the snow off their walks, or paint their houses.

External costs may exist, as well as external benefits. For example, when people drive to work, they create an externality by adding to air pollution. The cost is borne by those who breathe the polluted air.

Because of the effects on others, the government may wish to encourage activities which create external benefits and to discourage those with external costs. It can do so with the use of any of its three major tools: expenditures, regulations, or taxation. The government spends money for public health programs, for the immunization of the young. It has regulations on the types of automobiles which can be built, in order to reduce pollution. And taxes on gasoline or on polluting factories may likewise be used to discourage pollution.

The existence of an externality does not in itself make a compelling case for government action; the government should not be concerned with insignificant externalities or other trivial matters.[8] Thus, private incentives are generally enough to ensure that homes will be painted; the government does not usually intervene. (Government programs to clean up the slums are, however, partially justified on the basis of the external benefits.) Similarly, while some communities have local ordinances which require that lawns be mowed, they are only loosely enforced. Most homeowners have enough incentive of their own to mow their lawns, and external benefits are small. (Snow-removal ordinances are more common and more likely to be enforced. Can that be because of a greater benefit to passersby?) However, externalities (and our concern over them) may grow through time. While little was done about pollution two decades ago, major efforts are now directed toward cleaning up the air and water.

3. Merit Goods

Government intervention may also be based on the paternalistic view that people are not in all cases the best judges of what is good for them. According to this view, the government should encourage "merit" goods—those that are deemed particularly desirable—and discourage the consumption of harmful products. People's inability to pick the "right" goods may be the result of short-sightedness, ignorance, addiction, or manipulation by producers. (Recall Chapter 4's brief discussion of Galbraith's views on created wants.)

In some cases, the government attempts merely to correct ignorance in areas where the public may have difficulty determining (or facing?) the facts. The requirement of a health warning on cigarette packages is an example. But, in other instances, the government goes further, to outright prohibition, as in the case of heroin and other hard drugs.

The view that "the government knows best" is generally greeted with skepticism; the government intervenes relatively sparingly to tell adults what they should or should not consume. (Children are, however, another matter; they are not allowed to reject the "merit" good, education.) However, substantial government direction does occur in welfare programs, presumably on the ground that those who get themselves into financial difficulties are least likely to make wise consumption decisions. Thus, part of the assistance to the poor consists of food stamps and housing programs rather than outright grants of money. In this way, the government attempts to direct consumption toward housing and milk for the children, rather than (perhaps) toward liquor for an alcoholic parent.

4. Helping the Poor

The market is generally efficient in providing the goods and services desired by those with the money to buy, but it provides

---

[8]The government does not always adhere to this rule of thumb. Many laws and regulations can be found that scarcely seem necessary. For example, spitting against the wind was made unlawful in Sault Ste. Marie, and punching a bull in the nose was prohibited in Washington, D.C. It is rather difficult to imagine how those particular laws got on the books.

With a sufficiently grim imagination, we can perhaps guess how other unnecessary regulations were enacted, such as the Pittsburgh regulation against sleeping in a refrigerator, or the Arkansas law against the blindfolding of cows on public highways. These, and many other examples, may be found in Barbara Seuling's book *You Can't Eat Peanuts in Church and Other Little-Known Laws* (Garden City, N.Y.: Doubleday, 1975).

little for the poor. In order to help the impoverished and move toward a more humane society, programs have been established to provide assistance for old people, the handicapped, veterans, and the needy.

There is much resentment of the "welfare mess," and it does not all come from bigots who despise the poor. Because there were so many new programs introduced in a relatively brief period, particularly in the 1960s, it is perhaps inaccurate to speak of a welfare "system" at all. Recent presidents have struggled with this problem, and proposals for major reform have included Nixon's family assistance program (not enacted) and Carter's welfare proposals. The difficulty lies in how to reconcile conflicting objectives. How can a living income be provided to the needy without severely weakening the incentive to work? How can assistance be provided to abandoned mothers without giving fathers an incentive to desert their families? How can the poverty-striken be helped with housing without creating ghettos of the poor? There are no easy answers to such questions. But the search for solutions has been moved to a high priority. The reforms proposed by Carter were designed so that the poor who work would be better off than if they didn't work; they would not have their welfare benefits reduced by the amount of their earnings.

5. The Government and Economic Stability

Finally, if we go back to the beginning of the upswing in government activity—to the Depression of the thirties—we find that the primary motivation was not to affect the kinds of products made in the economy, nor specifically to aid the poor. Rather, the problem was one of the *quantity* of production. With unemployment rates running over 10 percent of the labor force year after year, the problem was to produce more—more of almost anything would help put people back to work.

The government role in providing a high level of employment and economic stability is so important that it will be a major topic of Parts 2 and 3 (Chapters 7 through 16).

TAXATION

The art of taxation consists of plucking the goose so as to obtain the largest amount of feathers with the least possible amount of hissing.
Jean Baptiste Colbert
Seventeenth-century French statesman

The major objective of taxation is to raise revenues—to obtain feathers without too much hissing. But other objectives are also important in the design of a tax system.

1. Neutrality . . .

In many ways, the market system works admirably. Adam Smith's "invisible hand" provides the consuming public with a vast flow of goods and services. As a starting point, therefore, a tax system should be designed to be neutral. That is, it should disturb market forces as little as possible, unless there is a compelling reason to the contrary.

For the sake of illustration, consider a far-fetched example. Suppose that blue cars were taxed at 10 percent, and green cars not at all. This tax would clearly not be neutral regarding blue and green cars. People would have an incentive to buy green cars; blue cars would practically disappear from the market. A tax which introduces such a distortion would make no sense.

This illustration is, of course, silly. But real taxes do, indeed, introduce distortions to some degree. For example, several centuries ago, houses in parts of Europe were taxed according to the number of windows. As a result, houses were built with fewer windows. To a lesser degree, the current property tax introduces perverse incentives. If you have your house painted and your roof repaired, the government's evaluation of your house (the *assessed value*) may be raised and your taxes thereby increased. Therefore, property taxes encourage you to let your property deteriorate.

The problem is that all taxes provide incentives to alter one's behavior in order to reduce their impact. So long as taxes must be collected, complete neutrality is impossible. The objective of the tax system must therefore be modest: to aim toward neutrality. As a starting point in the design of a tax system, the disturbance to the market that comes from taxation should be minimized.

2. . . . And Nonneutrality: Meeting Social Objectives by Tax Incentives

There is, however, an important modification which must be made to the neutrality principle. In some cases, it may be desirable to disturb the private market.

For example, the government might tax polluting activities, so that firms will do less polluting. The market is disturbed, but in a desirable way. Another example is the tax on cigarettes, which, in addition to its prime objective of raising revenue for the government, also discourages cigarette consumption. (Unfortunately, government policies are not always consistent. The government taxes cigarettes, forbids the advertising of cigarettes on TV, and requires health warnings on cigarette packages. But then the government turns around and subsidizes the production of tobacco.)

Taxation and regulation reflect different approaches aimed at correcting the failures of the private market. Regulation aims at overriding the market mechanism, forbidding or limiting specific behavior on the part of business. Taxation aims at using the basic market system, but making it work better. When there are externalities, such as pollution, the signals of the market are incomplete; businesses or individuals who pollute the air do not have to pay the cost. Taxation of externalities can improve the outcome of the market by making the signals facing businesses and individuals more complete; taxation makes them pay a penalty for polluting.

Of course, markets may not work very well because of beneficial externalities, rather than negative ones. In this case, the market signals may be made more accurate and complete by a government *subsidy*. For example, in order to reduce the nation's dependence on imported oil, President Carter combined a subsidy on small cars with a tax on "gas guzzlers" in his proposals to Congress.

A *subsidy* is the opposite of a tax. For example, a tax on automobiles requires a payment to the government for every automobile sold. A subsidy on automobiles would involve a payment by the government to the manufacturer (or to the purchaser) for every automobile sold (or bought).

3. Simplicity

To anyone who has wasted the first two lovely weekends of April sweating over an income tax form, simplicity of the tax system is devoutly desired. Of course, we live in a complex world, and the tax code must to some degree reflect this complexity. But, as a result of decades of tinkering, the United States income tax has become ridiculously complex. (See Box 5-1.) Indeed, it has become so complex that the Internal Revenue Service itself frequently gives incorrect answers to taxpayer inquiries. Some observers (including former Treasury Secretary William Simon) have recommended scrapping the old code and writing a new one from scratch.

4. Equity

Taxation represents coercion; taxes are collected by force if necessary. Therefore, it is important that taxes both be fair, and give the appearance of being fair. There are, however, two alternative principles for judging fairness.

BOX 5-1
MEET YOUR TAX CODE†

The Ways and Means Committee has before it this year a considerable list of proposed alterations in the nation's tax system. It is a fair bet, however, that the committee's tinkering will only further complicate that monument to obscurity, the Internal Revenue Code.

Decades of incessant tinkering, of putting in more and more kinks and convolutions, has produced a tangle that even tax experts cannot find their way through.

Abundant Bafflement

When the federal income-tax law was written in 1913 as a section of the Underwood Tariff Act, it provided for a tax of 1 percent on income over $4,000, rising to 6 percent on income over $500,000. There were few loopholes. It was a pure tax designed to raise revenue. Even so, the measure was ominously verbose—8,000 words.

In the sixty-three years since, that section of a tariff act has grown into a monstrosity. Today's revenue code, with its multitudinous deductions, credits, special-treatment provisions, and exceptions to exceptions, runs to something like 1.5 million words. While the code also covers a variety of other taxes, the greater part of it deals with corporate and personal income taxes. Treasury Department regulations explaining the provisions of the code sprawl over close to 6,000 pages in six hefty volumes. In addition, it takes 110 volumes to contain the Internal Revenue Service rulings on what the regulations mean.

Regulations and rulings galore are necessary, for the Internal Revenue Code's verbosity is matched by its obscurity. Section 341(E), which deals with collapsible corporations, is famous for the challenge it poses to a reader. Connoisseurs regard its opening sentence of 600 words as a masterpiece of thorny writing. But many other passages in the code can almost match it.

IRS instructions for filling out individual income-tax returns run to 150,000 words. The resulting taxpayer bafflement has made tax-return assistance a sizable industry. About half of the nation's 80 million tax filers use the

†Abridged from *Fortune,* March 1976, p. 143.

services of tax preparers. At the seasonal peak in the early spring, some 250,000 Americans are gainfully employed in helping other Americans cope with their tax returns.

Throw the Machine Away

When legislators in Washington recognize a tax problem they tend to go at it obliquely rather than head-on. An illustrative example was the congressional reaction to the disclosure that 155 taxpayers with incomes in excess of $200,000 had paid no federal income tax at all in 1967. The Ways and Means Committee felt obliged to do something quickly. But the committee did not proceed to tighten or abolish tax preferences that enable the rich to avoid taxes. Instead, the committee decided to impose what it called a minimum tax.

This proved to be exceedingly hard to comprehend—a major reason why the Tax Reform Act of 1969 was dubbed the Lawyers and Accountants Relief Act. The measure was also so ineffective that Congress felt constrained to rewrite it the following year. Each successive Congress has operated on this section again, and it is still weak.

Banker Walter Wriston, chairman of Citicorp, has come to the conclusion that "the tax machine has been so badly designed that no tinkering can help. It is time to throw the machine away." Both Wriston and [former] Secretary of the Treasury William Simon call for wiping away nearly all the deductions, preferences, credits, etc. and establishing a simple progressive tax, with hardly any ifs, ands, or buts in it. (Wriston would still allow deductions for state and local taxes, "to avoid paying taxes on taxes.") With nearly all avenues of tax avoidance closed off, rates could come way down.

Such an apocalyptic reform is probably not feasible in a complex economy pervaded by adaptions to present tax law. But certainly simplification of the Internal Revenue Code is long overdue. As Simon put it, "the present tax system is so riddled with exceptions and complexities that it almost defies human understanding."

The Benefit Principle Since the purpose of taxation is to pay for government services, taxes may be designed according to the benefit principle: Those who gain the most from government services should be required to pay the most. If this principle is adopted, then a question arises: Why not simply set prices for government services, which people can voluntarily pay if they want the services? In other words, why not charge a price for a government service, just as General Motors charges for cars? This approach may work—for example, for a toll road from which drivers can be excluded if they do not pay. But it will not work for public goods that benefit people even if they do not pay; for example, defense, disease control programs, a lighthouse, and air traffic control. It is the function of the government to determine whether total benefits make such programs worthwhile. Once the decision is made to go ahead, people must be required to support the program through taxes. If the benefit principle of taxation is followed, it is up to the government to estimate how much various individuals and groups benefit, and to set taxes accordingly. (Individual citizens cannot be allowed to provide the estimates of how much they benefit personally; they have an incentive to understate their individual benefits in order to keep their taxes down.)

Ability to Pay If the government sets taxes according to the benefit principle, it does not redistribute income; people are simply taxed in proportion to their individual benefits from government programs. If the government wishes to redistribute income, it can set taxes according to the _ability to pay._ The basic measures of the ability to pay are income and wealth.

If the government were to levy a progressive income tax and an inheritance tax

(and at the same time provide assistance to those at the bottom of the economic ladder), it would substantially redistribute income from the rich to the poor. But the world is not so simple. The government levies many other taxes as well, and when they are all taken together, it is not so clear that the government is taking a substantially larger percentage of the income of the rich than of the poor, as we shall see in the next section.

THE BURDEN OF TAXES: Who Ultimately Pays?

It is difficult to determine who bears the burden of many of our taxes. For example, consider the relatively simple social security tax. Half this tax is deducted from the take-home pay of the worker. This half is regressive. An employee receiving $10,000 per year pays a larger percentage in social security taxes than does an employee receiving $30,000. But what about the other half of the tax which is levied on the employer? Does the tax come out of the corporation's profits? Or is it passed on to the consumer in the form of higher prices? Or, possibly, this half may also fall on the worker: Without the social security tax, the employer might be willing to pay a higher wage.

And, if the question of tax burden—of who ultimately pays—is complicated for the social security tax, it is even more complex for many other taxes. We simply do not have a very precise idea of who ultimately bears the burden of taxes.

The burden, or "incidence," of all United States taxes—federal, state, and local—has been studied by Joseph Pechman and Benjamin Okner, two economists at the Brookings Institution (a Washington public policy research institution). In their study entitled _Who Bears the Tax Burden,_[9] they made several estimates reflecting differences

[9]Joseph A. Pechman and Benjamin A. Okner, _Who Bears the Tax Burden?_ (Washington: The Brookings Institution, 1974).

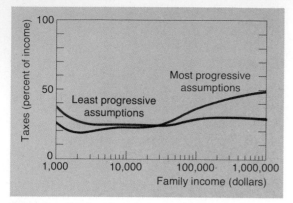

FIGURE 5-4 Total federal, state, and local taxes, as a percent of income.
The incidence of the combined federal, state, and local taxes depends on the assumptions. On the least progressive assumptions, with the corporation and property taxes being passed on in the form of higher prices and rents, the tax system is approximately proportional. (SOURCE: Joseph A. Pechman and Benjamin A. Okner, *Who Bears the Tax Burden?* Washington: The Brookings Institution, 1974, p. 4.)

of opinion among economists regarding tax burdens. Their results are summarized in Figure 5-4. The blue curve shows the burden when the most progressive assumptions are made; the red curve, the least progressive.[10] Somewhat surprisingly, on any of the assumptions made by Pechman and Okner, the United States tax system is not highly progressive. Indeed, if one were to accept Pechman and Okner's "least progressive" assumptions, it could be argued that our tax system is not progressive at all: The red curve is approximately horizontal. This lack of progressivity (in spite of the highly progressive income tax schedule, shown in Table 5-3) is due to two major factors: (1) proportional or even regressive taxes, such as the employees' half of the social security tax and a number of taxes at the state and local levels; and (2) the existence of tax "loopholes," which are of particular benefit to the wealthy in reducing their tax payments.

Tax Loopholes

"Loopholes" are provisions of the law which permit the reduction of taxes. (Thus, those who use the loopholes are acting perfectly *legally* to *avoid* taxes, and should be sharply distinguished from those who act *illegally* to *evade* taxes, perhaps by padding their deductions or understating their incomes.) The term *loophole* clearly implies that the tax provision is unfair, and, as there can be strong disagreement over just what *is* fair (Box 5-2), there is likewise some disagreement over just what constitutes a loophole. However, here are some of the items which are often put on the list.

1. Investment Tax Credit

When a corporation or individual acquires business equipment, it is permitted to deduct 10 percent of the price of that equipment from its tax bill. In some cases, this credit may be large enough to completely wipe out the tax obligation of the corporation or individual. (Thus, President Carter owed no income tax at all for the year 1976 because of the tax credit on equipment acquired by the family peanut business. He did, however, make a voluntary payment to the government in lieu of taxes.)

2. Domestic International Sales Corporation (DISC)

By setting up a subsidiary company, a corporation can defer the taxes on some of the profits from its export sales.

---

[10]According to the most progressive assumptions, property and corporation income taxes are paid by the well-to-do owners of property and corporations, and not passed on to the public in the form of higher prices. According to the least progressive assumptions (on which the red curve is constructed), corporation income taxes are passed on to the general public in the form of higher prices for the goods which corporations sell, and property taxes are passed on in the form of higher rents.

3. Depletion Allowances

Extractive industries, such as oil and copper mining, are allowed to deduct a fraction of the value of their sales in determining profits. Two arguments are used to defend these depletion allowances: They compensate the corporation for the reduction in the value of the mine (since there is less copper or oil left in the ground), and they help to attract investment into risky enterprises.

4. Tax-exempt Securities

If you buy state or local government bonds, the interest income you earn from them is exempt from federal income tax. Similarly, interest income from federal government bonds is exempt from state and local taxes. Thus, individuals and corporations (including banks) can reduce their income taxes by buying government bonds.

5. Capital Gains

When an asset is sold for more than it cost, the seller has made a *capital gain.* For example, if you buy General Motors stock for $1,000 and later sell it for $1,500, you have made a $500 capital gain. Capital gains are generally taxed at half the rate of ordinary income from wages or salaries.

6. Deduction of Interest

In calculating taxable income, individuals are permitted to deduct the interest which they pay on loans. This provision is of particular benefit to those who are making large interest payments on home mortgages.

The existence of these (and other) loopholes has led to much criticism. In 1976, Presidential candidate Jimmy Carter called the tax system a "disgrace to the human race" because of the many special exemptions and deductions. There are, however, three major complications that have so far prevented a comprehensive tax reform. First is the disagreement over just what is fair.

A *tax credit* is a subtraction from the tax payable. (For example, if a $1,000 machine is bought, the 10 percent investment tax credit means that $100 can be subtracted from the taxes paid to the government.)

In contrast to a tax credit, a *deduction* is a subtraction from taxable income. Suppose an individual pays $1,000 in interest on a home mortgage. This $1,000 can be deducted from taxable income. For someone in the 36 percent tax bracket, this results in a $360 reduction in taxes. (Note that the tax saving depends on the tax bracket. Thus, a $1,000 deduction reduces taxes more for someone in a 36 percent tax bracket than for a person in a lower tax bracket.)

During the 1976 Presidential campaign, Carter mentioned interest deductions (item 6) as one of the tax provisions that he wanted to change. His proposal led to strong objections from those who felt that it was only fair for the average family to get some tax break, and the item was quietly dropped from the list of tax reforms. Indeed, the dispute over what is fair inspired Senator Russell Long to a few lines of poetry. The typical attitude, he observed, is, "Don't tax you; don't tax me; tax the fellow behind that tree." (A 1977 poll found that the public favored tax reform by a 2 to 1 majority. But, the poll also revealed that, to most people, "tax reform" meant only "lower taxes.")

The second complication is the political problem. Clearly, those who benefit from loopholes have an incentive to lobby for their continuation.

Finally, reform is complicated by the fact that fairness is only one of the major objectives in a tax system. Most of the loopholes were put in expressly to promote national goals which the proponents considered important. For example, the investment tax credit was introduced, at President Kennedy's request, to stimulate investment. DISC was initiated to promote exports. The depletion allowance and capital gains treatment are justified as incentives to take risks.

Prior to the tax reform act of 1969, single people had a complaint. As the tax law was then designed, married couples got a tax break. For the married couple, each tax bracket was twice as wide as for a single person. Thus, for example, the single individual with an income of $15,000 was in the same tax bracket (that is, had the same marginal tax rate) as a married couple with an income of $30,000.

To meet the complaint of singles, the tax law was changed by the reform of 1969. No longer were brackets for married couples twice as wide as for single individuals. But this led to another complication. Consider two people (Jack and Joan), each with $15,000 in gross income, who married in 1977. After their marriage, they could no longer file as single individuals. And, as the tax brackets for marrieds were no longer twice as wide as for singles, their combined income of $30,000 pushed them up into a higher tax bracket. (Their marginal tax rate on additional income became 36 percent, compared with the 29 percent they would have paid as singles.)

Furthermore, this married couple faced other tax disadvantages. Rather than itemizing deductions for medical expenses, interest, etc., people are permitted to take a *standard deduction* in calculating their incomes subject to tax. For singles, the standard deduction (also known as the *zero tax bracket*) is $2,200; for a couple, it is $3,200, or only $1,600 per person. Finally, people are permitted a tax credit, with an upper limit of $180 for each single person and $180 per married couple.

As a result of these provisions of the tax law, Jack and Joan found their taxes increased when they married. Compared with their unmarried friends (Dick and Jane), they paid $1,018 more in tax in 1977, as shown in Table 5-5. To avoid such a "marriage tax," which must be paid each year, some couples threatened divorce, and some were even reported to have gone through with it. (As a result of criticisms, Congress reduced the marriage tax in 1977. For a couple with a combined income of $30,000, the marriage tax had been even higher—$1,286—in 1976.)

(To see why such apparently preposterous results can creep into the tax law, study problem 5-6, which illustrates how difficult, or even impossible, it may be to design a fair tax system.)

Tax-exempt securities are defended on the gound that they allow state and local governments to borrow at lower interest rates and thus ease the financial pressures on those governments. Interest-rate deductions are supported because they encourage home ownership and thus contribute to a stable society.

Indeed, the desire to achieve such national goals led to an ironic development during the first year of the Carter Presidency. Once he actually was in office, the candidate who had labeled the tax system a "disgrace" proceeded to propose a series of new credits and deductions, including:

- A home insulation tax credit, included in the energy proposals as a way to encourage fuel conservation

- A conservation credit, to allow a higher investment tax credit for energy-saving equipment

- A solar tax credit, to encourage conversion to solar heating

Each of these proposed credits is aimed at a worthy goal. But some of the arguments for special tax treatment are more convincing than others. Furthermore, the question

TABLE 5-5
The Marriage Tax

		Dick Jane (just friends)		Jack Joan (married)	
		Dick	Jane	Jack	Joan
1.	Gross income	$15,000	$15,000	$15,000	$15,000
1a.	Married couple's combined income			$30,000	
2.	Standard deduction (zero tax bracket)	$ 2,200	$ 2,200	$ 3,200	
3.	Personal exemptions	$ 750	$ 750	$ 1,500	
4.	Tax paid on [(4) = (1)−(2)−(3)]	$12,050	$12,050	$25,300	
5.	Gross tax	$ 2,645	$ 2,645	$ 6,128	
6.	Tax credit	$ 180	$ 180	$ 180	
7.	Net tax [(7) = (5) − (6)]	$ 2,465	$ 2,465	$ 5,948	
8.	Combined tax for two people	$4,930		$ 5,948	
9.	Marriage tax ($5,948 − $4,930)			$ 1,018	
10.	*Addendum:* Marginal tax rate on any additional income	29%	29%	36%	

should be asked: Is the tax system the best way to promote diverse national goals?

Unfortunately, there is no all-purpose answer to this question. Many economists favor the use of taxes for some purposes, say, to discourage pollution. But few favor using taxes to promote exports through the DISC. (Indeed, DISC is at the top of most lists for tax reform.) In taxation, as in so many areas of economics, the policymaker is left with the problem of balancing conflicting national goals.

Key Points

1. The defects and limitations of the market provide the government with an important economic role. The government affects the economy through expenditures, taxation, and regulation.

2. In dollar terms, government spending has skyrocketed since 1929. However, as a percentage of total output, the growth has been much slower. Indeed, if only purchases of goods and services are counted, the government's share of total output has been quite stable over the past two decades.

3. Of the federal expenditures, transfer payments have risen much more rapidly than expenditures for goods and services.

4. Personal income taxes, social security taxes, and corporate income taxes are the main sources of revenue for the federal government. At the state level, sales taxes are the most important tax. For localities, property taxes are most significant. States and localities also benefit from revenue sharing by the federal government.

5. Government regulatory agencies are active in many areas, controlling the prices of some industries (such as airlines), regulating monopoly, and protecting the public from misleading advertising, unsafe drugs, pollution, etc. A major problem with regulation is that the regulators are often under intense political pressure from the industry which they regulate. Thus it may be difficult to get regulation in the public interest, rather than in the interest of the industry.

6. There are a number of reasons for government activity, including:

- (*a*) Providing public goods that cannot be supplied by the market because their benefits cannot be denied to nonpaying individuals.
- (*b*) Dealing with externalities, such as controlling pollution.
- (*c*) Encouraging the consumption of "merit" goods, and discouraging or prohibiting harmful products.
- (*d*) Helping the poor.
- (*e*) Helping stabilize the economy.

7. A number of objectives are important in the design of a tax system:

- (*a*) In general, neutrality is a desirable objective.
- (*b*) In some cases, however, the government should alter market signals by taxation. For example, a tax can be used to discourage pollution.
- (*c*) Taxes should be reasonably simple and easily understood.
- (*d*) Taxes should be fair. There are two ways of judging fairness: the benefit principle, and ability to pay.

8. Tax incidence (that is, who ultimately pays the tax) is hard to determine. However, the United States tax system does not appear to be highly progressive, and may even be close to proportional (Figure 5-4).

9. There are a number of tax loopholes that are of particular benefit to those with high incomes.

Key Concepts

regulation	progressive tax	externality	investment tax credit
transfer payment	regressive tax	tax neutrality	depletion allowance
income tax	proportional tax	merit good	capital gain
marginal tax rate	revenue sharing	subsidy	
average tax rate	pure public good	tax loophole	

Problems

5-1 "That government governs best which governs least." Do you agree? Why or why not? Does the government perform more functions than it should? If so, what activities would you like it to reduce or stop altogether? Are there any additional functions which the government should undertake? If so, what ones? How should they be paid for?

5-2 "That government is best which is closest to the people. State and local governments are closer to the people than the federal government." Do you agree? Are there federal functions which might be turned over to the states? Are there federal functions which the states are incapable of handling? Are there functions which the federal government can do much better than the states or localities? Explain.

5-3 Explain the difference between a government purchase of a good and a transfer payment.

5-4 The patent law protects inventors and thus encourages private research. But the government also engages in research. For example, the government has agricultural experimental stations, and during the Second World War, the government developed the atomic bomb through the massive Manhattan Project. Why do you think the government engages in these two types of research, while leaving most research to private business? Does the government have any major advantages in undertaking research? Any major disadvantages?

5-5 Consider two views of the tax system:

(*a*) "The income tax is a mess. Homeowners get a tax break, but renters do not. The rich are able to escape some of their taxes by making large gifts to universities, the arts, and to charities. The only way to get equity into the system is to eliminate all deductions and exemptions, and make all income subject to tax."

(*b*) "The government can promote social goals, such as the support of education or the arts, through direct payments. It can also promote education and the arts by encouraging private giving. This is done by making gifts deductible from taxable income. Tax deductions may be an even more effective way of supporting education, the arts, and other desirable causes than direct government grants. Therefore, such deductions do not constitute 'loopholes.' Rather, they represent an efficient way of achieving important social goals."

Which of these arguments is stronger? Why?

***5-6** Design what you consider to be a fair personal income tax schedule, giving the average and marginal tax rates at various incomes. Provide schedules for single individuals and for married couples. In your system, how much tax would each of the following pay:

(*a*) A single individual with a $10,000 income

(*b*) A married couple, each of whom makes $10,000

(*c*) A single individual with an income of $20,000

(*d*) A married couple, with one partner making $20,000 and the other having no income.

Would the taxpayers in each of these four categories agree that your tax is fair? (As a background for this question, reread Box 5-2. And good luck!)

*This question is more difficult.

chapter 6
Business Organization and Finance

Christmas is over
and Business is Business
Franklin Pierce Adams

The government is an important participant in the United States economy, regulating business and providing such public goods as roads, health services, and defense. But the primary productive role is played by private business. Businesses use the resources of society—labor, land, and capital—to produce the goods and services that consumers, the government, and other businesses demand.

A topic in future chapters will be the behavior of businesses. How much do they produce? At what prices do they sell? What combination of land, labor, and capital do they use in the productive process? How do they respond to changing market conditions? Questions such as these are central subjects of any introductory study of economics. The purpose of this chapter is to provide background on the organization of businesses and the ways in which they obtain the money to finance expansion.

In addition to millions of farms, there were about 9 million other businesses in the United States in the late 1970s. By far the largest number were small entities, owned by an individual or a family. Such small businesses predominate in certain sectors of the economy, such as the restaurant business, many services (plumbers, electricians), and some retailing operations (although this is less true than it used to be, as a result of the growth of the supermarket and the retail chain). Some of them are here today, but will be gone tomorrow; small businesses are often high-risk ventures.

While most businesses are small, large corporations play a strategic role. They hire much of the labor force, use large quantities of raw materials, and make most of the profits. Each May, *Fortune* magazine publishes a report on the 500 largest corporations; they regularly make over half the total profits of all United States corporations.

96

BUSINESS ORGANIZATIONS

There are three types of business organization: the single proprietorship, the partnership, and the corporation. The single proprietorship and the partnership are the dominant forms of very small business, although even a one-person business may be a corporation. At the other end of the spectrum, large businesses are almost exclusively corporations. (There are exceptions. Large law firms, for example, are partnerships, and until recently, so were even the largest stock and bond brokerage houses.)

Single Proprietorships and Partnerships: Their Advantages and Problems

A single proprietorship is the easiest form of business to establish; there is little fuss or bother. If I decide to make pottery in my basement, I may do so. I can begin tomorrow, without going through legal and organizational hassles. (Not all businesses can be entered so informally. For example, state and federal laws restrict banking and insurance to corporations with substantial assets. And local zoning laws and regulations may block or complicate the establishment of even the simplest business.) Clearly, a single proprietorship has advantages for someone who wants to experiment with a new line of work—a fact that may explain why so many single proprietorships go out of business so quickly! The single proprietorship is flexible and uncomplicated; the owner has no one else to consult. The proprietor buys the materials needed, hires any help that is necessary and can be afforded, and undertakes to pay the bills. And the profits of the business belong to the owner, to be shared by no one (except the federal government, which collects its share in the form of personal income taxes paid by the owner).

But the single proprietorship has limitations. Most obviously, there are limits to how much one individual can manage. Consider a typical small business, the gasoline station. Clearly, there are problems for a single owner. While help can be hired to operate the pumps, there are advantages in having someone around who is "in charge." Yet one individual will find it a crushing burden to try to be present during the long hours when a gas station is open. The obvious solution is to take on a partner, who will be jointly responsible.

A partnership may involve two or more partners; some partnerships involve dozens of people. In a typical partnership, each partner agrees to provide some fraction of the work and some of the financing. In return, each partner receives an agreed share of the profits or suffers an agreed share of the loss. (These shares need not all be equal. For example, a "silent partner" is one who provides financial support, but does not participate in the actual day-to-day running of the business.) Again, the partnership is easily established; a simple oral agreement will do. This method is, however, not to be recommended; it is a way to lose both business and friend. A formal partnership agreement, drawn up by a lawyer, can prevent much grief.

Both the single proprietorship and the partnership are simple and flexible, but they have the following major limitations:

1. If a proprietorship runs into difficulty, the owner can lose more than his or her initial investment. Personal assets, including home and car, may be lost in order to pay the debts of the business. In short, a proprietor has *unlimited liability* for all the debts of the business. Similarly, there is *unlimited liability* in a partnership; the partners can lose their personal assets as well as the financial contributions initially made to the business. Indeed, there is a particular form of risk associated with the partnership. Each partner is liable for the obligations undertaken by the other partner or partners, and each partner runs the risk of being left "holding the bag" if the other partners are unable to meet their shares of the obligations of the partnership. Clearly, one should exercise great caution before taking on a dozen partners! (It is precisely because of this unlimited liability that partnerships are considered good form in the legal profession. A client has the assurance that *all* the partners will stand behind the acts of *each* partner.)

2. There is a problem of *continuity*. When a single proprietor dies, the business has no automatic continuing existence (although one of the children may take over the shop or farm and continue to run it). Continuity is an even more awkward problem in a partnership. Every time a partner dies or resigns, a whole new partnership must be formed. A new partnership agreement is likewise necessary whenever a new partner is admitted; and all partners must agree before any partner is allowed to sell his or her share of the partnership to a new party. These provisions are not surprising; after all, each of the partners will be liable for the acts of the new partner, and it is therefore only reasonable that each be given the right to veto the entrance of any new member.

3. There is the problem of *financing growth*. A partnership or proprietorship has a number of sources of financing: the personal wealth of the owner or owners; the profits made by the business which are plowed back to purchase new equipment or buildings; the mortgaging of property; and borrowing from banks, suppliers, friends, and relatives. But it may be difficult to borrow the money needed for expansion. Lenders are reluctant to take the risks of lending large amounts to a struggling new enterprise. Furthermore, it may also be difficult to bring in new owners to help with the financing. It is true that a carrot, in the form of a share of the profits, can be dangled in front of potential investors. But with the carrot comes a stick. In gaining a right to a share of the profits, a new partner also undertakes *unlimited liability* for the debts of the business. Clearly, outside investors will be reluctant to share in the partnership unless they have carefully investigated it and have developed an exceptionally high degree of confidence in the partners. This may make it very hard for a partnership to get the financing needed for expansion.

The Corporation

The major advantage of the corporate form of organization is that it *limits the liability* of its owners to their initial investment. When new investors buy shares of the common stock of a business, they thereby acquire partial ownership of the business without facing the danger of unlimited liability. If the business goes bankrupt and is unable to pay its debts, the owners lose no more than the purchase price of their shares. By reducing the risks of investors, the corporate form of business makes it feasible to tap a wide pool of investment funds. Thus, the corporation is the form of business most suited to rapid growth with the use of outside funds.

> Each *share of common stock* represents a fraction of the ownership or equity of a corporation.

Because corporations limit the liability of the owners, there is less legal protection for the creditors to whom the corporation owes money. If the corporation fails, creditors cannot lay claim to the personal assets of the owners. (Many corporations do, however, possess very large assets, cutting down the risks of the creditors to a very low level.) Corporations must inform those with whom they do business of this limited liability; they do so by tacking to their corporate title the designation "Inc." or "Incorporated" (in the United States), or "Ltd." or "Limited" (in the British legal system).

Originally, in Britain some centuries ago, corporation charters were awarded only rarely, by special grants of the king and the Parliament. These corporations were granted substantial privileges; some were given special rights to conduct business in the British colonies—the East India Company, for example. During the nineteenth century, however, there was a major revolution in business and legal thinking, and the modern corporation emerged. General incorporation laws were passed, granting to anyone the right to form a corporation. (See Box 6-1.) With a few important exceptions (such as banking, where governmental authorities retain control over the establishment of new banks), the establishment of a corporation is a relatively straightforward and uncomplicated legal procedure.

In addition to limited liability, the corporation offers the advantage of continuity. In law, the corporation is a fictitious "legal person."[1] When one of the stockholders dies, the corporation survives; the shares of

---

BOX 6-1
WHAT'S A "COMPANY LIMITED"?

In one of their lesser known nineteenth-century operettas (*Utopia, Limited*), Gilbert and Sullivan undertook to explain the new concept of a "Company Limited." It was, they said, an association (if possible, of peers and baronets):

> They start off with a public declaration
> To what extent they mean to pay their debts.

And, of course,

> When it's left to you to say
> What amount you mean to pay,
> Why, the lower you can put it at, the better.

Indeed, the best strategy for the founders of the company is to put up only a trivial amount of their own money—say, 18 pence:

> If you succeed, your profits are stupendous—
> And if you fail, pop goes your eighteen pence.

Of course, the company may fail:

> Though a Rothschild you may be
> In your own capacity
> As a Company you've come to utter sorrow—
> But the Liquidators say,
> "Never mind—you needn't pay,"
> So you start another Company to-morrow!

---

[1]In the late nineteenth century, this legal fiction was used by corporations to oppose government regulation. In a series of court cases, corporations argued that, as legal persons, they were shielded by the equal protection provisions of the Fourteenth Amendment to the Constitution.

the deceased are inherited by his or her heirs, without the corporation's organization being disturbed. The heirs need not be concerned about accepting the shares, since they are not liable for the corporation's debts. Furthermore, the corporation survives if some of the stockholders want to get out of the business. These stockholders can sell their shares to anyone willing to buy; there is no need to reorganize the company.

Corporation Taxes

The profits of a proprietorship or a partnership are taxed as the personal income of the proprietor or partners. When a corporation is established, taxation becomes more involved. From the viewpoint of the shareholder-owner, the corporate form of business organization may involve either a tax advantage or a tax disadvantage.

Consider an example. A corporation with 1 million shares outstanding makes pretax profits of $10 million, or $10 per share. The corporation is taxed as a separate entity; its total corporation profits tax might amount to $3 million. (The basic corporation income tax rate is 48 percent, but the effective tax rate is less than this percentage because of the investment tax credit and other detailed provisions of the tax law.) This leaves $7 per share in after-tax profits. Of this $7, the corporation might retain $5 for expansion of the business, and pay out the remaining $2 per share as dividends to the shareholders. In turn, the shareholders must include the dividends of $2 per share as part of their personal income, and pay personal income tax—at rates up to a maximum of 70 percent depending on their tax bracket. From the viewpoint of the shareholder-owner, the disadvantage of this arrangement is that dividend income is taxed *twice*. First, it is taxed in the year it is earned as part of the total profits of the corporation. Second, when it is paid out in dividends, it is taxed again as the personal income of the shareholder who receives it.

But there also may be a tax advantage. Consider the $5 in profits retained by the corporation for expansion. This income is taxed only *once*—and at an average rate of only 30 percent.[2] (There is a tax of $3 million on profits of $10 million.) For a wealthy shareholder in a high tax bracket, the 30 percent tax paid on the retained corporate profit is less than the owner would pay in personal income taxes if the business were a proprietorship or a partnership. Particularly for a new, growing business, there may thus be a tax incentive to incorporate. By keeping dividends low and plowing most of the profits back into the business, total taxes may be kept low.[3]

The double taxation of dividend income has drawn sharp criticism. Not only does a question of fairness arise, since profits going into dividends are taxed twice while profits retained for expansion are taxed only once. But a tax incentive is also provided for big corporations to grow even bigger. (Shareholders may be quite happy to have the corporation retain its earnings to finance growth, since they avoid the personal income tax which would be due if the corporation paid dividends. Although stockholders forgo dividend income in such circumstances, they own shares of a growing business.)

The "integration" of the corporate and personal income taxes, which would involve the reduction or elimination of double taxa-

---

[2]At least, it is taxed only once now. If, at some time in the future, it is paid out as dividends, it will then be taxed again as personal income. In this case, the second round of tax will be deferred, not avoided.

[3]The incentive to incorporate has been reduced by tax provisions which provide alternative ways of deferring taxes. Most notably, the Keogh plan permits the deferral of taxes on personal income put into a retirement fund. (After retirement, when the funds are used to provide the person with a pension, income taxes must be paid.)

tion on dividend income, was on the list of possible tax reforms studied by the Carter administration during its first year. However, it was not actually included in Carter's early tax proposals to Congress because of the desire to keep these proposals simple.

HOW A CORPORATION FINANCES EXPANSION

The corporation can obtain funds for expansion in the same ways as a proprietorship or partnership; that is, by borrowing from banks or plowing profits back into the business. But a corporation also has other options. It can issue common stock, bonds, or other securities.

Common Stock

When it sells additional shares of common stock, the corporation takes on new part-owners, since each share represents a fraction of the ownership of the corporation. As a part-owner, the purchaser of common stock not only receives a share of any dividends paid by the corporation, but also gets the right to vote for corporate directors who, in turn, choose the corporate officers and set the corporation's policies.[4]

Bonds

Rather than take on new owners by issuing additional common stock, the corpo-

ration may raise funds by selling *bonds*. A bond represents *debt* of the corporation; it is an I.O.U. that the corporation is obliged to repay, whether it is making profits or not. If the corporation doesn't pay, it can be sued by the bondholder.

A *bond* is a form of debt. The corporation (or government) that issues a bond undertakes to make periodic interest payments and to repay the face value or principal when the bond reaches maturity.

A bond is a long-term form of debt which does not fall due for repayment until 10, 15, or more years from the time it was initially sold (issued) by the corporation (or government). Bonds usually come in large denominations—for example, $10,000. The original buyer normally pays the corporation a sum equal to the face value of the bond; in effect, the original buyer is lending $10,000 to the corporation. (The original buyer can resell the bond at more or less than the face value, depending on the market for bonds.) In return for the $10,000, the corporation is committed to make two sets of payments:

1. Interest payments that must be made periodically (normally semiannually) during

[4]If its stock is diffused among a large number of shareholders, a corporation may, in practice, be run by a group of insiders made up of the directors and senior management. The small stockholder's problem is akin to that of the consumer. In both cases, the stakes are not sufficiently great for the individual stockholder or consumer to make his or her views known forcefully. If you own only a few shares of a corporation's stock, it is probably not even worth your time and your travel expenses to show up at the annual meeting. Furthermore, unless the corporation is doing very badly, you are likely to grant the management's request for your *proxy*; that is, the authorization to vote on your behalf at the annual meeting. (This does not mean that the management is immune from challenge. If the corporation's performance is weak, a dissident group may be successful in getting enough proxies to oust the old management.)

Several decades ago, A. A. Berle and Gardner C. Means pointed out the separation of ownership and control in their study *The Modern Corporation and Private Property* (New York: Commerce Clearing House, 1932). In a more recent work, R. J. Larner found that control was even more separated from ownership in 1963 than it had been when Berle and Means wrote. By 1963, the stockholding of 84.5 percent of the 200 largest corporations was so diffuse that no single family, corporation, or group of business associates owned as much as 10 percent of the stock. (Berle and Means had found the comparable figure to be 44 percent of the 200 largest corporations in 1929.) See R. J. Larner, "Ownership and Control of the 200 Largest Nonfinancial Corporations, 1929 and 1963," *American Economic Review*, September 1966, p. 780.

the life of the bond. If the interest rate is, say, 8 percent per annum on a bond with a $10,000 face value, the interest payment will be $400 (that is, 4 percent) every 6 months.

2. A payment of the $10,000 face value, or *principal*, when the date of maturity arrives. That is, the corporation must repay the amount of the loan at maturity.[5]

Since the corporation is committed to make the payments of interest and principal, a bond provides the purchaser an assured, steady income, provided the corporation avoids bankruptcy. Common stock, on the other hand, involves a substantial risk. During periods of difficulty, the corporation may cut the dividend, and the price of the stock may plummet. But, while bonds provide more safety than stocks, they offer less excitement. Unlike the owner of common stock, the bondholder cannot look forward to rising dividends if the company hits the jackpot. The bondholder will get no more than the interest and principal specified in the bond contract. Bonds are safe; they are also dull.

Some investors desire an intermediate security that will provide more safety than common stock while still offering a larger potential return than bonds. These investors may choose convertible bonds or preferred stock.

Convertible Bonds

Convertible bonds are like ordinary bonds, but have one additional feature. Prior to a given date, they may be exchanged for common stock in some fixed ratio (for example, 1 bond for 10 shares of common stock).

If the outlook for the corporation becomes very favorable, the convertible bondholder may exchange the bond for common stock, and thus own shares of the growing corporation. If, on the other hand, the company fails to prosper, the convertible bond may be held to maturity, when the bondholder will receive repayment of the principal.

Because the holder has the option of converting, the interest rate on convertible bonds is normally less than the rate on regular bonds, sometimes substantially less. Therefore, if you are thinking about buying convertible bonds, you have to weigh two conflicting considerations. The interest payments which you receive will be low. But you will have the right to convert into common stock, a right which may become very valuable in the event the business is successful.

Preferred Stock

Preferred stock, like common stock, represents ownership or equity, and not debt. The corporation is legally obligated to make interest payments to bondholders, but it is not legally required to pay dividends to preferred or common stockholders.

Preferred stockholders, however, have a claim on profits which precedes—or is "preferred" to—the claim of the common stockholder. The preferred stockholder has a right to receive specific dividends (for example, 10 percent of the face value of the preferred share) before the common stockholder can be paid any dividend at all. But, on the other hand, the preferred stockholder does not have the possibility of large gains open to the common stockholder. While the common stockholder may hope for rising divi-

---

[5]Intermediate-term securities—those issued with maturities between 1 and 7 years—are generally known as *notes* rather than bonds. They are identical to bonds except for their shorter maturities. Debt instruments with short terms of less than 1 year are called *bills* or *commercial paper*. These are different from bonds or notes, since they provide no explicit periodic interest payment. Rather, the purchaser makes a return by buying bills at a discount. For example, a purchaser buying a $100,000 bill now at a discounted price of $99,000 will get back $1,000 more than the purchase price when the bill reaches maturity.

dends if the corporation prospers, the preferred shareholder will at most receive the specified dividend. (A rare form of stock, the *participating* preferred, provides an exception to this rule. It gives the holder the right to participate in the growth of the company's dividends.)

In any year, the corporation may decide not to make any dividend payments to either the preferred or the common stockholders. Clearly, there is a potential problem here for the preferred stockholder. The voting control of the corporation is generally in the hands of the common stockholders. What is to prevent them from electing corporation directors who will eliminate all dividends for a number of years in order to be able to pay very large dividends in later years? If the preferred shareholders are confined to their specified dividend (of 10 percent or so), then they never will recapture the dividends lost in the previous years. Instead, the very large dividends will all go to the common shareholders, who will thus be enriched at the expense of preferred shareholders. To prevent this abuse, there are usually a number of specific protections for the holders of preferred shares. If dividends are not paid, preferred shareholders may receive the right to vote for company directors. And preferred shares may be *cumulative.* If no dividend is paid, the right to that dividend is passed on to future years. Unpaid preferred dividends accumulate, and must all be paid before the common stockholder is paid any dividend. Preferred stocks may be further "sweetened" by making them convertible into common shares at the option of the preferred shareholder.

As a general rule, all types of securities—common stocks, preferred stocks, and bonds—may be resold by the initial purchasers. Securities prices tend to reflect the judgment of buyers and sellers regarding the prospects of the corporation. Thus, for example, an announcement of a new product may make purchasers eager to buy the company's stock, and make present stockholders reluctant to sell. As a result, the price of the stock will be bid up. Purchasers also look at the position and performance of the company as indicated by a study of its financial accounts.

BUSINESS ACCOUNTING: The Balance Sheet and the Income Statement

Indeed, business accounts are valuable not only as a source of information for potential security buyers. They also are an important tool for helping management keep track of the company's position and performance. And businesses are required to keep accounts for taxation purposes.

There are two major types of business statement:

1. The *balance sheet*, which gives a picture of the company's position at a point in time; for example, on December 31 of last year.

2. The *income statement* (also called the *profit and loss statement*), which summarizes the company's transactions over a period of time, such as a year.

The income statement records the *flow* of payments into and out of the company's treasury. It is like a movie film that records the flow of water into and out of a bathtub. The balance sheet, on the other hand, is a still picture, showing the *stock* of water in the tub.

The Balance Sheet

The balance sheet lists the company's assets. Corresponding to the value of each asset, there must be an exactly equivalent amount either in the form of liabilities owed or in ownership. To use a simple illustration: If you have a car worth $6,000, for

TABLE 6-1
Ford Motor Company Balance Sheet, December 31, 1977
(millions of dollars)

Assets			Liabilities and net worth		
1. Current assets		10,872	5. Current liabilities		7,884
(a) Cash	1,489		(a) Accounts payable and		
(b) Marketable securities	1,883		accrued liabilities	6,438	
(c) Receivables	2,013		(b) Short-term debt	625	
(d) Inventories	4,914		(c) Other	821	
(e) Other current assets	573				
2. Land, plant, and equipment		5,001	6. Long-term debt		1,360
3. Other assets		3,368	7. Other liabilities		1,550
			8. Total liabilities (5 + 6 + 7)		10,794
			9. Net worth (4 − 8)		8,447
			(a) Capital stock	676	
			(b) Retained earnings	7,771	
4. Total assets (items 1 + 2 + 3)		19,241	10. Total liabilities and net worth (8 + 9)		19,241

Source: Ford Motor Company, *Annual Report 1977.*

which you still owe $4,000 to the bank, then $2,000 is the value of your ownership in the car. This fundamental equation also holds for a corporation:

> Assets = liabilities (what is owed)
> + net worth (the value of owner-
> ship)

Assets are listed on the left side of the balance sheet; liabilities and net worth are on the right. Because of the fundamental equation, the two sides must sum to the same total. *The balance sheet must balance.*

> The *net worth* of a corporation is the value of the stockholders' ownership. It is equal to assets minus liabilities

As an example, consider the simplified version of the balance sheet of the Ford Motor Company shown in Table 6-1. On the left-hand (asset) side, Ford has sizable assets in the form of cash (bank accounts), marketable short-term securities (such as government bills or commercial paper issued by

other corporations), and accounts receivable (say, the value of cars which have already been delivered but not yet paid for). Ford naturally has large inventories of materials, such as tires, paint, glass, and parts, and of completed automobiles. Ford also has major assets in the form of land, plant (buildings), and equipment.

On the other side of the balance sheet, most of the liabilities of Ford are short term: amounts which Ford has not yet paid for its steel and other supplies (accounts payable); wages and salaries not yet paid for work already performed (accrued liabilities); and short-term debt (such as money owed to banks). In addition, in 1977 Ford had an outstanding long-term debt of $1.4 billion. (If debt matures within one year, it is short term; in more than one year, long term.)

At the end of 1977, Ford's total assets were $19.2 billion, and its liabilities were $10.8 billion. The net worth, the ownership or equity of all stockholders, was therefore $8.4 billion. Of this, $676 million had been paid in originally by stockholders purchasing shares of the company. But by far the largest part, amounting to over $7.7 billion, represented retained earnings; that is, profits made over the years that had been plowed back into the business.[6]

At the end of 1977, there were 119 million shares of Ford common stock outstanding. (There were no preferred shares.) Thus, each share represented an equity, or *book value*, of $71 (that is, $8,447 million ÷ 119 million).

> The *book value* of a stock is the net worth per share. (It is calculated by dividing the net worth by the number of shares outstanding.)

If you are thinking of buying common stock of a company, its book value is one of the things that should interest you. If it has a high book value, you will be buying ownership of a lot of assets. But don't get carried away by a high book value. If these assets happen to be machinery and equipment that can be used only to produce a good with a falling demand, that high book value may not be worth very much; the assets may not earn much income in the future.

The Income Statement

While the balance sheet shows the assets, liabilities, and net worth of a corporation at a *point* in time, the *income statement* shows what has happened during a *period* of time—for example, during a calendar year. A simplified version of Ford's income statement for 1977 is shown in Table 6-2.

In 1977, Ford sold $37.8 million of cars, trucks, tractors, parts, etc. Costs of $34.8 million are subtracted from sales to calculate income (profit) before taxes of $3.0 million. Corporate income taxes were $1.3 million, leaving an after-tax profit of $1.7 billion, or about $14 per share. Of this after-tax profit, $359 million was paid in dividends to stockholders ($3.04 per share), and $1.3 million was retained by the company. (Observe that the retained earnings in Table 6-1 are much larger than those shown in Table 6-2. The reason is this: The income statement in Table 6-2 shows only the retained earnings during the one year, 1977. In contrast, the balance sheet in Table 6-1 shows the retained earnings accumulated over the entire lifetime of the company.)

Most of Ford's costs are reasonably straightforward. Ford pays wages to its work force, and buys steel, tires, parts, and materials from outside suppliers. [These costs are included in the large cost subcomponent of $32.3 in line 2(*a*).] But one cost item, *depreciation* [line 2(*b*)], needs to be explained. This cost arises because of the plant and equipment used by Ford to produce automobiles and other goods.

Depreciation

Consider the specific example of a machine acquired by Ford during 1977. This machine does not wear out during 1977; it

---

[6]"Retained earnings" may sound like a pool of funds which the corporation has readily available. However, this is generally not the case. Most retained earnings are not held in the form of cash; most are used to buy equipment or other items.

Suppose that, in the first year of its operation, a corporation earns $10,000, and retains it all. (It pays no dividend.) The $10,000 may be used to buy a new machine. Then, as a result, the following changes occur in the balance sheet:

Change in:			
Assets		**Net worth**	
Machinery	+$10,000	Retained earnings	+$10,000

The retained earnings have not been held in the form of idle cash; they have been put to work to buy machinery. The machinery shows up on the asset side. When the retained earnings are included in net worth, the balance sheet balances.

TABLE 6-2
Ford Motor Company Income Statement for the Year 1977
(millions of dollars)

1. Sales		37,841
2. Less: Costs		34,839
(a) Costs, excluding items below	32,300	
(b) Depreciation	629	
(c) Selling and administrative costs	1,286	
(d) Employee retirement plans	624	
3. Income (profit) before taxes (1 − 2)		3,002
4. Less: Income taxes		1,326
5. Net income (net profit) (3 − 4)		1,676
(a) Dividends paid	359	
(b) Retained earnings	1,317	

Source: Ford Motor Company, *Annual Report 1977.*

will continue to be used in coming years. It would therefore be misleading to count the full purchase price of the machine as a cost of production in 1977. Rather, it is appropriate to count just part of the price as a cost during 1977, with other fractions being allocated as costs during the coming years when the machine is still in use. The easiest technique for allocating costs involves *straight-line depreciation*, which spreads the cost of the machine (minus its scrap value, if any) evenly over its estimated lifetime. For example, if a machine costs $10,000 and wears out in 5 years (with no scrap value), straight-line depreciation is $2,000 per year for 5 years. More complicated are *accelerated depreciation* techniques, which involve the allocation of higher fractions to the early years than to the later years of the machine's lifetime. (See Figure 6-1.)

Depreciation accounting should not be considered an exact science. Not only does the useful lifetime of a machine depend on physical wear and tear, but it also depends on obsolescence, which cannot be accurately forecasted. Even if a machine could be permanently maintained in brand-new condition, it would eventually become obsolete;

that is, its useful life would end as new and more efficient techniques became available. (Obsolescence tends to be greatest for high-technology equipment. An early computer, built in 1946 at the University of Pennsylvania, contained 18,000 vacuum tubes, weighed 30 tons, and occupied a huge room, with other large areas needed for support. By the mid-1970s, a newly developed computer of equivalent capacity was smaller than a dime.)

But an even greater complication arises because of the tax laws. Note that depreciation is a cost which is subtracted before taxable income is calculated (Table 6-2). Thus, firms have an incentive to increase their depreciation costs by estimating short lifetimes for their machines; they thus reduce their before-tax income and hence their tax bill. To prevent the government's loss of tax revenues, the law specifies the lifetime over which various types of equipment can be depreciated. (The law also regulates the degree to which depreciation may be "accelerated.") Thus, depreciation figures may be more dependent on the tax law than on how fast a machine in reality wears out or becomes obsolete. (A company may keep

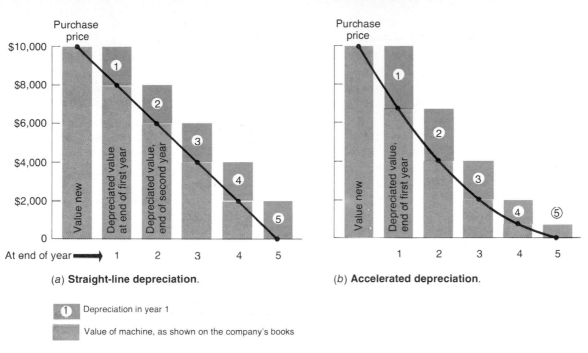

(a) **Straight-line depreciation.**

(b) **Accelerated depreciation.**

① Depreciation in year 1

Value of machine, as shown on the company's books

FIGURE 6-1 Depreciation ($10,000 machine, with 5-year life).
In straight-line depreciation, an equal amount of the machine's value is counted as a cost of production in each year of the machine's life. If accelerated depreciation is used, larger amounts of the machine's value are counted as cost of production in the early years than in the later years.

plant and equipment in use long after they have been completely depreciated on its books.)

FINANCIAL MARKETS

As we have seen, corporations may finance expansion by retaining their profits or by looking outside for sources of funds. They may borrow from banks, insurance companies, or other financial corporations. Or they may issue additional stocks or bonds. Financial markets and financial corporations occupy a strategic role in the economy because they help to determine which businesses will receive the finances for expansion.

Financial corporations, such as banks, savings and loan associations, and insurance companies, are *financial intermediaries* That is, they take small amounts of funds from a large number of people, pool these

funds, and lend them in larger amounts to businesses, governments, or individuals. For example, a savings and loan association may receive 100 small deposits with an average size of $300; with the combined total of $30,000, it makes a mortgage loan to someone buying a house. In doing this, the savings and loan (S&L) provides a useful service. The home buyer is saved the trouble of trying to locate the 100 individuals who would be willing to put up small amounts. The people who provide the funds are saved the nuisance of lending directly to the homeowner and of collecting on the loan every month. In addition to handling the paperwork, the S&L investigates the credit-worthiness of the potential home buyer, thus limiting the risk that the loan will not be repaid. Similarly, banks and insurance companies take funds from deposits or insurance policies, pool them, and lend them to businesses, governments, or individuals who meet their standards of credit-worthiness.[7]

Thus, a business that wants to borrow money may go to a bank or an insurance company. But what does a business do if it wants to raise money by selling its common stock? It may follow one of two courses. If it is a large corporation that already has many shareholders, it can give the present shareholders the rights or *warrants* to buy new stock at a specific price. Because this price is generally less than the current market price of the stock, the present stockholders have an incentive to exercise the rights (that is, to use the warrants to buy stock at the bargain price). Those who already have all the stock they want can sell the warrants to someone who wants to use them to buy stock at a bargain price. Thus, the corporation ends up by selling the new shares of its stock either to existing shareholders or to those who have bought the warrants.

Since a new company does not have a large number of present shareholders, it will use a different method of selling stock. It will approach an *investment bank*, a firm that merchandises securities. The investment bank looks for its profits in the markup between the price it pays to the company and the price at which it sells the stock to the public. The investment bank may simply undertake to sell as many shares as it can, up to the maximum the company is willing to issue. In this case, the company takes a risk: If buyers are unreceptive, few shares are sold and the company raises only a little money. However, if the investment bank is confident regarding the prospects of the company, it may *underwrite* the stock issue; that is, it *guarantees* the sale of the full issue of stock. If it is unable to find buyers for the whole issue, the investment bank will end up buying the shares itself. In order to limit its risk, the investment bank may bring in other investment banks to form a *syndicate* which jointly underwrites the new issue.

Investment banks may also underwrite corporation bonds. As part of their business, investment bankers keep close contact with pension funds and other large-scale purchasers of securities.

Financial Markets: The Objectives of Buyers of Securities

In some ways, the markets for stocks and bonds are similar to the markets for shirts, shoes, or automobiles. For example, just as the automobile dealer makes profits by the markup on cars, so the investment banker makes profits by the markup on stocks and bonds. But, in one very important way, the market for stocks and bonds is quite different from the market for shoes or cars. When you wish to buy a pair of shoes or a car, you can examine the available merchandise and make a reasonably good judgment as to its quality. You cannot make a perfect judgment, of course; you can't really be sure of the type of material used in the stitching in a shoe, and you can't really be sure that the brand new automobile will not turn out to be a lemon. Nevertheless, you can make a reasonably good judgment. But when you buy a common stock, you are, in effect, buying a future prospect—something which is clearly intangible and about which it may be very difficult to reach an informed and balanced judgment. Similarly, when you buy a bond, you are buying a set of promises made by the bond issuer to pay interest and principal on schedule.

Because of the uncertainty of the future,

---

[7]Several points of detail may be noted. First, funds placed in an S&L are technically called shares rather than deposits. However, they are so similar to a savings deposit in a bank that they may also be labeled deposits. Second, most of the funds which insurance companies receive for automobile, fire, and some other policies go to pay policyholders who have had accidents or fires. However, life insurance is different: Many policies involve savings programs for the policyholders. Such policies generate sizable amounts of funds that the insurance companies can lend to businesses.

leverage?

the purchaser will not simply choose the bond which has the highest prospective rate of return; the credibility of the promise of the company to repay is also important. Indeed, purchasers of securities have three considerations to balance: return, risk, and liquidity. *Return* is the percentage yield. For example, if a bond is purchased for $10,000 and it pays interest of $800 per year, then it yields 8 percent. *Risk* involves the chance that something will go wrong. For example, the company may go bankrupt and the bondholder may lose both interest and principal.

Finally, *liquidity* reflects the ability of the owner to get out of an asset on short notice, with little cost and bother. A deposit in an S&L is highly liquid. As a general rule, it may be withdrawn at any time for its full dollar value, with interest to the date of withdrawal. (Thus, in addition to handling paperwork and evaluating borrowers' credit-worthiness, S&Ls and other financial intermediaries provide their depositors with liquidity.) At the other end of the spectrum, real estate is very illiquid. If you have to sell your home on short notice, you may have to accept a price considerably lower than you would get with a more lengthy selling effort.

While investors look for a combination of high return, low risk, and high liquidity, they do not all weigh the three objectives equally. Some (particularly those with steady incomes who are saving for the relatively distant future) will weigh liquidity as relatively unimportant, while others (perhaps those whose children are about to enter college) will want to keep liquid investments on which they can draw in the near future. And different investors may have quite different attitudes toward risk.

The Objectives of Issuers of Securities

A company that sells stocks and bonds will also have a series of objectives to balance. It will try to obtain funds in such a way as to keep the *return* of the corporation's stockholders as high as possible; it will try to avoid *risk;* and it will try to assure the *availability* of money when it is needed.

A corporation balances risk and return when it chooses whether to sell stocks or bonds. In contrast with the view from the buyer's side, the corporation selling securities views bonds as having a higher degree of risk than common stock. If bonds are issued, interest payments must be met no matter how badly the corporation may be doing. Thus, large outstanding debt can put a corporation in a precarious position. If business slackens, it may be unable to meet large payments for interest and principal, and thus the corporation may face bankruptcy. There is no such risk with common stock, since the company can cut dividends in the event of a downturn in business.

But, while it is safer for a corporation to issue stock, there is a disadvantage: Additional stock involves taking on new part-owners. If the company does well, the rising profits will go partially to the new stockholders; the original stockholders must share their bonanza. In contrast, consider what happens if bonds are issued—that is, if the *leverage* of the corporation is increased—in order to buy new equipment or finance a new factory. After the required payment of interest on the bonds, any large profits from the new plant and equipment go only to the original stockholders. Thus, the more highly leveraged a corporation is, the greater is the uncertainty for its owners. Their potential gain is increased, but so is their potential loss, including the possibility of bankruptcy. (See Box 6-2.)

> *Leverage* is the ratio of debt to net worth. If this ratio is large, the corporation is highly leveraged.

As a group, stockholders and corporate managers tend to be optimistic. They consequently may try to maximize their expected

BOX 6-2
INDIVIDUALS MAY BE HIGHLY LEVERAGED, TOO

When Jimmy Carter arrived in Washington as the thirty-ninth President of the United States, he brought with him his close friend, confidant, and banker, Bert Lance. Like Carter, Lance was a Georgia boy who had made good; when he came to Washington, he estimated his net worth at $2.6 million.

Carter appointed Lance director of the Office of Management and Budget (OMB), a strategic post involving supervision of the spending proposals and spending activities of the various departments of the federal government. He was widely considered the second most powerful person in Washington. In his confirmation hearings before Congress, Lance presented a financial statement that told the secret of his success. But it also provided a hint of trouble to come. Bert Lance was highly leveraged. His assets were $7.9 million, but his debts were $5.3 million.

The major asset listed by Lance was a block of 190,000 shares of the National Bank of Georgia (NBG), for which he had paid over $17 per share, for a total cost of about $3.4 million. To help finance his purchases, he had borrowed $2.6 million from the Manufacturers-Hanover Bank of New York. If the price of the NBG stock went up, Lance would make a killing.

One problem was that in order to gain Senate confirmation for his new position as head of OMB, Lance had to agree to sell his NBG shares by the end of 1977. As he was a major shareholder, the market price began to fall in anticipation of his large sale. Within several months, the price of a share had slipped below $12. Lance found to his sorrow that leverage was a two-edged sword; his net worth had declined by more than a million dollars. Furthermore, because of losses from uncollectible loans, NBG suspended its dividends, depriving Lance of money which he needed to pay interest on his bank loans. Reporters became curious as to how he would handle his financial difficulties. They began to dig into his private affairs, turning up a number of questionable practices. Tales of Bert Lance's finances became the journalistic fad. As news of his financial adventures continued to appear in the papers, demands for his resignation grew. After defending himself at a hearing on Capitol Hill, Lance resigned and went back to Georgia.

gains by a high degree of leverage. Furthermore, limited liability provides an incentive for leverage. If things go well, the stockholders make, and keep, a large profit on their limited investment. If things go badly, the stockholders of course lose their small investment. But that is all they lose.[8] (If things go well, stockholders can earn many times their original investment. If things go poorly, they can lose their original investment only once.) Thus, a company may be highly leveraged in order to keep the potential gains in the hands of a few stockholders, while pushing off most of the risks onto a large number of bondholders (and others to whom the company owes money). Thus, even though a company takes risk into account when it issues stocks or bonds, it has a temptation to discount the importance of risk, since someone else will suffer much of the possible loss.

If corporate managers were free to leverage to their hearts' content, there might be disastrous instability in the economy. (When businesses go bankrupt, their employees may be thrown out of work, and other businesses to whom they owe money may also go bankrupt.) Fortunately, however, there are limits to leverage. As leverage increases, the increasing risks to bondholders (and other lenders) make them cautious. They become increasingly reluctant to buy that company's bonds unless they pay a very high interest. Indeed, if leverage becomes high enough, the company may find it impossible to sell bonds or to borrow from banks or others. Leverage is limited by the caution of lenders.[9]

(For some companies, lenders will be less concerned about leverage. If a company's sales grow steadily, it may safely have large debts. Thus, for example, it is sound for an electric power utility or telephone company to be deeply in debt.)

The final objective of corporations issuing securities is to assure the *availability* of money when it is needed. As a general rule, it is inadvisable to finance a new factory with short-term borrowing. It is unwise to have to keep repaying a short-term debt and borrowing money again each year to finance a factory over, say, a 20-year lifetime; in one of those years, borrowed funds may not be available. New factories should therefore be financed by long-term borrowing, by the issue of additional stock, or by retained profits.

In order to ensure the availability of money for unpredictable requirements that can arise, a corporation may arrange a *line of credit* at a bank. This involves a commitment by the bank to lend up to a specified limit at the request of the company. Similarly, builders may get commitments from savings and loan associations to provide mortgage money in the future. Such commitments allow builders to make firm plans for construction.

The Bond Market

Because security buyers balance risk and return, risky securities generally have to offer higher yields, or nobody will buy. This shows up in the bond market yields shown in Figure 6-2. Observe that the highest-grade corporate bonds, classified Aaa by

---

[8]In their early description of a "Company Limited," Gilbert and Sullivan clearly recognized the advantage of leverage. The company with an equity of only 18 pence would be very highly leveraged indeed. And profits on this 18 pence might well be "stupendous." (See Box 6-1.)

[9]However, the tax law gives corporations an additional incentive to increase their leverage. Interest paid on bonds and other loans can be subtracted as a cost in calculating taxable profits; consequently, interest payments reduce a company's tax. No such subtraction is permitted for dividends paid to stockholders.

This incentive for leverage constitutes a defect of the tax system, since leverage can contribute to financial instability. Thus, another reason (the incentive for leverage) may be added to the earlier argument on p. 100 for reform of the corporation tax.

Moody's Investors' Service, have lower yields than the more risky corporate bonds (Baa).[10] In turn, United States government bonds, which are free from risk of default, have lower yields than even the highest-grade corporate bonds. Note also that the gaps between these three sets of bonds (U.S. government, corporate Aaa, and corporate Baa) are not constant. Most conspicuously, the gap between corporate Aaa and Baa yields shot up during the early 1930s. As the economy collapsed into the Depression, bankruptcies mounted; many shaky firms went under. The risks associated with the holding of low-grade corporate bonds rose, and consequently their yields also rose. A similar, but less dramatic, increase in *risk premiums* took place during the recession of 1974, when the gap between the yields on corporate Aaa and corporate Baa bonds widened. (The gap between risk-free U.S. government bonds and corporate Aaa bonds also widened.)

> A *risk premium* is the difference between the yields on two grades of bonds because of differences in their risk.

While the most important reason for differences in bond yields is difference in risk, several other influences are at work. There are very large quantities of U.S. government bonds outstanding, and the market for these bonds is very active, with relatively small selling costs. (The gap is small between the "bid" price, at which bond dealers are ready to buy, and the "offer" price, at which they are ready to sell.) Thus, the lower yields on U.S. government bonds may also reflect a liquidity advantage; less loss is involved if the buyer has to turn around quickly and sell them. Finally, U.S. government bonds (sometimes simply called U.S. governments) pay interest that is exempt from state income taxes, a fact that also accounts for some of the gap between U.S. governments and taxable corporate Aaa bonds.

The biggest tax advantage, however, lies with the state and local government securities, whose interest is exempt from the large federal income tax. This important difference in tax treatment explains why yields on state and local government securities are lower than on U.S. governments even though the latter are free from the risk of default while state and local government securities are not. (In an extreme situation, the federal government has the constitutional right to print money to pay interest and principal on its bonds. State and local governments have no such right and may default on their debt, as the holders of New York City securities found to their sorrow in 1975.)

Finally, the most notable feature in the bond market is the general upward movement of all interest rates over the past two decades. This rise has been caused by the acceleration of inflation. When inflation is high, bondholders recognize that interest and principal will be repaid in the future when money is less valuable than at present. They therefore hesitate to purchase bonds unless interest rates are high enough to compensate them for the declining value of money. On the other hand, bond issuers and other borrowers are particularly eager to borrow during periods of inflation, since they too recognize that the loans will be repaid with depreciated money.[11] In their eagerness to borrow, they will tend to bid up the interest rate.

---

[10]In judging the quality of bonds, investors' services consider such things as leverage and the stability of a corporation's earnings.

[11]The advantages of borrowing during a period of inflation were explained in Box 1-2, which described the windfall to a homeowner with a large mortgage.

FIGURE 6-2 Long-term bond yields.
The differences between yields on different securities reflect primarily differences in risk.
(A notable exception is the low yield on state and local government securities, which
reflects their tax-exempt status.) The rising trend of all interest rates over the past two
decades has been caused by a rise in the rate of inflation.

The Stock Market

Stocks of major corporations already held by the public are usually bought and sold on the stock exchanges, the most famous being the New York Stock Exchange. Stockbrokers throughout the country maintain close contact with the exchanges, assuring that a potential buyer will be put in contact with the representatives of sellers and vice versa.

> A _broker_ acts as a representative of a buyer or seller, offering to buy or sell on behalf of clients.

Prices fluctuate on the stock exchanges in response to changes in demand and sup-ply. Stock purchasers are interested in such things as the current and expected future profits of the corporation. Thus, stock prices may rise rapidly during periods of prosperity.

In the 1920s, the desire to "get rich quick" in the stock market became a national mania. With stocks rising, many investors learned that individuals, too, could use leverage to increase their potential gains; they borrowed large sums to buy stocks in the expectation that their prices would rise. Then came the Great Crash of 1929. The Dow-Jones average of 30 major industrial stocks fell from 381 in 1929 to 41 in 1932 (Figure 6-3). Many investors were wiped out. The stocks of the best corporations in America shared in the disaster. From a price of $396 in early September 1929, General Electric fell to $168 in late November (fol-

FIGURE 6-3 The Dow-Jones industrial stock average, 1900–1977.
The biggest swing in stock prices, in percentage terms, took place during the expansive bull market of the 1920s and the sharp contraction (bear market) of 1929–1932. In the first two decades after World War II (1945–1956), average stock prices rose about sixfold. But between 1956 and 1977, there was no further gain; on average, stock prices were no higher in 1977 than in 1965.
[Note: The figure is a ratio (or semilog) chart, with equal vertical distances measuring equal percentage changes. For example, the distance from 100 to 200 is the same as the distance from 200 to 400.]

lowing the stock market panic), and to $34 by 1932. General Motors dropped from $72 to $36 to $8, and AT&T from $304 to $197 to $70.[12]

Another major upswing in the stock averages occurred in the 1960s, when the Dow-Jones went as high as 1,000. During the 1960s, the United States economy had the longest continuous expansion on record. Common stocks promised a share in the nation's prosperity. And they were widely looked on as a hedge against inflation. After all, stocks represent ownership of corporations, and in a period of inflation, the dollar value of a corporation's plant and equip-

ment should rise with the general increase in prices. This comforting viewpoint was plausible; but it was not borne out by unfolding events. From its 1966 high, the Dow-Jones retreated as inflationary pressures accelerated. During the 1970s, stock market participants came to the view that inflation was very unhealthy for the economy, and signs of accelerating inflation were generally followed by declines in stock prices. The stock market was also sensitive to changes in economic activity. For example, the stock market fell sharply during the severe recession of 1974–1975.

While the level of economic activity

---

[12]For some of the drama of the collapse, see John Kenneth Galbraith, *The Great Crash, 1929* (Boston: Houghton Mifflin, 1961); or Frederick Lewis Allen, *The Lords of Creation* (New York: Harper, 1935), Chap. 13.

influences the stock market, the stock market also influences the level of economic activity. A falling stock market may give rise to pessimistic business expectations, which in turn may discourage business executives from acquiring new factories and equipment. Moreover, when the price of its own stock is low, a business will be discouraged from issuing new stock to finance expansion. The sale of new stock involves giving up some part of future profits. Present owners (stockholders) will be reluctant to do so if they can raise little cash in return. On the other hand, if they can raise a lot of cash (that is, if the current market price of the stock is high), the present owners will find it more attractive to sell new stock and to invest the proceeds in the growth of the company. (For more precise details on this point, see Box 6-3.)

CAPITAL MARKETS: Two Important Problems

The economic function of the markets for financial capital is similar to the function of markets for goods: They help to determine *what* will be produced in the economy. For example, if a company develops a new product for which there is a large demand, its profits will likely rise, and it will have little trouble in raising funds for expansion by borrowing or by issuing stock. In this way, the company will be able to quickly produce the item in demand.

There are, however, special problems in the capital markets. First, because of problems of getting information, available finance may be directed into the wrong industries or to the wrong firms. Second, the operation of private capital markets does not assure that there will be the right total quantity of investment in the economy.

The Problem of Information: Will Funds Go to the "Right" Industries?

Because securities involve future prospects—a promise of either future interest payments or a share of future profits—they are particularly difficult to evaluate. If promises are being bought, then the money may go to the slickest talker. History is full of artful swindlers, ranging from John Law (whose Mississippi Company first provided speculative riches and then financial disaster to its shareholders in eighteenth-century Paris) to Bernard Cornfeld (whose Investors Overseas Service (IOS) lost the money of thousands of Europeans at the beginning of the 1970s).[13] Financing that goes into hairbrained schemes represents not only a loss to individuals, but also a loss to society of the projects which alternatively could have been financed.

Because it is so difficult for the average investor to evaluate the prospects of a company, there is a strong case for regulations which require the disclosure of information by those issuing securities. In the United States, these regulations are enforced by the Securities and Exchange Commission (SEC). Before offering securities to the public, companies are required to issue a *prospectus*, giving information on the present position and the future prospects of the corporation.[14] Publicly owned firms are required to make their accounts public and to announce publicly significant developments which may affect the price of their stock. (They are forbidden from leaking inside information to help their friends make a killing on the stock market.)

[13]Cornfeld's sales pitch became the title of a book on the IOS by Charles Raw, Bruce Page, and Godfrey Hodgson, *Do You Sincerely Want to Be Rich?* (New York: Viking, 1971). The victim's greed is the swindler's strongest ally.

[14]This requirement does not apply to state and local government bond issues. Following the troubles of New York, some underwriters began to require states and local governments to disclose much more information. They did so not only to protect their customers, but also to guard themselves from lawsuits.

BOX 6-3
HOW CHANGING STOCK MARKET PRICES CAN AFFECT GROWTH

While stock exchanges are involved primarily with purchases and sales of shares that are already held by the public, what happens on the stock market affects the ability of corporations to issue new stock and thus affects their ability to grow by purchasing new plant and equipment. In particular, a firm will find it more attractive to issue new stock if the current market price of its stock is above the book value.

To illustrate, suppose that a corporation with a net worth of $20 million has 1 million shares of stock outstanding. The stock has a book value of $20. If the price of the stock is high, the corporation may be able to issue an additional 1 million shares at a price much in excess of the book value; say, at $30 per share. With the inflow of $30 million in cash from the sale of the stock, the assets and net worth of the corporation both increase by $30 million. (Its liabilities remain unchanged.) Thus, its net worth rises from $20 million to $50 million. But, of course, there are now 2 million shares of its stock outstanding. It follows that the book value of its stock is now

$$\frac{\$50 \text{ million}}{2 \text{ million}} = \$25$$

Thus, by issuing new stock, the corporation has, at a single stroke, increased the book value of its stock from $20 to $25. The reason is that the new stock has been sold at a price above its initial book value. (Of course, if new stock is sold at a price *below* its book value, there will be the opposite result: Its book value will fall.)

But issuing stock at a high price in order to raise the book value is not necessarily a good idea. It is also important for the company to have a profitable use for its new funds. The point is this: When its stock price is high,

a firm finds it relatively attractive to issue new stock and thus raise funds to buy new plant and equipment. But when the market price of its stock is low, the corporation will hesitate to issue new stock because of the depressing effect on book value.

Indeed, a low stock price will not only discourage the issuance of new stock to finance growth, but it may also act as a drag on growth for two other reasons. The corporation may conclude that one of the best things that it can do with its retained earnings is to buy back some of its own cheap stock from the public at the current bargain price, thereby increasing the book value per share.† (This was done by a number of firms when their stock prices were very low during the 1970s.) Money which is thus spent to repurchase stock obviously cannot be used by the corporation to acquire additional factories or equipment.

The second reason that low stock market prices may deter growth is that a corporation may buy up the stock of other companies and take them over in order to use their plant and equipment. Why is this? Yale Prof. James Tobin has suggested the answer.‡ If other companies' stocks are selling well below book value, it may be much cheaper to acquire additional capacity by buying out other companies than by buying newly produced plant and equipment. If this happens, new investment is discouraged. Indeed, during the late 1970s, there was a rash of takeovers of this kind. (The takeovers of the late 1970s contrasted with the takeovers of the 1960s, when stock prices were high. In the sixties, most takeovers were not paid for in cash. Instead, the shareholders of the acquired company were paid off in newly issued stock of the new parent.)§

---

†A company can raise the book value by buying its stock when it is cheap, just as it did by selling its stock when it was dear (as in the earlier example in this box).

To see why, reconsider the corporation with 1 million shares outstanding, net worth of $20 million, and a book value of $20 per share. Suppose that the stock is selling for only $10 on the market, and the corporation buys back 500,000 shares. Because it uses $5 million in cash to buy the shares, its assets and net worth both fall by $5 million. Thus, its net worth falls from $20 million to $15 million. But, since there are now only 500,000 shares of stock left outstanding, the book value per share is $\frac{\$15 \text{ million}}{500,000} = \$30$. This is a clear increase over the original $20.

‡"Monetary Policy in 1974 and Beyond," *Brookings Papers on Economic Activity*, no. 1, 1974, pp. 219–232.

§For details, see "The Great Takeover Binge: It Could Rival the Craze of the 1960s, But Now the Giants Are Dealing in Cash," *Business Week*, Nov. 14, 1977, pp. 176–184.

The SEC has made the United States financial markets operate more efficiently, and it has prevented the type of financial buccaneering which marked the 1920s. (Cornfeld was induced to operate in Canada and Europe because of the strictness of SEC regulations.) Nevertheless, many investment projects are intrinsically risky. Thus, it is inevitable that large sums are sometimes channeled into projects that fail. For example, during the 1950s, the Ford Motor Company had a classic flop with its Edsel car. A number of large aircraft have also been money-losers, including an early jet airliner produced by General Dynamics. (Although the final results are not in, it appears that Lockheed's Tristar and the British-French supersonic Concorde will also be money-losers, in spite of their impressive technology.) In an uncertain world, each investment is an act of faith. The policy problem is to avoid investment decisions which are acts of *blind* faith.

Capital Markets and the Problem of Instability

When an economy is operating at full employment, it is producing all, or nearly all, that it can with its limited labor force and capital stock. If additional investment is undertaken in one area, such as the production of a supersonic airliner, cutbacks must be made elsewhere. Participants in the financial markets evaluate risks, and thus tend to channel funds to the companies whose prospects they consider brightest. Consequently, the markets tend to direct funds toward the most productive pattern of new investments.

But consider the problem when the economy moves down into a recession or a depression. Then, there are large amounts of unemployed labor and unused plant and equipment. The decision to build an additional bicycle plant, for example, is then not an alternative to another investment, such as additional machinery for the auto industry. They can both be built by putting the unem-

ployed labor and unemployed equipment back to work. Indeed, if the downward slide of the economy is severe, there are available resources to produce a lot of additional capital goods of all sorts—and additional consumer goods, too. The important question ceases to be *which* of the competing investments is better; for example, would it be better to invest in the auto industry *or* the bicycle industry? Rather, the full use of our potential requires that there be a movement back toward full employment. So the key question becomes: How do we get more investment in *both* the auto industry and the bicycle industry, and in other industries, too?

While the private financial markets do a reasonably good job in determining relative risks and rewards, and thus do a reasonably good job of determining *which* investments will be undertaken, they suffer major shortcomings in dealing with the problems of cyclical instability—the question of how much *total* investment should be undertaken. Consider what happened as the economy collapsed into the Depression of the 1930s. Stock market investors became panic-stricken as the Dow-Jones average plummeted. At the very low prices of the Depression, the stock market was no longer an attractive place for corporations to raise funds. Any issue of stock in those days meant that existing stockholders were practically giving away part of their ownership to the new buyers. Similarly, with the widespread difficulties of business, risk premiums on bonds rose sharply. For much of the 1930s, there was no overall shortage of investable funds—the riskless interest rate on federal government bonds was very low (between 2 and 3 percent). But funds were not cheap for many businesses because of extremely high risk premiums. As a result, investment was discouraged, and this added to the depth of the Depression.

Low stock prices and high borrowing costs were not the only reasons that investment dried up during the Depression. Many business executives were so frightened that they would not have undertaken expansion even if funds had been available at very low interest rates. Their pessimism and lack of investment were not the result of a lack of information. During the 1930s, business was indeed faced with appalling prospects; an individual with perfect information would still not have invested. Thus, while regulations requiring the disclosure of information can help direct investment funds into the most promising projects, additional information cannot be counted on to solve the problem of economic instability.

Because private financial markets do not necessarily result in a stable economy, the responsibility for stability has fallen to the federal government. How the government can fulfill this responsibility is the major topic of Parts 2 and 3 of this book.

Key Points

1. There are three forms of business organization: (*a*) single proprietorships; (*b*) partnerships; and (*c*) corporations.

2. Single proprietorships and partnerships are simple and flexible. On the other hand, the advantages of the corporate form of organization are (*a*) limited liability; (*b*) automatic continuity, even if one or more of the owners should die; and (*c*) better access to funds for financing growth.

3. A corporation can obtain financing by issuing common or preferred stock, and bonds (including convertible bonds).

4. There are two main types of business accounts. The balance sheet shows assets, liabilities, and net worth at a point in time. The income statement reports sales, costs, and profits during a period of time.

5. A financial intermediary takes small amounts of funds from individual savers and pools these funds to relend to businesses, governments, or individuals.

6. The purchaser of securities balances three important objectives: *high return, low risk,* and *high liquidity.*

7. A company that issues (sells) new securities also balances a number of objectives. It tries to keep the *return* of the corporation's stockholders as high as possible; it tries to avoid *risk;* and it tries to assure the *availability* of money when needed.

8. In general, bonds are less risky than common stocks for buyers of securities, and more risky for issuers of new securities. Corporations or individuals may increase their indebtedness in order to increase their leverage; that is, they may increase the ratio of debt to net worth. While this raises their potential gain, it also increases their risk of bankruptcy, since interest and principal payments are legal obligations.

9. Because stocks and bonds represent claims to future profits or interest payments, the evaluation of the issuer's prospects are extremely important for anyone buying a security. In order to protect the purchaser and to help direct funds into the projects where the returns are highest, the Securities and Exchange Commission (SEC) requires corporations to make relevant information available to the public.

10. Financial markets cannot be counted on to ensure the quantity of investment needed for full employment. The maintenance of a high level of employment is a responsibility of the federal government. (This role will be studied in future chapters.)

Key Concepts

single proprietorship
partnership
limited liability
corporation
incorporated (inc.)
share of common stock
equity (ownership)
dividend
double taxation of
    dividends
proxy
bond
principal (or face value)
convertible bond
preferred stock

cumulative preferred
    stock
balance sheet
income statement
assets
liabilities
net worth
short-term debt
long-term debt
retained earnings
book value
profit
straight-line depreciation
accelerated depreciation
obsolescence

financial intermediary
savings and loan association (S&L)
warrant
investment bank
underwrite
syndicate
yield (or return)
risk
liquidity
leverage
line of credit
risk premium
broker

Problems

6-1 Explain the advantages and disadvantages of incorporation.

6-2 Suppose you are an investment adviser, and a 50-year-old person comes to you for advice on how to invest $50,000 for retirement. What advice would you give? What advice would you give to a young couple who want to temporarily invest $10,000 that they expect to use for a down payment on a home 2 years from now?

6-3 For each of the following, explain why the statement is true or false:

(a) If liabilities exceed assets, net worth is negative.

(b) If additional stock is issued at a price in excess of the book value, the book value of the corporation's stock will rise.

(c) In general, dividends plus retained earnings are greater than corporate income taxes.

(d) Dividends paid in any year must be less than after-tax profits.

6-4 If a corporation increases its leverage, what are the advantages and/or disadvantages for:

(a) The owner of a share of the corporation's stock

(b) The owner of a $10,000 bond of the corporation

6-5 "While private enterprise does make some mistakes and invest in losing projects, it is less likely to do so than the government. After all, business executives risk their own money, while government officials risk the public's money." Do you agree? Can you think of any investment projects that the government has undertaken which were particularly desirable? Might they have been undertaken by private businesses? Why or why not? Can you think of any government investment projects which were particularly ill-advised?

6-6 In what ways do the interests of stockholders coincide with the interests of the managers of a corporation? Are there any ways in which their interests are in conflict?

*6-7 "High interest rates are needed to induce individuals or institutions to buy risky bonds. Similarly, high returns are required to induce corporations to invest in risky new ventures. Higher yields in response to risk are desirable, not only for the individual or corporation directly involved, but also for society. They discourage the waste of scarce resources on costly failures."

(a) Do you agree? Can you think of any exceptions, where the high risk premiums demanded by private investors discourage socially desirable expenditures? (Hint: We saw in Chapter 4 that the market mechanism does not necessarily work in a desirable way when there are externalities. Are there ever externalities in investment decisions?)

(b) In 1975, when New York City was in danger of default, the interest rate it had to pay to borrow money shot upward. Do you think that this increase was socially desirable? Argue the case for and against.

PART TWO
HIGH EMPLOYMENT AND
A STABLE PRICE LEVEL

The six chapters of Part 1 have set the stage for the study of economics, providing analytic and institutional background and outlining the major objectives of high employment, price stability, efficiency, an equitable distribution of income, and growth.

The focus of Parts 2 and 3 will be on the goals of high employment and price stability. These involve the overall aggregates of the economy. How many workers are employed in the economy as a whole? What is happening to the total quantity of output in the economy? What is happening to the average level of prices? Because they deal with economywide magnitudes, these questions are classified under the heading of *macroeconomics*. (*Makros* is the Greek word for "large.") In contrast, the objectives of efficiency and equity, which will be the principal topics of Parts 4 and 5, deal with the details of the economy. What specific goods are produced? Would we be better off if we produced more wheat and less butter? More bicycles and fewer cars? How is income divided between labor (in the form of wages and salaries) and capital (in the form of interest and profits)? Since these questions deal with the detailed relationships among various industries or groups in the economy, they go under the heading of *microeconomics*. (*Mikros* is the Greek word for "small," and appears in "microscope," the apparatus for looking at very small objects.)

As an introduction to Part 2 on macroeconomics, Chapter 7 describes how national output is measured. Chapter 8 addresses the question of why high unemployment can exist—and persist—in a market economy. Not surprisingly, much of the basic theory of unemployment can be traced back to the Depression of the 1930s and, in particular, to the pen of British economist John Maynard Keynes. Keynes argued that production fell and unemployment rose during the Depression because of *insufficient demand.* With the collapse in demand for automobiles in the early depression, autoworkers were discharged. When the demand for housing slackened, construction workers lost their jobs. When the demand for clothing declined, textile workers were laid off. Thus, the widespread increase in unemployment was due to an overall decline in the demand for the goods and services produced in the economy; that is, to a decline in *aggregate demand.* When people don't buy, workers don't work. The Keynesian theory of aggregate demand is explained in Chapter 8.

Chapters 9, 10, and 11 address the policy question: If aggregate demand is too low, what can be done about it? There are two important tools the authorities can use to control aggregate demand: fiscal policy and monetary policy. *Fiscal policy* involves changes in (1) government spending and (2) taxation. While the fine points must of course be left until the following chapters, the main way in which fiscal policies affect aggregate demand and employment may be stated quite simply. If, during a depression, the government undertakes a construction project (such as a dam), it thereby increases the demand for cement, steel, and other materials. Some people are put to work producing cement and steel, and others start to work directly on the construction of the dam. As a result, the unemployment rate will fall. The taxation side of fiscal policy works more indirectly. If the government cuts taxes, the public will have more income left after taxes, and they will tend as a consequence to buy more—more clothing, more washing machines, more vacations, and more of a whole host of goods and services. Again, people will be put to work producing clothing, washing machines, etc.

Monetary policy involves changes in the quantity of money. In our economy, there are two types of money. Most obviously, the dollar bills and coins which you have in your pocket are money; you can use them to buy lunch or go to a movie. But many purchases are not paid for with "pocket money." Payment by check is very common. Since balances in checking accounts are used so commonly to make purchases, they are counted as part of the total quantity of money. Because of the importance of checking-account money, a study of money involves an examination of how the banking system works (Chapters 10 and 11). The major idea behind monetary policy can be put quite simply. When people have more money in the form either of cash in their pockets or of balances in their checking accounts, they will tend to spend more. Thus, by taking steps to increase the quantity of money, the authorities can encourage spending.

Much of the basic macroeconomic theory dates from the Great Depression, when aggregate demand was too low and many workers were consequently unemployed. But problems can also exist on the opposite side. Aggregate demand can get too high. If people try to buy more than the limited available supply of goods, the result is inflation. Again, aggregate demand tools may be used by the authorities: fiscal and monetary policies can be adjusted, this time to restrain aggregate demand.

The chapters of Part 2 (especially Chapters 9 and 11) explain the basics of aggregate demand management. The propositions in these chapters are important; they have helped us manage our economy so that it has performed much better in the past 30 years than it did in the two decades between the two world wars. But our warning in Chapter 2 bears repeating: Theory necessarily involves simplification. And, when it is presented to beginning students, theory must be doubly simplified. Thus, the theoretical "road map" of Part 2 has been drawn with the bumps and potholes removed. But bumps and potholes do exist. While the economy in recent decades has performed well by historical standards, we have not been able to do better and better. Many problems remain unsolved. In particular, during the 1970s we have been unable to cure the twin problems of inflation and unemployment. These problems, and the difficult decisions which face the policymaker, will be the subject of Part 3 (Chapters 12 through 16).

But first, we must develop the simple story in Part 2.

chapter 7
Measuring National Product and National Income

In the modern economy, a vast array of goods and services is produced: cars, TV sets, houses, clothing, medical care, and food, to name but a few. One way of judging the performance of the economy is to measure the aggregate production of goods and services. A measure of total production does not, of course, give a complete picture of the welfare of the nation. When we acquire more and more goods, we do not necessarily become happier or more contented. Other things are important too: the sense of accomplishment which comes from our everyday work, and the quality of our environment. (See the Appendix to this chapter.) Nevertheless, the total amount which is produced is one of the important measures of economic success.

THE MARKET AS A WAY OF MEASURING PRODUCTION

The wide range of products poses a problem: How are we to add them all up into a single measure of national product? How do we add apples and oranges?

Market prices provide an answer. If apples sell for $10 per bushel and oranges for $20, the market indicates that 1 bushel of oranges is worth 2 bushels of apples. When market prices are used, oranges and apples can indeed be compared and added, as shown in the example in Table 7-1. In our complex economy, we can similarly add automobiles, clothing, TV sets, and the host of other goods and services to find the national product at market prices.

National product is the dollar value of final goods and services produced during the year.

Dollar Prices: The Elastic Yardstick

Dollar prices provide a satisfactory basis for calculating national product in any one year. But, if we wish to evaluate the

124

TABLE 7-1
Using Market Prices to Add Apples and Oranges

	(1) Quantity (bushels)	(2) Price (per bushel)	(3) Market value (3) = (1) × (2)
Apples	3,000	$10	$30,000
Oranges	2,000	$20	$40,000
		Total	$70,000

Market prices provide a way of adding different goods to get a measure of total production.

performance of the economy over a number of years, we face a second problem. The dollar is an elastic yardstick. Inflations can send the value of the dollar down (and infrequent deflations can send it up).

As the years pass, the market value of national product may rise for two quite different reasons. First, the *quantities* of apples, oranges, and other goods and services may rise. This increase is desirable; we have more and more goods and services at our disposal. Second, the *prices* of apples, oranges, etc., may rise. This increase is undesirable; it occurs because we have been unsuccessful in the battle against inflation. To judge the performance of the economy, *it is essential to separate the desirable increase in the quantity of output from the undesirable increase in prices.*

To do so, we use an *index of prices*, which measures inflation. For example, if the price of every good and service were

---

BOX 7-1
CONSTRUCTING A PRICE INDEX

In constructing a price index, goods and services are weighted according to their importance in total product. Suppose that since the base year, the price of mobile homes doubled, while the price of cars remained unchanged. An index of these two prices would not move up to a simple unweighted average of 150. Why?

Because people spend 10 times as much on cars as on mobile homes, cars are weighted 10 times as heavily as mobile homes in constructing an index, thus:

	(1) Base period price (by convention, set at 100)	(2) Price in period 2	(3) Weight	(4) Price × weight (4) = (2) × (3)
Autos	100	100	10	1,000
Mobile homes	100	200	1	200
		Total	11	1,200

The price index for period 2 is equal to the sum of column 4 divided by the sum of column 3; that is, $\frac{1,200}{11} = 109$.

2.

TABLE 7-2
Calculating Real GNP

Year	(1) Nominal GNP (billions of current dollars)	(2) Index of prices	(3) Real GNP (billions of 1972 dollars) $(3) = \frac{(1)}{(2)} \times 100$
1972	$1,171	100	$\frac{1,171}{100} \times 100 = \$1,171$
1974	$1,413	116.4	$\frac{1,413}{116.4} \times 100 = \$1,214$
1976	$1,692	133.8	?

Between 1972 and 1974, nominal GNP rose from $1,171 billion to $1,413 billion, or by $242 billion. But only $43 (= $1,214 − $1,171) billion reflected an increase in real production; the rest was inflation. As an exercise, calculate real GNP in 1976.

(Answer: $1,265 billion.)

compared with the prices in an earlier year (the *base* year) and found to be twice as high, the index of prices would be 200. (By convention, indexes are given in percentages, with the base year being assigned a value of 100.) In a more realistic situation, some prices rise more rapidly than others. In this case, the price index gives a *weighted average* of prices (Box 7-1).

Once we have this price index, we can use it to deflate current-dollar national product (Table 7-2, column 1) and find *constant-dollar* or *real* national product (column 3). (The specific measure of national product used in Table 7-2—gross national product, or GNP—will be defined in detail later in this chapter.) Between 1972 and 1974, prices rose on average by 16.4 percent. By dividing 1974's nominal GNP by the price index of 116.4 (and multiplying by 100 to compensate for the use of percentages), we find that

Nominal or *current-dollar* national product is measured at the prices existing when production took place.

Constant-dollar or *real* national product is measured at the prices existing in one specific base year.

1974 GNP of $1,413 billion was worth only $1,214 billion when measured in 1972 prices. Most of the increase in nominal GNP between 1972 and 1974 was caused by a rise in prices; there was only a small increase in the real output of goods and services.

Figure 7-1 shows nominal (current-dollar) and real (constant-dollar) GNP since the beginning of the Great Depression in 1929. The substantial difference between these two series is a reflection of inflation.

TWO APPROACHES: Expenditure and Income

Now let's turn from the important problem of inflation to the details of measuring national product. To begin, consider the simplest of all possible economies, in which the public consumes all the goods and services being produced. To illustrate, let's once more call on the basic circular-flow diagram introduced in Chapter 3 (Figure 3-3) and repeated here as Figure 7-2.

The performance of the economy can be measured by looking at either the upper loop or the lower loop. In the upper loop are the monetary expenditures by households buying the consumer goods produced by busi-

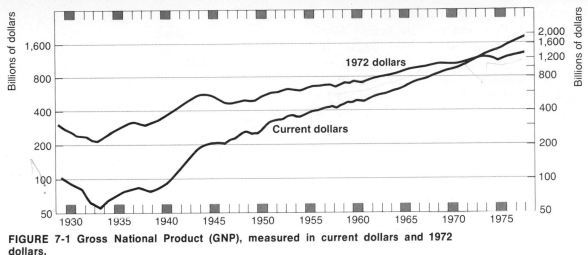

FIGURE 7-1 Gross National Product (GNP), measured in current dollars and 1972 dollars.
Much of the increased in current-dollar national product is the result of inflation. Observe that national product has grown more slowly in constant (1972) dollars than in current dollars.

ness. Where do these payments go? They are received (in the lower loop) by those who have provided the productive inputs: wages and salaries for the labor force; rents to the suppliers of land and buildings; and interest and profits to the suppliers of capital. Profits

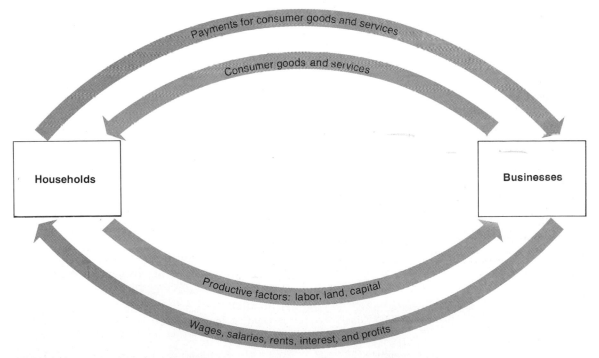

FIGURE 7-2 The circular flow of payments.
In the upper loop are the payments for the goods and services produced. In the lower loop, we see where the receipts of business go: to pay wages, salaries, rents, interest, and profits.

127

are a residual, left over after all other payments have been made. Thus, in this simple economy, the two loops give exactly the same total. We may look at the upper loop, which gives the market value of the national product. Alternatively, we may look at the lower loop, which measures *national income*.

> **National income** is the sum of all income derived from providing the factors of production. It includes wages and salaries, rents, interest, and profits.

NATIONAL PRODUCT: The Expenditures Approach

To calculate the upper-loop national product, all goods and services should be counted *once*, and *only* once. Government statisticians count the bread purchased by the consumer. But they do not also count separately the flour that was used in producing the bread, or the wheat that went into producing the flour. Similarly, they count the automobiles sold to consumers, but do not count separately the steel that went into the autos. To do so would involve counting the steel twice.

The bread and cars are *final products*; the wheat which went into the bread and the steel which went into the car are *intermediate products*. (See Box 7-2.) To avoid double counting, national product is found by adding up only expenditures on final products. These fall into several categories: personal consumption expenditures, government expenditures for goods and services, private

domestic investment and net exports (exports minus imports).

1. Personal Consumption Expenditures (*C*)

Consumption is the ultimate objective of economic activity, and personal consumption expenditures (*C*) constitute the largest component of national product. Consumer expenditures are divided into three main components: durable goods, such as cars or washing machines; nondurable goods, such as food or clothing; and services, such as medical services or haircuts. Details are provided in Table 7-3.

Bread, haircuts, and other goods and services purchased by the consumer are included in national product because they are final products. They are used up by consumers, and are not used for the production of other goods.

2. Government Purchases of Goods and Services (*G*)

The economy produces not only consumption goods and services, but a large volume of production also goes on through government auspices. The government hires contractors to build roads; the roads are produced. Workers are hired to keep up the parks which are open for the public's enjoyment; park services are produced. The government purchases aircraft and ships for the purpose of protecting the public. Court services are produced to provide justice and settle conflicts. Governments at all levels—federal, state, and local—undertake expenditures for the public good.[1]

While government expenditures on goods and services are included in national

---

[1] The inclusion of all government expenditures for goods and services in national product involves a problem. While some government purchases are for "final" use, other spending may reasonably be considered to result in intermediate products. A road, for example, can carry both vacation traffic (a "final" or consumption type of use) and trucks loaded with goods. Trucking is an "intermediate" stage in the productive process. Thus, it might be argued that only part of the spending for roads represents a "final" use, and that government spending for roads should not be included in national product insofar as the roads are used for business purposes. National product accountants have ducked the complicated problem of dividing government spending into "final" and "intermediate" categories. All government spending for goods and services is assumed to be "final," and is included in national product. Therefore, insofar as government provides intermediate goods and services to businesses, the official national product statistics represent an overestimate.

TABLE 7-3

The Composition of Personal Consumption Expenditures, 1977

Type	Billions of dollars	Percentage of total
1. Durable goods	179.8	14.8
(*a*) Automobiles and parts	83.8	6.9
(*b*) Furniture and		
household equipment	70.5	5.8
(*c*) Other	25.5	2.1
2. Nondurable goods	480.7	39.7
(*a*) Clothing	246.2	20.3
(*b*) Food and beverages	83.0	6.9
(*c*) Gasoline and oil	44.7	3.7
(*d*) Other	106.6	8.8
3. Services	550.7	45.5
(*a*) Housing	184.4	15.2
(*b*) Household operation	82.9	6.8
(*c*) Transportation	41.6	3.4
(*d*) Others	241.9	20.0
Total	1,211.2	100

Source. Survey of Current Business, April 1978.

product, transfer payments are not included. When the government pays people to work on the parks, it produces more attractive parks. But when the government makes transfer payments to the unemployed or to retirees under the social security program, nothing is produced by the recipient in exchange for the government expenditure. Government expenditures on parks are included in national product, but government social security payments are not.

3. Private Domestic Investment (*I*)

During a year, we produce not only consumption goods and services and governmental goods and services. We also produce capital goods (or "investment" goods) which will help in production in future years. Private domestic investment[2] (*I*) includes three major categories: (1) *plant* (that is, factories or other structures); (2) *equipment* (machinery, tools, etc.); and (3) *changes in inventories.*

Plant and Equipment The national product includes expenditures for new plant and equipment. The word "new" is emphasized. If a new factory is built or a machine produced, that factory or machine is part of the national product during the year of its construction. But a 10-year-old building or a 5-year-old machine sold by one firm to another is *not* included in national product. The building or machine is merely being transferred from one owner to another, and is not being produced this year.[3] (Renovations on an existing building during the current year are, however, included in national product.) Similarly, common stocks

[2]This category includes only private investment, since government investment (in dams, etc.) is included elsewhere as part of government expenditures for goods and services. It includes only domestic investment in the United States, since national product is being estimated. If General Motors builds a factory in Germany, its value is included in German national product, not in United States national product. (On the other hand, if Sony builds a plant in the United States, that plant is included in the private domestic investment of the United States.)

[3]For similar reasons, the purchase of secondhand cars or other secondhand durables is not included in the personal consumption category of national product.

BOX 7-2
VALUE ADDED

Consider more carefully the example of a loaf of bread sold to the final consumer for 60 cents. Behind the final sale is a whole series of transactions. Consider first the wheat that goes into a loaf of bread. Its value is 10 cents. That wheat has to be made into flour. After it is processed into flour, the value of the flour is 25 cents. Thus, the 10 cents' worth of wheat has a value of 15 cents *added* to it when it is made into flour. Similarly, value is added when the flour is baked into bread, and when the bread is delivered to the consumer.

How much has been produced? The answer: The 60-cent loaf of bread. In calculating national product, we must not add up all the sales of the first column, totaling $1.40. We have produced only 60 worth cents of bread.

The easiest way to measure product is to look at the final sale—the 60-cent loaf of bread sold to the consumer. Alternatively, we can arrive at the same result by adding up the value added at each stage in the productive process in column 3. Observe how these values do add up to the 60-cent price of the .

Stage of production	(1) Value of sales		(2) Cost of intermediate products		(3) Value added (1) − (2) = (3)
Intermediate goods:					
Wheat	10¢	−	0	=	10¢
Flour	25¢	−	10¢	=	15¢
Bread, at wholesale	45¢	−	25¢	=	20¢
Final good: Bread, at retail	60¢	−	45¢	=	15¢
Sum of value added					60¢

loaf of bread. This is so because, in these calculations, each intermediate good "cancels out"; that is, it appears twice, with a positive sign in column 1, and a negative sign in column 2. Value added at each stage of the productive process goes to the payment of income in the form of wages and salaries, rent, interest, and profits. Thus, summing the value added provides a lower-loop "income" measure, which can be used to check on the upper-loop measure of expenditures on final products.

Value added is equal to the value of a firm's product less the cost of intermediate products bought from outside suppliers.

Value added is not only a way of checking national product calculations; it also is a way of judging the importance of various industries. If we were to look only at final products, we would concentrate on automobiles, and ignore steel. Yet, the steel industry makes a very important contribution to the production of automobiles; this contribution can be measured by looking at value added in the steel industry. In 1977, major contributors to value added included the following industries:

Industry	Value added (billions of dollars)
Agriculture, forest, and fisheries	43
Mining	34
Construction	77
Manufacturing	392
Transportation	55
Communication	34
Electricity and other utilities	29
Wholesale and retail trade	252
Finance, insurance, and real estate	177
Other services	221

131

acquired by an individual or institution are not included in national product. They represent simply a transfer of ownership. Of course, if a corporation issues stock and finances the construction of a factory with the proceeds, the new factory is part of the national product. It has been produced during the current year.

Changes in Inventories We have seen that wheat that goes into bread is not counted separately in the national product, because its cost has already been included as part of the price of bread. But how about any wheat we produce above and beyond the amount we consume in the form of bread and pastries? What happens to it? The answer is that it is either exported (a possibility that we will consider in just a moment), or it is used to build up our inventories of wheat. Any such increases in our stocks of wheat represent something we have produced, and therefore they are included in our measure of national product.

Similarly, increases in inventories of steel are included in national product. But we do not include the steel which went into the production of refrigerators, since it is already included when we count consumer purchases of refrigerators. Nor is steel that went into a bridge counted separately, since it is already included in government expenditures. Nor is the steel used to make a machine, since it is already included in expenditures for plant and equipment.

Earlier, we said that in order to measure national product, we should measure final product. This is an acceptable and commonly used generalization. It is 99 percent right, and that is pretty good. But it is not precisely accurate: national product includes not only final product for the consumer, government, and plant and equipment sectors, but also the intermediate products that have been added to inventories. (The precisely correct statement is perhaps worth one last reiteration: We should measure everything once and only once.)

Changes in inventories can be either positive or negative. In a bad crop year, there may be less wheat on hand at the end of the year than at the beginning. We have taken more out of our stocks than we have put back in. In this case, changes in inventories are negative, and they are subtracted in measuring national product.

4. Exports of Goods and Services (X)

Wheat which we produce may be exported; if so, it should be included in national product. As such production does not appear elsewhere in the accounts, it is included in the separate item, exports of goods and services (X).

How a good, such as wheat, is exported is obvious; it is put in a ship and sent abroad. But how can services (such as haircuts and surgical operations) be exported? The answer is this. A tourist from Tokyo visiting Hawaii has all sorts of expenditures: for hotel accommodations, for bus fare, for haircuts, and for medical services. And the tourist may have come on a United States airliner. All these services have been provided by Americans. As they are paid for by the foreigner, they are considered exports of services even though the hotel, the bus, the barber shop, and the hospital physically remain in the United States. (Interest and dividend payments by foreigners to Americans are included among our exports of services. They represent payments by foreigners for the services provided by United States capital.)

5. A Subtraction: Imports of Goods and Services (M)

The production of wheat for export must be included in national product. On the other side, our consumers purchase Japanese automobiles. These purchases are part of the personal consumption expenditures category. But the car has not been produced in the United States; it should not be counted as part of our national product. Thus, a subtraction is made for cars imported from Japan (and other countries). Similarly, all other United States imports of goods and services (M) are subtracted when calculating national product.

National Product: A Summary Statement

From the above list, the formal statement of national product can be derived:

National product = personal consumption expenditures (C)

plus   government purchases of goods and services (G)

plus   private domestic investment (I)

plus   exports of goods and services (X)

less   imports of goods and services (M)

In symbols, this is written:

National product = $C + I + G + X - M$

GNP AND NNP: The Complication of Depreciation

The main outline of national product accounting has now been completed, but a number of details remain to be explained. One of the most important involves the measurement of investment.

When we count the full value of plant and equipment produced during this year, national product is overestimated. Why is this so? Because our existing plant and equipment have been operated for another year. As a consequence, they have deteriorated (depreciated). After calculating the total value of all plant and equipment pro-duced during the year, we should make an appropriate deduction for this depreciation. Only then will we get a true measure of how much our plant and equipment have increased during the year (Figure 7-3).

Thus, two definitions of investment should be distinguished.

> *Gross private domestic investment* (I_g) is equal to expenditures for new plant and equipment, plus the change in inventories.
> *Net private domestic investment* (I_n) is equal to gross private domestic investment, less depreciation. That is,
>
> $$I_n = I_g - \text{depreciation}$$

Corresponding to these two definitions of investment, there are two definitions of national product:

> *Gross national product* (GNP) =
> $$C + I_g + G + X - M$$
> *Net national product* (NNP) =
> $$C + I_n + G + X - M$$

From these definitions, it follows that:

NNP = GNP − depreciation

This relationship is illustrated in the first two columns of Figure 7-4.

In theory, NNP is the measure of national product that we should use; it takes into account the wear and tear on machinery during the year. Why, then, is there all this fuss over GNP instead of NNP in the newspapers and economics books? The answer: While NNP is the best measure conceptually, it is difficult to estimate with any great degree of confidence. Gross investment—the value of new plant, equipment, and inventories acquired by business—is relatively easy to measure. But the measurement of depreciation involves both conceptual and practical problems. How fast does a machine really

Initial stock of capital

Plus: New plant, equipment, and changes in inventories

Less: Estimates of deterioration and obsolescence of plant and equipment

Equals: Stock of capital at end of year

Gross investment

Depreciation

Net investment

Plant, equipment, and, inventories

Stock of capital at end of year

January 1

December 31

FIGURE 7-3 Net investment: a change in the stock of capital.
During the year the stock of capital increases by gross investment, less depreciation.

wear out? Will it become obsolete before it is physically worn out? If it will be scrapped in 10 years, does its value decline in a "straight line," by 10 percent each year? Furthermore, the national product accountant must begin with business accounts, and business estimates of depreciation may depend more on the technicalities of the income tax law than on the true rate at which plant and equipment lose their value. Because of these problems, the estimates of depreciation may be quite imprecise. Therefore, GNP is used more frequently than NNP by economists and the press.

THE SALES TAX COMPLICATION: Net National Product and National Income

Earlier in this chapter we described the circular flow of payments, with upper-loop payments being made for net national product and lower-loop payments representing

national income. In the very simple illustration used there, the two loops were equal, and net national product and national income were exactly the same size as a consequence. In our complex, real-life economy, they are closely related, but not precisely equal.

Net national product (NNP) is the total quantity of goods and services produced during the year, measured at market prices. *National income* (NI) is the sum of all income earned by those who provide the factors of production—that is, wages and salaries, rents, interest, and profits. How can they possibly be different? They may be different because the factors of production do not get all the returns from the sale of a good. Part goes to the government in the form of a sales tax.

Consider a package of razor blades priced, say, at $1.99. That $1.99 is divided among the various participants who bring

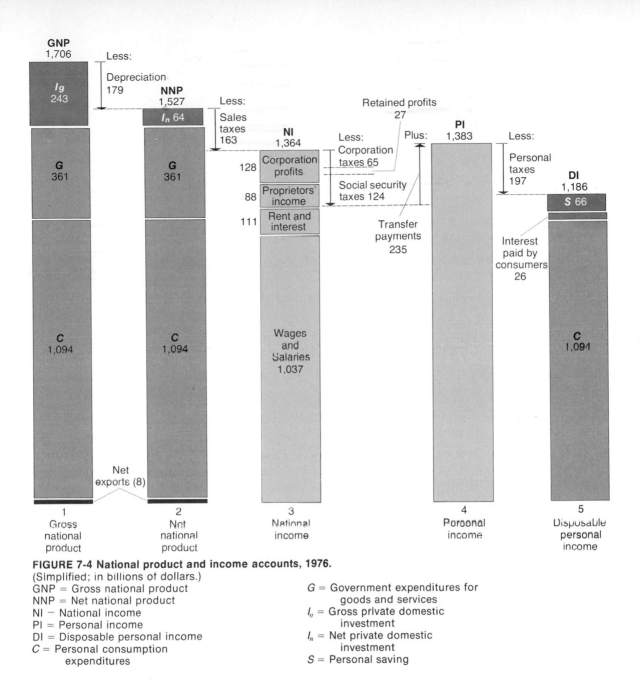

FIGURE 7-4 National product and income accounts, 1976.
(Simplified; in billions of dollars.)
GNP = Gross national product
NNP = Net national product
NI – National income
PI = Personal income
DI = Disposable personal income
C = Personal consumption
    expenditures

G = Government expenditures for
    goods and services
I_g = Gross private domestic
    investment
I_n = Net private domestic
    investment
S = Personal saving

the razor blades to market. It goes into wages and salaries, rents, interest, and profits of those who contribute to the production of the blades. The $1.99 is *part of national income*. But, when you get to the cash regis-

ter with your package of razor blades, you will pay more than $1.99. Approximately 10 cents (more or less, depending on the state in which you live) will be added in the form of a sales tax, making a total of $2.09. Because national product is measured at market prices, *it includes the whole $2.09.*

Thus, in Figure 7-4, sales taxes have to be subtracted from NNP in order to get the national income earned by the suppliers of productive resources.[4]

OTHER INCOME MEASURES

Thus far, we have seen that GNP includes consumption, government purchases of goods and services, gross investment, and exports less imports. The difference between GNP and NNP is depreciation, although this is difficult to measure precisely. We also saw that when sales taxes are subtracted from NNP, the remainder is national income, that is, the payments received from the provision of labor, land, and capital.

Personal Income (PI)

Now let's see what happens next. Although most of *national income* is received by households as their *personal income*, (PI), these two measures of income are not exactly the same.

The first reason is that not all national income flows through the business sector to households. Part of business profit is taken by the government in the form of corporate income taxes. Part of profit is retained by corporations to finance expansion. (Thus, dividends are the only portion of corporate profits which flow through to become personal income.) Finally, taxes are paid into the social security fund, and these taxes also fail to appear in personal income.

The second reason that personal income is not the same as national income lies in transfer payments. These are a source of personal income to households. But they are not derived from providing factors of production, and therefore are not included in national income.

Thus, to move from national income to personal income in Figure 7-4, we subtract corporation taxes, profits retained by corporations, and social security taxes. But we add transfer payments. Personal income is the measure which corresponds most closely to the everyday meaning of "income."

Disposable Personal Income (DI)

Not all personal income is available to the individual or family for personal use, however. The government takes a sizable chunk in the form of personal taxes. (These are mainly personal income taxes, but also include miscellaneous items, such as inheritance taxes.) After these taxes are paid, *disposable personal income* (DI) remains. It is divided three ways, among consumption, the payment of interest on consumer debt, and saving (*S*). Disposable income is an important concept, because consumers look at this income when they decide how much to spend.

---

[4]In Figure 7-4, proprietors' income is not broken down into its components of wages and salaries, interest and profits, and rents. National income accountants make no effort to separate (1) the income which farmers and the owners of other unincorporated businesses earn as a result of their labor from (2) the income they earn as profits from their farm or other business.

Figure 7-4 is simplified. In practice, there are errors in estimating the upper loop of national product and the lower loop of national income. Thus, in moving from NNP to national income, there is an adjustment not only for sales taxes, but also for a statistical discrepancy.

Key Points

1. The market provides a way of adding apples, oranges, automobiles, and the host of other goods and services produced during the year. Items are included in national product at their market prices.

2. However, market prices provide a misleading way of comparing the national product in two different years because the value of the dollar can shrink as a result of inflation. A rise in current-dollar national product may reflect a combination of an increase in prices and an increase in real production. In order to find the increase in real production, current-dollar GNP is deflated with a price index. (A price index is a weighted average of prices.)

3. There are two approaches to measuring the performance of the economy. The expenditures (upper-loop) approach involves the measurement of final product—consumption, government purchases of goods and services, investment, and exports less imports. The income (lower-loop) approach involves the measurement of wages and salaries, rents, interest, and profits.

4. In measuring national product, everything should be measured once, and only once. Intermediate products (such as wheat or steel) used in the production of other goods (such as bread or automobiles) should not be counted separately, since they are already included when we count the bread or automobiles.

5. Net investment equals gross investment minus depreciation. If net investment is positive, then more plant, equipment, and inventories are being manufactured than are being used up. Thus, the capital stock is rising (Figure 7-3).

6. $\text{GNP} = C + I_y + G + X - M$
$\text{NNP} = \text{GNP} - \text{depreciation}$
Because depreciation is hard to measure accurately, statisticans have more confidence in the measure of GNP than NNP, and therefore GNP is used more commonly.

7. Review Figure 7-4 for the relationships among NNP, national income, personal income, and disposable personal income.

Key Concepts

gross national product (GNP)
net national product (NNP)
price index
base year
weighted average
deflating with a price
  index
current-dollar GNP
constant-dollar GNP
upper-loop or national
  product approach

lower-loop or national
  income approach
final product
intermediate product
value added
consumption
investment
government purchases of
  goods and services
exports of goods and services
imports of goods and services

durable goods
nondurable goods
services
inventories
gross investment
net investment
depreciation
national income (NI)
personal income (PI)
disposable personal
  income (DI)

Problems

7-1 Consider a hypothetical economy in which the following quantities are measured (in billions of dollars):

Consumption expenditures	$1,000
Value of common stocks purchased	400
Gross private domestic investment	300
Government transfer payments	100
Sales taxes	50
Government purchases of goods and services	200
Corporate income taxes	200
Personal income taxes	100
Exports minus imports	10
Depreciation	75
Purchases of secondhand cars	100

(*a*) Calculate GNP. (Be careful. Not all the items are included.)

(*b*) Calculate NNP.

7-2 In Figure 7-1, compare the changes in real GNP and nominal GNP between 1929 and 1933. Which fell faster? From your finding, do you conclude that the average level of prices rose, or fell, or remained stable as the economy slid into the Great Depression?

7-3 The change in inventories can be negative. Can net investment also be negative? Explain.

7-4 Give an example of an import of a service.

7-5 Which of the following government expenditures are included in GNP?

(*a*) The purchase of an aircraft for the Air Force

(*b*) The purchase of a computer for the Treasury Department

(*c*) The payment of unemployment insurance benefits to those who have lost their jobs

(*d*) The salary paid to maintenance workers who mow the grass beside the highways

7-6 Last year the Anderson family members were involved in the following activities. What items are included in GNP? Explain in each case why the item is, or is not, included.

(*a*) They purchased a used car from their neighbor.

(*b*) They deposited $1,000 in a savings deposit at the bank.

(*c*) They purchased $2,000 worth of groceries.

(*d*) They flew to London for a vacation.

7-7 For 1976 (shown in Figure 7-4):

(*a*) Which was larger: government purchases of goods and services or gross investment?

(*b*) Approximately what percent of NNP was net investment?

(*c*) Approximately how large a percentage of national income were wages and salaries? Corporate profits? Rent and interest?

(*d*) Approximately what fraction of disposable income was saved?

Appendix

GNP AND ECONOMIC WELFARE

GNP is one of the most frequently used measures of economic performance. And major changes in GNP may indeed reflect severe problems or impressive gains. When the nation's real GNP fell by 30 percent between 1929 and 1933, many United States workers lost their jobs; the performance of the economy was clearly unsatisfactory. On the other hand, the very large increase in real GNP in Japan in recent decades has been associated with a rapid rise in the material standard of living.

Yet GNP has severe limits as a measure of economic welfare. In part, these limitations are due to the focus on market sales as a way of measuring output. While some products are included in GNP, other quite similar products are left out. When a professional carpenter builds bookcases, they appear in GNP; but if you build them for your own home, they are not included. A restaurant meal appears in GNP, but an equally delicious meal prepared at home does not (although the ingredients bought at the store are included.)[5] When someone tunes in the radio after a hard day's work, there is no GNP accountant present to measure the pleasure which the program provides.

On the other hand, some of the things which are included in GNP can scarcely be considered contributions to human happiness. When the cold war becomes more tense, rising armament purchases are included in GNP; yet we are no happier. If there is an increase in crime, additional expenditures for police, courts, and prisons are included in GNP. Yet society is scarcely better off than it was before the increase in crime. The production of automobiles is included in GNP, but there is no downward adjustment for the resulting pollution. Indeed, if people need medical attention as a result, GNP will go up. (Doctors' services are included in GNP.)

Naturally enough, economists are bothered by the shortcomings of GNP as a measure of well-being. During the past decade, a number of attempts have been made to deal with these inadequacies. These attempts fall under two main headings.

1. Emphasis on Additional Social Indicators

The first step is to downplay GNP as the measure of how the economy and society are performing, and to realize that it is only one of a number of important indicators of performance. In several countries, attempts have been made to present lists of social indicators that, taken together, can provide both a way of judging performance and a series of objectives for policymakers.[6] Important indicators of social well-being include such things as life expectan-

---

[5]The market is not the sole criterion of whether something is included in GNP. Since GNP is taken as a measure of the economy's performance, illegal products (such as heroin) are excluded from GNP on the ground that they are "bads" rather than "goods."

[6]Examples of such lists may be found in: Economic Council of Canada, *Eleventh Annual Review: Economic Targets and Social Indicators* (Ottawa, 1974); U.S. Department of Health, Education, and Welfare, *Toward a Social Report* (Washington, 1969); and Overseas Development Council, *The United States and World Development: Agenda 1977* (New York: Praeger, 1977).

cy, infant mortality rates, the availability of health care, the quantity of leisure, the quality of air and water (and other aspects of the environment), and the degree of urban crowding.

2. A Comprehensive Measure of Economic Welfare (MEW)

The second approach is more ambitious: to provide a comprehensive single measure of economic performance, including not only the standard national product measure, but also additions for the value of leisure and subtractions for pollution and other disadvantages of crowded urban living. Such a measure of economic welfare (MEW) has been presented by two Yale University economists, William Nordhaus and James Tobin.[7]

The difficulties they encountered were formidable. Indeed, the most interesting implication of their study is that a satisfactory index can't be constructed. To see why, consider the problem posed by leisure. As productivity has risen, the working population has taken only part of the gain in the form of higher wages and other measured incomes; a significant part of the gain has come in the form of a shorter workweek. Specifically, Nordhaus and Tobin calculated that the average number of leisure hours had increased by 22 percent between 1929 and 1965, while real per capita NNP had risen by 90 percent.

The question is, What should be made of these facts? Specifically, which of the following conclusions is correct?

1. Production per person has gone up by 90 percent, and we have gotten more leisure, too. Therefore, economic welfare has really improved by more than 90 percent; it has risen more than NNP.

2. Production per person has gone up by 90 percent. But leisure has risen by less than 90 percent; specifically, it has risen by only 22 percent. Therefore, overall welfare has risen by some weighted average of the 90 percent and the 22 percent. That is, overall welfare has improved by a smaller percentage than NNP.

It is far from clear which of these conclusions is "correct." Therefore, Nordhaus and Tobin presented two alternative estimates of MEW, reflecting the two alternative assumptions regarding leisure. These alternatives are shown in Figure 7-5, together with the growth of per capita NNP.

The choice between conclusions 1 and 2 is difficult; but it is only the beginning of the problems with evaluating economic welfare in a more comprehensive way. For example, observe that the Nordhaus-Tobin estimates of MEW do not drop during the Depression, and, indeed, they actually rise between 1929 and 1935. How can this be? Were we really becoming better off

---

[7]William Nordhaus and James Tobin, "Is Growth Obsolete?" in *Economic Growth, Fiftieth Anniversary Colloquium* (New York: National Bureau of Economic Research, 1972). (Tobin was a member of the President's Council of Economic Advisers during the Kennedy administration. Nordhaus was appointed a member when Jimmy Carter became President.)

FIGURE 7-5 Measures of economic welfare.
Nordhaus and Tobin found the measure of economic welfare to be *very* sensitive to the treatment of leisure. Measure 1 is based on the view that welfare has gone up by more than NNP, since we have gotten the increase in output, and more leisure, too. Measure 2 reflects the view that welfare has gone up by a weighted average of the increase in NNP and the (smaller) increase in leisure.

as the economy slid into the Depression? The explanation for this quirk: Nordhaus and Tobin have included leisure as an element of welfare, and leisure certainly increased as people were thrown out of work. But there is surely something wrong here. Leisure after a good day's work may be bliss; but enforced leisure following a firing is not so pleasant.

The ultimate test of economic success is the contribution which economic activity has made to the goal of human happiness. But to seek a single, summary measure of this contribution is surely to set out on an impossible task. In the words of Arthur Okun, a former chairman of the Council of Economic Advisers, the calculation of "a summary measure of social welfare is a job for a philosopher king."[8]

With all their warts and defects, we are stuck with the national product accounts. They are not very good, but they do have a rather precise meaning. And changes in GNP from year to year or from quarter to quarter do give us important information regarding the performance of the economy. GNP is one important and useful social indicator—but we should not view it as the last word.

[8]Arthur M. Okun, "Should GNP Measure Social Welfare?" *Brookings Bulletin* (Washington, Summer 1971).

chapter 8
Equilibrium with Unemployment: *An Introduction to Keynesian Economics*

The economic system in which we live . . . seems capable of remaining in a chronic condition of sub-normal activity for a considerable period without any marked tendency either towards recovery or towards complete collapse. Moreover, . . . full, or even approximately full employment is of rare and short-lived occurrence.

John Maynard Keynes,
The General Theory of
Employment, Interest and Money

Of all our economic problems, unemployment is perhaps the most vexing. Unemployment involves an obvious waste: The society forgoes the goods and services which the unemployed might have produced. Unemployed people suffer the demoralization, frustration, and loss of self-respect that come from enforced idleness.

Prior to the Great Depression of the 1930s, most economists did not consider unemployment to be one of the central problems of the economy. There were, of course, dissenters. Karl Marx believed that economic crises would become increasingly severe, with larger and larger numbers of workers added to the ranks of the unemployed. Sooner or later, capitalism would collapse because of its inherent defects. But Marx was outside the mainstream of economics. Most economists believed that there might be

short-term periods of severe unemployment, but that the market mechanism would bring about a speedy return to a high level of employment.

The decade of the 1930s shattered this confidence, and provided the backdrop for a new theory of unemployment. Not surprisingly, this theory was developed by a British economist. In contrast with the United States, where the Depression could be dated from 1929, Britain had suffered hard times extending back through the 1920s.

This new theory was put forward by John Maynard Keynes in his book *The General Theory of Employment, Interest and Money*.[1] The *General Theory* was a spectacular success; it ranks with Adam Smith's *Wealth of Nations* and Karl Marx's *Das Kapital* as one of the most influential economics books ever written. Acceptance of

[1](London: Macmillan, 1936.)

142

Keynes' theories was so widespread and so rapid as to justify the title "Revolution."[2] This is not to suggest that all of Keynes' ideas have stood the test of time. For example, few economists of the 1970s would agree with the early disciples of Keynes who dismissed money as playing only a minor role in the determination of national product. Nevertheless, Keynes' work continues to provide the foundation for the modern theory of employment.

Keynes' book is subtle and complex; many a graduate student has sweated over the more obscure passages of the *General Theory*. Nevertheless, his three most important propositions are relatively straightforward:

1. *Unemployment in the market economy*. In contrast with the prevailing classical school of economists (Box 8-1), Keynes argued that a market economy might have no strong forces moving it toward full employment. Indeed, a market economy might come to rest in an *equilibrium with large-scale unemployment*.

2. *The cause of unemployment*. Keynes argued that large-scale unemployment is the result of *too little spending* for goods and services. In other words, unemployment reflects an *insufficient aggregate demand*.

3. *The cure for unemployment*. To cure unemployment, aggregate demand should be increased. The best way to do that, said Keynes, is by increasing *government spending*.

The first two of these propositions will be explained in this chapter; the third will be deferred until Chapter 9.

KEYNESIAN THEORY: Aggregate Supply and Aggregate Demand

As a preliminary, let us consider more explicitly Keynes' argument about the importance of aggregate demand. If factories are closed and large numbers of people are out of work, not enough goods and services are being bought. If individuals, the government, or businesses go on a buying spree—if people buy more machines, more TV sets, more cars, more aircraft, and more computers—producers will respond by stepping up production of these goods; national product and employment will rise.

This is illustrated in Figure 8-2, on page 146. Starting at point *B*, with national product far below the level needed to ensure full employment, an increase in demand will cause output to rise. At this stage, when businesses have idle machines and equipment, and when there is a large pool of unemployed workers eager for jobs, the increase in demand will cause little or no rise in prices. Businesses will respond by producing more, not by charging higher prices. This is shown by the horizontal section of the aggregate supply function.

As demand continues to expand, the economy will sooner or later approach its capacity. Few workers and few machines will remain idle. If demand continues to increase, businesses will be unable to satisfy it by producing more and more. They will begin to raise prices. Thus, once the economy reaches the full-employment level of output, further increases in demand will cause inflation. Too much demand will be chasing too few goods. The economy will move up the vertical section (*AC*) of the aggregate supply function in Figure 8-2; the average level of prices will rise.[3]

---

[2]In 1947, Lawrence R. Klein (who was to become Jimmy Carter's chief economic adviser during the Presidential campaign of 1976) published a book entitled *The Keynesian Revolution* (New York: Macmillan, 1947; 2d ed., 1966).

[3]Recall from Figure 4-5 that a change in demand causes a movement along the supply curve. Demand determines what point on the supply curve will be observed.

BOX 8-1

CLASSICAL ECONOMICS:

Equilibrium with Full Employment

When Keynes argued that the market economy might have no strong tendency to move toward full employment, he was attacking the accepted theory of classical economists. According to them, a depressed economy would tend to move toward full employment, and would not reach equilibrium until full employment was restored. In other words, unemployment reflected a disequilibrium; it was the temporary result of disturbances to the economy.

To explain this classical view, suppose that the economy initially is at a position of large-scale unemployment—at point B in Figure 8-1. (This point is the same as point B in Keynesian Figure 8-2.) What market forces will be set in motion? In order to get a job, workers will be willing to accept lower wages. In order to sell products, manufacturers and other producers will cut prices. As prices fall, consumers buy more. Just as the demand for an individual good slopes downward to the right (as we saw in Chapter 4), so the aggregate demand for all goods and services slopes downward to the right (Figure 8-1). The general deflation, involving a fall in both wages and prices, will continue. The economy will move progressively from B to C to D, and will finally reach the full-employment equilibrium E.

But what could lead to the disturbance and unemployment in the first place? Just as there are "demand shifters" for the demand of an individual product (such as shoes), so there are demand shifters which can cause a movement in the aggregate demand curve. According to classical economists, a major shifter of aggregate demand is the quantity of money in the hands of the public. If people have a large amount of money, they will spend a lot; if they have only a little money, their aggregate spending will accordingly be low.

Thus, a classical explanation of the Depression goes something like this. In 1929,

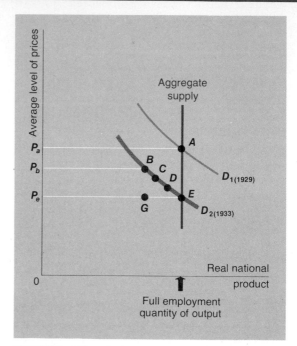

FIGURE 8-1 Classical theory and the unemployment problem.

there was a full-employment equilibrium at A, with aggregate demand D_1. Then, because of disturbances in the banking and financial system, the stock of money in the hands of the public fell by about 30 percent between 1929 and 1933. (How the money supply changes will be the major topic of Chapters 10 and 11.) As a result of the decline in the quantity of money, aggregate demand shifted to the left, to D_2. Prices began to fall, but they were sticky. They fell only from P_a in 1929 to the 1933 level of P_b, remaining above the level necessary for full employment (P_e). With prices remaining "too high," there was a surplus of goods; there was a general glut on the markets. Because producers could not sell the goods they were capable of making, the Depression persisted.

This classical approach leads to two possible solutions for a depression. First, the initial source of the disturbance might be eliminated. Steps might be taken to prevent a decline in the quantity of money in the first place, or to restore the quantity of money once it had fallen. Second, workers and businesses might be encouraged to accept lower wages and prices quickly, so the economy could move more rapidly to its new full-employment equilibrium E. The more willing workers and businesses were to accept lower wages and prices, the shorter would be the temporary period of unemployment. (For further detail on classical economics, see Appendixes 8-A and 8-B.)

Keynesians had three major objections to this classical explanation. According to Keynesians:

1. Wages and prices are not only sticky in the short run; they are likely to remain sticky *indefinitely*, because perfect competition does not prevail in the labor market or in markets for many goods and services. Wages will not move down (because of union contracts) and prices will not fall (because big business has the power to keep them up even in the face of slack demand).

Observe that the supply curve of classical economists was vertical. Once prices had a chance to adjust, a change in aggregate demand would result in a change only in the price level, not in the amount of output and employment. (E is directly below A in Figure 8-1.) On the other hand, the aggregate supply function of Keynesian economics (Figure 8-2) was quite different. If aggregate demand was low, prices would remain stable, and the economy would remain at an unemployment equilibrium like B. In short, Keynesians viewed downward price flexibility as a myth.

2. Furthermore, said Keynes, *even if* prices and wages were downwardly flexible, such flexibility wouldn't get the economy out of a depression. As prices and money wages both fall by, say, 20 percent, workers will find that their wages will buy no more. (Prices are 20 percent lower, but so are wages.) Thus, the quantity of goods purchased will remain stable at the depression level, and unemployment will persist. A fall in prices will cause a movement to G, not E (Figure 8-1).

Keynesians charged that classical economists were guilty of the *fallacy of composition*. A fall in the price of a good, such as shoes, will cause an increase in the quantity of the good sold. Classicists had argued that a general fall in prices would similarly cause a general increase in the quantity of goods sold. In so arguing, they had ignored the fact that a general fall in prices will be accompanied by a general fall in wages and other incomes that are derived from the sale of products. But such a fall in incomes will keep down consumption and aggregate demand.

The *fallacy of composition* involves the unwarranted conclusion that a proposition which is true of a *single* sector or market is necessarily true for the economy *as a whole*.

3. Finally, Keynesians were quite skeptical of the alternative classical recommendation for increasing employment in an economy at B: namely, increasing the money supply in order to increase aggregate demand from D_2 back to D_1. Keynesians believed that an increase in the money supply would be far less effective than an increase in government spending as a way of reviving aggregate demand.†

---

†This Keynesian-classical debate became too complicated to explain "who won" in an elementary text. For a treatment in much greater depth, see Paul Wonnacott, *Macroeconomics* (Homewood, Ill.: Richard D. Irwin, 2d ed., 1978). (Not surprisingly, Keynesians were right on some points, and classicists on others.)

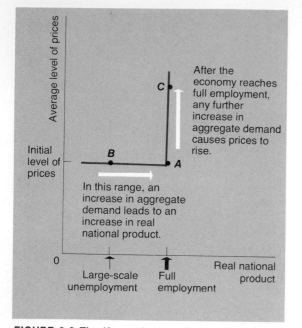

FIGURE 8-2 The Keynesian aggregate supply function.

The Keynesian aggregate supply function is a backward L. In the horizontal section—*BA*—prices are stable, and changes in aggregate demand cause changes in output. In the vertical section—*AC*—there is full employment, and an increase in aggregate demand leads to an increase in prices. Keynesian theory focuses on the segment *BA*, where there is large-scale unemployment.

(When the economy is at full employment, the unemployment rate will not be zero. At any time, some workers have voluntarily quit their jobs in order to find something better. Others have just entered the labor force and have not yet lined up their first jobs. In other words, even with "full" employment, there is some low level of *frictional* unemployment that reflects a normal process of job search rather than an insufficiency of aggregate demand.)

Writing in the 1930s, Keynes was preoc-cupied with the problem of unemployment. Keynes' theory was the theory of the Depression and how to get out of it. Thus, his primary focus was on the horizontal section of the aggregate supply function (*BA*), where changes in aggregate demand lead to changes in real output, not to changes in prices.[4] Indeed, in the basic Keynesian diagrams which appear later in the chapter (for example, Figure 8-7), the average price level is not even shown.

In order to tell whether the economy will be near *B* (with large-scale unemployment) or near *A* (with full employment), we need to determine aggregate demand. Keynes proposed that aggregate demand be analyzed by looking at its components, namely:

1. Personal consumption expenditures

2. Investment demand

3. Government purchases of goods and services

4. Net exports

The first two components of aggregate demand are considered in this chapter. (Government demand is studied in Chapter 9, and net exports in Chapter 16.)

PERSONAL CONSUMPTION EXPENDITURES

Of all the components of total spending, consumption is by far the largest. What do consumption expenditures depend upon? The factors that can affect an individual's consumption are numerous. The purchase of clothing depends on the weather. The purchase of automobiles depends in part on the

---

[4]During the 1970s, the United States economy has at times suffered simultaneously from large-scale unemployment and inflation. This experience of the 1970s is inconsistent with the simple Keynesian aggregate supply function of Figure 8-2, which suggests that the economy may suffer high unemployment (at point *B*) or inflation (at point *C*), but not both. In order to build up the theory of employment in relatively simple steps, we will use the basic Keynesian aggregate supply function (Figure 8-2) through the next few chapters, and return to the vexing problem of combined inflation and unemployment in Chapter 13.

state of roads. An extensive list of factors affecting consumption could readily be compiled. But of all the factors, one stands out as the most important. Consumption depends on the disposable income that people have left after they pay taxes.

The behavior of American consumers is shown in Figure 8-3. Low-income families confine their spending to little more than the necessities of life—food, clothing, and housing. But, even so, they find it hard to make ends meet. Observe that, at low-income levels, families' consumption spending exceeds their income. For example, families at G with disposable incomes of $5,000 (measured along the horizontal axis) on average consume about $6,000 (measured up the vertical axis). But how can low-income families possibly spend more than they have coming in? The answer: They do so by running up debts, or by drawing on their past savings. One group of low-income peo-

FIGURE 8-3 Consumption expenditures at different income levels, 1978.
Consumption depends on disposable income. Families with higher disposable incomes consume more than families with lower incomes. SOURCE: Department of Labor. Data updated to 1978 by authors

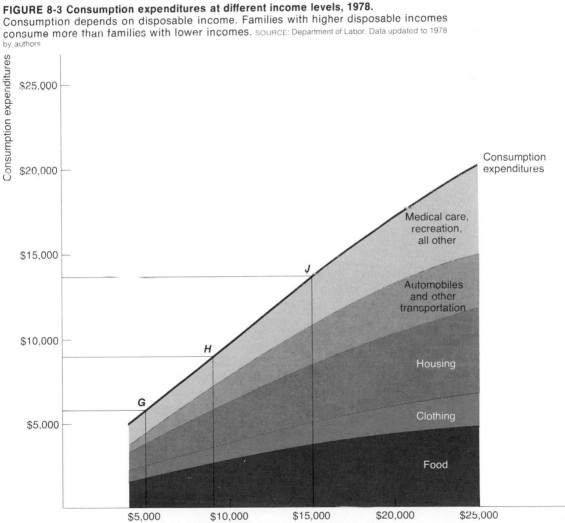

ple, those who are retired, have a particularly strong tendency to spend more than their current incomes; they draw on the assets they have accumulated during their working lives.

As the incomes of families rise, they find it easier to live within their current incomes. Thus, families at H with incomes of $9,000 on average spend $9,000 for consumer goods and services; they break even. As incomes rise, consumption also rises, but not so fast as income; at incomes above $9,000, families do not consume the full amount. For example, families at point J, with incomes of $15,000, consume considerably less than this amount and save the rest.

The relationship between disposable income and consumption has long been studied by economists and statisticians. In the middle of the nineteenth century, systematic relationships between income and consumption were observed by Prussian statistician Ernst Engel (who should not be confused with Karl Marx's benefactor and collaborator, Friedrich Engels). In particular, he noted that the fraction of income spent on food and other necessities falls as incomes rise. These relationships came to be known as Engel's laws, although the term "law" is somewhat of an exaggeration, since there are variations in consumer behavior from time to time and from place to place.

The relationship between disposable income and consumption became a central feature of Keynes' theory of unemployment. For the nation as a whole, consumption expenditures will also rise as incomes rise. The *consumption function* (that is, the relationship between the community's disposable income and its consumption expenditures) is illustrated in Table 8-1 and Figure 8-4.

(Figure 8-4 is drawn from the numbers in Table 8-1. For example, the first line of Table 8-1 states that consumption is $600 billion if income is $500 billion. This is shown as point A in the diagram, measured 500 units along the horizontal income axis, and 600 units up the vertical consumption axis.)

There are several important details in this diagram. The break-even point, at which consumption equals disposable income, may be found with the help of a 45°

TABLE 8-1
Consumption and Saving
(billions of dollars at constant prices)

	(1) Disposable income	(2) Consumption	(3) Marginal propensity to consume $(3) = \frac{\Delta 2\dagger}{\Delta 1}$	(4) Saving $(4) = (1) - (2)$	(5) Marginal propensity to save $(5) = \frac{\Delta 4\dagger}{\Delta 1}$
A	500	600		−100	
			$\frac{400}{500} = 0.8$		$\frac{100}{500} = 0.2$
B	1,000	1,000		0	
			$\frac{400}{500} = 0.8$		$\frac{100}{500} = 0.2$
C	1,500	1,400		+100	
			$\frac{400}{500} = 0.8$		$\frac{100}{500} = 0.2$
D	2,000	1,800		+200	

†Note: Δ1 means "change in disposable income"
Δ2 means "change in consumption"
Δ4 means "change in saving"

FIGURE 8-4 The consumption function (billions of dollars at constant prices).

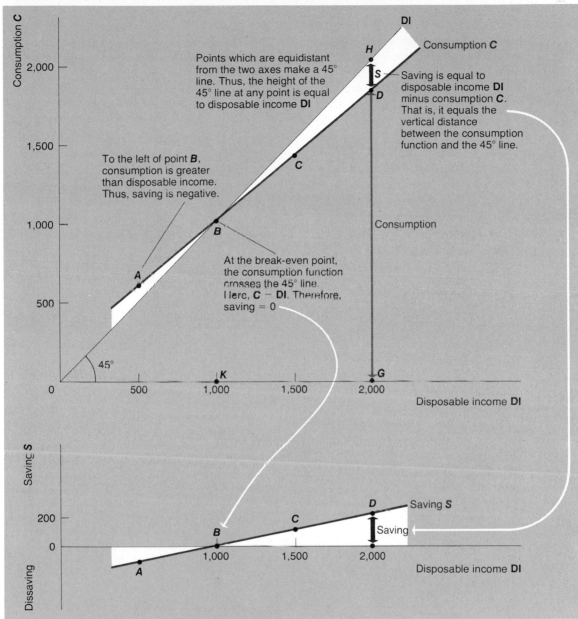

FIGURE 8-5 The saving function (billions of dollars at constant prices).
The saving function can be derived from the consumption function. Saving is the vertical distance between the consumption function and the 45° line.

line drawn from the origin. The 45° line has an important property: *Any point on the line is equidistant from the two axes.* Consider, for example, an economy in which disposable income is $2,000 billion, as shown by the point G on the horizontal axis of Figure 8-4. Then the vertical distance from G to point H on the 45° line is also $2,000 billion. Thus, this $2,000 billion disposable income may be measured either along the horizontal axis or as the vertical distance to the 45° line.

If income falls and we move to the left to point K, we can once again measure income as the height of the 45° line, in this case the height of point B. But point B is also the level of consumption (that is, B also lies on the consumption function). Therefore, point B, where the consumption function and the 45° line intersect, is the *break-even point.* At this point, consumption equals income.

Saving is what is left over after consumption expenditures; thus:[5]

Saving = disposable income − consumption

$$(8\text{-}1)$$

Drawing on this relationship, we may derive a saving function (Figure 8-5) directly from the consumption function. For example, if income is $2,000 billion, at point G, income is also measured by the height of H, while consumption is the height of D. The difference HD is saving, which is carried down to Figure 8-5. Similarly, other points on the saving function can be derived by taking the vertical distances between the consumption function and the 45° line in Figure 8-4. *The consumption function* (Figure 8-4) *and the saving function* (Figure 8-5) *are two alternative ways of illustrating precisely the same information.* (Notice point B in Figure 8-5, which corresponds to point B in Figure 8-4's consumption function. At this break-even point, where consumption equals income, saving is zero.)

The Marginal Propensity to Consume

Keynes was interested in explaining how consumption might change. He therefore introduced an important concept: the *marginal propensity to consume,* or MPC. Economists use the term *marginal* to mean "extra" or "additional." (As we shall see in a later chapter, marginal revenue means additional revenue, and marginal cost means additional cost.) Thus, the marginal propensity to consume is the additional amount consumed, as a fraction of additional disposable income. Formally,

$$\text{Marginal propensity to consume} = \frac{\text{change in consumption}}{\text{change in disposable income}}$$

Or, in abbreviated notation:

$$\text{MPC} = \frac{\Delta C}{\Delta \text{DI}} \tag{8-2}$$

where the Greek letter Δ means "change in."

If we think of a small $1 change in disposable income, this formula reduces to:

MPC = the fraction of an additional $1 in disposable income that is consumed   (8-3)

This is an obvious restatement of the idea: If your income increases by $1, and your consumption increases by $0.80 as a result, your MPC is 0.80.

Similarly,

$$\text{Marginal propensity to save} = \frac{\text{change in saving}}{\text{change in disposable income}}$$

[5]Strictly speaking, saving equals disposable income less consumption less interest paid by consumers, as we saw in Chapter 7. However, in order to keep the theory simple, the interest complication is ignored, and simplified Equation (8-1) is used when studying aggregate demand.

Abbreviated, this is:

$$MPS = \frac{\Delta S}{\Delta DI} \qquad (8\text{-}4)$$

Or:

MPS = the fraction of an additional $1
       in disposable income that is
       saved   (8-5)

In Table 8-1, the MPC and MPS are calculated in columns 3 and 5. Observe that

$$MPC + MPS = 1 \qquad (8\text{-}6)$$

This must be the case. If a person gets $1 more in income, whatever is not consumed is saved.

In Figure 8-6, the MPC is illustrated. It is equal to the vertical change in consumption, as a fraction of the horizontal increase in income. Thus, the MPC is equal to the *slope of the consumption function.* Consequently, if the MPC is constant (as it is in our illustration), the consumption function has a constant slope; it is a straight line.[6]

THE SIMPLEST EQUILIBRIUM: An Economy with No Government

Keynes' objective was to demonstrate that laissez faire market economies contain a fundamental defect; they may come to rest with a very high rate of unemployment. In order to explain this proposition as clearly as possible, we will look at a bare-bones economy, in which there is no international trade, no government, no depreciation, and no retained corporate profits. In this simplified economy, the differences among GNP, NNP, national income, and disposable income disappear. Furthermore, there are only two components of aggregate demand, namely, consumption C and investment I.

FIGURE 8-6 The marginal propensity to consume.
Since the slope of the consumption function gives the MPC, the consumption function is a straight line if the MPC is constant.

To make our task even simpler, we will initially assume that investment demand is a constant $100 billion. This $100 billion can be added to consumption demand to get aggregate demand, as shown in Table 8-2 (column 4) and in Figure 8-7. In this diagram, national product (NP) rather than disposable income DI is shown on the horizontal axis and on the 45° line. This substitution of national product for Figure 8-3's disposable income is legitimate, since NP = DI in the simple economy we are considering.

Equilibrium occurs where aggregate demand equals national product; that is, where the aggregate demand function cuts the 45° line. To see why this is the equilibrium, consider why a higher rate of output, B, would be unsustainable. The problem is illustrated in the magnified right-hand part of Figure 8-7. At output B, national product can be measured by the vertical distance to the 45° line; that is, national product is the height of the solid colored, plus shaded plus empty bars. But aggregate demand is

---

[6]The MPC plays a central role in Keynesian theory, as we shall see shortly. A companion (but much less important) concept is also sometimes used; namely, the *average* propensity to consume (APC). This is defined:
$$APC = \frac{\text{total consumption}}{\text{total disposable income}}$$

TABLE 8-2
Equilibrium National Product
(billions of dollars)

(1) NP National product (equals disposable income in this simple economy)	(2) C Consumption demand	(3) I Investment demand (assumed constant)	(4) AD = C + I aggregate demand (4 = 2 + 3)	(5) Relation of aggregate demand (4) to national product (1)	(6) Economy will:
500	600	100	700	Higher	Expand
1,000	1,000	100	1,100	Higher ↓	Expand
1,500	**1,400**	**100**	**1,500**	**Same**	**Stay at equilibrium**
2,000	1,800	100	1,900	Lower	Contract
2,500	2,200	100	2,300	Lower ↑	Contract

less than this—only the height of the solid colored and shaded bars. Thus, at output *B*, the amount we produce (national product) exceeds the demand for it (aggregate demand). What happens to the excess production (shown as the empty bar)? It remains unsold; it piles up on retailers' shelves and in warehouses. It represents *undesired inventory accumulation.* As unwanted goods accumulate, retailers, wholesalers, and other businesses cut back on their orders. Production falls. Moreover, it will continue to fall as long as aggregate demand lies below the 45° national product line. In other words, it will continue to fall until it reaches output *A*, where NP = AD and there is no further pressure of unsold goods. Therefore, *A* is the equilibrium quantity of output.

At a disequilibrium quantity of national product, such as *B*, it is important to distinguish between *actual investment* and *investment demand.* Actual investment—the quantity which shows up in the official

national product accounts studied in Chapter 7—includes all investment in plant, equipment, and inventories, whether that investment is desired or not. Thus, for an economy producing at *B*, the investment figure that appears in the national product accounts will be the shaded bar *plus* the empty bar. ("Empty bar goods" for which there is no demand, and which therefore pile up as *undesired inventory accumulation,* have clearly been produced during the year, and must therefore be included in the national product statistics.) In contrast with actual investment, investment demand (also known as *desired investment* or *planned investment*) is only the investment which businesses want; that is, the shaded bar.

Actual investment is the amount of new plant and equipment acquired during the year, plus the increase in inventories. All inventory accumulation is included, whether the inventories were desired or not.

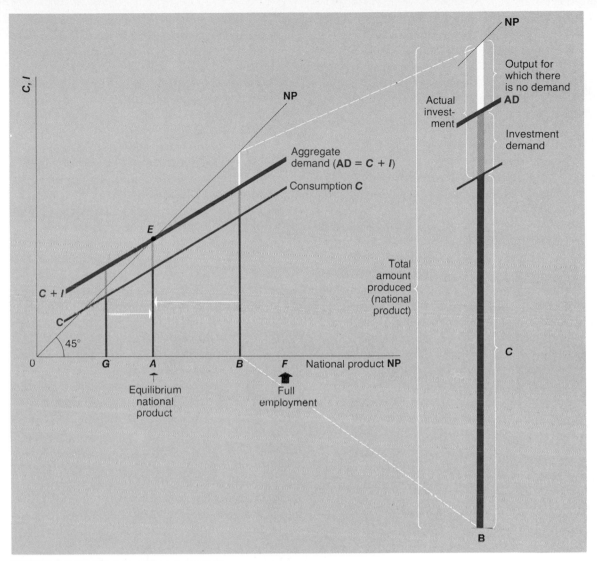

FIGURE 8-7 Equilibrium national product.
Point *E* represents equilibrium. Here, aggregate demand equals national product. A higher rate of production (for example, *B*) will not be stable, as we can see by looking at the magnified version of output *B*. National product equals the vertical distance to the 45° line. For most of this product, there is a market. Consumption demand takes the red bar. Investment demand takes the shaded bar. But for the empty bar, there is no demand. Unsold goods pile up in the warehouses. Businesses cut back on production. Output falls to its equilibrium, *A*.

Investment demand is the amount of new plant and equipment acquired during the year, plus additions to inventories which businesses wanted to acquire. It excludes undesired inventory accumulation.

Just as an output initially greater than equilibrium results in contraction, an output initially less than equilibrium generates expansion. Consider output *G*, where aggregate demand is higher than the 45° national product line. Goods will be snapped up by eager buyers. Retailers and wholesalers will find it difficult to keep goods in stock; inventories will fall below their desired levels. Retailers and wholesalers will step up their orders. Production will expand toward the equilibrium, A.

Equilibrium with Large-scale Unemployment

The key point stressed in Keynesian economics is that the equilibrium national product need not be at the quantity necessary to ensure full employment. Equilibrium national product is determined by aggregate demand (at A in Figure 8-7). On the other hand, the full-employment national product represents what the economy can produce with its current resources of labor, land, and capital; it is shown at point F. The situation which Keynes feared, and which he believed would be a common outcome of a free-market economy, is the one shown in this diagram: Aggregate demand is too low, and equilibrium product at A consequently falls far short of the full-employment quantity at F. (See the quotation from Keynes that introduces this chapter.)

CHANGES IN INVESTMENT DEMAND: The Multiplier

The basic Keynesian diagram (Figure 8-7) illustrates how the economy can reach an equilibrium at less than full employment. But it also can be used to illustrate how economic activity can change, with the economy periodically moving through boom and through recession. Indeed, Keynes directed two major criticisms at a laissez faire market economy. It would probably reach equilibrium with large-scale unemployment (Figure 8-7). But even if the economy did achieve full employment, this would probably be a temporary success. Unstable investment demand would cause large business fluctuations.

Consider what happens if investment demand increases. Suppose that business executives become more optimistic about the future. They will plan to expand their operations, undertaking more investment in plant and equipment. Suppose, specifically, that investment demand increases by $100 billion.

The results are shown in Figure 8-8. When the increase in investment demand is added, the aggregate demand function shifts upward by $100 million, from AD_1 to AD_2. Equilibrium once more occurs where aggregate demand and national product are equal; that is, where the aggregate demand function AD_2 cuts the 45° line at E_2. Thus, the increase in investment demand moves the equilibrium from E_1 to E_2. Something very important may now be observed. The equilibrium national product increases by more than the $100 billion increase in investment demand. Specifically, equilibrium national product increases by $500 billion.

How can that be? How can national product rise by more than the increase in investment? The answer is this: As businesses build more factories and order more equipment, people are put to work producing the factories and equipment. They earn more wages. As their incomes rise, they increase their consumption expenditures. Thus, the nation produces more capital goods (factories, equipment) *and* more consumer goods; national product rises by more than investment. As the equilibrium moves from E_1 to E_2, national product increases by $500 billion. This includes the $100 billion increase in capital goods production (shown as ΔI in Figure 8-8) that results from the initial upward shift in investment demand. And it also includes an increase of $400 billion in consumer goods (shown as ΔC) which results as incomes rise and consumers move along the consumption function from J to K.

Thus, the $100 billion increase in investment demand has a multiplied effect on

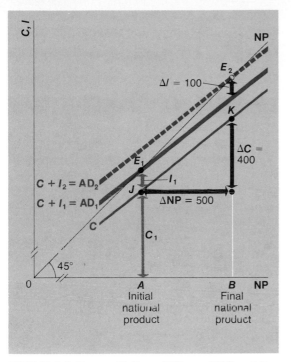

FIGURE 8-8 The multiplier. With an MPC = 0.8, a $100 billion increase in investment demand causes a $500 billion increase in national product.

The Multiplier Process: A More Detailed Look

The multiplier process may be better understood by looking in detail at what happens when $100 billion is spent to purchase capital goods. The direct result is a $100 billion increase in national product; more machines and other capital goods are produced. But this is not the end of the story. The $100 billion spent for plant and equipment goes in the form of wages, rents, profits, and other incomes to those who provide the labor, capital, and other resources used to produce the capital goods. In other words, disposable incomes are $100 billion higher. (Remember, we are dealing with a highly simplified economy in which there is no government to take a tax bite.) Consumers now spend most of this increase in disposable income, with the precise amount depending on their marginal propensity to consume (MPC). For example, if the MPC is 0.8, consumers will spend $80 billion more, as shown in the "second round" increase in the national product in Table 8-3.

national product. The relationship between the increase in national product and the increase in investment demand is known as the *investment multiplier*, or, more simply, as the *multiplier*. Formally, it is defined thus:

$$\text{Multiplier} = \frac{\text{change in national product}}{\text{change in investment demand}} \quad (8\text{-}7)$$

In our illustration, the multiplier is 5, since national product rises by $500 billion when investment demand increases by $100 billion.

TABLE 8-3
The Multiplier Process: Effect on National Product of Investment Expenditure
(billions of dollars)

		Effects on national product
First round:	Investment of	100.0
Second round:	Consumption of	80.0
Third round:	Consumption of	64.0
Fourth round:	Consumption of	51.2
Fifth round:	Consumption of	41.0
.		.
.		.
.		.
Total increase in national product		500.0
Of this total, consumption is:		400.0

But again, this is not the end of the story. When consumers spend $80 billion more for clothing, food, and other consumer goods, the incomes of textile workers, farmers, and others who produce consumer goods will rise by $80 billion. With an MPC of 0.8, these people will respond by consuming $64 billion more (that is, the $80 billion increase in income times the MPC of 0.8). Once more, national product has risen, this time by $64 billion. And so the story goes on, with each round of consumer spending giving rise to another, smaller round.

Observe that the total spending resulting from each dollar of initial investment expenditure forms the series $1 (1 + 0.8 + 0.8^2 + 0.8^3 \ldots)$. It can be shown[7] that such a series sums to:

$$\text{Sum} = \$1\left(\frac{1}{1 - 0.8}\right) = \$5 \qquad (8\text{-}8)$$

For each $1 increase in investment spending, national product rises by $5. Thus, with an MPC of 0.8, the multiplier is 5. More generally:

$$\text{Multiplier} = \frac{1}{1 - \text{MPC}} \qquad (8\text{-}9)$$

The size of the multiplier depends on the size of the MPC; that is, on the slope of the consumption function. The steeper the consumption function (that is, the higher the MPC), the larger will be the multiplier.

Several things must be stressed about the multiplier. First, it is very important,

because it is a fundamental building block of Keynesian economics. Second, and equally important, the multiplier takes the value $\frac{1}{(1 - \text{MPC})}$ *only* in the very simple economy under consideration here—most particularly, an economy with no taxes and no international sector. In a more realistic theory, with taxes, international trade, and other complications, there is still a multiplier process, but the multiplier is more complex than shown in this equation (as we shall see in succeeding chapters).

Finally, note how Table 8-3 corresponds to Figure 8-8. Each shows that a $100 billion increase in investment demand will cause a $500 billion increase in national product. This $500 billion is made up of the original $100 billion increase in investment, plus a $400 billion increase in consumption that results when people find their disposable incomes rising.

AN ALTERNATIVE APPROACH: Saving and Investment

We have now presented the building blocks of the simplest Keynesian theory. There is an alternative way of approaching this theory, by beginning with the saving function rather than the consumption function. As we have seen, the saving function (Figure 8-5) is an alternative way of presenting exactly the same information as in the consumption function (Figure 8-4). It is therefore not surprising that this alternative approach

---

*[7]Let c stand for the MPC. So long as c is less than 1 (in our case, 0.8), then the sum of the series

$$1 + c + c^2 + c^3 \ldots = \frac{1}{1 - c}$$

This can be shown by actually doing the division on the right side. In order words, divide 1 by $(1 - c)$, as follows:

$$
\begin{array}{r}
1 + c + c^2 \ldots \\
1 - c \overline{\smash{\big)}\ 1 } \\
\underline{1 - c } \\
c \\
\underline{c - c^2 } \\
c^2 \ldots
\end{array}
$$

leads to exactly the same conclusions: that equilibrium national product may fall short of the amount needed for full employment, and an increase in investment demand will lead to a multiplied increase in national product. But this alternative approach provides important additional insights into the way the economy works, and is therefore well worth investigating.

The Circular Flow of Expenditure: Leakages and Injections

To explain the saving-investment approach, we call once more on the circular flow of payments diagram, which was previously used in Chapters 3 and 7 (see especially page 127). Consider first a very rudimentary economy in which there is no investment demand, and in which consumers buy all the goods produced. Suppose

that producers sell $1,000 billion of goods during an initial period. In turn, they pay this $1,000 billion to households in the form of wages, salaries, rents, and other incomes. Suppose, further, that the households turn around and spend all their $1,000 billion incomes for consumer goods. Once more, the producers will sell $1,000 billion in goods and services, and once more they will pay $1,000 billion in incomes to the households. Round and round this $1,000 billion of payments will go; national product will be stable at $1,000 billion. This simplest of all economies is illustrated in Figure 8-9.

Now, let us introduce complications, starting with saving. Suppose that instead of consuming all their incomes of $1,000 billion, people decide that they would like to save $100 billion. They spend only $900 billion on consumer goods. Producers have

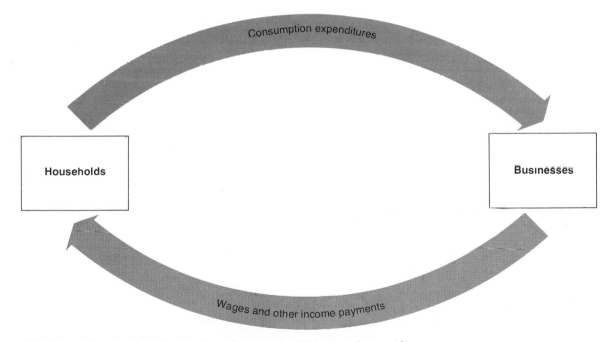

FIGURE 8-9 The simplest circular flow of payments. (All income is spent for consumer goods and services.)
The simplest economy is one in which people consume all their incomes. Incomes are used to buy consumer goods and services. In turn, the receipts from the sale of consumer goods and services are again paid out as incomes, in the form of wages, salaries, etc. Once more, people use all their incomes to buy consumer goods and services. Round and round the payments go.

manufactured $1,000 billion in goods, but they sell only $900 billion. Unsold goods pile up, and producers cut back on production. The circular flow of national product and income narrows. Thus, saving involves a leakage from the spending stream; it acts as a drag on national product and income.

But now, as an alternative, let us introduce investment demand instead. Suppose that businesses decide to increase their capital stock and that they order $100 billion worth of machinery. In response to the demand, $100 billion in machinery is produced. The machinery companies pay out the $100 billion in wages, salaries, and other incomes. Incomes rise, people consume more, and the circular flow of national product and income broadens. Investment acts as a *stimulus* to national product and income.

Thus, in terms of their effect on aggregate demand and output, saving and investment have offsetting effects. Saving is a *leakage* from the circular spending stream; an increase in the desire to save leads to a decrease in national product. Investment demand represents an *injection* into the circular spending stream; an increase in investment demand leads to an increase in national product. Equilibrium exists when the forces of contraction and expansion are in balance; that is, when saving equals investment (Figure 8-10).

The Equilibrium of Saving and Investment

This conclusion may be presented more formally with the use of the saving function, initially introduced in Figure 8-5 and repeated in Figure 8-11. Specifically, consider the case in which investment demand is $100 billion, as shown. Equilibrium will occur at *E*, where investment demand and saving are equal. At any greater quantity of income (such as *B*), the leakage from the circular flow of spending—in the form of saving—exceeds the injection of investment spending, and national product falls.

Saving and investment decisions are made by different groups. Households save

to buy a new car, to send the kids to college, or for retirement. Investment decisions are made by business executives; they buy additional plant and equipment when their profit prospects are good. Because of the cleavage between saving and investment decisions, *there is no assurance that, if an economy begins at full employment, desired investment and saving will be equal.* If desired investment is less than saving, as it is at the full-employment level of national product in Figure 8-11, national product will fall, and unemployment will result. The economy will reach equilibrium when income has decreased far enough (that is, to *A*) so that saving no longer exceeds investment demand.

Because the saving function can be derived directly from the consumption function, the saving-investment diagram represents exactly the same information as the consumption-investment diagram (Figure 8-7). To summarize these two approaches, we may recall that the condition for equilibrium can be stated in several different ways:

1. Equilibrium exists when national product is equal to aggregate demand (Figure 8-7).

2. Equilibrium exists when inventories are at their desired level; that is, when actual investment equals desired investment, and when there is no undesired buildup or reduction in inventories (Figure 8-7).

3. Equilibrium exists when desired investment and saving are equal (Figure 8-11).

The reason for unemployment may be expressed in two alternative ways. There will be an *unemployment equilibrium* if:

1. Aggregate demand is too low to buy the full-employment quantity of national product (Figure 8-7).

2. Desired investment falls short of saving when national product is at the full-employment level. (In Figure 8-11, note that at the full-employment quantity of output, investment demand is below the saving function.)

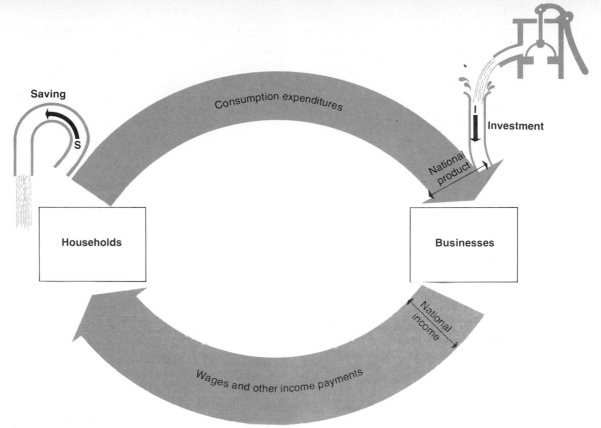

FIGURE 8-10 The circular flow, with saving and investment.
Investment expenditures work to broaden the spending stream. Leakages into saving narrow it. Equilibrium is reached when leakages from the stream (saving) are equal to injections (investment).

FIGURE 8-11 The equilibrium of saving and investment demand.
Output *A* represents the equilibrium, where saving = investment demand. At a greater national product, such as *B*, there will be a disequilibrium. Since the leakages from the spending stream (in the form of saving) are greater than the injections (in the form of investment), national product will fall toward its equilibrium *A*.

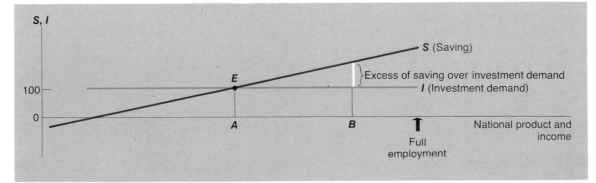

BOX 8-2
CHANGES IN THE DESIRE TO SAVE:
The Paradox of Thrift

Keynesian theory explains how equilibrium national product can change if there is a change in investment demand. And it also explains how equilibrium national product will change if there is an upward shift in the saving function (or, what amounts to the same thing, a downward shift in the consumption function).

Suppose that people become more thrifty; they save more out of any given level of income. This involves an upward shift in the saving function, as illustrated by the shift from S_1 to S_2 in Figure 8-12. At the initial level of national product, A, the leakage into saving (AG) will now exceed the injections in the form of investment demand (AE_1). Aggregate demand will fall short of national product, and unsold goods will pile up. Orders will be canceled, and national product will decrease to its new equilibrium, E_2. In the simple case where the investment demand is constant, the increase in the desire to save will have no effect on the equilibrium level of saving or investment; they are the same at BE_2 as they were at AE_1. The only effect is a decrease in output. Thus, Keynes argued that an increase in the desire to save has unfortunate consequences. It does not increase the equilibrium amount of investment, but rather, it increases the amount of unemployment.

But that is not the worst of it. In order to make the analysis simple, the demand for investment so far has been assumed constant. But that clearly need not be the case. The amount of investment can change, and indeed can change substantially. Specifically, investment demand may increase as the quantity of national product increases. As more and more goods are produced, there is a need for more machines and factories. In this case, investment demand may be drawn as an upward sloping function, as shown in Figure 8-13.

Now a shift in the saving function becomes particularly potent. A relatively small

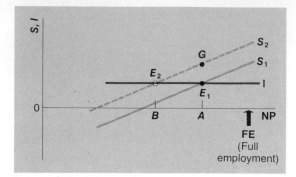

FIGURE 8-12 An increase in the desire to save.

increase in the desire to save, moving the saving function from S_1 to S_2, will cause a very large decrease in equilibrium national product, from A to B. Furthermore, the effects on the equilibrium amount of saving and investment are paradoxical. As a result of the *upward* shift in the saving function, observe that the amount of saving and investment in equilibrium *falls*, from AE_1 to BE_2. What happens is this: Beginning at the initial equilibrium of E_1, an increase in the desire to save causes an increase in leakages from the spending stream. Aggregate demand and national product fall. As they fall, businesses decide that they need fewer machines and factories. There is a decrease in the quantity of investment demanded. (The economy

FIGURE 8-13 The paradox of thrift.

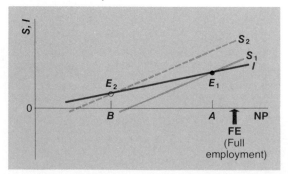

moves to the left along the investment demand function.) Equilibrium is restored only when national product has fallen enough so that people are content to save an amount which is no more than the diminished quantity of investment demand (at point E_2). Because the quantity of investment decreases as national product falls, and because national product must fall until saving is brought into equality with investment, saving will decline in the move from E_1 to E_2.

This is the *paradox of thrift*. An *increase* in the desire to save (a shift from S_1 to S_2) causes a *fall* in actual saving (from AE_1 to BE_2). Prosperity is increased by expenditure, not by saving.

Thus, Keynes in his *General Theory* echoed the words of eighteenth-century poet Bernard Mandeville, who argued in verse that if "Knaves Turned Honest" and abandoned luxurious living, the effects would be disastrous for the economy:

The price of Land and Houses falls;
Mirac'lous Palaces whose Walls,
Like those of Thebes, were rais'd by Play,
Are to be let . . .
The Building Trade is quite destroy'd,
Artificers are not employ'd. . . .

In short, private virtue may be social folly; saving causes unemployment.

(This passage, quoted in Keynes' *General Theory*,† was taken from Mandeville's allegorical poem *The Grumbling Hive: or Knaves Turned Honest*, originally published about 1705 and expanded and reprinted in 1714 with the title *The Fable of the Bees: or Private Vices, Public Benefits*. Keynes considered his *General Theory* to be in the iconoclastic tradition of the *Fable of the Bees*, a work which had been declared a nuisance by a grand jury in 1723 because of its praise of "private vices.")

The assumptions of the Keynesian theory, which lie behind the paradox of thrift, must be reemphasized at this point. The Keynesian analysis deals with the situation in which there is large-scale unemployment and prices are sticky; changes in aggregate demand lead to changes in output and no change in prices. In short, changes in aggregate demand cause the economy to move along horizontal section BA of the aggregate supply function shown in Figure 8-2. If, on the other hand, the economy is experiencing booming demand conditions, and is in the inflationary range of the aggregate supply function (AC), the Keynesian analysis of thrift must be completely reversed. An increase in the desire to save (decrease in the desire to consume) eases the macroeconomic problem. As consumption and aggregate demand fall, the inflationary forces are weakened. Furthermore, as the economy is fully utilizing its resources, with aggregate demand exceeding the amount which can be produced at existing prices, a decrease in consumption will release resources from the production of consumer goods. These resources will become available for the production of capital goods. Thus, an increase in the willingness to save will indeed add to the amount of factories and machinery produced; the real saving of society will be augmented. In a world of inflationary excess demand, the paradox of thrift does not hold.

†John Maynard Keynes, *A General Theory of Employment, Interest and Money* (London: Macmillan, 1936), p. 360.

The Multiplier: The Saving-Investment Approach

Just as the saving-investment diagram may be used to show an unemployment equilibrium, so it may also be used to illustrate the multiplier. This is done in Figure 8-14. Following an initial equilibrium at E_1, investment demand increases by $100 billion, from I_1 to I_2. Consequently, the equilibrium moves to E_2. Once again, observe that equilibrium national product increases by more than the investment demand. Indeed, income will increase until people are willing to save the full $100 billion injected into the spending stream by the new investment demand. (Only then will the leakages into saving be equal to the injections from investment demand.) With an MPC of 0.8, the marginal propensity to save (MPS) is 0.2, or one-fifth. Thus, people are not willing to save the additional $100 billion until income has increased by $500 billion. Once again, we see that equilibrium income rises by $500 billion.

The saving-investment approach provides an alternative equation for the multiplier.

FIGURE 8-14 The multiplier: saving and investment approach. With an MPS = 0.2, an increase of $100 billion in investment demand (from I_1 to I_2) will cause an increase of $500 billion in national product. That is

$$\Delta NP = \frac{\$100 \text{ billion}}{0.2} = \$500 \text{ billion}$$

Since income is either consumed or saved, we know that:

$$MPS = 1 - MPC \qquad (8\text{-}11; \text{ from } 8\text{-}6)$$

Thus, the two formulas

$$\text{Multiplier} = \frac{1}{1 - MPC}$$

and

$$\text{Multiplier} = \frac{1}{MPS}$$

are exact equivalents.

$$\text{Multiplier} = \frac{1}{MPS} \qquad (8\text{-}10)$$

Key Points

1. During the Great Depression between the two world wars, British economist John Maynard Keynes put forward a new theory of unemployment, arguing that:

(*a*) A market economy can come to rest at an equilibrium with large-scale unemployment.

(*b*) The cause of unemployment is insufficient aggregate demand.

(*c*) The most straightforward cure for unemployment is an increase in government spending. (This point is explained in Chapter 9.)

2. Keynes argued that, if the economy is suffering from large-scale unemployment, changes in total spending (aggregate demand) will cause changes in national product and employment. Prices and wages are sticky in a downward direction, and do not fall significantly during a depression (Figure 8-2).

3. The components of aggregate demand are:

(*a*) Personal consumption expenditures

(*b*) Investment demand

(c) Government purchases of goods and services

(d) Net exports (that is, exports minus imports)

4. Chapter 8 deals with a simple economy, involving only consumption and investment.

5. Consumption expenditures depend primarily on disposable personal income. As incomes rise, people consume more. The change in consumption, as a fraction of a change in disposable income, is known as the *marginal propensity to consume (MPC)*.

6. Equilibrium national product occurs where the aggregate demand function cuts the 45° line. Any higher level of national product would be unsustainable, since demand would fall short of production and unsold goods would pile up in inventories.

7. Equilibrium national product may fall short of the full-employment quantity.

8. An increase in investment demand raises national product and income. This induces people to consume more. In the simple economy, national product will increase by the rise in investment demand times the multiplier:

$$\text{Multiplier} = \frac{1}{1 - \text{MPC}}$$

But, because saving equals income minus consumption,

Marginal propensity to save $= 1 - \text{MPC}$

Thus, the multiplier may also be written:

$$\text{Multiplier} = \frac{1}{\text{MPS}}$$

9. There are several alternative ways of stating the condition for equilibrium. It exists when:

(a) Aggregate demand and national product are equal; that is, where the aggregate demand function cuts the 45° national product line (Figure 8-7).

(b) Inventories are at their desired level; that is, when actual investment equals desired investment and there is no undesired buildup or reduction in inventories (Figure 8-7).

(c) Desired investment and saving are equal (Figure 8-11).

Key Concepts

unemployment equilibrium
sticky wages and prices
frictional unemployment
aggregate demand
aggregate supply
fallacy of composition
consumption function
saving function
break-even point at which consumption equals income
45° line

marginal propensity to consume (MPC)
marginal propensity to save (MPS)
investment demand (or desired investment or planned investment)
undesired inventory accumulation
actual investment
multiplier
circular flow of spending
leakage
injection
paradox of thrift

Problems

8-1 Draw a diagram showing the consumption function, the aggregate demand function, and the 45° line. What quantity of NP represents the equilibrium? Explain why a higher NP would be unsustainable and would lead to a contraction of production. Explain also why a less-than-equilibrium NP would cause an expansion.

8-2 The consumption function and the saving function are two alternative ways of presenting the same information. The text explains how the saving function can be derived from the consumption function. Show how the consumption function can be derived from the saving function.

8-3 Draw a diagram showing investment demand and the saving function. What is the equilibrium national product? Explain why a higher national product would be unsustainable.

8-4 The mathematical formula for the multiplier $\dfrac{1}{1 - \text{MPC}}$ shows that a high MPC causes a high multiplier. By tracing the effects of $100 billion in additional investment through a number of "rounds" of spending, show that the multiplier is higher with an MPC of 0.9 than with an MPC of 0.8. (Use Table 8-3 on page 155 to start.)

8-5 "Saving and investment must always be equal. Therefore, an increase in the desire to save (an upward shift of the saving function) will cause an increase in investment." Do you agree or disagree? Explain.

8-6 What is the difference between actual investment and desired investment? What happens if desired investment is greater than actual investment? Why?

8-7 Consider an economy with the relationship between consumption and income shown in the table below.

(*a*) Fill in the blanks in the Saving column.

(*b*) Investment demand is originally $200 billion. Fill in the blanks in the Initial aggregate demand column.

(*c*) What is the equilibrium national product?

(*d*) Now assume that investment demand rises to $300 billion. What does this do to aggregate demand? (Fill in the Later aggregate demand column.) What is equilibrium national product now?

(*e*) Comparing your answers to *c* and *d*, find the multiplier.

Disposable income = NP (billions)	Consumption (billions)	Saving (billions)	Initial aggregate demand (billions)	Later aggregate demand (billions)
$1,000	$ 900	____	____	____
1,100	975	____	____	____
1,200	1,050	____	____	____
1,300	1,125	____	____	____
1,400	1,200	____	____	____
1,500	1,275	____	____	____
1,600	1,350	____	____	____
1,700	1,425	____	____	____
1,800	1,500	____	____	____

Appendix 8-A

SAVING AND INVESTMENT IN CLASSICAL THEORY

As we saw in Box 8-1, classical economists argued that market forces would cause the economy to move back toward full employment. Large-scale unemployment would create downward pressures on wages and prices; as wages and prices fell, more would be bought.

Classical economists also had a more specific argument, involving saving and investment. Like Keynes, they recognized that desired investment and saving would have to be equal for the economy to be in equilibrium. But, unlike Keynes, they did not believe that national product would have to fall if investment demand fell short of saving.

Rather, classical economists argued that the price mechanism tends to bring desired investment and saving into equilibrium—without unemployment. The key price that does this is the interest rate. This rate is the price or reward received by savers. It is also the price paid by corporations and others for funds with which they will construct buildings or engage in other investment projects.

Suppose that investment demand falls short of saving when the economy is at full employment. What will happen? According to classical economists, savers will have large quantities of funds. In their eagerness to acquire bonds and other earning assets, they will be willing to settle for a lower interest rate. As the interest rate falls, businesses will find it cheaper to borrow; they will be encouraged to undertake more investment projects. The rate of interest will continue to drop until desired investment and saving are brought into equality, as illustrated in Figure 8-15.

In other words, classical economists argued that there was something wrong with Keynes' plumbing. Savings do not simply leak from the economy (Figure 8-10). Rather, an increase in saving, through a fall in interest rates, will

FIGURE 8-15 Saving and investment in classical theory.
The *S* curve shows how much will be saved at various interest rates. The *I* curve shows how much businesses will borrow to finance investment projects at various interest rates. Classical economists argued that if saving exceeds investment demand, the interest rate will fall until saving and investment are equalized—without large-scale unemployment.

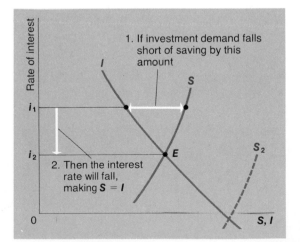

cause an increase in investment. Thus, the financial markets (where savers supply funds to investors) provide a pipe which connects saving and investment in Figure 8-10—that is, a pipe which brings saving leakages back into the spending stream in the form of investment demand.

In response, Keynes argued that classical economists were in error in assuming that the interest rate could fall enough to equate saving and investment at full employment. Suppose that at the full-employment level of income, the desire to save is S_2 rather than S in Figure 8-15. Then full employment cannot exist unless the interest rate becomes negative; that is, unless *lenders* pay interest to *borrowers*. But that is preposterous. Without a positive interest rate, people will be unwilling to lend money; they will lock it up in a bank vault instead. Because the interest rate cannot be negative, the financial capital markets cannot be counted on to ensure full employment.

(The S_2 and I curves, implying a negative rate of interest, appear on the only diagram in Keynes' *General Theory*.[8] Clearly, Keynes felt strongly about the errors of classical economists in arguing that a change in the interest rate would bring saving and investment into equality.)

The differences may be summarized. Classical economists argued that an *increase in saving*, by depressing interest rates, *will cause an increase in investment*, and thus stimulate growth. Saving is a benefit to society; it will make us better off in the future. In contrast, Keynes argued that an increase in the desire to save will cause *a decrease in national product and a higher rate of unemployment*. Thus, saving is antisocial (the paradox of thrift). Indeed, Keynes believed that it is more correct to argue that *investment demand causes saving* (as illustrated in Figure 8-14) than to argue that saving causes investment. Thus, said Keynes, classical economists had gotten things backwards.

[8] Keynes, *General Theory*, p. 180.

Appendix 8-B

SAY'S LAW

One strand of classical theory, known as Say's law after nineteenth-century economist J. B. Say, provided Keynes with the biggest target of all.

Say put forward the disarmingly simple idea that *supply creates its own demand.* When people sell a good or service, they do so in order to be able to buy some other good or service. The very act of supplying one good or service thus creates a demand for some other good or service. There can be too much supply for some specific product, such as shoes, but, if so, there is too much demand and not enough supply of some other product. Surpluses and shortages can exist in individual markets. But, for the economy as a whole, there cannot be an excess of supply over demand.

Keynes attacked Say's law with utter scorn:

I remember [British Prime Minister] Bonar Law's mingled rage and perplexity in face of the economists, because they were denying what was obvious. He was deeply troubled for an explanation.[9]

What were these classical economists denying? Following Say's law, they were denying the possibility that there could be a general glut on markets; that there could be a general inadequacy of aggregate demand.[10]

Keynes' attack was devastating; Say's law as an important doctrine was demolished. And it was also demolished by the facts. The 1930s demonstrated to even the most obtuse economist that a general glut was indeed possible.

---

[9]Keynes, *General Theory,* p. 350.

[10]According to Say's law, general gluts were impossible regardless of the average level of prices. Say's law was therefore inconsistent with the more sensible version of classical theory presented earlier in Box 8-1. (Recall that this theory recognized that so long as prices remained too high—at P_b rather than P_e—there could be inadequate aggregate demand at point B.)

chapter 9
Fiscal Policy

Fiscal policy has to be put on constant . . .
alert. . . . The management of prosperity is a
full-time job.
                                    Walter W. Heller[1]

In his *General Theory*, Keynes argued that chronic depression might be the outcome of laissez faire. The free private market does not ensure full employment. Furthermore, even if the economy were to achieve a high rate of employment, this happy situation would probably be temporary. The market economy tends to be unstable, either slowing down into a recession or speeding up into an inflationary boom.

But, in spite of the defects of the market economy, Keynes was not pessimistic. We are not, said he, inevitably condemned to suffer the economic and social costs of high unemployment or the disruptive effects of inflation. The government can deal with the root causes of these problems. Unemployment is the result of too little aggregate demand, as we saw in Chapter 8. Inflation is the result of too much aggregate demand;

prices rise when too much demand is chasing the available supply of goods. By taking steps to increase aggregate demand during a recession or depression, the government can increase the amount of national product and put the unemployed back to work. By restraining aggregate demand during periods of inflation, the government can slow down the rate of increase of prices.

This, then, was the policy message of the Keynesian revolution: the government has the ability—*and the responsibility*—to manage aggregate demand, and thus to ensure a continuing prosperity without inflation. The government can affect aggregate demand with *fiscal policies*—that is, by changes in *government spending* or *tax rates*. The principal purpose of this chapter will be to describe how the government can use fiscal policies to manage aggregate demand.

---

[1]Professor Heller, of the University of Minnesota, was the chairman of President Kennedy's Council of Economic Advisers. The quotation is from his book *New Dimensions in Political Economy* (New York: W. W. Norton, 1967), p. 69.

GOVERNMENT SPENDING

In the bare-bones economy discussed in Chapter 8, the government was completely ignored; there was no government spending or taxation. In order to proceed with simple steps, we will look first at the effects of government spending, and defer taxation until later.

Government expenditures for goods and services are a component of aggregate demand. People are employed building roads, teaching school, and maintaining parks. And the roads, educational services, and upkeep of parks are included in national product. When government demand is added to Chapter 8's bare-bones economy, then:

Aggregate demand (AD) =
    consumption expenditures (C)
  + investment demand (I)
  + government purchases of goods and
    services (G)

Thus, government spending (G) can be added vertically to consumption and investment demand, to get the aggregate demand line shown in Figure 9-1. Note that when government spending of $100 billion is added vertically to consumer demand plus investment demand, the equilibrium moves from point D to point E. The increase in national product, measured by the distance AB on the horizontal axis, is a multiple of the government spending. The *multiplier process works on government spending* just as it worked on investment expenditures. For example, when workers receive paychecks for road construction, a whole series of spending and responding decisions is set in motion. The workers spend most of their wages on consumption. Additional employees are hired by the consumer goods industries, and these employees also spend more as a consequence of their rising incomes.

FIGURE 9-1 The addition of government spending. Government spending is added vertically to consumption and investment demand in order to get aggregate demand. AD = C + I + G. Observe that the multiplier process works on government demand. Without government spending, the equilibrium would be at point D (as we saw in Chapter 8). With government spending, the equilibrium is at E. The increase in national product (AB = $500 billion) is a multiple of the $100 billion of government spending. As people's incomes rise, they move along the consumption function, consuming $400 billion more.

The process is similar to that illustrated earlier for the investment multiplier (Table 8-3).

In spite of the existence of government spending, aggregate demand in our economy may nevertheless still fall short of what is needed for full employment. Such was the case during the Depression of the 1930s. There were some government expenditures, yet the unemployment rate remained very high—more than 15 percent of the labor force. This situation is illustrated in Figure 9-2, where the full-employment national product is far to the right of the equilibrium, E.

In order to get to full employment, the government should spend more. The ques-

FIGURE 9-2 The recessionary gap, and fiscal policy for full employment.
At initial equilibrium *E*, there is large-scale unemployment. (National product *B* falls far short of the full-employment national product at *F*.) To reach full employment, government spending (*G₁*) should be increased by *HJ*, the amount of the recessionary gap. This will shift aggregate demand up to AD₂ and move the economy to a full-employment equilibrium at *H*. Note that *HJ*, the recessionary gap, is the vertical distance between the aggregate demand line (AD₁) and the 45° line, measured at the full-employment national product.

tion is, how much more? Observe that at the full-employment quantity of national product, the aggregate demand function (AD₁) lies below the 45° line. This shortfall of aggregate demand below the 45° line—distance *HJ*—is known as the *recessionary gap*.[2]

A *recessionary gap* exists when the aggregate demand function is below the 45° line at the full-employment quantity of national product.

It is the vertical distance from the 45° line down to the aggregate demand function (measured at the full-employment quantity of national product).

The *output gap* is the amount by which national product falls short of the full-employment quantity. It is measured along the horizontal axis. The output gap is larger than the recessionary gap, as can be seen in Figure 9-2.

In order to get to full employment, the aggregate demand function must be shifted up by this distance. Thus, *HJ* is the increase that is needed in government spending. Hence, we come to the first and most important rule of thumb for fiscal policy:

To reach full employment, government spending should be increased by *the amount of the recessionary gap*.

With this spending, the government shifts the aggregate demand function up by just enough to achieve full employment.

When the government increases its spending, once again the multiplier process is put to work. In Figure 9-2, note that an increase of government spending equal to the recessionary gap (*HJ*) will cause output to increase by an even larger amount, *BF*; that is, by enough to eliminate the *output gap* and restore full employment.

One final point should be emphasized. *For the full impact of the multiplier to occur, it is essential that taxes not be increased to pay for the additional government spending.* As we shall see shortly, an increase in taxes would remove purchasing power from the hands of the public, and thus inhibit consumption. This, then, is a key policy conclusion of Keynesian economics: During a depression, when a large in-

---

[2]Also sometimes called the deflationary gap. We avoid this term because a shortfall in demand tends to cause unemployment, not deflation. (The term *deflation* means a fall in prices.)

crease in aggregate demand is needed to restore full employment, government spending should not be limited to the government's tax receipts. Spending should be increased without increasing taxes. But if taxes are not raised, how is the government to finance its spending? The answer is, by borrowing. That is, by adding to the public debt. In a recession, deficit spending is not at all unsound. Indeed, it is just what is needed to stimulate aggregate demand and reduce unemployment.

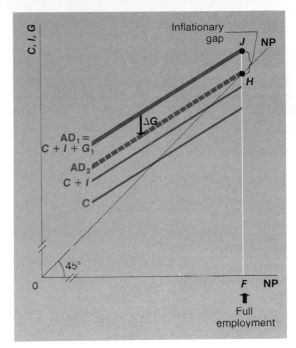

FIGURE 9-3 The inflationary gap.
At the full-employment quantity of output, aggregate demand may exceed the amount that the economy is capable of producing (J is above H). The excessive demand will cause inflation. To restrain inflation, aggregate demand should be brought down to AD_2. This can be done by a cut in government spending (ΔG) equal to the inflationary gap.

The government's *budgetary position* is calculated:

$$B = R - G$$

where B is the government's budget
R represents government revenues
G represents government expenditures

If the budget is positive ($R > G$), the government has a *surplus*.

If the budget is negative ($R < G$), the government has a *deficit*.

If $R = G$, the *budget is balanced*. (The term "balanced budget" is sometimes used loosely to mean that the budget is either in balance or in surplus—that is, $R \geq G$.)

Restrictive Fiscal Policy: The Suppression of Inflationary Pressures

During the 1930s, aggregate demand was too low; the economy was depressed. But this has not always been the case. Demand was very high during the Second World War and early postwar period; a rapid upward movement of prices was the result. Similarly, aggregate demand was too high during the last half of the 1960s, in large part because of government spending on the Vietnam war and on the Great Society programs. A new inflationary spiral was set off.

The situation where aggregate demand is too high is illustrated in Figure 9-3. At the full-employment national product, aggregate demand is *above* the 45° line. With

existing productive capacity, the economy cannot fill all the orders for goods. There is an *inflationary gap* (HJ); the pressure of excess demand will cause a rise in prices.

An *inflationary gap* exists when aggregate demand is above the 45° line at the full-employment quantity of national product. It is the vertical distance from the 45° line up to the aggregate demand function (measured at the full-employment quantity of national product).

The appropriate fiscal policy involves a sufficient *reduction* in government spending to bring aggregate demand down to AD_2. Specifically, the second rule of thumb for fiscal policy is this:

TAXES

Government spending is only one side of fiscal policy; the other side is taxation. Taxes do not show up directly as a component of aggregate demand. Instead, they affect aggregate demand indirectly by affecting consumption. (Taxes affect *disposable income*—the amount of income that consumers have left after they pay taxes. And changes in disposable income in turn affect consumption.)[3]

A Lump-sum Tax

In order to introduce tax complications one by one, we initially make a very unrea-

FIGURE 9-4 Effect of a $100 billion lump-sum tax.
If the MPC is 0.8, a lump-sum tax T of $100 billion causes the consumption function to shift down by $80 billion ($T \times$ MPC).

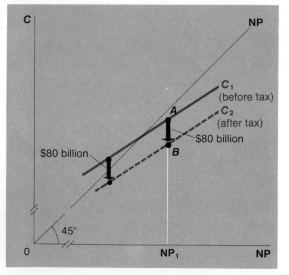

listic assumption—that taxes (T) are levied in a lump sum. That is, the government imposes taxes which involve a collection of, say, $100 billion, *regardless of the level of national product.*

How does this tax affect the consumption function? The answer is illustrated in Figure 9-4. Consider point A, any point on the consumption function C_1 which exists initially, before the imposition of the tax. Now suppose the government takes $100 billion from the public in taxes. At national product NP_1, people will have $100 billion less in disposable income after the payment of taxes. As a consequence, their consumption will decline. By how much? With a marginal propensity to consume (MPC) of 0.8, people will consume $80 billion less. (They will also save $20 billion less. Thus the $100 billion fall in disposable income is reflected in a $80-billion decline in consumption and a $20-billion decline in saving.) Therefore, point B on the after-tax consumption function C_2 is $80 billion below A. Similarly, every other point on the original consumption function also shifts down by $80 billion. The new after-tax function is parallel to the original consumption function, but $80 billion lower. In general,

When taxes are imposed and the consumption function shifts downward, aggregate demand will likewise shift downward. (When any component of aggregate demand shrinks, so does aggregate demand.) Thus, an increase in taxes represents an appropriate policy step when aggregate demand is too high and prices are rising. On the other

[3]Tax policies may also affect investment. For example, investment may be stimulated by the investment tax credit, which permits those who buy equipment to reduce their taxes by 10 percent of the cost of the equipment. In this chapter, we concentrate on the effect of taxes on consumption.

side, a *cut* in taxes represents a *stimulative* policy; the reduction in taxes will increase disposable income and shift the consumption function and aggregate demand *upward*.

Note that a change in taxes is almost as powerful a tool for controlling aggregate demand as a change in government spending. Almost, but not quite. An increase of $100 billion in government expenditures shifts aggregate demand up by the full $100 billion. But an increase in taxes of $100 billion shifts aggregate demand down by only $80 billion (100 billion times the MPC.) Because a dollar's change in government spending has a somewhat more powerful effect on aggregate demand than a dollar's change in taxes, an equal increase in both expenditures and taxes will have a net stimulative effect on aggregate demand. (See Box 9-1.)

Because government spending is more powerful, dollar for dollar, than a change in taxes, there is reason to turn to government spending when major changes are desired in aggregate demand.[4] And, indeed, economists did concentrate on the government spending side in their fiscal policy recommendations during the early Keynesian period. Since the early 1960s, however, tax changes have become more prominent in the management of aggregate demand. Thus, President Kennedy's program to "get the economy moving again" included a $10 billion cut in taxes. (This tax reduction was not enacted into law until 1964, after Kennedy's assassination.) Then, in 1968, a temporary tax surcharge was imposed to reduce the inflationary pressures associated with the Vietnam war and Great Society spending programs. In early 1975, taxes were cut in

order to stimulate the economy, which was suffering from the worst recession since the 1930s. Finally, when Jimmy Carter became President, one of his first policy proposals was for a $50-per-person tax rebate, aimed at increasing disposable incomes and aggregate demand. (This proposal was, however, withdrawn because of controversy over the desirability of stimulating aggregate demand in 1977.)

There are three reasons for this emphasis on tax changes as an important component of fiscal policy:

1. A tax cut is generally *less controversial* than an increase in government spending as a way of stimulating the economy. This is true in part because of skepticism over the ability of the government to spend money wisely, and because of fears that the government will grow bigger and bigger.

2. Tax changes may be put into effect *more quickly* than changes in government spending. For example, an increase in spending for highways, government buildings, dams, or other public works requires considerable planning, and this takes time.

3. Because the economy changes, the amount of fiscal restraint or stimulus should be adjusted from time to time. For example, while expansive policies were appropriate in the early 1960s, restraint became desirable as inflationary pressures accelerated after 1965. Again, stimulus was desirable in 1970; restraint by 1972; and stimulus again by 1974. If policies are to be adapted to the changing conditions in the economy, the initiatives we take today should be reversible in the future.

[4]This proposition is true only for government spending on goods and services, not for transfer payments. Unlike expenditures for goods and services, transfer payments do not constitute a component of aggregate demand, nor do they provide jobs directly. Like taxes, transfer payments affect demand indirectly by changing disposable income. Thus, like taxes, transfer payments have a less powerful effect on aggregate demand than government spending on goods and services.

To avoid excessive complexity, this chapter deals with the goods and services component of government spending and ignores transfer payments.

Tax changes are an important component of fiscal policy because they are *more easily reversed* than government spending. It is true that the public may be unhappy when previously cut taxes are reimposed. But they may be even more unhappy if government spending programs are eliminated. Furthermore, some government spending—for example, for roads, buildings, or dams—cannot be stopped without considerable waste. A half-finished bridge or dam is no good to anybody.

To summarize our policy conclusions thus far:

1. *To stimulate aggregate demand*, and thus combat unemployment, the appropriate fiscal policy involves an increase in govern-

ment spending and/or a cut in taxes; that is, *steps which tend to increase the government's deficit* (or reduce its surplus).

2. *To restrain aggregate demand* and thus combat inflation, it is appropriate to cut government spending and/or increase taxes; that is, take steps which *move the government's budget toward surplus*.

> A government deficit acts as a stimulus to aggregate demand. A surplus acts as a drag.

Adding Realism: A Proportional Tax

These two important policy conclusions have been illustrated by studying an extremely simple lump-sum tax. But this tax lacks realism. In the real world, tax collections rise and fall with national product and national income. This is obviously true of income taxes: the more people earn, the more taxes they pay. But it is also true of sales taxes. If national product and total sales rise, government revenues from sales taxes will likewise rise.

The tax system is complicated. Clearly, we cannot take all its complexities into account. We may, however, take a giant step toward realism by discarding the lump-sum tax and considering a tax that does rise and fall with national product. The one we consider is a *proportional tax*; that is, a tax that yields revenues which are a constant percentage of national product.

As we saw in Figure 9-4, a lump-sum tax shifts the consumption function down by a *constant* amount. But this is not true of a proportional tax. If national product doubles, tax collections will likewise double, and the depressing effects on the consumption function will also double. For example, if national product is NP_1 in Figure 9-5, a 20 percent tax will depress consumption from point B to D. But if national product is twice as high at NP_2, this same 20 percent tax will depress consumption by twice as much—from F to G.

Of course, a 30 percent tax depresses consumption even more than a 20 percent tax. (Consumption function C_3 lies below C_2.) In general, the heavier the tax, the more the consumption function rotates clockwise, as shown in Figure 9-5.[5]

Note two important effects of a proportional tax:

1. The higher the tax rate is, the more disposable income will be depressed and the lower the consumption function will be. Thus, an increase in the tax rate will reduce aggregate demand, and a cut in taxes will increase aggregate demand. On this first

FIGURE 9-5 A proportional tax: Effect on consumption.
When a proportional tax is imposed, the consumption function rotates clockwise around point A. The higher the tax rate, the more the consumption function rotates. As the tax rate rises from 20 to 30 percent, the consumption function becomes lower and flatter.

point, then, the effects of a proportional tax are similar to those of the lump-sum tax considered earlier. (But on the next point, they differ.)

2. In an economy with proportional taxes, the consumption function is flatter than in a tax-free economy. And the higher the tax rate, the flatter the consumption function becomes. But, as we saw in Chapter 8, the flatter the consumption function, the lower the multiplier. Moreover, the effect of a proportional tax in lowering the multiplier can be very substantial. Recall that, with no taxes and an MPC of 0.8, the multiplier was 5. But when a 25 percent proportional tax is introduced, the multiplier drops sharply, to only 2.5 (as explained in detail in Box 9-2).

[5]Note that the consumption function rotates around point A. Why is this so? By assumption, taxes are proportional to national product. Therefore, in the limiting case where national product is zero, taxes are likewise zero. Consumption is therefore unaffected. Thus, point A is on every consumption function, regardless of how high the tax percentage is set.

BOX 9-2
THE MULTIPLIER IN AN ECONOMY WITH TAXES

Taxes have a substantial effect on the multiplier process. Consider an economy with a marginal propensity to consume of 0.8 and a tax rate of 25 percent. Each $1 change in investment demand (or in government spending) will then have the following effect on aggregate demand.

	Change in national product for each $1 increase in investment demand
First round	
Increase of investment of	$1
Second round	
(a) Producers of investment goods have earned $1 more in first round	
(b) The government takes 25 cents in taxes, leaving disposable income of 75 cents	
(c) With MPC = 0.8, consumption as a consequence is $0.8 \times 75c$; that is,	$0.60 = \$1(0.6)$
Third round	
(a) Producers of consumer goods have earned 60 cents more in second round	
(b) The government takes 25 percent (or 15 cents) in taxes, leaving disposable income of 45 cents	
(c) With MPC = 0.8, consumption as a consequence is 0.8×45 cents; that is,	$0.36 = \$1(0.6)^2$
Fourth round	
Consumption is	$\$1(0.6)^3$
	.
	.
	.

Using formula on page 156, we find the sum of all rounds:

$$\$1 (1 + 0.6 + 0.6^2 + 0.6^3 + \ldots) = \frac{1}{1 - 0.6} = \qquad \$2.50$$

Therefore, the multiplier is 2.5.

(In more advanced texts, the multiplier formula for an economy with taxation is derived:

$$\text{Multiplier} = \frac{1}{s + t - st}$$

where s is the marginal propensity to save, and

t is the marginal tax rate; that is, the change in tax collections as a fraction of the change in national product.

This formula is not derived here in order to avoid preoccupation with algebra.)

LEAKAGES AND INJECTIONS: AN ECONOMY WITH GOVERNMENT SPENDING AND TAXES

The previous chapter explained a very simplified economy, with only consumption and investment, and no government sector at all. Such an economy reaches equilibrium when the leakages from the spending stream, in the form of saving, are just equal to the injections into the spending stream, in the form of investment.

When government spending and taxation are introduced, a similar proposition still holds: Equilibrium exists when leakages and injections are equal. But now there are more than one leakage and more than one injection. (See Figure 9-6.) Specifically, *government spending* represents an *injection* into the spending stream, similar to investment demand. When the government spends more for roads, buildings, etc., the producers of these roads and buildings earn higher incomes, and their consumption consequently rises. The circular flow of expenditures broadens as a result of this government spending. On the other side, *taxation* represents a *leakage*, similar to saving. Income

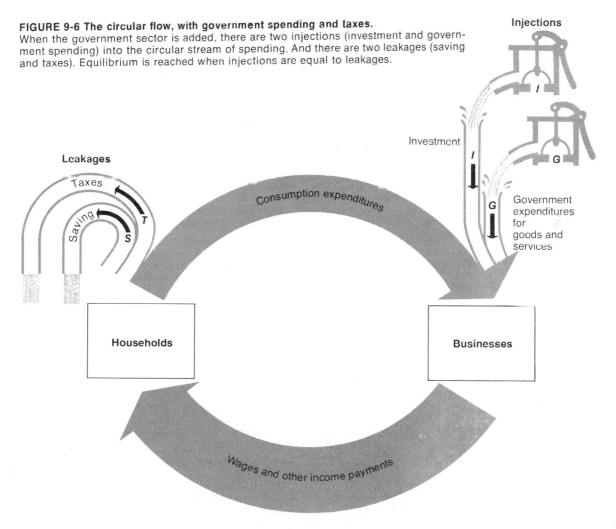

FIGURE 9-6 The circular flow, with government spending and taxes.
When the government sector is added, there are two injections (investment and government spending) into the circular stream of spending. And there are two leakages (saving and taxes). Equilibrium is reached when injections are equal to leakages.

extracted from the public in the form of taxation is not available for consumption expenditures. As consumption falls, the circular flow of expenditures narrows. As we have seen earlier, government spending provides a stimulus, while taxation acts as a drag on national product and income.

Thus, in the more complete economy with a government sector, the condition for equilibrium becomes more complex:

> Equilibrium occurs when the *leakages* (saving plus taxation) are equal to the *injections* (investment plus government spending).

BUILT-IN FISCAL STABILIZERS

Because taxes lower the size of the multiplier, they add to the stability of the economy. For example, in an economy with high taxes, there will be a small multiplier. Therefore, a fall in investment demand will cause only a moderate decline in national product. On the other side, an upswing in investment demand is unlikely to lead to a runaway boom in an economy with substantial taxes. The leakages into taxes will increase as national product rises, thus decreasing the strength of the expansion.

Tax revenues that vary with national product are therefore a *built-in* or *automatic stabilizer*. The way that taxes act to stabilize the economy is illustrated in Figure 9-7. In this diagram, taxes (T) are just adequate to cover government expenditure (G) when the economy is at the full-employment national product NP_1; the budget is balanced ($G = T$). Now if the economy swings down into a recession, to NP_2, tax collections fall, and the budget automatically moves into deficit. This provides a stimulus. With falling tax collections, disposable income is left in the hands of the public. Consumption falls less sharply than it would in a tax-free economy. Thus, the downward momentum

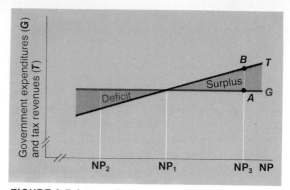

FIGURE 9-7 Automatic fiscal stabilization.
As national product rises from NP_1 toward NP_3, the government's budget automatically moves into surplus. This slows down the increases in disposable income and consumption and thus slows down the expansion. Conversely, the budget automatically moves into deficit during recessions as national product falls from NP_1 toward NP_2. The government deficit helps to keep up disposable income and consumption and thus alleviates the recession.

in the economy is reduced. Similarly, the tax system acts as a restraint on an upswing. As national product rises, tax collections rise and the government's budget moves toward surplus. The increase in disposable income is slowed down, and the upward momentum of the economy is weakened.

> An *automatic stabilizer* is any feature of the economic system which automatically tends to reduce the strength of recessions and/or the strength of upswings in demand, without policy changes being made. (Thus, an *automatic* stabilizer should be sharply distinguished from a *discretionary* policy action, such as a cut in tax rates or the introduction of new government spending programs.)

The degree of automatic stabilization depends on how strongly tax collections respond to changes in national product. Therefore, the degree of automatic stabilization provided by the tax system will be greater, the *higher* tax rates are, and the more *progressive* the tax system is. (Both the height and the progressivity of taxes work to make Figure 9-7's tax function steeper.)

There are also automatic stabilizers on the government expenditures side (not shown in Figure 9-7). With existing programs, unemployment insurance compensation and welfare expenditures automatically rise during a recession, sustaining disposable incomes and slowing the downswing.

While automatic stabilizers reduce the severity of economic fluctuations, they do not eliminate them. (Built-in stabilizers have been credited with reducing the amplitude of fluctuations in the United States by somewhere between one-quarter and one-half.)[6] The objective of discretionary fiscal policy is to reduce the fluctuations even more.

SOME COMPLICATIONS

The tendency for the government's budget to swing automatically into deficit during recessions, and automatically into surplus during inflationary booms, adds stability to the economy. It may therefore be looked on as a plus. But there are three important complications.

1. Fiscal Drag

When the tax system acts as a brake that slows down changes in aggregate demand, the resulting stability is not an unmixed blessing. True, the tax system reduces *unwanted* fluctuations in demand. But it can also exert a *fiscal drag* that slows down *desirable* increases in aggregate demand, and thus makes it more difficult to achieve full employment. The same stabilizing action which slows the descent into recession also slows the climb out of a recession.

Furthermore, once full employment has been achieved, the drag from the tax system can *slow down the healthy growth in demand needed to maintain full employment in an economy whose productive capacity is growing.* Reconsider Figure 9-7. The full-employment national product this year is represented by NP_1. Our growing productive capacity means that next year, full-employment national product will be greater—say, at NP_3. As output rises, tax collections rise. The result is a surplus that acts as a drag on aggregate demand, and that consequently may cause the economy to fall short of its potential (NP_3).

Fiscal drag is the tendency for rising tax collections to impede the healthy growth of aggregate demand that is needed for the achievement and maintenance of full employment.

It is worth emphasizing that automatic stabilizer and fiscal drag are two terms representing the same phenomenon: the built-in tendency for the tax system to stabilize the economy. Yet, the two terms sound as though they were poles apart. "Automatic stabilizer" is a mellow-sounding phrase; presumably, we should be all for it. "Fiscal drag" seems definitely bad; we should be against it. The difference in the use of the two terms comes, not from the way in which the tax system operates, but from the state of the economy. In an unstable economy, which tends to go first into a deep recession and then swing to the other extreme of an inflationary boom, the tendency of the tax system to slow down changes in aggregate demand is desirable. Therefore, it is appropriate to refer to the *automatic stabilization* provided by the tax system. But suppose that Keynes' original concern is valid. Assume,

---

[6]Peter Eilbott, "The Effectiveness of the Automatic Stabilizers," *American Economic Review*, June 1966, pp. 450–465. An international comparison is given in Bent Hansen, *Fiscal Policy in Seven Countries, 1955–1965* (Paris: Organization for Economic Co-operation and Development, 1969).

in other words, that the economy tends to stabilize at a high level of unemployment, with aggregate demand consistently falling short of the full-employment level. In such circumstances, we may speak of the *fiscal drag* exerted by the tax system.

Because of this dependence on underlying economic conditions, the term *fiscal drag* has appeared intermittently in the debate over macroeconomic policy. It first came to prominence in the Kennedy administration. During the late 1950s, there had been two quick recessions and two weak and incomplete recoveries. Kennedy and his advisers feared long-run stagnation. In order to "get the country moving," they decided to counteract fiscal drag.

Two policy tools were available. Returning to Figure 9-7, we observe that, as the full-employment national product grows from NP_1 to NP_3, the potential budgetary surplus AB is the measure of the fiscal drag. To eliminate this surplus:

1. Tax rates may be cut by enough to shift the tax function down so that it runs through point A.

2. Government spending may be increased by enough to shift the G function up so that it runs through point B.

The Kennedy administration decided on a compromise involving some tax cut and some increases in spending.

While fiscal drag may be a problem, these two ways of dealing with it (either by cutting taxes or increasing spending) are enough to bring joy to a politician's heart. It is therefore important to introduce one last term—one with a happy sound. The budget surplus AB generated by a growing economy is called a *fiscal dividend*. The fiscal dividend may be used for tax cuts or additional government spending.

> The *fiscal dividend* is the budget surplus, measured at the full-employment national product, that is generated by the growth of the productive capacity of the economy. (In Figure 9-7, distance AB represents the fiscal dividend created as productive capacity grows and the full-employment national product increases from NP_1 to NP_3.)

By the late 1960s, the term *fiscal drag* had fallen into disuse. The rapid escalation of spending for the Vietnam war and for domestic social programs, combined with the tax cut of 1964, greatly exceeded any surplus that might otherwise have been created by the growing economy. Budgetary deficits mushroomed. Aggregate demand became excessive and inflationary pressures grew. In these circumstances, the automatic tendency of the tax system to generate higher revenues was welcomed. What we needed was a drag, and that is what the tax system gave us. Indeed, inflationary pressures became so strong that even more restraint was needed. Thus, the income tax surcharge of 1968 was enacted.

In the middle 1970s, fiscal drag once more became part of macroeconomic policy discussions. Once again, the economy suffered from a high and persistent level of unemployment. Now, however, there was an added complication, in the form of inflation. Much of the increase in money income during that period reflected rising prices. But with higher money incomes, people were automatically pushed into higher tax brackets. (The personal income tax brackets shown in Table 5-3 are given in dollar terms. Therefore, a rise in money incomes moves people into higher tax brackets, even if their higher money incomes buy no more.) Thus, we were getting taxed more for two reasons. Taxes rose as our real incomes rose (regular fiscal drag). And tax rates rose as inflation pushed people into higher and higher tax brackets. Consequently, there was a double drag on the recovery of the economy out of the deep recession of 1974–1975. (During this period, discretionary policies to stimulate aggregate demand were inhibited by the fear of making inflation worse. The complexities of decision-making during a period of both high unemployment and high inflation are postponed until Chapter 13.)

2. Measuring Fiscal Policy: The Full-Employment Budget

Because the government's budget swings automatically toward deficit during recessions and automatically toward surplus during booms, the state of the budget cannot be taken as a measure of what has happened to *fiscal policy*. For example, when the budget moves into deficit during recession, this does not demonstrate that policymakers have accepted the teachings of Keynesian economics and have acted to stimulate the economy and offset the recession. They may have done nothing; the deficit may merely reflect a decline in the government's tax revenues as a result of the recession.

FIGURE 9-8 The full-employment budget.
A downward swing in economic activity from NP_1 to NP_2 causes the actual budget to move into deficit BC. Because the full-employment budget's revenues are measured at full employment national product (NP_1) regardless of the actual quantity of output, the full-employment budget is not affected by the recession. However, it does move into deficit (AE) as a result of a cut in tax rates (shown by the fall from T_1 to T_2).

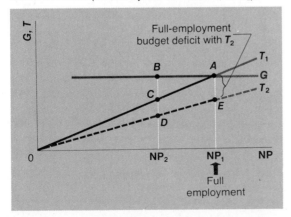

In order to determine whether fiscal policy is moving in an expansive or restrictive direction, some measure other than the actual budgetary deficit or surplus is therefore needed. The *full-employment budget* provides such a measure. In contrast with the actual budget, which measures actual government receipts less government expenditures, the full-employment budget indicates what the surplus or deficit would be with the current tax and spending legislation if the economy were at full employment.

The *full-employment budget* (also known as the high-employment budget) is defined thus:

$$B_{FE} = R_{FE} - G_{FE}$$

where B_{FE} is the full-employment budget.

R_{FE} represents full-employment receipts; that is, the receipts that the present tax laws would yield if the economy were at full employment.

G_{FE} stands for full-employment government expenditures; that is, actual expenditures less expenditures (payments to the unemployed, etc.) that are directly associated with unemployment in excess of the full-employment level (usually taken as 4 percent of the labor force).

The point of the full-employment budget is illustrated in Figure 9-8. Suppose the economy starts at NP_1, a position of full employment. With the present tax rate (represented by line T_1), government revenues are equal to government expenditures (G); the actual budget is in balance. (So is the full-employment budget. When the economy is at full employment, the two budgets are exactly the same.) Now suppose that the economy slips down into a recession; national product falls to NP_2. Tax revenues decline (to C); the actual budget automatically swings into deficit (*BC*). To the unwary, it might seem that the government has acted to stimulate the economy by budget deficits. But this is not so; the government has not yet made any policy change. If there were full employment, present tax rates T_1 would yield tax revenues of *A*. The full-employment budget is measured at the full-employment national product (NP_1) regardless of the actual national product. Therefore, the full-employment budget is still in balance after national product has fallen to NP_2. The full-employment budget accurately reflects what has happened to fiscal policy: nothing.

Now suppose that, with the economy at NP_2, the government takes discretionary steps to combat the recession by cutting the tax rate to T_2. How does this show up in the full-employment budget measure? At the full-employment national product, NP_1, the new tax rate T_2 would now yield revenues of *E*. Thus, the tax cut causes a full-employment budget deficit of *AE*. (It also causes an increase in the actual budget deficit, from *BC* to *BD*.) Similarly, an increase in government spending (an upward shift of *G*) would cause the full-employment budget to move into deficit (and the actual budget to move into greater deficit).

In summary, then:

1. A downward swing in the economy automatically causes the actual budget to move toward deficit, but not the full-employment budget.

2. A cut in tax rates or an increase in government spending causes both the actual and the full-employment budgets to move toward deficit.

3. Because the actual budget responds to changes both in the economy and in policy, it is a misleading measure of policy itself. Since the full-employment budget remains unchanged by changes in economic activity,[7] and shows only the effects of policy adjustments, changes in this budget indicate how fiscal policy has changed. (In the example in Figure 9-8, the full-employment budget moved into deficit as tax rates were cut from T_1 to T_2.)

We can see how misleading the actual budget would be as a measure of fiscal policy actions by comparing it with the full-employment budget in Figure 9-9. For example, during the recessionary years of 1960 and 1974, the actual budget moved sharply into deficit. But fiscal policy was not strongly expansionary, as the actual budget might falsely have suggested. The stable paths of the full-employment budget in 1960 and 1974 correctly show that very little change was occurring in fiscal policy.

Moreover, the full-employment budget figures can be used to identify some important changes in fiscal policy. Observe how the full-employment budget surplus declined in 1964, reflecting the expansionary tax cut of that year. On the other hand, in 1968 and 1969 there was a sizable swing in the full-employment budget from deficit to surplus, indicating the contractionary 1968 tax surcharge and cutbacks in spending programs. Finally, the sharp swing of the full-employment budget into deficit in 1975 reflected the expansionary tax cut and government spending designed to lift the economy out of the 1974–1975 recession.

But Figure 9-9 also shows some disquieting aspects of our fiscal history. Consider what happened in 1965 through 1967. The stagnation of the early sixties was a thing of the past; the economy was operating at a

---

[7]Because of the complexity of our economy, there are some exceptions (explained in more advanced works) where changes in economic conditions can affect the full-employment budget measure. Thus, the full-employment budget should not be looked on as a perfect measure of fiscal policy. But it is the best simple measure, and as an indicator of fiscal policy, it is clearly superior to the highly defective actual budget.

FIGURE 9-9 The full-employment budget and the actual budget, 1960–1977.
When the economy is operating below the full-employment level, tax revenues are depressed and the actual budget shows a larger deficit (or smaller surplus) than the full-employment budget. The full-employment budget shows changes in fiscal policy.

Sources: U.S. Department of Commerce and Federal Reserve Bank of St. Louis.

high level of employment, and inflation was beginning to gather momentum. The proper fiscal stance was restraint. Yet the full-employment budget slid into deficit. During these years, the government *destabilized* the economy, making the inflationary problem worse. The swing into a deeper deficit in 1972 also acted as a destabilizing force. It added inflationary pressures to an economy already operating close to its capacity.

Why were mistakes made? Some of the problems with fiscal management are complex, and must be put off until later chapters. But the principal problem in the 1965–1967 period was reasonably clear. Caught in the quagmire of an unpopular and frustrating war, President Johnson shied away from a tax increase to finance the higher government spending. The swing into deficit in 1972 also seems to have had political roots, apparently resulting from the desire of politicians to please voters with election-year spending.

3. A Policy Trap: The Annually Balanced Budget

Because the actual budget tends to swing automatically into deficit during recessions and is therefore a misleading indicator of policy, it sets a trap for the unwary and uninitiated policymaker. Suppose that the President and his advisers take a balancing of the (actual) budget as an important goal as they prepare their annual spending and tax proposals for Congress. What happens as the economy moves into recession? The budget automatically moves into deficit as a result of declining tax collections. If the authorities are determined to balance the budget, they have two policy choices: to cut government spending, or to increase tax rates. *Either step will depress aggregate demand and make the recession worse. By raising taxes or cutting expenditures, the government will offset the automatic stabilizers built into the tax system. Trying to balance the budget each year is a policy trap.*

One reason this trap deserves emphasis is because President Hoover fell into it during the early years of the Great Depression. As tax revenues fell and deficits mounted, Hoover was convinced that the elimination of deficits was essential to restore business confidence and hasten economic recovery. In 1932, he recommended that taxes be increased to get the budget back into balance. Congress agreed. The result was one of the largest peacetime increases in taxes in United States history. Fiscal policy was precisely the opposite of what was needed to promote recovery. Rather than the needed stimulus, the country got a large dose of restraint. The stage was set for the collapse into the deepest point of the Depression in 1933. And, ironically, the policy did not even succeed in its goal of balancing the budget. In part because of the added fiscal restraint, the economy collapsed; as it collapsed, tax revenues fell. The deficit persisted.

In Hoover's behalf, it should be noted that he was acting in line with the accepted wisdom of the day. Both Republicans and Democrats argued for "sound finance," meaning a balanced budget. For example, in his 1932 campaign, Roosevelt urged the government to "have the courage to stop borrowing to meet continuing deficits. Stop the deficits."[8] In Britain, the Treasury held the view that sound finance required the government to live within its means—a view based on historical experience. (In the century between the Napoleonic wars and the First World War, during which time the British Empire reached its peak of power, government surpluses resulted in a reduction of the national debt by one-quarter; that

is, from £0.8 billion to £0.6 billion. The British were able to avoid major wars and enjoy a rapid economic growth; as a result, their national debt fell from 200 percent of GNP to only 25 percent.)

The accepted wisdom of the day, which led to Hoover's blunder in recommending a huge tax increase, set the stage for the Keynesian revolution with its important message: Spending and tax policies should be aimed at the goals of full employment and price stability, and not at the goal of balancing the budget. *Fiscal policy should be designed to balance the economy, not the budget.*

But the widespread acceptance of Keynes' message has left two nagging worries. If the government runs whatever deficits are considered necessary to restore and maintain full employment, will we not eventually end up with a crushing burden of public debt? Isn't the government in danger of going bankrupt? And if the government is not held accountable for balancing the budget, how can it be expected to show restraint in its spending and taxing decisions? Will politicians be tempted to justify overspending by referring to the "needs of the economy"?

THE ISSUE OF RESTRAINT

Keynesian economics destroyed the old rule of an annually balanced budget. But to keep government spending under control, many people long for something to put in its place. In particular, some observers look on the concept of a "fiscal dividend" as dangerous. The concept itself may be valid, but telling

---

[8]Roosevelt took his strongest stand for fiscal conservatism in a Pittsburgh speech on Oct. 19, 1932. This speech became something of an embarrassment as the deficits mounted during his first administration. And, it inspired a story which circulated in Washington. When Roosevelt was returning to Pittsburgh several years later, he turned to one of his speechwriters for advice on how to explain away his earlier stand for a balanced budget. The reply was, "Deny you were ever in Pittsburgh."

This story apparently is a corruption of a somewhat similar event reported in Samuel L. Rosenman, *Working with Roosevelt* (New York: Harper, 1952), p. 87. (Incidentally, Rosenman was the one who coined the term "New Deal.")

Congress about it is something like introducing a 6-year-old to the cookie jar. It will just encourage Congress to indulge its appetite for new spending proposals. We may warn of the dangers of excess, but can we really expect restraint?

Because of disagreements over the proper role of the government in dealing with the problems of society, and also because of disagreements over the desirable level of aggregate demand, it is difficult to reach a consensus on any rule of thumb which will act as a constraint on government spending. And, in our complex and changing economy, no rule or guideline can possibly be appropriate for all conceivable situations. Nevertheless, a number of guidelines have been suggested. The first of these guidelines, involving the full-employment budget, is particularly important, as it has been endorsed by both Democratic and Republican presidents during the past two decades.[9]

1. Use the Full-Employment Budget as a Guide

The problem with the old balanced-budget rule was that it set the stage for destabilizing actions. (Remember: As the economy moves into recession and a budget deficit automatically appears, the old rule leads to tax increases or spending cuts that make the recession worse.) Such destabilizing actions can be avoided by the use of the full-employment budget as a policy guide. Since it does not automatically swing into deficit during recessions, it does not create a demand for tax increases or spending cuts. (Thus, the full-employment budget has two major uses: as a *way of measuring* fiscal policy; and as a *guide* to fiscal policy which avoids the trap of the annually balanced budget.)

There are two main ways of using the full-employment budget as a policy guide.

1(a). Aim for a balanced full-employment budget every year If the government balances the full-employment budget each year, then its expenditures are limited: They total no more than the tax revenues which would be generated by a full-employment economy. Restraint is achieved, while the destabilizing consequences of the old balanced-budget rule are avoided. The automatic stabilizers built into the economy reduce the amplitude of economic fluctuations.

But all this rule does is to allow the automatic stabilizers to work. It does not envisage a government going one step further and introducing fiscal stimulus to fight recessions. (Such stimulus—for example, a cut in tax rates—would violate the rule, since it would put the full-employment budget into deficit. Recall that precisely this case was illustrated in Figure 9-8). Thus, this first rule represents an unambitious strategy. Its aim is to avoid destabilizing actions, not to actively stabilize the economy. It therefore is reminiscent of the doctor's motto: *Primo non nocere,* or "First do no harm."

1(b). Balance the full-employment budget, but only when the economy achieves full employment The alternative approach is more ambitious in that it allows a government to take the initiative in managing the economy. One constraint the government must satisfy is that by the time full employment is reached, expenditures are to be limited to revenues and the budget is to be balanced. But, during recessions, taxes can be cut or spending increased in order to speed the return to full employment. In other words, the full-employment budget can be shifted into deficit during recessions. It need be returned to balance only when the economy reaches full employment.

[9]The Nixon administration explicitly endorsed the full-employment budget concept, and all Democratic administrations since 1960 have used the concept in the budget-making process. The Nixon administration leaned toward variant *1(a)*. Democratic administrations are less easily categorized, sometimes favoring variant *1(a)*, and sometimes *1(b)*.

2. The Cyclically Balanced Budget

Note that either of the two variants (1*a* and 1*b*) on the full-employment budget rule may leave the government with an actual budget which is in deficit on the average. Whenever the economy falls short of full employment, deficits are permissible in the actual budget, for which there may not be offsetting surpluses during periods of inflationary excess demand.

More long-term restraint can be provided by *cyclically balancing the actual budget.* According to this approach, there should be sufficient surpluses during good times to cover the deficits of the recessions. But, unlike the old annually balanced budget, the cyclically balanced budget envisions active fiscal management to combat instability, with taxes cut and spending increased during recessions, and opposite policies adopted during booms.

3. Place Limits on Government Spending

Another approach is to restrain government spending by limiting its overall level.[10] For example, one of Carter's commitments as a presidential candidate was to limit total federal government spending to no more than 21 percent of GNP.[11] (His first budget, presented in January 1978, came in above this figure, at 22 percent of estimated GNP, and we will have to wait to judge his longer-term success.) Since this proposal would limit spending, it implies that expansive fiscal policy actions will take the form of tax cuts.

Administrative Approaches

In recent decades, a number of administrative innovations have been introduced to improve the budget-making process and cut down waste in government expenditures. During the 1960s, a concerted effort was made to estimate the costs and benefits of government programs carefully in order to determine which were worth the costs and which were not. Unfortunately, the experiment with *cost-benefit analysis* was not a great success. In particular, the benefits of government programs proved hard to quantify. How is one to measure precisely the social gains from an additional $1 million spent on the police force in an urban area? There is a fundamental problem if a government agency is required to give a dollar estimate of the value of its own programs; it is likely to estimate the benefits to be comfortably greater than the costs.[12] Because government agencies were being asked to evaluate their own programs, the cost-benefit analyses of the 1960s were distinguished by their lack of distinction; most were not worth the paper they were written on.

During the 1970s, there have been two major innovations. One involved the budget-making procedures of the Congress. Traditionally, the President has made a comprehensive budgetary proposal to the Congress each year. The work on the President's budget proposal is coordinated and controlled by the Office of Management and Budget (formerly known as the Bureau of the Budget). But, prior to 1975, Congress had no similar mechanism to monitor its

---

[10]At the state level, attempts have been made to limit the size of government by limiting tax rates. Most notable has been the tax revolt in California. In 1973, Proposition 1 (a constitutional amendment to limit tax rates) was put on the ballot, but was defeated in spite of Governor Reagan's enthusiastic support. However, this setback for the proponents of a tax ceiling was temporary. In 1978, Proposition 13 (to limit property taxes to 1 percent of market value) was approved by a lopsided 2-to-1 majority—despite Governor Brown's opposition. In the month before the referendum, the proposition was given a boost when Los Angeles County sent out notices to 400,000 homeowners, raising their assessments by an average of more than 100 percent.

[11]After one year in office, he reiterated his intention to reduce federal spending to about 21 percent of GNP. See *Economic Report of the President*, January 1978, p. 9.

[12]This is, however, not always the case. Henry J. Aaron (who was appointed Assistant Secretary in the Department of Health, Education and Welfare in 1977) cites a number of studies which conclude that the benefits of some of the programs in the War on Poverty are less than the costs. Aaron argues that "research, insofar as it exercises independent influences on opinions about complex social questions, tends over time to be profoundly conservative in its impact." Aaron, *Politics and the Professors* (Washington, D.C.: The Brookings Institution, 1978), pp. 17, 30–34.

spending authorizations or to coordinate spending and taxation proposals. Instead, various parts of the budget went to different congressional committees. The pieces of the budget were voted on one by one. Yet the individual pieces, each of which may seem reasonable in isolation, do not necessarily add up to a coherent whole. In particular, they may be far off the size of the budget needed for economic stability. Therefore, in 1975, Congress set up its own budget committee, with special responsibility for monitoring and limiting the overall level of spending.

The second major innovation of the 1970s, *zero-base budgeting*, was introduced by President Carter. This technique, which had been developed and tested in some private corporations and some states (including Georgia when Carter was governor), requires every program to be critically evaluated "from the ground up." No program is to be continued simply because it exists. Thus, the objective of zero-base budgeting is to combat the deadweight of momentum in government spending. Zero-base budgeting differs from the practice of incremental budgeting, which focuses on the increments to be added to the previous year's budgets of the various departments and programs. (In an incremental-budgeting system, once a program is adopted, it tends to be continued even if it has outlived its usefulness.)

> *Zero-base budgeting* is a budgeting technique which requires items to be justified anew beginning at a zero funding base, without regard to expenditures in the past.

In addition to requiring that projects be justified anew, zero-base budgeting aims at ranking government programs in the order of their priority, to indicate which should be abolished if spending has to be cut. It is still too early to judge this approach, but some of the early reports have not been very encouraging. Perhaps out of fear of losing their jobs or of incurring the wrath of the beneficiaries of current programs, government officials have tended automatically to lump all the existing programs into the most desirable category, and to rank proposed new programs in a lower category. Such is the dead weight of the past!

THE PUBLIC DEBT

Whenever the government runs a deficit, it must borrow the money to pay for any expenditures in excess of its tax revenues. Thus, the adoption of Keynesian fiscal policies (involving deficit spending where needed to get the economy back to full employment) has created fears of a rising public debt that will become a crushing burden on future generations. Since the most rapid increase in the public debt took place during the Second World War, we may consider a specific issue: Who bore the economic burden of that war? The people of the time, or their children who inherited the huge government debt?

In order to explain and weigh the problems associated with a rising government debt, it is helpful to divide the discussion into two parts, looking first at the deficit spending, and then at the financial consequences of the debt itself. (Of course, this division is arbitrary. It is the deficit spending which necessitates the borrowing and the increase in the debt. But the division is useful in clarifying a complicated subject.)

Deficit Spending: What Is Its Opportunity Cost?

When the government spends, it makes a claim on productive resources. *If the economy is at full employment*, an increase in government spending must involve a reduction in production for the private sector of the economy. For example, when General Motors was making thousands of tanks to help fight the Second World War, it couldn't make cars at the same time.

Thus, military (or other government) production in 1943 came at the opportunity cost of giving up consumer goods in 1943. Therefore, in a fundamental sense, the burden of the war fell on the people at the time: It was they, and not we, who had to do without new cars. They were the ones who suffered, not only in terms of lives lost, but also in terms of consumer goods forgone.

But the conclusion that the burden of the war fell on the people of the early 1940s is only 90 percent correct; there is a missing element. If guns had not been produced to fight the war, more consumer goods could have been produced. But *more capital goods could have been produced, too.* Instead of turning out guns, ships, and planes, American industry could have produced more machines and built more factories. And if it had, the rising capital stock would have benefited not only the people of the 1940s, but future generations also. The capital stock could have been higher in 1945—and in 1975—had there not been the tremendous waste of war. Thus, because our capital stock—and therefore our income—is lower, *we* are still bearing some of the burden of that war.

(Quite a different set of conclusions follows if we look at deficit spending during a depression. With idle workers and machines, producing more goods for the government does not come at the expense of private consumption and investment. Indeed, because of the operation of the multiplier, we produce more consumer goods too. As more consumer goods are produced, investment demand is stimulated: To produce more cars and refrigerators, businesses need more machines and factories. Thus, deficit spending by the government *during a depression* involves a benefit rather than a burden to both present and future generations. It stimulates the production of more consumer goods for the current generation, and more capital stock for future generations.)

Effects of the Public Debt

But the government finances deficit spending by borrowing (selling bonds), thus adding to the public debt. What about this debt itself? Does it transfer a burden to future generations?

To answer this question, let us distinguish the payment of interest on the debt from the repayment of principal as bonds fall due. Consider the government debt which existed in 1947 because of the deficits of 1942. The first important point is that interest payments on this debt were not made by the people of 1947 to the people of 1942. Rather, they were made by *some* people in 1947 to *other* people in 1947. (Specifically, the taxpayers who financed the government's interest payments made the payments to bondholders who collected the interest.) Thus the existence of government debt (indeed, any debt) involves the transfer of funds from one group now to another group now; it does not involve a transfer from people in one period of time to people in another.

It should not, however, be assumed that this transfer from one group to another is costless or unimportant. There are three problems:

1. The transfer may lead to an *undesirable redistribution of income.* This depends on who holds the bonds and on who pays the taxes. (Of course, it also depends on what we consider the "socially desirable" distribution of income.)

2. When the government collects taxes to make interest payments, it creates an *excess burden.* When taxes are imposed, the public has an incentive to alter its behavior to avoid paying taxes. For example, people have an incentive to hire lawyers to search for tax loopholes and to divert their savings into tax-sheltered investments (that is, investments involving little or no taxation). As a result, the efficiency of the economy may be reduced. When money is taken out of one pocket and put into another, something is lost in the process.

3. The need for the government to make interest payments on a large debt may contribute to *inflation.* For example, inflation may occur when the government decides not to collect taxes to pay the interest, but simply to borrow and thus to run up its deficit.

> The *excess burden of taxes* is the decrease in the efficiency of the economy that results when people change their behavior to avoid paying taxes. (Thus it is distinguished from the *primary burden*, which is measured by the amount of taxes collected from the public.)

Finally, what happens as the debt falls due? Does the principal represent a burden when it is repaid? Two observations are important here. First, insofar as the debt is retired (paid off), this payment is just like an interest payment: It is a transfer of funds from one group *today* (the taxpayers) to

another group *today* (the bondholders). Second, and even more important, recent history shows that government debt is reduced only rarely. When bonds fall due, they are generally refinanced; that is, the government sells new bonds to raise the funds to pay off the holders of the old bonds that are coming due. Since the public debt is so seldom paid off, debt retirement is not a very important policy issue.

To issue debt with no intention of ever retiring it may seem like an unsound practice. But this is not necessarily so.[13] A government or a private corporation may safely have a continuing and growing debt if its ability to pay the interest is also increasing. What is important is that the debt not be out of proportion to the ability of the issuer to finance the debt payments in the future. In a growing economy with a growing tax base, the public debt may rise without getting out of proportion. Observe in Table 9-1 that, in spite of the rapid increase in the dollar amount of the public debt, it is now a much

TABLE 9-1
The Public Debt and Interest Payments, 1929–1977

Year	(1) Public debt†	(2) Gross national product	(3) Interest payments	(4) Public debt, as percentage of GNP (1) ÷ (2)	(5) Interest payments, as percentage of GNP (3) ÷ (2)	(6) Per capita public debt (current dollars)
	(billions of current dollars)					
1929	$ 16.5	$ 103.4	$ 0.7	16%	0.7%	$ 135
1941	56.3	124.9	1.1	45	0.8	422
1946	229.5	209.6	4.2	109	2.0	1623
1951	216.9	330.2	4.5	66	1.4	1406
1956	224.3	420.7	5.1	53	1.2	1334
1966	271.8	753.0	9.2	36	1.2	1383
1972	341.2	1171.1	14.6	29	1.2	1634
1977	587.6	1890.4	29.5	31	1.6	2709

†Outstanding debt of the federal government held by the public. This excludes debt of federally sponsored credit agencies, such as the Federal Home Loan Banks.

Source: Council of Economic Advisers, *Annual Report, 1978.*

[13]Indeed, a policy of repaying the public debt rapidly would be unsound. To pay off even a small fraction of the debt, the government would have to run large surpluses, and these might plunge the economy into a deep recession.

smaller percentage of GNP than it was at the end of the Second World War. And, in spite of the much higher interest rates now, the percentage of GNP that goes to pay interest on the debt is lower now than it was after the Second World War.

It is, however, important to be explicit about what Table 9-1 shows and what it does not show. It shows that in spite of the growth of the public debt, this debt is no larger *in relative terms* than it was in the past. But the table does not demonstrate that the debt is "problem-free." The three complications noted earlier (the redistribution of income, the excess burden of taxes, and the possible inflationary effects) apply to the current debt just as they applied to the debt of the 1940s. Indeed, the inflationary consequences of a growing debt do not by their very nature show up in Table 9-1. To see why, suppose that the government increases the debt (runs budgetary deficits) and thereby causes inflation. As a result, the dollar size of GNP is drawn up by the rise in prices. Because both the public debt and GNP are rising, the ratio of the two may not change much. (Indeed, the size of the debt relative to GNP may even fall.) But, in these circumstances, a stable or falling ratio of debt to GNP can scarcely be taken as reassurance that there is no problem. In fact, the increase in the debt has created a problem, in the form of inflation.

Can the Government "Go Broke"?

If it gets more and more deeply into debt, can the federal government, like a business corporation, go bankrupt? The answer is no, but the reason why it can't "go broke" should be carefully stated.

First, consider one common, but inaccurate, argument. It is frequently stated that the government cannot go bankrupt because it has the power to tax; thus, it has the power to extract from the public whatever amounts are necessary to service the debt. But there is surely something wrong with this argument. State and local governments also have the power to tax, yet they can go broke, as the holders of New York City securities discovered in 1975. (New York was unable to pay off its maturing debt.) Government in a democracy must face elections. Even dictatorships depend on public support. So there are practical limits to the height to which taxes can be raised. The holder of a government bond does not have a guarantee of repayment merely because the government has the right to tax.

The reason the federal government cannot go bankrupt is that it has an additional power even more potent than the power to tax. Bonds are repayable in money. The government has the power to print money to pay interest or principal—either directly or, more subtly, by pressuring or coercing the central bank (the Federal Reserve) to create money and lend it to the government to avoid default. In other words, a national government does not go bankrupt because bonds are repayable in something (money) which national governments can create. But if large quantities of money are created to help service the public debt, the consequence will be a rise in prices. (Recall what happened in the prisoner-of-war camp when large quantities of cigarette "money" suddenly came on the scene.) Thus, an excessive federal government debt has quite different consequences from an excessive corporate debt: It causes excess demand and inflation, not bankruptcy. Once again, the importance of a *moderate* government debt should be stressed. When the debt is moderate, its effects on aggregate demand need not be dangerous; it need not cause large, inflationary increases in demand. Indeed, a moderate stimulative effect on aggregate demand may be beneficial in keeping demand up to the full-employment level.

Key Points

1. An increase in government spending causes an increase in equilibrium national product. An increase in taxes causes a decrease in equilibrium national product.

2. When aggregate demand is low and the rate of unemployment is high, fiscal policy should be expansionary; that is, the government should increase spending and/or cut tax rates. These steps tend to increase the government's deficit.

3. When excess aggregate demand is causing inflation, fiscal policy should be restrictive; the government should cut spending and/or increase tax rates. These steps move the government's budget toward surplus.

4. Tax collections automatically rise as national product increases, and fall as national product falls. Thus, the government budget *automatically* tends to move into deficit during a recession, and into surplus during expansions. This tendency helps to reduce the amplitude of cyclical swings in aggregate demand, and thus provides built-in stability to the economy. But it can also involve fiscal drag, a tendency for rising tax collections to impede the healthy increase of aggregate demand that is needed for the achievement and maintenance of full employment in a growing economy.

5. Because the government's budget automatically responds to changes in national product, the actual budget cannot be taken as a measure of fiscal policy actions. The appropriate measure is the full-employment budget, which indicates what the surplus or deficit would be with current tax and spending legislation, if the economy were at full employment.

6. If the government attempts to balance the (actual) budget every year, it will fall into a policy trap, and take destabilizing actions. During a downturn in economic activity, when the budget automatically tends to move into deficit, the government will cut expenditures or raise taxes in an effort to balance the budget, thereby making the downturn worse. The Hoover administration fell into this policy trap in 1932, recommending a large tax increase, which the Congress passed.

7. This trap can be avoided if the full-employment budget (rather than the actual budget) is used as a policy guide. The full-employment budget has no tendency to swing automatically into deficit during recessions, and therefore it does not suggest (erroneously) that taxes should be raised. Thus, the full-employment budget has two major functions: (1) as a measure of fiscal policy; and (2) as a guide for fiscal policy.

8. Wars must be fought with the resources available at the time. In a fundamental sense, then, the burden of a war must be borne at the time it is waged. Nevertheless, future generations may be adversely affected. Insofar as war production involves a shift of resources away from investment, future generations will inherit a smaller capital stock.

9. A large government debt involves transfers from one group (taxpayers who finance the interest payments) to another group (the bondholders who collect interest). The interest payments on a large government debt can cause three problems:

    (*a*) They may involve an undesirable redistribution of income.

    (*b*) When taxes are imposed to pay the interest, there will be a loss of economic efficiency as people look for ways to avoid taxes.

    (*c*) If the government pays interest by borrowing rather than taxing, it can add to inflationary pressures.

Key Concepts

aggregate demand management
recessionary gap
output gap
budget surplus
budget deficit
inflationary gap
lump-sum tax
proportional tax
taxes as a leakage
government spending as an injection
automatic stabilizers
discretionary policy action
fiscal drag

fiscal dividend
actual budget
full-employment budget
full-employment receipts
full-employment government expenditures
annually balanced budget
cyclically balanced budget
cost-benefit analysis
zero-base budgeting
incremental budgeting
public debt
excess burden of taxes

Problems

9-1 Using a diagram, explain the difference between the recessionary gap and the output gap. Which is larger? How are these two measures related to the multiplier?

9-2 During the Great Depression, Keynes argued that it would be better for the government to build pyramids than to do nothing. Do you agree? Why or why not? Are there any policies better than pyramid building? That is, can you think of any policies which would give all the advantages of pyramid building, plus additional advantages? Explain.

9-3 During the Great Depression, the following argument was frequently made:

A market economy tends to generate large-scale unemployment. Military spending can reduce unemployment. Therefore, capitalism requires wars and the threat of wars if it is to survive.

What part or parts of this argument are correct? Which are wrong? Explain what is wrong with the incorrect part(s). Rewrite the statement, correcting whatever is incorrect.

9-4 In 1964 and 1975, tax cuts were used to stimulate aggregate demand. What are the advantages of using tax cuts, rather than an increase in government spending? What are the disadvantages? When restraint is needed, would you favor increases in taxes, cuts in government spending, or a combination of the two? Why?

9-5 A national program of medical insurance has been proposed by some members of Congress. Opponents argue that it would be prohibitively expensive. In response to this criticism, proponents sometimes put forward the following argument:

Because of the expense of a national medical program, its introduction should be delayed until the economy approaches full employment, when the government will have enough revenue to pay for it without severely unbalancing the budget.

Do you agree that this would be the best time to introduce a national medical program? Why or why not?

9-6 Assume that full employment initially exists and that the actual budget is in balance. If the economy then slips down into a recession, the actual budget and the full-employment budget will behave differently. (For help with this question, refer back to Figures 9-8 and 9-9.)

(a) If no fiscal policy adjustments are made to combat the recession, what will happen to the actual budget? To the full-employment budget? Explain why the two are different.

(b) Suppose, as an alternative, that the government takes strong fiscal policy steps to combat the recession. What will be the difference in the behavior of the actual budget and the full-employment budget then? Explain.

9-7 Attempting to balance the budget every year can set a trap for policymakers. Explain why a balanced-budget rule leads to incorrect policies during a recession. Does such a balanced-budget rule also lead to incorrect policies during an inflationary boom? Why or why not?

chapter 10
Money and the Banking System

Money, which represents the prose of life, and which is hardly spoken of in parlors without an apology, is, in its effect and laws, as beautiful as roses.
Ralph Waldo Emerson

Fiscal policy is the first major tool in the hands of the government for managing aggregate demand. Monetary policy, which involves control over the quantity of money in our economy, is the second. When people have more money, they tend to spend more; aggregate demand rises. Similarly, if the quantity of money falls, aggregate demand also tends to fall. By managing the quantity of money, the authorities can affect aggregate demand.

But there is also another reason why money is an important topic in macroeconomics. Money not only provides an opportunity to stabilize the economy; it can also represent a source of problems. Indeed, misbehavior of the monetary system has been associated with some of the most spectacularly unstable episodes in economic his-

tory. Two examples stand out. One involved the infamous German inflation in the years following World War I. In December 1919, there were about 50 billion marks in circulation in Germany. Four years later, this figure had risen to almost 500,000,000,000 billion marks—or an increase of 10,000,000,000 times! With so much money, it became practically worthless; prices skyrocketed. Indeed, money lost its value so quickly that people were anxious to spend whatever money they had as soon as possible, while they still could buy something with it.

The second illustration involves the United States experience in the Depression of the 1930s. Economists are still debating the exact causes of that depression and their relative importance.[1] But it can scarcely be denied that the misbehavior of the monetary

---

[1]As we saw earlier in Box 8-1, those in the classical tradition argue that a fall in the quantity of money was a major cause of the collapse into the Depression. For details, see Milton Friedman and Anna Schwartz, *A Monetary History of the United States, 1867–1960* (Princeton, N.J.: Princeton University Press, 1963), Chap. 7. Keynesians tend to be more skeptical. See, for example, Peter Temin, *Did Monetary Forces Cause the Great Depression?* (New York: W. W. Norton, 1976). The disagreements between Keynesians and classicists over the importance of money will be explained in Chapter 12.

and banking system played a role. As the economy slid down into the Depression, the quantity of money fell from $26.2 billion in mid-1929 to $19.2 billion in mid-1933—or by 27 percent. By the time Roosevelt became President in 1933, many banks had closed their doors, and many people with large deposits had been wiped out.

The coming chapters will investigate the *problems* and *opportunities* which the monetary system presents. Specifically, they will explore these questions:

1. Why are there forces within the monetary system that can destabilize the economy? What has been done in the past, and what more can be done in the future, to make the monetary system more stable?

2. How can money be managed to stabilize aggregate demand and reduce fluctuations in economic activity?

The purpose of the present chapter will be to explain how the monetary system works, and to provide a beginning in answering question 1. Future chapters (especially 11, 12, and 14) will provide greater detail on the first point (the problems) and explain the second (the opportunities).

THE FUNCTIONS OF MONEY

Without money, specialized producers would have to resort to barter. Because barter is so cumbersome, a monetary system will naturally evolve, even in the absence of a government—as the development of a cigarette money in the prisoner-of-war camp so clearly illustrated (Chapter 3).

Money has three interrelated functions:

1. First, money acts as the *medium of exchange;* that is, it is used to buy goods and services.

2. When money is used as a medium of exchange, it also becomes the basis for quoting prices. For example, a new car is priced at $6,000, and a pair of shoes at $30. Thus, money acts as the *standard of value.*

3. Finally, money serves as a *store of value.* Because it can be used to buy goods or services whenever the need arises, money is a convenient way of holding wealth.

Of course, money is not a perfect store of value, because its *purchasing power* can change. As we saw in Chapter 1 (Figure 1-4), prices of goods and services have risen rapidly, and the purchasing power of money has consequently declined.

The *purchasing power* of money is measured by the amount of goods and services which money will buy. During periods of inflation, a dollar buys less and less, and the purchasing power of money falls.

Furthermore, there is another major disadvantage in holding wealth in the form of money. A person who holds money earns no interest. Thus, beyond some relatively small amount of money needed for convenience, wealth is generally held in the form of interest-bearing securities, stocks, or real property (such as land or buildings).

MONEY IN THE UNITED STATES ECONOMY

> If it waddles like a duck,
> And quacks like a duck,
> Then it *is* a duck.
> **Anonymous**

Money is what money does. To define money, we should look at whatever is *actually used in transactions.* What is used by the householder paying the electric bill? By the customer at the supermarket? By the child buying candy? By the employer paying wages?

Coins and paper currency ($1 bills, $10 bills, etc.), which together are known as *currency,* are used in many transactions. But certainly not in all. Indeed, most payments are made by check. When you write a check, it is an order to your bank to make payment out of your checking account. (Formally, economists refer to checking accounts as *demand deposits.*) Thus, three items—coins, paper currency, and demand deposits—act as the media of exchange. They constitute the most basic and important concept of money, and they go by the symbol M_1. Unless otherwise specified, this is what economists mean when they speak of "money." Of the three components, demand deposits are by far the largest, amounting to about three-quarters of the total (Table 10-1). Thus, any discussion of money focuses on the banking system and on how the quantity of demand deposits can change.

> M_1 = currency + demand deposits

One technical complication regarding the data in Table 10-1 should be explained. Coins are issued by the United States Treasury. Paper currency is issued by the Federal Reserve. (Look at a dollar bill and you will see its formal name, "Federal Reserve Note," written across the top.) Demand deposits are liabilities (debts) of the commercial banks. When the quantity of money is calculated, currency and demand deposits are counted only when they are held by *the public*; that is, by individuals and non-bank institutions. Holdings by the federal government, the Federal Reserve, and commercial banks are not included in the money stock, since these are the institutions that create money. This exclusion makes sense. For example, if the Federal Reserve has $1 billion in Federal Reserve notes printed up and stored in its vaults, it makes little sense to say that the money stock has gone up by $1 billion. That currency gains significance and becomes "money" only when it passes out of the hands of the Federal Reserve and into the hands of the public.

M_2 and Near-Money

Money is important because it is used in transactions; it makes the exchange of goods and services work much more smoothly and efficiently than a barter system. But money is also important because it can affect aggregate demand. If you or I have more money, we are likely to spend more.

Once we concentrate on the effect of money on our spending, it is not clear that M_1 is unique. The line between M_1 and other similar assets is a fine one. Although savings deposits (generally) cannot be used directly to make payments,[2] they can be switched easily into demand deposits, which in turn can be spent. The spending patterns of someone with $10,000 in a savings account may not be very different from the spending of a person with $10,000 in a demand deposit.

Thus, when economists are investigating the effects of the banking system on aggregate demand, they frequently broaden

TABLE 10-1
Components of the Money Stock
(January 1978)

Component	Billions of dollars	Percentage of total
Coins } Paper currency }	89.2	26.4
Demand deposits	248.2	73.6
Total M_1	337.4	100.0
Time and savings deposits	474.6	
Total M_2	812.0	

[2]There are some exceptions, particularly in New England where "Negotiable Orders of Withdrawal" may be written against savings accounts. In all but name, these orders are checks. Consequently, the NOW accounts are, in fact, savings accounts against which checks can be written. The existence of such accounts blurs the distinction between "money" and other similar assets.

their horizons beyond the narrowly defined M_1. Specifically, they often use a second definition of "money," expanded to include savings and time deposits and designated as M_2. (Savings deposits are held by individuals. A time deposit is similar to a savings deposit, but is generally held by a business rather than an individual.)

> $M_2 = M_1$ + savings and time deposits in commercial banks.

It is possible to go beyond M_2 to consider other highly liquid assets or "near-monies" which can also affect spending. These include deposits in savings and loan associations, short-term government securities, and short-term debt issued by nonbank businesses.

> A *liquid asset* is an asset that can be converted quickly into money (M_1) with little fuss and cost, and at a stable dollar value.

BANKING AS A BUSINESS

Because checking deposits in banks constitute a large share of the money used in everyday purchases, banks occupy a strategic position in the economy. Never was this more clear than in the Great Depression, when many banks throughout the country went bankrupt. When Franklin Roosevelt became President in March 1933, the United States banking system was in a state of collapse. Monetary disruptions added to the other woes of the economy. Early 1933, with its chaotic banking conditions, marked the depth of the Depression.

But, while banks play a strategic role in the overall operation of the economy, they also have a particular significance to a small fraction of the population: the stockholders of banks. Banks, like manufacturing corporations or retail stores, are privately owned, and one of their major objectives is to make

profits for their stockholders. Therefore, two questions are relevant in an analysis of banking operations: How do they earn profits for their stockholders, and how can they be used by the authorities to stabilize the economy as a whole?

The Goldsmith: The Embryonic Bank as a Warehouse

The quest for profits led to the development of the modern bank. How this happened can be illustrated by dipping briefly into the history of the ancestors of banks—the medieval goldsmiths.

As their name implies, goldsmiths worked and shaped the precious metal. But they also undertook another function. As gold wares were extremely valuable, customers looked to the goldsmith for safe storage of their treasures. In return for the deposit of a valuable, the goldsmith would provide the customer with a warehouse receipt—the promise to return the valuable to the customer on demand. Thus, the goldsmiths performed a service for a rich elite that was basically similar to the service that a baggage checkroom at the airport performs for you or me. They stored packages for a fee, and returned them to the owner on demand.

When unique gold ornaments were deposited, the customer naturally wanted to get back precisely the item which had been left with the goldsmith. But goldsmiths held not only unique items for their customers; golden bars and golden coins were also deposited. In these cases, it was not essential to the depositor to get back *exactly* the same gold that had been deposited. And thus the basis for the development of banks was laid.

Fractional-Reserve Banking

To see how the banking business developed, let us look at the goldsmith's business in more detail. To do so, the balance sheet is a useful device. Recall the fundamental balance sheet equation presented in Chapter 6:

Consider an early goldsmith who had 10,000 "dollars" of his own money invested in a building. This investment showed up as a building on the left-hand asset side of the goldsmith's balance sheet, and as net worth on the right-hand side (Table 10-2). Now, suppose the goldsmith accepted $100,000 in gold coins for safekeeping. As the coins were in his possession, they appeared on the asset side. But the owners of the gold had the right to withdraw them at any time upon demand. Thus, the goldsmith had *demand deposit liabilities* of $100,000; he had to be prepared to provide the depositors with this much gold when they requested it. Thus, the early goldsmith had the balance sheet shown in Table 10-2.

At this stage, a fundamental question arose regarding the goldsmith's business. If it operated simply as a warehouse, holding the $100,000 in gold coins which the customers had deposited, it would not be very profitable. It would make only the small amounts that could be charged for safeguarding gold.

After some years of experience, the goldsmith might have noticed something interesting. Although he was committed to repay the gold of the depositors on demand, he did not actually repay them all at once in the normal course of events. Each week some of the depositors made withdrawals, but others added to their balances. There was a flow of gold out of his warehouse; but there was also an inflow. While there was some fluctuation in the goldsmith's total holdings of gold, a sizable quantity remained on deposit at all times.

Sooner or later a question therefore occurred to the goldsmith. Why not lend out some of this gold? Since the depositors did not all try to withdraw their gold simultaneously, he did not need to have all the gold on hand at all times. Some could be put to work earning interest. We can therefore imagine the goldsmith beginning to experiment by making loans. Undoubtedly he started cautiously, keeping a relatively large quantity of gold in his vaults. Specifically, suppose that he kept a large reserve of $40,000 in gold to pay off depositors in the event that a group of them suddenly demanded their gold back. He lent out the remaining $60,000 in gold, with the borrowers giving him promissory notes specifying their commitment to pay interest and repay the principal after a period of time. Then his balance sheet changed to the one shown in Table 10-3. The only difference was on the asset side: The goldsmith had exchanged $60,000 of gold for $60,000 in promissory notes (shown simply as "Loans").

In making loans, the goldsmith went beyond warehousing and entered the *fractional-reserve banking* business. That is, *he held gold reserves that were only a fraction of his demand deposit liabilities*. In

TABLE 10-2
Balance Sheet of the Early Goldsmith

Assets		Liabilities and net worth	
Gold coins	$100,000	Demand deposit liabilities	$100,000
Building	$ 10,000	Net worth	$ 10,000
Total	$110,000	Total	$110,000

The early goldsmith operated a warehouse, holding $1 in gold for every $1 in deposits.

TABLE 10-3
The Goldsmith Becomes a Banker

Assets			Liabilities and net worth	
Reserve of gold coins		$40,000	Demand deposits	$100,000
Loans		$60,000	Net worth	$10,000
Building		$10,000		
	Total	$110,000	Total	$110,000

Once the goldsmith had begun to lend the deposited gold and kept gold reserves equal to only a fraction of demand deposit liabilities, the business ceased to be a simple warehouse, and became a bank.

normal times, everything worked out well. He kept enough gold to pay off all depositors who wanted to make withdrawals. And he earned interest on the loans he had made.

As time passed and goldsmiths gained confidence in the banking business, they experimented by keeping gold reserves that were lower and lower fractions of their deposit liabilities. Sometimes they had only 10 percent in reserve, or even less. They had an incentive to reduce reserves, because each additional dollar taken out of reserves and lent out meant that additional interest could be earned. But, while the entry into fractional-reserve banking allowed goldsmiths to prosper, they faced two major risks in their new banking business.

1. Their loans might go sour. That is, they might lend to businesses or individuals who were unable to repay. Clearly, then, the evaluation of credit risks (the estimation of the chances that borrowers would be unable to repay) became an important part of goldsmithing—and of modern banking.

2. Because they kept reserves equal to only a fraction of their demand deposit liabilities, the goldsmith-bankers were counting on a reasonably stable flow of deposits and withdrawals. In normal times, these flows were indeed likely to be stable. But the goldsmith-banker could not count

on times being normal. If for some reason depositors became frightened, they would appear in droves to make withdrawals; in other words, there would be a *run* on the bank.

Bank Runs and Panics

During business downturns, people were particularly likely to become frightened, and look for safety. And what could be more safe than holding gold? In crises, then, the public tended to switch into gold—that is, they withdrew their gold from their bank deposits. But the banks, operating with gold reserves equal to only a fraction of their deposits, did not have enough gold to pay off all their depositors. A panic with a run on the banks was the result. Since banks did not have enough reserves to meet all their liabilities, every individual depositor had an incentive to withdraw his or her deposit before the bank ran out of gold and was forced to close. For all depositors as a group, this was self-destructive behavior: The run could push banks into bankruptcy, with some depositors losing their money forever. But individual depositors could not be expected to stay out of the lineup of those making withdrawals and thus to commit financial suicide for the common good. Indeed, each had a personal interest in being first in line to get back his or her gold deposit.

THE MODERN UNITED STATES BANKING SYSTEM

This account obviously has been an extremely simplified version of the history of banks. But it does help to explain why the United States banking system was periodically shaken with crises around the turn of the century. These banking crises added to the instability of the economy. Following the panic of 1907, a National Monetary Commission was established to study monetary and banking problems; the Federal Reserve Act of 1913 was the result.

The Federal Reserve

The Federal Reserve[3] (also known informally as the Fed) is the central bank of the United States. (It is the American equivalent of foreign central banks, such as the Bank of England, the Deutsche Bundesbank of Germany, the Bank of Canada, and the Bank of Japan.) As the central bank, the Federal Reserve:

1. Has the responsibility to control the quantity of money in the United States.

2. Issues paper currency (dollar bills).

3. Acts as the "bankers' bank." While you and I keep our demand deposits in the commercial banks, commercial banks in turn hold deposits in the Federal Reserve. While you and I—and business corporations—can go to the commercial banks for loans, commercial banks in turn can borrow from the Federal Reserve. The Federal Reserve also helps the commercial banks to make the system of payment by check work smoothly and inexpensively.

4. Supervises and inspects the commercial banks. (The Federal Reserve shares this function with other parts of the government, including the U.S. Treasury.)

5. Acts as the federal government's bank. The Federal Reserve holds part of the government's checking accounts and administers the sale and redemption of government bonds. The Fed may also act on behalf of the government in buying and selling foreign currencies (such as British pounds or German marks).

How the Federal Reserve carries out these responsibilities will be major topics in future chapters.

The Commercial Banks

In the United States, there are approximately 14,700 commercial banks—the ordinary banks where you and I hold our checking accounts. Some of these banks are very large. The Bank of America, the largest of all, has assets in excess of $80 billion and operates branches throughout California. (A *branch* is a building other than the head office where the bank accepts deposits.) Other banks are quite small, operating in small towns. In some states, banks are forbidden by law to open branches. But even where state law prohibits branches, some banks may become very large; for example, the large Chicago banks.

About two-thirds of the commercial banks—about 10,000—are *state* banks; that is, banks operating under state charter. The rest—about 4,700—are *national* banks, having received their charters of incorporation from the federal government. While the national banks are fewer in number than state banks, they tend to be larger; consequently, about 55 percent of all bank deposits are held by national banks.

National banks by law must belong to the Federal Reserve System. As member banks, they must adhere to the regulations laid down by the Federal Reserve, and they hold deposits in the Federal Reserve. State

---

[3]Details on the complicated organization of the Federal Reserve will be explained in Chapter 11.

All commercial banks

| Number | 14,718 | (100%) |
| Deposits | $861.9 | (100%) |

National banks

| Number | 4,701 | (31.9%) |
| Deposits | $476.4 | (55.3%) |

(All are members of the
Federal Reserve)

State banks

| Number | 10,017 | (68.1%) |
| Deposits | $385.5 | (44.7%) |

**State bank members of
Federal Reserve**

| Number | 1,019 | (7.0%) |
| Deposits | $152.4 | (17.7%) |

**Nonmembers of
Federal Reserve**

| Number | 8,998 | (61.1%) |
| Deposits | $233.1 | (27.0%) |

**Member banks of
Federal Reserve System**

| Number | 5,720 | (38.9%) |
| Deposits | $628.8 | (73.0%) |

FIGURE 10-1 Classification of commercial banks. (With number of banks and total deposits in billions of dollars, on June 30, 1977.)
A minority of United States banks are members of the Federal Reserve System, but they tend to be large and most deposits are held in them. SOURCE: Federal Reserve Bulletin, March 1978, pp. A16–A17.

banks may belong to the Federal Reserve System if they wish; about 1,000 have chosen to do so. Thus, fewer than half the banks in the United States belong to the Federal Reserve System (Figure 10-1). But almost all the larger banks are members, and consequently 73 percent of total deposits are held by member banks. Hereafter, we concentrate on banks that are members of the Federal Reserve System.

Two principal functions are at the heart of commercial banking: accepting deposits, and making loans to businesses and individuals. These functions show up clearly in the combined balance sheet of commercial banks that are members of the Federal Reserve, shown in Table 10-4. At the end of September 1977, their demand deposit liabilities of $260.3 billion constituted the largest component of the money stock of the United States. But banks also accept savings and time deposits; that is, deposits against which checks cannot normally be written, and which pay interest. In terms of their dollar volume, these deposits are even larger than demand deposits. But they play a less strategic role in the economy, since they are not used directly as a means of payment.

Unlike the goldsmiths and the early banks, modern commercial banks do not hold gold as reserves; gold is no longer the basic money of the United States or of other

TABLE 10-4
Combined Balance Sheet, Commercial Banks (Members of Federal Reserve System Only), September 30, 1977
(billions of dollars)

Assets		Liabilities and net worth	
(1) Reserves		(7) Demand deposits	$260.3
Currency	$ 8.3		
Reserve deposits		(8) Time and savings	
in Federal Reserve	25.6	deposits	376.5
(2) Other bank balances and		(9) Other liabilities	118.0
cash items	86.0		
(3) Securities		(10) Total liabilities	$754.8
U.S. government	92.7		
State and local			
governments	81.4		
		(11) Net worth	$ 58.1
(4) Loans			
Real estate loans	117.0		
Commercial and			
industrial loans	151.5		
Loans to individuals	92.8		
Other loans	73.7		
(5) Other assets	83.9		
		(12) Total liabilities	
(6) Total assets	$812.9	and net worth	$812.9

countries. Instead, banks hold two kinds of reserve: deposits in the Federal Reserve, and currency. Banks are *required by law* to keep reserves equal to specified percentages of their deposits. As part of its overall control over the banking system, the Federal Reserve can set required reserves between 7 and 22 percent of demand deposits, and between 3 and 10 percent of time deposits. Note that reserves, which appear on the *asset* side of the balance sheet, must meet the required percentages of the deposits appearing on the *liabilities* side of the bank's balance sheet. (For example, with a required reserve ratio of 15 percent, a bank with $100 million in demand deposit liabilities would have to hold $15 million of its assets in the form of reserves.)

Over half of all the banks' assets are held in the form of commercial, individual, and real estate loans (item 4 in Table 10-4).

Required reserves are reserves that commercial banks are required to hold in order to meet their legal obligations. These reserves are specified as percentages of demand and savings deposits. For commercial banks that are members of the Federal Reserve System, required reserves are held in the form of currency or deposits in the Federal Reserve.

The banks also hold substantial amounts of securities issued by the federal and state governments (item 3). Moreover, commercial banks keep deposits in other commercial banks that act as "correspondents" in other cities (included in item 2); such deposits in correspondents help banks carry out financial transactions in other cities. Finally, "other assets" of banks (item 5) include bank buildings, computers, and other equipment.

Secondary Reserves Even though bankers may generally count on a reasonably steady inflow and outflow of deposits, they must still protect themselves against temporary surges of withdrawals. *The reserves that banks hold to meet the reserve requirements laid down by the Federal Reserve do not provide an adequate cushion against such withdrawals.* Suppose, for example, that the required reserve ratio is 20 percent, and that the bank holds just barely enough reserves to meet this requirement. Then assume that owners of demand deposits withdraw $100,000 in currency. With a required reserve ratio of 20 percent, required reserves fall by $20,000 as a result of the withdrawal of $100,000 of deposits. But the bank's actual reserves fall by a full $100,000 when it pays out the currency, since currency is counted as part of the reserves. Thus, with actual reserves declining by $100,000 and required reserves by only $20,000, the bank's reserves are now $80,000 short of the legal requirement.

There are three ways in which a bank can protect itself against this danger. First, it may regularly hold *excess reserves* of currency and Federal Reserve deposits. For example, if the bank initially held $80,000 in excess reserves, this sudden withdrawal would create no problem. The holding of excess reserves is, however, expensive, since neither currency nor reserve deposits in the Fed yield interest.[4] As a result, banks generally hold only small amounts of excess reserves. (Typically, excess reserves are less than 1 percent of total reserves.)

> *Excess reserves* are reserves, in the form of currency or deposits in the Federal Reserve, that are in excess of those required.
>
> Excess reserves = total reserves − required reserves

Another way for the bank to protect itself is to hold *secondary reserves*; that is, securities that can be liquidated (converted into cash) on short notice. Because of their easy marketability, federal government securities are particularly appropriate as secondary reserves, especially if they mature in the near future. By holding 90-day federal government bills in its portfolio, a bank can obtain funds quickly, either by not buying new ones as the old bills mature or by selling bills on the market.

The third protection against a shortfall in reserves is the bank's *ability to borrow.* In difficulty, a bank may replenish its reserves by borrowing from the Federal Reserve. Or it may turn to the *federal funds market;* that is, a market in which banks with excess reserves lend to banks with inadequate reserves.

BANKS AND THE CREATION OF MONEY

The public's use of demand deposits as money would be reason enough to look carefully at the operation of banks. But banks claim attention for an additional reason—and one of great economic importance. In the normal course of their operations, banks create money. Most people have heard of this power in a vague and imprecise way. Banks are consequently looked on with a mixture of awe and resentment. How did they acquire this magical ability, and why should they have such extraordinary power? These attitudes reflect a lack of understanding of banking. There is, in fact, nothing magical in the process whereby money is created. Your local bank does not have a magical fountain pen with which it can create unlimited amounts of money out of thin air.

[4]There have been proposals—none of which has been passed by Congress—that the Federal Reserve pay interest on reserve deposits, to discourage banks from leaving the Federal Reserve System, and thus to protect the Fed's ability to control monetary conditions in the United States.

The operations of banks, and how they create money, can be understood most easily by looking at the balance sheets of individual banks. An individual commercial bank, like the aggregate of commercial banks shown in Table 10-4, has a list of assets and liabilities. To avoid being burdened with detail, we simplify the following tables by showing only the *changes* in the balance sheet of a bank. (Like the whole balance sheet, changes in the balance sheet must balance.) And to avoid untidy fractions, we assume that the required reserves of banks are a nice round figure—20 percent of their demand deposit liabilities. To simplify further, we assume that banks initially have no excess reserves.

Now, suppose that you find $10,000 left in a shoe box by your eccentric old uncle when he died. In a state of bliss, you rush to your local bank to put the $10,000 into your demand deposit account. As a result, your bank—call it bank A—has $10,000 more of currency on the asset side of its balance sheet (Table 10-5). And it also has $10,000 more in liabilities: you have a $10,000 claim on the bank in the form of a demand deposit. (This $10,000 deposit represents an *asset* to you; it is something you own. But this same $10,000 deposit is a *liability* to the bank; the bank must be prepared to pay you $10,000 in currency on demand.)

As a result of this deposit, what happens to the quantity of money in the United States? The answer: nothing. You initially held the $10,000 in currency; you exchanged it for $10,000 in demand deposit money. Once the deposit is made, the $10,000 in dollar bills ceases to be counted as part of the money stock, since it is held by the bank. (Remember the technical point regarding Table 10-1: Currency and demand deposits are included in the money stock only when they are held by the public, but not when

TABLE 10-5
Changes in Assets and Liabilities when Commercial Bank A Receives Your Deposit

Commercial bank A

Assets		Liabilities	
Reserves of currency	+$10,000	Demand deposits	+$10,000
Required $2,000 Excess $8,000			
Total	$10,000	Total	$10,000

Your balance sheet

Assets		Liabilities	
Currency	−$10,000	No change	
Demand deposit	+$10,000		
Total	0	Total	0

When commercial bank A receives your $10,000 deposit, its assets and liabilities both rise by $10,000. But your holdings of money do not change. You have merely switched from one type of money (currency) to another (a demand deposit).

they are held by the commercial banks, the Federal Reserve, or the United States Treasury.) The *composition* of the money stock has changed—there is now $10,000 more in demand deposits and $10,000 less in currency in the hands of the public. However, the total amount has not changed.

But this is not the end of the story, because the bank now has excess reserves. Its demand deposit liabilities have gone up by your $10,000 deposit; therefore, its *required* reserves have risen by $2,000 (that is, $10,000 × 20 percent). But its total reserves have risen by the $10,000 in currency that you deposited. Therefore, it now has $8,000 in excess reserves. Like the goldsmith of old, it is in a position to make loans to businesses and other customers.

Suppose that a local shoe store wants to increase its inventory of shoes, and approaches the bank for a loan of $8,000, an amount that just happens to equal the excess reserves of the bank. The bank agrees. Mechanically, what happens? The bank could, presumably, hand over $8,000 in dollar bills to the store owner (in exchange for the promissory note that commits the store to repay the loan). But the bank does not normally operate this way. Rather, when it makes the loan, it simply adds $8,000 to the demand deposit of the borrower. This is entirely satisfactory to the borrower, who can write a check against the deposit. As a result of this loan, the balance sheet of the commercial bank is modified, as shown in Table 10-6.

Now, what has happened to the money supply? Observe that *when the bank makes a loan, the stock of money in the hands of the public increases.* Specifically, there now is $8,000 more in demand deposit money. But what has the bank done? Nothing extraordinary. It has merely loaned out its excess reserves. (That is, it has loaned out *less* than was placed in its safekeeping when you made your original deposit.)

How a Check Is Cleared

So far, so good. But our story has just nicely begun. The shoe store borrowed from the bank in order to buy inventory, not to leave its money sitting idly in a checking account. Suppose that the shoe store (located in your home town) orders shoes from a Boston manufacturer, sending a check for $8,000 in payment. The shoe company in Boston deposits the check in its bank (bank B). This sets in motion the process of *check clearing*—which straightens out accounts between bank A in your home town and bank B in Boston (Figure 10-2). Bank B sends the check along to the Federal Reserve, receiving in exchange a reserve deposit of $8,000. Bank B's accounts balance, since its assets in the form of reserves have gone up by the same amount ($8,000) as its demand deposit liabilities to the shoe manufacturer. (The $8,000 reserve deposit represents an *asset* to bank B and a *liability* to the Federal Reserve.)

The Fed, in turn, sends the check along to bank A, subtracting the $8,000 from bank

TABLE 10-6
Bank A Makes a Loan

Assets			Liabilities		
Reserves of currency		$10,000	Demand deposits		
			of you		$10,000
Loan†		+$8,000	of shoe store†		+$8,000
	Total	$18,000		Total	$18,000

When the bank lends $8,000, demand deposits increase by $8,000. This represents a net increase in the money stock.

†Items resulting from the loan.

FIGURE 10-2 The clearing of a check.
In the check-clearing process, the bank in which the check was deposited (bank *B*)
acquires reserves, while the bank on which the check was drawn (bank *A*) loses reserves.

A's reserve deposit. Bank A balances its accounts by subtracting the $8,000 from the deposit of the shoe store which wrote the check in the first place.

Why a Bank Can Safely Lend No More than Its Excess Reserves

When the effects of the check clearing (in Figure 10-2) are added to bank A's earlier transactions (shown in Table 10-6), the net effects on bank A's balance sheet may be summarized in Table 10-7. Observe that, as a result of the check clearing, bank A's excess reserves have completely disappeared. (Its currency reserves rose by $10, 000 when you deposited the original $10, 000. Its reserve deposit in the Fed fell by $8,000 when the shoe store's check cleared. Thus, its net change in reserves is $2,000, just the amount required as a result of its $10,000 demand deposit liability to you.) This was the result of bank A's lending the shoe store an amount equal to its excess reserves. Thus, we come to a fundamental proposition:

A bank may prudently lend an amount *up to, but no greater than*, its excess reserves.

TABLE 10-7
Net Effects on Bank A
(Check clearing Combined with Earlier Transactions)

Assets		Liabilities	
Reserves	$ 2,000	Demand deposits of you	$10,000
Required $2,000			
Excess 0			
Loan	$8,000		
Total	$10,000	Total	$10,000

This table gives the combined effect on bank A of check clearing (Figure 10-2) and earlier transactions (Table 10-6). After the check is cleared, bank A has no excess reserves

The Multiple Expansion of Bank Deposits

We have seen how bank A's excess reserves are eliminated when the shoe store's $8,000 check clears. But observe (in Figure 10-2) that bank B now has excess reserves of $6,400; that is, the difference between the $8,000 increase in its actual reserves and the $1,600 increase in its required reserves. ($1,600 = 20 percent of the $8,000 increase in its demand deposit liabilities.)

Bank B may prudently lend up to the $6,400 of its excess reserves. In Table 10-8, we suppose that it lends this amount to the local camera store. When the loan is made, $6,400 is added to the demand deposit of the camera store. Because the amount of demand deposits held by the public goes up by $6,400, the *money stock increases by this amount.*

Assume that the camera store has borrowed the $6,400 to buy additional film. To pay for its purchases, it writes a check to Kodak. Kodak deposits the check in its Rochester, New York, bank—bank C. Once again, the check-clearing mechanism is set in operation. When bank C sends the check to the Federal Reserve, it receives a reserve deposit of $6,400 (Table 10-9). But when the check is sent along to bank B (the camera store's bank), that bank loses $6,400 in reserves, and no longer has any excess reserves.

Observe, however, that bank C now has excess reserves of $5,120, which it can lend out. When it does so, it will create a new demand deposit of $5,120, thus increasing the money stock once again. And so the process continues: As a result of your initial deposit of $10,000, there can be a chain

TABLE 10-8
Bank B Lends to Camera Store

Assets		Liabilities	
Reserve deposit	$8,000	Demand deposits	
		of shoe manufacturer	$8,000
Loan†	+$6,400	of camera store†	+$6,400
Total	$14,400	Total	$14,400

As a result of the second round of lending, the money stock increases by $6,400.

†Items resulting from the loan.

TABLE 10-9
The Creation of Money: After the Second Round

Bank B

Assets		Liabilities	
Reserves	$1,600	Demand deposits	
Required $1,600		of shoe manufacturer	$8,000
Excess 0			
Loans	$6,400		
Total	$8,000	Total	$8,000

Bank C

Assets		Liabilities	
Reserves	$6,400	Demand deposits	
Required $1,280		of Kodak	$6,400
Excess $5,120			
Total	$6,400	Total	$6,400

When bank C receives deposits and reserves of $6,400, it can prudently lend $5,120. And so the process continues.

reaction of loans, as shown in Figure 10-3 and Table 10-10. At each stage, the amount of loans that can be made (and the amount of deposits that can thereby be created) is 80 percent of the amount made in the previous stage. The total increase in deposits is the sum of the series: $10,000 + $10,000 × 0.8 + $10,000 × 0.8² . . . . If this series is taken to its limit—with an infinite number of rounds—then, by a basic algebraic proposition,[5] the sum is equal to $10,000/(1 − 0.8) = $50,000.

Thus, when the banking system acquires additional reserves, it can increase demand deposits by a multiple of the initial reserve increase. The demand deposit multiplier D is equal to the reciprocal of the required reserve ratio R:

$$D = \frac{1}{R}$$

For example, in our illustration, the required reserve ratio was 20 percent; thus, the initial acquisition of $10,000 in reserves made possible an increase in demand deposits of $50,000 (that is, $10,000 × 1/0.2). Alternatively, if the required reserve ratio were only 10 percent, the banking system would have been capable of creating up to $100,000 in demand deposits on the basis of $10,000 in reserves. Thus, when the Federal Reserve changes the required reserve ratio, as it is permitted to do within specified legal limits, it can have a powerful effect on the amount of loans which the banks can make, and on the amount of demand deposits which they can create. A few pages earlier, we emphasized that required reserves provide a bank with little cushion in the event of a withdrawal of deposits. That is not their primary purpose. Rather, the requirement that banks

[5]Mathematically, this is the same theorem used in the derivation of the multiplier in Chapter 8 (footnote 7). But the economic issues are quite different in the two cases. In the multiplier, the total effects of various rounds of *spending* are derived; here, changes in the *stock of money* are calculated.

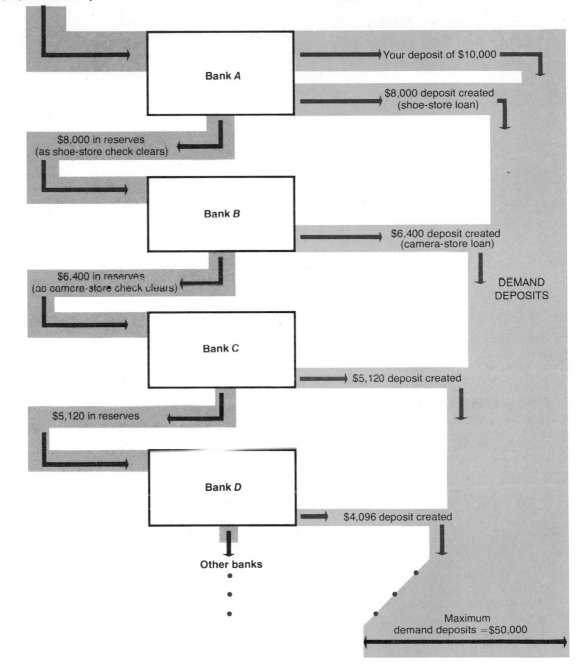

FIGURE 10-3 The multiple expansion of bank deposits. The banking system as a whole can do what no single bank can do. It can transform your original $10,000 in currency into as much as $50,000 in demand deposit money.

TABLE 10-10
The Multiple Expansion of Bank Deposits
A. The Chain Reaction

Bank	(1) Acquired reserves and demand deposits	(2) Required reserves (2) = (1) × 0.20	(3) Excess reserves = loans which banks can make (3) = (1) − (2)	(4) Changes in money stock (4) = (3)
A	$10,000 (yours)	$2,000	$8,000	$8,000
B	$8,000 (shoe manufacturer's)	$1,600	$6,400	$6,400
C	$6,400 (Kodak's)	$1,280	$5,120	$5,120
D	$5,120	$1,024	$4,096	$4,096
.	.	.	.	.
.	.	.	.	.
.	.	.	.	.
Maximum sum	$50,000	$10,000	$40,000	$40,000

B. Effects on Consolidated Balance Sheet of All Commercial Banks
(with maximum permissible expansion)

Assets		Liabilities	
Reserves	$10,000	Demand deposits	$50,000
Required $10,000			
Excess 0			
Loans	$40,000		
Total	$50,000	Total	$50,000

The commercial banking system as a whole can create a series of deposits on the basis of an initial $10,000 in reserves.

hold reserves is a way of *controlling the amount of loans they can make and the amount of money they can create.*

During the multiple expansion of deposits, the banking system as a whole does something which no single bank can do. *The banking system as a whole can create deposits equal to a multiple of the reserves which it acquires. But any single bank can create deposits* (by lending its excess reserves) *by an amount equal to only a fraction (80 per-cent) of the reserves which it acquires.*

Two Complications
With a required reserve ratio of 20 percent, $50,000 is the *maximum* increase in demand deposits following a $10,000 acqui-

sition of reserves by the banking system. In practice, the actual increase in demand deposits is likely to be considerably less, because of two complications:

1. Banks may decide not to lend out the maximum permitted, but to hold some excess reserves instead. During prosperous times, this is not an important complication. Because of the strong incentive of banks to make loans and thus increase their interest earnings, they hold only small amounts of excess reserves.

But, during a depression, bankers may become panicky. They may be afraid to make loans because they doubt the ability of borrowers to repay. They may decide to keep their funds secure by holding them as excess reserves. Thus, during the Great Depression, excess reserves skyrocketed, reaching about 50 percent of total reserves by 1940. This unwillingness of the banks to lend tended to keep down the amount of money in the hands of the public, and slowed the recovery.

2. As loans are made and people get more demand deposit money, they may want to hold more currency, too. In other words, they may withdraw cash from their deposits. Insofar as this happens, the reserves of the banks are reduced; the initial deposit of currency that started off the expansion is partially reversed. As a consequence, the total amount of monetary expansion is reduced.

When currency is held by the public, it is, in a sense, just ordinary money: The dollar I hold in my pocket is only a dollar. On the other hand, when currency is deposited in a bank, it becomes "high-powered." Although the dollar ceases to count directly in the money stock (since bank holdings of currency are excluded from the definition of money), that dollar bill is a bank *reserve*. On this reserve base, the commercial banking system can build a superstructure of as much as $5 of demand deposit money (if the required reserve ratio is 20 percent). The large amount of demand deposit money, built on a much smaller base of reserves, forms an inverted pyramid (Figure 10-4).

THE EFFECT OF COMMERCIAL BANK PURCHASES OF SECURITIES ON THE MONEY SUPPLY

Thus far, we have assumed that a commercial bank with excess reserves will lend out all these excess reserves to its customers in

FIGURE 10-4 The inverted monetary pyramid. On their reserve base of currency and reserve deposits, the commercial banking system can build a superstructure of demand deposits—of as much as $1/R$ times the base.

order to earn interest. But alternatively, banks can use these funds to increase their earning assets by purchasing securities, such as bonds issued by federal, state, and local governments or by private corporations. Such purchases of securities will also increase the money stock.[6]

To illustrate, suppose that, in the nth round in the monetary expansion chain, a bank acquires $1,250 in demand deposits and reserves. If the required reserve ratio is 20 percent, it will have $1,000 in excess reserves. Suppose that it uses these reserves to purchase a $1,000 government bond owned by the XYZ Corporation. Bank N pays for the bond by writing a check, which the XYZ Corporation deposits in bank O. Then the money stock as a consequence rises by $1,000; that is, by the $1,000 demand deposit which the XYZ Corporation

---

[6]This statement is generally true, but there are some possible exceptions. For example, if a bank buys a bond directly from the federal government, the money stock is not increased. The federal government gets a demand deposit in exchange for the bond. But demand deposits held by the federal government are not included in the money stock. (Recall the technical complication explained in the earlier section "Money in the United States Economy.")

now owns. The change in the money stock is thus exactly the same as it would have been if bank N had used these excess reserves to make a loan rather than to buy a bond. Moreover, as a result of this transaction, bank N loses its $1,000 of excess reserves, while bank O gains $1,000 of reserves. It is now bank O that finds itself with excess reserves ($800, to be precise). When it uses these reserves to make a loan or buy securities, the process of money creation continues.

Key Points

1. Money is important in the study of macroeconomics because:

(*a*) The authorities can take steps to alter the quantity of money, and thus affect aggregate demand. *Monetary policy* is the second great tool, along with fiscal policy, that can be used to manage aggregate demand. The details of monetary policy will be explained in Chapter 11.

(*b*) The monetary system has sometimes misbehaved; for example, during the panic of 1907 and the Depression of 1933. When the monetary system misbehaves, it can make the economy more unstable.

2. Money has three interrelated functions:

(*a*) As the medium of exchange
(*b*) As the standard of value
(*c*) As a store of value

3. Most economists define money as currency plus demand deposits (M_1). Demand deposits constitute about three-quarters of the total.

4. Savings and time deposits are close substitutes for M_1; a savings deposit can be easily switched into a demand deposit or currency, and then used to purchase goods or services. Because savings and time deposits can have an important effect on spending, some economists include them in a second definition of money (M_2). $M_2 = M_1 +$ savings and time deposits in commercial banks.

5. The Federal Reserve is the central bank of the United States. As such,

(*a*) It has the responsibility to control the quantity of money.
(*b*) It issues paper currency.
(*c*) It acts as the "bankers' bank."
(*d*) It supervises and inspects commercial banks.
(*e*) It acts as the federal government's bank.

6. Commercial banks have two principal functions: to accept deposits and to make loans. When a commercial bank makes a loan, it increases the money supply.

7. Commercial banks that are members of the Federal Reserve System are required to hold reserves in the form of currency or reserve deposits in the Federal Reserve. These reserves must meet required percentages of the commercial bank's demand and time deposit liabilities. The purpose of required reserves is to control the quantity of money that commercial banks can create.

8. When a *single* bank acquires additional deposits and reserves, it can safely lend out only a *fraction* of these reserves (that is, its *excess* reserves). But the commercial banking *system* (all commercial banks as a whole) can create deposits that are a *multiple* of any new reserves that it acquires.

9. The maximum increase in demand deposits that can be created by the banking system is:

$$\frac{1}{R} \times \text{the acquisition of reserves}$$

where R is the required reserve ratio

10. In practice, the increase is likely to be less than the maximum, since:

(a) Banks sometimes hold substantial excess reserves, especially during a depression. Bank unwillingness to lend excess reserves can keep down the quantity of money and slow down the recovery from a depression.

(b) As people get more demand deposit money, they are likely to want to hold more currency, too. When they withdraw currency from their deposits, the reserves held by the banks are reduced.

Key Concepts

monetary policy
medium of exchange
standard of value
store of value
purchasing power
currency
coin
Federal Reserve note
demand deposit
  (checking deposit)
savings and time deposits
M_1
M_2

near-money
liquid asset
fractional-reserve banking
balance sheet
demand deposit liability
promissory note
loan
bank run
Federal Reserve
central bank
commercial bank
national bank
state bank

member bank
required reserve ratio
required reserves
excess reserves
secondary reserves
federal funds market
check clearing
multiple expansion of bank deposits
demand deposit multiplier
"high-powered" reserves
monetary pyramid

Problems

10-1 (a) Suppose that a corporation that previously paid its workers in cash decides to pay them by check instead. As a result, it decides to deposit $100,000 which it has held in currency in its safe. Show how this deposit will affect the balance sheets of (1) the corporation, and (2) its bank (the First National Bank of Buffalo).

(b) Does this deposit of $100,000 affect the money stock? Why or why not?

(c) How much can the First National Bank of Buffalo now lend, if there is a required reserve ratio of 10 percent? If it lends this amount to a farmer to buy machinery, show the direct effect of the loan on the bank's balance sheet. Then show the First National Bank of Buffalo's balance sheet after the farmer spends the loan to buy machinery and the farmer's check is cleared.

(d) As a result of the original deposit (in part (a) of this problem), what is the maximum increase in demand deposits which can occur if the required reserve ratio is 10 percent? The maximum amount of bank lending? The maximum increase in the money stock?

10-2 Suppose that a bank receives a deposit of $10,000 and decides to lend the full $10,000. Explain how this decision can get the bank into difficulty.

10-3 If all banks are required to keep reserves equal to 100 percent of their demand deposits, what will be the consequences of a deposit of $100,000 of currency in bank A?

10-4 During the 1930s, banks held large excess reserves. Now they hold practically none. Why? If you were a banker, would you hold excess reserves? How much? Does your answer depend on the size of individual deposits in your bank? On interest rates? On other things?

10-5 Suppose that there is a single huge bank that holds a monopoly on all commercial banking in the United States. If this bank receives $100,000 in deposits, and if the required reserve ratio is 20 percent, how much can the bank safely lend? Explain (*Hint*: Study Table 10-10, Part B.)

chapter 11
The Federal Reserve and the Tools of Monetary Policy

> There have been three great inventions since the beginning of time: fire, the wheel, and central banking.
> **Will Rogers**

The Federal Reserve is the central bank of the United States, acting as the federal government's bank and the bankers' bank. As the central bank, it has one responsibility of prime importance. It *controls the quantity of commercial bank reserves*, and thereby controls the amount of demand deposit money that these banks can create. Its responsibility is to see that monetary conditions are consistent with the achievement of the goals of high employment and stable prices. If business is getting worse and the economy sliding into a recession, the job of the Federal Reserve is to expand the money stock, and thus support aggregate demand. And when business is booming and inflation threatens, the job of the Federal Reserve is to exercise restraint, to prevent an excessive monetary growth from fueling the fires of inflation. In this chapter, we examine the three principal policy tools in the hands of the Federal Reserve:

1. Open market operations; that is, purchases or sales of government bonds or shorter-term securities by the Federal Reserve

2. Changes in the discount rate; that is, the interest rate at which the Federal Reserve lends to commercial banks

3. Changes in required reserve ratios that the member commercial banks must hold as percentages of their demand and time deposits

Before explaining these tools in detail, let us look briefly at the organization of the Federal Reserve.

THE ORGANIZATION OF THE FEDERAL RESERVE

When the Federal Reserve Act was passed in 1913, the very concept of a central bank was controversial, in spite of the financial distur-

215

bances of previous years (including the panic of 1907). Those who opposed the creation of a central bank feared that it would involve a concentration of monetary power, with adverse political consequences. (This fear was not new. The Second Bank of the United States, which had acted as a rudimentary central bank in the early nineteenth century, had come to an abrupt end at the hands of Andrew Jackson, who attacked its political power. "The bank," said Jackson, "is trying to kill me, *but I will kill it.*"[1] And so he did.) The political controversies and compromises that surrounded the establishment of the Federal Reserve show up in its untidy organizational structure.

In order to diffuse power, the Federal Reserve was organized with 12 regional Federal Reserve Banks, in Boston, New York, Philadelphia, and other major cities (Figure 11-1). These 12 district banks handle most of the everyday operations of the Fed, including the clearing of checks and the issue of new currency. (If you look to the left of the President's picture on a dollar bill, you will find a seal which identifies the Federal Reserve Bank that issued it.) In Washington, overall coordination is provided by the seven-member Board of Governors of the Federal Reserve System (also known, more simply, as the Federal Reserve Board). During the history of the Fed, there have been numerous power struggles between the Board and the district banks. For example, the relative power of the Federal Reserve Bank of New York and the Federal Reserve Board was a matter of dispute between the two world wars. (During the 1920s, the

---

[1]Arthur M. Schlesinger, Jr., *The Age of Jackson*, abr. ed. (New York: Mentor, 1949), p. 42.

FIGURE 11-1 The Federal Reserve System. The United States is divided into twelve Federal Reserve districts, each with a Federal Reserve bank. (Alaska and Hawaii are part of the district served by the Federal Reserve Bank of San Francisco.)

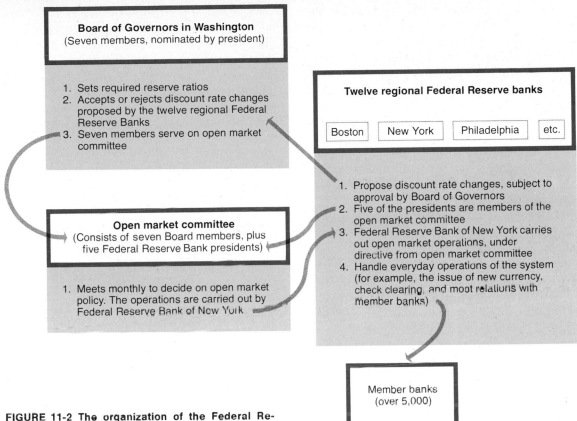

FIGURE 11-2 The organization of the Federal Reserve System.

Board was overshadowed by the forceful president of the Federal Reserve Bank of New York, Benjamin Strong. More recently, the Fed has been dominated by the chairmen of the Federal Reserve Board—most notably, William McChesney Martin who headed the Board from 1951 to 1970, and his successor, Arthur F. Burns, who was chairman until 1978.)

After many revisions in the Federal Reserve Act, the major current powers of the Board and the 12 regional Federal Reserve Banks are those listed in Figure 11-2.[2] Each of the principal tools of the Federal Reserve is treated differently:

1. *Changes in required reserve ratios of the commercial banks.* Power to change required reserve ratios is held by the Federal Reserve Board in Washington.

2. *Changes in the discount rate.* Proposals for change are made by the regional Federal Reserve Banks, but they must be approved by the Federal Reserve Board.

3. *Open market operations.* This tool, the most important of all, is controlled by the Federal Open Market Committee (FOMC), which consists of the seven members of the Board of Governors and five of the presidents of the 12 district Federal Reserve Banks. (The president of the New

[2]For more detail on the organization and operations of the Federal Reserve, see Board of Governors of the Federal Reserve System, *The Federal Reserve System: Purposes and Functions*, 6th ed. (Washington, D.C., 1974).

York Fed is a permanent member of the FOMC, with the other regional presidents serving on a rotating basis.) Meeting monthly in Washington, the FOMC issues directives to the trading desk in the New York Fed, which handles the actual purchases or sales of securities.

Although stock of the 12 Federal Reserve Banks is owned by the commercial banks that belong to the Federal Reserve System, the Federal Reserve is in every fundamental sense a public agency. Only three of the nine directors of each regional bank may be commercial bankers, while the other six are drawn from nonbank business and the general public. Furthermore, while the member commercial banks receive small, fixed dividends on their stock in their regional Federal Reserve Bank, by far the largest part of Federal Reserve profits is paid over to the United States Treasury. These profits, incidentally, are large. While the stabilization of the economy—and not profits—is the objective of the Federal Reserve, central banking is nevertheless an exceptionally profitable business.

The chairman of the Federal Reserve Board is appointed by the President of the United States, subject to congressional approval, as are the other six members of the board. In order to provide the Board with a degree of independence from partisan politics and thus to strengthen its ability to fight inflation and protect the value of the dollar, members of the Board are appointed for extended 14-year terms, with one position becoming vacant every 2 years. (The chairman serves for a 4-year term, beginning 1 year after the President's term begins.) Appointed by the President, but exercising monetary authority delegated by Congress, the Federal Reserve Board has had shifting relationships with the executive branch of government and Congress. During the Sec-

ond World War and its aftermath, the Federal Reserve cooperated closely with the U.S. Treasury in order to help finance the war. More recently, during the mid-1970s, the Federal Reserve has yielded to congressional pressure to state explicitly its objectives for growth of the money stock for the coming year, and to try to stick to these objectives.[3] (This pressure grew out of dissatisfaction with Federal Reserve policy in the early 1970s. In particular, critics charged that the rapid rate of growth of the money stock in 1972 and 1973 contributed to the inflationary boom. Then, when the Federal Reserve cracked down and sharply reduced the rate of growth of the money stock in 1974, the worst recession in almost four decades occurred.)

OPEN MARKET OPERATIONS

The Federal Reserve can increase the quantity of commercial bank reserves—and thereby increase the quantity of demand deposit money which the commercial banks can create—by purchasing U.S. government securities on the open market. That is, it puts in a bid on the securities market; the seller may be any commercial bank or any member of the general public who holds government securities and is willing to sell. Who the actual seller will be, the Fed does not know. But, whether the government security is sold by a commercial bank or by the public, the results are similar.

Suppose the Fed puts in a bid for a $100,000 Treasury bill (a short-term form of government debt, usually issued with a maturity of 90 days) and that General Motors is the seller. General Motors hands over the Treasury bill and gets a check for $100,000 in return. It deposits this check in its commercial bank (bank A). In turn, bank A sends the check along to the Federal Reserve, and has its deposit with the Fed increased by

[3]See Edward J. Kane, "New Congressional Restraints and Federal Reserve Independence," *Challenge*, November 1975, pp. 37–44.

TABLE 11-1
An Open Market Purchase: Initial Effects
(thousands of dollars)

Federal Reserve

Assets		Liabilities	
Government securities	+ 100	Reserve deposits of bank A	+ 100
Total	100	Total	100

Commercial bank A

Assets		Liabilities	
Reserve deposit	+ 100	Demand deposits of GM	+ 100
Required 20			
Excess 80			
Total	100	Total	100

The open market purchase increases bank A's reserves by $100,000. At this stage, the money supply has also increased by $100,000, because GM has a demand deposit of that amount.

Commercial bank A has excess reserves, and therefore a further expansion of the money supply can take place.

this amount. In other words, bank A's reserves increase by $100,000. The changes in the balance sheets of the Fed and commercial bank A are shown in Table 11-1.

At this initial step, the money supply has gone up by $100,000; GM's demand deposit is counted as part of the money supply. And the stage is set for a further expansion because of the new reserves held by bank A. Specifically, bank A now has $80,000 in excess reserves that can be loaned out. And a whole series of loans, similar to those already described in Chapter 10, can take place. Thus, with a 20 percent required reserve ratio, the $100,000 open market purchase makes possible a maximum increase of $500,000 in demand deposits—that is, an increase of $500,000 in the money stock. (Again, as explained in Chapter 10, this is a maximum. In practice, the actual increase will be less, insofar as the public decides to hold more currency along with its higher demand deposits, and insofar as commercial banks hold excess reserves.)

This, then, is the power of Federal Reserve open market operations. The Fed carries out the simple transaction of buying a government bond or Treasury bill, and the reserves of the commercial banking system increase as a result. Thus, the Fed makes possible a multiple increase in the nation's money supply.

Now suppose that the Fed buys the $100,000 Treasury bill from a commercial bank rather than from General Motors. The result is the same: The maximum increase in the money supply is once again $500,000, although the mechanics are slightly different. Table 11-2 shows the initial effects of an open market operation if the Fed buys the Treasury bill from the Chase Manhattan Bank. Chase sends the Treasury bill to the Fed and gets a reserve deposit in the Fed in exchange. At this initial stage, no change has yet taken place in the money stock. But note that Chase now has a full $100,000 in excess reserves, since its total reserves have gone up by $100,000 while its deposit liabilities, and therefore its required reserves, have not changed. Chase can safely lend out the full

TABLE 11-2

An Open Market Purchase: When a Commercial Bank Is the Seller

(Initial effects, in thousands of dollars)

Federal Reserve

Assets		Liabilities	
Government securities	+ 100	Reserve deposits of Chase Manhattan	+ 100
Total	100	Total	100

Chase Manhattan Bank

Assets		Liabilities	
Government securities	− 100	No change	
Reserve deposit	+ 100		
Required 0			
Excess 100			
Total	0	Total	0

If the Fed buys the government security from a commercial bank (say, Chase Manhattan), no change takes place in the money stock at this initial stage. However, Chase Manhattan now has a full $100,000 in excess reserves, which it can lend out.

$100,000 in excess reserves, creating a $100,000 demand deposit when it does so. Once again, the maximum demand deposit expansion is the series $100,000 + $80,000 + $64,000 + . . . , giving a total of $500,000.

In both examples of an open market purchase (Tables 11-1 and 11-2), note that when the Federal Reserve acquires an *asset* (the government security), its *liabilities* also go up. This is scarcely surprising, since the balance sheet must balance. The increase in Federal Reserve liabilities takes the form of reserve deposits, which act as the reserves of the commercial banks. Thus, we have a fundamental rule:

> When the Fed wants to increase the reserves of commercial banks and thus make possible an expansion of the money supply, it acquires assets.

(From the viewpoint of increasing com-

mercial bank reserves, it really doesn't matter *what* sort of asset the Fed acquires; any kind will do. You may illustrate this point by working out the balance sheet effects if the Fed buys a $1-million computer from IBM. But, of course, the Fed is a governmental body and must follow strict standards; it can't buy "any old asset." We could scarcely tolerate a Fed which accumulated the shaky personal I.O.U.s of politicians. Thus, outside of its purchases of computers and other necessary supplies, the Fed confines its purchases to the securities of the federal government.)

Restrictive Open Market Operations

Just as the Fed purchases securities when it wants to increase the money supply, so it sells securities when it wants to decrease the money supply. The numbers on the balance sheets are the same as in Tables 11-1 and 11-2, but the signs are the opposite.

But an actual open market sale might

lead to very tight monetary conditions. We live in a growing economy, in which productive capacity increases. It is appropriate that the money stock grow through time, in order to encourage aggregate demand to grow and keep the economy at full employment. Thus, restrictive policies by the Federal Reserve normally do not involve actual sales of securities. Rather, a *reduction in the rate of security acquisition*, aimed at reducing the rate of growth of the money stock, generally provides monetary conditions that are as tight as the Fed wishes in its fight against inflation.

OPEN MARKET OPERATIONS AND INTEREST RATES

When the Federal Reserve goes on the market to buy government bonds or shorter-term securities, it increases the demand for these securities. As a result, it puts upward pressure on their prices.

There is an important relationship between security prices and interest rates, which may be clarified by looking at government bills more closely. Unlike a government bond, which provides semiannual interest payments, a government bill involves no such explicit interest payment. It simply represents a promise by the government to pay, say, $100,000 on a specific date, usually 3 months after the date of issue. The purchaser obtains a yield by purchasing the bill at a *discount*; that is, for less than the full $100,000 face value. For example, a buyer who pays $99,000 for a 3-month bill gets back $1,000 more than the purchase price when the bill reaches maturity. Thus, the interest or yield on that bill is approximately 1 percent for the 3-month period—that is, 4 percent per annum. (By convention, interest is quoted at an annual rate, even for securities with less than 1 year to maturity.)

Now, suppose that the Fed enters the market, bidding for bills and pushing up their price to $99,500. At this price, how much can a bill purchaser make? Only $500, or about one-half of 1 percent for the 3 months; that is, 2 percent per annum. Thus, we see that:

> Security prices and interest rates *move in opposite directions*. A "rise in the price of Treasury bills" is another way of saying "a fall in the interest rate on Treasury bills." Similarly, a fall in the price of securities involves a rise in the interest rate.

Thus, when the Federal Reserve purchases government securities on the open market and bids up their prices, it is thereby bidding down interest rates. This is a general proposition that holds for long-term bonds as well as for short-term bills. (See Box 11-1.)

Secondary Effects

The secondary effects of the open market purchase also work toward a reduction of interest rates. As commercial bank reserves rise, the banks will purchase securities and step up their lending activities. The purchase of securities once again tends to push up security prices and push down interest rates. And, in their eagerness to make additional loans, banks may reduce the interest rate they charge. Specifically, they may shave their *prime rate*.

> The *prime rate* is the interest rate charged by banks on their least risky loans.

An open market purchase by the Fed has three important, interrelated effects: (1) it increases the money stock; (2) it makes more funds available for the commercial banks to lend; and (3) it lowers interest rates. The way in which these three forces can stimulate aggregate demand will be considered in detail in Chapter 12.

BOX 11-1
BOND PRICES AND INTEREST RATES

The relationship between bond prices and interest rates can be seen most easily by considering a *perpetuity*; that is a bond that has no maturity date and is never paid off. It represents a commitment by the government of the issuing nation to pay, say, $80 per year forever. [The United States Government does not issue such bonds, but examples may be cited—the famous British "consols" (the common abbreviation for their formal name, Consolidated Fund Annuities), and the not-so-famous "perps" issued by the Canadian Government.] Just as the semiannual interest or *coupon* payments on an ordinary bond remain fixed regardless of what happens to market interest rates after the bond has been issued, so the commitment of the government to pay $80 per year forever to the holder of the perpetuity remains in force, regardless of what happens to interest rates in the financial markets.

Like other bonds, perpetuities may be sold by their initial owners. A buyer willing to pay $1,000 for such a perpetuity would obtain an interest rate or yield of 8 percent; that is, $80 per year on the purchase price of $1,000. But if the price fell, and the buyer could get the perpetuity for $800, the annual $80 payment would provide a yield of 10 percent. Again, we see that a fall in the price of a security means a rise in the interest rate or yield that the security offers.

A bond with a specific maturity of, say, 10 years involves a much more complex calculation. As a background, note that if $100 is deposited in an account paying 10 percent per annum, the deposit will be worth $110 at the end of the first year. During the second year, 10 percent interest will be paid on this $110. That is, $11 interest will be added, raising the deposit to a total of $121 by the end of the second year. In general, after n years at an interest of i, a $100 deposit will grow to $100 (1 + i)^n$.

This procedure may be reversed. If the interest rate is 10 percent, a person should be willing to pay $100 *now* for the right to receive $121 in 2 years' time. That is, $121 to be received 2 years from now has a *present value* (PV) of $100. In general, if amount X is to be received n years from now, then:

THE FED'S SECOND TOOL FOR CONTROLLING THE MONEY SUPPLY: CHANGES IN THE DISCOUNT RATE

The Federal Reserve acts as the bankers' bank, as we have noted. Just as commercial banks lend to the general public, so the Fed may lend to commercial banks. In exchange for such a loan, the commercial bank gives the Fed its promissory note, secured by acceptable collateral (usually United States government securities). The interest rate on such loans is known as the *discount rate*.

The *discount rate* is the interest rate charged by the Federal Reserve on its loans to commercial banks.

$$PV = \frac{X}{(1 + i)^n}$$

In our example, $100 = \dfrac{\$121}{(1 + 0.10)^2}$.

A $100 bond with a 10-year maturity and coupon payments of $8 per year will pay the $8 each year until the tenth year, when the owner receives a final $8 plus the repayment of the face value of $100. If the market interest rate is, say, 9 percent, the PV or price of this bond is:

$$PV = \frac{\$8}{1.09} + \frac{\$8}{(1.09)^2} + \frac{\$8}{(1.09)^3} + \ldots + \frac{\$8 + \$100}{(1.09)^{10}}$$

$$= \$93.58$$

Or, in general,

$$\text{Price of bond} - \frac{C}{1 + i} + \frac{C}{(1 + i)^2} + \ldots + \frac{C + \$100}{(1 + i)^n}$$

where C is the coupon payment.

From this equation, we can calculate the price if we know the rate of interest (i), or we can calculate the interest rate if we know the price of the bond. The higher is the one, the lower is the other. Thus, once again we see that "an increase in the price of bonds" is another way of saying "a fall in the interest rate."

In Chapter 10, we saw how a commercial bank provides its customer with a demand deposit when it makes a loan. The transaction between the Fed and a member bank is similar.[4] When the Fed grants a loan to a bank, it increases that bank's reserve deposit in the Fed, as shown in Table 11-3.

Thus, such loans (or "discounts") add to the total reserves of the banking system.

Unlike open market operations, Fed lending is at the initiative of the commercial banks rather than the Fed. But the Fed has two ways of controlling the amount of discounting.

[4]The Federal Reserve can lend to nonmember banks in unusual circumstances, at an interest rate that is above the discount rate available to member banks.

TABLE 11-3
The Federal Reserve Grants a Loan
(thousands of dollars)

Assets		Liabilities	
Member bank borrowings	+ 100	Reserve deposits of member bank	+ 100
Total	100	Total	100

When the Fed lends to a member bank, bank reserves are increased.

1. It can refuse to lend to banks when they ask. Borrowing is intended as a temporary way of banks' bringing their reserves up to required levels when they have been run down by unexpected deposit withdrawals or other unforeseen circumstances. The Fed has made it clear that banks will not be permitted to borrow on a permanent basis. In order to keep a clean slate with the Fed, banks try to confine their borrowing to periods when it is really needed.

2. The Fed can change the discount rate. A higher discount rate makes it more expensive for the banks to borrow, and thus discourages such borrowing.

At one time, a change in the discount rate was also important as a signal of Federal Reserve intentions; a rise in the rate meant that the Fed wanted to cut back on the rate of monetary expansion taking place in the economy. Particularly in the years following World War II, discount rate changes took place infrequently, and they were considered as strong indicators of Federal Reserve policy when they did occur. But this has become less true in recent decades. Since 1955, the effect of the discount rate as a signal has been weakened by the number of small changes made to keep the rate close to market rates of interest (Figure 11-3). Nevertheless, the announcement effect was important in November 1978, when the rate was raised a full percent. The dollar had been falling in terms of other currencies, and the Fed wanted to give international financial markets a strong signal of its determination to fight inflation.

Criticisms of Discounting

Although the discount rate is one of the major tools in the hands of the Fed for controlling the quantity of money, the discounting procedure has been the target of two criticisms.

First is the argument that it reduces the effectiveness of open market operations. Suppose, for example, that the Federal Reserve wants to restrain the growth of the money stock. In its open market operations, it cuts down on the rate of purchase of securities, or it may even go so far as to sell them. This makes the commercial banks short of reserves; some of them find themselves falling below required ratios. Consequently, they may turn to the Fed, borrowing reserves under the discount procedure. Thus, the Federal Reserve with its left hand (discounting) may pump back the reserves which it is extracting with its right hand (open market operations).

In response, it is argued that discounting acts as a safety valve, allowing the Fed to follow tighter policies than it would otherwise dare. If there were no discounting, the Fed would have to tread lightly in restrictive open market operations, taking care not to put too much pressure on the commercial banks. Even though discounts involve some slippage, it may nevertheless be possible to get even tighter policies than in the absence of discounting: The Fed can safely push harder on the open market lever.

The second criticism is that the discount procedure may involve hidden subsidies to banks, since the discount rate is

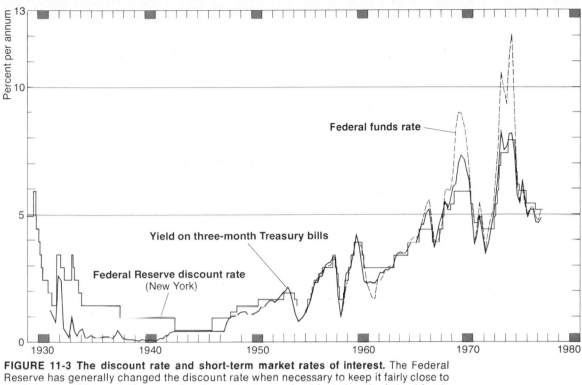

FIGURE 11-3 The discount rate and short-term market rates of interest. The Federal Reserve has generally changed the discount rate when necessary to keep it fairly close to market rates of interest. However, the discount rate remained far below the federal funds rate when short-term interest rates skyrocketed in 1969 and 1974.

sometimes significantly less than the market rate of interest a bank would have to pay to borrow elsewhere (such as in the federal funds market). This criticism was particularly strong in 1974, when the discount rate was much below most short-term interest rates, and when a single New York bank, the Franklin National, came to the Fed for over $1 billion in discounts. Unlike most banks, which depend on reasonably stable savings and demand deposits as their main sources of funds, Franklin had relied heavily on funds borrowed in the short-term financial markets. When short-term interest rates skyrocketed in 1974 and questions arose regarding Franklin's ability to survive, Franklin found itself unable to roll over its short-term

private borrowing; that is, it was unable to borrow new funds to repay short-term debts coming due. (Nobody wants to lend to a potential bankrupt—even if it is a bank.) In its desperation, Franklin turned to the Fed for massive loans. (Although these provided a temporary respite, Franklin did not survive as an independent institution. Its operations were taken over by the European-American Bank and Trust Co.)

One way of avoiding this second criticism would be to change the discount rate more frequently in order to keep it from lagging significantly below short-term market rates of interest. Such a proposal was made in a 1970 study by the Fed, but it was not acted upon. The simplest way would be to keep the discount rate at a fixed amount (say, $1/4$ percent) above the yield on short-term government bills. Such a *penalty rate*—that is, a rate in excess of an important market interest rate—would mean that banks would no longer be able to benefit by borrowing at a bargain from the Fed. (Historically, the Bank of England has had a penalty discount rate.)

THE FED'S THIRD TOOL FOR CONTROLLING THE MONEY SUPPLY: A CHANGE IN RESERVE REQUIREMENTS

The quantity of deposits that the commercial banks can create depends on the size of their reserves and on the required reserve ratio. Specifically, deposits can be created up to the amount of the reserves times $1/R$. Thus, an *increase* in R (the required reserve ratio) will *decrease* the amount of deposits that can be created.

The Federal Reserve Board has the legal power to change required reserve ratios within limits. Clearly, this is a very powerful tool. With total reserves of, say, $100 million, an increase in the required reserve ratio from 10 to $12^1/_2$ percent would reduce the maximum quantity of demand deposits from $1,000 million to $800 million.

The Federal Reserve learned the power of this weapon the hard way—as a result of one of its policy blunders during the Great Depression. Between August 1936 and May 1937, the Fed *doubled* required reserve ratios. The effects on the economy were softened because banks initially had large excess reserves. (Indeed, the ratios were raised to mop up excess reserves and put the Fed in a better position to prevent inflation.) But the economy nevertheless suffered a severe blow from the restrictive move. Banks felt compelled to cut back their loans. This derailed the recovery then in progress; unemployment shot up from 14.3 percent in 1937 to 19.0 percent in 1938. Since that unfortunate experiment, the Federal Reserve has stepped softly. As can be seen from Table 11-4, recent changes have been quite small, usually only one-half of 1 percent.

During the past decade, there has been a slight downward trend of required reserve ratios. This trend has, in part, been the result of Fed concern over defections of commercial banks from the Federal Reserve System. Lower reserve requirements permit the banks to hold more earning assets, and thus reduce their incentive to leave the System. (Nonmember banks do not have to meet Federal Reserve requirements, although they do have to meet state banking requirements, which are usually less exacting.)

MINOR MONETARY TOOLS

The Fed's three major weapons (open market operations, changes in the discount rate, and changes in reserve requirements) are *quantitative controls*; they help the Fed control the quantity of money in the United States economy. They are supplemented by (1) *selective* (or *qualitative*) controls, which can affect the supply of funds to specific markets, and (2) *moral suasion*.

Selective Control on the Stock Market: Margin Requirements

When you buy shares of common stock, you are subject to a *margin requirement* set by the Federal Reserve.[5] The objective of margin requirements is to limit speculative excesses in the stock market.

---

[5]The requirement applies to stocks traded on the major exchanges (such as the New York Stock Exchange), and to a list of stocks announced by the Federal Reserve Board. It does not apply to stocks of small corporations that fit neither of these categories.

TABLE 11-4

Required Reserve Ratios

(in percentages)

Effective date	For demand deposits† Highest	Lowest	For savings deposits‡
January 1963	16¹/₂	12	4
March 1967	16¹/₂	12	3
January 1968	17	12	3
April 1969	17¹/₂	12¹/₂	3
November 1972	17¹/₂	8	3
July 1973	18	8	3
December 1974	17¹/₂	8	3
February 1975	16¹/₂	7¹/₂	3
December 1976	16¹/₄	7	3
In effect, March 1978	16¹/₄	7	3

Legal limits within which Federal Reserve may set requirements

	Minimum	Maximum
Demand deposits, Reserve city banks	10%	22%
Demand deposits, other banks	7%	14%
Time and savings deposits	3%	10%

†Since November 1972, the highest required reserve ratio has applied to demand deposits in excess of $400 million in any one bank; the lowest demand deposit ratio has applied to deposits of less than $2 million. Prior to November 1972, the required reserve ratio depended on both the size of demand deposits and the location of the bank.

‡For details on time deposits, see the *Federal Reserve Bulletin*.

Margin requirements limit the amount that can be borrowed to purchase stocks or bonds. For example, if the margin requirement on stock is 60 percent, the buyer must put up 60 percent of the purchase price of the stock in his or her own money, and can borrow no more than 40 percent from a bank or stockbroker.

The stock market plays an important role in American capitalism. New issues of stock provide corporations with funds for expansion. And the owners of outstanding stock have liquidity and flexibility because they can readily sell; they are able to redirect their funds to dynamic new industries. But there is another side to Wall Street: it also is a substitute Las Vegas. Periodically, it appeals to the get-rich-quick passion. As stocks rise, people think that they have found the sure way to fortune.

What is the best way to get rich quick, if you "know" a stock will rise rapidly?

You borrow as much as possible and buy a large number of shares. For example, if you buy $5,000 worth of stock in an unregulated market, you may be able to borrow as much as $4,000 from your bank or broker; thus you are required to put up only $1,000 of your own money. If the stock doubles as expected, you can sell it for $10,000. After repaying your loan, you end up with $6,000 (less brokerage and interest costs)—or 6 times your initial investment of $1,000. The stock purchaser, like the business corporation, can gain *leverage* by borrowing money. (Leverage was explained in Chapter 6.)

This was the strategy of the 1920s. The tycoon and the grocery clerk alike became enthralled with the stock market as a shortcut to the good life. But the speculators of the twenties found that leverage was a two-edged sword. Suppose, in the above illustration, that the unthinkable happens; the stock goes down, not up. It does not have to go down very far before the bank or broker that loaned you the money becomes concerned with the safety of the loan: After all, 80 percent of the original value of the stock has been loaned. As the stock falls to 90 percent, then 85 percent, the lender no longer looks on the stock as adequate collateral for the loan. Consequently, the lender issues a *margin call*: More money must be put up by the stock owner, or the stock will be sold. If the owner has no more funds and cannot meet the margin call, the stock is sold. As a result, it falls further in price. This, in turn, causes other lenders to issue margin calls. Thus, heavy borrowing can make the stock market vulnerable to a cumulative wave of selling. The final act of the great stock market boom of the twenties was the collapse of the Dow-Jones average of industrial stocks from its 1929 peak of 380 to a low of 41 in mid-1932.

If the stock speculator were the only one to lose, we might dismiss this outcome as poetic justice—the speculator has taken a chance, and lost. But a stock market crash may have repercussions throughout the economy: Businesses will find it hard to raise the funds they need for expansion. And, as stock prices collapse, the holders of stocks will tend to cut back on their consumption expenditures, adding to a downswing. A healthy stock market bolsters the overall health of the economy. And a healthy stock market requires that stockholders be able to weather temporary setbacks without being forced to dump their stocks. They gain staying power by having their own money invested.

Following the great crash of 1929, the Fed in the 1930s was given the power to impose margin requirements, limiting the amount that can be borrowed to purchase stocks or bonds. Even a constant margin requirement (for example, 50 percent) adds stability to the financial markets by providing a significant range over which stocks may fall without triggering margin calls and a cumulative sell-off. But the Fed is also empowered to change the requirements. It can cut margin requirements to revive a low or declining market, and raise margin requirements to restrain a speculative burst. (In early 1978, the margin requirement on stocks was 50 percent, where it had been since early 1974.)

Selective Controls of the Past

During wartime periods, the Fed has been empowered to use other selective controls to keep down the demand for specific products. From 1941 to 1947, and again during the Korean war, the Federal Reserve controlled the amount that could be borrowed to purchase consumer durables. There were also selective controls on real estate credit during the Korean war. This power of the Federal Reserve to impose real estate and consumer credit controls was allowed to lapse by Congress at the end of the Korean conflict.

Other proposals have been made for the Federal Reserve to influence the amount of lending in specific markets. Most interesting, perhaps, is the suggestion that the Federal Reserve should positively encourage lending to certain sectors, such as housing or businesses in the ghettos. Banks that make such loans might be rewarded and encouraged by lowering the reserves they are required to keep.

The Federal Reserve has resisted these proposals, arguing that the control of the overall quantity of credit and money is difficult enough, and should not be complicated by also requiring the Fed to perform other, quite different functions. Furthermore, detailed control over the direction of credit is a political matter, more appropriately handled by Congress and the executive branch than by the partially independent Fed.

Moral Suasion

In addition to its formal weapons (such as open market operations or changes in the discount rate), the Federal Reserve may also attempt to influence the behavior of member banks in less formal ways. Specifically, it may resort to "jawboning"; that is, exhorting bankers to refrain from certain actions, or encouraging them to take others.

From time to time, for example, the Federal Reserve has recommended that banks reduce the amount of new loans they were making. The Federal Reserve has also recommended that banks keep higher capital accounts (net worth) in order to ensure their ability to weather storms. (A bank can increase its net worth by selling additional stock, or by retaining more of its profits rather than paying them out in dividends. An addition to net worth increases the amount by which a bank's assets exceed its liabilities. Thus the bank is protected if some of its assets disappear—for example, if some of its loans turn out to be uncollectable.)

There are a number of levers which the Federal Reserve can use in order to fortify its moral suasion and to ensure that the banks do not simply ignore its exhortations. For example, borrowing through the Fed's discount window is a privilege, not a right; if a bank ignores the recommendations of the Fed, it may find the Fed less willing to lend. Also, the Fed must approve certain bank activities, such as the opening of a branch in a foreign country. The Fed can refuse such permission if it feels that the capital position of the bank is inadequate.

Jawboning can, under certain circumstances, be quite effective; for example, it resulted in extraordinary bank compliance with the "voluntary"[6] program to restrain foreign loans during the mid-1960s. But the ability of the Federal Reserve to modify the course of events through moral suasion should not be exaggerated. After the experience of the late 1960s when the Fed recommended that banks keep down their volume of loans, a number of bankers swore (privately) that they would not be swayed by future exhortations. When they had held back, their competitors had stolen their business.

The scope for moral suasion is substantially less in the United States than in a number of other countries. In Britain and Canada, for example, there are only a very few banks. (Nationwide service is provided by an extensive network of branches.) In those two countries, the head of the central bank can meet face to face with representatives of all the banks in a single room, and moral suasion can be exerted in a more direct and emphatic manner than in the United States.

THE BALANCE SHEET OF THE FEDERAL RESERVE

Some actions of the Federal Reserve do not show up directly on its balance sheet (for example, moral suasion, or changes in reserve requirements). But other acts do— most conspicuously, its open market operations. Thus, the balance sheet of the Federal Reserve can provide insights into some of the Fed's activities.

The consolidated balance sheet of the 12 Federal Reserve banks is shown in Table 11-5. Two entries on the right side are particularly worth noting. First is the large amount of Federal Reserve notes outstanding. This is the result of the desire of the public to hold more currency as its overall holdings of money have increased. (While open market operations and other Fed policies affect the *amount* of money in the economy, the public is free to choose the *form* in which it wants to hold its money. When the public withdraws currency from the commercial banks, these banks in turn can get

---

[6]"Voluntary" must surely rank with "temporary" as one of the two most ambiguous words in Washington. Although the foreign loan restraints were declared to be "voluntary," it was clear they would become mandatory if there were significant violations. Indeed, in spite of a lack of violations, the program still became mandatory in 1968. (It was terminated in 1974.)

TABLE 11-5

Consolidated Balance Sheet of the 12 Federal Reserve Banks, Feb. 28, 1978

(billions of dollars)

Assets		Liabilities and net worth	
U.S. government securities	98.5	Deposits	
Member bank borrowings	0.3	Reserve deposits of member banks	25.8
Gold certificate account	11.7	U.S. Treasury	3.6
Other assets	21.7	Foreign and other	1.1
		Federal Reserve notes	90.7
		Other liabilities	8.4
		Total liabilities	129.6
		Net worth	2.6
Total	132.2	Total	132.2

In the Federal Reserve's balance sheet, U.S. government securities are the main asset, and Federal Reserve notes the largest liability.

more from the Federal Reserve by withdrawing some of their reserve deposits.)[7]

The second noteworthy item on the right side is the small net worth of the Federal Reserve. If the Fed were a private corporation, this would be cause for alarm. The slightest reversal in its fortunes might cause the value of its assets to dip below the amount of its liabilities, wiping out its net worth and threatening bankruptcy. But the Fed is no ordinary corporation. It is a part of the government, and a very special part, as it has the power to create money. Because of this special power, the Fed has an assured high flow of profits, and need not worry about building up its net worth. (The Fed is very profitable because it earns interest on the large holdings of government securities on the asset side, while it pays no interest on most of its liabilities, in particular, reserve deposits and Federal Reserve notes. As mentioned earlier, the Fed remits most of its profits to the United States Treasury.)

On the asset side of the Fed's balance sheet, United States government securities are by far the largest entry; these securities have been accumulated through past open market operations. Member bank borrowings are a very small item—only $303 million at the end of February 1978. Although these borrowings are generally low, they have shot up at times when banks were short of reserves, particularly in 1974. Finally, the gold entry in the Fed's balance sheet is left over from the historical role played by the Fed in the operation of the gold standard. As part of the gold standard arrangements, the Fed held gold as backing for the United States currency, and stood ready to buy and sell gold to the public. The gold standard

---

[7]When the public decides to hold more currency, bank reserves are reduced; the process is the opposite of the one in Chapter 10, when you deposited $10,000 and set the stage for a multiple expansion of bank deposits.

The large amount of Federal Reserve notes outstanding means that our earlier warning (in Chapter 10, in the "Two Complications" section) should be reemphasized. As the money stock is increased, there is a large leakage of currency from bank reserves into the hands of the public. As a consequence, actual money creation following an open market operation is generally much less than given in the formula for the maximum increase in demand deposits:

$$D = \frac{1}{R}$$

was drastically modified during the Depression of the 1930s, and was finally ended in 1971. The Fed and the United States Treasury no longer consider gold the ultimate money; indeed, they officially view it as similar to any other metal, such as copper or platinum.

WHAT BACKS OUR MONEY?

Money is debt. The largest component of the money stock (namely, demand deposits) is debt of the commercial banks. And Federal Reserve notes—the currency of everyday use—are liabilities of the Federal Reserve System.

In a sense, the money supply is backed by the assets of the banking system. Demand deposits are backed by the loans, bonds, and reserves held by the commercial banks. And Federal Reserve notes are backed by the assets of the Federal Reserve, mainly federal government securities. What, in turn, backs the government securities? The government's promise to pay, based in the first instance on its ability to tax, but in the final analysis on its ability to borrow newly created money from the Federal Reserve or to print money directly. (Recall the section in Chapter 9 entitled: "Can the Government Go Broke?")

Clearly, we have gone in a circle. Currency is backed with government debt; and government debt is ultimately backed by the ability of the federal authorities to print more currency. In a sense, the whole game is played with mirrors; money is money because the government says it is. Until a few years ago, Federal Reserve notes boldly proclaimed that "the United States of America will pay to the bearer on demand" the face value of the Federal Reserve note. And what would happen if an individual submitted a $1 bill and demanded payment? He or she would receive another $1 bill in exchange. This does not make much sense, and the bold proclamation has been eliminated from Federal Reserve notes. Now, we can say simply: A dollar is a dollar is a dollar.[8]

What, then, determines the value of a Federal Reserve note? Dollar bills have value because of (1) their relative scarcity compared to the demand for them, and (2) their general acceptability. So long as the Federal Reserve keeps the supply of money in reasonable balance with the demand for it, money retains its value even though it has no explicit backing with precious metal or any other tangible commodity.

Dollar bills are generally acceptable by such diverse people as the taxi driver, the house painter, and the doctor. They all know they can turn around and buy other goods and services with the dollar bills. In part, general acceptability is a matter of convention (as in the case of cigarettes in the POW camp). But convention and habit are reinforced by the status of currency as *legal tender*. Creditors must accept dollar bills in payment of a debt. (Coins are also legal tender, but only up to reasonable limits. The electric utility company is not obliged to accept 4,562 pennies if a customer offers them in payment for a bill of $45.62.)

> *Legal tender* is the item or items that creditors must accept in payment of debts.

The Federal Deposit Insurance Corporation

But how about demand deposits? What protects their role as part of the money stock? Unlike currency, demand deposits are not legal tender. A gas station is not obliged to accept a personal check, and usually won't do so.

[8]The correspondence between the U.S. Treasury and an irate citizen, who asked for redemption of a $10 bill and got two $5 bills in exchange, is reproduced under the title "A Dollar Is a Dollar Is a Dollar," *American Affairs*, April 1948; also reprinted in Lawrence S. Ritter (ed.), *Money and Economic Activity: A Selection of Readings* (Cambridge, Mass.: Houghton Mifflin, 1952), pp. 45–46.

People are willing to hold money in the form of demand deposits because of the convenience of paying many types of bills by check, and because they are confident that they can get currency for the deposits when they want it. But what assurance do depositors have of actually being able to get $100 in currency for every $100 they hold in demand deposits?

The first assurance lies in the assets of the commercial banks—their reserves and earning assets of loans and securities. If a bank finds that people are withdrawing more than they are depositing, it may cover the difference by selling securities on the financial markets, or using the proceeds of its loans or bonds as they come due. But bank assets may not always be enough; indeed, they proved to be woefully inadequate during the Depression of the 1930s. As the economy collapsed, many businesses could not repay their bank loans, and the value of bank assets shrank. As their assets fell to less than their deposit liabilities, the banks were driven into bankruptcy, and many depositors suffered heavy losses.

This situation clearly was dangerous because bank runs are contagious. Indeed, the contagion spread like wildfire in early 1933, and the banking system collapsed. In order to prevent a repeat of the 1930s, an important additional backing was therefore provided for bank depositors. The government set up the Federal Deposit Insurance Corporation (FDIC) to insure bank deposits up to a sizable limit ($40,000 per deposit, in 1978). For this insurance, the banks pay premiums to the FDIC. A similar institution (the Federal Savings and Loan Insurance Corporation, or FSLIC) guarantees savings and loan shares (deposits) up to the same limit. All federally incorporated banks and savings and loan associations (S&Ls) are required to belong to these insurance systems, and many state institutions also belong. Thus, the federal government stands behind the deposits of banks and S&Ls.

Why Not Gold?

There is an obvious problem with *fiat* money—that is, money that is money solely because the government says it is. The government or central bank can create such money at will. What, therefore, is to restrain the authorities from creating and spending money recklessly, generating a runaway inflation?

It is this question that provided a rationale for the gold standard. If the currency issued by the government and the central bank is convertible into gold, the authorities will not be able to create money recklessly. Like the goldsmith of old, they will have to keep a gold backing equal to a reasonable fraction of their currency liabilities. This was the original design of the Federal Reserve. The Federal Reserve was required to keep gold reserves behind its currency and deposit obligations in a manner analogous to the reserves the commercial banks were required to keep as a fraction of their deposit liabilities.

A country is on the *gold standard* when its currency is convertible into gold; that is, when the treasury and/or central bank stands ready to buy or sell gold at a fixed price (for example, 1 ounce of gold = $20.67). In such a country, gold coins circulate as part of the money stock.

Under the gold standard, the monetary system forms a large inverted pyramid built on a base of gold. On the base of its gold holdings, the Federal Reserve can build a structure of deposits and Federal Reserve notes, the size of which depends on the gold reserves that the Federal Reserve is required to keep. This structure, in turn, forms the base for an even larger superstructure of commercial bank deposits, the size of which depends on the required reserve ratio of banks. (See Figure 11-4.)

While the gold standard fulfills its ob-

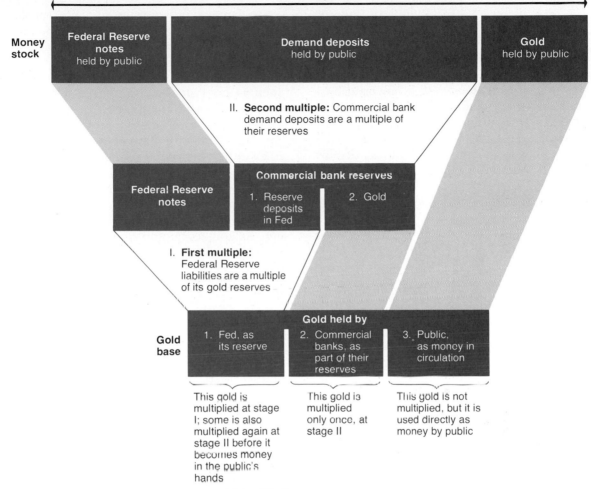

FIGURE 11-4 The gold standard pyramid (simplified).

jective of restraining reckless money creation, it has two serious flaws. First, the size of the superstructure of money tends to be kept in proportion to the gold base. This means that gold flowing into the central bank from gold mines or from foreign nations acts as a super open market operation. When the Fed buys gold, its purchase increases commercial bank reserves directly. (Recall that bank reserves increase whenever the Fed buys *any* asset.) Moreover, the gold improves the reserve position of the Fed itself. Therefore, the Fed is able to lend more to the commercial banks or buy more government securities on the open market. Thus, commercial bank reserves are increased in this indirect way as well. Consequently, a gold inflow can lead to a large increase in the money stock. Similarly, a gold outflow can have a very powerful contractionary effect. There is no assurance that a monetary system that responds to gold flows in this manner will provide the quantity of money needed for a full-employment, noninflationary economy.

The second difficulty is even more severe, and indeed, it was the reason for the collapse of the gold standard during the Depression. Because of the fractional-reserve system applying to both the commercial banks and the Federal Reserve, any tendency for the public to demand items lower in the pyramid had a powerful contractionary effect on the size of the money stock. We saw in Chapter 10 how your deposit of $10,000 in currency permitted a monetary expansion; a withdrawal of currency by the public likewise has a contractionary effect. But if the public withdraws gold, it is withdrawing the item at the base of the whole pyramid. In this case, the contractionary effect is particularly severe: Reserves have been removed from the Federal Reserve itself, and the Federal Reserve itself must take restrictive steps (such as reducing its loans to commercial banks) in order to meet its own required reserve ratios. In short, the money supply shrinks as part of the gold base is withdrawn.

During the Depression, people became frightened as unemployment and business bankruptcies shot upward. Being frightened, they tried to get their assets in the safest form possible; they withdrew currency from banks and switched from paper currency into gold. The monetary system thus came under strong contractionary pressures when the economy was already headed downward. When things became bad enough, the rules of the game were changed: Under legislation recommended by President Franklin Roosevelt, the American public was forbidden to hold gold (with a few

exceptions, such as for dental work). It wasn't until the beginning of 1975 that the public was allowed to hold gold again, and by then gold no longer played an important role in the monetary system.

The problem with the gold standard, then, is that it does not provide a steady and measured restraint. Rather, it exerts restraint in the form of a threat of disaster: If too much money is issued, there will be a crisis of confidence, a switch by the public away from paper money and into gold, and a collapse of the monetary structure. So long as the authorities are lucky (with gold flowing in from mines or from foreign countries), and so long as they follow farsighted policies aimed at avoiding any crisis of confidence, it is possible that the system will not work too badly. But in the period between the two world wars, the authorities were neither farsighted nor lucky. The gold standard added to the disaster of the 1930s. Any system which "kicks an economy when it is down" is basically destructive and should be discarded. (This was done in stages between 1933 and 1971.) In the words of British economist D. H. Robertson:[9]

The value of a yellow metal, originally chosen as money because it tickled the fancy of savages, is clearly a chancy and irrelevant thing on which to base the value of our money and the stability of our industrial system.

We cannot put our trust in a yellow metal; we have no choice but to put it in the officials of the Federal Reserve System, hoping that they manage our money wisely.

[9]D. H. Robertson, *Money*, rev. ed. (Cambridge: Cambridge University Press, 1948), p. 144.

Key Points

1. The Federal Reserve is responsible for controlling the quantity of money in the United States economy. It has three major quantitative tools at its command:

    (*a*) Open market operations

    (*b*) Changes in the discount rate

    (*c*) Changes in reserve ratios that must be met by commercial banks that are members of the Federal Reserve System

2. The Federal Reserve's untidy organizational chart is the result of an early controversy over the desirable degree of centralization. There are 12 regional Federal Reserve Banks, and a Board of Governors in Washington. For monetary policy, the most important institution of all is the Federal Open Market Committee, made up of the seven members of the Board of Governors plus five presidents of the regional Federal Reserve Banks.

3. When the Federal Reserve purchases securities on the open market, it creates bank reserves; when it sells securities, it eliminates reserves. Changes in reserves affect the amount of demand deposit money that commercial banks can create.

4. A purchase of securities by the Federal Reserve tends to bid up security prices. When this happens, the yields (interest rates) on securities are bid down.

5. A decrease in the discount rate encourages bank borrowing from the Fed. Such borrowing creates bank reserves.

6. When it decreases required reserve ratios, the Fed increases the quantity of demand deposits the commercial banks can create on any given reserve base.

7. Less important tools of the Federal Reserve include selective or qualitative controls (most notably, margin requirements for purchases of stocks) and moral suasion.

8. In the last analysis, there is nothing backing our currency: "A dollar is a dollar." Money retains its value because it is scarce. Even though it doesn't cost the Federal Reserve anything to create reserve deposits, and the costs of printing currency are small, the Fed does not create money recklessly. If it did so, there would be a wild inflation.

9. Under the old gold standard, the Fed was required to hold gold reserves equal to a fraction of its deposit and note liabilities. Since this system is based on gold, and gold "can't be printed," there was a restraint on irresponsible money creation. But the gold standard had two enormous defects. First, the amount of money that could be created on the available gold base was not necessarily the quantity needed for full employment with stable prices. The second defect was even worse. In a crisis of confidence, people exchanged other forms of money for gold. This caused a sharp contraction of the money supply. Because of its defects, the gold standard was abolished. The ability of the Fed to expand the money supply is no longer limited by its gold holdings.

Key Concepts

Problems

11-1 What are the three major tools of the Federal Reserve for controlling the quantity of money? Which of these tools affect the quantity of reserves of the commercial banks?

11-2 Suppose that the Federal Reserve purchases $100,000 in Treasury bills from commercial bank A. Explain how the balance sheets of the Fed and commercial bank A are affected. How much can commercial bank A now safely lend? (Assume that bank A's reserves were just adequate prior to the purchase by the Fed.)

11-3 Suppose that the Federal Reserve spends $1 million to buy a computer from IBM. Show the effects on the balance sheets of IBM, of IBM's bank, and of the Fed. If the required reserve ratio is 20 percent, how much can IBM's bank prudently lend as a result of this transaction?

11-4 Suppose that the price of a 3-month, $100,000 Treasury bill is $98,000. What is the yield on this bill? (Following the standard convention, quote the yield at an annual rate.) Now suppose that the price of 3-month bills falls to $97,000. What happens to the yield?

11-5 The Fed makes discounts at the initiative of the commercial banks. In what way do discounts reduce the control of the Federal Reserve over the money supply? In what way might the power of the Fed to grant or refuse discounts increase its control over the money stock?

11-6 "Counterfeiting is generally an antisocial act. But when there is a depression, all counterfeiters should be let out of jail." Do you agree or disagree? Explain why.

11-7 What backing do Federal Reserve notes have? Why are these notes valuable?

PART THREE
FIVE GREAT
MACROECONOMIC
QUESTIONS OF OUR TIME

art 2 of this book has introduced the two major tools of demand management: fiscal policy (involving changes in government spending and in tax rates) and monetary policy (open market operations, changes in required reserve ratios, etc.). By changing monetary and fiscal policies, the authorities can influence aggregate demand, aiming for the objectives of full employment and stable prices.

In the introduction to Part 2, the reader was warned that an effort would be made to keep the explanations simple. The "potholes" in the road map of economic policy were left out. But, while theory may be simplified, the real world remains complex. Although substantial progress has been made during the past 40 years in managing the economy to provide for full employment and stable prices, there have also been failures in the form of periodic recessions and stubborn inflation. We have done much better than our parents and grandparents did in the decades between the two world wars. But we do not seem to be moving on from one success to ever greater successes. The problem of recession has not been licked. Indeed, the recession of 1974–1975 was the most severe in more than three decades. Whether measured by the rate of unemployment, the rate of inflation, or the rate of growth of real national product, the American economy has performed less well during the 1970s than it did during the 1960s.

Nor is there unanimity on how we should proceed from here. Indeed, there are sharp controversies on some of the most basic issues of macroeconomics. The chapters of Part 3 will deal with five of the great macroeconomic questions of our time.

1. Monetary Policy and Fiscal Policy: Which Is the Key to Aggregate Demand?

Most economists believe that both fiscal policy and monetary policy are important tools for controlling aggregate demand. But there are substantial disagreements over which should be made the centerpiece of demand management policy. And there are strong views at the extremes, with some economists arguing that monetary policy is a weak and ineffective tool for managing aggregate demand, while others believe that fiscal policy has little effect on aggregate demand. This controversy is the subject of Chapter 12. We will conclude that the best approach generally involves a combined, cooperative use of both fiscal and monetary policies.

2. Aggregate Supply: How Can Inflation and Unemployment Coexist?

In Chapter 8, we introduced the simple Keynesian aggregate supply function. Up to the point of full employment, an increase in aggregate demand will lead to an increase in output, with prices remaining stable. After the full-employment point is reached, further increases in demand will cause inflation.

While this approach may have been adequate in dealing with the problems of the early Keynesian period, it will not do as a basis for policy in the modern economy, which has been afflicted simultaneously with high rates of unemployment and high rates of inflation. How can these two problems exist at the same time? How can we get the economy to full employment without unleashing the forces of inflation? These are the questions that will be discussed in Chapter 13.

3. Why Is the Economy Unstable?

Much time and ingenuity have gone into policies aimed at stabilizing economic activity and eliminating cyclical fluctuations in national product and employment. Yet the business cycle is a hardy bird; it refuses to pass into extinction. Why? What are the forces causing economic instability? Why have economic fluctuations been so persistent? These questions provide the subject of Chapter 14.

4. How Activist Should Policy Be?

The fourth topic has already been touched upon in the debate over budgetary strategy in Chapter 9. Those who argue that we should aim consistently for a balanced full-employment budget have set relatively modest goals: Our principal objective should be to avoid the destabilizing effects of trying to balance the actual budget every year. *Primo non nocere* should be our goal: Don't mess things up. Others argue that steady policy settings are not good enough; we should actively manage fiscal and monetary policies in order to stabilize the economy. This debate is studied in Chapter 15.

5. Fixed or Flexible Exchange Rates?

With one or two minor exceptions, we have confined the discussion to policies in a single country, the United States. Yet the countries of the world are interdependent; prosperity in one country affects its trading partners. The Depression of the 1930s caused worldwide distress; the prosperity of recent decades has likewise been an international phenomenon. The subject of Chapter 16 will be the ways in which inflation and employment in one country can be affected by its transactions with other countries.

An important facet of this topic is the exchange rate system. Should exchange rates be pegged by governments, or should they be allowed to fluctuate in response to changes in supply and demand? (An *exchange rate* is the price of one national currency in terms of another. For example, the price of the British pound in terms of United States dollars is an exchange rate. An exchange rate is *pegged* when it is kept fixed by one or more national governments.) During the past decade, this has been a hot topic for finance ministers and corporate treasurers, as well as for academic economists. At the beginning of the 1970s, the regime of pegged exchange rates set up at the end of World War II came apart at the seams. Since 1973, most important exchange rates have been *flexible*; that is, governments have allowed them to fluctuate in response to changing demand and supply conditions.

chapter **12**
Monetary and Fiscal Policy:
Which Is the Key to Aggregate Demand?

General [monetary] controls are a mirage and a delusion.
                                    Keynesian Warren Smith[1]

Money does matter and matters very much. Changes in the quantity of money have important, and broadly predictable, economic effects. . . . Substantial contractions in the quantity of money over short periods have been a major factor in producing severe economic contractions. And cyclical variations in the quantity of money may well be an important element in the ordinary mild business cycle.
                              Monetarist Milton Friedman[2]

The Keynesian Revolution of the 1930s and 1940s focused attention on the management of aggregate demand as a way to avoid a repeat of the Depression. Pushed aside was the classical viewpoint that the free market contains a self-adjusting mechanism that will naturally result in a return to full employment if the governmental authorities steadfastly pursue a policy of laissez faire.

But there was a second important aspect to the Keynesian revolution. Keynes drew attention to fiscal policy as a means of controlling aggregate demand. Specifically, the government should step up its spending and cut taxes during a depression, in order to move the economy back toward full employment. In contrast with classical economists,

who saw changes in the quantity of money as the principal cause of changes in aggregate demand, Keynes felt that money plays a secondary role; expansive monetary policy cannot be counted upon to get the economy out of a depression. Indeed, Keynes argued that, in the deepest pit of a depression, expansive monetary policies may be completely useless as a means of stimulating aggregate demand; an increase in the money stock may have no effect on spending.

In more normal times, Keynes was less negative regarding monetary policy. Indeed, the importance of money was suggested by the titles of his earlier works: *Monetary Reform* (1924) and *A Treatise on Money* (1930). Nevertheless, Keynes left a strong

---

[1]In *Staff Report on Employment, Growth, and Price Levels* (Washington: Joint Economic Committee, U.S. Congress, 1959), p. 401. By "general" controls, Smith meant tools that change the quantity of money, such as open market operations and changes in reserve requirements. (Smith was a professor of economics at the University of Michigan, and a member of President Johnson's Council of Economic Advisers.)

[2]In his "Comment on Tobin," *Quarterly Journal of Economics*, May 1970, pp. 319–320. (Until his retirement, Friedman was for many years a professor at the University of Chicago.)

240

legacy in favor of looking at fiscal policy as the primary tool to control aggregate demand. Consequently, a number of those who consider themselves solidly in the Keynesian tradition have assigned fiscal policy the central role in demand management, and monetary policies have been assigned a secondary, supporting role. Indeed, some Keynesians have gone as far as Warren Smith, who dismissed monetary policy as a "mirage and a delusion."

The inheritors of the classical tradition, in contrast, see money as the key determinant of aggregate demand. In the words of Milton Friedman, "Money is extremely important for nominal magnitudes, for nominal income, for the level of income in dollars. . . . "[3] Furthermore, Friedman is skeptical about the effectiveness of fiscal policy as a tool for controlling aggregate demand. The government budget can, of course, determine the allocation of resources; it can determine how much of the national income will be spent by the government, and how much will be left for the private sector. But Friedman does not believe that fiscal policy has an important effect on aggregate demand: "In my opinion, the state of the budget by itself has no significant effect on the course of nominal income, on inflation, on deflation, or on cyclical fluctuations."[4]

The gap between Smith and Friedman is wide. Not surprisingly, the vast majority of economists are somewhere between them. To the majority, both monetary and fiscal policies are important determinants of aggregate demand; neither should be dismissed as trivial. But the sharp disagreement between strong Keynesians (such as Smith) and strong classicists (such as Friedman) does point up several questions. What are the reasons for the disagreement? How important is money? How does it affect aggregate demand? If we wish to adjust the path of aggregate demand, should we look first to fiscal policy, or to monetary policy?

In Chapter 9, the Keynesian view of how fiscal policy can affect aggregate demand was described in some detail. In order to round out the discussion of fiscal and monetary policies, this chapter will explain:

1. The Keynesian view of how monetary policy can affect aggregate demand, and the circumstances in which the effect may not be very strong

2. The classical view on how monetary policy can affect aggregate demand, and why those in the classical tradition expect the effects of monetary policy to be both strong and predictable

3. The reasons why some of those in the classical tradition have doubts about fiscal policy; specifically, why they doubt that fiscal policy has the strong and predictable effect on aggregate demand suggested by the Keynesian theory outlined in Chapter 9

Toward the end of the chapter, we will explain the advantages of using a *combination* of monetary and fiscal policies as part of an overall strategy of stabilizing aggregate demand.

THE EFFECTS OF MONETARY POLICY: The Keynesian View

Keynes identified a three-step process by which a change in monetary policy could affect aggregate demand (Figure 12-1):

1. An open market operation and a change in the money stock can affect the rate of interest; e.g., an open market purchase by the Fed will tend to lower the interest rate.

[3]Milton Friedman and Walter Heller, *Monetary vs. Fiscal Policy: A Dialogue* (New York: W. W. Norton, 1969), p. 46. Although the debate in this booklet took place some years ago, it remains one of the clearest and simplest statements of basic differences within the economics profession regarding macroeconomic policy.
[4]Ibid., p. 51.

Keynesian economists trace the effects of monetary policy through three steps:
1. Monetary policy can affect the rate of interest.
2. Changes in the rate of interest can affect investment demand.
3. Changes in investment demand have a multiplied effect on aggregate demand and national product.

FIGURE 12-1 How monetary policy affects aggregate demand and national product: The Keynesian approach.

2. A change in interest rates can affect investment demand. With a lower interest rate, for example, business executives are encouraged to borrow money to buy new machines or to build new factories.

3. Higher investment demand will have a multiple effect on aggregate demand and national product.

The first step in the process—how an open market operation can affect interest rates—was explained briefly in Chapter 11. (More detail will be provided in Box 12-1.) The third step involves the familiar multiplier of Chapter 8. Here, we will fill in the gap in the middle, explaining step 2.

The Interest Rate and Investment Demand: The Marginal Efficiency of Investment

Businesses are interested in acquiring equipment or buildings because of the stream of returns such investments will pro-vide. Consider a very simple illustration, a machine costing $100,000 that will last forever. With it a manufacturer expects to produce and sell $50,000 more in goods each year. If the wages paid to workers to run the machine, plus the cost of material inputs, plus administrative costs, add up to $40,000 per year, the machine will provide a *return* (R) of $10,000 per year. In other words, the machine will provide a *rate of return* (r), or *yield*, of 10 percent per year on the initial investment of $100,000.

Alternatively, consider quite a different machine, which also costs $100,000 but has a useful life of only 1 year. Suppose that this machine generates enough in sales to cover labor, material, and administrative costs, plus an additional $110,000. Then this machine also provides a rate of return of 10 percent. That is, it provides enough to cover the $100,000 purchase price of the machine, and leave 10 percent over.

Both these illustrations are very simple. But they do provide examples of how the percentage rate of return may be calculated by taking into account:[5]

1. The initial price and expected life of the machine

2. The addition to sales expected as a result of the machine

3. Costs associated with running the machine, for labor, materials, etc.[6]

In making plans for capital expenditures for the coming year, the business executive will look first at the equipment or building that provides the highest expected rate of return. For a dynamic company in a growing industry, this rate may be very high indeed—20 or 30 percent per annum, or even more. In such cases, a corporation that is able to borrow will find it profitable to do so to acquire the new equipment.

Indeed, profits will be increased if the business continues to borrow to invest, *so long as the rate of return (r) from the investment exceeds the rate of interest (i) paid on the borrowed funds.* In such cases, the new plant or equipment will provide a flow of returns sufficient to cover the interest payments, and leave something over to add to profits. On the other hand, it would be a mistake to invest in plant or equipment with an expected rate of return below the rate of interest. More would be paid out in interest than would be contributed by the machine or building, and profits would suffer as a result. (Indeed, even if the firm has excess funds from retained profits and has no need to borrow to finance new plant and equipment, it would be a mistake to undertake investments with low rates of return. The money could more profitably be used to buy bonds and earn interest.) Thus, to determine whether to undertake an investment project, the business executive calculates *whether the expected rate of return on the plant or equipment is greater than the rate of interest.* (Of course, the executive lives in an uncertain world, and cannot be confident that the estimated rate of return will prove accurate. Therefore, the prudent executive will adjust expected yields downward to compensate for risks, and be on the safe side in making investment decisions.) Other businesses make similar calculations. Thus, for the economy as a whole, those investment projects will be undertaken whose (risk-adjusted) rates of return (r) exceed the rate of interest (i).

---

*[5]The formula for this calculation is a close cousin of the bond formula in Box 11-1. Specifically, if a machine has a life of n years, then:

$$\text{Price of machine} = \frac{R_1}{1 + r} + \frac{R_2}{(1 + r)^2} + \ldots + \frac{R_n + S}{(1 + r)^n}$$

where R_1 is the return in the first year, measured in dollars; R_2 the return in the second year; etc.
S is the scrap value of the machine at the end of its life in year n
r is the rate of return (measured as a fraction or percentage)
If we know the price of the machine and estimate the R's and S, we can solve for r.
In our simple example of a machine with a 1-year life (in which we implicitly assumed a scrap value of zero at the end of the first year), this calculation is:

$$\$100,000 = \frac{R_1}{1 + r} = \frac{\$110,000}{1 + r}$$

$$r = 0.1 = 10\%$$

[6]These costs do not include interest paid on funds borrowed to buy the machine. Interest costs come into the decision-making process at a later point, as we shall soon see.

TABLE 12-1
Expected Return on Investment

	(1) Expected rate of return (r) (percent per annum)	(2) Amount of investment expected to yield at least the return in (1) (in billions)
A	12%	$ 65
B	10%	$ 80
C	8%	$100
D	6%	$125

This decision-making process is illustrated in Table 12-1 and Figure 12-2. In Table 12-1, all investment projects for the economy are ranked according to their expected rates of return. For example, the highest-ranked $65 billion in projects are expected to yield returns of 12 percent or

FIGURE 12-2   The marginal efficiency of investment: The investment demand curve.
The investment demand (or MEI) curve slopes downward to the right. At a lower interest rate, more investment projects are undertaken.

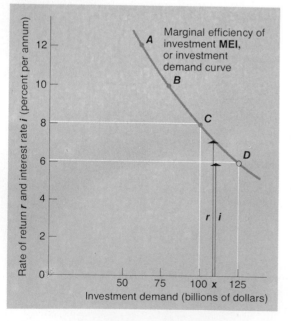

higher, and so all these projects will be undertaken if business can borrow at 12 percent or less. The next $15 billion in projects (for a cumulative total of $80 billion = $65 billion + $15 billion) will yield at least 10 percent, and so on. This schedule, commonly called the *marginal efficiency of investment* (MEI), is graphed in Figure 12-2. It shows how investment will increase as the interest rate falls. For example, if the interest rate is 8 percent, $100 billion of investment will be undertaken. (This amount yields at least an 8 percent rate of return.) But if the interest rate falls to 6 percent, investment will increase to $125 billion at point *D*. Therefore, a drop in the interest rate from 8 to 6 percent causes a $25-billion increase in investment.

The *marginal efficiency of investment* is the schedule or curve that shows possible investment projects, ranked according to their expected rates of return. It shows how much businesses will want to invest at various interest rates.

The advantage to businesses of undertaking additional investment when the interest rate falls from 8 to 6 percent may be seen more precisely by considering a specific project that ranks between *C* and *D*; for example, project *x*, which ranks in the 110th billion dollars of investment. The rate of return (*r*) on this project is just over 7 percent, as shown by the height of the MEI curve. With an interest rate (*i*) of only 6 percent, this project will more than cover interest costs. Consequently, it will add to profits. Similarly, the other projects between *C* and *D* become profitable when the interest rate falls from 8 to 6 percent.

The marginal efficiency of investment curve fits into the second step in the Keynesian approach to monetary policy, as illustrated in Figure 12-3.

Step 1
Open market purchase causes a fall in the interest rate

Step 2 Fall in interest rate causes increase in investment

r, i (%)

MEI

0

I_1

ΔI

Investment demand I

Investment increases

Step 3 The Multiplier

Investment (I), Saving (S)

ΔI

S

E_2

I_2

E_1

I_1

National product NP

NP_1 NP_2

Equilibrium national product increases by a multiple of the increase in investment. (This repeats the multiplier of Figure 8-14.)

FIGURE 12-3 How monetary policy works: Details on the Keynesian approach.
This figure fills out the details in Figure 12-1. In step 2, the amount of extra investment that is generated by a reduction in the interest rate depends on the MEI curve. In step 3, the multiplier effect of investment on national product depends on the marginal propensity to save (MPS); that is, the slope of the saving function. (Multiplier = 1/MPS) For details on step 1, see Box 12-1.

An expansive monetary policy operates as follows:

Step 1	Step 2	Step 3
Open market purchase→	Interest rate down→	Investment up→	National product up (the multiplier)

With a restrictive policy, the signs are the opposite:

Step 1	Step 2	Step 3
Open market sale→	Interest rate up→	Investment down→	National product down (the multiplier)

Problems with Monetary Policy

By this three-step process, open market operations can affect aggregate demand and national product. Why, then, the Keynesian skepticism regarding the possible effectiveness of monetary policy? The answer is: We cannot be sure that the responses at either of the first two steps will be very strong.

Keynes himself was particularly concerned that monetary policy would be ineffective at the very first step, and therefore could not be counted on as a way of getting out of the deep depression that existed when

the *General Theory* was written. Because the problem here is peculiar to a deep depression and has little relevance to the more normal conditions that have existed in recent decades, it is set aside in Box 12-1. The general point can, however, be summarized quite easily. During a deep depression, interest rates may be very low; for example, in the 2 to 3 percent range that prevailed during much of the Great Depression (as shown in Figure 6-2). In such circumstances, the ability of the Fed to push the rates down even further is not very great. Clearly, inter-

---

BOX 12-1
KEYNES ON THE INEFFECTIVENESS OF MONETARY POLICY DURING A DEPRESSION:

The Liquidity Trap

As we saw in Chapter 11, an open market purchase by the Federal Reserve involves a demand for a bond (or shorter-term government security). This increase in demand tends to pull up bond prices; that is, it pushes down interest rates. This short, direct explanation is all that is essential to fill in step 1 in the Keynesian monetary policy sequence shown in Figure 12-1—at least, it is all that is essential when discussing the past three decades, with their generally prosperous business conditions and their generally high interest rates.

But, to provide a complete explanation of Keynes' doubts about expansive monetary policy as a way of getting out of a depression, more detail is required. We need to look more closely at how monetary policy affects the rate of interest.

Keynes emphasized that the interest rate is a monetary phenomenon. The interest rate will reach its equilibrium, he maintained, when the demand and supply of money are equal; that is, when people are willing to hold the amount of money that exists in the economy.

One of the reasons that people hold money is to make purchases in the near future. The higher their incomes are, the more purchases they will plan to make, and the more money they will consequently want to hold. Thus, the demand for money depends partly on the size of national income.

But the demand for money also depends on the interest rate. Whenever money is held rather than used to buy a bond, the holder of money gives up the interest that could have been earned on a bond. If interest rates are very high, the treasurers of large corporations will try to keep as little money on hand as is conveniently possible, putting the rest into interest-earning securities. At an interest rate of 10 percent per annum, for example, $10 million earns $20,000 in interest per week—a tidy sum.

At lower rates of interest, less interest is forgone by holding money. Indeed, *if interest rates become very low, people may prefer to hold money rather than to buy bonds*. Why is this true? Because holding bonds is risky. If interest rates are very low, they may go up in the future. And, *when interest rates go up, the prices of bonds fall*.

---

est rates cannot be pushed all the way down to zero; at a zero interest rate, nobody would be willing to buy bonds. Indeed, as interest rates fall very low, bondholders increasingly consider bonds not worth holding for their very low returns, and they begin to unload them. Thus, the central bank can buy very large quantities of bonds while having only a minimal effect in pushing the interest rate down below its already low level. In such circumstances, expansive monetary policy fails in step 1.

In more normal times, open market op-erations can significantly affect the rate of interest, and the second step becomes the principal concern in the operation of mone-tary policy.

The Responsiveness of Investment to a Change in the Interest Rate

As Figure 12-2 is drawn, investment is quite responsive to a change in the rate of interest. For example, a fall in the interest rate from 8 to 6 percent will cause a 25 percent increase in investment demand, from $100 billion to $125 billion. An alter-

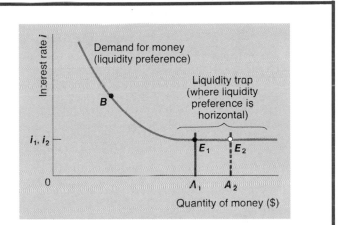

FIGURE 12-4 Monetary policy is in-effective (at step 1) if an increase in the quantity of money leaves the in-terest rate unaffected.

Just as it is unwise to hold General Motors stock if you think that its price will go down, so it is unwise to hold bonds if you think their prices are likely to fall

If interest rates get low enough, Keynes argued, people will be willing to hold *un-limited* amounts of money rather than take the risk of buying bonds. Thus, the demand for money—or, in Keynes' terminology, *liquidity preference*—becomes unlimited at low rates of interest, as shown by the flattening out of the curve in Figure 12-4.

Suppose that the economy is in a depression, and the rate of interest is already very low. The supply of money—that is, the amount of money in the economy (A_1)—intersects the demand (or liquidity preference) curve at initial equilibrium point E_1. Now suppose that the central bank increases the money stock to quantity A_2. What happens? The equilibrium between the demand and supply of money moves to E_2. At the old interest rate (i_1), people are willing to hold all the additional money rather than take the risk of buying any more bonds. The interest rate remains stuck; $i_2 = i_1$. The additional money is caught in the *liquidity trap* (the horizontal section of the liquidity preference curve). Because monetary policy cannot push down the rate of interest, an expansion of the money stock loses its punch.

Observe that this argument does not apply where interest rates initially are higher, for example at point *B*. Here, a change in the quantity of money will affect the interest rate, and monetary policy will get over the hurdle at the first step.

FIGURE 12-5 Monetary policy is ineffective (at step 2) if an interest rate reduction has little effect on investment.
If the MEI curve is steep, investment will not increase much when the interest rate falls. Therefore, the effect of monetary policy on aggregate demand is not very powerful.

native possibility is illustrated in Figure 12-5. Here, the investment demand (MEI) curve falls much more steeply than it did in Figure 12-2. Now, even with a sharp drop in the interest rate from 8 to 6 percent, investment is not increased very much by the expansive monetary policy—only by $5 billion.

The possibility that investment might be quite unresponsive to changes in interest rates was of considerable concern to economists during the 1940s and 1950s. Early studies of the MEI schedule suggested that it might, in fact, be almost vertical. Thus, in contrast with Keynes, who believed that monetary policy might be ineffective during a depression because of our inability to lower interest rates very much (step 1), some of his followers developed even broader skepticism regarding monetary policy. Even

if interest rates could be changed, they doubted that investment would be greatly affected (step 2). Thus, they doubted that monetary policy could be counted on to play much more than a secondary, supporting role to the main tool, namely, fiscal policy.

During the last two decades, there has been a movement back toward a more central position; the early fears that monetary policy is ineffective have dissipated somewhat. The early evidence that investment does not respond much to interest rates has not provided a conclusive case for dismissing the effects of monetary policy on investment, for two major reasons.

1. Statistical Problems in Measuring the Interest-Responsiveness of Investment Demand
First, it is not clear that the early studies were correct in concluding that interest rates do not affect investment demand very much. It is surprisingly difficult to identify the effects of interest rates on investment because so many other important changes are occurring at the same time. If investment doesn't fall much as the interest rate rises, there are two possible explanations: (1) The interest rate has little effect on investment (as early studies concluded); or (2) investment is influenced by the interest rate, but there are other offsetting influences. For example, investment may remain high or even rise during a period when rising interest rates are tending to depress it, because at the same time investment is being stimulated by increasing business optimism.[7] Investment may be very sensitive both to interest rate changes and to changes in business optimism, but you can't show the effect of either by looking only at how investment changes. More recent statistical work indicates that the early studies did not adequately deal with this complication, and consequently underestimated the responsiveness of investment to the rate of interest.

[7]Indeed, increased business optimism and rising interest rates do tend to occur at the same time. When business executives are optimistic, they are willing to bid up interest rates in order to acquire funds for expansion.

2. Credit Rationing: The Availability of Loanable Funds Furthermore, it is possible that investment might be affected by monetary policy even when investment demand is very unresponsive to changes in the rate of interest. This is illustrated with the use of Figure 12-6, which repeats the steep MEI curve of Figure 12-5.

Suppose that the initial equilibrium is at *A*, with $100 billion in investment. The central bank introduces a restrictive monetary policy: By selling securities on the open market, it pushes up interest rates and reduces commercial bank reserves. If the commercial banks initially have little or no excess reserves, they will be forced to cut back on their loans and other earning assets.

But we are assuming that even with higher interest rates—at, say, 10 percent rather than the original 8 percent—businesses are still quite eager to borrow and to invest; they are not discouraged much by the higher rate of interest. (In Figure 12-6, their demand to invest at *B* is $96 billion, almost as much as at *A*.) Banks will simply not be able to lend businesses as much as the businesses want, since to do so would run the banks down below their required reserve ratios. To protect their reserve positions, banks begin to refuse loan requests. In other words, they *ration* their available funds, lending less than credit-worthy customers want to borrow.

> *Credit rationing* occurs when banks are short of loanable funds. They therefore lend less than they would like to (if they had the funds), and less than credit-worthy borrowers want to borrow.

When this happens, investment is reduced, not because businesses show a lack of desire to invest, but because they are *unable to obtain financing.* The actual quantity of investment consequently falls short of the amount that businesses would like; the quantity of investment at *C* is to the left of

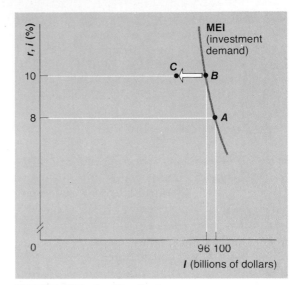

FIGURE 12-6 Credit rationing.
When the Federal Reserve reduces the quantity of bank reserves by an open market sale, commercial banks must reduce their loans or other earning assets to meet reserve requirements. As a consequence, they may ration credit, lending less than borrowers want and less than the banks would be willing to lend if they had ample reserves. Because of an inability to borrow, businesses are forced to cut back on investment. The effects of credit rationing are shown by distance *BC.*

the marginal efficiency of investment (MEI) curve. (This curve shows how much businesses will invest when they are able to obtain financing.) The distance *CB* reflects investment that doesn't occur because of the unavailability of funds. Thus, restrictive monetary policy works not only because of the discouraging effect of higher interest rates on investment (shown by the movement from *A* to *B*), but also because businesses are unable to invest because they cannot get funds (the movement from *B* to *C*).

The Asymmetrical Effect of Monetary Policy

A change in the availability of bank loans can contribute to the effectiveness of monetary policy as a tool for controlling aggregate demand. But it also adds to the list of reasons why monetary policy may be more effective in restraining aggregate demand during inflationary periods than in expanding demand during a recession. Specifically, there are three reasons why *restrictive* monetary policies may be more effective than *expansive* policies:

1. The Fed can be more confident of its ability to push interest rates up than of its ability to push them down. If interest rates are already low, the Federal Reserve may be unable to push them down very much further; interest rates cannot go to zero. On the other hand, there is no such limit on the height to which interest rates can be pushed by restrictive monetary policies.

2. Open market purchases by the Federal Reserve increase bank reserves, and thus make additional bank loans and an increase in the money stock *possible*. But the Fed cannot *force* the banks to lend. Indeed, when they were frightened during the Depression of the 1930s, banks held large quantities of excess reserves. On the other hand, banks *must* respond when open market sales reduce their reserves below the legally required ratio. They are forced to reduce their holdings of loans and securities, thus cutting back on the money stock.

3. A tight monetary policy can work by causing credit rationing. Businesses may be unable to borrow to finance investments, and thus may be pushed to a point to the left of the MEI curve (Figure 12-6). But the opposite is not true. No matter how expansive monetary policies become, businesses cannot be forced to borrow more than they want; they cannot be forced to a point to the right of the MEI curve.

Because of these asymmetries, monetary policy is sometimes compared to controlling investment demand with a string. If restrictive policies are adopted, the string tightens; investment is firmly drawn back. But the effects of expansive policies are much less certain. An expansive push on the monetary policy string makes an increase in investment possible. If the demand for investment is strong, investment in fact expands, keeping the string taut. In this case, monetary policy is powerful. But if business executives are pessimistic, they may not respond much to easier monetary conditions. They borrow little more, if any. Investment remains stagnant. The string goes limp. Monetary policy aimed at stimulating aggregate demand has little effect.

MONETARY POLICY: The Classical View

In contrast to Keynes, who started his analysis of aggregate demand by looking at its components (consumption, investment, government purchases of goods and services, and net exports), classical economists began from quite a different starting point. Their analysis was based on the *equation of exchange*:

$$MV = PQ \qquad (12\text{-}1)$$

where M = quantity of money in the hands of the public

P = average level of prices

Q = quantity of output (that is, real national product or real national income)[8]

Thus, PQ = national income or product, measured in nominal (dollar) terms

---

[8] In basic theoretical discussions, the fine points of the distinction between national product and national income are ignored, and the two terms are used interchangeably.

Besides Equation (12-1), there was also another version of the equation of exchange. This alternative version focused on total transactions (including intermediate sales), rather than just on the final payments included in national product. Here, we concentrate on the final-payments (or income) version of the equation of exchange, as it leads to the simplest comparisons between Keynesian and classical theory.

and   *V = income velocity of money,* that is, the average number of times that the money stock (*M*) is spent to buy final output during a year. Specifically, *V* is defined as being equal to *PQ/M*.

Suppose that the money stock is $100 billion. Assume that, in the course of a year, the average dollar bill and the average demand deposit are spent four times to purchase final goods and services. In other words, *V* is 4. Then, $100 billion times 4, or $400 billion, is the total spending for final output; aggregate demand (*MV*) equals $400 billion. In turn, this total spending (*MV*) equals the total quantity of goods and services (*Q*) times the average price (*P*) at which they were sold.

But how can the same dollar be used over and over to purchase final goods? Very simply. When you purchase groceries at the store, the $50 you pay does not disappear. Rather, it goes into the cash register of the store. From there, it is used to pay the farmer for fresh vegetables, the canning factory for canned goods, or the clerk's wages. The farmer or the clerk or the employee of the canning factory will in turn use the money to purchase goods. Once more, the money is used for final purchases. The same dollar bill can circulate round and round, adding to aggregate demand every time it is spent for final output.

The Quantity Theory of Money

The equation of exchange, by itself, does not get us very far, because it is a *tautology* or *truism*. That is, it must be true because of the way the terms are defined. Note that velocity is defined as *V = PQ/M*. Thus, by definition, *MV = PQ*. (Just multiply both sides of the first equation by *M*.)

But in the hands of classical economists, the equation of exchange became more than a tautology; it became the basis of an important theory. This theory—the *quantity theory of money*—was based on the proposition that *velocity (V) is reasonably stable.*

> The *quantity theory of money* is the proposition that velocity (*V*) is reasonably stable. Therefore, a change in the quantity of money (*M*) will cause nominal national product (*PQ*) to change by approximately the same percentage.

If, for example, the money stock (*M*) increases by 20 percent, then classical economists argue that velocity (*V*) will remain reasonably stable. As a consequence, nominal national product (*PQ*) will also rise by about 20 percent. In other words, a central proposition of classical economics is this:

1. A change in the quantity of money (*M*) is the key to changes in aggregate demand. A change in *M* will cause an approximately proportional change in nominal national product (*PQ*).

Those in the classical tradition also argue that:

2. In the long run (over periods of years and decades), real output (*Q*) tends to move toward the full-employment, capacity level.[9] Therefore, the long-run effect of a change in *M* is on *P*, not on *Q*. Most notably, a rapid increase in the quantity of money causes a rapid inflation.

3. In the short run (over periods of months or quarters), a change in *M* can have a substantial effect on both *P* and *Q*. For example, a decline in the quantity of money can cause a decline in output (*Q*) and the onset of a recession. And a rapid rate of growth of *M* can move a depressed economy back toward full employment, with *Q* rising.

[9]This classical proposition was explained in Box 8-1.

4. Monetary disturbances tend to be a major cause of unstable aggregate demand and of business cycles. If M is kept stable, a market economy will be quite stable.

5. Thus, the major macroeconomic responsibility of the authorities is to provide a stable money supply. Specifically, the money supply should be steadily increased at a rate that is adequate to buy the full-employment output of the economy at stable prices. As the capacity of the economy grows at something like 4 percent per annum, economists in the classical tradition argue that the authorities should adhere to a *monetary rule, increasing the money stock steadily at a rate of about 4 percent per annum.*

Because of their emphasis on money, modern economists who follow the classical tradition are frequently referred to as *monetarists.* Of these, Nobel prizewinner Milton Friedman is the most famous. Some of the main points of difference between Keynesians and monetarists are summarized in Box 12-2, although it is important to recognize that many present-day economists take an intermediate viewpoint.

Why Should Velocity Be Stable? The Demand for Money

The quantity theory may be traced back over 200 years, at least as far back as the essays on money and the balance of trade by British philosopher David Hume in the early eighteenth century. The early quantity theorists attributed the inflation of the time to the inflow of gold and silver money from the New World. The exact mechanism by which money affected aggregate demand and prices was not spelled out in detail by these early theorists. They believed that it was self-evident that, when people have more money, they tend to spend more. And when they spend more, with more money chasing a relatively fixed quantity of goods, prices rise.

More recently, and particularly in response to the Keynesian attack, classical economists have been more explicit about their theory. Velocity is stable, they argue, because there is a stable demand for money.

Specifically, people hold money because they want to purchase goods or services in the coming days or weeks. Money is held temporarily to bridge the time interval between the receipt of income and the payment of bills or the purchase of goods and services. The higher are people's incomes, the more money they will want to hold to make purchases. Similarly, the amount of money that a business firm wants to hold to pay its workers and suppliers depends on the size of its operations. Thus, the demand for money depends on the size of national product. And it is national product in current dollars (that is, PQ rather than simply Q) that is important in determining the demand for money. If prices are high, people will want to hold a lot of money to pay for expensive goods and services.

The demand for money shown in Figure 12-7 illustrates this relationship. The higher is current-dollar or nominal national product (measured up the vertical axis), the greater is the quantity of money demanded (measured along the horizontal axis). Suppose that the actual amount of money in the economy is initially at A_1, and the current-dollar national product is at B_1. Then the demand and supply of money will be in equilibrium, at point E_1. The quantity of money demanded, measured by the distance B_1E_1, will be equal to the quantity of money (A_1) actually in existence.

Now, suppose that an expansive monetary policy is followed, with the money supply increasing to A_2. At the existing national product (B_1), the stock of money that people have (B_1C) is greater than the amount they are willing to hold (B_1E_1); there is a temporary surplus of money of E_1C. With more money than they want, people spend it to buy more goods and services;

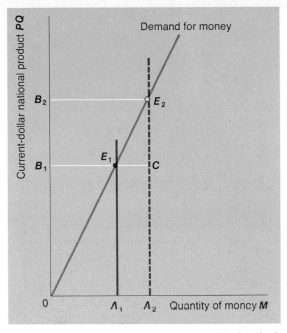

FIGURE 12-7 The demand for money: A classical view.
Those in the classical tradition argue that the demand for money is stable and depends primarily on current-dollar national product. If the stock of money which people hold exceeds the demand for money, then people will increase their spending.

aggregate demand goes up. If the economy is initially in a depression, with large amounts of excess capacity, output (Q) will respond strongly to the increase in money. But if the economy is already at or near full employment, the effect of an increase in aggregate demand will be a rise in prices (P). In either case, current-dollar national product (PQ) will go up. As this happens, people become willing to hold more money. The process continues until current-dollar national product rises to B_2, where the quantity of money and the demand for it are again in equilibrium at E_2. A change in the quantity of money tends to cause a proportional change in national product. Thus, the quantity theory of money is based on the view that there is a stable demand for money, similar to that shown in Figure 12-7. This is the theoretical underpinning of the proposition that velocity (V) is stable in the equation $MV = PQ$.[10]

CLASSICAL DOUBTS ABOUT FISCAL POLICY: Crowding Out

Classical economists emphasized the importance of money as a determinant of aggregate demand. Their views on fiscal policy were less unanimous. During the Great Depression of the 1930s, some of them recommended substantial increases in government spending as a way of increasing demand, output, and employment.[11] Others were quite skeptical about the effects of fiscal policy. For example, the British Treasury opposed additional government spending on the ground that it would do no good, since it would merely displace or *crowd out* private investment demand. (One of Keynes'

*[10]In Figure 12-7, the line showing the demand for money has a constant slope, and that slope is the velocity of money (V).

Here's why. The equation for the money demand line in Figure 12-7 may be written:

$$PQ = kM$$

where k is the slope of the line.

Therefore: $k = \dfrac{PQ}{M}$

which by definition equals V.

In other words, classical economists argue that V is stable because the demand for money approximates a straight line, such as the one shown in Figure 12-7.

[11]On fiscal policy views during the Depression, see J. R. Davis, "Chicago Economists, Budget Deficits, and the Early 1930s," *American Economic Review*, June 1968; and Herbert Stein, *The Fiscal Revolution in America* (Chicago: University of Chicago Press, 1969).

KEYNESIANS AND MONETARISTS:
Some Key Differences

In a complex debate with many participants, it is hard to summarize all the points at issue. But here are three of them (with references to where they are discussed in more detail).

Issue	Keynesian View	Monetarist View
1. Key to controlling aggregate demand	Fiscal policy (Chapter 9)	Monetary policy (Chapter 12)
2. Performance of market economy	(a) Market economy may reach long-lasting equilibrium with high levels of unemployment (Chapter 8).	(a) Market economy tends toward full employment in the long run (Box 8-1 and Chapter 13).
	(b) Market economy tends to be unstable (Chapter 14).	(b) Market economy tends to be reasonably stable at full employment *if* money growth is stable (Chapters 14 and 15).
3. Policy conclusions	Government has the responsibility to actively manage aggregate demand (primarily through fiscal policy) in order to: (a) get the economy up to the full-employment level, and then: (b) offset unstable movements in private sectors of economy, in order to keep the economy on a stable, full-employment growth path (Chapters 8 and 15).	Authorities should adhere to a monetary *rule*, increasing *M* steadily at the rate of growth of productive capacity (Chapter 15).

principal objectives in writing the *General Theory* was to combat this British Treasury view.) More recently, a similar position was taken by the United States Treasury during Gerald Ford's presidency. Treasury Secretary William Simon opposed tax cuts because he believed that larger government deficits would cause a decline in private investment demand.

> *Crowding out* occurs when an expansive fiscal policy (involving an increase in government spending or a cut in taxes) results in a fall in private investment demand.

Expansive fiscal policies may crowd out investment demand in the following way. When the government increases its expenditures or cuts taxes, its deficits rise. It therefore goes to the financial markets to borrow the money to cover the deficits. This additional borrowing tends to push up the interest rate. A higher interest rate, in turn, causes a movement along the marginal efficiency of investment (MEI) curve; investment demand decreases (Figure 12-8).

There is little question that some crowding out takes place; the issue is how strong the effect is. Keynesian economists tend to argue that investment demand is relatively unresponsive to interest rates (Figure 12-5), and that not much crowding out of investment takes place. Consequently, fiscal policy is a powerful tool for controlling aggregate demand (and monetary policy is weak). Monetarists, on the other hand, generally believe that the MEI curve is relatively flat (as shown in Figure 12-8), and that deficit spending by the government

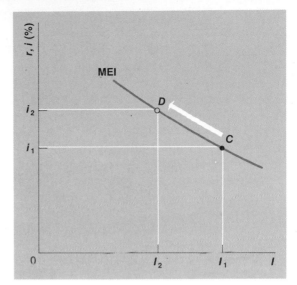

FIGURE 12-8   Crowding out: The monetarist view. Government deficits may push up the interest rate—from i_1 to i_2, for example. This causes a movement along the MEI curve from C to D, and investment demand decreases from I_1 to I_2.

tends to crowd out a relatively large amount of private investment.

In casting doubt on the effectiveness of fiscal policies, monetarists make one important qualification. If the government deficit is financed by issuing new money,[12] fiscal policy will have a powerful effect on demand. But monetarists attribute this effect to a change in the money stock, not to the government deficit itself. They see *pure fiscal policy* as having little effect on demand.

> *Pure fiscal policy* involves a change in government spending or tax rates, unaccompanied by any change in the rate of growth of the money stock.

---

[12]This obviously occurs if the government takes the line of least resistance and prints the money to cover its deficit. (This has not been a common practice in the United States, although it was done by both sides in the Civil War.)

There is also a more complicated route by which a government deficit can cause an increase in the money stock. When the government borrows to finance its deficit, interest rates tend to be pushed up and bond prices to be pushed down. The central bank may take steps to stabilize interest rates and bond prices. It can do so by purchasing government bonds on the open market. But open market purchases will increase the money stock by the process explained in Chapter 11.

STATISTICAL EVIDENCE

There is a sharp, clear difference of opinion between monetarists and Keynesians. To summarize: Monetarists argue that velocity is stable and that money is therefore the key to changes in aggregate demand. Some monetarists also argue that pure fiscal policy has little effect on aggregate demand. In contrast, Keynesians argue that fiscal policy has a powerful impact on aggregate demand; that velocity tends to be quite unstable;[13] and that monetary policy is less important than fiscal policy as a tool for controlling aggregate demand.

It would seem easy to settle this dispute. Simply look at the facts and see which theory is most in line with the observations of the real world. Unfortunately, this is easier said than done. We have already noted that there are problems in determining the slope of the marginal efficiency of investment schedule, one of the points at issue between Keynesians and monetarists. The difficulties in evaluating the facts may be understood more clearly by considering the full-scale counterattack on Keynesian economics launched by monetarists during the 1960s.

This counterattack was supported by two major statistical studies, the first by Milton Friedman and David Meiselman,

and the second by a group of economists at the Federal Reserve Bank of St. Louis.[14] The monetarists argued that Keynesian economics had been accepted and classical theory rejected on the basis of the theoretical case put forward in the *General Theory.* Yet nobody had stopped to study the facts seriously. It was true that considerable statistical work had been done to estimate the position and slope of the major functions that were featured in Keynesian theory, particularly the consumption function. But nobody had done a *comparative* study to find out which was more consistent with the facts—the classical theory or the Keynesian theory. The time had come, said Friedman and Meiselman, for somebody to conduct such a study. This they proposed to do.

The centerpiece of classical theory was the velocity of money; classical theory was based on the premise that velocity is reasonably stable. The central theoretical tool of Keynesian analysis was the marginal propensity to consume (MPC) and its algebraic cousin, the multiplier. For Keynesian policies to be useful, the MPC and the multiplier must be reasonably stable and predictable. According to Friedman and Meiselman, therefore, the debate came down to a basic question: Which is more stable, velocity or the multiplier? Looking at the statistical evidence for 1897 through 1958, they found the results to be "remark-

---

*[13]Keynes believed that velocity tends to be particularly pliable and variable during a depression. Reconsider the figure in Box 12-1. As the amount of money increases from A_1 to A_2, it is caught in the liquidity trap. People hold the additional money as idle balances. No change takes place in the interest rate, investment, or national product. In terms of the equation of exchange, PQ remains constant. But M is rising. What, then, is happening? The answer: Velocity is falling as fast as M is increasing, leaving PQ unchanged.

(Note that Keynes did not deny the equation of exchange. How could he, as velocity was defined in such a way that the equation was true by definition? But he believed that it was not *enlightening* as a way to analyze aggregate demand, because V can be unstable. Thus, he denied the basic proposition of the quantity theory. He argued that the best way to analyze demand was by looking at its major components: C, I, G, and net exports.)

[14]Milton Friedman and David Meiselman, "The Relative Stability of Monetary Velocity and the Investment Multiplier in the United States," in Commission on Money and Credit, *Stabilization Policies* (Englewood Cliffs, N.J.: Prentice-Hall, 1963), pp. 168–268; and Leonall C. Andersen and Jerry Jordan, "Monetary and Fiscal Actions: A Test of Their Relative Importance in Economic Stabilization," *Federal Reserve Bank of St. Louis Review,* November 1968, pp. 11–16.

The monetarist views of the St. Louis Fed are not shared by other parts of the Federal Reserve System. Indeed, at other Federal Reserve Banks and at the Federal Reserve Board in Washington, D.C., the St. Louis approach is sometimes referred to as "Brand X."

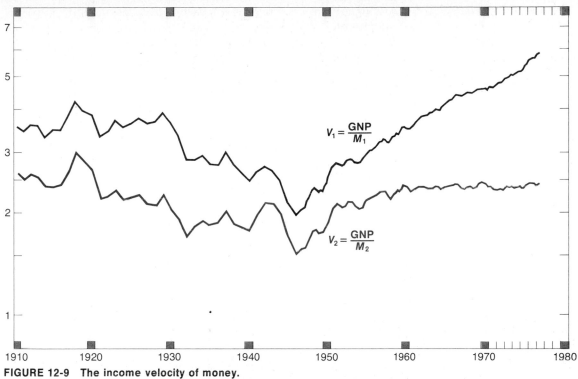

FIGURE 12-9 The income velocity of money.
The income velocity of money is the ratio of national product to the quantity of money. If M_1 (currency plus demand deposits) is taken as the definition of money, then there has been an upward trend in velocity (V_1) since the late 1940s. If M_2 (M_1 plus savings and time deposits) is taken as the definition of money, then velocity (V_2) has been quite stable for the past two decades.

ably consistent and unambiguous." The velocity of money was found to be decidedly more stable than the multiplier throughout that six-decade period—with one notable exception: the decade of the depressed 1930s. [Observe in Figure 12-9 that velocity dropped sharply as the economy collapsed into the Depression. This is true whether money is defined narrowly as currency and demand deposits (M_1), or more broadly to include time deposits (M_2).] The conclusion indicated by the Friedman-Meiselman results: Keynes' theory was not a "general" theory at all.[15] Rather, it was a specific

theory with relevance to the thirties. In the long-run test between Keynesian and classical economics, Friedman and Meiselman declared the classical theory to be the clear winner. Similar results were obtained by the St. Louis Fed.

Problems of Interpretation
Needless to say, these results did not persuade the partisans of the Keynesian viewpoint to give up their positions; the monetarist studies were vulnerable to counterattack. Most important, perhaps, was a fundamental problem that bedevils *any* sta-

[15]Keynes called his theory "general" because it dealt with conditions both of full employment and of large-scale unemployment. In contrast, he considered the classical theory "special," since it applied only to a fully employed economy.

tistical test of a theory. A theory is usually in the form of a cause-and-effect statement: "If the money stock is increased, this will cause an increase in aggregate demand"; or, to take an illustration from simple microeconomic theory, "If the price of a good rises, then consumers will, as a consequence, buy a smaller quantity." Yet, statistical evidence is merely a series of observations. The observed facts regarding money, aggregate demand, prices, and quantities purchased tell us simply *what* has happened, not *why* it has happened. Statistics do not show what caused what; they show only what things have happened together.

For example, if we observe that two items (*A* and *B*) are closely related, both rising and falling together, this observation does not, in itself, permit us to decide whether (1) *A* caused *B*, or (2) *B* caused *A*. (It is also possible that both *A* and *B* were caused by a third item, *C*.)

Now consider the Friedman-Meiselman and St. Louis statistical results. They found that changes in the quantity of money (*M*) and changes in nominal national product (*PQ*) were closely related over the period of six decades that they studied. They therefore concluded that the quantity theory was indeed upheld, that changes in the stock of money had a powerful and predictable effect on aggregate demand. What was the response of their critics? That no such powerful causal relationship had been demonstrated. While aggregate demand and changes in the quantity of money are indeed related, a significant part of this relationship is possibly the result of causation in the opposite direction. That is, *changes in aggregate demand can cause changes in the money supply.*

How could this be so? Consider an important, and relatively volatile, component of aggregate demand, namely investment. Suppose that businesses become optimistic regarding their future prospects, and decide to order new equipment. In order to finance their investment, they go to their banks, which respond by granting loans. The statistics will show an increase in investment and an increase in the money stock. But the driving force is the decision of businesses to invest, not the decision of the banking system to increase the quantity of money. So say the critics of Friedman and Meiselman.[16]

The Uncertain Lesson of Recent History

The difficulty of deciding that one theory is right and the other theory is wrong is increased by the conflicting lessons that may be drawn from recent history.

From the viewpoint of their proponents, the monetarist studies appeared at a good time. The events of the late 1960s tended to confirm the quantity theory and to cast doubts on the Keynesian view. In mid-1968, Congress imposed an income tax surcharge and placed a limitation on federal government spending in order to cool down the inflation generated by the Vietnam conflict. Economists using the Keynesian approach

---

[16]In this illustration, where the desire of businesses to invest causes an increase in the quantity of money, it is possible that the money stock will grow *before* the investment takes place; businesses may line up financing before the construction actually gets under way. Thus, even if the increase in the money supply occurs first, it may still be the effect rather than the cause. This point has been stressed by James Tobin, "Money and Income: Post Hoc Ergo Propter Hoc?" *Quarterly Journal of Economics*, May 1970, pp. 301–317. (Translation of the Latin title: "After This, Therefore on Account of This?")

Of course, it may be argued that the causal relationship is even more complicated than we have suggested. In the above example, the desire to invest led to borrowing and an increase in the money supply. But what would have happened if businesses had been unable to borrow? Would they have delayed or cut back on their planned investment? If so, there is a complex cause-effect relationship between investment and changes in the quantity of money. Investment causes changes in the quantity of money. But it is also true that changes in *M* cause investment in the sense that, without the change in *M*, the investment would not occur.

expected a powerful restrictive effect on aggregate demand. Indeed, there were fears that the Congress had engaged in "fiscal overkill" and that a recession would be caused by the sharp shift toward fiscal restraint. In order to soften the expected recession, the Federal Reserve eased monetary policy, allowing a rapid rate of growth of the money stock. (M_1 grew at an annual rate of almost 8 percent in the last half of 1968.) Thus, monetary policy was expansive, while fiscal policy was restrictive. And what happened? The economy followed the path set by monetary policy and continued to boom throughout late 1968. Indeed, the boom continued until after monetary policy was shifted sharply toward restraint in early 1969. Monetarists seemed vindicated, and Keynesians were shaken in their beliefs. Indeed, in the words of Profs. Alan Blinder and Robert Solow, the events of 1968 and 1969 threatened to send Keynesian economic advisers "scurrying back to their universities with their doctrinal tales [sic] between their legs."[17]

But the monetarist triumph was short-lived. By the early 1970s, the economy was not behaving the way the quantity theory said it should. And in 1975, a strong upswing in GNP took place in spite of a slow growth in the money stock. According to the quantity theory, this strong upswing should not have occurred with so little increase in the quantity of money—"the case of the missing money," in the words of Princeton's Stephen Goldfeld.[18] Recent history has not been kind to doctrinaire economists, whether Keynesian or monetarist.

THE CASE FOR USING MONETARY AND FISCAL POLICIES TOGETHER

The evidence provides little comfort for extreme Keynesians who focus their attention on fiscal policy and dismiss monetary policy as a "mirage and a delusion." And it provides little support to the rigid monetarists who see the quantity of money playing a predominant role in the determination of aggregate demand, irrespective of what is happening to fiscal policy.

Because we cannot count with any degree of certainty on the use of fiscal policy alone or monetary policy alone, there is a strong case to be made for using a combined strategy of monetary and fiscal expansion to combat recessions, and a combined strategy of monetary and fiscal restraint to fight inflation. By not putting all our eggs in one basket, we may reduce the uncertainty we would face if we were to rely exclusively on either monetary or fiscal policy.[19]

Furthermore, there are other reasons for favoring a combined monetary-fiscal strategy. During a boom in aggregate demand, restrictive steps are desirable. But restrictive actions are painful. A cut in government spending reduces programs that benefit various groups in the economy. An increase in taxes is clearly unpalatable. And a tighter monetary policy, involving higher interest rates and a reduced availability of loanable funds, can put a squeeze on housing construction and other types of investment. By using a combination of policies, the effect of each may be kept moderate and the adverse impacts diffused. Thus, we may avoid plac-

[17]Alan Blinder and Robert Solow, "Analytical Foundations of Fiscal Policy," in Blinder, Solow, and others, *The Economics of Public Finance* (Washington, D.C.: The Brookings Institution, 1974), p. 10.

[18]Stephen M. Goldfeld, "The Case of the Missing Money," *Brookings Papers on Economic Activity*, 1976, vol. 3, pp. 683–730.

[19]This intuitively plausible conclusion (that uncertainty is reduced by a combined use of both policy tools) requires statistical theory for a formal proof. Those with statistical training are referred to such a proof in William Brainard, "Uncertainty and the Effectiveness of Policy," *American Economic Review*, May 1967, pp. 411–425.

ing a very heavy burden on any single segment of the economy.

Similarly, a combined strategy is appropriate when expansion is needed. The problem of exclusive reliance on monetary policy as an expansive tool was noted earlier. If business executives are deeply pessimistic during a deep recession, expansive monetary policies may involve "pushing on a string." Monetary policies make additional investment possible, but they do not guarantee that it will take place. By using some fiscal expansion too, the chances of a recovery may be enhanced. But it is not desirable to place exclusive reliance on fiscal policies. In particular, it is undesirable to make increases in government spending the centerpiece of expansive aggregate demand policies. Spending programs undertaken today to expand aggregate demand will create a group of beneficiaries who, tomorrow, will strongly resist cutbacks in spending. Thus, programs undertaken today may be continued in the future, when stimulus is no longer needed and when, indeed, excess demand and inflation are becoming the principal macroeconomic problem.

A Complication: The Monetary-Fiscal Policy Mix and Economic Growth

But if the case for a combined monetary-fiscal strategy is strong, the way in which the two policies are fitted together can create adverse side effects. In particular, the rate of growth may be depressed. This danger arises both because of the way in which policy-making bodies have been set up in Washington (and also in other capitals), and because of the legacy of the Keynesian-classical debate.

Fiscal policies are in the hands of Congress and the President—decision-makers who are directly dependent on the public for their reelection. In the development of democracy, the power of the people's representatives over the budget represented an historic milestone. On the other hand, mon-

etary policies are in the hands of the Federal Reserve. Although the members of the Federal Reserve Board are nominated by the President and confirmed by Congress, and in this sense are responsible officials, they are one step removed from public accountability. This arrangement was no accident. The history of runaway inflations illustrated the danger of having the government itself create currency. Direct government control of the printing presses can create a powerful temptation for irresponsible spending. Thus, the Federal Reserve has been granted a degree of independence in its day-to-day operations as a way of strengthening its ability to combat inflation and maintain the value of the dollar.

Because fiscal policies are in the hands of politicians under constant pressures from their constituents for new programs and lower taxes, fiscal policies tend to be expansive. The central bank tends to be the major force for restraint; it may see its activities as the "only anti-inflationary game in town."

This division between fiscal and monetary policies is reinforced by the historic debate between Keynesians and classical economists. Keynes argued that aggregate demand in a market economy would frequently fall below the full-employment level, and that expansive fiscal policies were the way to deal with this problem. As a general rule, economists who specialize in fiscal policy are heavily influenced by Keynesian theory and put more emphasis on the goal of full employment than on the goal of price stability. When in doubt, they lean toward expansive policies. (Of course, numerous exceptions might be cited, but this is nevertheless true as a broad generalization.) On the other hand, monetary specialists tend to be more heavily influenced by classical economics and the quantity theory, with its emphasis on long-run policy making and its belief that the principal long-run effect of more expansive demand policies is on the price level (P) rather than on the quantity of real output (Q). Thus, monetary economists tend to stress the need for restraint (again, with numerous exceptions).

But what is the consequence of a policy mix that tends to combine fiscal expansion (government deficits) and monetary restraint (a low growth of M)? With the government having to borrow heavily on the bond market to cover its deficits and the central bank holding a tight rein on the money stock, interest rates are kept high. As a result, investment is discouraged. To put the same point somewhat differently, a portion of private saving is used to cover deficit spending by the government, rather than being used to finance investment. The rate of growth is depressed.

It is not clear exactly what can be done about this problem. One way of dealing with it is close consultation among the executive branch, the legislature, and the central bank in order to develop an overall package of monetary and fiscal policies that are conducive to growth. And, indeed, close contact and consultation does take place among representatives of the Treasury Department, the President's Council of Economic Advisers, the Office of Management and Budget, the Federal Reserve, and congressional committees. But each institution is subject to its own particular pressures. As a consequence, the effect on growth exerted by the monetary-fiscal policy mix may be expected to continue to be as important an issue in American economic policy in the future as it has been in the past.

Key Points

1. Most economists believe that fiscal and monetary policies both have substantial effects on aggregate demand. However, there is also a strong Keynesian tradition that puts the overwhelming emphasis on fiscal policy, while dismissing monetary policy as relatively unimportant. On the other side, there is a strong quantity theory (monetarist) view that money is the predominant force determining aggregate demand, and that fiscal policy has little effect.

2. Keynes proposed that the effects of monetary policy be analyzed by looking at three steps:
(1) The effect of monetary policy on the rate of interest
(2) The effect of the interest rate on investment
(3) The effect of a change in investment on aggregate demand (the multiplier)

3. Keynes himself believed that expansive monetary policies could not be counted on to get the economy out of the Depression of the 1930s because of a problem at the very first step. Interest rates were already very low, and could not be pushed down much further by an expansive monetary policy.

4. Some followers of Keynes had more general doubts about the effectiveness of monetary policies—not just in a depression, but also in more normal times. Specifically, they argued that a problem would arise at step 2 because investment is not very responsive to changes in the rate of interest. That is, the MEI schedule is steep (as shown in Figure 12-5).

5. But even if the MEI schedule is steep, restrictive monetary policies may reduce investment and aggregate demand by forcing banks to ration their loans.

6. Monetary policy may be more effective in restraining aggregate demand than in raising it. Monetary policy has been compared to controlling investment with a string.

7. Classical macroeconomics was based on the equation of exchange ($MV = PQ$) and on the proposition that velocity is stable (the quantity theory). Therefore, a change in M will cause current-dollar national product (PQ) to change by approximately the same percentage.

8. Classical economists believed that, in the long run, the principal effect of a change in the rate of growth of M would be a change in P (the price level). But in the short run, changes in the growth of M could also affect Q (real national product).

9. Indeed, those in the classical tradition believe that monetary disturbances are one of the principal causes of fluctuations in real output.

10. The view that velocity is stable is based on the belief that there is a stable demand for money. If, after a period of equilibrium, people get more money, their holdings of money will initially exceed their demand for it (Figure 12-7). They will use the surplus to buy goods and services, thus increasing current-dollar national product (PQ).

11. Some of those in the classical tradition doubt that fiscal policy will have a substantial effect on aggregate demand, unless the fiscal policy is accompanied by changes in M. (That is, they have doubts about *pure* fiscal policy.) These doubts are based on the belief that an increase in deficit spending will push up interest rates and therefore crowd out private investment.

12. Statistical evidence does not give a clear, unambiguous confirmation of either the strong Keynesian or the strong classical view. At times (for example, 1968), the evidence tends to support the quantity theory, and at other times (as in 1975), the evidence tends to contradict it.

13. Because of this (and for other reasons, too), it is undesirable to place exclusive reliance on either monetary or fiscal policies. Instead, it is wiser to use a combined monetary-fiscal strategy.

14. Because fiscal policy is made by elected politicians while monetary policy is made by the central bank, there is a tendency for fiscal policies to be expansive, while the burden of restraint falls on monetary policies. Because this combination means high interest rates, it tends to discourage investment and economic growth.

Key Concepts

marginal efficiency of investment (**MEI**)
rate of return
investment unresponsive to a change in the interest rate
credit rationing
availability of loanable funds
pushing on a string
equation of exchange
income velocity of money (V)

quantity theory of money
monetary rule
monetarist
crowding out
investment responsive to a change in the interest rate
pure fiscal policy
cause-effect relationship

Problems

12-1 In the Keynesian framework, there are three separate steps in the process by which monetary policy affects aggregate demand.

(*a*) What are these three steps?

(*b*) Keynes argued that expansive monetary policy would be ineffective in getting the economy out of the Depression of the 1930s because of a problem at one of these three steps. Which step? What was the nature of the problem?

(*c*) Some of the followers of Keynes argued that monetary policy is generally a weak and ineffective tool for controlling aggregate demand. They foresaw a problem at another one of the steps. Which step? What was the nature of the problem?

12-2 Suppose that a machine that will last forever costs $100,000 and yields a return of 10 percent. Now suppose that the price of the machine doubles to $200,000, while the amount that such a machine will produce remains the same, and the prices of outputs and inputs also remain unchanged. What happens to the yield on the machine?

12-3 The marginal efficiency of investment shows the expected rates of return of possible investment projects. For what reasons might expected rates of return on investment projects change through time? How would each of these reasons affect the MEI curve?

12-4 How do strong Keynesians and strong monetarists disagree on the way in which the MEI curve should be drawn? How does the way a strong Keynesian draws the MEI curve cast doubt on the effectiveness of monetary policy? How does the way a strong monetarist draws the MEI curve cast doubt on the effectiveness of fiscal policy in controlling aggregate demand?

12-5 Why might a restrictive monetary policy have more effect on aggregate demand than an expansive monetary policy?

12-6 "I accept the equation of exchange as valid. But I do not accept the quantity theory of money." Is it consistent for an economist to hold such a position? Why or why not?

12-7 How does a tight monetary policy combined with an expansive fiscal policy affect growth?

12-8 Suppose that the demand for money is initially equal to the quantity of money in existence. Then suppose that the quantity of money is doubled because of action by the central bank. According to a classical economist, what will happen?

*12-9 (Only for classes that have studied Box 12-1.) Suppose that the economy is in a depression, with a very low interest rate. Now suppose that the quantity of money is doubled. According to Keynes, what will happen?

chapter 13
Aggregate Supply: *How Can Inflation and Unemployment Coexist?*

The Keynesian revolution introduced modern macroeconomics, spreading the good news that depression and large-scale unemployment can be avoided. With the proper management of aggregate demand, Keynes argued, a high level of employment can be sustained. He debunked the Marxist view that wars and the threat of wars are necessary for economic prosperity in a capitalist economy. Any government spending, not only for the purchase of guns, will stimulate demand. And government spending on public works, education, or a host of other useful projects that come to mind will add to both the prosperity and quality of our society.

But the behavior of the economy depends on supply as well as on demand. In previous chapters, we have concentrated almost exclusively on aggregate demand. In this chapter, we look at aggregate supply.

Chapter 8 introduced the simple aggregate supply function of Keynesian theory, repeated here as Figure 13-1. According to this view, if there initially is a high rate of unemployment (at point A), an increase in aggregate demand will cause the economy to move toward B. At first, in the range AB, the increase in demand will be reflected entirely in an increase in output, and prices will remain stable. But if aggregate demand rises more than enough to provide full employment, prices will rise; the economy will move up the vertical section (BC) of the aggregate supply function. In other words, the economy may suffer the pains of either unemployment or inflation, but not both simultaneously.

In all probability, the reader has become increasingly uncomfortable with this view of the world: It doesn't seem to fit the facts very well. Indeed, in late 1974 and 1975, the economy suffered the worst rate of unemployment in more than three decades, while prices spiraled upward. There clearly is a conflict between the simple Keynesian

FIGURE 13-1 The simple Keynesian aggregate supply function.
The simple supply function is a backward L. Writing during the Depression, Keynes concentrated on the horizontal section (*AB*). Aggregate demand was too low; a rise in demand would increase real output from *A* toward *B*. Further increases in demand past point *B* would drive prices up. The policy objective was clear: Adjust aggregate demand to stay as close as possible to point *B*.

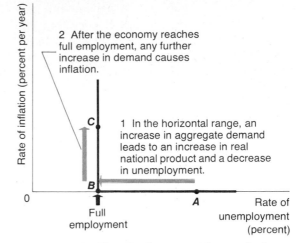

FIGURE 13-2 The simple aggregate supply function: A translation.
Before looking at the data, economists translate Figure 13-1 into this diagram. As unemployment—rather than output—is on the horizontal axis, an increase in demand will cause the economy to move to the left, from *A* toward *B*. Once full employment is reached, further increases in demand cause inflation and a movement from *B* toward *C*.

aggregate supply function and the facts. It is high time to look at the facts.

To do so, economists modify the simple Keynesian diagram, relabeling the axes with the two central macroeconomic problems: inflation and unemployment. When this is done, the idea behind Figure 13-1 can be used to draw Figure 13-2. In this figure, the initial point of large-scale unemployment (*A*) lies well to the right. Then, as aggregate demand and national output increase, the unemployment rate decreases and the economy moves to the left, toward point *B*. In the simplified Keynesian world we are now discussing, prices remain stable as the economy moves toward full employment. Therefore, both *A* and *B* are on the horizontal axis: When prices are stable, the rate of inflation is zero. But if there is a further increase in demand after the economy reaches full employment at *B*, prices begin to rise and the economy moves toward point *C*.

"Full employment" does not mean that the unemployment rate is zero; points *B* and *C* are not on the vertical axis of Figure 13-2. Even during periods of prosperity, some workers are unemployed because they have quit their old jobs to look for something better. Others have recently entered the labor force and are searching for appropriate work. Still others (such as construction workers) may have been temporarily laid off because of bad weather. Such *frictional unemployment* is not due to a lack of demand. Nor is *structural unemployment*, which results from changes in the location of industry or in the composition of output. For example, when textile production shifted from New England to the South, workers in northern textile towns lost their jobs and had difficulty finding new ones. Structural unemployment is longer-lasting and more painful than frictional unemployment; it requires either the establishment of new industries in the depressed area or the emigration of people to places where they can find jobs. During the 1960s, the government estimated that frictional and structural unemployment together totaled something like 4 percent of the labor force; thus, full employment was said to exist when 96 percent of the labor force was employed. (During the 1970s, this figure has been disputed—as we shall see later in this chapter.)

If the assumptions of the simple Keynesian aggregate supply function are correct, historical data should be "well-behaved"; that is, when the unemployment and inflation rates for each year are plotted, the points should lie on, or close to, the L-shaped function of Figure 13-2.

THE FACTS

Unfortunately, when we perform this experiment, a disaster results. In Figure 13-3, each point shows the inflation rate and the unemployment rate in one of the years since 1953. At first glance, there seems little systematic relationship at all between the rate of inflation and the rate of unemployment. Clearly, we do not have a nice L-shaped relationship. There were many years when inflation and high unemployment existed together.

The importance of this problem can scarcely be exaggerated. If the economy does not respond in a predictable manner to changes in aggregate demand, the basis for the demand management policies discussed in earlier chapters is undercut. During a recession, how can we be sure that expansive fiscal and monetary policies will not cause more inflation rather than more output? And, if we apply restraint during an inflationary boom, can we count on a reduction in the rate of inflation? Or will we

merely get less output? In other words, demand management policies require both a knowledge of how monetary and fiscal policies affect aggregate demand and a knowledge of how the economy responds to changes in aggregate demand. Making sense of the puzzle of Figure 13-3 is therefore one of the major tasks of macroeconomic theorists.

Making Sense of the Facts

The first thing that we can do to make sense of Figure 13-3 is to join the points chronologically. This is done in Figure 13-4. Lines are drawn joining consecutive years, and the three decades are color-coded: the 1950s are shown in blue, the 1960s in red, and the 1970s in dark blue. When this is done, some of the confusion disappears.

Two major points stand out:

1. During the 1960s, the data form a reasonably smooth curve. This is known as a Phillips curve, after British economist A. W. Phillips, who found that British data for 1861–1957 fitted a similar curve.[1]

> When the rate of inflation (or the rate of change of money wages)[2] is put on one axis and the rate of unemployment on the other, historical data sometimes trace out a smooth curve bending upward to the left (for example, the curve traced out by the United States data for the 1960s). Such a curve is known as a *Phillips curve*.

2. The observations for the 1970s are above and to the right of the Phillips curve traced out by the 1960s. If point *B* in Figure 13-2 may be considered macroeconomic heaven—with zero inflation and only 4 percent unemployment—then we have been heading northeast toward Hades, with high

[1]A. W. Phillips, "The Relation between Unemployment and the Rate of Change of Money Wages in the United Kingdom," *Economica*, November 1958, pp. 282–299.

[2]The original Phillips curve showed the rate of change of money wages (rather than inflation) on the vertical axis. Since money wages tend to rise rapidly during periods of high inflation, a similar curve is traced out whichever measure is put on the vertical axis.

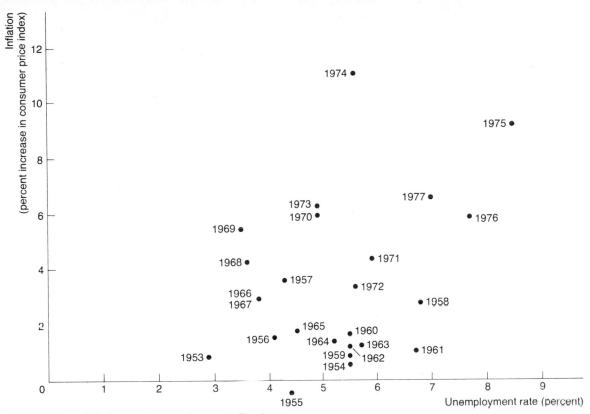

FIGURE 13-3 Inflation and unemployment. The facts.
When we actually plot the observations of recent years, we get a mess. There is no clear L
formed by the points. Indeed, they form no clear, simple pattern at all.

rates of both inflation and unemployment. To use an inelegant but common term, we have been suffering from *stagflation*.

Stagflation involves the combination of a high rate of unemployment (stagnation) and a high rate of inflation.

We thus have two questions before us. What is the nature of the curve observed during the 1960s? And why have things gotten worse during the 1970s, with higher inflation and higher unemployment? These two questions, and the policy problems they raise, will be the subjects covered in the remaining pages of this chapter.

THE PHILLIPS CURVE: Why Is It Curved?

According to the Keynesian approach illustrated in Figures 13-1 and 13-2, an increase in aggregate demand will lead to an increase in real output and a fall in unemployment until full employment is reached. Thereafter, a rise in demand will cause inflation. But the Phillips curves traced out by Phillips' British data and by the United States economy in the 1960s suggest that this is not the way that economies really work. There is no well-defined point of full employment, where rising aggregate demand ceases to cause an increase in output and shows up in higher prices instead. Rather, all increases

FIGURE 13-4 Inflation and unemployment: Making sense of the facts.
When the points are joined in chronological order, the 1960s form a curve. And the data
for the seventies are higher and further to the right.

in aggregate demand have an effect partly on output and employment and partly on prices. The economy moves upward and to the left along the Phillips curve. And, as the economy moves further and further to the left, the Phillips curve becomes steeper and steeper. In other words, a rise in demand is reflected more and more in a price increase and less and less in a fall in unemployment. Why should the economy respond in such a smooth, continuous manner to changes in demand?

Consider, first, the position of businesses. When large-scale unemployment exists, plant and equipment are also likely to be used at much less than capacity. If demand

increases in these circumstances, the primary response of businesses is to increase output rather than prices. An increase in output will allow the fuller utilization of plant and equipment and result in rising profits. Furthermore, businesses may be skeptical about their ability to make price increases stick. If they raise prices rapidly, their competitors—who also have excess capacity—will be only too eager to capture a larger share of the market.

As the expansion continues and plant and equipment are used more and more fully, businesses begin to respond differently to an increase in demand. They have relatively little excess capacity; the increase in demand does not offer them an increase in profits through a large rise in output. But they are increasingly in a position to raise prices. Higher prices no longer result in much loss of markets to competitors, since they are also approaching capacity and are not in a position to expand output rapidly to capture additional sales. Furthermore, as the unemployment rate falls, businesses find it harder to hire and keep workers: As the labor market tightens, businesses become increasingly aggressive in their bidding for workers, offering higher wages. As wage rates move upward, the costs of businesses rise; businesses respond by raising their prices.

Similarly, labor responds differently to increases in aggregate demand as full employment approaches. When there is large-scale unemployment, the workers' first concern is with jobs. If they are offered work, they are generally quick to take it without too much quibbling over pay. However, as economic expansion continues, the situation gradually changes: Workers become less and less concerned with getting and keeping a job and more and more aggressive in demanding higher pay.

These changing conditions, which affect both business and labor, do not come about suddenly at some well-defined point of full employment. On the contrary, the changes are gradual. As a result, the response of the economy to an increase in demand is smooth and continuous. Hence, the Phillips curve provides a more realistic representation of economic behavior than does the simple L-shaped function.

The Policy Dilemma of the 1960s: The Trade-off between Inflation and Unemployment

On the basis of Phillips' historical study and the unfolding situation in the United States, policy makers during the 1960s believed they faced a well-defined Phillips curve. This belief presented them with a policy dilemma. By adjusting aggregate demand, they could move the economy along the Phillips curve. But what point should they try to pick? A point like G in Figure 13-5, with low inflation and a high rate of unemployment? Or a point like H, with low unemployment but a high rate of inflation? Or some point in between? Facing a trade-off between the goals of high unemployment and price stability, what relative importance should they attach to the two objectives?

THE POLICIES OF THE 1960s: Trying to Deal with the Phillips Curve Dilemma

Dealing with the Phillips curve is not a pleasant task for any policy maker. At the beginning of the 1960s, following two quick recessions in the late Eisenhower years, the economy was at point G. When Kennedy came into office, he had promised to "get the economy moving," and he and his advisers fully intended to keep this pledge.[3] By using special tools to prevent *premature inflation* as aggregate demand was stimulated and the economy expanded, the Kennedy and John-

[3]In the early days of the New Frontier, Kennedy nevertheless hesitated to advocate an expansive fiscal policy. Tax cuts or increases in government spending did not fit in well with his famous call for sacrifice: "Ask not what your country can do for you; ask what you can do for your country." Furthermore, he was concerned that the Democrats' reputation as big spenders would make it difficult to get parts of his program through Congress. When a crisis arose over Berlin in the early days of his administration, there was a move within the White House to ask for a tax increase, as a way of challenging the American public to do its part. This move was blocked by Walter Heller, the chairman of the Council of Economic Advisers. The administration did not become publicly committed to a policy of fiscal expansion until 1962, when the President delivered the commencement address at Yale University, in which he attacked the "myths" of fiscal conservatism. For a readable account of economic policy making in the Kennedy administration, see Arthur M. Schlesinger, Jr., *A Thousand Days* (Cambridge, Mass.: Houghton Mifflin, 1965), chaps. 23 and 24.

FIGURE 13-5 The problem of the sixties: The inflation-unemployment tradeoff.
The Phillips curve presents policymakers with a dilemma. By adjusting aggregate demand, they can choose a point on the Phillips curve. But what point should they choose? *G* provides a low rate of inflation but high unemployment. *H* provides high employment but at the cost of substantial inflation. In 1961, the economy was at point *G*. The objective of the Kennedy and Johnson administrations was to reduce unemployment—but without increasing inflation. By restraining wage and price increases as aggregate demand expanded, they hoped to move the economy toward point *B*.

son administrations hoped to move toward point *B* in Figure 13-5, achieving full employment without touching off inflation. Two types of tools were used for this purpose: (1) labor market and regional development policies that would help workers find jobs more quickly and easily, and thus speed the movement to full employment; and (2) direct restraints applied to wages and prices, in order to suppress inflation.

> *Premature inflation* occurs when prices rise before the economy reaches full employment.

Policies to Help Workers Find Jobs

In order to reduce the unemployment rate, the Kennedy-Johnson administrations supplemented expansive fiscal policies with other programs aimed at matching workers and jobs. Most important were the following:

1. The Manpower Development and Training Act (MDTA) of 1962 provided on-the-job and other training for the unemployed, for young people, and for older workers with inadequate or obsolete skills. Thus, an attack was made on one of the paradoxes of our economy—the difficulty that employers have in filling jobs even when the unemployment rate is quite high.

2. Policies combatting discrimination in the labor market (most notably the Civil Rights Act of 1964) helped to reduce the barriers faced by blacks, women, and other groups seeking jobs.

3. Regional development programs were aimed at reducing structural unemployment by attracting industry to Appalachia and other depressed areas.

Wage-Price Guideposts[4]

To restrain wages and prices as expansive fiscal policies were applied, the Kennedy administration announced two basic guideposts:

1. On the average, prices should not be raised.

2. In general, wages in money terms should not rise by more than the increase in labor productivity in the economy as a whole, estimated in the early 1960s to be 3.2 percent per annum.

---

[4]The extensive literature on guideposts includes John Sheahan, *The Wage-Price Guideposts* (Washington: The Brookings Institution, 1967) and Craufurd Goodwin (ed.), *Exhortation and Controls: The Search for a Wage-Price Policy, 1945–1971* (Washington: The Brookings Institution, 1975).

> *Labor productivity* is the average amount produced by a worker. It is calculated by dividing real output by the number of workers employed.

These two guideposts are consistent. If wages are kept to their guideposts, no inflation need result. Since there is an increase in productivity, employers can afford to pay the higher wages and still keep prices constant on average. Labor can be paid more because labor produces more.

According to the guideposts, the increase in wages should be no more than the 3.2 percent increase in productivity in the economy *as a whole*, not the increase in productivity in a specific industry. In some industries, of course, productivity rises much more than in others. In the computer industry, for example, output per worker has soared by about 20 percent per year because of rapid advances in technology. It is neither equitable nor economically desirable for labor in such a rapidly improving industry to get wage increases in line with the productivity increases in that particular industry; the computer industry can get all the labor it needs without having to pay wage increases of 20 percent per annum. Therefore, most of the large increases in productivity in high-technology industries like computers should be reflected in *decreases* in price.

Similarly, on the other side, it is appropriate for industries with little or no productivity improvement to pay wage increases in line with the economy as a whole. Otherwise, they would be unable to hire and retain workers. But, with wages rising and productivity stable, these industries would have to raise their prices. Thus, the Kennedy guideposts recommended that prices *on average* remain stable; but some prices were expected to rise (in industries with small

increases in productivity) while other prices should fall (in high-technology industries).[5]

The government also recommended some exceptions to the basic 3.2 percent wage guidepost. In rapidly growing industries that were having trouble attracting adequate labor, wage increases of more than 3.2 percent per annum were desirable. Also, greater increases were permissible where wages had been particularly low.

These provisions made sense—to allow some price increases, and some wage increases in excess of 3.2 percent. But they complicated the enforcement of the guideposts, which contained no legal teeth. Rather, the guideposts were to be enforced by public opinion and presidential persuasion. But, once exceptions are recognized, it becomes difficult for the government to hold the line anywhere. In each case of wage or price increase, complex and debatable technical questions arise. (What has been the rate of increase in productivity in the industry? Were wages or profits abnormally low to begin with?)

Enforcement Problems During the 1960s, there were several critical phases in the enforcement of the wage-price guideposts. In order that a noninflationary wage settlement be reached in the steel industry, the Secretary of Labor became involved in the wage negotiations of 1962; the administration was gratified with the modest wage settlement, which it considered consistent with stable steel prices. But the ink was scarcely dry on the labor contract when the steel industry announced price increases. Kennedy felt he had been double-crossed; he was furious. He publicly denounced the steel corporations. The newspapers were quick to print his angry private reaction: He now recognized his father had been right all along—steelmen *were* a bunch of SOBs. (As the story originally appeared, Kennedy had

[5]The details of the guideposts are given in the Council of Economic Advisers, *Annual Report, 1962*, p. 189.

called into question the ancestry of *all* business executives. The President quickly corrected this point; it was only steelmen whom he had in mind. This correction did not make the steel executives any happier.) Faced with this Presidential outburst, the steel companies rolled back their prices.

A second—and fatal—major test for the guideposts came in 1966, when the airline machinists struck. Airline unions are in an enviable position: They hold high cards in bargaining for higher wages. A major element of airline costs consists of overheads in the form of interest and depreciation on aircraft. Because these high costs continue whether the planes are in the air or not, airlines are under tremendous pressures to settle quickly, and to grant high wage increases if necessary. Nevertheless, there are some constraints on the power of the airline unions. They cannot push up wages without limit: To do so would be to risk killing the goose that lays the golden egg. If wages become too high, airlines may be threatened with bankruptcy. (Thus, for example, when airlines were in financial difficulty in the mid-seventies, some pilots agreed to accept lower wages.) But there was no danger of bankruptcy in the early 1960s: With the upswing in the economy, airline profits were rising briskly.

But other restraints, in addition to the fear of "killing the goose," also operate in the airline industry. Because of the pervasiveness of government regulation over the airlines, the government can strengthen the bargaining position of the companies in dealing with the unions. This it did in 1966. Airlines that were still in operation were allowed to fly the scheduled flights of the struck airlines. And airlines that had been shut down by the strike were authorized to lend planes to those still operating. These steps, together with an agreement among

airlines for those gaining from the strike to pay the struck airlines, added to the bargaining power of the companies.[6]

As the strike dragged on, Congress began to debate legislation that would authorize the President to require the strikers to return to work. But the administration did not push for this authority. The strike was settled with a wage increase of 5 percent, which clearly exceeded the guidepost. (There was an attempt to justify the settlement by the high increase in productivity in the *airline* industry. But the logic of the guideposts required wage increases to be in line with the overall increase in productivity in the economy *as a whole*. Inflation could not be avoided if, for example, there were increases in wages of 20 percent in the computer industry, which other employers would be pressed to meet in order to keep qualified workers.)

The guideposts were coming apart. The end was accelerated by events in the construction industry, where settlements by 1965 and 1966 were running at average annual rates in excess of 6 percent.

As prices crept up, the logic of the wage guidepost was increasingly undermined. The consumer price index rose at an average rate of about 3 percent in 1966 and 1967. In these circumstances, workers could scarcely be expected to stick to a 3.2 percent wage increase. If they did so, their *real* wages would remain approximately constant; their higher money wages would do little more than compensate for the rise in prices. Yet real productivity was rising; more goods and services were being produced by the average worker. The maintenance of the 3.2 percent guideline would mean that labor would get none of the gains from rising productivity. Instead, productivity gains would all go to profits and other nonwage forms of income.

---

[6]For a discussion of how the agreement altered the balance of power between labor and management, see S. Herbert Unterberger and Edward C. Koziara, "Airline Strike Insurance: A Study in Escalation," *Industrial and Labor Relations Review*, October 1975, pp. 26–45. (The agreement was approved by the Civil Aeronautics Board.)

The *real wage* is measured by the quantity of goods and services that the wage will buy. It is found by adjusting the money wage for inflation. For example, if the money wage rises by 5 percent while prices rise by 2 percent, then the real wage has increased by 3 percent.

Thus, the wage-price guideposts of the Kennedy-Johnson era were designed to keep inflation from gathering momentum, not to deal with an existing inflation. Modifications might have been made. For example, wage increases might have been held to 3.2 percent plus some fraction (say one-half) of the previous year's increase in the consumer price index. (The government studied this approach, but never actually made it part of the wage-price policy.) Such a rule of thumb would have been consistent with a reduction in inflation. But, for such a wage guidepost to be credible, labor would have to have some assurance that inflation would, indeed, be reduced. As the 1960s wore on, inflationary forces gathered momentum; the guideposts became increasingly irrelevant.

Wage-Price Guideposts: Controversial Issues

The desirability of wage-price guideposts (or more formal legal controls on wages and prices) has been the subject of continuing and heated debate in the United States and other countries. Three main points are at issue.

1. Workability Skeptics point to the breakdown of the Kennedy-Johnson guideposts and to disappointing experiences with

similar policies in foreign countries.[7] Proponents point to the substantial successes of the 1960s: During the period when the wage-price guideposts were in force, the United States had an unusually long period of steady expansion. (Between early 1961 and late 1969, real GNP grew in every quarter, with the sole exception of the first quarter of 1967.) And, until excess demand was generated by Vietnam war spending, prices were reasonably stable; until 1966, the rate of inflation remained below 2 percent.

An *incomes policy* is a policy aimed at controlling inflation with the use of guideposts or other restraints on money wages and prices. (Wage restraints affect labor income. Price restraints affect other incomes, such as profits and rents.)

In more detail, the case against an *incomes policy* goes as follows. If the government proclaims guideposts, business and labor leaders can scarcely be expected to cooperate voluntarily. Labor leaders have to answer to union members who want higher wages, and business executives have to answer to their stockholders who want higher profits. Indeed, guideposts may be counterproductive. If the government has sanctified a 3.2 percent wage increase, how can any self-respecting labor leader settle for less? The 3.2 percent may become the floor from which bargaining will begin. And guideposts may also be counterproductive on the price side. Fearing that they may simply be a warning of more stringent controls to come, businesses may decide to "jump the gun." If prices are about to be frozen, won't a busi-

[7]For an evaluation of the early European experience, see Lloyd Ulman and Robert J. Flanagan, *Wage Restraint: A Study of Incomes Policies in Western Europe* (Berkeley: University of California Press, 1971). The authors reach a pessimistic conclusion: "Incomes policy . . . has not been very successful. . . . In none of the variations so far turned up has incomes policy succeeded in its fundamental objective . . . of making full employment consistent with a reasonable degree of price stability."

On the United Kingdom's experience, see also Hugh Clegg (a member of the early British Prices and Incomes Board), *How to Run an Incomes Policy, and Why We Made Such a Mess of the Last One* (London: Heinemann Educational Publishing, 1970); and Lawrence C. Hunter, "British Incomes Policy, 1972–1974," *Industrial and Labor Relations Review* (Cornell University), October 1975, pp. 67–84.

ness try to raise them now, while there is still time?

If the government backs up the guideposts with threats and admonitions—the so-called "open mouth" or "jawboning" approach that Kennedy had applied to the steel industry—enforcement is likely to be erratic and ineffective. If the government goes all the way to enact price and wage control laws, it may still find a problem of enforcement; goods in high demand may be channeled into *black markets* where prices are above the legal limits. (Indeed, since sellers are breaking the law, they may charge prices that are even higher than would exist in an uncontrolled market, in order to compensate for the risk of fines or imprisonment.) Finally, governments that use incomes policies may suffer from the illusion that they can indeed control prices in this way, and that they are therefore free to increase aggregate demand rapidly. If they do so, the incomes policies will collapse under the intense pressures of excess demand, and prices will shoot up.

On the other side, the case in favor of incomes policies has been neatly summarized by John Kenneth Galbraith: "Any idiot can argue the case against controls in the abstract. It is only that there are no alternatives." If direct action is not taken to restrain wages and prices, there is only one way to stop inflation: Restrain aggregate demand, and allow a painfully high rate of unemployment.

2. Allocative Efficiency
Opponents of guidelines and controls point out that they interfere with the function of the price system in allocating production. As we saw in Chapter 4, prices provide information and incentives to producers. When goods are scarce, prices rise, encouraging producers to make more. If prices are controlled, they no longer can perform this important role.

A particular problem arises because controls and guidelines may be enforced erratically. Responding to political pressures, the government may enforce price restraints most vigorously for goods that are considered essential. As a result of the relatively low prices, businesses will switch to the production of more profitable items. Thus, price controls may end up by reducing the production of the very goods the society considers particularly important.(Recall the discussion of rent control in Box 4-1.)

Proponents of incomes policies recognize this danger, but believe that it can be dealt with. It was partly to protect the allocative function that exceptions were permitted in the wage-price guideposts of the 1960s. And advocates of controls also generally propose that a government agency be given the authority to adjust legally permissible prices.

3. Economic Freedom
This last proposal is viewed with alarm by the opponents of incomes policies because of the economic power it would place in the hands of government officials. By denying price increases, they would have the power to force some companies into bankruptcy. Price and wage controls restrict the freedom of businesses and labor.

Furthermore, even less formal wage-price guidelines are subject to abuse. In wielding the jawbone, the president may find politically unpopular businesses (such as the steel industry) to be especially inviting targets. And public admonitions may be reinforced with harassment.

Proponents of controls tend to downplay these dangers and argue that they must be put in perspective. If no restraint is applied to wage and pricing decisions, the control of inflation will involve high rates of unemployment. The unemployed will be used as "cannon fodder" in the war against inflation. Thus, the freedom of business executives and labor leaders to do as they please must be weighed against the right of workers to have jobs.

THE TROUBLED SEVENTIES: Higher Inflation and Higher Unemployment

The history of the past two decades is disconcerting. The 1960s began with optimism and high hope that the Phillips curve dilemma could be solved with wage-price guidelines. Yet the opposite has happened. Rather than move to a point of high employment and low inflation, we have gotten the worst of both worlds during the seventies. What has gone wrong? How can we account for the simultaneous high rates of unemployment and inflation? Two principal explanations have been offered.

Cost-Push Inflation

The age of Keynesian economics is over; the macroeconomic revolution in fiscal and monetary management we owe to Keynes has run afoul of the microeconomic revolution in trade union and corporate power.

John Kenneth Galbraith

The first explanation involves the distinction between *demand-pull* and *cost-push* inflation.

> *Demand-pull* inflation occurs when demand is high and rising. Buyers bid eagerly for goods and services, "pulling up" their prices.
> *Cost-push* inflation occurs when wages and other costs rise and these costs are passed along to consumers in the form of higher prices. Prices are "pushed up" by rising costs. Cost-push inflation is also sometimes known as *market power* inflation.

As the economy enters a period of demand-pull inflation, with "too much money chasing too few goods," producers find that they cannot fill all their orders at the old prices, and prices are bid up. During such a period, production is high, unemployment is low, and prices rise. This is the traditional and most straightforward explanation of inflation. It lies behind the vertical section of the simple Keynesian aggregate supply function (Figure 13-1), and behind the increasingly steep section of the Phillips curve as the economy moves to the left when demand increases.

But suppose that strong labor unions and monopolistic companies have considerable power to set prices. Even when the demand for labor is low and the unemployment rate is high, a strong union may be able to use the threat of a strike to negotiate higher wages. Similarly, business firms with few competitors may raise their prices even though demand is sluggish. And businesses with higher costs of labor and material inputs may pass them along to the consumer in the form of higher prices.

It is possible that both demand-pull and cost-push forces will be at work together, and that inflation will be the result of both. But suppose, for the moment, that aggregate demand (measured in dollar terms) is stable, while inflationary pressures continue from the cost side. Prices continue to rise. With higher prices, the stable aggregate demand buys fewer goods, and people are thrown out of work as a result. In other words, rising prices are accompanied by a fall in output and a rise in the rate of unemployment.

Thus, while a combination of rising prices and rising unemployment seems paradoxical if we concentrate solely on demand-pull forces, it no longer is such a puzzle if account is taken of cost-push pressures. It is not surprising, then, that the cost-push explanation of inflation became prominent in the late 1950s, when inflation and unemployment increased simultaneously. (Both inflation and unemployment were higher in 1957–1958 than they had been in 1955–1956, as may be seen by referring back to Figure 13-4.)

The distinction between demand-pull and cost-push is summarized in Figure 13-6. With expansive monetary and fiscal policies,

Inflation (percent per annum)

PC$_2$

Cost push shifts whole Phillips curve up. If demand is held constant, fewer goods can be bought at the higher prices, and unemployment increases.

D

PC$_1$

C

E

B

Demand pull (higher inflation and less unemployment)

A

0

Unemployment rate (percent)

FIGURE 13-6 Demand-pull and cost-push inflation. By adjusting aggregate demand, the authorities can choose a point on the Phillips curve (PC$_1$). An increase in demand will move the economy along the Phillips curve from A to B, with higher inflation and lower unemployment. Cost-push shifts the whole Phillips curve upward, from PC$_1$ to PC$_2$. The authorities now have a less-pleasant choice. If they hold aggregate demand constant, fewer goods will be bought at the higher prices, and the economy will move to point C. High unemployment will occur along with the higher inflation. If they stimulate aggregate demand to keep unemployment low, there will be even more inflation at point D.

the authorities can cause a movement along the original Phillips curve (PC$_1$). With this pull of demand, there is more inflation and less unemployment. On the other hand, with cost-push, the whole Phillips curve shifts upward (to PC$_2$). The authorities now face an unpalatable choice. If, starting from point B, they keep aggregate demand stable in dollar terms, fewer goods will be bought at higher prices and unemployment will rise

(the movement from B to C). But if they increase aggregate demand to keep unemployment down, even higher inflation will result (at point D).

In the late 1950s, the debate over cost-push became heated.[8] In particular, it invited a search for culprits. Business executives blamed inflation on the aggressive and "irresponsible" bargaining of labor unions for higher wages (that had, in turn, forced businesses to raise prices). Labor blamed powerful corporations for pushing up prices in their greed for "fantastic profits."

Oil While labor and management blamed each other for cost-push inflation during the late 1950s, one cost-push culprit stood out in the mid-1970s: the Organization of Petroleum Exporting Countries (OPEC). In a brief period during 1973 and 1974, OPEC doubled and then redoubled the prices which importers had to pay for oil; and smaller increases were imposed in the following years.

Because of the importance of oil as a source of power for industry, as a fuel for our transportation system, and as a source of heat for our homes and factories, the skyrocketing price of oil had a powerful effect on the United States, and, indeed, on all oil-importing countries.[9] (Japan was perhaps the hardest hit of all, because almost all its oil is imported.) Businesses with higher costs for power, heating, and transportation tried to pass these higher costs along to consumers in the form of higher prices. The economy was subjected to severe cost-push pressures, with inflation accelerating into "double digits" (that is, above 10 percent) in 1974.

The sharp upward shift of the Phillips

[8]A detailed account of this early debate may be found in William G. Bowen, *The Wage-Price Issue: A Theoretical Analysis* (Princeton, N.J.: Princeton University Press, 1960). (Bowen later became president of Princeton.)

[9]For a discussion of the effects of higher oil prices on a number of countries (including the United States), see Edward R. Fried and Charles L. Schultze (eds.), *Higher Oil Prices and the World Economy* (Washington: The Brookings Institution, 1975).

curve led to a major policy disagreement in 1974 and 1975. On the one hand, the Ford administration and the Federal Reserve were worried at the prospect of runaway inflation and leaned toward tight aggregate demand policies. The rate of increase in the money stock was reduced, and the President recommended a tax increase in late 1974. (Thus, the Fed and the President apparently were aiming at a point such as *E*, below and to the right of point *C* in Figure 13-6.) But congressional concern over this strategy grew as the recession of 1974–1975 deepened, and the Congress moved to expand aggregate demand by cutting taxes in early 1975. During 1974 and 1975, the net result of the oil price shock and the policy response was a combination of high unemployment rates (averaging 7.1 percent) and high inflation rates (averaging 10 percent per annum). After 1974, the rate of increase in oil prices was much more moderate than in 1973 and 1974, a fact that helped reduce inflation during the sustained economic recovery that began in mid-1975.

In summary, this first explanation of stagflation depends on disturbances from the cost side: The Phillips curve can be temporarily shifted up by aggressive wage and pricing activities by unions and business, or by shocks from abroad, such as the increase in the price of imported oil.

PRICE EXPECTATIONS AND THE WAGE-PRICE SPIRAL: The Accelerationist Argument

The second explanation of simultaneous high rates of inflation and unemployment goes further, throwing into question the whole concept of a permanent curve such as that discovered by Phillips. According to this line of argument, the Phillips curve is stable only in the short run. It shifts whenever people's expectations of inflation change. In particular, it shifts upward as inflation gathers momentum. If the manag-

ers of monetary and fiscal policies aim for a low rate of unemployment, inflation will accelerate to higher and higher rates. (Hence, this is known as the *accelerationist* argument.)

The easiest way to explain this argument is to assume initially that prices have been stable for an extended period of time. On the basis of past experience, they are expected to remain stable into the indefinite future. The economy rests at point *G* on the initial Phillips curve (Figure 13-7), where the inflation rate is zero. Now suppose that the government decides that the unemployment rate at *G* is unacceptable; expansive fiscal and monetary policies are introduced

FIGURE 13-7 The acceleration of inflation: The wage-price spiral.

If demand is continuously increased by whatever amount is necessary to maintain the low rate of unemployment U_T, then the result is an ever-increasing rate of inflation. The economy moves successively to points *H, J,* and higher. (The original Phillips curve PC₁ shows how the economy responds to changes in aggregate demand during the short-run period when the initial wage contracts remain in force.)

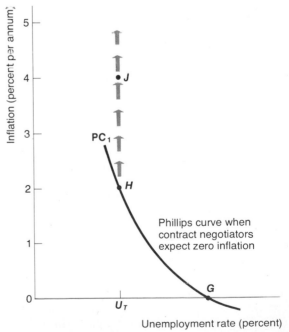

in order to increase aggregate demand and get the unemployment rate down to a target level of U_T.

What happens? To meet the higher demand, producers need more workers. Job vacancies increase, and those looking for jobs get them easily and quickly. Production increases and unemployment falls. In the face of higher demand, producers gradually begin to raise prices. But in the early stages of inflation, little change takes place in money wages. Most collective bargaining contracts are for 3 years, and union wages change only slowly as a result. Nonunion wages are also sticky. People may work on individual contracts that run for 1 or more years. And even where there is no written contract, it is customary to review wages only periodically—say, once a year. Thus, the initial reaction to the increase in demand is a relatively large increase in output, only a moderate increase in prices, and an even smaller increase in wages. The economy moves along the Phillips curve to point H (Figure 13-7).

But point H is not stable. The initial Phillips curve (PC_1) reflects wage contracts that were negotiated *on the assumption of stable prices.* But prices are no longer stable; and the contracts do not last forever. As new contract negotiations begin, workers observe that their real wages—the amount of goods and services their wages will buy—have been eroded by inflation. They demand a cost-of-living catch-up. So long as aggregate demand rises rapidly enough to keep the economy operating at full blast, the unions are in a good position to get their demands; with booming markets, employers capitulate to strike threats. And nonunion employees are likewise granted raises to keep them from quitting to look for more highly paid work. Because demand is high and rising, businesses can easily pass along the higher wages in the form of higher prices, and they do so. The rate of inflation accelerates; the economy moves to point J, above the origi-

nal Phillips curve. But, with a higher inflation rate, workers find that once again they have been cheated by inflation; once again their real wages are less than expected. At the next round of wage negotiations, they demand a larger cost-of-living catch-up. Moreover, as they have been twice burned, they may also demand something extra for future inflation, which they now begin to anticipate. The wage-price spiral gathers momentum. So long as demand is aimed at keeping unemployment at the low target rate of U_T, inflation will *continue to accelerate.*

Thus, the Phillips curve gives the wrong impression. It creates the illusion that there is a single trade-off between inflation and unemployment; in other words, that a low rate of unemployment can be "bought" with a moderate, steady rate of inflation. But, in fact, the cost is much higher: *an ever accelerating rate of inflation.* Wages and prices spiral upward, with higher prices leading to higher and higher wage demands, and higher wages being passed along in the form of higher and higher prices.

Limiting the Rate of Inflation

But ever accelerating inflation is intolerable. If prices rise faster and faster, sooner or later the whole monetary system will break down and the economy will revert to an inefficient barter system. (The rate required for a complete breakdown is very high indeed—thousands of percent per annum. But severe disruptions may be caused even by rates of inflation of 8 or 10 percent.) At some time, therefore, the monetary and fiscal policy makers will decide to draw the line; they will refuse to increase aggregate demand without limit.

To keep this illustration simple, suppose that the monetary and fiscal line is drawn sooner rather than later. As soon as the economy gets to point H, the government recognizes the danger of an ever accelerating inflation. It therefore switches aggregate demand policies. Instead of increasing aggregate demand by whatever amount is necessary to maintain a low target level of unemployment, the authorities limit aggregate demand to whatever degree is necessary to prevent inflation from rising above the 2 percent reached at H. In other words, the authorities change the policy target. Their primary objective is no longer to keep unemployment at the low level U_T, but instead, to keep inflation from rising above the 2 percent target level, I_T (Figure 13-8).

What happens? Workers still push for higher wages; the 2 percent rate of inflation is still eroding their purchasing power. But employers now are in a bind; they cannot easily pass along higher wages because of the restraint on demand. Labor conflicts and strikes result. And, in the face of restrained demand, output begins to fall and unemployment rises; the economy moves to the right, to a point such as L.

THE LONG-RUN PHILLIPS CURVE: Two Views

As demand is restrained, the economy moves to the right. But how far? Suppose demand is controlled in such a way as to keep inflation permanently at a rate of 2 percent. Where will the ultimate equilibrium be?

There are two schools of thought on this question. One school—which includes Profs. Edmund Phelps of Columbia University and Milton Friedman of Chicago[10]—argues that the economy will move all the way to N, to a point directly above the original equilibrium G (Figure 13-8). The other school believes that the economy will stop somewhere to the left of N, at a point like L or M.

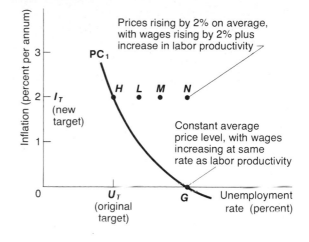

FIGURE 13-8 Limiting the rate of inflation.
If the managers of monetary and fiscal policies switch targets, limiting demand to prevent inflation greater than I_T, then the economy will begin to move to the right, to a point like L.

A Vertical Long-run Phillips Curve?

Consider first the views of Phelps and Friedman. Let us go back to the initial point, G (Figure 13-8). This represented a stable equilibrium. It was the result of an extended experience with a zero rate of inflation; both businesses and labor had a chance to adjust completely to the stable price level. If they now get a chance to adjust completely to a 2 percent rate of inflation (and this may take some time), then, according to Phelps and Friedman, the new equilibrium will be at N, where both labor and business are in the same real position as at G. At G, prices were stable, while nominal and real wages rose at the rate of increase in labor productivity (assumed to be 2.5 percent per annum in Table 13-1). Now, at N, real wages are also rising by the 2.5 percent increase in labor

[10]Milton Friedman, "The Role of Monetary Policy," *American Economic Review*, March 1968, pp. 1–17; Edmund S. Phelps, "Money Wage Dynamics and Labor Market Equilibrium," in Edmund S. Phelps (ed.), *Microeconomic Foundations of Employment and Inflation Theory* (New York: W. W. Norton, 1970), pp. 124–166; and Edmund S. Phelps, "Phillips Curves, Expectations of Inflation and Optimal Unemployment Over Time," *Economica*, August 1967, pp. 254–281.

TABLE 13-1

Example of Phelps-Friedman Equilibrium (after Wages Have Adjusted to Inflation)

Figures 13-8 and 13-9	(1) Prices	(2) Nominal wages	(3) Real wages
Point *G*, with zero inflation	Stable	Increasing by 2.5% per annum	Increasing by 2.5% per annum
Point *N*, with 2% inflation	Increasing by 2% per annum	Increasing by 4.5% per annum	Increasing by 2.5% per annum

Note that after adjustment for inflation, real wages increase at the same rate at *N* as they did at *G*. At both *N* and *G*, real wages can rise because of the increase in labor productivity, assumed to be 2.5 percent per annum.

productivity, but money wages are rising by an additional 2 percent per annum to compensate workers for the 2 percent annual increase in the prices they pay. The wage/price situation at *N* also leaves employers in the same real situation as at *G*: They pay 2 percent more for labor and for material inputs, but they are compensated by the 2 percent increase in their prices. Thus, their profits are the same in real terms. Consequently, they hire the same number of workers at *N* as they did at *G*. Thus, argue Phelps and Friedman, *N* lies directly above *G*, and the unemployment rate is the same at *N* as at *G*.

In other words, Phelps and Friedman argue that people have *no money illusion*. They are interested, not in wages and prices measured in dollars, but in what their wages or their sale of goods will bring in real terms. In the long run, the rate of inflation is basically irrelevant to the way the economy works, provided that rate of inflation is *constant* and *accurately recognized* by all contract participants.

> People have *money illusion* when their behavior changes in the event of a proportionate change in prices and money incomes.[11]

With a steady 2 percent rate of inflation, the economy moves eventually to *N*, where the unemployment rate and real wages are the same as at *G*. Alternatively, if the rate of inflation rises to 4 percent before monetary and fiscal policy makers draw the line to prevent more rapid inflation, the economy will eventually move to *R* (Figure 13-9); or, with a steady 6 percent rate of inflation, to *T*. All these are points of stable equilibrium; in each case, people have adjusted completely to the prevailing rate of inflation. (In contrast, point *H* was an unstable point because workers had not yet had a chance to renegotiate their wages to reflect the new inflation.) In other words, the points of long-run equilibrium trace out a vertical line; the long-run Phillips curve (PC_L) is *perfectly vertical*. In the long run, there is *no trade-off* between inflation and unemployment. By accepting more inflation, we cannot permanently achieve a lower rate of unemployment. We can achieve a lower rate of unemployment only during a temporary period of disequilibrium (at *H*). Unemployment gravitates toward the equilibrium or *natural* rate. This brings us back to the basic position of the classical quantity theory. In the long run, changes in aggregate demand (which are caused primarily by changes in the quantity

*[11] Strictly speaking, a phrase should be added to this definition: "and in the event that assets valued in money terms also change in the same proportion." (This addition does not substantially alter the argument.)

FIGURE 13-9   A vertical long-run Phillips curve?
If the negotiators of wages and all other contracts are free from money illusion, then there will be a complete adjustment to the prevailing rate of inflation over time. With steady increases in aggregate demand, the economy will gravitate toward the vertical long-run Phillips curve (PC_L). There is no long-run tradeoff between unemployment and inflation.

But the short-run Phillips curve is *not* vertical. For example, once contracts have adjusted completely to a 2 percent rate of inflation at *N*, then an unexpected disturbance in aggregate demand will cause the economy to move along the short-run Phillips curve (PC_2) running through *N*. Thus, a spurt in demand will cause an increase in output, a fall in unemployment, and some increase in inflation as the economy moves from *N* to *V*.

of money, *M*) will affect prices (*P*) and not the quantity of output (*Q*) or employment.[12]

> The *long-run Phillips curve* is the curve (or line) traced out by the possible points of long-run equilibrium; that is, the points where people have adjusted completely to the prevailing rate of inflation.

The *natural rate of unemployment* is the equilibrium rate that exists when people have adjusted completely to the prevailing rate of inflation.

Through each of the long-run equilibrium points (such as *N*, *R*, or *T* in Figure 13-9) there is a short-run Phillips curve, each reflecting contracts based on the prevailing rate of inflation. The short-run Phillips curve (PC_2) running through *N*, for example, is based on the expectation by contract negotiators that there will be a continuing rate of inflation of 2 percent per year. Suppose that after a number of years at *N*, the authorities adjust monetary and fiscal policies to make aggregate demand grow more rapidly. Faced with a high demand, businesses increase output, hire more workers, and begin to raise prices by more than 2 percent per annum. Their profits temporarily shoot up because workers are committed to the old labor contracts, based on expectations of 2 percent inflation. The economy moves along the short-run Phillips curve PC_2 to a point such as *V*, with a low rate of unemployment. But *V* is unstable for the same reason that *H* was unstable. Point *V* results from wage contracts that were agreed to when inflation was expected to be 2 percent. But actual inflation is 3 percent. Therefore, contracts will be adjusted during the next round of negotiations. When wage contracts are adjusted upward, an accelerating wage-price spiral will result if the authorities continue to follow expansive aggregate demand policies. Alternatively, if demand managers take steps to prevent any further increase in inflation, the economy will move to the right, back toward the long-run Phillips curve and the natural rate of unemployment.

In conclusion, note that there is some similarity between this *accelerationist* or

*[12]Thus, the vertical long-run Phillips curve of Figure 13-9 is the vertical aggregate supply function of classical economics (Figure 8-1), but in another guise.

natural rate theory and the earlier explanation of inflation based on cost-push. In each case, the Phillips curve shifts upward, and in each case, higher wage contracts can play an important role in the shift. But here the similarity stops. Cost-push theorists explain higher wages and higher prices on the basis of market power, and see strong unions and strong corporations as the culprits. Accelerationists, on the other hand, dismiss cost-push as an illusion. The apparent upward push of costs in the form of higher wages is not the result of union power; rather, it is the *lagged response* of wage contracts to the inflation brought on by excess demand. The government should not go looking for culprits in the form of powerful unions or powerful businesses. Rather, the culprit is right in Washington: the government itself (including the Federal Reserve), which has generated the inflationary demand in the first place.

FIGURE 13-10   An alternative view.
Many economists are convinced that there is a tradeoff between unemployment and low rates of inflation, even in the long run. The Eckstein-Brinner long-run Phillips curve, illustrated here, is an example of this view. Only at rates of inflation above 2½ percent does the long-run Phillips curve become vertical.

An Alternative View

Economists of the other school agree that inflation can accelerate. But they do not believe that the long-run Phillips curve is a perfectly vertical straight line. In particular, they argue that as inflation rates are brought down to very low levels, the long-run Phillips curve bends to the right. An example of such a long-run curve is provided in Figure 13-10, based on the work of Otto Eckstein and Roger Brinner.[13] (Because of the lack of unanimity among economists regarding the exact position and shape of the curve, it is wise to draw it with a very thick pencil, as we have illustrated with the shading in Figure 13-10.)

Such a curve implies two things. First, workers and others are concerned with their real incomes after adjustment for inflation. This proposition, which we have just explained for the Phelps-Friedman argument,

is what gives the long-run curve its vertical section above *A*.

Second, workers must be concerned with something else in addition to their real wages. (Otherwise, the curve would continue vertically down to the axis, as it does in the Phelps-Friedman version.) What can this something be? The answer is: their *money* wages. In particular, a cut in the money wage represents a humiliation that workers will strongly resist, regardless of what is happening to the level of prices and to real wages. But why should this unwillingness to accept lower money wages matter? After all, we live in a growing economy, with rising productivity and generally rising real wages. Thus, even in an economy with *zero* inflation, the average nominal wage will increase.

But not all industries are average. Even

[13]Otto Eckstein and Roger Brinner, *The Inflation Process in the United States* (Washington: Joint Economic Committee of the United States Congress, 1972).

in a growing economy, some industries decline. As their demand falls, they will discharge workers, adding to the rolls of the unemployed. This process may be slowed down if the industry cuts its prices relative to other prices. Its ability to do so depends in part on the wages it pays. If the rate of inflation is zero and average wages in the economy are going up by 2.5 percent, the declining industry will gain a wage advantage of only 2.5 percent by giving its workers no money wage increase at all. On the other hand, if the inflation rate is 2 percent and the average money wage increase is 4.5 percent, the declining industry may gain a 4.5 percent advantage by keeping nominal wages constant. The workers will not like their declining real wages; they may grumble, but they will go along rather than face unemployment. But they would not have acceded to a cut in nominal wages. Thus, by permitting workers to accept some decline in real wages gracefully without the humiliation of a nominal wage cut, a modest rate of inflation tends to maintain employment in declining industries. Consequently, there may be a less serious unemployment problem with a 2 percent inflation (at point B in Figure 13-10) than with a stable price level (at point C). In short, this money illusion—the unwillingness to take a money wage cut (regardless of what is happening to real wages)—provides a reason for believing that the long-run Phillips curve is not absolutely vertical in its lower reaches.[14]

Thus, in contrast to the vertical Phelps-Friedman long-run relationship (Figure 13-9), the Eckstein-Brinner curve of Figure 13-10 indicates that there *is* a long-run trade-off between inflation and unemployment. If the demand management authorities are very tough, and are determined to prevent *any* inflation, the rate of unemployment will settle at a very high figure—something like 8 or 9 percent per annum. If, on the other hand, they are willing to accept a moderate rate of inflation (of 2 or 2.5 percent), the economy should settle down to an unemployment rate in the 4 to 5 percent range.

Once again, points off the Eckstein-Brinner long-run Phillips curve are unstable. An attempt to maintain a very low rate of unemployment (say 3 percent) through demand management policies will lead to an ever accelerating inflation.

In spite of their differences over the lower part of the curve below a 3 percent rate of inflation, most present-day economists believe that the long-run Phillips curve is much steeper than the short-run curve. The reason is that the short-run curve shifts as people's expectations of inflation change. (In the words of Arthur Okun, "We are all accelerationists now."[15]) This raises the puzzle of how Phillips found his initial curve. After all, his data covered almost a century. But that century was quite different from the last two decades. While there was a very substantial amount of economic instability and price fluctuation, there was no long-run, strong upward movement of prices. (This was true not only of Britain, which Phillips studied, but also of the United

---

[14]Money illusion does not necessarily mean that those involved are too stupid to figure out what is happening. For example, many professors took a cut in real income in the mid-1970s, when prices were rising faster than their money incomes. By and large, this real cut was accepted. But it is not clear that university administrations would have avoided much stronger protests, had prices been constant and had the administrations tried to cut nominal salaries.

[15]Arthur Okun, "Inflation: Its Mechanics and Welfare Costs," *Brookings Papers on Economic Activity*, 1975, vol. 2, p. 356. Okun served as the chairman of President Johnson's Council of Economic Advisers. As an economist who had originally helped to popularize the Phillips curve in the United States, he was making a concession to Friedman that paralleled Friedman's earlier concession: "In one sense, we are all Keynesians now." [Friedman had, however, tacked on the qualification that "in another [sense], no one is a Keynesian any longer." From Milton Friedman, *Dollars and Deficits* (Englewood Cliffs, N.J.: Prentice-Hall, 1968), p. 15).]

States. Here, the average level of prices was about the same in the 1930s as it had been in the decade before the War of 1812.) Prices rose during booms and fell during recessions. Thus, strong expectations of inflation did not become deeply engrained. Contract negotiators were unsure whether the general movement of prices would be up or down; contracts contained no strong, built-in adjustment for inflation. Hence, Phillips found a reasonably stable curve covering a very long period.

In recent decades, however, the up-and-down price movements of history have disappeared. A basic inflationary trend has taken over; the average level of prices goes just one way: up. Hence, wage negotiators now build the expectation of further inflation into their contracts; the short-run Phillips curves are now higher than in the past.

FIGURE 13-11 The unwinding of inflation causes high unemployment.
Once inflation becomes built into contracts, it is painful to unwind. The short-run Phillips curve shown here reflects contracts based on 6 percent inflation. It takes a substantial period of demand restraint and consequent high unemployment at *V* before wage contracts are adjusted downward. (This diagram is consistent with both the Phelps-Friedman version of the long-run Phillips curve and the Eckstein-Brinner version. Above an inflation rate of about 2¹/₂ percent, both versions are vertical. Disagreement arises only below an inflation rate of 2¹/₂ percent, a range not shown here.)

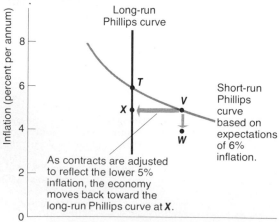

As contracts are adjusted to reflect the lower 5% inflation, the economy moves back toward the long-run Phillips curve at **X**.

THE PROBLEM OF UNWINDING INFLATIONARY EXPECTATIONS

The short-run Phillips curve represents a trap for policy makers. Those who decide on monetary and fiscal policies may think that they can achieve low rates of unemployment to the left of the long-run curve by expansive demand policies. In fact, they will be able to maintain a very low rate of unemployment only if they allow inflation to spiral ever higher.

But the problem is even worse than that. Once inflation becomes engrained in negotiators' expectations, it can be eliminated with demand-management policies only at the cost of a high rate of unemployment to the right of the long-run Phillips curve.

This is illustrated in Figure 13-11. Suppose that the economy has reached point *T*, with inflation consistently running at 6 percent per annum year after year. This point is stable; inflation will neither rise nor fall, and the unemployment rate will remain steady. Now, suppose that policy makers decide that 6 percent inflation is too high; they are determined to reduce it by restrictive monetary and fiscal policies.

As aggregate demand is restrained, businesses find their sales falling. Production is cut back and workers are laid off. The unemployment rate rises. Because of intensifying competitive pressures as businesses scramble to make sales, businesses no longer insist on such high price increases, and the rate of inflation begins to slacken off. But this does not happen quickly. Businesses are still committed to pay the hefty wage increases under the old labor contracts; their costs continue to rise even though demand is slack. As a result, the short-run effect of the restrained demand shows up most strongly in a fall in output and a rise in unemployment, and only to a small extent in lower inflation. The economy moves to point *V*, to the right of the long-run Phillips curve and on the short-run Phillips curve running through point T (reflecting wage contracts negotiated on the expectation that inflation would continue at 6 percent per annum).

Because it is off the long-run Phillips curve, point V is unstable. At the next round of wage negotiations, workers are willing to settle for more moderate wage increases because the rate of inflation is now only 5 percent. Their willingness to settle is reinforced by their desire to protect their jobs during a period of high unemployment. And employers take a strong bargaining stance because of disappointing sales and low profits.

With more moderate wage settlements, the economy moves from point V. If monetary and fiscal policies are kept tight, the rate of inflation will continue to drop; the economy will move to point W and progressively lower points. (The argument here is similar to that in Figure 13-7, except that everything is of course operating in the opposite direction.) On the other hand, if monetary and fiscal restraint is eased as the economy reaches 5 percent inflation, sales will begin to revive, unemployment will fall, and the economy will move back toward the long-run Phillips curve, at point X. (This argument corresponds to the earlier one in Figure 13-8.)

By following through the accelerationist argument, we can explain the high rates of unemployment and inflation of the 1970s. During the late 1960s, demand inflation was allowed to gather steam, both because of the desire to get unemployment down and because of government spending for the Vietnam war. The inflationary momentum was accelerated by the expansive monetary and fiscal policies of 1971–1972. Then, when high inflation rates became a matter of grave concern, demand was restrained. But inflation did not respond quickly to the tighter policies. Rather, unemployment shot upward while inflation receded only slowly from its very high rates. (Indeed, inflation was increased by skyrocketing oil prices.)

WHERE DO WE GO FROM HERE?

To explain how we got into this mess does not explain how we get out. Nevertheless, we may identify three important policy issues: (1) What are the implications of the past two decades for demand management policies? (2) What, if anything, can be done to ease the transition to a lower rate of inflation? (In other words, is there any way of reducing inflation that is less painful than sweating it out of the economy with tight monetary and fiscal policies and the high unemployment rate illustrated in Figure 13-11?) (3) What can be done to reduce the natural or equilibrium rate of unemployment in the economy? (That is, what can be done to shift the long-run Phillips curve to the left?)

Aggregate Demand: The Importance of Steady Growth

Whether one adheres to the Phelps-Friedman view of a vertical long-run Phillips curve or agrees with Eckstein and Brinner that the long-run curve bends as it approaches the horizontal axis, there is a strong advantage in aiming for a *stable* rate of growth of aggregate demand.

This point is illustrated in Figure 13-12. If the increase in demand is stable, a point (such as A) on the long-run Phillips curve will be observed continuously. Consider, now, the unstable situation, with the economy swinging back and forth from point C to point B in alternate years. Which is better, 2 years at A, or 1 year at C plus 1 year at B?

Over the 2-year period, the *average* rate of inflation is the same with the unstable economy as with the stable one; 1 year at 5 percent and 1 year at 3 percent will average out to the 4 percent at A. Because the average rate of inflation is 4 percent in either case, contracts continue to reflect this rate; the economy stays on the short-run Phillips curve shown. But note that the *average rate of unemployment is higher* with the unstable

FIGURE 13-12   Instability and the average rate of unemployment.

In terms of inflation, 2 years at *A* (with 4 percent inflation) is equivalent to 1 year at *B* (5 percent inflation) plus 1 at *C* (3 percent inflation). But in terms of unemployment, the 2 years at *A* are preferable. The 5 percent unemployment rate at *A* is less than the 5 ½ average that would result from 1 year at *B* (4 percent) and 1 year at *C* (7 percent).

alternative. Because of the bow in the short-run Phillips curve, the drop in unemployment between *A* and *B* (by 1 percent) is less than the rise between *A* and *C* (2 percent). Thus, the average rate of unemployment in an economy swinging from *B* to *C* (namely, 5.5 percent) is greater than the average rate at *A* (5 percent). This leads to an important conclusion: *Stability will contribute to a low average level of unemployment.*

Because of the importance of stability, *we cannot put "virtuous" conduct in the bank.* If we decide to follow a very restrictive demand policy and live with a high rate of unemployment, we will not acquire a "right" to an equivalent amount of compensating employment during an expansionary period in the future. Whatever the trend of demand, there is an advantage in *stability* in this trend. On this, all economists can agree. But the statement raises an important question: If everybody wants more stability, why don't we get it? The problem of instability will be the subject of Chapter 14.

There is less unanimity over what the *trend* of aggregate demand should be. Those in the Friedman-Phelps school argue that

the trend of aggregate demand is irrelevant in determining the rate of unemployment; the long-run Phillips curve is vertical all the way down to the axis. The unemployment rate with zero inflation is the same as with a steady 3 percent inflation. Since we can't achieve a lower rate of unemployment by accepting 1 or 2 percent inflation, we should aim for stable prices. Other economists, including most of those in the Keynesian tradition, believe that the long-run Phillips curve bends to the right as it approaches the axis, and that a moderately inflationary trend of aggregate demand (involving, say, 1 or 2 percent inflation) can contribute to a high rate of employment. Unfortunately, the question of whether we should ultimately aim for 2 percent inflation or 1 or 0 percent is not very important at present, since inflation rates of 6 percent or more are being forecasted into the indefinite future. Rather, the issue is whether some way can be found to bring the inflation rate down without putting the economy through the restrictive wringer, with high rates of unemployment.

Bringing the Inflation Rate Down: Proposals to Ease the Transition

High unemployment rates and high inflation rates exist together because expectations of inflation have been built into contracts. Breaking these inflationary expectations with tight aggregate demand policies is a painful process. It is only through the hardship of unemployment—or the threat of it—that the market persuades individuals and institutions to reduce their demands. However, two proposals have been made to reduce wage and price increases in a less painful manner.

1. Incomes Policies   One proposal is to use incomes policies, with the government intervening in the wage and price-making decisions in order to reduce inflation quickly.

During the 1970s, the debate over incomes policies repeated much of the earlier debate of the 1960s, with the effectiveness of such policies being a major point of dispute. New proposals to improve the effectiveness of guideposts included the Tax-based Incomes Policy (or TIP). According to this concept, the government would use the tax system to encourage compliance. For example, under the proposal of Henry Wallich and Sidney Weintraub, companies that granted wage increases in excess of an announced guidepost would be penalized with higher corporate income taxes.[16] Arthur Okun proposed an alternative. Rather than using the stick of higher taxes on those who violated the guidepost, he suggested offering the carrot of tax cuts for those who complied. The TIP proposals attracted considerable attention, particularly during the early Carter administration. Critics doubted that TIP would be effective enough to justify the complications it would introduce into the administration of the tax system.

In terms of incomes policies actually used during the 1970s, the most important occurred in the first Nixon administration. During the first half of 1971, the economy was at a point like C in Figure 13-12, with unemployment (at 6 percent) and inflation (at 4 percent) running well above their averages for the previous decade. In order to break the inflationary psychology, President Nixon in August 1971 imposed a 90-day freeze on wages, prices, and rents, followed by less rigid controls which lasted through 1972. These wage and price controls were accompanied by expansive monetary and fiscal policies aimed at reducing the rate of unemployment.

Like other experiments with incomes policies, these controls were controversial; they raised many of the issues discussed earlier with respect to the Kennedy-Johnson wage-price guideposts. In one way, they

seemed to work very well: The inflation rate dropped sharply in late 1971 and 1972, and the unemployment rate declined slightly. But inflation soon spiraled up again after the controls were relaxed: The rate of inflation by 1973 (6.2 percent) exceeded that of 1971. And by 1975, both inflation (at 9.1 percent) and unemployment (at 8.5 percent) were far above their 1971 levels. Consequently, there are two conflicting views of this episode:

(a) The wage-price controls worked, breaking the inflationary momentum and laying the basis for stable prices without going through the costs of an extended period with high rates of unemployment. But the successes of 1971 and early 1972 were blown when monetary and fiscal policy makers became too ambitious. They allowed aggregate demand to rise rapidly in 1972 and 1973, pulling inflation up to a very high rate. In other words, the freeze was a success, but it was soon wiped out by the mistake of allowing demand to increase too rapidly.

(b) The controls were not really a success at all, but merely a short-run illusion. They temporarily suppressed price increases but did not alter underlying trends. When the freeze was ended, prices quickly regained lost ground.

During the closing years of the Nixon administration and the Ford presidency, aggregate demand policies became the only major weapon against inflation; wage and price controls were avoided (with the notable exception of price controls on fuels—oil, gasoline, and natural gas).

During his 1976 election campaign, Jimmy Carter announced his intention to ask Congress for standby authority to im-

---

[16]Henry C. Wallich and Sidney Weintraub, "A Tax-Based Incomes Policy," *Journal of Economic Issues*, June 1971, pp. 1–19. At the time the proposal was made, Wallich was a professor at Yale, and Weintraub a professor at the University of Pennsylvania. (In 1974, Wallich became a member of the Board of Governors of the Federal Reserve System.)

pose wage and price controls. After his election (but before his inauguration), his statement provided businesses with an incentive to "jump the gun" by establishing higher prices that would be taken as the starting point in any control program. Indeed, the desire to jump the gun was widely interpreted as a contributing factor in the price increase announced by the steel industry soon after election day. (As steel companies had traditionally been a target of controls and guideposts, it was not surprising for them to try to protect their position.) In order to reduce such price increases motivated by the expectation of controls, Carter announced that he would not, after all, ask for standby price-control authority. During his first year in office, efforts to limit inflation were confined to low-keyed and informal discussions with business and labor, and to statements that the administration hoped that business and labor would show restraint. "Wishboning," the critics called it. It was not very effective; during Carter's first year in office, the already high inflation showed signs of accelerating.

2. Indexed Wages?

Inflation is a way of disappointing expectations.
                                    Joseph Kraft

A second possible way of easing the transition to a lower rate of inflation is to deal with the inflationary expectations that are built into wage contracts. For example, with an inflation rate of 6 percent per year, workers may demand wage increases of 9 percent per annum to compensate for the inflation and provide the 3 percent increase in real purchasing power that is their goal. Such contracts, running over a 3-year period, mean that inflation will persist even in the face of restrictive demand policies and very high rates of unemployment.

Thus, there is a vicious circle: Inflation exists because people expect it, and people expect it because it exists. Why not break this circle by providing workers with protection against inflation? In our example, this could be done by having a basic wage increase of 3 percent, with the provision that workers will also get increases to compensate for whatever changes in the cost of living occur during the lifetime of their contract. Workers should be happy with this *indexing* or *escalator clause*, because it protects wages not only against the present inflation, but also against the possibility of even high inflation in the future. Such a contract should speed the adjustment to a lower level of inflation. Progress made in reducing inflation will be reflected quickly in a lower cost-of-living adjustment to wages. A rapid deceleration of inflation becomes possible. Thus, the tying of wages to the consumer price index is an attractive proposal; it attacks a very difficult and dangerous problem at its root. But unfortunately, we cannot be certain it would solve the problem of inflationary momentum; indeed, it might make the inflation much worse.

> Wage contracts are *indexed* when they contain an *escalator clause* that provides for additional money wages to compensate for increases in the consumer price index.

The reason is this: If all wages are indexed, wage negotiations focus on real incomes. Suppose, in the various negotiations that take place, people negotiate real wage and salary increases of 4 percent on average. (That is, they negotiate increases of 4 percent plus whatever change occurs in prices.) But suppose, also, that labor productivity is going up by only 2 percent. Then such contracts are inconsistent with what the economy can actually produce.[17] If in-

[17]For a limited period, workers might gain as the share of wages in national income rises at the expense of other shares, such as profits. But a quick glance back at the relative income shares in Figure 7-4 shows that this cannot continue very long before profits disappear altogether. And if profits are squeezed, investment will decline, reducing the productivity gains from which future wage increases can be paid.

consistent contracts had been made in nominal dollar terms, the inconsistency would be "solved" by inflation: Prices would rise until people end up with less in real purchasing power than they expected when they negotiated their money wages. But, with indexed wages, there is no such simple solution. Wages will rise ever more rapidly, chasing an impossible target. An open inflationary spiral can result. In other words, if an indexation scheme is to be widely adopted, it is essential that there be some mechanism to prevent the total claims on national product from exceeding what the economy can actually produce.[18] Otherwise, indexation can become part of the cause rather than part of the cure for inflation.

This problem with indexation is formidable. We all like to believe that our individual contribution is particularly worthy, and that we each deserve a larger share of the economic pie. Thus, wage negotiators have a tendency to push for a real wage increase greater than the average increase in productivity for the economy as a whole. And this problem has become more acute in the past decade. Between 1950 and 1968, average productivity per worker increased by about 2.5 percent per annum. But in the decade since, the increase has fallen to an annual rate of about 1.5 percent.[19] Thus, if indexing were generally adopted, some way would have to be found to keep negotiated real wage increases down to a level that many workers would consider pitifully small.

What Can Be Done to Reduce the Equilibrium Rate of Unemployment?

Even if we were to get a smooth transition to an equilibrium at a lower rate of inflation, our macroeconomic problems would not be solved. There would still be a sizable amount of unemployment due to frictional and structural causes. Indeed, estimates of the equilibrium or natural rate of unemployment—below which inflation will begin to accelerate—have been revised upward substantially during the past two decades. During the early years of the Kennedy administration, the 4 percent unemployment target was considered achievable without unleashing inflationary pressures.[20] But by the middle seventies, the Council of Economic Advisers was suggesting that the natural rate had risen by 1 percent or perhaps more.[21] And some recent statistical work has concluded that the natural rate of unemployment may now be as high as 6 percent.[22] Two explanations have been put forward for the apparent upward creep in the rate of unemployment that can be achieved without accelerating inflation.

The first is based on the change in the composition of the labor force. Compared with the sixties, the labor force in the 1970s contained a larger percentage of teenagers,

---

[18]Partly on the basis of the favorable Brazilian experience with indexation, Milton Friedman suggested the indexing of wage contracts in the United States. But the indexing system in Brazil had a special, built-in mechanism to control inflation. Wages were not adjusted for actual inflation, but rather, for the inflation rate predicted by the government. Not surprisingly, the predicted rate was generally less than the actual rate proved to be. Thus, the indexing system was used as a means for shaving real wages. It was, in a sense, a cross between an indexing system and a system of wage-price controls. The Brazilian experience therefore does not provide a good test of what would happen in the event of a full indexation of wages.

[19]One of the reasons for this fall apparently has been environmental protection and other government regulations, which have required business investment that does not increase output as conventionally measured. On the important topic of lagging productivity in the United States economy, see Council of Economic Advisers, *Annual Report, 1978*, pp. 146–149; and Edward F. Denison, "Effects of Selected Changes in the Institutional and Human Environment upon Output per Unit of Input," *Survey of Current Business* (U.S. Department of Commerce), January 1978, pp. 21–44.

[20]Council of Economic Advisers, *Annual Report, 1962*, pp. 44–47.

[21]Council of Economic Advisers, *Annual Report, 1975*, pp. 94–97.

[22]Phillip Cagan, "Reduction of Inflation and the Magnitude of Unemployment," in William Fellner (ed.), *Contemporary Economic Problems, 1977* (Washington: American Enterprise Institute, 1977), p. 16.

who have higher unemployment rates than adults (Figure 13-13). As teenagers became a larger fraction of the labor force, the overall unemployment rate tended to rise. But because of changes in the birthrate over the past two decades, the percentage of teenagers in the labor force will decline in the early 1980s, and this drop should tend to reduce the overall rate of unemployment somewhat.[23]

The second explanation is that improvements in unemployment insurance and welfare tend to keep up the incomes of those thrown out of work. As a consequence, they are less desperate to take the first job that comes along. Frictional unemployment rises as those out of work engage in a more leisurely search for jobs.[24] It is not clear what, if anything, should be done about this: The objective of reducing unemployment comes into conflict with the goal of reducing the hardship of those unemployed. Nevertheless, it does underline the need to keep incentives in mind when designing government programs, and in particular, to try to avoid peculiar situations where people may actually be better off not working.

But what can be done to reduce the equilibrium rate of unemployment? First, steps to reduce discrimination against blacks and women can help by reducing the high rates of unemployment of those groups. Second, government training programs have been greatly expanded over the past 15 years under such programs as the Comprehensive Employment and Training Act (CETA). The purpose of such programs is clear: to help the chronically unemployed prepare themselves for useful work. Unfortunately, early studies of these programs suggest that they have been expensive and only moderately successful. (More comprehensive studies of CETA are currently under way.) It is hard to see training programs as *the* solution to hard-core or teenage unemployment, although they may be *part* of a solution.

The Government as the Employer of Last Resort? A much more ambitious approach would be for the government to act as the *employer of last resort*; that is, the government would stand ready to offer jobs to those who want work but are unable to find it in the private sector.

Although the government now has no such commitment to provide last-resort jobs, it has taken some steps in that direction with the Public Service Employment Program, which was expanded into an $8.4 billion program to provide 725,000 jobs during President Carter's first year in office. A stronger proposal was contained in the original 1976 version of the Humphrey-Hawkins bill (officially known as the Full Employment and Balanced Growth Act). That bill would have committed the government to offer whatever jobs were needed to get the unemployment rate down to a target of 3 percent per annum.

Proposals to make the government the employer of last resort are very controversial. (Indeed, they are so controversial that the last-resort provisions were dropped from later versions of the Humphrey-Hawkins

[23]Some economists have argued that the increasing participation by women in the labor force has also tended to push up the unemployment rate. However, others believe that there is no necessary relationship between women's participation and the equilibrium unemployment rate. On this controversial point, see Clair Vickery, Barbara R. Bergmann, and Katherine Swartz, "Unemployment Rate Targets and Anti-inflation Policy as More Women Enter the Workforce," *American Economic Review,* May 1978, pp. 90–94.

[24]For example, Stephen T. Marston has concluded that the average job seeker who is drawing unemployment insurance looks between 20 and 30 percent longer before taking a new job than does the average uninsured job seeker. Stephen T. Marston, "The Impact of Unemployment Insurance on Job Search," *Brookings Papers on Economic Activity,* 1975, vol. 1, pp. 13–48.

In Canada, there was a major liberalization of unemployment insurance in 1971. Canadian studies indicate that this added almost 1 percent to the unemployment rate.

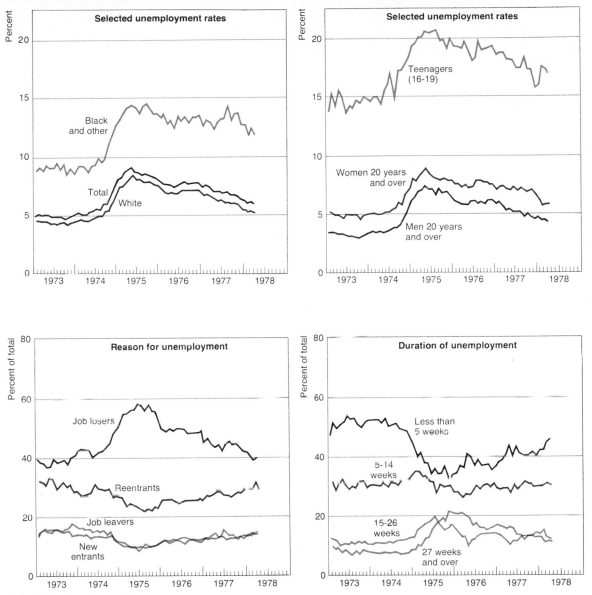

FIGURE 13-13   Unemployment.
Unemployment rates vary greatly among different groups in the economy. Blacks consistently have an unemployment rate that is about twice as high as that of whites. Women have higher unemployment rates than men. And teenagers have the highest unemployment rates of all. Even during the prosperous year of 1973, the teenage unemployment rate was still almost 15 percent. And during the recession of 1974–1975, it rose to more than 20 percent.

The lower two figures show how the nature of unemployment changes during a recession. During good times (such as 1973), most of the unemployed are not people who have been fired or laid off (job losers). Rather, most are those who have quit or are entrants into the labor market who have not yet found jobs. But during the recession of 1974–1975, more than half the unemployed were job losers. During the recession, note how the duration of unemployment increased.

bill.) On the positive side, government projects might give the unemployed something useful to do. For example, the unemployed might do maintenance jobs in the cities, or carry out conservation and public works projects similar to those of Roosevelt's recovery program in the 1930s.

On the other side, two related objections are made. The first is the cost of such a program. The expenditure of $8.4 billion for 725,000 jobs in Carter's first year works out to more than $11,500 per job. The second objection is that a government program of last-resort employment might weaken incentives to work in the private sector; thus, a larger and larger government sector might become an increasing burden on the private sectors that have to support the government with their tax payments. In particular, unless wages in last-resort jobs were kept below wages in the private sector, people would have no incentive to move out of the last-resort jobs and into private employment. But proponents of last-resort jobs have shown little sensitivity to this problem. In the original Humphrey-Hawkins bill, for example, "fair" rates of pay for public employment jobs were defined extremely generously. This led Charles L. Schultze (who later became Carter's chairman of the Council of Economic Advisers) to criticize the bill since it could lead to the following peculiar outcome:

A person can turn down a private industry job and still be eligible for a "last-resort" job. . . . An unskilled laborer earning, say, $2.50 an hour in private industry can afford to quit, remain unemployed for four to six weeks . . . then claim a "last-resort" job paying . . . $3.50 to $4.50 an hour, and come out way ahead.[25]

Indeed, since private employers might have to match the high government wage scales in order to retain workers, a poorly designed program of last-resort employment might significantly contribute to cost-push inflation, and thus make it even more difficult to achieve the twin objectives of high employment and stable prices.

In aiming for these two goals, there seems to be no simple solution. This is a problem with which we will have to struggle in the decades ahead.

[25]Testimony before the United States Senate, Subcommittee on Unemployment, May 1976.

Key Points

1. The data for recent decades do not fit a simple L-shaped aggregate supply function; indeed, they show little consistent relationship between unemployment and the rate of inflation.

2. However, during the 1960s, the annual observations do trace out a Phillips curve. The observations for the 1970s are above and to the right of this curve.

3. The Kennedy-Johnson administrations invoked wage-price guideposts to keep the average level of prices stable as the economy expanded. Until 1965, prices were indeed reasonably stable. Thereafter, the guideposts were violated with increasing frequency, and inflation gathered momentum.

4. Wage-price guideposts and other forms of incomes policies are controversial on three principal grounds:

> (*a*) Are they effective?
> (*b*) Do they adversely affect allocative efficiency?
> (*o*) Are they consistent with economic freedom?

5. Two major explanations have been offered for the simultaneous high rates of inflation and unemployment of the 1970s—that is, for the upward shift in the short-run Phillips curve:

> (*a*) Cost push, particularly in the form of higher oil prices
> (*b*) Higher wage settlements, which include catch-ups for past inflation and/or protection against expected future inflation

6. Insofar as expectations of inflation are built into wage and other contracts, the short-run Phillips curve will be unstable; there will be a different curve for every expected rate of inflation.

7. Phelps and Friedman argue that there is no "money illusion." In the long run, people adjust completely to a steady, expected rate of inflation. As a consequence, there is no long-run trade-off between inflation and unemployment; the long-run Phillips curve is a vertical straight line.

8. While other economists agree that the long-run Phillips curve is vertical once inflation exceeds 2 or 3 percent per annum, they believe that it bends to the right as inflation drops below 2 or 3 percent. Thus, the acceptance of small rates of inflation can help to achieve low rates of unemployment.

9. Regardless of which of these two views is correct, the long-run average rate of unemployment will be lower, the more stable is the path of aggregate demand.

10. Using restrictive aggregate demand to reduce inflation can result in very high rates of unemployment. Two proposals have been offered to ease the transition to a lower rate of inflation:

> (*a*) Incomes policies. These raise the same three controversial issues noted in key point 4.
> (*b*) Indexed wages. These might work, but they raise the danger of an explosive inflation—if real wage settlements exceed the rate of productivity increase.

11. Proposals to decrease the equilibrium rate of unemployment include:

> (*a*) Steps to reduce discrimination against blacks and women
> (*b*) Training programs for the unemployed
> (*c*) A program in which the government acts as the employer of last resort

The third proposal is particularly controversial because of its cost and because of the difficulty of designing incentives for people to move out of last-resort employment and into the private sector.

Key Terms

frictional unemployment
structural unemployment
Phillips curve
stagflation
policy dilemma
trade-off
premature inflation
guideposts
incomes policies

productivity
real wage
jawboning
black market
demand-pull inflation
cost-push inflation
shift in the Phillips curve
acceleration of inflation
wage-price spiral

contracts adjusted for inflation
money illusion
long-run Phillips curve
natural rate of unemployment
tax-based incomes policy (TIP)
indexed wage
escalator clause
employer of last resort

Problems

13-1 During the first year of Carter's administration, suggestions that wage-price guideposts might be imposed led to strong objections from labor unions and business executives. Why should labor be against wage-price guideposts if they make possible a combination of low inflation and low unemployment? Why might business executives oppose wage-price guideposts?

13-2 Why does the (short-run) Phillips curve bend more and more steeply upward as it goes to the left? That is, why isn't it a straight line?

13-3 Explain why expansive demand policies aimed at a low rate of unemployment might cause a wage-price spiral and an accelerating rate of inflation.

13-4 What difference does it make whether the long-run Phillips curve is vertical (as Phelps and Friedman argue), or curved toward the lower end (as Eckstein and Brinner suggest)? What policies would be appropriate in the one case, but not in the other? As long as inflation is running above 5 percent per annum, is this controversy important?

13-5 A steady increase in aggregate demand will result in a lower average rate of unemployment over an extended period of time than will a stop-go policy, which involves alternate periods of restrictive and expansive policies. Why?

13-6 If the Phillips curve (such as that shown in red in Figure 13-4) is stable only in the short run, how did Phillips originally find a curve for Britain that was stable for almost a full century?

*13-7 Would you favor the government's acting as the employer of last resort? Why or why not? If you are in favor, what jobs would you give to those hired under a last-resort program? How much would you pay them? Would you place any time limit on how long they can work for the government under this program?

If you are opposed, do you have any alternative proposals to reduce unemployment below 6 percent (where some economists expect inflation to begin to accelerate)? What are the advantages and disadvantages of your proposals?

chapter 14
Why Is the Economy Unstable ?

A recession is when your neighbor is out of work. A depression is when you're out of work.
Harry S. Truman

Although we all want a stable, steady growth of the economy, we don't get it. Business conditions rarely stand still. Moderate expansions often give way to inflationary booms; and inflationary booms give way to recessions. This chapter asks the question: Why? Why has the economy been unstable? What disturbing forces are at work within the economy, and what shocks come from the outside? And why have the tools of fiscal and monetary management been inadequate to eliminate economic instability? Indeed, why do the activities of the federal government and the Federal Reserve sometimes make business fluctuations worse?

FLUCTUATIONS IN BUSINESS ACTIVITY

National product accounting is a relatively modern invention; it is only since 1929 that the United States government has collected GNP data on a regular basis. But, by using historical statistics on production and finance (railroad and canal shipments, blast furnace output, bank clearings, etc.), we can trace the ups and downs of American business from the beginning of the Republic. Figure 14-1 shows estimates of business activity since 1835, as compiled by the Cleveland Trust Company.

Of all the fluctuations in our history, the largest took place between 1929 and 1944. First came the collapse into the Great Depression, with real GNP falling by more than 30 percent between 1929 and 1933. This was followed by a long and painful recovery, interrupted by the recession of 1937–1938. It was not until the huge demand for munitions during World War II that the economy fully recovered. After the war, there was a temporary drop in output as factories were converted from guns and ammunition to peacetime products. Since that time, there have been a series of recessions: in 1948–1949, 1953–1954, 1957–1958, 1960–1961, 1969–1970, and 1973–1975. The fluctuations in economic activity are irregular; no two recessions are exactly alike. Nor are any two expansions. Some expansions

295

FIGURE 14-1 Business activity, 1835 to 1977.
Business activity fluctuates irregularly. The biggest swing occurred between 1929 and 1945, with the economy first collapsing into the Great Depression and then rising to a peak of war production. Earlier booms were associated with such events as the California gold rush and railroad building. Early recessions generally came in the aftermath of wars, or as a result of financial disturbances, such as the panic of 1907 which led to the founding of the Federal Reserve. SOURCE: Cleveland Trust Co.

last for years, the 1961–1969 expansion being the most notable example. Others are short-lived, such as the expansion of 1958–1959, which quickly gave way to a new recession. The economy is not a pendulum swinging regularly at specific intervals. If it were, the analysis of business fluctuations would be much simplified: The movement of a pendulum is easily predicted.

Four Phases of the Business Cycle

Because business fluctuations are so irregular, it is perhaps surprising that they are called "cycles." But they all have the same four phases (Figure 14-2).

The key to identifying a business cycle is to identify a *recession*—the period when economic activity is declining. But this immediately raises a problem of definition: How far down does the economy have to go

before a recession is declared? There is political as well as economic significance in the answer: No administration wants to be blamed for creating a recession. A private research organization—the National Bureau of Economic Research (NBER)—is the guardian of the keys; it declares what is, and what is not, a recession. Its major test is historical: Is a current downswing as long and severe as declines of the past that have been tagged as "recessions"? But fortunately, as we saw in Chapter 1, there is also a simpler test:

A *recession* occurs when real gross national product declines for two or more consecutive quarters.[1] (The quarterly data used in this test are seasonally adjusted, a procedure explained in Box 14-1.)

---

[1]There is no similar, accepted definition of a depression. Because the depression of the 1930s was so deep and long-lasting, unemployment would have to be severe and persistent before we should talk of a depression. Perhaps the definition should require that unemployment be at double-digit levels (that is, 10 percent or more) for a full 2 years.

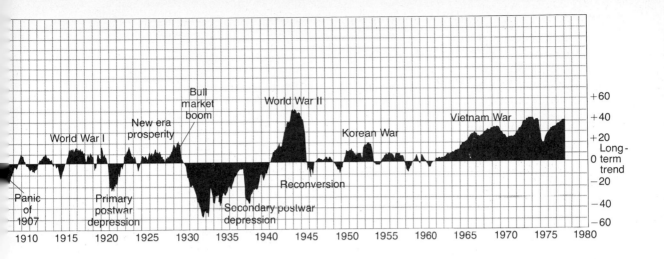

(Every decline of the past which the NBER has identified as a recession has met this simple definition.)

As production declines during a recession, business profits drop and unemployment rises. The increase in unemployment generally lags behind the change in output; most businesses are reluctant to lay off or fire workers.

The recession ends with the *trough*; that

FIGURE 14-2 Four phases of the business cycle.
Periods of expansion and recession alternate, with peaks and troughs in between. The National Bureau of Economic Research identifies each recession, the peak month that precedes it, and the trough month that ends the recession. Not every expansion reaches a high degree of prosperity with a low unemployment rate; an expansion sometimes ends prematurely and a new recession begins.

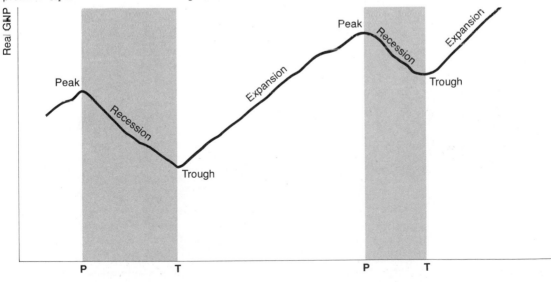

BOX 14-1
SEASONAL ADJUSTMENT OF ECONOMIC DATA

Not all ups and downs in economic activity are problems. Crops grow by the calendar; harvests are gleaned in the summer and autumn months. The month-to-month swings in food production reflect a law of nature with which we learn to live. And retail sales boom in December, only to collapse in January.

Such regular month-to-month swings are not our concern. The decline in retail sales in January is the result of high Christmas buying; it is not a symptom of a coming recession. In order to identify a recession, we must remove the seasonal effects; that is, we must *seasonally adjust* our data on production, sales, etc. The following technique is used.

From past information, suppose the statistician discovers that December sales of toys typically run at three times the average monthly rate, only to drop to one-half the average monthly rate in January. The raw data for toy sales can then be seasonally adjusted by dividing December's sales by 3 and multiplying January's sales by 2. (In fact, more complicated techniques than this are used; but this is the general idea.) Similarly, quarterly data for GNP or monthly indexes of industrial production can be adjusted to remove seasonal fluctuations, and help to identify the underlying movements in the economy.

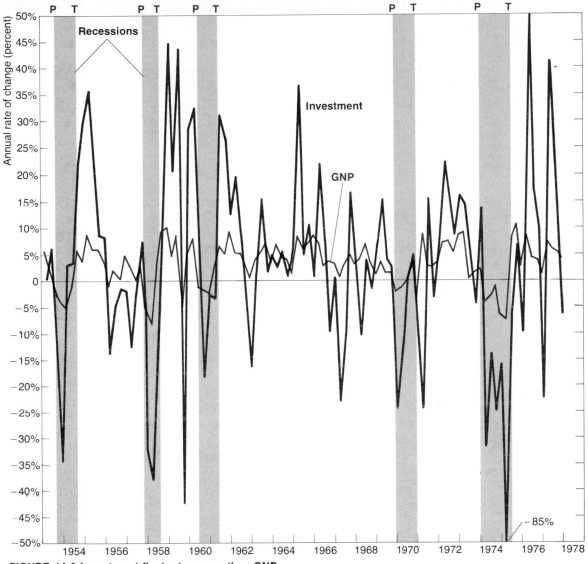

FIGURE 14-3 Investment fluctuates more than GNP.
This diagram shows the quarter-to-quarter changes in real GNP and real investment. Investment usually changes by a much greater percentage than GNP. (It is conventional to show quarterly changes at annual rates. For example, if investment rose from 100 in one quarter to 101 in the next quarter, this change would be 1 percent per quarter, or 4 percent at an annual rate. This diagram follows this convention, showing annual rates of change. Data were seasonally adjusted.)

is, the month when economic activity is at its lowest. This is followed by the *expansion* phase. Output increases, and profits, employment, wages, prices, and interest rates generally rise. Historically, the *peak* or upper turning point was often associated with a financial panic, such as the panic of 1907 or "Black Tuesday"—October 29, 1929, when the stock market crashed. Recent peaks have been less dramatic, with one notable exception. The economic peak in late 1973 coincided with war in the Middle East, an oil embargo, and skyrocketing oil prices.

The Sources of Instability

Instability does exist, then. But why?

An obvious way to approach this question is to look at each of the major components of aggregate demand: investment, consumption, net exports, and government purchases of goods and services. In the following pages, each of these components will be considered in turn, to see why they might fluctuate from month to month or year to year. We will then turn to a disconcerting possibility mentioned earlier—that government policies, on either the fiscal or monetary side, may have contributed to instability.

Of the major components of national product, investment claims first attention: It

has been the most unstable. Figure 14-3 shows how investment fluctuates by a greater percentage than GNP.

INVESTMENT DEMAND: The Accelerator

Investment demand depends on a number of variables. One of them—namely, the interest rate—was considered in Chapter 12. There, we looked at how monetary policy can affect the interest rate and thus influence investment and aggregate demand.

But, while interest rate changes can give an important insight into how monetary policy works, they are scarcely the most important cause of changes in investment. Historically, investment has usually risen in periods when interest rates were rising (in other words, investment has risen in spite of rising interest rates); and investment has fallen when interest rates were sliding

TABLE 14-1
The Acceleration Principle

Time	(1) Yearly sales of bicycles (in thousands)	(2) Desired number of machines (column 2 ÷ 10 thousand)	(3) Net investment (change in column 2)	(4) Gross investment (column 3 + replacement of 2 machines)
Phase I: Steady sales				
First year	200	20	0	2
Second year	200	20	0	2
Phase II: Rising sales				
Third year	220	22	2	4
Fourth year	240	24	2	4
Phase III: A leveling off				
Fifth year	250	25	1	3
Sixth year	250	25	0	2
Phase IV: Declining sales				
Seventh year	230	23	−2	0
Eighth year	210	21	−2	0
Phase V: A leveling off				
Ninth year	200	20	−1	1
Tenth year	200	20	0	2

Investment fluctuates much more than consumption. Net investment depends on the *change* in consumption.

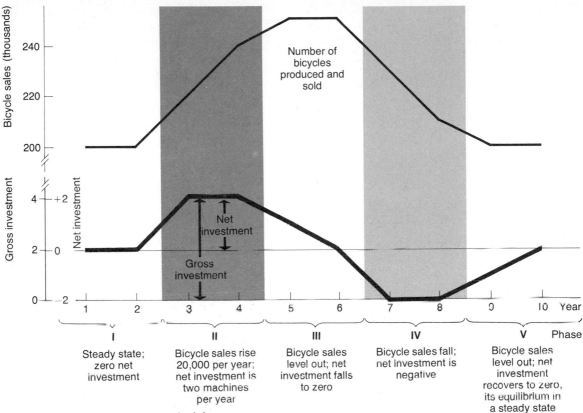

FIGURE 14-4 The acceleration principle.

Phase I: Steady state; zero net investment

Phase II: Bicycle sales rise 20,000 per year; net investment is two machines per year

Phase III: Bicycle sales level out; net investment falls to zero

Phase IV: Bicycle sales fall; net investment is negative

Phase V: Bicycle sales level out; net investment recovers to zero, its equilibrium in a steady state

downward. The major engine that drives investment is not interest rates, but something else.

Suppose we approach this question (about the major cause of changes in investment) by putting ourselves in the business executive's shoes. Why should we want to invest? Why, for example, should we want to acquire more machines?

The simplest answer is that businesses want more machines because they want to produce more goods. Consider the numerical illustration in Table 14-1 and Figure 14-4. Suppose initially that a bicycle manufacturer sells 200,000 bicycles every year, and that one machine is needed for every 10,000 bicycles produced. Assume also that the manufacturer initially has the 20 machines needed to produce the 200,000 bicycles. So long as the demand for bicycles

remains stable (as shown in Table 14-1, Phase I, years 1 and 2), there is no need for additional machines; there is no net investment.

That does not, however, mean that machine production is zero. Suppose that a machine lasts for 10 years, with 2 of the original 20 machines wearing out each year. So long as the demand for bicycles remains constant at 200,000 per year, then gross investment will continue to be 2 machines per year. (That is, 2 machines will be purchased to replace the 2 that wear out each year.)

Now, suppose that the demand for bicycles starts to grow in Phase II. In the third year, sales increase by 10 percent, from 200,000 to 220,000. As a consequence, the manufacturer needs 22 machines; 2 additional machines must be acquired. Gross investment therefore rises to 4 machines—2 replacements plus 2 net additions. An increase in sales of only 10 percent has had an *accelerated* or magnified effect on investment: Gross investment has risen from 2 to 4 machines, or by no less than 100 percent. (This magnified effect on investment provides an important clue as to why investment fluctuates so much more than GNP in Figure 14-3.) Then in the fourth year, with the *growth* of sales remaining constant at 20,000 units, gross investment remains constant at 4 machines per year.

Next, see what happens in Phase III. In the fifth year, demand begins to level out. As growth slows to 10,000 bicycles, only one additional machine is needed. Both net and gross investment *decline* as a result of the *slowing of the growth* of bicycle sales. We emphasize: An actual decline in sales is not necessary to cause a decline in investment. (Sales did not decline in the fifth year; they merely grew more slowly than in the fourth year.) Then, when the demand for bicycles levels out in the sixth year, there is no longer a need for any additional machines; net investment drops to zero, and gross investment falls back to two. Then, if bicycle sales begin to decline in Phase IV (year 7), the number of machines which the manufacturer needs will decline; the machines which are wearing out will not be replaced. Net investment becomes negative, and gross investment can fall to zero.

This example of the acceleration principle illustrates a number of important points:

1. Investment (in machines) fluctuates by a much greater percentage than consumption (of bicycles).

2. Net investment depends on the *change* in consumption.

3. Once consumption begins to rise, it must continue to grow steadily if investment is to remain constant. A reduction in the growth of consumption will cause a *decline* in investment (year 5). But very rapid rates

of growth of sales may be unsustainable. Therefore, a very rapid upswing in economic activity contains the seeds of its own destruction. As the rate of growth of consumption slows up, investment will tend to fall off.

4. It is possible for gross investment to collapse, even though there is only a mild decline in sales (year 7).

5. For investment to recover, it is not necessary for sales to swing upward. A reduction in the rate of decline of sales is sufficient (year 9). Thus, a decline in economic activity contains the seeds of recovery.

This illustration was simplified, but the validity of its major points may be shown in a few examples. If business slackens off and fewer goods are shipped, the amount of trucking declines. Consequently, the demand for new trucks will decline sharply; in the face of even a mild decline in total trucking, there is no need to replace the trucks being worn out. Or consider what happens when the birthrate declines. Construction of schools is cut back. (New schools are needed primarily to accommodate an increase in the student population.) The accelerator applies to other forms of investment (like school buildings, teacher training, and factories) as well as to machines.

The accelerator also applies to inventory investment, and this can add to the instability of the economy. Merchants may attempt to keep their inventories in proportion to sales. Thus, when sales increase, orders to the factory may be increased even more in order to achieve a desired buildup of inventories. Similarly, when sales fall, orders to the factory may be cut back even more in order to reduce inventories. Indeed, swings in inventory investment have been such important contributors to all recessions of the past 30 years (except that of 1969–1970) that these recessions are often referred to as "inventory recessions." In Figure 14-5,

FIGURE 14-5 Inventory changes.
Inventory investment fluctuates sharply. With the exception of the 1969-1970 recession, inventory investment became negative in every recent recession. (Data are seasonally adjusted, with changes shown at annual rates.)

note that in each recession except that of 1969–1970, inventory investment became negative. (That is, businesses reduced their inventories.) Nevertheless, inventory investment does not always act as a destabilizing force. There is no need for retailers to keep any rigid relationship between their sales and inventories. Indeed, the effects of temporary spurts in sales may be cushioned by the existence of inventories: Retailers may meet the increased demand by running down their inventories.

Modification of the Simple Accelerator: Lags in Investment

Even in the case of a manufacturing operation, it is an oversimplification to assume that a rigid relationship exists between sales and the number of machines; to assume, in our example in Table 14-1, that one machine is needed for every 10,000 bicycles produced. In reality, the *capital/output ratio* is not fixed. Instead of acquiring new machines, a firm can run its factories overtime when demand increases. And, at the end of

10 years, an old machine does not suddenly disintegrate; it wears out gradually. During a boom, older machines can be kept in use beyond their normal retirement age.

> The *capital/output ratio* is the value of capital (machines, factories, etc.) divided by the value of annual output.

What should be taken into account by businesses in deciding whether to buy new machinery or to "make do" by patching up old machinery or scheduling overtime? One important consideration is how long an increase in sales is expected to last. If it is just a temporary spurt and will quickly subside, expensive new machines should not be ordered. They may not be received quickly enough to meet the bulge in demand, and may add to idle capacity during the next downturn. Thus, the immediate response to increases in sales may be to schedule overtime, and to wait and see before ordering new machines. As a result, there are significant delays in the response of investment to changes in sales.

From the point of view of our current question regarding the causes of economic instability, these delays represent both an advantage and a disadvantage. In the short run, they add to stability: Businesses do not rush out to buy new machines with every little increase in sales. But, over longer periods, lags can add to the force of an upswing or a downswing. If high levels of sales continue for some time, businesses conclude that prosperity is permanent; orders for new machines are placed. Once this happens, competitors may become concerned: If they don't jump on the bandwagon, they may lose their place in a growing market. A boom psychology can develop. Although it is initially slow to respond, investment demand can gain considerable momentum.

Interactions between consumption and investment can add to the momentum of the economy.[2] As more machines are ordered, incomes rise in the machinery-producing industries. As incomes rise, people consume more. As they buy more consumer goods, business optimism is confirmed—the rising sales are "for real." As a consequence, orders for plant and equipment may be increased even more.

When the lessons of the simple accelerator model (listed earlier as points 1 through 5) are modified by the effect of time lags, we can identify three stages in the response of investment to a reduction in the rate of growth of sales:

1. In the very short run (of a few weeks or months), there will be little if any effect on investment in plant and equipment. Inventories are temporarily allowed to increase, cushioning the effects of changes in demand. There are also other "cushions": Overtime is canceled, and the opportunity is taken to retire machines that have been kept in service past their normal lifetimes.

2. If sales continue to be weak, business executives begin to fear the worst. Rather than accumulate higher and higher inventories, they cut back sharply on their production. And as production falls, they slash new orders for machines. Momentum is added to the downswing as laid-off workers reduce their consumption.

3. But consumption demand does not continue to decline indefinitely. While some purchases may easily be postponed, consumers try to maintain their expenditures for food and other necessities. Furthermore, as durable goods (such as refrigerators and autos) wear out, consumers become increasingly anxious to replace them. As the decline in consumer spending moderates, investment in machinery and buildings begins to recover. (However, the recovery may be delayed by the desire of retailers, wholesalers, and manufacturers to work off excessive inventories.)

Each of these three stages is important, and each contains its own valuable lesson. These lessons are, respectively:

1. Investment is not volatile in the face of small and temporary reductions in the rate of growth of sales.

2. If sales remain weak for some time, investment falls. Feedbacks between falling investment and falling consumer demand add to the downward momentum of the economy.

3. But the downward movement does not continue forever. Even in the worst depressions, economic activity does not collapse toward zero. The accelerator process generates natural forces of recovery, once the rate of decline of consumption slows down.

---

[2]The relationship between consumption and investment was explored more formally in a well-known early article by Paul A. Samuelson, "Interactions between the Multiplier Analysis and the Principle of Acceleration," *Review of Economic Statistics*, May 1939, pp. 75–78.

Three similar forces are in operation during the recovery phase of a cycle: a slow initial response; a gathering momentum; and the seeds of a coming decline. Here, however, one important distinction must be made. If the increase in demand can be kept moderate and steady, the natural rebound into recession may be avoided: While consumption will not fall indefinitely in a recession, it can rise consistently and steadily at a constant rate during an expansion. A *moderate* growth in consumption need not turn around into a recession. For this reason, a moderate growth can be more healthy and lasting than a business boom.

One final observation ties back to the discussion of monetary policy in Chapter 12. In an expansion, businesses must decide how much new machinery to order, and how much they will "make do" by scheduling overtime and keeping old machines in production. In this decision, a relevant consideration is the cost of new machines. There are two important types of cost: (1) the price of the machine itself; and (2) the price of the financing—that is, the interest rate. Here, of course, is where monetary policy comes in. By pushing up interest rates, open market sales can raise the cost of acquiring new machines or buildings or inventories; thus, they can slow down an investment boom.

CONSUMPTION DEMAND

In percentage terms, consumption fluctuates by much less than investment during business cycles. Indeed, consumption generally fluctuates by a smaller percentage than total GNP (Figure 14-6). Nevertheless, changes in consumer expenditures, particularly on durables, can add to the severity of business fluctuations.

Consumer durables, such as cars or washing machines, have some of the characteristics of the machinery used by industry. They have extended useful lives of 5, 10, 15 years, or even more. Because durables do not

wear out suddenly, consumers have considerable discretion as to when they replace such items. If consumers face financial difficulties, or if they are pessimistic about the future, they can defer the purchase of new cars and other durables. As a consequence, purchases of consumer durables fluctuate more than the purchases of items like food.

Consumer durable purchases may add to the downswing in economic activity. For example, as the economy slid into the worst recession in more than three decades in 1974, auto sales (in current dollars) fell to $41.9 billion from the $49.7 billion of 1973. Worries over the availability and cost of gasoline contributed to this decline. Consumer durables may also add momentum to the recovery: By 1976, car sales rose to $61.5 billion. Rising consumer optimism was one of the reasons for this increase. But it was also partly due to the condition of many cars on the road. After keeping their old cars past normal trade-in age in 1974 and 1975, many car owners were eager to replace their aging vehicles by 1976.

Thus, consumer durable purchases, like investment, carry the seeds of a turnaround. After a period of falling and low sales, existing durables begin to wear out, and the consumer is increasingly anxious to replace them. Alternatively, after several years of booming auto sales, a decline may be the natural result: With so many relatively new cars in their possession, consumers retire from the market.

How Consumer Behavior Acts as a Stabilizing Influence

During a business upswing, consumption increases, thus adding to the strength of the boom. If consumers didn't spend more, there wouldn't be the mutually reinforcing feedbacks between investment and consumption.

But, in another sense, consumer behavior adds to the stability of the economy. While it is true that consumption rises in a boom, it goes up proportionately less than

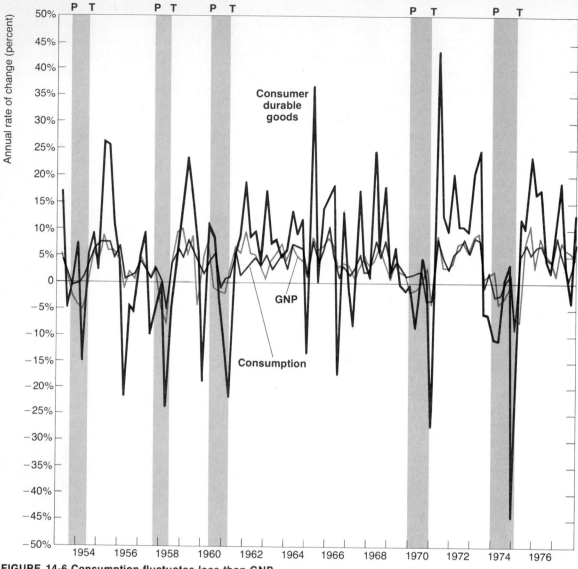

FIGURE 14-6 Consumption fluctuates less than GNP.
Total consumption expenditures fluctuate less than GNP. But one component of consumption—durable goods—fluctuates more than GNP.

disposable income; the rest of income is saved. The leakage out of the income stream and into saving provides an important element of stability. (Like the leakage into taxes, the leakage into saving acts as an automatic stabilizer.)

Similarly, consumer behavior contributes to stability during a business slump. Consumption falls, but by less than income.

Indeed, during a particularly sharp slump, large numbers of consumers spend more than their incomes—they *dissave*, either by drawing on past savings or by borrowing.

NET EXPORTS

Net exports (that is, exports minus imports) can be a disturbing force. Or they can act as a stabilizer, reducing the amplitude of fluctuations originating elsewhere in the economy.

The relationship between international trade and the domestic economy will be considered in detail in Chapter 16; for the moment, we will hit the high points. International trade can be a source of instability for two reasons. First, major changes can occur in the market for internationally traded commodities. Most conspicuously, the quadrupling of the price of oil by the Organization of Petroleum Exporting Countries in 1973 and 1974 provided a shock to the United States economy. Second, business cycles in one country have a tendency to spread to others. A boom in Western Europe, for example, will stimulate the United States economy. As Western Europeans buy more of a whole range of products, they will also buy more American goods, thereby increasing United States exports. And an increase in United States exports sets off a multiplier process, just as an increase in investment demand does. (It doesn't matter whether there is a $100 million purchase of United States machines by American businesses or by Europeans. In either case, income will be generated in the American machinery industry, and this income will be spent and respent in the multiplier process described in Chapter 8.)

While changes in our exports have a multiplied effect on the United States national product, the existence of imports reduces the magnitude of our fluctuations. Like saving and taxes, imports represent a stabilizing leakage from the domestic spending stream. The higher the *marginal propensity to import*, the lower will be the multiplier and the more stable will national product tend to be. For example, when United States incomes rise, Americans generally buy more cars—including more Japanese and German vehicles. If imported cars were not available, Americans would buy the products of Detroit instead. Incomes in Michigan would rise even more rapidly; the expansion would

be even stronger at home. Similarly, imports moderate a recession. As incomes decline, our imports of cars and other products also decline. Since some of the sales losses fall on Japan and Germany rather than Detroit, the downswing in American GNP is moderated.

> The *marginal propensity to import* is defined as the change in imports divided by the change in national product.

Because one country's imports represent another's exports, international trade has contrasting effects on the two trading partners during a business upswing. An expansion originating in the United States causes an increase in the nation's imports. Since these rising imports are exports of a foreign country (such as France), expansion occurs in that country as well. But, to the United States, the imports represent a leakage; they slow down the domestic expansion.

GOVERNMENT SPENDING: States and Localities

Of the components of national product, government spending is still to be considered. The spending of the federal government will be studied in later sections that deal with fiscal policy. But we should also look briefly at the activities of state and local governments. Their operations are generally not included under the heading of fiscal policies because they have neither the *incentive* nor the *ability* of the federal government to stabilize the economy with changes in spending or tax rates. Their policies are designed with other objectives in mind.

They lack the incentive to try to stabilize the economy because the state or locality itself gets only a small fraction of any of the stabilizing benefit of its actions. To understand why, recall that, even for a nation, part of the stimulative effect of an expansive policy leaks out to foreign countries in the form of greater imports. For a state, the leakage to "foreigners" (that is, other countries or other states) is much larger. For example, as the state of Maine increases its spending, incomes in that state rise. Consumption expenditures also rise as a result. But many of the goods consumed in Maine are produced in other states. Thus, as Maine's consumption rises, much of the stimulus will go to production in other states. Prosperity in any one state is closely dependent on the level of prosperity in the nation as a whole; no individual state is in a position to buck the trend. The same proposition obviously also applies to localities to an even greater extent.

Furthermore, a state or local government does not have the ability to pursue active stabilization policies, because it is subject to financial constraints that do not apply to the federal government. Unlike the federal government, a state or locality does not have the ultimate ability to print money to service its bonds. Therefore, the holder of a state or city bond will rightly worry about the risk of default. During a recession, skittishness in the bond markets can severely limit the ability of the state or locality to borrow; indeed, as the recession reduces tax revenues, concern may grow about the state or local government's ability to handle even its existing level of indebtedness. Thus, pressure from the financial markets may drive states or localities into *destabilizing* fiscal actions. Most notably, New York City teetered on the brink of bankruptcy in 1975, when the severe recession and lagging tax revenues drew attention to the underlying weakness of the city's budget. New York found it impossible to issue new bonds on the financial markets. As a result, the city was forced to restrain spending, an action that tended to make the recession worse.

However, two important factors kept total state and local spending up as the economy declined in 1974 and 1975. First,

tax revenues of most states and localities held up very well in spite of the recession. In part, this strength was due to the increase in property tax receipts: With the rapid inflation in housing prices, assessments increased and property tax collections rose from $46 billion in 1973 to $52 billion in 1975. Second, the federal government stepped up grants to states and localities (from $41 billion in 1973 to $54 billion in 1975) in order to help them sustain their spending and avoid destabilizing cutbacks. As a result, overall state and local government spending expanded substantially between 1973 and 1975 (from $180 billion to $227 billion), providing needed stimulus to the economy. Thus, in spite of New York's troubles, overall spending by state and local governments acted as a stabilizing influence during the sharp recession of the midseventies.

FISCAL AND MONETARY POLICIES: The Ambiguous Record

Since the Depression of the 1930s, economists and government officials have given much thought to the use of fiscal and monetary policies to stabilize the economy. The theory presented in Part 2 of this book suggests that in the face of a recession, expansive fiscal and monetary policies can maintain aggregate demand and make the downturn more mild. Similarly, restrictive fiscal and monetary policies can restrain inflationary excess demand.

But when we look at the record of recent years, as we shall do in just a moment, it is not clear that fiscal and monetary policies have fulfilled the high hopes held for them. Changes in these policies seem to have been procyclical about as often as they have been countercyclical.

In one way, even the ambiguous record of recent years is not too bad—particularly if we compare it with what happened in the period between the two world wars, when

A *countercyclical* monetary or fiscal policy is one that reduces the amplitude of business cycles.

A *procyclical* monetary or fiscal policy is one that increases the amplitude of business fluctuations. ("Procyclical" refers to results, not intentions. The authorities may have been trying to stabilize the economy, but may have made mistakes.)

major policy errors contributed to the Depression. For example, a large tax increase, aimed at balancing the budget, was imposed in 1932; the result was a deepening of the Depression. It was to attack such folly, and to warn of the policy trap into which policy makers would fall if they tried to balance the government budget every year, that Keynes wrote his *General Theory*. Similarly, there were major blunders on the monetary side. Monetary policy was tightened in 1931, contributing to the decline of over 25 percent in the quantity of money between 1929 and 1933 and adding to the depth of the Depression. Again in 1936 and 1937, the Fed blundered. Fearing inflation, it doubled the reserve ratios that banks were required to keep; this move pushed the recovering economy back into recession.

In recent decades, we have avoided mistakes of such magnitude, and in this sense recent policy has been a success. But, if we look at the record more closely, it is not clear how much policies on average have contributed to stability. Figure 14-7 includes measures of monetary and fiscal policies since 1960, together with inflation rates, unemployment rates, and rates of growth of real GNP. For reasons explained in Chapter 9, the full-employment budget of the federal government is taken as a measure of fiscal policy. The most common measure of money, M_1 (consisting of currency plus demand deposits), is taken as an indicator of monetary policy.

The following case can be made that monetary and fiscal policies have helped to stabilize the economy. During the early 1960s, the economy was slack. In order to stimulate aggregate demand, the rate of growth of the money stock was stepped up in the early 1960s, and taxes were cut in 1964. Then, when inflation became a major problem in the late 1960s, fiscal policy moved in a restrictive direction with the tax surcharge of 1968, and monetary policy was tightened in the following year (with the rate of growth of M_1 declining from 7.4 to 3.9 percent). Then, to combat the 1970 recession and promote recovery in 1971, the full-employment budget was shifted from surplus to deficit, and the rate of growth of the money stock was accelerated. Finally, fiscal policy was moved sharply in an expansive direction in 1975 to promote recovery.

On the other side, it can be argued that many of the policy changes of the past two decades did more harm than good. Even the tax cut of 1964, which was hailed as a success at the time, may be questioned. It came when the economy was already well on the way to recovery. And it added to the inflationary pressures that accumulated in the late 1960s. Then, when the monetary restraint of 1969 was added to the fiscal restraint of 1968, aggregate demand was suppressed too much; the result was recession, which began in late 1969. In 1972, when the economy was already recovering nicely, additional fiscal stimulus was applied (with the full-employment budget moving deeper into deficit) and the rate of growth of the money stock accelerated. The expansive policies were overdone, and inflationary pressures grew. To restrain the inflation, fiscal policies became less expansionary in 1973, and monetary expansion was slowed down. A further tightening of monetary policy occurred in 1974. Once again, there was an overreaction; the result was a sharp fall in real GNP in 1974. According to this line of argument, economic instability is

(a) **Fiscal policy:** The full-employment budget

(b) **Monetary policy:** Changes in the money stock (M_1)

(c) **The rate of inflation**

(d) **The unemployment rate**

(e) **The growth of real GNP**

FIGURE 14-7 The record of the past two decades: Policies and results.
During the past two decades, there have been substantial changes in fiscal policy (as measured by the full-employment budget) and in monetary policy (as measured by changes in M_1; that is, currency plus demand deposits). The shift toward a more rapid expansion of the money stock between 1960 and 1963, plus the tax cut of 1964, contributed to the expansion of the economy. However, it is difficult to judge whether changes in monetary and fiscal policies have on average increased or decreased economic instability in the past decade. [Note: All series except the full-employment budget are seasonally adjusted. Percentage rates of change (in parts *b*, *c*, and *e*) are at annual rates.]

SOURCES: Department of Commerce, Board of Governors of the Federal Reserve System, and Federal Reserve Bank of St. Louis.

TABLE 14-2
Fiscal Policy in Selected Countries, 1955–1965:
Percentage of Business Cycle Eliminated

Country	(1) Eliminated by discretionary policy	(2) Eliminated by automatic policy	(3) Total percentage eliminated
Belgium	5	16	21
France†	− 35	48	13
Germany†	14	12	26
Italy‡	− 17	32	15
Sweden	5	n.a.	n.a.
United Kingdom	− 10	− 3	− 13
United States	17	32	49

Of the seven countries studied, Hansen found that discretionary fiscal policies (column 1) contributed significantly to stability only in Germany and the United States. In France, Italy, and the United Kingdom, fiscal policy was destabilizing (as shown by the negative signs in the first column).

   †1958–1965.
   ‡1956–1965.
   n.a., Not available.
   Source: Bent Hansen, *Fiscal Policy in Seven Countries, 1955–1965* (Paris: Organization for Economic Co-operation and Development, 1969), Table 2.6, p. 69. The figures pertain to central governments only.

partly attributable to mistakes in monetary and fiscal policies.

Doubts about the results of aggregate demand policies are not confined to the United States. For example, in an early study of a number of European countries plus the United States,[3] Bent Hansen found that discretionary fiscal policy changes were as likely to destabilize the economy as to stabilize it. His results are summarized in Table 14-2. (They indicate that automatic stabilizers work; for example, falling tax collections during a recession tend to maintain disposable income and consumption. It is the effect of discretionary policy changes, shown in the first column of Table 14-2, that are important for the policy debate.) Perhaps most disconcerting of all, one of the worst records was turned in by the United Kingdom, the home of John Maynard Keynes. (We will return to the British experience in Chapter 16.)

Three major reasons have been put forward for the mediocre performance of the managers of monetary and fiscal policies:

1. Lags in the operation of policies, and uncertainty over just how quickly the policies will work, make it difficult to stabilize the economy.

2. Policy makers have other goals in addition to economic stability. The pursuit of the other goals may destabilize the economy.

3. Just as there are traps facing the fiscal policy maker (if an attempt is made to balance the budget annually), so there are traps for the monetary policy maker.

LAGS IN THE OPERATION OF POLICIES: The Helmsman's Dilemma

Monetary and fiscal policies may destabilize the economy because they are ill-timed.

[3]Bent Hansen, *Fiscal Policy in Seven Countries, 1955–1965* (Paris: Organization for Economic Co-operation and Development, 1969).

They may fight the battles of last year, and be inappropriate to deal with the problems of the present, and, more important, those of the future.

There are three lags that make it difficult to time economic policies correctly. To illustrate, suppose that the economy begins to slide down into a recession. This fact may not be recognized for some time. It takes time to gather statistics on what is happening in the economy. Initial signs of weakness may be dismissed as temporary disturbances; not every little jiggle in economic activity grows into a recession or boom. Thus, the first lag is the *recognition* lag, which occurs between the time the weakness in the economy begins and the time when it is recognized. Furthermore, even after the decline is recognized, policy makers take some time before they act; this is the *action* lag. For example, congressional hearings must be held before taxes are cut. And spending programs must be designed before they can be implemented. Finally, after action is taken, there will be some delay before the major *impact* on the economy is felt. For example, when government spending finally is increased, the various rounds of consumer spending in the multiplier process take some time. And, for monetary policy, there is a lag between the open market purchase that pushes down interest rates and the actual investment that is stimulated as a consequence. These, then, are the types of lag: the *recognition* lag, the *action* lag, and the *impact* lag.

Consider how the existence of these lags can lead to incorrect policies and add to the instability of the economy. Suppose, for example, that the ideal path of aggregate demand is shown by the solid line in Figure 14-8. But actual demand follows the dashed curve. Starting at point *A*, aggregate demand starts to slip below the desired level; the economy begins to move into a recession. However, this problem is not recognized for some time—not until point *B*. Even then,

taxes are not cut immediately; action does not take place until point *C*. But, by this time, it may be too late. There is a further lag before the action affects demand (between points *D* and *E*), and by then the economy has already recovered. Fuel is added to the inflationary fire. Then, as the severity of inflation is recognized, policies are shifted in a restrictive direction. But once again there are lags; the policies can come too late, making the next recession worse.

The slowness of the economy to respond, and the momentum that the economy can accumulate in its downswing or upswing mean that the problem of the policy maker can be compared with that of the helmsman of an ocean-going ship. The helmsman may turn the wheel, but a large ship does not respond to the helm immediately. Suppose a ship heads out of New York harbor, intending to go due south past the eastern tip of Cuba on the way to the Panama Canal. If the helmsman finds his course drifting to the east, he can correct it by turning the wheel to starboard.

His problem is, by how much? If he turns the wheel just slightly, the ship will continue on its easterly course for some time; it does not respond quickly. In his anxiety, he may turn the wheel more sharply. Clearly, the more sharply the wheel is turned, the more quickly the ship will return to its course of due south. But, if the wheel has been swung hard right, a new problem will arise. Once the ship points due south, it will be turning with considerable momentum; it will not stay on the southerly course even though the wheel is swung smartly back to the center. The ship will now be drawn in a westerly direction by its momentum. In his panic, the helmsman may be tempted to swing the wheel back hard to port. If the helmsman swings the wheel sharply to get back on course quickly, he will overcorrect. We can imagine the voyage of the anxious mariner—zigzagging down the Caribbean.

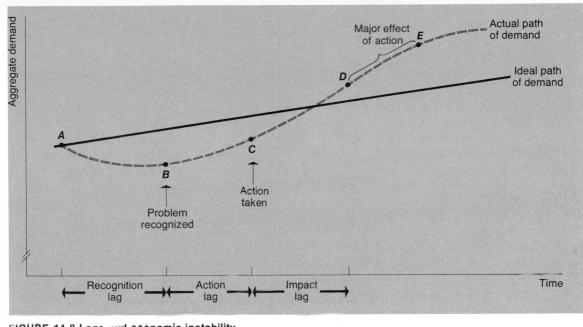

FIGURE 14-8 Lags and economic instability.
Because of the recognition, action, and impact lags, it is possible that policy adjustments will make things worse. Expansive steps aimed at fighting the recession at point *C* may add to a later inflationary boom at *E*. Similarly, policies aimed at restraining an inflationary boom may make the next recession worse.

But, of course, ships do not zigzag all over the ocean. With some practice, the helmsman learns not to lean too hard on the wheel. And he learns to move the wheel back to the center *before* the ship gets back to its intended course; the ship's momentum will complete the turn.[4]

Policy making involves the same problems as steering a ship—with a few more added for extra excitement. One of the additional complications is that the helm and the rudder of the economic ship are connected by elastic bands and baling twine. Unlike the mechanism connecting the ship's wheel to the rudder, the mechanism connecting monetary and fiscal policies to aggregate demand does not work in a precise, highly

predictable manner. Furthermore, the economic policy maker may have to chart a course across turbulent and stormy seas. During the decade of 1965–1975, for example, there were large shocks to the United States economy: first, the war in Vietnam; then the inflationary pressures on food prices stemming from Soviet crop failures and large-scale American grain exports in 1972 and 1973; then the oil embargo and the quadrupling of oil prices in 1973 and 1974. If the ship is being guided across placid seas, the policy maker has the luxury of turning the wheel meekly and slowly, so as not to overcorrect. But in stormy waters, this is not good enough; a meek application of policies will be overwhelmed by other

---

[4]The importance of allowing for momentum is also understood by slalom skiers, who begin each turn before they reach the gate, not when they reach it.

forces. This, then, is the helmsman's dilemma: How hard should the wheel be swung, and how soon should it be moved back toward center?

Particularly in the making of fiscal policy, delays have long been recognized as a significant problem. For example, President Kennedy initially proposed a major tax cut in 1962; it did not become law until 1964. And the 1968 income tax surcharge was not enacted until almost a year after it was requested by President Johnson. Several proposals have been made to shorten the action lag and thus to reduce the danger that delayed policies will destabilize the economy. Most notably, both the Kennedy and Johnson administrations recommended that the president be given the power to change income taxes across the board by as much as 5 percent, with the Congress retaining the right to override the decision. But this proposal involved the sensitive issue of congressional power over taxes, and Congress declined to grant the president the requested authority. Furthermore, the possibilities of the president's getting such authority faded even further in 1974 and 1975. In the early days of his administration, President Ford asked for a tax increase to help in the fight against inflation. But the Congress was concerned with the recession, and cut taxes instead. Congress felt that it could not even trust the president to decide whether taxes should be raised or lowered; in such circumstances, it was unlikely to grant the president additional power.

DESTABILIZING GOVERNMENT ACTIONS: The Problem of Conflicting Goals

The government may take actions that destabilize the economy because it has other pressing objectives. Most notably, government expenditures during wartime generally are so high that they cause rapid inflation. But inflation in such circumstances does not necessarily mean that the government is making a mistake. The inflation of the 1940s was not too high a price to pay for the defeat of Hitler.

Is There a "Political" Business Cycle?

Another objective of policy makers—namely, the desire to get reelected—may also contribute to economic instability. Office holders obviously want the voters in a mellow mood when they enter the polling booths: Economic prosperity can contribute to the chances of reelection.[5] There is a temptation for policy makers to overstimulate the economy in an election year, since the favorable effects on output and employment tend to show up relatively quickly, while the adverse effects in terms of inflation tend to be delayed—with luck, until after the election.

While there has been much speculation on the existence of a political business cycle,[6] the facts are mixed. Sometimes the economy is indeed stimulated in the year before the election; 1951 and 1952, 1964, 1967 and early 1968, 1971 and 1972, and

---

[5]Yale Prof. Ray Fair has concluded that the important economic factor in elections is not the position of the economy, but rather, the direction in which it is headed; in other words, it is better for the economy to be rising from a lower level than to be stable at a higher level. Thus, Roosevelt's reelection in 1936 was no particular paradox. While the unemployment rate was still sky-high at 16.9 percent, it was down significantly from the 23.6 percent of 1932. Ray Fair, "Growth Rates Predict November Winners," *New York Times*, Jan. 25, 1976, and "The Effect of Economic Events on Votes for President" (New Haven, Conn.: Yale University, Cowles Foundation Discussion Paper no. 418, mimeographed, Jan. 19, 1976).

[6]For example, Assar Lindbeck, "Stabilization Policy in Open Economies with Endogenous Politicians," *American Economic Review*, May 1976, pp. 1–19; William D. Nordhaus, "The Political Business Cycle," *Review of Economic Studies,* April 1975, pp. 169–190; and Edward R. Tufte, *Political Control of the Economy* (Princeton: Princeton University Press, 1978).

1975 and 1976 are all examples. But it is hard to make too much of two of those examples—in both 1951–1952 and 1967 through early 1968, stimulus was associated with a military conflict whose unpopularity helped to drive the incumbent president from office. Furthermore, there are examples on the other side. Most notably, the Eisenhower administration was reluctant to propose stimulation in the late 1950s. And in 1975 and 1976, President Ford opposed stimulative fiscal measures. (However, they were passed by the Congress in spite of his objections.) In addition, the timing of the 1964 tax cut can scarcely be considered an election gimmick on the part of the administration. It had been recommended long before, in 1962.

In the light of the inconclusive evidence on election-year stimulation, attention has focused on 1972, for two reasons. First, there was an unusual coincidence of elections in that year in Canada, Germany, Italy, Japan, and the United States, with France following in early 1973. This coincidence may have contributed to the close international synchronization of the business cycle between 1971 and 1975.[7] Second, the United States election of 1972 was unusually interesting, since the events preceding and following it eventually forced President Nixon from office.

In 1972, both fiscal and monetary policies were set for economic stimulus. The full-employment budget was in substantial deficit, and the money supply in 1972 increased by almost 9 percent, compared with an annual average of just over 6 percent in 1970–1971. There were widespread, and plausible, rumors that the White House was putting pressure on the Fed to keep monetary conditions easy prior to the election. The most explicit charge of political motivation appeared in an article in *Fortune* magazine:

The committee [the Federal Open Market Committee, or FOMC] also knew that the Administration's desire to [follow an expansive policy that would] prevent interest rates from rising rapidly was linked to the coming election.

In the circumstances, the dispute between [Federal Reserve Chairman Arthur] Burns and the FOMC majority [in favor of the less expansive policy of letting interest rates rise] became fairly tense at times. At one point, frustrated by his inability to convince the committee of the need to hold down interest rates, Burns left a meeting in obvious anger. He returned in about an hour, announcing: "I have just talked to the White House."

The effect of this declaration on the committee must have been quite dramatic. . . .

Burns eventually succeeded in persuading the FOMC to continue providing that stimulus throughout 1972.[8]

This spectacular story is hard to evaluate because of denials by people who were present at the FOMC meetings in 1972.[9]

Ultimately, motivation is very hard to prove; and motives are complex. On the question of whether the Federal Open Market Committee was influenced by pressures from the White House, it is appropriate to give the committee the benefit of the doubt, particularly when there were plausible alternative explanations of the large monetary expansion in 1972. First, the lowest rate of unemployment reached through the first 10 months of 1972 was 5.5 percent, more than 1.5 percent above the average for 1966 through 1969, when the inflationary wave of the 1960s had been set off. Looking at one of

---

[7]This possibility was suggested in a study for the Organization of Economic Co-operation and Development (OECD) by a group of economic experts. OECD, *Towards Full Employment and Price Stability* (Paris: OECD, 1977), p. 52.

[8]Sanford Rose, "The Agony of the Federal Reserve," *Fortune*, July 1974, pp. 186–188.

[9]See, for example, the denial by board member Andrew Brimmer, *Fortune*, August 1974, p. 113.

the most important economic indicators (namely, the unemployment rate), the Fed could believe that there was additional slack in the economy, and that a continuation of expansive policies was in order.

Furthermore, the initial estimates of the growth of the money stock, which formed the background of decision making in 1972, turned out to be underestimates; the Fed was operating on the basis of faulty data. Thus, the strongest criticism of the Fed for following excessively expansionary policies in 1972 can be made only with the advantage of hindsight. Policy makers have no such advantage. Quite apart from political motivation, there are adequate alternative explanations (the 5.5 percent unemployment rate, and faulty data on the money stock) that can account for the policies of 1972.

MONETARY POLICIES: The Trap of an Interest Rate Objective

The ultimate objectives of the Federal Reserve are full employment and price stability. But obviously the Federal Reserve does not control the level of employment and prices directly; rather, it adjusts the levers of monetary policy—open market operations, the discount rate, and reserve requirements. It is only by influencing the quantity of money and interest rates that the Fed affects employment and prices.

In formulating its policy, the Federal Open Market Committee (FOMC) has a decision to make: Should it give the trading desk at the New York Federal Reserve Bank instructions to aim for a certain level of interest rates? Or should the trading desk be ordered to concentrate on the quantity of money? Or some combination of the two? A controversy has raged over this question for decades; complex issues are involved. One aspect of the controversy is directly relevant to this chapter on instability: *If the Federal Reserve becomes preoccupied with maintaining a specific interest rate, it can destabilize the economy.*

To see why, suppose that the Federal Reserve has a strong interest rate goal. Say, for example, that it wants to keep the interest rate on bonds fixed at 6 percent per annum. Then suppose that an upturn in the economy occurs; business executives become more optimistic and undertake additional investment. To finance their new plant and equipment, they borrow. As a result of the additional demand for funds, interest rates are bid up and bond prices fall. If the Fed wants to stabilize interest rates and bond prices, it now has to buy securities on the open market. But such open market purchases increase bank reserves and lead to an increase in the money supply. As a consequence of more money and stabilized interest rates, there is an additional increase in aggregate demand. And, as demand rises, businesses are encouraged to revise their investment plans upward once more; the expansion gathers momentum. There is a cumulative upward movement, with higher demand causing an increase in the money stock, and the increase in the money stock in turn causing a further increase in demand. (Similarly, there can be a cumulative downward movement if the Federal Reserve attempts to stabilize interest rates in the face of declining investment demand. The Fed will sell securities to prevent a decline in interest rates, and the open market sale will add to the downswing.)

A substantial one-way movement of the economy is not necessarily bad. Indeed, if the economy is bumping along with very high rates of unemployment, a strong upswing is desirable. In this case, a decision by the Fed to keep interest rates from rising can contribute to a recovery. But a policy of interest rate stabilization may also cause a healthy expansion to run away into an inflationary boom, or a mild decline to turn into a major recession.

Some Illustrations

The idea that business fluctuations may be associated with fluctuations in the money supply is not new. Indeed, prior to the Keynesian revolution, business-cycle theorists concentrated on monetary and financial disturbances as principal causes of economic fluctuations. (Much of this literature focused on the vulnerability of banks in a fractional-reserve system, and on the threat of panics and bank runs explained in Chapters 10 and 11.) The idea that attempts to stabilize interest rates can destabilize aggregate demand goes back at least to the beginning of this century, to the writings of Swedish economist Knut Wicksell.[10] But there are some surprisingly new illustrations of this old problem. (For some recent illustrations of the relationship between business cycles and other financial problems, see Box 14-2.)

Perhaps the clearest example occurred during the 1940s. In order to help the Treasury borrow cheaply to finance the war debt, the Federal Reserve promised to keep interest rates pegged (fixed) at a low level. To do so, it had to buy securities, thus losing control over bank reserves and the money supply. This lack of control contributed to the inflation of the 1940s, and became a particular problem during the Korean war. In order to gain control over the money stock and restrain inflation, the Federal Reserve argued that it should be released from its commitment to the Treasury to keep interest rates low. The Treasury at first objected, but finally agreed in the Treasury-Federal Reserve Accord of 1951.

The second illustration of interest rate stabilization involves the policies of 1972. It adds one more explanation to our earlier discussion of why the money supply expanded rapidly in that year. This illustration requires some background. In the face of continuing inflation, the Nixon administration introduced wage and price controls in August 1971. One problem with controls is that they may be considered unfair. Unions, in particular, fear that controls will be used to limit wages, but not profits and other incomes. Therefore, if controls are to have broad public support, they must be applied to all forms of income, including interest and dividends. The responsibility for supervising interest and dividends went to Chairman Burns of the Federal Reserve, who had been an early advocate of government restraints on wages and prices.

This was an unfortunate choice. Burns was now wearing two hats, and the two jobs were in conflict. In support of the wage-price program, his responsibility was to keep down interest rates. As chairman of the Federal Reserve, his responsibility was to control the money supply. But if an explosion of the money supply were to be avoided as the economy strengthened, a rise in interest rates would have to be permitted; vigorous open market purchases could not be used to keep interest rates down. And what actually happened? Interest rates were held down, and the money supply rose rapidly during 1972.

This episode illustrates a very important problem which must be solved unless wage-price controls are to end up causing even higher rates of inflation. Indeed, willingness to answer the following questions may be taken as a test of whether the proponents of wage-price controls are serious or not: Are wage and price controls politically acceptable if they do not include a ceil-

---

*[10]Knut Wicksell, *Lectures on Political Economy* (New York: Augustus M. Kelly Reprints of Economic Classics, 1967), vol. 2, pp. 127–208.

Appendix 8-A explained why classical economists believed that changes in interest rates could help to restore full employment. More generally, they believed that changes in interest rates would help to stabilize investment and aggregate demand. For example, during a boom, interest rates would be bid up because of the eagerness of businesses to borrow to finance new investment. Rising interest rates would remove some of the incentive to invest, thereby moderating the boom. Thus, changes in interest rates could act as an automatic stabilizer, performing the function for classical economics that taxes perform in Keynesian economics.

And, just as the automatic stabilizer of Keynesian economics can be canceled out if policy makers fall into the trap of trying to balance the government's budget every year, so the automatic stabilizer of classical economics can be canceled out if the central bank keeps interest rates from changing.

BOX 14-2
FINANCIAL INSTABILITY IN A RECESSION

We have seen that some economic forces favor a turnaround as a recession deepens. For example, after an extended period of low purchases, consumers must eventually reenter the market to replace their worn autos, lawnmowers, and washing machines. Similarly, after a period of decline, investment begins naturally to pick up, as the accelerator example illustrates. There is, however, a complicating factor that can make a developing recession worse: the financial instability of business corporations. During normal times, there is a relatively small and steady rate of bankruptcy. While bankruptcies often involve personal tragedy, they generally do not inflict a high cost on the economy. Indeed, a modest rate of bankruptcy is necessary for a healthy economy, since it weeds out incompetent managers; thus it acts as an incentive for greater efficiency among the survivors and releases resources for use in the growing, dynamic sectors of the economy. The problem is that during a severe recession, bankruptcies come in waves, sweeping away the competent along with the incompetent. Most businesses involve substantial risks; the role of the entrepreneur is to weigh risks and make prudent decisions. But when business is bad, the prudent as well as the foolish can be forced to the wall. And as they go bankrupt, businesses may take their suppliers with them; suppliers have counted on their bills being paid. The business dominoes fall.

While financial instability jumps from the financial section to page 1 of the newspapers during a sharp recession, the seeds of the problem may have been sown in the preceding boom, particularly if inflationary forces were strong at that time. If prices rise rapidly, prudent businesses generally make only moderate profits. The gravy goes to the financial buccaneers who borrow all they can to leverage their operations to the limit. (Leverage was explained in Chapter 6.) The greatest gains are often in real estate. With large borrowings, real estate operators see their wealth soar as the prices of land and buildings rise while debts remain constant. As the boom rolls on, real estate operators try to borrow more and more, to increase their leverage. But, when the bubble bursts, leverage comes back to haunt them; the most highly leveraged are the first to fall.

Several policy issues are raised by the danger of a domino effect of bankruptcies. First, what can be done ahead of time to strengthen the financial system? Financial problems of the recession may reflect the excesses of the preceding boom; thus, it is important to avoid speculative excesses by maintaining sound, steady growth. And, once a downswing has begun to develop, it is important to keep it from gathering momentum.

But what should be done when bankruptcies are imminent? During the recession that opened the decade of the 1970s, two large corporations teetered on the brink of financial disaster—the Penn Central Railroad and Lockheed Aircraft. (Interestingly, the problems of these two corporations were not the result of financial buccaneering in the preceding prosperity. Penn Central had been in deepening trouble for some time. Lockheed was faced with large losses on its jumbo jet. In each case, however, the recession precipitated the crisis.) These two companies performed strategic economic functions that the government considered essential. Although the Penn Central was allowed to go into bankruptcy, the government ensured that its operations would continue—first under the supervision of the court, and then under the new Consolidated Railroad Corporation (Conrail). And the government stepped in to prevent the bankruptcy of Lockheed by guaranteeing up to $250 million of its loans.

(In other words, the government guaranteed that private lenders to Lockheed would be repaid. Without this guarantee, Lockheed would have been unable to borrow.)

While this rescue of Lockheed helped to keep the recession from getting worse, it raised a serious question: Is there a double standard in the economy, with "socialism for the rich," and no similar government rescue for small businesses? One reason for this double standard is easy to find. A very large corporation is the equivalent of a large number of small businesses: A single large "domino" can create as much shock as a series of small bankruptcies.

The problem of what, if anything, to do directly about corporate bankruptcies remains difficult and controversial. But in one area there is general and long-standing agreement. Through the Federal Deposit Insurance Corporation (FDIC), the government since the 1930s has undertaken to protect the depositors of banks up to large limits. This insurance also protects the banks themselves against a crisis of confidence, in which panicky depositors withdraw their funds.

In spite of this special protection for the banks, banking was one of the trouble spots during the 1974–1975 recession. During the past two decades, banking has been very dynamic; banks have discovered new ways of raising money and doing business. For example, they now compete more actively for funds by offering certificates of deposit, which are similar to short-term government bills. And banks have been out to conquer new worlds, both domestically (with such innovations as bank credit cards) and internationally (with more active foreign loan and foreign exchange departments). Many of these innovations are desirable; they add to the efficiency of the economy. But there also has been an unhealthy emphasis on bank "performance"; banks felt pressure to show consistent year-to-year gains in profits. And, as a result, some became infected with the "go-go" spirit of the sixties. Some made substantial commitments to Real Estate Investment Trusts (REITs). Others took fliers in areas in which they had no particular expertise, including the foreign exchange market.

The prosperous years masked the problems; a general buoyancy of the economy will save the imprudent—temporarily. The cracks appeared as the economy moved into recession during 1974. Franklin National, the twentieth largest bank in the nation, failed.† And substantial losses were suffered by Real Estate Investment Trusts sponsored by other large banks, including none other than David Rockefeller's Chase Manhattan. (The Chase REIT lost $166 million in 1975.) There was no danger of widespread collapse of the banks themselves. But stories of bank difficulties became common in the financial press. And the jitters were international in scope: Franklin's problems were followed about a month later by the failure of a German bank (Herstatt), which had lost heavily in its foreign exchange trading. (It had bought currencies it expected to rise, but they had fallen instead.)

It is perhaps too strong to argue—as did the former New York State Superintendent of Banking—that "Bankers aren't *supposed* to be smart. They're supposed to be safe."‡ But it is important that restraint be exercised during a period of prosperity. And it is essential that supervisory agencies use sharp pencils and critical standards during such trouble-free times; during the next recession, it may be too late.

---

†Franklin's crisis began in May 1974, when it was unable to borrow to refinance its short-term debt that was coming due. It was kept afloat for several months by loans from the Federal Reserve. (Recall the discussion of discounting in Chapter 11.)

There was an ironic note in the difficulties of Franklin. The spring 1974 issue of *The Bankers' Magazine* carried a series of articles called "The Wide World of Banking." One of these articles was by Italian financier Michele Sindona, the chairman of Franklin's International Executive Committee. Sindona's article was entitled "Survival of the Fittest."

‡Elliott B. Bell, as quoted in *Business Week*, Sept. 8, 1975, p. 9.

ing on interest rates? If there is an interest rate ceiling, will the money supply expand rapidly, increasing aggregate demand and demolishing the controls in a wave of demand-pull inflation?

The 1974–1975 Recession The third illustration, involving monetary policy during the very sharp decline in the economy in late 1974 and early 1975, was much more complicated. It did not involve an attempt by the Fed to keep interest rates constant. Rather, it showed what can happen when the Fed concentrates on interest rates, and does not let them adjust quickly enough in the face of very rapid changes in economic conditions.

The decisions of the Federal Open Market Committee during this period are shown in Figure 14-9; they involved targets both for an interest rate (specifically, the federal funds rate on short-term loans between banks) and for changes in the quantity of money (both M_1 and M_2). Central banking is not a precise business; the targets were set not as specific figures, but as ranges within which the interest rate and money supply should be kept. Notice what happened after July 1974. The interest rate objective was generally met, while increases in the quantity of money fell far short of the objectives.

During this period, interest rates were not fixed by the Fed; note how rapidly the target range for the interest rate fell after July. What the experience suggests is the following: The Fed underestimated the sharpness of the recession. It therefore underestimated the speed with which business demand for investment and for bank loans would fall. It therefore overestimated the expansion of the money supply that would occur at any given interest rate. That is, the Fed chose interest rate and money supply targets that were inconsistent. In the face of the inconsistent instructions, the trading

FIGURE 14-9 Federal Reserve targets and results: 1974 to early 1975.
The shading in the upper diagram shows the interest rate objectives of the Federal Open Market Committee (FOMC). The two sets of shading in the lower part show the FOMC objectives for changes in M_1 and M_2. As the economy slid rapidly into a deep recession in late 1974 and early 1975, the Federal Reserve generally kept interest rates within the target range but fell short of the money supply objectives. (In part b, a negative rate of change means that the money stock was declining. Thus, in January 1975, M_1 decreased at an annual rate of almost 3 percent.)

desk at the New York Federal Reserve Bank adhered to the interest rate target, and allowed the growth of the money stock to fall far below target. The low rate of growth of the money stock contributed to the depth of the recession.

This is an important problem. The Fed is likely to underestimate the strength of a cyclical swing when it is particularly strong; indeed, the recession of 1974–1975 was unusually severe. But this is precisely the time when adherence to an interest rate target will lead to errors on the money supply side which make the fluctuation worse. In other words, the more severe the fluctuation is, the more likely it is that the Fed will make the instability even worse if it concentrates on the interest rate target.

The Fed's performance during the recession led to criticisms from a wide spectrum of economists. Keynesian Paul Samuelson wondered if the economy was headed into "A Burns Depression?" Monetarist Milton Friedman wanted to know, "What Is the Federal Reserve Doing?"[11] As a result of doubts about the Fed's performance during the recession, the Congress in 1975 insisted that the Federal Reserve announce its monetary targets, and explain to a congressional committee any failures to meet these targets.

*This more difficult section may be omitted without loss of continuity.

[11]The quotations are the titles of columns in *Newsweek*. Samuelson's column appeared on March 3, 1975, and Friedman's column on March 10, 1975.

(a) Federal open market committee range for the interest rate on federal funds

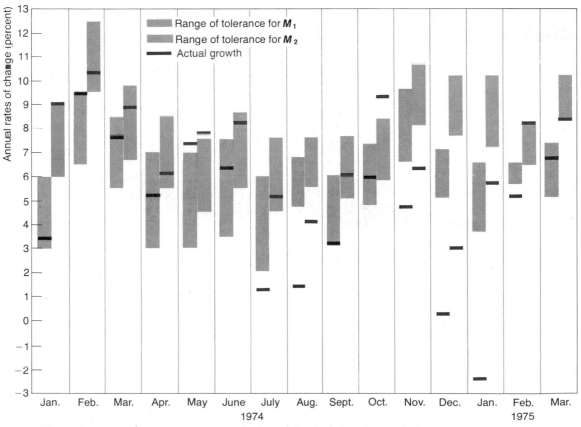

(b) Federal open market committee ranges of tolerance for changes in M_1 and M_2

Key Points

1. Business activity moves irregularly, with both large and small fluctuations. The largest fluctuation took place between 1929 and 1944, when the economy collapsed into the Great Depression and then rose to a peak of war production.

2. There are four phases to a business cycle. A *recession* occurs when seasonally adjusted real GNP falls for two or more consecutive quarters. The recession ends with the *trough*; that is, the month when economic activity is at its lowest point. This is followed by an *expansion* phase, which reaches a *peak* before the next recession begins.

3. Investment tends to fluctuate more widely than other segments of GNP. The *accelerator* principle illustrates why. Investment depends on the change in sales, and investment demand can change by a large percentage in the face of relatively small movements in sales. The accelerator also helps to explain why turning points occur in the business cycle. Investment can fall even in a growing economy, if the rate of growth of sales slows down; an actual decline in sales is not necessary. During a recession, investment can recover when sales decline at a slower rate; an actual upturn in sales is not necessary.

4. While the acceleration principle illustrates important forces that help to determine investment demand, it represents a simplification. In practice, there may be delays in the response of investment to changes in sales. These delays contribute to the stability of the economy in the face of small disturbances. But they mean that, once an expansion or contraction gets going, it can gather momentum.

5. The record of fiscal and monetary policies is not impressive. It is not clear whether fiscal and monetary policies have, on average, decreased or increased the amplitude of business fluctuations.

6. The existence of time lags is one of the reasons why it is difficult to design countercyclical policies. The *recognition* lag is the interval before changes in economic conditions are recognized. The *action* lag is the interval between the time a problem is recognized and the time when fiscal and monetary policies are adjusted. The *impact* lag is the interval between the time when policies are changed and the time when the major effects of the policies occur. Because of lags, policies implemented today will have their effects in the future, when they may be too late.

7. Policy makers have many goals in addition to economic stability. Competing goals, such as the winning of a war, can lead to policies that destabilize aggregate demand. The desire to be reelected may tempt policy makers to adopt overly expansive policies.

8. We saw in Chapter 9 that there is a trap for the unwary fiscal policy maker. An attempt to balance the budget every year can destabilize the economy. There is a similar trap for the unwary monetary policy maker. If the central bank attempts to keep interest rates stable, it may destabilize aggregate demand.

Key Concepts

business cycle

recession

trough

expansion

peak

seasonal adjustment

accelerator

marginal propensity to import

countercyclical policy

procyclical policy

recognition lag

action lag

impact lag

conflict of goals

political business cycle

the pegging of interest rates (1940s)

the Treasury-Federal Reserve Accord of 1951

Problems

14-1 In Figure 14-1, the Cleveland Trust Company has listed a number of important events associated with periods of prosperity. Choose three of these events, and explain why each contributed to prosperity. (Take one example from the 1835–1865 period, one from 1865–1900, and one from the twentieth century.)

14-2 Using the data shown in Table 14-1 and Figure 14-4, draw a new chart, showing bicycle sales and gross investment in the same "percentage change" way that GNP and investment are plotted in Figure 14-3. Does this example confirm the message of investment instability in Figure 14-3? Why or why not?

14-3 Complete the table below of the acceleration principle, assuming that one machine is needed to produce every 1,000

automobiles. Assume that a machine lasts 10 years. Assume also that one tenth of the initial number of machines is scheduled for retirement in each of the next 10 years.

14-4 Suppose, alternatively, that there is a lag in investment. The number of machines desired in any year is calculated by taking the average number of autos produced in that year and the previous year. (In other respects, follow the assumptions of Problem 14-3.) Then recalculate the table in Problem 14-3. Does this change in the assumption make investment demand more or less stable?

14-5 Suppose that you are in business and that demand for your product has recently increased. You now have to choose among (1) turning away some of your new customers, (2) scheduling overtime, (3) add-

Year	(1) Yearly sales of autos	(2) Desired number of machines	(3) Net investment	(4) Gross investment
1	100,000			
2	100,000			
3	90,000			
4	80,000			
5	80,000			
6	80,000			
7	90,000			
8	100,000			
9	100,000			

ing a new shift, or (4) expanding your factory and the number of your machines. Explain the important considerations in choosing among these four choices.

14-6 In discussing countercyclical fiscal policy, attention is focused on the federal government rather than on state and local governments. Why?

14-7 Step by step, explain why a decision of the Federal Reserve to keep interest rates stable can cause an upward movement of the economy to gather momentum. In what circumstances might it be desirable to keep interest rates stable? In what circumstances might it be undesirable to keep them stable?

chapter **15**
Fine Tuning or Stable Policy Settings?

If something works, don't fix it.
Edith Bunker,
"All in the Family"

In Chapter 14, the ambiguous record of fiscal and monetary policies was reviewed. It is not clear whether we should judge the aggregate demand policies of the last two decades as a success or a failure. In part, the answer depends on the question: Successful compared with what? Certainly, compared with the decades between the two world wars, the economy has performed well during the sixties and seventies. The answer also depends in part on which years we consider. During the first half of the 1960s, there was a strong and healthy expansion. But the performance of the economy in the late 1960s and the 1970s was less impressive. Inflation accelerated in the late 1960s. And there have been two recessions in the 1970s (including the severe 1974 recession).

The mediocre performance of the economy during the past decade revitalized an old debate, which goes back to the early days of the Keynesian controversy in the 1930s. (For a quick review of the main points at issue between Keynesians and monetarists, refer back to Box 12-2.) On the one side are those in the activist Keynesian tradition, who argue that fiscal and monetary policies should be managed to help achieve the goals of a high level of employment and reasonably stable prices. As the economy heads toward recession, expansive policies should be adopted; as the economy heads toward an inflationary boom, restraint should be exercised.

On the other side are the monetarist inheritors of the classical tradition, who argue that activist, *discretionary* monetary and fiscal policies are more likely to do harm than good, no matter how well-intentioned policy makers may be. Consequently, they argue that discretionary policies should be avoided; instead, permanent monetary and fiscal policy settings should be chosen and maintained regardless of the short-term fluc-

325

tuations in economic activity. In other words, policy rules should be followed. It is of course important that the rules be chosen carefully and, in particular, that they be consistent with economic stability. Thus, it would be a mistake to follow a rule of stabilizing interest rates, because, as we saw in Chapter 14, doing so might destabilize aggregate demand. Likewise, the old gold standard involved a poor set of rules. Because banks under this system kept fractional reserves in the form of gold, a large superstructure of money could be built on a relatively small base of gold reserves, a practice that made the banking system vulnerable to runs. Similarly, it would be a mistake to establish a rule requiring a balanced budget every year; such a rule would create the policy trap described by Keynesians. However, there are policy rules that avoid such traps. Specifically:

1. The Federal Reserve should aim at a consistent increase in the money supply, at something like 4 or 5 percent per year. This increase would provide the money needed to purchase the expanding national output at stable prices.

2. The government should balance the full-employment budget each year. Such a rule would allow automatic stabilizers to work, but would rule out discretionary countercyclical fiscal policy actions.

Since the advocates of fixed rules are generally in the classical or monetarist tradi-

tion, they emphasize the first rule, involving a steady increase in the money supply.

As in Chapter 12, the sharp contrast between Keynesians and monetarists may be illustrated by comparing the statements of Keynesian Warren Smith and monetarist Milton Friedman. The flavor of the activist, hands-on-the-helm Keynesian view was given by Smith:[1]

The only good rule is that the budget should never be balanced—except for an instant when a surplus to curb inflation is being altered to a deficit to fight deflation.

Friedman explicitly criticized this activist policy of attempting to "fine-tune" the economy:[2]

Is fiscal policy being oversold?
Is monetary policy being oversold? . . .
My answer is yes to both of those questions. . . .
Monetary policy is being oversold. . . .
Fiscal policy is being oversold. . . .
Fine tuning has been oversold.

This chapter has three objectives: (1) to explain the activist Keynesian approach to economic stabilization in more detail than in the early chapters, (2) to explain the monetarist case against discretionary policies and in favor of policy rules, and (3) to explain some problems with setting policy rules.

AIMING FOR A STABLE, HIGH-EMPLOYMENT ECONOMY: The Activist Keynesian Approach

As we have seen (especially in Chapter 8), Keynes believed that a market economy would suffer from two major diseases. The equilibrium toward which the economy moved would probably be one of inadequate

[1]Warren Smith, statement to a meeting of Treasury consultants, 1965, as quoted by Paul A. Samuelson, *Economics*, 10th ed. (New York: McGraw-Hill, 1976), p. 234. For another illustration of the activist viewpoint, see the quotation from Walter Heller that introduced Chapter 9.

[2]Milton Friedman and Walter Heller, *Monetary vs. Fiscal Policy* (New York: W. W. Norton, 1969), p. 47.

aggregate demand and high unemployment. And, even if the economy did get to a position of full employment, it would be unlikely to stay there, primarily because of the instability of investment demand. In short, demand would tend to be both *inadequate* and *unstable*.

In the early days of the Keynesian revolution, inadequacy of aggregate demand was considered the more important problem. This was scarcely surprising, because of the depth and persistence of the Great Depression. *Secular stagnation* was the biggest worry of early Keynesian writers.[3] However,

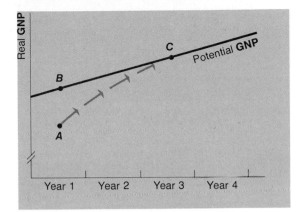

FIGURE 15-1 The Keynesian strategy: An active policy.
The activist Keynesian strategy is to move quickly to the full-employment or potential GNP path. Fiscal and monetary policies should then be fine-tuned to combat instability and keep the economy as close as possible to the potential GNP path.

Secular stagnation occurs when aggregate demand is consistently too low for many years. Consequently, large-scale unemployment persists, and it may even become increasingly severe.

since the late 1940s, the emphasis of Keynesian thinking has shifted away from the problem of secular stagnation and toward the problem of instability. This change was the result of two related developments. First, the economy did not lapse back into depression in the period after World War II; it went through bouts of inflation as well as periodic recessions. There was no long-run lack of demand. Second, there were developments in economic theory, particularly with respect to consumption, that suggested that the long-term growth of aggregate demand would not be so low as had been feared. (Developments in consumption theory are explained in the Appendix at the end of this chapter.) Nevertheless, concern continued over both the adequacy and the stability of aggregate demand. Therefore the policy problem, as seen by Keynesian economists, was (1) to stimulate aggregate demand to the full-employment level, and then

(2) to adjust or fine-tune it whenever needed to combat business fluctuations.

This Keynesian strategy is illustrated in Figure 15-1. Suppose that the economy in year 1 begins at a position of high unemployment; the actual production of the economy, at A, is well below the potential at full employment (B). Of course, the potential output of the economy does not remain constant. As time passes, the labor force grows, the capital stock increases, and technology improves. Thus, the full-employment or potential path of the economy trends upward. The objective of policy in year 1 should be to aim the economy toward the full-employment path. But full employment cannot be achieved immediately; there are lags in the implementation and effect of policy. Thus, policy in year 1 should be aimed at stimulating the economy so that it approaches full employment at some time in the reasonably near future, as shown by the arrows in Figure 15-1.

[3]Most notable was Alvin Hansen, a Harvard professor who popularized Keynes in the United States with his prolific writing and persuasive teaching. One of his early books was entitled *Full Recovery or Stagnation?* (New York: W. W. Norton, 1938).

FIGURE 15-2 The Keynesian strategy in practice, 1962–1966.

The blue parts of the diagram are taken from the Council of Economic Advisers' Report published in early 1962. They show the gap between the actual and potential GNP, and illustrate how various future paths (A, B, and C) would affect the gap. The red parts of the diagram show the outcome; they are taken from the CEA report 5 years later. Although the economy had not moved quickly back to its potential path, the gap had been eliminated by late 1965.

An Example

By going back to the early 1960s, we can find a specific illustration of this Keynesian strategy. The dark blue parts of Figure 15-2 are taken from the annual report of the Council of Economic Advisers (CEA), published in January 1962.[4] Dotted lines show three possible outcomes. A, the most favorable, would eliminate the *GNP gap* within 2 years. On the other hand, a growth path toward C would not involve any relative improvement; the GNP gap would remain just as wide in 1963 as it was in 1961. The policy problem was to try to make the economy follow path A, or adhere reasonably close to it.

> The *GNP gap* is the amount by which actual GNP falls short of potential GNP.

The outcome in the following years is shown in the red parts of Figure 15-2, which are taken from a diagram in a later CEA report.[5] The red curve showing actual GNP traces out a very impressive performance. Although the GNP gap was not eliminated within 2 years, it was eliminated within 4; by the end of 1965, the economy was right on target. What remained now was to fine-tune the economy, keeping it as close as reasonably possible to the potential growth path.

There were, of course, problems. One was the tendency of prices to rise before full employment was achieved. The wage-price guideposts discussed in Chapter 13 were designed to deal with this problem. The second was the well-recognized problem of lags: How do you adjust policies when the actions taken today do not affect the economy until some future time, when they may no longer be appropriate?

Forecasting

One way to deal with the problem of lags is to forecast where the economy is heading. If forecasts can be made with reasonable accuracy, the policy makers will be able to "lead" their moving target.

In developing a forecast for the coming months and year, economists in and out of government use a number of techniques, most of them involving the use of computers. Typically, econometric (statistical) techniques are applied to past information on consumption, income, etc., to estimate how the economy behaves. For example, how is consumption related to income? Based on past relationships, future consumption is estimated. Typically, forecasters also estimate future investment, government expenditures, and net exports. The path of investment is forecasted on the basis of

---

[4]Council of Economic Advisers, *Annual Report, 1962*, p. 52. (Minor changes have been made in the Council's diagram. For example, the price base has been switched from 1961 to 1958, to make the blue parts of the diagram comparable with the red parts.)

[5]Council of Economic Advisers, *Annual Report, 1967*, p. 43.

current and expected future interest rates and other important influences. The president's budget and spending authorizations by Congress are used to estimate the probable course of government spending. When such pieces are fitted together, it is possible to make a projection of GNP. For this purpose, a number of models of the United States economy have been developed. They include the MPS model (of the Massachusetts Institute of Technology, the University of Pennsylvania, and the Social Science Research Council), Otto Eckstein's Data Resources, Inc. (DRI) model, and Lawrence Klein's model at the Wharton School, to name a few.

Econometric models provide a useful starting point for forecasts, and are particularly helpful in cross-checking the various components of aggregate demand (consumption, investment, government spending, and net exports) to make sure that they are consistent. However, models have a major limitation: Essentially, they provide mechanical projections (although the mechanisms of the models are very complex and impressive). The economic future depends on many forces, some of which are not easy to incorporate in formal models. Thus, forecasters generally adjust the initial results of their econometric models to allow for additional factors that they consider important. The final result is a "judgmental" forecast—using the results of models, but with modifications. This combined method has worked reasonably well. A common evaluation is that "econometric models don't predict well; but econometricians do."

In adjusting the raw output of econometric models, forecasters use the results of various surveys of future intentions; for example, the Commerce Department and the McGraw-Hill Economics Department's questionnaires regarding investment intentions; Conference Board surveys of capital appropriations by businesses; and surveys of consumer attitudes, including those done by the University of Michigan Survey Research Center.

Turning Points One of the hardest problems in forecasting is to tell when a turning point will take place—when an expansion will reach a peak and a decline will begin, or when a recession will hit the trough and a recovery begin. But such turning points are very important. If an upswing will end in the next several months, now is the time to consider more expansive policies.

What is needed, then, is something that will signal a coming turn. The search for *leading indicators* has been centered in the National Bureau of Economic Research, under the leadership of Arthur F. Burns (who spent much of his career at the NBER), Geoffrey Moore, and Victor Zarnowitz. A number of leading indicators have been identified; they include such items as common stock prices, new orders for durable goods, and the average number of hours worked per week. An index of leading indicators is published monthly by the Department of Commerce in *Business Conditions Digest.*

A *leading indicator* reaches a turning point (peak or trough) before the economy as a whole changes direction. (New orders for durable goods are an example.)

As Figure 15-3 shows, leading indicators have been helpful: They have predicted every recession since 1948. But, even when they correctly signal a future recession, they don't tell *when* it will occur; they don't provide the same period of advance warning each time. (Note that the leading indicators provided a 23-month warning of the 1957 recession, but only a 4-month warning of the 1953 recession.) And, worse still, they sometimes send out false signals, indicating a downturn even though the economy in fact continues on its upward course. (Note 1950 and 1962.) This false signal problem has led to a common quip: Leading indicators have signaled seven of the last five recessions.

FIGURE 15-3 Index of leading indicators.
The curve shows the behavior of the leading indicators. The P and T notation along the top
dates the peaks and troughs of the economy as a whole; the recessions in between are
shaded. Note that a signal from the leading indicators *usually* means a coming turn—but
not always. For example, the indicators turned down in 1950, but there was no recession
on the horizon. The figures show the number of months by which the indicators led the
turning points in the economy. Sometimes there is a long warning: 23 months elapsed
between the time when the indicators turned down in 1955 and when the economy as a
whole began to decline in 1957. But sometimes the indicators give as little as 4 or 5
months warning of a coming recession (in 1953 and 1973).

Accuracy of Forecasts An idea of the
accuracy of forecasts is provided in Figure
15-4, which shows the annual projections of
current-dollar GNP by the Council of Economic Advisers (CEA). On average, actual
GNP has differed about 1 percent from projected GNP.[6] Of course, the worse the forecasting error, the worse the resulting economic policy will tend to be. Note, in particular, the relatively large error in 1965–1966
when current-dollar GNP grew by about $1\frac{1}{2}$
percent more per annum than expected; this
was the period when inflation became a
serious problem. But the inflation of the
1960s should not be attributed just to forecasting errors or to a failure of economic
analysis. The main problem was political.
Trapped in an unpopular war, President
Johnson for several years overruled the recommendations of his economic advisers that
taxes be increased to restrain inflation.[7]
When the tax surcharge of 1968 was finally
enacted, it was long overdue; inflation had
gathered considerable momentum.

[6]Comparing actual changes with projected changes does not do complete justice to the CEA projections. These
projections are based on the assumption that certain monetary and fiscal policies will be followed. In fact, policy
changes may occur, and these changes may alter GNP. Thus, the projection may have been accurate on the basis of the
assumptions made, but be thrown off by policy changes. Similarly, deviations may have occurred because of major
strikes or other unanticipated special events.

[7]Doris Kearns, *Lyndon Johnson and the American Dream* (New York: Harper & Row, 1976), p. 296.

FIGURF 15-4 The accuracy of projections by the Council of Economic Advisers, 1963–1977.
In most years, actual GNP ends up within 1 percent of projected GNP. However, projections are occasionally further off the mark. In 1966, for example, the projected change in current-dollar GNP was only 6.9 percent. But the actual change turned out to be 8.6 percent.

THE CASE AGAINST ACTIVISM

Part of the case against discretionary policies was outlined in Chapter 14. Because there are lags in the implementation of monetary and fiscal policies, and additional lags before aggregate demand responds, the policy maker has a tendency to play the part of the anxious mariner, swinging the policy wheel too late and too hard. Skeptics of fine tuning doubt that forecasting can be made sufficiently accurate to eliminate the danger of overreaction by monetary and fiscal policy makers.

This danger is increased by a second related problem, arising because of another type of lag. While the lags studied in Chapter 14 involved delays *before* aggregate demand changes, this other lag occurs *after* aggregate demand changes; it involves the differing speeds with which real GNP and prices respond to changes in demand. Specifically, when aggregate demand rises, the

short-run effect on real output is generally powerful. Unless producers are already straining hard against their capacity limitations, they respond to an increase in demand by producing more. However, as time passes, the higher demand tends to be reflected more and more in terms of higher prices and less and less in terms of real output. In other words, when aggregate demand is stimulated, the favorable output effects come quickly; the unfavorable price effects come with a delay. This creates a temptation to stick with expansive fiscal and monetary policies for their short-term benefits.

Figure 15-5 illustrates the criticisms that monetarists direct at the activist Keynesian approach. The first step in this approach is to estimate potential GNP. There is a tendency to be optimistic, to overestimate potential GNP and the amount by which unemployment can be reduced by expansive demand policies. Such an overly optimistic estimate is shown by the blue potential GNP line in Figure 15-5. The red line shows the sustainable long-run path consistent with a steady rate of inflation and with the equilibrium (or "natural") rate of unemployment.

Now let us see what the critics fear if activists are in charge of policy. Beginning at A, the economy is recovering from a recession. Monetary and fiscal policies are set for expansion of aggregate demand. Real output is rising rapidly, the unemployment rate is falling, and inflation (with its delayed response) is still slowing down because of the previous period of slack. Everything seems to be going well; the expansive policy settings are retained. But, without anyone's

noticing, the economy moves past B, crossing the sustainable path. When this happens, the seeds of a more rapid inflation are being sown, although the inflationary result will not appear for some time. (As the curve in the lower diagram shows, inflation does not begin to accelerate until time C.)

If the error in estimating the potential GNP path has been large, the economy may never actually reach it. The expanding demand shows up increasingly in terms of inflation, and less and less in terms of real output. Expansive fiscal and monetary policies can increase aggregate demand, but they do not control whether the higher demand will cause higher output or higher

FIGURE 15-5 Policy activism: The case against.
Because of the delayed response of prices and overly ambitious goals, aggregate demand will be overstimulated, say the critics. When inflation finally does become an obvious problem, then policy-makers will overreact.

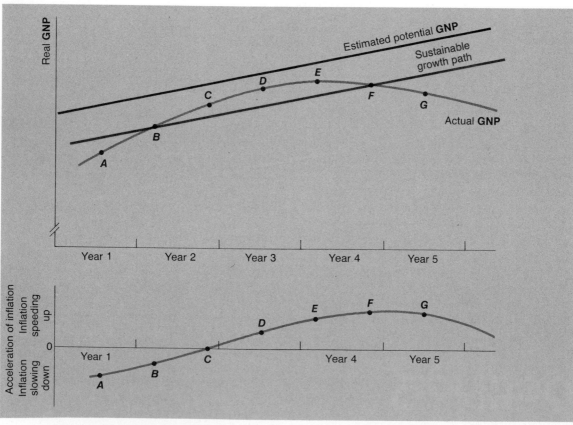

prices. Between *C* and *D*, a sharp policy debate is likely. Those focusing on the potential GNP path argue that to reach the real output target, aggregate demand should be increased even more. But, as inflation is by now accelerating, others urge caution. As time passes and inflation gets worse and worse, those urging restraint eventually win the debate. And, with inflation by now rising rapidly, the policy adjustment may be abrupt. Furthermore, the previous overexpansion is already generating contractionary forces (because of the acceleration principle of Figure 14-4). Thus, the economy may fall into a sharp recession. But, as always, inflation responds with a lag; it remains serious even though tight policies have been introduced. As a consequence, everything seems to be going wrong during the period between *E* and *G* (just as everything went right during the expansion between *A* and *B*). The economy is headed into a recession and unemployment is rising, yet inflation is still getting worse. As the unemployment rate rises higher and higher while inflation decreases very little, more and more people argue that demand restraint simply won't stop inflation. Inflation has become "built in," and it is widely believed that nothing much can be done about it with monetary and fiscal policies. (Jawboning or formal price and wage controls are sometimes seen as a way out of inflation.) Aggregate demand policies are therefore turned in an expansive direction, in order to increase output and reduce unemployment. A new upswing begins. But inflation has accelerated more as a result of the period of excess demand than it

has fallen as a result of the period of slack.[8] Thus, each upswing begins with a higher rate of inflation than the previous one.

This, then, is the case against activism. And just as the case in favor of activism can be supported with real-world diagrams (Figure 15-2), so the critics can point to real-world evidence of failures of discretionary policies. First, they note that recent recoveries have indeed begun with higher and higher rates of inflation. Inflation was about 1 percent in the early recovery year of 1961; about 4 percent in the early recovery of 1971 and 1972; and about 7 percent in the early recovery of 1975 and 1976.

Second, real-world examples similar to Figure 15-5 may be found. Specifically, consider Figure 15-6. The original estimates of potential GNP, made at the time, indicated that actual GNP in 1972 was still well below potential. Expansive monetary and fiscal policy settings were maintained through 1972 to stimulate the economy. And, even at the peak of the expansion in 1973, original estimates of potential GNP showed the economy well below the potential path.

But the 1971–1973 expansion ended in an inflationary burst. With the advantage of hindsight, we may conclude that the potential GNP path was overestimated at the time. Indeed, later, more realistic estimates of potential GNP are shown in red. These estimates indicate that actual GNP had reached the potential by the end of 1972, and that the further rapid expansion in early 1973 contributed to inflation.[9]

Thus, argue the monetarists, the tendency to overestimate potential GNP makes it

---

[8]Recall from Chapter 13 (Figure 13-12) that the short-run Phillips curve is bowed, and that, therefore, inflation accelerates more strongly as a result of excess demand than it decelerates as a result of slack.

[9]The downward revisions of the potential GNP path were presented in Council of Economic Advisers, *Annual Report, 1977*, pp. 54–55. Although the CEA expressed reservations regarding the original estimates of potential GNP at the beginning of 1974, these estimates continued to be used as late as 1975 in official documents. For example, in September 1975, the Congressional Budget Office (CBO) published a diagram similar to the blue parts of Figure 15-6, showing a GNP gap throughout the 1972–1973 period. Thus, as late as 1975, the CBO was implying that expansive policies had not been carried far enough in 1972 and 1973. (See CEA, *Annual Report, 1974*, p. 65; and CBO, *Recovery: How Fast and How Far?* September 1975, p. 36.)

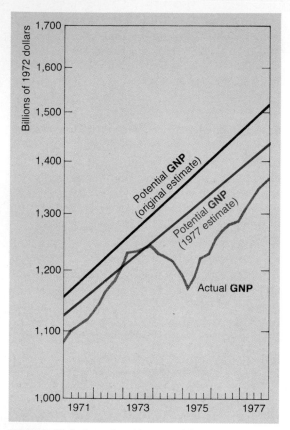

FIGURE 15-6 Actual and potential gross national product, 1971–1977.
According to estimates of potential GNP at the time (shown in blue), actual GNP in 1973 still fell short of the potential. Later revisions of potential GNP (shown in red) indicate that the economy had reached its potential by the end of 1972, and was overheating by early 1973. SOURCES: Council of Economic Advisers, *Annual Report, 1977*, p. 55; *Annual Report, 1978*, p. 85.

an inappropriate target for economic policy; inflationary overexpansion may result. Rather, the objective should be a *stable increase in GNP*. Accordingly, they recommend that aggregate demand be increased at a stable rate of, say, 5 percent per year. It is true, of course, that if the real potential of the economy fails to grow by this 5 percent figure, aggregate demand will outrun productive capacity and inflation will result. But the

inflation will be mild: A 1 percent shortfall in the growth of capacity will cause 1 percent inflation. Such a policy, they argue, will avoid the excesses of fine tuning: expansive monetary and fiscal policies that are aimed at an unattainable real output goal, but result in rapid inflation. In short, monetarist policy rules are aimed at achieving a stable growth in current-dollar GNP.

POLICY RULES: The Freedom Issue

Some of the proponents of policy rules base their case on political as well as economic considerations. Specifically, they believe that policy rules will result in less interference by government officials in the free enterprise system. Several decades ago, Chicago Prof. Henry C. Simons made rules a cornerstone of his *Economic Policy for a Free Society:*[10]

In a free enterprise system we obviously need highly definite and stable rules of the game, especially as to money. The monetary rules must be compatible with the reasonably smooth working of the system. Once established, however, they should work mechanically, with the chips falling where they may. To put our present problem as a paradox—we need to design and establish with the greatest intelligence a monetary system good enough so that, hereafter, we may hold to it unrationally—on faith—as a religion, if you please.

The search for monetary rules compatible with a smooth working of the economy led to the proposal that the money supply be increased at a steady rate, year in and year out.

THE CASE AGAINST POLICY RULES

On behalf of discretionary policy making, four basic criticisms can be made of fixed rules: (1) In practice, there cannot be—

[10]Henry C. Simons, *Economic Policy for a Free Society* (Chicago: University of Chicago Press, 1948), p. 169.

nor should there be—rigid rules that are followed regardless of the consequences. (2) Even though there is much to be said for a stable rate of growth of nominal aggregate demand, monetary and fiscal policy rules will not provide it. (3) Rule-makers generally recommend rules aimed at providing barely enough aggregate demand to keep prices stable. The result may be an unnecessarily high rate of unemployment. (4) Paradoxically, efforts to follow stable policy settings can, in practice, lead to abrupt changes in policies.

Policy Rules as a Will-o'-the Wisp

Monetarists argue for policy rules that should be followed regardless of current conditions. In Simons' view, they should be followed regardless of how the chips fall. But this rigid position can scarcely be taken literally. After all, evidence regarding economic institutions and economic behavior must be taken into account in establishing any rule; not to do so would be foolish. Yet these institutions and patterns of behavior change. And when they do, any rule based on them should be reconsidered—not held steadfastly, like a religion. There used to be a monetary "religion" based on the gold standard. But its application led to disaster. Indeed, as Simons himself observed, "The utter inadequacy of the old gold standard, either as a definite system of rules or as the basis of a monetary religion, seems beyond intelligent dispute."[11] But that is exactly the point—rules cannot be maintained regardless of the evidence, regardless of how the chips fly.

As Paul Samuelson has observed, a set of rules is "set up by discretion, is abandoned by discretion, and is interfered with by discretion."[12] Indeed, it is impossible to establish a rule that will prevent a repetition of the greatest destabilizing acts of governments in the past. In the midst of military conflicts, governments will bend or discard rules. No religion of finance will stand in the way of the religion of victory. Monetary rules do not exist in a vacuum. They involve questions of alternatives, of evidence, of analysis—not of theology. No rule is rigid.

Would a Monetary Rule Make the Growth of Aggregate Demand More Stable?

In order to make their case, those who favor a policy rule put forward two related propositions: (1) that discretionary policies tend on average to destabilize the economy; and (2) that a rule would lead to greater stability. Chapter 14 and the early pages of this chapter have illustrated how difficult it is to come to a firm conclusion on the first point. An impressive case can be made on either side, depending in part on whether the early 1960s or the 1970s are chosen for study.

Argument over the second point (that a rule will lead to greater stability) is muddied by the failure of advocates to come to a consensus as to what the rule should be. Most monetarists believe that the traditional definition of money as M_1 (consisting of demand deposits and currency in the hands of the public) is the correct basis for policy; M_1 should be increased steadily. There are, however, dissenters (most notably, Milton Friedman) who believe that the key concept

---

[11] *Economic Policy for a Free Society*, p. 169. The gold standard got things backward, putting greater emphasis on the long-run trend of demand than on short-run stability. In the long run, there was a restraint on the amount of money that could be built on any given gold base, and the base changed only gradually as new gold was mined. But the restraint depended on a threat. If too large a superstructure were built, then there would be a crisis of confidence, and people would demand gold in exchange for paper currency and bank deposits. Since the threats on occasion became reality, the gold standard at times contributed to short-run instability.

[12] "Principles and Rules in Modern Fiscal Policy," *Collected Papers of Paul A Samuelson* (Cambridge, Mass.: MIT Press, 1966), vol. 2, p. 1278.

is the second definition of money. That is, M_2 (which includes time deposits in commercial banks) should be increased at a constant rate.

This is a significant problem, since the two magnitudes do not grow at the same rate. During short periods, they have not moved in closely parallel directions; and over the longer run, M_2 has tended to grow more rapidly than M_1. These discrepancies—and the division among monetary economists—have been met with sarcasm by their opponents: Monetarists are not sure what money is, but whatever it is, it's magic.

Insufficient Aggregate Demand?

Monetarists generally propose rules that will allow aggregate demand to rise no more rapidly than the productive capacity of the economy. This would provide the basis for a stable economy, including stable prices. Their debate with Keynesians involves both the *stability* and the *trend* of aggregate demand.

The desirability of a trend involving zero inflation depends on the nature of the long-run Phillips curve; monetarists generally argue that it is vertical right down to the axis (Figure 13-9) so that zero inflation in the long run exacts no cost in terms of higher unemployment. Many Keynesians disagree, arguing that the curve bends as it approaches the axis (Figure 13-10), and that, therefore, the monetarist proposal would involve an unnecessarily high rate of unemployment. Because of the high rates of inflation of recent years, there is no recent statistical evidence on this matter. Older statistical evidence going back to the 1930s does not provide support for the monetarist view that the long-run Phillips curve goes straight down to the horizontal axis.[13] Thus, the monetarist prescription (that we move to-

ward a stable, noninflationary rate of growth of aggregate demand) involves the danger of a permanently high rate of unemployment. Consequently, even if we wanted to try such an approach, it would be prudent to reconsider this policy if the unemployment rate rose as the inflation rate was worked down close to zero. Such a procedure is, however, generally opposed by monetarists on two grounds. First, if you are going to reconsider the rule as you go along, it really isn't a rule. Second, inflationary expectations are themselves a major contributor to the inflationary momentum, since they get built into wage contracts. If the government and the central bank are going to fight inflation effectively, they must take a firm, credible position in order to convince the public that inflation will indeed be reduced. An announced policy of reconsidering as you go along is scarcely credible.

In other words, critics of monetary rules fear that monetarists would keep the trend of aggregate demand too low, creating high unemployment. Monetarists believe that their critics are unlikely ever to stop inflation, because they lack the will.

The Paradox of Gradualism: Economic Policy in the Early Nixon Years

No government can commit itself to follow policy rules regardless of how the chips fall; governments are elected to use their best judgment. To return to our earlier analogy, no helmsman will lash the wheel permanently in place, regardless of where the ship may head. But, if the distinction between rules and discretionary policies disappears upon examination, an important policy issue nevertheless remains: Should policy makers attempt to fine-tune the economy, adjusting fiscal and monetary policy settings frequently with an ambitious objective of maintaining a high-employment,

---

[13]Some of this older evidence is reviewed in Paul Wonnacott, *Macroeconomics*, rev. ed. (Homewood, Ill.: Richard D. Irwin, 1978), Appendix 13-B.

stable economy? Or should they make policy adjustments relatively infrequently, keeping an emphasis on the long-run performance of the economy? Should the helmsman turn the wheel vigorously and often, in order to keep the ship on course? Or should the wheel be generally held in the straight-ahead position, with adjustments being made only infrequently and gradually? In short, the important policy debate is not between fine tuning and *fixed* policy rules. Instead, it is between fine tuning and *gradual, less frequent* changes in economic policy.

Some of the problems of gradualism were illustrated during the early years of the Nixon administration. During the preceding Kennedy-Johnson years, Keynesianism had been at its zenith. Kennedy spoke of getting the country moving again; fiscal stimulus was proposed as a means for doing so; and, as full employment approached, fine tuning became the order of the day. Then, when Nixon took office, a significant change in emphasis took place. While the administration certainly did not go all the way to embrace a policy rule, and indeed rejected the "Friedmanite" label, the chairman of the Council of Economic Advisers (Paul McCracken) did characterize his approach as being "Friedmanesque." Rather than move quickly to the ultimate aggregate demand objectives, the administration spoke in terms of gradualism. And George Shultz, the Director of the Office of Management and Budget, in early 1971 characterized current policy: "Steady as you go." Certainly there was at least a hint of stable policy settings.

But what happened? As the economy recovered slowly from the trough of the recession in November 1970, the unemployment rate remained high. By the middle of 1971, the seasonally adjusted unemployment rate was still what it had been in late 1970—about 6 percent.

Pressures mounted to "do something." The result was a very abrupt shift, with a new economic policy being introduced in August of 1971. Wages and prices were frozen; taxes were cut to stimulate domestic spending; and strong international measures were taken to stimulate aggregate demand. (The international measures will be discussed in Chapter 16.)

Thus, we face dangers on either hand.[14] If we attempt to fine-tune the economy, we may overreact to small and transitory disturbances. But, if "steady as you go" becomes our watchword, very strong political pressures may build up as the chips continue to fly; the result may be a very abrupt change in policy indeed. The Nixon administration fell victim to the second danger. Although it advocated gradualism, it ended up with one of the sharpest policy shifts of recent decades.

THE OUTCOME OF THE DEBATE

While monetarist rule-makers remain in the distinct minority, some important changes have occurred during the 1970s as a consequence of their criticisms of activist policies and as a consequence of the disappointing results with aggregate demand management:

1. There has been increased awareness of the problem of lags and the dangers of destabilizing the economy if policy actions are taken too late. (Although monetarists helped to highlight this problem, they were not alone in recognizing it. Indeed, concern over policy lags can be traced back through Keynesian literature.)

2. Because of these lags, there is substantial distrust of abrupt changes in monetary or fiscal policies, involving either a

---

[14]Economists thus are condemned by their profession to argue, "On the one hand . . . ; on the other hand . . . ." After a briefing by the chairman of the Council of Economic Advisers, Harry Truman sarcastically observed that "what we need around here is a one-armed economist."

sharp change in the rate of growth of the money stock, or a sharp change in the full-employment budget. Such sharp changes may add to future problems.

3. In making policy, the importance of paying attention to the long-term consequences is more widely recognized. In particular, because aggregate demand has a lagged effect on prices, policies aimed at the control of inflation cannot promise quick results; anti-inflation policies should be made with the long run in mind.

These three changes show up in policy actions and in statements by senior officials, both in the United States and in other countries. Most notable was the action taken by the Congress in 1975 as a result of its concern over the abrupt changes in monetary policy in preceding years. As we noted in Chapter 14, Congress has insisted that the Federal Reserve announce its monetary targets and explain any failures to meet these targets. A number of foreign countries, such as Germany and Canada, have also adopted

monetary policies aimed at a stable growth of the money stock.

Perhaps the most remarkable criticism of short-term aggregate demand management came from British Prime Minister James Callaghan in a speech at a conference of his Labour Party in September 1976:

We used to think that you could just spend your way out of a recession and increase employment by cutting taxes and boosting government spending. I tell you, in all candour, that that option no longer exists, and that insofar as it ever did exist, it only worked by injecting bigger doses of inflation into the economy followed by higher levels of unemployment as the next step. That is the history of the past 20 years.

And Gerald Bouey, the Governor of the Bank of Canada, stressed in a 1976 speech that:

A longer-run approach to policy is essential. . . . We must keep an eye on the far horizon, on where we want our economy to be a number of years from now.

Key Points

1. The mediocre record of monetary and fiscal policies in recent years has enlivened an old debate between Keynesians and monetarists: Should aggregate demand policies be actively adjusted in the quest for high employment and stable prices? Or should monetary and fiscal rules be established?

2. The activist Keynesian approach involves several steps. First, the full-employment or potential path of GNP should be estimated. Second, if actual GNP is significantly below potential GNP, aggregate demand should be expanded until the potential path is approached. Thereafter,

fiscal and monetary policies should be adjusted as needed to combat fluctuations.

3. This strategy was followed with success during the first half of the 1960s. But aggregate demand became too high and inflation accelerated when President Johnson delayed in asking for a tax increase to finance large military and domestic spending.

4. Monetarists believe that discretionary policies are likely to do more harm than good, and therefore they recommend that policy rules be followed. Most important is the rule that the money stock be increased by a fixed percentage, year after year, regardless of current economic conditions. Monetarists distrust discretionary policies because:

(a) There are lags before aggregate demand can be adjusted, as explained in Chapter 14.

(b) There is also another important lag: The price effects of a change in aggregate demand lag behind the output and employment effects.

(c) Keynesians tend to be overly optimistic in estimating the potential path of real GNP.

(d) Because of the lags and overoptimism, expansive policies tend to be continued too long. Then, when inflation becomes a clear and present danger, policy makers tend to overreact, causing a fall in aggregate demand and a recession. But inflation does not respond quickly to the lower aggregate demand. The restrictive policies are therefore deemed a failure, and another round of expansive policies is begun. Consequently, discretionary policies are likely to cause instability and an inflationary bias in the economy. Each recovery tends to begin with a higher rate of inflation than the previous one.

(e) Policy rules will result in less interference by government officials, and therefore in more economic freedom.

5. The 1972–1975 period tends to confirm at least some of these monetarist reservations. (Review Figure 15-6.)

6. A number of counterarguments can be made against the monetarist case and in favor of discretionary policies:

(a) In practice, no government will follow policy rules regardless of the short-run consequences (how the chips fall) and competing objectives (such as wartime finance).

(b) Monetary rules do not ensure a stable increase in aggregate demand. Disagreements among monetarists over the use of M_1 or M_2 as the basis of the monetary rule illustrate the difficulties in picking a rule that will in fact stabilize demand.

(c) Rule-makers tend to propose rules that will keep the trend of aggregate demand too low. An unnecessarily high rate of unemployment will be the result. (Compare this with key point 4(d), the monetarist view that activist policies will give the economy an inflationary bias.)

(d) Efforts to follow stable, gradual policies may paradoxically lead to abrupt policy shifts. For example, the gradualist approach of the early Nixon years led to growing criticisms of "do-nothing" policies in the face of continued weakness in the economy; gradualism ended with the abrupt policy changes of August 1971.

7. In spite of these counterarguments, important changes in attitudes have occurred as a consequence of the monetarist criticisms of fine tuning and the disappointing results with aggregate demand management:

(a) The problem of lags is more clearly recognized.

(b) Abrupt changes in monetary and fiscal policies are distrusted.

(c) The importance of keeping long-term objectives in mind is more widely recognized.

Key Concepts

policy activism
discretionary policy
policy rule
fine tuning
secular stagnation

potential GNP
GNP gap
sustainable growth
leading indicator
gradualism

Problems

15-1 Explain the various steps in the activist Keynesian strategy.

15-2 Why is it important for activists to be able to forecast economic developments? What methods are available for forecasting aggregate demand?

15-3 Critics have sometimes said that, by simply quoting this year's change in GNP, you could do as well as an economic model builder in predicting next year's change in GNP. If you had done this in the period between 1963 and 1977 (shown in Figure 15-4), how would the accuracy of your forecasts have compared with those of the Council of Economic Advisers? Would you be able to claim a smaller error in any specific year or years? Should people be impressed by this claim?

15-4 What case do monetarists make against the Keynesian activist approach?

15-5 What case in turn can be made against monetary or other policy rules?

15-6 Why do Samuelson and others argue that a policy rule is impossible? Why is a rule a "will-o'-the-wisp"?

Appendix

SECULAR STAGNATION IN EARLY KEYNESIAN THEORY

Although Keynesians continue to worry about the problems of inadequate demand in the long run and unstable demand in the short run, their emphasis has shifted substantially over the past four decades. In the late 1930s, fears of secular stagnation—a long-run inadequacy of aggregate demand—were understandable. Aggregate demand had indeed been inadequate for a full decade. (It was only the abnormal spurt in the demand for weapons in World War II that finally pulled the economy out of the prolonged Depression of the previous decade.) But in recent decades, it has become increasingly difficult to argue that aggregate demand has on average been too low. The long-run trend of recent years has been one of substantial inflation. Thus, Keynesians have become more concerned with short-run instability than long-run stagnation.

In this appendix, we double back to the early Keynesian period to see why economists feared there would be secular stagnation. There are two reasons for going back to what is, obviously, a very dated discussion:

1. Most forecasting models are built on the Keynesian framework. Yet, when this framework was used in its simple form at the end of the Second World War, it led to very misleading forecasts. It is important to know what went wrong, in order to have a sound basis for current forecasting.

2. The explanation for the errors of forecasting in the forties will require a modification of the theory of the multiplier, presented in Chapters 8 and 9.

At the end of the Second World War, most economic forecasters predicted a postwar recession or depression—unless the government provided continuing stimulus with large-scale spending.

In retrospect, these fears of a postwar depression seem grossly exaggerated. (Indeed, GNP in 1946 turned out to be $190 billion, in contrast with the standard forecast of about $170 billion. And unemployment was only about one-third the forecasted amount.[15]) But forecasters do not have the advantage of hindsight; they must take their stand on the basis of information presently available. At the end of the Second World War, there were four reasons for fearing a collapse of the economy. First, there had been a sharp recession following the First World War; history might repeat itself. Second, with the coming of peace, the economy would revert to its natural peacetime state. And what was that? The prewar decade suggested that it was one involving high levels of unemployment. Third, with the coming of peace, government spending was being cut back. Finally, the new Keynesian theories warned of secular stagnation. It is this last point on which we will focus.

To see why Keynesian theories warned of secular stagnation, let us refer back to the Keynesian framework presented in Chapter 8.[16] The theory of aggregate demand was constructed on the foundation of the consumption

---

[15]A postmortem on these early forecasts is provided by Michael Sapir, "Review of Economic Forecasts for the Transition Period," *Conference on Research in Income and Wealth*, vol. XI (National Bureau of Economic Research, 1949); and Lawrence Klein, "A Post-Mortem on Transition Predictions of National Product," *Journal of Political Economy*, August 1946, pp. 289–308.

[16]One of the most explicit statements that large-scale unemployment is the natural state of the market economy may be found in Alvin H. Hansen, *Full Recovery or Stagnation?* (New York: Norton, 1938).

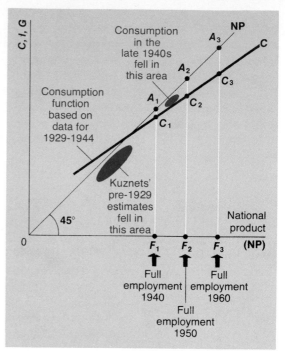

FIGURE 15-7 The fear of the forties: Secular stagnation. With this consumption function, the gap (AC) between consumption demand and the full-employment national product grows as the capacity of the economy grows.

function. What did that function look like? Keynes' theories suggested a function of the general form used in earlier chapters and shown in Figure 15-7. Furthermore, the available statistical evidence supported this view. The consumption data which had been collected for the period between 1929 and 1944 gave a series of observations that fitted such a consumption function closely; the theory was confirmed by the facts. Or so it seemed.

Consider the implications of this consumption function. Assume for the moment that there is no government spending or net exports. Then, for there to be full employment, investment spending must fill the vertical gap between the consumption function and the 45° line at the full-employment national product. In 1940, for example, investment must be C_1A_1 if there is to be full employment. And what happens as time passes? With investment and technological improvement taking place, the productive capacity of the economy increases: The national product required for full employment will move to the right through time. As this happens, the amount of investment required to fill the gap between consumption demand and productive capacity will grow— from A_1C_1 to A_2C_2 to A_3C_3 and beyond. Investment demand will have to grow both in absolute size and *as a fraction of national product.* Can investment demand be counted on to rise this rapidly? Hansen and other early Keynesians believed that the answer was no. Indeed, investment might even fall below its historical levels. There were no large new investment projects in sight comparable with, say, the building of the railroads. And the United States no longer had a frontier in the West to tame and build up. Consequently, Hansen concluded that the government would have to engage in ever higher spending in order to fill the shortfall between private demand and potential GNP, or there would be large-scale unemployment. The natural state of a market economy is one of depression.

The Long-run Consumption Function to the Rescue

But the economy did not suffer a depression after World War II. And the reasons were not merely the cold war and continued government spending for defense and other purposes. As the economy expanded, consumption was much above the old consumption function fitted to data from 1929 to 1944; the observations for the late forties were in the red area above the consumption function in Figure 15-7. The fears of secular stagnation faded in the light of the vigorous consumer demand of the late 1940s.

Why did this happen? Why was consumer demand so high during the late forties? Was it a fluke? Was it due to special factors?

There were undoubtedly some special factors. Private cars had not been produced during the war, and consumers were eager to replace their aged vehicles. Similarly, there was a large replacement demand for a whole series of consumer durables. Furthermore, many young families were getting settled after the disruptions of the war, and they had long lists of desired purchases.

But, in spite of these special features, the late forties did not represent a fluke. Rather, the fluke lay in the 1929 to 1944 data that economists had used to estimate the consumption function shown in Figure 15-7.

Contrary to what that consumption function suggested, consumption over the long run has been a stable fraction of income. In other words, the long-run consumption function C_L runs approximately through the origin, as illustrated

FIGURE 15-8 Consumption and disposable income, 1929–1977. Over the past five decades, consumption has traced out a straight line running approximately through the origin.

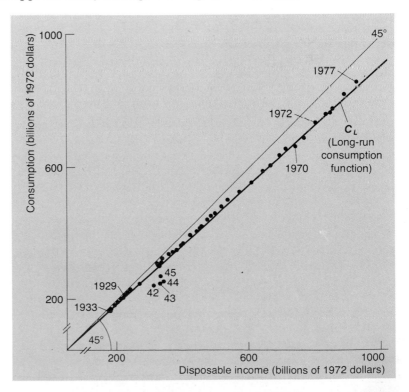

in Figure 15-8 (which is drawn with data for the past half-century). But it did not require the observations of recent decades to discover this. Rather, it was discovered by Nobel prizewinner Simon Kuznets, who went backward into history to estimate national income and its components in the late nineteenth and early twentieth centuries. He found that there had been sizable saving despite the low incomes in the 1800s. Just as the points for the late forties lay above the right-hand portion of the misleading 1929–1944 consumption function C in Figure 15-7, so Kuznets' early estimates lay below the left end.

During the late 1940s, economists did not, of course, have our advantage of the observations of the most recent three decades shown in Figure 15-8. But the observations for the late forties were coming in, and Kuznets' data had become available. Moreover, even before any of this information became available, C in Figure 15-7 could have been rejected as a long-run relationship between income and consumption. In the old days, when income was, say, at one-half the 1940 level, there was *some* saving and investment; consumption was less than income during the nineteenth century. Therefore, C could not be the long-run consumption function. Why had the 1929–1944 data, on which it was based, been so misleading?

An answer was suggested by a young graduate student at Harvard University, James Duesenberry (now a professor at the same institution).[17] He argued that consumption depends not only on current income, but also on the previous high level of income to which people have become accustomed, and on the consumption habits they have formed. This means that the consumption function observed during an economic decline is different from the one seen during a long-run period of gradually increasing incomes. Specifically, as the economy slid down into the Great Depression and incomes fell, consumers did not cut their spending down to the historical levels observed in the nineteenth century (point H in Figure 15-9). Rather, they had become accustomed to a high level of consumption, and they tried to maintain their standard of living. They cut back relatively little on their consumption, moving from point A to point B along the relatively flat short-run consumption function C_{S_1}. Then, during the later 1930s as income recovered toward its former 1929 level, consumers retraced their steps along the relatively flat short-run consumption function toward point A. Thus, said Duesenberry, people move along a flat short-run consumption function during a decline and an early recovery, because they are trying to maintain the standards achieved during the previous period of prosperity.

But, as the recovery continues and people's incomes reach new highs, there is a return to the normal long-run relationship, with consumers saving a stable fraction of their incomes. They move along the long-run consumption function from A to F (Figure 15-9). Once they have gotten to F and have become accustomed to their new affluence, they will not readjust back to A in the event of a new recession. Rather, they will try to keep consumption close to the level at F; they will move to the left along a new, relatively flat short-run consumption function (C_{S_2}) to G.

[17]James S. Duesenberry, *Income, Saving, and the Theory of Consumer Behavior* (Cambridge, Mass.: Harvard University Press, 1949).

FIGURE 15-9 Consumption in the short and the long run.
During a period when incomes are declining, people try to maintain their previous standard of living. Consumption moves to the left along a relatively flat short-run consumption function (C_S). During prosperity, as people reach new highs of income, they consume a constant fraction of their income, moving along the long-run consumption function (C_L).

Thus, Duesenberry contended that there is a whole series of short-run consumption functions along which people move during recessions and early recovery. The height of the short-run consumption function depends on the previous high income to which people have become accustomed. In other words, the short-run consumption function shifts upward to higher and higher levels as incomes rise during prosperity. Each new recession, starting from a higher level of income than the one before, involves a higher short-run consumption function.[18] Duesenberry labeled this upward shift the *ratchet effect*.

The period of the Great Depression was special because the economy stayed below its previous high (of 1929) for so long. Consequently, the economy moved back and forth along a single short-run consumption function for a whole decade. This misled early Keynesians into believing that the relatively flat consumption function traced out during the Depression[19] represented the fundamental relationship between consumption and income. But, as we have seen, Kuznets' long-run historical data and data for recent decades trace out a straight line from the origin.

This distinction between the long-run and short-run consumption functions means that we should be careful in using the multiplier presented in Chapters 8 and 9. While the multiplier does indeed equal $1/(1 - \text{MPC})$ in a simple economy without taxation, it should not be regarded as a constant. The response of consumption to income is higher in the long run than during a short-run business cycle; that is, the MPC is higher. Therefore, *the multiplier is larger in the long run than in the short.*

[18]Other explanations of consumer behavior have been put forward by Albert Ando and Franco Modigliani, who suggest that consumers respond to changes in wealth, and by Milton Friedman, who argues that consumers spend in line with what they perceive as their normal income (the "permanent income hypothesis").

[19]The data for 1942 through 1944 were misleading for a different reason. Although incomes were high during the war, consumption was kept down by the unavailability of goods (such as new cars) and by patriotic drives to encourage saving and the purchase of war bonds. Thus, the wartime observations fell in the vicinity of W in Figure 15-9, below and to the right of the long-run consumption function. These observations tended to confirm the erroneous view held at the end of the war that C_{S_1} was "the" consumption function. (Note that W would be close to a extension of C_{S_1}.)

chapter 16
Fixed or Flexible Exchange Rates?

As for foreign exchange, it is almost as romantic as young love, and quite as resistant to formulae.

H. L. Mencken

Economic efficiency requires specialization. It is efficient to grow wheat and corn in the Midwest, and to grow cotton in the South. And the scope for specialization goes far beyond the boundaries of any single country. Even such a large nation as the United States can gain by international specialization. It is efficient for the United States to export wheat and to import bananas. The United States exports about 9 percent of its national product—items such as wheat, aircraft, and computers. In return, we import such things as automobiles, coffee, cameras, and oil.

The way in which international specialization can contribute to a high standard of living fits into the study of economic efficiency in Part 4; we therefore defer the detailed consideration of international trade and efficiency to Chapter 25. In this chapter, we will study the monetary and macroeconomic aspects of international transactions.

What happens if the United States spends more abroad than foreigners spend here? What complications are introduced into monetary and fiscal policies by international transactions? What can be done to minimize international disturbances to the United States economy?

EXCHANGE RATES

In many ways, international trade is like domestic trade; it adds to economic efficiency because of comparative advantage and economies of scale. But there are two major complications that make international transactions different from domestic trade:

1. Domestic trade involves a single currency. For example, when a New Yorker purchases Florida oranges, both the consumer and the producer want the payment to be made in the same currency; namely, U.S.

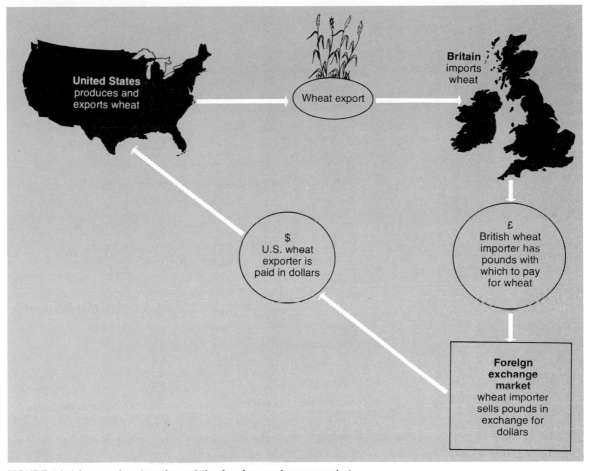

FIGURE 16-1 International trade and the foreign exchange market.
International trade normally involves more than one national currency. The British importer wants to pay in pounds; the United States exporter wants to receive payment in dollars. Consequently, the British import results in a transaction on the foreign exchange market, with pounds being sold for dollars.

dollars. But consider a British importer of United States wheat. The wheat is resold to British flour mills, which pay for it in British pounds (£). The British importer therefore has pounds with which to pay for the wheat. But the United States exporter wants to receive payment in dollars. Therefore, the British importer will go to the *foreign exchange market* in order to sell pounds and buy the dollars needed to pay for the wheat, as illustrated in Figure 16-1. (Foreign exchange markets are located in financial centers, such as London and New York.)

A *foreign exchange market* is a market in which one national currency (such as the U.S. dollar) is bought in exchange for another national currency (such as the British pound).

An *exchange rate* is the price of one national currency in terms of another national currency. For example, the price £1 = $2 is an exchange rate, and so is $1 = 250 yen. (The yen is the currency of Japan.)

2. International trade is complicated by barriers that do not exist in trade between states, provinces, or cities within the same country. Most notably, national governments impose *tariffs* (also known as *duties*) on many imports. Tariffs protect domestic producers by giving them an advantage over foreign competitors. The consumer, however, suffers: Prices of imports are increased by tariffs. And, when the prices of imported goods rise, domestic producers may also raise their prices, since they can now do so without losing business to foreign competitors.

A *tariff* is a tax imposed on a foreign good as it enters the country.

Other barriers also impede international trade. For example, the United States government imposes a *quota* on the amount of sugar that can be imported in order to protect domestic sugar producers.

A *quota* is a limit on the quantity of a good that can be imported.

Tariffs and other restrictions on trade will be studied in Chapter 26. Here, we concentrate on the first point—foreign exchange transactions, and the complications they raise for domestic stabilization policies.

THE FOREIGN EXCHANGE MARKET

Because there are more than a hundred countries in the world, the foreign exchange markets involve many currencies, and transactions can be quite complicated. In order to keep the discussion simple, let us concentrate on United States transactions with a single country, the United Kingdom.

Like the market for wheat or oranges, the market for *foreign exchange* can be stud-

Foreign exchange is the currency of another country. For example, British pounds or Japanese yen are foreign exchange to an American. United States dollars are foreign exchange to a Briton or German.

ied by looking at demand and supply. The demand for British pounds by those now holding dollars arises from three types of transactions:

1. American imports of British goods. For example, when an American buys a British car, a demand for British pounds is created. (The American wants to pay in dollars, but the British auto company wants payment in pounds.)

2. American imports of British services. For example, an American tourist may stay in a British hotel and eat in a British restaurant. In order to pay the hotel or restaurant, the American first buys pounds with dollars; in other words, the tourist creates a demand for pounds in exchange for dollars.

What is the difference between an import of a good and an import of a service? The good physically enters the United States; the car is unloaded at an American port. In the case of a service, there is no such physical transfer of a good to the United States; obviously, the hotel room and the restaurant stay in London. But in either case, a demand for pounds is created.

3. American acquisitions of British assets. For example, if an American corporation wants to invest in Britain by building a new factory there, it will need pounds to pay the British firm that constructs it.

The demand for pounds, like the demand for wheat, depends on the price. Suppose that, instead of being worth $2, the British pound had the much higher price of $3. What would this mean? British goods and services would be more expensive to

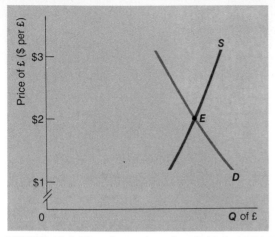

FIGURE 16-2 The demand and supply for British pounds.
The equilibrium exchange rate is determined by the intersection of demand and supply. The demand for pounds in terms of dollars depends on (1) United States imports of British goods; (2) purchases of British services by Americans; (3) purchases of British assets by Americans. The supply of pounds depends on (1) British imports of United States goods; (2) British purchases of United States services; (3) British purchases of United States assets.

Americans. If the price of the pound were $2, a British hotel room costing £10 would cost an American $20; but if the price of the pound were $3, that same room would cost $30 in U.S. money. As a result, American tourists would be less likely to go to Britain, and Americans would be less likely to buy British cars. Thus, when £1 costs $3, the quantity of pounds demanded is less than when a pound costs $2, as illustrated by the demand curve (D) in Figure 16-2.

Now consider the other side of the market, the supply of pounds in exchange for dollars. When British residents want to buy something from America, they must offer pounds in order to get dollars; a supply of pounds is created. Thus, the supply of pounds depends on:

1. British imports of United States goods

2. British imports of United States services

3. British acquisitions of United States assets; that is, British investment in the United States

DISEQUILIBRIUM IN THE EXCHANGE MARKET

The demand for pounds may exactly equal the supply at the existing exchange rate. It is possible, for example, that at an existing exchange rate of £1 = $2, the demand and supply curves intersect, as shown at the initial equilibrium E in Figure 16-3.

But we live in a changing world. Even if the demand and supply are initially in equilibrium, one or both curves may shift as time passes. Suppose that the demand for pounds decreases from D_1 to D_2. It might do so for any of a number of reasons; anything that decreases the United States demand for British products will cause a leftward shift of the demand for pounds. For example, the Japanese may become strong competitors of the British, producing cars that cut into British sales in the American car market.

As a result of the shift in the demand curve, the initial price of $2 per pound is no longer an equilibrium. In the face of this change, the British government has the option of taking any one (or a combination) of the following steps:

1. It can keep the exchange rate fixed at $2 by intervening in the exchange market. In order to be able to stabilize exchange rates, governments hold *reserves* of foreign currencies. In this example, the British government can keep the price of the pound at $2 by selling some of its United States dollar reserves to purchase the surplus quantity of pounds, *GE*.

Foreign exchange reserves are foreign currencies held by the government or central bank.

349

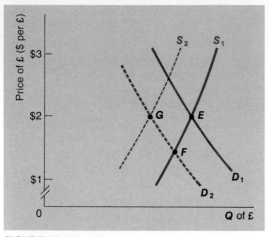

FIGURE 16-3 A shift in the demand for pounds.
If the demand for pounds shifts to the left from D_1 to D_2, there will be a surplus of pounds (*GE*) at the old exchange rate. The British can eliminate this surplus by one or a combination of the following steps: (1) The purchase of surplus pounds in exchange for dollars by British authorities. (This will work only temporarily, however, because British holdings of dollar reserves are limited.) (2) A change in the exchange rate to its new equilibrium, *F*. (3) A reduction of the supply of pounds (to S_2) by British restrictions on imports and other international transactions. (4) Restrictive aggregate demand policies in Britain, which also reduce British imports and supply of pounds.

It may be that the initial disturbance is only temporary. In the face of declining export sales, the British car manufacturers may respond vigorously, bringing out new models and recapturing their share of the United States market. In this event, the official intervention in the foreign exchange market will smooth out the temporary aberration. But not all shifts in demand and supply are temporary. The Japanese may prove to be tough competitors, and the British car manufacturers may be lethargic; the shift from D_1 to D_2 may represent a permanent change. In this case, the British government cannot maintain the original exchange rate of £1 = $2 indefinitely by buying pounds in exchange for dollars. Why? Because its holdings of dollars are

limited; sooner or later it will run out of dollar reserves.

Thus, in the face of a permanently lower demand for pounds, the British government must move to one of its other options:

2. It may allow the exchange rate to move to the new equilibrium, *F*.

3. In order to maintain the price of £1 = $2, the British government may reduce the supply of pounds to S_2 by taking direct action affecting international transactions. For example, it can limit the amount of United States assets that Britons are legally permitted to acquire. It may limit British imports of goods by the imposition of additional tariffs or quotas. Or it may reduce British expenditures for United States services by limiting the amounts that British tourists are allowed to spend in the United States.

4. The British government may reduce the supply of pounds more indirectly by adopting restrictive monetary and fiscal policies. Such policies will reduce British imports—and consequently the supply of pounds on the foreign exchange market—for two reasons. First, tighter policies will slow down British economic activity and reduce incomes. As a result, consumption will fall, including the consumption of imports. Second, the tighter policies will reduce British inflation. And, as British goods become more competitive in price, British consumers will be encouraged to buy domestic goods instead of imports.

(The lower British inflation will also affect exports: More competitive British goods will capture a larger share of the United States market. As Americans buy more British goods, the demand for pounds will increase, helping to eliminate the gap between the demand and supply at the exchange rate of £1 = $2.)

Since the end of the Second World War in 1945, the central debate in international finance has been over which of these four options should be used to deal with disequilibrium in the exchange markets. In the early postwar period, a number of European countries, including Britain, leaned toward the third option (direct restrictions). This tool, however, has a grave defect: By interfering with international transactions, it reduces the efficiency of the world economy. Thus, in recent decades, most of the debate has involved the other three options—official intervention in the exchange markets, changes in exchange rates, and changes in domestic policies. It is not necessary to make a sharp choice among these options; many intermediate arrangements are possible, involving a combination of these three strategies. Indeed, the design of intermediate arrangements has been the dominant concern in international financial negotiations; hence, it is one of the important topics we cover in this chapter.

But first, we will look at the historical gold standard, where reliance was placed on the fourth option. Exchange rates were kept stable, and international equilibrium was maintained by changes in aggregate demand in the various nations.

THE CLASSICAL GOLD STANDARD

Prior to the First World War (and again briefly in the period between the two world wars), most of the major trading countries of the world adhered to the international gold standard. To be on the gold standard, a country must fulfill these conditions:

1. The monetary unit must be defined in terms of a specific quantity of gold. (For example, prior to the Great Depression, the United States government specified that 1 ounce of gold was equal to $20.67.) The

authorities must stand ready to exchange gold for paper currency, or paper currency for gold, at the official price.

2. The government must allow gold to be exported or imported freely.

These two conditions suffice to keep exchange rates stable. Suppose the United States sets the official price of gold at $20 per ounce, and the British set the price at £10 per ounce.[1] These gold prices imply an exchange rate (or *mint parity*) of £10 = $20; that is, £1 = $2. International flows of gold will keep the exchange rate close to this rate.

> The *mint parity* is the exchange rate that can be calculated from the official prices of gold in two countries under the gold standard.

To see why, suppose that market forces temporarily push the price of the pound up to $2.10. Such an exchange rate would be inconsistent with the official prices of gold in the two countries; it would provide an opportunity for a foreign exchange trader to make a profit by taking the following steps:

1. With £100, buy $210 on the exchange market. Put aside $10.

2. Use the remaining $200 to buy 10 ounces of gold in the United States at the official price of $20 per ounce.

3. Ship the 10 ounces of gold to the United Kingdom.

4. Sell the gold to the United Kingdom Treasury or Bank of England at the official price, getting £100.

5. Take the £100 and repeat the same steps.

This *arbitrage* results in a profit, amounting to the $10 put aside during the initial step, less the costs of handling, ship-

---

[1] Although the dollar price of gold used in this example is close to the actual price prior to 1933, the price of gold in terms of pounds does not correspond to the historical price. We use £10 per ounce to keep the arithmetic simple.

Arbitrage is any set of transactions aimed at making a profit because of an inconsistent set of prices. (In our example, the exchange rate of £1 = $2.10 was inconsistent with the official prices of gold in America and Britain.)

ping, and insuring the gold. Note that arbitrage tends to eliminate the inconsistency between the exchange rate and the official prices of gold in the two countries. In step 1 of the operation, the arbitrageur sells pounds to buy dollars. This sale pushes down the price of the pound to $2.09, $2.08, and lower. The price will not, however, fall all the way to the mint parity of £1 = $2. Arbitrage will stop when the discrepancy between the exchange rate and the mint parity barely covers transportation and other costs. The exchange rate at which arbitrageurs will just barely be able to cover the costs of shipping gold from the United States is known as the American *gold export point*. With a low cost of shipping, it might be something like £1 = $2.02. There is also another *gold point*, at which it will be scarcely worthwhile to ship gold from the United Kingdom to the United States—at something like £1 = $1.98. Under the gold standard, arbitrage tends to keep the exchange rate within the narrow band set by the gold points. Within this band, the exchange rate is free to move in response to changes in demand and supply.

A *gold point* is an exchange rate at which an arbitrageur can barely cover the costs of shipping, handling, and insuring gold. (Beware of confusion regarding a gold point: A gold point is an *exchange rate*, not a price of gold.)

If the gold standard is to operate as a system for international adjustment—if, in other words, we are to have assurance that gold won't continuously flow out of one country and into another—then countries must follow an important "rule of the gold standard game." Together with the two conditions noted early in this section, this rule provides a third cornerstone of the international gold standard:

Each country should permit its money stock to change in the same direction as the change in its gold stock. That is, when a country's gold stock is rising, it should allow its money supply to increase, and vice versa.

Actually, this third condition will be *automatically* met if the monetary authorities follow a passive, do-nothing policy. Why is this so? Under the old gold standard, commercial banks used gold as part of their reserves, and so did central banks. (Recall the latter part of Chapter 11, especially Figure 11-4.) When gold flowed into a country, it might go directly to the commercial banks, thereby increasing their reserves and making possible an expansion of the money stock. Or the gold might be purchased by the central bank. But the acquisition of gold by the central bank, like the purchase of any asset, resulted in an increase in commercial bank reserves, as shown in Table 16-1. With excess reserves, the commercial banking system could then expand the money stock. And, just as an inflow of gold caused an automatic increase in the quantity of money, so an outflow of gold caused an automatic decrease.

The Adjustment Mechanism of the Gold Standard

How did the classical gold standard work to prevent a continuing flow of gold from one country to another? Economists foresaw the following sequence of events.

Suppose that Britain begins to import much more than it exports. Gold will then flow from Britain to the United States to pay for the excess British imports. The United

TABLE 16-1
Initial Effects on Money Stock of a Gold Inflow
(thousands of dollars)

Assets		Liabilities	
Federal Reserve			
Gold	+ 100	Reserve deposits of member banks	+ 100
Total	+ 100	Total	+ 100
Commercial Bank A			
Reserve deposit	+ 100	Demand deposits of arbitrageur	+ 100
Required 20 Excess 80			
Total	+ 100	Total	+ 100

This table shows the effects when an arbitrageur imports gold, sells it to the Federal Reserve, and deposits the proceeds in commercial bank A. Note the similarity to Table 11-1, which illustrated an open market purchase. In both cases, the commercial banks obtain excess reserves, permitting a further expansion of the money stock.

States money stock will automatically rise; the British money stock will automatically fall. Aggregate demand will rise and prices will be bid up in the United States; aggregate demand and prices will fall in Britain. As British goods become cheaper compared with United States goods, British exports will rise and imports will fall. The British loss of gold to the United States will stop.

> An international *adjustment mechanism* is a set of forces that works to reduce surpluses or deficits in international payments.
> A country has a *deficit* when its foreign expenditures exceed its foreign receipts.
> A *surplus* exists if its receipts exceed its expenditures.[2]

Problems with the Gold Standard

The international gold standard provided exchange-rate stability during much of the nineteenth century, when international trade and investment grew rapidly. But the gold standard also had major defects:

1. The process of adjustment may be very painful. For example, gold may flow out of a country that is suffering a depression. The gold standard causes a reduction in the money supply, which further depresses aggregate demand and increases unemployment. In other words, there may be a *conflict* between the *expansive policies* needed for domestic prosperity, and the *restrictive policies* required if the gold outflow is to be reduced.

The gold standard may also make the domestic situation worse in the country receiving gold. The automatic increase in the money supply may add to inflationary pressures that already exist.

2. A country receiving gold may take steps to reduce the inflationary impact of the gold inflow. It can do so by breaking the key "rule of the game" (which requires that the money stock be permitted to change when the gold stock changes). By engaging in open market sales, the central bank can reduce the quantity of money by the same

[2]The Appendix to this chapter explains the balance-of-payments accounts.

amount that the gold inflow increases it. By *sterilizing* gold in this manner, the central bank can combat inflation. In practice, many countries violated the "rule of the game" under the old gold standard.[3]

> A gold flow is *sterilized* when the central bank takes steps to cancel out the automatic effects of the gold flow on the money supply.

But, when a surplus country engages in this practice, it interferes with the adjustment process. Insofar as this country is successful in preventing inflation, it puts an additional burden on the deficit country (the country losing gold). That country will now find it even more difficult to achieve the price advantage in foreign markets that it requires to stop its gold outflow. Consequently, it will have to cut back on its money supply and suppress its aggregate demand even more sharply.

Thus, under the gold standard, the burden of adjustment may be unevenly divided. Surplus countries feel free to sterilize gold inflows. The fact that this slows down the adjustment process and allows the gold inflows to continue may be of no particular concern to them. But the deficit countries enjoy no such luxury. They have to take deflationary action before they run out of gold. Thus, the gold standard has a *deflationary bias*: There is greater pressure on the deficit countries to reduce domestic aggregate demand than on the surplus countries to increase it.

3. As we saw in Chapter 11, the gold standard can lead to very unstable monetary conditions. Under the fractional-reserve system of banking, a large quantity of money is built on a relatively small base of gold. The monetary system is therefore vulnerable to a crisis of confidence and a run on the available gold stock. Such a crisis of confidence came during the Great Depression of the 1930s, and the gold standard collapsed. One country after another announced that it would no longer convert its currency into gold.

In summary: (1) The international adjustment process under the gold standard could be painful. It might involve changes in a country's money supply that would make its domestic problems of inflation or unemployment worse. (2) The burden of adjustment might fall more heavily on deficit than on surplus countries, giving the system a deflationary bias. (3) Domestic monetary systems built on gold might be subject to panics and bank runs, which would add to instability.

THE ADJUSTABLE PEG: The IMF System, 1945–1971

In 1944, toward the end of the Second World War, senior financial representatives of the allied countries met at Bretton Woods, New Hampshire. This conference designed an *adjustable peg* system of exchange rates for the postwar world and established a new organization, the International Monetary Fund (IMF) to help make the new system work.[4]

The Bretton Woods system was designed to provide some of the exchange-rate stability of the old gold standard, while avoiding its major defects. Specifically, under the Bretton Woods system, exchange rates were generally to be kept stable within a narrow band ($\pm$ 1 percent) around an officially declared par. For example, for most

---

[3]A.I. Bloomfield, *Monetary Policy under the International Gold Standard* (New York: Federal Reserve Bank of New York, 1959), p. 50.

[4]The Bretton Woods conference also established a second important international organization, the International Bank for Reconstruction and Development (IBRD), to provide financial assistance for the rebuilding of war-torn countries and for economic development.

of the post-1945 period (specifically, from 1949 to 1967), the pound was *pegged* at an official price or *par value of* £1 = $2.80.

The *par value* of a currency (under the IMF system prior to 1971) was the official price of the currency, specified in terms of the United States dollar or gold.[5]

The founders of the IMF recognized that some provision would have to be made for international adjustment in the event of deficits or surpluses. Recall from the discussion at the beginning of this chapter (and Figure 16-3) that there are only four major ways for Britain to deal with a disturbance in the foreign exchange market. It may:

1. Change tariffs or other restrictions on imports or other international transactions.

2. Keep the price of pounds stable by buying surplus pounds with dollars (or selling pounds in the event of a shortage).

3. Change domestic aggregate demand policies in order to shift the demand and supply curves for pounds in terms of dollars.

4. Change the exchange rate.

The IMF system represented a compromise, with each of these steps playing a part. Increases in tariffs or other restrictions on imports (option 1) were considered generally undesirable, but were permitted in emergencies (including the severely disrupted period after World War II). But the main reliance was intended to be on the other three options.

Exchange-rate disturbances might be temporary, reflecting such things as strikes, bad weather that affects crops, or other transitory phenomena. In such circumstances, changes in exchange rates were considered undesirable: A fall in the price of the currency would be reversed in the future when the transitory events passed, and such swings in exchange rates were judged to perform no useful function. Rather than allow exchange rates to move, countries should fill temporary deficits by using foreign exchange reserves to intervene in the foreign exchange market (option 2). (For example, the British could use their reserves of dollars to buy pounds and thus prevent a fall in the price of the pound.) Because temporary swings might be quite large, the IMF was empowered to lend foreign currencies to deficit countries in order to help them stabilize their currencies on the exchange markets. (Thus, the word "Fund" is an important part of the title of the IMF. The IMF obtained the funds to lend to deficit countries by contributions from its member countries.) But no country has unlimited quantities of foreign exchange, and there are limits to the amount the IMF is willing to lend. Therefore, a country can intervene in the exchange market to support the price of its currency only as a temporary, stopgap measure to deal with short-run disturbances. Sales of foreign exchange cannot be a permanent solution to a continuing deficit.

Some disturbances in the exchange market are not transitory; some shifts in the demand or supply curves for foreign exchange will not reverse themselves in the future. In such cases, more fundamental steps than exchange market intervention must be taken, such as changes in domestic aggregate demand management (option 3). For example, if a country is following excessively expansive aggregate demand policies, the resulting inflation may price its goods out of world markets and cause international payments deficits. In such cases, a more restrictive domestic demand policy is appropriate in order to improve the international payments position and also to contribute to domestic stability. The IMF can require a

[5]As we shall see shortly, the United States fixed the price of the dollar in terms of gold, while other countries generally pegged the prices of their currencies in terms of the dollar.

country seeking a loan to introduce such restraint in monetary and fiscal policies.

But an adjustment in domestic demand is not always a desirable way of dealing with an international payments problem. As we have seen in the discussion of the gold standard, a deficit country might already be suffering from domestic recession; restrictive aggregate demand policies to solve the international payments problem would just make the recession worse.

In such circumstances, where the first three options had been ruled out or proved inadequate, the country was in a *fundamental disequilibrium*, and the Bretton Woods system approved the use of the only remaining option: Change the exchange rate. For example, the British *devalued* the pound from £1 = $4.03 to a new par of £1 = $2.80 in 1949, and again lowered the par value in 1967 to $2.40. On the other side, the Germans *revalued* their currency (the Deutsche Mark, or DM) upward in 1961 and 1969.

> A country *devalues* when it lowers the par value (the official price) of its currency.
> A country *revalues* when it raises the par value of its currency.

In summary, then, the IMF system involved a combined approach. In extreme cases, direct restrictions on imports or other international payments could be used to suppress deficits. Temporary deficits could be dealt with by selling foreign currencies on the exchange market, thus supporting the price of the home currency. (A country in temporary surplus could likewise buy foreign currencies to keep down the price of its currency.) Or domestic aggregate demand policies might be changed; policy changes were particularly appropriate if they also eased domestic problems of inflation or unemployment. Finally, if there was a fundamental disequilibrium, the par value of the currency could be changed. Thus exchange rates were pegged, but adjustable.

THE IMF SYSTEM: The Problem of Adjustment

For several decades, the IMF system worked reasonably well—well enough to provide the financial background for the recovery from the Second World War, and for a very rapid expansion of international trade. But it contained major flaws that caused a breakdown at the beginning of the 1970s.

In practice, there were defects in the policy of changing par values to deal with "fundamental disequilibriums." When a country begins to run a deficit or surplus, it is uncertain whether the deficit or surplus will be transient (in which case it can be covered with sales or purchases of foreign currency), or whether it represents a fundamental disequilibrium (in which case a change in the par value is appropriate). The IMF agreement itself provided no help in this regard: At no place did it define a fundamental disequilibrium.

Since a fundamental disequilibrium involves a surplus or deficit that will persist, one simple test is to wait and see whether in fact it does persist. But waiting can be a nerve-wracking experience. In particular, deficits involve the loss of foreign exchange reserves. And, as reserve losses increase, *speculators* add to the problem. As soon as speculators become convinced that the deficits will continue—and that the British, say, will therefore eventually be forced to devalue—they have an incentive to sell pounds. (For example, if a speculator sells pounds at the current price of $2.80, and the British do devalue the pound to, say, $2.40, the speculator can buy the pounds back for $2.40, making a profit of 40 cents on each pound.) Thus, speculators may add a flood of pounds for sale on the foreign exchange market. To keep the pound from dropping in price, the British authorities have to buy up these excess pounds, using their reserves of U.S. dollars to do so. Thus, the entry of speculators into the market speeds up the loss of British foreign exchange reserves and puts increased pressure on the authorities to devalue. This may then become a case of *self-fulfilling expectations*: The expectation by speculators that the pound will be devalued leads them to take an action (sell pounds) that increases the likelihood that the British authorities will, in fact, have to devalue.

> A *speculator* is anyone who buys or sells a foreign currency (or any other asset) in the hope of profiting from a change in its price.

We have noted that with devaluation speculators reap a windfall gain (of 40 cents per pound in our example). But this is just a transfer from the British authorities who lose exactly the same amount by fighting the speculators. (When the speculators sold, the British authorities bought the same pounds at $2.80. After the devaluation, they sell them back at $2.40, for a loss of 40 cents.) Ultimately, it is the British taxpayer who bears this loss. Why, then, do the authorities fight speculation as it builds up? Why don't they quickly devalue? The answer is that they are still unsure whether a devaluation is really necessary. And they hope to end speculation by restoring confidence that the pound will not be devalued. (If potential speculators can be convinced that no devaluation will occur, they will have no incentive to sell pounds.) To restore confidence, the authorities firmly declare their determination to defend the pound.[6] But once government leaders have staked their reputation on the defense of the currency, it is very difficult for them to back down and change its par value. Therefore, in practice, devaluations tended to be infrequent and long delayed under the IMF system. And, once they came, they tended to

be large, so that the government would not have to go through the painful experience again in the near future. Thus, the system of adjustable pegs did not work out as hoped. In fact, for long periods the system was one of *rigid pegs* as officials committed themselves firmly to the existing exchange rates. Then, when pressures became intolerable and changes had to be made, *jumping pegs* were the result, with drastic adjustments being made.

On the other side, surplus countries were even more reluctant to increase the exchange value of their currencies. As an upward revaluation of the currency will raise the price of domestic goods on the world market, it will be opposed by export businesses. And surplus countries are in a relatively good position to stand pat: Whereas deficit countries face a limit on the reserves they can lose before they run out, there is no such limit on the reserves a surplus country can accumulate. When a country revalues its currency, it is because of other, less obvious pressures.

To illustrate, consider what happens if Germany runs a surplus in its international payments; the demand for marks exceeds the supply. In order to keep the DM from rising, Germany will sell marks for United States dollars. But the German authorities must get the marks from somewhere. There are two main sources. The government may get them by running a budget surplus; that is, by increasing taxes or cutting spending. But this is scarcely a palatable option; the public dislikes both tax increases and spending cuts. The alternative is for the central bank to provide the marks to buy dollars. But if this happens, the reserves of German banks will increase: The purchase of United States dollars by the Bundesbank (the German central bank) will have the same effect on

---

[6]Even if the officials are almost sure that the pound will be devalued tomorrow, they must declare today that it will not be. What choice do they have? If they admit that it may be devalued (or even if they refuse to comment), speculators will pour pounds into the market, and they will reap even greater profits at the expense of the government when the devaluation does occur.

German bank reserves as a purchase of gold or an open market purchase of government bonds. Thus a balance-of-payments surplus tends to cause inflation. Consequently, the fear of inflation may push a country into an upward revaluation of its currency, in order to reduce or eliminate its surplus. In particular, this has been true of Germany, where there is a strong fear of inflation because of the lasting memories of hyperinflation following the First World War. In order to combat the inflationary effects of an international surplus, Germany raised the par value of the mark in 1961, and again in 1969.

But most surplus countries were very reluctant to raise the par value of their currencies. Japan was the prime example of a country that declined to revalue in spite of its large surpluses during the 1960s.

Thus, the IMF system turned out to be quite rigid. Countries tended to defend their existing par values strongly, thereby removing an important method of international adjustment. As a result, some countries were pushed back toward an emphasis on changes in domestic aggregate demand as a way to adjust (as under the gold standard). The British, for example, engaged in a series of "stop-go" domestic policies, restricting aggregate demand when their foreign exchange reserve position became serious, and turning the policy settings to "go" when their international position improved. Thus, a strong destabilizing force was introduced into domestic economic policy.

Suggestions for Improving the Adjustment Process

By the late 1960s, governments were considering proposals to modify the IMF system to provide for greater exchange-rate flexibility. Most notable was the proposal for a *crawling peg*. Under such an arrangement, countries would not wait for tremendous pressures to build up on their exchange rates

before making changes. When moderate international deficits or surpluses occurred, countries would adjust their par values frequently, and by small amounts. For example, in the face of a surplus, Germany might raise the par value of the mark by 0.25 percent per month—or a total of 3 percent per annum—until the surplus was reduced or eliminated. Such a small change would provide little incentive for speculators. (Indeed, if interest rates in Germany were kept 3 percent below United States interest rates, speculators would make no gain by buying marks: The gain from the rise in the value of the mark would be canceled out by the lower interest that could be earned on German securities.)

A second proposal was to allow a band of exchange-rate fluctuation wider than the 1 percent on either side of par permitted by the IMF rules. (During the 1950s and 1960s, countries generally followed even stricter procedures than permitted by the IMF, intervening to keep exchange rates within 0.75 percent of the official par.) As we shall see, the *wider band* was actually used between late 1971 and the breakdown of the pegged exchange-rate system in early 1973.

THE U.S. DOLLAR AND THE ADJUSTABLE PEG: The Problems of Liquidity and Confidence

Under the old IMF system, countries kept their exchange rates pegged. This involved a problem, since there are fewer independent exchange rates than there are countries. In a very simple world of two countries, say the United States and Britain, there is only one exchange rate. (Of course, this rate may be quoted either way. For example, $1 = £0.50 is just another way of stating that £1 = $2.) In general, in a world of n countries, there are only $n - 1$ independent exchange rates.[7] This fundamental fact of international fi-

---

[7]In a three-country world—Britain, France, and the United States—it may seem that there are three independent exchange rates: between the pound and the dollar, between the franc and the dollar, and between the franc and the pound. But in reality, there are only two (that is, $n-1$). Knowledge of any two exchange rates tells what the third will be. For example, if the price of the pound is $2 and the price of the franc is 20 cents, it follows that the pound is worth 10 times as much as the franc. That is, £1 = 10 francs.

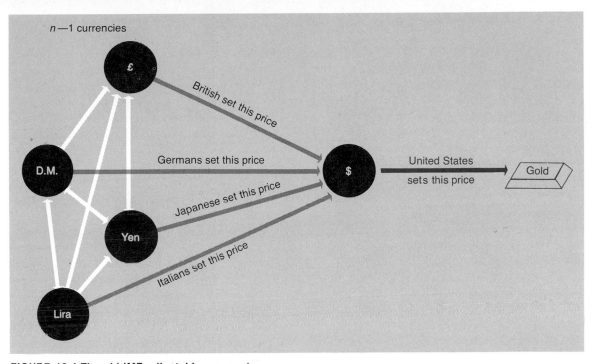

FIGURE 16-4 The old IMF adjustable-peg system.
Each of the $n-1$ countries set its exchange rate with the United States dollar (dark blue arrows). These $n-1$ exchange rates determined all exchange rates, including those in white. The United States, as the nth country, set only the price of gold.

nance posed two interrelated questions for the designers of the IMF system:

1. If an exchange rate—such as the rate between the British pound and the U.S. dollar—wanders to the edge of the permissible band, does Britain or the United States have the responsibility of intervening in the foreign exchange market to stabilize it?

2. In the case of fundamental disequilibrium, the exchange-rate parity might have to be altered. Does the United States or Britain make the decision to alter the parity? And which country chooses the new par?

The IMF solution to the first question was as follows: Other countries tied their currencies to the United States dollar, and the United States in turn undertook to keep the dollar convertible into gold.[8] This determined the entire set of exchange rates between countries (Figure 16-4). As far as exchange rates were concerned, the United States was the odd man out. Every other country was responsible for an exchange rate. As the nth country, the United States had no such responsibility.

The answer to the second question followed from the answer to the first. Since

[8]That is, the United States undertook to buy or sell gold to foreign central banks or treasuries at the official price of 1 ounce = $35. In technical terms, the IMF system involved the *gold exchange standard*, which exists when countries peg their currencies either to gold or to another currency (like the dollar) that in turn is pegged to gold.

But, although all currencies were thus pegged to gold either directly or indirectly, this system was a far cry from the classical gold standard. The United States government made no commitment to sell gold to the public; indeed, between the Great Depression and 1975, United States citizens were forbidden by law to hold gold. Furthermore, exchange parities were to be adjustable, not fixed firmly as under the gold standard.

Britain was responsible for keeping the pound pegged in terms of dollars, the ball was in the British court when the decision came to change the parity. (Provisions were made, however, for international consultations in the IMF regarding the new parity to be chosen.)

Thus, the United States had a unique role in the IMF system. The dollar was at the center, with other currencies being pegged to it. Other countries maintained pegged exchange rates, and they took the initiative in choosing new parities when exchange rates were adjusted. The United States was thus placed squarely in the center of one of the thorniest problems of the IMF system: How much *international liquidity* should there be, and how should additional liquidity be created?

> *International liquidity* is the total amount of reserves held by the various nations.

International Liquidity

Under the adjustable peg system, a country held its international reserves in

1. Gold

2. Foreign exchange, especially dollars

3. The country's reserve position in the IMF; that is, the contribution that the country had made to the IMF, and that it had an unconditional right to withdraw

For the United States—with its responsibility to keep the dollar convertible into gold—gold formed the primary reserve. Other countries had the responsibility of stabilizing their currencies relative to the dollar, and they therefore kept sizable amounts of dollars to be used as needed to intervene in the exchange markets. (Some countries, and particularly France, also held large portions of their reserves in the form of gold. For a discussion of French policies, see Box 16-1.)

In his 1960 book, *Gold and the Dollar Crisis*, Prof. Robert Triffin of Yale University argued that there was a fundamental problem with reserves in the IMF system.[9] As international trade expanded, countries would want more reserves. How could reserves be increased? By digging more gold, or by increases in foreign holdings of U.S. dollars.

The prospects for large increases in the supply of gold were not promising. Furthermore, it is not very sensible to dig gold out of one hole in the ground (in the mines of South Africa, the Soviet Union, or Canada) merely to bury it in another hole (in Fort Knox or in the vaults of the New York Fed). Thus, if countries were going to get the reserves they needed, their foreign holdings of dollars would have to increase. But how does a foreign country get more United States dollars? By running a surplus with the United States. In other words, the United States would have to have deficits. But, as American deficits continued and foreign dollar holdings became larger and larger compared with the relatively stable United States stock of gold, the ability of the United States to convert the dollar into gold would increasingly come into question. There would inevitably be a crisis of confidence, a run on United States gold by foreign governments, and a collapse of the IMF system.

In brief, the IMF system would not last. The United States could eliminate its deficit, giving the world a *liquidity crisis*, with inadequate reserves. Or this nation could continue to run deficits, with the predictable result of a *crisis of confidence* and a run on United States gold. Triffin suggested a solution: The IMF should be turned into an international central bank, capable of creating an international reserve that would supplant the United States dollar. This reserve could be methodically created to meet growing needs for liquidity.

[9]Robert Triffin, *Gold and the Dollar Crisis* (New Haven, Conn.: Yale University Press, 1960).

BOX 16-1

THE IMF, THE DOLLAR, AND DE GAULLE:

Deficits without Tears

As seen by the United States, the IMF system involved special responsibilities and special burdens. As the dollar was the principal reserve currency, the United States had a particular responsibility to keep the purchasing power of the dollar stable, and thus to provide a stable basis for the international financial system. And this country had a special problem. Because the United States was the nth country, it had little control over its exchange rates and over the international adjustment process.

From Paris, the world looked different. Led by President de Gaulle, the French government during the 1960s believed that there were fundamental defects in the IMF system. But, far from placing undue burdens on the United States, the IMF system gave this country an absurd advantage. When any other country ran a deficit, it had to use its reserves of foreign exchange to support the price of its currency on the exchange market. The United States was quite different. When the price of the United States dollar fell on the exchanges, this meant that other currencies were rising in terms of dollars. To keep the prices of their currencies down within the limits permitted by the IMF, the other countries therefore had to sell their currencies in exchange for dollars. In other words, a United States deficit was reflected, not in a loss in American reserves and constraints on American policies, but rather, by an *increase in U.S. dollar holdings by foreign countries*. By buying United States dollars, foreign countries automatically financed United States deficits. The United States could run "deficits without tears."

The French were particularly concerned with the freedom that the IMF system gave the United States to invest in foreign countries. Suppose that an American corporation wanted to acquire a French factory. It would sell dollars and buy francs to pay for the factory. In order to keep the exchange rate pegged, the French authorities would have to enter on the other side of the market, buying the dollars and selling the francs being demanded by the United States company. In other words, the IMF system required the French authorities to provide the francs with which United States companies could finance their takeover of French industry. To the French, this was ridiculous.

The French could have dealt directly with this problem by forbidding American investment in French industry; a national government has such a right. But this prohibition would not have been a satisfactory solution. Unable to set up shop in France, United States industry could move to Belgium. Because Belgium and France were partners in the European Economic Community (the EEC, or "Common Market"), goods produced in Belgium could be shipped duty-free to France. Thus, there was a formidable problem for the French government. It could finance a United States takeover of French industry. Or it could refuse to do so, and see its markets lost to Belgian workers employed in American-owned plants financed by the Belgian government.

What was needed, then, was a fundamental change in the IMF system. The system had to be redesigned to reduce the United States to the same position as other countries, with its reserves limiting its ability to run deficits. In the French view, this could be done by restoring the classical gold standard. Payments deficits should be settled in gold by all countries, including the United States. In order for there to be enough gold to permit a return to the gold standard, the French recommended that the price of gold be raised.

To enforce discipline on the United States, the French government decided not to hold large amounts of dollars. When it had to intervene in the foreign exchange markets to sell francs and keep the price of the franc down near its par value, it obtained dollars. But it then presented the dollars to the United States Treasury to be exchanged for gold. This move caused tension between de Gaulle and the Kennedy-Johnson administrations. If countries insisted in switching out of dollars and into gold, there wouldn't be enough gold to go around.

But, in the end, French intransigence regarding gold played little role in the demise of the IMF system. In the spring of 1968, French students rioted, setting the stage for a large increase in French wages, a rise in French prices, and a rapid deterioration of the French international payments position. Much of the French gold reserve was drained away to foreign countries to cover French deficits. Although it was certainly the last thing the French students had in mind when they began to throw cobblestones, they provided a reprieve to the United States government. For a time, pressures on United States gold stocks were relieved.

(Other surplus countries, particularly Germany and Japan, declined to join the French in demanding United States gold. They did not agree with the French view that the old gold standard should be restored. And Germany and Japan had more important things at stake. Germany was afraid that, if it asked for American gold, the United States would withdraw troops from Europe to reduce its international payments problems. Japan was concerned that requests for United States gold would cause this country to restrict imports from Japan to protect its international payments position. Thus, during the late 1960s, there was a twilight period of dollar convertibility. Technically, the dollar was still convertible into gold. But, in practice, the two major holders of dollars did not feel free to ask for gold.)

Special Drawing Rights

Toward the end of the 1960s, an international consensus developed that something had to be done about the problem outlined by Triffin. Another reserve had to be created as an alternative to dollars, so that the United States would no longer have to run deficits to provide reserves for the rest of the world. After a series of hard negotiations, the IMF was empowered to create Special Drawing Rights (SDRs), which could be used by nations to cover balance-of-payments deficits.

SDRs consist of bookkeeping accounts in the IMF owned by national governments, somewhat similar to the deposits that individuals hold at commercial banks. But the mechanism for creating SDRs is much simpler than the open market operations by which a central bank creates money within a domestic economy. The IMF creates SDRs in the easiest possible way: It directly adds SDRs to the accounts of the various nations with the IMF. Nothing is received in exchange. The SDRs are allocated, or distributed, to the various member nations of the IMF in proportion to their quotas; that is, in proportion to the contributions they have made to the IMF.

A country can use its SDRs to cover its deficits in several ways, but the simplest is the following. Suppose that Italy has a weak international payments position. It can directly approach other countries, such as the United States and Germany; these countries may agree to provide Italy with dollars and marks in exchange for a transfer of SDRs from the Italian account in the IMF to the United States and German accounts. In turn, the Italians can use the dollars and marks to pay for imports, or for intervention in the foreign exchange market to support the price of the lira.

Between 1970 and 1972, about $10 billion worth of SDRs were created by the IMF and distributed to the members. According to the initial design, the SDR was equal to a specific amount of gold. (Originally, 35 SDRs were equivalent to 1 ounce of gold.) Thus, the SDR was frequently referred to as "paper gold." However, with the collapse of the pegged exchange rate system and the abandonment of an official price of gold by the United States in the early 1970s, SDRs were modified. They are now kept equivalent, not to a specific amount of gold, but rather to a basket of 16 major national currencies, including the dollar, the pound, the franc, and the mark. Between 1973 and 1978, no additional SDRs were created. The replacement of the adjustable peg system with a floating exchange rate system meant that countries had less need for reserves.

THE BREAKDOWN OF THE ADJUSTABLE PEG SYSTEM, 1971–1973

In 1971, the old adjustable peg system began to come apart. During the early part of that year, the United States economy was recovering from recession. But the recovery was painfully slow, in part because of the large leakage of United States demand into imports. (Recall that expenditures on imports increase production and employment in foreign countries rather than in the United States.) Although merchandise imports in the second quarter of 1971 were only 5 percent of total GNP, no less than 20 percent of the *increase* in United States aggregate demand was spent on imports in that quarter.

There was a growing concern in Washington that imports were increasing so rapidly because the value of the dollar was too high; American goods had been priced out of world markets. Yet, as the nth country, the United States had little control over this situation. Instead, the value of the dollar was determined by other countries pegging their currencies to it (as we saw in Figure 16-4). In spite of substantial United States deficits during the 1960s—and foreign complaints about these deficits—other countries had on average *devalued* their currencies with respect to the dollar; that is, they had *raised* rather than lowered the exchange value of the dollar. Thus, their decisions had been making the United States payments position even weaker. Moreover, as the nation's deficits mushroomed in early 1971, doubts rose regarding the ability of the United States to maintain convertibility of the dollar into gold.

In August 1971, the United States introduced a new economic program, involving a sharp break with the past. On the domestic side, wage and price controls were imposed to suppress inflation during the recovery. On the international side, the United States suspended the convertibility of the dollar into gold and imposed tariff surcharges in order to pressure foreign countries into raising the prices of their currencies (that is, into lowering the value of the dollar.) In the uncertainty that followed, a number of countries abandoned their fixed pegs and allowed their currencies to *float* on the exchange markets.

A *floating* or *flexible* exchange rate is one that is allowed to change in response to changing demand or supply conditions.

If governments and central banks withdraw completely from the exchange markets, the float is *clean*. A float is *dirty* when governments or central banks intervene in exchange markets by buying or selling foreign currencies in order to affect exchange rates.

In December 1971, an attempt was made to patch up the pegged exchange-rate system at a conference at the Smithsonian Institution in Washington. The new pegged rates chosen by most of the participants generally involved higher prices of their currencies; thus, the United States achieved its goal of dollar devaluation. (The United States also reduced the price of the dollar in terms of gold—the only price over which it had direct control.) In order to provide for more flexibility than in the old system, wider bands around the chosen pegged rates were permitted; the exchange rate could vary 2.25 percent above or below the chosen peg before countries were obliged to intervene to prevent further exchange-rate movement.

But the Smithsonian patchwork did not last. In 1972, the British let the pound float. As stresses on the exchange-rate system increased in early 1973, other countries abandoned the pegs of the Smithsonian Agreement, and a general system of floating exchange rates resulted.

FLEXIBLE EXCHANGE RATES:
Advantages and Disadvantages

The major advantage of flexible exchange rates is that they avoid the problems of the adjustable peg (or of the gold standard). That is, changes in exchange rates provide for international adjustment; countries do not have to tailor their domestic policies to balance-of-payments needs. And exchange-rate adjustments can take place gradually, without involving crises of confidence and huge speculative flows.

But on a number of points, flexible exchange rates have been criticized:

1. Fluctuations in exchange rates may disrupt international trade and investment. (It is a matter of dispute whether this disruption is greater than under the IMF system.)

2. Critics point to the back-and-forth

movement of exchange rates since 1973 (Figure 16-5), arguing that such fluctuations have served no useful purpose. But supporters of flexible rates respond that the post-1973 period has been unusual in terms of the magnitude of disturbances. In particular, increases in the international price of oil caused large changes in international payments. It is doubtful that the IMF system could have survived such shocks.

3. Exchange rate movements can contribute to domestic problems. For example, if a country has a weak international payments position, its currency will *depreciate*. True, this contributes to international adjustment: As the price of the home currency falls, exports become cheaper to foreigners, who consequently buy more, and imports become more expensive, discouraging their purchase. But, it is precisely this increase in the price of imports that causes a problem: It adds to domestic inflation. In the United States, a falling price of the dollar added to inflationary pressures in 1973 and 1978.

A floating currency *depreciates* when its price falls in terms of other currencies. (Note that a pegged currency is devalued; a floating currency depreciates.)

A floating currency *appreciates* when its price rises in terms of other currencies.

4. When exchange rates are allowed to float, an important discipline over monetary and fiscal policies is lost. Under the IMF adjustable peg system, the fear of balance-of-payments deficits and losses of reserves provided a restraint on inflationary policies.

Proponents of floating exchange rates recognize that exchange rate flexibility may reduce discipline in domestic policies. But they doubt that international discipline is desirable. Countries moving into a recession may have balance-of-payments deficits. One of the main themes of this chapter has been that if countries try to maintain their exchange rates in such circumstances by restricting aggregate demand, they will make the recession worse.

The evolution of the international monetary system over the past half century has reflected changing attitudes and objectives. As the gold standard gave way to the adjustable peg, and the adjustable peg to flexible exchange rates, less emphasis was placed on exchange rate stability as a way of providing a stable framework for international trade and investment. More emphasis was placed on exchange rate changes as part of the international adjustment process, and on the desirability of designing aggregate demand policies to stabilize the domestic economy rather than exchange rates.

FIGURE 16-5 Selected exchange rates, 1971–1977.
Exchange rates have moved substantially during the 1970s. In early 1973, most currencies (with the notable exception of the Canadian dollar) rose in terms of the United States dollar. Between 1971 and 1978, the prices of the yen and the mark increased in terms of the United States dollar, particularly during 1978. (By late 1978, the dollar prices of both the yen and the mark had doubled.) Part b shows changes in the weighted average price of the United States dollar in terms of other currencies. In calculating the average, foreign currencies are weighted according to the amount of trade of each country with the United States. (In both parts, changes are measured from the exchange rates existing at the end of 1970.)

(a) Selected foreign currencies

(b) The United States dollar

Key Points

1. International trade is different from domestic trade because:
   (a) Imports are often subjected to special taxes (tariffs).
   (b) International trade involves more than one national currency.

2. A foreign exchange market is a market for one national currency in terms of another. The demand for a foreign currency depends on:
   (a) Imports of goods
   (b) Imports of service
   (c) Acquisitions of foreign assets

   Similarly, a nation's supply of a foreign currency depends on:
   (a) Exports of goods
   (b) Exports of services
   (c) Acquisitions of its assets by foreigners

3. Suppose that after a period of equilibrium in the foreign exchange market, the demand for pounds in terms of dollars shifts to the left. The British government can deal with this change in the relationship between demand and supply by one or a combination of the following steps:
   (a) By intervention in the exchange market; that is, by selling United States dollars to buy up the excess pounds
   (b) By changing the exchange rate (or permitting it to change in response to market forces)
   (c) By reducing the supply of pounds through restrictions on imports or other international transactions
   (d) By restricting aggregate demand in Britain, and thus reducing the supply of pounds originating from British imports

4. Under the classical gold standard, the adjustment mechanism worked through changes in aggregate demand. Suppose, for example, that a country had a competitive advantage with low-priced goods, and consequently exported a lot and imported only a little. Gold would flow in. This flow would automatically increase the quantity of money. Aggregate demand would be stimulated and prices would rise. With higher prices, the country would lose its competitive advantage; its exports would fall and its imports would rise.

5. There were a number of defects in the classical gold standard:
   (a) The change in aggregate demand caused by an international gold flow might make it more difficult to meet the domestic objectives of full employment and stable prices.
   (b) Surplus countries might sterilize their gold inflows to prevent inflation, thus putting a greater burden of adjustment on the deficit countries.
   (c) Because domestic currency was convertible into gold, the monetary system was vulnerable to a crisis of confidence and a run on the available gold stock. This defect contributed to the collapse of the international gold standard during the Great Depression of the 1930s.

6. At the end of the Second World War, the IMF system was established, involving pegged but adjustable exchange rates. In the event of a fundamental disequilibrium, a country could devalue or revalue its currency. There were three major problems with this system: the confidence problem, the adjustment problem, and the liquidity problem.
   (a) There could be a crisis of *confidence* when a devaluation was expected. Speculators had an incentive to sell the currency before its official price was reduced (that is, before the currency was devalued).

(*b*) In order to discourage speculation, authorities generally denied
that devaluation was being considered. Once they had made a
commitment not to devalue, exchange rates tended to be rigid, leaving the system without
an adequate *adjustment* mechanism. (Deficit countries tended to
have continuing deficits, and
surplus countries, continuing
surpluses.)

(*c*) At least until the first Special
Drawing Rights (SDRs) were created in 1970, increases in *liquidity* depended on United States
deficits. When the United States
ran deficits, foreign countries acquired reserves in the form of
U.S. dollars.

7. The adjustable peg system broke
down in the 1971–1973 period, leading to
the present system of flexible or floating
exchange rates. The new economic policy of
the United States in 1971 was one of the
important events in this breakdown. The
United States suspended the convertibility
of the dollar into gold and imposed temporary import surcharges to encourage other
countries to revalue their currencies in terms
of the dollar.

8. Flexible exchange rates avoid some
of the problems of the gold standard or the
adjustable peg. Countries can tailor their
aggregate demand policies to the domestic
objectives of full employment and stable
prices, rather than to the balance of payments.

Criticisms of flexible exchange rates include the following:

(*a*) Fluctuations in exchange rates
may disrupt trade.

(*b*) A depreciation of the currency
will make imports more expensive, and thus add to inflation.

Key Concepts

exchange rate
foreign exchange
foreign exchange market
imports of goods
imports of services
acquisition of foreign assets (that is, investment in foreign countries)
foreign exchange reserves
official intervention in the exchange market
gold standard
mint parity
arbitrage
gold points
"rule of the gold standard game"
deficit
surplus
gold sterilization
adjustable peg
 par value

fundamental disequilibrium
devalue
revalue
speculator
rigid peg
adjustment problem
"stop-go" policy
crawling peg
wider band
*n*th country
liquidity problem
reserve currency
Special Drawing Right (SDR)
confidence problem
flexible or floating exchange rate
clean (or dirty) float
depreciation of a currency
appreciation of a currency

Problems

16-1 Suppose that after a period of equilibrium, the demand for the British pound falls on the exchange markets. What alternatives does the British government have to deal with this change?

16-2 Under the old gold standard, suppose that the United States keeps the price of gold fixed at 1 ounce = \$10. Suppose that the British keep the price fixed at 1 ounce = £2. Now suppose that the exchange rate is £1 = \$6. Explain how a profit can be made by arbitrage.

16-3 Under the old gold standard, why does a gold flow automatically cause a change in the money stock?

16-4 What is the nth country? Why did the United States end up as the nth country? What special problem or problems does the nth country have?

16-5 Why might a country follow a "stop-go" policy under a pegged exchange-rate system?

Appendix

INTERNATIONAL PAYMENTS ACCOUNTS

The United States balance-of-payments accounts provide a record of transactions between residents of the United States and other countries. A system of double-entry bookkeeping is used. That is, a set of accounts with two sides (+) and (−) is constructed, and any single transaction affects both sides equally. Thus, if government statisticians had perfect information on all international transactions, the complete transactions of the United States would always balance. By convention, an export of an American good is shown on the positive or "credit" side of the United States balance of payments, and an import of a foreign good is put on the negative or "debit" side. (One word of warning is necessary. As we shall see, a positive or credit item is not necessarily "desirable"; nor is a negative or debit item necessarily "undesirable.")

To illustrate how the double-entry bookkeeping works, consider a simple case where a United States business imports $100,000 in parts from a German manufacturer. The imports show up on the negative side of the United States balance of payments. But something else also happens. The American importer has to pay for the parts. Suppose, to make things easy, that the importer pays with a check, which the German manufacturer deposits in its New York account. (For convenience, a German business engaged in international transactions may keep bank accounts in the United States as well as Germany.) Then Table 16-2 shows the effects of this single transaction on the United States balance-of-payments accounts. Note that an increase in German assets (bank accounts) in the United States appears on the positive side. This must be so, to make the accounts balance.

TABLE 16-2
An International Transaction:
Effects on the United States Balance of Payments

Positive items (credits)	Negative items (debits)
Increase in German assets in United States $100,000	United States import of parts $100,000

Each international transaction—such as this import of German parts—affects both sides of the United States balance of payments equally. As a consequence, the two sides of the balance of payments sum to the same total.

The complete (but simplified) balance-of-payments accounts of the United States are shown in Table 16-3. These accounts are divided under four main headings. First are *current account* figures (category I), which include exports and imports of goods and services, and unilateral transfers (gifts). Current account items should be sharply distinguished from *capital account* items, which represent changes in U.S. holdings of foreign assets, or changes in foreign holdings of assets in the United States. Some of these items represent official reserve assets (category IV), but most are other assets (category II), many of which are owned by private corporations. Logically, the third

TABLE 16-3

United States Balance-of-Payments Accounts, 1977

(billions of dollars)

Positive items (credits)			Negative items (debits)		
I. Current account					
1. Exports of goods and services		177	4. Imports of goods and services		192
(a) Merchandise exports	120		(a) Merchandise imports	152	
(b) Travel	6		(b) Travel	7	
(c) Receipts from U.S. investments abroad:	25		(c) Payments for foreign investments		
from direct investments	13		in United States	12	
from other investments	12		by private sector	6	
			by U.S. government	6	
(d) Other	26		(d) Other	21	
			5. Unilateral transfers, net		5
			(a) U.S. government grants	3	
			(b) Other	2	
II. Capital account, excluding reserve items					
2. Increase in foreign nonreserve assets		14	6. Increase in U.S. nonreserve assets abroad		26
in United States			(a) Direct investment	5	
(a) Direct investment in			(b) Other long-term	10	
United States	2		(c) Short-term	11	
(b) Other long-term	5				
(c) Short-term	7				
III. Statistical discrepancy					
			7. Statistical discrepancy		3
IV. Changes in reserves					
3. Increase in foreign official assets		35	8. Changes in U.S. reserve assets		0
in United States			(a) Gold	0	
(a) U.S. government securities	32		(b) SDRs	0	
(b) Other	3		(c) Reserve position in IMF	0	
			(d) Foreign currencies	0	
Total		226	Total		226

Source: Department of Commerce, *Survey of Current Business.*

category—the statistical discrepancy—should not appear at all in a perfect set of accounts. But it does appear, because the other items have not been measured precisely.

Now consider the accounts in more detail. Item 1*a*, merchandise exports, includes the products such as wheat, computers, and aircraft exported by the United States in 1977. Travel (1*b*) represents our sales of travel services to foreigners. Receipts from past American investments abroad (1*c*), involving dividend and interest payments, amounted to $25 billion.

Note that *returns* to investments, in the form of dividends and interest, appear in the current account. But investment itself appears in the capital accounts. The reason is this: If General Motors builds a new plant in Germany, United States-owned assets abroad rise. Therefore, this investment belongs in the capital accounts (specifically, in item 6*a*). But when GM receives dividends from its foreign subsidiaries, this does not involve a change in ownership. GM receives the dividends, but still owns the foreign subsidiaries. Thus, the dividends go in the current account (1c). Similarly, interest from a foreign bond appears in the current account. (But, if the foreign bond were paid off, that would represent a change in asset holdings, and would appear in the capital accounts.)

In the capital accounts (category II), several subcategories may be distinguished. *Direct investment* in the United States occurs when there is an increase in ownership by foreigners who control the business; for example, when Volkswagen establishes production facilities in the United States, that appears as direct investment (2a). Similarly, on the other side, when Ford builds an engine plant in Wales, that also appears as direct investment (6a). Other long-term investment (2b and 6b) does not involve control. Individuals or corporations are acquiring foreign bonds, or stocks of companies they do not control. Short-term investment (2c, 6c) involves the acquisition of debt with less than 1 year to maturity.

Increases in foreign official assets in the United States (item 3) represent dollars held by foreign governments and central banks, mostly in the form of U.S. Treasury bills.

On the other (debit) side of the accounts, increases in United States reserve assets may take the form of gold, SDRs, our reserve position in the IMF, and foreign currencies. For example, if the United States were to acquire gold, that would show up under item 8a. (In balance of payments accounting, gold is considered a "foreign" asset.) Note that an acquisition of gold by the United States appears as a *negative* or *debit* item in this nation's balance of payments. (Remember our earlier warning: Positive doesn't necessarily mean "good," or negative, "bad.") By going back to a very simple transaction, we can see why this must be so. Suppose that an American manufacturer exported $1 million of machinery, and the foreign country paid with $1 million in gold. The machinery export appears on the positive side of the United States balance of payments. To make the accounts come out right, the acquisition of gold by the United States must appear on the negative side.

But, if the two sides of the balance of payments must be equal, what do we mean when we talk of the balance of payments being in "deficit" or "surplus"? When such terms are used, we must be excluding certain items from the calculations. One standard way of calculating the balance of payments is to exclude changes in reserves (category IV), taking the net amount of categories I, II, and III. In effect, this involves "drawing a line" after category III, and counting only the items above this line. According to this definition of the balance of payments—known as the *official reserve transactions balance* or *official settlements balance*—the United States had a deficit of $35 billion in 1977. Of all the balance-of-payments figures, this is probably the most meaningful. As a first approximation, it measures the surpluses or shortages that would exist in foreign exchange markets at existing prices in the absence of official intervention. But even this balance has lost much of its meaning in the post-1973 period, since changes in demand and supply for foreign exchange often show up as changes in exchange rates, rather than changes in reserves. In other words, if we want to consider developments in international payments, *any* single summary figure that can be derived from the balance-of-payments accounts is incomplete. We would also have to look at movements of exchange rates. Thus, the Advisory Committee on the Presentation of the Balance of Payments Statistics in 1976 recommended, and the government agreed, to discontinue the publication of the summary figures of the United States balance of payments.[10] The official reserve transactions balance of the United States is no longer considered significant enough to be published in the balance-of-payments accounts (although it can be calculated, as we have done).

Balances of some of the sectors of the international payments are, however, still published. These include the *balance on merchandise account* (item 1*a* minus 4*a*), which shows the difference between the value of the goods we have exported and those we have imported. (If exports exceed imports, there is a surplus; if imports exceed exports, there is a deficit.) Similarly, *the balance on goods and services* (item 1 minus 4) gives the difference between the exports and imports of goods and services. Finally, the *balance on current account* (item 1 minus 4 and 5) shows the balance on all noncapital account transactions. That is, it shows how much more we are earning abroad than we are spending or giving away, and consequently it shows the net amount of assets we are accumulating abroad. If the current account is positive, the amount of foreign assets we are accumulating exceeds the amount of assets that foreigners are acquiring in the United States.

---

[10]Report of the Advisory Committee on the Presentation of the Balance of Payments Statistics, *Survey of Current Business*, June 1976, p. 18.

The standard definition of the U.S. balance of payments in the 1960s—the so-called *liquidity balance*—is no longer used, and is too complicated to explain here.

PART FOUR
MICROECONOMICS:
Is Our Output Produced Efficiently?

Parts 2 and 3 have been focused on unemployment and inflation, the two great problems in macroeconomics. Now that we have taken this broad overview of the economic "forest," we turn to a more detailed examination of the "trees." Thus, the *microeconomic* analysis that follows in Parts 4 and 5 will involve an examination of the individual firms that produce goods and services (like Ford Motor Company or the Florida orange grower) and the individual consumers who purchase cars and oranges. This study of the economy "in the small" is directed to the three questions: *What* is produced? *how* is it produced? and *for whom* is it produced? In Part 4 we will deal with the first two questions, just introducing the question of *for whom*, which will be taken up in detail in Part 5.

In Part 4 our focus will be on efficiency. One might well ask: "Because Parts 2 and 3 were concerned with unemployment, were they not also devoted to the question of efficiency?" The answer is a clear yes. Historically, unemployment has been a major source of economic inefficiency. Idle labor and idle capital have meant the loss of output that could have been produced. We have also seen that severe inflation causes inefficiency. If the price system breaks down as a consequence of inflation and no longer gives the clear signals on which business planning must be based, decision-making deteriorates and the nation's output is less as a consequence.

Recognizing that these sources of inefficiency are important, we now turn our attention in Part 4 to the additional reasons why our economy is inefficient. To isolate these new sources of difficulty, we shall assume away the two great macroeconomic problems of inflation and unemployment. In other words, we now assume that there is no general rise in prices, nor large-scale unemployment. Even if these extremely favorable assumptions were realized, there would still be reasons why we might not be making the most of our productive ability. Specifically, we might be producing too much of one good and not enough of some other. That is one of the major problems to be studied in Part 4.

chapter 17
Demand and Supply:
The Concept of Elasticity

When you have nothing else to wear
But cloth of gold and satins rare,
For cloth of gold you cease to care—
Up goes the price of shoddy.

Gilbert and Sullivan,
The Gondoliers

To begin the study of microeconomics, we pick up the analysis of the demand for and supply of an individual good where we left it in Chapter 4. A brief review of that chapter is provided on pages 377–379 in Box 17-1, entitled "Remember?" If you don't remember, we strongly recommend that you reread Chapter 4.

ELASTICITY

First, we introduce an important idea used to describe demand or supply—the concept of *elasticity*. As we shall see, this concept is needed to analyze a number of economic questions; for example: "Who bears the burden of a sales tax?" or, "Why are food prices unstable?"

The Elasticity of Demand: What Happens to Total Revenue as Price Changes?

Suppose you are the manager of Fenway Park, home of the Boston Red Sox. You have been selling tickets for $4 each, but because of the huge salaries that two of your star outfielders have negotiated, you are losing money. The owners who have employed you may be millionaires, but they are concerned, and they press you to take action to increase your total revenue. Specifically, they suggest that you raise the ticket price to $5. This suggestion bothers you—particularly when it leaks out to the newspapers. Not only do the sportswriters denounce the "greed" of the owners; they also argue that higher prices will backfire, causing fans to stay away in droves. As a consequence, gate receipts (total revenue) will be lowered, or so the sportswriters say.

Who is right—the sportswriters or the owners? You cannot be sure. The two possibilities are illustrated in Figure 17-1. To read this diagram, we must first show total revenue geometrically. For example, if the initial equilibrium is at E_1 in panel *a*, what is total revenue? The answer is $100,000;

375

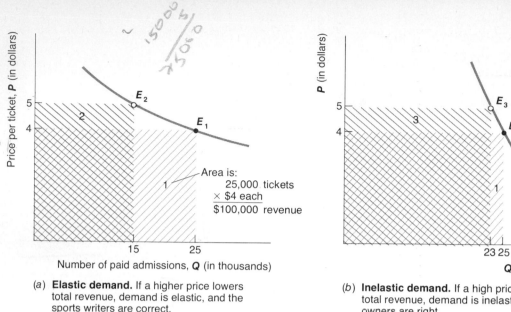

(a) **Elastic demand.** If a higher price lowers total revenue, demand is elastic, and the sports writers are correct.

At original equilibrium E_1, price is $4, 25,000 tickets are sold, and total revenue is $100,000, shown as area 1. When price is raised to $5, 15,000 tickets are sold (at E_2), and total revenue *falls* to $75,000, shown as area 2.

(b) **Inelastic demand.** If a high price raises total revenue, demand is inelastic, and the owners are right.

Although we start from the same initial equilibrium E_1 with $100,000 total revenue, the result of a price increase in this case is quite different. Since ticket sales hold up well in spite of the higher price, total revenue *increases* to $115,000.

FIGURE 17-1   Managing Fenway Park: The elasticity of demand and total revenue.

that is, the base Q (25,000 fans) times the height P ($4 a ticket). This is also the area of rectangle 1 (shaded in blue). Similarly, we can sketch into the diagram the rectangles measuring the total revenue at other points on the demand curve.

> *Total revenue* is the rectangle enclosed to the southwest of a point on the demand curve.

Now let us return to our original question: Can you increase your total revenue by raising the price? If you face the demand curve shown in panel *a*, a price increase will backfire. The quantity demanded responds strongly to the rise in price. In technical terms, demand is described as *elastic*. Observe that as you move up the demand curve from E_1 to E_2, total revenue falls from $100,000 to $75,000. However, if you face the

demand curve shown in panel *b*, the price increase will work: Attendance holds up well in spite of the higher price. As you move up the demand curve from E_1 to E_3, total revenue increases from $100,000 to $115,000. Because the quantity demanded is relatively unresponsive to the change in price, demand is described as *inelastic*.

> In general: If a change in price causes total revenue to move in the opposite direction (for example, if a rise in price causes a fall in total revenue), then demand is *elastic*.
>
> If a change in price causes total revenue to move in the same direction, then demand is *inelastic*.

Elasticity: The Responsiveness of Quantity Demanded to Price

In comparing panels *a* and *b*, we see that elasticity is just a way of describing the responsiveness of demand to a change in

BOX 17-1
REMEMBER?

Demand . . .

The quantity of apples demanded depends on the price of apples . . .

and other influences (such as the price of oranges and bananas, changing tastes, or changing consumer income).

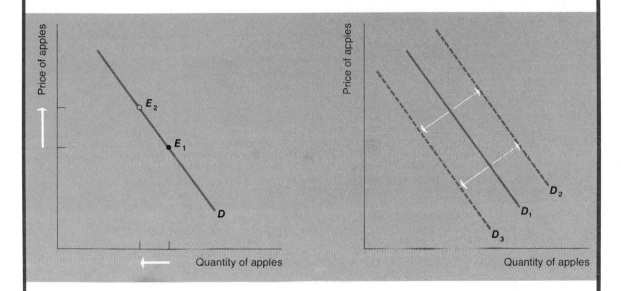

In this panel, we see that if the price of apples rises, the quantity demanded falls. Such a movement along a given demand curve is described as a "decrease in the quantity demanded."

In this panel, we see that if one of the *other* influences changes, the demand curve shifts. For example, if income rises, the demand curve shifts from D_1 to D_2. On the other hand, if income falls, the demand curve shifts to D_3. This leftward shift in the curve is described as a "decrease in demand."

(continued on next page)

$\triangle P \uparrow, R \downarrow$ elastic
$\triangle P \uparrow, R \uparrow$ inelastic

Supply . . .

The quantity of apples supplied depends on the price of apples . . .

and other influences (like the weather, the price of fertilizer and other inputs, changing technology, and the prices of other possible outputs like wheat).

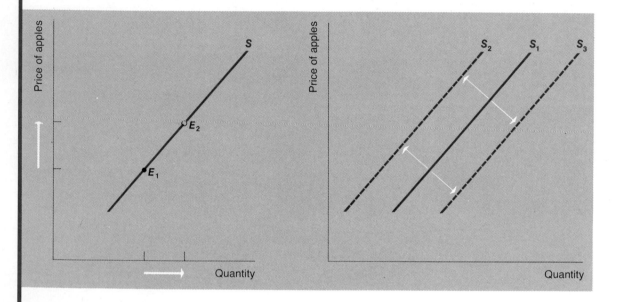

In this panel, we see that if the price of apples increases, equilibrium moves up the supply curve. Such a movement is referred to as an "increase in the quantity supplied."

In this panel, we see that if one of these other influences changes, the supply curve shifts. For example, if the price of fertilizer rises, the supply curve shifts from S_1 to S_2.

On the other hand, if there is particularly good weather, then the supply curve shifts to S_3. Such a shift in the supply curve is described as an "increase in supply."

Supply and Demand together determine price

Equilibrium price and quantity occur at E, where the supply and demand schedules intersect.

Note: Neither curve shifts so long as other influences on supply and demand do not change ("other things equal"). But . . .

suppose that other influences do change. For example, suppose that consumer income rises, so that demand shifts from D_1 to D_2. Then equilibrium moves from E_1 to E_2 (with more sold at a higher price).

price. For both curves, the price change is the same: an increase of $1. But the response of quantity demanded varies greatly. In the case of inelastic demand in panel b, there is little response, while in the case of elastic demand in panel a, there is a very large response. More specifically, in moving from E_1 to E_2 in panel a, total revenue falls because the quantity demanded decreases by 40 percent, which is more than the 25 percent increase in price. This suggests an alternative way to define elasticity: Demand is elastic if the quantity changes more rapidly than price. Thus, we have the following definitions:[1]

Elasticity of demand, ϵ_d

$$= \frac{\% \text{ change in quantity demanded}}{\% \text{ change in price}} \quad (17\text{-}1)$$

If ϵ_d is greater than 1, demand is *elastic*.
If ϵ_d is less than 1, demand is *inelastic*.

Figure 17-2 emphasizes this idea of elasticity as a measure of the response of the quantity demanded; in this illustration, the response is to a price reduction. As an analogy, think of elasticity as a measure of how much the demand curve "stretches" to the right (along the quantity axis) in response to the price reduction. Visualize the demand curve as a rubber band hanging limp, completely unstretched, in panel a. In the next four panels, it is stretched to the right into positions of increasing elasticity until, in panel e, it is extended into a position of full stretch (complete elasticity).

Panels b and d are similar to the two panels of Figure 17-1. Now let us consider the three cases (in panels a, c, and e) that we have not encountered before. Elasticity of the completely vertical demand in panel a is zero because there is a zero change in quantity demanded in response to any price change. In other words, the numerator in the elasticity ratio given in Equation (17-1) is zero. At the other extreme, elasticity of the completely horizontal demand in panel e is

*[1]Any numerical evaluation of elasticity between two points on a demand curve involves a minor technical problem that we illustrate with the following calculations. If we let ΔQ represent "change in Q," the percentage change in quantity in Equation (17-1) may be written $(\Delta Q/Q)$ (100%). And if we similarly rewrite the percentage change in price as $(\Delta P/P)$ (100%), our elasticity formula becomes:

$$\frac{(\Delta Q/Q) \ (100\%)}{(\Delta P/P) \ (100\%)} = \frac{\Delta Q/Q}{\Delta P/P}$$

This is a recasting of elasticity as a ratio of *relative* changes. This can be used to evaluate the elasticity of demand as we move from E_1 to E_2 in Figure 17-1a as follows:

$$\epsilon_d = \frac{10,000/25,000}{1/4} = 1.60$$

(Actually, since price is reduced, ΔP is negative, and therefore ϵ_d is negative too. However, this negative sign is usually dropped.)

But one problem remains. In this calculation we used the initial E_1 values of $Q = 25,000$ and $P = 4$. But now suppose we had moved from point E_2 to E_1 on the demand curve. Initial values would now be those at E_2; in other words, $Q = 15,000$ and $P = \$5$. You can confirm that this would result in the different calculation of $\epsilon_d = 3.33$. Obviously, we would like an elasticity description of the demand curve between E_1 and E_2 that is the same whether we start at E_1 or E_2. So, rather than take either of the P, Q combinations used above, we take the average of the two; in other words, the average quantity $\overline{Q}$ and average price $\overline{P}$. Thus, elasticity of demand is calculated to be

$$\epsilon_d = \frac{\Delta Q/\overline{Q}}{\Delta P/\overline{P}}$$

$$= \frac{10,000/[(25,000 + 15,000)/2]}{1/[(5 + 4)/2]} = 2.25$$

As we expected, this falls between our two previous calculations of 1.60 and 3.33. Because this value exceeds 1, demand is elastic.

infinitely large. Because the change in price in the *denominator* (in this same equation) is zero, that ratio is infinitely large.

In panel *c*, quantity increases at the same rate as price falls; hence the numerator and denominator in Equation (17-1) are the same and elasticity is 1. This is referred to as *unit elasticity*.[2] Note how total revenue remains constant in this case.

In Figure 17-2, the flatter the curve, the more elastic. Can we conclude that this is always true? The answer is yes, *if the curves being compared pass through the same point* (like J in Figure 17-2). This conclusion is significant enough to reemphasize:

> If two demand curves pass through the same point, the flatter one is the more elastic.

This idea is important to remember. But it is also important to recognize that when two demand curves do *not* pass through the same point, flatness alone does *not* indicate elasticity. An example is provided in Figure 17-3, which illustrates the demand for bananas in the small Swedish economy and in the large United States economy. Although United States demand is flatter, both curves have exactly the same elasticity. (In both

*[2]An elasticity of 1 can be confirmed by using the averaging method explained in footnote 1.

FIGURE 17-2 Elasticity as the degree of horizontal (quantity) stretch.

The two important questions that elasticity answers are:	Inelastic	Unit elasticity	Elastic
1. How responsive is the quantity demanded to a price change?	Relatively unresponsive.		Relatively responsive.
2. What happens to total revenue?	It moves in the same direction as price. (That is, as price falls, so does total revenue.)	It remains constant. (In this example, it is $100,000 at *any* point on the demand curve.)	It moves in the opposite direction to price. (As price falls, total revenue increases.)
Examples:*	Salt (0.1), coffee (0.25).	China and tableware (1.1).	Millinery (3.0); foreign travel, in the long run (4.0).

*For specific estimates of demand elasticity, including the bracketed estimates given here, see H. S. Houthakker and L. D. Taylor, *Consumer Demand in the United States* (Cambridge: Harvard University Press); H. Schultz, *Theory and Measurement of Demand* (Chicago: The University of Chicago Press); and M. Spencer and L. Siegelman, *Managerial Economics* (Homewood, Ill.: Irwin).

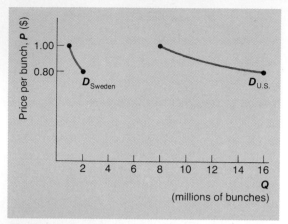

FIGURE 17-3 A case where flatness does not indicate elasticity.
The United States demand curve is flatter (that is, its slope is less), but the elasticity of the two curves is identical. The reason is that if the price falls by 20 percent, the quantity doubles in both cases. (In Sweden, it increases from 1 to 2, whereas in the United States, it increases from 8 to 16.)

cases the quantity demanded increases by 100 percent when price falls by 20 percent.)[3]

ELASTICITY OF SUPPLY

Just as elasticity of demand indicates the responsiveness of buyers to a change in price, so elasticity of supply indicates the responsiveness of sellers. Supply is elastic if producers respond strongly to price changes, or inelastic if they respond weakly. The formula for supply elasticity is similar to the formula for demand elasticity in Equation (17-1):

$$\text{Elasticity of supply, } \in_s$$
$$= \frac{\% \text{ change in quantity supplied}}{\% \text{ change in price}} \qquad (17\text{-}2)$$

Figure 17-4 shows five examples of supply elasticity. They range from the completely inelastic lack of response in panel *a* to the completely elastic response in panel *e*.[4] And if we again view elasticity as degree of stretch to the right, we can visualize the completely inelastic supply curve in panel *a* being stretched to the right into the completely elastic position in panel *e*. Once again, as in the case of demand, there is a simple rule connecting flatness and elasticity: *If two supply curves pass through the same point* (such as point ⌐ in Figure 17-4), *the flatter one is the more elastic*. But otherwise, elasticity cannot be judged merely by flatness.

In contrast with demand (which traces out a curve if the elasticity is one), supply with unit elasticity is a straight line. More-

---

*[3]There are two other illustrations of why flatness and elasticity are not the same. The first is provided in Figure 17-2c. As we move left to right along this curve, elasticity remains constant (at a value of 1), but the curve becomes more and more flat. The second is provided in Problem 17-3, where it is shown that as we move along a straight-line demand curve (with, of course, constant flatness), elasticity keeps changing.

[4]To calculate a precise elasticity value, say between points A and B on the supply curve in panel d, we use the same approach as in our calculation of demand elasticity (in footnote 1).

$$\in_s = \frac{\Delta Q / \bar{Q}}{\Delta P / \bar{P}} = \frac{100/[(400 + 300)/2]}{1/[(9 + 8)/2]} = 2.43$$

Thus, this supply is confirmed to be elastic.

But, despite the great similarity in the calculations, there is one respect in which elasticity of supply and demand are quite different. Elasticity of demand indicates whether or not total revenue rises when we move to a new equilibrium on a demand curve. But there is no similar interpretation for supply: If we move to a lower-priced equilibrium on a supply curve (say from B to A in Figure 17-4d), price and quantity both decrease; hence total revenue must fall regardless of the elasticity of supply.

(a) $\epsilon_s = 0$.
Completely
inelastic.

(b) $\epsilon_s < 1$.
Inelastic.

(c) $\epsilon_s = 1$.
Unit
elasticity.

(d) $\epsilon_s > 1$.
Elastic.

(e) $\epsilon_s = \infty$.
Completely
elastic.

FIGURE 17-4   Different elasticities of supply.

over, if extended, it would pass through the origin, as shown in panel c of Figure 17-4. (On such a line, P always changes at the same rate as Q. For example, if P doubles, Q also doubles. Hence, in this case the numerator and denominator in Equation (17-2) must be equal, and elasticity of supply is 1.) The straight-line supply curve shown in panel b is inelastic because, if extended, it would pass through the Q axis. (You should prove this in Problem 17-4.) Similarly, the supply curve in panel d is elastic because it would pass through the P axis. This, then, is the simple key to deciding whether a straight-line supply is elastic or inelastic: If extended, does it pass through the P or Q axis?

WHY ELASTICITY IS IMPORTANT: Who Bears the Burden of a Commodity Tax?

We will now illustrate how this concept of elasticity can be applied to answer important economic questions. The first question is: How do the elasticity of demand and supply determine who bears the burden of a sales tax? To answer this, consider the supply and demand for a good shown in Figure 17-5a. The initial equilibrium before the tax is at E_1, with 10 million units sold at a price of $3. Suppose now that the government imposes a sales tax of $1 per unit, which it collects from sellers. Who bears the burden of this tax?

The effect of this tax, levied on sellers, is to shift the supply curve upward from S_1 to S_2 by the full $1 amount of the tax. To confirm this, consider any quantity supplied—say, 13 million units. Point A on the supply curve S_1 tells us that before the tax, sellers would have to receive $4 per unit to induce them to sell 13 million units. This means that *after* the tax, they must receive $5 (at point B) in order to enable them to pay the government the $1 tax and still have the same $4 left. Thus, point B is on the new, after-tax supply curve S_2. And no matter what point we consider on S_1, the corresponding point on S_2 is always $1 higher. Thus, the entire supply curve shifts upward by the amount of the tax arrow from S_1 to S_2.

As a result of the tax, the equilibrium moves from E_1 to E_2, and the price rises from $3.00 to $3.20. Thus, buyers bear 20 cents of the burden; they pay 20 cents more. Sellers bear the remaining 80 cents of the burden. Their selling price has risen by 20 cents—from $3.00 to $3.20—as a result of the tax. But $1 goes to the government. Thus, the tax causes the return to the seller to fall from $3.00 to $2.20. The two arrows on the far left show how the $1 tax is split up into the 20-cent burden on buyers and the 80-cent burden on sellers.

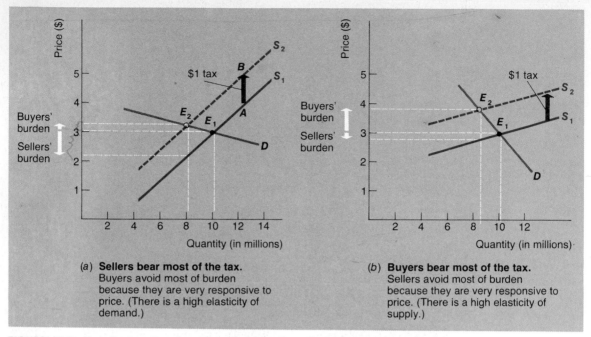

FIGURE 17-5 How the burden of a sales tax depends on the elasticity of demand and supply.

In part *a*, equilibrium of S_1 and D result in before-tax price of $3. As a result of the tax, supply shifts from S_1 to S_2 and the new equilibrium price is $3.20. Buyers pay 20 cents more—the burden of the tax that they bear. Sellers receive $2.20 (that is, the $3.20 market price less the $1 tax that they must pay the government). Thus they receive 80 cents less than the original $3—and this is the burden they bear. In part *b*, supply is more elastic than demand, and consequently the after-tax price rises to $3.80. In this case, buyers bear 80 cents of the burden, and sellers only 20 cents.

The reason that buyers bear a lighter share of the burden in this case is because they respond more to changes in price than do sellers. (Demand is more elastic than supply.) However, in panel *b* the reverse is true. Here, sellers are more responsive to changes in price. (Supply is more elastic than demand.) As a result, sellers bear the lighter burden of the tax.

These conclusions can best be summarized if we think of two groups in a market, one buying, the other selling. Suppose one group (it doesn't matter which) takes the view: "We aren't that keen on exchanging this good. If the price moves against us, we can back away. In responding to price changes, we're flexible, sensitive, *elastic.*" Suppose the other group feels: "We have no choice; we must exchange this good. Even if price moves against us, we can't back away. We're inflexible, unresponsive, *inelastic.*" It is no surprise that this second group will bear most of the burden of a tax and will, in other situations as well, be in the more vulnerable position.

THE DETERMINANTS OF ELASTICITY

What makes the demand for a specific good elastic or inelastic? Here are some of the important influences.

Elasticity of Demand

1. *Luxuries versus Necessities* Luxuries tend to have an elastic demand, necessities an inelastic demand. For example, luxuries like hats have an elastic demand because purchasers can back away from the market and stop buying them if their prices rise. But essentials such as electrical power or salt have an inelastic demand because purchasers can't avoid buying them, or can do so only with substantial inconvenience.

2. *Percentage of Income* Big items in a budget tend to have a more elastic demand than small items. To cite an extreme example, the demand for houses is more elastic than the demand for toothpicks. Purchasers may spend a week trying to negotiate a 1 percent lower price on a new house. But they won't even notice a 50 percent increase in the price of toothpicks. For small items like toothpicks, consumers become very insensitive to price.

3. *Substitutability* Items that have good substitutes tend to have a more elastic demand than those that do not. To illustrate, consider sugar and salt, items which are alike in many respects. Both are necessities, and both are small items in any budget. Yet sugar has a more elastic demand than salt because it has substitutes (such as honey), but salt does not. (Thus, salt has a low elasticity for all of the first three reasons.)

4. *Time* The passage of time may have an important influence on elasticity. The longer the time period, the more elastic the demand becomes for most goods. The reason is that it may take time for a price reduction to become known and for buyers to adjust to it. For example, if the price of ski equipment is reduced by 20 percent, some potential buyers may not hear about the lower price for 3 months, and hence may not actually get around to new purchases until the next ski season. Even those who hear of the new price may be unable to take immediate advantage of it because they have already made other plans and cannot get away to ski. In brief, any lag in time between a price reduction and the resulting purchases means that demand becomes more elastic as time passes. (In international trade, there are often even greater time lags involved because of greater distance. Accordingly, foreign demand for our goods often responds even more slowly to a change in price than does domestic demand.)

Another reason demand may be more responsive in the long run is that in the short run, purchasers may temporarily be "locked in" technologically so that they cannot immediately take advantage of a price reduction. For example, purchasers of peripheral components for computers may have little choice but to keep buying these from the original manufacturer in order to keep them compatible with the rest of their equipment. In the short run, they have little defense against a change in price by the manufacturer. Demand may consequently be less elastic in the short run, with these purchasers not responding to price until they again decide on how their whole computer system is to be replaced. As another example, if you own an exotic foreign car, you may find yourself in much the same situation. Once you have bought the car, you may be almost completely vulnerable (inelastic) in your dealings with the only garage in town that can service it. Your response to high service charges will occur only when you eventually buy a new car.

Elasticity of Supply

The elasticity of supply depends on the ability of producers to back away from the market if prices fall, and on their ability and willingness to expand sales if prices rise. Thus, elasticity of supply depends on:

1. The Cost and Feasibility of Storage Goods that are costly to store will have a low elasticity of supply. Goods that will soon rot will be thrown on the market regardless of price; their elasticity of supply will be very low.

2. The Characteristics of the Production Process Does an item have a close *substitute* in production? (That is, can the labor, land, and equipment used to produce it be readily switched into the production of another good?) If so, then supply will be elastic. For example, compare the elasticity of supply for wheat and for all grains taken together. In the face of a fall in the price of wheat, a producer may be able to respond by shifting fairly easily into a substitute grain like corn; thus the supply of wheat is somewhat elastic. But if the price of all grain falls, a farmer may have much more difficulty in shifting out of grain production because there are no close substitute activities. Instead, the farmer will have to move into a less closely related activity, like raising beef. Thus the supply of grain, taken as a whole, is less elastic than the supply of wheat.

In contrast with substitutes (such as wheat and corn), other goods may be *joint products*, like hides and beef. (When you produce one, you get the other.) The decision to butcher a steer is influenced by the price of beef, but hardly at all by the price of hides. Once the steer has been butchered, the (relatively unimportant) hide will be sold regardless of the price. Consequently, the supply of hides is inelastic—because hides are a relatively unimportant joint product.

3. Time Time may influence supply elasticity, just as it influences demand elasticity. In fact, this idea has already been encountered in our discussion of rent control in Chapter 4. In Figure 17-6, we illustrate further with the example used by the great English economist Alfred Marshall in his discussion of the influence of time on supply almost a century ago. Suppose demand for a perishable commodity like fresh fish suddenly rises from D_1 to D_2. The

FIGURE 17-6 How a price increase is moderated by supply response.

(a) **Immediate effect.**
On the first day, supply is completely inelastic. Thus the shift in demand from D_1 to D_2 results in a very large price increase, to P_2.

(b) **Short-run effect.**
Supply now has some elasticity, since the catch of fish can be increased by hiring more labor and using existing boats more heavily. Thus the price rise is moderated to P_3.

(c) **Long-run effect.**
Supply now has even greater elasticity, since there is now time for new boats to be built. As a result, more fish are sold and price settles down further to P_4.

386

immediate effect on the first day in panel *a* is for price to rise to P_2. The reason is that after the boats return for the day, the quantity supplied will not be influenced by price. Fresh fish is not a storable commodity; there are no inventories carried over from day to day, from which additional supplies can be drawn in the event of rising prices. Nor will fish be stored if the price is low. (In Marshall's day, refrigeration was not widely available.) Today's catch, Q_1, will be sold regardless of price. However, during the ensuing days, as the fishing companies increase their crews and temporarily draw old boats back into service (perhaps along with other vessels previously running pleasure cruises), supply does respond to higher price. (The average daily catch of fish increases.) Thus, supply becomes more elastic in panel *b*, and price settles back somewhat to P_3. But this is not the eventual equilibrium, since more time will be required for all the necessary responses to increased price (such as the construction of new fishing boats). When this happens, there is a much more elastic long-run supply response, as shown in panel *c*, and it results in a long-run equilibrium involving even larger sales and an even smaller price increase at P_4.

FIGURE 17-7 Short-run instability of farm price and income.
In a normal year, inelastic demand D and supply S_1 result in equilibrium at E_1. But if there is a bumper crop and Q_2 is put on the market, equilibrium is at E_2 and price falls from P_1 to P_2. Because demand is inelastic, total farm income is lower at E_2 than at the normal equilibrium E_1. But if there is a poor crop Q_3, equilibrium is at E_3 and farm income rises above the normal level.

ELASTICITY AND THE SPECIAL PROBLEMS OF AGRICULTURE

Since the Great Depression of the 1930s, the government has supported the prices of many farm crops. For example, the support price of wheat was $2.25 in 1977, and $2.35 in 1978. If farmers in 1977 could not sell their wheat in the private market for at least $2.25, the government stood ready to buy it at this price.[5] Why did the government make this guarantee to farmers, when it did not do

so to other producers? One reason was that agriculture has historically suffered from two special problems: Agricultural prices have been unstable, fluctuating up and down from year to year; and they have shown a tendency to fall (compared with the prices of other goods).[6] To understand each of these problems, we ask: "What would happen to agricultural prices if there were no government intervention in these markets?" As we shall see, the concept of elasticity is very important in providing an answer.

Year-to-Year Price Instability

In Figure 17-7, we show how inelastic demand and supply may result in very un-

[5]The program was, in fact, more complicated than this. The government stood ready to lend farmers $2.25 a bushel, provided they put up their wheat as collateral. If, after 11 months, farmers were unable to sell their wheat at a price above this, the loan came due, and farmers forfeited their grain to the government rather than repay the loan. In addition, the government made direct payments to farmers to bring their total return up to $2.90 per bushel.

[6]Of course, with inflation, depressed price does not mean that there has been a fall in agricultural prices, measured in dollars. They have only shown a tendency to fall, relative to other prices. Relative prices are the subject of the microeconomic chapters of Parts 4 and 5. (The average level of prices was studied in Parts 2 and 3.)

stable farm prices and income in the short run. (Demand for farm products is relatively inelastic because people must satisfy their appetite for food no matter what happens to price.) The (immediate) supply that reaches the market after harvest in a normal year is represented by S_1. It will also be very inelastic—indeed, completely inelastic (as shown) if the products are perishable or there are no storage facilities. Thus, in a normal year, equilibrium is at E_1 with price P_1. But with a bumper crop and resulting supply S_2, equilibrium shifts to E_2 and price falls to P_2. In this example, a bumper crop cuts price by a third! Worse yet for farmers: The inelasticity of demand has meant

---

BOX 17-2

TO FLORIDA CITRUS GROWERS, A FREEZE IS A BLESSING†

Cold Eases the Fears of a Bumper-Crop Surplus Resulting in Money Loss

The freezing weather in Florida's citrus belt will reduce this year's previously predicted bumper crop . . . but ironically it will ease the worries of growers who had feared they would lose money because of the surplus.

"Nature has bailed us out of a bumper crop," a spokesman for the Florida Citrus Commission said yesterday in a telephone interview. "The growers were going to lose money, but now the problem has been taken care of and an oversupply situation has been corrected."

*   *   *

Does this newspaper report imply that the demand for Florida's citrus fruit is elastic or inelastic?

†Rona Cherry, in *The New York Times*, Jan. 23, 1977, with permission.

388

that their income has been reduced (from the rectangle enclosed to the southwest of E_1 to the smaller rectangle to the southwest of E_2). Similarly, you can confirm that a poor crop that results in equilibrium at E_3 will raise farm income. (See Box 17-2.) In short, because demand and supply are inelastic, relatively small variations in crop yield result in large price fluctuations (between P_3 and P_2). Moreover, the better the crop, the lower is farm income.

Long-run Downward Trend in Price

This second farm problem is best understood by briefly considering our economic history. If we go back far enough, farming was our largest activity, with the majority of the population working on the soil. With old-fashioned techniques of agricultural production, an individual family could do little more than produce enough for itself.

But, with improvements in agricultural methods and technology, productivity increased. A typical farm family could produce progressively more food: enough for two families, then three, then four, and so on. Of course, as that happened, the number of people required on the farm to produce food fell to a smaller and smaller fraction of the population. This decline had effects that reached far beyond the farm. In fact, one of the essential requirements of our industrial development was the success of farmers in producing a food supply beyond their own needs. Without this capability, the labor force necessary for a developing industry would never have been released from the task of grubbing a bare living out of the soil. It was no accident that the industrial revolution in Britain in the eighteenth century was preceded by a revolution in agricultural productivity. And that agricultural revolution has continued: The American farm family today supplies food for itself and for over 25 city families as well.

But this has been a mixed blessing for farmers, and once again elasticity is the key to understanding why. In panel a of Figure 17-8, E_1 represents the initial equilibrium in an earlier period, at the intersection of long-run supply S_1 and demand D_1, with demand being relatively inelastic because food is a necessity. Over many decades, D has been shifting to the right from D_1 to D_2 because of (1) the increase in the total food-consuming population and (2) the rising income of that population. But the effects of rising income have been fairly modest. Although consumers purchase more of almost everything as their incomes rise, their expenditures on food are less responsive than their expenditures on many other goods. With rising income, people may double their expenditures on clothes and triple their expenditures on vacations, but they increase their food consumption by only a small amount.[7] After all, how much more can anyone eat?[8]

On the other hand, over these same decades there has been an even greater shift in supply (from S_1 to S_2 in panel a) because of rapid improvements in farm technology, such as the development of new chemical fertilizers that have greatly increased yield per acre. With supply shifting more rapidly

---

[7]In fact, expenditure on some very special products (so-called inferior goods) falls as income rises. Potatoes were cited as an example in Chapter 4. As income rises, consumers can afford to switch from potatoes to meat.

[8]Technically, the *income* elasticity of demand for food is low. (As we noted in Chapter 8, this low income elasticity of demand for food was observed by nineteenth-century statistician Ernst Engel; hence, it is sometimes known as Engel's Law.) Just as price elasticity describes how demand responds to price changes, income elasticity describes how demand responds to income changes. Formally,

$$\text{Income elasticity of demand} = \frac{\text{percentage change in quantity demanded}}{\text{percentage change in income}} \qquad \text{[Compare with Equation (17-1).]}$$

When we use the simple term "elasticity," we are referring to price elasticity.

to the right than demand, price has fallen to a new equilibrium at E_2. But, as price falls, farmers—and even more important, their children—leave the farm to go into more highly paid activities in the city. And because they do, the proportion of the population on the farm falls. (Of course, this outflow of people from the farm also means that farm output rises less rapidly than it otherwise would, and that the price reduction is not so severe.)

This, in a nutshell, is the history of American agriculture: Because productivity has outrun demand, the proportion of the population on the farm has fallen. By becoming more and more efficient, American farmers are doing a great service to the public in terms of providing large quantities of food at a very low price. But their very success in doing so has meant that our farmers are producing themselves—or their neighbors—out of jobs.

Are We Moving into a New Era in Agriculture?

The problem of oversupply and depressed price in American agriculture would be even more severe were it not for our large exports of food products. These exports became particularly important in the early 1970s as a result of crop failures in the Soviet Union and other parts of the world. Indeed, the buoyant demand for agricultural goods on world markets pulled up the international prices of wheat, soy beans, and other items, drawing the United States price of food up as well. (Along with the increased price of oil, the higher price of food was an important influence contributing to the acceleration of inflation in the 1973–1974 period.) Is this the first indication that we are moving into a new era of food shortage rather than surplus? Specifically, will the future world problem switch from the traditional one of supply outrunning demand,

FIGURE 17-8   The long-run trend in agriculture.
The classic problem of agriculture in part a has been that supply has shifted to the right more rapidly than demand; hence, price has fallen. This situation may repeat itself in the future or it may change, as some people now predict, to the situation shown in part b. There, shifts in supply do not keep pace with shifts in demand, and price rises.

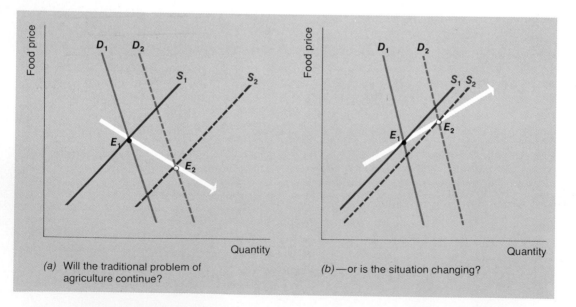

(a) Will the traditional problem of agriculture continue?

(b)—or is the situation changing?

shown in Figure 17-8a, to the new problem, shown in panel b, where supply shifts less than demand, and food price rises rather than falls?

The argument that future food supply will lag behind demand has been advanced by a number of observers. Some of the reasons put forward are not very convincing. For example, the claim that we are facing a food crisis because the world is running out of land seems to have little foundation. In fact, recent studies indicate quite the contrary: Only about half the world's arable land is now being used, and much of the unused acreage has good agricultural potential.[9] Moreover, recent advances in technology have allowed us to increase output by expanding our use of other inputs (like fertilizer) rather than land. For example, between 1957 and 1977 the acreage of United States land used to grow peanuts remained the same, but our output of peanuts almost quadrupled. If this process continues, our future requirements for additional land may not be so great as is often supposed.

However, it is not so easy to dismiss some of the other reasons that food supply may lag behind demand. One is that productivity improvements in agriculture may not continue at their past rapid rates. While it is very difficult to predict productivity, there is some reason for concern. It seems unlikely that we will be able to continue to expand fertilizer production at past rapid rates because of limited supplies of oil and gas, key inputs in fertilizer production. A second concern is whether the serious crop failures in foreign countries during the 1970s were the result of unfavorable trends in the world's climate. But on this issue, even weather experts are divided; some believe

our climate is warming up, others believe it is cooling off, while others believe that neither is happening and that, instead, the weather is just fluctuating. Finally, to decide whether the future situation will be the one shown in panel a or panel b of Figure 17-8 requires projecting world food demand as well as supply. This projection requires an answer to the difficult question: Will the rapid population increases in the less-developed countries continue, or will these countries begin to follow the lower birthrate patterns recently observed in the industrialized parts of the world?

Clearly, it is extraordinarily difficult to predict any such future developments, as economists have discovered over the past two hundred years. (The early English economist Thomas Malthus argued that population tends to outrun the supply of food, and that therefore the wage rate naturally gravitates to the starvation level. But Malthus has been proven wrong over the past two centuries: The "iron law of wages" has been broken, and real incomes have risen spectacularly.) Of one thing we can be sure: The inelasticity of demand for food will mean strong upward pressure on price if we are now entering a period of food scarcity, or strong downward pressure on price if we are returning to the traditional surpluses.

(By the late 1970s, the American agricultural problem seemed to be shifting back from scarcity to surplus. As a result of three bumper years, the price of wheat fell about 50% between 1974 and 1977. In fact, the price was so low by 1977 that farmers were selling their wheat to the government for the guaranteed $2.25 price, and the government stockpile of wheat was increasing rapidly.)

[9]This is the conclusion reached by the Food and Agricultural Organization of the United Nations (FAO) in a 1969 study, *Provisional Indicative World Plan for Agricultural Development.* In another study, Leroy L. Blakeslee, Earl O. Heady, and Charles F. Framingham (*World Food Production, Demand and Trade,* Ames: Iowa State University Press, 1973) have estimated that only 3.4 billion of the world's 7.8 billion acres of potentially productive land are under cultivation.

A FINAL PERSPECTIVE ON AGRICULTURE:
Is Falling Price the Sign of a Sick Industry?

Not necessarily. To see why, suppose that the price of a good you are producing has been cut in half. But, because of your higher productivity, you are now producing three times as many units as before (at the same total cost). Your profit will be rising, rather than falling.

For a real-world example, consider IBM. Computer technology has developed at an incredible rate over the past three decades. An electronic chip that can be held on the end of your finger will now do more than the early computer which contained hundreds of tubes and occupied a large room. Because of such rapid improvements in computer technology, IBM has been able to cut computer prices drastically. (According to one estimate, the computing power of new machines has increased so much more rapidly than their price that by 1965 the cost of computing power had fallen to just over one-tenth the 1954 level.) Yet, over the same period, IBM's profits increased.

For the American farmer, prices have also fallen—at least in relative terms. By the 1965–1975 period, the ratio of prices farmers received to the prices they paid had fallen to 70 percent of the 1910–1914 average (that is, to 70 percent of *parity*). In other words, the prices farmers paid for inputs such as fertilizer and machinery and for consumer goods rose more rapidly than the prices which farmers received for wheat, cotton, peanuts, and so on. (Government price guarantees had prevented any further erosion of the relative prices facing farmers.) But during this same period, the productivity of the farmer increased many times. For this reason, farmers have not suffered as much as we might think if we just look at the low price they receive.

Key Points

1. Demand elasticity indicates what happens to *total revenue* as price falls. If demand is elastic, total revenue rises; if it is inelastic, total revenue falls.

2. Demand elasticity is also a measure of the *responsiveness* of quantity demanded to price: the more responsive, the more elastic. Goods with high demand elasticity include large-budget items and items with close substitutes.

3. If two curves pass through the same point, the flatter one is the more elastic. But if they do not pass through the same point, there is no such simple relationship between flatness and elasticity.

4. Elasticity of supply measures the responsiveness of quantity supplied to price; again, the more responsive, the more elastic. Goods with high supply elasticity include items that can be easily and cheaply stored and goods with close substitutes in production.

5. As time passes, the elasticities of both demand and supply tend to increase.

6. In any market, the group that is unresponsive to price (whether it be buyers or sellers) will be in the more vulnerable position because it is less willing to back away from the market in the face of an unfavorable price change. For example, the relatively unresponsive (inelastic) group will bear more of the burden of a sales tax.

7. Year-to-year fluctuations in food prices are made more severe by inelasticity of demand. This same inelasticity means that a bumper crop may lower farm income, while a poor crop may raise it.

8. The downward trend in farm prices relative to other prices has occurred in the past because of rapidly improving farm technology and our limited appetite for food. As a consequence, supply has tended to outrun demand. It is not clear whether this will continue, or whether the situation will be reversed, with food prices rising in the future.

Key Concepts

elastic demand
inelastic demand
unit elasticity of demand
total revenue as a $P \times Q$ rectangle
relationship of elasticity to total revenue

elasticity of supply
burden of a sales tax
joint products
price instability (and its relation to
   elasticity)

Problems

17-1 Fill in the blanks.
Curve with greatest elasticity is _____
Next greatest elasticity is _____
Next greatest is _____
Lowest elasticity is _____
Unit elasticity is _____

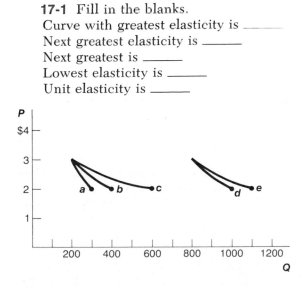

17-2 (*a*) Why didn't we define elasticity much more simply, as just the flatness of a curve; that is, $\Delta Q/\Delta P$? (Hint: Plot exactly the same demand curve as in Figure 17-1*a*, but change the scale in which you measure price. Specifically, measure price in quarters, not dollars, so that the height of E_1 and E_2 is now four times as great. What happens to the flatness of D?)

(*b*) "Flatness is a poor measure because it depends on the arbitrary scale in which P (or Q) is measured." Is this statement true or false?

393

*17-3 Using the formula in footnote 1 (page 380), calculate the elasticity of the section *AB* in the demand shown below. Do the same for the section *CE*. Consider the following statement: "Since *AB* and *CE* have the same flatness, but different elasticity, this shows once again that flatness does not necessarily reflect elasticity." Is it true or false?

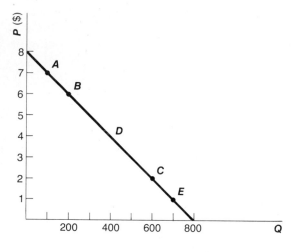

17-4 In the diagram below, *S* represents any straight-line supply that, if extended, would pass through the *Q* axis. To show that *S* must be inelastic, draw a straight line to pass through the origin and any point *R* on the supply *S*. What is the elasticity of line *OR*? What, therefore, can be concluded about the elasticity of supply *S*?

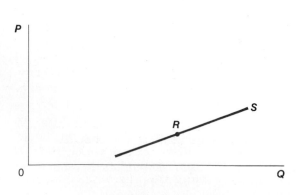

17-5 The mechanics of tax collection can vary. Sometimes a tax is collected from sellers (as in Figure 17-5*a*), sometimes from buyers. Redraft Figure 17-5*a* on the assumption that buyers, rather than sellers, pay the tax initially. Does this change affect the incidence of the tax? In other words, does it affect how buyers and sellers share the burden?

17-6 List several items that you think have high elasticity of demand, and several with high elasticity of supply. In each case, explain why you have classified the item the way you have.

17-7 Suppose you wish to impose a sales tax that will have minimum impact on the real income of the poor. What sort of goods would you tax, and how would their supply and demand elasticities compare?

*17-8 (Based on footnote 1 in this chapter.) In this diagram,

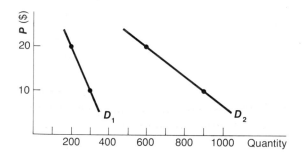

(*a*) What is the (price) elasticity of demand D_1 as price falls from $20 to $10? As price rises from $10 to $20?

(*b*) How does the elasticity of D_1 compare with that of D_2?

(*c*) Now suppose income has doubled and that demand has consequently shifted from D_1 to D_2. Calculate the income elasticity of demand. (See footnote 8 in this chapter.)

chapter 18
Demand and Utility

"Producers dance to the consumers' tune."

Reprise from Chapter 4

What is the tune that consumers play? Why do they demand certain products, but not others? What does a demand curve tell us about how consumers think and feel? Once we have answered these questions, we will be better able to understand how much consumers can be damaged by a fall in production. For example, how much are consumers hurt when a Florida freeze reduces the orange crop?

Before proceeding with a detailed study of the market demand of all consumers as a group, we should first look at the demand curves of individual consumers. Such individual demand curves lie behind the market demand curves that we have used in Chapters 4 and 17.

(In this example, two individuals represent the millions of consumers in the economy.) Bill Jefferson's demand in panel *a* shows how much he is willing and able to buy at various prices. Similarly, Barbara Washington's demand is shown in panel *b*, indicating her quite different view on the desirability of this product. At any given price, say $1, we horizontally add the quantities demanded by each consumer in order to get the corresponding point on the market demand schedule in panel *c*. (The individual demand curves are labeled with a small *d*, and the market demand with a capital *D*.)

Now let us look more closely at the demand schedule of one of these individuals.

MARKET DEMAND AS THE SUM OF INDIVIDUAL DEMANDS

The total market demand for a good or service is found by summing the demands of all individuals, as illustrated in Figure 18-1.

DEMAND REFLECTS MARGINAL UTILITY

A good is purchased because someone, somewhere, wants it. A demand for a product exists because it provides someone,

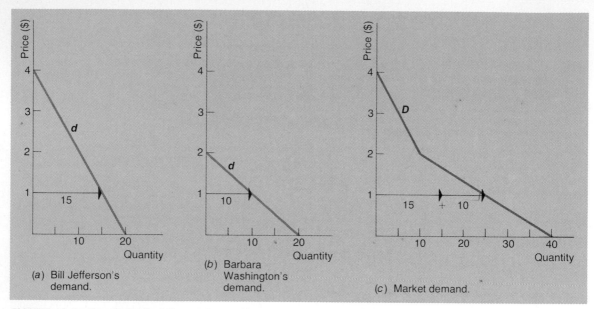

FIGURE 18-1   How individual demands combine to make up market demand.
To derive total quantity demanded at each price (for example, $1), horizontally add the quantities demanded by all individual consumers.

somewhere, with satisfaction or utility. Indeed, *marginal utility* is the key concept underlying demand. By definition:

> *Marginal utility* is the satisfaction an individual receives from consuming one additional unit of a good or service.

To illustrate, consider Lori Escaf, a student who is considering how many skiing lessons she should purchase this month. We ask her to evaluate how much utility or satisfaction she would receive from one lesson, from a second, and a third. Her reply might be: "The first lesson would clearly give me the most satisfaction; after studying, I'm just dying to get away from it all for a day. The second would give me considerable pleasure, but not quite so much. And less again for the third, since my appetite for skiing gets a bit jaded after a while. And so on."

The message she is giving us is the simple one sketched out in Figure 18-2: Her

marginal utility decreases as more units are consumed. Since eventually this must be true for every good or service, it is sometimes referred to as the *law of diminishing marginal utility*. But be careful with this "law." Although marginal utility must ultimately fall, it may rise at first. The first ski lesson may yield only pain, and skiing may not be enjoyable until the second, third, or fourth lesson. But eventually, as more and more lessons are purchased, marginal utility must fall: If you take 10 lessons in one month, the tenth will provide less satisfaction than the ninth. (For simplicity, we will deal with an example where marginal utility declines from the very first unit.)

So far, Figure 18-2 is imprecise (since we haven't yet put a unit of measurement on the marginal utility axis). Therefore, we press Escaf to be more specific about how highly she values each lesson. She is at a loss to do so until we point out that her evaluation of each lesson should be reflected in how much she would be willing to pay for it.

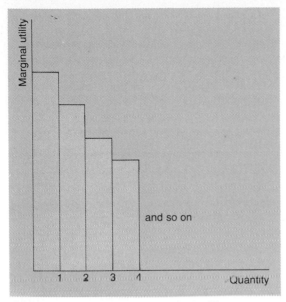

FIGURE 18-2 Diminishing marginal utility.
Each additional purchase provides less additional satisfaction.

above $20, I won't buy any lessons. At $20 I'll buy one, because that's what I think it is worth. Only if the price falls to $17 will I buy two lessons. And only if the price falls all the way to $13 will I buy three."

Thus, when we asked her to give us her marginal utility schedule, the best estimate she could come up with was her demand schedule. This relationship between demand and marginal utility is an important one[1] (and one we shall use frequently in the balance of this book). It can be expressed

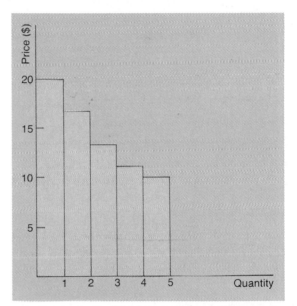

FIGURE 18-3 Diminishing marginal utility, as reflected in the willingness to buy at various prices.
The marginal utility schedule in Figure 18-2 may be quantified by asking the consumer: "How much would you be willing to pay for each additional unit?"

Pursuing this line of reasoning, we ask her: "What would you be willing to pay for the first lesson?" When she replies, "Oh—$20," we continue: "And what would you be willing to pay for the second?" (More precisely, we might ask, How low would the price have to fall before she would be willing to buy two lessons?) In this case, her reply is $17. In this way, we get her to provide the information shown in Figure 18-3.

But since Escaf is very bright, she suddenly realizes: "Figure 18-3 is just my demand schedule. It must be. At any price

---

*[1]Although marginal utility and demand are very closely related, they are not precisely the same; we have slipped over a theoretical technicality here.

The problem is that marginal utility may be measured precisely in dollar terms only when the marginal utility of money, our measuring rod, is itself constant; otherwise, a measuring rod is being used that stretches or shrinks. Suppose, for example, that the price of cars falls and people spend less money on automobiles, leaving more for the purchase of other goods. As people increase their purchases of other goods, they get less marginal utility from each additional purchase. Therefore the marginal utility of money falls (because, after all, the utility of money depends on the utility of goods that money will buy). Thus, our measuring rod—namely, the marginal utility of money—is not constant.

While this is a sticky theoretical problem, it does not alter the conclusions which will be reached in the following chapters. (They can be established rigorously by theoretical techniques more advanced than those used in this book.) For this first course, we must be content to illustrate, rather than prove, a number of important propositions.

thus:

> The height of a demand curve indicates the marginal utility of the good.

Equilibrium for the Consumer: How Much of a Good to Buy?

Figure 18-3 represents Lori Escaf's marginal utility of skiing lessons, and as such, it also represents her demand. If all skiing lessons sell for $10, how many will she buy? To answer this, consider her first lesson. Since she values it at $20 (its marginal utility) and it costs her only $10, she will obviously buy it. Similarly, she will also buy the second, third, and fourth lessons because she also values them above their $10 cost. But she will stop when she purchases the fifth because the $10 utility it provides is just equal to its $10 cost.[2] She has struck upon a reasonable rule:

> Consumer equilibrium involves increasing the purchase of a good until its marginal utility just falls to the level of its price.

(See Box 18-1 for more detail on consumer equilibrium.)

CONSUMER'S SURPLUS

Note that Lori Escaf is indifferent to the purchase of the fifth lesson, since it costs exactly the maximum amount she is willing to pay: $10. But this was not true of the fourth. For that lesson she also paid $10, even though she was willing to pay as much as $11. In other words, that fourth lesson provides *more benefit* or marginal utility ($11) than its *cost* ($10). She gets a surplus, or excess of benefit over cost, amounting to $1 on this fourth lesson. Similarly, she gets

---

BOX 18-1
EQUILIBRIUM FOR THE CONSUMER: *How to Choose between Goods?*

In this chapter, we are focusing on how a consumer reacts in buying a single good. But at the same time, it is important to think of the consumer as facing a choice *between* goods. Should a consumer use his given income to buy more carrots and fewer apples, or vice-versa? In making this decision, he should push his purchase of each good to the point where the marginal utility received from the last dollar spent on carrots is equal to the marginal utility received from the last dollar spent on apples. To confirm this, suppose he has not done so. Specifically, suppose his marginal utility (per dollar of expenditure) is greater on carrots than on apples. In this case, he can make his given income go farther (provide more utility) by switching a dollar of expenditure from apples to carrots; the utility received from the additional carrots exceeds the utility lost on apples. And it will be in his interest to continue to switch purchases in this way until these marginal utilities are equalized. (Notice that they will equalize, because the marginal utility of carrots will fall as he buys more, while the marginal utility of apples will rise as he buys fewer.)

We can state this theorem in general: A consumer will be in equilibrium if he extends his purchases in every direction to the point where *the utility he receives from the last dollar of expenditure on one good is the same as that received from the last dollar spent on any of the others.* In this way, he maximizes his utility from a given income. (The consumer's choice between alternatives is considered in greater detail in Appendix 18-A.)

---

[2]Since the cost of the fifth item is $10, just equal to its marginal utility, she will not really care whether she gets the fifth lesson or not. By convention, economists assume that this last, "don't care" unit is, in fact, purchased.

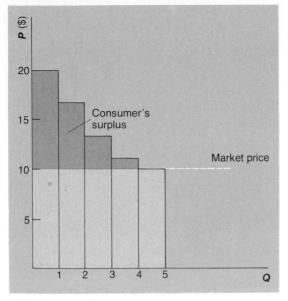

FIGURE 18-4 Consumer's surplus.
The purchaser is willing to pay as much as $20 for the first unit. But she has to pay only the actual market price—$10. She thus receives a surplus of utility, or "consumer's surplus," over and above what she pays for this first unit. Similarly, there is consumer's surplus on the second, third, and fourth units, shown by the darker shading.

an even higher *consumer's surplus* (of $3) on the third lesson. For all purchases, she gets the darker blue consumer's surplus area shown in Figure 18-4.

> *Consumer's surplus* is the net benefit a consumer gets from being able to purchase a good. It is the difference between the maximum amount the consumer would be willing to pay and what actually is paid.

Now that we can visualize demand as a series of marginal utility bars, we hereafter approximate it with a smooth curve. With the above analysis of an individual's demand in hand, we can now turn to the market demand in Figure 18-5. (Remember, market demand is the sum of the demands of all individuals.)

Buyers are, of course, better off when the price falls. This not very surprising proposition may be illustrated by looking at what happens to consumers' surplus when the price decreases. Indeed, in Figure 18-5 we see that there are two reasons why consumers as a group benefit when the price falls from $10 to $6, and the quantity purchased consequently increases from 400 to 600 units. First, each of the 400 units they originally bought for $10 now costs $4 less; consumers thus save $1,600 (that is, 400 × $4) on the original 400 units, as shown by area 1. Second, the price reduction induces consumers to purchase 200 units more, so for the first time they now enjoy consumers' surplus on these units as well. To illustrate, consider one of these additional units, say

FIGURE 18-5 If market price falls from $10 to $6, consumer's surplus increases by the shaded area 1 + 2.
At a $10 price, 400 units are purchased. When price falls to $6, there is now a $4 saving on each of these units, for a total of $4 × 400 = $1600, shown as area 1. This is the increase in consumer's surplus on the original purchases. But at this low price of $6, 200 more units are purchased, and there is now a consumer's surplus on these as well, equal to area 2. Thus the increase in consumer's surplus on both accounts is the entire blue area (1 + 2). To confirm this conclusion, note that consumer's surplus at the original $10 price was area 3 (just as in Figure 18-4). But at a $6 price, consumer's surplus is area 3 + 1 + 2, for an increase equal to the shaded area 1 + 2.

the five-hundredth. The $8 the buyer would be willing to pay for this unit is shown by the height of the demand curve, that is, by the height of the empty bar plus the solid bar. But since this unit costs the buyer only $6 (the height of the empty bar), he enjoys a surplus of $2, shown by the solid bar. If we were to sketch in the other similar solid bars, the result would be the shaded triangle 2. This represents the increased consumers' surplus because of the *new* purchases.

Thus, we conclude that because of the lower price, the consumers' situation has improved (consumers' surplus has increased) by the whole shaded area (1 + 2) in Figure 18-5. Consequently:

> If the market price *falls,* there will be an *increase* in consumers' surplus equal to the horizontal area between the old and new price, and to the left of the demand curve.

And, of course, the same basic proposition applies to a price increase:

> If the market price *rises*, there will be a *decrease* in consumers' surplus equal to the horizontal area between the new and the old price, and to the left of the demand curve.

THE FLORIDA FREEZE: Applying the Analysis of Chapters 17 and 18

To understand how our new analytical tools can be applied to a specific problem, consider the various effects of the record cold winter of 1977 that froze part of the Florida citrus crop. (The Florida freeze, already mentioned in Box 17-2, is now illustrated in Figure 18-6.) This freeze reduced the harvest coming onto the market in that year from the expected bumper supply S_1 to S_2. This in turn meant that prices were

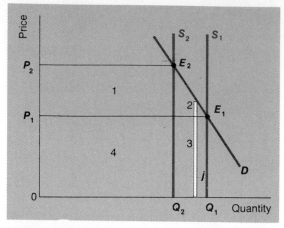

FIGURE 18-6 How Florida citrus freeze benefited producers but damaged consumers and the nation as a whole.
The bumper crop of S_1 in 1977 would have resulted in equilibrium E_1, with price P_1. But because of the frost, the supply coming onto the market in that year was reduced to S_2. Consequently, equilibrium was at E_2, with price P_2. Producers' total revenue without the freeze (at E_1) would have been areas 3 + 4 (the rectangle to the southwest of E_1). But with the freeze shifting equilibrium to E_2, revenue was area 1 + 4 instead. Note that area 4 is common to both; thus producers gain area 1 from the freeze but lose area 3. Consumers have their surplus reduced by area 1 + 2 as a result of the increased price. For the nation overall, we must consider the effect on both groups:

Consumers	lose 1	lose 2
Producers	gain 1	lose 3
Sum indicates nation will	lose 2	lose 3

This overall loss to the nation of area 2 + 3 is easily confirmed. Consider *j*, one of the cases of fruit that froze. The marginal utility it would have provided is the height of the thin bar. Visualize similar bars throughout the range between Q_2 and Q_1, each representing the utility that one of the frozen cases of fruit would have provided. Their sum (area 2 + 3) represents the total loss of utility due to the freeze. *Warning.* Area 1 is a loss to consumers and a gain to producers. In canceling it out in the tabled calculations above, we assume that area 1 is valued similarly by the consumers losing it, and the producers receiving it—or at least similarly enough not to upset our conclusion. (This complication will be considered in Chapter 21.)

higher, with equilibrium at E_2 rather than E_1. Here is how each group was affected:[3]

Producers benefited. Because demand

---

[3]To simplify this illustration, picking, shipping, and other costs of getting the oranges to market are ignored.

for citrus fruits is inelastic, producers' revenue increased; they gained more from the higher price than they lost from their reduced harvest. (Of course, if citrus demand had been elastic, producers would have lost.)

Consumers lost. Because price rose, consumers' surplus was reduced by area 1 + area 2. Specifically, consumers were worse off because they were paying a higher price and because they had less fruit to eat.

With producers benefiting and consumers losing, it is not immediately obvious how the nation as a whole was affected, on balance. However, a moment's reflection leads us to the following conclusion:

On balance, the nation lost. Our real income was reduced because we had fewer oranges. Because oranges froze, we as a nation were worse off.

The various effects of a crop loss may now be summarized. Producers gain. (If demand were elastic, they would lose.) But consumers and the nation overall lose (regardless of demand elasticity.)[4]

Now let us return to our conclusion that producers benefit from a freeze, and examine this more carefully. If you are an individual producer, it will not be in your individual interest to let your crop freeze. Nothing you can do individually will affect price; and whatever the price may be, the more you have to sell the better. But it will be in the interest of *all* producers if there is a general freeze, because the resulting scarcity *will* affect price. This raises the question: If producers cannot get Mother Nature to restrict their supply, is it not in their interest to work together to do it themselves? Unfortunately, from the nationwide view, the answer may be yes. The main reason hindering producers from doing precisely this is that they may have difficulty in organizing to restrict supply. In turn, this problem may lead them to look instead to the government to introduce and enforce collective supply restrictions—for example, a government restriction on the number of acres that a farmer may plant. This limitation will raise price and may also raise farm income, but what it does to consumers and the nation as a whole is quite another matter.

From our discussion in this chapter, it is evident that a demand curve can tell us a great deal even if we do not know its exact shape and location. Of course, if we know its shape and location, we will know still more about the effects of a price change. But precise information is difficult to obtain and must be estimated. (Some of the problems in estimating demand are considered in Appendix 18-B.)

[4]If a good is produced for export (for example, Brazilian coffee), the nation as a whole may gain from a freeze. Thus, when frosts in Brazil reduced coffee supplies, prices soared in 1977. Brazil as a nation gained. The reason is that domestic producers benefited from the higher price. True, consumers lost, but they were mostly in foreign countries, not Brazil. In such cases, it may be in the national interest to restrict supply, as Brazil did during the 1930s by dumping coffee into the ocean.

Such supply restrictions should, however, be approached cautiously, even if a narrow national viewpoint is taken. In the long run, the demand elasticity may be much higher than in the short run. In other words, if coffee prices are kept high for a long period, people may switch to tea and decide that they prefer it.

Key Points

1. Marginal utility is the satisfaction derived from consuming one more unit of a good or service.

2. The height of the demand curve reflects marginal utility (approximately).

3. Consumers benefit when price falls. Specifically, the change in consumers' surplus is the horizontal area to the left of the demand curve enclosed between the old and the new price.

4. When a crop is destroyed (by rot, frost, or whatever) producers may lose or benefit, depending on whether demand is elastic or not. The only firm conclusion is that consumers—and the nation overall—will lose.

Key Concepts

individual demand
market demand
marginal utility
law of diminishing marginal utility

relationship of demand to marginal utility
consumers' surplus
choices between goods
effect of price change on consumers' surplus

Problems

18-1 Suppose each of three individuals has unit elasticity of demand for a particular good. Without drawing any diagrams, can you guess what the elasticity of the total market demand for this good will be?

Now draw diagrams showing how the market demand should be constructed. Is it flatter than an individual demand? Is it therefore more elastic? Explain.

18-2 Using your own example, explain why marginal utility eventually must fall.

18-3 Explain consumers' surplus in your own words to someone who has not yet read this chapter. Specifically, explain the two ways in which consumers will be affected by an increase in the price of bread.

18-4 Suppose that a substantial part of a lettuce crop spoils en route to market because of the producers' negligence. Will these producers suffer a loss as a consequence? Explain. How will consumers and the nation as a whole be affected?

Appendix 18-A

THE THEORY OF CONSUMER CHOICE: INDIFFERENCE CURVES

The demand curve is an important tool for analyzing consumer behavior. But there is another approach, which uses the concept of an *indifference curve*. This approach highlights an important principle introduced in Chapter 2 and emphasized in Box 18-1: Economic behavior involves a *choice between alternatives*. Consider an individual consuming unit—a single individual or household. Suppose, for simplicity, that the household is consuming only two goods, food and clothing. The indifference curve concept may then be illustrated with Figure 18-7 and Table 18-1.

Suppose that the household begins with any point chosen at random in Figure 18-7; say, point A, representing 3 units of food and 2 units of clothing. Then, to draw the indifference curve through A, we ask the following question: What other combinations of food and clothing would leave the household equally well off?

The household may inform us that it would just as soon be at point B (with 2 units of food and 3 of clothing) as at A. In other words, if the household starting at A were asked to give up one unit of food in return for one more unit of clothing, it would respond that it doesn't care whether such a change takes place or not. The household is indifferent between points A and B. Then we may draw an indifference curve connecting points A and B.

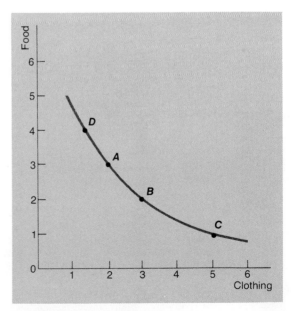

FIGURE 18-7   An indifference curve.
An indifference curve joins all points where the household has the same level of satisfaction or utility.

TABLE 18-1
Combinations among Which the Household Is Indifferent

Combination	Food	Clothing	Amount of additional clothing required to induce household to give up 1 unit of food
A	3	2	
B	2	3	1
C	1	5	2

> An *indifference curve* connects various points among which a household is indifferent. That is, each point on an indifference curve represents the same level of satisfaction or utility.

Now let us continue the experiment, asking the household under what conditions it would be willing to give up one more unit of food. In moving downward to the right from point *B*, the household recognizes that it is getting short of food, and has a lot of clothing. Therefore, the household is willing to give up another unit of precious food only in return for a large amount (say, 2 units) of clothing. Point *C*, representing 1 unit of food and 5 of clothing, is on the same indifference curve as *A* and *B*. Because the household is increasingly reluctant to give up food as its quantity of food declines, the indifference curve has the bowed shape shown.[5] (That is, it is convex to the origin.) Similarly, if the family moves in the other direction (upward to the left on the indifference curve), it has more food and less clothing. As a consequence, it is willing to give up only a small amount (two-thirds of a unit) of its precious clothing to get an additional unit of food. (This is illustrated by the move from point *A* to point *D*.)

This indifference curve is reproduced as u_1 in Figure 18-8. But recall that our starting point, *A*, was a point chosen at random. Therefore, we can also draw an indifference curve starting at any other point. For example, by starting at points *F* and *G*, we can draw indifference curves u_2 and u_3. Thus, there is a whole family of indifference curves, which form an *indifference map.*

Whereas all points on a single indifference curve represent the same level of satisfaction, points on another indifference curve represent a different level of satisfaction. On which of the three indifference curves would the household prefer to be? The answer is u_3, because this curve is farthest out from the

[5]In technical terms, the *marginal rate of substitution* of clothing for food rises as the quantity of food decreases. The marginal rate of substitution is shown in the last column of Table 18-1.

> The *marginal rate of substitution* of clothing for food is the amount of clothing which must be provided to compensate for the loss of one unit of food.

Although indifference curves are usually bowed, as illustrated, this need not always be the case. For example, a two-car family might be indifferent among the choices of (*A*) two Chevs, no Fords; (*B*) one Chev, one Ford; or (*C*) no Chevs, two Fords. Then, with Chevs on one axis and Fords on the other, the indifference curve joining points *A*, *B*, and *C* is a straight line. Thus, the indifference curve is a straight line if the two goods are perfect substitutes.

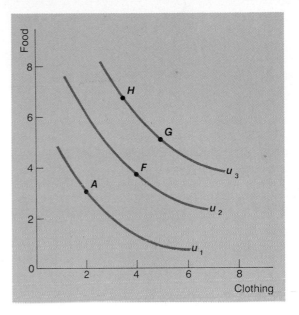

FIGURE 18-8 A system of indifference curves: An indifference map.
There is a whole set of indifference curves for the household, each curve representing a different level of utility. Thus, u_2 involves a higher level of utility than u_1, and u_3 a still higher level.

origin. On this curve, the household gets a higher level of utility or satisfaction than on u_2. To verify this, note that no matter where on u_2 the household may be (say F), it can find a point on u_3 (like G) that is preferred because it leaves the household with more of both goods. (And because other points like H are equivalent to G, they must also provide a higher level of utility than F.)

Incidentally, this illustrates the technique used by economists (and others) to show three variables in a diagram with only two dimensions. The three variables are the quantity of food, the quantity of clothing, and the household's utility. We can visualize this system of indifference curves as mapping out a utility hill, with each curve representing a contour line showing points with equal utility, just as a geographer's contour line shows points with equal height above sea level. And, just as the geographer's contour lines cannot cross, so the indifference curves of a household do not cross. As the household moves from the origin to the northeast, it moves up the utility hill to higher and higher levels of satisfaction.[6]

Consumer Choice

As we have seen, the indifference map reflects the household's *desires*; the household prefers G to F in Figure 18-8, and is indifferent between H and G. But the household's behavior depends not only on what the household *wants* but also on what it is *able* to buy.

---

[6]One advantage of the indifference curve approach is that we don't have to worry about the units of measurement up the utility hill. We know that curve u_3 represents more utility than curve u_2, but we don't need to measure *how much* more. Indeed, avoiding the problems with the measurement of marginal utility (to which we referred in footnote 1, p. 397) was one of the main arguments for the indifference curve approach presented by Nobel prizewinner J. R. Hicks in his *Value and Capital* (London: Oxford University Press, 1939).

FIGURE 18-9 **The equilibrium of a household with a budget limit.**
KL represents the household's budget limit. Each point on this line represents a combination of food and clothing that can be purchased, and that just barely exhausts the household's budget. Equilibrium involves moving along this budget line to the point (E) where the line is tangent to the highest achievable indifference curve.

What the household is able to buy depends on three things: its money income, the price of food, and the price of clothing. If the household's income is \$100, while the price of food is \$10 per unit and clothing is \$20, then the various options open to the household are illustrated by the *budget line KL* in Figure 18-9.

> The *budget line* (or *income line*) shows the various options of a household with a given money income and facing a given set of prices.

If the whole \$100 is spent on food at \$10 per unit, the household can buy 10 units, as shown by point K. At the other extreme, if the household spends its whole \$100 on clothing at \$20 per unit, it can buy 5 units, as shown by point L. Similarly, it can be shown how any other point on the straight line KL will exactly exhaust the budget of \$100. (As an exercise, show that this is true for point M.)

With this budget limit, the household purchases the combination shown at E. That is, it moves along the budget line to the point where the line is tangent to the highest possible indifference curve, in this case u_3. Any other feasible purchase (like M) is less attractive because it leaves the household on a lower indifference curve (u_2 rather than u_3).

> Consumers maximize their satisfaction or utility by moving along their budget line to the highest attainable indifference curve. This is achieved at the point of tangency shown in Figure 18-9.

In conclusion, we reemphasize that the budget line and the indifference map are drawn independently of one another. The indifference map shows what the household wants; in constructing the indifference map, no attention is paid to what the household can actually afford. What it can afford is shown by the budget line. When the indifference map and the budget line are brought together, the choice of the household is determined.

Effect of a Price Change

Figure 18-10 illustrates how the household will respond to a fall in the price of clothing. With clothing priced at $20 per unit, we saw that the original budget line was KL and the initial equilibrium was E_1. Now suppose that the

FIGURE 18-10 The effect of a fall in the price of clothing.
As the price of clothing falls, the budget line rotates counterclockwise around point K. As a result, there is an increase in the quantity of clothing purchased. This may alternatively be illustrated by the movement along the demand curve in the lower diagram.

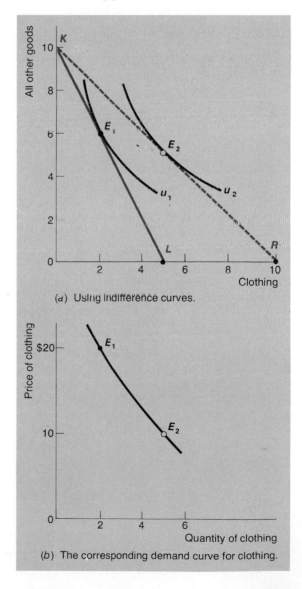

(a) Using indifference curves.

(b) The corresponding demand curve for clothing.

407

price of clothing falls to $10. This causes the budget line to move to *KR*. (If all $100 is spent on clothing, the household can now buy 10 units at point *R*. But because we assume that the price of food does not change, the new budget line still ends at point *K*, as before.)[7]

> A change in the relative prices of clothing and food results in a change in the slope of the budget line.

Faced with the new budget line *KR*, the household again searches for its highest possible indifference curve, finding it at the point of tangency E_2. The two points of equilibrium, E_1 and E_2, correspond to similar points on the demand curve of the household, shown in Figure 18-10*b*.

Observe that the household's real income increases when the price of clothing falls; E_2 is on a higher indifference curve than E_1.

[7]Because we are dealing with a simple example with only two goods (food and clothing), food may be interpreted as representing all other goods. In showing the relationship between the indifference curve diagram and the demand curve in Figure 18-10, it is customary to write "all other goods" on the vertical axis.

Appendix 18-B

STATISTICAL DIFFICULTIES IN ESTIMATING A DEMAND CURVE: THE IDENTIFICATION PROBLEM

There are various methods of estimating demand for a specific product. A sample of consumers may be surveyed to determine how each one would react to a price change. Alternatively, a firm may test-market, reducing (or increasing) its price in one city and examining how its sales there compare with its sales in similar cities where the price has been held steady.

The third method of estimating demand, and the one we consider here, is to observe how much of the good was purchased in the past at various prices. We would hope to observe a "scatter" of observations as in Figure 18-11a—if we were lucky. It would then be a simple task to fit a straight line to these observations. (We would actually use a special statistical technique to do this, but that is not the problem we wish to address. For present purposes, you can think of fitting a straight line by eye, using a ruler.)

In panel b, we examine the underlying demand and supply curves that gave rise to these four observations. Through the entire period of observation, the demand curve remained stable at D. But the supply curve shifted. Thus, our 1975 observation was the result of the intersection of the demand curve and the 1975 supply curve S_{75}. The 1976 observation was the result of the intersection of that same demand curve and supply, which had now shifted to S_{76}. Similarly, the shifting supply curve in 1977 and 1978 accounts for the observations in those years.

Now we see why we were lucky in our scatter of observations in panel a. They were generated in panel b by a *stable* demand curve and a *shifting* supply curve, and therefore we were able to "identify" demand. Our tentative conclusion (which will turn out to be correct) is that demand is identified by shifts in supply. (As an exercise, set up an example where supply is identified by shifts in demand.)

FIGURE 18-11   Special case when demand is easily estimated.

(a) Scatter of observations.

(b) How these observations were generated: Supply shifts while demand remains stable.

409

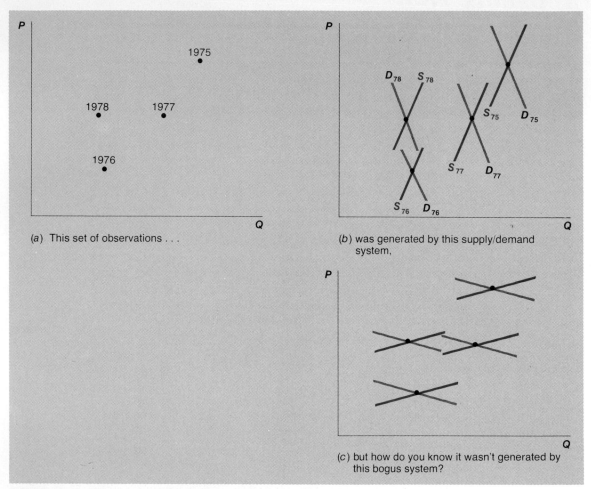

FIGURE 18-12 When demand estimation requires a special approach.

But we will usually not be so lucky. Consider the more typical case shown in Figure 18-12 where the set of observations in panel *a* has been generated by the shifting supply and demand curves shown in panel *b*. Since both demand and supply shift in panel *b*, the result in panel *a* is a scatter of observations that gives us neither demand nor supply, but some apparently incomprehensible combination of both.

To emphasize the difficulty in this problem, in panel *c* we show a completely bogus supply and demand system that could also have generated the scatter in panel *a*. When all we have to work with is what we see in panel *a*, how in the world can we decide whether this scatter has been generated by the true, inelastic supply/demand system in panel *b* or the completely bogus elastic system in panel *c*? Or by some other bogus system?

If we have no further information, this problem is indeed a hopeless one. But, if we can get more information, we may be able to identify both demand and supply. Specifically, we require information both on how supply shifts

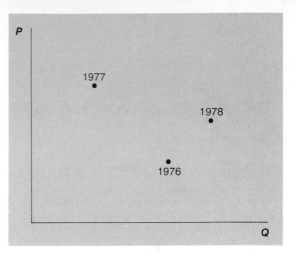

FIGURE 18-13 Can demand be identified?
This scatter seems hopeless. Without further information, it is.

(since this is what identifies demand), and on how demand shifts (to identify supply).

Although the solution to this problem requires a fairly complex statistical technique, a highly simplified example will illustrate the basic idea. Consider the three observations in Figure 18-13. Without further information, we can make no more sense out of them than we can out of the scatter in Figure 18-12a. (Specifically, as an exercise you should show how this scatter could have been generated by several supply/demand systems, and that there is no way of knowing which is the true one.)

But now let us see how we *can* identify the true underlying supply/demand system if we have additional information on how each curve shifts. Suppose we know that demand shifts with income. In other words, recalling the analysis of Chapter 4, suppose that an increase in income results in a parallel shift to the right of the demand curve. Then we examine the figures on income and discover that it was the same in 1976 and 1977, but rose in 1978. Accordingly, we conclude that the demand curve remained in the same position in 1976 and 1977, but shifted to the right in 1978.

Suppose we also know that supply shifts as a result of strikes; that is, since a strike will reduce the quantity supplied, it will shift the supply curve to the left. Moreover, in examining data on labor disputes in this industry, we discover that a strike occurred in 1977, but not in 1976 or 1978. Accordingly, we conclude that the supply curve was in the same position in 1976 and 1978, but had temporarily shifted to the left in 1977.

In the light of this additional information, there is now only one combination of supply and demand curves that could have generated the observations in Figure 18-13. As an exercise, you should try to discover it yourself and check it against the solution shown in Figure 18-14. Since it is the only system of supply and demand curves that could have generated this scatter, it must be the one that *did* generate it. Try as you like, you cannot find a bogus system capable of producing these observations. Thus, knowledge

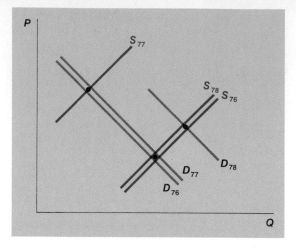

FIGURE 18-14 How demand (and supply) can be identified.

With knowledge that there was a parallel shift to the left in supply in 1977 and a parallel shift to the right in demand in 1978, this becomes the only supply and demand system that can be fitted to the three observations in Figure 18-13.

about how supply and demand shift has allowed you to eliminate bogus possibilities and to pin down or identify both supply and demand.

To sum up: We started out trying to estimate demand from the apparently incomprehensible scatter of observations in Figure 18-13. But, with some additional information on what causes demand and supply to shift, we were able to estimate demand in Figure 18-14 (the D_{76}/D_{77} location, except during the high-income year when it shifted to D_{78}). As a special bonus, we were also able to estimate supply (the S_{76}/S_{78} location, except during the year of a strike, when it shifted to S_{77}).

Of course, this simplified illustration can only provide a certain "feel" for the identification problem. In practice, estimating supply and demand (like estimating most other economic relationships) involves additional complications. For example: Each curve may shift in response to several influences (rather than just one). Thus, the demand for beef shifts not only with income but also with the price of pork. This sounds like "too much" information. Nevertheless, it can be used to estimate demand and supply by an econometrician (economic statistician), using the appropriate statistical techniques.

Problem

18-5 Using Figure 18-14, illustrate our earlier claim that shifts in supply identify demand, and that shifts in demand identify supply. In particular, show graphically the scatter that we would have observed, and what we would (or would not) be able to identify, if:

    (*a*) There had been no income increase in 1978.

    (*b*) There had been neither an income increase in 1978 nor a strike in 1977.

chapter 19
Costs and Supply

" . . . and consumers dance to the producers' tune."
Reprise from Chapter 4

We now examine the tune that producers play. They provide us with some goods at low cost, other goods at high cost, and still other goods not at all because their cost would be prohibitive. Thus, supply reflects costs. Specifically, we shall show that the height of a supply curve reflects *marginal cost,* just as the height of a demand curve reflects marginal utility. Furthermore, we shall show how a change in producers' profit ("producers' surplus") can be read off a supply curve, just as a change in consumers' surplus can be read off a demand curve.

COSTS AND SUPPLY IN THE SHORT RUN

Figure 19-1*a* illustrates how total costs of a firm rise as its output increases. The numbers behind this diagram are set out in the first five columns of Table 19-1. (For the moment, ignore the last two columns in this table.) Notice in Figure 19-1*a* that even

before the firm starts producing (that is, when its output is still zero), it faces $35 of costs. For example, interest on borrowed funds and depreciation of equipment will be costs even if nothing is produced. These are called *fixed costs* (or overhead) because they do not vary as output increases; in this diagram, there is always this same $35 of fixed cost, regardless of what output may be.

But when this firm starts to produce, it will incur other costs as well, and these will vary with output. For example, the greater its output, the more labor it will hire and the more materials it will buy. Accordingly, any costs above and beyond the original $35 of fixed costs are called *variable costs.* Initially, to keep the analysis as simple as possible, we shall view the firm as using only two inputs: capital (its fixed cost) and labor (its variable cost). Of course, in the long run, a firm can vary not only its labor but also its capital by adding more machinery and buildings. Later in the chapter, we shall deal

413

(a) Total cost=fixed cost+variable cost.

(b) Marginal cost: the increase in total cost.

FIGURE 19-1   Short-run costs of a hypothetical firm (drawn from Table 19-1).
Total cost is the sum of fixed cost and variable cost, as shown in part a. Marginal cost indicates how much total cost is increasing, as shown by the set of blue bars in part a or in part b.

with this case; but for now, we concentrate on the short run, the period in which the firm can vary the size of its labor force but continues to use a fixed amount of capital.

Total cost is the sum of both fixed and variable costs; that is, the combined height of the two wide arrows in Figure 19-1. In particular, we are interested in how total cost increases, as shown by the blue bars, or "stairsteps." Thus in producing its first unit of output, the firm's costs rise by $24, represented by the first blue bar in Figure 19-1a. In producing the second unit, its costs rise by $16, represented by the next bar. Economists call each such bar _marginal cost_ (while business executives usually call it _incremental cost_). By definition:

Marginal cost is the increase in total cost caused by the production of one more unit.

Note how similar this concept is to marginal utility (the increase in utility because one more unit is consumed).

Each of the blue marginal cost bars in panel a of Figure 19-1 is now assembled on its own in panel b. (This schedule can be viewed as "what would be left" if the supporting red bars in panel a were removed and the blue bars were allowed to settle down to the baseline.)

Although marginal cost may fall at first, it must eventually rise with output, because of the law of diminishing returns. To ex-

TABLE 19-1
Short-Run Costs of a Hypothetical Firm*

(1)	(2)	(3)	(4)	(5)	(6)	(7)
Quantity *q*	Fixed Cost *FC*	Variable Cost *VC*	Total Cost *TC = FC + VC*	Marginal Cost *MC* = change in total cost	Average Cost** *AC = TC ÷ q*	Average Variable Cost** *AVC = VC ÷ q*
0	35	—	35			
1	35	24	59	59 − 35 = 24	59 ÷ 1 = 59	24 ÷ 1 = 24
2	35	40	75	75 − 59 = 16 etc.	75 ÷ 2 = 38 etc.	40 ÷ 2 = 20 etc.
3	35	60	95	20	32	20
4	35	85	120	25	30	21
5	35	115	150	30	30	23
6	35	155	190	40	32	26
7	35	210	245	55	35	30

*Columns (1) through (5) are graphed in Figure 19-1, and columns (6) and (7) in Figure 19-3.
**Rounded to the nearest dollar.

plain this law, consider the example of a firm producing TVs with a given stock of machinery. As it initially hires more labor, each additional worker increases the firm's output by a substantial amount. But ultimately, as its labor force grows and its equipment is operated closer and closer to capacity, an additional worker will add only a small amount to the firm's output. All the new employee can do is work on odd jobs or spend most of the time standing around waiting for one of the machines to be free. In other words, there has been a decrease in the *marginal product of labor* (defined, as we would expect, as the additional output a firm can produce because it has hired one more worker).

The law of (eventually) diminishing returns: If more of one factor (labor) is employed while all other factors (like capital) are held constant, eventually the marginal product of that factor (labor) must fall.

In Part 5, we shall see that this is a key principle in our explanation of wages and other income payments. For now, it is important because it explains why marginal costs must ultimately rise. In our example, the TV firm operating at close to capacity is still able to increase its output by hiring more workers; but, because the added labor results in a lot of wasted motion (a falling marginal product of labor), the marginal cost of producing another TV rises.

How Marginal Cost Determines the Quantity Supplied

In Figure 19-2 we reproduce the rising portion of the marginal cost curve from Figure 19-1*b*. We shall now show that this is the key to defining the firm's supply curve (just as the marginal utility schedule is the key to the individual's demand curve).

To confirm this important proposition, suppose market price is $40, as shown by the horizontal price line. (When we make this

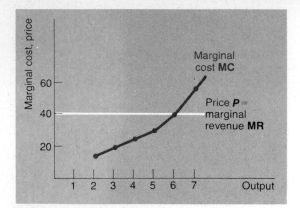

FIGURE 19-2 Marginal cost as the firm's supply curve: a first approximation. (Marginal costs are for the firm shown in Figure 19-1).
Marginal cost MC is equal to price *P* at an output level of 6 units. Since this output maximizes profit, it is the amount that this firm will supply.

supposition, we are of course assuming perfect competition, with the firm having no control over price.) This price line is also labeled the firm's marginal revenue. By now we can guess that, by definition:

> *Marginal revenue* is the increase in total revenue from the sale of one more unit.

It is easy to confirm that marginal revenue will be this constant $40 price. The reason is that total revenue will be $40 from the sale of 1 unit, $80 from the sale of 2, $120 from 3, and so on. No matter how many units the firm may be selling, its total revenue will always increase by $40 if it sells 1 unit more.

Given this $40 price and the marginal cost schedule shown in Figure 19-2, how many units will the firm produce? The answer is 6. The reason is that any decision to produce at a higher output level, say 7, would be a mistake, since the $55 marginal cost of producing that seventh unit exceeds the $40 price at which it can be sold. On the other hand, if the firm is at an output level below 6, say 4, expansion will be in its interest (the marginal cost of the fifth unit is

$30, and it can be sold for $40). But at 6 units, there is no tendency to expand or contract production, because marginal cost MC has risen to the level of price (that is, marginal revenue). Consequently, this is the equilibrium output for the firm, because at this point its profit is at a maximum. (As an optional exercise, you can confirm this by calculating profit at each possible output level, as in Appendix 19-A).

If price rises from $40 to $55, you can visualize the horizontal price line shifting up to this new, higher level. The firm will respond to this higher price by increasing its output to 7 units, where MC is again equal to price. Or, if price falls to $30, it will supply 5 units; and so on. Notice that what we are doing is defining this firm's supply response; that is, how much it would supply at various prices. As price rises, it simply follows its marginal cost curve up; or if price falls, it follows its MC curve down. Thus, MC defines the supply curve of the individual firm—subject to one important complication to which we now turn.

Does Marginal Cost Always Determine the Quantity Supplied?

The answer is no, not quite. Why? Because it is not certain the firm will produce anything at all. If it does, MC does indeed determine the quantity supplied. Otherwise, the quantity supplied will be zero. The critical question therefore is: How far can price fall before the firm will close down and stop producing altogether?

To throw light on this question, two new concepts are useful: *average cost* (AC), defined as total cost divided by output; and *average variable cost* (AVC), defined as variable cost divided by output. These two new curves (calculated in the final columns of Table 19-1) are shown, along with MC, in Figure 19-3. Note that the MC curve cuts the AC curve where AC is at a minimum. This must be the case, for reasons explained in Box 19-1.

Now consider what happens if the price falls to $30. To identify its best level of output, the firm finds where MC equals the $30 price; this is at 5 units. Observe that, at this point, average cost is at a minimum and is equal to price. The best the firm can do with a price of $30 is to cover its average costs. It will barely break even; profits will fall to zero.[1] But because it is breaking even, the firm will continue to produce.

Next, suppose price falls even lower, say to $25. If the firm produces at all, its output would be 4 units, at point J, where MC equals the $25 price. But this output would involve operating at a loss, since J lies below the AC curve. (Specifically, the $25 price the firm receives does not cover the $30 average cost of producing each unit.) But even though this firm is operating *at a loss* at J, it will still continue to produce. The reason is that its $25 selling price more than covers its average *variable* costs. (That is, point J lies above AVC.) Therefore, it can completely cover its variable costs and still have some revenue left over to partly cover its fixed costs. And it is better to cover these fixed costs partially than to shut down and not cover them at all.[2] Thus, so long as a firm is at least covering its variable costs, it will continue to produce. That remains true so long as price is above the $20 level at K; but if price falls below this, the firm will not even be able to cover its variable costs, and it will close down. (The full calculations for each of these cases are set out in Table 19-3 in Appendix 19-A.)

Thus, *in the short run* (in the period when the firm is working with a fixed capital stock and cannot avoid its fixed cost commitments), the firm will react to any given price by supplying a quantity that can be read off its marginal cost curve, provided it is operating at a point on its marginal cost curve above AVC. In brief:

FIGURE 19-3 Drawing the firm's cost curves, and showing how they define its short-run supply. Marginal cost is reproduced from Figure 19-2. Average cost AC and average variable cost AVC are taken from columns 6 and 7 in Table 19-1. The firm's short-run supply curve is shown as the heavy curve. It is that portion of its MC curve that lies above its AVC curve.

The firm's short-run supply curve is that part of its marginal cost curve that lies above its average variable cost curve.

This discussion may be summarized by describing the plight you may find yourself in someday if you are operating at a point like J. For example, suppose that you have inherited a house in another city, which you wish to rent out. You have to pay $200 a week of fixed costs (taxes, etc.) and $40 a week of variable costs (electricity, fee for the rental agent, etc.). If you can get only $100 rent, should you rent the house or leave it vacant? The answer is: Rent it. True, you will incur a loss, but since the $100 price you will receive more than covers your $40 of variable cost, you will at least have $60 left over to cover some of the fixed costs, like the tax payment. And that's better than leaving the house vacant and being stuck with

---

[1]Profits are shown in detail in column 8 of Table 19-3, in Appendix 19-A.
[2]Remember: Bygones are bygones. The firm is saddled with those fixed costs no matter what it does; they are water under the bridge. (Hence, they are sometimes referred to as "past" or "sunk" costs.)

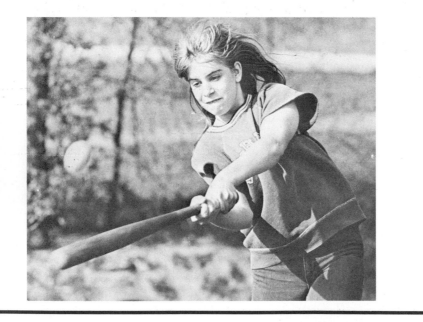
all the fixed costs. In brief, your loss will be less if you rent it than if you leave it vacant. Of course, in the long run you will not want to keep such a house, since you are suffering a loss. But in the short run—that is, until you can sell the house—you are stuck.

All you can do is your best, which is to minimize your loss by renting it out.

But, of course, in the long run, you are not stuck with the house; you can sell it. Your reaction as a supplier will be quite different.

COSTS AND SUPPLY IN THE LONG RUN

All the costs we have discussed so far apply to the short run, since they describe a firm with a fixed capital stock of plant and equipment. But over the long run, the size of the firm can change. It may expand by acquiring new plant and equipment; or it may shrink by not replacing plant and equipment as they wear out (or by selling plant and equipment). Thus, costs which are *fixed* in the short run become *variable* in the long run, and as a result, the costs shown in Figure 19-3 are no longer an adequate guide.

Suppose that a firm starts out as a small operation, with a small factory and only a few machines. Then, after it is successfully established, it expands into a new, larger factory, with many new machines. The original short-run cost curve (SAC$_A$ in Figure 19-4) will no longer be relevant; the firm will now be on a new short-run cost curve (SAC$_B$). With a larger plant and more equipment, average costs will be lower for any quantity of output greater than q_1; not surprisingly, it is desirable to have a large plant in order to produce a large output. (But for small output levels below q_1, it is of course not desirable to have a large plant; in other words, SAC$_B$ is higher than SAC$_A$. The reason is that the firm incurs a lot of expenses in acquiring a large plant, but some of this plant cannot be fully utilized.)

But there are not just these two possible sizes of plant; there are many. In Figure 19-5, four short-run cost curves are chosen from the whole family of such curves, with each representing a different quantity of plant and equipment. (The short-run average cost curves SAC$_A$, SAC$_B$, etc., begin with S to emphasize their short-run nature.)

Over the long run, the firm will choose the size of plant and equipment (and therefore the SAC) which *minimizes* its cost. Hence, for example, if it plans an output q_3, it will choose the plant and equipment re-

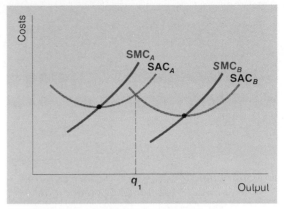

FIGURE 19-4 Cost in the short and long run.
SAC$_A$ shows short-run average cost with a given fixed capital stock *A*. If the firm wishes to produce more than q_1 in the long run, it can reduce costs by expanding its capital stock and moving to short-run average cost SAC$_B$.

quired to operate on short-run curve SAC$_C$; similarly, to produce q_4, it will choose the quantity of plant and equipment required for SAC$_D$; and so on. The long-run average cost curve (LAC) forms an "envelope" that just barely encloses all the SAC curves from below. (It may be easy for us to draw this curve, but see Box 19-2 for the problems encountered by the economist who first had the idea.) Because there are many short-run SAC curves, rather than just the four illustrated, LAC forms a smooth curve. It shows the lowest average cost at which each output can be produced over the *long run,* that is, the period in which producers have the freedom to adjust the quantity of capital they will use. It provides a summary of the relevant information from all the SAC curves.

Scale Effects in Production

Now that we have made the important distinction between long- and short-run costs, we can distinguish clearly in Figure 19-6 between two important economic concepts:

1. The law of diminishing returns This law applies to a situation where capital

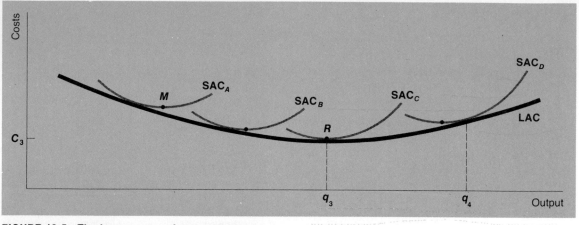

FIGURE 19-5 The long-run envelope cost curve.
The SAC curves are the short-run average cost curves that apply if capital stock is fixed at
various levels, *A, B,* etc. LAC is the long-run average cost curve that encloses all of them
from below. It is the appropriate curve for a firm that is free to select any level of capital
stock. To produce q_3, it would thus select capital stock *C* and keep its average cost down
to the lowest possible level C_3. Similarly, to produce q_4, it would select capital stock *D* (and
therefore operate on SAC$_D$).

is held constant. As we saw in our TV
example, it states that, with capital held
constant, marginal costs eventually must
rise (as shown by arrow *f*).

2. Economies of scale This concept
applies to a situation where all inputs (both
labor and capital) can be increased; in other
words, we move along LAC. For the firm
shown here, economies of scale exist, so that

this move results in a reduction in average
cost; that is, LAC falls (as shown by arrow
e).[3]

In brief, although one of these ideas
describes rising costs and the other describes falling costs, they are not in contradiction. The reason is that the law of diminishing returns applies if one factor (capital)
is held constant, while economies of scale

*[3]Formally, economies of scale are not defined in terms of the average cost curve. The formal definition, given
earlier, may be repeated:

Economies of scale exist when a doubling of all inputs more than doubles output.

There is, however, a close connection between this definition and the shape of the LAC curve. Consider an
illustration, where 10 units of labor and 1 unit of capital can be used to produce 100 units of output. At a cost of labor
of $10 and a cost of capital of $50, the total cost of 100 units will be $10 × 10 + $50 × 1; that is, $150. Thus, the
average cost is $1.50.

Now, suppose that the quantity of both inputs is doubled, to 20 units of labor and 2 of capital. If the price of labor
and capital remains constant, the total cost of production becomes $10 × 20 + $50 × 2; that is, $300. If there are
economies of scale, this doubling of inputs *more than doubles* output from 100 to, say, 240. Thus, the average cost is
now only $1.25 (that is, $300 ÷ 240). As output increases, average cost falls.

Indeed, if the prices of inputs remain constant, economies of scale will result in a falling average cost curve. (If,
however, the prices of inputs rise as larger quantities are used, the LAC may begin to rise before economies of scale are
exhausted. Thus, economies of scale and a falling LAC are not precisely the same thing. But they are very closely
related.)

FIGURE 19-6   How a firm can face both economies of scale and diminishing returns.
This firm faces diminishing returns, as shown by arrow *f*. (Its marginal cost curve SMC$_A$ rises in the short run, so long as its capital stock is fixed at level *A*.) For this firm, there are also economies of scale, as shown by arrow *e*; its average cost LAC falls as it increases its use of *all* factors.

FIGURE 19-7   A firm's long-run supply curve.
The firm's LAC curve is reproduced from Figure 19-5. LMC is the corresponding long-run marginal cost curve that intersects LAC at its minimum point *R*. Long-run supply is the heavy line; that is, the portion of LMC lying above the shutdown point *R*.

describe a situation where all factors are variable.

Long-run Supply

In Figure 19-7, LAC is the long-run average cost (or envelope) curve for a firm. The corresponding long-run marginal cost curve (LMC) is also shown, with this LMC intersecting the average curve LAC at its minimum point. (Remember: In business or baseball, marginal and average curves are always related in this way.) In most respects, the analysis of long-run costs and supply runs parallel to the preceding analysis of short-run costs and supply, and details need not be repeated. For example, long-run supply is determined by long-run marginal cost (LMC), provided price is high enough to keep the firm from shutting down altogether. It is only in defining the long-run shutdown point that we must take special care.

What is the long-run shut-down point? The answer is *R*, where average cost LAC reaches a minimum. This is the break-even point; if price is at this level, the firm will operate at *R*, just barely covering all its costs. But at any price below this, the firm will incur a loss, and will stop producing.

This is, of course, different from the short-run situation, where a firm may continue to produce at a loss because it is stuck in the industry. In the long run, it is not stuck. Eventually, it will have to make a decision on whether it should replace its plant and machinery when they wear out. If it is operating at a loss, it will choose not to replace plant and machinery. (In other words, there are no fixed costs in the long run.) Therefore, at any price below P_1 in the long run, this firm will eventually leave this industry, and its supply will disappear. Thus:

> The firm's long-run supply curve is that part of its long-run marginal cost curve that lies above its long-run average cost curve.

This long-run supply is shown as the heavy curve in Figure 19-7. A comparison of long- and short-run supply is given in Box 19-3.

For the rest of this book, we shall typically drop the letter *L* (for "long") and *S* (for "short") and use the abbreviated terms MC and AC. These will represent long-run curves unless we specify otherwise.

LAC min → break even pt.

THE ECONOMIST'S DEFINITION OF COST

When economists talk about taking all costs into account, they use a much broader definition of cost than accountants do. To illustrate, suppose a friend who operates a store has asked you to analyze her business. Her breakdown of costs in column a of Table 19-2 seems to confirm her view that she has a good thing going. With revenue of $102,000 and costs of $74,000, she is earning an accounting profit of $28,000.

But you dig more deeply. You discover that she could earn a $24,000 salary by taking up a standing offer of a job from an insurance company. This is an *implicit cost* because it is not paid out of pocket. But we must include it, as we have done in column b, or we would not have an adequate picture of the true costs involved in operating this business (that is, the cost of all the resources used, including her own talent and energy). And we would not be able to judge whether she is doing as well in this business as she could in another activity (namely, working

BOX 19-3
RECAP: SHORT-RUN AND LONG-RUN SUPPLY BY THE FIRM

In Figure 19-8, the long-run cost curves (and in particular, the long-run supply curve LMC) are reproduced from Figure 19-7. Suppose the firm is initially operating at point R. We also draw in its short-run cost curves, and in particular, its short-run supply SMC. Now suppose that price rises from P_1 to P_2. In the short run (so long as the firm does not change its capital stock), the firm moves up its short-run supply curve from R to K, thus increasing its output from q_1 to q_2. But if P_2 continues in the long run, the firm will increase its capital stock, thus moving to point T on its long-run supply curve and, in the process, expanding its output by an even greater amount to q_3. This is another illustration of why supply is more elastic in the long run than in the short run. (Long-run supply tends to be elastic for an additional reason. Not only will existing firms expand their plants in the face of higher price, but new firms may also enter the industry. A further review of long-run versus short-run supply is given in Problem 19-3.)

FIGURE 19-8 A comparison of long-run and short-run supply.

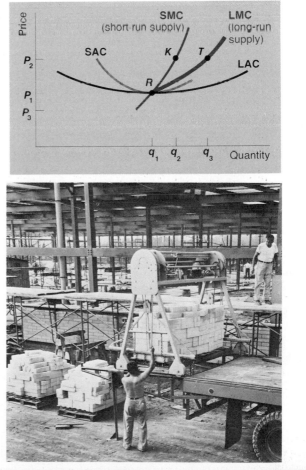

TABLE 19-2
The Evaluation of Costs and Profit

(a) By accountants		(b) By economists		
Total revenue	$102,000	Total revenue		$102,000
Costs (out-of-pocket)		Explicit (out-of-pocket) costs		
Labor $10,000		Labor	$10,000	
Materials 59,000		Materials	59,000	
Rent 5,000		Rent	5,000	
Total $74,000	$74,000			
		Implicit costs (income foregone)		
		Owner's salary	$24,000	
		Interest	1,000	
		Normal profit	2,000	
		Total costs	$101,000	$101,000
Accounting profit	$28,000	Economic (above-normal) profit		$ 1,000

for the insurance company mentioned before).

This implicit salary for her own effort illustrates the concept of *opportunity cost*, that is, what has to be given up. By definition:

> The opportunity cost of an input is the return that it could earn in its best alternative use.

Opportunity cost also roughly indicates how much an input must be paid to keep it in its present use. For example, if your friend doesn't earn her opportunity cost (her potential salary in insurance), she will have an incentive to shift out of her present activity into the higher-return insurance business.

You also discover that your friend has other opportunity costs which must also be included in column *b*. For example, she has about $30,000 of her own money tied up in this business. What would be her best alternative use of this money? She indicates that she would lend out part of it, thus earning $1,000 in interest. She would use the rest to buy part-ownership of a company in which she could earn a $2,000 profit. This last item—the opportunity cost of capital—is called *normal profit.*

Whenever we draw a cost curve in this book, we include not only explicit out-of-pocket costs, but also implicit costs such as normal profit. Therefore, in our example, costs are the full $101,000 shown in column *b* of Table 19-2. This broad definition means that costs tell us how much all the resources employed by a firm could be earning elsewhere. Since her $102,000 of revenues exceed this $101,000 cost, she has earned above-normal profit of $1,000. (In economics, the word "profits" means *above-normal* profits unless otherwise stated.) It is this $1,000 "bottom-line" profit figure that allows you to judge that your friend does indeed have a good thing going: Her business not only provides her with an appropriate $24,000 income for her own effort and an appropriate return for the capital she has invested; it also provides her with $1,000 in addition. If present firms in an industry are making such (above-normal) profits, there is an incentive for other entrepreneurs to move their capital into the business, to get in on a good thing.

> *Economic profit* is above-normal profit; that is, profit after opportunity costs have been taken into account.

Now suppose that salaries in other jobs increase. Specifically, suppose the insurance company increases its offer to your friend from $24,000 to $27,000. This increases the $24,000 salary item in implicit costs by $3,000; and when column *b* is accordingly recalculated, the $1,000 of (above-normal) profit is changed to a $2,000 loss. Your friend is no longer able to earn as much in this enterprise as in her best alternative activity. And (assuming she views this alternative line of work as equally interesting), she will have an incentive to move.

Thus, economic profit (or loss) is defined in such a way that it provides a signal, indicating whether resources are being attracted into (or repelled from) an activity.

PRODUCER'S SURPLUS

Just as we examined in detail in the last chapter how a price change will affect *consumer's surplus*, we shall now consider how a price change will affect *producer's surplus*, that is, economic (above-normal) profit.

Figure 19-9 illustrates a perfectly competitive firm, with supply reflecting its marginal cost schedule (MC). At the initial price of $500, the firm supplies 30 units and receives a total revenue of area 1. If price rises to $700, the firm responds by moving up its supply curve from *R* to *T*, supplying 40 units for a total revenue of areas 1 + 2 + 3. Thus, its revenue increases by areas 2 + 3.

But its costs also rise. To see how much, we sketch in the marginal cost for each of the additional units produced (shown by the vertical bars). The sum of all these marginal costs—namely, area 2—indicates how much the firm's total costs rise as its output increases from 30 to 40. Since the firm's revenue increases by areas 2 + 3, but its costs rise by area 2, its profit (or producer's sur-

FIGURE 19-9 As price rises (and the firm moves to a new equilibrium on its supply curve), producer's surplus increases by the shaded area
At initial price $500 and equilibrium *R*, 30 units are supplied for a total revenue of 30 × 500 = $15,000, shown as area 1. At a price of $700, equilibrium moves from *R* to *T*, and 40 units are sold, for a total revenue of $28,000, or areas 1 + 2 + 3. Total revenue thus increases by area 2 + 3. But of this, area 2 represents increased costs. Increased profit (producer's surplus) is therefore area 3.

plus) increases by area 3. Note that this is the area between the old price of $500 and the new price of $700, and to the left of the supply curve. In general:

> If market price rises (falls) and the producer moves to a new equilibrium on the supply curve, the increase (decrease) in producer's surplus is the horizontal area between the old and new price, and to the left of the supply curve.

Although this conclusion has involved just one firm, Appendix 19-B shows it is also true for all firms taken together. Thus, producers' surplus for an industry can be read off the industry supply curve in exactly the same way.

Appendix 19-B also shows how the supply curve for a particular product can be derived by horizontally adding the supply curves of all individual producers, just as market demand was derived in Figure 18-1 by horizontally adding the demands of all consumers.

As already noted, producer's surplus represents economic (above-normal) profit. For an alternative way of illustrating economic profit, see Appendix 19-C.

Key Points

1. A firm's short-run supply is determined by its short-run marginal cost curve, provided that the price is at least high enough to cover its short-run variable costs.

2. A firm's long-run supply is determined by its long-run marginal cost curve, provided that the price is at least high enough to cover its long-run average costs.

3. In measuring costs, economists use an "opportunity cost" definition. Thus, they include the explicit costs that accountants calculate, plus implicit costs, such as the normal profit on capital invested in the enterprise.

4. After all such opportunity costs have been covered, any remaining profit (that is, above-normal profit) provides an indication of how much more is being earned in this activity than elsewhere. Thus, if present firms are making such profits, resources will tend to move into this industry. On the other hand, if present firms are not covering their opportunity costs (that is, if they are suffering a loss), resources will tend to move out.

5. When price changes and there is a consequent move to a new equilibrium on the supply curve, producers' surplus (profit) will increase. This change in producers' surplus is represented by the area to the left of the supply curve between the old and the new price, in the same way as the change in consumers' surplus in Chapter 18 was represented by the area to the left of the demand curve between the old and the new price.

Key Concepts

marginal cost
fixed cost
variable cost
total cost
average cost
average variable cost
marginal product of labor
law of diminishing returns
dependence of supply on marginal cost
marginal revenue
relationship of marginal cost to average cost
break-even point
shutdown point

short-run versus long-run costs
envelope cost curve
economies of scale
short-run versus long-run supply
accountants' versus economists' definition of cost
explicit versus implicit costs
opportunity cost
normal versus above-normal (economic) profit
producers' surplus
effect of a price change on producers' surplus

Problems

19-1 Which of the schedules (short-run AC, AVC, MC; long-run AC, MC) will the firm need to know before deciding how much to supply in the short run? In the long run? In each case, explain why.

19-2 "In the long run, all costs are variable." Do you agree? Explain, using machinery as an example of a fixed cost.

19-3 (*a*) Consider a firm operating at point R on the SAC and LAC curves in Figure 19-8. Does its short-run supply extend below R? If so, how far? Why?

(*b*) Suppose price falls to P_3. Explain how the firm (with the benefit of hindsight) would review its original decision to enter this industry. What would its output be in the short run, and in the long run? Is this another illustration of why supply is more elastic in the long run than in the short run?

19-4 "A firm that is facing diminishing returns (rising costs) cannot be facing economies of scale (falling costs)." Do you agree? Explain.

19-5 Explain why economists define costs to include normal profit. If additional profit exists, what does this tell us?

19-6 If a farmer in Kansas provides a statement of his costs to his income tax accountant, are there any opportunity costs he may miss? Explain.

Appendix 19-A

SHORT-RUN PROFIT CALCULATIONS FOR A PERFECTLY COMPETITIVE FIRM

The costs of our hypothetical firm in Table 19-1 are reproduced in the first four columns of Table 19-3. In the other columns we show how this firm will select its output level to maximize profit (or minimize loss) if it is faced with various market prices.

If price is $40, total revenue is shown in column 5 as simply the $40 price times the number of units produced. Then profit is calculated in column 6 from the figures set out in columns 4 and 5. For example, if output is 2 units, profit is $5. (That is, $80 of total revenue in column 5 less $75 of total cost in column 4.) Alternatively, at an output level of 1 unit, profit is −19 (that is, a $19 loss), resulting from $40 of total revenue less $59 of total cost. The result of all such calculations in column 6 confirms our conclusion in Figure 19-2 that an output level of 6 units will maximize profit.

If price is $30, the arrow in column 8 shows that the firm will produce 5 units of output at a zero profit. (Its total cost in column 4 is $150, exactly the same as its total revenue in column 7.) This zero profit level is the best the firm can do. Thus $30 is its break-even price.

If price is $25, the best the firm can do is to minimize its loss at a $20 level by producing 4 units. It does not close down because its $100 total revenue more than covers its $85 of variable cost in column 3, thus leaving it $15 to partly cover its fixed cost. This result is better than shutting down and not covering *any* of its fixed cost.

TABLE 19-3
How a Perfectly Competitive Firm Will Select Its Profit-Maximizing (or Loss-Minimizing) Output in Response to Four Hypothetical Prices

(1)	(2)	(3)	(4)	(5)	(6)	(7)	(8)	(9)	(10)	(11)	(12)
				Best output (shown by arrow) if:							
				Price = $40		Price = $30		Price = $25		Price = $20	
Quan-tity (Q)	Fixed cost (FC)	Vari-able cost (VC)	Total cost (TC = FC + VC)	Total reve-nue (TR)	Profit (+) or loss (−) (TR − TC)	Total reve-nue (TR)	Profit (+) or loss (−) (TR − TC)	Total reve-nue (TR)	Profit (+) or loss (−) (TR − TC)	Total reve-nue (TR)	Profit (+) or loss (−) (TR − TC)
1	35	24	59	40	−19	30	−29	25	−34	20	−39
2	35	40	75	80	5	60	−15	50	−25	40	−35
3	35	60	95	120	25	90	− 5	75	−20	60	−35 ←
4	35	85	120	160	40	120	0	100	−20 ←	80	−40
5	35	115	150	200	50	150	0 ←	125	−25	100	−50
6	35	155	190	240	50† ←	180	−10	150	−40	120	−70
7	35	210	245	280	35ˋ	210	−35	175	−70	140	−105

†Profit is also at a maximum at 5 units of output. In cases like this, we assume that the firm selects the larger output.

If price is $20, the firm has two equally unattractive options. It can produce 3 units at a loss of $35, with its $60 revenue just barely sufficient to cover its $60 of variable costs. Or it can close down completely, in which case it would run the same $35 loss (the fixed cost that it cannot avoid). Twenty dollars is its "shutdown" price; at any price below this, it cannot even cover its variable costs and it will close down.

Appendix 19-B

SUPPLY AND PRODUCERS' SURPLUS FOR AN INDUSTRY

The first three panels of Figure 19-10 display the long-run supply curves of three firms, representing the large number of firms in an industry. The supply of firm A is reproduced from Figure 19-7; this firm is prepared to supply even at a relatively low price. Firm B is different in one important way; it does not supply at all until price rises to P_2 (since its minimum long-run average cost is P_2). Firm C will not supply at all until price rises even higher—to P_3.

Supply for the Industry

At price P_1, the only firm producing will be firm A. Thus total industry supply in the last panel is just arrow f, the quantity supplied by firm A. Price is not high enough to induce firms B and C to produce. But, as price rises, industry supply is suddenly augmented at P_2 as firm B starts to produce and supplies the quantity indicated by arrow g. As price rises above P_2, market supply becomes the sum of the supplies of firms A and B. Finally, at price P_3, firm C is just barely attracted into production, and market supply is shown by the three arrows representing the supplies of all three firms. To sum up: The

FIGURE 19-10 Industry supply as the horizontal sum of individual firms' supplies.
At P_1, market supply is arrow f from firm A, the only firm producing at that low a price. At P_2, A's supply is augmented by arrow g from firm B, since B is barely induced into production. At price P_3, firm C also starts to produce (arrow k). Thus, at any price, market supply S is the horizontal sum of the supplies of all individual firms.

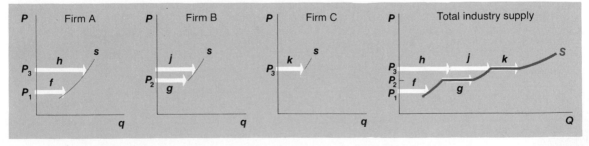

industry supply curve is the heavy line in the last panel, representing the horizontal sum of the supplies of all the individual firms.[4]

Producers' Surplus for the Industry

In Figure 19-11 we show how the producers' surplus for these firms and for the industry increases as price rises from P_1 to P_3. For example, producer's surplus increases for firm A by area 3 (defined exactly as in Figure 19-9). Similarly, the increase in producer's surplus for firm B is shown as the shaded area in the next panel. There is no surplus for firm C, since it has just entered the industry and is barely able to cover its costs. Finally, the last diagram confirms that the increase in producers' surplus for the whole industry may simply be read off the industry supply curve, using the same approach as in Figure 19-9: It is the area between the old price P_1 and the new price P_3, and to the left of industry supply.

A Further Possible Problem in Defining Industry Supply

In certain special circumstances, industry supply may involve an additional complication, not discussed in Figure 19-10. To illustrate, consider the case of a metal-fabricating industry made up of a number of competitive firms located in a small city near Chicago. Suppose that the industry supply is S_1 in Figure 19-12a. (This is exactly the same sort of supply curve as S in the last panel of Figure 19-10, constructed by summing the individual supplies of all firms.) When demand shifts from D_1 to D_2, we would expect equilibrium to shift from E_1 to T, with price rising from P_1 to P'. But this doesn't happen, because as the industry grows, the costs facing each firm fall. This may occur, for example, because the supplier that is shipping unprocessed steel to this industry is now delivering to many more firms and is consequently able to reduce its charges to each.

[4]If there are many potential firms like B, and if the threshold price P_2 that will induce them to enter the industry is close to initial price P_1, long-run supply will be very elastic.

FIGURE 19-11   Increase in producers' surplus for individual firms and for the industry as price rises.
As price rises from P_1 to P_3, the producer's surplus of firm A increases by area 3. Since B doesn't start to produce until price rises to P_2, it earns its surplus (area 4) only because price rises above this. (C has no surplus, since at price P_3, it can barely cover its costs.) The sum of these areas is 5, which is also seen to be the area between P_1 and P_3, and to the left of the industry supply curve S.

(a) **Favorable shift in costs.** Initial equilibrium of S_1 and D_1 is at E_1. With a shift in demand to D_2, the apparent new equilibrium is at T, with price rising from P_1 to P'. However, expansion of this industry results in a downward shift in costs, and supply shifts down to S_2 as a consequence. Equilibrium is thus at E_2, and price falls rather than rises. Long-run supply S^* results from joining all points such as E_1 and E_2.

(b) **Unfavorable shift in costs.** As a result of a shift in demand to D_2, apparent new equilibrium is at T. But in this case, expansion of the industry raises costs and hence shifts supply up to S_2. The new equilibrium is therefore actually at E_2, with price increasing all the way up to P_2. Again S^* results from joining all points such as E_1 and E_2.

FIGURE 19-12 How effects that are external to the firm affect the long-run industry supply.

This reduction in the costs of the metal-fabricating firms shifts supply down in Figure 19-12a from S_1 to S_2, with the new equilibrium at E_2 rather than at T. If we join all points like E_1 and E_2, the result is the supply curve S^* that takes into account all effects; that is, the entry of new firms, the expansion of existing firms, and the cost reductions that occur because the industry is expanding.

Another example is an industry that may initially have little or no skilled labor available. But, as it expands, a skilled labor force may be created, as young people in the course of their education decide to acquire skills in this now prominent, rapidly expanding industry. Firms hiring from such a skilled labor force may find their costs reduced because they no longer have to spend as much on training programs. A final example might be a high-technology industry. The larger the number of firms in an expanding industry, the greater the chance of new technological discoveries that reduce cost.

Two points are worth noting. First, the cost effects that shift S_1 to S_2 are often described as *external to the firm*, but *internal to the industry*. The reason is that they occur, not because of the expansion of one firm, but rather, because of the expansion of the whole industry. Second, if supply S^* is falling, as in panel *a*, increased demand *lowers* price, rather than raising it.

Now let us turn to panel *b* of Figure 19-12, where we show the less favorable possibility—where external effects make the supply curve rise more rapidly than it would otherwise. In this case, costs for each firm (and hence industry supply) shift *up* because the industry is expanding. Suppose there is a pool of skilled personnel that is adequate for an industry producing at the low output level Q_1. What happens if this labor pool does not expand as the industry grows? (Suppose the industry is watchmaking and young people don't want to learn this skill.) As output of this industry increases and firms hire more labor, they must turn to unskilled workers. As a consequence, their labor force is no longer entirely skilled but, instead, becomes a mixture of the skilled and unskilled. As a result, costs rise. Thus, supply shifts from S_1 to S_2, and S^* in this case is steeper than S_1. We conclude that in this case increased demand has raised price by even more than we would otherwise expect.

Such effects that are external to the firm may be important in practice, and will be mentioned again later. But for now, such complications are assumed away.

Appendix 19-C

ALTERNATIVE WAYS OF SHOWING PROFIT

Figure 19-13 presents two equivalent ways of showing the profit of a perfectly competitive firm facing market price P_2.

1. Profit as Producer's Surplus

Before examining profit when price is P_2, suppose that price is initially P_1. Then in panel a we see that the firm's profit is zero. (The best it can do is produce at E_1, its break-even point.)

When price rises from P_1 to P_2, the firm's equilibrium shifts from E_1 to E_2 and its profit (producer's surplus) increases by the blue area between the old and new price and to the left of its supply curve. Since its profit at E_1 was zero, this increase in profit also represents its total profit at its new equilibrium E_2.

2. Profit as the Difference between Price and Average Cost

Panel b illustrates the second way of showing a profit when price is P_2 and the firm is operating at E_2. The price received per unit (that is, average revenue) is P_2. The average cost per unit is C, the height of the AC curve at output level q_2. The difference between the two (P_2C) is the firm's per unit profit. When this is multiplied by the number of units it sells (q_2), the result is its total profit, shown as the shaded area.

FIGURE 19-13 Alternative measures of (economic) profit.

(a) **As producer's surplus.** Total profit equals producer's surplus above the break-even point.

(b) **As a difference between AC and price.** Total profit also equals profit per unit (P_2C) times the number of units (q_2).

chapter 20
The Perfectly Competitive Market

Under perfect competition, the business dodoes, dinosaurs and great ground sloths are in for a bad time—as they should be.

R. H. Bork and W. S. Bowman, Jr.

Chapter 18 described the behavior of buyers and Chapter 19 the behavior of sellers. We can now bring the two sides together, and examine how markets work. In this chapter we continue to assume that markets are perfectly competitive: There are many buyers and many sellers, with no individual buyer or seller having any influence over price. This is the simplest form of market, and it exists in a number of sectors of the United States economy. (For example, many agricultural markets are perfectly competitive.) Furthermore, when we understand how a perfectly competitive market works, we will then be able to study the more complex forms of markets, such as monopoly or oligopoly.

THE PARADOX OF VALUE

With the last two chapters as a background, consider a puzzle that bothered Adam Smith

when he wrote his *Wealth of Nations* in 1776. One of the most valuable commodities is water; we simply cannot do without it. If necessary, we would be prepared to sell everything we own to acquire it. In contrast, we could easily do without things like diamonds or champagne; we would hardly notice the loss. Yet water sells for a low price, while champagne sells for a very high price. Is the world upside down?

The solution to this troublesome puzzle may be found by applying the analysis of the last two chapters. Before reading on, see if you can solve this puzzle for yourself.

To provide the solution, the supply and demand curves for water and champagne are brought together in Figure 20-1. In the case of water, demand and supply result in a low price, P_W. True, demand for water is very great; but it is so plentiful (it can be supplied at such a low price) that we continue to consume more and more of it, until at equi-

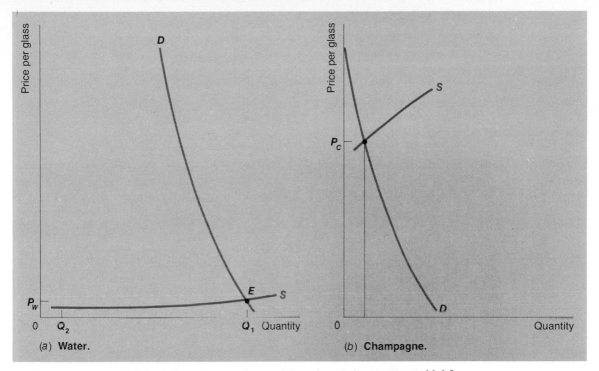

FIGURE 20-1 How can price of water be so low and the price of champagne so high?
In panel *a*, *D* and *S* result in equilibrium at *E*, with the low price P_W and low marginal utility of water $Q_1 E = P_W$. On the other hand, in panel *b*, the high cost of supplying champagne means that its price is at the much higher level P_C and its marginal utility is also at this higher level. If we view *only the last unit consumed*, champagne is more valuable than water. But when we consider *all units consumed*, our conclusion is reversed. For example, the glass of water at Q_2 that keeps someone from dying of thirst has a value beyond measure. (We do not have space to show the height of the demand curve above Q_2.) All units of water, including those at the margin and those inside the margin, provide us with far more utility than all the units of champagne. In this sense, water is far more valuable.

librium *E* we are consuming glasses of water on which we place a low valuation. (Remember that marginal utility is given by the height of the demand curve, and at consumption level Q_1 this is only $Q_1 E$.)

On the other hand, in the case of champagne, demand and supply result in a high price. True, the demand for champagne is not great. But it sells at a high price because its supply is restricted by its high cost of production. Consequently, only the most enthusiastic buyers consume it, and on the last unit they consume, they enjoy a margin-

al utility of P_C. We conclude that the higher price of champagne is telling us that, *at the margin* where we look at only the last units consumed, *champagne is more valuable* (provides a higher marginal utility) *than water*.

But this is obviously only part of the story. The *total* value of water to society is our valuation, not just of the last glass we drink, but of *every* glass we drink, and the ones that keep us from dying of thirst are very valuable indeed. In fact, our valuation of one of those first glasses of water, say at

Q_2, is extremely high; it is given by the height of the demand curve at Q_2, and we don't have enough room at the top of the diagram to show it. But the same is not true of champagne; the utility of the very first glass of champagne *can* be shown in Figure 20-1. The *total value* to society is the utility we receive from *all the units we consume*; in this sense, water is much more valuable than champagne. Thus we conclude that, *overall*, water is more valuable to us than champagne, even though its price is lower (its value *at the margin* is less). The paradox is resolved.

This water/champagne paradox provides a prelude to our discussion of markets because, as we shall see, the question of whether or not markets are working well involves a careful focus on what is happening at the margin. But this water example should help you to remember that there is another important issue: The units *before* we get to the margin may be very important indeed.

The other fundamental message is the very simple one we first encountered in Chapter 4: If we wish to make any sensible statement about price, looking at demand alone is not good enough. (Note how misleading a comparison of only the very large demand for water and the limited demand for champagne would have been.) We must also look at supply. Again, we cannot say it better than Alfred Marshall: We must examine both blades of the scissors.

PERFECT COMPETITION AND ECONOMIC EFFICIENCY

Before examining in detail how the competitive market works, we make two assumptions.

Two Important Assumptions

Thus far, we have made no distinction between the benefit a good provides to those who buy it (its *private benefit*), and the benefit it provides to society as a whole (its

social benefit). Often the two are the same. For example, the benefit to society of beefsteak is the benefit enjoyed by those who buy it and eat it; those who don't eat it, don't enjoy it. But this isn't always the case. For example, the benefit to society of services provided by professional gardeners may include not only the satisfaction enjoyed by those who buy these services, but also the satisfaction of other individuals in the neighborhood. But for now, we assume away this complication; we assume that the purchaser gets all the benefit from the good. Thus:

Assumption 1. Social benefit is the same as private benefit. More precisely, the marginal benefit of a good to society as a whole (which we shall call MU_s) is the same as its marginal benefit (marginal utility) to those who buy it (MU). Either of these can be read off the market demand curve.

$$MU_s = MU \qquad (20\text{-}1)$$

We make a similar assumption about cost:

Assumption 2. Social cost is the same as the private cost of producers. More precisely, the marginal cost of a good to society as a whole (MC_s) is the same as its marginal cost to producers (MC). Either can be read off the supply curve.

$$MC = MC_s \qquad (20\text{-}2)$$

Again this is often true: For example, the cost to society of producing wheat is just the cost incurred by wheat producers. But again there are exceptions: The cost to society of paper may not only be the private cost incurred by the firm producing it, but also the cost to other firms or individuals downstream who suffer if the papermill dumps polluting wastes into a river.

Such exceptions to these two assumptions are clearly important, and will be the focus of our attention in Chapters 23 and 24. Nonetheless, in many cases these assumptions are reasonably true; such cases will be considered in this chapter.

The Idea of Economic Efficiency

In the previous two chapters, we have seen how the individual consumer picks the best quantity to buy, and how the individual producer picks the best quantity to sell. In either case, the activity is expanded until *its marginal cost equals its marginal benefit.* This principle is so fundamental in economics that it is not only the acid test of whether individuals (like consumers and producers) are operating at their best level. It is also the test of whether or not the economy as a whole is operating efficiently. In fact, the idea of efficiency in economics is based on precisely this concept:

Efficiency requires that an activity be run at a level where its marginal cost equals its marginal benefit.[1]

If this condition is not met, a better solution can be found by either expanding or contracting this activity until its marginal cost does equal its marginal benefit. In other words, if this condition is not met, there is an efficiency loss. (This is a loss in *allocative* efficiency. For example, if we are producing to the point where marginal cost has risen above marginal benefit, we should produce less of this item, and transfer resources to the production of some alternative good or service.[2])

Why the Perfectly Competitive Market Is Efficient

Figure 20-2 illustrates how the decisions of many consumers and many producers in a perfectly competitive market lead to an efficient outcome. Note in the middle panel that supply and demand are equal at an equilibrium output of 100 units and a $10 price. At this equilibrium, the quantity purchased by each consumer is shown in the panels on the left, while the quantity sold by each producer is shown in the panels on the right. (In the early pages of Chapter 18, we used just two consumers (Bill Jefferson and Barbara Washington) to represent the many buyers in a competitive market. We follow a similar procedure here, using just three consumers and three producers to represent the very large number of consumers and producers who participate in this market.)

Consider the situation of an individual consumer who extends consumption until the last unit provides a personal benefit (marginal utility) of $10, shown by the vertical bar. For this consumer, marginal cost is the amount paid for one additional unit; that is, the price. By consuming up to the point where marginal utility equals price, the consumer is thus equating his marginal benefit and marginal cost (as we saw in Chapter 18).

For an individual firm in perfect competition, price represents marginal benefit. Since the firm continues to produce up to the point where marginal cost equals price (as we saw in Chapter 19), the firm is also equating its marginal cost and marginal benefit.

Thus, in a competitive market:

Consumers purchase until
$$MU = P \tag{20-3}$$
Firms produce until
$$P = MC \tag{20-4}$$
Therefore,
$$MU = MC \tag{20-5}$$

[1]A more complete statement of economic efficiency will be developed in Box 20-1.

[2]Recall the distinction between *allocative* efficiency and *technical* efficiency in Chapter 1. Throughout the present discussion, we slide over technical efficiency: We assume that good managers avoid outright waste in the productive process by using the lowest-cost methods available. For example, in Table 19-1, 4 units cannot be produced for any less than $120. Thus, our focus in this discussion of efficiency is not on the technical question of eliminating wasted motion in production; rather, it is on the allocative question of whether we are producing the right quantities of various goods.

FIGURE 20-2   Individual consumers and producers in a competitive market.
In panel *b*, market demand *D* reflects the individual demands in panel *a*, while market supply *S* reflects the supplies of individual firms in panel *c*. The perfectly competitive solution, where *S* and *D* intersect, is at a price of $10 and an output of 100 units. The bars in panel *a* show how each consumer extends his purchases until marginal utility MU equals the $10 price; and the bars in panel *c* show how each firm produces to the point where its marginal cost MC is equal to this $10 price. Since each consumer's MU is equal to each producer's MC, any change in production or consumption would result in an efficiency loss.

These three equations are illustrated in the three panels of Figure 20-3. Note especially that benefits are equal to costs at the margin in panel *c*, suggesting an efficient outcome. In fact, all that is necessary to ensure this is to call on the two assumptions stated in the previous section, that private and social evaluations are the same on both the benefit and the cost side. Then it follows from statement (20-5) above that, in a perfectly competitive market,

$$MU_s = MC_s \qquad (20\text{-}6)$$

That is,

Marginal social benefit =
marginal social cost

We do indeed have an efficient outcome from the point of view of society as a whole.

If private and social evaluations are the same on both the benefit and cost side, the perfectly competitive equilibrium is efficient from an overall, social point of view.

This proposition is so important that it is emphasized in Box 20-1.

NONEFFICIENT LEVELS OF OUTPUT

To confirm that, subject to specified conditions, the competitive market is efficient, let us return to the competitive equilibrium of Figure 20-2. Suppose you are a bureaucrat or czar who has arbitrarily ordered that, instead of the equilibrium quantity of 100 units, 20 more units are to be produced and con-

FIGURE 20-3 The competitive market: The equalization of marginal utility and marginal cost. (An elaboration of Figure 20-2b.)

sumed. Try as you like, you cannot avoid a loss on those additional units. On the one hand they must cost more than $10; regardless of the firm (or firms) you select to produce them, that firm will have to move *up* its supply curve to a higher marginal cost level. At the same time, those additional units will be consumed by an individual (or individuals) who values them at less than $10; regardless of whom you may select to consume them, that individual will be moved further *down* his demand curve to the right, to a lower marginal utility. With the cost of each additional unit greater than $10, and the benefit it provides less than $10, there will be a net loss.

We can arrive at exactly the same conclusion using only the market supply and demand curves in the center panel of Figure 20-2, as reproduced in Figure 20-4. Suppose that output is expanded beyond the efficient, competitive level of 100, say to the 140 units shown in panel *a*. To show the efficiency loss that results, consider a typical unit, *c*, of this additional output. Its benefit is shown by the empty bar (the height of the demand curve); but its cost is even larger, as shown by both the empty bar and the solid bar (the height of the supply curve). Thus the net loss on this unit alone is the solid bar, and the sum of all similar losses on all the other excess units of output in the range between 100 and 140 is shown by the red triangle.

On the other hand, suppose that for some reason output is less than the efficient level of 100 units. Let us say it is 60 units, as shown in panel *b* of this diagram. To show the efficiency loss that results, consider one of the units that is no longer produced, say *d.* Since its cost would have been the empty bar (under the supply curve) and its benefit the empty bar *plus* the solid bar (the height of the demand curve), the net benefit to society of producing it would have been the solid bar. Or to put the same point another way, society incurs the loss of this solid bar because this potentially beneficial unit is not

FIGURE 20-4 Inefficient levels of output.

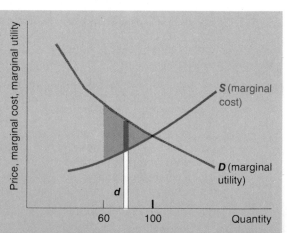

(a) **Too much.** Output is increased beyond the perfectly competitive equilibrium of 100 units (where **S** and **D** intersect) to 140 units. On each of these additional units there is an efficiency loss because marginal cost (the height of the supply curve) exceeds marginal utility (the height of the demand curve). The total efficiency loss from all such units of excess output is the shaded red triangle.

(b) **Too little.** Output is restricted to only 60 units, less than the perfectly competitive level of 100. On each of these 40 units foregone, marginal utility (the height of the demand curve) would have exceeded marginal cost (the height of the supply curve). There is therefore a loss because these potentially beneficial units are not produced, and this loss is shown as the shaded red triangle.

produced. And the sum of all such losses through the range of restricted output from 100 down to 60 is the shaded red triangle. The rent control program described earlier in Box 4-1 provided an illustration of a market in which too little is produced. When the government sets a low price, suppliers provide less than the equilibrium quantity, and the decline in quantity involves an economic loss similar to that shown in Figure 20-4b.

This idea of an efficiency loss (sometimes called a deadweight loss) is so important to the study of microeconomics that you should be sure you have mastered Figure 20-4 before proceeding. In particular, we emphasize:

> An *efficiency loss* occurs whenever there is a move away from the output where marginal benefit is equal to marginal cost.

(A further discussion of efficiency is provided in Box 20-2 and in the appendix to this chapter.)

THE MARKET PRICE AS A SCREENING DEVICE

Every economy must have some rationing device to determine who will consume a scarce good and who will not. In our economy, market price plays that role by acting as a barrier that must be overcome by buyers. In panel *a* of Figure 20-5, we see a competi-

---

BOX 20-2
PARETO AND THE ELIMINATION OF DEADWEIGHT LOSS

With a bit of extra effort and imagination, we can increase our understanding of the important idea of efficiency.

A change that will make one individual better off without hurting anyone else is called a *Pareto-improvement*, after the great Italian economist Vilfredo Pareto who first developed this idea. If we have made all such Pareto-improvements, we arrive at a Pareto-optimum. This is exactly what economists mean by an efficient solution. It means that all deadweight losses have been eliminated, that is, all possible Pareto-improvements have been made.

The idea of a Pareto-improvement can be illustrated in Figure 20-2. Suppose that initially Brandeis has 1 less unit of output than we have shown there (namely, 14 units), while Chan has 1 more (21). A Pareto-improvement is now possible because we can make Chan better off without hurting anyone else (that is, without hurting Brandeis, the only other person who will be involved). Here is how: Let Chan sell that 1 unit to Brandeis for $10. Chan benefits from this transaction. (Because he values his twentieth unit at $10, he values his twenty-first unit—the one he is giving up—at less than $10. So he benefits when he receives $10 for it.) At the same time, Brandeis has not been hurt because he values the unit he receives (his fifteenth) at exactly the same $10 that he pays for it.

This Pareto-improvement is possible because, initially, all producers and consumers did not value their last unit equally. But with this transaction, we have reached the perfectly competitive solution in Figure 20-2, where all consumers and producers *do* value their last unit equally (at $10). That is, the MU for all consumers is equal to the MC for all producers. So any further Pareto-improvement is impossible. Therefore this perfectly competitive solution is Pareto-optimal (that is, efficient).

tive market in which 1,000 units are sold at a $15 price. In panel *b*, we see that this price has blocked out all potential consumers except those prepared to pay at least $15. In panel *c*, we see that this same $15 price also acts as a barrier to potential sellers, blocking out all but the lowest-cost producers. Unenthusiastic buyers and high-cost sellers are turned back, excluded from the market because of one simple criterion—they are unwilling to meet the market price.

FIGURE 20-5   Price as a barrier that screens buyers and sellers in a competitive market.

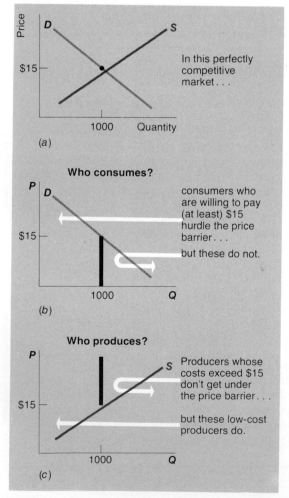

HOW COMPETITIVE MARKETS FOR SEVERAL GOODS ANSWER THE QUESTION, HOW MUCH OF EACH WILL BE PRODUCED?

Figure 20-6 illustrates how a competitive market acts as a mechanism for shifting production from one good (pork) to another (beef) in response to changing consumer tastes. Initially, equilibrium for each good is shown at E in the two panels. Given consumers' initial preferences as reflected in D_B and D_P, this is an efficient allocation of resources; just the right amount of each good is being produced. For example, at the beef output level Q_B, its marginal benefit D_B is equal to its marginal cost S_B.

But now suppose consumer preferences change, with the demand increasing for beef and decreasing for pork. D'_B now reflects the increased utility of beef, while D'_P reflects the decreased utility of pork. Equilibrium in each panel shifts from E to E'. The increase in beef output is the competitive market's response to the increase in beef demand; similarly, the decrease in pork output is the competitive market's response to the decrease in pork demand.

But this new allocation of resources is also efficient, given the new pattern of consumer tastes. (For example, at new beef output Q'_B, its marginal benefit D'_B is equal to its marginal cost S_B.) In shifting resources in this way, the perfectly competitive market has moved the economy from one efficient allocation of resources to another.

PREVIEW: Problems with the Free Market

Thus far, we have provided a very rosy picture of how well free markets work. The examples of inefficient outcomes occurred when the government intervened to overrule the workings of a competitive market: When the government czar dictated output, too much was produced, and when the government set a rent ceiling, too little housing was

442

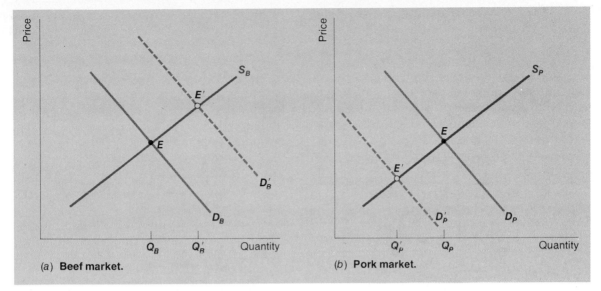

FIGURE 20-6 How a perfectly competitive market allocates resources efficiently to satisfy changing wants.
With demand for beef in panel a at D_B and demand for pork in panel b at D_P, the perfectly competitive market results in efficient output levels Q_B and Q_P. (For example, beef output Q_B is efficient because marginal benefit D_B is equal to marginal cost S_B.) When the utility consumers derive from these two goods changes (for example, when beef demand increases to D'_B, and pork demand decreases to D'_P), the perfectly competitive market results in expanded beef output Q'_B and reduced pork output Q'_P. These are the new efficient levels of output, given the change in consumer tastes.

produced. Indeed, up to this point, the analysis has had a very strong laissez faire message: The government should leave the market alone, its wonders to perform.

But this gives a distorted view of the United States economy. In particular, for the free market to result in an efficient outcome, all four basic conditions listed in Table 20-1 must be met.

But, in practice, these conditions may

TABLE 20-1
How Four Basic Conditions Can Be Violated

	Condition	Will be violated if:	Considered in Chapter(s):
(20-1)	$MU_S = MU$	There are benefits to others than purchasers (neighbors enjoy a well-kept garden, for example)	24
(20-2)	$MC = MC_S$	There is pollution or other costs not borne by producers	23
(20-3)	$MU = P$	A single buyer has some influence over price (as may occur if there are only a few buyers)	28
(20-4)	$P = MC$	A single seller has some influence over price (as may occur if there are only a few sellers)	21, 22

443

be violated. (Table 20-1 shows the chapters that deal with cases where the conditions are violated.) When they are violated the economy, left alone, will operate inefficiently. In this case, government intervention may make the economy work *more* efficiently, not less. Furthermore, even when all four conditions are met, the outcome will not necessarily be quite as good as the previous pages suggest, as we shall now see.

A RESERVATION ABOUT THE PERFECTLY COMPETITIVE SOLUTION: It Depends on the Distribution of Income

Returning to Figure 20-2, suppose that Abel has a higher income than Brandeis, and this is the reason why he has the greater demand

for this good. (Remember, demand depends both on desire for the product *and* ability to pay.) In Figure 20-7 we reproduce Figure 20-2, making only one single change: We suppose that the incomes of Abel and Brandeis are reversed. Brandeis now has a high income and hence a high demand, while Abel now has a low income and hence a low demand, as shown in the white section. (Since nothing else need change,[3] the rest of Figure 20-7 has a shaded background.) In this diagram, just as in Figure 20-2, a perfectly competitive market yields an efficient solution. But it is a quite different solution. There is no way that economists can judge which of the two solutions is better. All we can say is that both are efficient.

Abel and Brandeis, of course, will each have a clear opinion on which is better: Abel

[3]Market price need not be exactly the same $10 as in Figure 20-2; but this is an unimportant detail that does not affect the argument.

FIGURE 20-7 Another efficient, perfectly competitive solution.
This figure is similar to Figure 20-2, except that Brandeis is now rich and Abel is poor. Consequently, Brandeis now has the greater demand and accordingly consumes the greater quantity (60 units). This solution results from perfect competition and is therefore efficient, just like the one in Figure 20-2. Which is better? The individuals concerned will have a strong view about this, with Abel preferring Figure 20-2 and Brandeis preferring Figure 20-7. But an economist examining this from the point of view of society as a whole cannot judge, because it is impossible to compare Brandeis' utility gain in moving from Figure 20-2 to Figure 20-7 with Abel's utility loss.

prefers Figure 20-2, where he gets most of this good (65 units), while Brandeis will prefer Figure 20-7, where *he* gets the lion's share. But from the overall point of view of society as a whole, there is no way to judge. True, if we could meter the heads of these two individuals and thus be able to say that, in moving from Figure 20-2 to Figure 20-7, Brandeis's utility gain exceeds Abel's utility loss, we might judge the pattern in Figure 20-7 superior. But this we cannot do, since *there is no known way of comparing the utility of one person with the utility of someone else.*

To sum up: For each possible distribution of income, there is a different perfectly competitive solution. Each of these solutions is efficient; but we cannot demonstrate that one is better than the rest. The question of how income should be distributed is one that economists alone cannot answer (although we will throw more light on it in Chapter 31).

*ANOTHER RESERVATION: When a Competitive Market Provides Misleading Signals

We have now dealt with the basic features of perfectly competitive markets. But there are a number of additional complications. For example, prices act as signals to which both consumers and producers react; but what happens if producers get the wrong message?

To illustrate this problem, recall from Figure 17-7 how a small shift in the supply of an agricultural product (perhaps because of crop failure or disease in a herd) will result in a substantial change in price. This instability may be compounded by the fact that there is typically a time lag (delay) between the decision to produce and the eventual delivery of the finished good to market. For example, wheat must be planted

in the fall or spring for harvest in the summer; and the decision to breed cattle is often made several years before beef is delivered to market.

In this situation, an initial disturbance may set off a recurring cycle of price fluctuations, with price high one year, low the next, high the next, and so on. The idea is a simple one (and can be understood without necessarily consulting its detailed exposition in Box 20-3). Suppose that because of some initial disturbance, the price of hogs is unusually high. As a consequence, farmers expand hog production. When these hogs come to market at a later date, the result will be an oversupply, and the price will fall. In turn, the depressed price will induce farmers to switch out of hogs, and this shift will lead in the next period to a shortage, raising the price up again to an abnormally high level. Thus the cycle continues as long as producers misread the market price signals and erroneously use today's price in making their production decisions. Even though this market is perfectly competitive, it follows a cyclical pattern and therefore does not work well. (The losses that result from this cyclical pattern are detailed in the next section.)

*THE ROLE OF SPECULATION IN REDUCING PRICE INSTABILITY

There are several ways in which the cyclical pattern may be broken. First, after perhaps two or three price changes, farmers may recognize what is happening and accordingly stop making the erroneous assumption that today's price provides a good prediction of tomorrow's price. (Indeed, theoreticians who argue that there may be severe, continuing "cobweb" fluctuations have been criticized on the ground that they assume that farmers never learn.) The other possibility is that someone else recognizes this cobweb

*Note to instructors: In a short course, the rest of this chapter may be omitted without loss of continuity.

BOX 20-3
THE COBWEB CYCLE

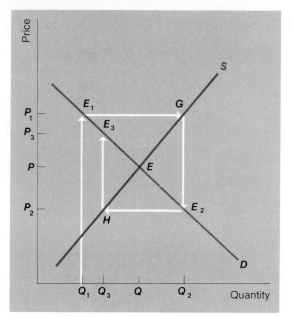

Suppose that equilibrium has traditionally been at E, where long-run supply S and demand D intersect. If there is no shock to this system, price will continue at P, with production at Q. But now suppose that in the initial period some disturbance (perhaps a disease) reduces the total number of hogs coming onto the market to Q_1. Also suppose that no more hogs can be produced for a year, so that the immediate supply is inelastic at quantity Q_1. In other words, immediate supply can be visualized as the tall arrow running vertically up from Q_1 and intersecting demand at the equilibrium point E_1. As a result, price is at the high level P_1.

In this initial year, farmers must decide on how many hogs to produce for the next year. Facing the very favorable price P_1, they respond by moving to point G on their supply curve, thus producing quantity Q_2. But when this large quantity comes on the market in the second year, the completely inelastic immediate supply (shown by the arrow pointing down toward Q_2) now results in a new equilibrium E_2, with low price P_2.

Of course, in this second year, farmers must decide what to produce for the third year. Facing low price P_2, they respond by selecting point H on their supply curve. But when this small quantity Q_3 is eventually produced and comes on the market in the third year, it results in an equilibrium at E_3, with price at the relatively high level P_3. Price, production, and consumption continue to bounce back and forth until the system again settles down to a long-run equilibrium at E.

But things could conceivably be even worse. We leave you to confirm (Problem 20-8) that if supply S is elastic enough (and/or demand D is inelastic enough), the cycle will not converge to E, but instead will "explode," with price fluctuations becoming larger and larger.

The cobweb example provides a good illustration of a *dynamic problem*; that is, a problem in which *time must explicitly be taken into account*. Specifically, supply has a dynamic (time) element, since next year's supply depends on this year's price.

pattern and takes action that is not only personally profitable, but that also modifies the cycle and thus benefits society as a whole.

Suppose that price in a hog cycle has risen in the first year and fallen in the second year. Now a bright individual suddenly realizes, "I've seen this happen before. This is that hog cycle again. Because price is low this year, a lot of farmers will be getting out of pork, and the price will be going up next year. I'm going to buy some of this year's cheap pork, refrigerate it, and sell it next year."

This will be a profitable venture (if the costs of storage, etc., are not too high), since the individual has discovered a way of putting into practice the advice any stockbroker will give: Buy cheap and sell dear. But this action will not only benefit the purchaser; it will also moderate the cycle. Why? The purchase of pork when it is cheap creates an additional demand that prevents its price from falling quite so far. And when pork is sold later at a high price, the additional supply prevents the price from rising quite so far. Thus the cycle is moderated by *speculation.*

> *Speculation* involves the purchase of an item in the hope of making a profit from a rise in its price (or the sale of an item in the expectation that its price will fall).

Basically, the case for speculation is as simple as that. But to nail it down more precisely, consider how the stabilization of price is beneficial from the point of view of society as a whole. Specifically, imagine the instance where not one, but many, speculators store pork in year 2 when price is low for sale in year 3 when it is high. Moreover, for simplicity, assume initially that there are no storage costs, nor any interest charges on borrowed money.

Panel a of Figure 20-8 shows the demand curve for pork, reproduced from Box 20-3. Year 2 is illustrated: In the absence of speculation, equilibrium is at E_2, with low price P_2 and high output Q_2. Panel b shows year 3, with the same demand curve, but with lower production Q_3; in the absence of speculation, equilibrium is at E_3, and the price is a high P_3. Now consider the behavior of speculators. They buy when the price is low in year 2, in order to sell in year 3 when the price is high. Specifically, they withdraw units from the market in year 2, store them, and thus increase the supply coming onto the market in year 3. This raises price in year 2 and lowers it in year 3. This speculation will continue until it is no longer profitable; in other words, to the point where prices are equalized over time ($P'_2 = P'_3$) and the cyclical swing has been eliminated.[4] Why? Because, as long as the price is lower in year 2 than in year 3, some speculator will have an incentive to buy pork in year 2 for resale in year 3. The quantity that speculators transfer from year 2 to year 3 is shown by the arrow below each panel.

Notice how beneficial price stabilization has been. True, reduced consumption in year 2 has reduced utility then, as shown by the red area in panel a; but there has been an even greater blue increase in utility in panel b, because of the increase in consumption in year 3. The reason for this difference is that units are being withdrawn from a "relatively sated" public in year 2 and provided to a "relatively starved" public in year 3. The difference between these two areas is a net benefit from speculation.

Of course, if this is a benefit that results from eliminating a cycle, it is also a loss from having a cycle rather than stable prices in the first place. This then provides a

---

[4]For this conclusion to hold firmly, speculators must be able to foresee the next year's price exactly. In the real world, with its uncertainties, speculation will not eliminate price swings completely.

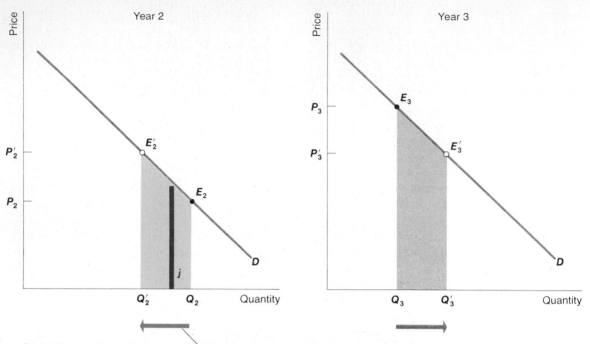

Speculation involves withdrawing this amount from market in year 2 . . . and transferring it to year 3

FIGURE 20-8   How speculation may have the beneficial effect of stabilizing price.
Without speculation, equilibrium in year 2 is at E_2 and in year 3 at E_3. (This particular example of fluctuating price is drawn from the cobweb cycle in Box 20-3, but it could equally well have been the result of other influences, such as varying weather conditions.) Speculation involves reducing the supply on the market in year 2 from Q_2 to Q'_2 (as shown by the arrow) and transferring it to year 3, thus increasing the supply then by this same amount, from Q_3 to Q'_3. This raises price in year 2 and lowers it in year 3 until, in theory, the two are equal. (That is, until $P'_2 = P'_3$.) A typical unit of reduced consumption in year 2 will reduce utility by bar j in panel a; and the total loss from all such units of reduced consumption is the total red area. Similarly, the gain from increased consumption in year 3 is the blue area. The difference in these two areas is the beneficial effect of speculation.

second major reservation about perfectly competitive markets: A failure of the timing and signaling mechanism may lead to price instability, as in the cobweb example. And if this is not ironed out by speculators, the free movement in price allowed by a perfectly competitive market may become a disadvantage—even though it is a great advantage in other circumstances (for example, in Figure 20-6).

So far, speculators emerge from this discussion very much the heroes of the piece, but only because we have assumed that they predict the future correctly. But, of course, they may guess wrong, and if they do, their actions will result in a loss both to

themselves and to society. For example, if they store today on the expectation that price will be higher next year, but if in fact price turns out to be lower instead, they incur an obvious loss themselves. Moreover, from the viewpoint of society as a whole there is also a loss, because their sales next year will further depress the price then, making the fluctuation worse. Thus, their individual success and their potential benefit to society depend on their ability to predict the future.

Finally, speculators can also provide a benefit when price fluctuations are due to other causes. Our example has involved a cobweb cycle, but a similar gain could be achieved if speculation irons out price fluctuations that result from changing weather conditions.[5]

*GOVERNMENT AGRICULTURAL PRICE SUPPORTS

1. To Stabilize Price and Consumption

> **And let them gather all the food of those good years that come, and lay up corn under the hand of Pharaoh, and let them keep food in the cities.**
>
> **And that food shall be for store to the land against the seven years of famine, which shall be in the land of Egypt; that the land perish not through the famine.** Genesis 41:35–36

One of the arguments in favor of the government's providing a guaranteed price for wheat and other agricultural goods is that this will do precisely what speculators do—iron out fluctuations in price and quantity consumed. For example, suppose that the government guarantees price at a moderate, average level. Then, in bumper-crop years when the market price falls below this guaranteed level, farmers will sell their wheat to the government, thereby moderating the drop in market price. Moreover, the government will then be able to sell these accumulated stocks of wheat to the public during lean years, thus moderating the price increase that occurs then.

This idea of an "ever-normal granary" has had a renewed appeal recently because of international developments. It is not only a United States crop failure that can send our food prices shooting skyward. A crop failure in some other part of the world can do the same thing. Thus, the rapidly rising food prices of the early 1970s were a result of crop failures in the Soviet Union and elsewhere, and the increases in the government-guaranteed price which fol-

lowed were designed partly to rebuild United States stocks to cover such contingencies. The objective was to accumulate buffer stocks not only to stabilize price, but also to prevent starvation in foreign countries that might encounter crop failures in the future.

Although this provides a case for government price guarantees, difficult questions remain. For example: Why can't private speculators do the job of stabilizing price? If they can see a future shortage developing, why wouldn't they buy cheap now in order to sell dear in the future period of scarcity, and in the process moderate the price fluctuation?

To some degree, the question of who can do the better job of stabilizing price—private speculators or the government—reduces to the question of who can better predict future price. It is not clear why we should expect people in the government to be better forecasters, since they are good at winning elections, whereas private speculators are good at predicting future price. (Speculators who are poor at predicting lose money and go into some other business.) On the other hand, a government price guarantee does something that private speculators cannot do: It provides farmers at planting time with a guarantee of the price they will eventually receive.[6] And, provided this price is set at about the right level (admittedly, a tall order), this will be a more effective way of inducing the right production response from farmers. Furthermore, the government has an advantage not open to private speculators: access to large funds at a low interest rate.

However, the biggest problem with government price supports is that they frequently involve another objective, above and beyond just stabilizing price, as we shall see.

---

[5]To make this analysis more realistic, we should recognize that there are storage and interest costs, along with a profit margin for speculators to compensate them not only for their time and effort, but also for the risk they face. (Remember: The speculator who guesses wrong takes a big loss.) This means that speculation will cease before P'_2 and P'_3 are equated in Figure 20-8, with a gap remaining between these two prices sufficient to cover these items. Although this would modify the analysis, it would not change the principal conclusions.

[6]Remember, private speculators only moderate price; they do not guarantee it in advance.

2. To Raise Average Price

To isolate one issue at a time, assume that the problem of price instability does not exist; food is being produced at an efficient level of output, and the government has already stored away an ever-normal granary to cover the risk of bad crops here or abroad. In these circumstances, suppose the government introduces a price guarantee designed to raise, rather than stabilize, farm price (and hence farm income). Farmers respond to a high guaranteed price by producing more and the government must buy up the surplus. There are two major effects. First, farm output has been increased beyond its initial perfectly competitive (and efficient) level, so that there is an efficiency loss. At the same time, there is also a large transfer of income. This transfer goes to farmers (who sell more at a higher price). It is paid for by consumers (who pay a higher price for food) and taxpayers (who have to pay for the surplus stocks the government buys up).[7]

How, then, does one defend the idea of a price guarantee designed to raise farm income? One argument is that it will help cure farm poverty. But a price guarantee that subsidizes a bushel of wheat, rather than a poor farmer, is a very ineffective way of curing poverty, since it subsidizes the wealthy high-volume farmer much more than the poor low-volume farmer. The problem is not just that wealthy farmers get more income from the government than poor farmers; they often get a much larger *proportion* of their income from government

payments.[8] This raises the question: Wouldn't it be far better to subsidize the poor farmer directly with some sort of income supplement (taking care to design it, like the negative income tax in Chapter 32, so that it would not destroy the incentive to work)?

We conclude that in analyzing government farm policies, the reason for a price guarantee is a crucial issue. If the price guarantee is designed only to stabilize price by accumulating an ever-normal granary, then a substantial argument can be made in its favor. But if, in addition, it is designed to raise the average level of farm prices, it becomes much more difficult to justify. Moreover, this issue is complicated by the fact that the real objective of price supports is often to raise price, but they are promoted on the ground that they would stabilize price. How, then, does one determine which objective is being pursued? A simple answer seems to be: If the accumulated surplus does not grow beyond the amount which may be needed to cover future crop failures, the policy may be judged as stabilizing and efficient. But if the surplus grows beyond this level (or, equivalently, has to be kept down to this level by contrived disposal programs or by limits on production), price supports have been raising farm income. And if higher farm income is judged a desirable objective, we should search for more appropriate policies—policies that would more successfully cure farm poverty, without further enriching the already affluent large farmer.

---

[7]The government has taken steps to reduce the cost to consumers by introducing a two-price system. Thus, in 1977, the government undertook to support the market price at $2.25, and at the same time undertook to pay farmers directly the amount needed to bring their total return up to the target price of $2.90. By making such direct payments, the government provided farmers with $2.90 per bushel, while allowing the price to users to fall below that level.

[8]It has been estimated that in 1968, farmers with total sales of over $100,000 had an average income of $39,578, of which $8,867 (or 22.4 percent) was received in direct payments from the government. Farmers with sales between $2,500 and $5,000 had an average income of $6,832 (since many of the smallest farmers also had non-farm sources of income), with only $588 (that is, 8.6 percent) coming from direct government payments. [Source: Luther G. Tweeten, "Agricultural Policy," in American Enterprise Institute, *Food and Agricultural Policy* (Washington: AEI, 1977), p. 52.]

In order to channel government assistance to the less affluent farmers, 1973 legislation limited the payments to any single farmer to $20,000 per year.

Key Points

1. The efficient level of output from the point of view of society as a whole is where marginal social cost is equal to marginal social benefit.

2. If social costs are the same as private costs (and social benefits the same as private benefits), a perfectly competitive market will generally result in an efficient level of output. Thus, perfect competition eliminates deadweight loss from the economy; it allocates resources efficiently to satisfy human wants.

3. However, the wants that will be satisfied depend on how income is distributed. For each distribution of income, there is a different perfectly competitive result. And economics cannot clearly tell us which one is best.

*4. Another problem with a perfectly competitive market is that·its price signals may be misread, and price may fluctuate as a result. An example is the hog cycle that occurs if producers erroneously assume that price this year is a good indication of what price will be next year.

*5. Private speculation or government price guarantees may be beneficial in a perfectly competitive market if they reduce price fluctuations.

*6. If price supports are designed to raise (rather than stabilize) price, they become much more difficult to justify. They introduce inefficiency into the system, and they are a high-cost, relatively ineffective way of curing farm poverty.

Key Concepts

price reflects marginal, not total, value
economic efficiency
private versus social benefit
private versus social cost
why perfect competition is efficient
efficiency loss
how price rations scarce goods
how price changes production patterns
efficiency and the distribution of income

when market signals mislead
*cobweb cycle
*dynamic problems
*speculation
*when speculation is efficient, when not
*agricultural price guarantees
*when guarantees are efficient, when not
*how guarantees transfer income

Problems

20-1 Apply the analysis of this chapter to show the triangular efficiency loss from rent control. (Refer back to Box 4-1.)

20-2 Critically evaluate: "Economists know the price of everything, but the value of nothing. They tell us that gold has a higher price than food. But we know that food has the higher value, because without it we would starve."

20-3 What condition must be met if resources are to be efficiently allocated? Explain why inefficiency occurs if this condition is not fulfilled.

*Drawn from optional, starred sections of this chapter.

20-4 "A perfectly competitive price that all buyers and sellers take as given is the key link in orchestrating production and consumption in an efficient way." Do you agree? If so, illustrate.

20-5 "Why study perfect competition? There are few goods produced in this sort of a market." Comment.

20-6 According to Adam Smith, the pursuit of private gain leads to public benefit. Under what circumstances is this not true?

*20-7 Under perfect competition, suppose that consumer demand shifts from oranges to apples. What happens to output of these two goods? Do these changed output levels represent an efficient allocation of resources? Why? Diagrammatically show the efficiency losses that would occur if outputs did not change in response to demand.

*20-8 Redraw the cobweb diagram in Box 20-3, starting with these two changes: make S more elastic, and locate E_1 much closer to E. Does the resulting cycle settle down to E? How do you compare your result with Box 20-3?

*20-9 What are some of the pros and cons of government-guaranteed prices for farmers?

*20-10 If speculators guess wrong and buy a good in year 1 to sell in year 2 when it is even more plentiful and cheap, would their activities result in an efficiency gain or loss? Illustrate with a diagram. Would speculators realize a profit or loss?

Appendix

ILLUSTRATING THE EFFICIENCY OF PERFECT COMPETITION WITH INDIFFERENCE CURVES[9]

This chapter has shown that perfect competition will result in efficiency in a simple economy in which there is no pollution or any other externality. To illustrate this point, demand and supply curves were used (Figure 20-3). We now show the same conclusion in an alternative way, using indifference curves (explained in Appendix 18-A) and the production possibilities curve (introduced in Chapter 2).

We saw in Appendix 18-A how the household picks its best position by choosing the point where the budget line is tangent to the highest attainable indifference curve. A similar argument applies to producers, as illustrated in Figure 20-9. Suppose that producers are originally at point A, making 500 units of clothing and 1,300 units of food. Suppose also that the prices of food and clothing are both $10 per unit. Then the money income of the producers totals $18,000 (= $10×500 + $10×1,300). The income or budget line of the producers will be the line L_1. As we saw in Appendix 18-A, the slope of this line reflects the relative prices of food and clothing.

Note that point A is not the highest possible income that producers can make when they face prices of $10 per unit for both food and clothing. By moving to point E, they can produce 1,000 units of each good, making a total income of $20,000, as represented by income line L_2. This is the best they can do.

[9]This appendix requires Appendix 18-A as a background.

FIGURE 20-9 How producers maximize their incomes.
The line representing producers' income goes through the point at which production is taking place. Its slope depends on the relative prices of the two goods. Producers attain the highest income line by producing where the slope of the production possibilities curve is the same as the slope of the income line; that is, at the point of tangency, E.

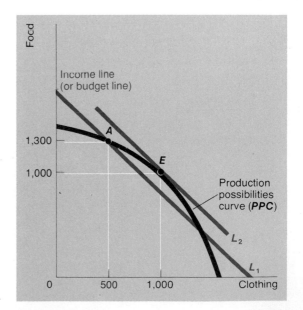

Now let's put this theory of producer behavior in Figure 20-9 together with our earlier theory of consumer behavior in Figure 18-9. In a perfectly competitive economy, in which every producer and every consumer takes prices as given, equilibrium is at E in Figure 20-10. On the one hand, producers maximize their income by moving along the production possibilities curve to the point (E) of tangency with the highest attainable income line L. At the same time, consumers maximize their utility by also moving to point E—because this is where the income (budget) line L is tangent to the highest attainable indifference curve (U_2). Thus the community as a whole achieves an efficient solution, because it is producing at the point on its production possibilities curve that generates the highest attainable level of utility (U_2). This, then, is our alternative illustration of the proposition established in Chapter 20: A competitive economy leads to an efficient solution.[10]

*[10]There must be a slight catch somewhere. This analysis suggests that there is a single (unique) efficient solution (at E)—and we already know from Chapter 20 that there is not. (For each income distribution there is a different efficient solution.) This puzzle is resolved by noting that in Figure 20-10 we draw indifference curves for the *community as a whole*, rather than for an individual household (as in Figure 18-8). And there are severe problems involved in defining such a community indifference system: There is no simple way of "adding up" the preferences of all the individuals in the nation. To illustrate, consider the simple, extreme case of a two-person economy: If I have all the income, then my preferences are the ones that count; if you have all the income, then it is your preferences that count. In other words, a community's preferences depend on who has the income. This means that there is no unique community indifference system. Nor, as a consequence, is there any unique efficient equilibrium; the equilibrium depends on how the nation's income is distributed.

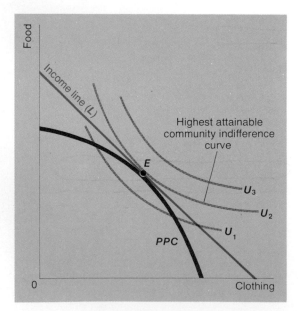

FIGURE 20-10 The competitive equilibrium.
The competitive equilibrium occurs at E. Producers pick the point where the PPC is tangent to the highest attainable income line. Consumers pick the point where the income line is tangent to the highest attainable indifference curve. At this point, E, the production possibilities curve and the indifferent curve are tangent. The maximum level of utility U_2 is achieved, given the productive capacity of the economy (shown by the PPC).

We emphasize again that this efficient solution results from producers on the one hand and consumers on the other responding independently to the competitive market prices reflected in the slope of the income line L.[11] This in turn raises the final, key question: Why does the competitive market generate the relative prices shown by L? To answer this question, suppose that initially the relative prices are those shown by line L_1 in Figure 20-11. (The lower slope of L_1 reflects a lower relative price of clothing.) Facing these relative prices, producers respond by producing at A, the point that maximizes their incomes. But, as consumers, people try to consume at B, the point of tangency between the income line and indifference curve U_3. However, they are in fact unable to reach point B, since the economy is incapable of producing the combination of food and clothing represented by this point. As a consequence, markets are out of equilibrium. The quantity of clothing demanded by consumers (C_B) exceeds the quantity supplied by producers (C_A); the price of clothing consequently rises. At the same time, the quantity of food demanded (F_B) is less than the quantity supplied (F_A); the price of food falls. As the relative prices of food and clothing change, the income line moves from L_1 toward L, and producers respond by moving from A toward E. This movement continues until the income line becomes L; it is only then that demand and supply are brought into equilibrium, at point E. Thus, the equilibrium prices are indeed those reflected in line L.

*[11]To illustrate what can go wrong if producers do not act as perfect competitors, suppose that the producers of clothing form a monopoly; then they will restrict the supply of clothing. In other words, the economy moves to the left of E in Figure 20-10, and it is no longer possible to reach indifference curve U_2. Consequently, the nation's level of satisfaction falls.

FIGURE 20-11 How markets adjust from an initial point of disequilibrium.
If the relative price of clothing is originally below its equilibrium (that is, prices are those reflected in L_1 rather than L), producers will want to produce at A, and consumers will want to consume at B. As a result, there will be a shortage of clothing ($C_B - C_A$) and a surplus of food ($F_A - F_B$). Consequently, the relative price of clothing will rise until prices fully adjust to their equilibrium, shown by the slope of the income line L.

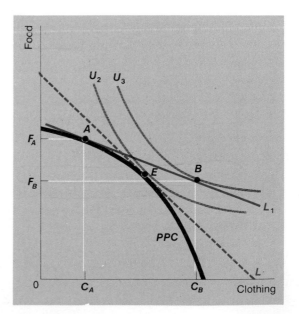

chapter 21
Monopoly

The chief agency on which defenders of the market economy have relied to keep self-interest within useful bounds and prevent it from becoming oppressive is the system of free competition. Without it free exchange between unequals could still be a tyranny and its freedom a sham.

John Maurice Clark

In some markets, perfect competition prevails. There are many buyers and many sellers, with none affecting price. At the other end of the spectrum, other markets are monopolies, each having only one seller. (The Greek word *monos* means "single," and *polein* means "to sell.")

WHY DOES MONOPOLY ARISE?

There are four important reasons why there may be only one firm selling a good:

1. *Control over an Input or Technique.* A firm may control something essential that no other firm can acquire. One example is the ownership of a necessary resource; an oft-cited illustration was Alcoa's control over bauxite supplies that allowed it essentially to monopolize the sale of aluminum before World War II. Another example is the ownership of a patent, which allows the inventor exclusive control over a new prod-

uct or process for a period of 17 years, (Patents are designed to encourage expenditure on research by allowing the inventor to reap a substantial reward.) When an existing firm owns a patent or exclusive control over a resource, new firms might like to enter the industry; but since they cannot, the industry remains monopolized.

2. *Legal Monopoly.* It is sometimes illegal for more than one company to sell a product. Examples include the U.S. Postal Service: It is illegal for a company to set up in competition with the post office in the delivery of letters (but not in the delivery of packages). Similarly, private bus companies are sometimes given the exclusive right to service a community.

3. *Natural Monopoly.* A natural monopoly develops not because it is guaranteed by law, but, instead, because it is the natural result of special cost conditions. An example is American Telephone and Telegraph

456

(AT&T). Because of the cost advantage that monopolist AT&T enjoys, no other firm would want to install telephone lines in a community already serviced by AT&T. Since this is one of the most interesting forms of monopoly from an economic point of view, it is the one we shall concentrate on in this chapter.

4. *Collusive Monopoly.* Several producers may get together to form a single, unified marketing operation in order to charge a higher price. (This form of monopoly is introduced at the end of this chapter, and is discussed in detail in Chapter 22.)

The prevalence of monopoly depends in part on how broadly a market is defined. In the early 1970s, Boeing had a temporary monopoly of the jumbo jet market, but not of the broader market for airliners; at that time the 747 still had no competition from other jumbo jets, but it did have to compete with smaller aircraft. (Even in jumbo jets, Boeing's monopoly was short-lived, as other manufacturers developed somewhat similar planes.) The telephone company has a monopoly of telephone service, but not of the broader market for communications where it must compete with the mails and the telegraph company. Indeed, in the very broadest sense, every producer competes with every other producer for the consumer's dollar. If you buy a new hi-fi, you may cut down on long-distance telephone calls to help pay for it. Thus, in a very broad sense, the telephone company competes even with the producer of hi-fi equipment.

But, if markets are defined in a reasonably limited way, significant areas of monopoly exist—in telephones, water, local gas service, and local electrical service, to name a few. Nonetheless, the importance of monopoly should not be overstated. *Oligopoly,* where the industry is dominated by only a few sellers, is much more important in the United States economy. Indeed, some of the largest sectors of our economy are oligopolies, including industries such as automobiles, computers, aircraft, heavy construction equipment, large electrical generators, and steel. In spite of the importance of oligopoly, it is appropriate to consider monopoly first. Monopoly is the simpler form, and it provides a necessary background for the study of oligopoly.

NATURAL MONOPOLY: The Importance of Cost Conditions

Figure 21-1 illustrates how important cost conditions may be in determining the number of producers in a market. The two panels show two products with identical demands, but with different costs facing an individual producer.

In the industry shown in panel *a*, a typical firm's long-run average cost curve (AC) reaches a minimum at only 10 units of output, a very small portion of the total market. As a consequence, total market demand cannot be satisfied by one firm operating at its minimum cost. Instead, the least costly way of servicing this market is with many firms, and it is no surprise that perfect competition results.

In panel *b*, AC has the same minimum value of $100, but the big difference is the much larger volume of output necessary for a firm to achieve this low cost. Unlike panel *a* where AC reaches a minimum and turns up at a very small volume, in panel *b* AC continues to drift down. The least expensive way of servicing the market is with one firm, and the stage is set for monopoly. By definition:

> *Natural monopoly* occurs when the average cost of a single firm falls over such an extended range that one firm can produce the total quantity sold at a lower average cost than could two or more firms.

What makes a natural monopoly? Why might costs continue to fall through much or all of the range needed to satisfy market demand? The answer is: high fixed cost

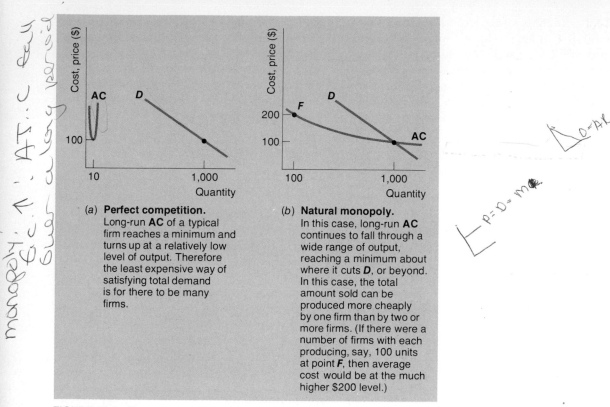

(a) **Perfect competition.**
Long-run **AC** of a typical firm reaches a minimum and turns up at a relatively low level of output. Therefore the least expensive way of satisfying total demand is for there to be many firms.

(b) **Natural monopoly.**
In this case, long-run **AC** continues to fall through a wide range of output, reaching a minimum about where it cuts **D**, or beyond. In this case, the total amount sold can be produced more cheaply by one firm than by two or more firms. (If there were a number of firms with each producing, say, 100 units at point **F**, then average cost would be at the much higher $200 level.)

FIGURE 21-1 How cost conditions can lead to natural monopoly.

(overhead). Local telephone, electric, water, and gas services are all examples of natural monopoly, because the fixed cost in running telephone or electric wires, or in laying water and gas pipes, is very high relative to variable cost. (To illustrate what happens when fixed costs dominate, set fixed cost in Table 19-1 at $1,000, rather than at just $35, and recalculate average cost. Notice how AC continues to fall as this $1,000 of fixed overhead is spread over a larger and larger number of units of output.)

To verify that panel *b* tends to result in monopoly, suppose that initially a few firms are each producing 100 units at point *F*. This low volume will result in a high average cost ($200) for each firm. An aggressive firm will discover that by increasing its output, it can lower its cost, and hence offer its product at a lower price than its competi-

tors. Thus it can squeeze them out of business. In such a case of natural monopoly, competition tends to drive all firms but one out of the market.

The obvious attraction to the consumer of such price competition during the period in which the industry is being "shaken down" and the number of firms reduced is likely to disappear once the successful firm has eliminated all its competitors and has emerged as a monopoly. As the only remaining supplier, it will have considerable control over the price. Once it has eliminated its competition and has indicated that it will greet any new firms entering this industry with whatever price cutting is necessary to drive them into bankruptcy, it can raise the price with little fear of present or future competition. Consumers of this product are at the mercy of this firm, except insofar as they are prepared to restrict their purchases. An important question therefore is this: How high will the monopoly set the price? But before answering this question, we need to make one more important distinction between perfect competition and monopoly.

THE DIFFERENCE IN THE DEMAND FACING A PERFECT COMPETITOR AND A MONOPOLIST

The perfect competitor in panel *a* of Figure 21-2 must take the market price as given. For example, an individual farmer never thinks of asking 1 cent a bushel more for his wheat, because he knows he wouldn't get it; and he will never offer to sell for 1 cent less, since he can sell all his wheat for the going market price. *The farmer has no "market power." As an individual producer among many, he is unable, by reducing the quantity he supplies, to have any noticeable influence on price.* To confirm this statement, suppose market price is $2, as determined by market supply and demand in panel *b*. The farmer's response to this price in panel *a* is to supply 2,000 units. Now suppose he tries supplying only half that quantity; that is, 1,000 units. This move will reduce market supply in panel *b*, shifting *S* to the left, but by such a small amount (1,000 bushels) that this action won't even be noticed in the market. (If you try to draw the new supply curve, you will find you are just drawing a line over the old supply *S*.) Consequently, market price in panel *b* remains the same. The farmer has tried to raise the price, but this attempt to exercise market power has failed miserably. As an individual seller, he has no influence whatsoever over price, and this is reflected in the completely elastic demand curve he faces in panel *a*.

Now consider the monopoly, shown in panels *c* and *d* of Figure 21-2. In panel *d*, total market demand is exactly the same as in the competitive case above. The only difference is that this market demand is now being satisfied by a single monopoly firm; in other words, *the demand facing the individual firm in panel c is exactly the same as the total market demand in panel d.*

As a result, the monopolist can indeed affect price. To confirm this, suppose that the monopoly firm is initially selling at a $2 price. Because it is the only seller, the firm alone is supplying all the 2 million units sold (shown at point *A* in either panel *c* or panel *d*). Now suppose the company tries to influence price by cutting its sales in half, from 2 million to 1 million units. The result is that price rises to $3; the firm moves from *A* to *B* on the demand curve. By restricting output, it is able to raise price. (Alternatively, the firm could have made exactly this same move from *A* to *B* by quoting a $3 price, in which case buyers would purchase 1 million units.)

In short, the monopoly firm has market demand within its grasp. It is free to move along the market demand curve from a point like *A* to *B*, selecting the one that suits it best. On the other hand, the perfect competitor has no control over price; instead, the company (or individual) faces its own completely elastic, individual demand curve, and all it can do is select the quantity to sell. While the monopolist can raise the price, the perfect competitor must take price as given. The monopolist is a "price maker," while the perfect competitor is a "price taker."

WHAT PRICE DOES THE MONOPOLIST SELECT?

Any firm, monopolist and competitor alike, will maximize profit by selecting the output where marginal cost (MC) is equal to marginal revenue (MR). As already recognized (in Figure 19-2), *marginal revenue for the perfectly competitive firm is the given market price at which it sells.* (For example, marginal revenue for the perfectly competitive firm in Figure 21-2*a* is $2; its marginal revenue schedule is identical to its completely elastic

MC = MR
comp: MR = P
mon: B MR < P

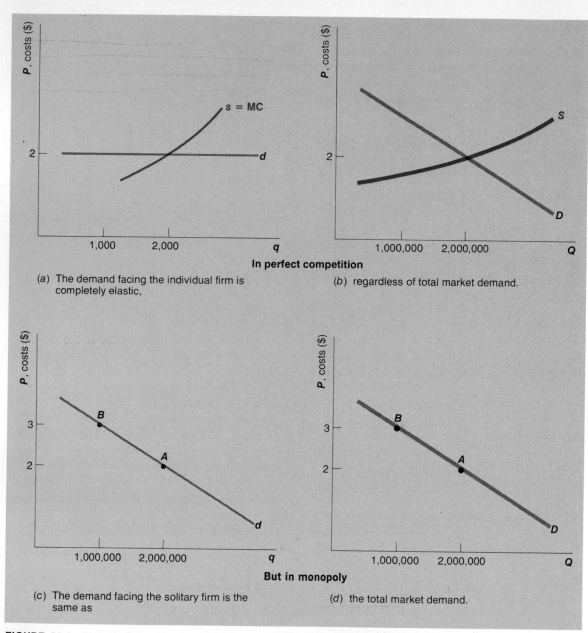

In perfect competition

(a) The demand facing the individual firm is completely elastic,

(b) regardless of total market demand.

But in monopoly

(c) The demand facing the solitary firm is the same as

(d) the total market demand.

FIGURE 21-2 The difference in the demand facing the monopolist and the perfect competitor.
Note that market demand is shown with a heavy line and marked with a capital *D*, whereas demand facing an individual firm is shown with a light line and marked with a small *d*.

demand curve.) But *for the monopolist, marginal revenue is not equal to the selling price*. This is such an important point that it deserves a detailed example.

What Is the Marginal Revenue of a Monopolist?

Suppose the monopoly firm in Figure 21-3 moves from *B* to *C* along its demand curve. At *B* it was selling 1 unit at a $50 price, but now at *C* it is selling 2 units at a price of $45 each. (Its average revenue AR is $45.) What is its marginal revenue, that is, the additional revenue it receives because it is selling 2 units rather than 1? We can readily calculate the answer. The monopoly's total revenue from selling 1 unit was $50. When it sells 2, its total revenue is $90. Thus, its marginal revenue from the sale of the second unit is $90 − $50 = $40. Note that the marginal revenue ($40) is less than the price ($45). There is a good reason why. In order to sell the second unit, the monopolist has to cut the price—including the price on the first unit. As a consequence, marginal revenue is reduced. This establishes an important conclusion:

> For a monopolist, marginal revenue is *less than price.*

Table 21-1 shows the marginal revenue for the monopolist at each level of output. Total revenue is given in column 3, while

FIGURE 21-3 Why a monopolist's demand (AR) and marginal revenue (MR) differ. (Figures are drawn from Table 21-1.)
At point *B*, the monopoly sells 1 unit for $50. At point *C*, it sells 2 units for $45 each, for a total revenue of $90. The sale of the second unit increases its total revenue by $90 − $50 = $40. Its marginal revenue is thus $40. (Another way to calculate this is to note that the monopoly receives a $45 price on the sale of the second unit; but from this it must deduct the $5 decrease in the price of the first unit, from $50 to $45.)

column 4 shows how this total revenue changes for each successive unit sold. The resulting marginal revenue schedule is graphed in Figure 21-3. Note that even though the selling price (on the demand curve) does not fall to zero in the range shown, marginal revenue falls below zero.

The demand and marginal revenue curves are stepping stones in answering the

TABLE 21-1
How Marginal Revenue for a Monopolist Is Derived from Demand (Average Revenue) Information

(1) Quantity (*Q*)	(2) Price (*P* = AR)	(3) Total revenue (*P* × *Q*)	(4) Marginal revenue (MR)
1	$50	$ 50	$50
2	45	90	(90 − 50) = $40
3	40	120	(120 − 90) = 30
4	35	140	(140 − 120) = 20
5	30	150	(150 − 140) = 10
6	25	150	(150 − 150) = 0
7	20	140	(140 − 150) = −10

(handwritten at top: monopoly demand curve = A.R = P.)

(handwritten at left margin: P = MC.)

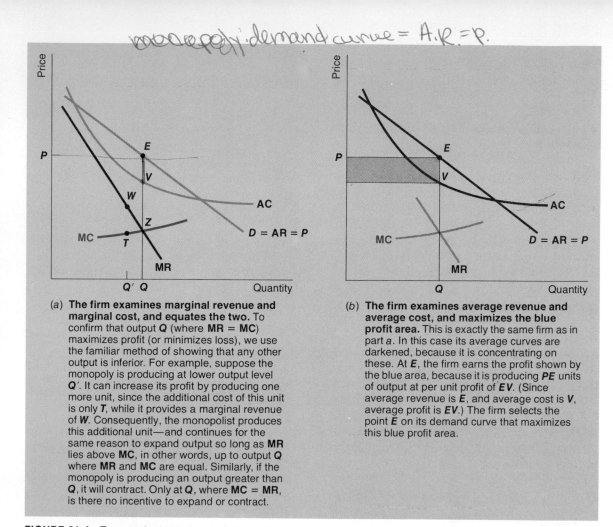

(a) **The firm examines marginal revenue and marginal cost, and equates the two.** To confirm that output **Q** (where **MR = MC**) maximizes profit (or minimizes loss), we use the familiar method of showing that any other output is inferior. For example, suppose the monopoly is producing at lower output level **Q′**. It can increase its profit by producing one more unit, since the additional cost of this unit is only **T**, while it provides a marginal revenue of **W**. Consequently, the monopolist produces this additional unit—and continues for the same reason to expand output so long as **MR** lies above **MC**, in other words, up to output **Q** where **MR** and **MC** are equal. Similarly, if the monopoly is producing an output greater than **Q**, it will contract. Only at **Q**, where **MC = MR**, is there no incentive to expand or contract.

(b) **The firm examines average revenue and average cost, and maximizes the blue profit area.** This is exactly the same firm as in part *a*. In this case its average curves are darkened, because it is concentrating on these. At **E**, the firm earns the profit shown by the blue area, because it is producing **PE** units of output at per unit profit of **EV**. (Since average revenue is **E**, and average cost is **V**, average profit is **EV**.) The firm selects the point **E** on its demand curve that maximizes this blue profit area.

FIGURE 21-4   Two equivalent views of the profit-maximizing equilibrium of a monopoly.

question: How high does a profit-maximizing monopolist set price?

Monopoly Output and Price

As we saw in Chapter 20, the best choice for anyone making an economic decision is to *equate marginal cost and marginal benefit.* But for the monopolist, marginal benefit is marginal revenue. Thus, to maximize profit, the monopolist picks the output *(Q) where marginal cost equals marginal revenue,* as shown in Figure 21-4, panel *a*.

For profit maximization, the firm chooses the output where

$$MC = MR$$

What price does the firm charge? The demand curve indicates the prices at which various quantities can be sold. Thus, to sell quantity *Q*, the monopoly selects price *P*. This choice is most simply referred to as the selection of the profit-maximizing point on the demand curve.

(handwritten at bottom: how MR = MC)

Of course, in this case of monopoly (just as in perfect competition), the firm must address another important question: Should it be in business at all? The answer is yes. In selling Q units, it makes a per unit profit of EV (the difference between its selling price E on the demand curve and its average cost V on the AC curve). Thus, a profit for a monopolist will exist so long as E lies above V, that is, so long as the demand curve cuts through (overlaps) the average cost curve.

The monopoly's *total* profit is the shaded area shown in panel b of Figure 21-4, that is, the per unit profit (EV) times the number of units sold (PE). (This area is shaded in blue to represent profits, in contrast to losses which will eventually appear in red.) Thus, these two panels show the monopoly firm maximizing profit in two exactly equivalent ways: In panel a, it equates MC and MR. Alternatively, in panel b, it selects the point E on its demand curve that maximizes the blue profit area. We shall use these two approaches interchangeably. The approach in panel b has been introduced because it clearly shows the profits which the firm is attempting to maximize. Moreover, it captures both conditions that a firm must satisfy: It ensures (1) that the marginal condition MC = MR will be met, and (2) that the firm will not be operating at a loss (in which case it would go out of business in the long run).

The monopoly firm maximizes its profits (and thus picks the best position for itself) by choosing the output where MC = MR. But an important question remains: How should this output level be judged by society as a whole? Specifically, will the output chosen by the monopolist lead to economic efficiency?

IS MONOPOLY EFFICIENT?

The answer is no: A monopoly will produce too little output, and the nation's resources will be misallocated as a consequence.

But before we show the reason for such allocative inefficiency, note that monopoly may also be technically inefficient; the firm may not be operating on its lowest possible cost curve. Because it has no competition, a monopoly may relax its cost controls, and resources may be wasted as a consequence. In drawing our diagrams, we assume away this kind of inefficiency. (Thus we assume that the firm is always operating on its lowest possible AC curve.) But *technical inefficiency in monopoly industries is a very important cost to society*, and should not be forgotten.

Now let us return to the more subtle problem of allocative inefficiency (or just "inefficiency," for short). To illustrate why a monopoly will produce too little output, consider the two industries shown in Figure 21-5. The demand curves for these two products are identical; moreover, the marginal cost curves for producing these two goods are also identical, as shown.[1] The only difference is that the market in panel a is serviced by a large number of perfectly competitive firms, while the market in panel b is serviced by a monopolist. These two panels illustrate the important difference between a perfectly competitive industry and a monopolized industry.

For the perfectly competitive industry in panel a, the marginal cost curve for the industry (MC) is the supply curve, and equilibrium is at E_C. Output Q_C is produced and sold at price P_C. But if this industry is monopolized as in panel b, equilibrium will be at E_M, with lower output Q_M and higher price P_M. Thus:

---

[1]The only costs shown are marginal costs, because we focus on the issue of resource misallocation, which involves examining what happens at the margin. (We assume that producers in either panel a or b are at least covering their average costs.)

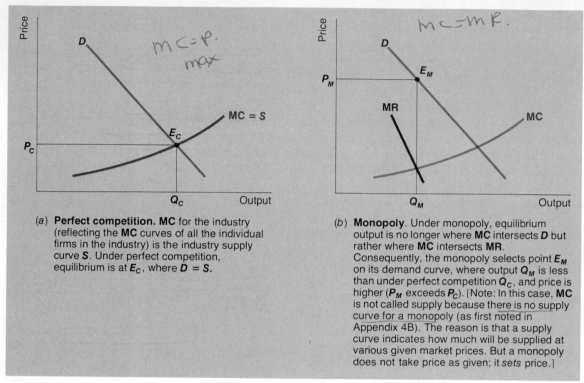

(a) **Perfect competition. MC** for the industry (reflecting the **MC** curves of all the individual firms in the industry) is the industry supply curve **S**. Under perfect competition, equilibrium is at E_C, where **D = S**.

(b) **Monopoly**. Under monopoly, equilibrium output is no longer where **MC** intersects **D** but rather where **MC** intersects **MR**. Consequently, the monopoly selects point E_M on its demand curve, where output Q_M is less than under perfect competition Q_C, and price is higher (P_M exceeds P_C). [Note: In this case, **MC** is not called supply because there is no supply curve for a monopoly (as first noted in Appendix 4B). The reason is that a supply curve indicates how much will be supplied at various given market prices. But a monopoly does not take price as given; it *sets* price.]

FIGURE 21-5   The results of monopoly: restricted output and higher price.

The monopolist sells less than the perfectly competitive output, and at a higher price.

On both counts consumers suffer: At point E_M in panel *b*, they pay a higher price and enjoy less of this good than they would under perfect competition at point E_C. On the other hand, the monopoly benefits: Because it can raise its price, it has an opportunity for profit not available to perfect competitors. So far, in trying to evaluate monopoly, we are faced with the typical dilemma of the policymaker; monopoly damages one group (consumers) but benefits another (the producer). How can we determine its overall net effect on society as a whole?

We know that the answer must be: There is an efficiency loss because of mo-

nopoly. Since Q_C in panel *a* is the perfectly competitive output, it is efficient. Therefore, the lower level of output Q_M in the monopoly case must involve an efficiency loss; that is, a deadweight loss to society as a whole. This is confirmed in panel *a* of Figure 21-6, where the competitive equilibrium E_C and the monopoly equilibrium E_M of Figure 21-5 are reproduced in one diagram. The red efficiency loss under monopoly is established here in exactly the same way as in Figure 20-4*b* and is left as an exercise. (To check your answer, see the caption to Figure 21-6*a*.)

The reason for this inefficiency is seen in panel *b* to be this: The marginal benefit to society (that is, marginal utility) of a good is reflected in its market demand, regardless of whether the industry servicing that demand is competitive or monopolized. The marginal cost of a good to society is also shown; it is the marginal cost of its production. Efficiency requires that a good should be produced to output level Q_C where these two are equal. This is what happens under perfect competition (right-hand arrow).

But if this market is serviced by a monopoly, the firm will sell less, since it equates MC and its *individual* marginal benefit, which is not the same as the benefit to society. That is, its individual benefit is its marginal revenue, and not the marginal utility of the good to consumers (demand). Thus, when a monopolist makes a decision on the basis of self-interest, rather than society's interest, it is no surprise that society suffers. Adam Smith's "invisible hand" fails in its task.

A final interpretation is that this efficiency loss under monopoly occurs because one of the conditions in Box 20-1 has been violated. Which one? Notice that at monopoly output Q_M in panel *a* in Figure 21-6, price P_M is about three times as large as MC. Thus the monopolist does not equate P and MC, and condition (20-4) in Box 20-1 is violated. In the rest of this chapter and in the next, this is the question we will continue to pursue: What happens if all but one of the conditions for an efficient solution in Box 20-1 hold, but condition (20-4) is violated?

A Reservation

The previous discussion seemed to lead to the clear judgment that the society is harmed if a perfectly competitive industry is monopolized. This conclusion is generally correct. But it's not absolutely airtight, for two reasons. One is the rather difficult concept set out in Box 21-1. The other involves the distinction between the *efficiency effect* and the *transfer effect* of a monopoly.

The efficiency effect is the reduction in efficiency associated with the production of a quantity that is too small. This effect is measured by the red efficiency loss shown in Figure 21-6*a*. The transfer effect occurs because the higher price charged by the mo-

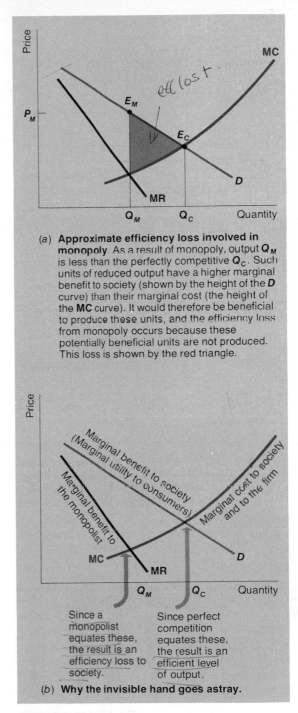

(a) **Approximate efficiency loss involved in monopoly** As a result of monopoly, output Q_M is less than the perfectly competitive Q_C. Such units of reduced output have a higher marginal benefit to society (shown by the height of the **D** curve) than their marginal cost (the height of the **MC** curve). It would therefore be beneficial to produce these units, and the efficiency loss from monopoly occurs because these potentially beneficial units are not produced. This loss is shown by the red triangle.

| Since a monopolist equates these, the result is an efficiency loss to society. | Since perfect competition equates these, the result is an efficient level of output. |

(b) **Why the invisible hand goes astray.**

FIGURE 21-6 Monopoly vs. perfect competition.

BOX 21-1
THE THEORY OF THE SECOND BEST

The conclusion that the monopolization of an industry results in a misallocation of resources is generally correct, but not always.

To understand why, consider an industry, X, in an economy whose other industries (Y_1, Y_2, Y_3, ...) are all perfectly competitive. If X is monopolized, not enough of good X will be produced, and too much of Y_1, Y_2, Y_3, ... This is the standard conclusion.

But now suppose that all other industries (Y_1, Y_2, Y_3, ...) are themselves monopolized. Then, if X is perfectly competitive, there will be too little of each of the other goods (Y_1, Y_2, Y_3, ...) produced, and too much X. What happens if industry X is now monopolized? This will reduce its output, and bring it back closer into line with other industries; thus, the allocation of the nation's resources may actually be *improved*.

We may thus identify the *problem of the second best*. The first best economy is one in which all industries are competitive. In such circumstances the monopolization of an industry will make the economy less efficient. But in a second best world—one in which some industries are *already* monopolized—it is unclear whether monopoly in yet another industry will make the economy more or less efficient. There is no simple answer to this question; the *theory of the second best* is quite complex.

> The *theory of the second best* is the theory of how to get the best results in remaining markets when one or more markets have monopoly or other imperfections about which nothing can be done.

A second best argument is sometimes made in support of government policies to monopolize an agricultural industry. (See the milk example at the end of this chapter.) Since the rest of the economy is pervaded by monopoly, so the argument goes, monopolizing agriculture may improve the nation's resource allocation. By and large, economists remain unimpressed with this argument and continue to recommend that we aim at the "first best" competitive solution by reducing monopoly abuse wherever it may be found. Hence, the theory of the second best is introduced here, not as a reason for encouraging monopoly in any specific sector, but rather, as a warning that the economic world is seldom as simple as we might hope, and therefore policies are seldom as clear-cut.

---

nopolist involves a transfer from consumers who pay the higher price to the monopolist who pockets it. In concentrating on the efficiency effect, we have thus far ignored the effect of the transfer. That is, we have implicitly assumed that the utility the monopolist gains from, say, an additional $100,000, is roughly equal to the decline in consumers' satisfaction when they lose this sum. But it is possible that this assumption is wrong. The monopolist may get more utility from this transfer than consumers lose. (Suppose, for example, that the product is something like a Rolls Royce. The consumers who buy it are so wealthy they hardly notice the $100,000 extra cost. But if the owners of the monopolistic firm are widows and orphans, they may get enormous satisfaction from the additional $100,000 in profits.) In this case, the act of transferring income would provide a *net benefit*. Moreover, it is conceivable that such a benefit might offset the efficiency loss shown in red in Figure 21-6*a*. Then our unfavorable judgment on monopoly would be upset.

While this argument is logically possible, it is also somewhat strained; it seems to reflect the exception, rather than the rule.[2] Therefore, most economists would be prepared to argue that the monopolization of an industry typically results in a net loss to society.

In passing, it should be pointed out that this problem of whether the $100,000 is of equal benefit to buyers and sellers arises in evaluating almost any economic policy, whether it be controlling monopoly price, limiting pollution, or opening trade with foreign countries. Any such policy results in a change in some market price, and hence a transfer of income between buyers and sellers. Thus, any normative conclusion (on whether the policy is desirable or not) requires a working assumption of how people compare in their valuation of income. Anyone unprepared to make a reasonable working assumption on this score is restricted to positive economics—to an analysis of economic events, policies, and institutions, without any judgment on whether they have been beneficial to the community as a whole.

GOVERNMENT ANTIMONOPOLY POLICIES

In order to protect consumers, the government has from time to time instituted policies to deal with monopoly. These have included:

1. Setting up a regulatory agency to control the price a monopolist sets.

2. Operating a monopoly under government ownership.

3. Enforcing antitrust laws to split up a monopoly into two or more smaller firms, or to prevent several firms from merging to form a monopoly. (The objective in this case has been to protect not only consumers, but also competing firms.)

The first two points are considered in this chapter, and the third in Chapter 22.

Price Regulation: The Attempt to Get a Monopolist to Act like a Perfect Competitor

Some significant sectors of the economy are monopolies. It makes sense to have only one set of telephone or electrical wires running down the street; telephone and electricity service are natural monopolies. So, too, are local gas, sewage, and water services. Some of these (for example, water or sewage services) are provided by a government corporation. Others (such as telephones) are provided by privately owned corporations. In this case, the government may regulate price. When it does so, where should it set the price?

To shed light on this question, consider the monopolist shown in Figure 21-7. (This diagram reproduces the cost curves in Figure 21-6, with the addition of the average cost curve AC.) We have already seen that a monopoly that is free to quote its own price will select point E_1 on its demand curve (at an output Q_1 where MC = MR), rather than the socially desirable, efficient point E_2 (where MC = D = marginal utility). An appropriate government policy would be to move it down its demand curve from E_1 to E_2. In theory, this result can be accomplished very simply by setting the maximum price that the firm can charge at P_2, the price at which its MC curve intersects the demand curve. This is called *marginal cost pricing*.

Since the monopoly firm is now prohibited from raising price, it is forced to act like

[2]Indeed, a negative transfer effect seems more likely: A dollar is probably worth more to the typical consumer than to the typical monopolist.

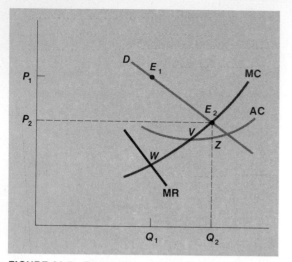

FIGURE 21-7 Regulating monopoly price: The easy case.
Without price regulation, the monopoly firm maximizes its profit by selecting point E_1 on its demand curve. (At this point, output is Q_1, where MR = MC.) If the government sets maximum price at P_2, the firm moves down its demand curve to point E_2, with its output increasing to Q_2. This is the efficient output where the marginal benefit to society (D) is equal to marginal cost (MC). The efficiency gain from this policy comes from the elimination of the original triangle of monopoly inefficiency E_1E_2W. (This is the efficiency loss shown in red in Figure 21-6a.) This policy also reduces monopoly profit. (Since initially the monopolist maximized profit by selecting point E_1, any other point on the demand curve—including E_2—involves less profit.)

a perfectly competitive firm, taking price as given. Like the perfect competitive firm, it will produce to point E_2, where its MC curve rises to the level of its given price P_2. Since E_2 is also the efficient point where MC = D = MU, this policy has eliminated the original efficiency loss due to monopoly.[3]

In summary, consider how well marginal cost pricing solves the monopoly abuses of producing too little at too high a price. The monopoly is forced to reduce its price,

and consequently it also increases its output. In addition, its monopoly profit has been reduced, though not necessarily eliminated. (Per unit profit of E_2Z still remains.)

Unfortunately, dealing with monopoly in practice is often not so easy. Although marginal cost pricing still allows a profit in the example shown in Figure 21-7, in other circumstances it may lead to a loss. In such a case, marginal cost pricing is not a satisfactory policy, since it involves setting a price ceiling that would eventually drive the firm out of business. Such an industry requires some other form of regulation. This more difficult situation is dealt with in Box 21-2.

THE SPECIAL CASE OF DISCRIMINATING MONOPOLY: Letting a Monopolist Act like a Monopolist—in Spades

The argument so far is that a monopolist should not be allowed to set a high price. But there is one interesting exception to this general rule.[4] Figure 21-8 shows the demand for the services of a doctor in a small town, along with her average costs (which, as always, include her opportunity costs; that is, what she could earn elsewhere). If she must quote a single price to all patients, she will decide not to go into this community. The reason is that her demand D does not overlap AC, so there is no single price she can select that will cover her costs. In short, even though she would be a monopolist and have the power to quote price, she would have no single price worth quoting. The best she could do would be to select a point like E on her demand curve, thus setting her fee at P and selling quantity Q.

---

[3]This presents a puzzle: A government price ceiling *increases* efficiency in this example, but a government ceiling on rents *reduces* efficiency (as noted in our discussion of Figure 20-4b). How is this possible? The answer: The ceiling on rents moves an industry away from an efficient, perfectly competitive equilibrium. But in Figure 21-7, a price ceiling moves an inefficient monopoly at E_1 toward an efficient equilibrium at E_2.

Clearly, government intervention can be a powerful tool, since it can move a market away from its free-market equilibrium. While this can be damaging if the free market is initially competitive, it can be beneficial if the free market is initially monopolized. For this reason, economists oppose a price ceiling in some circumstances, but favor it in others.

[4]This example was developed by Joan Robinson in *The Economics of Imperfect Competition* (London: Macmillan, 1933), p. 203.

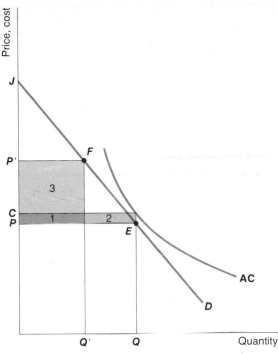

FIGURE 21-8 **When discriminating monopoly may be justified.**
If the doctor (the potential monopolist) can charge only one price, she will not move into this town, because D is not great enough to overlap AC. Any point such as E that she might select on D would thus leave her operating at a loss, shown by area 1 + 2, and she would stay away. On the other hand, she will move into town if she is allowed to discriminate, charging low fee P to the poor and high fee P' to the rich. On her Q' of services sold to the rich, she can increase her income by area 1 + 3 (that is, she can capture part of the consumers' surplus of the rich). This additional income more than offsets her original loss 1 + 2, so she can now earn a profit and hence decides to move in. She benefits from discriminatory pricing because she is able to earn a higher income here than elsewhere. And her patients also benefit because of the remaining consumers' surplus that her presence provides. (Although she has captured some of their consumers' surplus, they still have some remaining.)

But she would still not cover her costs, because her price P would be less than her average cost C. (Specifically, her total loss, compared with what she could earn elsewhere, would be areas 1 + 2; that is, Q units sold at a loss of CP on each.)

Under such circumstances, this community goes without a doctor, thus losing po-

tential consumers' surplus PJE. Obviously, if there were some way for her to acquire part of this consumers' surplus, it would be profitable for her to move in, and the community would benefit as well. She can do this if she is allowed to discriminate among her patients, selling her service at a higher price to some than to others. To illustrate, suppose she starts at initial position E, charging one price P to all her patients and incurring losses 1 + 2. She can do better by discriminating; that is, by charging her first Q' patients (the wealthy ones) a higher fee, P'. This increases her income from these wealthy patients by areas 1 + 3, more than offsetting her original losses 1 + 2. Therefore, she is now able to more than cover her costs; with a higher income here than she could earn elsewhere, she decides to stay in town.

In short, if she cannot discriminate, she will be forced to take an abnormally low income, and this community will lose a doctor. But if she is allowed to discriminate, she will move in. This is beneficial for her and for her patients. In fact, it even benefits those patients who must pay the higher fee, because her presence provides them with a consumers' surplus ($P'JF$) that they would otherwise have to forgo. Price discrimination is therefore justified in this case, because it benefits everyone concerned.

Even if price discrimination is desirable, it may not be possible in some cases. To make different prices stick, the discriminating monopolist must be able to divide the market, thus preventing individuals who buy at the low price from turning around and selling to those who are charged the high price. In the doctor example, market division is no problem. A patient who buys a low-priced operation cannot turn around and sell it to a sick friend. On the other hand, it may not be possible for a bus company to discriminate among its adult customers, charging some $10 and others $20. The reason is that those who are able to buy cheap $10 tickets may resell them to the others for some price (say $15) that benefits both groups. (But the bus company can discriminate between adults and children, since an adult is unable to use a child's ticket.)

Finally, it should be reemphasized that price discrimination is desirable in Figure 21-8 only because the monopolist would be out of business otherwise (D does not overlap AC). But price discrimination is not justified in the normal case of monopoly where D does overlap AC and the monopolist is consequently able to earn a monopoly profit by quoting a single price. Indeed, an earlier section of this chapter explained why such a monopolist should not be given the freedom even to quote a single price, let alone several. This is the type of monopoly that we shall concentrate on hereafter in this book—the classical case in which the firm is able to produce profitably without discriminating and where the exercise of monopoly power is damaging to the public interest.

*GOVERNMENT MARKETING PROGRAMS: Helping Competitors to Act like a Monopolist?

> Things are seldom what they seem,
> Skim milk masquerades as cream.
>
> Gilbert and Sullivan,
> *H.M.S. Pinafore*

Figure 21-7 showed how a government regulatory agency may be able to increase the efficiency of an industry by forcing a monopoly firm (or individual) to act like a perfect competitor, in the process driving the firm down its demand curve. But in some cases, the government acts in the opposite direction: A competitive industry may be provided with a marketing organization that allows the competitors to act like a monopolist and thus move up their market de-

*Instructors of short courses may omit this section.

BOX 21-2 UNFORTUNATELY, DEALING WITH MONOPOLY IS OFTEN NOT SO SIMPLE

In Figure 21-9 we show the case in which average costs keep falling through an even greater range of output than in Figure 21-7. (Demand is similar in these two diagrams; the only difference is that in Figure 21-7, average cost reaches a minimum and turns up to the *left* of the demand curve, but in Figure 21-9 it reaches a minimum to the *right* of the demand curve.) In this instance, the regulation of monopoly price involves substantial problems.

Average Cost Pricing

Suppose that we try to apply the guideline that worked so well in Figure 21-7, and again try to drive the monopoly firm down its demand curve from its original profit-maximizing equilibrium at E_1 to the efficient point E_2, where MC = D. As before, we attempt to do so by regulating price at P_2. Unfortunately, this policy will no longer work, because it will turn the monopoly into a money-loser and eventually drive it out of business. (At output level Q_2, price P_2 is not enough to cover average cost.) The lowest we can set the price without forcing the monopolist to give up is P_3, which will result in a new equilibrium at E_3. Since at this point price is barely high enough to cover average cost, the firm just breaks even. This policy is called *average cost pricing*. Once again, the regulatory agency takes away the monopoly's power to select a point on its demand curve; the agency makes the decision on the appropriate point and makes it stick by regulating price.

Finally, the effect on efficiency of average cost pricing is shown in panel *b* of Figure 21-9. If it were possible to move the monopoly all the way down its demand curve from E_1 to E_2, the result would be the now familiar triangular efficiency gain shown as areas 4 + 5. But since average cost pricing allows us to move this firm only part way—from E_1 to E_3—the gain is limited to area 4.

Therefore, we conclude that since this

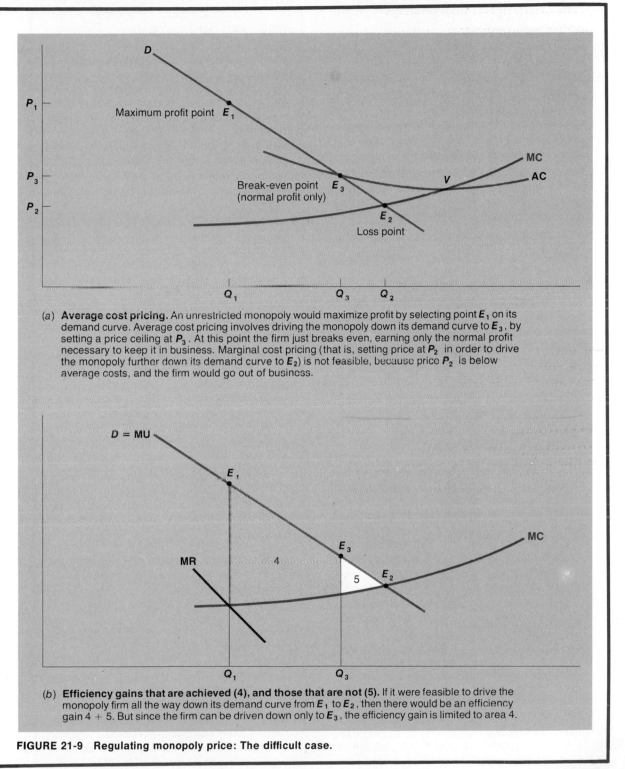

(a) **Average cost pricing.** An unrestricted monopoly would maximize profit by selecting point E_1 on its demand curve. Average cost pricing involves driving the monopoly down its demand curve to E_3, by setting a price ceiling at P_3. At this point the firm just breaks even, earning only the normal profit necessary to keep it in business. Marginal cost pricing (that is, setting price at P_2 in order to drive the monopoly further down its demand curve to E_2) is not feasible, because price P_2 is below average costs, and the firm would go out of business.

(b) **Efficiency gains that are achieved (4), and those that are not (5).** If it were feasible to drive the monopoly firm all the way down its demand curve from E_1 to E_2, then there would be an efficiency gain 4 + 5. But since the firm can be driven down only to E_3, the efficiency gain is limited to area 4.

FIGURE 21-9 Regulating monopoly price: The difficult case.

BOX 21-2 (cont'd)

policy of average cost pricing increases monopoly output from Q_1 to Q_3, it results in a *gain in allocative efficiency.* (Remember that unless we state otherwise, the word "efficiency" means "allocative efficiency.") Unfortunately, however, this policy, and any of the others discussed in this box, may lead to a *loss in technical efficiency* (that is, the firm may not operate on its lowest possible cost curve). After all, why should the firm in Figure 21-9 strive hard to lower its costs, when a reduction in costs will result in a lowered regulated price? Why shouldn't the firm's executives be allowed generous expense accounts, since such costs are simply passed on to consumers in the form of higher prices? No matter what the firm does, it can't make a profit; so why should it tightly control its costs? (At best, it can earn a temporary profit only between the date it reduces its costs and the date the regulatory agency gets around to reducing its price.)

Government Subsidy (with Marginal Cost Pricing)

Another possible government policy to deal with the monopoly in Figure 21-9 is to force it all the way down its demand curve from E_1 to efficient point E_2 by *marginal cost pricing*, while at the same time paying the firm a lump-sum *subsidy* necessary to cover its loss. In other words, a regulated price of P_2 drives the firm down its demand curve to point E_2 (thus capturing the entire possible efficiency gain 4 + 5), while the subsidy keeps the firm in business.

Although this policy may be attractive in theory, it raises such problems in practice that it is seldom used. (Subsidies to privately operated urban transit systems, however, have been justified along these lines.) For one thing, it is difficult for the public to understand why a government committed to controlling the market power of monopoly should end up subsidizing it. The point that the government is also regulating price (and thus eliminating monopoly profits) is difficult to explain to the public. Moreover, the policy of

taking money out of the monopolist's pocket with one hand (the regulated price) while putting it in with the other (the subsidy) may strike the public as being inconsistent, even though it is not. In addition, the general problem in price regulation reappears here. So long as the government is committed to subsidizing the costs of a monopolist, how can those costs be controlled? A firm may be very successful in holding costs down so long as it has to meet the test of the marketplace where the cost of failure is bankruptcy; but it may be far less successful in controlling its costs when it no longer faces that test. Finally, a government that has to get a subsidy passed by a log-rolling Congress ("I'll vote for the subsidy in your district if you'll vote for the subsidy in mine") may end up with a compromise subsidy that has little relationship to the original efficiency objective.

Government Ownership

The political problems involved in granting a subsidy are less severe if the government owns the monopoly, which it can then operate in the public interest at efficient point E_2. Again, taxpayers must subsidize the loss that results. Government-owned urban transit systems are often cited as examples. (Government subsidies cover more than half the costs of the typical large urban public transportation system.)

Additional complications involved in pricing urban transport and other government services are studied in greater detail in Chapters 23 and 24. For now, this warning is in order: Once again, things may not work out as well in real-world practice as in theory. Even if the government does run this monopoly, it may not operate it at the most efficient point E_2, since its objective in operating the enterprise may not be to increase efficiency so much as to redistribute income. (For example, the government may be trying to redistribute income from taxpayers to the large number of voters who use the urban transport system.) Finally, the same problem arises here as in the other policies discussed in this section: So long as this firm receives whatever subsidy is necessary to cover its costs, why should it strive to keep costs down?

mand curve—something they cannot do acting alone. As one might expect, the effects are those typical of any monopoly: Producers enjoy a benefit, consumers incur a cost, and there is an overall efficiency loss.

Figure 21-10a shows a competitive industry before any attempt is made to monopolize it. Industry equilibrium is shown (on the right) at E_1, with market price $80. At the same time, the situation of an individual firm is shown with the thin lines on the left. The firm is in equilibrium at F_1, producing 100 units and just covering its costs.

In panel b, this industry is monopolized when a marketing association is formed that allows all producers to speak with one voice and quote a higher price. Suppose the price the association decides on is $140, well above the competitive $80 level. On the right-hand side of this panel, we see that the industry consequently moves up its demand curve from E_1 to E_2. Thus, to make this higher price stick, the association must, like any monopolist, reduce sales from 1,000 units to 600. This cut implies that the individual firm on the left must decrease its output from 100 to a quota of 60. Therefore the firm moves from F_1 to F_2. Despite the fact its output has been reduced, its increased price now allows it to earn a profit (shown as the blue area).

The monopolization of this industry has had the expected results. Producers benefit from their newfound profit, while consumers lose because of increased price. On balance, there is an overall efficiency loss (which is left for you to show in Problem 21-9).

However, in panel b of Figure 21-10, we see that there are strong pressures for such associations to come apart. While it is in the collective interest of all firms to restrict their output in order to raise price to $140, at this high price it is in the interest of the individ-

ual firm to expand output. In fact, at the $140 price set by the association, the individual firm has an incentive to produce, not at F_2, but at B, the output where MC cuts the set price. The problem, then, for the industry association is how to compel each individual firm to operate in the collective interest at F_2, rather than attempt to pursue its own interest at B. This discipline is essential: If some firms start to produce more than their quota, more than 600 units will come onto the market, and price will fall. Moreover, getting existing firms to stick to their quotas is not the only problem: The entry of new firms, attracted by the above-normal profits, would also drive price down.

The problem of enforcing quotas and restricting entry often leads perfectly competitive producers of agricultural goods in the United States and elsewhere to seek a government marketing agency to do what a private producers' association may not be strong enough to accomplish. Since even a government agency may have difficulty in enforcing a quota on output, limitations are often placed, instead, on the acreage a farmer can plant (in the case of United States tobacco producers)[5] or on the number of hens that a poultry farm can maintain (in the case of Canadian egg producers). But such a quota system, even when enforced by government regulations, may spring leaks. For example, a number of Canadian egg producers have been found with more hens than their quotas allow. Unbelievably, two of these individuals who "came up with egg on their face" were members of the board of directors of the marketing board that had set the quotas! There can be no clearer illustration of the problems of restricting output when producers' collective and individual interests are in conflict.

In the United States, there have been a number of examples of voluntary producers'

[5]For other U.S. agricultural products, strict acreage limits are not enforced. But farmers are required to "set aside" (that is, to idle) some acres in order to be eligible for government loans and deficiency payments. For example, in 1978, farmers were required to set aside 20 percent of their wheat acreage to be eligible for loan and deficiency payments on their wheat.

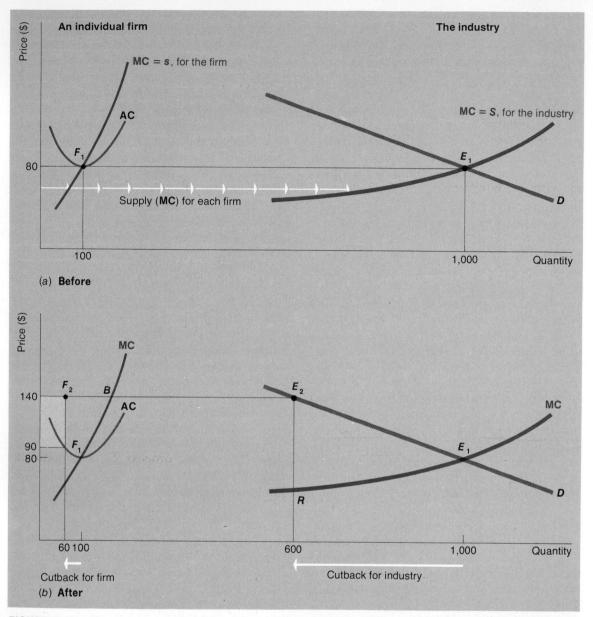

(a) Before

(b) After

FIGURE 21-10 Effect of a producers' association or government marketing program on an individual firm and the industry.

Panel *a* illustrates a competitive industry (similar to the one shown in Figure 21-1*a*). Market equilibrium is shown on the right at E_1 where $D = S$. (Industry supply is the horizontal sum of the individual supply curves, as shown by the arrows.) Market price is $80, and there are 1,000 units supplied. (The individual firm on the left supplies 100 of these units.)

In panel *b* this industry is monopolized when a producers' association or government marketing agency moves the industry from equilibrium E_1 to E_2. It does so by quoting a price of $140, with industry sales reduced as a consequence from 1,000 units to 600. In turn, the sales of the individual firm on the left must be reduced from 100 units to a quota of 60. This means that the firm moves from equilibrium F_1 to F_2 where it makes the $3,000 profit shown as the blue area. (On each of its 60 units, it earns a $50 profit.) But the problem is that although this reduction in output has raised profits all around, each firm facing the given $140 price would like to increase its output. The firm shown would like to move from F_2 to B, where MC = price. But additional output would drive market price down; the industry would slide down its demand curve from E_2 toward E_1. Moreover, with this price reduction, the profits of individual firms would also be reduced. (Of course, when there are thousands of firms in an industry—as in agriculture—a few can violate their quotas without disturbing price. But not many.) Thus disciplining firms to stick to their quotas is critically important. For this reason, producers often favor a scheme run by the government.

associations. To cite one: By 1910, milk producers in certain regions of the country had privately banded together to gain bargaining power over their price. Their success was always limited by their inability to firmly control output coming onto the market, so that by the early 1930s they had become relatively ineffective. Under the pressure of very low milk prices in 1935, the government introduced its present system of "milk marketing orders," which guarantee the farmer a minimum price (depending on the location and the eventual use of the milk). But there were unfortunate side effects when the government thus became involved in propping up price for a group of producers: The milk suppliers had an incentive to make political campaign contributions to politicians with potential influence over their marketing program. Promises of large campaign contributions by milk producers before the 1972 presidential election were followed by a price increase for the industry, and this action became a major subject of investigation by the Watergate special prosecutor.

DO FIRMS REALLY MAXIMIZE PROFITS?

The best of all monopoly profits is a quiet life.
J. R. Hicks,

So far, it has been assumed that producers maximize their profit. But it should be recognized that they sometimes pursue quite different objectives. Sometimes, they may decide on a policy because it makes them look good to their stockholders. Sometimes, with the objective of growing larger, they may expand output beyond the profit-maximizing point (provided they achieve some reasonable level of profit). Sometimes, in the interest of safety, they may swing in the other direction, and "think small," only undertaking expenditures that will yield a high profit, but dropping more risky expenditures that would yield a lower profit. Or sometimes they may follow a policy of "no

change" solely because they enjoy the quiet life. For example, if they are earning large profits, why should they worry about changing their output and price just because their cost curves have shifted slightly? Or why should they worry about the minor loss incurred if they hire a few relatives?

Why not construct our economic theory using one of these other assumptions instead? For some of these assumptions, we can't construct a theory because the objective is not specific enough. (For example, 10 business executives in identical circumstances, each pursuing the quiet life, might come up with 10 different decisions on output and price.) And even when a theory can be constructed, it will have the same flaw as profit maximization: It will not describe all economic decision-making. So we use profit maximization because this assumption is simple and precise enough to allow us to "get off square 1" and construct a theory, and because it generally describes economic decision-making at least as well as any alternative assumption. But we recognize that in some cases it will not hold. Even when it does, it may only be part of the story, since other objectives may also influence the decision-making process. So we should be appropriately modest in making claims for our conclusions.

Of course, if we have evidence that certain firms are pursuing some other objective (such as rapid growth), we may be able to adjust our profit-maximization conclusions in some reasonable way. For example, since high-growth firms tend to produce a larger output than profit-maximizing firms, we might ask: What does this greater output imply about price to the consumer? What are its effects on efficiency? How would producers respond to price regulation? And so on. The answers to some of these questions are straightforward, but others are not so clear. If we wanted to clarify them, we might even go one giant step further and construct a whole new theory from scratch, based on some other assumption than profit maximization. But that's a story for a more advanced course.

Key Points

1. Monopoly means that there is a single seller. This situation may occur when a firm controls something essential to the production or sale of a good—like a patent, resource, or government license. Or it may occur if a number of firms combine in order to speak with one voice, so that they will be able to quote the industry price.

2. Another important reason for monopoly is that a firm's costs may fall over such a wide range of output that total market demand can be most inexpensively satisfied by a single firm. This is a natural monopoly. Even when there are many firms in such an industry initially, they will tend to be eliminated by competition, with the large firm that emerges able to undercut any present or future competitors.

3. A monopoly can do something a perfectly competitive firm cannot: Because it faces a demand curve that slopes downward to the right, it can quote the price at which it will sell.

4. Marginal revenue (MR) for a monopolist is not the same as price. The MR curve lies below the demand curve.

5. A monopolist maximizes profit by equating MC with MR, not with price. As a consequence, monopoly results in an inefficiently low level of output.

6. One government policy to control monopoly is to set the maximum price the monopolist can charge. Facing this given price, the monopolist is forced into the price-taking role of the perfect competitor, and consequently increases output to a more efficient level.

7. Just as this policy of forcing a monopolist to act like a perfect competitor may increase efficiency, a government policy that helps perfect competitors to act like a monopolist will reduce efficiency. Oft-cited cases include marketing programs for agricultural products.

8. A case can sometimes be made for allowing a monopoly to price-discriminate, that is, to charge a higher price to one group than to another. (A doctor in a small town, say, may charge a higher price to her wealthy patients.) Such discriminatory pricing may be justified if the good or service could not otherwise be produced.

Key Concepts

patent
legal monopoly
natural monopoly
collusive monopoly
oligopoly
market power
monopolist's demand
monopolist's marginal revenue
monopoly inefficiency

how monopoly raises price and lowers output
marginal cost pricing
average cost pricing
discriminating monopoly (when justified, and when not)
government monopolization of an industry
objectives other than maximizing profit

Problems

21-1 Consider an industry in which the discovery and development of advanced machinery and technology mean that, as time passes, average costs for a firm tend to drift lower and lower. That is, through time the average cost for an individual firm moves from AC_1 to AC_2 in the following diagram. What do you think would happen in such an industry? Explain why. From the point of view of society as a whole, does the falling cost involve any advantages? Any disadvantages? In your view, how do these compare?

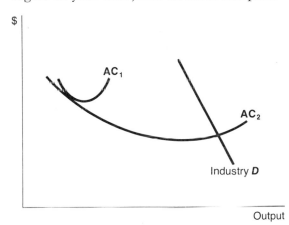

21-2 (*a*) If the firm with AC_2 in the diagram for problem 21-1 is not regulated, would you expect that all the monopoly profits would go to the firm's owners? If not, who else do you think might eventually capture a share of these profits?

(*b*) Draw in the marginal cost curve. Is it desirable to regulate price? Why? Show the level at which you would set regulated price. Defend this decision.

21-3 Which of these producers do you think is closer to being a monopoly?

(*a*) American Motors or Rolls Royce

(*b*) The producer of bread in a small town or the producer of the wheat used in it

(*c*) A community's large chain store or its corner grocery store

21-4 Given the cost conditions in the following diagram, name the price that would be set by a monopoly that is:

(*a*) Maximizing its profit

(*b*) Operating as a nonprofit organization

(*c*) Run by the government at an efficient output level

If (*a*) and/or (*b*) are not efficient, explain why.

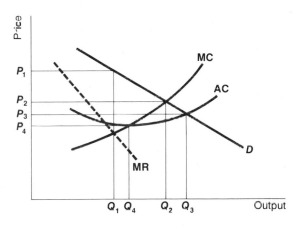

21-5 Do you agree with this statement? "Compared to the monopolist, the farmer has an easy job; he doesn't have to worry about setting price. He can just take it as given."

21-6 Does output Q in Figure 21-4*b* yield the monopolist the largest possible profit *per unit of output*? Explain.

21-7 Evaluate the following policy recommendation: "The sole objective in dealing with monopoly is to eliminate excess profits. And this is easy to do. Just examine the firm's current operations, calculate its average cost (including normal profit), and set price at this level."

21-8 The following diagram shows the demand and the costs the government faces in providing a public utility service (say electricity) in a certain city.

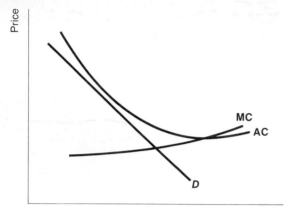

(a) If the government is interested only in maximizing its profit (minimizing its loss), show the price it will set and how much it will produce and sell. Also show its profit or loss.

(b) From an overall economic point of view, is this the most efficient level of output? If not, show what the most efficient level is and explain why. What price does the firm set to achieve this output level, and what happens to its profit or loss?

(c) Suppose that this public utility is allowed to set discriminatory prices. It decides to charge the public a higher rate for its initial purchases while still continuing to charge the rate it set in question *(b)* for any additional purchases. Could this lead to an efficient level of output? What happens now to the loss previously incurred by the public utility?

(d) Do you see now why public utilities are sometimes allowed to set discriminatory rates?

(e) In the section "The Special Case of Discriminating Monopoly," it was observed that for successful discrimination, a firm must be able to divide its market and prevent resale among buyers. The doctor has no great problem in dividing the market. How about the public utility selling electricity?

*21-9 Show and explain the overall efficiency loss from the monopolization of the industry in Figure 21-10*b*. Is income transferred as a consequence? If so, from whom to whom? Is it possible to argue that the monopolization of this industry is beneficial to society if the satisfaction which farmers receive from $1 of additional income is greater than the satisfaction which consumers receive from $1? Explain.

*21-10 Show the profit that the firm in Figure 21-10*b* would capture if it could get away with producing at point *B*. Is this a long-run equilibrium if all firms try to do the same? Explain.

*21-11 How might an agricultural marketing association be defended by using the theory of the second best?

*21-12 The British Columbia Milk Board sells milk at a price more than 10 percent above the free-market level. The board has also made it illegal to sell reconstituted milk (powdered milk mixed with water and fresh milk). The reason given for this action is to protect the consumer from an inferior product. Yet, in tests, consumers cannot distinguish between this milk and fresh milk, and it would cost far less. Is the marketing board protecting consumers or some other group?

chapter 22
Markets Between Monopoly and Perfect Competition

People of the same trade seldom meet together, even for merriment and diversion, but the conversation ends in a conspiracy against the public, or in some contrivance to raise prices.

Adam Smith,
Wealth of Nations

Monopoly represents the clearest form of market power; the monopolist is alone in the marketplace and has power to choose the price at which sales are made. But, if we look at such giants of American business as General Motors, IBM, and General Electric, we find that most of them are not monopolists. General Motors competes with Ford and Chrysler; IBM has Control Data and Burroughs to contend with; and General Electric competes with Westinghouse (in the electrical generator market) and with Pratt and Whitney (in the jet engine market). Oligopoly—where the market is dominated by a few large sellers—is more significant in the United States economy than outright monopoly.

In this chapter we discuss oligopoly, concentrating on the difficult policy questions it raises, and the various measures the government can use to control it. We also describe another kind of market that lies between monopoly and perfect competition: monopolistic competition. This will complete our discussion of the basic market forms.

OLIGOPOLY

The degree to which an industry is dominated by a few sellers is measured by the *concentration ratio.* This is the proportion of an industry's sales that is captured by its four largest firms. For example, Figure 22-1 shows that the auto and breakfast food industries are each dominated to a remarkably high degree by the four largest firms. (But also notice that there are some industries, like sporting goods, which are not.) While there seems to have been some slight trend over the last 30 years toward increased concentration in the American economy, with large firms getting somewhat larger shares of the market, there is little tendency for single producers to eliminate their competitors and emerge as monopolists from the competitive struggle. Thus, oligopoly is a stable form of market organization. It is not merely a temporary stop on an inevitable road to monopoly. What forces account for this stability? Why do a few firms grow so large, while none goes all the way to become a monopolist?

479

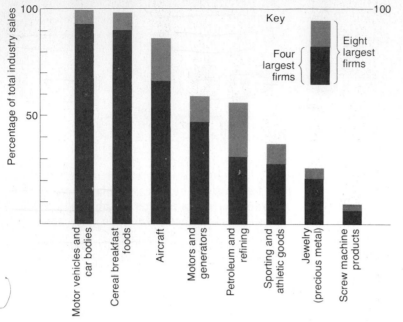

Key

Four largest firms {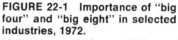

Eight largest firms

FIGURE 22-1 Importance of "big four" and "big eight" in selected industries, 1972.
SOURCE: Bureau of the Census, *1972 Census of Manufacturers.*

Part of the answer lies in the nature of costs. In many industries, there are advantages of large-scale production; there is a decline in average cost as output rises. A plant designed to produce 500,000 cars per year can operate at a much lower average cost than a plant designed to produce 100,000. But costs do not continue to fall forever. A plant which produces 2 million units cannot operate at a lower average cost than a 1-million-unit plant.

When costs fall over a considerable range, they encourage the development of large firms. But when costs eventually begin to rise while production is still far short of the total quantity sold in the market, they discourage any large firm from growing even larger and developing into a monopoly. Thus, cost conditions may lead to *natural oligopoly:*

Natural oligopoly occurs when the average costs of individual firms fall over a large enough range so that a few firms can produce the total quantity sold at the lowest average cost.

This definition is illustrated in Figure 22-2*b,* where natural oligopoly is compared with perfect competition and natural monopoly.

But it is not just cost conditions that account for the persistence of oligopoly. Oligopoly represents a balance of forces that encourage concentration and those that work against it.

One of the strongest forces working toward larger and larger corporations is the advantage of *market power.* The larger a firm becomes by internal growth or by buying out and absorbing its competitors, the greater its power to set price without great concern about its competitors. Thus, a firm in natural oligopoly—with no incentive to expand because of costs—may nonetheless seek to expand in order to acquire more market power.

On the other side, the government provides a countervailing force against monopoly. The desire to protect consumers and competitors has led Congress to pass antitrust laws that prevent firms from establishing a monopolylike position.

FIGURE 22-2   Natural oligopoly compared with perfect competition and natural monopoly.

(a) **Perfect competition.**
Long-run **AC** curve turns up at relatively low level of output.

(b) **Natural oligopoly.**
Intermediate case: Long-run **AC** reaches its minimum at a sizable fraction of the total market. Several large firms will be able to get at or close to minimum cost, but small firms will have high average costs and will find it difficult to compete.

(c) **Natural monopoly.**
Long-run **AC** curve continues to fall, not reaching a minimum until about where it cuts **D**, or beyond.

The *product differentiation* which exists in many oligopolistic markets also discourages monopolization. General Electric and Pratt and Whitney jet engines are similar, but not identical, and IBM computers are similar, but not identical, to Control Data's. A buyer with satisfactory experience with Ford cars may strongly prefer a new Ford to a Chevvy. It is such product differentiation that helps smaller firms (such as American Motors) to survive alongside giants. (While product differentiation is a significant characteristic of many oligopolistic markets, it is not important to them all. In the basic steel industry, for example, the product of one company is pretty much the same as another's.)

THE OLIGOPOLIST AS A PRICE SEARCHER

We have seen that oligopoly lies in the broad area between the polar cases of monopoly and perfect competition. At either of these two polar extremes, the firm is free of worry over how its competitors will react if it changes its price or output. The monopolist (by definition) has no competitors worth worrying about. On the other hand, the perfectly competitive firm need not worry because it is only one of many, many small competitors. Since it provides only a miniscule part of the total market supply, its decision to change output will not even be noticed by the other firms. In contrast, in an oligopoly, the individual firm is very much aware of its few large competitors, and must worry about their reactions. If it reduces price, will its competitors follow? Will its action set off a price war? And where may this lead? In an oligopoly, the firms are mutually *interdependent*; each is concerned about the reactions of its competitors. The oligopolist is very conscious of competition.

In perfect competition, firms are *price takers*. The individual firm has no influence over price, which is determined by the impersonal forces of demand and supply. In monopoly, the firm is a *price maker*. By selecting a point on its demand curve, it chooses the price at which it wishes to sell. In oligopoly, the firm is a *price searcher*. Although it has some influence over price, this is limited by the possible reactions of its competitors.

Because the oligopoly is in competition with a few large firms capable of vigorously responding to its actions, it must develop a marketing strategy. The world of oligopoly can resemble a chess game, with move and countermove. And, like a chess game, the outcome may be unpredictable. Once we enter the world of oligopoly, we leave behind the simple, definite solutions of both monopoly and perfect competition. Ever since Augustin Cournot's nineteenth-century study of duopoly (two sellers), it has been recognized that the search for an equilibrium price can be quite complex; oligopoly is one of the least satisfactory areas of economic theory.

For this reason, it is not possible here to do more than emphasize a few highlights. The first topic involves the situation where oligopolists recognize their common interest in raising prices and collude to act as though they were a monopoly. The second topic will be the case where oligopolists abandon this common interest in pursuit of their own individual interests and the collusive arrangement comes apart.

Collusion

In the United States, collusion is against the law. The reason for such laws may be seen by looking at the economic effects of a cartel, the most formal type of collusion, where firms get together to gain the advantages of monopoly.

A *cartel* is a formal agreement among firms regarding pricing and/or market sharing.

As a simple example of collusion, consider a market where there are three similar firms. Although they maintain their own separate corporate identities, with their own plants and their own sales forces, suppose they get together to agree on a common price. In their collective interest, what is the best price to choose? The answer: the price which a monopolist would pick; that is, the price which will maximize their combined profits. Specifically, this price is determined in Figure 22-3 as follows. The marginal cost curves of the three firms are added horizontally (as shown by the arrows) to give the combined marginal cost curve for the industry. The highest profit is made at the point in panel *b* where this marginal cost curve cuts the industry's marginal revenue. (MR may be calculated from *D* for an industry, just as it was for a firm in Table 21-1.) The collusive price is therefore set at $100, directly above the intersection of the industry's MC and MR.

This cartel benefits producers, who have maximized their collective profit. (The profit each realizes is shown by the blue area.) But from the viewpoint of society, this collusive arrangement presents the same problem as a monopoly. Too little is produced. For an efficient allocation of the resources of society, output should be raised from 600 units to 900, where marginal cost intersects the demand (marginal utility) curve. The efficiency loss from collusive pricing is shown by the red triangle. (To confirm this loss, review Figure 20-4*b*.) Thus in collusive oligopoly, just as in monopoly, Adam Smith's "invisible hand" again fails, as Smith himself recognized. (See the quotation from Smith that introduces this chapter.)

The Breakdown of Collusion: The Incentive to Cheat

While the cartel chooses a price in the same way as a monopolist does, it faces a problem that is absent in monopoly. Because the cartel consists of more than one

FIGURE 22-3 Collusion by three oligopolists.

This example of three colluding oligopolists is very similar to the milk marketing program shown in Figure 21-10b. The most substantial difference is that in the earlier case the large number of milk producers had little hope of managing and enforcing a private agreement, so they turned to the government. But in this present cartel case, there are only three producers, so there is at least some hope of arriving at an agreement and making it stick. MC for the industry is shown in panel b as the horizontal sum of the MC curves for the three individual firms. MR for the industry is calculated from industry demand. The maximization of industry profit requires that output be set at 600 units (where industry MC = MR) and that price be fixed at $100. In other words, the cartel selects point E on its demand curve. How is the market of 600 units divided among the three firms? The simplest solution is to set a quota of 200 units for each, as shown in panel a. Thus each firm produces at point F, where it earns the blue $4,000 profit that results from the sale of 200 units at a $20 profit on each. (This $20 unit profit is the difference between the $100 selling price and the $80 average cost.) The problem is that the individual firm facing a price set at $100 would prefer to sell more than its 200-unit quota. (It can sell an additional unit for $100, while its MC is only slightly more than $40.) But if it does so, more than 600 units will be produced, and in panel b industry price will fall. If firms thus forget their *collective* interest in favor of pursuing their *individual* interest, the price-fixing arrangement comes apart.

firm, some way must be found of dividing the market. Observe that the only way that the price can be maintained at its profit-maximizing level of $100 is by restricting output to 600 units. (An attempt to sell any more will lead to downward pressure on price; that is, the industry will slide down its demand curve to the right.) There are a number of ways that participants can agree

to limit sales. The market may be divided equally among all members (in this example, 200 units each), or it may be divided according to historical market shares, or by geographical area. For example, in the 1920s, two European firms agreed to carve up the market for explosives. Dynamite was allowed exclusive rights in certain continental European markets, in exchange for leaving British Empire markets to Nobel. (This was the firm of the same Nobel who established a peace prize.)[1]

From the viewpoint of the cartel members, the problem with such arrangements is that they tend to be unstable. Each member of the cartel has an incentive to cheat by selling more than its allotted share. (It is "cheating" as viewed by the other members of the cartel, but not as viewed by the public. More production will lower price and reduce the red efficiency-loss triangle.) Observe in panel *a* of Figure 22-3 that the first firm's marginal cost is only slightly more than $40, while the market price is $100. If the firm can steal a sale away from its competitors, it will increase its profit by almost $60. Thus, it has an incentive to step up sales efforts, or to give secret price rebates in order to win customers. (Even if a firm grants a 20 percent rebate on the selling price of $100, the returns from the sale will still far exceed the MC.) So the problem is seen to be this: Each member of a cartel has a collective interest to keep sales down in order to keep the price up. But each member has an individual interest, in conflict with the other members, to sell more than its allotted share. If individual interests come to dominate, firms will produce beyond their quotas, and the cartel's price will collapse in a price war as firms fight over market shares. Because of the strength of the individual interest, cartels have tended to come apart after short and stormy histories.

Moreover, when there is a complete breakdown in a cartel, the struggle over markets may intensify. This is particularly true if the cost advantages of large-scale production have increased as a result of technological change. In this case, a natural oligopoly may be evolving into a natural monopoly. In the absence of government intervention, only one firm will ultimately survive. The question is, which one? Each firm wants to be the victor; each has an incentive to try to gain an advantage over its rivals by expanding rapidly to gain the lower costs from large-scale production. Excess supply is likely, with firms pushing frantically for sales. The result may be cutthroat competition; that is, selling at a price below average cost and below marginal cost in order to drive rivals out of business. In this struggle, the prize will probably go to the firm with the "deepest pockets" (the largest financial resources) which enable it to sustain the short-term losses while it is cutting the throats of its rivals.

A CASE STUDY: The International Oil Cartel

The most conspicuous and successful collusive arrangement of recent decades has been the Organization of Petroleum Exporting Countries (OPEC), an organization made up of most of the oil exporters, including a number of nations in the Middle East, Indonesia, Nigeria, and Venezuela. In late 1973 and early 1974, OPEC succeeded in doubling and then redoubling the price of crude oil (from less than $3 per barrel to more than $10). In the following years, OPEC not only made the higher price stick, but jacked it up even further. The result was far and away the greatest peacetime transfer of wealth among nations in history.

---

[1]There are other ways of carving up a market. In the 1930s, Westinghouse agreed to pay General Electric a 2 percent royalty for the patent right to produce an improved light bulb, provided Westinghouse sold not more than one-third as many bulbs as GE. But if Westinghouse tried to increase its sales beyond this quantity, it had to pay a savage 30 percent royalty. You can imagine how effectively this agreement froze the relative shares of the market going to Westinghouse and GE.

Another form of collusion is a *bidding cartel*. For example, in isolated cases, some antique dealers in Britain have met together before the auction of a valuable item to set the maximum price that they would bid. Thus, one of their number would buy the antique for a bargain price at the expense of the seller. Why were the other dealers prepared to stop bidding at this low price? The answer: They knew that it would soon be their turn to get a bargain purchase.

Yet many economists thought OPEC would fail. It raised the price astronomically, but it seemed to have no system for setting production quotas. How could it get away with this? The answer: There were a number of special features of the international oil market that made OPEC much stronger and more stable than the typical collusive arrangement.

1. The low elasticity of demand for oil—particularly in the short run—provides OPEC with substantial market power. It can raise price without a sharp short-run reduction in the quantity demanded. Thus, inelastic demand provides a price-fixing cartel with a golden opportunity: By raising price, it can raise total revenue. And there is another advantage of inelastic demand. Because sales hold up well in the face of rising price, there is less temptation for cartel members to squabble over market shares.

Why is the short-run demand for oil inelastic? The answer is that, in the short run, it has *no substitute*: We simply do not have time to develop other forms of energy like solar or atomic power. Moreover, oil is *essential*. In the great gasoline shortage of 1973, people in some states waited in line for hours before dawn for gasoline stations to open; some even hoarded gasoline in oil drums in their backyards. Thus we became painfully aware of our dependence on oil. But our dependence is nothing compared with that of the Europeans and, even worse, the Japanese, who are in an extremely vulnerable position because they must import practically all their oil. At all times of the day and night, 365 days a year, the shipping lane between the Persian Gulf and Japan is punctuated every few miles with a gigantic tanker carrying the huge volume of oil necessary to fuel Japanese industry. In brief, the oil-importing countries have had little choice but to buy OPEC oil despite its high price.

There is a third reason that the demand for oil is inelastic: Although it is an essential item, it often represents a minor fraction of total costs. This is particularly true in manufacturing: Factories seldom shut down because the price of oil increases.

2. Not only was the elasticity low, but the demand curve for oil had also shifted out rapidly during the boom of 1972 and 1973. By the time OPEC began hiking the price, demand was both inelastic and high.

3. At the same time, the OPEC *supply* of oil was being curtailed—for noneconomic reasons. Because of the Arab embargo on sales to the United States and other countries supporting Israel in the 1973 Yom Kippur war, OPEC's oil exports fell by about 25 percent in the period when it was making its most substantial price increases. Although this was a politically motivated reduction in supply, it had an important economic side effect: By keeping oil in short supply, it helped make the rapid price increases stick.

4. One very large oil producer, Saudi Arabia, does not need the money from large-scale oil production. Its population is very small, and it has vast funds saved from past oil sales. Therefore, it can comfortably support the high oil price by cutting back production. Notice in Figure 22-4 how far below capacity the Saudis had decreased their production by 1975. (In addition, note how the other four low-population nations in OPEC had done the same.)

5. The international oil companies, which buy oil from OPEC members, were very much concerned over maintaining their sources of supply. They were therefore hesitant to switch away from a supplier with a high price to one with a somewhat lower price. As a consequence, they were reluctant to encourage price cutting among OPEC members by playing one member off against another.

6. Competition among OPEC members is also inhibited by the chemical characteristics of oil from different sources. Refineries

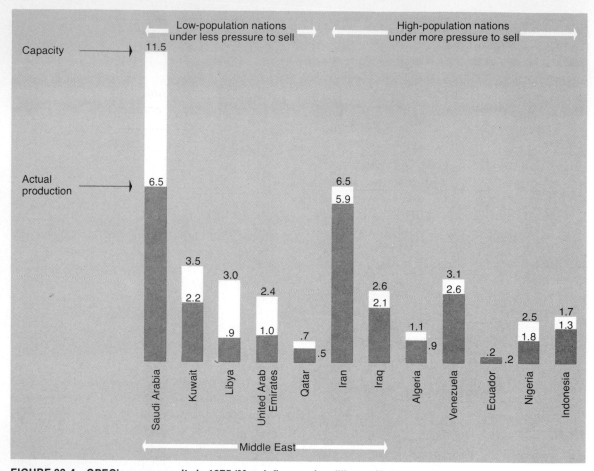

FIGURE 22-4 OPEC's overcapacity in 1975 (March figures, in millions of barrels a day).
Because of their low population, the five countries on the left were under less pressure to
sell oil. Their willingness to cut back production below capacity meant that OPEC was
able to control the oversupply problem that often destroys a cartel.

designed for oil from a particular source may not be able to use oil from other sources.

In spite of these influences that reduced the pressure to cut prices, there have been strains within OPEC. In particular, there is a conflict of interest between members whose oil is showing signs of depletion (Iran, Venezuela) and those (most notably Saudi Arabia) whose wells are expected to produce for decades to come. Iran and Venezuela have an interest in getting as high a price as possible while they still have oil. On the other hand, Saudi Arabia has an interest in not spoiling the market for oil in future decades. (Note that a high price of oil now encourages the long-run development of substitute forms of energy, and thus tends to weaken the demand for oil in the 1990s and beyond.)

This divergence in interests has caused

disputes within OPEC over oil prices. For example, at the OPEC meeting in late 1976, most members wanted a 15 percent price increase in 1977, while Saudi Arabia held out for 10 percent. Because of the Saudis' huge productive capacity, they were able to make their views prevail; the 1977 price increase was only 10 percent.

ELEMENTS OF STABILITY IN AN OLIGOPOLY

We have seen that one of the ways oligopolists can try to avoid price wars is to form a cartel and agree formally on price. But within the United States, cartels are illegal. How, then, do American oligopolists reduce the pressure of price competition? How do they avoid price wars and arrive at a reasonably stable—and profitable—price? (Obviously, it is important for oligopolists to find answers to these questions. Equally matched giant competitors may face mutual exhaustion if they decide to slug it out by trying to capture markets with prices below average costs. In their exhaustion, they have a mutual interest in coming to a *modus vivendi*—to live and let live.)

The Kinked Demand Curve

The best way to understand the idea of a kinked demand curve is to put yourself in the position of one of the three large oligopolists in an industry. If you cut your price, the other two competing firms are likely to take your act as a challenge. Since neither can afford to let you take away a share of its market, it is therefore likely to meet your price cut with a price cut of its own. On the other hand, if you raise price, your competitors may consider this a golden opportunity. By keeping their own selling price stable, they will be able to capture a share of your sales. You therefore perceive that your competitors are behaving in a nonsymmetrical way: If you drop your price they will follow you, but if you raise your price they will not.

Figure 22-5 shows how this sort of behavior can lead to price stability. In this market, the three firms are assumed to be of equal size; each initially has one-third of total sales. Suppose your firm is the one illustrated. You know that if you change price and if your competitors follow, you will retain your present one-third of the market. Thus you will move along the relatively vertical demand curve labeled d_f. (Note that at any price, say P_2, the quantity you sell on d_f is one-third of the total sales shown on the market demand curve D.) However, d_f is relevant only if you quote a price *below* the existing price at E_1. If you quote a price *above* this—say P_3—your competitors will *not* follow. Instead, they will stand pat and will cut into your market, as shown by the red arrow.

Therefore, if you drop your price below E_1, you face demand d_f, while if you raise your price above E_1, you face demand d. In other words, the expected behavior of your competitors presents you with the kinked demand curve shown by the heavy lines in Figure 22-5. Faced with this demand curve, how do you maximize profit? The likely answer: Select point E_1 where the kink occurs. Thus, you don't rock the boat. You continue to quote the price P_1 that you and your competitors have been quoting, and you service your safe traditional share of the market. Your profit is shown as the shaded blue area. (Experiment with other points on your kinked demand curve above and below E_1 and note that in each case your profit area is less. Moreover, also shift AC up or down a bit, and notice that E_1 remains your profit-maximizing point. Thus you tend to keep your price stable even though your costs change.)

The idea of a kinked demand curve was first developed in the 1930s, and it has had continuing appeal as a way of explaining why oligopoly prices are stable, and in particular, why they often remain firm during recessions when demand declines. For example, the price auto manufacturers charge dealers tends to be relatively firm during a recession. (There are, nevertheless, exceptions. In 1974, auto manufacturers offered rebates—in effect, price reductions—in order to increase their lagging sales.)

The kinked demand curve has, however, been controversial. In the first place, the argument is incomplete; while it may explain price stability, it does not explain how price is established in the first place. For example, in Figure 22-5, price remains at P_1 because it started out at P_1. But how did it get to be P_1 in the first place? It just sits there in this diagram unexplained, like the "smile without the cat" in *Alice in Wonderland.* The second difficulty with the kinked demand idea is that prices are not as rigid as the theory suggests. As already noted, automobile prices did indeed fall during 1974.

FIGURE 22-5 Kinked demand curve.
Suppose that you have two equally large competitors, and your initial equilibrium is at E_1. If your competitors were to follow any price change you might make, the demand curve you would face would be d_f; regardless of the price you might quote, you would retain your basic one-third share of the market. (For example, if you were to quote price P_2, you would sell 10 units.) Unfortunately, however, you do not face d_f throughout its entire range, because your competitors will not always follow your price change. They will follow only if you reduce price, so the only portion of d_f that is relevant is the heavily lined section below E_1. What demand curve do you face if you raise price? Since your competitors do not follow you in this case, they will cut into your share of the market (as shown by the red arrow). Thus, the demand you face will be d. To sum up: If your competitors follow your price change down but not up, you will face the heavy, kinked demand curve.

Furthermore, the 1970s have been marked by many increases in oligopoly prices, an outcome which the kinked demand curve would not predict. How, then, do we explain the price changes that do occur in oligopolistic industries?

Price Leadership

One explanation of orderly changes in oligopoly prices may be found in price leadership. Just as firms come to the conclusion that price cuts may be self-defeating, they may also decide that it is desirable to follow a firm that takes the first step and raises price. If all other companies follow, the price increase will stick—to the mutual benefit of each of the firms.

To illustrate the leadership concept in Figure 22-5, suppose that you are a price leader. Then the demand curve you face no longer has a kink. Instead, it is the line d_f throughout its entire length, because your competitors will follow your price change both down *or* up. In these circumstances, you will be able to lead the industry up to a new, higher price, provided you are confident that the other firms will indeed follow your lead.

If your leadership is thus assured, the result may approach that of a cartel. As leader, you will select the price that will maximize your own profits, and your choice should be approximately the price that will maximize profits for the industry as a whole. However, as there is no formal agreement, the problem of "cheating" may be substantial. The leader may find others shaving prices (or providing rebates) in order to increase their market shares. For example, during this century, giant U.S. Steel has sometimes acted as price leader, and has not reacted to under-the-table price cuts by some smaller firms. (It was better to ignore them than to retaliate and thereby lead the whole industry into a round of price cutting.) Consequently, these smaller firms were able to take advantage of U.S. Steel's

price umbrella to cut into its markets: In 1910, U.S. Steel held almost half the market; but by the 1950s, its share had fallen to about one-third. Thus, while the giant in an industry may have a decided advantage from lower costs, the smaller firms may also have a major advantage: They may be able to compete aggressively without provoking competitive responses from the giant.

In practice, it may be quite difficult to identify any clear pattern of price leadership. There may be no consistent price leader; first one company may take the initiative in changing prices, then another. General Motors does not always announce its new model prices first; the initiative is sometimes exercised by Ford or Chrysler. And price leadership may be quite tentative. One firm may announce a price increase, to see if others follow. If they don't, the price will be rescinded. (This sort of "trial and error" pricing may just be a way for the firm to test whether or not it can act as a price leader.)

Finally, even when oligopolists follow a pattern of price leadership, we cannot be certain that they are exerting monopoly power. If costs have generally risen by, say, 10 percent, an oligopolist may raise price by about 10 percent in the expectation that others will follow. Price leadership has apparently occurred; yet the firms may merely be defending themselves against rising costs, rather than exploiting monopoly power at the expense of the public. (For a way in which oligopolists may end up quoting the same price even though there is no price leadership, see Box 22-1.)

NON-PRICE COMPETITION

Under certain circumstances, firms may fear that price reductions are dangerous; they could touch off a price war. And, even where they have no such fears, they may find that

BOX 22-1
FOCAL POINT PRICING

Thomas Schelling's noneconomic example illustrates how independent firms may end up quoting the same price even though they do not collude:

You are to meet someone in New York City. You have not been instructed where to meet; you have no prior understanding with the person on where to meet; and you cannot communicate with each other. You are simply told that you will have to guess where to meet and he is being told the same thing and that you will just have to try to make your guesses coincide.

You are told the date but not the hour of this meeting; the two of you must guess the exact minute of the date for meeting. At what time will you appear at the chosen meeting place?†

Of the thousands of possible choices, Schelling discovered that a majority of people selected the information booth at Grand Central Station, and almost all chose high noon. Both are "focal points" because they provide the best guess of what the other party will do. So too with price: A retailer who wants to guess the price that competitors will charge in the range of say, $11.20 to $12.40, may well select the focal point $11.95. This price is based on the familiar tradition of "charging $12 but making it seem like $11." Thus, with no communication whatsoever between firms, this $11.95 focal point may become the industry price.

†Thomas C. Schelling, *The Strategy of Conflict* (Cambridge: Harvard University Press, 1960), p. 56.

other ways of competing are more attractive than cutting price.

Advertising

One form of non-price competition is advertising. The firm that advertises has a simple objective: to make people want its product and buy more. That does not mean, however, the more advertising the better. Since advertising must be paid for, it also shifts up the cost curve. At some point, the firm will find that enough advertising is enough; any further expenditures would not pay for themselves in terms of increased sales.

In an oligopoly, the primary goal of advertising may be to capture the competitor's market. Thus, for example, the primary effect of Chrysler's advertising is to take sales away from General Motors or Ford. And those two companies, in turn, advertise to take sales away from their rivals.

Advertising also increases the total market demand for the product. Thus, a monopolist such as AT&T advertises to increase the demand for long-distance calls. And some associations of perfect competitors advertise to increase market demand, even though no single producer would find it profitable to advertise. (For example, the orange growers' association advertises to encourage people to drink orange juice.) But the most heavily advertised products lie in the battleground between perfect competition and monopoly, where an advertiser can gain both by taking sales away from competitors and by increasing the total demand for the product.

The social value of advertising is a controversial issue. On behalf of their industry, advertising agencies make the following points:

1. Advertising helps the consumer to make better decisions. It informs the public of new products and of improvements in old products. By informing consumers of what is available, it reduces "search costs." For example, advertising may tell consumers where the bargains are, so they can save time and effort in shopping.

2. Advertising helps new producers to compete. By informing the public of a new product, it helps the producer to expand sales toward a high-volume, low-cost level. (A closely related point is that advertising stimulates research; if new products could not be advertised and sold in huge quantities, the cost of their research and development could not be covered.)

3. Advertising supports our communications industry. Radio and TV are financed by advertising revenues. Even the mundane classified ads play a significant role in the support of newspapers.

4. Advertising results in higher-quality products: The goodwill built up from past advertising of a brand name product may be an asset of great value for a firm—an asset it will be careful not to damage by turning out a shoddy product. Moreover, advertising acts as a guarantee of quality in another way: Producers are restrained from false advertising by fear of action by the Federal Trade Commission.

5. By encouraging the public to spend more, advertising stimulates production and creates jobs.

On the other side, critics respond:

1. Most advertising represents a waste. The heaviest advertising takes place in oligopolistic markets. Firm *A* advertises to steal customers from firm *B*, and *B* advertises to cancel out the effects of *A*'s advertising. After advertising, *A* and *B* share the market in roughly the same way as before. Little has changed, except that costs have gone up. So consumers pay more for this product merely because it is advertised.

2. Where advertising is not a self-canceling waste, it is often pernicious, creating frivolous wants, distorting tastes, and increasing the materialism of a materialistic society.

3. Advertising often misinforms. For example, if a firm falsely claims that its headache remedy is best (when in fact it is less effective than competing products), consumption purchases may be distorted. In this case, the cost of advertising includes both the waste in resources that go into making this claim and the cost to people who buy a less effective product.

4. Much advertising is offensive and debases our society. We cannot listen to radio or TV without being bombarded with tasteless ads.

5. Advertising is a poor way to pursue the goal of full employment. If aggregate demand is too low, it should be increased by expansive fiscal and monetary policies.

It is difficult to compare these conflicting claims (except on point 5, where the case for advertising is particularly weak). Our conclusion is that the statement that advertising involves "*all* loss" is too extreme, and so is the statement that advertising involves "*no* loss whatsoever." What do you think?

Other Ways in Which Firms Compete

In addition to advertising, there are other forms of non-price competition. A firm can hire a larger sales staff in order to beat the bushes for customers. Or, it can spend more on research, development, or design to improve the quality or attractiveness of its product. (This step may be welcomed by the consumer. But efforts to increase the appeal of a product may get out of hand, particularly in an industry where governmental price regulation limits companies to non-price competition. Lewis Engman, the former chairman of the Federal Trade Commission, has observed that the typical airline commercial is "like an ad for a combination bawdy house and dinner theater.") The typical oligopolist, such as the auto or appliance manufacturer, is locked in a struggle to match the competitors' price, and advertising, and sales force, and improvements in design and quality. Little wonder that the world of the oligopolist seems more competitive than that of the farmer, who may operate in a "perfectly competitive" market, but who never even thinks of a neighbor as a competitor. (But remember: According to the economist's definition, farming is the more competitive industry, since a single farmer has no influence whatsoever over price.)

BARRIERS TO ENTRY

If several large oligopolistic firms (like the auto companies) have been competing in the past by making huge expenditures on design improvements and advertising, it may be almost impossible for a new firm to break into the industry unless it too has vast sums to spend. There are other barriers to entry into an industry as well. For example, existing firms may be associated with widely recognized brand names. (In some countries, the brand name "Kodak" is almost synonymous with "camera," and how do you compete with that?) In other cases, existing firms may have patents, without which production may be difficult or impossible.

But the single most important barrier to entry is the fact that, in most oligopoly industries, costs fall over a wide range of output. In other words, economies of large-scale production make it very difficult for a small firm to compete. In order to get started, a new firm must have "deep pockets"; it must have the financial resources to set up a productive facility large enough to move it quickly into the high-volume, low-cost range of production. (For this reason, new competition in oligopolistic markets often comes, not from struggling new firms, but rather from giants from another industry. For example, Xerox was faced with major new competition when IBM and Kodak entered the market for office copiers.)

If such barriers to entry are low or nonexistent, new firms freely enter. The result is no longer oligopoly (with a few sellers), but, instead, a quite different market form.

MONOPOLISTIC COMPETITION: Low Barriers to Entry

If the average cost curve stops falling and starts to rise when the firm is producing only a small fraction of the total industry sales, there is no cost advantage in being a giant in the industry, and many competitors successfully enter. This situation sounds like perfect competition, but it is not if firms are producing a differentiated product. In this case, the result is *monopolistic competition*. Because each firm is selling a somewhat different product, each has some control over price; if it raises its price slightly, it won't lose all its customers. Thus, it does not face the perfect competitor's perfectly horizontal demand curve. Instead, its demand curve slopes downward to the right—but not much. Because of the existence of many competitors, its control over price is not

great. In other words, the demand curve facing the individual producer is quite elastic, as illustrated in Figure 22-6.

> *Monopolistic competition* exists when there are many sellers of differentiated products. The demand curve facing the individual competitor is quite elastic, but not perfectly so.

Product differentiation need not involve a physical difference. Retail trade is an example. Different stores sell very similar products; indeed, they may sell the same brand names—Gillette razors, Kellogg's corn flakes, etc. But the individual stores differ in an important respect: They are in different locations. The consumer may be willing to pay slightly more for one store's Kellogg's corn flakes than for another's because it is closer. Because of its location, the first store has some control over price, al-

FIGURE 22-6 Equilibrium for a typical firm in monopolistic competition.

(a) **In the short run.** The firm faces a sloping demand d_1 because its product is differentiated. Short-run equilibrium is at E_1, with the above-normal profit shown in the shaded area. This attracts new firms into the industry, shifting this firm's d to the left until a new equilibrium is reached at E_2 in panel b.

(b) **In the long run.** This is a long-run equilibrium because above-normal profits have been eliminated by the entry of new firms. (Note: In these two panels, **AC** is the same. The only thing that changes is demand, which shifts to the left from d_1 to d_2 as a result of the new entrants.)

though not a great deal. It if charges a much higher price, buyers will bypass it to go to the less expensive (though less convenient) competitor.

It is relatively easy to get into retailing; a vast pool of funds is not necessary to buy a corner store or to run a gas station. Where existing firms are making large above-normal profits, new entrants will come in, tending to eliminate these excess profits, as illustrated in Figure 22-6. Initially, the typical firm shown in panel *a* is operating at E_1 and earning the shaded profit. But, as new competitors enter and capture some of its sales, the demand curve it faces shifts to the left. New firms continue to enter, thus shifting its demand curve to the left, until demand is tangent to the average cost curve as shown in panel *b*. Faced with this new demand curve, the best the firm can now do is to select the point of tangency E_2, where it earns no excess profit. (Any other point on the demand curve would leave it operating at a loss.) Thus, free entry tends to eliminate above-normal profits for the run-of-the-mill firm in monopolistic competition. (If a firm enjoys some specific advantage, such as special management skills, it will continue to earn above-normal profits.)

Observe in panel *b* that monopolistic competition seems to involve inefficiency. At the firm's output of 80 units, MC ($50) is not equal to price ($90), so there is no reason to expect an efficient allocation of resources. Consumer demand could be satisfied at lower cost if there were fewer firms, each producing more (that is, if the typical firm in panel *b* were to increase its output from 80 units to 100, where its average cost is at the minimum $85 level). If the industry were reorganized in this way, wouldn't the result be a more efficient allocation of resources?

The answer is: Not necessarily. True, cost would be lower, and this would be an advantage for society. But there would also be a disadvantage: Since there would be fewer firms, consumers would have less choice. For example, a reduction in the number of retail stores would mean that those remaining could sell a larger volume, thus lowering their costs (and prices); but it would also mean that some customers would have to travel farther to shop. Perhaps the convenience of local stores is worth the slightly higher price we have to pay.

In short, when a product is differentiated, it becomes difficult to pin down the idea of efficiency as simply as we did with an undifferentiated product (in Box 20-1). As a practical matter, no economist argues that the government should undertake broad regulations of firms operating in monopolistic competition. It is hard to make a federal case out of inefficiences (if any) that arise from monopolistic competition.

The characteristics of the major types of market structure are summarized in Table 22-1.

POLICIES TO DEAL WITH MARKET POWER: Some Problems

While monopolistic competition raises no major policy problems, the same is not true of oligopoly. In dealing with oligopolists, the government seeks to prevent them from developing monopoly power. As one measure, legislation has made the takeover of one firm by another illegal if it is expected to lessen competition substantially. Collusive price fixing is likewise against the law. Furthermore, a number of regulatory agencies have been established to control prices in oligopolistic industries. For example, the Civil Aeronautics Board (CAB) controls airline fares.

But the task of developing policies to deal with market power is not easy. It is not certain that breaking up large firms or controlling them will improve the performance of the economy. A number of problems complicate the life of the policymaker.

TABLE 22-1
Types of Market Structure

Type of market	Number of producers and type of product	Entry	Influence over price	Examples
Monopoly	One producer; product with no close substitute	Difficult or impossible	Substantial (price maker unless price regulated by government)	Telephone service
Oligopoly	(a) Few producers; little or no product differentiation	Difficult	Some (price searcher)	Steel Aluminum
	(b) Few producers; differentiated product	Difficult	Some (price searcher)	Autos Computers Cigarettes
Monopolistic competition	Many producers; differentiated product	Easy	A little	Most retail trade
Perfect competition	Many producers; undifferentiated product	Easy	None (price taker)	Wheat Some other agricultural products

1. Advantages of Large Size

Although size brings the danger that the consumer will be exploited with monopoly pricing, it also can bring benefits. This is most clearly true in the case of a "natural monopoly," where a single large firm has lower costs than a number of smaller firms. If such a natural monopoly is broken up, costs will rise, resulting in an economic loss for society. For example, splitting up the local telephone company would increase competition, but it would also substantially increase costs. (Think of the cost of installing two or three sets of telephone lines in every community.) The proper way to deal with the telephone monopoly is therefore through price regulation, not by splitting it up in an attempt to establish competition in local telephone service.[2] [The principle that costs should be considered before a firm is broken up has not always been recognized by the courts. For example, in the Alcoa case of 1945, Judge Learned Hand stated that the purpose of the antitrust laws is to "perpetuate and preserve, for its own sake and *in spite of possible cost*, an organization of industry in small units which can effectively compete with each other." (Italics are added.)]

Another advantage of large firms is that they can afford research and development. Thus, they can be a source of rapid economic growth. In his classic defense of large firms, Joseph Schumpeter wrote:

As soon as we go into details and inquire into the individual items in which progress was most conspicuous, the trail leads not to the doors of those firms that work under conditions of comparatively free competition but precisely to the

---

[2]While it can be argued that one company should provide all the telephone service, it is not clear that one company should provide all that service *and* manufacture telephones as well. The Justice Department has brought suit to require AT&T to split off Western Electric, a subsidiary that manufactures phones and other equipment.

doors of the large concerns—which, as in the case of agricultural machinery, also account for much of the progress in the competitive sector—and a shocking suspicion dawns upon us that big business may have had more to do with creating that standard of life than keeping it down.[3]

Although large firms can finance research, this point should not be exaggerated; it is surprising how many innovations come from smaller firms. For example, the oxygen furnace (one of the major twentieth-century innovations in basic steel) was invented, not by a giant United States firm, but by a small Austrian firm which was less than one-third the size of a single plant of U.S. Steel. Furthermore, the American steel industry was slow to adopt the new technology; it did so only under severe competitive pressures from imported steel during the 1960s. It was competition, not size, which accounted for technological change in this case.

2. When Is Competition "Unfair?"

In order to prevent the elimination of competitors, the government may take steps to limit cutthroat competition and other predatory acts. But it is difficult to know where cutthroat competition ends and legitimate competition begins. Competition which causes a few bankruptcies can play a useful function in weeding out the incompetent. But if a firm is allowed to drive *all* its competitors into bankruptcy, the result is monopoly—a most unfortunate consequence if it does not bring lower costs, but results only in a concentration of market power. The tough question is this: How can the government introduce regulations that will protect an industry from cutthroat competition without protecting it from *healthy* competition as well?

Consider, for example, the Civil Aeronautics Board (CAB), which was established to limit ruinous competition among airlines. By and large, economists agree that for much of its history, it has gone far beyond this and limited even healthy competition, thus keeping airline fares excessively high. The strongest evidence was provided on the Los Angeles–San Francisco run where Pacific Southwest (a local, within-state airline not subject to CAB regulations) charged a price far below that of the national airlines. As a result, the national airlines were also forced to cut their prices, so that by the mid-1970s the fare on this run was one-third to one-half less than on interstate routes of similar length. (Price competition did not erode profits on the San Francisco–Los Angeles run, since lower fares were offset by higher volume; that is, by fewer empty seats.) The CAB's role in keeping air fares high was further illustrated in 1974, when it rejected an application by a private British airline (Laker) to provide service between New York and London for $125 each way, or little more than a third the economy rate then charged by other airlines.

However, during the last half of the seventies, steps were taken to permit more price competition among airlines, both within the United States and internationally. In 1977, Laker's application was approved and other airlines followed in cutting prices. In part, this relaxation of regulation was due to a broad coalition against high regulated prices, which included Senator Kennedy and important members of both the Ford and Carter administrations. In part, it was the result of a 1975 Department of Transportation study that debunked the airlines' claim that an end to price regulation would result in a wholesale termination of airline service to smaller cities. The airlines' argument was that they needed high prices on the heavily traveled routes in order to make the profits necessary to cover losses on the less traveled routes. The Department's study estimated that only 29 of the 394 American cities then serviced would lose their airline service if prices were no longer regulated.

---

[3]Joseph Schumpeter, *Capitalism, Socialism and Democracy* (New York: Harper, 1942), 3rd ed., p. 82.

This history of CAB controls seems to lead us, then, to a fairly skeptical view of regulation. (For reasons for even further skepticism, see Box 22-2.) But don't forget: Regulation may be an extremely valuable weapon in the government's antimonopoly arsenal. As stated earlier, it may be the best way of dealing with natural monopoly. So we conclude that regulation in itself is not necessarily either good or bad. Each case depends on the answers to a number of questions: Are the regulators acting in the interests of consumers or of the producers in the industry? Are they keeping prices down or up? And are they regulating a natural monopoly (like telephones) or a naturally competitive industry (like the parking lots in Box 22-2)?

3. What Constitutes Collusion?

If cutthroat (or "unfair," or "antisocial") competition is hard to identify, so is collusion. There may be exceptional cases, of course, where collusion has clearly taken place. For example, competitors may get together with the specific intention of fixing price and splitting up the market. In such cases, they can be sent to jail for their efforts. (See the electrical manufacturers' conspiracy, Box 22-3.)[4] But what is to be done in more complex cases, where oligopolists with a common interest arrive at the same price without even so much as a wink or a nod because all firms follow when one announces a price change? Certainly we cannot make it illegal to quote the current market price. If a firm is only "meeting the price competition," how can it be condemned? After all, doesn't a perfectly competitive producer (like the wheat farmer) also sell at the going market price? Similar prices do not prove collusion.

The courts have struggled with this tough problem for decades, not always with consistent results. In the early (1927) International Harvester case, the Supreme Court ruled that price leadership is not illegal unless there is a clear agreement between firms:

. . . the fact that competitors may see proper, in the exercise of their own judgment, to follow the prices of another manufacturer, does not establish any suppression of competition or show any sinister domination.

Yet, by 1946, the Supreme Court was ready to hold cigarette manufacturers guilty of price fixing even though they were not involved in any price agreement.

4. Conglomerate Mergers

The takeover of a competitor in the same market ("horizontal" merger) will tend to lessen competition. So may the takeover of a supplier or a customer ("vertical" merger). But how about takeovers in other fields—the "conglomerate" mergers which were so popular in the go-go days of the 1960s, when International Telegraph and Telephone (IT&T), Ling-Temco-Vought, Litton, and others were flying so high? IT&T, for example, acquired Avis (car rental), Sheraton (hotels), Continental Baking, Grinnel (automatic fire sprinklers), Hartford Fire Insurance, and many, many others. (During the stock market boom of the mid-1960s, stock purchasers responded enthusiastically to rapidly growing firms, bidding up the price of their stock to astronomical levels and thus encouraging their further expansion.)

Dealing with conglomerate mergers is a difficult problem. Size itself can be considered objectionable, especially if one considers the political implications of the great concentrations of economic power held by conglomerates. (IT&T, in particular, did not provide reassurance on this point when it

[4]This case, and a number of other business ventures which ended badly, are described in John Brooks, *The Fate of Edsel and Other Business Ventures* (New York: Harper & Row, 1962).

BOX 22-2
THE PARABLE OF THE PARKING LOTS

Producers have a natural interest to narrow the market and raise the price.

Adam Smith

Henry Manne, professor of law at the University of Miami, tells a simple parable to illustrate the problems of government regulation:†

Once upon a time in a city not far away, thousands of people would crowd into the local football stadium on a Saturday afternoon. The problem of parking was initially solved by a number of big commercial parking lots whose owners formed the Association of Professional Parking Lot Employers (APPLE). But, as time passed and crowds grew, every plumber, lawyer, and schoolteacher who owned a house in the neighborhood went into the parking business on Saturday afternoon, and cars appeared in every driveway and on most lawns. Members of APPLE viewed the entry of these "amateurs" into their business with no great enthusiasm, especially since some were charging a lower fee. Stories began to circulate about their fly-by-night methods, and the dents they had put in two cars were given wide publicity (even though, on investigation, it was discovered that denting was an equally serious problem in the commercial lots).

At a meeting of all members of APPLE, emotions and applause ran high as one speaker after another pointed out—in some cases, in a very statesmanlike way—that parking should be viewed, not as a business, but as a profession governed by professional standards. In particular, cutthroat price competition with amateurs should be regarded as unethical. The one concrete proposal, quickly adopted, was that APPLE members should contribute $1 per parking spot "to improve their public image, and put their case before the proper authorities."

No accounting was ever made of this money, but it must have been spent wisely,

since within a few months the city council passed an ordinance to regulate industry price and to require that anyone parking cars must be licensed. But it turned out to be difficult for an independent house owner to get a license; it required passing a special driving test to be "professionally administered" by APPLE, a $25,000 investment in parking facilities, and $500,000 in liability insurance. Since every commercial lot found its costs consequently increasing by 20 percent, the city council approved a 20 percent increase in parking fees. (Within a year, APPLE had requested that the city council guarantee the liability insurance, so that people would have no fear of parking in commercial lots. One argument put forward by an APPLE spokesman was that this idea was similar in its intent to recent congressional legislation setting up an insurance scheme for stockbrokers.)

On the next football afternoon, a funny thing happened on the way to the stadium. Since police were out in large numbers to enforce the ordinance, driveways and lawns were empty and long lines of cars were backed up waiting to get into each commercial lot. The snarl was even worse after the game. Some people simply gave up waiting for their

†"The Parable of the Parking Lots," *Public Interest*, no. 23 (Spring 1971), pp. 10–15. Abbreviated with the author's permission.

cars and had to return to retrieve them next day. (There was even a rumor that one car was never found.)

Under political pressure to "do something," the city council sent a stern letter to APPLE threatening to impose "heavy regulation" on the industry unless it was able to "shape up." In response, APPLE decided to go ahead with a "statistical-logistic study of the whole socioeconomic situation" by two computer science professors at the local university. Their report cited the archaic methods of the industry and pointed out that what each firm needed was fewer quill pens and more time on a computer.

As the parking lots began to computerize their operations, it became quite clear that in the face of these rising costs, a further increase in parking fees was required. The increase was quickly approved by city councillors relieved that, in the modernization of the industry, they had finally found a solution. But, unfortunately, it was no solution after all. The problem, it turned out, was not so much deciding which car should be moved where, as actually moving it—and that continued to be done by attendants who had become surly and uncooperative because of the pressure they were facing.

Relief, however, did appear in two forms. First, many people got fed up with the hassle and started watching the game on TV. Second, small boys who lived in the houses closest to the stadium went into the car wash business on Saturday afternoon. They charged $5, but it was worth the price, since they guaranteed a top-quality job. (In fact, they guaranteed that they would spend at least 2 hours on it.) And they always had as many cars as they could handle, even on rainy days—in fact, especially on rainy days.

became involved in schemes to influence a presidential election in Chile.)

But conglomerates may offer substantial benefits, since mergers may provide economies of scale in production, management, or marketing. Moreover, firms with large resources may significantly increase competition if they enter a new industry by buying out one of the smaller firms. (There will then be, say, four major competitors in the industry rather than the previous three.)

Therefore, it is no surprise that government policy toward conglomerates has been rather ambivalent. Some restraints have been exercised; to cite one instance, a court settlement has required IT&T to give up Avis Rent-A-Car. But no broad attack has been made on conglomerates, perhaps because the issue lost much of its urgency during the 1970s when these firms were treated very roughly by a falling stock market and the incentive for further takeovers was reduced. (But another takeover "binge" nevertheless occurred in the late 1970s; see p. 116.)

ANTITRUST LEGISLATION IN THE UNITED STATES: A Summary

> Th' trusts . . . are heejous monsthers built up bc th' enlightened intherprise iv th' men that have done so much to advance progress in our beloved country. . . . On wan hand I wud stamp thim undher fut; on th' other hand not so fast.
> **Peter Finley Donne's characterization of Theodore Roosevelt**

With such complications in the background, it is not surprising that antitrust legislation and enforcement have had a complex history. (On its last business day in early 1969, the outgoing Johnson Administration launched an antitrust case against IBM. The case is now, 10 years later, still underway. If the transcript thus far were lined up, it would take about 30 feet of shelf space. And that represents only the government's half of the case; IBM's defense is just beginning.

BOX 22-3
THE GREAT ELECTRICAL EQUIPMENT CONSPIRACY, AND OTHER MISDEEDS

In the 1950s, the manufacturers of heavy electrical equipment conspired to set prices, thereby raising the cost of almost every power-generating station built in the United States during that period. Senior officials from General Electric, Westinghouse, and 27 other firms ended up in court. Two million dollars in fines were eventually paid, and seven executives each spent 30 days in jail. (In fact, the personal cost to those involved was even more devastating. Almost as soon as the Justice Department began its investigation, the salary of one GE vice-president was cut from $127,000 to $40,000 a year. While he was recovering from that shock, he was fined $4,000 and sent to prison for 30 days. When he got out, GE eased him out of the company altogether.)

Here is how *The Wall Street Journal* described the conspiracy in a passage that strangely echoes the words of Adam Smith, written over two centuries ago and quoted at the beginning of this chapter.

Many of the meetings took place at the conventions of the National Electrical Manufacturers Association and other trade groups. Rather typically, after a conventional and perfectly lawful meeting of some kind, certain members would adjourn for a rump session and a few drinks in someone's suite. It seemed natural enough that mutual business problems would be discussed—specifications, for example—and like as not prices would come up. In time it was easy enough to drift from general talk about prices into what should be done about them—and finally into separate meetings to fix them for everyone's mutual benefit.†

One scheme they used was a complicated form of bidding cartel (somewhat like the antique dealers' cartel in footnote 1 in this chapter). The firms agreed in advance on a "phase of the moon" bidding system involving a 2-week rotation, with each firm knowing whether it should bid low or high on any contract and taking its turn in being the low bidder. (As in most collusive schemes, the pressures to cheat were considerable, and for this reason General Electric finally dropped out. As one executive put it, "No one was living up to the agreements. . . . On every job someone would cut our throat; we lost confidence in the group.")

In 1976 in another case, 47 executives from 22 companies pleaded no contest to federal charges of fixing the prices of cardboard boxes. Included were no less than the president of Container Corporation of America (annual sales: about $1 billion). He was fined $35,000 and had to spend 15 days in jail (more precisely, 15 nights, since the judge allowed him out to work during the day).

†*The Wall Street Journal*, Jan. 10, 1961.

500

While it cannot yet be considered a lifetime occupation, involvement in the IBM antitrust case is no short-term commitment.) Because of the complexities of antitrust legislation, it is not possible to do more than note the highlights.

The Sherman Antitrust Act (1890)

In response to the wave of mergers and the growing concentration of United States industry in the late nineteenth century, Congress passed the Sherman Act. It was direct and to the point. "Every contract, combination in the form of a trust[5] or otherwise, or conspiracy in restraint of trade" was declared illegal. It was likewise illegal to "monopolize, or attempt to monopolize, or combine or conspire . . . to monopolize" trade.

Teddy Roosevelt became the first "trust-busting" President. The surge of legal activity initiated during his presidency led to the breakup of Standard Oil and the American Tobacco Company in 1911.

The Clayton Act (1914)

The Clayton Act spelled out some of the missing details of the Sherman Act. Among its provisions, the Clayton Act:

1. Prohibited *interlocking directorates* designed to lessen competition. (An interlocking directorate exists when a director sits on the board of two or more competing firms.)

2. Prohibited the takeover of another company by the purchase of its common stock, if that takeover "substantially lessens competition." (However, this provision was evaded by firms that purchased the physical assets of the other company instead. This loophole was not closed until the Celler-Kefauver Anti-Merger Act in 1950.)

3. Prohibited *tying* contracts; that is, contracts which require purchasers to buy other items in a seller's line in order to get those they really want. (Such a tying contract, or "full-line forcing," allows a firm with one particularly appealing product to use it to monopolize the sale of other products.)

The Federal Trade Commission Act of 1914

The Federal Trade Commission (FTC), a permanent board of five members, was set up in 1914 to deal with "unfair methods of competition." It was empowered to hold hearings and issue cease-and-desist orders where it found unfair competition. Unfortunately, however, the law did not define what "unfair" meant, and the courts made it clear that they, and not the FTC, would pass judgment on this question. Consequently, the FTC's power was sharply limited. (It does, however, retain a role in controlling market power. For example, since 1973 it has been engaged in a suit against Exxon and other oil companies, charging anticompetitive practices. Like the IBM case, the Exxon suit shows signs of dragging on and on and on.) Currently, a primary function of the FTC is to control misleading advertising and the misrepresentation of products.

These three acts, the Sherman Act, the Clayton Act, and the FTC Act, have formed the cornerstone of United States antitrust policy. (The electrical equipment conspiracy was prosecuted in 1960 as a violation of the Sherman Act.)

The Robinson-Patman Act (1936)

This act, and also the Miller-Tydings Act, are included in this survey because they

---

[5]The word "trust" has a long history. Before the Sherman Act, a favorite way to limit competition was to put common stock of different firms into a "trust," with an agreement for collective action and profit sharing. (The word "antitrust" is now used broadly to refer to any action against a powerful firm or group of firms.)

illustrate how antitrust legislation may decrease, rather than increase, competition. The Robinson-Patman Act was designed, not to protect the consumer, but instead to protect small firms in an industry from larger (often more efficient) competitors. In the words of co-sponsor Wright Patman, the act's objective was to "give the little business fellows a square deal" by curbing price cutting by large discount and chain stores. (It was therefore sometimes called the Chain Store Law.) Specifically, it was designed to prevent large stores from buying from suppliers at quantity discounts unless such discounts were justified on the basis of actual cost economies. It also prohibited stores from selling to the public "at unreasonably low prices." Its major effect was to impede, though not prevent, the efficient development of retail trade.

The Miller-Tydings Act (1937)

This is another law which puts the interests of small business above those of the buying public. It exempted "fair trade" contracts from antitrust laws, when such contracts are permitted by state law. (Under a fair trade contract, the manufacturer of a name-brand good could fix the price that retail stores charge the public.) During the 1960s and 1970s, manufacturers found it increasingly difficult to enforce such contracts, and, under heavy public attack, the fair trade exemption was ended.

A Final Word: The "Rule of Reason" and "Workable Competition"

United States antitrust legislation was launched on a wave of hostility toward the growing giants of the late nineteenth century, and toward their predatory, anticompetitive methods. But, since the days of the nineteenth-century "robber barons," there have been relatively few pure black and white situations. Antitrust history is largely a struggle with difficult gray areas.

At an early stage, in the 1920 U.S. Steel

case, the Supreme Court enunciated the "rule of reason." The Court held that mere size was no offense; giant U.S. Steel was let off because the Court judged that it had not actually exercised monopoly power. But standards change. By 1945, the Court held that guilt does not require any overt act. In the Alcoa case of that year, the Court decided that even if a firm's actions might be otherwise reasonable, these actions are nevertheless illegal if they help the firm to maintain a monopoly position. For example, one reasonable business policy is to expand plant capacity in anticipation of increased demand. But precisely this action was judged to make Alcoa guilty, because it tended to block out potential new firms:

> . . . [Alcoa] insists that it never excluded competitors; but we can think of no more effective exclusion than progressively to embrace each new opportunity as it opens, and to face every newcomer with new capacity already geared into a great organization, having the advantage of experience, trade connections and the elite of personnel.

Between the permissive U.S. Steel decision in 1920 and the much tougher Alcoa decision in 1945, the pendulum had obviously swung a long way.

In the face of the need to balance the complex considerations of market power, tacit collusion, economies of scale, and the other issues which monopoly and oligopoly raise, it may be too much to hope for a final solution. Perfect competition is the perfect answer only in textbooks. In the real world, we must settle for "workable competition," where we gain many of the advantages of large-scale business, but curb the more flagrant abuses. Harvard Prof. Richard Caves has compared antitrust laws with traffic laws. Going 58 miles an hour in a 55-mile zone represents no calamity. But the police are there to catch the speeder who goes 80. The fact that we *might* get caught makes most of us drive a little more carefully.

Similarly, the electrical machinery and cardboard-box cases described in Box 22-3 remind business executives that there is a cell awaiting the flagrant offender; they are likely to be more careful as a result.

Moreover, fear of prosecution by the government is not the only discipline a business faces. A firm may also be sued by a competitor who has been damaged by anticompetitive practices. In such a civil antitrust suit, the court is allowed to award the injured party up to three times the amount of the damage incurred. For example, after the electrical equipment executives were sentenced to jail on *criminal* charges of price fixing, their companies were also taken to court in almost 2,000 *civil* suits, and as a consequence, they had to pay an estimated $400 million to $600 million.[6] Obviously, this "treble damage" clause provides a substantial incentive for private firms to act as investigators in unearthing antitrust violations.

CONCLUSIONS: Chapters 21 and 22

When market prices are not set in a perfectly competitive way, tough problems are posed for policymakers, and society faces the possibility of substantial deadweight efficiency losses. (Table 22-2 shows one authority's informed guess of how large losses may be. Notice that his estimate includes both the cost to society of allocative inefficiency (because monopolists and oligopolists produce too little output) and the cost of technical inefficiency (because firms are often not producing on their lowest possible cost curves). The total estimated efficiency cost for the United States exceeds 6 percent of our GNP. This may not sound like much, but in fact it is a whopping sum. (In 1978, 6 percent of GNP amounted to more than $120 billion.)

TABLE 22-2
Guestimated Cost to Society because Perfectly Competitive Pricing Does Not Prevail

	Estimated 1966 cost as a percentage of GNP
Allocative inefficiency due to resource misallocation: By monopolists and oligopolists in unregulated sectors	1.5%
In regulated sectors	0.6
Technical inefficiency due to inadequate cost control by firms insulated from the discipline of competition	2.0
Waste from advertising and other promotional efforts	1.0
Other	1.1
Total	About 6.2% of GNP

Source: F. M. Scherer, *Industrial Market Structure and Economic Performance* (Chicago: Rand McNally, 1970), p. 408.

[6]Giant, wealthy IBM is a favorite target for such suits. For example, in the early 1970s, Telex Corporation won an award of over $350 million from IBM, a decision that earned Telex's lawyer a $50-million fee—a good return for the 100-hour workweek he had averaged for 18 months. (Among other things, he and his staff had to wade through *30 million pages* of documents provided by IBM.) But there was a sour ending. An appeals court reversed the judgment against IBM, and Telex refused to pay the lawyer's fee. The result: The lawyer sued Telex, his former client, and in return Telex sued the lawyer for leading the company into imprudent litigation against IBM. At last report, the legal snarl had still not been resolved.

Key Points

1. Many American markets are oligopolies, dominated by a few firms. In any such market, there is a substantial incentive for firms to collude so that they can act like a monopolist in raising price and restricting output. Such monopolization of an industry would lead to an inefficient allocation of the nation's resources.

2. An important example of a collusive agreement is OPEC, the cartel of oil exporting countries. In 1973 and 1974, this organization more than quadrupled the world price of oil. The result was the greatest peacetime transfer of wealth in history.

3. Our antitrust laws prohibit American firms from forming cartels, and from engaging in other forms of collusion that restrict competition. Nonetheless, there are forms of tacit collusion (such as price leadership) that are difficult to prosecute, but that may allow oligopolists to exercise monopolylike power.

4. Oligopolists often find price competition damaging, and prefer to compete in other ways. They may try to capture sales from rivals by large advertising expenditures, or by expenditures on research to develop better products.

5. When there are no barriers to entry (like patents or economies of large-scale production) and many small firms enter an industry, the result is monopolistic competition. This is like perfect competition except that firms are selling differentiated products. For this reason, each firm has some small control over price. (It faces a slightly sloping demand curve rather than the completely flat demand facing a perfect competitor.) Price *could* be reduced below the level that occurs in monopolistic competition, but only at the cost of providing consumers with less variety. Therefore, little case can be made for government control measures.

6. Although government regulation of industry price may be the appropriate policy in dealing with a natural monopoly, it involves major problems in other industries, such as the airline industry, where it has raised fares rather than lowering them.

7. Passing and enforcing antitrust laws raise many difficult questions. (For example, how do you know when firms are colluding?) Nonetheless, these laws have improved the competitive tone of American business, because violations can lead to jail sentences, to fines, or to civil suits from competitors for triple damages.

Key Concepts

concentration ratio
natural oligopoly
product differentiation
collusion
cartel
incentive to cheat
cutthroat competition
kinked demand

price leadership
competition by advertising
competition in product quality
monopolistic competition
mergers: horizontal, vertical, and conglomerate
antitrust policy
workable competition

Problems

22-1 What is the difference between the monopoly-like collusion involved in the cartel in Figure 22-3, and the monopolization of the milk industry in Figure 21-10? Why should the monopolization of an industry be outlawed in the first case, yet condoned—in fact, organized—by the government in the other?

22-2 If there are only four large firms in your industry, explain why collusion would be in your economic interest as a producer. Explain how consumers of your product would be affected. Describe the problems involved in arranging a collusive agreement and in making it stick. Would the agreement be legal?

22-3 What do you think would happen to the world price of oil if:

    (*a*) Huge deposits of oil were discovered off the California coast?

    (*b*) Huge new deposits of oil were located off the Saudi Arabian coast?

    (*c*) Saudi Arabia were to withdraw from OPEC?

    (*d*) There were a major breakthrough in nuclear energy, with fusion (hydrogen) power expected to be a major source of electricity by 1995?

    (*e*) The United States government were to impose a $1 per gallon additional tax on gasoline?

    (*f*) All countries were to raise gasoline taxes by $1 per gallon?

22-4 "Agricultural prices are unstable, but other prices are stable." Evaluate this statement in the light of our discussion of kinked demand and our earlier analysis of agriculture in Chapter 17. To what degree do you believe this difference justifies agricultural price supports?

22-5 On balance, do you think that advertising is beneficial or damaging to society?

22-6 By how much would the price of cars have to fall to compensate you for your restricted choice if one of the companies went bankrupt?

22-7 Until a recent court decision, lawyers who cut their fees below the level allowed by their state bar association could be disbarred. How would you evaluate this regulation from an economic point of view?

22-8 It sounds like a good idea to forbid any firm from predatory price cutting that would drive its competitors out of business. But consider the two examples below. In each case, do you think that the price-cutting action should be judged illegal (as it sometimes has been)?

    (*a*) An efficient firm with lower cost charges a lower price, and thus drives its less efficient competitors out of business. (Under our competitive system, the more efficient take business away from the less efficient. Do you think this is a good system? If the less efficient are not driven out of business, what happens to the cost of producing goods?)

    (*b*) In a natural monopoly with economies of scale, the large expanding firm finds its costs are falling; hence, it lowers its price and drives its small competitors out of business.

Do you see now why enforcing antitrust laws is a difficult business?

22-9 Which of the following agreements between firms in an industry do you judge desirable? Undesirable?

   (*a*) An agreement to convert to the metric system at exactly the same time

   (*b*) An agreement to reduce output by 10 percent to end a glut on the market

   (*c*) An agreement to quote the same price

   (*d*) An agreement by the railroads to lay the same width of track

22-10 Manufacturers of cigarettes and producers of perfume both advertise. Do you think waste is involved in either case? In one more than the other? Discuss the possible benefits from advertising and the possible damage in each case.

22-11 Suppose that, for the last 10 years, a government agency has regulated the prices of hotel rooms, thus preventing price competition among the big companies like Hilton and Sheraton. Suppose, also, that in return, these companies have maintained hotels in many smaller cities. The government is now considering an end to this regulation. As an adviser to this industry, draw up a brief on how dangerous this action would be. Now switch roles, and criticize the brief. In your view, which is the stronger case? Do you think this example is similar to airline regulation?

chapter 23

Problems of the Environment:
Pollution and Congestion

The fact that the nation's commitment to environmental cleanup will impose massive costs is in itself no reason to retrench on the commitment. But their very size does make costs a central factor in the design of control policy. The difference between inefficient and efficient control policies can mean scores, perhaps hundreds, of billions of dollars released for other useful purposes over the next several decades.

Allen V. Kneese and Charles L. Schultze

Pollution comes in many forms. Water pollution fouls our water, damages our recreational resources, and poisons fish; and poisoned fish poison people. But an even more serious problem may be air pollution. Although experts are not yet in agreement on its effects, it has been estimated that poisonous fumes may be reducing the life expectancy of the residents of big cities by 3 years or more. In response to these problems, Congress has passed a number of control measures.

THE COSTLY JOB OF CLEANING UP

As expanded and amended in the early 1970s, the Water Pollution Control Act and the Clean Air Act:

1. Limit the pollutants a firm may discharge into a waterway or into the air. [The Environmental Protection Agency (EPA)

has the responsibility for setting and enforcing these limitations.]

2. Provide subsidies to municipalities for building waste disposal plants; and provide subsidies (in the form of tax reductions) to firms installing pollution control equipment.

3. Limit the pollutants emitted by new-model cars.

There is no question that these policies have been effective in reducing pollution. For example, by 1978 auto manufacturers had reduced carbon monoxide and hydrocarbon emissions from their new models by 80 to 90 percent from the uncontrolled levels of the mid 1960s. Also, water pollution had been reduced between 25 and 50 percent (depending on the measure). Consequently, there are now boutiques in Cleveland along the Cuyahoga, a river that once caught fire

507

because of its heavy dose of pollutants. And as even a critic concedes: "From the Appalachians to the Cascades, shy mountain streams that used to make their escape from paper-mill towns rafted with foam and stinking black with sulfite liquor now manage to sparkle a bit in the sunlight. Crab traps once more dangle from hardware-store ceilings of little towns up the Hudson ...."[1] Furthermore, similar progress has been made in other countries. People no longer suffocate in a London smog, and salmon are reappearing in the Thames.

But now the easy battles have been won and the cleanup program is becoming increasingly costly. One well-known cost involves the jobs that are lost when a plant is forced to close down because it cannot meet pollution-control standards. In addition, there are other costs that are not so well recognized, but are very important and are borne by the entire public:

1. We pay a higher price for many goods because producers often pass on the cost of pollution control to consumers. One such good is paper, which costs us more because of the costs that paper mills face in cutting down their emissions. And we pay hundreds of dollars more to buy a car (and more again each year to operate it) because it now has a cleaner exhaust.

2. We pay higher taxes because of the subsidies granted to firms and municipalities installing pollution-control equipment.

Consequently, the cost of pollution control touches us all—and it is a very large tab: It has been estimated that by the early 1980s we will be spending $40 to $60 billion a year to meet the cleanup standards set in the early 70s.[2]

Because pollution is so costly to control, an important question is whether the present methods are the least expensive ones available. The answer is no; and one of our objectives in this chapter will be to explain why. A second objective will be to outline a better

[1]Tom Alexander, *Fortune*, November 1976, p. 129.

[2]For sources of these estimates, see footnote 6, p. 81. For details on the costs of pollution control in the 1967-1975 period, see Edward F. Denison, "Effects of Selected Changes in the Institutional and Human Environment upon Output per Unit of Input," *Survey of Current Business* (U.S. Department of Commerce), January 1978, pp. 21-44.

BOX 23-1
WHY NOT CONTROL POLLUTION BY ENDING ECONOMIC GROWTH?

All that a no-growth policy can accomplish is to *end the increase* in pollution. Unlike other policies, it holds no promise whatsoever of reducing pollution below its existing heavy levels. Thus it would be inferior to our present policies, which have allowed us to reduce pollution—by a quarter or a half, according to some estimates. (To have achieved such a reduction in pollution by just controlling GNP would have required a massive cut in GNP.)

We therefore conclude that regulating GNP would be an extraordinarily expensive, yet ineffective, way of curing pollution. It is like killing a rat by burning half your house down. Even if you cure the problem, the side effects are appalling. Better by far to find a cure specifically designed to deal with the problem: If the problem is a rat, get a trap; if the problem is pollution, find a policy that directly reduces it.

policy. (A worse policy, and one that is sometimes recommended, is dealt with in Box 23-1.) Finally, before proceeding, we have one more preliminary observation. Although some people suggest that we *eliminate* water and air pollution, a moment's thought makes it clear that this is an impossible objective. Even if we were to bring United States industry to a halt by closing down every plant that did any polluting whatsoever, rainwater would still wash pollutants from a million country barnyards and city streets into our streams. Since it is not possible to eliminate pollution, the practical question is: How far should we cut it back?

POLLUTION: An External Cost

When pollution exists, private and social costs differ. For example, the costs of chemicals to society include not only the private or *internal cost* of production faced by the chemical firm, but also the cost to those who live downstream and must put up with wastes released into the river. While the chemical firm has to bear any internal production cost, any cost downstream is "external" to its operation, since this cost must be borne by others. Hence, this cost downstream is an *external cost*, or a *cost spillover.*

To analyze this problem, first consider the simplest possible example: Suppose that each unit of a good must be treated with a fluid that is then released into a river. In this case, each unit of output involves a constant external pollution cost, shown as the red arrow in Figure 23-1. This diagram also shows that when this external cost is added to the internal cost borne by producers (the hollow arrow MC), the result is the arrow MC_S, the marginal cost of this good to society.

FIGURE 23-1 With pollution, private and social costs differ.
The marginal cost to society of a good (the pink arrow MC_S) includes both the marginal *internal* cost to the producing firm (the hollow arrow MC) plus a marginal *external* cost not borne by the producing firm (the red arrow).

CONTROLLING POLLUTION: The Simplest Case

When there is such an external cost, even perfect competition results in a misallocation of resources, as shown in Figure 23-2. In this figure, MC and MC_S are reproduced from Figure 23-1, and we also show demand D representing, as before, the marginal benefit of this good. The perfectly competitive equilibrium is at E_1, with output Q_1 where demand D is equal to supply S_1, with S_1 reflecting internal, private costs only (since these are the only costs faced by firms making the supply decisions). Since E_1 equalizes only marginal benefit with marginal *private* cost S_1, it is not efficient. An efficient solution requires that marginal benefit be equal to marginal *social* cost, and this occurs at E_2, at the smaller quantity of output Q_2. Thus, we conclude that in a free, competitive market, firms produce too much of a polluting good (Q_1, rather than the efficient amount Q_2).[3] It is in society's interest to cut

[3]In terms of our earlier analysis in Box 20-1, a free market does not lead to an efficient solution because marginal private cost MC is not equal to marginal social cost MC_S [that is, condition (20-2) in that box is violated].

FIGURE 23-2 Free-market efficiency loss when there is an external cost.
Demand for this good *D* represents its marginal benefit (either private or social). But its private and social costs are *not* the same because of some external cost like pollution (the red arrow). *Before the antipollution tax* , industry supply is S_1, reflecting the private (internal) costs of production facing sellers. This supply equals demand at E_1, with output at Q_1. But this output is inefficient because the marginal social costs of all units between Q_1 and Q_2 exceed their marginal utilities. For example, the last unit Q_1 is not worth producing; its benefit (the hollow arrow under the demand curve) is less than its two costs to society (the hollow arrow plus the red arrow). *After the tax*, producers are forced to face both the internal *and* external costs, so that their supply curve shifts up from S_1 to S_2. (This supply shift in response to a tax is exactly the same as in Figure 17-5.) *D* and S_2 now yield an equilibrium at E_2, with output Q_2. This is efficient because marginal social cost and benefit are equal. The efficiency gain from reducing output from Q_1 to Q_2 is the elimination of the red triangle. However, if the government arbitrarily limits output further, from Q_2 to say Q_3, then we will consequently be losing units of this good with a potential benefit (given by the height of the demand curve) that exceeds their cost (given by the height of the marginal social cost curve). The total efficiency loss that results is triangle FE_2G. (If output is reduced even further, then this triangular loss becomes even larger.)

back its production and to use the labor and capital to produce something else.

To confirm that Q_1 is an inefficient quantity of output, note that the benefit from the last unit produced is the hollow arrow under the demand curve. But its cost would be even greater, since it includes both its private cost (this same hollow arrow, as defined under the MC curve) and its external cost, shown by the red arrow. Hence, this

red arrow represents the net loss involved in producing this unit. Since there is a similar loss involved in the production of each of the other excess units between Q_2 and Q_1, the total efficiency loss is given by the shaded red triangle.

In this case, the cure is a relatively simple one: Impose a per unit tax on producers equal to the marginal external cost (that is, the solid red arrow). Note that such a tax imposes a cost on producers equal to the cost of their pollution on others. Thus, the tax "internalizes" the externality; the producer is forced to face the external cost along with the internal cost. This increased cost to producers from the tax shifts the supply curve up from S_1 to S_2, with the new equilibrium at E_2 where demand and new supply S_2 intersect. The new output of Q_2 is efficient because marginal *social* cost and benefit are equal. Finally, the efficiency gain from this tax policy is the red area, the original efficiency loss that has now been eliminated.

An alternative policy for fighting pollution is merely to set an arbitrary limit on output. This limitation may or may not help to solve the problem; in fact, it may even be worse than doing nothing at all. For example, if output is arbitrarily limited to Q_3, as an exercise you can show that there would be a loss to society of triangle FE_2G. (To confirm, see the caption to Figure 23-2.) Since this loss exceeds the original red loss, the cure in this case is worse than the original problem. You should also be able to show that an even stiffer restriction on output will result in an even greater efficiency loss. Thus, there is an advantage in using the market mechanism, rather than setting an arbitrary limit on output. If the costs of pollution can be estimated and a tax of this amount imposed, the right amount of pressure can be applied to the market to push it back from the initial Q_1 to the efficient output Q_2. (For an example of the costs of completely eliminating pollution—in this case, noise and air pollution around an airport—see Box 23-2.)

BOX 23-2
ELIMINATING AIR AND NOISE POLLUTION—JAPANESE STYLE

For more than 6 years after the completion of the new Tokyo airport at Narita, farmers and radical students prevented any planes whatsoever from landing there. Their method was simple: On the land at the end of the runway, they built a high steel tower that prevented planes from landing or taking off. But just consider the cost of this action. First, there was the cost of interest and depreciation on the airport. Second, more than $7 million of wages and salaries had to be paid annually to the cleaning and servicing personnel who kept the airport in a constant state of readiness for the opening that was delayed, and delayed, and delayed. . . .

Eventually, the Japanese police tore down the steel tower. Rioters countered by ransacking the airport's control tower, and destroying much of the navigational equipment. Finally, in May 1978, on the twelfth attempt, the airport was opened. But by then it was in a state of military seige, surrounded by fortresses built by its opponents, and protected by 14,000 riot police behind a cordon of barbed wire.

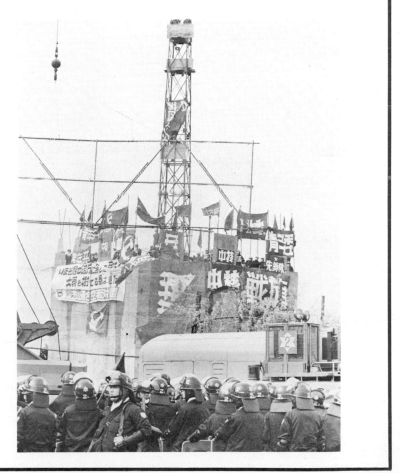

*CONTROLLING POLLUTION: A More Complex Case

In practice, policymakers face a number of complications omitted from our earlier example. In any particular air space (say, over Los Angeles) or any particular body of water (such as Lake Erie), the problem is not just one polluting industry (as in Figure 23-2), but many. Second, pollution and output are not locked together in the fixed way we assumed in earlier diagrams (where each additional unit of output generated a constant amount of pollution). In the more typical case, pollution may vary: A good may be produced with either a high level of pollution (if wastes are dumped uncontrolled into the water or air) or a low pollution level (if wastes are somehow treated, or if less polluting fuels are used).

Consider a firm that installs purifying equipment to treat its wastes or uses cleaner, but more expensive, fuels. This firm reduces pollution, but at a cost. This cost of reducing pollution for all firms in an area is shown in Figure 23-3 as the curve MCR. (R stands for reducing pollution.) It is drawn by first graphing point Q_1, the amount of pollution that will occur if it is not restricted in any way. As pollution is cut back, we move to the left up the MCR curve. At first, cleanup costs are low as the easy battles are won. (Pollution unit Q_2 can be eliminated at the low cost shown by the short red bar.) But the more pollution is reduced (that is, the more we move to the left in this diagram), the higher becomes the cost of further cleanup (the higher MCR becomes).

Until the last few decades, there were few restrictions on pollution. Therefore, any firm that could save costs by dumping its pollutants (rather than treating them) did so, and the result was a pollution level of about Q_1. Thus some of our lakes and rivers became public sewers.

FIGURE 23-3 The effect of a pollution tax.
Q_1 is the amount of pollution that would occur in the absence of any control measures. As we move from this point back to the left along MCR, we see the cost of reducing pollution by one more unit (for example, by installing pollution-control equipment). Thus if pollution has been restricted all the way back to Q_4, any further reduction would involve very expensive pollution-control measures, involving a cost shown by the tall red bar. If pollution tax T is imposed, firms voluntarily reduce pollution to Q_3. For example, a firm will eliminate pollution unit Q_2 because it is less expensive (short red bar) to do so than to pay the pollution tax T. On the other hand, firms will not reduce pollution to the left of Q_3 because the cost of doing so (for example, the tall red bar) is more than the cost of paying the tax and continuing to pollute.

*GOVERNMENT POLLUTION-CONTROL MEASURES

Now let's suppose the government wants to cut pollution in half—from Q_1 to Q_3. Consider the policies which might be used.

1. A Pollution Tax

Assume that the government levies a pollution tax (sometimes called an effluent fee). Specifically, in Figure 23-3, suppose that tax T is charged for each unit of pollution emitted by a firm. Then firms eliminate

*Note to instructors of short courses: At any subsequent point you may leave this chapter without losing background essential for future chapters.

pollution in the right-hand tail of the MCR curve. It costs them less to stop (the short red bar) than to continue to pollute and pay the pollution tax T. But pollution is reduced only to Q_3, where the tax line intersects MCR. To the left of this point, it is more expensive to stop polluting than to pay the tax. For example, it would be more costly for the polluter to clean up pollution unit Q_4 (at a cost shown by the height of the tall red bar) than to pay the tax. So the firm pays the tax, and continues to pollute.

2. Requiring Each Firm to Reduce Its Emissions

One might well ask: Why go to all the trouble of setting the pollution tax in Figure 23-3 when pollution could be cut by the same amount merely by requiring every firm to reduce its emissions by half? The answer is that this simpler approach would involve heavier cleanup costs, as we shall now show.

Not all firms face the same costs in reducing pollution. With a tax, pollution is cut down in the least-cost way, by firms to the right of Q_3. (Firms to the left of Q_3 continue to pollute.[4]) However, if all firms are required to cut their pollution in half, firms to the left of Q_3 must now also participate—at the high cost illustrated by the tall red bar.

Thus, the advantage of a pollution tax is that it "lets the market work." With firms reacting to the tax signal, pollution is reduced by firms that can do so least expensively, and society devotes fewer real resources to the cleanup task. The savings may be substantial. Kneese and Schultze have estimated that *a pollution tax would cost society 40 to 90 percent less than a policy of requiring all firms to reduce pollution by the same fraction.*[5]

Which Policy Does the Government Use?

Surprisingly, the government relies on controls rather than on a pollution tax. (In fact, a bill to set such a tax died in congressional committee in 1969.) Instead, pollution limits are set for individual firms. Not only does this policy involve enormous, unnecessary cleanup costs. In addition, it is very difficult and costly to administer. (It has been estimated that serious pollution occurs at no less than 55,000 sites in the United States.)

By the mid-1970s there was a second problem. The government had set air and water standards with little regard for the cost of reducing pollution (MCR). Instead, it was concentrating on what was technologically possible given existing pollution-control knowledge, and some of the measures were extremely expensive. Moreover, the Clean Air Act, as amended, was designed to "protect and enhance" the quality of the nation's air—a worthy objective, except that the legislation was interpreted to mean that the air should not be allowed to deteriorate significantly *anywhere.* So even the states with the cleanest air were having problems attracting new firms. This blocked one avenue for reducing the overall pollution problem, namely, shifting firms from overloaded, highly polluted areas into regions with low pollution levels (where at least some of the pollutants could be "washed away" by natural processes).

Moreover, because pollution regulations were so severe, by the mid-70s many firms were in violation of air or water standards, and were expending more of their efforts in fighting these regulations in the halls of Congress or the courts than in trying to find a pollution cure. In some cases, these

---

[4]This may sound unfair, since these polluters escape the cleanup costs. But remember: They have to pay a tax.
[5]Allen V. Kneese and Charles L. Schultze, *Pollution, Prices, and Public Policy* (Washington: The Brookings Institution, 1975), pp. 90, 99.

firms seemed to be counting on the government to provide them with an eleventh-hour exemption to the law. To cite one example, in 1977 the auto companies started producing engines for the 1978 models that violated the emission standards set for 1978. (This was referred to as "nuclear diplomacy," that is, the assumption by one party (the auto industry) that the other party (the government) would not take the legal action that would close down the industry—an action with appalling consequences.) The result was that Congress relaxed the standards.

Similarly, a threat to close seven plants, employing 24,000 workers in Ohio's Mahoning Valley, induced the EPA to exempt them from water-emission restrictions. Such flip-flops tended, at a minimum, to erode the credibility of the controls. And they meant that standards were not being set in an even-handed way, but instead, were being defined by a government under pressure to make last-minute changes. Such examples illustrate a final problem with controls: Each firm has an incentive to argue that the costs of reducing its pollution are too high, and that it should be given an exemption. The government is not in a good position to evaluate such claims. On the other hand, with a pollution tax, the incentive for each firm is to look for ways to eliminate pollution in order to avoid paying the tax.

An Alternative Policy? Subsidizing Pollution-Control Equipment

By the mid-70s, the federal government was providing matching grants, totaling about $1 billion a year, to municipalities installing waste treatment plants. The government was also providing subsidies in the form of tax reductions to firms installing pollution-control equipment. How effective is such a subsidy scheme?

In the first place, such subsidies will be effective only if the equipment that is in-stalled does a good job of reducing pollution. One of the problems has been that after the government subsidizes the new installation, it pays little or no attention to how efficiently it is operated. Second, this sort of subsidy puts all the emphasis on end-of-pipe treatment; that is, on the reduction of pollution as it is about to be discharged into the environment. But if a subsidy is justified for end-of-pipe treatment, it should be similarly justified for *any* reduction in pollution, regardless of how it may be achieved—for example, by the use of less powerful chemicals. Moreover, there is evidence that, in some cases, such alternatives may be far less costly. For instance, the 3M Company spent only $1 million to introduce a less polluting process; by the mid-70s, this process had saved the company over $10 million in waste disposal and other costs.

It may be concluded, therefore, that an end-of-pipe subsidy is too narrow an attack on the problem. And it will involve a cost to society if some firms do not use the lowest-cost method of controlling pollution, but instead, switch to the end-of-pipe method solely because it is subsidized. The principle is a simple one. It is better to tell firms what to do than to give them detailed instructions on how to do it. (A regulation made as far back as the eighteenth century B.C. illustrates this principle perfectly. Hammurabi, King of Babylonia, set out a very simple building code. If a house fell down and killed an occupant, the builder was put to death. All details for meeting this regulation were left to the builder.)

RECYCLING

One of the most promising ways to deal with pollution is to recycle wastes, rather than dump them into the environment. Beer cans that are reprocessed to be used again do not deface the landscape. Wastes that are recycled into the production process do not foul our rivers.

BOX 23-3
POLLUTION CONTROL: Problems and Perspective

In Figure 23-3, tax *T* limits pollution to Q_3. An even higher emission fee would cut pollution back even more. The question we address in this box is: How far do we want to cut pollution back? In other words, how high should we set the pollution tax?

The Problem of Setting the Right Pollution Tax

In Figure 23-4 we reproduce MCR from the previous diagram, and also now show MCP, the marginal cost of pollution to society. These two curves should not be confused. MCR is the cost of *reducing* pollution—for example, the cost of pollution-control equipment. On the other hand, MCP is the cost of *having* pollution; that is, the cost to us of foul air and contaminated water. The shape of MCP in Figure 23-4 reflects the fact that so long as pollution is at a very low level, its marginal cost is low. The first units of waste that are dumped into a stream generally break down and are absorbed by the environment. Similarly, the smoke from a campfire in a deserted area has no perceptible effect on the air. But as pollution builds up, additional emissions become increasingly costly.

Given these two curves, the best target is to cut back pollution to the point where MCP = MCR. At any other level, there will be a loss to society, which can be most dramatically illustrated by the case where pollution is left completely uncontrolled and consequently increases from Q_3 to Q_1. For all units of pollution to the right of Q_3, MCP is greater than MCR, so it is a mistake to let this pollution occur. To evaluate the cost of this mistake to society, consider one typical unit of this excess pollution, say unit Q_2. The cost of eliminating this unit of pollution (the empty arrow defined under the MCR curve) is less than the cost of letting it continue (the two arrows under the MCP curve). Therefore, the

FIGURE 23-4 Efficiency loss from leaving pollution uncontrolled.
MCR is reproduced from Figure 23-3. We also show MCP, the environmental cost of additional units of pollution. The best target level is to restrict pollution to Q_3, where MCR = MCP. To do so, a pollution tax is set at T_3.

net cost of allowing this unit of pollution to continue is the solid red arrow. If we sum the similar costs on all such units through the range Q_3 to Q_1, the result is the triangular red area—the loss to society of leaving pollution uncontrolled.

On the other hand, a policy of cutting pollution back below Q_3 also involves a loss to society. For example, if pollution is reduced to Q_4, one more unit involves little environmental cost (the height of the MCP curve above Q_4); but it is exceedingly costly to eliminate (the height of the MCR curve). Again we conclude that setting an arbitrary limit on pollution, say at Q_4, is not the best solution. Instead, the best target, Q_3, can be found only by taking both the cost of pollution (MCP) and the cost of removing it (MCR) into account. (Once this target pollution level

BOX 23-3 (continued)

is determined, the necessary cutbacks can be achieved by setting pollution tax T_3.)

Unfortunately, this approach is not as easy as it may sound; one reason is the difficulty in estimating MCP. As already noted, scientists who fear the possible effects of air pollution do not yet agree on how severe its cost may be in terms of human life. But even if they could resolve this issue, it is very difficult to put a value on a human life. (See Box 24-2.) Since we can therefore only be very imprecise about MCP, our estimate of Q_3, the right limit on pollution, will also be very imprecise.

Finally, we now use Figure 23-5 to illustrate why pollution-control policy is a much more pressing issue today than in the past, and why it will likely be an even more pressing issue in the future.

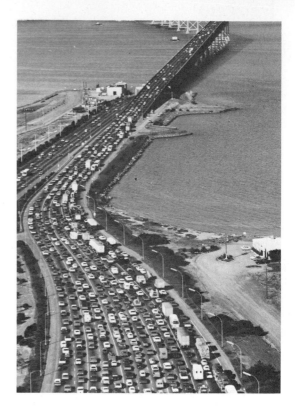

FIGURE 23-5   Pollution in perspective.
If we had not begun to deal with this problem, then unrestricted pollution would have increased (with growing GNP) from the past Q_{1960} to the present Q_{1980} to the future Q_{2000}. As a result, the loss to society of leaving pollution unchecked in each of these years is shown as the rapidly growing set of triangles marked 1960, 1980, and 2000. (Note that each of these triangles is defined between the relevant MCR and MCP curves in exactly the same way as in Figure 23-4.)

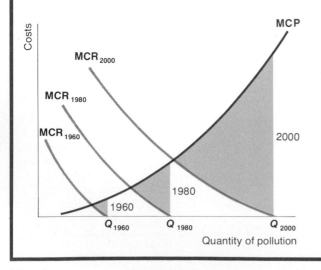

The Pollution Problem in Historical Perspective

Why are we so concerned now with pollution, while a few decades ago we were almost totally unconcerned? Is the problem worse, or have we just awakened? And if it is getting worse, what can we expect 20 or 30 years from now?

In Figure 23-5, MCP is shown, along with MCR for three periods. MCR_{1960} cuts the baseline at Q_{1960}, the level of pollution that would have occurred had it been left completely unrestricted at that early date. Similarly, the other MCR curves indicate uncontrolled pollution levels Q_{1980} and Q_{2000} at those later dates. The red triangle marked 1980 shows the loss from a policy of leaving pollution uncontrolled today. (It is defined just as the red loss is in Figure 23-4.)

Now consider our situation in 1960. At that time, there were fewer factories clustered along any river and fewer cars spewing fumes into city air. So pollution was less severe. The result of leaving this pollution uncontrolled was the relatively small loss shown as the red triangle marked 1960. In those days, people did not think much about this problem.

Now let us look ahead to the future, to the year 2000. If industrial activity keeps growing as in the past (doubling in real terms every 15 or 20 years), unrestricted pollution will grow to Q_{2000}, and the loss from failing to deal with it will be the huge red triangle 2000. There are several reasons why this loss builds up so rapidly. First, uncontrolled pollution will tend to grow as output grows. Second, it may grow even faster, since more powerful chemicals and other materials are used as technology changes. For both these reasons, the MCR curve shifts rapidly to the right. Finally, in the view of many experts, the MCP curve becomes steeper and steeper: The cost of pollution not only rises, but it does so at an increasingly rapid rate.

We emphasize that Figure 23-5 is not a prediction of the future; it is merely a picture of what the future would have looked like if we had not taken action.† In this respect, it is similar to the public health problem in the nineteenth century. With the growth of industrial cities, lack of adequate sanitation produced an explosive health problem that could equally well have been described by a frightening diagram like Figure 23-5. The response to this challenge was the public health programs that prevented the "prophecy" in such a diagram from coming true. Similarly, pollution-control legislation can help to ensure that the prophecy in Figure 23-5 does not come true.

---

†Moreover, in this diagram as in any other economic model, we have oversimplified. For example, we have assumed that pollution does not accumulate; in other words, that the cost of pollution depends only on how much occurs in the year in question. But pollution *does* accumulate. Heavy metal emissions from past years are with us today because they do not decompose with time. The same is true of certain pesticides that decompose very slowly. Our future problem could therefore be even more severe.

Figure 23-6 illustrates the potential benefits from recycling. The basic idea behind this diagram is the concept of *material balances*: On the left, production "sucks in" the materials it requires. They include both new materials drawn up through pipe *a* and recycled materials returned to the production process through pipe *c*. These materials pass through the production/consumption process and reappear in different form as "total materials out" on the right side of the diagram. Some of these residual, "left-over" materials (such as chemical wastes) result from production, while some (like beer cans) are residuals from consumption.

This figure provides a framework for thinking about three important issues:

1. Our economic system is grafted onto our environment, with changes in one affecting the other. Thus, as our economic system expands, strains on the environment tend to increase both because more material is drawn up through pipe *a* and because more pollutants are dumped back into the environment through pipe *b*.

2. The natural processes of our environment can absorb a limited amount of pollution. For example, a stream can dilute a certain amount of waste material. For most pollutants, problems arise only if residuals are dumped back into the environment too rapidly.

3. We can help to cure the pollution problem by more recycling, that is, by redirecting more of the residuals into pipe *c* rather than pipe *b*. Moreover, any success on this score will have a highly desirable side effect. The more our production/consumption requirements can be satisfied by materials recycled through pipe *c*, the fewer natural resources will have to be drawn from the environment through pipe *a*. In brief, recycling helps to solve two important problems at once: the problem of pollution and the problem of conserving natural resources. We will return to a more detailed discussion of natural resources in Chapter 30.

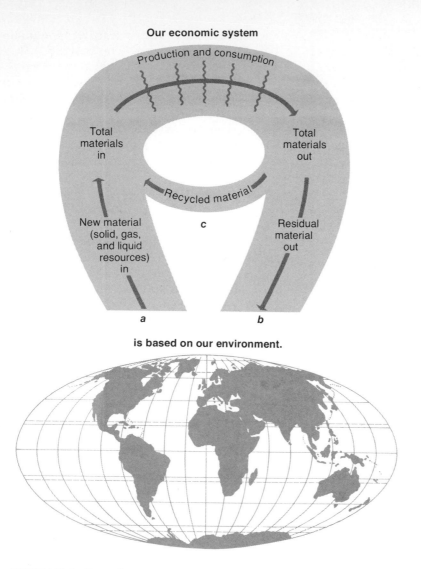

Our economic system

Production and consumption

Total materials in

Total materials out

Recycled material

c

New material (solid, gas, and liquid resources) in

Residual material out

a

b

is based on our environment.

FIGURE 23-6 Recycling and the environment.
The economic system in the upper half of this diagram uses the environment by extracting resources from it through pipe *a* and returning residuals back to it through pipe *b*. On the left, "total materials in" include both resources drawn from pipe *a* and recycled material from pipe *c*. On the right, total materials out that result from production and consumption are disposed of either by returning them into the environment through pipe *b* or recycling them through pipe *c*. For any given level of production and consumption, increased recycling (that is, diverting materials from pipe *b* to pipe *c*) involves two benefits: It reduces the residuals dumped into the environment through pipe *b*, *and* it reduces the natural resources we must draw out of the environment through pipe *a*.

*CONGESTION AND THE AUTOMOBILE

Parking is such sweet sorrow.
Sid Caesar

Congestion, like pollution, involves external costs. An individual who decides to drive a car during congested periods takes into account costs like gasoline, and also the personal costs of aggravation and delay.

Since the driver must face both these costs, they are internal costs. But the individual does not take into account the external costs—the increased aggravation and delay that other drivers encounter because one additional car is on the road, making traffic jams a little more dense and parking spots a bit harder to find.

The problem is illustrated in Figure 23-7.[6] During nonrush hours, drivers equate

[6]In this example, only one type of auto externality—congestion—is considered. Clearly, the problem would be more complex if other auto externalities (like air pollution) were considered at the same time.

FIGURE 23-7 Traffic congestion and the case for tolls.
During nonrush hours, equilibrium is at E_1 and there are fewer than 60 cars on this stretch of highway. Traffic runs smoothly, and one more car does not cause congestion delay; in other words, there are no external costs (MC and MC_s coincide.) But during rush hours, drivers put a higher value on using the highway, so that the marginal benefit MB shifts to the right to MB_2 and more than the critical number of 60 cars are put on the road. Because the highway is now congested, traffic is delayed, and private MC is no longer flat. Instead it rises, since each driver wastes his *own* time in the traffic jam. But in addition *other* drivers also suffer increased delay because his car is put on the road. This external cost must be added to MC to get marginal social cost MC_s. Private decisions by drivers equating MC and MB_2 will result in equilibrium at E_2, with 90 cars on the road. But this is 10 more than the efficient number (80) where marginal social cost (MC_s) equals MB_2. Moreover, the cost of these 10 excess cars on the road is easy to show. The last one (the ninetieth car) provides the benefit shown by the hollow arrow under MB_2. But the cost of having it on the road is the private cost (the hollow arrow under MC) *plus* the external cost to the other drivers (the red arrow). Thus, the net cost of this excess car is the red arrow. When similar costs for the other excess cars are summed, the result is the red triangular loss. If a toll equal to T is imposed on each car during rush hours, then the private cost MC shifts up to MC*. Private decisions equating MC* with MB_2 now result in an efficient equilibrium at E^*, with 80 cars on the road. The efficiency gain from this policy is the elimination of the previous red triangular loss.

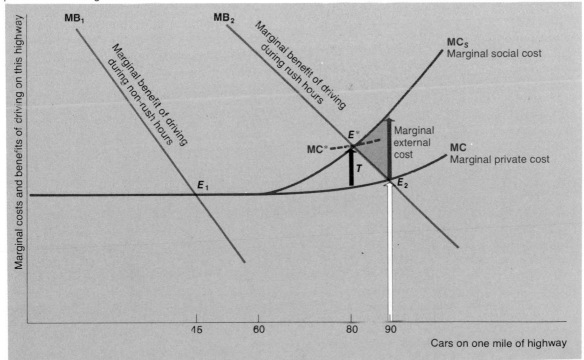

the marginal costs (MC) and marginal benefits of driving (MB₁). Forty-five cars are driven at equilibrium E_1. Traffic moves smoothly, and drivers face no congestion problems. Now look at what happens during rush hours, when drivers put a high value on using the highway. (Many must get to work, and driving is the most convenient way.) Marginal benefit shifts to the right, equilibrium is at E_2 with 90 cars on the road, and congestion is now a problem. First, the driver faces a higher private marginal cost (MC) because of the additional time required to reach his destination.[7] Second, one more car makes the congestion worse, so that other drivers also face an additional burden of aggravation and delay. This is the external cost of the individual driving, shown as the solid red arrow in Figure 23-7. Of course, when this cost is added to the driver's private MC, the result is the marginal cost to society of having one more car on the road (MC$_S$).

The rush-hour problem is that decisions by drivers are based only on *private* cost MC rather than *social* cost MC$_S$. Thus equilibrium is at E_2 with too many cars on the road, and with an efficiency loss shown by the colored triangle (as detailed in the diagram's caption). A tax or toll equal to the external cost (the gap between MC and MC$_S$) will ensure that each driver takes into account not only his own costs, but also the external cost of his decision on other drivers. Only then will equilibrium be at E^*, with an efficient, smaller number of cars.

[Actually, tolls should be introduced only if their benefit (the elimination of the triangular shaded area in Figure 23-7) exceeds their cost of collection, including traffic delays at toll booths. These delays are often reduced by building reverse bottlenecks; that is, widening the road to provide space for a large enough number of toll booths to keep traffic moving. There is even some possibility that delays might eventually be avoided altogether by replacing toll booths with an electronic device or a TV camera that would read off the license plate of each passing car, along with the time of day. Then drivers would be sent a bill—like a phone bill—at the end of each month.]

Note that, as in the case of pollution, the efficient solution does not involve eliminating congestion, but only reducing it. (In Figure 23-7, traffic is reduced to only 80 cars, not to 60.) Also note that the appropriate toll varies with the time of day. Thus, when MB₂ reflects the desire to travel in rush hours, the efficient toll is T. But when MB₁ reflects the more limited desire to travel in nonrush hours, no toll is required. In other words, the appropriate toll is determined by the pressure of drivers to use the highway. Once set, the toll then relieves that pressure.

In describing such a toll, we have considered only the objective of efficiency. Of course, another objective of a toll may be to raise money to pay for the road. But in a congested area, a toll should not be set with just this money-raising objective in mind. Instead, it should be set to ensure that the road will be used efficiently. An example will illustrate this point: Suppose that there are two bridges into a city, and that they are just barely able to handle the traffic without tie-ups. If a toll is set on each bridge to cover its costs, there will be no toll on the old bridge that has already been paid for, but a high toll on the new bridge. As drivers consequently switch from the new to the old bridge, a traffic jam is created where none existed before.

Finally, there have been a number of other suggestions for reducing auto congestion. Each would reduce the problem, although generally in a somewhat less efficient way than a toll. These include proposals to: (1) Increase the tax on gasoline. This

---

[7]Because the driver does not pay for this time, it is not an accounting cost. But, the waste of time does involve an opportunity cost: what the driver could have done with this time if he were not stuck on the highway.

would reduce congestion by reducing the cars on the road anywhere, at any time. But this is a less effective policy since it does not deal directly with the problem of congestion on specific highways at specific times.[8] (2) Induce people to form car pools by levying a toll not on the car, but rather on the empty seats in it. (3) Provide a further incentive for car pools by reserving fast lanes on superhighways for cars with more than, say, two passengers. (But this has raised a problem for the police: How do you tell at a distance whether a passenger is really a passenger, or one of the mannequins motorists sometimes transport to allow them to use these special lanes?)

[8]Although a gasoline tax is not the most effective policy to reduce congestion, it does help. And of course it also has two other important justifications: It reduces pollution, and it reduces our demand for imported oil, thus making it less profitable for OPEC to raise prices so rapidly.

Key Points

1. Pollution is an example of an external cost, a cost that is borne not by the individual or firm directly involved in the activity, but instead by somebody else.

2. With the Clean Air Act and the Water Pollution Control Act, the government has imposed controls on the amount of pollutants firms can release into our air or water.

3. An alternative system of charging a pollution tax would generally have been superior, because it would have been a less costly way of reducing pollution. (The reductions in pollution would have been undertaken by the firms that could do so at the least cost.)

4. Such a pollution tax would also have been superior to another government policy that has been used: Subsidizing firms (or municipalities) that install pollution-reducing equipment. Such a subsidy is too narrow an approach to the problem because it attacks pollution only at the "end of the pipe." Hence, opportunities to reduce pollution in less costly ways may be missed.

5. Recycling production or consumption wastes back into the production process helps solve two problems: First, less polluting waste is dumped into the environment. Second, fewer natural resources need to be extracted from the environment to support our present production and consumption levels.

6. Highway congestion is another example of an external cost, because other drivers suffer delays and aggravation when an individual drives into a jammed-up road. Again, the most efficient policy is some form of tax, such as a toll, on this activity (provided the cost of collecting the toll does not outweigh the gains).

Key Concepts

internal (private) cost
external cost
social cost
inefficiency of free market
how a tax may increase efficiency
internalizing an externality
marginal cost of reducing pollution (MCR)
marginal cost of having pollution (MCP)
pollution tax

pollution limits for individual firms
subsidization of pollution-control equipment
recycling
material balances
how the environment absorbs some pollutants
traffic congestion
how tolls affect efficiency

Problems

23-1 In 1977, after almost a week of oil spill, an oil blowout in the North Sea was finally capped by a high-priced, high-living American named Red Adair. Draw a diagram like Figure 23-1 to show the various costs involved in offshore drilling for oil. Determine whether the following costs are external or internal: (*a*) the expenditure by the oil companies on installing and operating drilling rigs; (*b*) the cost to the companies of hiring Red Adair; (c) the loss of marine life and the damage to beaches if oil spills occur that cannot be capped in time.

23-2 "When faced with a problem, economists have a natural inclination to suggest a solution that somehow utilizes the powerful magic of the price system; thus their solution for pollution control is a tax. On the other hand, lawyers have a natural inclination to set up regulations, and pass judgment on a case-by-case basis. And because lawyers make our laws, this is what has happened." Discuss.

23-3 Do you agree with these statements? Explain.

(a) "Pollution taxes are immoral. Once a firm has paid its tax, it has a license to pollute. And no one should have this license."

(b) "Imposing a physical limit on the emission of a pollutant is like saying that you can do just so much of a bad thing and pay no penalty, but the moment you step over this line you will pay a large penalty."

(c) "There is no point in insisting on crystal-clear discharges into a river as muddy as the Mississippi."

(d) "Since it is impossible (and in any case, undesirable) to eliminate all polluting activities, the cost of pollution can be reduced if some polluting ac-tivities are moved into geo-graphic regions where the environment can absorb most of the pollutants without notice-able effect."

23-4 Use Figure 23-6 to explain the various effects on the environment when cars were made smaller during the decade of the 1970s.

23-5 We have seen that the target rate of pollution is not zero. Do you think that the target rate of crime should be zero, or not? In other words, do you think we should expand crime prevention and hire police until the crime rate is driven to zero?

23-6 Show why completely eliminating congestion by cutting traffic back to 60 cars in Figure 23-7 would be worse than taking no action at all. Is it always true that the complete elimination of an externality is worse than no action whatsoever?

***23-7** Do you see any similarity between rush-hour tolls and peak-load (rush-hour) increases in the price of electricity? What do you think the efficiency effect of setting a high price for peak-load electricity would be?

***23-8** The government of an Italian city (which happened to be run by the Communist Party) subsidized the local public trans-portation system so that it could offer free rides, but only during morning and evening rush hours. Would such a subsidy work toward an efficient outcome? Why or why not? (Be careful! This is a complicated ques-tion.) Could there be objectives other than efficiency in this type of subsidy?

chapter 24
Public Goods

There are certain goods that have the peculiarity that once they are available no one can be precluded from enjoying them whether he contributed to their provision or not. These are the public goods.
Robert Dorfman

External, spillover effects can be either bad or beneficial. Our earlier example of a bad external effect was the dumping of chemical wastes into a river that damaged people living downstream. The goods and services we now consider involve beneficial external effects, that is, benefits enjoyed by someone other than the buyer. Examples already cited include the homeowner who plants a beautiful garden that neighbors also enjoy; or the individual who is vaccinated, thus protecting others from the spread of the disease.

EXTERNAL BENEFITS AND RESOURCE MISALLOCATION

If there are any spillovers, whether they be costs or benefits, the free market will result in a misallocation of the nation's resources. In Figure 23-2, we have seen that if a good

has a spillover cost, a free, competitive market will result in too much output. In Figure 24-1, we now show that if a good has a spillover benefit, then (as we would expect) a free, competitive market will result in not enough output. (Before reading the detailed confirmation in the caption to Figure 24-1, you should try to prove this yourself. Hint: there are now external benefits to be added to the demand curve rather than the external costs that were added to the supply curve in Figure 23-2.) In this diagram we also show another expected result: A good with an external benefit should be subsidized (just as a good with an external cost should be taxed). When, for example, we subsidize vaccinations, we are "internalizing an externality" in much the same way as when we taxed a polluter in the last chapter.[1] In that earlier example, the polluter who paid the

[1]Because it is less complicated to administer, the government subsidy of vaccinations is typically in the form of a reduction in their cost (often to zero), rather than a grant paid to those who acquire them. But either form of subsidy has a similar effect in encouraging people to acquire more.

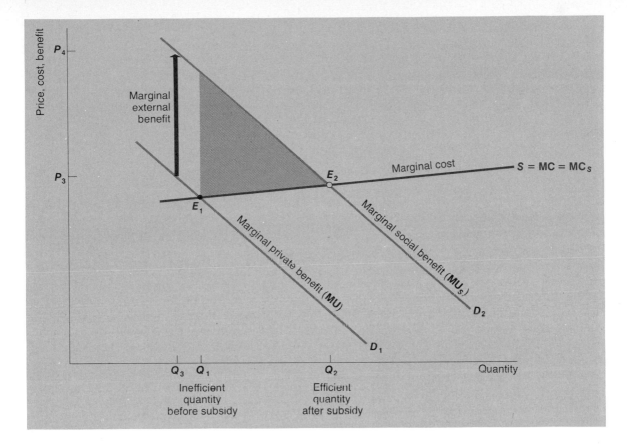

FIGURE 24-1 Efficiency loss when there is an external benefit.
In this diagram we consider a product—like vaccinations—that has external benefits but
no external costs. The height of the market demand D_1 reflects how the actual purchasers
value the vaccinations (that is, their own internal benefit because they don't get the
disease). But there is also an external benefit (the arrow) enjoyed by nonpurchasers
because the disease isn't passed on to them. When these two benefits are taken into
account, the result is the marginal social benefit curve (MU$_S$).

A free, perfectly competitive market results in equilibrium at E_1, where marginal cost
is equal to marginal *private* benefit (since this is the only benefit going to those who make
the purchasing decisions.) But the resulting quantity (Q_1) is not efficient. Instead,
efficiency requires that marginal cost should be equal to marginal *social* benefit, and this
occurs at E_2, at a higher level of output Q_2. Thus we conclude that a free market does not
produce enough of a good with external benefits. Specifically, the red triangle shows the
efficiency loss if output is at the free market level Q_1. All units of output between Q_1 and Q_2
have a benefit—the height of D_2—that exceeds their cost shown by the height of S. Thus
producing them would result in a net benefit. In other words, *not* producing them results
in a net loss—as shown by the red triangle. Alternatively, referring back to our earlier
analysis in Box 20-1, we can confirm that inefficiency results because condition (20-1) is
violated. One possible way to eliminate this inefficiency is to provide purchasers with a per
unit subsidy equal to the external benefit arrow, thus shifting the demand curve up from
D_1 to D_2. (Demand shifts in this way because, for example, the individual initially prepared
to pay only P_3 for unit Q_3 will now be prepared to pay P_4—that is, his original P_3 plus the
subsidy provided by the government.) With this shift in demand, a competitive market will
do the rest. Its new equilibrium will be at E_2, where supply and new demand D_2 intersect.
Thus efficient output Q_2 is achieved. Finally, the efficiency gain from this subsidy is the red
area, the original efficiency loss that has now been eliminated.

tax was made to "feel internally" the external damage caused. On the other hand, the purchaser of a vaccination who receives a subsidy is allowed to "enjoy internally" the external benefit this action provides to others. In either case, *the private firm or individual acts only after taking external effects into account.* This is as it should be.

Externalities may sometimes be internalized even without government action, but strictly as a result of private market forces. A private real estate firm will sometimes purchase a whole block of houses in a run-down neighborhood, renovating them all. The expenditure on each house raises the value of that house, and also provides a spillover benefit by raising the value of the other houses in the block as well. Hence, when the firm resells the whole block, it will capture both these benefits. Thus, while it may not find the purchase and renovation of one house profitable, the purchase of the whole block may be—merely because the private firm is able to capture the spillover effects.

As another example, if a firm constructs a ski lift on a mountain, it will be able to sell tow tickets. These receipts will be an internal benefit to the firm. But it will also generate an external benefit in the form of greater business for the restaurant at the base of the mountain. The internal benefit to the ski-lift company from ticket sales may be insufficient to justify constructing the lift. But if the firm can internalize the externality by buying the restaurant, it may be profitable to build the lift.

This suggests an alternative approach to spillovers: Allow economic units to join into large enough bodies so that decision-makers will take externalities into account. For example, heavy industry in a large city may result in a spillover cost of air pollution in the suburbs. If the city is expanded to include the suburbs, this cost will be internalized: All pollution will then have to be taken into account by the new, larger city government. Such an expansion of a city may also internalize externalities on the benefit side. For one thing, the city may decide to finance an orchestra or a theatrical company that cannot be justified unless the benefits provided to the suburbs can also be taken into account. (Note that this is only one argument for increasing city size. There are also many arguments for decreasing the size of some cities. We are merely pointing out one economic influence that should be taken into account.)

Now consider a flood-control dam in a river valley. If a farmer were to build such a dam, he would enjoy an *internal* benefit since his own crops and buildings would be protected from floods. But such a benefit would be trivial compared with the enormous cost of constructing the dam. So no individual farmer would build it. Nonetheless, the dam would provide very large *external* benefits in the form of flood control for the thousands of other farmers in the valley. So it is well worth building. But if it is to be built at all, it will have to be built by a large group of farmers acting together—or by the government. This introduces the idea of a public good.

PUBLIC GOODS

One definition of a public good is "anything the government provides." But this is too broad a definition for our purposes,[2] since it includes all sorts of activities that could be undertaken privately but are provided by the government instead. (Public transport systems and the U.S. Postal Service are exam-

[2]In fact, it is very difficult to define a public good. There are several definitions, each with some particular advantage over the others. For an alternative definition and further discussion, see the essay by Peter Steiner in Solow and Blinder, *The Economics of Public Finance* (Washington: The Brookings Institution, 1974).

ples.) Since we are not interested in so broad a definition, we begin with the more narrow idea of goods that cannot be provided by the private market.

Since the idea of external benefits is important to our definition of a public good, we now compare in detail two of our previous examples. The first is hiring a gardener. Most of the benefits are *internal*, that is, they go to the family that hires the gardener to work on its own property. Therefore the market works, at least to a degree: People do have gardening done, although the amount falls short of the efficient level.

Compare this with the example of a flood-control dam in a river valley. There are two important differences in this case. First, most of the benefits from the dam are external, since they go to thousands of farmers in the river valley. For this reason, the market doesn't work at all: If a dam is to be built, the government must do it. But there is another, more subtle difference: Once the government has built the dam, an individual farmer's benefit from it is the same as if he had built it himself.[3] This, then, is our concept of a public good: It provides an individual with a benefit that does not depend on whether or not that person is the actual purchaser. Another illustration is the lighthouse, mentioned in Chapter 5. Once it is built, no sailor can be excluded from using its services.

A *pure public good* is one from whose benefits people are not excluded, regardless of who pays for the good.

The distinction between a public good and an ordinary private good is shown in the next two diagrams. An example of an ordinary good is provided in Figure 24-2, with the first two panels showing each individual consumer's marginal utility. In each case, the consumer would actually have to purchase and acquire the good in order to realize utility from it. As we saw in Figure 18-1, total market demand in panel *c* is obtained by a horizontal summation of the individual demands (marginal utilities) in panels *a* and *b*.

Figure 24-3 shows the alternative case of a pure public good, where *all* individuals can benefit from *each* unit produced. For example, consumer A gains utility a_1 from the first unit. But this same unit also provides consumer B with utility b_1. Since both individuals benefit from this first unit (both can, for example, see the warning beam from the same lighthouse), the utility provided by this first unit is $a_1 + b_1$, as shown in the last panel. Thus, for such a pure public good, marginal social utility (MU_S) is found by adding the individual utilities *vertically* (in contrast with the horizontal addition for a pure private good).[4]

But it is important to recognize that the resulting marginal social utility (MU_s) is not a demand curve. Nobody would buy the first unit if its price were $a_1 + b_1$. But, if it can be produced at this cost or less, the first unit should be produced. And if the second unit can be produced for $a_2 + b_2$ or less, it should be produced too; and so on.

---

[3]Notice that this is not true of gardening, where the benefit to an individual *does* depend on who has the gardening done—himself, his neighbor, or someone far down the street.

[4]We have here dealt with the two extreme cases: a pure private good, which provides utility only to the purchaser, and a pure public good, which provides utility regardless of who pays for it. There are, of course, many intermediate cases, where the purchaser gets most of the benefit, but others get some benefit. These intermediate cases were covered in our discussion of external benefits in the first section of this chapter.

Of course, there may be some individuals who get zero utility from a public good. Some may even get negative utility from it. An example is the army. While most people place a positive value on the defense service it provides, some place a negative value on it. (Any negative valuations should of course be taken into account in evaluating MU_s.)

(a) Consumer A's demand (A's marginal utility).

(b) Consumer B's demand (B's marginal utility).

(c) Market demand (marginal social utility).

FIGURE 24-2   A pure private good.
We horizontally sum individual demands in parts *a* and *b* to get market demand in part *c*. (At a price of $9, *A* buys 1 unit. If the price falls to $8, *B* also buys a unit. If the price falls to $7, *A* buys a second unit; and so on.) With a pure private good, there are no external benefits. Therefore, the market demand curve in part *c* represents the marginal social utility of this good.

FIGURE 24-3   A pure public good.
For a pure public good, we vertically add the individual marginal utilities in parts *a* and *b* to get the marginal social utility in part *c*. (The reason is that both consumers benefit from each unit.) With a pure public good, we thus stack utilities vertically (one on top of the other), whereas with a private good in Figure 24-2, we added utilities horizontally (putting one beside the other).

(a) Consumer A's marginal utility.

(b) Consumer B's marginal utility.

(c) Marginal social utility MU_S.

The Problem of Evaluating the Benefits of a Public Good

Suppose that the final panel of Figure 24-3 shows the benefits of building a system of flood-control dams on a river. Let us now examine in more detail our earlier claim that this public good must be provided by the government. If it should be produced (that is, if the first dam costs less than $a_1 + b_1$ to build), why can't it be provided by private enterprise? After all, since the two farmers value it at $a_1 + b_1$, why doesn't some entrepreneur collect this amount from them and build the dam? (The entrepreneur would be collecting more than the cost of the dam and therefore could even pocket a profit.)

To answer this question, note that our two farmers A and B actually represent thousands of farmers in the valley. (For other public goods as well, there are also very large numbers of consumers.) Thus you can visualize MU_S as the vertical sum not of two individual marginal utility curves, but, instead, of thousands of them, with each of them being relatively insignificant. Now suppose that you are one of these individuals, and the private entrepreneur who is promoting this project asks you for your valuation of the dam. Specifically, he asks how much you would be willing to contribute to its construction. What would you reply? Clearly, you would have a strong incentive to understate your benefit, because you realize that it is very unlikely that your answer will influence the decision on whether the dam is built. You will either get a dam or not, depending on how the other thousands of farmers in the valley respond. The only thing your reply will affect is the amount you will be contributing toward the dam's construction, and it is in your interest to minimize this amount. So you reply that you believe a flood-control system is exactly what this valley needs, and you believe your neighbors would value it very highly. But while your neighbors would gain, you ex-

pect very little benefit yourself; you personally are willing to pay very little for it.

You can now rest assured that your reply will have little effect on the decision to build the dam. Moreover, if it is built (as you hope), it will cost you very little. Yet you cannot be excluded from enjoying its services: If the dam prevents a flood, your buildings and land will be protected. The problem, of course, is that you will not be the only one with an incentive to understate your benefit. Every other individual in the valley will also have exactly the same incentive, so that the entrepreneur will get a seriously biased response, and will accordingly decide not to build a dam that should be built.

So individuals who want a dam cannot get it built by any sort of private market process. Their only recourse is to vote for a government that will build it *by collecting the necessary taxes* from themselves and their neighbors. Thus the decision gets made and backed up by the power of the government.

Decision-making: Private versus Public

Private and public decision-making differ in several important respects. First, it is more difficult to reverse an expenditure in the public sector. Recall that in the private market economy, if we don't want big cars after all, we can stop buying them next year, and they will stop being produced. The reason is that an auto company would sooner admit its mistake than continue to lose money on it; hence the saying: "Don't throw good money after bad." In short, business executives will admit their mistakes to save their jobs. Not so in the public sector, where admitting mistakes may *cost* politicians their jobs: If a government expenditure program is dropped, the opposition party may be able to use this "admission of error" to throw the government out in the next election. Furthermore, politicians who do not personally suffer out of pocket when they continue questionable expenditures. Therefore, politicians are less likely to admit a mistake and reverse a public expenditure.

(Because of this tendency, government expenditures have a very long life expectancy. Consequently, some critics have suggested "zero-base budgeting." This requires that any government expenditure be periodically revaluated from the ground up, to ensure that once it ceases to be justified, it will, like a private business expenditure, be dropped. This procedure is quite different from our tradition of taking existing government expenditures as given and concentrating the political struggle in Congress on where *additional* funds should be allocated.)

Another important private-public difference is that in the private sector, you get to vote (with your dollars) on, say, whether or not color TVs should be manufactured. In other words, if you are willing to buy a TV, you will encourage the production of TVs. In the public sector, you vote for a dam (in theory) by voting for a political party committed to building it. But in practice, it is not this simple; in fact, you may not get to vote on the issue at all. The reason is that in an election, you vote for a party with a *whole set* of policies. And you, like most other voters, may be voting for this party because of some other completely unrelated issue, like its policy toward China. It is therefore quite possible that the voters who have elected a government that has promised a dam don't really want the dam after all. (For a further complication in the political process, see Box 24-1.)

Thus, there are all sorts of problems involved in government decision-making. But the question still remains: *On economic grounds,* should the dam be built? In trying to answer this, the government may be as unable as the private entrepreneur to get a very satisfactory estimate of the benefits of the dam. For example, if the government asks you what value you would place on it,

and you believe that you will be taxed according to your reply, you will have the same strong incentive to understate that you had when you were asked by the private entrepreneur. On the other hand, if you believe the government will build the dam without increasing your taxes, it will be in your interest to overstate your valuation (to increase the chance that the dam will be built). Thus, estimates by individuals of what the dam is worth tend to be very unreliable, regardless of who is collecting them.

To sum up, the task of estimating the benefits of a public good seemed very cut and dried in Figure 24-3: Just get the individual MU curves and sum them vertically. In practice, however, these curves may remain a mystery because (1) individuals may not be quite sure how highly they value the good; and (2) even if they did know, they wouldn't tell you.

Benefit-Cost Analysis

Although the government is unlikely to get a very good estimate of the value of a public good by asking its potential users, it may still be able to go some distance in evaluating benefits. For example, the government can make estimates of the increase in crops which would result from a flood-control dam. It can do so by examining past records to determine how frequently floods occur and the value of the crops lost in each flood. Such an evaluation of benefits, along with an evaluation of the cost of the dam, is known as *benefit-cost analysis.*

However, one problem with this sort of approach is that, unless it is treated with care, it may be used to justify projects that the government has decided to build on purely political grounds, without great regard to economic costs. For example, a dam may have been promised to a key group of voters in the last election campaign. And anyone in the government with the task of justifying this dam may be able to do so by underestimating its construction costs and

BOX 24-1
A PROBLEM OF PUBLIC CHOICE

In making decisions, our elected representatives may have a number of motives. For example, they may try to provide what a majority of the public wants, or what they think the public *should* want. Or they may be just trying to maximize their chances of being reelected. But even if they have the sole objective of providing what a majority wants, there may be no simple way of doing this.

This is best seen by considering a population of only three individuals, faced with a choice among three options, *A*, *B*, and *C*. Suppose that the following table shows how each individual would rank each of these options. For example, the first column tells us that individual 1 prefers option *A* to option *B*, and *B* to *C*.

Preferences of Three Individuals for Alternative Policies *A*, *B*, and *C*

	Individual		
Choice	1	2	3
First choice	A	B	C
Second choice	B	C	A
Last choice	C	A	B

In choosing among the options, what is the will of the majority?

If these individuals vote first between options *A* and *B*, a majority (individuals 1 and 3) will vote for *A*. With *A* the choice so far, the only remaining question is how it compares with *C*. In voting between these two, the majority (individuals 2 and 3) prefer *C*. So *C* is the final choice, reflecting the apparent will of the majority.

But now suppose that these individuals had happened to vote first between *B* and *C*. In this case, *C* is immediately rejected because individuals 1 and 2 prefer *B*. Thus the preference of the majority isn't clear at all; *C* may be the final choice or immediately rejected, depending on how the voting is set up.

Thus we conclude that in a world in which individual preferences differ, an important determinant of the final choice may be the political process itself (in this example, the political decision on which options will be voted on first). In the face of such ambiguity, the party or individual that controls the voting procedure may be able to control the result.†

†For much more detail on the voting problem, see Kenneth Arrow, *Social Choice and Individual Values* (New York: John Wiley, 1951).

adding more and more benefits until the project is justified. These benefits might include the recreational services of the new lake and the human lives saved by flood control. While these may be important benefits, the value placed on them must be highly arbitrary. For example, what is a human life worth, in dollars and cents? (On this difficult question, see Box 24-2.)

There may be an additional complication in getting an accurate estimate if, as often happens, the engineers who expect to construct the dam are also the ones who are evaluating its benefits. They then face a

BOX 24-2
THE ETERNAL PUZZLE: What Is a Human Life Worth?

The simple answer: An infinite amount. The miner trapped underground has a life which is priceless. Yet, we don't value our own lives this way. Were they to have infinite value, safety concerns would dominate all others. We would live as close as possible to our work and never drive a car, let alone take a long plane trip to earn something as trivial as a few thousand dollars.

One method used to evaluate a life is the individual's earnings potential—the expected amount the individual would have earned over the rest of his or her lifetime. By this measure, a life lost at age 30 is worth far more than a life lost at 60. Using this approach, the National Highway Traffic Safety Administration was using a value of $270,000 for the average life lost in the late 1970s. (At the same time, the British Department of Environment was using $100,000, a figure that is much lower, of course, because British earnings are less. But does that mean a British life is worth less?) In any case, such figures surely underestimate, since they measure the value of a *livelihood*, not a *life*.

An alternative approach is to start by asking, "What's the valuation of an individual who actually 'puts his life on the line'?" That is, how much more than the average wage must be offered to induce a worker to take a high-risk job like that of a lumberjack or doorkeeper? We can answer this question by looking at how much higher wages are in these risky occupations. (But there are several problems here: The higher wage tells us only how the relatively risk-immune workers who take these jobs value their lives, and this value may be far less than the valuation of the vast majority of the population who value their lives more highly, and consequently won't take such risky jobs. Second, this estimate is meaningful only if the individuals who take these jobs understand the risks they are taking. And they may not. For example, did you know that police officers and firefighters have jobs that are many times safer than lumberjacking or doorkeeping?) Using this approach, and also taking into account the family's valuation of a life lost, the resulting estimates run from a few hundred thousand dollars to a million and a half.

Finally, whenever an expensive safety regulation is imposed, one can calculate how highly a life must be valued to justify the expense. It has been estimated that some recent federal on-the-job safety standards are so costly to meet that they can be justified only if a human life is valued at between $10 million and $50 million.

We can draw two conclusions from this wide difference in valuation (the $270,000 used in setting highway safety standards and the $10 million to $50 million necessary to justify some on-the-job safety standards). First, we are not imposing strict enough standards on the highway (where we value a life too low), and/or we are imposing too strict standards on the job (where we value a life too high). In other words, if we change our safety standards (raising them on the highway and lowering them on the job), we can save the same number of lives at lower cost. Second, the extremely wide range of these estimates tells us something we knew all along: It is very difficult to answer the question, "What is a life worth?"

conflict of interest. On the one hand, they are responsible to the public for estimating benefits as accurately as possible. On the other hand, they have a substantial personal interest in inflating the estimated benefits in order to justify the dam, and thus to create future income and employment for themselves.

Public Expenditures: Too Large or Too Small?

The above discussion suggests that government expenditures may be excessively large. But John Kenneth Galbraith takes the opposite view, judging public expenditures to be inadequate. One reason he cites is that goods provided by the private market are advertised (with their consumption increased as a consequence), while goods provided by the government are not. Therefore, we overspend on autos, but underspend on roads; we overspend on cosmetics, but underspend on public health. As Galbraith puts it:

> The family which takes its . . . air-conditioned, power-steered, and power-braked automobile out for a tour passes through cities that are badly paved, made hideous by litter, blighted buildings, billboards, and posts for wires that should long since have been put underground. They pass on to a countryside that has been rendered largely invisible by commercial art. They picnic on exquisitely packaged food from a portable icebox by a polluted stream and go on to spend the night at a park which is a menace to public health and morals. Just before dozing off on an air mattress beneath a nylon tent, amid the stench of decaying refuse, they may reflect vaguely on the curious unevenness of their blessings. Is this, indeed, the American genius?[5]

Although Galbraith seems to be in direct conflict with those who think that public expenditure is excessive, both may be

[5]John Kenneth Galbraith, *The Affluent Society* (Boston: Houghton-Mifflin, 1958), p. 253.

partly right. It may be that we spend too much on certain public expenditures, but not enough on others.

THE ENVIRONMENT: A Public Good?

As Galbraith's comment emphasizes, protecting our environment should be one of our important economic objectives. There are several ways in which we can do so.

The first is to tax any firm (or individual) doing damage to the environment for whatever reason. If a firm is polluting our air or water or defacing our landscape by strip mining, say, it should be taxed, as we concluded in our discussion of pollution in Chapter 23.

But suppose that the environment is deteriorating of its own accord; no firm or individual is at fault in any way. For exam-

---

BOX 24-3
A REVIEW OF MARKET STRUCTURE IN THE LAST FIVE CHAPTERS:
How a Typical Firm's Costs Compare with Total Market Demand

Figure 24-4 shows how the kind of market that develops (whether it be monopoly, perfect competition, or whatever) is heavily influenced by the range over which the firm's average costs continue to fall. To highlight this point, we consider five different goods in the first five panels of this diagram. (We discuss the sixth panel later.) In almost all respects, these five goods are identical. In each case, total market demand is exactly the same, and average cost AC reaches a minimum at the same height, C. (This is also true in panel e, although we don't have room to show it.) The only difference in these five goods is a crucial one. As we move left to right from panel to panel, AC reaches a minimum at increasingly large levels of output. Thus, in panel a, AC reaches a minimum at a very small output level, while in panel e, the minimum value of AC is so far to the right that it cannot even be shown in the diagram.

In the case of perfect competition in panel a, market demand can be satisfied at minimum cost by a large number of producers. There is little role to be played by the government, since this market is generally efficient when left to its own devices. (We assume here that there are no complications, such as serious price fluctuations over time, or important externalities. If externalities do exist, the government should tax to discourage external costs, or subsidize to encourage external benefits.)

Panel b is the case of natural oligopoly, where market demand can be satisfied at minimum cost by just a few firms. In such a market, a strong case can be made for the vigorous enforcement of antitrust laws to prevent collusion or the merger of these firms into a monopoly.

In the case of natural monopoly in panel c, market demand can be satisfied at lower cost by one firm than by several. Here, the application of antitrust legislation to split up a single firm makes little sense, since the split would raise costs. A preferred approach is price regulation, which allows the monopoly to produce at low cost, but prevents it from charging a high monopoly price.

In panels d and e, costs have finally outrun demand. At no point do D and AC any longer overlap, so there is no single price a firm can charge and still cover its costs. The appropriate government policy in either case is "hands off." If the gap between demand and costs is small enough, as in panel d, a discriminating monopolist (say, the doctor in Chapter 21) may be able to cover her costs if she is allowed to charge ple, suppose that a species of wildlife is dying off in the wilderness. In this case, the proper approach is to recognize that the preservation of this species is a public good. Since no individual values the species highly enough to incur the cost of personally preserving it, the only way such a policy can be implemented is by the government's action. And if the government does act, everyone can enjoy the resulting benefits.

How large would these benefits be? This question is not easy to answer. While most people would put some value on the preservation of a wildlife species, it is very difficult to say how much. As Harvard's Richard Caves has put it: "How highly should we value wombats, if they are so far from civilization that no one will ever see them, let alone eat them?" One answer is that we may place some value on them, even

different prices to different consumers. Since her service will not be available otherwise, the government should allow her to follow this policy.

But in panel *e*, cost outruns demand by such a large amount that even a discriminating monopolist cannot cover the cost of producing this good. In fact, the product will not even appear on the market; there is no economic justification for its production.

In panel *f*, we show a public good. In this case, we examine how its cost compares with the marginal social benefit curve, MU$_S$. (For specific detail, see problem 24-1*b*.) If the market is left to its own devices, no individual will purchase this good. If it is to be purchased at all, it must be by the government.

FIGURE 24-4   The relationship of the costs of a single producer and total market demand.

| (a) Perfect competition (see Figure 22-2a). | (b) Natural oligopoly (see Figure 22-2b). | (c) Natural monopoly (see Figure 22-2c). | (d) Discriminating monopoly (see Figure 21-8). | (e) Nonexistent good. | (f) Public good (see Figure 24-3). |

An appropriate government role is to

| Leave the market alone | Enforce antitrust legislation | Regulate price | Allow monopolist to discriminate | Leave the market alone | Provide the good itself |

though we don't ever see them, just as we may place a value on an air-conditioning system even in a summer in which we never actually turn it on. This phenomenon is described as "option demand"—the desire to have an option, whether or not we ever exercise it. Thus we may have an option demand for a wildlife species that we may or may not ever view. Similarly, we may have an option demand for public parks in which we may or may not ever picnic. This idea of option demand is very important in evaluating.environmental benefits.

Yet Caves' basic point is well taken: In discussing environmental protection, it is important to take a hardheaded view of the benefits and costs involved. For example, consider a caribou population that would be disturbed by a proposed oil pipeline. A major cost would be involved in the extreme event that the pipeline were to cause the caribou to become extinct, since this action could not be reversed by future generations. But if there is no such risk of extinction, what is the difference between reducing the population of caribou by X percent and reducing the population of cattle by X percent, as we do when we slaughter them for meat? (Both policies provide obvious benefits: killing cattle provides food, while laying pipelines is essential to provide heat and power.)

Once again we conclude, as we did in Chapter 23, that keeping environmental damage down to an appropriately low level makes more sense than trying to avoid any damage whatsoever.

Key Points

1. If a good provides an external benefit, a perfectly competitive market will provide less than the efficient level of output. The government can induce the expansion of output to the efficient level by subsidizing buyers of this good by the amount of the external benefit. This "internalizes the externality," because buyers then personally enjoy not only the benefit the good provides to themselves, but also an amount equal to the benefit it provides to others.

2. No individual farmer would ever consider building a flood-control dam, because of its high cost and the fact that the benefits he himself would receive would be trivial compared with the benefits that would go to thousands of neighboring farmers. This, then, is the general idea of a public good: It is a good that will not be produced by the private market, but must be produced, if it is to exist at all, by the government.

3. A more precise and narrow definition is that a pure public good is nonexcludable in consumption: Once the dam is built, no one can be excluded from enjoying its flood-control services.

4. Building such a dam will be justified if its cost is less than the benefit it provides to all the public.

5. In practice, there may be major problems involved in evaluating these benefits. Even if people have a clear idea in their own minds of what the benefits would be, they are unlikely to tell any government official (or, for that matter, any private entrepreneur). Therefore, an alternative approach of benefit-cost analysis is often used. Thus, for example, the benefit of flood control is estimated by looking at past records of how often floods have occurred and the damage they have done to crops. But it still remains extraordinarily difficult to estimate some of the benefits (like saving human lives) and some of the costs (like damaging runs of migratory fish).

6. There are two important ways to protect the environment. When it is being damaged by, say, a polluting firm, the proper approach is to tax that firm (as we saw in Chapter 23). But when the environment is deteriorating of its own accord (for example, if a wildlife species is becoming extinct), the preservation of the environment may be viewed as a public good. Thus, government protection of the environment is justified if the costs of this protection are less than the benefits it provides to all individuals in society.

Key Concepts

external benefits
how a subsidy affects efficiency
internalizing an external benefit
internalizing an external cost
a pure public good
marginal social utility for a private good and
  for a public good

private versus public decisions
relative nonreversibility of public expenditure
zero-base budgeting
benefit-cost analysis
why the environment is a public good
option demand

Problems

24-1(a) Draw a diagram like Figure 24-3c, and also draw in a completely horizontal marginal cost curve at a height just above a_2. Now show the number of units of this public good that the government should provide. (For example, how many dams should the government build in a flood-control network?)

(b) In Figure 24-4f, extend MU_S to the right. Also extend AC to the right until it reaches a minimum, and then draw in the corresponding MC curve. How many units of this good should the government provide?

24-2 If a freeway is to be built into a city, discuss the benefits and costs that you think should be estimated. Explain why preparing such an estimate might be a difficult task.

24-3 Do you think national defense is a public good? Why? Do you think estimating its benefits would be difficult? Why?

24-4 Suppose you are working for a government in the tropics, and a proposal is being considered to spray a wide area of territory for malarial mosquitoes. A critic states that such an expenditure is not justified, since if it were justified, a private entrepreneur would already have seized this opportunity. What position do you take?

24-5 (Review of the last two chapters). Suppose the only three individuals who would benefit from a public good have the demand (marginal utility) schedules shown at the top of page 538. Assume also that each unit of this good involves a production cost of C and an external cost of K. Should this good be produced? If so, at what output level?

24-6 Suppose that, instead of the per

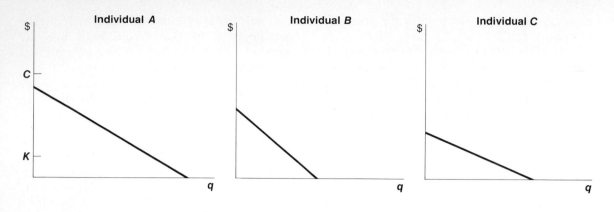

Individual A   Individual B   Individual C

unit subsidy to the *buyer* shown as the red arrow in Figure 24-1, the government provides exactly the same subsidy to the *seller*. Show the effect. Does this subsidy increase output to the efficient level? How does this policy compare with the policy of subsidizing the buyer?

chapter 25
The Gains from International Trade

Our interest will be to throw open the doors of commerce, and to knock off its shackles, giving freedom to all persons for the vent of whatever they may choose to bring into our ports, and asking the same in theirs. Thomas Jefferson

Economic gains come from specialization. One of the reasons for the high material standard of living in the United States is our high degree of specialization. Steel is produced near the coalfields of Pennsylvania, wheat is produced in the Western states, and citrus fruits are grown in California and Florida. By such specialization, we are able to increase our total output of goods.

Just as specialization within the United States makes our economy more efficient, so, too, specialization among the United States and other countries contributes to our efficiency. Specifically, international trade and specialization bring the same benefits as domestic specialization, first noted in Chapter 3: namely, the gains from *comparative advantage* and *economies of scale*. International trade also opens domestic producers up to increased competition and thus reduces their market power. Consequently, Americans purchase goods more cheaply both from foreign firms and from domestic pro-

ducers who must keep their prices down in order to meet foreign competition.

The major objective of this chapter will be to consider each of these benefits from trade in detail. But before doing so, we ask two questions.

WITH WHOM DO WE TRADE? WHAT DO WE TRADE?

The answers are provided in Table 25-1. From the first column, it is evident that the most important United States trading partner is Canada. (This is no surprise, since distance and transport costs are natural deterrents to trade, and they are at a minimum in our trade with Canada.) Japan is also a key trading partner, followed by the large countries in the European Economic Community and Latin America.

The right-hand side of the table indicates that our trade is spread over a wide variety of goods. Our exports include such

539

TABLE 25-1
United States Merchandise Trade Pattern in 1977
(in billions of dollars)

With whom do we trade?		What do we trade?	
Exports: 1977 U.S. sales to:		Exports	
Canada	$ 28.3	Grains	$ 10.3
Japan	10.6	Other agricultural products	14.1
European Economic Community (EEC)	26.5	Nonagricultural industrial supplies	29.9
Western Europe, except the EEC	7.6	Machinery	33.5
Eastern Europe	2.9	Civilian aircraft	2.8
Latin America	17.9	Autos and parts	13.0
Australia, New Zealand, and South		Other consumer goods	8.9
Africa	3.8	All other	8.1
Other countries in Asia and		Total $120.6	
Africa	23.0		
Total	$120.6		
Imports: 1977 U.S. purchases from:		Imports	
Canada	$ 29.7	Coffee, cocoa, and sugar	$ 5.5
Japan	18.5	Other foods, feed, and beverages	8.5
European Economic Community	22.1	Petroleum and products	45.0
Western Europe, except the EEC	6.1	Other industrial supplies and	
Eastern Europe	1.1	materials	36.0
Latin America	21.2	Machinery	13.4
Australia, New Zealand, and South		Autos and parts	18.8
Africa	2.8	Other consumer goods	21.8
Other countries in Asia and		All other	2.6
Africa	50.1	Total $151.6	
Total	$151.6		

Source: Survey of Current Business (U.S. Department of Commerce), June 1978, Part 2, pp. 24–30.

diverse items as grain from Iowa and aircraft from Seattle. And our imports include base metals and other materials essential to American industry (not to mention coffee, which seems to have become essential to American consumers, judging from our willingness to buy regardless of its skyrocketing price in 1977). And, for a nation on wheels, autos and oil account for an important part of our trade. (Our auto trade with Canada alone accounted for roughly $8 billion in exports and imports—largely because of the 1965 duty-free Auto Pact described in Box 3-4.)

Over time, trade has been growing, and for some items, very rapidly. For example, between 1972 and 1977 our imports of oil and its products increased from less than $5 billion to $45 billion. (This rapid growth was the result of both an increase in the

quantity of oil imported and a large increase in its price.) Similarly, in that same brief period, the value of our grain exports roughly tripled.

This, then, describes *what* and *with whom* we trade. Now let us return to the advantages we reap from trade. We consider three basic sources of gain: (1) increased competition, (2) economies of scale, and (3) comparative advantage.

MARKETS BECOME MORE COMPETITIVE, AND HENCE MORE EFFICIENT

Consider the monopoly firm in Figure 25-1. Initially, in the absence of international trade (panel *a*), it has the United States market all to itself. If there is no government regulation, it will be able to set a monopoly

(a) **Without trade (like Figure 24-4c).** Without trade, home market demand can support only one low cost producer. The result: a natural monopoly.

(b) **With trade (like Figure 24-4b).** With trade, market demand is greater, but the number of producers is also greater, because it now includes both American and foreign firms. The result: a natural oligopoly.

FIGURE 25-1 How international trade breaks down monopoly power.

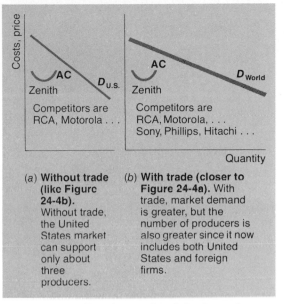

(a) **Without trade (like Figure 24-4b).** Without trade, the United States market can support only about three producers.

(b) **With trade (closer to Figure 24-4a).** With trade, market demand is greater, but the number of producers is also greater since it now includes both United States and foreign firms.

FIGURE 25-2 How international trade makes an oligopoly more competitive.

price. In panel *b*, we see what happens when trade is opened up. The potential demand facing the American producer is much larger, as shown by the total world demand curve. Therefore, the American firm is now able to go after foreign markets as well as the domestic market. But, it is no longer able to take the United States market for granted, since it faces stiff competition here from foreign producers. Thus, foreign trade can transform a natural monopoly in the domestic market (panel *a*) into a natural oligopoly in the world market (panel *b*). In the process, this firm's monopoly control of the United States market is broken, and its ability to exercise market power by charging a high price is reduced. As we have seen, any lowering of price toward a more competitive level results in an improved allocation of resources, with corresponding efficiency gains.

On the other hand, if the industry is originally a natural oligopoly, international trade can make it substantially more competitive. Observe in Figure 25-2 that a United States firm with about one-third of the domestic market in panel *a* will—after trade is opened up—have only a small fraction of

the much larger world market in panel *b*. Again, increased competition will tend to keep down price. Furthermore, the United States consumer may also gain because the domestic producer is forced to compete in non-price aspects, such as quality or design. Thus, the United States automobile industry has been encouraged to produce smaller cars, as a result of competition first from Volkswagen (in the late 1950s) and, more recently, from Datsun, Toyota, and Honda.

ECONOMIES OF SCALE

In the face of economies of scale (involving falling average costs as output expands), there are two additional potential gains from trade.

New Products Become Available

Specifically, international trade may make it profitable to produce goods which otherwise would not be produced at all. Figure 25-3*a* (which repeats Figure 24-4*e*) illustrates such a product. Demand is too low in the domestic economy to allow this

(a) Without trade (reproduced from Figure 24-4e).

(b) Same good, with trade (like Figure 24-4c).

Without trade this good will not be produced,

but with trade, it will be produced.

FIGURE 25-3 How international trade may create new products.
The AC curves in these two figures are identical. But because of trade, the demand curve in part b is much farther to the right.

good to be profitably produced. But when the foreign market becomes available, demand becomes large enough to cover average costs (a rising D overlaps AC) and the item is introduced. An example is the 747 jumbo jet, introduced by Boeing at the beginning of the 1970s. If there had been no hope for sales to foreign airlines, Boeing would not have been able to cover the enormous design and tooling costs necessary to produce such an aircraft; at the very least, its introduction would have been delayed. Perhaps it would not have been produced at all.

Existing Goods Can Be Produced More Efficiently

Where there are economies of scale, trade results not only in the introduction of new products, but also in the more efficient production of old products. For example, European producers have been able to manufacture automobiles at larger volume and lower cost since the establishment of the European Economic Community. (By removing trade barriers, this agreement allows a manufacturer in any one EEC country to sell freely to consumers in all EEC countries.)

COMPARATIVE ADVANTAGE

Now suppose that there are no economies of scale; instead, suppose costs are constant. (The average cost curve is horizontal.) The theory of comparative advantage tells us that even in these circumstances, gains can be realized by international trade.

The basic idea of comparative advantage has already been introduced in Chapter 3. Even though the doctor cited there may be more skillful (that is, may have an absolute advantage) in both medicine and gardening, she does not do her own gardening. Instead, she concentrates on medicine, the activity in which she has a comparative advantage. By specializing in this way, she can acquire far more gardening service than if she were to take the time to do it herself.

The international analogy is this: Even though the United States may be better (that is, have an absolute advantage) in producing both wheat and transistor radios, it may be in our interest to concentrate on wheat and other products in which we have a comparative advantage, and leave transistor radios to other countries. By specializing in wheat, we may be able to acquire more radios through trade than we could produce ourselves.

The idea of comparative advantage was developed in the early nineteenth century by David Ricardo, an English economist, financier, and member of Parliament. In his simplified illustration of this idea, Ricardo assumed that markets were perfectly competitive, that there were no transport costs, that all production costs were constant, and that the only input was labor. He also assumed that there were only two countries (we shall call them America and Europe) producing two goods (we shall call them food and clothing).

Absolute Advantage

As a preliminary, Table 25-2 shows the case where each country has an *absolute*

TABLE 25-2
Illustration of Absolute Advantage:
Hypothetical Output per Worker in Europe and America

	Clothing	Food
America	3 units	2 units
Europe	4 units	1 unit

In the first column, Europe has an absolute advantage in clothing production because a worker can produce 4 units, compared with only 3 in America. In the second column, America has an absolute advantage in food, because a worker here can produce 2 units, compared with only 1 in Europe. Both countries together can produce more total output when America specializes in food and Europe specializes in clothing.

To confirm, suppose specialization has not occurred; in other words, suppose that each country is initially producing both goods. Now suppose that they begin to specialize—America in food, Europe in clothing. Therefore, a worker in America is switched out of clothing and into food production. At the same time, a worker in Europe is switched in the opposite direction (out of food and into clothing). As a result of these two switches:

	Clothing output changes by	Food output changes by
In America	−3	+2
In Europe	+4	−1
Therefore, net world output changes by	+1	+1

TABLE 25-3
Illustration of Comparative Advantage:
Hypothetical Output per Worker in Europe and America

Product	Clothing	Food
America	6 units	3 units
Europe	4 units	1 unit

In Europe, one worker can produce either 4 units of clothing or 1 unit of food. Thus, the opportunity cost of 1 unit of food in Europe is 4 units of clothing. In America, a worker can produce either 6 units of clothing or 3 of food. The opportunity cost of food in America is therefore 6/3 = 2 units of clothing. (Notice how we calculate this opportunity cost by taking the ratio of the figures in the American row, just as we calculated the European cost (4/1) from the figures in the European row.) Since the opportunity cost of food in America is less than in Europe, America has a comparative advantage in food and specializes in this good.

To confirm that this specialization will increase total world output, again suppose that each country is initially producing both goods. Now suppose they begin to specialize: America switches one worker out of clothing and into food, and Europe switches two workers out of food and into clothing. Then:

	Clothing output changes by	Food output changes by
In America	−6	+3
In Europe	+8	−2
Therefore, net world output changes by	+2	+1

advantage in the production of one good. In the first column, we see that a clothing worker in Europe can outproduce a worker in America (4 to 3), so by definition Europe has an absolute advantage in clothing. Similarly, in the second column we see that America has an absolute advantage in food, since an American worker can outproduce a European worker (2 to 1). The most efficient allocation of resources is to have America specialize in food and Europe in clothing.

So far, it seems that each country specializes in the good in which it has an absolute advantage. But this is not always so. We shall now show that the key to

specialization is *comparative advantage*, rather than absolute advantage.

Comparative Advantage

Table 25-3 illustrates the more difficult case where one country, America (like the doctor in Box 3-3), has an absolute advantage in the production of both goods. [An American worker outproduces a European worker in both clothing (6 to 4) and food (3 to 1).] Nonetheless, America, like the doctor, will not try to satisfy its requirements by producing both goods itself. Instead, it will specialize in one and buy the other from Europe, as we shall now explain.

Our first step is to calculate the opportunity cost of, say, food in each country. First, in Europe: The second row of Table 25-3 tells us that a European worker who is now producing 1 unit of food could, instead, be producing 4 units of clothing. In other words, in Europe *the opportunity cost of 1 unit of food is 4 units of clothing.* Since prices tend to reflect costs, we would expect these two goods to exchange in Europe for this same 1:4 ratio (that is, in the absence of international trade, 1 unit of food will exchange in Europe for 4 units of clothing).

On the other hand, what is the opportunity cost of food in America? The first row of Table 25-3 tells us that an American worker who is producing 3 units of food could instead be producing 6 units of clothing. In other words, in America the opportunity cost of (a unit of) food is $6/3 = 2$ units of clothing. Consequently, we would expect the two goods to exchange in America at this same 1:2 ratio; that is, before trade, 1 unit of food will exchange for 2 units of clothing.

Since the opportunity cost of food in America is less (2 units of clothing versus 4 in Europe), we say that America has a comparative advantage in food. By definition:

> A country's *comparative advantage* is the good that it can produce relatively cheaply; that is, at lower opportunity cost than its trading partner.

A similar set of calculations using the figures in Table 25-3 shows that in clothing, Europe has a lower opportunity cost, and hence a comparative advantage.[1].

With this concept of comparative advantage in hand, our last step is to show that both countries will benefit if they specialize in their product of comparative advantage and trade for the other—at any price ratio between the 1:2 price ratio which would prevail in an isolated America and the 1:4 in Europe. Although we do not have enough information to determine precisely what that price ratio will be,[2] let us suppose it is 1:3; that is, 1 unit of food exchanges internationally for 3 units of clothing. (This ratio is often called the terms of trade.) Also suppose that, initially, each country produces both goods. America can now benefit by specializing in its product of comparative advantage, food, and trading to satisfy its clothing needs. Specifically, for each American worker taken out of clothing production, America loses 6 units of clothing. But, instead, that worker now produces 3 units of food, which can then be traded (at the 1:3 international price ratio) for 9 units of clothing—for a clear gain of 3 units of clothing. Similarly, Europe also gains by specializing in its product of comparative advantage, clothing, and trading it for food.[3]

To sum up this example, both countries gain from trade. America benefits by specializing in food (its comparative advantage) and trading for clothing. At the same time, Europe benefits by specializing in clothing (its comparative advantage) and trading for food. The reason that there are gains from trade is that the cost ratios in the two rows of Table 25-3 (namely 4/1 and 6/3) are different. (If these ratios are the same, there will be no comparative advantage and no gain from trade.)

---

[1] In Europe the opportunity cost of clothing is 1/4 of a unit of food (1/4 of a unit of food must be given up to acquire 1 unit of clothing). Similarly, in America the opportunity cost of clothing is $3/6 = 1/2$ unit of food. With its lower opportunity cost of clothing, Europe has a comparative advantage in clothing, and specializes in it. [Notice from these calculations in this simple two-country, two-product example that America's comparative advantage in one good (food) means that Europe must have a comparative advantage in the other (clothing).]

[2] Remember, price is determined by both cost (supply) and demand, and the ratios we are working with here only describe cost. To determine price precisely, we would also have to know about demand—for example, how strongly Europeans demand food (the American export) and how strongly Americans demand clothing.

[3] In switching a worker from food to clothing production, Europe loses 1 unit of food. But that worker produces 4 units of clothing instead, and this output can be traded (at the 1:3 international price ratio) for $4/3 = 1\frac{1}{3}$ units of food—for a clear gain of $\frac{1}{3}$ units of food.

FIGURE 25-4 Gains from trade.

American production possibilities curve AC is derived from the first row in Table 25-3, on the assumption that there are 200 million workers in America. If they all work at producing clothing (6 units each) the 200 million workers will produce 1200 million units of clothing and no food at point *A*. On the other hand, if they all produce food (3 units each) they will produce a total of 600 million units of food and no clothing at point *C*. Finally, suppose that half the American workers produce food and half produce clothing. Then the 100 million clothing workers will produce 6 units each, for a total of 600 million units of clothing, while the 100 million food workers will produce 3 units each, for a total of 300 million units of food. This combination of outputs is plotted as point *B*. (The constant figures in the first row of Table 25-3 ensure that the American

production possibilities curve *AC* will be a straight line.) Suppose that without trade, America produces and consumes at point *B*. When trade is opened, America can (1) *specialize* in food, by shifting production from *B* to *C*, and (2) *trade* 300 units of food for 900 units of clothing, thus moving from *C* to *D*. For America, production is still on production possibilities curve *AC* (as it must be), but trade now allows us to consume beyond this curve at *D*. The American gain from trade is our increase in clothing consumption from the original 600 units at point *B* to the 900 units at point *D*. (Our consumption of food does not change. Of course, America need not necessarily end up at point *D*. For example, in moving up the trade arrow, it may stop at a point short of *D*. Then its gains from trade would be both increased clothing, and increased food.) Figure 25-5b shows gains with a curved PPC.

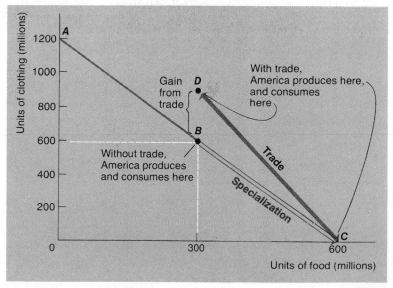

The gain to the United States from trade may be illustrated in another way. Figure 25-4 shows the American production possibilities curve, derived from the United States figures in the first row of Table 25-3, assuming that there are 200 million workers in America. (For example, if they all work at producing clothing, each of the 200 million workers will produce 6 units for a total of 1,200 million units of clothing, as shown as point A.) The production possibilities curve is a straight line because the opportunity cost of food in America remains constant as we move down the production possibilities curve. No matter what the level of food output may be, producing 1 more unit always costs 2 units of clothing.

Before trade, we will produce and consume at a point on the production possibilities curve, such as B. With trade, we can benefit by the following two steps.

1. *Specialize.* Shift production from B to C, as shown by the double arrow. That is, produce 300 more units of food by giving up 600 million units of clothing. Thus we concentrate on food, the good in which we have a comparative advantage.

2. *Trade.* Trade these 300 million additional units of food (at the 1:3 international price ratio) for 900 million units of clothing. This second step is shown by the heavy single arrow.

As a result of this specialization and trade, our consumption can rise from point B to point D. In other words, we can consume 300 more units of clothing, which is our *real income gain* (or efficiency gain) from trade.

Comparative advantage thus leads to gains from trade. But why does comparative advantage exist? Why does America have a comparative advantage in wheat? One major reason is our large endowment of highly productive land, especially in the Midwest. On the other hand, a country like India, with

its huge pool of unskilled labor, tends to have a comparative advantage in activities that require a great deal of labor. Thus, comparative advantage depends on resource endowments. It also depends on skills built up over the past. For example, our highly developed technology gives us a comparative advantage in producing such high-technology items as computers and jumbo jets.

TRADE AND TECHNOLOGICAL CHANGE: Their Similarities

In a closed economy with no trade, a country cannot get beyond its production possibilities curve (PPC). But with trade, consumption outside the PPC becomes possible. True, production is always limited by the PPC, but consumption can be greater because of the gain from trade. In other words, international trade is the way for countries to break out of their production limitation and reach a point of consumption and real income beyond it. (In Figure 25-4, America breaks out of its production limitation AC and consumes at point D beyond.)

Figure 25-5 shows the important way in which international trade and technological change are similar. Both can move us from point B to a higher point of consumption, such as D. But, while technological change achieves this by an outward shift in the production possibilities curve, trade achieves it by allowing us to consume at a point beyond our production possibilities curve.

Trade and technological change are also alike in another significant respect. Though they generally provide a benefit to the nation as a whole, they do not necessarily benefit each and every individual within the nation. Naturally, then, some individuals may object vehemently to trade or to technological change. For example, when textile machinery was introduced, workers feared that it would eliminate their jobs. (Some workers did indeed lose their jobs, even though ma-

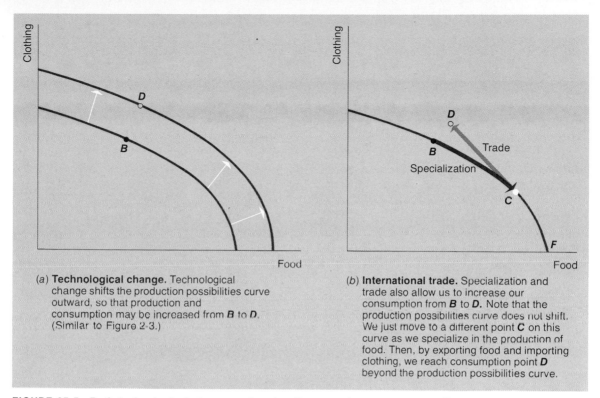

(a) **Technological change.** Technological change shifts the production possibilities curve outward, so that production and consumption may be increased from **B** to **D**. (Similar to Figure 2-3.)

(b) **International trade.** Specialization and trade also allow us to increase our consumption from **B** to **D**. Note that the production possibilities curve does not shift. We just move to a different point **C** on this curve as we specialize in the production of food. Then, by exporting food and importing clothing, we reach consumption point **D** beyond the production possibilities curve.

FIGURE 25-5 Both technological change and trade allow us to increase consumption.

chinery has ultimately made possible much higher productivity and jobs at much higher pay.) Early workers on occasion threw wooden shoes (in French, *sabots*) into the machinery; hence, the word "sabotage" was coined. Similarly, international trade may temporarily displace textile workers, if production is shifted from textiles (where some markets have been lost to imports) to computers or jumbo jets (where we have a comparative advantage and can export). Once again, those who are harmed may object vehemently. In this case, they need not throw their shoes into the machinery; laws that restrict imports are the way to seek protection. Thus, trade restrictions and sabotage are similar in one respect: Both prevent a general improvement in the standard of living in order to protect a specific group.

The temporary unemployment that follows either trade or technological change is a problem, but one that is frequently exaggerated. Workers displaced by technological change tend to be fairly quickly absorbed elsewhere, as are workers displaced by imports. This has been historically true in the United States. It has also been true in Europe, where the Common Market (the European Economic Community) has opened up trade among countries on a very large scale, but temporary unemployment has been less than expected.

[Before leaving Figure 25-5, note two other points illustrated in panel *b*. First, there are gains from trade even when opportunity costs are not constant; that is, when the production possibilities curve is not a straight line. Second, although trade induces a country to specialize, often it will not specialize completely. (In panel b, America moves from B to C, but not all the way to F.)]

INTERNATIONAL TRADE AND EFFICIENCY

While this analysis has illustrated the general case for trade, it is a bit abstract since it lumps all American exports into a single food category and all imports into a single clothing category. Moreover, the only prices that exist are relative, barterlike prices. (For example, the price of 1 unit of food is 3 units of clothing.) Now, let us return to the more familiar world of supply and demand, where

goods are sold for dollars. (For example, the price of a bushel of wheat is $2.20.) Here, we shall no longer think in abstract terms of only two goods, with food representing all United States exports and clothing representing all its imports. Instead, we examine one specific American export item (wheat) and one specific United States import item (woolens). In this more familiar frame of reference, we shall illustrate how trade increases efficiency.[4]

Efficiency Gain on a Typical Export: Wheat

Figure 25-6 shows the United States demand and supply curves for wheat. With-

[4]Our analysis can be used only to illustrate conclusions, rather than prove them. (Proof requires more complicated techniques.)

FIGURE 25-6 Detailed effects of the export of an individual good—wheat.
With trade, price increases from P_A to P with Q_1Q_2 exported. Part of these exports come from reduced consumption (Q_1Q_A), with a typical unit shown as e. The consumer's valuation of this lost unit of consumption is shown as the hollow bar; the gain from exporting it instead is the export price P, that is, the hollow bar plus the solid bar. Thus the net gain on this unit is the solid bar, and the net gain on all such units of reduced consumption (in the range Q_1Q_A) is blue triangle 3. Exports also come from increased production (Q_AQ_2), with a typical unit shown as f. The cost of producing this unit is the hollow bar, while its benefit is the export price P, that is, the hollow bar plus the solid bar. Thus the net gain on this unit is the solid bar, and the net gain on all such units of increased production (in the range Q_AQ_2) is the blue triangle 4. Thus, the efficiency gain from exporting is both these areas (3 + 4). Because price has risen, producers gain at consumers' expense. The transfer from consumers to producers is illustrated by the wide white arrow on the left.

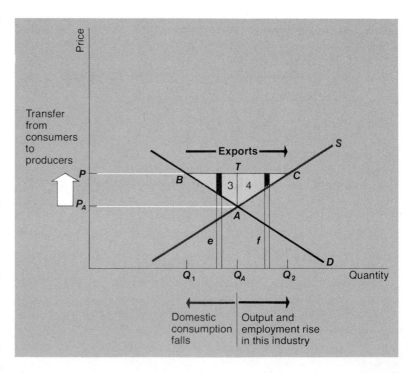

548

out trade, equilibrium in the domestic market is at point A, where the nation's supply and demand intersect. Thus we produce Q_A at price P_A. At the same time, the price in the rest of the world is at the higher level P, reflecting the higher costs of producing wheat in foreign countries.

When trade is opened, United States producers discover that they can sell abroad at this higher price P, and they begin to do so. Moreover, since they can sell at P abroad, they will be unwilling to sell at any lower price in the home market. Thus the domestic price rises to the world level P. (In a more realistic situation, the American price rises to the foreign price, less transportation costs. But in this simple illustration we assume that transport costs and other similar complications do not exist.)

American producers, facing this more attractive price, expand their output. Specifically, they move up their supply curve from A to C, increasing their output from Q_A to Q_2. But, of course, consumers view this higher price quite differently. They move up the demand curve from A to B, thus reducing their consumption from Q_A to Q_1. In short, Q_2 is now produced in the United States, and Q_1 is consumed. The difference $(Q_1 Q_2)$ is the amount the United States exports. Thus, these exports come partly from increased production and partly from reduced domestic consumption. We now examine each of these effects in turn.

Consider first one of the units of reduced consumption $Q_1 Q_A$, say unit e. The consumer's valuation of this lost unit of consumption is shown as the hollow bar under the demand curve. (Recall that demand reflects marginal utility.) But our gain from exporting this unit is the export price P that we receive for it, that is, the hollow bar plus the solid bar above. Hence, the net gain from exporting it, rather than consuming it, is the solid bar. The sum of all such solid bars throughout the relevant range $Q_1 Q_A$ is the blue triangle 3. This is the gain from

switching goods from consumption to a more highly valued use, namely, export.

Next, consider one of the units of increased production for export $Q_A Q_2$, say unit f. The cost of producing it is the hollow bar under the supply curve. (Recall that supply reflects marginal cost.) Our benefit from producing it is the export price P received for it, which is the hollow bar plus the solid bar. So the net gain from producing it for export is the solid bar. The sum of all such solid bars through the relevant range $Q_A Q_2$ is the blue triangle 4. This is the efficiency gain from expanding production for export.

The total gain from exporting is shown as the sum of both these effects; in other words, the total blue area in Figure 25-6. In simple terms, this gain tells us that we can sell wheat to foreigners for more than it costs us to produce it, or more than we lose by switching it away from our own consumption.

Of course, this shaded area will represent an efficiency loss if our producers are not allowed to export. It shows that interference in a competitive world market can be damaging, just as we have seen that interference in a competitive home market can be damaging.

Efficiency Gain on a Typical Import: Woolens

A parallel analysis illustrates the gain from importing a specific item. Figure 25-7 shows the United States supply and demand curves for an import-competing product like woolens. Without trade, equilibrium in the domestic market is at point A, with price P_A and quantity Q_A produced and consumed. At the same time, the price in the rest of the world is at the lower level P, reflecting the lower costs of production there.

When trade is opened, United States consumers can buy imported woolens at this lower price P. Since they will be unwilling to buy from American producers at a higher price (like P_A), the domestic price will fall to

Transfer from producers to consumers

FIGURE 25-7 Detailed effects of the import of an individual good—woolens.

With trade, price decreases from P_A to P, with HJ imported. This reduces home production by $Q_A Q_5$, with one such typical unit shown as j. The cost of importing it is the import price shown as the hollow bar. The cost saving because it is no longer produced at home is the hollow bar plus the solid bar. Thus the net benefit from importing it is the solid bar—and the benefit on all such units of reduced production (over the relevant range $Q_A Q_5$) is the blue triangle 1. Imports also result in increased consumption of $Q_A Q_6$, with a typical unit shown as k. The cost of acquiring it is the import price P, shown as the hollow bar, while it provides benefit (marginal utility) equal to the hollow bar plus the solid bar. Thus the net gain on this unit is the solid bar, and the net gain on all such units of increased consumption (in the range $Q_A Q_6$) is the blue triangle 2. Thus the efficiency gain from importing this good is the entire blue area. Because price has fallen, consumers gain at producers' expense. This transfer from producers to consumers is illustrated by the wide white arrow on the left. Finally, note that output and employment fall in this import-competing industry, but rise in the export industry shown in Figure 25-6. When both these effects are taken into account, there is no reason to expect either a large increase or decrease in employment as a result of trade. (The point of international trade—like technological change—is not to increase employment, but rather to increase our real income.)

the world level P. At this lower price, United States consumers increase their purchases. Specifically, they move down their demand curve from A to J, increasing their consumption from Q_A to Q_6. At the same time, domestic producers respond to lower price P by moving down their supply curve from A to H, thus reducing their output from Q_A to Q_5. In short, Q_5 is now produced in the United States, while Q_6 is consumed; the difference $(Q_5 Q_6)$ is the amount imported. Thus, United States imports result both in decreased production and increased consumption.

First, consider one of the units of decreased production $Q_A Q_5$, say unit j. The cost of importing it is the price P we must pay for it, shown as the hollow bar. But as a consequence, we save the cost of producing it, which is the hollow bar plus the solid bar (that is, the marginal cost as defined under the supply curve). Thus, the net gain from importing it, rather than producing it more expensively at home, is the solid bar. And the sum of all such solid bars over the relevant range Q_5Q_A is blue triangle 1. This is the gain from allowing imports to displace inefficient, high-cost domestic production.

Now consider one of the units of increased consumption Q_AQ_6, say unit k. Its cost is the import price P shown by the hollow bar. But the consumer values it as the hollow bar plus the solid bar (its marginal utility defined under the demand curve). The net benefit from this unit of increased consumption is thus the solid bar, and the sum of all such benefits is the blue triangle 2. This is the efficiency gain from allowing consumption to expand in response to a bargain international price.

The total efficiency gain on both accounts is the whole blue area in Figure 25-7. In simplest terms, this area shows that we can benefit by buying a low-cost import because it allows us to cut back our own inefficient, high-cost production; and it also allows us to increase our consumption of a bargain-priced good.

HOW INTERNATIONAL TRADE ADVERSELY AFFECTS SOME GROUPS

While trade leads to an overall gain in efficiency, it is important to emphasize again that not all groups benefit. For example, in Figure 25-6, trade brings an increase in the United States price of wheat. This increase benefits wheat farmers at the expense of consumers, with this transfer shown by the wide white arrow to the left of the diagram. (This is an important graphic device that will be used to show transfers throughout the rest of this book.) On the other hand, an import in Figure 25-7 results in the opposite sort of transfer. Because it lowers price, it benefits consumers at the expense of producers.

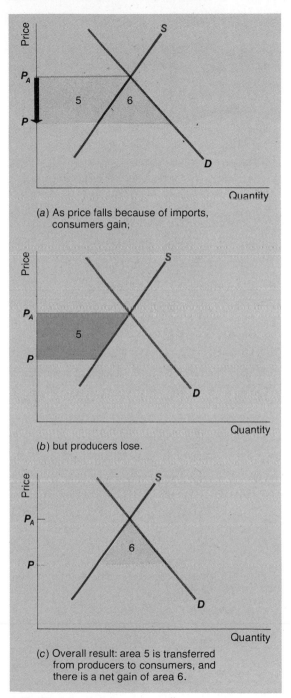

(a) As price falls because of imports, consumers gain,

(b) but producers lose.

(c) Overall result: area 5 is transferred from producers to consumers, and there is a net gain of area 6.

FIGURE 25-8 Detailed effects of an import of woolens. (An alternative to Figure 25-7.)

These benefits and losses to each group as a result of imports are shown more precisely in the alternative analysis set out in Figure 25-8. Each panel in this diagram reproduces the United States supply and demand curves for woolens from Figure 25-7. The gain to the nation's consumers from a lower price involves both a reduced cost on their original purchases and a benefit from increased consumption. Together, these increase consumers' surplus by the blue area enclosed to the left of the demand curve in panel *a*. At the same time, producers are damaged both because they receive a lower price and because they lose sales to imports.[5] Together, these reduce producers' surplus, as shown by the red area enclosed to the left of the supply curve in panel *b*. Because this area 5 also appears as a blue gain in panel *a*, it is a transfer from the producers who lose it in panel *b* to the consumers who receive it in panel *a*. (This technique of identifying a transfer is important because it can be used on a wide variety of problems; for example, see Problem 25-8.) At the same time, area 6 in panel *a* is a blue gain *not* offset by a red loss. This is the efficiency gain, and it appears as the blue triangle in panel *c*. This is, of course, exactly the same efficiency gain we first showed in Figure 25-7.[6,7]

As a current example of how imports affect various groups in the United States, consider our recent large imports of textiles from the Far East. The effect on American textile producers was clear. They were damaged because these imports depressed the domestic price of textiles. At the same time, it was clear to American consumers that they were benefiting from a lower textile price. What was not always clear, however, was the net effect on the nation as a whole. But this analysis suggests that the overall effect was favorable, since the benefit to consumers more than offset the loss to producers.

Again, note the important warning that we introduced earlier and that we now wish to raise here as well. In arriving at these conclusions, we have assumed that the consumers' valuation of a $1 increase in income is roughly the same as the producers' valuation of a $1 reduction in income—or at least that they are sufficiently close so that our conclusions are not upset.

Key Points

1. In this chapter, a strong case has been made for international trade. (In the next chapter, we study the case for tariffs and other restraints on trade.)

2. There are three major sources of benefit from trade: (*a*) greater competition, (*b*) economies of scale, and (*c*) comparative advantage.

3. When trade is opened, countries specialize in certain products, increasing their

---

[5]For a review of the basic idea of how consumers' surplus changes as price changes, see Figure 18-5, page 399. For a similar review of how producers' surplus changes (a concept we will also now be frequently using), see page 425.

[6]The method of Figure 25-8 can also be used to explain Figure 25-6 more fully. Specifically, as price rises in Figure 25-6:

(a) Consumers' surplus falls by $PBAP_A$

(b) Producers' surplus rises by $PCAP_A$

(c) Thus, the net effects are a *transfer* of $PBAP_A$ from consumers to producers, and an *efficiency gain* of ABC.

[7]*Note to instructors:* To a substantial degree, our analysis of transfer and efficiency effects in the balance of this book will be based on diagrams similar to Figure 25-7. But those who wish to supplement this with diagrams similar to Figure 25-8 will find several detailed in the Instructor's Manual.

output of these goods. If there are economies of scale, costs fall as a result of this output increase.

4. Even if costs do not fall with rising output, trade will be beneficial if countries specialize in the goods in which they have a comparative advantage, that is, in those products in which they are relatively most efficient. We saw this not only in the Ricardian case where cost is constant, but also even in cases where cost (supply) rises as output increases (for example, Figure 25-6). This means that trade and specialization are still beneficial even though they result in rising marginal costs.

5. Because trade lowers the prices of goods we import and raises the prices of goods we export, it hurts some while bene-fiting others. Consumers of imports benefit, while consumers of exported goods are harmed. (To some degree, but not complete-ly, these are the same people, so that this transfer partly "washes out.") In addition, producers of exports benefit, while produc-ers of import-competing goods are hurt.

6. International trade is similar in many respects to technological change. Both increase real income by allowing a nation to consume more: Trade allows a country to consume beyond its production possibilities curve, while technological change shifts the production possibilities curve out. Trade and technological change can involve the same sort of short-run unemployment, as some present jobs disappear and workers shift to new, more productive jobs.

Key Concepts

specialization
increased competition
economies of scale
greater availability of products
absolute advantage
comparative advantage

opportunity cost
gain from trade
trade compared to technological change
exports: efficiency, transfer, and employ-
    ment effects.
imports: efficiency, transfer, and employ-
    ment effects

Problems

25-1 "Foreign competition makes an industry more competitive." Should this result be viewed as an advantage or a disadvantage by (a) consumers of this good; (b) producers; (c) the nation as a whole?

*25-2 Suppose that the production of both X and Y involves economies of scale. Is it possible for both countries to benefit if Europe specializes in one and America specializes in the other? Explain your answer. Does this answer still hold if the cost curves for each good are identical in the two countries? (Hint: Review the discussion of economies of scale in Chapter 3.)

25-3 Return to Table 25-2, where costs are constant. (a) Change the "northwest" number 3 to 5. Does Europe now have an absolute advantage in either good? A comparative advantage in either? Draw a diagram like Figure 25-4 to show the potential American gain from trade (again assuming that there are 200 million workers in the United States and the international price ratio is 3:1). (b) Now change that same northwest number 5 to 8. Which country now has a comparative advantage in food? In clothing? Are there potential gains from trade? Why or why not?

25-4 As a result of crop failures abroad in 1972–1973, world grain prices rose dramatically, and in response, United States grain exports increased. Consumers claimed that the resulting higher food prices in the United States were damaging to our economy, while producers claimed that they were beneficial. How would you evaluate these claims?

25-5 The following diagram shows the situation of Europe (the rest of the world) corresponding to the United States situation in Figure 25-5b. Identify clearly:

    (a) How Europe specializes when trade is opened.

    (b) How Europe trades. Fill in details of how much of each good Europe exports or imports.

    (c) Are there any lines or curves in this diagram that must be similar to those that appear in Figure 25-5b?

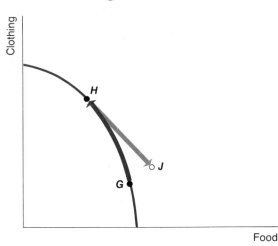

    (d) Does Europe gain from trade? If so, how much?

    (e) Return to Figure 25-5b. Can you explain why America specializes only to C, rather than to F?

25-6 "Economists say that international trade and technological change are similar—but they are wrong. Technological change increases our real income by making us more productive. Trade does not." Evaluate this statement.

25-7 (This problem looks ahead to Chapter 26.)

    (a) Suppose that the United States and Europe become involved in a trade war, with each imposing such heavy restrictions on imports that trade between the two is eventually cut off altogether. Use Figure 25-5b and the diagram in Problem 25-5 to show the gains or losses each would suffer. Is it true that a trade war is a zero-sum game (what one country wins, the other loses)? Or is it like any other kind of war, with losses on both sides?

    (b) Use two diagrams like Figures 25-6 and 25-7 to show in more detail how the United States would be affected by such a trade war.

25-8 To see how the analysis of Figure 25-8 can be applied to an entirely different problem, suppose the government decides to raise farm income, not by buying wheat, but,

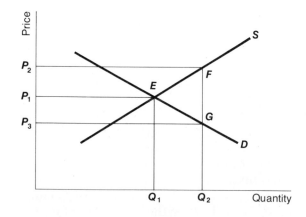

instead, by the "deficiency payments" scheme in the diagram shown here: If the free-market price that farmers receive is below P_2, they will be paid the difference or "deficiency" for every bushel they sell. (In the United States, the government uses a combination of price supports and deficiency payments.) Farmers respond to this guaranteed price of P_2 by moving up their supply curve from the initial equilibrium at E to F, thus increasing output from Q_1 to Q_2. But when this large output is delivered to market, price falls to P_3. (The demand curve tells us that this is the price consumers will pay for quantity Q_2.) Then the government settles up with the farmers, writing them checks for the deficiency P_2P_3 on each bushel of wheat, or a total sum of P_2FGP_3.

(a) With a series of colored diagrams like the panels in Figure 25-8, show how each of these three groups benefits or loses: consumers; producers; the U.S. Treasury. (How much of the taxpayers' money does the Treasury pay out on this program?) By comparing these effects, indicate the transfers that take place, and in a final diagram, show the net, overall efficiency effect of this policy.

(b) Confirm this efficiency effect by noting how this policy affects output, and applying Figure 20-4.

chapter 26
Tariffs and Other International Trade Issues

Protectionism is the institutionalization of economic failure.

Former British Prime Minister Edward Heath

Despite the gains from trade explained in the previous chapter, no country today completely follows a policy of free trade. Instead, every nation erects barriers to restrict imports, such as tariffs (taxes imposed on imported goods as they enter a country) or quotas (limits on the number of units that can be imported).

True, since the 1930s we have made substantial progress in reducing these trade restrictions. In the Kennedy Round of trade negotiations in the 1960s, the United States and the other Western industrial countries cut their tariffs by about 35 percent. And again, in the late 70s, we were engaged in negotiations to reduce trade barriers, with the target this time being a tariff cut of about 40 to 50 percent.

But negotiating trade barriers downward has been a long and arduous process. Despite these efforts, each country still retains substantial tariff and quota protection. There are two basic reasons: (1) Tariffs may

be introduced for noneconomic reasons. For example, a tariff may be imposed to protect an industry which might be essential to national defence in case of an emergency. (2) A country may restrict imports for special economic reasons, some of which are fallacious, but some of which may contain a kernel of truth.

NONECONOMIC EXPLANATIONS OF TARIFFS

The government may protect an industry for either military or political reasons. Consider each objective in turn:

1. An Industry May Be Essential for National Defense

Two centuries ago, Adam Smith argued that national defense is an important goal. In pursuing this objective, he maintained, we should be willing to protect our defense industries even if such protection involves an economic cost (that is, even if foreign countries have a comparative advantage in producing weapons). This argument remains powerful more than two hundred years later. As an extreme example, we do not buy tanks from the Russians, even though it might be cheaper to do so (and even though the Russians might conceivably agree to sell). For military reasons, defense industries are essential.

(An important distinction can be made between consumer goods and weapons. Trade in consumer goods is mutually beneficial; both trading partners obtain more goods and therefore enjoy a higher standard of living. In the military area, however, we cannot say, "the more weapons the better." Defense depends on a country's *relative* strength compared with other countries. Indeed, if all countries have more weapons, we all may be worse off, not better off. Therefore, in the case of military equipment, no general case can be made that trade is beneficial.)

In protecting our defense industries, an important problem arises: Where do we draw the line? Do we protect just our military aircraft industry, or do we go one step beyond and protect our aluminum industry because it provides an input essential for military aircraft? We conclude that although this defense argument makes sense in many cases, it can be abused, since almost every industry makes some small, indirect contribution to national defense.

2. People Vote for Their Present Jobs

International trade means that jobs are lost in industries whose sales fall because of competition from imports. But new jobs are created in export industries. The problem is that people are more concerned about their present jobs that they may lose than the possibility of new jobs in an export industry. (After all, who knows for sure who will actually get these new export-based jobs?) So workers who don't want to take risks vote against increased trade; that is, they vote for the tariffs and other trade restrictions that protect their current jobs. Thus, too much attention is paid to the employment loss from increased imports, and not enough to the employment gain from increased exports.

But even if we look only at imports, we remember from Figure 25-8 that the losses to producers from increased imports were more than offset by gains to consumers. By pointing this out, why can't a politician sell the idea of allowing imports to come in more freely?

The answer is that individuals tend to think and vote as producers, not consumers. To illustrate why, suppose that the import in question consists of shirts. The large benefits to consumers from increased imports of shirts are distributed widely to millions of purchasers, with each benefiting by such a small amount that nobody is likely to switch votes on this account. (Instead, consumers vote on issues which they view as more important.) On the producers' side, however, things are different. Here, fewer individuals are affected by increased shirt imports, but the effect on each individual—on both the management and labor side—is much more substantial. For people in this industry, the possible loss of a job will be important enough to determine how they vote. In brief, producers vote for a tariff, while consumers use their votes on other issues. Therefore, the interest of consumers in free trade tends to be inadequately represented. (For a criticism of a policy that ignores the interests of consumers, see Box 26-1.)

A further reason that shirt producers may be able to exert strong political pressure is that they are not spread out all over the United States, as consumers are. Instead, they are concentrated in a few states or congressional districts. For members of Congress representing such districts, one very good way of getting political support may be to push for import restrictions on shirts. If they do, the shirt producers in these districts are likely to vote for them, while they will lose few votes of consumers. [Moreover, this is not just a political sleight-of-hand. From the narrow point of view of shirt-producing districts, duty-free imports of shirts may indeed be undesirable. The reason is that such districts bear much of the loss from duty-free imports (the red area in panel *b* in Figure 25-8). At the same time, they receive little of the benefit (the blue area in panel *a*), because most consumers live elsewhere. So for these districts, losses from increased shirt imports may exceed gains.] Thus, it is no great surprise if the members of Congress from shirt-producing districts go to Washington committed to restricting imports of shirts. On getting there, they meet other members with similar problems: They too may be seeking protection for the goods produced in their own districts. The result is logrolling: The members from shirt-producing districts agree to vote to protect the products of other districts, in return for the promise of other

members to vote for restrictions on shirt imports.

The result is continuous pressure in Congress for protection for industries that compete with imports. And when imports on a wide variety of goods are restricted, the shirt producing constituencies may well be damaged after all because of the higher prices of a wide range of imported goods. But the members from these districts may still be popular locally because they are remembered for their support for the protection of the shirt industry, rather than for their support for the protection of other goods.

Thus it is no surprise that some two hundred years after the case for free trade was clearly stated by Adam Smith, protection still lives on. In fact, we might have even more severe trade restrictions except for two things: (1) More and more producers in export industries are recognizing how strong an interest they have in freer trade; and (2) the president is elected by all the people and carries a brief for the country as a whole. And most presidents in recent years have supported international initiatives to reduce tariffs.

ECONOMIC ARGUMENTS FOR PROTECTION

To meet the strong case for international trade which dates back to Smith and Ricardo, advocates of protection have put forward a number of economic arguments. Some of these are fallacious, amounting to little more than weak rationalizations for protection, while others are stronger. The weakest arguments are considered first.

1. "Buy American because it keeps our money at home."

This argument is sometimes expanded to. "If I buy a transistor radio from Taiwan, I get the radio, and Taiwan gets the dollars. But when I buy a radio made in the United States, I get the radio and the dollars stay here." The fallacy in this argument is that the Taiwanese do not work hard to produce radios for export merely for the joy of holding dollars. Like you or me, they want to earn dollars to buy things. To a large degree, they use dollars to buy food, machinery, or other products from the United States. Thus, while we buy radios with money in the first instance, we are ultimately buying radios with machinery and food. And, as we saw from the illustration of comparative advantage in Chapter 25, gains can come to both the United States and Taiwan from such specialization. [1]

2. "We can't compete with cheap foreign labor."

The reason wages are higher in America than in most foreign countries is that we are more productive. (Recall Box 25-1.) When we take into account both influences (our

higher wages and our higher productivity), it does not necessarily follow that our costs are higher, and that we consequently cannot compete. True, we cannot compete with cheap labor in other countries in activities of their comparative advantage. But we can compete in activities of our comparative advantage, where our higher productivity more than offsets our higher wage. And this is where we should be concentrating. (On the argument that we will be unable to compete with foreign producers, see also Box 26-2.)

If we look at the other side of the coin, here is how this argument for protection is often stated in foreign countries: "We can't compete with American labor, because it is more productive." Of course, the reply in this case is that, although United States labor productivity is higher, our wages are also higher, so our costs are not lower across the board. True, other countries will not be able to compete in activities where our productivity is particularly great and where we consequently have a comparative advantage. But they can compete successfully in those other goods in which they enjoy a comparative advantage (that is, where their wage advantage exceeds our productivity advantage).

3. "Tariffs should be tailored to equalize costs at home and abroad."

This recommendation may sound plausible, but it misses the whole point of international trade: *Gains from trade are based on cost differences between countries.* (It is to our advantage to import bananas, oil, or radios precisely because they can be produced more cheaply abroad than at home.) Thus, if we succeed in the (very difficult) task of tailoring tariffs to make costs precisely equal at home and abroad, there will be no incentive left for trade, and the potential

---

[1] Chapter 16 discusses the situation where American expenditures in foreign countries are substantially greater or less than foreign expenditures in the United States.

THE PETITION OF THE CANDLEMAKERS

Sometimes the argument that we can't compete with cheap foreign labor appears in the slightly different form: "We can't compete with cheap foreign goods." This idea has never been more effectively criticized than by Frederic Bastiat over a hundred years ago. Here is his satirical description of an appeal by French candlemakers to the government to protect them from the free sunlight that was supposedly ruining their business:†

We are subjected to the intolerable competition of a foreign rival, who enjoys, it would seem, such superior facilities for the production of light, that he is enabled to inundate our national market at so exceedingly reduced a price, that, the moment he makes his appearance, he draws off all custom from us; and thus an important branch of French industry, with all its innumerable ramifications, is suddenly reduced to a state of complete stagnation. This rival is no other than the sun.

Our petition is, that it would please your honorable body to pass a law whereby shall be directed the shutting up of all windows, dormers, skylights, shutters, curtains, in a word, all openings, holes, chinks, and fissures through which the light of the sun is used to penetrate into our dwellings, to the prejudice of the profitable manufactures which we flatter ourselves we have been enabled to bestow upon the country; which country cannot, therefore, without ingratitude, leave us now to struggle unprotected through so unequal a contest. . . .

Does it not argue the greatest inconsistency to check as you do the importation of coal, iron, cheese, and goods of foreign manufacture, merely because . . . their price *approaches zero*, while at the same time you freely admit, and without limitation, the light of the sun, whose price is during the whole day *at zero*?"

†Abridged from Frederic Bastiat, *Economic Sophisms* (Princeton: D. Van Nostrand Co., Ltd., 1964), pp. 56–60.

gains from trade will be lost. In short, all that tailored tariffs accomplish is to strangle trade.

While these three arguments for tariffs are fallacious, the following arguments do contain at least some element of truth.

4. "If we buy cars from Detroit rather than from Japan, employment will rise in Detroit rather than in Japan."

This statement may be true, particularly if there is large-scale unemployment in Detroit. Why, then, does it not provide a very strong case for restricting trade, ranking in importance with the efficiency argument for free trade in the last chapter? The answer is that this argument is based on the assumption that if we restrict our imports, our trading partners will not reduce their imports from us—a very questionable assumption indeed. To see why, suppose we restrict our imports so that American purchases are switched from Japan to Detroit. (This is often called a "beggar-my-neighbor" policy because we would be trying to solve our unemployment problem by shifting it onto the Japanese.) In this case, how do we prevent the Japanese from retaliating by restricting their imports of our goods, and thus shifting the unemployment problem back to us?

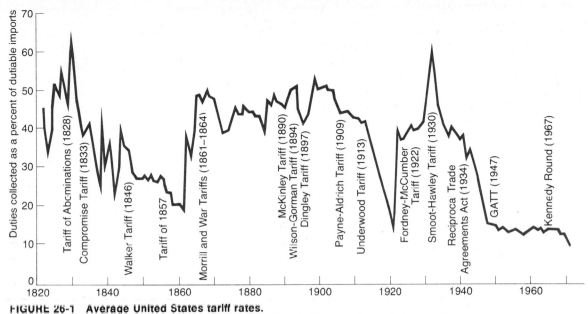

FIGURE 26-1   Average United States tariff rates.
The United States has had high tariffs sometimes and low tariffs other times. But since the mid-'30s, the trend has been down, so that now our tariffs average less than 10 percent. Increasingly, the focus is on how non-tariff barriers restrict trade.

SOURCE: Data from Statistical Abstract of the United States.

In periods of worldwide recession, all countries are tempted to initiate a beggar-my-neighbor policy of increased protection; it is a tempting policy for them for exactly the same reason that it is a tempting policy for us. If all attempt to solve unemployment this way, the result will be a general disruption of trade, possibly leading to an increase, rather than a decrease, in unemployment. Thus, the United States tariff increases in the Smoot-Hawley tariff of 1930 (combined with foreign retaliation) contributed to the worldwide depression. The Roosevelt administration undertook to reverse this destructive trend by pushing for the Reciprocal Trade Agreements Act, and by negotiating lower tariffs. (See Figure 26-1.)

If there is large-scale domestic unemployment, the cure should be sought in domestic monetary and fiscal policies (as discussed in Parts 2 and 3), not in mutually destructive beggar-my-neighbor trade restrictions.

5. "Restricting trade will diversify a nation's economy."

This is true; just as trade leads a country to specialize, restricting trade leads to the opposite: diversification. And isn't it a good thing for a country to diversify—to avoid putting all its eggs in one basket?

The answer is, perhaps. But countries, like individuals, can gain from specialization even though there are risks involved. The existence of risks, such as the possibility of an oversupply of teachers, or lawyers, or doctors, does not mean that individuals are foolish to prepare for specialized occupations.

At the national level, an example of a high degree of specialization is Ghana's dependence on cocoa exports. For such a country, whose exports are highly concentrated on one or a few products, risks can be reduced by diversification. And diversification, in turn, may be encouraged by protecting new industries. But even for a country like Ghana, the argument must be balanced against the advantages of specialization—the gains from trade. Moreover, taking risks may bring substantial benefits. After all, the price of cocoa may rise, and in this case the more specialized Ghana is, the more it will benefit from this price increase. (Specialized oil producers have recently done exceptionally well.)

Finally, for an advanced industrial country like the United States, policies to diversify the economy are unnecessary: No matter how freely we may trade and specialize, our activities are still likely to remain remarkably diversified. The evidence is that we would not give up the production of a whole category of goods (like industrial products) to concentrate on another (like agricultural products). Indeed, it would be unlikely that we would give up one industry (say electrical machinery) in order to specialize in another (autos). Instead, the evidence suggests that trade leads to specialization in *certain kinds* of machinery, and *certain kinds* of cars. Except for a few countries with highly specialized natural resources, trade does not generally result in a very narrow range of production activities.

6. "We need to protect our infant industries."

The basic idea here is this: We may not be able to compete with other countries in an industry with economies of scale until this industry is well established and operating at high volume and low cost. This can be a real problem if the industry is one in which we have a comparative advantage, where we would eventually be able to produce very cheaply. Thus, it is argued, we should use a tariff to protect such an industry from being wiped out by tough foreign competition during the delicate period of its infancy.

Although this line of reasoning is logi-

cally valid, it raises two important, practical questions: (1) How do you know that the only advantage of the foreign country is that its industry is already established? For example, if a country is thinking of protecting an infant watch industry, how does it know that the only advantage of the Swiss is that their industry is already established? Maybe the Swiss have basic advantages in watchmaking. If so, then a watchmaking industry established elsewhere may never be able to compete. (2) When does an infant subsidy become an old-age pension? The typical industry which asks for protection as an infant never seems to grow up, but instead becomes chronically dependent on its tariffs. Such industries can become a real problem. Once established, they influence many votes, so protection continues to go to them, rather than to the real infants who have not yet hired a large enough labor force to give them voting clout.[2]

7. "Restricting imports may reduce the price we have to pay for them."

In the discussion of monopoly in Chapter 21, we saw how a single seller could increase market price by restricting sales. Using a corresponding argument, we will show in Chapter 28 that a single purchaser (a monopsonist) can *reduce* market price by restricting *purchases*. The same may be true for a country in international trade: If it is a large enough purchaser of a good, it may be able to reduce the price of that good by restricting its purchases (imports). For example, if we impose a tariff or quota to restrict our imports of a European good, we may be able to lower the price we pay to the Europeans for that good. This is sometimes referred to technically as *improving our terms of trade* (that is, reducing the number of units of exports we must give up in order to acquire a unit of imports).

While the United States is a large

[2] A third practical question is this: If such an industry will eventually be a profitable one, why shouldn't those individuals who establish it cover any initial losses out of their future profits? The answer may be that they are unable to raise the capital necessary to get them through this initial period of losses.

enough purchaser to affect world price by such a restriction on its imports, this policy is of limited applicability. (It is most important for oil: The Carter administration hopes to keep the international price of oil from rising rapidly by cutting imports of oil, imposing tariffs if necessary.) But tariffs will not improve our terms of trade if our trading partners can effectively retaliate by imposing their own tariffs. And some of our trading partners, especially the Europeans, are now in a sufficiently strong position to do precisely this. In other words, just as we can use our market power to reduce the price of our imports, other trading nations can use their market power to reduce the price of their imports (our exports). In the face of downward pressure on the price of both our imports *and* our exports, our terms of trade may not improve after all. The volume of trade may simply be restricted.

Free Trade versus Protection: A Summary

This discussion illustrates that one should never judge an issue by adding up the number of arguments for and against it. There are only a few arguments for free trade, but they are very impressive indeed: Free trade increases competition in our domestic market, and increases pressure on our firms to innovate. It provides consumers with a wider selection of goods. And it allows firms to fully exploit comparative advantage and economies of scale. Thus, it raises our standard of living.

On the other hand, there is a whole battery of arguments for protection. But in summing them up, we first note that some are downright illogical. Moreover, even those that have some element of truth are of limited practical importance in determining United States policy. (See the "tariffs increase employment," "diversity," and "terms of trade" arguments.) This leaves the noneconomic arguments, such as the necessity of having a defense industry. But even here, tariff protection is hardly necessary,

since this industry is already protected by the fact that the United States government is the buyer, and it purchases mostly from domestic firms rather than from foreign suppliers.

THE DEVELOPMENT OF TRADE POLICY IN THE UNITED STATES AND ELSEWHERE

Figure 26-1 illustrates how United States tariff policy has fluctuated dramatically in the past. Historically, liberalizing our trade has been a story of "two steps forward and one back." However, more or less steady progress has been made since the depths of the Depression. In 1934, the Reciprocal Trade Agreements Act provided for *bilateral* (two-way) negotiations in which the United States would bargain down tariffs with another country. Then, in 1947, the United States and 22 other nations signed the General Agreement on Tariffs and Trade (GATT). This was based on the idea of *multilateral* negotiations in which all participating countries would lower their tariffs. Since 1947, United States policy has, by and large, been to concentrate on this multilateral approach and to bargain down tariffs in GATT. (An important exception was the bilateral 1965 Auto Pact, in which the United States agreed to eliminate auto tariffs with Canada only.)

The European Economic Community (EEC)

In the late 1950s a remarkable change took place in Europe with the formation of the European Economic Community (EEC). In this agreement, Germany, France, Italy, Holland, Belgium, and Luxembourg (later joined by Britain, Ireland, and Denmark) agreed to (1) form a common market by introducing free trade among all participating countries; (2) impose a common tariff against goods coming into the EEC from other countries; and (3) introduce other measures of economic coordination, such as a common policy of agricultural price supports.

One of the reasons for the formation of the EEC was that the founding countries eventually wanted to move some distance toward political union. But they also had a strong economic motive as well: to gain the benefits of freer trade. In Appendix 26-B, we illustrate these gains and also note that they are tempered by losses to the Europeans because the United States and other countries are not included in this "free-trade club."

It has been very difficult to assess how much recent European economic growth has been due to the EEC, and how much has been due to other influences. It is also difficult to assess how the EEC has affected outside countries like the United States. On the one hand, by inducing more rapid European growth, it has made Europe a better potential customer for our exports. On the other hand, because the United States is not an EEC member, American firms now face the special problem of being outsiders in competing in the European market. (For example, before the EEC, American and German firms faced the same tariff barriers in selling in the French market. But since the EEC has been formed, our firms still face a tariff when going into the French market. But competing German firms do not.)

The Kennedy Round

By the early 1960s, there were several good reasons for the United States to promote the idea of a new round of multilateral tariff reductions within GATT. By reducing all tariffs (and in particular, the United States tariff and the new common European tariff) such a move would (1) reduce the United States problem of being an outsider in its trade with Europe; (2) promote closer political ties with Europe; and (3) provide the familiar gains from freer trade to all participants. The result of this initiative was the Kennedy Round of negotiations which,

as already noted, resulted in the 1967 agreement in GATT to cut existing tariffs on average by about 35 percent.

However, following this major success, pressure has once again built up to reintroduce protection, especially in the form of non-tariff restrictions on trade.

Non-Tariff Barriers (NTBs)

The most familiar type of non-tariff barrier (NTB) is a quota that limits the quantity of a good that can be imported. (Appendix 26-A shows why a quota may have many of the same effects as a tariff.) There are also many other, more subtle NTBs. For example, a country may impose complex and costly customs procedures or quality standards that deter imports. Or, it may have stiff health standards that must be met by imports. This last restriction raises the possibility that some NTBs may be justified. The gains to our health from such stiff standards may be worth the cost of reducing foreign imports. But this nagging question still remains: Are such standards being raised to improve our health, or to protect domestic producers?

Thus it is often difficult to judge whether an NTB is justified. Furthermore, it is often difficult to prove that a country is in violation of its GATT agreements if it raises an NTB. As a consequence, countries that wish to stiffen protection are increasingly turning to NTBs. This, along with tariff reductions such as the Kennedy Round, has meant that NTBs are becoming increasingly visible and important as deterrents to trade. As the new post-Kennedy Round of GATT negotiations got under way in the 1970s, there were two major targets: remaining tariffs *and* NTBs.

THE MULTINATIONAL CORPORATION (MNC)

No discussion of trade policy would be complete without some reference to two important phenomena: rapid technological change (see Box 26-3) and the rise of the multinational corporation.

Multinational corporations (MNCs) are firms with their head office in one country and subsidiaries in other countries. For example, Ford produces cars not only in the United States, but also in Britain, Germany, and other countries. And other countries have their multinationals too, like Royal Dutch Shell.

Why does an American company go multinational? The traditional answer is that some firms go abroad to develop a source of a necessary raw material. But there are other important reasons as well. Once an American firm has developed a new product for the domestic market at great research and development costs, it will want to sell it worldwide. (And it will be able to do so cheaply, to the degree that its research, development, and other overhead costs have already been covered.) Moreover, an American company that has decided to sell its product in, say, Europe may also decide to produce it there, if this is cheaper than producing it in the United States and paying the shipping costs (including both the transatlantic transport cost and any European tariff).

Alternatively, United States firms may go abroad in search of lower wages: For example, they may go to Korea or Taiwan to produce goods with heavy labor requirements. This has recently led to the complaint by American labor that the multinationals are "exporting American jobs." In particular, labor has asked: "Why should the MNCs be allowed to transfer their technological know-how abroad, especially when much of it has been developed with the assistance of government funds provided by United States taxpayers?"

Multinational companies reply that the existence of their foreign subsidiaries also creates jobs in the United States. For example, auto engines, transmissions, and other parts are produced in the United States for export to General Motors factories that assemble cars in Canada. (About one-fourth of United States exports are such shipments by American firms to their foreign subsidiaries.) Second, the American public that owns shares of MNCs benefits from the billions of dollars of profit they earn on their foreign operations. Third, the goods they are producing in low-wage countries will be manufactured there regardless. If they are not produced by subsidiaries of United States firms, they will be produced there by foreign-owned firms.

Economists also add that in transmitting technology between countries, MNCs raise productivity and income elsewhere. Morever, this is a two-way street: Just as foreign countries benefit when American MNCs transmit their technology abroad, Americans also benefit when foreign MNCs transmit their technology to their subsidiaries in this country. In addition, because of the ease with which they can transfer production across borders, MNCs may make it easier for countries to get established quickly in their activities of comparative advantage. In other words, by making specialization easier, MNCs help increase world income.

However, the growth of multinational corporations has raised problems, mostly for the host countries in which the MNCs have established subsidiaries. For example, there is some concern that a large multinational may be able to acquire monopoly power in the host country's market. (On the other hand, the entry of a multinational may *reduce* the market power of an existing *domestic* monopolist.) Host countries are also concerned about the issue of political independence. For example, it is often felt that many of the most important decisions for host countries are not made there at all, but are instead made in foreign head offices. Furthermore, it is more difficult for a host country's government to deal with a MNC

BOX 26-3
CHANGING TECHNOLOGY IN THE INTERNATIONAL ECONOMY

Rapid technological change has complicated the traditional free-trade versus protection argument in the following way: In a stable, static world the most profitable course for a country is to concentrate on its comparative advantage. But in a world of rapid technological change, comparative advantage keeps changing. As a country switches from industry to industry in pursuit of its comparative advantage, the benefits of specialization may be eaten up by recurring turnaround costs (in the form of installing equipment and retraining labor in new industries.)

After the Second World War, this argument was used to explain why some countries doubted their ability to benefit from growing trade with the technological leader, the United States. A simple analogy will illustrate: A rich and innovative man hires someone to fix his car, and pays well for the job. But as soon as the employee has bought the necessary tools and mastered the job, the rich man announces he has discovered a brilliant way to do it himself. Now he wants the employee to look after the electrical system in his house. As soon as the employee masters this, the rich man announces that he has invented a completely automatic, trouble-free electrical system so he can shift the employee into some other activity.

Throughout this process, the employee's wage may rise rapidly, since it is very profitable to be associated with a man of such wealth and genius. But the employee still faces problems. First, he is spending a lot of money in tooling up for new jobs, and is exhausting himself in learning how to handle them. Second, he may begin to wonder: "Given my employer's genius at replacing me, where will this all end? Will I eventually be shining his shoes for $50,000 a year?" So the employee begins to ask whether it would not be better to opt out of this game, even though quitting would mean a loss of income.

This sort of example was used to illustrate a problem faced by our trading partners. They agreed that free trade with us might maximize their income. But our rapid technological progress meant that their activities of comparative advantage were constantly changing, and made some of their economists wonder: "Is the real income gain from trade worth the turnaround costs? And who wants to be a fifth wheel anyway?"

This argument has recently become far less compelling because our trading partners (especially Germany and Japan) have reduced the technological gap and, in some activities, have even taken the technological lead. Instead, the argument now appears in somewhat different form, as follows: With the development of the international economy, any technological change that occurs in one country can be copied, within a brief period, by producers in another country. An American innovation in product X may give us a comparative advantage in this good, but it will last only until the production of X is copied in some other country with lower labor costs. At this point, the United States moves on to producing and exporting another good in which it has made an even more recent technological breakthrough. Thus the comparative advantage of the United States is in technologically advanced activities, and these keep changing. Notice that this new interpretation focuses on the heavy turnaround costs incurred by the technologically advanced country. To return to our earlier analogy: The Europeans and Japanese have not, as they might have feared, ended up shining our shoes. Instead, they began by producing shirts and radios. But now they have moved up into producing cars and TVs, leaving shirts and radios for the new emerging industry in less developed places like Taiwan and Hong Kong.

than a domestic firm, because the MNC can more easily exercise the option of simply leaving the country to produce somewhere else. Finally, the image of multinationals has not been improved by the behavior of companies like Lockheed. In an attempt to secure foreign defense contracts, Lockheed made payments to a number of politically influential people abroad. (No less than a former Japanese prime minister and a prominent member of the Dutch royal family were touched by this scandal.)

Key Points

1. Trade restrictions, such as tariffs or quotas, result in an efficiency loss. (The gains from trade, discussed in Chapter 25, are eroded as trade is reduced.)

2. Trade restrictions on a good also transfer income from consumers to producers. An important reason why countries have trade restrictions is that producers are able to exercise more political power than consumers.

3. While many statements on the long list of economic arguments for protection are fallacious, some have a degree of economic merit. A less developed country, now concentrating on natural resources, may protect an industry in order to diversify its economy, thus reducing its economic risks. An even stronger case can be made if the industry in question is a "promising infant," that is, an industry of comparative advantage if only it can be firmly established. (The problem is, however, that such infant support frequently becomes an old-age pension.)

4. Since the United States is important enough as a buyer to affect the world price of a good, we might be tempted to impose a tariff for this reason. (By reducing our purchases of imports, we might induce a reduction in the price we have to pay for them.) But we can improve our terms of trade in this way only if other similarly large countries do not retaliate by imposing their tariffs on *our* goods. This is in general a very questionable assumption, particularly since EEC countries now act together in setting a common tariff.

5. The same risk of foreign retaliation arises if we impose a tariff to try to cure a United States unemployment problem. Since this tariff would simply shift our unemployment problem onto our trading partners, their likely reaction in self-defense would be to impose their own tariffs against our goods, thereby reducing employment in our export industries.

6. Multinational corporations transmit new technology across national borders. Moreover, because they can switch activities from country to country, they may make it easier for countries to find their activities of comparative advantage quickly. For example, they often allocate labor-intensive activities to low-wage countries.

7. This in turn has led them into conflict with United States unions that have accused them of exporting jobs. MNCs have also been criticized by host countries in which their subsidiaries are located. To illustrate: There is frequently political resentment that important economic decisions for host countries may not be made there at all, but instead in some head office located in a foreign country.

Key Concepts

tariff

quota

Kennedy Round

political arguments for protection

military arguments for protection

economic arguments for protection

beggar-my-neighbor policy

diversification versus specialization

infant industry protection

terms of trade

tariff retaliation

bilateral versus multilateral negotiations

General Agreement on Tariffs and Trade (GATT)

European Economic Community (EEC)

non-tariff barrier (NTB)

the multinational corporation (MNC)

subsidiary

incentives to move abroad

Problems

26-1 Explain in nontechnical terms:
- (*a*) Why countries gain from trade
- (*b*) Why and under what special circumstances they may nonetheless benefit economically by imposing some restrictions on imports
- (*c*) Two fallacious arguments for restricting imports, with your explanation of why they are wrong

26-2 In 1977, exports were equal to about 9 percent of United States GNP. They are more important for a number of other countries where they account for even higher proportions of GNP (over 20 percent in Great Britain, Sweden, and Canada). Do you think the relatively low American percentage makes trade unimportant for the United States? Which of these four countries trades most in *absolute* terms? Do you think United States exports and imports are unimportant for our trading partners? (About 70 percent of Canadian exports and 30 percent of Japanese exports go to the United States.) Finally, if the United States were, like Europe, split up into several countries, what would happen to the export/GNP ratio of each of these new countries?

26-3 Here is another argument in the free-trade versus protection debate: "Tariffs are desirable because the government can raise revenue this way; consequently, other taxes can be reduced."
- (*a*) How do you evaluate this argument?
- (*b*) Does it follow that the higher the tariff, the higher the revenue the government collects?

26-4 "Advertisers can try to persuade consumers to buy a good; but they cannot force them to buy. However, trade barriers involve the coercive power of the state: They can force consumers to buy the domestic product rather than the foreign product (unless the buyers are willing to do without altogether). Therefore, if we wish to protect the sovereignty of the consumer, trade barriers are a greater danger than advertising." Evaluate this statement.

26-5 Do you agree or disagree with the following quotation: "Consumers not only fail to vote in their economic interest. Worse yet, they often don't even understand what their economic interest is. For example, consumers often react automatically to patriotic appeals like 'Buy American,' rather than ask critical questions like: 'Does the firm that is asking me to do this really have patriotic motives, or is it just trying to sell me an overpriced product?'" Do you think we should be more suspicious of people who make such patriotic appeals?

26-6 (*a*) By recasting Figure 25-8, show the effect of a "prohibitive" United States tariff that completely eliminates our import of a good.

(*b*) By developing a similar diagram, explain the effects of a foreign tariff that prevents us from exporting a good.

(*c*) What are the effects if *we* prohibit our exports of this good? Why, then, might our government impose such a restriction? (In the face of rapidly rising world prices of soybeans in the early 1970s, we did indeed limit our exports of this good.)

26-7 "Transport costs are like tariffs. Both deter trade. If either were reduced, countries would reap increased benefits from trade. Raising tariffs is much the same as going back to shipping goods in old, expensive clipper ships." Do you agree? Why or why not?

26-8 Do you think it would pay Australian cement manufacturers to spend a lot of money to promote a tariff on cement? Why?

26-9 For many decades, American textile manufacturers have complained that they have been losing out to Japanese manufacturers. More recently, Japanese manufacturers have in turn been complaining that they have been losing out to producers in countries like Korea and Taiwan. How would you explain to these Japanese manufacturers what is happening?

Appendix 26-A

THE EFFECTS OF A TARIFF OR QUOTA THAT REDUCES IMPORTS

Effects of a Tariff

Typically, a United States tariff will not end our import of a good (as in Problem 26-6*a*), but will only reduce it. In Figure 26-2, we consider this more realistic case.

Point *A* is the "no-trade" equilibrium while *J* is the free-trade equilibrium, with imports *HJ*. Now suppose that we impose a tariff *t* that reduces but does not eliminate this trade. In this case we would (correctly) expect an equilibrium somewhere between *A* and *J*, at a point like *K*. Thus our tariff *t* raises price from the free-trade level *P* to *P_t*, shifts our equilibrium from *J* to *K*, and reduces our imports from the free-trade level *HJ* to *RK*.

The effects on all parties concerned are shown in the last three panels in this diagram. As the United States price rises from *P* to *P_t*, consumers' surplus is reduced by the red area enclosed to the left of the demand curve in panel *b*, while producers benefit from an increase in producers' surplus (the blue area 3 enclosed to the left of the supply curve in panel *c*). But now there is another effect, not encountered before, that is shown as area 4. This is the benefit to the

United States Treasury because it is now collecting revenue from the tariff it has imposed. (A tariff t, equal to RF, is collected on each of the RK units imported—for a total revenue of area 4.)

Since the two blue benefits in panel c also appear as red losses in panel b, they are transfers. Specifically, area 4 is a transfer from consumers (who lose) to the Treasury (that benefits), while area 3 is a transfer from consumers to producers. But not all the red loss to consumers in panel b is canceled out by blue gains in panel c. The balance is the net efficiency loss to society, shown as the two red triangles in panel d.[3] We conclude that a tariff results in an efficiency loss and a transfer from consumers to producers. Moreover, when a tariff only reduces (rather than eliminates) an import, there is another transfer as well—from consumers to the Treasury collecting the tariff revenue.

Effects of a Quota

Trade may be restricted by a tariff or by a non-tariff barrier (NTB) like a quota. Such a restriction limits the number of units of a good that can be imported, and has many effects similar to a tariff. For example, in Figure 26-2 we saw that a tariff t raised price in the United States market from P to P_t, and thus reduced imports from HJ to RK. An equivalent, even more direct way of reducing imports by the same amount would be simply to ban any imports above and beyond RK; in other words, impose a quota limitation of RK. If we do this, the new equilibrium will again be at the same point K, just as it was with the tariff.

Therefore a quota of RK is sometimes referred to as the "quota equivalent of tariff t." It leads to the same inefficiency in resource allocation as tariff t. Specifically, it raises price in the United States market, and so induces high-cost domestic production and decreased consumption. But there is one big difference. Recall that with a tariff, the higher price the consumer pays for imports goes to the United States Treasury in the form of the duty it collects (area 4 in Figure 26-2c). But *with a quota, no such revenues are collected*. Therefore, this amount goes not to the Treasury, but instead to whoever is lucky enough to acquire the quota right to import. If these rights, or import licenses, are granted by the United States Government to American importers, this windfall income 4 goes to the importers rather than to the Treasury. But if the quota rights somehow end up in the hands of the foreign firms that sell this good in the United States market, *this income goes to them rather than to the U.S. Treasury.* Consequently, this is a loss to the United States, and this sort of quota becomes a much more costly protectionist device for America than a tariff.[4] (For an example of how costly, see Box 26-4).

[3]These two efficiency effects are marked 1 and 2 because they correspond to the two triangular efficiency effects first encountered in Figure 25-7. [Of course, colors are reversed because in that earlier diagram trade was being opened (so there were efficiency gains), whereas in this diagram trade is being restricted (so there are efficiency losses). As an exercise, you should be able to confirm that triangle 1 in Figure 26-2d is the efficiency loss that results because inexpensive imports have been replaced by higher-cost domestic production, while triangle 2 is the efficiency loss that results because consumers have been prevented from purchasing this good at the lowest possible price.]

[4]One solution to ensure against this loss would be for the United States government to auction off these quota rights. Since the total revenue raised by the U.S. Treasury from this sale would be about area 4, such a quota would have effects similar to those of the tariff in Figure 26-2.

FIGURE 26-2 Effects of a tariff.

(a) The domestic American supply is **S**. Under free trade, there is (by assumption) a completely elastic world supply at price **P**. Therefore, the total supply on the American market (from both domestic and foreign sources) is **SHJ**. This intersects American demand **D** at point **J**, the free-trade equilibrium involving imports of **HJ**. But when tariff **t** is imposed, the world supply shifts up by this same amount **t**. (Foreign suppliers now require their original **P**, plus an amount **t** to compensate them for the tariff they must pay at the United States border.) With this upward shift in foreign supply, the total supply on the American market (from both domestic and foreign sources) becomes **SRK**. This intersects American demand **D** at point **K**, which is the new equilibrium under the tariff. Note that price has increased from **P** to **P**$_t$, by the amount of the tariff. Imports have decreased from **HJ** to **RK**, and American consumption has decreased by the red arrow below the baseline. At the same time, American output has increased by the blue arrow, hence employment in this industry has increased.

(b) Because price rises, consumers lose.

(c) But producers gain 3 and the treasury gains 4.

(d) The result is transfer 3 from consumers to producers, transfer 4 from consumers to the treasury, and an overall efficiency loss 1 + 2.

ESTIMATED COST TO THE UNITED STATES OF THE IMPORT QUOTA ON RAW SUGAR, 1970†

It has been estimated that, under free trade, Americans could have purchased sugar at $110 a ton, and that equilibrium would have been at J. This would have involved United States imports of HJ, that is, $11.6 - 2.9 = 8.7$ million tons.

But, because an import quota of 5.2 millions tons was imposed, the total supply in the United States market was curve S' (the domestic supply curve S plus imports limited to 5.2 million tons). This intersected United States demand at equilibrium K. Thus, the quota not only reduced imports from HJ to RK (the quota limit). It also raised price by $51 (that is, from the $110 free-trade level to $161). So it was the equivalent of a $51 tariff.

Now let's see how various groups were affected. Area 3 was a $227-million transfer from consumers who were damaged by the higher sugar price to American producers who benefited from it. But because it was only a transfer from one American group to another, it was not a loss to the United States. The other three areas, however, did represent American losses. Area 1 was an efficiency loss of $79 million because low-cost imports were displaced by higher-cost domestic production. Area 2 was an efficiency loss of $10 million because sugar could not be purchased at the $110 world price by American consumers who valued it above $110 (but below $161). Finally, area 4 was also a loss to the United States, a $265-million transfer of income from American consumers to the foreign holders of import rights. (American consumers paid $51 per ton more for imported sugar, and foreign holders of quota rights received $51 per ton more for this same sugar.)

The total loss to the United States there-

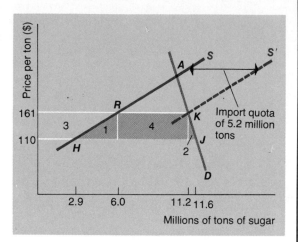

fore was areas $1 + 2 + 4 = $79 million + $10 million + $265 million = $354 million. Note in this case how the two efficiency losses were relatively small compared with the $265 million transfer of income from United States consumers to foreign quota holders.

Finally, suppose that the United States had not imposed this quota of RK, but had, instead, levied a $51 tariff. These two policies would have been equivalent in the sense that they would both have led to equilibrium at K, with imports of RK. Moreover, under either policy, effects 1, 2, and 3 would also have been the same. The difference would have been effect 4: Under a tariff, this $265 million transfer from the American consumer would have gone as tariff collections to the United States Treasury (and hence, would not have been a loss to the United States). On the other hand, under the quota, this transfer went to foreign quota holders, and hence was a loss to the United States.

†Data drawn from Ilse Mintz, *U.S. Import Quotas, Costs and Consequences* (Washington: American Enterprise Institute for Public Policy Research, February 1973).

This analysis throws light on an interesting recent policy issue. Rather than administer tariffs or quotas on our imports of textiles and color TVs, the United States has pressed hard to get certain countries to agree to impose so-called "voluntary" quotas on their firms exporting to the United States. As a consequence, we have lost income 4 to these foreign firms exporting to us (as well, of course, as costs 1 and 2 that follow from any form of protection). Why, then, do we pressure foreign countries to impose these quotas? Why don't we impose our own import restrictions ourselves? The reason is that if we were to impose trade restrictions, then, according to GATT (the General Agreement on Tariffs and Trade), we would be subject to retaliation by the foreign country. (Because foreign producers get the windfall from export licenses—as illustrated in Box 26-5—"voluntary" export quotas are less damaging to foreign economies than American import quotas or tariffs. Thus foreign countries may agree to quotas on their exports to the United States, rather than risk unilateral United States imposition of import restrictions.)

Problems

26-10 In March 1977, the U.S. International Trade Commission recommended that the President reduce the United States quota on sugar imports by a third. The President rejected this recommendation. Do you agree or disagree with his decision? Explain.

26-11 Using a multipanel diagram like Figure 26-2, explain the effects of the voluntary Japanese quota on TV exports to the United States in 1977 that reduced their sales of TVs to this country by just over 40 percent.

Appendix 26-B

THE EFFECTS OF THE EUROPEAN ECONOMIC COMMUNITY (EEC)

What happens when a group of countries form a common market, such as the EEC or one of the common markets recently created in Africa or Latin America?

Economic Effects on a Member Country

Many of the economic motives for a country joining a common market like the EEC are straightforward and have already been discussed; the expected benefits include those that come from exploiting economies of scale and comparative advantage in a larger market. Such benefits from increased trade flows between market partners are referred to as the benefits from *trade creation*. But because other countries are excluded from this common market, there is now one additional important complication: *trade diversion*. This problem occurs when one country (say, Britain) *switches* its purchases from an excluded country (like the United States) to a country within the common market (like Germany).

Trade diversion occurs because a member country like Britain applies *preferential* (discriminatory) treatment to its imports: Those from its European partners enter duty-free, while imports from outsiders like the United States must still pay a tariff. We can show why this import tariff may induce the British to switch their purchases from the United States to Germany by adding only one twist to our previous analysis in Figure 26-2. This is seen in Figure 26-3, which shows how a country like Britain was affected when it joined the EEC. (So far, we have been drawing diagrams like Figure 26-2 only for the United States. We emphasize that Figure 26-3 is drawn for Britain.)

Suppose that Britain's cheapest foreign source of supply for this good has always been the United States, at a price of $2=£1. Under free trade, the British equilibrium in panel *a* would have been at *J*, with imports *HJ* from the United States. But suppose that the British historically have had a 50 percent tariff *t*, so that their equilibrium has been at *K* rather than *J*, with domestic British price at £1.50 and imports from the United States of only *RK*. On these imports, the British Treasury has been collecting *RKBC* of tariff revenue (a per unit tariff *t* on *RK* units).

As already noted, if the British were to remove their tariff on imports from *all* countries, their new equilibrium would be at *J*, with imports *HJ* from their lowest cost source (the United States). Moreover, the price in Britain would fall by the full amount of the tariff *t*.

But the British don't drop their tariff on imports from all countries, but only from EEC countries. Thus, all British imports from the United States must still pay a tariff. Approaching the British dock, the American good has a price tag of £1, which is less than the £1.10 price of the good from Germany (Britain's next cheapest source of supply). That is what these goods cost the

574

FIGURE 26-3 Some of the effects on the British when they joined the Common Market.

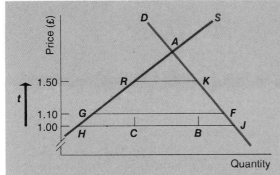

(a) With completely free trade, equilibrium in the British market would be at *J*, with price £1.00 and *HJ* imported from the least cost source—the United States. If the British impose a 50 percent tariff on imports from all countries, equilibrium shifts to *K*, with price £1.50 and *RK* imported from the United States. Finally, when the British join the European Economic Community (EEC) and allow duty-free imports from Europe, but not from the United States, equilibrium shifts from *K* to *F* and price falls from £1.50 to £1.10. This is the price at which Britain can acquire this good from, say, Germany, the cheapest European source. The effects on various British groups of this last step (entry into the EEC) are shown in panels *b*, *c*, and *d*.

(b) As British domestic price falls by Δ*P*, consumers gain.

(c) But producers lose 3; and the British Treasury no longer collects tariff revenue 4.

(d) The result is overall efficiency gains 1 and 2, but loss 5.

British nation as a whole. But that is not how they appear to the individual British consumer, who doesn't get to compare their prices until *after they have gone through British customs*. At this point, the United States good has acquired a £1.50 price tag (because of the tariff), while the tariff-free German good still has its original £1.10 price tag. In short, the German good is more expensive for the British nation as a whole, but it is less expensive for the individual British purchaser who makes the decision to buy it. So the British buy from Germany, paying the £1.10 price. The new equilibrium in the British market is shown at F. Thus, Britain's membership in the EEC has lowered price in the British market from £1.50 to £1.10, and Britain has now stopped buying from the United States and imports GF from Germany instead.

The last three panels in Figure 26-3 show the effects on various groups in Britain. In panel b, the British price reduction is seen to benefit consumers by the blue area enclosed to the left of the demand curve; in panel c, it is seen to damage British producers by red area 3 enclosed to the left of the supply curve. Of course, there is also a loss to the British Treasury (thus, indirectly, to the British taxpayer). Since British imports now enter duty-free, the British Treasury loses its previous tariff revenue of $RKBC$ in panel a, now shown as red area 4.

The transfers among the British producers, consumers, and treasury that this policy would bring (that is, those areas that appear both in blue in panel b and in red in panel c) are left as an exercise. More interesting is the overall effect on efficiency, as shown in panel d. Areas 1 and 2 are net gains since they appear as a blue benefit in panel b, but not as a red loss in panel c. As before, these represent increased efficiency in production and consumption and can be interpreted just like areas 1 and 2 in Figure 26-2. On the other hand, area 5 is a net loss since it appears as a red loss in panel c, but does not appear as a blue gain in panel b. This is the efficiency loss from trade diversion. Specifically, it is the cost to the British nation of acquiring this good from Germany at a cost of £1.10 rather than from the United States, the cheapest source, at a cost of £1. It is a cost that is difficult for the public to see because it only shows up in the form of lost tariff revenue to the British Treasury.

In short, because the British now have a discriminatory tariff, some of their imports are diverted from the least expensive source (the United States) to a more expensive source (Germany), and the British nation as a whole incurs loss 5 as a consequence. But it also reaps benefits 1 + 2 because its domestic price is less distorted than before; in other words, in falling from £1.50 to £1.10, British price has moved at least some distance toward the free-trade level of £1. Moreover, the more competitive the price from the partner source (Germany), the greater are benefits 1 + 2 and the smaller is loss 5. (To confirm, redraw panel d, assuming that the Germans are more competitive, supplying at a price of £1.05. Note how benefits 1 + 2 become larger, and loss 5 becomes smaller.)

The Effects of the Common Market on Outsiders Like the United States
It is not just the British who face a cost when they divert their imports from the United States to Germany. An even more obvious cost falls on us,

because we have lost an export market in Britain. Recall that the shaded area in Figure 25-6 was the net benefit to the United States if an export market is opened. Obviously, there is a similar triangular loss when an existing export market is suddenly closed. On the other hand, to the degree that the EEC has increased European growth, it has made its members better customers for United States products. (In addition, the EEC has agreed to reduce some of its tariffs against our goods to compensate us for some of the markets we lost.)

Problem

26-12 In response to American complaints that the Common Market damages United States exports, European leaders have pointed out that all they are doing in Europe is what the 13 colonies did in America two centuries ago: simply bringing together a group of countries (colonies) to trade freely. Are the British, in providing free access to German imports (and thus discriminating against the United States), any different from, say, the Virginians who, for the last two hundred years of United States history, have provided free access to New York imports (and in this special sense have discriminated against Europe)?

What do you think?

PART FIVE
MICROECONOMICS:
How Income Is Distributed

n Part 5, the central topic is income distribution: *For whom* is the nation's output produced? More specifically, we shall be asking questions like: What determines the income that labor receives in the form of wages? What determines the interest and profit of capital owners and the rental income of landowners? Why does the heavyweight champion earn millions of dollars for every fight, while a nurse earns only a few thousand a year? And what policies can the government introduce if it wishes to change the nation's income distribution?

To answer such questions, we shall be turning our attention from the markets for goods and services to the markets for labor, capital, and other factors of production. Fortunately, many of the principles developed in analyzing the markets for goods in Part 4 can be applied with appropriate modifications to factor markets. It will be no great surprise to find that factor markets are like product markets. Sometimes they operate efficiently; sometimes they do not. Therefore, while much of Part 5 will be new, much will be the application of the tools we developed in Part 4 to a challenging new set of problems.

In leaving Part 4, we reemphasize one of its important messages. Almost any government policy, from the regulation of a monopoly to the imposition of a tariff, will change a market price. And when a price changes, there are two effects:

an *efficiency* effect, and a *transfer* from one group to another. (For example, a price rise worsens the position of buyers and improves that of sellers; thus it involves a transfer from buyers to sellers.) When an economic policy is assessed, both these effects should be taken into account.

In the analysis of product markets in Part 4, the focus was on the question of efficiency. But we have seen that a policy that increases efficiency cannot be judged on this ground alone; its transfer effect must also be recognized. When we shift our major focus to income distribution in Part 5, a similar conclusion is reached: Any policy designed to transfer income cannot be judged on this ground alone; its effect on efficiency must also be carefully examined. In the box that follows, we illustrate the two concepts of efficiency and income transfer by reviewing several diagrams from Part 4.

But whether or not you embark on this detailed review, you should look at the diagrams in Figures 1 and 2 to get the general idea of their message. Figure 1 provides two cases where transfer effects (white arrows) are exactly the same, but efficiency effects (shaded triangles) are completely different. On the other hand, Figure 2 shows two policies with exactly the same efficiency effects (blue triangles), but completely different transfers (white arrows). Clearly, if we look at one effect but not at the other, we may get a very incomplete picture.

WHY BOTH EFFICIENCY AND TRANSFER EFFECTS MUST BE CONSIDERED

An Important Message from Part 4

To see how similar transfer effects can be accompanied by different efficiency effects, we reconsider the commodity tax in Figure 1. Then, to show how similar efficiency effects can be accompanied by different transfer effects, we will reconsider monopoly in Figure 2.

Reprise: The Commodity Tax on a Good That Pollutes and on One That Does Not

Panel a of Figure 1 shows the effect of a commodity tax on a good with no polluting side effects. Panel b shows this same tax applied to a good that does involve pollution, with the tax set at a level equal to the pollution cost. Otherwise, these two panels are identical. In both panels, the commodity tax will involve exactly the same set of transfers, shown by the broad white arrows. The reason that the transfers are identical is that in both cases, the tax shifts supply from S_1 to S_2, and equilibrium from E_1 to E_2. As a consequence, in each case consumers lose because the price they pay rises from P_1 to P_2, and producers lose because the price they receive (after paying the tax) falls from P_1 to P_3. But while consumers and producers lose, the United States Treasury gains in the form of increased tax receipts. Thus, in each panel, the broad white upward arrow shows the transfer from consumers to the United States Treasury, while the arrow pointing down shows the transfer from producers to the Treasury.

But, while transfers are the same in each case, the efficiency effects are quite different. Without pollution (panel a), the tax causes a red triangular loss of efficiency. But in the face of pollution (panel b), this same tax causes a blue triangular efficiency gain. The reasons are detailed in the caption to Figure 1—but the basic idea is simple: In either case, the tax reduces output from Q_1 to Q_2. If there is no pollution (panel a), this output reduction results in an efficiency loss because it moves the economy away from the efficient

output level at Q_1. But when pollution exists (panel b), the efficient output level is not Q_1, but rather Q_2; and the output reduction induced by the tax moves the economy *toward* this point, thus generating an efficiency gain.

Another way of seeing how this policy can improve efficiency in panel b but not in panel a is this. In panel b's case of pollution, the tax provides a benefit that does not exist in panel a: the benefit to the public of having a polluting activity curtailed. These two panels contain an important message: In two sets of circumstances, a policy can have identical transfer effects, but completely different efficiency effects.

Reprise: The Problem of Monopoly

Figure 2 illustrates two ways in which monopoly output may be increased, thus increasing efficiency. In panel a, the familiar policy of price regulation is reproduced from Figure 21-7. The monopoly's initial equilibrium is at E_1. A policy of marginal cost pricing (that is, setting maximum price at P_2) will force the monopoly down its demand curve from E_1 to E_2, with the resulting transfer from the monopoly to consumers, as shown by the broad white arrow. In the process, monopoly output is increased from Q_1 to the efficient quantity Q_2, with the blue efficiency gain being the result.

Whereas in panel a the efficiency gain results from controlling the monopoly price, in panel b exactly the same efficiency gain is achieved by allowing the monopoly complete pricing freedom—including the freedom to charge different prices on different units. Suppose the monopoly is able to divide up its market and thus engage in price discrimination, just like the monopolist in Figure 21-8. However, where that earlier doctor-monopolist could divide the market into just two segments and thus quote only two prices, suppose that this present monopoly is in a strong enough position to quote a different price on each transaction. In other words, in dealing with the very first buyer, this monop-

FIGURE 1
Transfers the same, efficiency effects different:
The effects of a commodity tax . . .

(a)
. . . if there is no pollution (based on Fig. 17-5)

(b)
. . . if pollution does exist (based on Fig. 23-2)

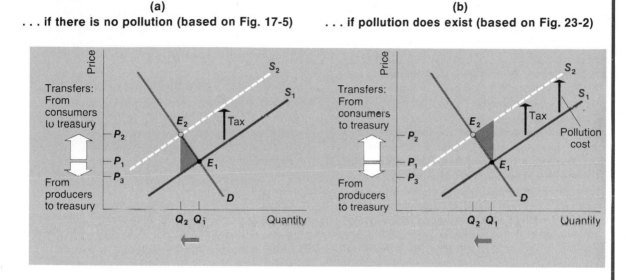

In both panels a and b: Before the tax, equilibrium of S_1 and D occurs at E_1, with price P_1 and output Q_1. The tax shifts supply up to S_2, thus shifting equilibrium to E_2. Consequently, output is reduced to Q_2 and price is increased to P_2.

(a)   (b)

Transfer Effects	**Transfer Effects**
The burden of the tax is divided between consumers and producers. Consumers lose because the price they pay rises from P_1 to P_2. Producers lose because the price they receive (after tax) falls from P_1 to P_3. (Producers actually receive P_2, but out of this, they must pay the tax of P_2P_3.) Thus, two transfers may be identified: the transfer of P_1P_2 per unit from consumers to the treasury, and the transfer of P_1P_3 from producers to the treasury.	Exactly the same as in panel (a).

Efficiency Effect	**Efficiency Effect**
In this case, there are no externalities, so that D represents marginal benefit (utility) to consumers *and* to society, while S_1 represents marginal cost to producers *and* to society. Since D and S_1 are equal at output Q_1, this is the efficient output level. Since the tax reduces output below this level to Q_2, it results in an efficiency loss. (This red triangular loss is exactly the same as the one in Fig. 20-4b.)	Because pollution costs exist, the marginal cost of this good to society is S_2 rather than S_1. Since S_2 intersects marginal benefit D at E_2, Q_2 is the efficient level of output. By reducing output from Q_1 to this efficient level Q_2, the tax generates an efficiency gain, shown by the blue triangle.

oly refuses to sell even 1 unit unless it receives the maximum price that the buyer is prepared to give up, namely, the narrow price arrow *a*. The monopoly then turns to the next buyer and similarly extracts *b*, the maximum price that second consumer is willing to pay. The monopoly continues to work its way down its demand curve, exercising the ultimate degree of market power by squeezing every last nickel from every consumer along the way.† Because it can thus price each unit all the way up to its demand curve, it is able to convert its demand curve into a marginal revenue curve. For example, price *b* on the monopoly's demand curve is also a point on its marginal revenue curve, because its additional revenue from selling the second unit is *b*.

Such a monopoly will not stop at E_1, but instead, will continue to *F*, where its marginal cost MC now equals its new marginal revenue *D*. (To confirm this, observe that a monopoly selling at point E_1 will receive a marginal revenue equal to the arrow $Q_1 E_1$. Since its marginal cost is only $Q_1 W$, it will continue to expand production.) Therefore, in panel *b* the monopoly increases its output from Q_1 to Q_2, just as in panel *a*. Hence, there is exactly the same blue efficiency gain.

By now, of course, you may be very uneasy about the way the monopoly in panel *b* is able to benefit from discriminatory pricing. The large transfer from consumers to the monopoly in panel *b* is shown by the broad white arrow. (The height of this arrow is the average of the price increases the monopoly is now charging its original customers.)‡ Note how this contrasts with the transfer in panel *a*, which was in exactly the opposite direction because the monopoly was forced to lower its price.

[Note that there is one big difference between the discriminating monopolist discussed here and the discriminating monopolist in Figure 21-8. In that earlier diagram, the

doctor-monopolist was not able to produce at all unless she could discriminate. (Her *D* was always below AC.) And it was better for consumers to be able to buy her services at a high price than not to be able to buy them at all. But there is no such justification for discrimination here, since the monopolist in Figure 2*b* is initially able to produce profitably at E_1 without discriminating.]

Panel *b* also illustrates why *monopoly profits provide a poor indication of how monopoly distorts resource allocation* (that is, how it reduces efficiency). When the monopoly in panel *b* increases its profit by price discrimination, this does not increase the monopoly distortion in resource allocation. Quite the contrary: It eliminates this distortion altogether.

The message of Figure 2 may be recapped. The outcomes of the two panels involve exactly the same blue efficiency gain. But the transfers are completely different. Whereas the forced reduction in price in panel *a* transfers monopoly profit back to consumers, the unfettered exercise of monopoly power in panel *b* allows the monopolist to profit even more at the expense of consumers.

Conclusions

Any economic policy can have two effects: a transfer, and an efficiency effect. If we consider only one of these effects, we will miss an important part of the total picture. For example, if we should look only at the transfer effects in Figure 1, we would conclude: There is no difference between these two cases. And we would miss the completely different effects on efficiency. Or, if we should look only at the efficiency effects of the two policies in Figure 2, we would conclude that they are the same. And we would miss their completely different transfer effects.

---

†Since one individual may appear in several locations on the demand curve, the monopoly must be able not only to quote a different take-it-or-leave-it price to each individual, but also, in dealing with one individual, to quote a different price for each purchase. Obviously, no firm does discriminate so completely. But the basic idea in this analysis still holds for firms that price-discriminate to a less complete degree. (For example, surgeons may have a widely varying set of rates.)

*‡But on all the additional $Q_1 Q_2$ units the monopoly sells, price is lower than the original P_1. Isn't this then a transfer from the monopoly to consumers? The answer is no. There can be no transfer to consumers unless they actually benefit in some way, and here they do not, since on each and every one of their purchases, the monopolist has extracted a price just equal to the utility they receive.

FIGURE 2
Efficiency effects the same, transfers different

(a)	(b)
Regulating monopoly price (based on Fig. 21-7)	**Allowing the monopolist to discriminate completely (reference Fig. 21-8)**

Original equilibrium is at E_1, with the monopoly selling output Q_1 at price P_1.

(a)

A price ceiling set at P_2 drives the monopoly down its demand curve from E_1 to E_2.

(b)

This discriminating monopoly will price "right up to its demand curve," charging the first buyer a, the second b, and so on. This allows it to convert its demand D into a marginal revenue curve. Hence, when it works its way down to E_1 it does not stop, since its marginal revenue (Q_1E_1) is still higher than its marginal cost (Q_1W). Instead it will continue to produce to F, where these two *are* equal.

Transfer Effect

Since the price consumers pay is lowered from P_1 to P_2, there is a transfer from the monopolist to consumers shown by the broad white arrow.

Transfer Effect

Since the monopoly is able to squeeze a higher price (a, b, etc.) out of its original consumers, there is a transfer from consumers to the monopoly. (In fact, all the original consumers' surplus is transferred to the monopoly.)

Efficiency Effect

Output is increased from Q_1 to the efficient level Q_2, where marginal cost equals marginal benefit D. The resulting efficiency gain is shown in blue.

Efficiency Effect

Exactly the same as in panel a.

chapter 27
Wages in a Perfectly Competitive Economy

Last week a premature blast went off
And a mile in the air went big Jim Goff.
. . . .
When the next payday came around
Jim Goff a dollar short was found
When he asked "What for," came this reply
"You're docked for the time you was up in the
        sky."

Thomas F. Casey, "Drill Ye Tarriers, Drill"

The wage rate is the price of labor; and the market for labor is somewhat similar to the market for a good, such as wheat. It is, of course, far from being completely the same. Labor is not just a commodity; labor involves *people*. Thus, major policy issues arise in labor markets which do not appear in the markets for other inputs or for final products. For example, if a manufacturer wishes to abuse a machine, that is pretty much his own business; the cost will come when the machine wears out quickly, and no major issue of public policy will arise. Not so for labor. If the mine owner wishes to abuse workers by sending them to hazardous, dust-filled mines, the health of human beings is obviously affected. The government has the right—and the responsibility—to intervene to set health standards. Or consider another example. Some business executives have peculiar quirks with respect to their products. In the early days of the automobile, Henry Ford's attitude was, "You can have any color of car you want—so long as it is black." No question of public policy arose; Ford paid for his views by a loss of sales to competitors who were willing to give consumers their choice of colors. In contrast, personal quirks in the market for labor can be pernicious. If an employer just doesn't like black workers, the government may reasonably intervene to enforce nondiscriminatory hiring. Machines and other inanimate objects have no rights; but workers do.

Although the labor market is different in these respects from other markets, it may still be analyzed with some of the familiar tools we have already developed. What influences affect labor demand? What influences affect supply? In what circumstances does a free labor market result in an efficient wage and employment level, and in what circumstances does it not? Can the government intervene in the labor market to transfer income to labor, just as it sometimes intervenes in a product market to transfer income from one group to another? And when it does, what effect does its intervention have on efficiency? These are the questions studied in this chapter.

Here, we assume that labor markets are perfectly competitive, because we must understand this case before we can fully appreciate what happens when labor markets are not competitive (the issue addressed in the next chapter). Thus in this chapter we assume that workers have not formed a labor union to raise wages. There are so many buyers of labor service (employers) and so many sellers (workers) that none can affect the price (wage rate).

In the United States, real hourly wage rates are now approximately five times as

> The *real* wage rate is the nominal (or dollar) wage rate adjusted for inflation. The statement that the real wage is five times as high now as in 1900 means that an hour of labor time will now buy five times as many goods and services as in 1900.

high as they were in 1900. They have increased because of rising labor productivity.

We begin our analysis of labor markets by examining this close relationship between wages and productivity.

LABOR DEMAND AND PRODUCTIVITY

In this chapter, we shall focus on the labor market for an *industry*. But, to set the stage, we first examine labor demand by a single firm—for example, the hypothetical firm with a given stock of plant and machinery shown in Table 27-1.

In column 2 we see how this firm can increase its physical output by hiring more labor. In column 3, the marginal physical product of labor is calculated, as we would expect, by noting how much total product in column 2 increases as each additional worker is hired. For example, hiring the second worker increases output from 9 to 17, or by 8 units.

But the firm is even more interested in how its revenue increases as it hires more

TABLE 27-1
Marginal Productivity of Labor†

(1) Number of workers per day	(2) Total physical product per day	(3) Marginal physical product (change in column 2 because one more worker is hired)	(4) Price per unit of product	(5) Value of marginal product, that is, marginal productivity of labor (MPL) (5) = (3) × (4)
1	9	9	$10	$90
2	17	8	$10	$80
3	23	6	$10	$60
4	27	4	$10	$40
5	29	2	$10	$20

In this hypothetical example, marginal physical product falls continuously as we move down column 3. In other words, there are diminishing returns to labor throughout. While the pattern does not have to look like this (for example, there might initially be increasing returns), we know from the law of diminishing returns (Chapter 19) that marginal physical product must eventually fall.

†Shown for a hypothetical firm with a given capital stock and selling in a competitive market at a constant price.

labor. This is shown by the marginal productivity of labor schedule (MPL) in column 5, For example, hiring the second worker yields $80 of additional revenue, or the 8 additional units that worker produces times the $10 price of each unit. (Notice that we are assuming that the firm not only hires in a competitive *labor* market, but also sells its output in a competitive *product* market, where price is constant at $10). In its decision-making, the firm will be concerned with the *value* of labor's contribution in column 5. This is graphed in Figure 27-1.

> The *marginal physical product* of labor is the additional number of units of output a firm can produce because it has hired one more worker. The *marginal productivity of labor* is the dollar value of its marginal physical product.

FIGURE 27-1 A firm's demand for labor is the marginal productivity of labor (column 5 of Table 27-1).
Each point on the MPL curve represents a point on the firm's demand curve. For example, point *T* on the MPL curve is also on the demand curve, because at a wage rate of $60, the firm hires three workers. Similarly, point *V* on the MPL curve is also on the demand curve, because at a wage rate of $80, the firm hires two workers.

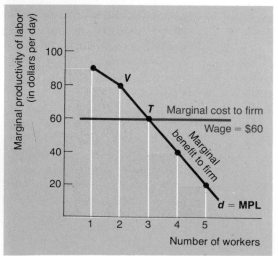

How many units of labor will the firm hire? If the daily wage paid to each worker is the $60 shown by the red line in Figure 27-1, this firm will stop hiring when it has employed three workers. (The fourth won't be hired because that worker would provide only $40 of additional revenue but would cost $60 to hire.) In general, a firm in a perfectly competitive labor market will maximize its profit by hiring labor to the point where its marginal benefit (MPL) is equal to its marginal cost (the wage rate).

> In a perfectly competitive equilibrium, a profit-maximizing firm will hire labor to the point where the marginal productivity of labor equals the wage rate.

It now takes only one final step to show that the marginal productivity curve for the firm represents its demand for labor. We have already seen that point *T* on its MPL curve is also a point on its demand curve (since, at a $60 wage, the firm will hire three workers). Similarly, any other point on this MPL curve, say *V*, is also a point on the firm's demand curve. (At an $80 wage, the firm will hire only two workers.) With each point on the MPL curve representing a point on the demand curve, the two curves coincide.

Finally, you should now work through Problem 27-1 to see how the firm's income is divided between the wages it pays to labor and the amount it has left over to pay interest, profit, and rent to other factors of production. This will be a useful introduction to this chapter's discussion of how income is divided.

What Causes a Shift in Labor Demand?

An equivalent way to pose this question is: What causes a shift in the marginal productivity of labor schedule in column 5 of

Table 27-1? First, the price of the firm's product (column 4) may change. If it rises from $10 to $15, then all the marginal productivity figures in column 5 will correspondingly rise, causing the demand for labor to shift upward to d_2 in Figure 27-2. Examples of such a shift in demand include the increased demand for carpenters resulting from an increase in the price of houses, and the increased demand for farm labor following an increase in the price of wheat. Both these examples illustrate the *derived demand* for labor. Labor may be demanded, not for its own sake directly, but instead to produce something else.

> *Derived demand* exists when a good or service is demanded because of its usefulness in producing some other good or service. Thus, there is a derived demand for labor to produce cars, and for land to grow wheat.

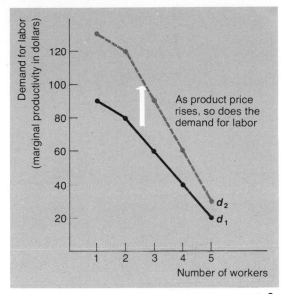

FIGURE 27-2 The firm's derived demand for labor. d_1 is the marginal productivity of labor when product price is $10. (It is calculated in column 5 of Table 27-1, and has already appeared as d in Figure 27-1.) d_2 is the marginal productivity of labor if product price rises to $15. (This is a recalculation of column 5 in Table 27-1, with $15 replacing $10 in column 4.)

Another reason for an upward shift in the demand for labor (that is, an increase in the MPL values in column 5 of Table 27-1) is that labor may become physically more productive. In other words, its marginal physical product in column 3 may increase. Such an increase can result from an expanded use of *capital* or an improvement in *technology*. For example, if additional machines are installed in a factory (more capital), the existing work force may be able to produce more. If a new type of machine is designed or a better layout for the factory is discovered, technology is improved, and workers consequently may be able to produce more. Often changes in the quantity of capital come hand in hand with changes in technology. When a new, larger aircraft is introduced, the airlines that purchase it are able to use improved technology. But they also increase their capital stock, because they replace small aircraft with the new,

larger ones. For both reasons, the productivity of pilots increases.

(Some improvements in technology result in a lower demand for labor in specific industries. For example, when new weaving machinery was introduced during the industrial revolution, some textile workers lost their jobs. But in the long run, even such "labor-saving" improvements bring increased demand for labor and higher wages in the economy as a whole, as we shall see later in Box 28-2.)

The Labor Market for an Industry

Now let us turn from the labor demand by a firm to the labor demand by an industry. In a perfectly competitive economy, the demand for labor by an industry will be the sum of the demands by the individual firms in somewhat the same way that the market demand for a good (in Figure 18-1) is the

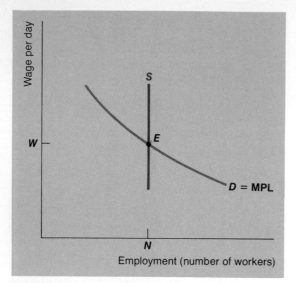

FIGURE 27-3 Determination of an industry's wage rate.
In a perfectly competitive labor market, the wage rate *W* is determined by the intersection of the demand and supply curves for labor.

sum of the demands of individual consumers.[1] Such an industry demand curve for labor (*D*) is shown in Figure 27-3. What about supply? For the moment, we assume that the number of workers seeking employment in this industry is constant (*N*); in other words, labor supply is the completely inelastic curve *S*. (This assumption will be relaxed later in this chapter.) Given these *S* and *D* curves, the equilibrium occurs at *E*, with wage *W*.

MARGINAL PRODUCTIVITY AND THE DIVISION OF INCOME

One of our major interests in Part 5 is to see how the nation's income is divided, and the marginal productivity of labor curve (the demand for labor) can throw light on this issue. Specifically, in this section we shall show how the income share going to labor and the income share going to other factors of production in an industry can be read off the MPL curve shown in Figure 27-4.

The first step is to show the value of the industry's total output.[2] The first worker produces output with a value of *a* in Figure 27-4, the second produces *b*, and so on to the last worker, who adds *j*. Thus, the total value of output is equal to the shaded areas 1 + 2. (We assume that nothing can be produced unless some labor is employed.)

What part of this total goes to labor? The answer is area 2, since wage *W* is paid to the *N* units of labor. Thus, if the labor

FIGURE 27-4 An industry's marginal productivity of labor curve and the distribution of income (based on Figure 27-3).
Total income earned by all factors of production is area 1 + 2. Of this, area 2 is paid to labor, and area 1 goes to other factors of production.

---

[1]In fact, the industry's demand for labor is not exactly the horizontal sum of the demands by the individual firms. To see why, note that if the wage rate falls, each firm hires more workers, as shown by the individual labor demand curves. But this increased hiring results in increased industry output, which depresses the price of that output. This in turn shifts the labor demand curve of each individual firm. (Remember, each of these curves was drawn on the assumption that output price remained constant.)

In short, the individual demand curves we are trying to sum do not remain fixed. In assuming away this problem, we recognize that the statements we make from now on will only be approximations. (As one might expect, there are many other examples of such complicated "feedbacks" in economics.)

[2]More precisely, the industry's value added, that is, the value of the industry's output after deducting the costs of all its inputs purchased from other industries (like the cost of steel to the auto industry). Throughout this analysis we define value of output in this value added sense.

market is competitive, we can summarize how the value of the industry's output is distributed in the following two statements:

> Labor receives income equal to the wage rate times the number of workers employed. This is represented by the rectangle enclosed to the southwest of the equilibrium point on the labor demand curve (marginal productivity of labor curve).

Area 1 is what remains after labor is paid. It is what employers have left to distribute to other factors of production: interest and profit to capital, rent to land, and so on. Thus:

> After labor is paid, all other factors of production together receive the triangular area enclosed to the northwest of the equilibrium point on the labor demand curve.

These two conclusions can now be used to analyze some of the effects of an important—and controversial—government policy: the minimum wage.

THE EFFECT OF A MINIMUM WAGE

Since the Fair Labor Standards Act was passed in 1938, the United States has had a legislated minimum wage in most, but not all, industries. The objective has been to raise labor income: to ensure that people receive a living wage, and thus to reduce the poverty problem. What effect has this legislation had? To answer this question as simply as possible, we initially assume that the minimum wage applies to all industries.

Industries that already pay a wage above the legislated minimum will not be affected.[3] Accordingly, we concentrate on a

typical industry that *is* affected. In Figure 27-5a, the original supply and demand for labor generate initial equilibrium E_1, with employment N_1 and wage W_1. If a minimum wage is set above this, at, say W_2, firms facing more expensive labor cut back their hiring from N_1 to N_2, and equilibrium shifts to E_2. The result is that $N_2 N_1$ workers are involuntarily unemployed, seeking work but unable to get a job.

How are various groups in the economy affected? In particular, does this legislated increase in the wage rate achieve its objective of increasing labor income? The answer is: Not necessarily, because it has two conflicting effects. On the one hand, labor income increases because the wage rate rises; but on the other hand, labor income decreases because employment falls. Specifically, according to the first of our two summary statements on income distribution, labor's initial income at E_1 was areas $5 + 7$, but at the new equilibrium E_2, labor income has become areas $5 + 4$. Thus, labor's income has increased by area 4 (workers who still have a job receive a higher wage). But it has decreased by area 7 (workers who have lost their jobs no longer receive any wage). Both these effects are shown in panel *b* of Figure 27-5.

What happens to the income of other factors of production? Initially, income to other factors was areas $3 + 4 + 6$ (the triangular area to the northwest of equilibrium E_1 in panel *a*). But at the new equilibrium E_2, this income shrinks to area 3. Thus, other factors lose income $4 + 6$, as shown in panel *c*.

From this analysis we see that a minimum wage will not necessarily transfer income from other factors of production to labor. True, it does reduce the income of other factors in panel *c*; but it does not

---

[3] Exceptions may occur if there are accepted differentials in wages among industries. Then raising wages of workers on the bottom end of the scale to the minimum level may also raise wages of workers higher up the scale. The question of why wage differentials exist is an important one that recurs throughout the next three chapters. (The critical student may wonder how wages can possibly differ among industries if labor markets really are competitive. The answer is that there are many different types of labor. Skilled workers are paid more than the unskilled, whether labor markets are perfectly competitive or not.)

FIGURE 27-5 Effects of a minimum wage in competitive conditions.

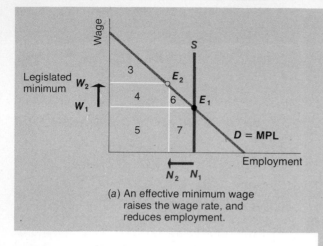

(a) An effective minimum wage raises the wage rate, and reduces employment.

(b) Labor gains and loses: Gain 4 goes to workers who still have jobs. But those who no longer have jobs lose 7.

(c) Other factors of production lose.

(d) Net result: An efficiency loss. That is, losses in the panels above that are not offset by blue gains.

necessarily raise the income going to labor in panel *b*, since the red losses and blue gains there may cancel out. Obviously, the elasticity of demand for labor is the key: If it is inelastic, then labor income overall will rise; but if it is elastic, then total labor income will fall.

But in either case, there will be individuals in the labor force who suffer—namely, those who lose their jobs. Who are these individuals? The answer tends to be: blacks and other minority groups who tend to be "last hired, first fired", and teenagers who lack work experience and skills. A minimum wage raises very special problems for teenagers. They may find it very difficult to get jobs; often they end up in part-time employment. In addition, they may be unable to get into the on-the-job training programs that are so important for their future careers. (We return to this issue in detail in Chapter 29.) Because of the high teenage unemployment rate (more than double the rate for adults), a number of economists have suggested a lower minimum wage for teenagers than for adults. But this measure has been opposed by organized labor on the ground that employers might lay off high-wage adults, who may have families to support, in order to hire low-wage teenagers. This remains a controversial issue, and attempts to make the teenage minimum less that the adult minimum have not so far been very successful—although the vote has been close. By a tense, one-vote margin, the House of Representatives in 1977 defeated an amendment to allow employers to pay teenagers less than the legal minimum wage for adults for a period of 6 months.

Finally, in panel d of Figure 27-5 we see how a minimum wage results in a red efficiency loss. (As before, this is any area that appears in the panels above as a loss to one group without being a gain to another.) To confirm this, observe that the thin red bar shows the nation's output forgone because worker j is left unemployed by the minimum wage; and the total red area is the output forgone because of all the workers who have lost their jobs. This is the now familiar efficiency loss that results when a market—in this case, a labor market—is moved away from its perfectly competitive equilibrium.

In evaluating the United States minimum wage legislation, several important qualifying observations should be added to this analysis. If workers are risk-averse, they may prefer the situation before the minimum wage (when a low-paying job was easy to find) to the situation afterward, when they may either have a higher wage or lose their jobs entirely. Thus, because it increases the risk facing the labor force, the cost of a minimum wage may be greater than Figure 27-5 suggests.

On the other hand, there is a good reason why its cost may be *less* severe. Our diagram is based on the assumption that all jobs are subject to this legislation—that workers who lose their jobs have "nowhere else to go" and become unemployed. But in the United States a few other jobs are available: For example, in 1975, 6 to 7 percent of our labor force was in jobs not covered by the minimum wage legislation.

Finally, when we relax the perfectly competitive assumptions that we make about labor markets in this chapter, our efficiency conclusion may change dramatically. As we shall see in the next chapter, a minimum wage applied in noncompetitive markets may raise, rather than lower, efficiency.

*DISCRIMINATION IN THE LABOR MARKET: An Introduction

Demand and supply curves can be used to identify some of the consequences of racial discrimination (although discrimination also clearly involves social, moral, and political issues which cannot be dealt with in such a simple framework). What happens if employers tend to favor whites for the better positions, and offer only inferior jobs to blacks, even though they may have equal skill and training? Although the example we use is discrimination against blacks, the analysis also applies to discrimination against women or any other group.

The initial situation in a competitive labor market for an industry that does *not* discriminate is shown in the left panel of Figure 27-6a. Wage W is paid to N workers—N_W whites and N_B blacks. No distinction is made between them; that is, in hiring workers, employers are "color-blind." Now what happens if discrimination is introduced into this market? Specifically, consider an extreme form of discrimination, where employers no longer hire blacks to do the same jobs as whites. In other words, employers cut blacks out of the main labor market, hiring them instead for low-productivity, dead-end jobs.

As a consequence, there are now the two

---

*Instructors in short courses may omit this slightly more difficult section without loss of continuity. Another, simpler example of discrimination appears later in Box 28-3.

separate labor markets shown in part *a* of this diagram—the one on the left for whites, and the one on the right for blacks. (This is an example of a *dual labor market*.) In the main labor market, supply shifts from S to S_W because this market is now "whites only"; the wage rate consequently rises from W to W_W. In the black labor market shown on the right, demand for labor D is low, reflecting the fact that the only jobs available are low-productivity tasks. Supply in this market is S_B, representing blacks who now have nowhere else to go. Consequently, the wage rate is W_B, substantially less than the wage W that blacks received before discrimination.

The effects of such discrimination on each group and on the overall efficiency of the economy are the following:

1. *Black workers lose*. Because their wage rate falls from W to W_B, their total wage income falls from area 3 to area 6. (They may also suffer higher unemployment, which does not show up in this diagram.)

2. *White workers gain*. Because their wage rate rises from W to W_W, their total wage income rises by area 1 (that is, from area 4 to areas 4 + 1).

3. *Owners of other factors of production lose*. Specifically, the income earned by capital and other non-labor factors of production in the main labor market decreases by areas 1 + 2. (Their income before discriminatory action was areas 7 + 1 + 2, while their income afterward is 7.) Of this, area 1 is a transfer from them to white workers receiving a higher wage.[4] (Their loss 2 may be roughly offset by new income 5 that they earn in the ghetto market).

4. *There may be little effect on whites overall*. Because non-labor factors (like capi-

tal) are owned mostly by whites, there may be little effect on all whites taken together. True, white wage earners gain area 1; but this represents merely a transfer from other white-owned factors.

5. *There is an efficiency loss*. When we turn from the transfer effects to the efficiency effects shown in part *b* of this diagram, we see that the total product of the economy falls. As black workers are forced out of the main labor market, production falls by the red area. This is only partially offset by their new (blue) production in the ghetto market into which they have been segregated. The difference is the reduced total output of the economy, that is, the efficiency loss from this policy of discrimination.

6. *This efficiency loss is born by blacks*. Because there is little net effect on whites overall, blacks suffer essentially all the efficiency loss from discrimination.[5]

Estimates on how important some of these effects may be are given in Box 27-1.

This analysis has provided us with only an introduction to discrimination, rather than the last word. Some of our conclusions depend on the assumptions we have made. For example, when we relax the assumption that labor markets are perfectly competitive, some conclusions must be modified (as we shall see later in Box 28-3). Moreover, the labor market is only one of the places where discrimination occurs. (For a discussion of discrimination in the housing market, see Box 27-2.)

THE SUPPLY OF LABOR FOR AN INDUSTRY

In our discussion of labor markets so far, we have made the simplifying assumption that

---

[4]This leads to the following puzzle: While discrimination may be in the economic interest of white *workers*, this analysis suggests that it is not in the interest of *employers* representing other factors of production (such as their own capital, stockholders' capital, etc.). Why, then, do employers continue to discriminate? One possible answer will be given later in Box 28-3.

[5]To confirm this, notice that the reduction in black income (from area 3 to 6 in panel *a*) is essentially the same as the efficiency loss—the red area less the blue area in panel *b*.

FIGURE 27-6   An introduction to the economics of labor-market discrimination.

(a) How discrimination affects wages and incomes.

In a color-blind market *without discrimination,* equilibrium is at **E** in the left panel. The wage received by all workers is **W,** with N_W whites and N_B blacks employed. *With discrimination,* blacks are forced into the ghetto market on the right, where equilibrium is E_R. Thus black wages fall from **W** to W_B and the wage income of black workers falls from area 3 to area 6. Meanwhile, the forced departure of blacks from the main labor market on the left reduces labor supply there from **N** to N_W, thus raising wages of whites from **W** to W_W, and raising the wage income of white workers by area 1 (that is, from area 4 to areas 4 + 1).

(b) The efficiency effects of discrimination

As a result of the forced departure of black labor from this main labor market, there is lost output of the red area under the marginal productivity curve. This is more than . . .

the output (blue area) produced by black labor when it is hired in this low-productivity ghetto market. Efficiency loss is the difference in these two areas—the reduced output of black labor because it is shifted from high- to low-productivity jobs.

the labor force of an industry is given; in other words, that labor supply is completely inelastic. But typically, the supply of labor for an industry is not constant, because labor may be induced by a high wage to move in from other industries. In particular, relatively unskilled workers move freely among industries. (In contrast, the highly skilled are less mobile because of relatively strong ties to their special industry: A nuclear physicist cannot easily switch to brain surgery.)

The movement of labor into an industry is illustrated in Figure 27-7. As the wage rate rises from W_1 to W_2, the labor supplied to this industry increases from N_1 to N_2 as workers are drawn in from other industries by this increasingly attractive wage rate. As a specific example, the labor supply curve tells us that when the wage rate rises to W_3, worker a is drawn into this industry. In

order to attract him, the wage probably has to be slightly above his previous wage.[6] But his previous wage was also his previous

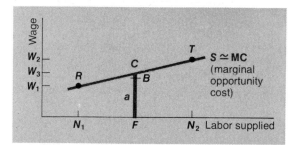

FIGURE 27-7   Supply of labor for an industry.
The rising supply curve for labor shows how an increase in the wage paid by an industry increases the number of workers seeking jobs there. Moreover, the height of the supply curve at any point like C roughly reflects the opportunity cost of hiring another worker (a) in this industry—that is, his productivity in his previous job. Thus, the supply curve for labor reflects the opportunity cost of hiring one more worker (just as the supply curve for a product reflects the cost of producing one more unit of output.)

[6]For example, worker a, who is willing to move into this industry when its wage reaches W_3, may have been earning FB in his previous job. The reason he doesn't move until the wage reaches W_3 is that he requires incentive BC to compensate him for the fact that he liked his previous location better, and that he incurs economic and

BOX 27-2
DISCRIMINATION IN THE HOUSING MARKET†

Blacks have a lower standard of living not only because discrimination in the labor market lowers their wage. In addition, discrimination in the housing market often raises the price blacks have to pay, as illustrated in this diagram.

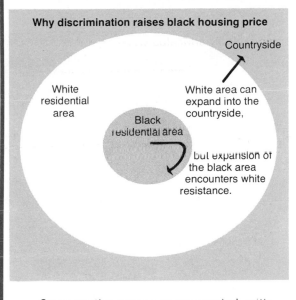

Why discrimination raises black housing price

Countryside

White residential area

Black residential area

White area can expand into the countryside,

but expansion of the black area encounters white resistance.

Suppose the races are segregated, with blacks in the central core area and whites in the suburbs beyond. Any increase in the white population can be accommodated by an expansion of new housing into the surrounding countryside. But an expansion of black population encounters resistance—in

particular, the reluctance of whites near the boundary to rent or sell to blacks. Moreover, population pressure in the black area may build up as blacks move into the city from depressed rural areas, especially in the South. (This migration is much less now than it was several decades ago.) This pressure raises the price blacks have to pay to the point where whites near the border are finally willing to rent or sell to blacks. Thus, blacks pay more than whites—with the difference in price being the amount that whites require to overcome their reluctance to deal with blacks. (How can a houseowner sell to blacks at a higher price than whites? The answer is that the owner quotes a price above the market value, and accepts a lower bid if it is made by a white, but not if it is made by a black.)

Exceptions to this pattern may occur. Indeed, prices in the white area next to the black core may even temporarily fall if panicky whites try to sell quickly. (In the past, such panic was sometimes induced by real estate agents who engaged in the now illegal practice of "block-busting." This is the practice of selling one or two houses in an all-white block to blacks, and then using high-pressure scare tactics to play on the fear of the remaining whites to stampede them into quick sales "while there is still time." The incentive for real estate agents to engage in this practice was the commission they made from the rapid turnover of homes.)

†This discussion of housing draws on Edwin Mills, *Urban Economics* (Glenview, Ill : Scott Foresman, 1972), pp. 169, 170.

psychological costs in moving. Note that for some people, this incentive may be zero or even negative: Some people who are footloose or adventurous (or who find the new location more attractive) may move even if they have to take a slight cut in pay. Thus, strictly speaking, the "transfer price" *FC* necessary to induce a worker to move may not be exactly the same as the wage in his previous job (*FB*). Indeed, in some cases, a considerable differential may be necessary—for example, to attract construction workers to Alaska. However, this complication does not substantially weaken the main point: The height of the supply curve roughly reflects opportunity cost.

FIGURE 27-8 Why a perfectly competitive labor market is efficient.
(*a*) At the perfectly competitive employment level N_1, there is an efficient number of workers· in this industry—because *S* (the marginal cost of another worker) is just equal to *D* (the marginal benefit of another worker). (*b*) N_2 is inefficient. There are too many workers in this industry—individuals like *f* whose productivity here (the empty bar) is less than his productivity elsewhere (empty bar plus solid bar). An example is the feather-bedding contract discussed in the next chapter. (*c*) N_3 is also inefficient. There are too few workers in this industry. Employment should be increased by hiring workers like *g*, whose productivity here (the empty bar plus the solid bar) exceeds his productivity elsewhere (the empty bar). Examples occur if a union raises the wage rate above the perfectly competitive level or if a single employer (monopsonist) offers a wage below the perfectly competitive level. [The triangular efficiency loss in this panel is a smaller area than the efficiency loss from inadequate employment in Fig. 27-5*d*. The reason: In that earlier diagram we assumed that the labor supply for an industry was completely inelastic; workers could not move from one industry to another. Here, we make no such assumption (the labor response *S* does have some elasticity).]

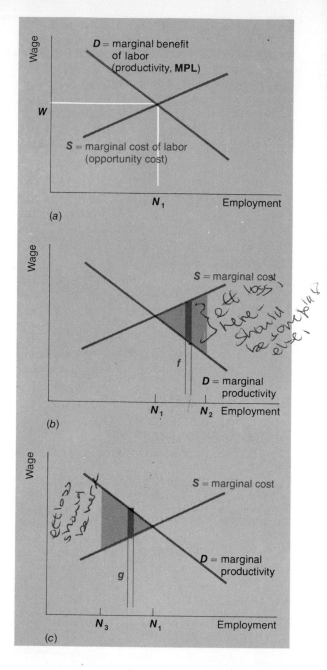

marginal productivity. (Remember, his previous employer would have equated *a*'s marginal productivity and wage rate.) So the height of the bar FC roughly represents the value of the output *a* was producing in his alternative activity—his opportunity cost. Thus, we conclude that:

> The height of an industry's labor supply curve provides a rough measure of the opportunity cost to society when another worker is hired in that industry.

THE "INVISIBLE HAND" IN A PERFECTLY COMPETITIVE LABOR MARKET

Does Adam Smith's "invisible hand" work in factor markets as it did in product markets? Specifically, if a labor market is perfectly competitive and is left alone, will it lead to an efficient result?

Panel *a* of Figure 27-8 illustrates the employment level N_1 and wage *W* in a

perfectly competitive labor market. This is efficient because it satisfies our criterion; the marginal benefit of any activity (in this case, hiring labor) must be equal to its marginal cost. This is confirmed in panels *b* and *c* by showing that any other solution is inefficient. (This analysis can be developed very briefly because it is so similar to our demonstration that a perfectly competitive market *for a good* yields an efficient result, in Figure 20-4.)

On the one hand, suppose that for some reason employment is greater than N_1, say N_2 in panel *b*. Let f represent one of these units of "excess employment." The benefit from employing this worker in this industry is his marginal productivity, as given by the empty bar under the labor demand curve. But the cost of employing him is the value of the output he no longer produces in his alternative activity: This is given by the empty bar plus the solid bar under the supply curve. The difference is the solid bar, which is the efficiency loss to society because he is in this industry rather than a higher-productivity job elsewhere. The total efficiency loss to society for all such excess workers in the range N_1N_2 is the red triangle.

On the other hand, at employment N_3 in panel *c*, there are too few workers in this industry. To confirm, consider one worker *g* who might be employed in this industry, but is not. The cost of employing him here is the value of his output in his alternative activity, shown by the empty bar under the supply curve; but the benefit from employing him is his marginal productivity in this industry, shown by the empty bar plus the solid bar under the demand curve. The difference is the solid bar which represents his greater productivity in this industry than elsewhere; this is the output that is lost because he is not employed here. Finally, the total efficiency loss to society is the red triangle—the sum of all such losses over the range N_3N_1.

In brief, this efficiency loss occurs because workers are not hired in this industry even though they would be more productive here than elsewhere.

To sum up: There is an efficiency loss if employment in this industry is greater or less than the free, perfectly competitive level N_1 in panel *a*. (For futher detail on this point, see Box 27-3.) Thus this analysis confirms the clear analogy between the labor market for an industry, where perfect competition generates efficient employment and wage rate, and a product market (discussed in Chapter 20) where perfect competition generates efficient output and price. But, as before, we can make no claim that perfect competition is "best." It satisfies only one of our important objectives: the *elimination of deadweight inefficiencies*. But it does not address the question: How equitable is the resulting distribution of income between labor and other factors of production? (We return to this very difficult question in Chapter 31.)

While perfectly competitive labor markets are efficient in theory, complications arise in practice. One has already been noted in our discussion of discrimination. Another complication is any external spillover cost or benefit. (An externality raises problems in a labor market just as in a product market. For an example of a spillover in a labor market, see Problem 27-8.) But the most substantial complication of all is that, in practice, labor markets seldom are perfectly competitive. Buyers and sellers of labor often exercise market power. When they do, there is no longer any reason to expect that a free market will lead to an efficient result, as we shall see in the next chapter.

Box 27-3
ADAM SMITH'S "INVISIBLE HAND" IN THE LABOR MARKET

Our analysis of Smith's "invisible hand" in a product market in Figure 20-3 is extended to a factor market in Figure 27-9. If all individual employers and employees make decisions that are in their own self-interest, the result will be in the public interest (at least in the sense that the outcome is efficient). In panel *a*, producers hire labor up to the point where they maximize their profit. In panel *b*, workers pursue their own self-interest by offering their labor services to this industry so long as the wage they receive (*W*) is greater than their reward elsewhere. The result in panel *c* is an efficient one for society, made possible because of the key role played by a competitive market wage rate. It is the employers' reaction to a given market wage in panel *a* and the workers' reaction to that same wage in panel *b* that bring MPL and MC together in panel *c*. So long as no single individual on either side of the market can influence *W*, it is the key link in orchestrating the actions of employers and employees in an efficient way.

FIGURE 27-9 How the pursuit of private benefit in a perfectly competitive labor market results in an efficient outcome for society as a whole. (Compare with Figure 20-3.)

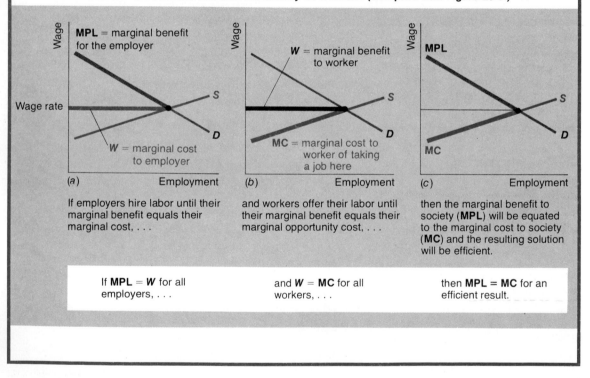

(a) If employers hire labor until their marginal benefit equals their marginal cost, . . .

(b) and workers offer their labor until their marginal benefit equals their marginal opportunity cost, . . .

(c) then the marginal benefit to society (**MPL**) will be equated to the marginal cost to society (**MC**) and the resulting solution will be efficient.

If **MPL** = *W* for all employers, . . .

and *W* = **MC** for all workers, . . .

then **MPL** = **MC** for an efficient result.

598

Key Points

1. Demand for labor reflects the marginal productivity of labor. In a competitive labor market where no individual buyer or seller of labor has any influence over the wage rate, a firm will hire labor until the marginal productivity of labor equals the wage rate.

2. Demand for labor in an industry, say textiles, may shift because of an increase in the price of textiles. Thus, the demand for labor is "derived" from the demand for textiles. Or, labor demand may shift as a result of increased use of capital or because of the discovery of new techniques.

3. If labor markets are competitive, an effective, economywide minimum wage will reduce employment and will therefore result in an efficiency loss. The elasticity of demand for labor will determine whether, on balance, the total income of labor will increase or decrease.

4. If employers in a perfectly competitive labor market discriminate by segregat-ing blacks into low-wage, low-productivity jobs, the wages of whites will rise, while the returns to other factors of production will fall. There will be a loss to society as a whole, because blacks are less productive than they would be in an integrated labor market. (Similar effects follow if any other group is subjected to discrimination.)

5. The supply of labor for an industry reflects the (approximate) opportunity cost of labor, that is, the output workers could have produced in other industries.

6. Adam Smith's "invisible hand" works in a perfectly competitive labor market just as it does in a perfectly competitive product market: If all market participants (employers and employees) pursue their individual economic gain, the result will be an efficient solution for society as a whole. The assumption of perfect competition is essential for this efficient result; neither buyers nor sellers of labor can influence the wage rate (the issue addressed in the next chapter).

Key Concepts

real wage
marginal physical product of labor
marginal productivity of labor (MPL)
why labor demand reflects MPL
derived demand
share of income paid to labor

share of income paid to other factors
minimum wage
labor market discrimination
opportunity cost of labor
why labor supply reflects opportunity cost
labor market efficiency

Problems

27-1 In Figure 27-1 we concluded that, at a $60 wage, this firm hires three workers.

(*a*) What, then, is its total revenue? (Use the background data in Table 27-1.) How much remains after its wages have been paid; that is, how much does the firm have left over to pay interest, rent, and profit to its other factors of production?

(*b*) Geometrically, show (*i*) the firm's total revenue; (*ii*) the part of this revenue that it pays to labor; and (*iii*) the part that is left for other factors of production.

27-2 The firm's MPL curve in Figure

27-1 is drawn on the assumption of a given $10 price for the firm's output. But now suppose that because of decreased consumer demand for this output, its price falls to $7. Show graphically what happens to the firm's MPL curve. Does the firm change its employment? If so, by how much? Is this a further illustration of how "producers dance to the consumers' tune"?

27-3 "If you accept the Galbraithian argument that the demand for goods is contrived by advertising, then the demand for labor to produce these goods is similarly contrived." Explain why you agree or disagree.

27-4 Because of a special commonwealth association, Puerto Rico has many close economic ties with the United States. What do you think of the idea of imposing the United States minimum wage in Puerto Rico? In answering this question, keep this in mind: Because of low labor productivity and a rapidly growing labor supply, Puerto Ricans have historically had a wage rate substantially lower than in the Continental United States.

Would such a common minimum wage result in a more severe unemployment problem in Puerto Rico or the Continental United States? In your view, should the Puerto Ricans have a minimum wage below the U.S. level? What do you think of the idea of setting a minimum wage in Puerto Rico low enough so that it would not cause any unemployment there? If it were set at this level, would it achieve the objective of reducing poverty by raising wages?

27-5 If the government wants to increase labor income by imposing a minimum wage, should elasticity of demand for labor be very high or very low in order to make this policy successful? Why?

27-6 The efficiency loss that occurred in Figure 27-6 can be viewed as the result of the division of the labor market into two segments—black and white—with different productivity levels in each. Explain why a similar efficiency loss is involved, at least to some degree, in the United States labor market because of its geographical divisions. (Because workers find it difficult and costly to move, they often stay in low-wage and low-productivity areas, rather than move into higher-productivity areas.) Is it therefore true that barriers to labor mobility impose a cost on the economy? Do you see now why a policy of increasing labor mobility raises the efficiency of the economy even when it doesn't reduce unemployment—which of course it will also tend to do?

27-7 "The wage rate acts as a screening device that determines where scarce labor will be employed and where it will be not." Following Figure 20-5, illustrate this idea. (Use the example of labor that is hired to build apartment buildings but not hired to hoe field corn.)

27-8 Suppose that the people in a large city judge that there are external benefits involved in hiring musicians for a symphony orchestra. (Musicians are thought to make an important indirect contribution to the cultural life of the community merely by living there—in addition, of course, to the direct contribution they make whenever they play in a concert.) If a symphony orchestra is being organized by a private entrepreneur who requests a subsidy from the city government, what would you recommend?

chapter 28
Wages in Imperfect Labor Markets

Trade unionism is not socialism. It is the capitalism of the proletariat.

George Bernard Shaw

In this chapter we recognize the importance of noncompetitive influences that exist in the labor market. On the one hand, workers in many industries are organized into unions so they can speak with one voice in influencing wage rates and working conditions. Noncompetitive conditions frequently exist on the employers' side of the market as well. An extreme example is a firm that is the principal employer of labor in a small town.

One reason unions are formed is to provide workers with bargaining power, often to offset bargaining power that employers already exercise. When market power exists on both sides of the market, the result is *bilateral (two-way) monopoly*. This is the situation that we wish to study eventually. But, in order to work up to this, we first address two preliminary questions: What happens if there is market power only on the supply side of the labor market? And what happens if there is market power only on the demand side?

First, what happens if workers form a union that becomes the single monopoly seller of labor services?

LABOR UNIONS: The Exercise of Market Power on the Supply Side of the Market

The modern labor union serves its members in many roles. It negotiates for pleasanter, healthier, and safer working conditions, and procedures for dealing with workers' grievances. Thus it adds to the status and dignity of labor. The union also provides its members with some degree of job protection—often in the form of a seniority system. (Those longest on the job are the last to be laid off.) The union may also become a social forum for its members. But one of its central roles is to exercise bargaining power in order to raise the income of its members. It does so either directly by negotiating higher wages, or indirectly by negotiating such fringe benefits as pensions, health insurance, or paid vacations. (We use the term

601

"wages" to include all such benefits.) Moreover, some union policies designed to open jobs for younger members (such as reducing the workweek or introducing compulsory retirement) may also indirectly raise wages by restricting the labor supply.

Craft versus Industrial Unions

There are two kinds of unions in the United States.

1. *Industrial unions*, such as the United Auto Workers, draw their membership from a specific industry.

2. *Craft unions*, such as the plumbers' or carpenters' unions, draw their members from *any* industry, provided the workers have a common skill.

Both types of unions engage in collective bargaining over wage rates.

> *Collective bargaining* is any negotiation between a union and management over wages, fringe benefits, hiring policies, job security, or working conditions.

In addition, craft unions may attempt to influence wages indirectly by restricting the supply of labor. This approach involves two steps: (1) negotiating with employers to hire only union members; and then (2) limiting union membership either by direct restrictions or by imposing such barriers to entry as high initiation fees or long periods of apprenticeship.

(Can you now see why the charge is sometimes made that the American Medical Association (AMA) has acted like a craft union? To become a doctor requires a medical degree, and, during the first half of this century, many of the existing medical schools were closed down because they were decertified by the AMA. The stated motive of AMA's tough certification requirements was to improve the quality of medical service. But, without passing judgment on this score, consider how this difficult certification affected the supply of doctors, and therefore their incomes.[1]

Before examining the detailed economic effects of unions, we first briefly review the long struggle to establish unions in the United States.

A Brief History of American Unions

You must offer the American working man bread and butter in the here and now, instead of pie in the sky in the sweet by and by. Charles Killingworth, describing Samuel Gompers' philosophy

The beginning of the American union movement dates back to an era in which a relatively powerless labor force lived in poverty, or near to it. In the last third of the nineteenth century, the Knights of Labor emerged, basing its appeal on becoming the one great organization that might speak for all labor. Like the labor movement in England and a number of other European countries, the organization sought to make labor a unified force for bringing about radical political change.

But American workers have never been sympathetic to such a political objective. Accordingly, the Knights disappeared, to be replaced in the 1880s by the American Federation of Labor (AFL), led by Samuel Gompers and devoted to the bread-and-butter issues of improving wages and working conditions, rather than to pursuing a political class struggle.[2] And this remains an important characteristic today. American labor does not always vote along party lines. While it frequently votes Democratic, it also on occasion supports the Republicans. Thus

---

[1]During the past 15 years, the AMA has reduced its opposition to rapid increases in the supply of doctors. Indeed, there is reason to expect that a surplus of doctors may develop in the coming decades.

[2]When asked what labor wanted, Gompers had a simple answer: "More."

FIGURE 28-1 Major trends in United States union membership (relative to total employment).
American union membership remained low until the mid thirties, then rose rapidly until the end of World War II. Since then, union membership has grown less rapidly than the labor force.

SOURCE: U.S. Department of Labor, Handbook of Labor Statistics.

American labor has not followed the common pattern (in England and some other European countries) of formal, close association with one political party.

Since these beginnings, the history of the American union movement can be broken up into the three periods sketched in Figure 28-1: (1) an initial low-membership period until about 1935; (2) rapid growth for the next decade, until roughly the end of World War II; and (3) the period since.

The Period before the Great Depression Until the mid-1930s, unions developed in a hostile climate. On the one hand, business executives strongly resisted any attempts to unionize their firms, and would frequently retaliate against pro-union workers by firing them and then blacklisting them with other potential employers. They would also sometimes use so-called *yellow-dog contracts*, in which a worker had to sign a commitment not to join a union in order to get a job.

An important question was how the courts would treat labor-management disputes. In particular, in light of the Sherman and Clayton antitrust acts, would they view unions as restraints on trade? Judgments either for or against unions seemed possible: On the one hand, a union could be viewed as a restraint on trade, since it is a combination of workers seeking to raise wages, just as a collusive oligopoly is a combination of sellers seeking to raise price. On the other hand, the Clayton Act seemed to exclude unions by stating that "labor is not an article of commerce." By and large, the courts' judgments during this early period did not favor labor.

For several reasons, union growth was thwarted during the 1920s and early 1930s as employer resistance to unionization increased. Employers introduced paternalistic schemes providing labor with generous benefits in an attempt to show workers that they would do better outside a union than in. Moreover, the AFL lost some ground because it remained firmly committed to the idea of craft unionism on which it was founded. Therefore, it did not adequately appeal to the increasing number of unskilled workers in mass-production industries, such as steel and autos.

The Period of Rapid Growth before and during the Second World War

In the depths of the Depression in the 1930s, several pro-labor acts were passed, culminating in the 1935 Wagner Act (National Labor Relations Act). This act had three important provisions:

1. It made it clear that workers had the legal right to form unions.

2. It prohibited employers from a number of unfair labor practices, such as firing or blacklisting pro-union workers.

3. It established the National Labor Relations Board (NLRB) to control unfair labor practices by employers and to resolve disputes among unions. For example, the NLRB is empowered to hold elections in which workers decide which of two or more competing unions will represent them.

There is no question that the Wagner Act achieved its objective of removing the barriers to union growth: During the decade that followed, the proportion of the labor force that belonged to unions almost tripled. There was a second important reason for this growth. In 1936, several union leaders, led by John L. Lewis, split away from the AFL because of its concentration on craft unions. They formed the Congress of Industrial Organizations (CIO), a collection of *industrial* unions. Between 1936 and 1945, the CIO had great success in unionizing such mass-production industries as autos and steel.

The Postwar Period

Since World War II, unions have ceased to grow at the rapid rate of the preceding period. In fact, although their membership has increased moderately, it has not grown as rapidly as the labor force, so that the percentage of workers in unions has actually declined. There are several reasons for this.

First, heavy industry (where union membership tends to be most solidly concentrated) has had declining employment relative to other sectors of the economy. There also has been a shift in industrial jobs to the South, where unionism is weaker than in the North. In addition, attitudes toward unions have undergone change. Postwar unemployment rates have been much lower than during the 1930s, and this decline has weakened the commitment to unions. (During the Depression, workers felt desperately powerless and looked to unions for protection.) And unions may have overplayed their hand during the Second World War. During the early war years, unions had added muscle in the form of a rapidly increasing membership. By 1944 they were flexing that muscle in a series of strikes that many of the public viewed as damaging to the war effort. The feeling that unions were becoming too powerful contributed to the passage of the Taft-Hartley Act in 1947, in the face of stiff union opposition.

The Taft-Hartley Act

Just as the Wagner Act 12 years earlier had dealt with "unfair" employer practices, the Taft-Hartley Act now attempted to outlaw "unfair" union practices. For example, it prohibited closed shops in industries engaged in interstate commerce. (Only union members can be hired in a closed shop; thus a closed shop provides a union with veto power over who can be hired.) The Taft-Hartley Act also prohibited jurisdictional strikes (conflicts between unions over whose members will do specific jobs). It also forbade the "checkoff" of union dues unless workers agree to it in writing. (With a checkoff, employers collect dues for the union by deducting them from workers' paychecks.) In addition, the Taft-Hartley Act included provisions to increase the financial responsibility of union leaders. For example, it required pension funds to be kept separate from other union funds, and required union leaders to provide both their own membership and the National Labor Relations Board with detailed information on how union funds are spent. The act also contained a provision to delay strikes which "imperil the national health or safety." Specifically, the president was empowered to seek a court *injunction* in such circumstances to require strikers to return to work for an 80-day "cooling-off" period.

But the most controversial provision of the Taft-Hartley Act was contained in its famous section 14(b). This recognized the right of states to prohibit contracts which require workers to join unions. Some 20 states (mostly in the South) have done so, passing right-to-work laws which forbid compulsory unionism (and thus make the closed shop and the union shop illegal.) Union leaders consider section 14(b) to be overtly anti-union, and they have worked hard for its repeal. Indeed, opposition to 14(b) is considered an acid test of whether a politician is pro-union or not. (Candidate Jimmy Carter straddled this issue in his 1976 presidential campaign. He committed himself to sign a repeal of 14(b) if Congress passed such a repeal. But he made no positive commitment to push such a repeal through Congress.)

A *closed shop* means that a firm can hire only workers who are already union members.

A *union shop* permits the hiring of non-union members, but requires workers who are not yet members to join the union within a specified period (such as 30 days).

A *right-to-work law* makes compulsory union membership illegal. It thus outlaws the closed shop and the union shop in favor of the *open shop* (in which a firm can hire workers without requiring them to join a union).

The Landrum-Griffin Act This act was passed in 1959 by a Congress that was concerned over union corruption and wished to increase the restraints on union leaders. Among other stipulations, union officials were prohibited from borrowing more than $2,000 of union funds; the embezzlement of union funds became a federal offense; and restrictions were placed on ex-convicts seeking union offices. This act also sought to make union decisions more democratic by strengthening the power of members to challenge their leaders through the ballot box: It required regularly scheduled elections of union officers by secret ballot, with every member being eligible to vote. Moreover, a member's right to participate in any union meeting was guaranteed, and any member was given the right to sue a union that tried to withhold any of these privileges. While it is difficult to judge how effective this legislation has been in limiting union corruption, one conclusion can be reached: It has still not completely solved the problem. (For recent evidence of union corruption—and violence—see Box 28-1.)

By the mid-1950s, the success of the CIO in unionizing workers on the basis of industry rather than craft had led the AFL to move at least some distance in this direction. Accordingly, by 1955 it was possible for the two to resolve their differences and rejoin forces in the new AFL-CIO. Most unions today are members of this giant umbrella organization, with the major exceptions being the United Auto Workers (who left the AFL-CIO in 1968), the Teamsters and the United Mine Workers.

The Economic Effects When a Union Negotiates Higher Wages: A First Approximation

Since unions bargain over wages (and working conditions) for their members, they must be included in any realistic analysis of the labor market. In this section we consider the effects of a union that exercises its market power to raise the wage rate. We begin by assuming that employers have no market power on the other side of the market. In other words, employers take the wage rate as given. But we emphasize that because of this assumption, our conclusions will represent only a first approximation. As we shall see, these conclusions will change substantially if employers can also influence the wage rate.

Suppose that, with no union, equilibrium in a perfectly competitive labor market for an industry is at point E_1 in Figure 28-2. Now assume that this industry is unionized, that is, that the workers who supply labor form a monopoly (a union) that speaks for them with one voice. Moreover, suppose that the union raises the wage rate from W_1 to W_2. (The enforcement of this wage requires "union discipline." Members must not be allowed to offer their labor services for less than W_2.) Faced with wage W_2, employers react by reducing employment from N_1 to N_2 (with the displaced workers having to find jobs in other industries). Thus, because the union has raised wages, the market equilibrium in this industry has

moved from the perfectly competitive equilibrium E_1 to E_2.

Now consider the transfer and efficiency effects of this policy. The transfer is shown by the white arrow to the left of this diagram. Because of the increased wage, workers who still have jobs in this industry benefit, while other factors of production lose. At the same time, there is an efficiency loss shown by the red triangle (as detailed in Figure 28-2's caption.) This loss occurs because employment has been reduced below its perfectly competitive, efficient level at N_1, and displaced workers have had to move to industries where their productivity is lower.

But again, notice that, in arriving at any conclusion like this on efficiency in Part 5, we must make assumptions similar to those we made in the chapters of Part 4. For example, we assume that perfectly competitive conditions exist elsewhere in the economy. And we also keep in mind that, although we can make the statement that the move from E_1 to E_2 is inefficient, we cannot make the stronger statement that this move "is damaging overall to the economy" without making some assumption about how the winners and the losers compare in their evaluation of income. Remember: As always, efficiency is desirable; but it's not the whole story.

Finally, note that the similarity of labor and goods markets, first noted in the previous chapter, continues to hold. In particular, Figure 28-2 shows that the monopolization of a labor market is similar to the monopolization of a product market in Figure 21-6a, except, of course, that now we are talking about wage and employment of labor rather than the price and quantity of a product.[3]

---

*[3]However, there is an important reason why we cannot analyze monopoly in a labor market in exactly the same way as we analyze monopoly in a product market. In a product market, a monopoly firm will take into account any loss of sales and reduction in output that result from its high price. But in a labor market, it is not clear how fully a union will take into account any reduced employment that results from its high wage. This may be particularly true if the industry is growing and if the high wage does not displace any of the *current* union members, but instead reduces only the number of *new* workers coming into the industry. This difficulty prevents us from determining the level of W_2 by applying the standard analysis of monopoly in Chapter 21, where MC is equated to MR. (The union may not care much about the MC and MR of additional new workers.) Therefore we cannot be specific about how much a union will try to raise the wage rate.

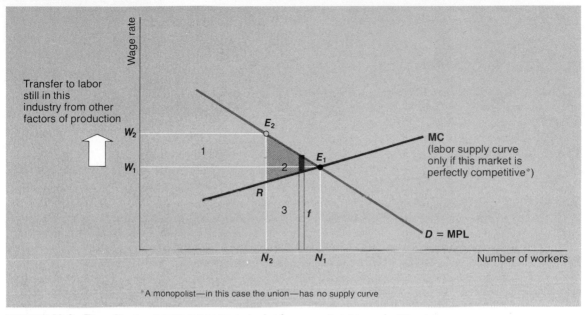

Transfer to labor
still in this
industry from other
factors of production

*A monopolist—in this case the union—has no supply curve

**FIGURE 28-2   The effects of unionizing an industry in a previously competitive labor
market.**

When a union is formed, equilibrium shifts from the perfectly competitive point E_1 to E_2.
(The union raises the wage rate to W_2, and employers respond by reducing employment to
N_2.) As a result, there is a transfer from other factors of production to the workers who still
have jobs in this industry. This transfer is shown by the white arrow. (Specifically, it is
area 1).

There is an efficiency loss shown by triangle 2. This efficiency loss is explained by
following the analysis outlined in Figure 27-8c. Consider one of the workers in the range
between N_1 and N_2 who has been laid off—say worker f. His productivity in this industry
was the height of the demand curve; that is, the empty bar plus the solid bar. But his
productivity in an alternative industry—his opportunity cost—is given by the height of the
MC curve; that is, by the empty bar. So when he loses his job in this industry and must take
a job elsewhere, the lost productivity is the solid bar. And the lost productivity from all
such workers in the range $N_1 N_2$ who must shift to lower productivity jobs is triangle 2.

[Why is the efficiency loss only area 2, in contrast to the efficiency loss of areas 2 *plus*
3 from a minimum wage (Figure 27-5)? After all, both policies—a minimum wage and a
union—raise wages and therefore reduce employment in a competitive industry. The
answer is that workers who lose their jobs in the unionized industry shown here can get
lower-paying jobs elsewhere. Therefore their lost productivity in this industry (2 + 3) is
partially offset by their productivity in another job (3). However, with the minimum wage in
Figure 27-5, their lost productivity 2 + 3 is not offset by any productivity gain elsewhere.
(With an economy-wide minimum wage, workers who lose their jobs cannot find
lower-paying jobs elsewhere; they remain unemployed, and produce nothing.)]

Featherbedding: The Economic Effects

**Any idiot can decide whether to hire one
or two boys to wash his car. But the
head of Britain's largest car company
can't decide whether 1,000 or 2,000
workers should be employed on an assembly line.**   Overheard in an English pub

A union seeks not only to raise the
wages of its members. It may strive also to
protect their jobs. This second objective may
become very important, particularly if employment is shrinking. (For example, consumer demand for the product may be falling off, or laborsaving machines may have
been introduced into the industry.)

BOX 28-1

THE PROBLEM OF UNION CORRUPTION AND VIOLENCE

The Rise and Fall of Jimmy Hoffa

1957 President of International Brotherhood of Teamsters

1964 Convicted of fraud, misuse of union funds, and jury tampering

1967 Jailed

1971 Released

1976 Disappeared

Violence dates back a long way in American labor history, to the early days of unions when employers hired "goon strikebreakers" and workers replied with violence of their own. Today, most American union leaders are involved neither in violence nor in financial corruption. But instances of these activities still do occur frequently enough to remain a major problem and a blot on the union movement. For example, in the late 1960s, Joseph Yablonski challenged W. A. (Tony) Boyle for the leadership of the United Mine Workers. After losing the election, Yablonski threatened to expose irregularities within the union. On December 31, 1969, an intruder murdered him, his wife, and his daughter in their sleep. In 1974, Boyle was convicted of arranging this murder, and was sentenced to three life terms in jail. (In a retrial in 1977 and 1978, he was convicted again.)

But there is no better illustration of violence and corruption than the life of Jimmy Hoffa, a man entangled in both. In the early 1960s, as president of the International Brotherhood of Teamsters, he was one of America's most powerful labor leaders. Less than 15 years later, he was gone—without even a decent funeral.

In 1957, Hoffa became president of the Teamsters when his predecessor (David Beck) was sent to prison for larceny, embezzlement, and income tax evasion. One of John Kennedy's campaign promises in 1960 was that he would prosecute Hoffa for corruption. In 1964, as a result of investigations initiated by Attorney General Robert F. Kennedy, Hoffa was convicted on various counts of jury tampering, fraud, and misuse of union funds. Following unsuccessful appeals, he began jail terms of 8 and 5 years in 1967. After his parole had twice been denied, his sentence was commuted by President Nixon in 1971.

In 1975, while engaged in an effort to regain his position in the union, Jimmy Hoffa disappeared without a trace.

There are two principal ways that a union may approach the problem of shrinking employment. One is to negotiate a reduction in the number of hours in a standard workweek; if all workers work fewer hours, no worker need be fired. (Moreover, if the union is able at the same time to negotiate a sufficient increase in the per hour wage rate, its members need suffer no income reduction. In this case, they would be working less for the same pay.)

The second way that a strong union may deal with falling employment is to use its bargaining strength (by striking, if necessary) to force employers into a featherbedding agreement. One example is the agreement that standby musicians be hired when nonunion musicians are performing. Another example occurs when advertisers provide newspapers with type that is already completely set. The newspapers may still have to hire union members to set this type again. This "bogus type" is never used.

> *Featherbedding* is the employment of labor in superfluous jobs.[4]

But perhaps the most famous example of all was the job of railroad fireman. In the old days of steam locomotives, he would shovel coal to keep the fire burning. Yet his job remained guaranteed by a union contract even after the introduction of the diesel engine, which had no fire. Although the railroad companies tried to eliminate this unnecessary job as early as 1959, they did not succeed until 1972. Then, in 1977, the railroad companies attempted also to eliminate the job of rear brakeman, a task that they similarly viewed as unnecessary. But this raised a complicated safety issue,

since a rear brakeman rides the caboose, watches out for shifting loads on the cars, and flags a warning when the train has to come to a sudden stop. Clearly, this example raises a difficult question: Is this really an issue of featherbedding, or of safety?

But some examples, such as "bogus type," are featherbedding pure and simple. What is the effect of such superfluous work? The answer is that it generally keeps employment in that industry higher than the perfectly competitive, free-market level.[5] Specifically, it keeps employment at N_2 in Figure 27-8b on p. 596, rather than allowing it to fall to the competitive level N_1. And it leads to an efficiency loss which is at least as great (and often greater) than the red triangle shown in that earlier diagram. (That triangular efficiency loss was based on the assumption that employers hire more workers, but still use them as productively as possible. However, many featherbedding contracts require employers not only to hire more workers, but also to assign them to low- or zero-productivity tasks, such as the setting of "bogus type." This makes the efficiency loss even greater.)

Is this judgment on featherbedding too severe? After all, without it workers would face the serious dislocation involved in switching jobs. Moreover, some older workers may be unable to find employment elsewhere. Isn't featherbedding a way of introducing compassion into the economic system? In some circumstances the answer is yes, but it is a bad way to do it. Far better to ease labor's shift into other jobs than to have society carry an overhead of unproductive employment into the future. (A common way of negotiating the end to a featherbedding clause is for the company to guarantee that all the specific individuals now holding

---

[4]Featherbedding as defined by the Taft-Hartley Act (payment for work not actually performed) is illegal. Here we are concerned with a broader definition that includes cases where workers are on the job, but the work is contrived. (That is, the job would not exist were it not guaranteed by the union-management contract.)

[5]This is not always the case, however. The "bogus type" requirement contributed to the death of newspapers in a declining industry. It therefore may have resulted in fewer newspaper jobs (even though it may have kept up the number of typesetting jobs).

jobs will continue to be employed. They are in effect given "tenure" within the firm, and guaranteed that their wages will not be cut. They may be shifted to other, more productive jobs, thus reducing the efficiency loss. They may even be kept in their old featherbedded jobs. But the important point is that the firm does not have to hire replacements when these current workers retire. In this case, the efficiency loss from featherbedding is gradually eliminated as workers retire and are not replaced. More on the relation between efficiency and compassion is provided in Box 28-2.)

Why Our Judgment on Unions So Far Has Been Too Harsh

So far the unions have not fared well in this discussion. In fact, the discussion to this point could be viewed as the case against unions, and an overstated one at that. True, on the issue of guaranteeing employ-

---

BOX 28-2
THE CONFLICTING OBJECTIVES OF COMPASSION AND EFFICIENCY

Two centuries ago, at the beginning of the industrial revolution in Britain, laborsaving machinery was introduced into the textile industry. Displaced workers in those days had much bleaker prospects than today: It was far less clear that other jobs could be found; and without a job, families faced severe malnutrition or even worse. Consequently, there were riots in which workers (the Luddites) broke into the factories, destroying the new laborsaving machines. While sympathizing with their plight, we must ask ourselves: Suppose they had succeeded? Suppose laborsaving machinery had been banned, and their primitive handcrafting jobs guaranteed? If they and their heirs had been completely successful in thwarting technological change, wouldn't our situation today be very much like theirs two centuries ago? And if so, what progress would we have made against the problem that concerned them most: poverty?

Although laborsaving machinery may create transitional unemployment, it creates far better jobs in the long run. When bulldozers are introduced, whole armies of workers with shovels lose their jobs. But in the long run, this is highly beneficial both to society *and to most of the workers who initially lose their jobs*. Displaced ditchdiggers get jobs in new, growing industries (automobiles, electronics, etc.). These jobs exist because the introduction of bulldozers and other machines increases our ability to produce, and therefore raises our income and purchasing power. Even the former ditchdiggers who end up driving the bulldozers benefit, since they earn a far higher wage rate. (True, they have to learn a skill, but this effort pays off handsomely.)

In short, society benefits because the labor force is engaged in more productive activities than ditchdigging. Because machines now perform menial jobs, we produce more. This example illustrates why we should not automatically choose compassion over efficiency, but instead, should search for policies that combine both. Historically, economic progress—our increased level of efficiency—is the reason that we now have the income to be able to afford more compassion than we could have two hundred years ago. It is the reason why we are now wealthy enough to ensure people against the extremes of poverty that had to be faced in earlier, less productive eras. The point is a simple one: We should exercise compassion, but not in a way (like featherbedding) that thwarts progress because it locks in inefficiency.

ment (featherbedding), our criticism will still stand. But on the union role of raising wages, we shall now discover that we may have been too critical. The reason is that in analyzing imperfect labor markets one step at a time, we have so far looked only at what happens when market power exists on the *supply* side of the market. Now we shift the spotlight and ask: What happens when market power exists on the *demand* side of the market? The answer is no surprise: This also introduces inefficiency. Indeed, we shall discover that when employers exercise market power on the demand side of the market, the unionization of workers on the supply side may be a desirable offsetting influence.

MONOPSONY: Market Power on the Demand Side of the Labor Market

Employers typically quote the wage rate at which they will hire. In doing so, they frequently do not act like perfect competitors who take a market wage as given, but instead act like a monopsonist (a single buyer) who can use market power to keep the wage rate down. While monopsony power is often exercised in complicated ways (see Box 28-3), we begin by looking at the problem in its simplest form.

We initially assume exactly the same perfectly competitive market that we began with in Figure 28-2, with equilibrium at E_1 reproduced in Figure 28-3. But this time, instead of introducing monopoly on the supply side (a union), we introduce monopsony (a single buyer) on the demand side. What happens if employers band together to lower the wage rate (while workers on the other side of the market act as perfect competitors, taking this wage rate as given)? Specifically, suppose that employers quote a wage W_2 below the perfectly competitive wage W_1. In response, some workers leave this now unat-

FIGURE 28-3 Effects when a perfectly competitive labor market is monopsonized.
When a monopsony is formed, equilibrium shifts from the perfectly competitive point E_1 to E_2. (Because the monopsonist quotes lower wage W_2, fewer workers offer their labor services—and employment falls from N_1 to N_2.) As a result there is the efficiency loss shown by the red triangle, as some workers shift into lower-productivity jobs in other industries. Finally, the lower wage results in a transfer from labor to other factors of production, as indicated by the white arrow on the left.

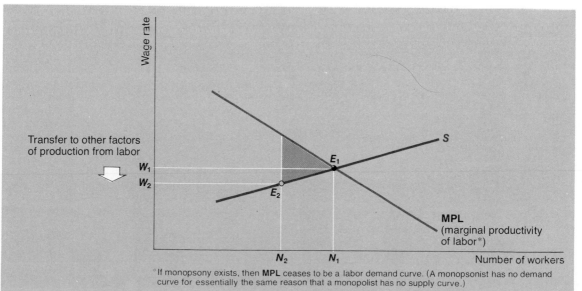

*If monopsony exists, then **MPL** ceases to be a labor demand curve. (A monopsonist has no demand curve for essentially the same reason that a monopolist has no supply curve.)

tractive industry for other jobs; in other words, they move down their supply curve from E_1 to a new equilibrium at E_2.

The transfer effect is shown as the white arrow to the left of this diagram. Workers are paid a lower wage, and other factors of production benefit as a consequence.[6]

At the same time, there is the red triangular efficiency loss, because employment has been reduced below its perfectly competitive efficient level at N_1; this is the same effect first detailed in Figure 27-8c. Specifically, this efficiency loss follows because workers between N_1 and N_2 who leave this industry go to less productive jobs elsewhere.

How does monopsony in the labor market arise? There are several possible answers: There may be just one firm hiring labor in a small town. Or, employers may band together to form a bargaining association to depress wages and thus increase their own income. Here we see another example of Adam Smith's "invisible hand" gone astray: The monopsonist's pursuit of private benefit does *not* lead to public benefit. Quite the contrary: It leads to the efficiency loss shown by the red triangle in this diagram.

In reality, there are few cases in which monopsony occurs in its pure form (only one buyer). There is more likely to be a small group of employers, that is, an oligopsony (few buyers). Each quotes a wage rate and exerts some influence over it. This may be a strong or a weak influence. On the one hand, competition with other employers in the labor market may keep the wage close to the competitive level W_1. But if the few oligop-

[6]Note to instructors: Figure 28-3 (and others in this chapter) may be supplemented with a multipanel analysis (similar to Figure 27-5) that shows how each group in the economy is affected. Details are given in the *Instructor's Manual.*

FIGURE 28-4 How monopsony (the reserve clause) depressed baseball salaries. (Figures in $000s, rounded.)
SOURCE: Sports Illustrated; Associated Press, December 9, 1976.

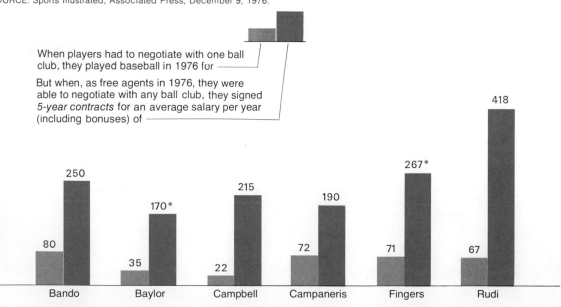

When players had to negotiate with one ball club, they played baseball in 1976 for ⎯

But when, as free agents in 1976, they were able to negotiate with any ball club, they signed *5-year contracts* for an average salary per year (including bonuses) of ⎯

Bando 80 / 250
Baylor 35 / 170*
Campbell 22 / 215
Campaneris 72 / 190
Fingers 71 / 267*
Rudi 67 / 418

*Annual average over a *six* year contract

sonists collude (either overtly or by such covert means as "wage leadership"), the wage may be depressed well below W_1—at or near the level W_2 that a monopsonist would choose.

Although monopsony in its pure form (only one buyer) is rare, there has been one notable example: the monopsony power that the owners of baseball clubs used to have in buying the services of their players.

Monopsony and Baseball Salaries

I don't understand why grown men play this game anyhow. They ought to be lawyers or doctors or garbage men. Games should be left for kids. Ted Turner, Atlanta Braves owner

One reason grown men play baseball is because of the high income it offers, especially since the monopsony power of club owners like Ted Turner was broken in 1976. Before this, the "reserve clause" had made each club owner a monopsonist, since a player could not sign a contract with anyone else. But, beginning in 1976, a play-er in certain circumstances could become a free agent and negotiate with other clubs. Figure 28-4 shows what happened. A comparison of the before-and-after salaries of these players indicates the remarkable way that the monopsony power of the reserve clause had depressed players' salaries.[7]

(Certainly the reserve clause was bad for the players. But was it bad for the game? Baseball club owners argue that, without the reserve clause, teams in large cities like New York will be able to use their larger gate receipts to "buy a world series" by bidding away all the superstars from smaller cities like Cincinnati. Games will become lop-sided. Thus, competition among clubs for players will destroy competition between teams on the playing field and ruin the game. And the owners point to the World Series of 1977 and 1978 as omens of things to come. Both were indeed won by the New York Yankees, rich in superstars signed from other clubs; one of these, Reggie Jackson, hit three home runs in the final 1977 Series game. The owners also contend that the salaries that result are unfair, since the su-

---

[7]In a bizarre sidelight, Charles Finley, the owner of the Oakland Athletics, sold three of his best players to other clubs for a total of $3\frac{1}{2}$ million just before they were to become free agents. But the baseball commissioner declared this a no-sale, so that when the players did eventually become free agents and signed contracts with other clubs, Finley lost them without receiving a dime in return. He subsequently lodged a suit against the baseball commissioner for the $3\frac{1}{2}$ million he had lost.

BOX 28-3
MONOPSONY AND DISCRIMINATION IN THE LABOR MARKET

Monopsonists who are using their market power to depress the wage rate of their entire labor force may go one step further and reduce even more the wage paid to a specific subset of their workers (for example, blacks). To illustrate, consider the monopsonistic firm that has used its market power to depress the wage rate in Figure 28-3 from the perfectly competitive level W_1 to W_2. It may then go one step further and increase its profit even more by offering blacks an even lower wage. (This case is unlike the perfectly competitive example of discrimination in Figure 27-6 in one important respect: Here discrimination *is* in the interest of the employer who practices it.)

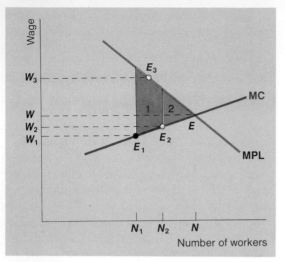

FIGURE 28-5   How inefficiency may be reduced if a union raises wages in a monopsonized labor market.
Suppose that before the union, the monopsonist had set the wage rate at W_1, below the perfectly competitive level W. With equilibrium at E_1, there was an efficiency loss of $1 + 2$. When the union raises the wage to W_2, equilibrium moves from E_1 to E_2, some employment is restored, and the efficiency loss from monopsony is reduced to area 2. In other words, this increased wage improves efficiency by area 1. And because it raises the wage rate, it also transfers income from the monopsonist to labor. However, the union may try to push the wage up past the competitive wage W, for example to W_3. Insofar as it succeeds, equilibrium will be shifted away from E toward E_3, and efficiency will be reduced once again.

The actual wage is likely to lie somewhere in the range between W_1 and W_3, the rates that each party would like to set if it had unlimited power to do so. (But these may not be the wage rates that the parties actually quote to *begin* negotiations. For example, the company may initially quote a wage below W_1 as a bargaining ploy—to allow it apparently to "compromise" later when it accepts what it really wants—a wage near W_1. Of course, labor may do the same, quoting an initial wage above W_3. Consequently, in the early stages of any negotiation, there may be an exceedingly large gap between the bargaining position of the two parties—and the public may get the erroneous impression that there is little hope for a settlement.)

perstar who can draw the crowds is paid far too much relative to the first-class player who is also very valuable to his team. Do you think the owners are primarily promoting their own interest, or do they have a point?)

The Effects of Unions Reconsidered

We are now in a position to show why our criticism of unions, which held if markets were initially competitive, is no longer necessarily justified if markets have monopsonistic elements.

Figure 28-5 shows that a union that raises wages may actually raise, rather than lower, the level of overall efficiency in the economy. This will occur, for example, if there is initially a monopsonist who has already lowered the wage rate from the competitive level W to W_1. At this lower wage, fewer workers have been offering their labor services to this industry. Therefore, this monopsony has lowered employment in this industry from N to N_1 (shifted equilibrium from E to E_1) with a consequent efficiency loss of areas $1 + 2$. If a union is now formed and raises the wage rate from W_1 to W_2 (shifting equilibrium from E_1 to E_2), the efficiency loss is reduced from areas $1 + 2$ to just area 2. In other words, there is an efficiency gain of area 1. (Of course, formation of this union has also benefited union members by recapturing some of the income they had been previously losing to the monopsonist.)

This analysis suggests that the following case can be made for unions:

In labor markets dominated by monopsonistic elements, with employers quoting wage rates, it is in the workers' interest to form a union so they can bargain collectively with one voice. Then the wage rate can no longer be quoted by employers making a take-it-or-leave-it offer like W_1. Now workers have a representative sitting at the bargaining table who can counter with the same sort of take-it-or-leave-it offer to management, as follows: "If you do not accept our wage claim, then we will strike your firm, withdrawing all workers from the job and closing down your operations." Thus the union allows workers to speak from the same sort of position of strength that employers often enjoy, and the actual wage will be one that is negotiated between union and management. Only in this way can labor exercise what Galbraith calls _countervailing power_ to prevent the wage from being depressed to a level like W_1 in Figure 28-5. And if labor thus raises its wage from W_1 to W_2, this will be not only in its own interest; in addition, from the overall social point of view, this higher wage will increase efficiency by area 1.[8] Moreover, union practices like picketing are simply a means of increasing the union's countervailing position of strength by ensuring that the union is effectively speaking for all labor, and that the employer cannot hire substitute labor. In other words, such measures make the workers' take-it-or-leave-it threat as credible as management's."[9]

A Complication

Such is the case for unions. But it cannot be used to justify all exercise of market power. If a union gets very strong and pushes the wage up beyond W toward W_3, equilibrium will shift away from E toward E_3 and efficiency will once again be reduced.

Thus, the typical policy problem in the labor market is not that one side has market power and the other does not, but rather, that the relative power of the two may be highly imbalanced. If the government is pursuing the objective of making labor markets more efficient, it should take care when reducing the bargaining power of only _one_ group and not the other. In this case, it must keep a sharp watch on the exercise of bargaining power on the other side of the market as well, to ensure that the problem of imbalance is not being made worse.

This discussion also allows us to sharp-

en up our earlier conclusion about a minimum wage. If a minimum wage raises the wage rate in Figure 28-5 from an existing very low level like W_1 toward the competitive level W, employment and efficiency in this labor market will be increased, rather than decreased. On the other hand, if it is set at a higher level and therefore raises the wage rate _away from_ W and toward W_3, employment and efficiency will be reduced. Therefore, a useful guideline for a minimum wage is to set it near the competitive wage level in most industries. (This guideline is difficult to put into practice because competitive wage rates are difficult to estimate, and they differ among industries.)

BILATERAL MONOPOLY: Relative Bargaining Power

When power exists on both sides of the market (as in Figure 28-5), the two participants will be pushing in opposite directions. While the employer is trying to keep the wage rate down to W_1 or W_2, the union is trying to push it up to a point like W_3. The outcome will depend on the bargaining power of the two sides; we cannot tell by looking at the MC and MPL curves precisely where the final solution will be.

Which Side Has the Stronger Bargaining Position?

To see the importance of bargaining power, suppose that there is only one company in a mining town and that it is facing an ineffective union that represents only a minority of the workers. In this case, the company will be in by far the stronger

---

[8]This is another example of the theory of the second best, first encountered in Box 21-1. Strictly from the point of view of _efficiency_, economists agree that the best solution is for all buyers and sellers in all markets to have no influence over price, that is, to be price takers in perfectly competitive markets. But suppose there is only a single employer in a small town, who will inevitably be able to exercise some monopsony influence over the wage rate. The "first best" solution (perfect competition on both sides of the market) is simply not possible, no matter how desirable it might be. Instead, we must look for a second best solution. This may involve workers forming a union in order to influence price and thus counterbalance the power that the monopsonist already enjoys on the other side of the market.

[9]Although labor and management are in conflict over the wage-rate issue discussed here, there are many other issues on which their interests coincide. For example, both the steelworkers' union and the steel companies oppose the importation of cheap foreign steel.

bargaining position, and is likely to be successful in imposing a wage near W_1. On the other hand, if there is one union facing several employers, the union may have the stronger monopoly position, and it may succeed in negotiating a wage near W_3. It is sometimes suggested that this is the situation in the auto industry (although Ford and GM can scarcely be considered weak bargaining adversaries).

If the United Auto Workers (UAW) judges that its negotiations with the industry are not proceeding in a satisfactory way, it typically threatens to pull its workers out on strike in one of the auto companies, say Ford. If it does so, Ford workers on strike will get income support from a union strike fund drawn from workers from all the auto companies. But the company being struck (Ford) does not get the same sort of support from the other companies in the industry.[10] True, Ford may get moral support from the other firms, but they still go on selling cars and cutting into Ford's market. And therein lies Ford's problem. If it is shut down by a strike and unable to produce cars, it will find that its share of the market is being eroded and that its profits are falling. In fact, a strong union may have the power to drive a company bankrupt—and sometimes this does happen, although not by design.

(Workers rightly regard driving a firm out of business as "overkill," since this would destroy their jobs. Consequently, a union will not pick as its target one of the financially weak companies in an industry; American Motors is not a prime target of the UAW. If a firm is already close to bankruptcy, a strike threat may be very ineffective. It may be met only by the resigned observation: "We can't add to our present offer. If we have to pay higher wages, we will go out of business; and if you strike, that will also drive us out of business. There is simply nothing more we can do." And if the firm is not bluffing, the negotiations end there. Consequently, the union will select as its target a company that is reasonably sound financially, one that can be hurt a great deal by a strike without being driven bankrupt.)

Strikes

The bargaining position of either side can also depend on its ability to outlast the other in a long strike. For example, the credibility of a strike threat by a union depends in part on the size of its strike fund. If this has been depleted by earlier strikes, the company will be in a good position to sit back and take the attitude: "You can't afford a strike. Here is our offer (close to W_1). Take it or leave it." (In practice, the company is likely to camouflage this message in diplomatic phrases. It does not want to put the union leaders in a humiliating position where they feel forced into an unwanted strike to save face and keep their union jobs.) On the other hand, the inventory of finished goods held by a company is an important determinant of its bargaining strength. If it has a large inventory, the company will still be able to sell its product even if a strike closes down production. But if its inventory is low and its market position is consequently in jeopardy, its bargaining position will be weak. In this case the union may be able to take the attitude: "Here is our offer (close to W_3): Take it or leave it." It is no accident that companies try to build up inventories, and that unions try to build up strike funds before critical wage negotiations begin.

Strikes are costly to both sides: to labor in the form of lost wages, to management in the form of lost sales and profits. To illustrate this more precisely, suppose that, in the absence of a strike, the wage is W in Figure 28-6, with employment N. Then a strike that reduces employment to zero involves a tem-

---

[10]Sometimes, industries make exceptions. For example, if one airline is struck, the others have agreed to share their revenue with it, in order to increase its strength in resisting union demands. Thus they hope to prevent the union from picking the companies off one at a time.

porary cost in terms of lost output valued at areas 1 + 2. (Recall Figure 27-4.) Labor loses income 1 (its wage W times employment N) while the income lost by other factors is the remaining area 2. (Note that this is only the short-run cost of a strike, since it applies only so long as labor and other factors of production do not seek employment elsewhere.)

Since both parties face such a substantial potential loss from a strike, it is often assumed that when a strike does occur, it is the result of an error in judgment by at least one of the conflicting parties. For example, labor may have become publicly committed to one position and management to another, with each feeling that it cannot back down. Unfortunately, the decision to strike is not so simple. There are two good reasons why each side may judge that it is better to allow a strike to occur than to concede to the other.

First, the wage that is settled on *after* a strike is usually more attractive for each side than its opponent's final offer on the eve of the strike. This is detailed in Figure 28-7. A strike occurs because there is still a gap between the union's last offer and the last offer of management. In ending the strike some weeks or months later, the two sides will usually settle on a compromise wage in between. But precisely because it is a compromise wage, it will be more attractive for each side than its opponent's last offer before the strike. Thus, achieving a more attractive wage is an incentive for each side to accept a strike rather than to capitulate.[11]

The second incentive is that a strike may be the best way for each side to establish its long-run credibility: A strike threat means nothing if the opponent discovers it is only a bluff. For example, if management learns that under no circumstances will the union strike, it will simply quote its desired

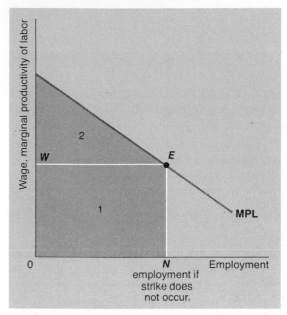

FIGURE 28-6 Short-run cost of a strike to labor and other factors of production.
Without a strike, the value of total output in this industry is area 1 + 2 (the marginal productivity of *all* workers). Labor earns area 1, and other factors of production earn 2. But *if a strike does occur,* both these income areas are lost.

wage W_1 in Figure 28-5. Then it need not budge, since it can be sure that the union will not go on strike and therefore must eventually come around to accepting this low wage. Similarly, if a union discovers that it is dealing with a management that is only bluffing and will not allow a strike to occur, it can quote its preferred wage W_3 and sit back until management capitulates. Thus, each side may allow a strike to occur in order to prove that it is not bluffing—to prove that when it says, in future negotiations, that "this is our last offer; failing this, the strike goes on," its opponent will listen.

If by now you have concluded that collective bargaining has some of the characteristics of a poker game, you are right.

[11]Sometimes it is pointed out after the strike is over that one contender has been able to move the wage rate in its favor by only a trivial amount, say 5 cents per hour. True, this may not seem like much (for example, for the union). But, in reality 5 cents an hour will be a very great deal if *it raises the base on which all future wage increases are calculated.* (In this case, labor will get that extra 5 cents an hour permanently.)

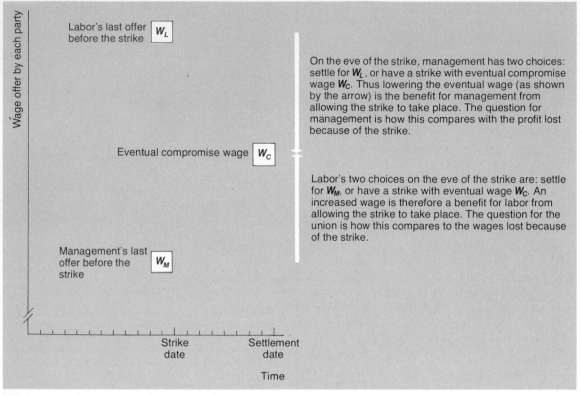

On the eve of the strike, management has two choices: settle for W_L, or have a strike with eventual compromise wage W_C. Thus lowering the eventual wage (as shown by the arrow) is the benefit for management from allowing the strike to take place. The question for management is how this compares with the profit lost because of the strike.

Labor's two choices on the eve of the strike are: settle for W_M, or have a strike with eventual wage W_C. An increased wage is therefore a benefit for labor from allowing the strike to take place. The question for the union is how this compares to the wages lost because of the strike.

FIGURE 28-7   Why each party may be willing to see a strike occur.

For this reason, it is a mistake to believe that a wage rate is determined solely by impersonal economic forces. These forces do set the background and define the limits within which the negotiated wage will fall. But frequently the specific wage that emerges is very much the product of the bargaining skills of the participants.

The Cost of a Strike When There Are Spillovers

The only cost of a strike we have considered so far is the cost of lost output in the industry where the strike actually takes place. For example, in Figure 28-8a, the value of lost output when the rubber tire industry is on strike is shown as area 3

(exactly the same as areas 1 + 2 in Figure 28-6). But the loss may not end here: As tire supplies are depleted, auto production may be delayed or dislocated. This disruption involves a cost to the auto industry and inconvenience to the car-buying public. Since these are costs that are not incurred by any firm or individual in the tire industry, they are spillover (or external) costs of the strike and are shown as area 4. In short, if a rubber workers' strike occurs, it will involve both internal cost 3 to the tire industry plus external cost 4 elsewhere in the economy.

In panel b we see that the situation could be far worse. If one or more auto companies is eventually forced to shut down, the value of the lost output in the auto

FIGURE 28-8 Spillover cost of a strike.
(a) When a strike occurs in tire production, area 3 shows the internal cost to the industry, in terms of the lost output of tires. Area 4 shows the additional external cost to the public, and in particular to the auto industry where production is dislocated because tire supplies have dried up. (b) If the shortage of tires becomes so severe that auto companies have to lay off workers, the spillover cost of a strike (area 4) may be far more severe than the internal cost to the tire industry (area 3).

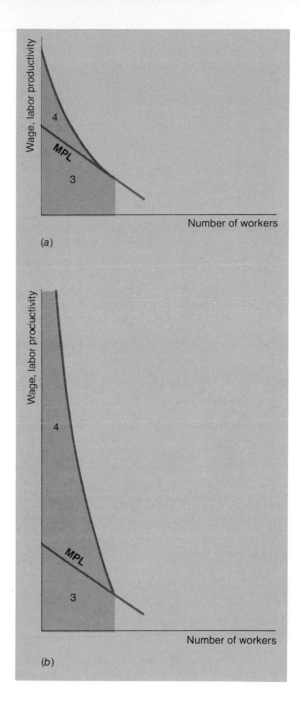

industry and the inconvenience to the public (area 4) may far exceed the value of the lost output in the tire industry (area 3). In this case, there is even less reason to expect Adam Smith's "invisible hand" to lead to an efficient solution. The cost of a strike to society (areas 3 + 4) overwhelms the cost (3) to those who actually make the strike decision (that is, labor and management in the tire industry).

Other illustrations abound. When truck drivers (members of the Teamsters Union) go on strike, the spillover cost (in terms of dislocated production or rotting crops that cannot be delivered to market) far exceeds the cost of lost income in the trucking industry. When mine workers go on strike, the external cost to steel companies and electrical power stations that can no longer acquire coal to burn far exceeds the cost of lost income in the mining industry. (For another example, see Box 28-4).

Thus, the public (especially labor and management in the auto industry) has a stake in any strike decision in the tire industry. But *it is not represented in these negotiations.*[12] The attitude of the public may be summarized thus: "While labor and management in this industry are fighting over how area 3 is to be divided, we are losing area 4. Something is very wrong."

While this is a valid criticism of the collective bargaining system, it should be

---

[12]Except perhaps indirectly. For example, a threat by the auto companies to buy steel from Japan may exert pressure on the steel industry and the union to settle without a strike.

BOX 28-4
AN EXAMPLE OF A SPILLOVER: How a Canning Strike Hurt Farmers

In the summer of 1976, near the peak of a record crop of fruits and vegetables ripe for canning, more than 30,000 cannery workers went on strike in California. Lost wages and productivity in the canning factories were only a small part of the cost of this dispute. By the time it was settled, farmers had been forced to lay off 15,000 field workers who would have harvested the crop. Almost $10 million worth of tomatoes (or about 5 percent of the harvest) rotted in the fields, as did over $10 million worth of clingstone peaches (almost 15 percent of the crop) and about $5 million of apricots (30 percent of the harvest). In total, the strike cost the California economy roughly $260 million and represented a financial disaster for many of the state's small farmers. Moreover, because so much of the nation's supply comes from California (over 50 percent of the fruits and 85 percent of the nation's tomatoes are canned there), the American consumer also had to bear a cost in the form of higher prices.

kept in perspective. Strikes may be costly to society, but they are relatively infrequent. Most contracts are signed without a strike. The American worker, on average, spends less than 1 day a year on strike; more time is spent on coffee breaks than on strikes.[13] And

[13]Frequent wildcat strikes involving sudden walkouts by small groups of workers can be much more disruptive than a full-scale strike that follows a breakdown in union-management contract negotiations. Wildcat strikes may be the result of unions that are too weak to prevent their members from taking actions that harm the workers in the industry as a whole.

Fortunately, wildcat strikes are uncommon in the United States. But they have been a major problem in Britain, and indeed have contributed to the decline of the British automobile industry. For example, when British Leyland was struggling against a rapid decline in its market share in early 1978, six vehicle inspectors walked off the job in a dispute over the condition and color of the overalls that the company had provided them. Forty other inspectors stopped work in sympathy, and as a consequence 3,600 workers had to be temporarily laid off. Car production worth $3 million was lost, and the company's share of the market shrank even further.

ways may be sought to solve disputes without striking.

Procedures to Prevent Strikes

As noted earlier, the Taft-Hartley Act empowered the President to seek a court injunction in order to enforce an 80-day "cooling off" period, delaying a strike which threatens the national health or safety. Such a court injunction provides further time for labor and management to negotiate a settlement. (However, an injunction does not guarantee against a strike after the 80-day period. Furthermore, it does not even guarantee a temporary respite: Strikers may defy the court and refuse to work for the cooling off period).

To assist deadlocked negotiations, the Federal Mediation Service has been established. *Mediation* (or *conciliation*) involves the appointment of an impartial third party to study the situation and suggest a compromise settlement. But this mediator cannot make any binding recommendation on how the dispute will be settled.

A second, more forceful technique is *voluntary arbitration,* a voluntary agreement by both labor and management to submit their conflict to an impartial third party. After hearing evidence and arguments from both sides, this arbitrator will then propose a solution which both parties have *bound themselves in advance* to accept. (Provisions for voluntary arbitration are included in most collective bargaining agreements, as a way of settling disputes over the interpretation of the terms of the agreement.)

A third, and much more drastic, approach is sometimes suggested: *compulsory arbitration*, whereby the government *forces* both parties to submit their dispute to an arbitrator, who then decides on a binding settlement. Although this seems like a simple solution, it has tended to cause bitterness and hostility in countries which have relied on it.

DISPUTES INVOLVING PUBLIC SERVICE EMPLOYEES

The most damaging strikes are usually those with large external or spillover costs. These costs tend to be particularly great in public sector employment. When New York transit workers go on strike, lost income of the transit authority (area 3 in Figure 28-8*b*) is trivial compared with the spillover cost of tying up economic activity in the city (area 4). Serious spillover costs similarly result from a strike of garbage collectors or firefighters.

Since public service employees face a monopsony employer (the government), it can be argued that, unless they unionize, the government can exercise too much market power in setting their wage rate: They must accept whatever "take-it-or-leave-it" contract the government offers. In order to improve their bargaining position, public service employees have recently been organizing at a remarkably rapid rate: Membership in public service unions increased from just over 1 million in 1960 to more than 6 million in 1978. By 1978, the American Federation of State, County and Municipal Employees (AFSCME) had grown to more than 1 million members, and had become the largest of the unions affiliated with the AFL-CIO. The gap between public service wages and salaries and those in the private sector had already been essentially closed, and questions increasingly arose as to whether public sector employees were being overpaid—not underpaid—compared with those in the private sector.

For several reasons it may be argued that once public service employees do form a strong union, the balance of market power tips too far in their direction.

1. The threat of a strike by public service employees becomes a very potent weapon. Whereas a strike in the private sector puts pressure on employers to settle because of the income they will lose, a strike in the public sector—such as a sanitation or transit workers' strike—puts pressure on the employer (the government) because of the votes it may lose from an irate, suffering public.

2. A government typically may find it easier than a private employer to raise the funds necessary to pay a higher wage bill. For example, it may increase taxes or simply borrow, an apparently painless way to resolve any labor dispute. An even easier way to avoid a strike may be to increase employee pensions. This measure involves the present government in little taxation or borrowing, since it is only a commitment to pay employees in the future when they retire. Thus, it may appeal to politicians whose major concern is to win the next election. But, as New York City has proved, such a policy has painful long-run consequences: By 1975, "the chickens had finally come home to roost." Wage and pension commitments (combined with other major problems, such as large welfare expenditures) drove the city to the brink of bankruptcy, where it was saved only by state and federal government aid.

3. In private industry a strike may drive a firm out of business. Thus, strikers run the risk that their jobs may disappear, and this prospect acts as a restraint on labor demands. But there is far less restraint of this kind in the public service. True, a strike may cost the government an election. But this is a serious problem only for the government officials who are voted out of their jobs. It is far less of a threat for public service workers whose jobs are likely to exist no matter who wins the next election. This tends to put a public service union in a strong bargaining position.

4. Public employees (and their dependents) may become a significant percentage of the voting population. This tends to weaken the resistance of elected officials to their demands.

At every level of government—federal, state and local—strikes of public service workers are generally illegal. Nonetheless, some civil servants (particularly at the local level) do walk off the job or withdraw their services in more subtle ways, such as reporting in sick. Should they be allowed the right to strike? It is easy to answer no: If firefighters go on strike, people may die in fires. If trash collectors go on strike, pollution may threaten public health. If the police go on strike, criminals may have a field day. In the face of such a strike threat, a government may feel almost forced to meet labor demands. Surely no group of individuals should hold this sort of power over the public.

Unfortunately, however, the problem is not quite so simple. If workers are not allowed to strike, they may reasonably demand some other mechanism for achieving a fair wage. One possibility is to provide civil servants with salaries equal to those in comparable private sector jobs. (This policy has been explicitly adopted by the federal government.) Although this is a promising approach, it provides neither a simple nor a complete solution. One difficulty is considered in Problem 28-6; another is the problem of defining what is meant by a "comparable" private sector job. And what downward adjustment, if any, should be made to salaries because of the greater job security and attractive pensions which public employees enjoy?

Key Points

1. Labor markets are often imperfect. Workers form unions to exercise monopoly power on the supply side of the market. On the other side of the market, employers may exercise monopsony power. Examples include a government that hires public service employees and a private firm that is the only major employer in a small town.

2. If markets initially are perfectly competitive and a newly formed union raises the wage rate, the result will be a transfer to labor from other factors of production. There will also be an overall efficiency loss because some workers are not hired in this industry even though they would be more productive here than elsewhere.

On the other side of the market, if employers acquire monopsony power and lower the wage below its perfectly competitive level, there will be the same sort of efficiency loss. But, whereas the efficiency effects of monopoly and monopsony will be similar, their transfer effects will be in opposite directions. When a monopsonist lowers wages, the transfer is *from* labor *to* other factors of production.

3. If a labor market is already monopsonized by a single employer, it no longer necessarily follows that efficiency will be reduced if a union is formed to raise the wage rate. In fact, if the union's market power is used only to offset the market power of the employer, efficiency can be *increased.*

4. Unions have other objectives in addition to raising wage rates. They may seek better working conditions or a feather-bedded contract that guarantees job security. Such a contract reduces efficiency because employers are forced to hire workers in jobs where their productivity is low—or even zero.

5. Bilateral monopoly occurs when market power exists on both sides of the labor market: Unions with monopoly power bargain with employers with monopsony power. The wage that results will fall between the high wage an unopposed union would seek and the low wage an unopposed monopsonist would offer. But, within these limits, it is impossible to predict precisely where the wage rate will be set. However, it will be heavily influenced by the bargaining power and expertise of each side. (For example, a large union strike fund will increase the union's bargaining power, while a large inventory of finished goods will increase the bargaining power of management).

6. Labor and management may each consider a strike better than accepting the other's before-strike offer, in spite of the cost of a strike to labor in the form of lost wages, and to management in the form of lost output and profit. The reason is that strikes are usually settled at a compromise wage rate somewhere between the last offer of management and the last offer of labor on the eve of the strike. And each party may view the other's last offer as less attractive than striking for a compromise wage.

7. Membership in public service unions has grown rapidly in recent years. Such a union may have a strong bargaining position, particularly if it provides an essential service. To avoid a strike, a government employer may be willing to tax or borrow to meet a wage claim that would drive a private employer out of business.

Key Concepts

industrial union
craft union
collective bargaining
closed shop
union shop
right-to-work law
open shop
transfer and efficiency effects of a union
featherbedding
transfer and efficiency effects of monopsony

bilateral monopoly
why a union may decrease or increase
  efficiency
relative bargaining power of union and
  management
losses to each side from a strike
why strikes occur
spillover costs of a strike
Taft-Hartley injunction
mediation
arbitration: voluntary and compulsory

Problems

28-1 "Monopsonization of a labor market may have exactly the same effect on efficiency as the formation of a union." Is this possible? Explain. Would the transfer effects be the same in the two cases? (If you have studied Figure 2 in the introduction to Part 5, use the present example to show how the same situation can occur in a labor market, namely, how two policies can involve identical efficiency effects, but entirely different transfers.)

28-2 In the case of monopsony, which efficiency condition in Box 27-3 has been violated? Explain.

28-3 In Figure 28-5, suppose that the initial wage rate in a unionized labor market is at W_3. If employers form a bargaining association and successfully negotiate a lower wage rate, show how efficiency is affected. Consider two cases: What happens if the association negotiates the wage down to W_2? Down to W_1?

28-4 Do you think that, as capital accumulates, the bargaining power of workers vis-a-vis management increases or decreases? Which workers can more effectively threaten to strike—workers who would be leaving bulldozers idle, or workers who would be laying down their shovels?

28-5 Which union in each of the following pairs has the greater bargaining power? In each case, explain why.

(a) A union of workers on the New York subway or a union of workers who build the trains

(b) A firefighters' union or an elementary teachers' union

(c) An elementary teachers' union or a university professors' union

(d) An airline pilots' union, or an intercity bus drivers' union

28-6 "Tying wage increases in the public sector to wage increases in private industry will not necessarily equalize wages. All it will do is keep them the same if they start out equal. If public sector wages are initially less than the private sector wages, tying wages in this way only guarantees that inequities will be preserved." Do you agree? Do you think it is fair to pay both public and private employees the same wage if public employees have a greater guarantee of job security?

*28-7 Explain how the theory of the second best applies to labor forming a union in a market that is already monopsonized.

chapter 29
Other Incomes

All economic analyses begin with the cultivation of the earth. . . . To the economist, . . . the green plain is a sort of burial place of hidden treasure, where all the forethought and industry of man are set at naught by the caprice of the power which hid the treasure. . . . Thus is Man mocked by earth his stepmother, and never knows as he tugs at her closed hand whether it contains diamonds or flints, good red wheat or a few clayey and blighted cabbages.
George Bernard Shaw

About three-quarters of United States national income goes to labor in the form of wages and salaries. The remaining quarter goes to the owners of other productive factors—in particular, capital and land. Now we examine these other forms of income.

Income from capital is earned in several forms. First, interest income is earned by those who provide *debt capital*, that is, those who lend money to businesses (or others) to finance the purchase of machinery or the construction of new buildings. (One way to lend a firm money is to buy its bonds. Another way is to lend money to a bank or other financial intermediary which in turn lends it out to the firm.) Second, profit income is earned by those who own *equity capital*, that is, those who own small businesses outright, or who own shares of a corporation's stock. Although the individual who is buying stocks and bonds may view them quite differently, in this chapter we emphasize the similar role they play. Both represent a way in which people can con-

tribute to the expansion of the nation's capital, and earn an income in return.

Income is earned not only on physical capital, such as machinery and buildings, but also on *human capital*. An example is the human capital you are now accumulating in the form of an education. Your expenditure of time and money today will increase your productivity in the future and hence increase your income. Thus, an investment in human capital involves an expenditure today that is expected to pay off in the future, just like an investment in a machine or some other form of physical capital. (But, as we shall see, you shouldn't be too optimistic about this payoff.)

INTEREST: The Return to Debt Capital

To begin, let's suppose that firms finance investment only by borrowing. Borrowing takes place in the market for loanable funds where lenders (suppliers of funds) and borrowers (demanders of funds) come together.

Like a competitive commodity market, a perfectly competitive market for loans can be analyzed with supply and demand curves.

The Demand and Supply of Debt Capital

Figure 29-1 shows the demand curve for loans by firms seeking the money to purchase plant and machinery. (People who need loans to buy houses or cars also participate in this market.) Just as we have already seen that the demand for labor depends on the marginal productivity of labor, so too the demand for loans depends on how productive that money will be when it is invested, that is, the *marginal efficiency of investment* shown in this diagram. Thus, bar *a* on the left represents the investment with the highest possible return—15 percent. (To give an oversimplified illustration, a 15 percent return would result if a firm that purchased a machine for $1 million were to earn $150, 000 per year on it forever.) The next most attractive investment is *b*, which can earn a $14^{1}/_2$ percent return; and so on. The result is the marginal efficiency of investment curve (MEI). This curve also represents the demand for loans. For example, if the interest rate is 10 percent, then Q_1 of loans will be demanded: Firms will wish to invest in all the high-return opportunities to the left of *V*, but none to the right where the return has fallen below the 10 percent cost of borrowing money.

This demand for loanable funds is reproduced in Figure 29-2, along with the supply of funds by lenders. This supply indicates how much businesses and households are willing to provide at various interest rates.[1] For example, the 6 percent interest rate that would just barely induce individual *f* to save and lend reflects how highly he values this money in its alternative use—current consumption. (Individuals who value current consumption more highly won't be induced to save and lend until the interest rate rises above 6 percent. Therefore, they appear further to the right in this supply schedule.) In a perfectly competitive capital market, equilibrium will be at *E*, where demand and supply intersect; thus the rate of interest will be 8 percent.

It is important to emphasize that this 8 percent interest rate reflects the height of the demand curve at *E*. In other words, the marginal efficiency of investment is 8 percent. We can take $1 worth of goods today and invest it to produce $1.08 of goods next year. *Since capital is productive, present goods can be converted into a larger amount of future goods.*

FIGURE 29-1 The marginal efficiency of investment and the demand for loans.
Investment opportunities are ranked in order, starting with those yielding the highest return on the left. The resulting MEI schedule is also the demand for loans. For example, if the interest rate is 10 percent, then firms will demand Q_1 of loans. They keep borrowing to point *V*, where the marginal benefit of borrowing (the MEI schedule) is equal to the marginal cost (the interest rate).

[1]In this analysis, we ignore a number of macroeconomic complications, including the effects of the banking system on the supply of loans. These complications were studied in Chapters 10 to 12. Chapter 12 also provided additional detail on the marginal efficiency of investment. See especially pp. 242–244.

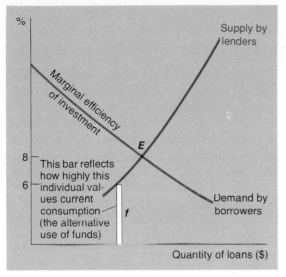

FIGURE 29-2   The market for loans.
The demand for loans is reproduced from Figure 29-1.
It reflects the marginal efficiency of investment. The
supply of loans depends on how highly lenders value
money in its alternative use—consumption. The equilibrium is at *E*, with an 8 percent interest rate.

> Through investment, present goods can be
> *exchanged for* a larger amount of future
> goods. Thus, present goods are *worth more*
> than future goods, with the interest rate tell-
> ing us how much more.

How Risk Affects the Interest Rate a Borrower Must Pay

So far, we have been talking as though,
at any point in time, there is only one
interest rate. But of course there are many. A
very large and financially sound corporation
will be able to borrow at a relatively low
interest rate, since lenders view this loan as
relatively risk-free. But a company in shaky
financial condition will have to pay a higher
interest rate to compensate lenders for the
greater risk they have to take in this case.
Thus, the interest rate shown in Figure 29-2
may be viewed as the "base rate of interest"
that applies to a risk-free loan; as such, it is
the best simple measure of the marginal
efficiency of investment. Even though we
continue to concentrate on this base rate, we
should keep in mind that it reflects a whole
array of interest rates on loans of varying
risk.

As we have seen in earlier chapters, an
important question in product or labor markets is: What happens if the government
intervenes to impose some restriction? This
is also an important question in the capital
market (the market for loans).

Effects of an Interest Rate Ceiling

Figure 29-3*a* shows what happens in a
perfectly competitive capital market when
the government imposes a ceiling on the
interest rate that can be charged by banks.
Original equilibrium (before the ceiling) is
shown at E_1, with the interest rate at i_1. If the
government now sets a ceiling rate below
this, say at i_2, savers will be discouraged
from saving and lending. In other words,
they will move down the supply curve from
E_1 to E_2. At the same time, borrowers would
like to respond to the low interest rate by
moving down the demand curve from E_1 to
F, borrowing more. But they cannot, because lenders aren't supplying enough. As a
result, the market no longer clears: E_2F is
the shortage of funds, that is, the unsatisfied
demand of borrowers who cannot find loans.

One of the arguments sometimes put
forward in favor of an interest rate ceiling is
that it will reduce the burden of debt on
relatively poor individuals and small firms
that must borrow. And the lower interest rate
does result in a transfer from lenders to
borrowers, at least to those borrowers lucky
enough to get loans. (This transfer is shown
by the white arrow to the left of panel *b*.) But
there is no guarantee that this redistribution
will "help the poor." Some of the largest
borrowers who get the "bargain" loans may
be the rich (who borrow to buy big homes
and engage in business ventures). And some
of the borrowers who are left unsatisfied
may be the poor, who suffer greatly as a
consequence.

Moreover, this interest rate ceiling has two unfavorable effects on efficiency. The first is the familiar red efficiency loss shown in panel *b*. The interest rate ceiling has reduced loans by ΔQ, with a typical investment project that has been "knocked out" shown as *g*. The cost to society of this loan would have been the empty bar under the supply curve (the cost to the lender of having to reduce consumption). The benefit would have been the empty bar plus the solid bar under the demand curve (the productivity of the investment). Thus, this loan would have resulted in the net benefit shown by the solid bar. Or, to put the same point the other way around, this solid bar is the loss involved because this particular loan does not take place. And the total efficiency loss from the interest rate ceiling is the sum of similar losses on all the other loans that are eliminated in the range ΔQ; in other words, the red triangle. Thus a principle previously established in the market for goods and for labor—that displacing a perfectly competitive equilibrium will result in an efficiency loss—has now similarly been shown to hold in a perfectly competitive market for investment funds as well.[2]

But there is a second efficiency loss that may be even more serious. Because of the interest rate ceiling, demand for loans exceeds supply, so that loans must somehow be rationed. It may be first come, first served, or some more complex procedure. But whatever this procedure, the efficiency loss will be limited to the red triangle *only if* those who are rationing funds provide them to *exactly the right set of borrowers*. In other words, borrowers like *g* must be refused, while the more productive borrowers like *j* still get loans. But there is no guarantee that this will happen. Both are trying to borrow,

and if *g* comes up with the more convincing application and gets the loan and *j* does not, there has been a "rationing error," an additional source of efficiency loss.

Moreover, the rationing error may be even worse than this if *j* loses out, not to *g*, but, instead, to an even lower-productivity applicant like *h*. In fact, *h*'s productivity is so low that he would not even seek a loan at the free-market interest rate i_1. The only reason *h* is even applying is because of the attraction of the artificially low interest rate. If *h* gets funds rather than *j*, the efficiency loss from this rationing error—the reduction in the nation's output—is the difference in *j*'s (tall bar) productivity and *h*'s low productivity.

This problem may be summarized as follows: In a free capital market, the interest rate is a price that allocates funds to the most productive investment projects. But when an interest rate ceiling is imposed, some other allocating device must be used, and there is then a risk that the wrong set of projects will get the funds. This adds another efficiency loss above and beyond the red triangle in panel *b*.

(Moreover, this is a general problem that applies to other cases of price fixing as well, such as our earlier example of rent control. We leave it to you as an exercise to show that the problem is not only that controls result in fewer apartments for people to rent. In addition, the wrong people may end up in these apartments. For example, a retired couple may continue to hang on to a choice New York apartment even though they now spend 9 months a year in Florida and would give up the apartment if they had to pay the higher free market rent.)

Once again we conclude: If we wish to transfer income from the rich to the poor,

---

[2]Of course, if monopoly elements exist, the free-market interest rate will not be efficient. In these circumstances, an interest rate ceiling may *increase* efficiency. This could occur, for example, if the banks have been colluding, or if there are other imperfections in the market that have kept interest rates above the competitive level. In this case, a ceiling that brings the interest rate back down toward the competitive level will increase efficiency.

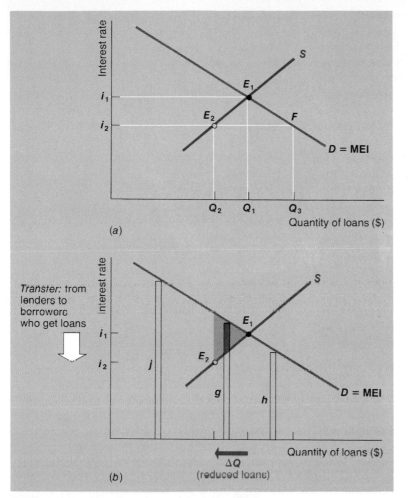

FIGURE 29-3 Effects of an interest rate ceiling.

Panel *a* shows how an interest rate ceiling reduces loans and leaves investment demand unsatisfied. Before the ceiling, equilibrium in a competitive capital market is at E_1, with Q_1 of investment funds loaned out at interest rate i_1. When a ceiling of i_2 is imposed, borrowers are attracted by the lower rate and seek Q_3 loans. (Borrowers try to move down their demand curve from E_1 to F.) But only Q_2 are available. (Lenders, discouraged by the reduced interest return, move down their supply curve from E_1 to E_2.) Thus, equilibrium shifts from E_1 to E_2, loans are reduced from Q_1 to Q_2, and there is $Q_2 Q_3$ unsatisfied demand for loans.

Panel *b* illustrates the transfer and efficiency effects of this policy. By lowering the interest rate that lenders receive and borrowers pay, the interest rate ceiling results in a transfer from lenders to borrowers who get funds. This transfer is shown by the white arrow on the left. In addition, the ceiling has two possible efficiency effects. First, economically justified projects like *g* will be "knocked out" by the shortage of funds. The resulting efficiency loss is shown as the red triangle. Furthermore, if those who are rationing funds err and provide them for the "wrong" (that is, less-productive) projects, there will be a further efficiency loss: For example, a high-productivity project like *j* may lose out to a lower-productivity project—perhaps even to a project like *h* that would not even be considered were it not for the artificially reduced interest rate. The cost of such a rationing error is the difference in the height of *j* and *h*.

changing a market price like the interest rate may be an unwise way to do it. In the first place, an interest ceiling may be an ineffective form of transfer because it may not move income from the rich to the poor at all. (The statement that "borrowers benefit, therefore the poor benefit" involves two possible errors: First, borrowers as a group may not benefit, since some no longer get funds. Second, borrowers may not be poor.) Moreover, an interest ceiling may have damaging effects on efficiency. Isn't it better for the government to do any transferring directly, by taxing the rich and subsidizing the poor? The answer is yes, *provided* the government can do so without incurring large efficiency losses of a different sort. (This issue will be discussed in detail in Chapter 32.)

NORMAL PROFIT: A Return to Equity Capital

So far in this chapter we have focused on borrowing as a source of funds for investment projects. Now let's broaden our analysis to include "equity finance," that is, funds a firm raises by selling its stock. (A third source of funds is retained earnings.) Those who buy stock obtain a share of the ownership and future profits of the firm (rather than its promise to repay at a certain interest rate).

It is now important to recall our earlier distinction (in Chapter 19) between two kinds of profit. First, *normal profit* reflects opportunity cost—the return necessary to induce and hold funds in one activity rather than another. Second, *above-normal profit* is any additional return beyond this. It is analytically convenient to defer discussion of above-normal profit to a later section and to concentrate here on normal profit: For those who provide equity funds, what is their normal profit? That is, what is the opportun-

FIGURE 29-4 The market for investment funds (a generalization of Figure 29-2).
Whereas Figure 29-2 showed only business borrowing, the diagram here shows two ways that business may raise funds: by borrowing or by equity finance (the sale of stock). *D* is the demand for funds (in either debt or equity form) to finance new investment, while *S* is the corresponding supply of funds. In equilibrium, the base rate of return—in the absence of risk—would be *r*. But in a risky world, the return any specific business must actually pay for the funds it raises will be *r* plus an appropriate amount to compensate the lender for risk.

ity cost of these funds? The answer is the return the funds could earn in their best alternative use. But the alternative to buying stock is to buy interest-bearing securities. Thus, normal profit is the base rate of interest plus an appropriate premium for risk. (Risk in this case may be substantial because the entire amount that is put into the ownership of a firm may be wiped out.[3])

We can now recast Figure 29-2 in the more general form shown in Figure 29-4, which represents the total market for investment funds. Now, *D* includes the total demand by business for investment funds (whether these funds are raised by borrowing or by the sale of stock), while *S* is the corresponding supply. The resulting equilibrium *Q* is the quantity of both debt and equity funds provided by savers to those who invest.

---

[3]Profit is sometimes described as a reward for risk taking. But it is more than this, since it must also include a base rate of return needed to attract funds away from interest-bearing alternatives.

THE ROLE OF FACTOR PRICES

In the last three chapters, we have examined the pricing of two factors of production (labor and capital). It is now appropriate to pause briefly to consider how these factor prices influence both the individual firm's decisions and the allocation of resources across the economy as a whole.

How Factor Prices Influence Decisions by Individual Firms

In its decision-making, a firm must address several issues; on the one hand, it must decide on how much labor it will employ and how much machinery and other capital equipment it will utilize. But at the same time, it must also decide on which goods to produce and how much of each. To illustrate, if the wage rate rises, the firm will tend to hire less labor and more capital. (It substitutes a relatively less expensive factor of production, capital, for a more expensive one, labor.) Moreover, because of the higher wage it has to pay, it may also reduce the output of its final products, especially those requiring a great deal of labor. (As a further example of how factor and product decisions are interrelated, suppose the price of one of its products rises. In response, the firm will increase its output of this good by hiring more factors of production and/or by shifting production away from one of its other outputs.) In short, the firm's decisions on what to produce and the amount of factors to employ are not separate decisions. Instead, they are all *elements of one overall decision.*

How Factor Prices Influence the Allocation of Scarce Resources Throughout the Economy

Just as the price of a good acts as the screening mechanism for deciding who will consume it and who will not (see Figure 20-5), so a factor price acts as a monitoring device to determine how a scarce resource will be used. For example, the wage rate acts as a screen to determine the particular activities in which our scarce labor will be employed. In a competitive, fully employed economy, a wage rate rising with productivity conveys a clear message to those producers who can no longer afford to hire. The message is: Society can no longer afford to have its scarce labor employed in your activity; there are now too many other, more productive pursuits. This may seem harsh, but in the long run it is the sure and beneficial sign of economic progress. Think back, for a moment, to all the things that labor used to do in America, and no longer does. At our current high wage rates, it doesn't pay to hire workers to hoe field corn anymore, as in the "good old days." And household servants have almost vanished.

Similarly, we have seen how the interest rate is a market price that acts as a screen to determine in which particular activities investment will take place. And when that screening device is replaced by another (for example, the bank rationing that occurred with the interest rate ceiling in Figure 29-3), investment funds no longer tend to go into the most productive activities.

THE RETURN TO HUMAN CAPITAL

Income is earned not only by investment in machinery and other physical capital, but also by investment in *human capital*—the acquisition of skills, training, and education.[4] In many essential respects, an investment in human capital is similar to an investment in physical capital: Current consumption is reduced in the expectation of higher future income and consumption. For example, students give up the income they

[4]For a sample of the work by three of the early contributors in this field, see G. S. Becker, *Human Capital: A Theoretical and Empirical Analysis, with Special Reference to Education* (New York: National Bureau of Economic Research, 1964); Jacob Mincer, *Schooling Experience and Earnings* (New York: National Bureau of Economic Research, 1974); and T. W. Schultz, *The Economic Value of Education* (New York: Columbia University Press, 1963).

could make if they were not busy studying; they live frugally in the hope that the education will pay off in higher income after graduation. Similarly, apprentices may be willing to work for abnormally low wages if they are receiving training that is likely to lead to a better job in the future.

Who pays for the investment in human capital? In the case of education, the investment is undertaken by the individuals who pay tuition and spend their time studying. But governments also invest: Federal, state, and local governments all help to finance education. One justification for these expenditures is that it is only fair to provide educational opportunity for all. Another justification is that education provides not only a benefit to those who acquire it, but also spillover benefits to others in society as well. For example, if a highly educated chemist discovers a more effective fertilizer, it may not only increase the discoverer's own income, but may also benefit consumers who will enjoy lower food prices. In the face of such spillover benefits, the unaided free market may not provide enough investment in human capital, so the government also contributes.

On-the-job apprenticeship or training in industry also represents an investment in

BOX 29-1
WHO SHOULD INVEST IN APPRENTICESHIP TRAINING?

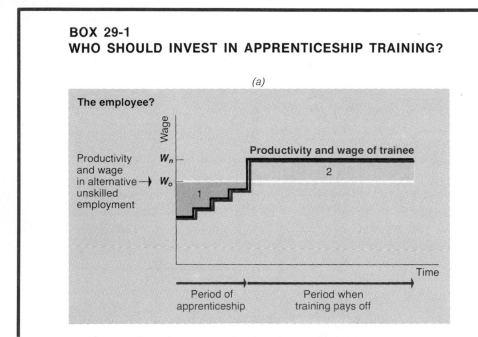

(a)

In panel *a*, the trainees' wage (the red line) is always kept the same as their productivity (the dark blue line). Therefore the employers make no investment. The total cost of the investment (area 1) is borne by the trainees who take a lower wage during the apprenticeship than the wage W_o that they could earn in alternative jobs. They also get all the later payoff from the investment (area 2), since the wage W_n then is higher than the W_o they would earn without training.

In panel *b*, the trainees bear none of the cost of the investment. Their wage remains the same W_o that they would have earned in other jobs. It is now the employers who pay the total cost (area 1), since they get less productivity from the trainees during the apprenticeship period (dark blue line) than the wage they pay human capital. There are several ways the initial cost of this investment may be covered. For example, individual workers may accept a low wage during the apprenticeship period when their productivity is still low. (The possibility of using this arrangement is limited by the minimum wage laws.) Alternatively, employers may pay apprentices a standard wage and thereby bear the initial costs of this investment. But this option raises a serious problem for employers, since they are investing in an asset (skill or training) which they do not own. (See Box 29-1.) The workers are not slaves, and they can always quit and go to work elsewhere, tak-

ing the training with them. (Of course, the ease with which they can do so depends on how specific their expertise is to the company that trained them.) This is another reason why there may be underinvestment in human capital: Employers may not invest as heavily in training programs as they would if workers would guarantee to stay on the job and thus allow employers to "get their money back."

Human Capital and Discrimination

The problem of low income for a minority may reflect far more than present discrimination by employers. It may also be the

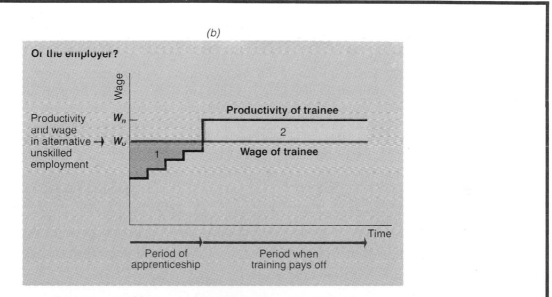

(b)

Or the employer?

them (red line). In theory, employers also get the later payoff from this investment (area 2) when the productivity of the trainees exceeds their wage.

But the problem as seen by employers is that they may not get this later payoff, since workers may leave once their training is completed. Specifically, workers may be attracted away by another employer offering higher wage W_n—that is, the wage that their services are now worth. This risk reduces the incentive for employers to undertake investment in human capital, even though it would yield high returns to society in terms of greater labor productivity.

(These two panels represent the two sharpest alternatives. But in practice, other more complicated arrangements are often introduced. For example, even employers who pay the whole training cost (as in the second panel) almost always give the trainees some of the eventual payoff 2, in order to encourage them to stay.)

result of the past inability of the minority to acquire human capital. Such a group may be caught in a vicious circle. To illustrate: Past discrimination has meant that blacks have been paid lower wages; as a consequence, they have been unable to provide equal educational opportunity for their children; therefore they continue to be paid lower wages—even by employers who no longer discriminate. One way of breaking this vicious circle is to ensure equal educational opportunity for blacks. Indeed, to make up for past discrimination, special efforts are now being made under affirmative action programs to get blacks, other minorities, and women into training programs and positions where they can accumulate human capital. Whether affirmative action should extend to reverse discrimination—whereby minorities and women are hired by business (or admitted to universities) ahead of more qualified white males—is a very controversial legal, moral, and social question, which has reached the Supreme Court. (In the 1978 Bakke case, a California medical school was sued by a rejected white applicant who claimed to have better qualifications than some nonwhites who had been admitted. The Court ordered Bakke admitted, but upheld the principle of affirmative action.)

Measuring the Return on Human Capital: What Is a University Education Worth?

Acquiring a university education involves a cost for a student in terms of fees and expenses, plus the income that could have been earned by working instead. What is its future payoff? Panel *a* of Figure 29-5 indicates that the average annual income of those with a university education was roughly $4,600 greater in 1969 than the income of those with only a high school education. But by 1974–1975, this gap had narrowed to roughly $3,200, showing that the economic value of a college education has been falling. Moreover, this has been partic-

ularly true for the younger group of recent graduates in panel *b*, where the income gap has shrunk even more dramatically.

Why were the financial rewards for a university education falling? The most important reason was the increased supply of university-trained people. Unprecedented numbers were being graduated, both because of the population bulge at the university age level and because an increasing proportion of that population was going to university. At the same time, the demand for university graduates was not increasing at the same pace—partly because of shrinking job opportunities in education, one of the areas of employment that require a university degree. (Elementary schools, high schools, and universities had already staffed up earlier to handle the population bulge.)

But why were the rewards for education falling more rapidly in the younger age group—those just out of college? One reason is that the search for jobs is more intense at this level. In contrast, many college graduates who have been working for years have mastered special skills that make them particularly valuable to their companies; as a consequence their salaries keep rising.

Now suppose we wish to calculate a percentage rate of return on a human investment like a university education (just as we would calculate a percentage rate of return on a physical investment like machinery). The first task would be to estimate the initial cost of this investment: the tuition and other costs of going to a university, plus the income forgone. This cost would then be compared with the estimated benefits in the form of higher lifetime earnings.

Unfortunately, these calculations involve a number of serious difficulties. Can we really say that the higher income of university graduates (like the $3,200 on the right side of Figure 29-5*a*) is all due to their university education? The answer is no. One reason for their higher earnings is that they are, on average, more talented and hard-

FIGURE 29-5 How much more do university graduates make? Average annual income of men working full time. To remove the effect of inflation, all incomes are expressed in 1967 dollars.

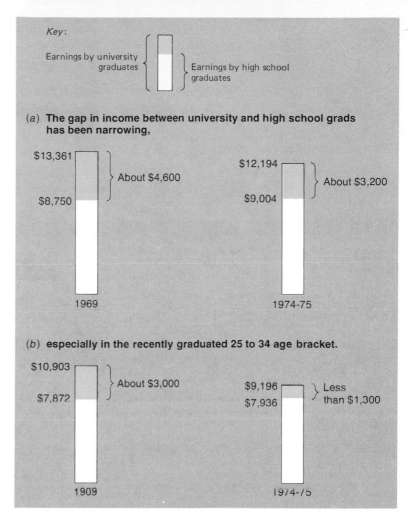

Key:

Earnings by university graduates { } Earnings by high school graduates

(a) **The gap in income between university and high school grads has been narrowing,**

$13,361
$8,750
} About $4,600
1969

$12,194
$9,004
} About $3,200
1974-75

(b) **especially in the recently graduated 25 to 34 age bracket.**

$10,903
$7,872
} About $3,000
1969

$9,196
$7,936
} Less than $1,300
1974-75

SOURCE: R. B. Freeman, "The Decline in the Economic Rewards to College Education," *Review of Economics and Statistics*, February 1977, p. 18. Other figures quoted in the text are drawn from this same source, as well as P. Taubman and T. Wales, "Education as an Investment and as a Screening Device," in F. T. Juster (ed.), *Education, Income and Human Behavior* (New York: McGraw-Hill, 1975).

working. Thus, even if they had no university education, they would still earn more. Thus one task is to figure how much of this $3,200 to attribute to a university education rather than to greater talent and perseverance.[5] A second difficulty is that the *private* rate of return to the individual ac-

quiring an education is not the same as the *social* rate of return to the nation as a whole. (For adjustments in the private rate necessary to estimate the social rate, see Box 29-2.)

Studies that attempt to take these complications into account indicate that the private rate of return to an individual from

---

*[5]This introduces a very important statistical problem that is often encountered in economics, sometimes in more complicated contexts. Obviously, if we attribute the full $3,200 income difference to education, we will overstate its influence; similarly, if we attribute the full $3,200 difference to talent, we will overstate *its* influence. The problem is that the two influences (education and talent) are closely related (correlated), since individuals with one also tend to have the other. Moreover, the more closely these two influences are related (that is, the more severe is the problem of "collinearity"), the less reliable statistical estimates become. (In the extreme case, if these two influences were perfectly correlated so that the most talented individuals were also invariably the most educated, statistical estimation would break down completely. It would become impossible to unscramble how much of the higher income was due to talent and how much to education.)

acquiring an undergraduate degree is about 8 to 10 percent per year, while the social rate of return is probably less—perhaps as low as 4 percent. (For those who incur the much heavier cost of continuing on to a Ph.D., the private rate of return on this extra effort is only about 2 percent.) Moreover, these studies confirm that the returns to a university education have been falling over time, because of both a decrease in its benefits (as shown in Figure 29-5) and an increase in its costs (such as tuition). Indeed, the rate of return on this particular form of human capital seems to have fallen below the rate of return on investment in physical capital.

Of course, one should also take into account the additional benefits of a university education as "consumption," rather than "investment." For example, it provides many individuals with a greater appreciation of history and literature. One might also evaluate the benefits a well-educated individual receives from having a more interesting and challenging job. (Even if the income were the same, it would be pleasanter to design a bridge than pour the cement.) Then, too, jobs may come with what the British call "perks" (perquisites). For example, expenses-paid business trips often also provide some pleasure. But on the other hand, those at the top often work very hard, under great pressure.

The Complex Nature of Wages and Salaries

In Chapter 27, we concentrated on explaining a simple base wage rate that might be paid to unskilled workers. In this chapter, we have seen that the wage or salary payment that others receive may reflect not only this base wage rate, but other components as well. For example, an individual's income may be higher because of education. Or, it may be higher because of some specific talent or ability: Billie Jean King and Jimmy Connors were born with a great natural ability to hit a tennis ball; others are born with a special talent for solving equations.

Figure 29-6 illustrates why the earnings of different individuals can vary. An initial point of reference is provided on the left by the base income of $10,000 earned by an unskilled laborer with no special talent or training. The remaining three individuals are business consultants. Consultant *A* is educated up to an M.B.A. and has 9 years' experience. He earns $18,000 income; this is also what he could earn in an alternative occupation. (This includes the $10,000 base wage plus an $8,000 return on his education and experience.) In other words, $18,000 is his income, and also his opportunity cost. Individual *B* has exactly the same education and experience as *A*, and the same $18,000

opportunity cost. But her income is another $14,000 higher because she has a special flair for sorting out business problems, and her customers are willing to pay for this talent. Finally, individual *C* has exactly the same education, experience, and opportunity cost as *A* and *B*. But he has an even more incisive mind in dealing with business problems; he is widely regarded as the "best in town." His income consequently is a hefty $61,000.

Three components of income can be distinguished:

1. The $10,000 base income for unskilled work.
2. The $8,000 extra income that these consultants could earn in other jobs because of their education and experience.

Components 1 and 2 represent opportunity cost.

FIGURE 29-6 Dividing income into its components.
We suppose these three business consultants have the same qualifications—an MBA plus 9 years experience—and the same $18,000 opportunity cost, shown by the red dashed line. Any surplus income above this is rent, shown in light blue. Thus *A* earns no rent, *B* earns $14,000 rent, and *C*—with the greatest natural talent for the job—earns $43,000 rent.

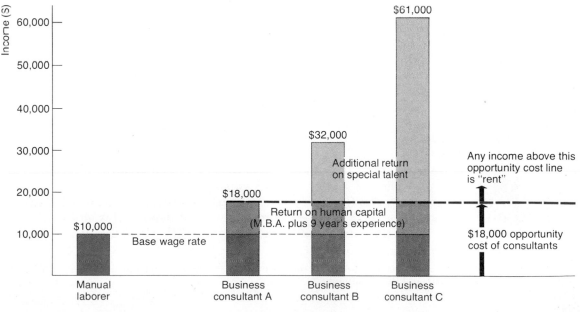

3. Additional returns to those with special talents.

This third item falls under the economists' broad definition of rent:

> Economists use the term *rent* in a broad sense, to identify the return to any factor of production in excess of its opportunity cost.

RENT

What do Beverly Sills, Jack Nicklaus, and an acre of Iowa farmland have in common?

The answer to this question is: Like business consultant *C* (Figure 29-6), they all earn an economic *rent* because of their superior quality. Sills has an exceptional voice. Nicklaus plays outstanding golf. An acre of Iowa land yields record-making quantities of grain.

FIGURE 29-7   Rent based on differences in quality of land (based on wheat price of $3 per bushel).
Marginal land *C*, which is just barely fertile enough to cultivate, earns no rent. High-productivity land *A* earns the highest rent.

Rent on Agricultural Land, based on Difference in Quality

Figure 29-7 shows three plots of land with no alternative use but to grow a crop. In other words, their opportunity cost is zero. It therefore follows from the preceding definition that any income they earn is rent. In this special case, then, the economist's and the public's definition of rent coincide: It is the income earned by land.

Relatively poor land *C* has such low productivity that with a wheat price of $3 a bushel, it has only just been brought into cultivation. The value of the wheat it produces is barely sufficient to cover costs of fertilizer, machinery, the farmer's time, and other inputs. Therefore it earns no income—no rent. Land *B* is higher-quality, more fertile soil that grows enough wheat per acre to pay for other inputs and leave $60 per acre; that is, its rent is $60 per acre. Land *C* is even more productive and earns a rent of $150 per acre.

Of course, the rent on these plots of land depends on the price of wheat. Suppose that because of crop failures elsewhere in the world, the price of wheat rises from the initial $3 a bushel (in Figure 29-7) to $4. The result is shown in Figure 29-8. Land *C*, which previously earned no rent, now does. And the rents earned by plots *A* and *B* increase. Land *D* is now the marginal land, just brought into cultivation and earning a zero rent.

*Another Example of Rent: The Income from Mineral Deposits

A mineral deposit may also earn an economic rent. To confirm this statement, recast Figure 29-7 and 29-8 as follows. Mineral deposit *A* is a rich vein of ore, easy to reach. Mineral deposit *B* is also a rich vein of ore, but difficult to reach and extract.

*Note to instructors of short courses: The rest of this chapter is made up of optional sections. Any of the starred sections may be omitted without losing continuity.

FIGURE 29-8 How rents increase when the price of wheat increases.
This figure is the same as Figure 29-7 except that the price of wheat has risen from $3 to $4 per bushel. Because of this increased price, all existing plots of land earn greater income—that is, greater rent. Moreover, less productive plot *D* is brought into cultivation for the first time.

Deposit *C* is of poorer quality and so difficult to reach that it is initially (in Figure 29-7) barely being mined. In Figure 29-8 we see how an increase in the price of ore increases the rent earned on each of these deposits and induces the mining of low-yield deposit *D* for the first time.

*Rent on Land because of Its Location

Land may yield economic rent not only because of its fertility, but also because of its location. To illustrate, land *A* in Figure 29-9 is in the prime business district of a city and can be used in a highly productive way. A business may wish to locate there for a variety of reasons: It may want to be close to suppliers and competitors so that it can easily keep up with new developments and innovations in the industry. Or, it may wish

to hire in the large labor pool that exists in this area of high-density population. Or, it may wish to be close to the population center in order to reduce the cost of transporting its product to market. For all these reasons, location *A* earns a rent. Land *B* is less attractive since it is not in this prime district, and it earns a smaller rent. Finally, land *C* earns no rent because it is even farther away and therefore involves even higher costs of inconvenience and transportation.

These blocks in Figure 29-9, just like the bars in Figure 29-7, give us a picture of how rents compare. And because the selling price of land depends on the rent it can earn (as we shall shortly see in more detail), these blocks also give us a picture of how land prices over an urban area will compare. (Although the heights of the blocks have been drawn to reflect rents and land values, they may also provide some rough indication of where the tallest buildings will be constructed. The reason is that constructing each additional square foot of office space eventually becomes more and more expen-

FIGURE 29-9 Rent based on differences in the location of land.
Compare with Figure 29-7. Because of its greater convenience and lower transport costs, land *A* earns a higher rent than land *B*. Land *C*, in a relatively poor location, earns no rent.

sive as a building gets higher and higher. Consequently, if land is cheap, you buy more land and build sideways. But if land is expensive enough, you conserve it by building up. Thus, buildings tend to be tallest in the prime, most expensive locations.)

*Above-Normal Profit as a Rent

Since above-normal profit is defined as a return above opportunity cost, it is, by definition, a rent. Although it can arise in perfect competition (see the Appendix), the most obvious examples occur in the case of oligopoly or monopoly. To cite one example, the above-normal profit earned by a monopoly (and illustrated by the shaded area on page 462) is often referred to as a monopoly rent. Since it exists because entry by new firms into the industry is restricted, it is a rent on whatever restricts entry. For example, it may be rent on a government license that is granted to one firm (or a few) and that blocks out other potential competitors. Or, it may be rent on a patented product that other firms cannot copy.

*HOW RENTS ARE CAPITALIZED

If land plots A and B in Figure 29-7 are put up for sale, we would expect A to sell for a higher price; it will be more valuable because of the higher rent it will earn. This is generally true. Higher rents result in higher land values. But can't we be more precise about how the value of land is determined?

If you had the money and you were interested in buying land B in Figure 29-7, how much would you be willing to pay for it? Bear in mind that, as an alternative, you can always purchase bonds (or stocks) instead, and earn a rate of return of, say, 6

percent. In this case you should be willing to pay about $1,000 for land B. This gives you the same rate of return on your land purchase ($60 on $1,000, or 6 percent) as on the alternative placement of your funds in bonds. Moreover, the competition of other potential buyers who feel the same way will ensure that the price of land B will settle at about this $1,000 level—so long as the rent on B is expected to remain at about $60 per year.

But when the rent on land B doubles in Figure 29-8 to $120, its value will change; it will also roughly double to about $2,000, with the rate of return left unchanged at 6 percent (that is, a $120 return on $2,000). To describe this process, we say that an increase in rent is capitalized in the value of the asset (land).[6]

This leads us to be even more skeptical of any government program to assist farm income by raising commodity prices. Such a policy may have little effect on the income to labor engaged in farming. Instead, its major effect may be merely to raise rents (as shown in Figures 29-7 and 29-8) and consequently the value of farmland. Thus, typical farmers benefit from the government program because they *own* farmland, not because they are *working* their farms. Moreover, it is a once-and-for-all benefit that they can capture by selling their farmland for an inflated price and retiring to Florida with the proceeds.

Of course, this inflated value of farmland makes it very difficult for anyone to raise the money necessary to enter farming. Thus a government program that is designed to "help out the small farmer" may, in fact, keep many small farmers out of farming altogether. Moreover, serious problems arise

---

[6]There are many complications: The price of land will be affected not only by present rents, but by expected *future* rents too. For example, if a single year's rent increases by 20 percent, the price of land may increase by more than 20 percent if people expect rents to continue rising.

Further detail on how an income flow (like rent or interest) is capitalized in the value of an asset (like land or a bond) is provided in Box 11-1. (The "capitalization of an income flow" is just another way of saying "the calculation of the present value of an income flow.")

even for those who do raise the necessary funds to get into farming by borrowing heavily on a big mortgage. They will be able to earn a living—and make those big mortgage payments—only if the government price-support program continues. So these farmers *of necessity* become strong supporters of the government program; without it, food prices would fall, and they would no longer be able to make their mortgage payments. (And if they are consequently forced to sell their farmland, they would have to do so at a very large loss. Remember that falling food prices mean falling land values.) In short, one of the problems with government support programs is that they become very difficult to reverse: When they are introduced, they benefit one group—those who initially own the land. But when they are reversed, they damage another group—those who own the land at this later date.

(Of course, government price supports are not the only reason that farm prices and land values may be inflated; in 1973, crop failures abroad had exactly the same effect. Farmers who bought land at inflated prices at that time were caught in the same sort of vise: By 1977, when farm prices had come down, many were unable to meet payments on their mortgages and faced bankruptcy. They had little choice but to become strong advocates of price supports.)

Another government agricultural program is the restriction placed on the acreage of land planted in a certain crop, such as tobacco. This has raised tobacco prices and the value of restricted tobacco land. As a consequence, the original owners of this land have reaped thousands of dollars of windfall gain per acre. In a similar example, the sale of milk in British Columbia is restricted; as a consequence, the quota right to sell milk from one cow has now risen to the point where it is worth twice as much as the cow itself.

Moreover, examples are not limited to agriculture. The number of taxis in New York is limited: A driver must have a "medallion" to operate a cab. Because this requirement makes taxis scarce in New York, the fares collected by each taxi are greater. But the increased income (rent) tends to be capitalized in the value of a medallion. As a result, by 1977 the price of a medallion had risen to $42,000, that is, to almost *ten times* the cost of the cab itself. (See Box 29-3.) Thus, someone who wants to own and operate a cab in New York faces the same problem as the Midwestern farmer. He may be able to do reasonably well once he gets into the business, but how in the world does he raise the money to get started in the first place?

Finally, taxi medallions raise this issue: Rather than let the medallion owners benefit from the policy of restricting the number of cabs, would it not have been better for New York to auction off the rights to operate cabs only for 1 or 2 years at a time? Then the city would have been able to collect the rents. Moreover, individual drivers could now enter the industry far more easily. They would have to buy only the right to operate a cab for 1 or 2 years, rather than the far more expensive right to operate it permanently (the cost they now incur when they buy the medallions).

*Taxing Rent

Rent has always been a natural target for taxation. In fact, about a century ago, Henry George built a powerful single-tax movement based on the idea that nothing should be taxed but land rents. (His book *Progress and Poverty* sold millions of copies, and he almost won an election for mayor of New York.) Why, asked George, shouldn't we tax land rents, since they represent a pure windfall? Owners obviously don't produce the land, nor do they work for their rental incomes. Instead, they just hold ownership in the land and become wealthy from "unearned increments" as the population increases and rents rise. George argued that

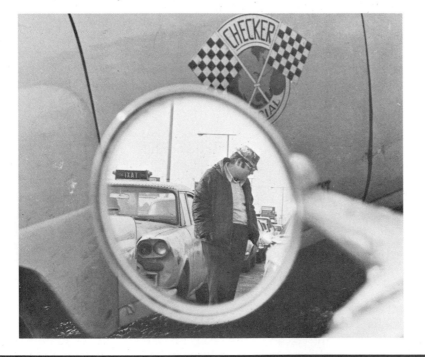

the land rents belong to the public as a whole and should be taxed away from the owners and used for public purposes.

George's case was based not only on equity, but also on efficiency. A levy on land rents is one of the few taxes that will not distort resource allocation. For example, if half the rent on land is taxed away, it will still remain in cultivation. What else can the owner do with it? And because the quantity of land in use is not affected, there is no reason to expect an efficiency loss. [Compare this with a tax on any other factor of production. For example, a tax on labor income (wages) would tend to affect the incentive to work and might thus affect the amount of labor used in the economy.]

However, George's proposal to tax land

rent raises a number of serious difficulties. First, if present owners paid a high price for their land, rents are not a windfall to them at all, but just a reasonable return on their large initial expenditure on land. The only windfall is to the previous owners who sold the land for a high price. But how can they be taxed? They may already be in Bermuda, beyond the reach of the taxing authority. Second, in practice it may be impossible to separate the rent on land from the return to buildings or other improvement on the land. (If you tax a landlord's income, you will be taxing *both*.) But to an economist, the return to buildings is not a "rent" at all. Instead, it is a return to capital, and it cannot be taxed without causing distortion and inefficiency. For example, a tax on the returns from apartment buildings will discourage building construction and maintenance, just as rent control was shown to do in Chapter 4. Finally, a tax on land clearly cannot be the only tax in an economy in which government expenditures are as large as they are today.

Key Points

1. Those who provide the nation's capital receive income in several forms. Those who own businesses receive a profit income. Those who lend money to businesses to purchase plant or equipment receive an interest income.

2. In a perfectly competitive capital market, the interest rate is determined by the demand and supply of loanable funds. Demand reflects how productive these funds will be when they are invested (the marginal efficiency of investment). Supply reflects how highly savers value money in its alternative use —consumption.

3. Because capital is productive, present goods can be exchanged for even more future goods. Therefore, present goods are worth more than future goods. The interest rate indicates how much more.

4. The interest rate also acts as a screening device that allocates funds to investment projects with the highest productivity. A government ceiling that lowers the interest rate below its perfectly competitive level results in two kinds of efficiency loss: It reduces the total funds available for investment, and may result in these funds being allocated to the wrong set of projects. It also results in a transfer from lenders to those borrowers who are able to get loans.

5. Income is earned not only on machinery and other forms of physical capital, but also on human capital, that is, on skills, training, and education. The individuals who own the human capital are not the only ones who bear the initial cost of the investment. Governments also invest by subsidizing education, and businesses invest by subsidizing training programs. An inadequate past opportunity to accumulate human capital is one significant reason why the income of minority groups is depressed.

6. The return from an investment in a university education has been estimated as about 8 to 10 percent for the individual who acquires it, and about 4 percent for society as a whole.

7. Economists define rent as the return to any factor of production above its opportunity cost. Those with superior talents in any occupation, whether it be business consulting or basketball, earn a rent.

8. Land also earns a rent—except for plots that are not cultivated or have just barely been brought into cultivation. The most fertile plots earn the largest rent. If the price of wheat (or whatever other product is grown on the land) increases, rents on all cultivated plots of land rise and new plots are brought into cultivation.

*9. Rent is also earned on land because of its location. Mineral deposits similarly earn rent, with the richest, most accessible deposits earning the highest rents. Above-normal profits earned by a firm are also a form of rent. In the case of monopoly, these rents are typically due to something (such as a patent or a government license) that blocks entry by potential competitors.

*10. The higher the rent earned by an asset (like a plot of land), the higher its value; this illustrates how rents are "capitalized." It has important implications for any agricultural price support policy that raises rents and therefore the price of farms. Although it obviously benefits those who own farms, it won't necessarily increase the income of those who want to buy farms and work them. Quite the contrary: It tends to discourage new entrants by increasing the initial cost of buying a farm.

Key Concepts

debt and equity capital
physical and human capital
marginal efficiency of investment (MEI)
why present goods are worth more than future goods
base (risk-free) rate of interest
transfer and efficiency effects of an interest rate ceiling
misallocations due to rationing of funds
normal and above-normal profit
substitution between factors of production

interest rate as an allocator of investment funds
human capital and discrimination
affirmative action programs
private and social returns to education
economists' broad definition of rent
rent on land due to fertility
*rent on land due to location
*monopoly rent
*capitalization of rent

Problems

29-1 (Review of Chapters 27 and 29.) Why are wages and salaries higher in the United States than in most other countries? Why are our other forms of income also higher? The highest per capita incomes are not in the United States or Western Europe, but in some of the smaller states along the Persian Gulf. Why?

29-2 "In a world in which labor is free to switch jobs, there will be inadequate investment in human capital in the form of job training." Do you agree? Explain why or why not. How might our minimum wage

laws be changed to reduce this problem? Would such changes raise other problems?

29-3 Explain why the armed services have subsidized the university education of students who sign up to serve for several years after graduation. (Is your answer similar to one of the cases illustrated in Box 29-1?)

29-4 Why might a firm pay a very high salary to attract an executive from a competing firm?

29-5 In Figure 29-6, does consultant *A* receive more income than a manual laborer

*The star indicates discussion in an optional section of this chapter.

because of rent? Does *B* receive more than *A* because of rent? Explain your answer.

29-6 The public's idea of rent does not coincide with the economist's definition. How are the two concepts different? Give an example of (*a*) a return which an economist considers rent, but the public does not; (*b*) a return which the public considers rent, but the economist does not; and (*c*) a return which both consider rent.

29-7 Do you think that rent is an important or an insignificant part of the income of the following:
    (*a*) Robert Redford
    (*b*) An elevator operator
    (*c*) Muhammed Ali
    (*d*) A textile worker

29-8 Are these statements true or false? "An increase in the price of oil not only stimulates the search for oil. It also brings previously uneconomic sources of oil into production. But it does not affect rent on existing oil fields." If these statements are false, correct them.

*29-9 Suppose that all the agricultural land within 100 miles of Kansas City is equally fertile. Suppose, also, that all corn must be sold in Kansas City, and that the cost of transporting it there depends only on distance. What would you expect the pattern of land rent over this area to be?

*29-10 Suppose New York City imposed its taxi restriction by allowing only a restricted set of *individuals* (Smith, Gonzales, etc.) to drive cabs. Would rents be generated in this case? If so, who would earn these rents?

*29-11 The number of doctors is limited because anyone practicing medicine must have a license. Are rents generated in this case? To whom do they go? Is the objective of licensing to affect doctors' income, or is there some other reason?

*29-12 According to Henry George's single-tax idea, taxes on land rent would not affect efficiency even if they reached rates of 50, 90, or 95 percent. Do you agree? Why or why not? Does George's argument apply to other forms of rent? For example, would a 95 percent tax on above-normal profits affect efficiency? Why or why not?

Appendix

ABOVE-NORMAL PROFIT AS A RENT IN PERFECT COMPETITION

Above-normal profit is not limited to imperfectly competitive markets. It may exist in perfect competition as well, as illustrated in Figure 29-10. Skip row 1 for the moment and consider the second row. (This diagram is based on Figure 19-11, which should be reviewed before you read on.) Blue area 5 in panel *d* shows producers' surplus (or rent) in the long run if market demand shifts from *D* to *D'* and price consequently rises from initial P_1 to P_3.[7] (Producers' surplus, rent and above-normal profit are three ways of describing the same thing: a return above opportunity cost.) Note that relatively efficient firm *A* earns a higher rent (area 3 in panel *a*) than firm *B*, which doesn't even produce initially and starts up only when price rises to P_2. Moreover, both *A* and *B* are more efficient than marginal firm *C*, which just barely gets into production at P_3 and earns no rent.

---

[7]It is assumed that at initial P_1 there is no producer's surplus going to any firm.

FIGURE 29-10   How rent (producers' surplus) shrinks in the long run: The concepts of rent and quasi-rent.
Row I: Initially, equilibrium is at *E* in panel *d*. Only firm *A* is producing; *B* and *C* have not yet started up. Now suppose that demand shifts from *D* to *D'*. The supply response will be quite different in the short run (row I) and in the long run (row II). In the short run, before new firms *B* and *C* have time to get into production, market supply in panel *d* is relatively inelastic; it reflects only firm *A*'s supply response. Consequently price rises all the way to P_4—and this high price generates the large short-run rent for firm *A* shown as area 9.
Row II: In the long run, *B* and *C* begin to produce in response to the high price. As a consequence, supply in panel *d* becomes more elastic than in the short run, and price falls back to P_3. This reduces firm *A*'s rent to area 3. In this new long-run equilibrium, the three firms earn varying amounts of rent, just like the three plots of land in Figure 29-7.

This idea of rent as a return based on quality differences (with no rent earned at the margin) is of course the same idea encountered in the case of rent on land. In particular, the blue areas in panels *a, b* and *c* are similar to the three bars in Figure 29-7, or to the three blocks in Figure 29-9. In those earlier diagrams, rent went to the land that was more productive; here, it goes to the producers who are more efficient. For example, rent area 3 may go to firm *A* because its high degree of management expertise allows it to operate with lower costs than its competitors.

Just as the second row shows the eventual long-run equilibrium, row 1 illustrates the earlier equilibrium in the short run, that is, equilibrium in the period before firms *B* and *C* have time to enter this industry. Therefore, supply in the short run (S_S in panel *d*) is less elastic than in the long run (S_L below).

Because these new firms B and C have not yet got into production, the only supply response is by existing firm A. As a result, the shift in demand from D to D' results in a much greater rise in price in the short run (from P_1 to P_4) than in the long run (from P_1 to P_3 below).

Because short-run price P_4 is so high, it generates a very large rent for existing firm A (shown as area 9). But in the long run, some of this rent disappears: It is squeezed out in the second row as new firms B and C enter this attractive industry and price settles back to P_3. The only rent A continues to earn in the long run is area 3.

Thus, we conclude that while a competitive market is efficiently allocating the nation's resources, it may generate very large rents for those with some high-quality asset like management talent. It may also generate very large short-run rents for those who, like producer A, are lucky enough to be in just the right place at just the right time.

Problem

*29-13 What do you think of this statement? "An enterprise can have income left over (that is, above-normal profit) to exercise social responsibility only if it has a monopoly position. Business executives who boast that they have been using corporate funds in a socially responsible way are asking for an investigation by the Antitrust Division of the Justice Department."

chapter 30
Natural Resources, Conservation, and Growth

The . . . economy of the future might . . . be called the "spaceman economy," in which the earth has become a single space ship, without unlimited reservoirs of anything.

Kenneth Boulding

Land is one of our most valuable natural resources. Furthermore, it has one very important characteristic: When it is used, it is not "used up" (provided, of course, that we give the soil reasonable care and protection). In other words, the amount that will be available in America next year will be the same, whether or not we use it today. But this is not true of most other natural resources. The amount of iron ore that will be available in the future depends on how much we use today. And the amount of timber that we can cut 10 years hence depends on how much we cut today.

We now turn to these other resources, like iron ore or timber, where the future supply does depend on the current rate of use, and where questions of conservation are therefore important. Are we using these resources up too fast? Are we taking the attitude: Why should I worry about posterity—what has it ever done for me? Do our expanding industrial requirements, along with our finite and shrinking resource supplies,

put us on a collision course that will soon bring us to our knees, as some observers have predicted? And what can economics tell us about how rapidly we should be using up our scarce natural resources?

THE EFFICIENT USE OF RESOURCES: An Introduction

A simple market for a privately owned natural resource (timber) is illustrated in Figure 30-1. Here, S reflects the direct cost of currently harvesting timber—the wages of lumberjacks, the cost of hauling, etc. But another cost of cutting it this year is that it will not be standing there to cut and sell next year. Supply curve S' takes into account both these costs. For example, the price required to induce the owner of unit a to sell today—the *reservation price*—includes the empty bar (the harvesting cost) *plus* the solid bar (the amount necessary to compensate for the future reduction in the available harvest).

The demand for timber D, like the demand for any other input, depends on its marginal productivity—for example, the productivity of timber as it is used by the construction industry. Equilibrium in a competitive timber market will be at E, with price P and quantity Q of timber cut. This is efficient, because the marginal benefit of cutting timber (its marginal productivity, given by the height of D) is equal to the marginal cost [the height of S', which includes both the cost of harvesting (QF) and the cost of having a reduced stand available in the future (FE)].

An important reason why this competitive market provides an efficient solution is that we have assumed that the forests are privately owned. There are owners with *property rights* who have an interest in *taking the future into account*. Thus, they have a clear incentive to see that the cutting takes place in a sensible manner—that is, in a way that takes full account of future costs FE (and that also recognizes other conservation concerns like protecting the small trees that will make up the "next generation" harvest).

If forests were common property that anyone could cut down, the result would be quite different. You can guess, quite correctly, that uncontrolled cutting might be a conservation disaster: Anyone could operate a chain saw in the free forest, and the only cost that would be taken into account would be the harvesting (cutting and transporting) cost S. Individuals cutting down trees would have little regard for the loss to future harvests. ("If I don't cut it now, someone else will.") Too much would be cut down

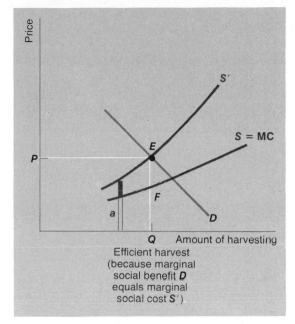

FIGURE 30-1 Market for a privately owned natural resource.
The supply S' of this natural resource depends not only on the marginal cost of harvesting (as illustrated by the hollow bar) but also on the necessary compensation to the owner for the reduced crop available for harvest in future years (the solid bar). Provided that the resource is privately owned, both these costs will be taken into account and the equilibrium will be at the efficient point E.

today, and valuable timber would be sold at too low a price.

PROBLEMS WITH A COMMON PROPERTY NATURAL RESOURCE: FISH

To see why conservation may become a serious problem when there are no property rights, consider the case of fish. Whereas many forests are the property of individuals or corporations, the oceans are not. The result is shown in Figure 30-2. To emphasize the importance of the ownership issue, let's assume that demand and supply are exactly the same here as in Figure 30-1. (For this reason, this diagram could also be used to show what would happen if our forests were not owned.) Since people who fish do not own the schools of fish, they have little reason to take into account the damage they are doing to future catches. (After all, each individual takes too small a catch to affect the future fish population.) So they respond according to supply curve S rather than S', and make their decision strictly in terms of the current cost of harvesting, without regard to how their actions affect future catches. The result is an equilibrium at $\tilde{E}$ rather than E. Too many fish are caught.

The efficiency loss that results because fish are a common property resource is shown as the red triangle. This is easily

---

BOX 30-1
WHAT INFLUENCES AN OWNER'S RESERVATION PRICE?

Some of the major influences on reservation price are: (1) The *expected future price* of the natural resource. The greater the expected price of timber next year, the greater the owner's incentive to leave timber standing ("in the bank," so to speak). Therefore, the higher will be the reservation price required to induce its harvest today. (2) The *expected future cost* of harvesting the resource. The higher the expected cost of cutting the timber next year, the less incentive the owner will have to defer its harvest until then, so the lower will be the reservation price. Obviously, if this expected future cost is high enough, it could eat up the entire future price of the timber, thus eliminating its future value. In these circumstances, the owner has no incentive at all for leaving timber uncut. In this case, S' coincides with S in Figure 30-1. (3) The *interest rate*. The higher the interest rate, the greater the valuation of present goods relative to future goods and the greater the incentive to acquire timber today, when it is highly valued. In other words, the higher the interest rate, the lower the reservation price. (4) The *age of the forest*. If the forest is "fully mature" (that is, if any growth is just offset by the rotting of aged trees), the owner will realize no growth in the timber by leaving it standing for another year. Consequently, there is no incentive for leaving the timber uncut. So long as only mature trees are culled out, S' again coincides with S in Figure 30-1.

For simplicity, we have been assuming that the owner's decision is only whether to cut the timber this year or next year. But, of course, the issue is not so clear. Instead, the problem is to find the efficient pattern of harvesting over each of the next *n* years. And if the owner is engaged in replanting the forest (rather than simply letting it grow up itself, as we assume here), this is another important cost to be taken into account.

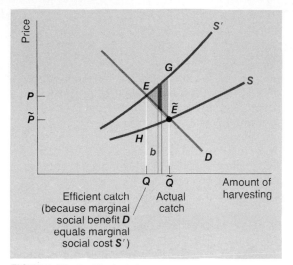

FIGURE 30-2 Market for a common property resource.
This case is exactly the same as the one shown in Figure 30-1, but with one exception. Here the natural resource is not privately owned. (Anyone can catch fish in the ocean.) Since there are no owners to take the future into account, the supply response is S rather than S'. Equilibrium is thus at $\tilde{E}$ rather than E, and the harvest is at $\tilde{Q}$ rather than the efficient level Q. The result is the red efficiency loss.

confirmed by considering b, one of the "excess" fish caught. The marginal benefit of catching b is shown as the empty bar under the demand curve, while its marginal cost (including the effect on future catches) is shown as the empty bar plus the solid bar defined under the S' curve. Thus the net loss from catching this fish is the solid bar, and the sum of the losses on all the other "excess" fish caught over the range $Q\tilde{Q}$ is the red triangle.

A possible solution is to tax those who catch fish according to the damage they do to future catches—in other words, tax them (or charge them a fishing fee) high enough to raise their supply curve from S to S'. This would result in the efficient catch Q.[1] (Notice how close this is to our analysis of

external costs in Chapter 23. See also Problem 30-2.)

In Chapter 25, we cited the advantages of free trade in goods. In that discussion we saw a number of impressive reasons why an "open border" may be in a nation's interest. But in the case of extracting a natural resource like fish, there is a problem with an open border. In fact, free and unrestricted access of all comers to a fishing area can destroy a nation's conservation attempt to control the catch made by its own people. Thus, recent attempts by a number of countries to extend their property rights over fish by expanding their territorial limits should be judged not only in terms of the obvious issue of whether domestic or foreign fishing boats will get this year's catch, but also in terms of the more subtle issue of whether this policy is aimed at conserving the resource. (The difficult task of conservation is complicated by the fact that fish swim. No matter how carefully a nation may protect them, they may get caught outside its territorial waters.)

The question of territorial rights has now become an important policy issue, involving many countries (including the United States) in international disputes. Indeed, it led Britain and Iceland close to military conflict in their recent "cod wars." The dispute was initiated by Iceland's unilateral extension of its territorial waters to a 200-mile limit. The reason given was that its population of cod had fallen by one-third, and it was concerned that overfishing might lead to a disaster like the near disappearance of herring a few years before. (The seriousness of the threat to the cod population was a controversial issue. As the *Economist* pointed out, cod and herring are different kettles of different fish: The short-lived herring can be decimated by one bad spawning season, but cod have about 8 years to spawn.) British fishing boats, long accustomed to fishing off

[1]For other policies to reduce a harvest to a more efficient level, see Box 30-2.

BOX 30-2
POLICIES TO DEAL WITH A COMMON PROPERTY RESOURCE

The problem is: How can harvesting be restricted today in order to prevent a damaging shortage tomorrow? To illustrate, we turn from commercial ocean fishing to sport fishing—say, for bass or trout in an inland lake (where there may be exactly the same case for conservation).

1. The option we have already suggested is for the government to impose a price restraint by levying some sort of tax or fishing fee. The requirement for a fishing license is one example. (Even more appropriate, were it not for difficulties in its administration, would be a fixed charge per fish caught.)

2. The second option is for the government to impose various *non-price restraints*. Examples abound: It may limit each person's catch. Or, it may limit the fishing season, prohibiting any fishing whatsoever at certain times. (The off-season is typically defined to minimize the disturbance to spawning.) In other cases, more peculiar non-price restraints have been imposed. In certain areas of Alaska, salmon fishing is illegal unless it is done in a boat no more than 32 feet long, and the maximum number of nets each person can use is carefully specified.

3. A third option, which may be feasible for a small lake but not for an ocean, is to put fishing rights under *private ownership*. The idea is to get the new owner to preserve his asset by reducing the catch from $\tilde{Q}$ to Q in Figure 30-2. (He might do so, for example, by charging a fee of EH on each fish caught.) This "creation of a property right" is sometimes cited as a way of allowing a free market that would not work well otherwise to allocate resources efficiently.

But, in practice, this policy raises two difficulties. The first is a transfer problem: How do you deal with the new owner, who now can reap the ownership benefits from a resource which was previously publicly owned? (One possibility is for the government to auction off fishing rights to private owners. The government would thus reap the ownership benefits.) The second problem is this: In controlling the fishing in a lake, the new owner will have monopoly power (unless there are many other lakes with other competing owners nearby). How, then, can we be sure that this monopolist will cut back the catch from $\tilde{Q}$ only to Q, the desirable level from a conservation point of view? Why won't the owner, like any other profit-maximizing monopolist, exercise market power to cut back the catch even further? If this occurs, private ownership will not bring an efficient solution after all.

the coast of Iceland, continued to do so. Iceland sent out gunboats to cut the British fishing nets. When an Icelandic gunboat fired shots toward a British ship, it was rammed and forced back into harbor. In good nineteenth-century tradition, the British sent in the Royal Navy, in a scene that approached the dimensions of an old Hollywood movie.

Disagreements over the extension of territorial waters from 12 to 200 miles also arose within the United States, between two groups of fishermen. Those on the East Coast favored an extension to 200 miles; they wanted protection from competing foreign boats off the East Coast. But an extension was opposed by tuna fishermen on the West Coast who were less concerned with foreign competition off the United States coast than with being able to range south, fishing off the coast of Latin America. (They recognized that, if the United States extended its territorial waters, they would not be able to object to a similar extension by Latin American countries. In fact, the United States did extend its territorial waters to 200 miles in 1977.)

*The Idea of Maximum Sustainable Yield

While the preceding analysis has highlighted the important issue of common property versus private ownership of resources, in many respects it is an oversimplification of the resource problem. In Figure 30-3 we examine some other important resource issues. This diagram shows how the *growth* in a hypothetical fish population (on the vertical axis) depends on the *size* of the population (on the horizontal axis). Point D indicates that the maximum size of the population is 10 million fish. In this case, the

ocean is so loaded with fish that the population cannot increase: For each new fish, an existing one must die. If there is no fishing, the fish population will grow toward this number, but not beyond.[2] But there is no reason why a hungry human race should be particularly interested in this "no fishing" solution. (There is little satisfaction in knowing that the sea is as full of fish as it can possibly get.) Instead, let us consider a point like C that does involve fishing. Here the fish population is $X_C = 2$ million, and is increasing by $Y_C = 1^{1}/_3$ million per year. At this point, we can take out the natural increase of $1^{1}/_3$ million fish year after year without reducing the 2 million population. Hence, this curve is referred to as the *sustainable yield* curve, or more simply, the *yield* curve.

> *Sustainable yield* is the amount of a renewable resource (like fish) that can be harvested and still leave the population constant.

The highest point on this curve, M, represents the *maximum sustainable yield*. This is a point of particular interest, showing the maximum we can fish out on a continuing basis without depleting the parent stock. But to harvest fish at this maximum rate requires a parent population of 5 million. Preventing the resource from falling below this 5-million level is roughly what economists mean by conservation.

Of course, for some resources and in some periods, conservation efforts may not be necessary. The situation long ago, before large-scale commercial fishing, is illustrated by a point like K, with the ocean almost as full of fish as it could get. As human population and our demands on the seas increased,

---

*Instructors of short courses may omit this section.

[2]To confirm this statement, note that if we are at some other point, such as K, the fish population will grow (by the height of K). This growth means that, in the next period, the population will be greater, causing a movement to the right, which will continue as long as the yield curve lies above the axis.

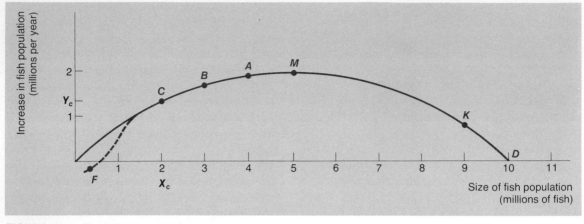

FIGURE 30-3   Sustainable yield curve.
This curve shows the tendency of a fish population to increase. For example, point *C* indicates that a population of 2 million fish will grow by 1⅓ million per year. This is the number we could catch and still leave the population intact. At first this curve rises. The larger the fish population, the greater its possible increase. However, this increase reaches a maximum at point *M*, where a fish population of 5 million generates an annual increase of 2 million. This 2 million is the *maximum sustainable yield*, the largest number we could catch per year and still leave the fish population constant. To the right of *M*, the yield curve falls as the ocean becomes increasingly crowded with fish. When the population of fish reaches 10 million (point *D*), the ocean is saturated. It can support no further increase. Because of limitations of food supply or the development of natural predators, the fish population will stabilize—even if no fishing at all takes place.

the fish population was reduced by heavier commercial fishing. However, so long as the fish population remained above 5 million (that is, to the right of the maximum sustainable yield at *M*), there was no conservation problem. As we harvested more, the fish population fell, but it became more able to regenerate itself. (That is, the natural increase became greater, as shown by the height of the curve.) It is only if the fish population falls to 5 million that we begin to encounter potential problems. If at this point we continue to harvest more than the natural increase, we will continue to reduce the fish population (shift to the left of *M*).

But now, with each such shift, the fish population becomes less able to regenerate itself. (Each shift to the left puts us on a lower point on the yield curve.) If we do not exercise discipline over our catches, we may risk extinguishing a whole species, just as we very nearly extinguished the buffalo. (And fishing out an ocean is not just a theoretical possibility. As already noted, this almost happened with herring in 1969 as a result of the development of larger, more efficient fishing boats. And the introduction of sonar for chasing down whales has endangered the whale population.)[3]

To sum up: Once harvesting begins to

[3]If the yield curve is like the dashed curve in Figure 30-3, heavy fishing may do irreversible damage to the species. To illustrate: Suppose that we have fished out the population down to about a quarter-million fish, and are consequently at point *F*. Fish cannot find other fish to spawn. There is no longer a natural increase. Instead, there is a natural decrease in population. (*F* lies below the horizontal axis.) Thus, once we have reached a point like *F*, the population will eventually die out on its own even if we stop fishing altogether. Clearly, the first rule of conservation should be to prevent such irreversible disasters.

deplete the population, it is important to try to identify the maximum sustainable yield (M) and the population (5 million) on which it is based. These figures will provide the approximate targets for efficient harvesting and conservation of the population.[4]

THE CONSERVATION OF NONRENEWABLE RESOURCES

> The characteristic conclusion of the Doomsday Models is very near the surface. It is, in fact, more nearly an assumption than a conclusion, in the sense that the chain of logic from the assumptions to the conclusion is very short and rather obvious. . . . The imminent end of the world is an immediate deduction from certain assumptions, and one must really ask if the assumptions are any good.   Robert Solow

Even with a resource like fish that is renewable (it can reproduce itself), a too rapid harvest can eventually exhaust the resource supply. But resource exhaustion becomes an even more serious specter if the resource is *non*renewable (it cannot reproduce itself). Examples include oil and copper ore. (Although new oil supplies may be created, the eons of years necessary to do so mean that, for all practical purposes, we consider oil nonrenewable.)

There is a certain finite quantity of each nonrenewable resource, and if we continue to use up some constant amount each year, we will ultimately exhaust the available supply. Moreover, this day of reckoning will tend to come even sooner because, with

population growth, the amount we extract is not staying constant, but is growing instead.

Simple Projections Spell Disaster

When you project the present rate of world population growth, you find that our requirement for nonrenewable resources is on a collision course with their available supply. Within the next hundred years or so, something must change. A number of models have been developed to show that, on our finite planet, today's trends in population growth and resource use cannot continue long into the future. For example, a computer-based study in 1972 concluded that:

If the present growth trends in world population, industrialization, pollution, food production, and resource depletion continue unchanged, the limits to growth on this planet will be reached sometime within the next one hundred years. The most probable result will be a rather sudden and uncontrollable decline in both population and industrial capacity.[5]

If present trends continue, by the middle of the twenty-first century disaster will be upon us—or, more precisely, upon our grandchildren.

But does it make any sense to assume that present trends will continue for a century? After all, if we are prepared to project present trends, we can bring the world to an end much more dramatically than this, and we don't need a computer to show it. Any simple illustration will do. For example, if we project from a period in which the fruit fly population is growing, we can in a matter

---

*[4] The correct target need not be precisely M. On the one hand, the target may be shifted slightly to the right of M in order to reduce the costs of fishing. (By letting the fish population grow, we make the fish easier and cheaper to find.) On the other hand, the interest rate tends to pull the target to the left of M. The reason: In taking so many fish out of the sea today that we deplete the population from 5 million to, say, 4 million, we consume fish now at the cost of an even greater quantity of fish in the future. This sort of trade may be justified if we value fish more highly today than in the future. The interest rate tells us that this is in fact the case.

Because these two influences—the cost of catching fish and our higher valuation of present fish—are pulling us in two opposing directions, we can still regard M as a good approximate target.

[5] Donella H. Meadows and others, *The Limits to Growth* (New York: Universe Books, 1972), p. 29.

of a relatively few years bury the earth 2 miles deep in fruit flies. Any such projection provides an illustration, not of good economics or biology, but of the mathematical magic of mechanically compounding a rate of growth.[6] A far more challenging and rewarding intellectual exercise is to ask: Why will the population of fruit flies eventually stop growing? Why will major changes in our present economic and social system occur?

Adjustments as Resources Become Scarcer

What changes can we expect in our present pattern of life as a growing population presses on a shrinking resource supply?

Change 1. Substitution in Production As demand presses on available supply, the price of resources rises and producers substitute other inputs. For example, the price increases that occur as the supply of oil is depleted will make people turn to other sources of energy, such as solar energy, wind energy, or alcohol. (They may not yet be economical, but they are becoming so as the prices of oil and natural gas continue to increase. Indeed, Brazil is already making use of significant amounts of alcohol as a supplement for gasoline.)

Change 2. Induced Innovation The higher the price of oil, the greater the economic incentive to improve existing substitutes and to develop new ones. Thus, it is not just a case of switching to known substitutes. In addition, substitutes not yet known may be discovered. Think of how the development of plastics has reduced our requirement for base metals.

Change 3. Substitution in Consumption As the price of energy rises, consumers buy smaller cars, turn down their

thermostats, and insulate their homes more thoroughly. As forests have been cut down and quality wood has become more expensive, consumers have turned to furniture made with veneers rather than solid wood.

Change 4. Changes in Population Growth Population growth cannot be projected far into the future because the rate of population increase will be modified by the economic pressures that build up. As our planet becomes more crowded, bringing up children becomes more expensive—and this may influence the typical couple's decision on family size. Moreover, the population growth rate may fall for other reasons that have little to do with economics. In the highly industrialized countries, birthrates have recently been dropping because of changing social attitudes toward the family and children, and because of the development of birth control methods. True, most of the world's population is still in the less developed countries, where the rate of increase is still high. Reasons for this continued high rate include poverty (parents view children as a way of providing for their old age), a decline in death rates (because of better medical services), and religious or social objections to birth control. But these influences are likely to weaken. Living standards are rising (slowly), and death rates cannot continue to fall as rapidly as in the past.

With the increasing scarcity of resources, there is still a major problem. But it is not the problem of some future resource Doomsday. (There are far more plausible reasons than resource scarcity for the human race to face Doomsday before the year 2100—particularly if we are unable to control the use of nuclear weapons.)

What, then, is the nature of the resource problem? Basically, it is one of cost and technology. Oil provides an example. Ener-

---

[6]To confirm the magic of compound growth, consider this: We will give you a million dollars, if you will give us just 1 cent today, 2 cents tomorrow, 4 cents the next day, and so on for just one month.

gy substitutes are available, but they are costly. Technology (along with increasing oil scarcity) determines when existing substitutes will become economical and how rapidly new substitutes will be developed. A second example is one of our most essential resources, but one that we frequently take for granted: fresh, clean water. If we run out of it, we will be forced to tap a more expensive source of supply than our lakes and rivers: the ocean, where the supply is unlimited. But the use of seawater would involve the enormous cost of purifying and transporting it. Our problem is to keep these potential future costs in mind when we make decisions today, to ensure that we do not use our resources carelessly and wastefully. The more intelligently we conserve resources and the more we develop substitutes, the less the future cost of resource scarcity will be.

The interesting question, in the case of either economics or fruit flies, is therefore not, What would happen if current trends were to continue for 100 years? but rather, What is the likely process of adjustment? And even more to the point, What is the best path of adjustment? What can we do to make the process of adjustment work smoothly in terms of encouraging the discovery and development of substitutes? And finally, are we pricing resources high enough today to protect our interests tomorrow? (For a detailed analysis of this question, see Box 30-3.)

FURTHER OBSERVATIONS ON ECONOMIC GROWTH

In Chapter 1, several arguments for growth were considered:

1. Unemployment is likely to be less severe in a rapidly growing economy.

2. Growth makes it easier to solve the poverty problem. Growth brings an across-the-board increase in income that lifts many families out of poverty; it is a "rising tide that lifts all boats." Moreover, growth makes it easier to change the *relative* position of the boats—to increase the percentage of the nation's income that goes to the poor. It is far easier to provide for the poor if the total income pie is growing than if it is not (and any gains to the poor must be taken from someone else).

3. Growth increases not only our own future income, but also the income of our children.

However, as already noted, this third point should not be overstated. If history is any guide, technological improvements will make our children wealthier than we are, no matter what growth policy we follow. As MIT's Robert Solow points out: "Why should we poor folk make sacrifices for those who will in any case live in luxury in the future?"

Moreover, growth has recently been criticized on other grounds as well: It depletes our resources and increases the pollution in our environment. Do these arguments justify slowing growth (or, as some suggest, setting a target growth rate of *zero*)? In Chapter 23, we argued that a non-growth policy was a poor way to attack the pollution problem, both because ending growth would involve an enormous cost and because it would be relatively ineffective since it would not deal directly with the pollution problem. (It would only prevent pollution from growing, but it would not cut it back.) There are similar reasons for being skeptical of a no-growth policy to conserve our resources. It would involve great cost, and it would not directly attack the problem of resource scarcity. (Even if we were to end growth completely, we might still continue to deplete our resources at too rapid a rate.) Better by far to deal specifically with the resource problem by encouraging the discovery and development of substitutes, and by ensuring that resources are priced high

BOX 30-3 THE EFFICIENT PRICING OF A NONRENEWABLE RESOURCE

How high should a nonrenewable resource be priced in order to ensure that our future requirements can be met? Although this is a difficult question to answer, we can isolate some of the important issues by considering the following simplified example. Suppose we have a limited quantity of a metal that will be completely replaced in 2 years by a cheaper plastic substitute of equal quality. The objective, then, is to completely use up the available supply of the metal in the next 2 years in the most efficient way. (Because cheaper plastic will then become available, there is no need to save any metal beyond this date.) How should it be priced this year and next year to achieve this objective?

The answer is to select metal prices P_1 and P_2 in the 2 years as shown in Figure 30-4, so that the following two conditions are met:

1. The quantities used in the 2 years should exactly add up to the total available supply Q. In other words, $Q_1 + Q_2 = Q$.

2. Price P_2 should be higher than P_1 by a gap AB equal to the interest rate. Thus, if the interest rate is 5 percent, P_2 should be 5 percent higher than P_1.

Why does this price pattern result in the efficient allocation of this resource over time? The answer is that efficiency requires that we value the marginal productivity of a ton of metal the same in both years. (Otherwise we would be able to increase output by switching a ton of metal from one year to the other.) But hasn't this efficiency criterion been violated, since the marginal productivity of a ton of metal this year (as defined under demand curve D_1) is bar Q_1A, while its marginal productivity next year is the higher bar Q_2C? The answer is no: *We value these two marginal productivities equally because they are earned in two different years.* Remember from Chapter 29 that we value goods this year more highly than goods next year (with the interest rate measuring the difference). When we accordingly raise the value of this year's Q_1A by the interest rate, we see that it is worth exactly the same as next year's Q_2C. (Indeed,

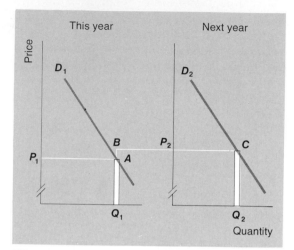

FIGURE 30-4 Efficient pricing pattern for a nonrenewable resource over 2 years.
Efficient pricing requires that the gap AB between prices in the 2 years be equal to the interest rate. Efficiency also requires that the amount of the resource used up ($Q_1 + Q_2$) be equal to the total quantity available. (Note that there is no reason for D_1 and D_2 to be the same; in fact, they are quite different in Figure 30-5. Note also that each P represents price of the resource *after* extraction costs have been deducted.)

it was precisely to make these values equal that we separated P_1 and P_2 by the rate of interest.)

To sum up the message of Figure 30-4: The fixed supply of this resource is efficiently allocated if we use Q_1 this year and Q_2 next. This is what will occur in a competitive market if prices are P_1 and P_2 in the 2 years. We make no claim that this is the price pattern that will necessarily prevail; in fact, it may not. For example, if the supply of this resource is controlled by a small number of producers (as in the case of oil), they may, like any other oligopolists, use their market power to set prices above P_1 and P_2. [True, higher prices will mean that some of this resource will not be used up by the end of next year, when it will be displaced by substitutes. But the oligopolists will still have maximized profits because of the increased price on the amount that they actually *do* sell. This is an obvious extension of our conclusion (in Chapter 22) that it may be profitable for colluding oligo-

FIGURE 30-5 Efficient pricing pattern for a nonrenewable resource over a longer period.
This figure extends Figure 30-4. The efficient pattern of price and resource use over time may be viewed as fitting a price "staircase" PP' to the demand curves, with the restriction that $Q_1 + Q_2 + Q_3 \ldots$ be equal to the fixed remaining supply. As before, the height of each step in this staircase is the interest rate.

polists to raise price, even though they sell less as a consequence.]

In Figure 30-4, it has been assumed that the resource will be completely replaced by a substitute in 2 years. In Figure 30-5, this analysis is extended to the case where the resource is replaced after a longer period. (If we were ambitious enough, we could obviously have extended this diagram to cover, say, 20 or 300 years.)

The resource in Figure 30-5 is replaced by a substitute after year 4. This does not necessarily mean that a substitute eliminates all demand in succeeding years. In fact, there is still demand for the metal in year 5, namely, D_5. But the point is that it lies below P_5. It follows that the end of our use of this resource may occur not only if a substitute is found, but also if demand shrinks in the future because public taste turns against it. For example, home furnaces were quickly converted away from coal about half a century ago, not only because oil and gas substitutes were developed, but also because no one wanted to shovel coal any more, especially before breakfast.

There are three crucial but highly unpredictable influences that will affect the efficient pricing pattern:

1. If existing deposits of the resource turn out to be less plentiful than expected, there will be less Q to distribute over time, and the price "staircase" PP' will rise. On the other hand, if new deposits are discovered, there will be more Q available, and the price staircase will fall. (Unfortunately, the problem is even more complicated than this: Not only does the resource price depend on new discoveries. In addition, new discoveries also depend on resource price, because a high price stimulates the search for the resource.)

2. Price staircase PP' will shift if demand turns out to be different from what is expected. For example, if future demand is greater than expected, the price staircase will rise.

3. The price staircase will fall (or rise) if substitutes are developed more (or less) rapidly than expected; and it is very difficult to predict just when the development of substitutes will, in fact, occur. For example, it is very difficult to estimate when—if ever—hydrogen fusion will provide a major source of energy. But the best rate of use of oil depends very much on whether this substitute will become available in the early twenty-first century.

Another complication is that, for some resources like oil, it may be easier to develop substitutes for some of its uses (energy) than for others (plastics production).

Thus, in practice, it is very difficult to pin down specifically the efficient pricing and allocation pattern for any resource. But this box has highlighted some of the important considerations that should be taken into account.

enough to induce us to cut back adequately on their use.

In short, slowing growth is not a specific enough policy to cure any single specific problem (like resource depletion, pollution, or congestion). But there is one argument that can be made for slowing growth: Although it would not solve any *one* of these problems, it would tend to make *all* of them less severe.

Finally, in assessing the growth-versus-antigrowth debate, a helpful question to ask is this: Would the arguments now used against growth have applied equally well a hundred years ago? If so, has our growth over the past century been a mistake? Indeed, there are some who argue that, if we could, we should turn back the clock; but many others would disagree. This is a judgment that you will have to make for yourself.

OIL: The Efficiency and Transfer Effects of the OPEC Price Increase

Our discussion in this chapter of the conservation of a nonrenewable resource now allows us to add an important dimension to our analysis in Chapter 22 of how OPEC (the Organization of Petroleum Exporting Countries) has raised oil price. Specifically, we can now say more about the efficiency and transfer effects of this recent rapid price increase. (The question of how OPEC developed into a strong enough organization to dictate such a large price increase is addressed in Box 30-4.)

The Effect on Efficiency

In Figure 30-6 we show the inelastic world demand for OPEC oil, reflecting the marginal productivity of oil in the consuming countries.[7] The marginal cost MC of extracting oil from many of the Middle East countries is so low (25 cents a barrel or thereabouts) that it may be ignored. Finally, we show how the colluding OPEC producers raised price from the original level P_1 to P_2.

How can such an enormous price increase be justified? OPEC's reply is that, from the point of view of overall efficiency (see Figure 30-1), conservation requires that oil users be charged enough to cover an adequate reservation price. This includes not only the relatively insignificant cost of extracting oil (MC), but also the far more important compensation to the oil producing countries because they no longer have as much "black gold" in the ground for future use. Therefore they argue: "Initially oil consuming nations did not pay us an adequate reservation price. As a result, they wastefully used this valuable resource. The price increase was simply the action necessary to prevent such wasteful use, and thus protect the world's future supply of oil."[8]

The reply of the oil importing countries is easy to predict: "True, conservation required some increase in price to a level above P_1. But the price increase of more than four times—all the way up to P_2—is ridiculous. Oil is not in the future crisis-supply situation that such a price implies. There are still vast reserves left in the Middle East, and every year new reserves are being discovered—for example, in the North Sea and Mexico. Moreover, additional large quantities of oil exist, although in forms that are difficult to extract (such as the oil in United States shale and in the Canadian tar sands, where a new technological breakthrough could greatly increase the world supply). Finally, by early in the next century

---

[7]As already pointed out, the world demand for oil has been increasing each year. For this and other reasons, we would like ideally to set up a whole sequence of diagrams, one for each year, as in Figure 30-5. But to simplify, we use one diagram and assume that demand has remained roughly the same each year, at *D* in Figure 30-6.

*[8]And they might add, along the lines suggested in Figure 30-5, "Conservation requires not only that we set the price high enough to begin with, but also that *we keep raising that price each year.*

we may develop completely new forms of atomic energy (fusion) that will substantially displace oil as a source of energy. In short, price P_2 is far higher than conservation requires. In raising price this much, the OPEC members are not primarily interested in the *efficient* use of this resource. Instead, their objective is the same as that of any old-fashioned monopolist: They have raised price in order to *transfer income from us to them*."

The Transfer Effect

What we are witnessing today in . . . oil and raw material prices is virtually the same as what is going on between trade unions and employers associations on the national level. It is a struggle for the distribution and use of the national product, a struggle for the world product. Helmut Schmidt, then Minister of Finance and later Chancellor of the Federal German Republic

The transfer from the United States and other oil importing countries to OPEC that has resulted from the oil price increase is shown roughly as area 1 in Figure 30-6. (On sales of Q_2 to oil importing countries, OPEC increased price from P_1 to P_2.) It is difficult, in such a diagram, to portray adequately the importance of this loss to us and benefit to the OPEC members. By the mid-1970s the transfer amounted to some $80 billion dollars a year, or about 2 to 3 percent of the total income of the oil importing countries.[9] The United States share of this burden was about $30 billion.

To sum up: In previous chapters, we have examined transfers within the United States—between American producers and consumers, or between American labor and

FIGURE 30-6 Effects of OPEC's increase in the price of oil.
The OPEC price increase from P_1 to P_2 caused the oil-consuming countries to purchase less than they would have otherwise; that is, Q_2 rather than Q_1. Thus they moved up their demand curve from E_1 to E_2. OPEC spokesmen argued that they raised prices in order to efficiently conserve the world's future supplies of oil. But in the opinion of the oil-consuming countries, a major objective of OPEC was to transfer area 1 (about $80 billion per year) from us to them.

capital. In such cases, we have been properly concerned with the "bottom line," which shows the efficiency effect—the net effect of the policy after all transfers have been canceled out. But the oil price increase is quite different because it involves an *international* transfer between countries. In this case, we still have some interest in the overall efficiency effect, that is, the net effect on the world as a whole. But we may also be very much concerned with the effect on the United States. So we focus on that transfer 1, the loss incurred by the United States (and other oil consuming countries). Thus, from the American point of view, color area 1 a very dark red.

---

*[9]Whereas the financial transfer occurs as soon as the oil is sold, the real transfer of goods may be spread out over time. To the degree that members of OPEC use these oil receipts to import automobiles, military aircraft, machinery, etc., there is an immediate transfer of goods. But part of OPEC's income is not spent in this way but, instead, simply accumulates in bank accounts in New York, London, or elsewhere. In this case, the real transfer occurs in the future when the bank deposits are used to buy physical goods.

BOX 30-4
COULD WE HAVE PREVENTED OPEC FROM GETTING SUCH A STRANGLEHOLD OVER OIL PRICE?

A number of observers believe that there were two occasions when action on our part might have prevented OPEC from initially seizing market power over the price of oil. The first came in May 1970 when the Libyan government ordered a production cutback in order to force an oil company to pay a higher price. At this point the United States government could have taken the initiative in convening the oil companies to ensure that any oil company cut off from its supplies by Libya or any other country could be supplied by the companies drawing oil from other Middle East sources. This action would have left the Libyans out in the cold: The oil company they were pressuring would have had a guaranteed supply of oil, while the Libyans would have lost their oil revenue. They would have also noticed how this lost revenue was diverted to other, competing Middle Eastern suppliers. At that time OPEC was still weak and far less prepared than it is today for a confrontation. Such an experience for the Libyans would have clearly underlined the cost that an oil producing country could expect if it tried to raise price.

A second opportunity presented itself in the following year. We have already seen that buyers facing a monopoly of sellers can protect their interests by forming a monopsony on their (buying) side of the market. This is essentially what the oil companies tried to do in facing monopolist OPEC in 1971: In a remarkable example of solidarity, they sent a message to OPEC demanding joint negotiations—collective bargaining by all the oil companies on one side, and all the OPEC members on the other. In other words, they were attempting to set up a bilateral monopoly, organizing power on their side of the market in order to offset OPEC's power on the other side of the market. (To back up their position, the oil companies also agreed secretly on an insurance scheme to guarantee that none would be cut off from supplies. But this effort came a year too late.†)

It came as no surprise when the OPEC members viewed this initiative with hostility. The crucial question was: Which side would the United States government support? From an economic point of view, the answer was clear: Since this action by the oil companies was designed to slow down OPEC's increase in the price of oil, it was in the economic interest of the United States to support it. But the United States government did not provide that support, largely for political reasons. There was a strong desire to maintain friendly relations with Iran and Saudi Arabia, which were viewed as important keys in containing Russian influence in the Middle East. (With larger oil revenues, countries like Iran and Saudi Arabia would become more prosperous, thus more able to resist Russian influence. Moreover, their governments would be less likely to be overthrown by elements hostile to the U.S.) American officials at that time were also very much concerned that the oil producing countries, if pressed too hard, might cut off oil supplies. So the U.S. government did not strongly support the oil companies, and the OPEC members easily rejected the idea of collective bargaining.

Since then, alternative suggestions have been put forward on how the major oil consuming nations might bargain collectively with OPEC, rather than simply accept OPEC's quoted monopoly price. But even if the oil importing countries were able to combine in some way and thus transform the oil market into a bilateral monopoly, one problem would remain: So long as OPEC can effectively threaten to cut off our oil supplies, how can we expect to substantially lower price?

†For more detail, see U.S. Senate, Subcommittee on Multinational Corporations, *Multinational Oil Corporations and U.S. Foreign Policy*, Report to the Committee on Foreign Relations (Washington: Government Printing Office, 1975), pp. 126–131.

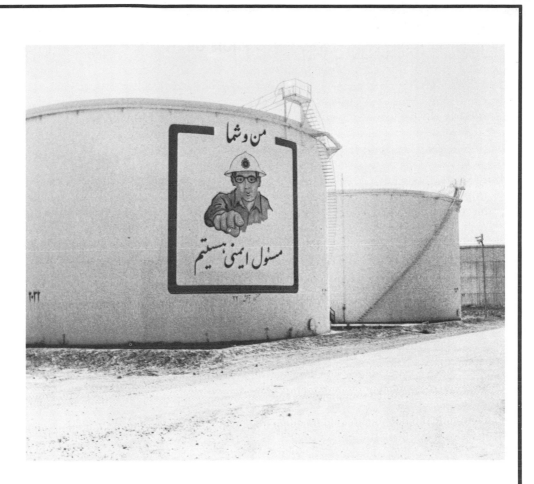

To clarify this point, consider the bilateral monopoly scenario: OPEC refusing to sell oil unless we pay, say, $20 a barrel, and the oil consuming countries refusing to buy oil unless we can get it for, say, $4 a barrel. Just as in labor negotiations, resulting price will depend very much on the credibility of each participant's threat to withdraw from the market and "not make a deal."

Could OPEC make good a threat not to sell? This would be very difficult: While the Saudis and the other low-population countries may have become wealthy enough to be able to "turn off the taps" temporarily, Iran and other OPEC members with large populations and heavy financial requirements would be hard-pressed to follow suit. There seems no way that OPEC could stop the flow of oil short of some collective arrangement for temporarily sharing and living off past accumulations of wealth.

But, whereas it would be difficult for OPEC to stop selling, it would be downright impossible for the consuming countries to stop buying. Therefore, our threat to walk away from the bargaining table would not be credible. There is no way that a democratic government in Europe or Japan could refuse to buy oil and thus allow its people to "freeze in the dark." Thus, OPEC would still hold the stronger basic bargaining position.

Key Points

1. If a resource (such as timber) is privately owned, its supply will reflect not only the current cost of harvesting or extracting it, but also the amount necessary to compensate the owner for the adverse effect of present harvests on future resource supplies.

2. If a resource (such as fish) is not privately owned, private fishing fleets will take no account of how this year's harvest will affect future harvests, and the result is an efficiency loss: Too much is harvested today.

3. In an attempt to limit the current catch of fish, the government may impose various restrictions, such as fishing licenses or off-season limits on fishing. In the case of ocean fishing, some governments have extended their territorial waters to limit the catch of foreign vessels. (It is difficult, however, to sort out how much of this territorial extension is a desire to conserve and how much is a desire to protect domestic vessels from foreign competition.)

4. Special problems arise when a resource is nonrenewable. (Timber and fish are renewable because they reproduce themselves. But resources like oil and copper do not.) If current rates of consumption continue, we must someday exhaust our nonrenewable resources. This simple observation has led to a number of "Doomsday studies" that predict the collapse of our economic system. However, a problem with many of these studies is that they generally take inadequate account of price adjustments. As such resources become increasingly scarce, their prices rise; this encourages conservation and stimulates the search for substitutes. An important question is: Are today's prices of nonrenewable resources high enough to ensure that existing supplies will not be used up too quickly and that the development of new substitutes will be encouraged?

5. OPEC has attempted to defend its rapid price increases with a similar sort of conservation argument. While most observers agree that conservation concerns have justified *some* oil price increase, much of the spectacular jump that occurred in the 1970s may be viewed as the exercise of monopoly power—the transfer of huge sums from the oil consuming nations to OPEC.

Key Concepts

renewable resource
nonrenewable resource
reservation price
privately owned resource
common property resource
territorial limits

sustainable yield curve
maximum sustainable yield
economic growth, pros and cons
conservation effect of increased oil price
transfer effect of increased oil price

Problems

30-1 In the early American frontier society, with an unlimited amount of fully mature forest (in which new growth was balanced by the rotting of old trees), cutting in one year did not reduce the timber available in later years. In that case, did it matter whether this resource was common property or privately owned? Does it matter today? Explain.

30-2 Is the potential extinction of a fish species another example (like pollution in Figure 23-5) of a problem that exists only because of the world's growing population? Can it also, like pollution, be viewed as an example of an external cost, where actions taken by one group (fishermen today) damage another group (fishermen tomorrow)?

30-3 Suppose 50 boats are fishing in an ocean area. Would there be any reason for the government to allow the boat owners to sign an agreement restricting the amount each catches? Is it possible that restricting the catch, which began as a conservation measure, may become a means of exercising market power? Explain. Can you think of any other examples of monopolists who might defend their use of monopoly power by calling it a conservation measure?

30-4 The problem of efficient timing in harvesting timber is illustrated in the dia-

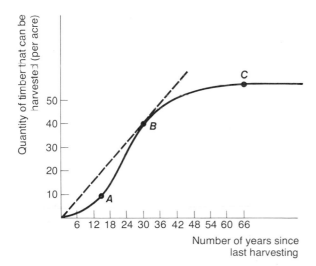

gram below. For example, point A on the yield curve indicates that if we wait 15 years before harvesting again, an acre will yield 10 units of timber. Which point represents a forest in which there is no longer any timber growth? (In other words, for every new tree that grows, an old one rots.) Would you cut off the timber every 15, 30, or 66 years? Explain. (Assume that cutting and replanting costs are negligible.)

30-5 Doomsday models typically project a constant rate of growth of population and resource usage, and hence forecast disaster. What economic forces tend to cause a change in the use of raw materials? What forces affect the rate of population growth?

30-6 Equity among generations seems to suggest that we should not sacrifice much for our children, since they are likely to be wealthier than we are regardless of what we do. But what do you think of the following counterargument? Historically, each generation has sacrificed for the next. Is it fair for any generation to opt out of this process and thus become a "free rider," receiving benefits from the previous generation, but making no attempt to pass on benefits to the next?

30-7 Suppose there is an unexpected technological breakthrough so that we can expect to be able to produce energy (equivalent to a barrel of oil) for only $6 by 1985. What do you think would happen to the price of oil now?

*__30-8__ In Figure 30-5, explain why it is inappropriate to push conservation too far. Specifically, explain why it would be a mistake to cut back consumption 1 unit below Q_1 in year 1 in order to conserve that unit for use in year 5. Also, show why it would be a mistake to ignore conservation concerns and use 1 *more* unit than Q_1 in year 1.

chapter 31
Income Inequality

Should a disc jockey earn twice as much as a United States senator? Should the president of a corporation earn five times as much as the President of the United States? Should a basketball player earn ten times as much as a violinist with the Boston Symphony? The United States income distribution is riddled with such glaring differences. In this chapter we shall look at the income of Americans to see whether such examples are the exception or the rule. How unequal are American incomes, overall?

Our second task will be to address the question: What is a *fair* distribution of income? Is it the income distribution that results from the free play of market forces? Or, is it an equal income for all? Or, is it some compromise between the two?

The place to begin is with a review of why income differences arise in the first place.

REVIEW: Why Do Incomes Differ?

In the preceding chapters, we have seen how market forces provide some people with larger incomes than others. For example, the high income of a surgeon is in part a return to human capital—compensation for the years of forgone income and hard study involved in acquiring a medical degree, and the necessary further study beyond. It may also be partly a *rent* on greater-than-average *innate talent*, or "gift." Of course, other individuals have gifts of quite a different sort; star athletes and entertainers also earn very large rents. Income differences also arise because of wealth; those who own stocks, bonds, and other forms of property receive income from them. (In fact, there are even greater differences in wealth than in income. The poorest half of our population holds only about 6 percent of the nation's wealth, and the poorest quarter holds almost none at all.[1]) In addition, income differences may arise because of the exercise of *market power*. People who find themselves in a monopoly position may be able to profit handsomely in terms of increased income. (Some of the surgeon's high income may be the result of the restricted supply of medical school graduates.)

While these reasons for income differences reflect the workings of the economic marketplace, there are other reasons which are far less related to the market, if at all. One specific surgeon's income may be lower because of a personal decision to sacrifice income for leisure. (The individual may have chosen to live and practice in a resort area, and to take off every afternoon to fish in the summer and ski in the winter.) An individual in a minority group may have a lower income because of discrimination. Some income differences may be the result of just plain luck. The quarterback who permanently injures his elbow and must retire from the game suffers an income loss from a vicious tackle that has nothing whatsoever to do with the marketplace. Of course, luck can raise income: Being "the right person at the right time" is a surefire way of earning a windfall income. When there is an oil blow-out, it must be capped immediately, and Red Adair commands a very large income because he is known as the "world's best." (See Box 31-1.)

Of all the causes of income differences, can we say which is most important? According to a recent—and surprising— study by Jacob Mincer, the answer is loud and clear: human capital. He concludes that *differences in human capital explain roughly 60 percent of the differences in American income.*[2]

HOW MUCH INCOME INEQUALITY IS THERE?

> **It's the rich whot gets the gryvy,**
> **It's the poor whot gets the blime.**
> **English ballad, World War II**

Are wide individual differences in income the exception or the rule? When we look at the income of all Americans, how much inequality is there?

In Table 31-1 column *a*, we see that if government taxes and all transfer payments (including social security benefits) are excluded, the poorest fifth of the population receives less than 1 percent of the nation's income (in fact, only 0.3 percent) At the

[1]Lester Thurow, "Toward a Definition of Economic Justice," *The Public Interest*, Spring 1973, pp. 56–80 (Table 2).

[2]"Education, Experience, Earnings and Employment," in F. Thomas Juster (ed.), *Education, Income and Human Behavior* (New York: McGraw-Hill, 1975), p. 73. This study was based on 1959 data for white urban males.

BOX 31-1
DON'T PHONE RED ADAIR UNLESS YOU ARE PREPARED TO PAY

When he answers the phone, there is a $5,000 charge.

If he advises on a problem, there is another $10,000 charge.

But it is only if he goes to work that the cash really starts to flow. For the job of capping the 1977 North Sea oil spill (a job that took his team less than a week), he was paid $6.6 million.

But before you think of competing for his job, ask yourself this: Do you *really* want to handle dynamite as close to burning oil wells as Red Adair does?

TABLE 31-1
Income Distribution of United States Families in 1976
(before taxes and transfers)

(a) Income distribution			(b) Cumulative income distribution			
Population	**Share of total income**		**Population**	**Share of total income**		**Point in Figure 31-1**
Low 20%	gets 0.3%		First 20%	gets	0.3%	H
Second 20%	gets 7.2		First 40%	gets 0.3 + 7.2 =	7.5	J
Third 20%	gets 16.3		First 60%	gets 7.5 + 16.3 =	23.8	K
Fourth 20%	gets 26.0		First 80%	gets 23.8 + 26.0 =	49.8	L
High 20%	gets 50.2		Total	gets 49.8 + 50.2 =	100.0	M

Source: Congressional Budget Office, *Poverty Status of Families under Alternative Definitions of Income,* Background Paper no. 17, rev. (Washington: Congress of the United States, June 1977), p. 24.

other extreme, the highest-income fifth of the population receive over half the nation's income. This unequal distribution is illustrated with a *Lorenz curve.* The first step is to rearrange the data in panel *a* of Table 31-1 into cumulative form in panel *b.* For example, in the second row, the poorest 40 percent of the population earn 7.5 percent of the nation's income. [To get this figure, we add (accumulate) the first two numbers in panel *a.*] This point, labeled *J,* is then plotted in

Figure 31-1, along with other points that are similarly calculated. The result is the Lorenz curve of United States income.

To get some feel for how much inequality exists in this distribution of income, we ask: What would this Lorenz curve look like if all families received exactly the same income? In that case, we would observe point *F* instead of point *J* (40 percent of the population would receive 40 percent of the income). And instead of point *K* we would

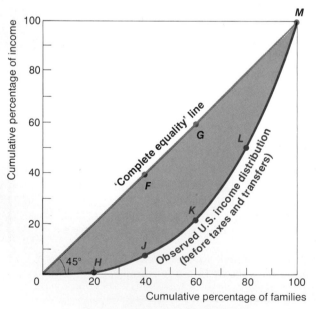

FIGURE 31-1 Lorenz curve showing income distribution of United States families in 1976 (before taxes and transfers).

If every family had exactly the same income, the American income distribution would follow the 45° straight line. The actual income distribution is shown by the curve that lies below this—with the red slice between the two showing the amount of income inequality. In Figure 31-2, we show how a substantial part of this inequality is removed by government tax and expenditure policy. (Note that we define income per family and not per person. As discussed in Chapter 1, a per-person definition makes no sense. For example, an infant earns a zero income but that gives no indication of how well off it may be.)

observe point *G* (60 percent of the population would receive 60 percent of the income). When we join all points like *F* and *G*, the result is the "complete equality" line *OFGM*, that is, the 45° straight line drawn from the origin. Thus the degree of income inequality is shown by the amount of bow in the Lorenz curve; that is, by the size of the red slice between the curve and the 45° line.

In fact, inequality is not as serious a problem as this diagram suggests. One reason: Even if each family were earning exactly the same lifetime income, the Lorenz curve would still not coincide with that 45° line. We would still observe some "inequality slice." The reason is that, during any single year, we would observe some families that are young (so still have a low income), and some families that are in their earning prime (with a higher income). Inequality exists in that year for these families, even though they have exactly the same lifetime income.

Nonetheless, even when such influences are fully taken into account, a substantial degree of inequality exists. Society's response is to reduce this inequality by government taxation that concentrates more heavily on the rich, and government expenditure that concentrates more heavily on the poor.

HOW MUCH INEQUALITY DOES THE GOVERNMENT NOW ELIMINATE?

The degree to which government taxes and transfer payments reduce inequality in the nation's income distribution is shown in Figure 31-2. The colored area is exactly the same as in Figure 31-1. But here it is broken down into a light area that shows how much the government reduces inequality and a darker area that shows how much still remains.

Curve *a* is a reproduction of the before-taxes-and-transfers curve graphed in Figure 31-1. Curve *b* shows the major shift toward equality that occurs as a result of social insurance, including social security and unemployment insurance. (Social security and other government programs that shift this curve are discussed in detail in the next chapter.) Curve *c* shows the further shift that results from cash transfers (such as Aid to Families with Dependent Children). Curve *d* shows the shift as a result of transfers-in-kind, where the government provides goods (such as food) or services instead of cash. The final shift to curve *e* shows the effect of taxation. When all programs are considered, the overall picture is one of a government that is redistributing income substantially from the rich to the poor, in the process eliminating roughly a third of the income inequality.[3] (Oft-heard claims that the government is not very effective in changing the nation's income distribution have frequently been based on calculations that do not take some of these programs, such as in-kind transfers, into account.)

One surprise in this diagram is that taxation, often supposed to be a great income redistributor, has much less impact than spending programs. Certainly taxes are a large enough item in our income to make a big difference. But they do little redistributing because, on balance, they are not very progressive. (As we have seen in Chapter 5,

[3]Perhaps more than this. Remember that we could achieve complete equality of lifetime incomes and still leave the Lorenz curve with a bow below the 45° line.

Another reason why even more inequality may have been eliminated is that curve *e*, based on government figures, may be on the low side. Edgar Browning (in "How Much More Equality Can We Afford?" *The Public Interest*, Spring 1976, p. 93) has calculated that as early as 1972, the low-income fifth of the population received 11.7 percent of the total income (rather than the 7.2 percent figure graphed in curve *e*). Moreover, according to Browning's figures, the gap between the Lorenz curve and the 45° line is similarly reduced throughout the rest of its range.

On the other hand, such calculations may err on the other side and overstate the effectiveness of government programs in reducing poverty. The precise reason is discussed in Chapter 32, footnote 5.

income taxes are progressive, taking a larger proportion of income from the rich than the poor. But these taxes are offset to a substantial degree by other regressive taxes and the existence of loopholes for the relatively wealthy.)

Finally, if we look at the nation's income distribution (curve *e*) between, say, the early 1960s and the early 1970s, we find that inequality is being reduced at a substantial, but far from spectacular, rate. Most of this change is caused by what's happening at the extremes: a rise in the income share of the bottom fifth of the population and a decline in the share of the top fifth.[4]

In reducing income inequality, have we gone too far? Or not far enough? Should we aim at some target distribution of income? Is there, in principle, such a thing as a fair or equitable distribution for society?

WHAT IS AN EQUITABLE INCOME DISTRIBUTION?

> See how the fates their gifts allot,
> For A is happy—B is not.
> Yet B is worthy, I dare say,
> Of more prosperity than A!
>
> If I were fortune—which I'm not—
> B should enjoy A's happy lot,
> And A should die in miserie—
> That is, assuming I am B.
>
> **Gilbert and Sullivan,**
> ***The Mikado***

A search for an equitable or just distribution of income for society will lead us into treacherous intellectual terrain from which some of the world's noted philosophers have been unable to escape with reputations intact. Although, in this elementary treatment, we cannot expect to arrive at any definitive answer, we can at least isolate some of the important issues and questions of debate.

But to begin with, we reemphasize two important points made in Chapter 1.

First, *equity and equality are two different concepts.* In our Lorenz curve description of income distribution, we have addressed only the question of equality; How equal *are* incomes? This is an empirical question. We can answer it by looking at the facts—by examining how much each American family earns. On the other hand, the question of equity is not what incomes are, but rather what they *should be.* What income distribution is fair and just? This is an ethical issue on which people are not unanimous. Some believe that equity is equality, that all should be paid the same income. On the other hand, some believe that equity is not equality, that, for example, the individual who works harder or more effectively should be paid more.

> *Equal* means "of the same size." *Equitable* means "fair." The two are not necessarily the same.

Second, we reemphasize that government policy cannot be designed to achieve equity alone; instead it must take into account other (conflicting) goals as well. But to sharpen our idea of equity, suppose for now that this is our only concern. *On grounds of equity alone,* what should our target distribution of income be?

Of the many possible answers to this question, we now consider three: first, the distribution that results from the free play of the economic market place; second, a completely equal distribution of income; and third, some compromise between the two.

---

[4]Edgar Browning, "How Much More Equality Can We Afford?" Table 3.

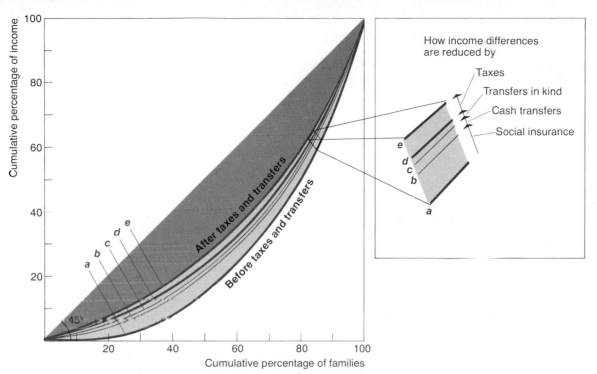

FIGURE 31-2 How government taxes and expenditures reduce United States income inequality (1976).

Taxes and transfers by all levels of government in 1976 reduced income inequality in the United States by about one third. Taxes, which shifted the curve from *d* to *e*, were a relatively unimportant form of equalization compared to government expenditure programs; the most important of these was social insurance (social security and unemployment insurance), which reduced inequality from curve *a* to curve *b*.

SOURCE: Congressional Budget Office, *Poverty Status of Families under Alternative Definitions of Income,* Background Paper no. 17, rev. (Washington; Congress of the United States, June 1977), p. 24.

Is the Free Market's Distribution of Income Equitable?

Whatever is, is right.

Alexander Pope, *Essay on Man*

In economics, few would agree that whatever is, is necessarily right. *The free market does not do an entirely satisfactory job of distributing income.* Consider a monopolist who amasses a huge sum by successfully cornering the world's supply of a good, selling some at a very high price, and letting the unsold balance rot. In such cases it is very difficult to argue that the free market distributes income in a fair, equitable way.

But our reservations about the free-market distribution are far more fundamental than this, and apply even when markets are perfectly competitive. Such markets will, under certain conditions (no externalities, etc.), efficiently allocate factors of production in a way that will maximize the total income pie. In the process, they determine a set of prices of both goods and factors of production—the wages of labor, rents on land, etc. Thus they both maximize the nation's income pie and determine how it will be divided. But when we say that free competitive markets are efficient, we are only saying that they do a good job of maximizing the total output pie. We make no claim whatsoever that they divide that pie up in a fair, equitable way.

Of course, efficiency is an important objective. It is clearly desirable to have an economic system in which deadweight losses have been eliminated and the national pie is consequently maximized. But remember: That national pie is being maximized for *those who have the income to pay for it*. Thus, competitive markets maximize our output, but that output may include luxuries for the rich and too few necessities for the poor. Even the strongest supporters of the free market, while championing its efficiencies, will still vote for aid to widows and the destitute. This point is important enough to repeat: The provable virtues of a free, perfectly competitive market have to do with its efficiency, not its equity.

Perhaps the best illustration is this: In a perfectly competitive economy, rents on land efficiently direct the nation's scarce land into its most productive uses. (If rents are forced below the competitive level, land will be used in wasteful ways.) But the payment of these rents to those who own the land does not necessarily give us a fair and equitable distribution of income. We can see this point by considering an extreme example of land that has been inherited by the idle rich. Why should they earn an income many times that of the able and hardworking people whom they have hired to manage and work this land? Indeed, it is very difficult to argue that a free market, even a perfectly competitive one, will necessarily provide an equitable distribution of income.

Equality as a Target

The idea that we should aim for complete equality has an immediate appeal to the average citizen and to the philosopher alike. (See Box 31-2.) But the more we think about it, the less simple it all becomes. In fact, the considered reaction of many people is that anyone who sacrifices valuable leisure for hard work should get some reward: It is basically unfair to pay the same income to those who work and to those who do not. If individual A works only part-time and spends the remaining time at home asleep, it is only fair to pay A less than individual B, who works full-time.[5]

This argument can be pushed one step further: Consider individual C, who is just plain lazy, and consequently is totally unproductive. Is it fair to pay C for sleeping on the job, when we don't pay A for sleeping at home? Therefore, it's not just work that should be rewarded, but how hard you work. And it is even more than just hard work; it is also the nature of the job. Paying steelworkers a higher wage to build skyscrapers does not seem unjust. Instead, it seems like a fair return for the risk they are taking.

To illustrate a further reason for concluding that complete equality is not necessarily just or equitable, consider an individual who is working full-time and is also studying hard on weekends and in her spare time to accumulate human capital, say a degree in accounting. Fairness and equity suggest that when she trades her valuable leisure for hard work, she should someday be rewarded; her income tomorrow should be increased as a reward for her accumulation of human capital today. Similarly, should not the accumulation of physical

---

[5]This conclusion not only has an intuitive appeal; it can also be supported with the following, more technical argument. Anyone who decides on shorter working hours is taking some of his or her potential income in the form of leisure, rather than cash. Therefore, income should be defined broadly to include both income taken in the form of cash and income taken in the form of leisure. Fairness requires that an individual who takes a lot of income in one form—leisure—should get less in the other form—cash.

capital also be rewarded? Is it unjust if someone who saves (that is, who sacrifices consumption today) is rewarded with greater consumption tomorrow?

The important conclusion of this section is this: <u>Considerations of *equity alone* do not lead us to set complete equality as our objective.</u> We are skeptical of this target just as we were skeptical earlier of the free-market determination of income. Therefore, we now consider some compromise between the two.

A Compromise between the Free Market and Complete Equality

It is easy to conclude that both the free-market and complete-equality solutions involve serious inequities. What is far more difficult is to say where in the broad range in between we should aim. We will not be able to answer that question. But here are some suggestive ideas for you to consider as you grapple with it (and you must, as a voter.)

Make It a Fair Race, . . .

Suppose we think of participating in the economy as being in a race in which each runner's income is determined by his finish. The egalitarian view that "justice is income equality" implies that the government should equalize all rewards at the end of the race: Give everyone a bronze medal—no golds, and no last-place finishers left empty-handed. As the Dodo in *Alice in Wonderland*, put it, "Everybody has won, and all must have prizes." We have already seen that this "complete-equality" solution involves serious inequities.

An alternative view is that the responsibility of the government is only to ensure that the race is fair. Disadvantages should be eliminated: No one should start with a 50-yard handicap because of being a woman, or a black, or the child of a father who is not influential. In this race, everyone has a right, but it is the right of equality of opportunity, not equality of reward. In brief, everyone should have the right to an equal *start*—but not to an equal *finish*.[6]

The idea of equal opportunity has an immediate appeal, but defining it unfortunately is not simple. Buried in any definition of a fair race is a judgment of which disadvantages are unfair and should be removed, and which disadvantages should not. Disadvantages of race, color, and ethnic background clearly should be removed. But should compensation be made for disadvantages arising from differences in natural ability? Does it make any more sense to penalize an individual in the economic race for more natural business talent than to penalize a runner for strong legs? If we were to embark on such a penalty or handicap system, we would end up in the world of Kurt Vonnegut's Handicapper General, who weighs down ballerinas with bags of bird-shot (see Box 31-3).

. . . but Modify the Rewards It is quite possible to have a fair race, yet still have a bad system of rewards. For example, suppose the winner were to be given the Olympic Stadium and the loser were to be thrown (Roman style) to the lions? Believing in a fair economic race does not prevent us from modifying its rewards—in other words, from using government taxes and transfer

[6]The issue of rights is an important one in this debate. Since everyone has certain other rights (the right to vote, freedom of speech, etc.), why should each of us not have the right of equal access to the marketplace? In other words, why shouldn't we be given equal (dollar) votes to spend there? In practice, it would be prohibitively costly to give everyone this right: An equal division of the pie would greatly shrink its size. But even if this cost did not exist, we can see that there would still be a fundamental philosophical problem. In the economic race, which should be the "inalienable right": the right to an equal start, or the right to an equal finish?

(At best, the concept of an inalienable right is a slippery one. For example, in many countries the right to vote isn't inalienable at all. Even in some democracies, it's taken away from a small group, including some convicted felons. In England this disenfranchised group includes the king, the queen, and members of the House of Lords.)

BOX 31-2 RAWLS ON EQUALITY

Harvard philosophy professor John Rawls has argued that income equality is a desirable goal—except in special circumstances. His analysis starts in an extremely promising way. A consensus on the fair distribution of income is extremely difficult to achieve because everyone has a particular ax to grind: Those with high incomes support a system in which inequality is allowed, because it lets them keep their higher income. On the other hand, those with low incomes are more likely to advocate equality because it will improve their position. Rawls therefore suggests that, to get an objective view, people must be removed from their present situation and placed in an "original position" where they decide on what the distribution of income should be, without knowing the specific place they themselves will eventually take in this distribution. What income distribution will they choose?

Although the details of Rawls' argument are often complex, the essentials may be simplified in a few sentences. The typical person in the original position will argue something like this: "Whatever income distribution is chosen, with my luck, chances are that I'll end up on the bottom end of it. So I will vote for the income distribution that will leave me, the low man on the totem pole, as well off as possible." Since everyone is similarly situated in the original position, Rawls argues that all will reason in the same way. He concludes that a consensus will develop in favor of an equal distribution of income—unless there is an unequal distribution that leaves *everyone* better off. This is what Rawls calls the *difference principle.*†

While Rawls' approach will generally lead to equality, there are special circumstances in which it will not. Indeed, it is important to understand when, in his world, equality will be chosen and when it will not. We now

TABLE 31-2
When Rawls' Theory Leads to Inequality: An Example‡

	Income of all individuals but one	Income of last individual
Option A (equality)	$ 5,000	$5,000
Option B (inequality)	$10,000	$5,100 ★

★Option B chosen because everyone is better off

illustrate with two extreme examples. (When you understand them you will see that the argument applies in less extreme cases as well.) Suppose people in the original position are choosing between the two income distributions shown in Table 31-2. Option A is a completely equal distribution in which everyone's annual income is $5,000. (Perhaps taxation of any income above this level is so prohibitive that everyone stops earning at this point.) Now suppose it is possible to move to Option B, where everyone's income is $10,000 except for the last individual, whose income is $5,100. (Suppose that this move is possible because the prohibitive tax is removed and people respond by earning more.) Because everyone benefits, Rawlsian logic leads to a move from A to B, a move *away from equality.*§ Most people would agree. So far, Rawls's theory is not controversial: In the circumstances shown in Table 31-2, Rawls, like almost everyone else, would allow for a great deal of inequality.

In Table 31-3, we consider the more likely situation, where we are faced with options A and C. As before, the move away from equality (in this case, from A to C) benefits almost everyone by $5,000. But now we recognize that any such substantial change is likely to leave at least one person worse off. (Note in the last column how the income of the last individual is reduced by $100.) In this case,

†In his *Theory of Justice* (Cambridge: Harvard University Press, 1971), Rawls was concerned with more than just income distribution: "All social values—liberty and opportunity, income and wealth, and the bases of self-respect—are to be distributed equally unless an unequal distribution of any, or all, of these values is to everyone's advantage." (p. 63).

‡Whereas we focus on the bottom individual, Rawls' focus is on a typical individual in the bottom group. But this does not seriously affect his conclusion or our evaluation of it.

§In this discussion, envy is not taken into account; it is assumed that nobody's happiness is reduced by the knowledge that someone else has become richer.

TABLE 31-3
When Rawls' Theory Leads to Equality: An Example

	Income of all individuals but one	Income of last individual
Option A (equality)	$ 5,000	$5,000*
Option C (inequality)	$10,000	$4,900

*Option A chosen because a move to C would damage the last individual.

Rawls argues that people in an original position would choose option A: With their concern about ending up at the bottom end of the totem pole, they would focus on the figures in the last column and prefer A with its $5,000 income to C with its $4,900 income. Thus, according to Rawls, people would choose equality.

It is here, when he is putting forward a strong argument in favor of equality, that Rawls' theory is open to criticism. Ask yourself: If you were in Rawls' original position, without knowledge of where you would eventually end up, which option would you choose? Would you join the consensus Rawls expects in favor of A? Most people would find C difficult to resist. The miniscule risk of being $100 worse off seems trivial in comparison with the near certainty of being $5,000

better off. This seems to be a risk well worth taking. Indeed, those who would select Rawls' option A are those who would *avoid risk at almost any cost.* Indeed, how in the world would you find anyone so risk-averse? (Observe that the risk you would be taking in choosing income distribution C rather than A would be the same as your risk at the racetrack or the stock exchange if you were to bet $100 for a chance to win $5,000, with odds *in your favor* of 100 million to one.†† Who would not join the queue?)

Thus people in an original position would not necessarily vote for equality option A over C, as Rawls contends. Accordingly, it is when he is arguing for equality that his argument is weakest. The difficulty is that his analysis is based on the assumption that the only concern is with what is happening in the last column in those two tables††—that is, with that last, poorest individual. (Specifically, the choice is based on *maxi*mizing the *min*imum income; hence, this is often referred to as the *maximin* criterion.) But why should we completely ignore the vast majority and be totally preoccupied with that last individual?

In a later reconsideration of the maximin criterion,§§ Rawls concluded that although he still viewed it as attractive, "a deeper investigation . . . may show that some other conception of justice is more reasonable. In any case, the idea that economists may find most useful . . . is that of the original position. This perspective . . . may prove illuminating for economic theory."

††Why those odds? There are about 100 million families (or unattached individuals) in the United States. In moving from option A to C, they would all "win" $5,000—except for the one who would lose $100.

*††Experiment: Change the two numbers in the first column any way you like (just so long as you keep the figure for option A smaller than for option B). Rawls' decision will remain unaffected. This is true whether you make the example less extreme or more extreme. To illustrate: If you happened to vote, like Rawls, for option A in Table 31-3, just change the $10,000 in the southwest corner to $100,000 or even more. Won't you eventually come around to option C and give up voting in a Rawlsian way?

*§§See John Rawls, "Some Reasons for the Maximin Criterion," *American Economic Review, Proceedings,* 1974, pp. 141–146.

Rawls' theory had an immediate appeal to those who believe in income equality because it seemed to be a more scientific support of their position than the traditional argument for equality. According to that earlier argument, complete equality is a desirable target because it would maximize the total utility of all individuals in society. But this conclusion follows only if it can be assumed that all individuals have the same capacity to enjoy income—technically, only if everyone has the same marginal utility of income schedule. (If this assumption does not hold, we can increase total utility by moving away from complete equality—by transferring some income away from those who are less able to enjoy it to those who are more able to enjoy it.) Unfortunately, there is no way we can confirm or deny this assumption; remember, there is no way to meter people's heads to compare the satisfaction they receive.

So this traditional marginal utility argument does not provide a very scientific support for income equality. Nor, as we have seen in this box, does Rawls' theory. Just like the older theory, it has a weak link. (In Rawls' theory, the weak link is the assumption that the only concern is for the individual who turns out to be lowest on the totem pole.) Moreover, many of those who believe in equality became less enthusiastic about Rawls' theory when they discovered that it allows for a very substantial degree of inequality—as we have seen in Table 31-2 and as Rawls himself has reiterated. (See, for example, John Rawls, "Some Reasons for the Maximin Criterion," p. 145.)

BOX 31-3
KURT VONNEGUT ON WHY ONLY HORSES AND GOLFERS SHOULD BE HANDICAPPED†

The year was 2081, and everybody was finally equal. They weren't only equal before God and the law. They were equal every which way. Nobody was smarter than anybody else. Nobody was better looking than anybody else. Nobody was stronger or quicker than anybody else. All this equality was due to the 211th, 212th, and 213th Amendments to the Constitution, and to the unceasing vigilance of agents of the United States Handicapper General. . . .

George [Bergeron, whose] intelligence was way above normal, had a little mental handicap radio in his ear. He was required by law to wear it at all times. It was tuned to a government transmitter. Every twenty seconds or so, the transmitter would send out some sharp noise to keep people like George from taking unfair advantage of their brains. . . .

On the television screen were ballerinas. . . . They weren't really very good—no better than anybody else would have been anyway. They were burdened with sashweights and bags of birdshot and their faces were masked, so that no one, seeing a free and graceful gesture or a pretty face, would feel like something the cat drug in. George was toying with the vague notion that maybe dancers shouldn't be handicapped. But he didn't get very far with it before another noise in his ear radio scattered his thoughts. . . .

George began to think glimmeringly about his abnormal son who was now in jail, about Harrison, but a twenty-one-gun salute in his head stopped that. "Boy!" said Hazel, "that was a doozy, wasn't it?" It was such a doozy that George was white and trembling, and tears stood on the rims of his red eyes.

Two of the eight ballerinas had collapsed to the studio floor, were holding their temples. . . .

The television program was suddenly interrupted for a news bulletin. It wasn't clear at first as to what the bulletin was about, since the announcer, like all announcers, had a serious speech impediment. For about half a minute, and in a state of high excitement, the announcer tried to say, "Ladies and gentlemen—"

He finally gave up, handed the bulletin to a ballerina to read. . . . "That's all right—" Hazel said of the announcer, "he tried. That's the big thing. He tried to do the best he could with what God gave him. He should get a nice raise for trying so hard."

"Ladies and gentlemen—" said the ballerina, . . . "Harrison Bergeron, age fourteen . . . has just escaped from jail, where he was held on suspicion of plotting to overthrow the government. He is a genius and an athlete, is under-handicapped, and should be regarded as extremely dangerous."

A police photograph of Harrison Bergeron was flashed on the screen. . . . Harrison's appearance was Halloween and hardware. Nobody had ever born heavier handicaps. . . . Instead of a little ear radio for a mental handicap, he wore a tremendous pair of earphones, and spectacles with thick wavy lenses. The spectacles were intended to make him not only half blind, but to give him whanging headaches besides.

Scrap metal was hung all over him. Ordinarily, there was a certain symmetry, a military neatness to the handicaps issued to strong people, but Harrison looked like a walking junkyard. . . .

†Abridgement of "Harrison Bergeron" from the book WELCOME TO THE MONKEY HOUSE by Kurt Vonnegut Jr. Copyright (c) 1961 by Kurt Vonnegut Jr. Originally published in FANTASY AND SCIENCE FICTION. Reprinted by Permission of DELACORTE PRESS/SEYMOUR LAWRENCE.

payments to reduce the income differences that result.

To the authors, this idea of a fair race and a modified system of rewards that reduces (but does not eliminate) income inequality seems to be an appealing principle. But again, the idea is not as simple as it sounds. Is not an individual's economic life less like a standard race than like a relay race? Moreover, a relay race with no beginning or end? The race you run depends on the start you get in terms of your whole background, including your family wealth. A first reaction is that it should not be like this. To keep the race fair, everyone should be started off equally, without any advantage of inherited wealth. Should we therefore tax away all inheritances and, for the same reason, gifts?

This is a difficult proposal to defend, even on equity grounds. Consider two men with equal incomes. One spends it all. The other wishes to save in order to pass wealth on to his children. Is it fair to impose a tax that prohibits him from doing so? And, in broader terms, is not charity a virtue? What can one say of a society that prevents gifts to family or friends?

Conclusions: Can We Pin Down the Idea of Equity?

Unfortunately, the answer is no. The perplexing problem of equity yields no clear solution. The only conclusions we have been able to reach are both negative ones:

Equity is not complete equality of income; nor is it the income distribution that the free market generates. So we are left somewhere in between. We conclude that, in terms of equity considerations alone, we should move from a free-market distribution some distance, but not the whole way, toward equalizing incomes. To further complicate matters, any such move tends to involve an efficiency cost in terms of a shrinking national pie. (Guaranteeing people an income regardless of what they do tends to erode their incentive to work, a problem that will be detailed in the next chapter.) Because of this efficiency cost, it is desirable to stop short of the degree of equality which would be chosen if equity were the sole objective.

In practice, we have already moved some considerable distance toward equalizing incomes, as Figure 31-2 illustrates. It is possible that we have not yet moved far enough; and it is also possible that we have moved too far. This question of how the nation's income should be distributed is likely to remain an issue of continuing debate. But it is important that the dispute about how the national income pie should be divided does not become so heated and exhausting that the total size of that pie is substantially reduced. To use an earlier analogy: If all participants had spent their energies in a squabble about how the race should be run and how the rewards should be divided, no one would have broken the 4-minute mile.

Key Points

1. Large differences exist in the incomes of individual Americans. Some have high incomes because of their human capital, wealth, native talent, market power, or just plain luck. Others have low incomes because they enjoy none of these advantages or for some other reason. For example, they may suffer from discrimination, or they may have sacrificed income for leisure.

2. If we examine the United States income distribution before government taxes and transfers are taken into account, we observe a remarkable degree of income inequality. The poorest 20 percent receive only 0.3 percent of the nation's income pie, while the richest 20 percent get over half that pie.

3. However, roughly a third of this inequality is eliminated by government transfer expenditures that are concentrated heavily on the poor, and by progressive taxes that draw heavily from the rich. (However, our tax system is not as progressive as is often supposed, and it does far less equalizing than government expenditures.)

4. The most effective government expenditure in equalizing income is social insurance (social security and unemployment insurance). But other government expenditures, both in cash and in kind, also play an important role.

5. Equality is a question of fact: How equal are incomes? On the other hand, equity is a matter of judgment: What should

relative incomes be? It is difficult to argue that either a completely equal distribution of incomes or the unequal free-market distribution is equitable. A desirable target seems to lie somewhere in between.

6. While it is very difficult to be more precise than this, two rough guidelines have been suggested. First, keep the economic race as fair as possible. In other words, give everyone an equal opportunity. For example, the government should ensure that no one starts at a disadvantage because of race or sex.

7. But equal opportunity need not result in equal reward. Even if everyone could be given an equal start, there is no reason to expect that all will finish in a tie. Some will get greater rewards than others. Thus, the second responsibility of the government is, where necessary, to modify rewards—that is, to reduce income inequality by taxes and transfer payments.

8. Finally, even if we could determine an equitable income distribution, it does not follow that the government should continue to redistribute income up to this point. The reason is that the act of redistributing income (changing the division of the national pie) affects the incentive to work and hence the level of efficiency (the size of that pie). So a compromise should be selected between the conflicting objectives of equity and efficiency.

Key Concepts

cumulative income distribution (Lorenz curve)
social insurance
cash transfers
transfers in kind
difference between equity and equality

limitations of the free market as a distributor of income
*Rawls' difference principle
*maximin
difference between equalizing opportunity and equalizing reward

Problems

31-1 Explain to your very bright roommate (who is not taking economics) why some Americans have much higher incomes than others.

31-2 Mark McCormack is, in his own words, an "engineer of careers." His company grossed $35 million in 1976 from a 15 to 40 percent agent's fee for managing 250 tennis stars (Bjorn Borg) and golfers (Jack Nicklaus, Arnold Palmer). Others have also tried to set themselves up as agents in this way, but have not succeeded on this handsome a scale, if at all. Do you think McCormack's huge income is the result of (a) only luck; (b) luck and other reasons; or (c) just other reasons? If you answer (b) or (c), explain what the other reasons might be.

31-3 Does the marketplace generate a rental income for those with high reputation (just as for those with great skill)?

31-4 Do you agree with the following statement? (If not, explain why.) "Free-market prices of factors of production help to maximize the total national income pie and also divide that pie in an equitable way."

*31-5 Is this statement true or false? If false, correct it. "Rawls' maximin principle is to *maximize* the *minimum* possible income. But this is the preference only of people who are unwilling to risk any of their income in the hope of acquiring more. Many people are not like this, including all those individuals who bet a small part of their income (at the races or Monte Carlo) in the hope of winning more."

*31-6 In 1899, John Bates Clark wrote (in the *Distribution of Wealth*) that "free competition tends to give to labor what labor creates [that is, the marginal product of labor], to capitalists what capital creates [that is, the marginal product of capital] and to entrepreneurs what the coordinating function creates." This sounds as though everyone gets what he or she deserves; that is, free competition distributes income in an equitable way. Do you agree? In your view, what does a free competitive market do well, and what does it do not so well?

chapter 32
Government Policies to Reduce Inequality: *Can We Solve the Poverty Problem?*

Welfare has been indicted for encouraging family dissolution, promoting illegitimacy, degrading and alienating recipients, papering over the sins of a society that generates poverty, shielding the dissolute and lazy from their just deserts, failing to support life by providing too little assistance, and fostering sloth by providing too much. Conservatives, liberals, and radicals unite in attacking the welfare system but divide over its specific faults.
Henry J. Aaron

Although Americans may differ on the question of how far we should go in reducing income inequality in general, there is one specific issue on which the overwhelming majority agree: Nobody should starve; nor should children grow up in abject poverty. Yet, in 1976, poverty was still a fact of life for *about 1 in 12 American families.* You can confirm the effect this has on people by driving from a wealthy suburb of any large American city into a depressed core area. In the United States, overall wealth stands in stark contrast to the poverty faced by those who are insufficiently fed, housed, and clothed. In the mid-1960s the poverty problem was recognized to be so important that, in introducing new legislation, the United States government declared a "war on poverty," introducing a series of bills to improve the lot of the poor.

This chapter is a study of the poor—the individuals who appear in the bottom left-hand corner of the Lorenz income curve in Figure 31-1. Who are the poor? Why are they poor? What programs has the government introduced to fight the war on poverty? Are we winning that war, or do these programs add up to what is commonly called a "welfare mess"? And finally, can existing programs be streamlined and made more effective?

POVERTY

The economic definition of poverty is "inadequate income." But this does not mean that poverty is strictly an economic condition. It is often also a state of mind, a condition in which the individual feels helpless and unable to cope. Therefore, poverty is a subject for sociologists and political scientists, as well as economists. One of the difficulties encountered in studying poverty is the chicken-or-egg problem: Are people unable to cope because they are poor? Or are they poor because they are unable to cope? Undoubtedly the answer is, "Both."

> *Poverty* exists when people have inadequate income to buy the necessities of life. In 1978, it was defined, for an urban family of four, as an income of about $6,600.

How the Poverty Line Is Defined

In defining the poverty line—officially known as the "low-income line"—the government starts with the idea that food is the first essential in a poverty budget. Accordingly, the Department of Agriculture calculates the cost of a diet that satisfies the requirements of minimum nutrition. (As in any such definition of subsistence or bare necessity, judgment is very important. To illustrate: About $80 in 1959 prices, spent on just the right combination of things like lard, soybeans, orange juice, and beef liver, will provide a medically balanced diet for one person for a year. Moreover, this menu will be healthier than the present diet of some well-to-do Americans. But who would you get to eat it? Consequently, the Department of Agriculture does not base its calculations on this, but instead uses a reasonably acceptable, but not luxurious, diet.) Finally, since low-income families typically spend about one-third of their income on food, this food cost is multiplied by 3 to arrive at the official low-income line. In 1978, it was about $6,600 for the typical urban family of four.[1] (The precise figure varies, depending on the size of the family, its location, and so on. Thus the poverty line for an urban family of six members was roughly $8,800; but for the same family living on a farm, the poverty line was reduced to just over $7,500. For more detail, see Table 1-1.)

Of course, the poverty line has to be adjusted upward periodically to take account of inflation. And historically over the long term, it tends to rise for another reason as well: Our concept of poverty keeps shifting up. The poverty income of about $6,600 in 1978 would have been regarded in colonial times as a very handsome income indeed (even after full adjustment is made for inflation). In fact, it would still have been considered a good income as late as the 1930s. When President Roosevelt spoke of one-third of the nation living in poverty at that time, he implied a poverty-line income in the 1930s that was far lower, and that would buy far less, than the poverty income of 1978. So upward adjustments in the definition of poverty do occur. But beware: If the definition of poverty is made too flexible, the concept becomes meaningless. If, for example, poverty is defined as the income of the bottom one-tenth of the population, there is no hope of curing it: By definition, 1 in 10 Americans will *always* be poor, no matter how much we may raise everyone's income. And the statement that 1 American family in 10 is living in poverty will tell us absolutely nothing about how serious the problem is, or how successful we have been in curing it.

Who Are the Poor?

Table 32-1 shows how poverty is related to race and location: A nonwhite is more than twice as likely to be living in poverty as a white,[2] and a person living in the South is more than twice as likely to be poor as an individual living in the North. Poverty falls unevenly in other respects as well. For ex-

---

[1] In order to recognize the many dimensions of this problem, wouldn't it be more meaningful to define poverty, not in terms of inadequate income, but rather, in terms of inadequate food, shelter, clothing, and so on? One of the difficulties with this idea is that it would include in the ranks of the poverty-stricken many Americans who have more than enough income to afford a proper diet, but haven't the judgment to buy it.

[2] It is not true, however, that there are more nonwhite poor than white poor in the United States. Without reading further, can you see why? (The answer is, there are more white poor, because most of the population is white.)

ample, the larger the family size, the more likely it will be poor. Someone with less than 8 years of education is about four times as likely to be poor as someone who has finished high school; and going on to complete a university education almost (but not quite[3]) guarantees one against poverty. People living in the core area of a big city are more likely to be poor than those living in its suburbs. (Part of the reason is that many of those who have been able to afford to move from the core to the suburbs have already done so.) But poverty is not limited to the core areas of big cities: A heavy incidence falls on farms and in small towns and cities as well. Finally, a fatherless family is about eight times as likely to be poor as a family with a resident father. In fact, in the early 1970s, almost half the nation's poor lived in fatherless families.

GOVERNMENT POLICIES TO REDUCE POVERTY

Federal, state, and local social welfare expenditures (defined broadly to include social security and aid to education) grew from $77.2 billion in 1965 to $286.5 billion in 1975, an almost fourfold increase in one decade. By 1975, almost 20 percent of United States GNP was devoted to such expenditures.[4] What are these programs, and how successful have they been?

Policies to Reduce the Causes of Poverty

The public usually thinks of antipoverty policies as the transfer of large sums to the poor, and most of our expenditures are indeed of this form. But these outlays relieve only the *symptoms* of poverty: They make it more bearable without providing much hope that the problem will be cured (that is, that the poor will be able to increase their earnings). A more promising long-run approach to poverty is to attack its *causes*. For example, expenditures on education or training are designed to cure one of the causes of poverty: inadequate human capital. The objective is to allow people to accumulate this capital in order to provide for their own support in the future. (Although it is usually more promising to attack the causes of a problem than its symptoms, this is not always the case. In extreme cases of "clinical" poverty, where individuals have such a low innate capacity or skill that no amount of training will allow them to earn a living, straight support programs may be the more effective form of assistance.)

In this section, we consider policies that attack the causes of poverty.

1. *Subsidizing investment in human capital.* Federal, state, and local governments subsidize education in various ways. The provision of free elementary and secondary schooling is the most important, but there are also other programs that provide job training. For example, the Comprehensive Employment and Training Act (CETA) provides federal subsidies for training unemployed workers.

TABLE 32-1
Incidence of Poverty by Race and Region
(percentage of population in 1976)

By race		By region	
Whites	7.3%	South	12.1%
Nonwhites	16.1%	West	8.2%
		Northeast	5.7%
		North Central	5.9%

Source: Congressional Budget Office, *Poverty Status of Families under Alternative Definitions of Income*, Background Paper no. 17, rev. (Washington: Congress of the United States, June 1977), pp. 11, 13.

[3]In 1972, 2.2 percent of college graduates were living below the poverty line.
[4]Congressional Budget Office, *Poverty Status of Families under Alternative Definitions of Income*, Background Paper no. 17, rev. (Washington: Congress of the United States, June 1977), p. 1.

2. *Antidiscrimination Policies.* Another cause of poverty is job discrimination, which reduces the income of blacks, other minorities, and women. The Equal Pay Act (1963) requires that women be paid the same as men for equal work, and the Civil Rights Act (1964) outlaws discrimination in hiring, firing, and other employment practices.

3. *Dealing with Unemployment and Disability.* The most important government policies to cure unemployment are, of course, policies designed to keep the economy operating at a high-enough level of output. Permanent disability cannot be cured, but some of it can be prevented by adequate safety standards, the responsibility of the Occupational Safety and Health Administration. (When unemployment or disability do occur, workers are covered in each case by government insurance programs.)

4. *Other Policies.* The Work Incentive Program (WIN) subsidizes the training and employment of people on welfare. It also enables parents to take jobs by providing day-care facilities for children. This provision is particularly important in reducing the incidence of poverty in that increasingly important group of families with only one parent in the home.

Policies to Reduce the Symptoms of Poverty: Income Maintenance Programs

Even if it is not possible to cure a disease, it is very important to provide the patient with relief from the symptoms. While we are in the process of developing long-run cures for poverty (such as upgrading human capital and ending discrimination) we also provide income maintenance programs for those in poverty. (And, as we can see in Table 32-2, large payments are made to the elderly under Social Security and other government pension plans.) We now consider a few of these assistance programs in detail.

Social Security Social security is by far the most important income maintenance program. Payroll taxes are collected from self-employed individuals, employees, and employers, and are used to finance retirement and other benefits. Because these benefits go to all retired participants in the program whether they are poor or not, it is not, strictly speaking, an antipoverty program. Nonetheless, many of the aged would be in poverty without social security.

Aid to Families with Dependent Children (AFDC) This is an example of a program that is designed specifically to deal with the poverty problem: A family cannot qualify unless it is poor. (Moreover, in some areas a family cannot qualify if an able-bodied man is in the home. While this provision has the desirable objective of encouraging able-bodied fathers to go to work, it sometimes drives them out of the home instead. They may feel that the simplest way for them to support their dependents is to leave, and thus allow their families to qualify for welfare.)

In-kind Assistance While the programs like AFDC in category B in Table 32-2 provide the poor with benefits in *cash*, the programs in category C provide benefits *in kind*; that is, they provide the poor with some good or service. These are the most rapidly growing welfare programs. Between 1965 and 1975 there was a *sixteenfold increase* in these forms of assistance. Food stamps and housing subsidies are two examples.

Food stamps: This program allows the poor to buy vouchers from the federal government, which they can use to buy food. The subsidy they receive is the difference between the low price they pay to the government for the vouchers (food stamps) and the value of the vouchers in buying food at the grocery store.

TABLE 32-2
Government Expenditures on Income Maintenance Programs, Fiscal Year 1976
(in billions of dollars)

A. Cash social insurance		$124.0
Social security and railroad retirement	$ 73.7	
Government pensions	22.7	
Unemployment insurance	18.5	
Workers' compensation	3.8	
Veterans' compensation	5.3	
B. Cash assistance		$ 18.0
Veterans' pensions	2.7	
Supplemental Security Income	6.0	
Aid to Families with Dependent Children	9.3	
C. In-kind transfers		$ 41.5
Food stamps	5.3	
Child nutrition	2.0	
Housing assistance	2.3	
Medicare		
Hospital insurance	12.3	
Supplemental medical insurance	4.7	
Medicaid	14.9	
Total		$183.5

Source: Congressional Budget Office, *Poverty Status of Families under Alternative Definitions of Income*, Background Paper no. 17, rev. (Washington: Congress of the United States, June 1977), p. 22.

The poorer the family, the lower the price it pays for the vouchers, that is, the greater the subsidy it receives. Thus, as a family's income rises, its subsidy falls; when its income reaches a certain level, the subsidy is cut off altogether.

There is a good reason for this provision: It ensures that food stamps will go only to the poor. But it has a very unfortunate side effect: The incentive to go to work is eroded. (Some of the income earned by taking a job must be spent on higher-priced food.) By itself, this effect may not be too important. But many of the other subsidies in categories B and C in Table 32-2 are also reduced as a family's income rises. When the effect of all these subsidies is taken into account, the accumulated impact on the incentive to work may be very great indeed. The poor may well wonder: "Why go to work to earn a living when it means that we lose several subsidies? Specifically, why

earn an additional $1,000 of income, if it means that we will have our food subsidy reduced by, say, $400, our housing subsidy by $250, and our Medicaid by $250 (for a total reduction of $900)? It's just as though we had to pay a $900 tax on this $1,000 of additional income." Technically, we say that such a family is paying a 90 percent implicit tax on its additional income. But the tax may be even higher than this. If, for example, this family were to lose another $200 of subsidies, the implicit tax the welfare program imposes on them would exceed 100 percent; going to work would make them worse off.

> The *implicit tax* built into a welfare program is calculated by examining the *subsidies lost* when a family earns another $1 of income. (If its subsidies are reduced by 46 cents, the implicit tax is 46 percent.)

Public housing: This form of in-kind assistance was first introduced in 1937, and it has been modified on numerous occasions since. But the basic idea is this: A local government is subsidized by the federal government to acquire land (usually in the slums), to clear it, and to build housing. (More recently, this program has also allowed local governments to buy existing houses as well.) This housing is then rented out to low-income tenants who pay 25 percent of their income in rent, with the federal government paying the rest. Thus, the more a family earns, the more it must pay for its housing. Consequently, this program, just like food stamps, erodes the incentive to work. (For other government housing subsidies, see Box 32-1.)

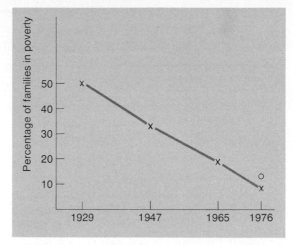

FIGURE 32-1   How the percentage of the population below the poverty line is shrinking over time.
By the standards of the mid-70s, the proportion of the population in poverty has been steadily reduced over time.

SOURCE: The 1929 figure is a very rough approximation that follows from the fact that average real income in 1929 was at about the poverty level as presently defined. The 1947 figure is from the 1964 Economic Report of the Council of Economic Advisers. The other figures are from Congressional Budget Office, *Poverty Status*, pp. xiv and xv. [There has been some disagreement about these estimates. For example, the Bureau of the Census estimate for 1975 (shown with the empty dot) is higher; but it did not take into account income received in kind, such as food and medical services.]

ASSESSING THE PRESENT PACKAGE OF WELFARE MEASURES

Are We Winning the War against Poverty?

In spending vast sums, are we making headway against the poverty problem? Figure 32-1 suggests that the answer is yes, at least to some degree. By present poverty standards, one in two Americans was poor in 1929; by 1947, the figure was one in three; by 1965, it was less than one in five; and by 1976, it was one in twelve.[5] But the problem is: How do we know how much of this has been due to the antipoverty program, and how much has been due to the fact that, with technological change and the accumulation of capital, our income has been rising and thus has automatically reduced poverty?

Because this question is so difficult to answer, it is appropriate to be modest in making claims about the effectiveness of the poverty program. Moreover, there are two respects in which this program can be criticized: It is neither very equitable nor very efficient. (Its inefficiencies will be discussed

*[5]If we examine the 1976 income of United States families before taxes and transfers are taken into account, 27 percent of them are below the poverty line. [See Congressional Budget Office, *Poverty Status of Families under Alternative Definitions of Income*, Background Paper no. 17, rev. (Washington: Congress of the United States, June 1977), p. xv.] Taxes and transfers reduce this to only 8.3 percent. This sounds like clear evidence that government action drastically reduces poverty. But this conclusion does not follow quite so simply. The reason: If transfer payments did not exist, there would be a greater incentive to work. Without welfare to fall back on, people would feel they had little choice but to work. With more people working, there would be less than 27 percent initially below the poverty line. So the effect of government taxes and welfare payments is to reduce poverty by less than the figures (from 27 percent to 8.3 percent) suggest. (Incidentally, this same reservation holds in interpreting Figure 31-2. If government programs did not exist, more people would work and the initial income distribution *a* would have less of an inequality bow. For this reason, government programs tend to reduce inequality by less than the lightly shaded slice between curves *a* and *e*.)

BOX 32-1
HOUSING SUBSIDIES: Who Benefits?

Many voters believe that better housing is an important social goal—better housing for the poor, and better housing for the average citizen too. Of the numerous incentives for housing, the most notable is a provision which allows homeowners to reduce the income tax they have to pay. (In calculating their taxable income, they are permitted to deduct the property taxes and interest payments on their mortgages.) The idea is to encourage people to own their own homes. As a consequence, more houses are built, and existing houses are kept in better repair. Far from being an antipoverty program, this policy benefits wealthy owners of big homes more than the poor who own small homes or none at all.

Another government housing policy is urban renewal, which is designed to improve slum housing, revitalize downtown business areas, and attract middle-class residents from the suburbs back into the big cities. This program involves federal subsidies to local governments to tear down central city slums and rebuild these core areas. But this policy has generated heated controversy: Its supporters view it as the last hope of saving the big cities, while its critics point out that, initially at least, it resulted in many more dwellings being torn down than constructed. As a consequence, the central city poor found that their housing supply was shrinking. Another reason for the shrinkage was the success of this program in its important objective of attracting back the middle class from the suburbs: Thus, much of the new available space was occupied by the nonpoor. To ensure that the poor will be better accommodated, attempts have been recently made to guarantee that any renewal program includes specified amounts of low-income housing.

later; see, for example, Box 32-2. For now we consider its inequity.)

Inequities in the Present System

If we return to Table 32-2, two messages stand out clearly: First, governments are spending a great deal of money on transfer expenditures. Second, there is a whole hodgepodge of programs. (Although some coordination of diverse programs has taken place, a great variety still remains.) Inequity arises because some families qualify for more of these programs than other equally poor families. By drawing on several of these programs, some poor families are lifted not only to the cutoff poverty level, but well above it, while other families are left substantially below it. In some cases, welfare recipients end up with a higher income than some of the workers who pay taxes to support them. (Little wonder that these workers become vocal critics of welfare.) To top it all off, the poor sometimes feel that the welfare workers who administer these programs hold far too much arbitrary power over them, while some welfare workers in turn view these programs as a nearly hopeless administrative tangle. On receiving the *Public Assistance Handbook*, former Senator Clifford P. Case declared: "I was appalled to receive a package of regulations weighing almost six pounds, as thick as the Washington, D.C. telephone directory. Leaving the human element aside, this handbook is the best possible evidence that the present welfare program is a bureaucratic nightmare."[6] In view of these problems, why not replace the whole checkered pattern of policies with a single program that guarantees each family the same minimum income (adjusted, of course, for differences such as family size)?

A GUARANTEED MINIMUM INCOME: A Cure for the Poverty Problem?

"You can't solve a problem by throwing money at it."

Overheard in Washington, D.C.

Why not eliminate poverty in one stroke by setting a minimum income at the poverty level? If any family's income were to fall below that level, the government would cover its shortfall with a direct grant. What would this cost? If we add up the shortfall in income of all families below the poverty line, the sum is likely to be substantially less than 1 percent of the United States GNP.[7] Considering what we are already spending, why not just commit ourselves to this sort of relatively modest increase in expenditure, and end poverty at a single stroke?

Unfortunately, it is not so easy.

Inefficiencies in a Subsidy Program

The problem is that a program that raises the income of the poor by $10 billion will cost us far more than $10 billion. Waste is involved because such a program has adverse effects on incentives.

Disincentives for Those Paying for the Subsidy The first adverse incentive applies to those who pay the higher taxes necessary to finance this scheme. The heavier the tax rate, the more likely it is that an individual will ask, "Why am I working so hard when the government gets such a large slice of what I earn?" Studies done on this subject fail to show as substantial an effect as one would expect. One reason is that although a higher tax makes working less attractive (by reducing the reward), it also

---

[6]Quoted in Henry J. Aaron, *Why Is Welfare So Hard to Reform?* (Washington: The Brookings Institution, 1973), p. 11.

[7]In *Equality and Efficiency: The Big Tradeoff* (Washington: The Brookings Institution, 1975) p. 108, Arthur Okun estimated that the shortfall in 1973 amounted to about $9 billion, a figure that was well below 1 percent of GNP. (Our discussion in this chapter draws heavily on Okun's book.)

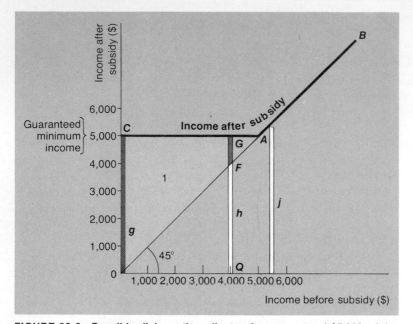

FIGURE 32-2 Possible disincentive effects of a guaranteed $5,000 minimum income.
The 45° line *OAB* is the no-subsidy line. For example, at point *F* on this line, family *h* that
earns $4,000 (measured left to right) would end up with $4,000 (measured up). On the
other hand, heavy line *CAB* shows income with the subsidy. Family *h* is paid a $1,000 (solid
bar) subsidy necessary to raise it to the guaranteed $5,000 level, while family *g* (which
earns no income) must be paid a full $5,000 subsidy. This program erodes the incentive to
work. Why should *h* keep working when he can quit and join *g* and still have his family's
income guaranteed at the same $5,000 level? Worse yet, if *j* dislikes his job, why should he
keep working? If he quits and also joins *g*, his income will be reduced only slightly (from
$5,400 to $5,000).

makes working more necessary (for anyone trying to maintain previous levels of spending); and these two effects tend, to some degree, to offset each other. But even though high taxes may not have a large effect on the incentive to work, they do encourage the search for tax loopholes. And as higher-income individuals engage in (or hire lawyers to engage in) socially unproductive efforts to minimize their tax payments, there is a consequent waste imposed on society. As Arthur Okun puts it: "High tax rates are followed by attempts of ingenious men to beat them, as surely as snow is followed by little boys on sleds."[8]

[8]Okun, *Equality and Efficiency*, p. 97.

Disincentives for Those Receiving the Subsidy

Now let's turn to those at the bottom end of the income scale who will receive this subsidy. Here one would expect more substantial incentive effects, for the reasons shown in Figure 32-2. (In this diagram we concentrate on what happens at the bottom end of the income scale, and disregard for now any taxes that may be paid in this low-income range. And to simplify further, we use a "round figure" poverty line of $5,000.) Families are plotted along the horizontal axis according to how much income they originally earn. Thus, family *h* with a $4,000 earned income is plotted at point *Q* along the horizontal axis. Income after the implementation of this policy is measured up the vertical axis. If no subsidy were to be paid to family h, its "income after" would also be $4,000, as shown by the empty bar. In other words, family h would be shown by point F on the 45° line, where its before and after incomes are equal. Hence this 45° line may be called the "same-before-and-after" line, or just the "no-subsidy" line.

But, of course, our minimum income program does pay family h a subsidy—specifically, the $1,000 solid bar FG that is necessary to raise its income to the minimum $5,000 poverty level. Since the income of any other family below the poverty line is similarly subsidized up to this $5,000 level, the "income after subsidy" line is the heavy line CAB. Shaded area 1 represents the shortfall income gap that the government must fill at an additional cost that we have already noted is likely to run to less than 1 percent of our GNP—*provided* people continue to work and earn as much after the subsidy is introduced as they did before.

The problem is that, because they are being subsidized, some people will *not* work as hard as before. For example, the father of family h may realize: "If I don't work at all, the government will still guarantee us the same $5,000; so why should I work?" And if he stops working, that $4,000 of income he earned disappears. The position of that family on the horizontal axis therefore shifts to the left, from situation h to situation g. At this point, nothing is being earned, that family has become totally unproductive, and it must be subsidized by the full $5,000 solid bar. Therefore, in order to raise this family's income by the original $1,000 shortfall, the government ends up by paying out $5,000 (which, of course, it has to raise from the public in taxes). This example illustrates what Arthur Okun refers to as "transferring income with a leaky bucket": Although $5,000 has been raised in taxes, it has increased this family's income by only $1,000. The other $4,000 has "leaked away" because the family has stopped working.

This leakage also represents the efficiency loss that results from this income distribution policy. (The original income this family produced was the $4,000 empty bar at h, but this is now lost to society because no one in the family any longer works.)

Disincentives that Apply to the Nonpoor Disincentive effects may apply not only to poor families like h with initial incomes below the $5,000 support level; they may also apply to nonpoor families like j with incomes above $5,000. Suppose the breadwinner in family j has been earning the $5,400 shown, in a boring and unpleasant job. The subsidy program will now offer a tempting option: Go fishing, and receive a $5,000 income from the government. If this happens, family j also shifts to the left into position g, where it too qualifies for the full $5,000 subsidy. So the government has to subsidize not only those with initial incomes below the $5,000 poverty level, but *also* some with incomes above the poverty line, for whom this program was never intended.

In short, when the government attempts to fill an income gap by such a simple subsidy, its cost may far exceed the initial income shortfall that it set about to cure. The reason is that this subsidy disturbs incentives, and some people stop working. From the point of view of the government that is paying out these subsidies, this problem appears in two forms: On the one hand, many poor families like h may absorb more subsidy than expected; on the other hand, a whole new and unexpected group of families like j may appear on the scene, hat in hand. Moreover, when a family like j goes onto the antipoverty program, the overall efficiency loss to society is particularly severe. It is the empty bar at j—the $5,400 of income that is no longer produced because the breadwinner is off fishing.

The reason that this policy is so inefficient is that the portion CA of the "income

BOX 32-2   THE LACK OF WORK INCENTIVES IN OUR EXISTING WELFARE SYSTEM

Originally, Aid for Families with Dependent Children (AFDC) involved an implicit tax of 100 percent: If a family earned another $1 of income, its AFDC payment was reduced by $1. Now, however, its AFDC payment is reduced by about 66 cents (depending on its income level). In other words, the implicit tax in AFDC is now about 66 percent. Although this seems to leave some modest incentive to work, the poor often qualify for other welfare programs as well. Because most of these are also tied to income, they too involve an implicit tax. Thus, when such programs as Medicaid, food stamps, and housing assistance are also taken into account, the total welfare package involves an implicit tax that frequently exceeds 75 or 80 percent—in some cases even 100 percent.† So, a poor family that qualifies for several programs may have little or no incentive to work. (Moreover, "reforms" that have been debated by Congress have involved implicit tax rates that sometimes run as high as 120 to 130 percent. Families that earn another $1 in income would lose $1.20 or $1.30 in welfare benefits. In this case, they would have a strong economic incentive to stop working.)

†In practice, these implicit tax rates are very complicated to calculate, and depend on the income level of the recipients. Henry J. Aaron found that those who received four selected types of assistance in 1972 faced an implicit tax rate that was "high and capricious," running as much as 73 percent in the $4,000 to $8,000 income range, and over 100 percent in the $8,000 to $9,000 range. See Henry J. Aaron, *Why Is Welfare So Hard to Reform?* (Washington: The Brookings Institution, 1973), pp. 33 and 34. In 1977–1978 Aaron was an Assistant Secretary of Health, Education, and Welfare, with responsibility to work on welfare reform.

after subsidy" line is completely horizontal, leaving the poor *no* incentive to go to work. (The implicit tax they face is 100 percent: For every additional $1 they earn, their subsidy is reduced by the same $1.) Thus, in terms of efficiency, it provides an even greater antiwork bias than the present welfare system. (For detail on the lack of work incentives in our present system, see Box 32-2.)

What sounded like a simple solution to poverty—filling the income gap with an additional government expenditure of less than 1 percent of our GNP—is not an efficient solution. If such a program were tried, much more would have to be poured into the gap because of its antiwork incentives.

Does a Subsidy Program Involve Noneconomic Costs?

The economic cost of a subsidy program is the output the nation loses because people

work less. But there may be social costs as well.

1. One of the many reasons that fathers remain in the home and support their families is the fear of what might happen if they were to leave. If a government welfare program guarantees child support and removes this fear, won't some fathers feel more free to leave? (Worse yet, as we have already seen, some programs like Aid for Families with Dependent Children may provide an incentive for fathers to leave.) So welfare programs have implications that go far beyond economics; they may be important in shaping our social structure, and in particular, the future status of the family unit.

2. Does welfare encourage a problem it is designed to cure: the "culture of poverty"? Does it encourage dependency and destroy pride and self-respect? Being the breadwinner may be one of the few sources of pride and self-respect for those with low-paying, no-promise jobs. If welfare provides as adequately for their families as they can, does it make them feel like so much excess baggage and destroy their self-respect? What pride is left for a man if his wife tells him she can get as much from welfare as he is able to earn?

How Did We Get Caught in the Welfare Trap?

It's enlightening to stand back for a moment and consider how we worked ourselves into our present situation, in which we are spending enormous sums to cure poverty, but are inadequately encouraging people to escape from it. Suppose we start from a situation in which all forms of assistance are paid out regardless of the recipient's income; like government support of public education, they benefit the rich and poor alike. Precisely because these policies benefit all income groups, they would be viewed as not "sharp" enough to deal with poverty. Therefore, to focus on the poor (and to keep costs down), we would add programs that would provide assistance only to the poor—specifically, programs that would pay each family according to its degree of poverty: The poorer the family, the more assistance it would receive. Thus, we would introduce programs like food stamps or housing assistance that would depend on the recipient's income. But these are precisely the programs that involve an implicit tax, and that therefore erode the incentive to work. So many people work less, and the nation's output is reduced. To some degree, we begin to "spin our wheels." The more we subsidize, the more subsidy may be required.

THE KEY TRADE-OFF: Equity versus Efficiency

It all seemed so simple. As we look back over Parts 4 and 5, the following clear mes-

sage seemed to be emerging: Intervene in product or factor markets to increase efficiency. (For example, intervene to tax polluters, or to regulate monopoly price.) If this intervention also has favorable equity effects, so much the better; then there are no conflicts, and the appropriate policy choice is a simple one. (For example, it is easy to endorse ending discrimination in the labor market because this increases efficiency and also equitably transfers income to those who have faced disadvantages because of their color or sex.) However, such cases are the exception, rather than the rule; conflicts typically do arise. The search for efficiency in product and factor markets does not necessarily lead us to an equitable income distribution. Therefore, to achieve equity, we should rely on direct government transfers rather than inefficient interventions into factor or product markets (like the imposition of an interest rate ceiling).

Unfortunately, it's not so easy after all, because of one weak link in this argument: Direct government transfers may not be very efficient either. In particular, government spending on the poor erodes the incentive to work and reduces national output. So we are still left with the trade-off between the objectives of equity and efficiency: The size of the national pie is reduced if we try to carve it up in a more equitable way.

This is not a recommendation that we go back to transferring income by the inefficient market interventions we have criticized in earlier chapters. Not only are they inefficient. Worse yet, as a means of raising the income of the poor, they are often ineffective. (An interest rate ceiling benefits rich borrowers as well as poor, and in fact, may leave many relatively poor borrowers out in the cold completely.[9]) The message remains: The way to raise the income of those in poverty is by direct government transfers to those who are in poverty. But we had better find a better way of doing it than the

[9]As another example, farm price guarantees benefit the rich farmer without lifting many poor farmers out of poverty.

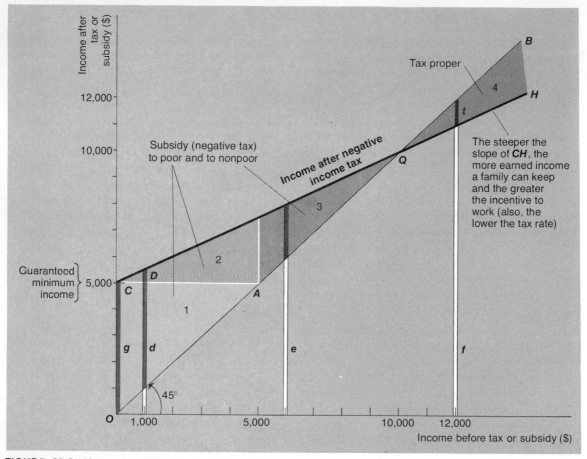

FIGURE 32-3 How a negative income tax might work. Compare with Figure 32-2.

Family *g* with a zero earned income is paid the solid bar grant of $5,000. But what do we do with family *d* with $1,000 of earned income? If we make the same mistake we made in Figure 32-2 and raise this income up only to that same $5,000 (by a $4,000 grant), then this will leave no incentive for this family to keep working to earn that $1,000. So to provide an incentive to work we grant this family $4,500 instead (as shown by the solid bar), thus bringing its total up to $5,500 at point *D*. If we continue in this way, always providing a $500 incentive for families to earn an additional $1,000 of income, we move up heavy line *CDQ* to cut-off point *Q* where no subsidy is paid. Moreover, if we continue to allow families to keep half of any additional income they earn, we will tax incomes above this level down from *QB* to *QH*. Thus, red area 4 shows us how any income above $10,000 is subject to a tax. (For example, family *f* with a $12,000 income pays the $1,000 tax *t*). At the same time, blue area 1 + 2 + 3 shows us how any income below $10,000 is subsidized ("taxed in reverse"). Hence the name: negative income tax.

simple subsidy programs we have been discussing so far. In particular, we should search for a way that is *equitable* (and that, unlike our present welfare package, treats all the poor alike). And a way that is also *efficient*—in other words, that does not destroy the incentive to work.

THE NEGATIVE INCOME TAX: Can We Combine Equity and Efficiency?

How can we guarantee families a minimum income (for example, $5,000) without destroying their incentive to work? This is the essential question, and it is not an easy one to answer. To arrive at some clues, let's put our last diagram back on the drawing board in Figure 32-3. This new diagram has the same frame of reference as Figure 32-2, except that it is extended to the right to allow us to take account not only of families that receive a subsidy, but also of higher-income families that pay the government a tax. The 45° "same-before-and-after" line OQB now represents the "no-subsidy, no-tax" line where families would be if the government neither subsidized nor taxed them.

Design of a Negative Income Tax

To see how a negative income tax would work, we begin by assuming, as before, that the minimum income level is set at $5,000. But now, rather than subsidizing incomes just up to the line CA by filling gap 1 as we did in Figure 32-2, we instead subsidize incomes up to the heavy line CQ by filling the gaps $1 + 2 + 3$. By giving the "income-after" line CQ an upward slope, we give people an incentive to work: The higher the income they earn (the farther they move to the right in this diagram), the greater the income they get to keep (the higher they rise on line CQ). In this way we attempt to plug the big leak in the bucket (people quitting work to go on welfare).

But this has apparently become a very expensive program for the national treasury, since the subsidy is now area 1 plus areas 2 and 3. Specifically, the government now provides an even greater subsidy (areas $1 + 2$) to poor families earning incomes below the $5,000 poverty level. Moreover, it also provides subsidy 3 to nonpoor families with incomes all the way up to $10,000—roughly one-third of American families in the mid-1970s (the base period of this analysis). Of course, families earning even higher incomes pay a tax. For example, a family earning $12,000 pays the $1,000 tax shown as the red bar t. Thus, heavy line CQH shows how we subsidize all the way up to point Q, and tax beyond. (Although this line need not have a constant slope, in our simple example we assume that it does: Any family gets to keep half of any additional income it earns.[10])

Furthermore, the apparent high cost of this program is not limited to just filling new gaps $2 + 3$. In addition, the U.S. Treasury loses the previous taxes collected from many nonpoor families in the $5,000 to $10,000 income range. (Before, they were taxed; now, they are subsidized.) And this leads to some extraordinary conclusions. A policy that we instituted initially to benefit poor families with incomes below $5,000 not only benefits nonpoor families in the $5,000 to $10,000 range, but does so for two separate reasons: First, it pays them a subsidy; and second, it relieves them of a previous tax. Moreover, it will also reduce taxes of some families in the income range even above $10,000.[11] Benefiting such families was scarcely our objective when we set out to cure poverty incomes below $5,000!

When one takes into account all these considerations, doesn't the negative income tax come out badly in comparison with the simple subsidy scheme in Figure 32-2? Why would anyone recommend it? The answer is that it has more favorable built-in incentive effects. The negative income tax should be a far less leaky bucket than a simple subsidy scheme (or our present welfare system). This point is worth considering in detail.

How the Negative Income Tax Reduces the Leaks in the Welfare Bucket

By providing families with the incentive of keeping half of any of the additional income they earn, the negative income tax would induce them to get out and earn more, and thus "move to the right" in Figure 32-3. Since this would reduce (and in some cases, perhaps even eliminate) the subsidy some families receive, the cost of this scheme

---

[10]In other words, those with earned incomes of less than $10,000 (who are subsidized) face a 50 percent implicit tax, while those with incomes above $10,000 face a 50 percent tax proper (on all income over $10,000).

[11]To confirm this statement, consider a family with income just barely over $10,000. In Figure 32-3, it will pay a miniscule tax that is less than the tax it pays at present.

would be less than the blue subsidy area in Figure 32-3 may have initially suggested. Moreover, the cost of this scheme might be reduced even further by the addition of special features. For example, the line *CQH* might be lowered by, say, $1,000. This would maintain the same incentive to work (the same slope of *CQH*), but would enormously reduce the cost of the scheme (the subsidy areas 1 + 2 + 3). The one problem is that those at *C* doing no work would now receive less than the $5,000 poverty minimum. But this problem might be reduced by providing a guaranteed $5,000 income to those who are aged, infirm, or disabled and *cannot* work. (If these people can be clearly identified, a guaranteed income would involve no inefficiency; it would not affect the work these people do, because they are unable to work regardless.)

The Negative Income Tax Does Not Resolve All Conflicts

We can now see how the design of any negative income tax scheme involves tension among three objectives:

1. To set the minimum income level (*C*) high enough so no one will be left destitute.

2. To give *CQH* enough slope to provide people with a strong incentive to work. (Indeed, many would view the slope of *CQH* in Figure 32-3 as being too low and therefore providing inadequate incentive to work. Since people can keep only half of any additional income they earn, they spend half their time working for the government.)

3. To keep the subsidy areas 1 + 2 + 3 small, in order to keep the cost of the program down and avoid heavily subsidizing the nonpoor.

Since these three objectives are in conflict, it is impossible to achieve them all. In particular, the way to achieve the second objective is to make line *CQH* steeper. But a greater slope means that either *C* must be lower or subsidy areas 1 + 2 + 3 must be larger. Thus objective 2 conflicts with objectives 1 and 3.

Summary

While the negative income tax does not resolve all conflicts, it nonetheless does look like a promising approach. Obviously, in passing judgment on it in the future, a crucial question will be: What precisely are the incentive effects of this scheme compared with alternative welfare programs? Early results of experiments, in which samples of families have actually been put onto a negative income tax, are still difficult to evaluate;[12] full returns are not yet in. But if expectations about its favorable effects on incentives are confirmed by these experiments, the negative income tax may be a promising way of reducing some of the conflict between efficiency and equity. On the one hand, it would go some distance in achieving efficiency by providing a greater incentive to work than our present welfare package.[13] At the same time, it would also move us toward a greater degree of equity in several ways: (1) It would guarantee a minimum income for all; (2) it would replace the wide variety of existing welfare programs with one consistent policy that would treat all alike; and (3) it would also satisfy another equity objective of most Americans because it would leave those who work with a higher income than those who do not.

But two major problems would still remain. First, what are the noneconomic effects[14] of a negative income tax? Second,

[12]For detail on the most prominent of these experiments, see Joseph A. Pechman and Michael Trimpane (eds.), *Work Incentives and Income Guarantees: The New Jersey Negative Income Tax Experiment* (Washington, D.C.: The Brookings Institution, 1975).

[13]We emphasize that it must replace *all* existing welfare payments, except those going to the aged and others unable to work. (If other subsidies like food stamps were to remain, they would continue to erode work incentives.)

[14]Preliminary evidence from a Seattle-Denver experiment implies that a negative income tax may increase the incidence of family breakups. On the other hand, the New Jersey experiment suggests that it may increase the number of young adults finishing high school.

what would it cost? Some of its supporters would say that by moving people to the right in Figure 32-3 to a higher earned income level, this policy would cost less than the direct grant program in Figure 32-2—perhaps even less than our present welfare package. But others are not so sure.[15] Nonetheless, on balance the negative income tax may be one of the more promising approaches for transferring income without incurring serious inefficiencies.

Key Points

1. Poverty is defined as inadequate income to buy the necessities of life. A specific poverty-line figure is determined by calculating the minimum cost of a nutritious and reasonably edible diet and multiplying that figure by 3. In 1978 the poverty line for a nonfarm family of four was about $6,600. By this standard, as many as 1 in 12 American families were living in poverty. But this was still a big improvement on the 1965 figure of about 1 in 5.

2. Blacks are more likely to be poor than whites, and Southerners more likely to be poor than Northerners. The less an individual is educated, the greater the risk of poverty. The problem exists in cities, towns, and farms, with the areas least affected being the suburbs of big cities. Poverty is a particularly serious problem in fatherless families.

3. Transfer expenditures by federal, state, and local governments increased almost fourfold between 1965 and 1975; consequently, about 20 percent of the United States GNP in 1975 was being spent on transfers.

4. In the long run, the most promising government antipoverty policies are those that deal with the causes rather than the symptoms of poverty. These policies include subsidizing investment in human capital (both education and on-the-job training),

and eliminating employment discrimination against minorities and women.

5. Government income maintenance programs include social security, which is paid to poor and nonpoor alike. But there are also many programs, like Aid to Families with Dependent Children, food stamps, and housing assistance, that are designed specifically for the poor. The problem with these programs is that when the poor earn more income, there is a reduction in the subsidies they receive (an implicit tax). This reduces their incentive to work, thus lowering the nation's output and level of efficiency.

6. The whole package of present programs is also inequitable. Some of the poor are not lifted up to the poverty line, while others who qualify under several of these programs are lifted above it—indeed, in some cases, even above the income earned by some of the people who pay taxes to support the antipoverty program.

7. Why not, then, replace this present system with a single policy that would lift all the poor up to the same minimum income level? The answer is that the poor, with their incomes thus guaranteed, would have little or no economic incentive left to work. With lost potential output, the economy would operate at a low level of efficiency. Thus, the conflict between greater equality and effi-

---

[15]For example, there are many nonpoor families in the $5,000 to $10,000 income range that do not now receive any payment from the government, but they would under a negative income tax. The concern is that their incentive to work might be reduced, and this might add substantially to the cost of the program. (Initial results of the experiments on the negative income tax suggest that it may reduce the willingness to work overtime and the amount of paid work that wives do.)

ciency persists: As we try to carve up the national pie more equally (by raising the income of the poor), the total size of that pie is reduced.

8. A negative income tax may be one method of reducing, but not entirely elimi-nating, this conflict. Under this policy, families would be allowed to keep part of any additional income they earn; this provision in turn would leave them with an incentive to work. The program would also guarantee every family a minimum income.

Key Concepts

definition of poverty line
groups most affected by poverty
causes of poverty
symptoms of poverty
government policies to increase human capital
government policies to eliminate discrimination
Work Incentive Program
Social Security
Aid to Families with Dependent Children
food stamps

public housing
implicit tax in a welfare system
inequities in our welfare system
disincentive effects of a guaranteed minimum income
possible noneconomic costs of a welfare system
the "welfare trap"
the efficiency effects of a negative income tax
conflicting objectives in a negative income tax

Problems

32-1 What is meant by an implicit tax rate of 90 percent? Of 105 percent? What is the effect of such a tax rate?

32-2 Let's review the efficiency losses from our income redistribution policy in Figure 32-2. What is the efficiency loss if this subsidy induces the breadwinner of family *h* to go fishing? The breadwinner of family *j*? What is the efficiency loss if the breadwinner of family *j* takes a day off each week to go fishing? What is the efficiency loss from subsidizing a family like *g* that originally earned no income?

How do you think the efficiency loss would change if the minimum income level were set at $6,000, rather than $5,000?

32-3 Explain to your bright roommate

(who is taking economics but hasn't yet reached this chapter) exactly what you mean by a "leaky bucket."

32-4 Let's see if we can't reduce the costs to the government of the negative income tax in Figure 32-3. The incentive to work in that diagram is the $500 a family can keep out of each additional $1,000 it earns. Now suppose that the amount it can keep is reduced from $500 to $300.

    (*a*) Redraw Figure 32-3 to take this into account.

    (*b*) What has happened to the incentive to work?

    (*c*) What has happened to the implicit tax in this welfare proposal?

(*d*) Are your answers to *b* and *c* related in any way? If so, how?

(*e*) What has happened to the total amount of subsidy the government must pay? (Be careful.)

(*f*) Has this transfer bucket (sometimes referred to, in perhaps the worst pun of the century, as the "Okun bucket") become leakier or less leaky?

(*g*) Now regraph this policy making one further change: Set the poverty level at $4,000, rather than $5,000. Again answer questions *b*, *c*, and *e*. What are the pros and cons of the two policies you have graphed?

32-5 Suppose you are designing a negative income tax. Graph your answers to each of the following questions:

(*a*) What do you consider a reasonable minimum family income (*OC* in Figure 32-3)?

(*b*) What do you consider to be the maximum reasonable implicit tax rate? How does the slope of *CQ* in your diagram therefore compare to *CQ* in Figure 32-3?

(*c*) From your answers to *a* and *b*, calculate the break-even level of income (like the $10,000 at *Q* in Figure 32-3).

(*d*) Do you think the tax proper (on families to the right of the break-even point *Q*) should be greater or smaller than the implicit tax on families to the left of *Q*?

(*e*) Explain the possible "public finance problem" in your scheme. In other words, do you think your scheme would make it difficult for the government to collect enough taxes from those to the right of *Q* to cover the costs of subsidizing those to the left of *Q*? As real incomes rise, would this public finance problem become more serious, or less? Would you agree with the view that we should institute a negative income tax someday, with the only question being how soon we can afford it?

chapter 33
Marxism and the Economic Systems of the Soviet Union and Yugoslavia

> In proportion as capital accumulates, the lot of the laborer be his payment high or low, must grow worse. **Karl Marx, *Das Kapital***

Historically, one of the major criticisms of the free enterprise system has been that it does not distribute income in an equitable way—largely because of the income payments that go to private owners of physical capital ("capitalists"). Moreover, many critics believe that the economic and political power held by capitalists limits the government in its attempts to redistribute income. Hence, their solution is to replace our system with one that is fundamentally different—specifically, with a "socialist" system in which capital is owned by the state on behalf of all the people.

This chapter begins with a discussion of the ideas of Karl Marx, whose writings over a century ago have proved to be the most influential and durable criticisms ever leveled against the free enterprise system. This is followed by an examination of the socialist systems of the Soviet Union and Yugoslavia, two illustrations of the many alternative ways in which the philosophy of Karl Marx can be put into practice.

KARL MARX

> ... the capitalist gets rich ... at the same rate as he squeezes out the labor power of others, and then forces on the laborer abstinence from all life's enjoyments. **Karl Marx, *Das Kapital***

Today about one-third of the world lives under some form of Marxist-communist economic system. In addition, there are many followers of Marx who do not support any of the existing communist states, but who believe his ideas should be implemented in a different way. Clearly, this means that whether or not Marx was right, he certainly was one of the most influential thinkers in history.

Marx's criticism of the free market was based on two theories, both accepted by many orthodox economists of his day: (1) the labor theory of value, and (2) the theory that wages tended toward a socially defined subsistence level. According to the labor theory of value, the value of any good is determined by the amount of labor that goes into producing it. (But be careful: As Marx recognized, this value must include both the labor time directly involved in producing the good and the labor time spent on, or "congealed in," the machinery used to produce the good.) Marx then asked: With labor being the source of all value, does it receive the total value of the nation's output in return for its effort? His answer was: No, all labor receives is a low wage representing only a fraction of what is produced. The rest is a "surplus value" that goes to the employer or capitalist (the owner of the capital equipment with which labor is combined). Marx's conclusion: Because this surplus value should go to labor, the working class is being exploited.

Surplus Value and the Class Struggle

According to Marx, this exploitation of the proletariat (workers) by the bourgeoisie (capitalists) results in a class struggle, and much of his effort was devoted to appealing to workers of his day to organize themselves to fight this struggle. In his words, "Let the ruling classes tremble at a Communist revolution. The proletarians have nothing to lose but their chains. They have a world to win. Working men of all countries, unite!"[1] In his view, the capitalist class would continue to accumulate more and more capital and use it increasingly to exploit labor. Thus there would be ". . . an accumulation of misery, corresponding to the accumulation of capital." Marx's cure was a revolution (which he viewed as inevitable[2]) in which the workers would seize power and abolish the ownership of capital by private individuals: "By despotic inroads on the rights of property [workers would] centralize all instruments of production in the hands of the State."[3] Finally, after this new socialist system has been firmly established, the state will wither away, leaving Marx's ideal communist society.

Socialism is an economic system in which the "means of production" (capital equipment, buildings, and land) are owned by the state.[4]

In countries like the Soviet Union, *communism* means an idealistic system in which all means of production and other forms of property are owned by the community as a whole, with all members of the community sharing in its work and income. The Soviet Union makes no claim to having achieved communism. Rather, it claims to be working "through socialism towards communism."

In the West, communism has a quite different meaning. It refers to the present economic and political system of countries like the Soviet Union.

[1]Karl Marx and Friedrich Engels, *Manifesto of the Communist Party* (Peking: Foreign Languages Press, 1975), p. 77. Note that Marx went far beyond an analysis of economic forces to prescribe what should be done to change them. (Marx and the Marxists strongly deny the suggestion by some economists that a "value-free" economics is possible.)

*[2]If this revolution is the inevitable result of an historical process governed by unchangeable economic laws, as Marx believed, what's the point of exhorting workers to struggle hard to achieve it? One possible answer: Even an inevitable event may be speeded up.

Another related problem with Marxist philosophy is that it seems inconsistent to argue, as Marx did, that humans cannot escape from economic laws through the first stages of history; yet, with the revolution, they do escape from these laws.

[3]Marx and Engels, *Communist Manifesto*, p. 59.

[4]"Socialism" has become an emotion-laden word that is now used loosely in a wide variety of meanings. To the campus radical, it is a tool for attacking the shortcomings of American society. To the American millionaire, it is a plot to deprive the wealthy of their hard-earned fortunes. To the Swedish politician, it means a mixed economic system, combining substantially free markets and a large degree of private ownership with a highly developed social welfare system. To Nobel prizewinner Friedrich Hayek, it represents a tragic step along "the road to serfdom." To the British Fabian Socialist, it means the gradual evolution of a more humane economy, with a more equal distribution of income. With such confusion on its meaning, it is little wonder people have difficulty in debating the virtues and vices of socialism.

How the Critic Has Been Criticized

Marx's critics have pointed out that many of his predictions have proved false. For example, there is little evidence that any existing states, such as that of the Soviet Union, are withering away, even though the Soviet state has existed for more than 60 years. [The idea that the state would "wither away" ranks as one of the most curious in the history of economic and political thought. One need not be as cynical as Lord Acton ("Power corrupts; absolute power corrupts absolutely") to be skeptical of the idea that those who have struggled hard to gain power will be prepared to give it up voluntarily.] Second, as capital has accumulated, there has not been the accumulation of misery that Marx predicted. Quite the contrary; misery has been reduced. And for good reason: Over the long run, the accumulation of capital has raised the demand for labor, and thus has raised, rather than lowered, the wage rate.[5] (Remember: Workers driving bulldozers are paid more than workers with shovels.)

Yet, there is a gap between what the nation produces and what labor is paid. We have referred to it as payments to other factors of production. Marx called it surplus value. In particular, he focused his attack on the payments going to owners of capital. Was he justified in dismissing these payments as simply the exploitation of labor?

How Are Capital Costs to Be Covered?

Here we must be very careful. Part of the cost of capital is the payment for the labor time spent on producing machinery. As Marx recognized, this is an appropriate payment to labor; therefore it is not surplus value. But Marx did regard as surplus value the other important component in the cost of capital: the interest (or profit) that is paid to those who provide the funds to finance investment. Remember: Investment requires that someone, somewhere, defers consumption. And in our system, the interest rate is the reward to people who voluntarily defer their consumption.

The Marxist contention is that it is precisely these payments that make our system inequitable. Moreover, Marxists maintain, it is possible to set up a system without such an interest rate incentive; the government simply ensures that people defer consumption by taxing away part of their income, and uses the proceeds for investment. Then the ownership of capital is held by the state on behalf of the people, rather than by the individual capitalists who hold it in our system.

While this system may achieve Marx's objective of ending income payments to capitalists, it raises several new problems. First, raising investment funds by such a system of involuntary savings (that is, by taxing the public) may "hurt" more than our

---

[5]While many Marxists concede that workers' income has risen in *absolute* terms, they reinterpret Marx's prediction to mean that workers would become poorer, not in any absolute sense, but *relative* to other classes in society. But even this weaker claim is difficult to support from historical data.

Another argument that many Marxists now make is that although capitalists may have been unable to exploit labor in Europe and North America to the degree that Marx predicted, they have succeeded in exploiting labor in the less developed countries (LDCs), which have become the modern economically subjugated proletariat. While there is not space here to discuss this issue in detail, we cite two reasons why we should be skeptical of any general charge that we exploit the LDCs when we do business with them. First, our investment in the LDCs is not, as sometimes supposed, a "zero-sum game" in which they lose what we gain. Instead, foreign investment typically provides both a profit to investors and a benefit to the host countries, where foreign investors often bid up wages and also pay out part of their profits in taxes to host governments. Second, our trade with the LDCs isn't a zero-sum game either. As we saw in the Comparative Advantage section in Chapter 25, it is quite possible for both parties to gain from trade. (In particular, beware of the argument that we exploit the LDCs when we trade more with them, and that we also exploit them when we trade *less* with them—for example, when we impose high tariffs on their goods.)

system of voluntary savings. This could occur, for example, if taxation draws funds from everyone, including not only the rich, but also the relatively poor—people who, in our system, are not (and should not be) forced to save because their current needs are so pressing.

Second, can investment decisions made by salaried government officials be as flexible and generate as much innovation as decisions made by the owners of capital? The investment decision involves both evaluating existing investment opportunities (which plant should be expanded?) and developing new ones (what new products should be developed?). Don't capital owners in our system have a much greater incentive to do this? (In your future examination of how the two systems compare, here are two good questions to keep in mind: Which of our innovations are the Soviets using? And which of their innovations are we using? Or, if you consider that unfair because of the United States head start, compare the Soviet Union with Italy or Japan.)

Finally, consider the practical problems encountered in allocating investment funds to various sectors across the economy, as is typically done in communist countries in a 5-year plan. To illustrate, first consider what happens in our free enterprise system if there is a major new discovery of, say, copper ore in Montana. To finance its development, the companies involved increase their borrowing, and the interest rate rises slightly. In response to this, marginal investments elsewhere in the nation are cut back. Thus, funds for this development are raised from all over the country, as a result of a large number of individuals and firms reacting to a market interest rate. In comparison, what occurs in a communist country that, 6 months ago, set its 5-year investment targets for each sector? Do the planners sit down and go through the planning process all over again? For a big enough discovery, they

might. But for a less significant one, they might simply say: Let's wait until the next planning period to develop it.

The Role of Profit

Normal profit may be viewed as a return to capital, just like the interest rate (the big difference being that one is paid to equity capital while the other is paid to debt capital). But above-normal profit is an additional return beyond this. In a free enterprise economy, it goes to entrepreneurs. Is this justified? To throw light on this issue, consider two reasons why above-normal profit may arise: It may be a monopoly profit, or it may be a profit from a successful innovation.

Above-Normal Monopoly Profit Many non-Marxist economists would agree that this sort of profit should be reduced or eliminated by "trustbusting" or regulation. But the Marxists charge that we are naive if we believe that we can effectively deal with monopoly in our present economic and political system. The reason, Marxists argue, is that in our system, monopolists can translate their economic power (money) into political power (votes) via political campaign contributions. And this power allows them to thwart antimonopoly action. In short, our elected officials are too often committed to the interests of the rich and the powerful, rather than to the interests of the public. Thus, Marxists contend, the only effective way to deal with this problem is to change the system and to prevent the accumulation of wealth that makes such political corruption possible.

There is, of course, an element of truth in this Marxist criticism of our system—more, perhaps, than we like to admit. But the question is one of alternatives: If a system is to be set up based on the "public interest," how is that elusive concept to be defined? What better way is there to define it than by elections? It is scarcely satisfactory to say that the Communist Party by definition represents the will of the people. (The Communist Party in the Soviet Union is also known as the Bolshevik Party, literally the majority party. It has consistently taken the view that it *automatically* represents the majority.[6]) In Western countries, the prevailing view is that it is far better to let voters choose among two or more alternative political parties; it is better to reform our existing political system than to replace it.

Above-Normal Profit from Innovation

There are other reasons (besides monopoly) why a firm may earn an above-normal profit. Perhaps it has introduced a technological improvement that allows it to manufacture its product at lower cost. Or, it may have developed a new product that better satisfies consumer tastes. True, in the long run, such above-normal profit may disappear as competitors follow suit. But nonetheless, it still provides the incentive that keeps business innovating and responding to changing consumer tastes. In short, this sort of profit opportunity is what makes our system go; it determines what will be produced and how. Since we judge that it is inappropriate for all this profit to go to the innovator or entrepreneur, we tax away part, but not all, of it. (Some incentive to innovate must be left.) However, many Marxists take the view that although this profit system may have worked well enough in our early stages of development,[7] it is no longer satisfactory. The whole incentive system should be changed and the economy directed in

some other way. Precisely how, of course, is the big question.

Moreover, this question is not answered by Marx's recommendation: "From each according to his ability; to each according to his need." This may sound good, but in practice it is a totally impractical guideline: If individuals define their own needs, the sum will always outrun a nation's ability to produce; and if needs are defined by someone who dictates them, two questions remain: Who is to decide? and How does that person decide who needs what?[8]

For one of the most important practical examples of how concrete production decisions are made in an economy using an alternative method to our profit system, let us now consider the Soviet Union.

THE COMMAND ECONOMY OF THE SOVIET UNION

The first country to attempt to put Marx's philosophy into practice was the Soviet Union, and for almost 30 years it was the only communist nation of any significance.

In 1917, the repressive and decaying czarist regime in Russia was overthrown by a moderate group led by Kerensky; in turn, Kerensky was overthrown by a small, militant group led by Lenin, a Marxist revolutionary. (The Germans, intent on destroying Russia as an enemy in the First World War, had transported Lenin from his exile in Switzerland, across Germany to the Russian border in a sealed railway car.) But it was only after Lenin's Red Russians had defeat-

---

[6]One criticism of Marxism is that it provides inadequate guidelines for dealing with the conflicts among individuals or among groups that arise in a society. Indeed, Marx didn't even address the question of how conflict would be resolved after the revolution, because, by assumption, conflict will no longer exist then. It has been suggested that this is one explanation for the paradox that has occurred in the Soviet Union: Although this system may be devoted in *theory* to the idea of greater freedom, it has been far from successful in achieving it.

[7]Marx himself was a great admirer of how well the profit system had worked in developing rapid economic growth during the early stages of the industrial revolution.

[8]In the Soviet Union, this guideline was eventually modified to: "From each according to his ability, to each according to his *work*." Work has been interpreted not only in terms of time and effort expended, but also in terms of what is done. (Musicians and politicians in Russia get a much higher income than equally hardworking bricklayers.)

TABLE 33-1

How the Soviet System of Public Ownership and Central Planning Differs from Our System

Basic issues	Soviet system	Modified free enterprise
1. Is ownership of productive assets held by the state or by private individuals?	State ownership (with some exceptions, for example, in parts of agriculture and retail trade)	Private ownership (with exceptions like the post office, some utilities, and some transport systems)
2. How are prices and outputs determined?	Largely by central planning agency	Largely in individual markets, in response to profit motive
3. How much freedom of choice do consumers have?	In theory, free choice in spending income; but in practice, items of desired style, size, etc., may be difficult to obtain	Essentially free choice in spending income, with producers more responsive to a wide variety of tastes

ed the White Russians in a bitter civil war and had turned back an invasion by Western countries trying to purge Russia of its new communist regime, that the communist leaders could turn their attention fully to the design of a new kind of economy.

As it has developed, that economy has differed from ours in two major respects: (1) Productive assets are predominantly owned by the state rather than private individuals; and (2) many production decisions are made by a central authority. Our discussion of each of these is summarized for easy reference in Table 33-1.

Public versus Private Ownership

In the United States, the basic pattern is private ownership—with some exceptions (for example, school buildings, and public works like the Tennessee Valley Authority). On the other hand, in the Soviet Union, the basic pattern is public ownership, with exceptions. For example, there is private ownership in the Soviet Union of some retail and wholesale business. In addition, over one-third of the houses in cities and virtually all houses on farms are owned by private individuals. Moreover, private ownership in agriculture extends beyond housing. For example, each family working on a collective farm can still have the use of a small plot of land and the livestock and equipment to go with it. Finally, of course, there is private ownership of personal assets like clothing and household tools.

But otherwise, assets in the Soviet Union are predominantly owned by the state. These assets include the "means of production" that, in Marx's view, were used to exploit labor: factories and industrial machinery, natural resources, and all transport and banking facilities.

Central Planning in the Soviet Economy

The second big difference in the two systems is that the important decisions on what will be produced in the Soviet Union are made by a central planning agency (GOSPLAN). In comparison, in our economy most such decisions are made by a host of individual producers responding to a profit incentive. (But not all; a number of our production decisions, such as the number of military aircraft or schools that will be built, are made by federal, state, or local governments.)

In a complex planning system, the Soviet government decides on a 5-year plan which establishes the desired rate of growth, including the necessary supporting level of investment. Within this broad framework, a more detailed plan is drawn up for each year, specifying output targets throughout the economy. This decision is not made in an entirely arbitrary way by government planners; instead, it is the result of an elaborate set of consultations, in which each firm and industry suggests amendments to its targets. Nonetheless, these targets are eventually set by the planners, and each plant manager is given a specific quota to fulfill. And, as in our system, the manager will face an array of incentives (bonuses, promotions, etc.[9]) to reach or exceed that quota and to make a profit. Profits do exist in the Soviet Union, and can be calculated just as in any economy where the prices of all outputs and inputs are given. But profits tend only to be a piece of accounting information and are often not even a very meaningful one at that, since they are calculated from output and input prices that are set by planners and may not mean too much. The point is that *profits do not provide the same incentive to produce as in our system; therefore, they do not play the same key role in allocating resources.* To illustrate: The central planners may decide to contract an activity that is profitable in order to expand one that is unprofitable—a pattern exactly the opposite of what happens in our system. The plant manager is a hired official carrying out a directive of what to produce (and occasionally offering advice), rather than an entrepreneur making decisions about what output will be.

The surprising thing about such a highly complicated planning system is not that it sometimes works badly, but that it works as well as it does. Consider the problem that arises if the target for steel output, say, is increased. Because steel production requires machinery, the target in the machinery industry must also be increased. But machinery production requires steel, so the steel target much be increased again. In turn, this results in a second-round increase in the machinery target, and so on, and on. Because steel is an input for machinery production and machinery is an input for steel production, one target cannot be arbitrarily set without regard to the other. Moreover, this interdependency illustrates only the simplest possible "loop" in the economic system. In reality, a complex economy like that of the Soviet Union is characterized by a myriad set of much more complicated loops, with the output of one industry being (directly or indirectly) used as an input of almost all the others. Thus, one output level cannot be set in isolation.

It is sometimes assumed that if there is an economic problem, it can be solved by planning. Some may be solved, but others cannot; moreover, the act of planning introduces a number of problems of its own. In theory, feeding appropriate mathematical techniques[10] into computers should make it possible to "get the plan right," that is, to come up with a consistent set of outputs. But in practice, the economy is too complex and unpredictable to be adequately treated in this way, and bottlenecks frequently occur. For example, what happens if the production of steel is inadequate to meet the needs of the machinery industry and other steel-using industries? Such a bottleneck would raise even greater problems for Soviet planners if they did not have the political power to impose a very simple solution: In the face of a shortage, let the consumer do without. If

---

[9]There is no shortage of incentives in the Soviet system. In fact, incentives for individual workers in the Soviet Union are similar to (and, indeed, sometimes even greater than) those available to American workers. Russian workers are paid higher wages in some occupations than in others; moreover, high piecework rates (that is, bonuses for additional units produced) are more frequently used as an incentive in the Soviet Union than in the United States. Often, highly productive workers are granted tangible rewards, such as free, government-financed holidays. And there are other incentives which may seem odd to us but appear to have a certain appeal in the Soviet Union; for example, highly productive workers are decorated and cited as "Heroes of Socialist Labor."

[10]Such as the input-output analysis developed by Wassily Leontief at Harvard University.

steel is in short supply, put it into the production of industrial machinery rather than home refrigerators. With this set of priorities, it is no surprise that Soviet performance in heavy industry is better than in consumer goods and housing.

Growth in the Soviet Economy

The example just given is but one reflection of the Soviet emphasis on industrial growth at the expense of the consumer. In addition, planners impose a high growth rate by diverting a large proportion of income away from consumption and into investment. Since investment accounts for about 30 percent of GNP in the Soviet Union, compared with roughly 15 percent in the United States, it is no surprise that Soviet growth has exceeded that of the United States. (Between 1960 and 1974, Soviet growth was 4.9 percent per year, compared with 3.8 percent in the United States.) But a higher growth rate in the Soviet Union must be interpreted with great care. It reflects the fact that its leaders have the political power to divert a very large slice of income from consumption into investment; it does not necessarily prove that the communist system is a relatively efficient way of generating growth. To illustrate this point: Japan is a noncommunist free-market economy that has been investing roughly the same large 30 percent slice of its GNP, and Japanese growth has far exceeded that of the Soviet Union. (One argument used to explain relatively rapid growth in both the Soviet Union and Japan is that growth is easier for a country that can copy advanced technology developed elsewhere; it becomes much more difficult when that country becomes a world leader and has to develop its own.)

One of the major ways the Soviet planners divert income away from consumption is by imposing a tax on consumer goods that

accounts, on average, for about one-third of their price. The Soviets have found this tax to be a useful device in at least two respects: First, they can make the overall tax system more progressive by raising the tax on luxuries and lowering it on necessities. Second, this tax finances the heavy Soviet level of investment and takes money out of the hands of the public, thus reducing consumer purchasing power. Consequently, the problem of shortages of consumer goods is reduced, though not avoided.

The Position of the Soviet Consumer

Consumers tend to be the forgotten people in the Soviet system—for several reasons. We have already seen that they are forced (via heavy taxation) to sacrifice current consumption to finance rapid growth; and they are also forced to shoulder much of the burden of inefficiency when bottlenecks develop. But there is another cost in the Soviet command economy that they also have to bear. To understand it, consider again the manager whose major concern is to satisfy a given output target, say, for producing nails. If planners have set the quota in terms of tons, the manager will most easily satisfy it by producing large nails.[11] On the other hand, if that quota is defined as a certain number of nails, the manager will tend toward producing small ones. In neither case will this nail production satisfy the consumer, who wants a selection of various kinds. Of course, the consumer may be able to make a wrong-sized nail do in a pinch. But what does a person with big feet do if shoe producers meet their quota by concentrating on small sizes? (In the last decade, Soviet leaders have paid more attention to consumer goods. For example, auto production has increased substantially, in cooperation with the Italian automaker, Fiat.)

[11]In an old cartoon in the Russian periodical *Krokodil*, about 100 men are pulling a cart laden with a huge nail 100 yards long. When a bystander asks; "What is it for?" the reply is, "We don't know, but it fulfills our complete quota of 50 tons of nails."

The Interplay of Economic and Political Systems

The Soviet system of political dictatorship is quite consistent with Marx's prediction that the overthrow of the capitalist system would be followed by a "dictatorship of the proletariat." One of the interesting questions is whether a centrally planned economy like the Soviet system would work at all with the degree of political freedom that we enjoy. In some sense, the more economic commands that come from a central authority, the more dictatorial a system becomes. This is an important issue because a major Soviet criticism of our system, and one that sometimes contains considerable truth, is that economic power corrupts political institutions. But if the Soviets' alternative economic system requires an even worse form of government, what sort of cure is that?

Better Macroeconomic Balance?

The Soviets seem to be able to do a better job of curing unemployment than we do, since they can set their target outputs at a level to closely approximate full employment. But, while they face less overt (obvious) unemployment, they have a greater problem with "disguised" unemployment, that is, workers on the job who seem to be producing something, but who are in fact contributing little or nothing to the national product. An example is the labor used to produce undersize shoes that never get worn; while this may appear to be productive employment, it is, in fact, wasted effort. An oft-cited failure of our economy was Ford's decision in the 1950s to develop a new car called the Edsel. Its failure represented a loss not only to Ford, but to the nation as a whole, in terms of wasted resources. In the Soviet Union, such a failure would not have occurred. Instead, the public would have bought the Edsel. It might not have been quite what people wanted, but they would not have had much choice. In the United States an incorrect decision results in a loss to producers and short-run unemployment in an industry; both of these can be identified and evaluated. On the other hand, a similarly erroneous decision in the Soviet Union results in a loss to consumers that may not be so obvious and so easy to measure, but may be just as real.[12] And this suggests another important question to keep in mind in your future comparison of the Soviet and American systems: Do Edsel-type goods still exist in the Soviet Union, or are they disappearing?

Which is the worse problem—the Soviets' disguised unemployment, or our overt unemployment? Our problem of overt unemployment may be less damaging in the long run, because it is obvious to all. Therefore a government is brought under pressure to reduce it. (There may be no similarly strong pressure to reduce disguised unemployment, precisely because it *is* disguised and therefore may go unrecognized.) How-

[12]Or is it? After all, what difference does it make whether the public is driving an Edsel or a Mercury? In terms of the basic transportation they provided, they were quite similar cars; the main difference was in styling. This brings into focus again a fundamental criticism of our free enterprise system: What is the point of satisfying existing consumer desires when they are the result of advertising and the other methods producers use to manipulate consumers?

As pointed out earlier, this is an argument that sounds good, but in practice raises serious problems. First, who is to say which desires are basic, and which are contrived? (In the last analysis, almost everything, from good music to dill pickles, is an acquired rather than a "basic" taste.) Second, although we may wish to reform advertising and the other means that are used to influence tastes, what is wrong, at any point in time, in satisfying *existing* consumer desires? This approach may not be ideal, but isn't it better than having someone or some group decide on what our desires should be?

Our democratic political system provides an interesting parallel. It is set up to respect the public's existing political preferences, even though they may have been formed by political parties using advertising and other forms of "manipulation." This may not, in theory, be an ideal system, but in practice we judge it better than a system in which "basic" or "ideal" political preferences are determined for the public by some individual or group.

ever, in another respect, the Soviet problem of disguised unemployment may be less damaging: The individuals involved are at least working, and hence *feel* productive even though they are not. So its psychological and social effects are less serious.

Are the Two Systems Becoming More Similar?

It is frequently suggested that our free enterprise system and the Soviet command economy are converging—for several reasons. First, we have been attempting through our tax and welfare system to reduce income differences; at the same time, the Soviets have been allowing greater differences in income in their system. A major reason is that the Soviets are becoming increasingly aware of the desirability of increasing efficiency; and this means conserving scarce factors like human capital by paying a high return to the high-productivity individuals with a lot of it. So scientists receive a much higher income than clerks, and skilled workers earn much more than unskilled workers.[13] As a result, human capital is becoming a significant source of income differences in the Soviet Union, as well as in the United States. (Recall Jacob Mincer's evidence, presented in Chapter 29, that about 60 percent of American income differences are due to human capital.) Because of this growing importance of *human capital*, a socialist policy that deals only with *physical capital* (by putting it in the hands of the state) is no longer an adequate way to treat the problem of serious income inequality. This raises the question: Will the appeal of socialism to those who believe in equalizing incomes become less strong than in Marx's day?

A second respect in which the Soviet and American economic systems are becoming more similar is that our government is intervening more in production decisions, while the Soviet government is intervening less. Why is our government intervening more? With economic growth, there is an increase in the spillover costs, like pollution, that require government control. Also, with our increased income, we are better able to afford the things governments provide, including not only public goods (like highways and parks), but also welfare payments (like unemployment insurance and subsidized medical services).

At the same time, the Soviet government is intervening less: The Soviets seem to be moving at least some distance away from their highly controlled planned economy to a less centralized system that depends more on the market. Since the mid-1960s, the Soviet government has introduced a number of reforms along the lines suggested by E. Liberman of Kharkov University. These reforms are designed to increase the efficiency of the Soviet system by making the producer more concerned with making a profit (say, by cutting costs) and less concerned with merely fulfilling a production quota. For example, producers can now take orders from customers specifying the color, size, and style of a product, and managers who produce shoes of an unwanted size or style are penalized if their product cannot be sold. In addition, a firm's management is now given some limited authority in changing price. This decentralization of decisions from planners to individual producers has brought production more closely in line with consumer demand, and closer to a free enterprise model.

But, despite this evidence of Soviet-American convergence, great differences in philosophy and practice remain. One important question in the future will be: How far

[13]In fact, the differences in wages are even more pronounced in the Soviet Union than in the United States. But this is a bit misleading because many Soviet services (like medical care) are free, and many others (like housing) are heavily subsidized. As a result, there are smaller differences in real income in the Soviet Union than simple wage comparisons suggest.

will the Soviets go in decentralizing their system and making it more sensitive to the market? Some clues may be provided by considering the case of Yugoslavia. This is a communist economy that has been designed to respond to pressures of the marketplace. Hence it may give us some idea of the direction in which the Soviet Union may be heading.

THE SOCIALIST MARKET ECONOMY OF YUGOSLAVIA

By the end of the Second World War, Soviet armies had swept the Germans out of the countries of Eastern Europe, imposing communist political and economic systems in their wake. Since that time, the history of these countries has been marked by a long and sometimes unrewarding struggle for political and economic reform. The story of Yugoslavia is somewhat different. That country was liberated from the Germans, not by the Soviet army, but instead by a Yugoslavian guerrilla movement. The civil war that followed was won by Marshall Tito, a communist who nonetheless was sufficiently independent to break politically with Moscow in 1948. He was then able to introduce his own kind of communism, which can best be described as "market socialism." Like the Soviet or any other Marxist system, it involves state ownership of productive assets. But Yugoslavia has a less centralized economy than the Soviet Union. The decision on what will be produced depends more heavily on market signals from consumers than on commands from central planners.

Before we consider how the Yugoslavs have introduced a greater degree of freedom in the marketplace, it is important to keep their economy in perspective by noting the respects in which their government still does exercise a high degree of control. First, although many prices vary as a result of market pressures, they typically do so only within specified limits; moreover, in some sectors there is complete price control by the government. Second, the government imposes a high rate of growth. (As in the Soviet Union, it taxes away roughly one-third of GNP and directs it into investment.) Third, the government determines which sectors will grow more rapidly than others by allocating investment funds to each. However, within each sector there is, typically, considerable competition among enterprises for available funds. Finally, the Yugoslavs, like the Soviets, draw up a 5-year plan. But theirs is less in the Soviet style of setting target outputs in each sector than in the French style of simply indicating what output levels are likely to be. Thus, a steel firm can see the expected level of output in industries (like machinery and home appliances) that use steel. It can then use this information to make its own decision on how much steel to produce.

The Greater Degree of Market Freedom in Yugoslavia

In Yugoslavia, a firm may be owned by the state, but it is operated by its workers,[14] who elect a manager to make day-to-day decisions. The manager acquires labor and other factors of production and sells the firm's output in more-or-less free markets,

---

[14]This system of "workers' self-management" is also designed to give workers in Yugoslavia a sense of participation. Alienation of workers was one of the major criticisms that the Yugoslavs had of the Soviet system.

Worker alienation has also been a long-standing socialist criticism of free enterprise systems. Recently, attempts have been made in Western countries to allow workers greater participation in management decisions. For example, in 1976 the West Germans passed a law which gives workers the same representation as stockholders on the supervisory boards of large companies. (However, ultimate control is still held by stockholders.)

with the objective being to earn profits, which in turn go to the workers.[15] The enterprise may succeed or it may not, depending on its ability to earn profits by responding to changes in consumer tastes and other market pressures. And, within limits, the firm can change its price.

Because production decisions are influenced by the profit motive and are sensitive to consumer wants, the Yugoslav system achieves some of the efficiencies of ours.[16] But (no surprise) it consequently also encounters some of our problems. First, managers who are in a monopoly position soon discover that they can exploit this position: They can increase their workers' profits by restricting supply and raising price.[17] Thus the efficiency losses of monopoly may arise in such an economy, just as they do in ours. Second, workers' income depends on earnings from the enterprise, rather than on just a formal wage. And since the financial success of enterprises varies, so does workers' income. Thus, worker ownership introduces incentives to labor to work harder (thereby increasing efficiency); but it also results in an uneven distribution of income that many socialists view as inequitable. Even in this socialist state, *there is still a basic conflict between the objectives of efficiency and equity.* (In order to keep their incomes more equal, the Yugoslavs in 1972 imposed limits on income differences among workers.) Third, compared with the Soviets, the Yugoslavs face a greater problem of overt unemployment (though a smaller problem of disguised unemployment). The reason is that, in Yugoslavia, profits determine whether an enterprise will prosper or not, and if it does, it may expand. Hence, regions that have profitable enterprises may have no problem in absorbing a growing labor force and thus maintaining full employment. But regions with unprofitable firms that do not grow may face an unemployment problem. There is no Soviet-type command for production to expand in these areas.

Special Problems

In Yugoslavia, there is still a relatively healthy, small-scale, privately owned sector where new firms are set up by private individuals, just as in our system. But, if we concentrate on the rest of the economy where capital is publicly owned, an important question (common to any socialist econ-

---

[15]In Yugoslavia, it is not clear what sort of profit is maximized. From the point of view of overall economic efficiency, total profit of the enterprise should be maximized. But there is an incentive in Yugoslavia to use the quite different criterion of maximizing *average profit per worker* (since this gives each worker-owner the largest possible profit).

[16]But there is still evidence that the Yugoslav system falls considerably short of its objective of satisfying consumers. In a celebrated case in 1977, police broke up a ring that was smuggling blue jeans into Yugoslavia, using a wire strung across the Idria River. When this wire was cut, 1,200 pairs of jeans were backed up into the hands of the "Italian connection" on the other side.

*[17]At first, socialist theoreticians were optimistic that the monopoly problem could be solved by setting up a system in which planners would announce prices. This would force producers into the role of price takers. As a consequence, they would produce to the point where their marginal cost is equal to price. At the same time, consumers would also take market price as given, and would consume to the point where their marginal utility is equal to price.

But how would a planner decide on the price to announce? If the price that has been previously announced does not equate producers' supply and consumers' demand, the planner changes it until it does. With producers and consumers all acting as price takers, wouldn't such a socialist system provide the efficiency of perfect competition—even better than our imperfectly competitive free enterprise system? The answer is: Not necessarily. The profit-seeking manager who has monopoly power will still be able to exercise it. As the only producer, the manager just reduces the supply. The planner will then observe that supply is falling short of demand, and will raise price to the monopoly level the producer is seeking. In other words, a monopolist who figures out how the system works will not take price as given, even if it is announced by a central planner.

omy) is: Who sets up new enterprises? In Yugoslavia, existing firms develop new product lines and open up new branches. But how are *new* firms established?

This is a major issue because the entry (or even just the threat of entry) of new firms into an industry may reduce or prevent monopoly abuse, thus increasing the efficiency of the economy. Moreover, new firms may mean an even greater variety of new products to satisfy consumer demand more effectively, as well as new jobs in regions of severe unemployment. New firms in our system are formed by entrepreneurs who know they will own them and earn profits from them. But where private ownership is not allowed, what then? In Yugoslavia, new firms may be set up by a local community using government-supplied funds. But the problem is that the initiator loses control of the enterprise as soon as it is established and passes into the hands of its workers—so the incentive to exercise such an initiative is reduced.

CONCLUSIONS

In previous chapters we have seen how, in our system, redistributing income via government transfer payments affects incentives—in particular, the work incentive of those receiving the payments. In this chapter we have seen how, in the Soviet and Yugoslavian systems, the more drastic socialist policy of redistributing income by giving the ownership of capital to the state will also affect incentives—in this case, the incentives to initiate and innovate. Thus, there is no system that will work perfectly in theory, solving all our problems at once. Consequently, judgment on which economic system is better depends on the answer to this question: In *practice*, which system

does a better job of solving the basic economic problem of transforming resources into the satisfaction of human wants? As you evaluate this issue for yourself in the future, remember that the standard criticism of socialism is that it does not do a particularly good job of satisfying these wants. And also remember the basic criticism of free enterprise: It does a far worse job of satisfying the wants of the poor than of the rich.

Another criticism of free enterprise is that large corporations often exercise too much economic and political power—power that should be exercised by the government on behalf of the people. But if socialists cure this problem by transferring a great deal of economic power (specifically, the ownership of capital) to the government, does too much power then fall into the hands of the state?

Finally, we must distinguish between the physical capital that a socialist state brings under government ownership and control, and the human capital that cannot be dealt with in this way: the skills, experience, and expertise we carry around in our heads. Labor is no longer the largely unskilled commodity that Marx observed over a hundred years ago; labor now exists at widely varying skill levels. Consequently, our nation's capital today is in the hands not only of those who own physical plant and machinery, but also of those who own human capital. And these people range all the way from semiskilled workers to managers and those who work in scores of professions. As a result, it is now much more difficult to argue that society is simply divided into two groups: those who exploit (the capitalists) and those who are exploited (the workers). Most workers are also "capitalists"—some because they own physical capital, but most because they own large quantities of human capital.

Key Points

1. Most of the physical capital in our free enterprise system is owned by individuals; under socialism it is owned by the state on behalf of all the people. The theoretical appeal of socialism is that it eliminates one of the major causes of inequality in our system: the power and income enjoyed by those who own capital.

2. The two major economic characteristics of the system that exists in the Soviet Union today are: (*a*) physical capital is owned publicly rather than privately; and (*b*) investment and output levels are determined by a central planning authority.

3. One of the advantages of Soviet economywide central planning is that industry output targets can be set at a level that keeps unemployment low. But there are disadvantages. Central planning results in a great accumulation of power in the hands of the central political authorities. And the more that such power is centralized, the greater the risk that this power will be abused. A key question is: Could a Soviet-style command economy be run without political dictatorship?

4. A further problem with economywide planning is that it is extremely difficult to administer and therefore often results in bottlenecks and other inefficiencies. As a consequence, central planning tends to re-sult in higher levels of disguised unemployment, with workers engaged in unproductive activities, such as producing goods that poorly satisfy consumer tastes.

5. In recognition of this problem, the Soviets have recently been attempting to make their system more sensitive to "messages from the marketplace." This approach has brought them closer to Yugoslavia's economic system.

6. Yugoslavia is, like Russia, a socialist country in which productive capital is owned by the state. But it differs from Russia because much less economic decision-making is done by a central authority and much more is handled by individual enterprises responding to profits and subject to market pressures.

7. For this reason, the Yugoslavian economy is closer to our system; as a consequence, the government encounters some of the same problems that we face (such as unemployment). Moreover, the fact that the Yugoslavs' capital is publicly owned means that they face a problem common to the Soviet Union or any other socialist country: how to attain the high levels of innovation and initiative that exist in a free enterprise system, where persons who own capital take great risks in order to earn future profits.

Key Concepts

capitalist
labor theory of value
subsistence level of wages
surplus value
proletariat
bourgeoisie
socialism
communism

Gosplan
5-year plan
output target
overt versus disguised unemployment
Soviet/American convergence
Liberman reforms
Yugoslav market socialism
management of firms by workers

Problems

33-1 What did Marx mean by "surplus value"? Does it include some, all, or none of the costs of capital that must be paid by firms undertaking investment?

33-2 What are the two forms of unemployment? Which is worse in the Soviet system? Which is worse in our system? Explain.

33-3 In your view, what is the most important difference between the Soviet and the Yugoslav systems?

33-4 Do you agree with the following statement? Because many workers are hostile to capital, they oppose a rapid accumulation of it—either by a firm or by the nation as a whole. Thus they fail to understand their own interest, which is to be working with more rather than less capital. (The more capital, the higher their wage will be.)

33-5 Give your own concrete example to explain how a bottleneck may occur in a centrally planned economy. Does socialism require central planning? Explain.

33-6 Do you think the free enterprise and socialist systems will ever converge into an "ideal" system? Explain.

33-7 Do we acquire more new technology from the Japanese, British, and Germans, or from the Russians and Czechs? Are there several reasons for your answer? Explain.

33-8 "Under unrestricted free enterprise, a stupid, shiftless individual who has inherited a great deal of land can charge a maximum rent, and through the diligent pursuit of idleness, become very wealthy—indeed, far wealthier than the intelligent, hardworking person who rents the land. Something is wrong." Do you agree?

Now consider three alternative solutions to this problem, carefully criticizing each:

(*a*) Put a ceiling on rent. This would transfer income from landlords to tenants.

(*b*) Charge the maximum rent, but have the land owned by the state, with all income going to the state.

(*c*) Let landlords continue to own the land and charge maximum rents. But place a heavy percentage tax on their income.

Which solution is closest to the socialist blueprint? Which is closest to our modified free enterprise system?

33-9 One standard criticism of socialism and communism is that they promise more, but deliver less. Do you agree? Explain.

Glossary

(Not all these terms appear in the text; some are included because they occur frequently in readings or lectures. Page numbers shown after the definitions provide the primary references for the terms. For additional references, see the index).

ability-to-pay principle. The view that taxes should be levied according to the means of the various taxpayers, as measured by their incomes and/or wealth. Compare with *benefit principle.* (p. 89)

absolute advantage. A country (or city or individual) has an absolute advantage in the production of a good or service if it can produce that good or service with fewer resources than other countries (or cities or individuals). See also *comparative advantage.* (p. 40)

accelerationist. One who believes that an attempt to keep the unemployment rate low by expansive demand policies will cause more and more rapid inflation. (p. 277)

accelerator. The theory that net investment depends on the change in sales. (p. 300)

accounts payable. Debts to suppliers of goods or services. (p. 104)

accounts receivable. Amounts due from customers. (p. 104)

action lag. The time interval between the recognition that adjustments in aggregate demand policies are desirable and the time when policies are actually changed. (p. 313)

adjustable peg system. A system where countries peg (fix) exchange rates but retain the right to change them in the event of fundamental disequilibrium. (In the adjustable peg system of 1945–1973, countries generally fixed the prices of their currencies in terms of the United States dollar.) (p. 354)

ad valorem tax. A tax collected as a percentage of the price or value of a good.

aggregate demand. Total expenditures on consumer goods and services, government goods and services, (desired) investment, and net exports. (p. 146)

allocative efficiency. Production of the best combination of goods with the best combination of inputs. (p. 14)

annually balanced budget principle. The view that government expenditures should be limited each year to no more than government receipts during that year. (p. 183)

antitrust laws. Laws designed to control monopoly power and practices. Examples: Sherman Act, 1890; Clayton Act, 1914. (p. 499)

appreciation of a currency. In a flexible exchange-rate system, a rise in the price of a currency in terms of another currency or currencies. (p. 364)

arbitrage. A set of transactions aimed at making a profit from inconsistent prices. (p. 352)

arbitration. Settlement of differences between a union and management by an impartial third party (the arbitrator) whose decisions are binding. (p. 621)

arc elasticity of demand. The elasticity of demand between two points on a demand curve, calculated by the formula

$$\frac{\Delta Q}{Q_1 + Q_2} \div \frac{\Delta P}{P_1 + P_2} \qquad \text{(p. 382n)}$$

asset. Something that is owned. (pp. 103–104)

automatic stabilizer. A feature built into the economy which tends to reduce the amplitude of fluctuations. For example, tax collections tend to fall during a recession and rise during a boom, slowing the change in disposable incomes and aggregate demand. (Thus they are an automatic fiscal stabilizer.) Interest rates tend to fall during a recession and rise during a boom because of changes in the demand for funds. These changes in interest rates tend to stabilize investment demand. (Thus they are an automatic monetary stabilizer.) (pp. 178, 317)

average-cost pricing. Setting the price where the average-cost curve (including normal profit) intersects the demand curve. (pp. 470–472)

average fixed cost. Fixed cost divided by the number of units of output.

average product. Total product divided by the number of units of the variable input used.

average revenue. Total revenue divided by the number of units sold. Where there is a single price, this price equals average revenue. (p. 461)

average total cost. Total cost divided by the number of units of output. (p. 416)

average variable cost. Variable cost divided by the number of units produced. (p. 416)

balanced budget. (1) A budget with revenues equal to expenditures. (2) More loosely (but more commonly), a budget with revenues equal to or greater than expenditures. (p. 171)

balanced budget multipler. The change in equilibrium national product divided by the change in government spending when this spending is financed by an equivalent change in taxes. (p. 174)

balance of payments. The summary figure calculated from balance-of-payments credits less balance-of-payments debits, with certain monetary transactions excluded from the calculation. (There are various ways of defining monetary transactions; thus, there are various balance-of-payments definitions. The most common excludes official reserve transactions.) (p. 371)

balance-of-payments accounts. A statement of a country's transactions with other countries. (p. 370)

balance-of-payments surplus (deficit). A positive (negative) balance of payments. (p. 371)

balance of trade (or balance on merchandise account). The value of exports of goods minus the value of imports of goods. (p. 372)

balance sheet. The statement of a firm's financial position at a particular time, showing its assets, liabilities, and net worth. (p. 103)

band. The range within which an exchange rate could move without the government's being committed to intervene in exchange markets to prevent further movement. That is, under the adjustable peg system, governments were obliged to keep exchange rates from moving outside a band (of 1 percent either side of parity). (pp. 354, 358)

bank reserve. See *required reserves.*

bank run. A situation in which many owners of bank deposits attempt to make withdrawals because of their fear that the bank will be unable to meet its obligations. (p. 199)

bankruptcy. (1) A situation in which a firm (or individual) has legally been declared unable to pay its debts. (2) More loosely, a situation in which a firm (or individual) is unable to pay its debts.

barrier to entry. An impediment that makes it difficult or impossible for a new firm to enter an industry. Examples: patents, economies of scale, accepted brand names. (p. 492)

barter. The exchange of one good or service for another without the use of money. (p. 35)

base year. The reference year, given the value of 100 when constructing a price index or other time series. (p. 125)

beggar-my-neighbor policy. A policy aimed at shifting an unemployment problem to another country. Example: an increase in tarriffs. (p. 560)

benefit-cost analysis. The calculation and comparison of the benefits and costs of a program or project. (pp. 186, 530)

benefit principle. The view that taxes should be levied in proportion to the benefits which the various taxpayers receive from government expenditures. Compare with *ability-to-pay principle.* (p. 89)

bilateral monopoly. A market structure involving a single seller (monopolist) and a single buyer (monopsonist). (p. 615)

bill. See *Treasury bill.*

blacklist. A list of workers who are not to be given jobs because of union activity or other behavior considered objectionable by employers. (p. 603)

black market. A market in which sales take place at a price above the legal maximum.

bogus type. Type that is set but not actually used. The setting of bogus type is a way of protecting typesetters' jobs when ready-made type is already available (for example, from a newspaper advertiser). (p. 609)

bond. A written commitment to pay a scheduled series of interest payments plus the face value (principal) at a specified maturity date. (p. 101)

bourgeoisie. (1) In Marxist doctrine, capitalists as a social class. (2) The middle class. (3) More narrowly, shopkeepers. (p. 699)

boycott. A concerted refusal to buy (buyer's boycott) or sell (sellers' boycott). A campaign to discourage people from doing business with a particular firm.

break-even point. (1) The output at which costs just equal revenues and therefore profits are zero. (p. 417) (2) The level of disposable income at which consumption just equals dispos-

able income and therefore saving is zero. (p. 149)

broker. One who acts on behalf of a buyer or seller. (p. 113)

budget deficit. The amount by which budgetary outlays exceed revenues. (p. 171)

budget line (or income line). The line on a diagram which shows the various combinations of commodities which can be bought with a given income at a given set of prices. (p. 406)

budget surplus. The amount by which budgetary revenues exceed outlays. (p. 171)

built-in stabilizer. See *automatic stabilizer.*

burden of tax. See *incidence of tax* and *excess burden of tax.*

business cycle. The more or less regular upward and downward movement of economic activity over a period of years. A cycle has four phases: recession, trough, expansion, and peak. (p. 297)

capital. (1) Real capital: buildings, equipment, and other materials used in the production process which have themselves been produced in the past. (p. 22) (2) Financial capital: either funds available for acquiring real capital *or* financial assets such as bonds or common stock. (3) Human capital: the education, training, and experience which make human beings more productive. (p. 631)

capital consumption allowance. See *depreciation.*

capital gain. The increase in the value of an asset over time. (p. 91)

capitalism. A system in which capital is privately owned.

capitalized value. The present value of the income stream which an asset is expected to produce. (p. 223)

capital market. A market in which financial instruments such as stocks and bonds are bought and sold. (p. 107)

capital-output ratio. The value of capital divided by the value of the annual output produced with this capital.

capital stock. The total quantity of real capital.

cartel. A formal agreement among firms to set price and/or market shares. (p. 482)

categorical grant. A federal grant to a state or local government for a specific program. Such a grant requires the recipient government to pay part of the cost of the program. (p. 80)

cease-and-desist order. An order from a court or government agency to an individual or company to stop a specified action. (p. 501)

central bank. A banker's bank, whose major responsibility is the control of the money supply. A central bank also generally performs other functions, such as check clearing and the inspection of commercial banks. (p. 200)

central planning. Centralized direction of the resources of the economy, with the objective of fulfilling national goals. (p. 703)

certificate of deposit (CD). A marketable time deposit.

ceteris paribus. "Other things unchanged." In demand-and-supply analysis, it is common to make the *ceteris paribus* assumption; that is, to assume that none of the determinants of the quality demanded or supplied is allowed to change (with the sole exception of price). (p. 53)

check clearing. The transfer of checks from the bank in which they were deposited to the bank on which they were written, with the net amounts due to or from each bank being calculated. (p. 206)

checkoff. The deduction of union dues from workers' pay by an employer, who then remits the dues to the union. (p. 605)

circular flow of payments. The flow of payments from businesses to households in exchange for labor and other productive services and the return flow of payments from households to businesses in exchange for goods and services. (p. 158)

classical economics. (1) In Keynesian economics, the accepted body of macroeconomic doctrine prior to the publication of Keynes' *General Theory.* According to classical economics, a market economy tends toward an equilibrium with full employment; a general deflation of wages and prices can help to restore full employment; a market economy tends to be stable if monetary conditions are stable; and changes in the quantity of money are the major cause of changes in aggregate demand. (p. 144) (2) The accepted view, prior to about 1870, that value depends on the cost of production. [In the late nineteenth century, this was replaced with the "neoclassical" view that value depends on both costs of production (supply) and utility (demand).]

class struggle. In Marxist economics, the struggle for control between the proletariat and the bourgeoisie. (p. 699)

clean float. A situation where exchange rates are determined by market forces, without intervention by central banks or governments. (p. 363)

closed economy. An economy with no international transactions.

closed shop. A business that hires only workers who are already union members. (p. 605)

cobweb cycle. A switching back and forth between a situation of high production and low price and one of low production and high price. A cobweb cycle can occur if there are long lags in production and if producers erroneously assume that price this year is a good indicator of price next year. (p. 446)

collective bargaining. Negotiations between a union and management over wages and working conditions. (p. 602)

collective goods. Goods which, by their very nature, provide benefits to a large group of people. (p. 527)

collusion. An agreement among sellers regarding prices and/or market shares. The agreement may be explicit or tacit. (p. 482)

commercial bank. A privately owned, profit-seeking institution that accepts demand and savings deposits, makes loans, and acquires other earning assets (particularly bonds and shorter-term debt instruments). In the United States, a commercial bank may receive its charter from the federal government (in which case it is a *national bank*), or from a state government (a *state bank*). (p. 200)

common stock. Each share of common stock represents part ownership in a corporation. (p. 98)

communism. (1) In Marxist theory, the ultimate stage of historical development in which (*a*) all are expected to work and no one lives by owning capital, (*b*) exploitation has been eliminated and there is a classless society, and (*c*) the state has withered away. (2) A common alternative usage: the economic and political systems of China, the Soviet Union, and other countries in which a Communist party is in power. (p. 699)

company union. A union dominated by the employer.

comparative advantage. If two nations (or cities or individuals) have different opportunity costs of producing a good or service, then the nation (or city or individual) with the lower opportunity cost has a comparative advantage in that good or service. (p. 41)

competition. See *perfect competition.*

competitive devaluations. A round of exchange-rate devaluations in which each of a number of countries tries to gain a competitive advantage by devaluing its currency. (Not all can be successful; each must fail to the extent that other countries also devalue.)

complementary goals. Goals such that the achievement of one helps in the achievement of the other. (Contrast with *conflicting goals.*) (p. 17)

complementary goods. Goods such that the rise in the price of one causes a leftward shift in the demand curve for the other. (Contrast with *substitute.*) (p. 54)

concentration ratio. Usually, the fraction of an industry's total sales made by the four largest firms. (Sometimes a different number of firms—such as eight—is chosen in calculating concentration ratios, and sometimes a different measure of size—such as assets—is chosen.) (p. 479)

conflicting goals. Goals such that working toward one makes it more difficult to achieve the other. (p. 17)

conglomerate merger. See *merger.*

consent decree. An agreement whereby a defendant, without admitting guilt, undertakes to desist from certain actions and abide by other conditions laid down in the decree.

conspicuous consumption. Consumption whose purpose is to impress others. A term originated by Thorstein Veblen (1857–1929).

constant dollars. A series is measured in constant dollars if it is measured at the prices existing in a specified base year. Such a series has been adjusted to remove the effects of inflation (or deflation). Contrast with *current dollars.* (p. 126)

constant returns (to scale). This occurs if an increase of x percent in all inputs causes output to increase by the same x percent.

consumer price index (CPI). A weighted average of the prices of goods and services commonly purchased by families in urban areas, as calcu-

lated by the U.S. Bureau of Labor Statistics. (p. 12)

consumers' surplus. The net benefit that consumers get from being able to purchase a good at the prevailing price; the difference between the maximum amounts that consumers would be willing to pay and what they actually do pay. It is approximately the triangular area under the demand curve and above the market price.

consumption. (1) The purchase of consumer goods and services. (p. 129) (2) The act of using goods and services to satisfy wants. (3) The using up of goods (as in capital consumption allowances).

consumption function. (1) The relationship between consumer expenditures and disposable income. (p. 149) (2) More broadly, the relationship between consumer expenditures and the factors that determine these expenditures. (p. 345)

convergence hypothesis. The proposition that the differences between communistic and capitalistic societies is decreasing. (p. 707)

corporation. An association of stockholders with a government charter which grants certain legal powers, privileges, and liabilities separate from those of the individual stockholder-owners. The major advantages of the corporate form of business organization are limited liability for the owners, continuity, and relative ease of raising capital for expansion. (p. 98)

correlation. The tendency of two variables (like income and consumption) to move together.

cost-benefit analysis. See *benefit-cost analysis.*

cost-push inflation. Inflation caused principally by increasing costs—in the form of higher prices for labor, materials, and other inputs—rather than by rising demand. Contrast with *demand-pull inflation.* (p. 275)

countercyclical policy. Policy which reduces fluctuations in economic activity. (p. 309)

countervailing power. Power in one group which has grown as a reaction to power in another group. For example, a big labor union may develop to balance the bargaining power of a big corporation. A term originated by Prof. John Kenneth Galbraith of Harvard.

craft union. A labor union whose members have a particular craft (skill or occupation). Examples: electricians' union, plumbers' union. Contrast with *industrial union.* (p. 602)

crawling peg system. An international financial system in which par values would be changed frequently, by small amounts, in order to avoid large changes at a later date. (p. 358)

credit instrument. A written promise to pay.

credit rationing. Allocation of available funds among borrowers when the demand for loans exceeds the supply at the prevailing interest rate. (p. 249)

creeping inflation. A slow but persistent upward movement of the average level of prices (not more than 2 or 3 percent per annum).

cross-section data. Observations taken at the same time. For example, the consumption of different income classes in the United States in 1979.

currency. (1) Coins and paper money (dollar bills). (p. 195) (2) In international economics, a national money, such as the dollar or the yen. (p. 347)

current dollars. A series (like GNP) is measured in current dollars if each observation is measured at the prices that prevailed at the time. Such a series reflects both real changes in GNP *and* inflation (or deflation). Contrast with *constant dollars*. (p. 126)

current liabilities. Debts that are due for payment within a year.

customs union. Agreement among nations to eliminate trade barriers (tariffs, quotas, etc.) among themselves and to adopt common barriers to imports from nonmember countries. Example: the European Economic Community. (p. 574)

cutthroat competition. Selling at a price below both average and marginal cost, with the objective of driving competitors out of the market (at which time prices may be raised and monopoly profits reaped). (p. 484)

cyclically balanced budget. A budget whose receipts over a whole business cycle are at least equal to expenditures over the same cycle. Unlike an annually balanced budget, a cyclically balanced budget permits countercyclical fiscal policies. Surpluses during prosperity may be used to cover deficits during recessions. (p. 186)

debasement of currency. Reduction of the quantity of precious metals in coins.

debt instrument. A written commitment to repay borrowed funds.

declining industry. An industry whose firms make less than normal profits. (Firms will therefore leave the industry.)

decreasing returns. This occurs if an x percent increase in all inputs results in an increase of output of less than x percent.

deflation. (1) A decline in the average level of prices; the opposite of inflation. (p. 11) (2) The removal of the effects of inflation from a series of observations by dividing each observation with a price index. The derivation of a constant-dollar series from a current-dollar series. (p. 126)

deflationary bias. Such a bias exists in a system if, on average, monetary and fiscal authorities are constrained from allowing aggregate demand to increase as rapidly as productive capacity. (The classical gold standard was criticized on the ground that it created a deflationary bias.) (p. 354)

deflationary gap. See *recessionary gap.*

demand. A schedule or curve showing, *ceteris paribus,* how much of a good or service would be demanded at various possible prices. (p. 50)

demand curve. The curve relating the quantity of a good demanded to its price, *ceteris paribus.* (p. 50)

demand deposit. A bank deposit withdrawable on demand and transferable by check. (p. 196)

demand deposit multiplier. See *money multiplier.*

demand management policy. A change in monetary or fiscal policy aimed at affecting aggregate demand.

demand-pull inflation. Inflation caused by excess aggregate demand. (p. 275)

demand shift. A movement of the demand curve to the right or left as a result of a change in income or any other determinant of the quantity demanded (with the sole exception of the price of the good). (p. 53)

demand shifter. Anything except its own price that affects the quantity of a good demanded. (p. 53)

depletion allowance. A deduction, equal to a percentage of sales, which certain extractive industries are permitted in calculating taxable profits. (p. 91)

depreciation. (1) The loss in the value of physical capital due to wear and obsolescence. (2) The estimate of such loss in business or economic accounts; that is, a capital consumption allowance. (p. 107)

depreciation of a currency. A decline in the value of a floating currency measured in terms of another currency or currencies. (p. 364)

depression. An extended period of very high unemployment and much excess capacity. (There is no generally accepted, precise numerical definition of a depression. This text suggests that a depression requires unemployment rates of 10 percent or more for 2 years or more.) (p. 296n)

derived demand. The demand for an input that depends on the demand for the product or products it is used to make. For example, the demand for flour is derived from the demand for bread. (p. 587)

devaluation. In international economics, a reduction of the par value of a currency. (p. 356)

dictatorship of the proletariat. In Marxist economics, the state after a revolution has eliminated the capitalist class and when power is in the hands of the proletariat. (p. 706)

differentiated products. Similar products that retain some distinctive difference(s); close but not perfect substitutes. Examples: Ford and Chevrolet automobiles, different brands of toothpaste. (p. 493)

diminishing returns, law of eventually. If technology is unchanged, then the use of more and more units of a variable input (together with one or more fixed inputs) must eventually lead to a declining marginal product for the variable input. (p. 415)

discounting. (1) The process by which the present value of one or more future payments is calculated, using an interest rate. (See *present value.*) (p. 222) (2) In central banking, lending by the central bank to a commercial bank or banks. (p. 222)

discount rate. (1) In central banking, the rate of interest charged by the central bank on loans to commercial banks. (p. 222) (2) Less commonly, the interest rate used in discounting.

discretionary policy. Policy which is periodically changed in the light of changing conditions. The term is usually applied to monetary or fiscal policies which are adjusted with the objectives of high employment and stable prices. Contrast with *monetary rule.* (p. 326)

disposable (personal) income. Income that households have left after the payment of taxes. It is divided among consumption expenditures, the payment of interest on consumer debt, and saving. (p. 136)

dissaving. Negative saving.

dividend. The part of a corporation's profits paid out to its shareholders.

division of labor. The breaking up of a productive process into different tasks, each done by a different worker (for example, on an automobile assembly line). (p. 33)

dollar standard. An international system in which many international transactions take place in dollars and many countries hold sizable fractions of their reserves in dollars. Also, other currencies may be pegged to the dollar. (p. 358)

double taxation. The taxation of corporate profits first when they are earned and second when they are paid out in dividends. (p. 100)

dumping. The sale of a good at a lower price in a foreign market than in the home market—a form of price discrimination.

duopoly. A market in which there are only two sellers. (p. 482)

econometrics. The application of statistical methods to economic problems.

economic efficiency. See *allocative efficiency* and *technical efficiency.*

economic integration. The elimination of tariffs and other barriers between nations. The partial or complete unification of the economies of different countries.

economic rent. The return to a factor of production in excess of its opportunity cost. (p. 638)

economics. (1) The study of how people acquire material necessities and comforts, the problems they encounter in doing so, and how these problems can be reduced. (p. 3) (2) Frequently, a narrower definition is used—the study of the allocation of scarce resources to satisfy human wants. (p. 31)

economies (diseconomies) of scale. See *increasing (decreasing) returns.*

economize. To make the most of limited resources; to be careful in outlay. (p. 21)

effluent charge. A tax or other levy on a polluting activity based on the quantity of pollution discharged. (p. 510)

elastic demand. Demand with an elasticity of more than one. A fall in price causes an increase in total expenditure on the product in question, because the percentage change in quantity demanded is greater than the percentage change in price. (p. 376)

elasticity of demand. The price elasticity of demand is

$$\frac{\text{Percentage change in quantity demanded}}{\text{Percentage change in price}}$$

Similarly, the income elasticity of demand is

$$\frac{\text{Percentage change in quantity demanded}}{\text{Percentage change in income}}$$

The unmodified term "elasticity" usually applies to price elasticity. (pp. 380, 390)

elasticity of supply. The (price) elasticity of supply is

$$\frac{\text{Percentage change in quantity supplied}}{\text{Percentage change in price}}$$

(p. 382)

elastic supply. Supply with an elasticity of more than one. A supply curve which, if extended in a straight line, would meet the vertical axis. (pp. 382–383)

emission fee. See *effluent charge.*

employer of last resort. The government acts as the employer of last resort if it offers jobs to those who are willing and able to work but cannot find jobs in the private sector. (p. 290)

employment rate. The percentage of the labor force employed.

endogenous variable. A variable explained within a theory.

Engel's laws. Regularities between income and consumer expenditures observed by nineteenth-century statistician Ernst Engel. Most important is the decrease in the percentage of income spent on food as income rises. (p. 148)

entrepreneur. One who organizes and manages production. One who innovates and bears risks.

envelope curve. A curve that encloses, by just touching, a series of other curves. For example, the long-run average-cost curve is the envelope of all the short-run average-cost curves (each of which shows costs, given a particular stock of fixed capital). (p. 420)

equation of exchange. $MV = PQ$. (p. 250)

equilibrium. A situation where there is no tendency for change. (p. 51)

equity. (1) Ownership, or amount owned. (2) Fairness.

escalator clause. A provision in a contract or law whereby a price, wage, or other monetary quantity is increased at the same rate as a specified price index (usually the consumer price index). (p. 288)

estate tax. A tax on property owned at the time of death.

Eurodollars. Deposits in European banks, denominated in United States dollars.

excess burden of a tax. The decrease in efficiency that results when people change their behavior to reduce their tax payments. (p. 189)

excess demand. The amount by which the quantity demanded exceeds the quantity supplied at the existing price (that is, a shortage). (p. 53)

excess reserves. Reserves held by a bank in excess of the legally required amount. (p. 203)

excess supply. The amount by which the quantity supplied exceeds the quantity demanded at the existing price. A surplus. (p. 52)

exchange rate. The price of one national currency in terms of another. (p. 347)

exchange-rate appreciation (depreciation). See *appreciation (depreciation) of a currency.*

excise tax. A tax on the sale of a particular good. An *ad valorem tax* is collected as a percentage of the price of the good. A *specific tax* is a fixed tax per unit of the good.

exclusion principle. The basis for distinguishing between public and nonpublic goods. If those who do not pay for a good can be excluded from enjoying it, then it is a nonpublic good. (p. 84)

exogenous variable. A variable not explained within a theory; its value is taken as given.

externality. An adverse (or beneficial) side effect of production or consumption for which no payment is made. Also known as a *spillover* or *third-party effect.* (p. 61)

externally held public debit. Government securities held by foreigners.

Fabian socialism. Form of socialism founded in Britain in the late nineteenth century, advocating gradual and evolutionary movement toward socialism within a democratic political system.

factor mobility. Ease with which factors can be moved from one use to another.

factor of production. Resource used to produce a good or service. Land, labor, and capital are the three basic categories of factors. (p. 22)

fair return. Return to which a regulated public utility is or should be entitled.

featherbedding. Make-work rules designed to increase the number of workers (or the number of hours) on a particular job. (p. 609)

federal funds rate. The interest rate on very short term (usually overnight) loans between banks. (p. 203)

fiat money. Paper money that is neither backed by nor convertible into precious metals but is nevertheless legal tender.

final product. (1) Products that have been acquired for final use and not for resale or for further processing. (2) The economy's output of goods and services after all double counting has been eliminated. (p. 128)

financial intermediary. Institution that issues financial obligations (such as demand deposits) in order to acquire funds from the public. The institution then pools these funds and provides them in larger amounts to businesses, governments, or individuals. Examples: commercial banks, savings and loan associations. (p. 107)

financial market. A market in which financial instruments (stocks, bonds, etc.) are bought and sold. (p. 107)

fine tuning. An attempt to smooth out mild fluctuations in the economy by frequent adjustments in monetary and/or fiscal policies. (p. 326)

firm. The decision-making business unit which organizes and directs the production of goods or services. A firm may direct the activities of one or more plants.

fiscal drag. The tendency for rising tax collections to impede the healthy growth of aggregate demand that is needed for the achievement and maintenance of full employment. (p. 179)

fiscal policy. The adjustment of tax rates or government spending in order to affect aggregate demand. (p. 168)

fiscal year. A 12-month period selected as the year for accounting purposes.

Fisher equation. See *equation of exchange.*

fixed asset. A durable good, expected to last at least a year.

fixed cost. A cost that does not vary with output. (p. 413)

fixed exchange rate. An exchange rate that is held within a narrow band by monetary authorities. (p. 355)

fixed factor. A factor whose quantity cannot be changed in the short run.

floating (or flexible) exchange rate. An exchange rate that is not pegged by monetary authorities but is allowed to change in response to changing demand or supply conditions. If governments and central banks withdraw completely from the exchange markets, the float is *clean.* (That is, the exchange rate is *freely flexible.*) A float is *dirty* when governments or central banks intervene in exchange markets by buying or selling foreign currencies in order to affect exchange rates. (p. 363)

focal-point pricing. This occurs when independent firms quote the same price even though they do not explicitly collude. They are led by convention, rules of thumb, or similar thinking to the same price. (For example, $19.95 for a pair of shoes.) (p. 490)

forced saving. A situation where households lose control of some of their income, which is directed into saving even though they would have preferred to consume it. This can occur if the monetary authorities provide financial resources for investment, creating inflation which reduces the purchasing power of households' incomes (and therefore reduces their consumption). Alternatively, forced saving occurs if taxes are used for investment projects (such as dams).

foreign exchange. The currency of another country. (p. 348)

foreign exchange reserves. Foreign currencies held by the government or central bank. (p. 350)

forward price. A price established in a contract to be executed at a specified time in the future (such as 3 months from now). See also *futures market.*

fractional-reserve banking. A banking system in which banks keep reserves (in the form of currency or deposits in the central bank) equal to only a fraction of their deposit liabilities. (p. 197)

freedom of entry. The absence of barriers that make it difficult or impossible for a new firm to enter an industry. (p. 492)

free good. A good or service whose price is zero, because at that price the quantity supplied is at least as great as the quantity demanded.

free-market economy. An economy in which the major questions "What?" "How?" and "For whom?" are answered by the actions of individuals and firms in the marketplace rather than by the government. (p. 47)

free trade. A situation where no tariffs or other barriers are imposed on trade between countries.

free-trade area (or free-trade association). A group of countries that agree to eliminate trade barriers (tariffs, quotas, etc.) among themselves, while each retains the right to set its barriers on imports from nonmember countries. Compare with *customs union.*

frictional unemployment. Unemployment that is not due to a lack of aggregate demand but rather occurs because some workers have quit their jobs to look for something better and because entrants and reentrants into the labor force spend a reasonable time looking for jobs. (The term is also sometimes applied to temporary layoffs attributable to other nondemand causes, such as bad weather.) (p. 146)

full employment. (1) A situation in which there is no unemployment attributable to insufficient aggregate demand; that is, where all unemployment is due to frictional or structural causes. (2) A situation where all who want to work can find jobs with reasonable promptness.

full-employment budget (or high-employment budget). Full-employment government receipts (that is, the receipts which would be obtained with present tax rates if the economy were at full employment) minus full-employment government expenditures (that is, actual expenditures less expenditures directly associated with unemployment in excess of the full-employment level). (p. 181)

full-line forcing. See *tying contract.*

fundamental disequilibrium (in international economics). A term used but not defined in the articles of agreement of the International Monetary Fund. The general idea is that a fundamental disequilibrium exists when an international payments imbalance cannot be eliminated without increasing trade restrictions or imposing unduly restrictive aggregate demand policies. (p. 356)

futures market. A market in which contracts are undertaken today at prices specified today for fulfillment at some specified future time. For example, a futures sale of wheat involves the commitment to deliver wheat (say) 3 months from today at a price set now.

gain from trade. Increase in income that results from specialization and trade. (p. 545)

game theory. Theory dealing with conflict, in which alternative strategies are formally analyzed. Sometimes used in the analysis of oligopoly.

general equilibrium. Situation where all markets are in equilibrium simultaneously.

general equilibrium analysis. Analysis taking into account interactions among markets. (p. 59)

general price level. Price level as measured by a broad average, such as the consumer price index or the GNP deflator.

Giffen good. A good whose demand curve slopes upward to the right.

Gini coefficient. A measure of inequality derived from the Lorenz curve. It is the area between the curve and the diagonal line divided by the entire area beneath the diagonal line. It can range from zero (if there is no inequality and the Lorenz curve corresponds to the diagonal line) to one (if there is complete inequality and the Lorenz curve runs along the horizontal axis).

GNP deflator. The index used to remove the effects of inflation from GNP data. (p. 126)

GNP gap. Amount by which actual GNP falls short of potential GNP. (pp. 170, 328)

gold certificate. Certificate issued by the U.S. Treasury to the Federal Reserve, backed 100 percent by Treasury gold holdings.

gold exchange standard. International system in which most countries keep their currencies pegged to, and convertible into, another currency which, in turn, is pegged to and convertible into gold. (p. 360)

gold point. An exchange rate at which an arbitrager can barely cover the costs of shipping, handling, and insuring gold. (p. 352)

gold standard. System in which the monetary unit is defined in terms of gold, the monetary authorities buy and sell gold freely at that price, and gold may be freely exported or imported. If central banks follow the "rule of the gold standard game," they allow changes in gold to be reflected in changes in the money stock. (p. 351)

gold sterilization. A gold flow is sterilized when the central bank takes steps to cancel out the automatic effects of the gold flow on the country's money supply (that is, when the "rule of the gold standard game" is broken). (p. 354)

good. Tangible commodity, such as wheat, a shirt, or an automobile. (p. 22)

Gresham's law. Crudely, "Bad money drives out good." More precisely: If there are two types of money whose values in exchange are equal while their values in another use (like consumption) are different, the more valuable item will be retained for its other use while the less valuable item will continue to circulate as money. (p. 38)

gross (private domestic) investment. Expenditures for new plant and equipment, plus the change in inventories. (p. 133)

gross national product (GNP). Personal consumption expenditures plus government purchases of goods and services plus gross private domestic investment plus net exports of goods and services. The total product of the nation, excluding double counting. (p. 133)

holding company. A company that holds a controlling interest in the stock of one or more other companies.

horizontal merger. See *merger*.

human capital. Education and training which make human beings more productive. (p. 23)

hyperinflation. Very rapid inflation. (p. 12)

identification problem. The difficulty of determining the effect of variable *a* alone on variable *b* when *b* can also be affected by variables *c, d*, etc. (p. 409)

impact lag. The time interval between policy changes and the time when the major effects of the policy changes occur. (p. 313)

imperfect competition. This exists in a market when any buyer or seller is large enough to have a noticeable effect on price. (p. 49)

implicit (or imputed) cost. The opportunity cost of using an input that is already owned by the producer. (p. 424)

import quota. A restriction on the quantity of a good that may be imported. (p. 564)

incidence of a tax. The amount of the tax ultimately paid by different individuals or groups. (for example, how much does a cigarette tax raise the price paid by buyers, and how much does it lower the net price received by sellers?) (pp. 383, 581)

income-consumption line. The line or curve traced out by the points of tangency between an indifference map and a series of parallel budget (income) lines. It shows how a consumer responds to a changing income when relative prices remain constant.

income effect. Change in the quantity of a good demanded as a result of a change in real income with no change in relative prices. The change in the quantity of a good demanded as a result of a change in real income resulting from a change in the price of the good after the *substitution effect* of the change in relative prices has been eliminated.

income elasticity of demand. See *elasticity of demand*.

income line. See *budget line*.

incomes policy. A government policy (such as wage-price guideposts or wage and price controls) aimed at restraining the rate of increase in money wages and other money incomes. The purpose is to reduce the rate of inflation. (p. 286)

income statement. See *profit-and-loss statement*.

increasing returns. This occurs if an increase of *x* percent in all inputs results in an increase in output of more than *x* percent.

incremental cost. The term which business executives frequently use instead of "marginal cost."

incremental revenue. The term which business executives frequently use instead of "marginal revenue."

indexation. The inclusion of an *escalator clause* in a contract or law. (p. 288)

index number. A weighted average of prices (or other variable), with the base year being assigned a value of 100. (p. 125)

indifference curve. A curve joining all points among which the consumer is indifferent. (p. 403)

indifference map. A series of indifference curves, each representing a different level of satisfaction or utility. (p. 405)

industrial union. A union open to all workers in an industry, regardless of their skill. (p. 602)

industry. The producers of a single good or service (or closely similar goods or services). (p. 49)

inelastic demand. Demand with an elasticity of less than one. See also *elasticity of demand*. (p. 376)

infant-industry argument for protection. The proposition that new domestic industries with economies of scale or large requirements of human capital need protection from foreign producers until they can become established. (p. 562)

inferior good. A good for which the quantity demand declines as income rises, *ceteris paribus*. (p. 54)

inflation. A rise in the average level of prices. (p. 11)

inflationary gap. The vertical distance by which the aggregate demand line is above the 45 degree line at the full-employment quantity of national product. (p. 171)

inheritance tax. Tax imposed on property received from persons who have died.

injection. Spending for a GNP component other than consumption. (p. 177)

injunction. Court order to refrain from certain practices or requiring certain action. (pp. 605, 621)

innovation. A change in products or in the techniques of production.

inputs. Materials and services used in the process of production.

interest. Payment for the use of money. (p. 101)

interest rate. Interest as a percentage per annum of the amount borrowed.

interlocking directorate. Situation where one or more directors of a company sit on the boards of directors of one or more other companies that are competitors, suppliers, or customers of the first company. (p. 501)

intermediate product. A product which is used as an input in producing another good or service. (p. 128)

internalization. A process that results in a firm (or individual) taking into account an external cost (or benefit) of its actions. (p. 510)

international adjustment mechanism. Any set of forces which tends to reduce surpluses or deficits in the balance of payments. (p. 353)

international liquidity. The total amount of international reserves (foreign exchange, SDRs, etc.) held by the various nations. (p. 360)

inventories. Stocks of raw materials, intermediate products, and finished goods held by producers or marketing organizations. (p. 132)

investment. Accumulation of capital. See also *gross investment, net investment.*

investment bank. A firm that merchandises common stocks, bonds, and other securities. (p. 108)

investment good. A capital good. Plant, equipment, or inventory.

invisible. An intangible; a service (as contrasted with a good).

"invisible hand." Adam Smith's phrase expressing the idea that the pursuit of self-interest by individuals will lead to a desirable outcome for society as a whole. (p. 7)

iron law of wages. The view (commonly held in the nineteenth century) that the high human birthrate creates a tendency for the supply of labor to outrun the productive capacity of the economy and the demand for labor. As a consequence, it was an iron law of nature that wages would be driven down to the subsistence level. (Any excess population at that wage would die from starvation, pestilence, or war.) (p. 69)

jawbone. Persuade; attempt to persuade, perhaps using threats. (p. 274)

joint products. Products produced together. Example: meat and hides. (p. 56)

joint profit maximization. Formal or informal cooperation by oligopolists to pick the price that yields the most profit for the group. (p. 482)

jurisdictional dispute. Dispute between unions over whose workers will be permitted to perform a certain task. (p. 605)

key currency. A national currency commonly used by foreigners in international transactions and by foreign monetary authorities when intervening in exchange markets. Examples: the United States dollar, and, historically, the British pound. (p. 360)

Keynesian economics. The major macroeconomic propositions put forward by John Maynard Keynes in *The General Theory of Employment, Interest and Money* (1936): A market economy may reach an equilibrium with large-scale unemployment; steps to stimulate aggregate demand can cure a depression; and fiscal policies are the best way to control aggregate demand. Contrast with *classical economics.* (p. 143)

kinked demand curve. A demand curve which a noncollusive oligopolist faces if its competitors follow any price cut it makes but do not follow any price increase. The kink in such a demand curve occurs at the existing price. (p. 487)

labor. The physical and mental contributions of people to production.

labor force. The number of people employed plus those actively seeking work. (p. 10)

labor-intensive product. A good whose production uses a relatively large quantity of labor and relatively small quantities of other resources.

labor participation rate. See *participation rate.*

labor theory of value. Strictly, the proposition that the sole source of value is labor (including labor "congealed" in capital). Very loosely, the proposition that labor is the principal source of value. (p. 699)

labor union. See *union.*

laissez faire. Strictly translated, "let do." More loosely, "leave it alone." An expression used by the French physiocrats and later by Adam Smith, meaning the absence of government intervention in markets. (p. 7)

land. This term is used broadly by economists to include not only arable land but also the other gifts of nature (such as minerals) which come with the land. (p. 22)

law of diminishing marginal utility. As a consumer gets more and more of a good, the marginal utility of that good will (eventually) decrease. (p. 396)

law of diminishing returns. See *diminishing returns, law of eventually.*

leading indicator. A time series that reaches a turning point (peak or trough) before the economy as a whole. (p. 329)

leakage. (1) A withdrawal of potential spending from the circular flow of income and expenditures. (p. 177) (2) A withdrawal from the banking system that reduces the potential expansion of the money stock. (p. 211)

leakages-injections approach. The determination of equilibrium national product by finding the size of the product at which leakages are equal to injections. (p. 178)

legal tender. An item that, by law, must be accepted in payment of a debt. (p. 231)

leverage. The ratio of debt to net worth. (p. 109)

liability. (1) What is owned. (p. 103) (2) The amount that can be lost by the owners of a business if that business goes bankrupt. (p. 98)

life-cycle hypothesis. The proposition that consumption depends on expected lifetime income (as contrasted with the early Keynesian view that consumption depends on current income).

limited liability. The amount an owner-shareholder of a corporation can lose in the event of bankruptcy. This is limited to the amount paid to purchase shares of the corporation. (p. 98)

line of credit. Commitment by a bank or other lender to stand ready to lend up to a specified amount to a customer on request. (p. 111)

liquid asset. An asset that can be sold on short notice, at a predictable price, with little cost or bother. (p. 109)

liquidity. Ease with which an asset can be sold on short notice, at a predictable price, with little cost. (p. 109)

liquidity preference. The demand for money (that is, the willingness to hold money) as a function of the interest rate. (p. 246)

liquidity preference theory of the interest rate. The theory put forward by J. M. Keynes that the interest rate is determined by the willingness to hold money (liquidity preference) and the supply of money (that is, the stock of money in existence). Contrast with *loanable funds theory of interest.* (p. 246)

liquidity trap. In Keynesian theory, the situation where individuals and businesses are willing to hold all their additional financial assets in the form of money—rather than bonds or other debt instruments—at the existing interest rate. In such circumstances, the creation of additional money by the central bank cannot depress the interest rate further, and monetary policy cannot be effectively used to stimulate aggregate demand. (All additional money created is caught in the liquidity trap and is held as idle balances.) In geometric terms, the liquidity trap exists where the liquidity preference curve is horizontal. See also *speculative demand for money.* (p. 246)

loanable funds theory of interest. The theory that the interest rate is determined by the demand for and the supply of funds in the market for bonds and other forms of debt. Contrast with the *liquidity preference theory of interest.*

lockout. Temporary closing of a factory or other place of business in order to deprive workers of their jobs. A bargaining tool sometimes used in labor disputes; the employer's equivalent of a strike.

logarithmic (or log or ratio) scale. A scale in which equal proportional changes are shown as equal distances. For example, the distance from 100 to 200 is equal to the distance from 200 to 400. (Each involves a doubling.)(p. 114)

long run. (1) A period of time long enough for the quantity of capital to be adjusted to the desired level. (p. 419) (2) A period long enough for equilibrium to be reached. (3) Any extended period.

Lorenz curve. A curve showing cumulative percentages of income or wealth. For example, a point on a Lorenz curve might show the percentage of wealth owned by the poorest half of the families. (The percentage of wealth or income is shown on the vertical axis, and the percentage of families on the horizontal axis). Such a curve can be used to measure inequality; if all families have the same wealth, the Lorenz curve traces out a diagonal line. See also *Gini coefficient.* (p. 668)

lump-sum tax. A tax of a constant amount. The revenues from such a tax do not change when income changes. (p. 172)

M_1. The narrowly defined money stock; currency (paper money plus coins) plus demand deposits held by the public (that is, excluding holdings by the federal government, the Federal Reserve, and commercial banks). (p. 196)

M_2. The more broadly defined money stock; M_1 plus savings and time deposits in commercial banks (excluding large certificates of deposit). (p. 197)

M_3. An even more broadly defined money stock; M_2 plus deposits in mutual savings banks, savings and loan shares (deposits), and credit union shares (deposits).

macroeconomics. The study of the overall aggregates of the economy (such as total employment, the unemployment rate, national product, and the rate of inflation). (p. 122)

Malthusian problem. The tendency for population to outstrip productive capacity, particularly the capacity to produce food. This is the supposed consequence of a tendency for population to grow geometrically (1, 2, 4, 8, etc.) while the means of subsistence grows arithmetically (1, 2, 3, 4, etc.). The pressure of population will tend to depress the wage rate to the subsistence level and keep it there, with the excess population being eliminated by war, pestilence, or starvation. A problem described by Thomas Malthus in his *Essay on the Principle of Population* (1798). (p. 69)

managed float. A dirty float. See *floating exchange rate.*

marginal. The term commonly used by economists to mean "additional." For example: *marginal cost* is the additional cost when one more unit is produced; *marginal revenue* is the addition to revenue when one more unit is sold; *marginal utility* is the utility or satisfaction received from consuming one more unit of a good or service.

marginal efficiency of investment. The schedule or curve relating desired investment to the rate of interest. (p. 242)

marginal physical product. The additional output when one more unit of an input is used (with all other inputs being held constant). (p. 586)

marginal productivity. The dollar value of the marginal physical product of an input. (p. 586)

marginal propensity to consume (MPC, *c*). The change in consumption expenditures divided by the change in disposable income. (p. 150)

marginal propensity to import. The change in imports of goods and services divided by the change in GNP.

marginal propensity to save (MPS, *s*). The change in saving divided by the change in disposable income. 1 - MPC. (p. 150)

marginal rate of substitution. The slope of the indifference curve. The ratio of the marginal utility of one good to the marginal utility of another. (p. 404)

marginal revenue product. The additional revenue when the firm uses one additional unit of an input (with all other inputs being held constant).

marginal tax rate. The fraction of additional income paid in taxes.

margin call. The requirement by a lender who holds stocks (or bonds) as security that more money be put up or the stocks (or bonds) will be sold. A margin call may be issued when the price of the stocks (or bonds) declines, making the stocks (or bonds) less adequate as security for the loan. (p. 228)

margin requirement. The minimum percentage which purchasers of stocks or bonds must put up in their own money. For example, if the margin requirement on stock is 60 percent, the buyer must put up at least 60 percent of the price in his or her own money and can borrow no more than 40 percent from a bank or stockbroker. (p. 227)

market. An institution in which purchases and sales are made. (p. 47)

market economy. See *free-market economy.*

market failure. The failure of market forces to bring about the best allocation of resources. For example, when production of a good generates pollution, too many resources tend to go into the production of that good and not enough into the production of alternative goods and services.

market mechanism. The system whereby prices and the interaction of demand and supply help to answer the major economic questions "What will be produced?" "How?" and "For whom?" (p. 47)

market power. The ability of a single firm or individual to influence the market price of a good or service. (p. 49)

market share. Percentage of an industry's sales accounted for by a single firm.

market structure. Characteristics which affect the behavior of firms in a market, such as the number of firms, the possibility of collusion, the degree of product differentiation, and the ease of entry.

measure of economic welfare (MEW). A comprehensive measure of economic well-being. Per capital real national product is adjusted to take into account such nonmonetary influences on welfare as leisure and pollution. (p. 140)

median. The item in the middle (that is, half of all items are above the median and half are below).

medium of exchange. Money; any item that is generally acceptable in exchange for goods or services; any item that is commonly used in buying goods or services. (p. 195)

member bank. A commercial bank that belongs to the Federal Reserve System. (p. 201)

mercantilism. The theory that national prosperity can be promoted by a postive balance of trade and the accumulation of precious metals.

merger. The bringing together of two or more firms under common control through purchase, exchange of common stock, or other means. A *horizontal merger* brings together competing firms. A *vertical merger* brings together firms which are each others' suppliers or customers. A *conglomerate merger* brings together firms which are not related in any of these ways. (p. 497)

merit good. A good or service which the government considers particularly desirable and which it therefore encourages by subsidy or regulation (such as the regulation that children must go to school to get the merit good of education). (p. 85)

microeconomics. The study of individual units within the economy (such as households, firms, and industries) and their interrelationships. The study of the allocation of resources and the distribution of income. (p. 374)

military-industrial complex. A loose term referring to the combined political power exerted by military officers and defense industries; those with a vested interest in military spending. (In his farewell address, President Eisenhower warned against the military industrial complex.)

minimum wage. The lowest wage that an employer may legally pay for an hour's work. (p. 589)

mint parity. The exchange rate calculated from the official prices of gold in two countries under the gold standard. (p. 351)

mixed economy. An economy in which the private market and the government share the decisions as to what shall be produced, how, and for whom. (p. 47)

model. The essential features of an economy or economic problem explained in terms of diagrams, equations, or words or a combination of these.

monetarism. A body of thought which has its roots in classical economics and which rejects much of the teaching of Keynes' *General Theory.* According to monetarists, the most important determinant of aggregate demand is the quantity of money; the economy is basically stable if monetary growth is stable; and the authorities should follow a monetary rule involving a steady growth of the money stock. Many monetarists also believe that the effects of fiscal policy on aggregate demand are weak (unless accompanied by changes in the quantity of money), that the government plays too active a role in the economy, and that the long-run Phillips curve is vertical. (The most famous monetarist is Milton Friedman, a retired University of Chicago professor.) (p. 253)

monetary base. Currency held by the general public and by commercial banks plus the deposits of commercial banks in the Federal Reserve. (p. 211)

monetary policy. Central bank policies aimed at changing the quantity of money or credit conditions; for example, open market operations or changes in required reserve ratios. (p. 215)

monetary rule. The rule, proposed by monetarists, that the central bank should aim for a steady rate of growth of the money stock. (p. 326)

money. Any item commonly used in buying goods or services. Frequently, M_1. (p. 195)

money illusion. Strictly defined, people have money illusion if their behavior changes in the event of a proportional change in prices, money incomes, and assets and liabilities measured in money terms. More loosely, people have money illusion if their behavior changes when there is a proportional change in prices and money incomes. (p. 280)

money income. Income measured in dollars (or, in another country, income measured in the currency of that country).

money market. The market for short-term debt instruments (such as Treasury bills).

money multiplier. The number of dollars by which the money stock can increase as a result of a $1 increase in the reserves of commercial banks. (p. 208)

money stock (or supply). Narrowly, M_1. More broadly and less commonly, M_2 or M_3. (p. 196)

monopolistic competition. A market structure with many firms selling a differentiated product, with low barriers to entry. (p. 493)

monopoly. (1) A market in which there is only a single seller. (2) The single seller in such a market. A *natural monopoly* occurs when the average total cost of a single firm falls over such an extended range that one firm can produce the total quantity sold at a lower average cost than could two or more firms. (p. 457)

monopsony. A market in which there is only one buyer. (p. 611)

moral suasion. Appeals or pressure by the Federal Reserve Board intended to influence the behavior of commercial banks. (p. 228)

most-favored-nation clause. A clause in a trade agreement which commits a country to impose no greater barriers (tariffs, etc.) on imports from a second country than it imposes on imports from any other country.

multinational corporation. A corporation that carries on business (either directly or through subsidiaries) in more than one country. (p. 564)

multiplier. The change in equilibrium national product divided by the change in investment demand (or in government expenditures, tax collections, or exports). In the simplest economy (with a marginal tax rate of zero and no imports), the multiplier is $1 \div$ (the marginal propensity to save). (p. 154)

municipals. Bonds issued by local governments. (p. 112)

national bank. A commercial bank chartered by the national government. (p. 200)

national debt. (1) The outstanding federal government debt. (2) The outstanding federal government debt excluding that held by federal government trust funds. (3) The outstanding federal government debt excluding that held by federal government trust funds and the 12 Federal Reserve Banks. (p. 187)

national income. The return to all factors of production owned by the residents of a nation. (p. 128)

national product. See *gross national product* and *net national product*.

natural monopoly. See *monopoly*.

natural rate of unemployment. The equilibrium rate of unemployment. The rate of unemployment to which the economy tends when those making labor and other contracts correctly anticipate the rate of inflation. The rate of unemployment consistent with a stable rate of inflation. (p. 281)

near-money. A highly liquid asset that can be quickly and easily converted into money. Examples: a savings deposit or a Treasury bill. (p. 196)

negative income tax. A reverse income tax, involving government payments to individuals and families with low incomes. (The lower the income, the greater the payment from the government.) (p. 692)

negotiable order of withdrawal (NOW). A check-like order to pay funds from an interest-bearing savings deposit. (p. 196)

neocolonialism. The domination of the economy of a nation by the business firms or government of another nation or nations.

net exports. Exports minus imports. (p. 133)

net (private domestic) investment. Gross (private domestic) investment minus depreciation. (p. 134)

net national product. (NNP). Personal consumption expenditures plus government purchases of goods and services plus net private domestic investment plus net exports of goods and services. GNP minus depreciation. (p. 133)

net worth. Total assets less total liabilities. (p. 104)

neutrality of money. Money is neutral if a change in the quantity of money affects only the price level without affecting relative prices or the distribution of income.

neutrality of taxes. See *tax neutrality*.

New Left. Radical economists; Marxists of the 1960s and 1970s.

nominal. Measured in money terms. Current-dollar as contrasted to constant-dollar or real. (p. 126)

noncompeting groups. Groups of workers that do not complete with each other for jobs because their training or skills are different.

non-price competition. Competition by means other than price; for example, advertising or product differentiation. (p. 489)

non-tariff barrier. Impediment to trade other than tariffs. Example: import quota. (p. 564)

normal good. A good for which the quantity demanded rises as income rises, *ceteris paribus*. Contrast with an *inferior good*. (p. 54)

normal profit. The opportunity cost of capital and/or entrepreneurship. (Normal profit is considered a cost by economists but not by business accountants.) (p. 424)

normative statement. A statement about what should be. Contrast with a *postive statement*. (p. 29)

NOW account. A savings account against which a negotiable order of withdrawal may be written. (p. 196)

Okun's law. The observation that a 3 percent change in real GNP (compared with its long-run trend) has been associated with a 1 percent change in the opposite direction in the unemployment rate. (Named after Arthur M. Okun.)

old age, survivors, and disability insurance. Social security.

oligopoly. A market in which there are only a few sellers who sell either a standardized or differentiated product. A *natural oligopoly* occurs when the average total costs of individual firms

fall over a large enough range that a few firms can produce the total quantity sold at the lowest average cost. (Compare with *natural monopoly*.) (p. 480)

oligopsony. A market in which there are only a few buyers.

open economy. An economy which has transactions with foreign nations.

open market operation. The purchase (or sale) of government (or other) securities by the central bank on the open market (that is, not directly from the issuer of the security). (p. 218)

open shop. A business that may hire workers who are not (and need not become) union members. Contrast with *closed shop* and *union shop*. (p. 605)

opportunity cost. The amount that an input could earn in its best alternative use. The alternative that must be foregone when something is produced. (pp. 24, 424)

output gap. The amount by which output falls short of the potential or full-employment level. The recessionary gap times the multiplier. The GNP gap. (p. 170)

panic. A rush for safety, historically marked by a switch out of bank deposits into currency and out of paper currency into gold. (p. 199) A *stock-market panic* occurs when there is a rush to sell and stock prices collapse. (p. 113)

paradox of thrift. The paradoxical situation, pointed out by Keynes, where an increase in the desire to save can result in a decrease in the equilibrium quantity of saving. (p. 160)

paradox of value. The apparent contradiction, pointed out by Adam Smith, when an essential (such as water) has a low price while a nonessential (such as a diamond) has a high price. (p. 434)

Pareto improvement. Making one person better off without making anyone else worse off. (Named after Vilfredo Pareto, 1848–1923.) (p. 441)

Pareto optimum. A situation where it is impossible to make any Pareto improvement. That is, it is impossible to make any individual better off without making someone else worse off.

parity price. The price of a farm product (such as wheat) that would allow a farmer to exchange it for the same quantity of nonfarm goods as in the 1910–1914 base period. (A concept of fair price used in American agricultural policy since the Agricultural Adjustment Act of 1933.) (p. 392)

partial equilibrium analysis. Analysis of a particular market or set of markets, ignoring feedbacks from other markets.

participation rate. Number of people in the civilian labor force as a percentage of the civilian population of working age.

partnership. An unincorporated business owned by two or more people. (p. 97)

par value of a currency. Up to 1971, under the IMF adjustable peg system, the par value was the official price of a currency specified in terms of the United States dollar or gold. (p. 355)

patent. Exclusive right, granted by the government to an inventor, to use an invention for a specified time period. (Such a right can be licensed or sold by the patent holder.)

payroll tax. A tax levied on wages and salaries, or on wages and salaries up to a specified limit. Example: social security tax.

peak. The month of greatest economic activity prior to the onset of a recession; one of the four phases of the business cycle. (p. 299)

peak-load pricing. Setting the price for a good or service higher during periods of heavy demand than at other times. The purpose is to encourage buyers to choose nonpeak periods and/or to raise more revenue. Examples: electricity, weekend ski tow.

pegged. Fixed by the authorities, at least temporarily. Examples: pegged interest rates (1941–1951), pegged exchange rates (1945–1973).

perfect competition. A market with many buyers and many sellers, with no single buyer or seller having any (noticeable) influence over price. That is, every buyer and every seller is a *price taker.* (p. 49)

permanent income. Normal income; income that is thought to be normal. (p. 345n)

permanent-income hypothesis. The proposition that the principal determinant of consumption is permanent income (rather than current income). (p. 345n)

perpetuity (or "perp"). A bond with no maturity date that pays interest forever. (p. 222)

personal consumption expenditures. See *consumption.*

personal income. Income received by households in return for productive services and from transfers prior to the payment of personal taxes. (p. 136)

personal saving. Loosely but commonly, disposable personal income less consumption expenditures. More strictly, disposable personal income less consumption expenditures less payment of interest on consumer debt. (p. 135)

petrodollars. Liquid United States dollar assets resulting from payments for oil received by the members of the Organization of Petroleum Exporting Countries (OPEC).

Phillips curve. The curve tracing out the relationship between the unemployment rate (on the horizontal axis) and the inflation rate or the rate of change of money wages (on the vertical axis). (p. 267) *Long-run Phillips curve*: the curve (or line) tracing out the relationship between the unemployment rate and the inflation rate when the inflation rate is stable and correctly anticipated. (p. 281)

planned investment. Desired investment; investment demand; ex ante investment. (p. 152)

plant. A physical establishment where production takes place.

policy dilemma. This occurs when a policy that helps to solve one problem makes another worse. (p. 269)

political business cycle. A business cycle caused by actions taken to increase politicians' chances of reelection. (p. 314)

positive statement. A statement about what is (or was) or about how something works. Contrast with a *normative statement.* (p. 29)

poverty level (or poverty standard). An estimate of the income needed to avoid poverty. (p. 15)

precautionary demand for money. The amount of money that households and businesses want to hold to protect themselves against unforeseen events.

preferred stock. A stock that is given preference over common stock when dividends are paid; that is, specified dividends must be paid on preferred stock if any dividend is paid on common stock. (p. 102)

premature inflation. Inflation that occurs before the economy reaches full employment. (p. 270)

present value. The value now of a future receipt or receipts, calculated using the interest rate, *i.* The present value (PV) of X to be received n years hence is $X \div (1 + i)^n$. (p. 223)

price ceiling. The legally established maximum price. (p. 62)

price discrimination. The sale of the same good or service at different prices to different customers or in different markets, provided the price differences are not justified by cost differences, such as differences in transportation costs. (p. 468)

price-earnings ratio. The ratio of the price of a stock to the annual (after-tax) earnings per share of the stock.

price elasticity of demand (supply). See *elasticity of demand (supply)*.

price floor. (1) The price at which the government undertakes to buy all surpluses, thus preventing any further decline in price. (p. 449) (2) The legally established minimum price.

price index. A weighted average of prices, as a percentage of prices existing in a base year. (p. 125)

price leadership. A method by which oligopolistic firms establish similar prices without overt collusion. One firm (the price leader) announces a new price, confident that the other firms will quickly follow. (p. 489)

price line. See *budget line*.

price maker. A monopolist (or monopsonist) who is able to set price because there are no competitors. (p. 482)

price mechanism. See *market mechanism*.

price parity. See *parity price*.

price searcher. A seller (or buyer) who is able to influence price. (p. 481)

price support. A commitment by the government to buy surpluses at a given price (the support price) in order to prevent the price from falling below that figure. (p. 449)

price system. See *market mechanism*.

price taker. A seller or buyer who is unable to affect the price and whose market decision is limited to the quantity to be sold or bought at the existing market price. A seller or buyer in perfect competition. (p. 481)

price-wage flexibility. The ease with which prices and wages rise or fall (especially fall) in the event of changing demand and supply. (p. 144)

prime rate of interest. The interest rate charged by banks on loans to their most credit-worthy customers. (p. 221)

procyclical policy. A policy that increases the amplitude of business fluctuations. ("Procyclical" refers to results, not intentions.) (p. 309)

producers' surplus. Net benefit that producers get from being able to sell a good at the existing price. Returns to capital and entrepreneurship in excess of their opportunity costs. Rents on capital and enterpreneurship. Measured by the area left of the supply curve between break-even price and existing price. (p. 425)

product differentiation. See *differentiated products*.

production function. The relationship showing the maximum output that can be produced with various combinations of inputs.

production possibilities curve. A curve showing the alternative combinations of outputs that can be produced if all productive resources are used. The boundary of attainable combinations of outputs. (p. 23)

productivity. Output per unit of input.

profit. In economics, return to capital and/or entrepreneurship over and above normal profit. (p. 424) In business accounting, revenues minus costs. (Also sometimes used to mean profit after the payment of corporate income taxes.)

profit-and-loss statement. An accounting statement that summarizes a firm's revenues, costs, and income taxes over a given period of time (usually a year). An income statement. (p. 105)

progressive tax. A tax that takes a larger percentage of income as income rises. (p. 77)

proletariat. The working class, especially the industrial working class.

proportional tax. A tax that takes the same percentage of income regardless of the level of income. (p. 77)

proprietors' income. The income of unincorporated firms. (p. 136)

prospectus. A statement of the financial condition and prospects of a corporation, presented when new securities are about to be issued. (p. 115)

protective tariff. A tariff intended to protect domestic producers from foreign competition (as contrasted with a revenue tariff, intended as a source of revenue for the government). (p. 558)

protectionism. The advocacy or use of high or higher tariffs to protect domestic producers from foreign competition.

proxy. A temporary written transfer of voting rights at a shareholders' meeting. (p. 101)

proxy fight. A struggle between competing groups in a corporation to obtain a majority vote (and therefore control of the corporation) by collecting proxies of shareholders.

public debt. See *national debt.*

public good. See *pure public good.*

public utility. A firm that is the sole supplier of an essential good or service in an area and is regulated by the government.

pump priming. Short-term increases in government expenditures aimed at generating an upward momentum of the economy toward full employment.

purchasing power of money. The value of money in buying goods and services; 1 ÷ the price index.

purchasing power parity theory. The theory that changes in exchange rates reflect and compensate for differences in the rate of inflation in different countries.

pure public good. A good (or service) with benefits that people cannot be excluded from enjoying, regardless of who pays for the good. (pp. 83, 527)

qualitative controls. In monetary policy, controls that affect the supply of funds to specific markets. (p. 226)

quantitative controls. In monetary policy, controls that affect the total supply of funds and the total quantity of money in an economy. (p. 226)

quantity theory (of money). The proposition that velocity is reasonably stable and that total spending therefore will be strongly influenced by the quantity of money. (p. 251)

quota. A numerical limit. For example, a limit on the amount of a good that may be imported. (p. 570)

random sample. A sample chosen from a larger group in such a way that every member of the group has an equal chance of being chosen.

rate base. Allowable capital of a public utility, to which the regulatory agency applies the allowable rate of return.

rate of exchange. The price of one national currency in terms of another. (p. 347)

rate of interest. Interest as a percentage per annum of the amount borrowed.

rate of return. (1) Annual profit as a percent of net worth. (2) Additional annual revenue from the sale of goods or services produced by plant or equipment, less operating costs (labor, materials, etc.) and depreciation, as a percent of the depreciated value of the plant or equipment. (3) Discount rate at which the present value of future returns (additional revenues less operating costs) from new plant or equipment equals the acquisition price of that plant or equipment. (p. 243)

rationing. (1) Strictly, a method for allocating the right to acquire a good (or service) when the quantity demanded exceeds the quantity supplied at the existing price. (2) More loosely, any method for allocating a scarce resource or good. In this sense, we may speak of the market *rationing by price.*

ratio scale. See *logarithmic scale.*

real. Measured in quantity terms; adjusted to remove the effects of inflation. (p. 126)

real capital. Buildings, equipment, and other materials used in production, which have themselves been produced in the past. Plant, equipment, and inventories.

recession. A cyclical downward movement in the economy, as identified by the National Bureau of Economic Research. A downward movement in the economy involving at least two consecutive quarters of decline in seasonally adjusted real GNP. (p. 296)

recessionary gap. The vertical distance by which the aggregate demand line is below the 45 degree line at the full-employment quantity of national product. The output gap divided by the multiplier. (p. 170)

recognition lag. The time interval between the beginning of a problem and the time when the problem is recognized. (p. 313)

regression analysis. A statistical calculation of the relationship between two or more variables.

regressive tax. A tax that takes a smaller percentage of income as income rises. (p. 77)

regulation Q. A limit on interest rates that commercial banks may pay on deposits.

rent. (1) In economics, any payment to a factor of production in excess of its opportunity cost. (p. 638) Other common definitions: (2) The return going to the owners of land. (3) Payments by users to the owners of land, buildings, or equipment.

required reserves. The amount of reserves that a

bank legally must keep. For members of the Federal Reserve System, these reserves are held in the form of currency or deposits with a Federal Reserve Bank. (p. 202)

required reserve ratio. The fraction of deposit liabilities that a bank must keep in reserves. (p. 202)

reservation price of a resource. The cost of harvesting the resource today plus the amount necessary to compensate for the reduction in the quantity of the resource available in the future. (p. 649)

restrictive agreement. Agreement among companies to restrain competition through practices such as price fixing or market sharing.

retail price maintenance. Practice whereby a manufacturer sets the minimum retail price of a product, thereby eliminating price competition among retailers of that product. (p. 502)

return to capital. See *rate of return*.

revaluation of a currency. An increase in the par value of the currency. (p. 356)

revenue sharing. Grant by the federal government to a state or local government. *General revenue sharing* involves grants whose use is (practically) unrestricted. (p. 80)

revenue tariff. See *protective tariff*.

right-to-work law. State law making it illegal to require union membership as a condition of employment. State prohibition of closed shops and union shops. (p. 605)

risk premium. The additional interest or yield needed to compensate the holder of bonds (or other securities) for risk. (p. 112)

roundabout production. The production of capital goods and the use of these capital goods in the production of consumer goods. The production of goods in more than one stage.

rule of 70. A rule that tells approximately how many years it will take for something to double in size if it is growing at a compound rate. For example, a deposit earning 2 percent interest approximately doubles in $70 \div 2 = 35$ years. In general, a deposit earning x percent interest will double in about $70 \div x$ years.

satisficing theory. The theory that firms do not try to maximize profits but rather aim for reasonable target levels of profits, sales, and other measures of performance.

saving. See *personal saving*.

saving function. (1) The relationship between personal saving and disposable income. (2) More broadly, the relationship between personal saving and the factors (like disposable income) that determine saving. (p. 149)

Say's law. The discredited view that supply in the aggregate creates its own demand (regardless of the general price level). (p. 167)

SDRs. See *special drawing rights*.

seasonal adjustment. The removal of regular seasonal movements from a time series. (p. 298)

secondary boycott. Boycott against a firm to discourage it from doing business with a second firm, in order to exert pressure on the second firm (which may be in a strong position to withstand direct pressure).

secondary reserves. Bank holdings of liquid assets (Treasury bills, etc.) that can readily be converted into primary reserves (currency or reserve deposits).

second best, theory of the. The theory of how to get the best results in remaining markets when one or more markets have defects about which nothing can be done. (p. 466)

secular trend. The trend in economic activity over an extended period of many years.

selective controls. See *qualitative controls*.

sell short. See *short sale*.

shortage. (1) The amount by which quantity supplied is less than quantity demanded at the existing price; the opposite of a surplus. (2) Any deficiency. (p. 52)

short run. (1) The period in which the quantity of plant and equipment cannot change. (2) The period in which the quantity of plant cannot change. (3) The time period taken to move to equilibrium. (4) Any brief time period.

short sale. (1) The sale of a borrowed asset (such as a stock), to be repurchased and returned to the lender at a later date. (The purpose is to make a profit if the price falls prior to the repurchase date.) (2) A contract to sell something at a later date for a price specified now.

single-tax proposal. The proposal of Henry George (1839–1897) that all taxes be eliminated except one on land. (George argued that all returns to land represent an unearned surplus.)

snake. An agreement among some Western European countries to keep their currencies within a narrow band of fluctuation (the snake). Prior to 1973, they allowed their currencies to move jointly in a wider band with respect to the dollar (the *snake in the tunnel*). (Since 1973, the snake has not been tied to the dollar.)

socialism. An economic system in which the means of production (capital equipment, buildings, and land) are owned by the state. (p. 699)

soil bank program. A government program under which the government pays farmers to take land out of production (in order to reduce crop surpluses).

special drawing rights (SDRs). Bookkeeping accounts created by the International Monetary Fund to increase the quantity of international reserves held by national governments. SDRs can be used to cover balance-of-payments deficits. (p. 362)

speculation. The purchase (or short sale) of an asset in the hope of making a quick profit from a rise (fall) in its price. (pp. 357, 447)

speculative demand for money. The schedule or curve showing how the rate of interest affects the amount of assets that firms and households are willing to hold in the form of money (rather than in bonds or other interest-bearing securities). A key concept in the Keynesian theory of an unemployment equilibrium. See also *liquidity trap.* (p. 246)

spillover. See *externality.*

stagflation. The coexistence of a high rate of unemployment (stagnation) and inflation. (p. 267)

standard of value. The item (money) in which the prices of goods and services are measured. (p. 195)

state bank. A commercial bank chartered by a state government. (p. 201)

sterilization of gold. See *gold sterilization.*

store of value. An asset that may be used to store wealth through time; an asset that may be used to finance future purchases. (p. 195)

structural unemployment. Unemployment due to a mismatch between the skills or location of the labor force and the skills or location required by employers. Unemployment due to a changing location or composition of jobs.

subsidy. A negative tax.

subsistence wage. Minimum living wage. A wage below which population will decline because of starvation or disease. (p. 68)

substitute. A good or service that satisfies similar needs. Two commodities are substitutes if a rise in the price of one causes a rightward shift in the demand curve for the other. (p. 54)

substitution effect. The change in the quantity of a good demanded because of a change in its price when the real income effect of the change in price has been eliminated. That is, a change in the quantity demanded as a result of a movement along a single indifference curve. See also *income effect.*

sunspot theory. The theory put forward in the late nineteenth century that cycles in sunspot activity cause cycles in agricultural production and hence cycles in business activity.

superior good. A good whose quantity demanded rises when incomes rise. A *normal good.* (p. 54)

supply. The schedule or curve showing how the price of a good or service influences the quantity supplied, *ceteris paribus.* (p. 51)

supply of money. See *money stock.*

supply shift. A movement of the supply curve of a good (or service) to the right or left as a result of a change in the price of inputs or any other determinant of the quantity supplied (except the price of the good or service itself). (p. 55)

supply shifter. Anything that affects the quantity of a good or service supplied except its own price. (p. 55)

surplus. (1) The amount by which quantity supplied exceeds quantity demanded at the existing price. (2) Any excess or amount left over. Contrast with *shortage.* (p. 52)

surplus value. In Marxist economics, the amount by which the value of a worker's output exceeds the wage; the share of output appropriated by capitalists. (p. 699)

sustainable yield. The amount of a renewable resource (like fish) that can be harvested while still leaving the population constant. (p. 653)

sympathy strike. A strike by a union that does not have a dispute with its employer but rather is trying to strengthen the bargaining position of another striking union with that union's employer.

syndicate. An association of investment bankers to market a large block of securities. (p. 108)

tacit collusion. The adoption of a common policy by sellers without explicit agreement. (p. 490)

target price. Agricultural price guaranteed to farmers by the government. (If the market price falls short of the target price, the government pays farmers the difference.) (p. 450n)

tariff. A tax on an imported good. (p. 556)

tax-based incomes policy (TIP). An incomes policy backed up with tax penalties on violators or tax incentives for those who cooperate. (p. 287)

tax incidence. See *incidence of a tax.*

tax neutrality. (1) A situation where taxes do not affect relative prices. (2) A situation where the excess burden of taxes is zero.

tax shifting. This occurs when the initial taxpayer transfers all or part of a tax to others. (For example, a firm that is taxed may charge a higher price.) (p. 383)

technical efficiency. Providing the maximum output with the available resources and technology, while working at a reasonable pace. The avoidance of wasted motion and sloppy management. (p. 14)

terms of trade. The average price of goods sold divided by the average price of goods bought.

theory of games. See *game theory.*

theory of public choice. Theory of how government spending decisions are made and how they should be made.

third world. Countries that are neither in the "first" world (the high-income countries of Western Europe and North America, plus a few others such as Japan) nor in the "second" world (China and the countries of Eastern Europe). Low- and middle-income countries other than those run by Communist parties.

time preference. The desire to have goods now rather than in the future. The amount by which goods now are preferred over goods in the future.

time series. A set of observations taken in successive time periods. For example, GNP in 1974, in 1975, in 1976, etc.

TIP. See *tax-based incomes policy.*

total revenue. Total receipts from the sale of a product. Where there is a single price, that price times the quantity sold. (p. 376)

transactions demand for money. The amount of money that firms and individuals want to cover the time between the receipt of income and the making of expenditures. (p. 252)

transfer payment. A payment, usually made by the government to private individuals, that does not result from current productive activity. (p. 76)

Treasury bill. A short-term (less than a year, often for 3 months) debt obligation of the U.S. Treas-

ury. It carries no explicit interest payment; a purchaser gains by buying a bill for less than its face value. (p. 221)

trough. The month of lowest economic activity prior to the beginning of a recovery; one of the four phases of the business cycle. (p. 296)

turnover tax. A tax on goods or services (whether they are intermediate or final products) whenever they are sold.

tying contract. Contract which requires the purchaser to buy another item or items in a seller's line of products in order to get the one that is really wanted. (p. 501)

underwrite. Guarantee by an investment banker that the whole new issue of stock will be sold. (An investment banker unable to sell all the underwritten stock must buy the remainder.) (p. 108)

undistributed corporate profits. After-tax corporate profits less dividends paid. (p. 136)

unemployment. The inability of people who are willing to work to find jobs. More generally, the underuse of any resource. (p. 10)

unemployment rate. The percentage of the labor force unemployed. (p. 10)

union. An association of workers, formed to negotiate over wages, fringe benefits, and working conditions. (p. 601)

union shop. A business where all nonunion workers must join the union within a brief period of their employment. Compare with *closed shop* and *right-to-work law.* (p. 605)

unit elasticity. Elasticity of one. If a demand curve has unit elasticity, total revenue remains unchanged as price changes. A straight-line supply curve with unit elasticity will, if extended, go through the orgin. (pp. 381–382)

unlimited liability. Responsibility for debts without limit. (p. 97)

value added. Value of the product sold less the cost of intermediate inputs bought from other firms. (p. 130)

velocity of money. The average number of times per year that the average dollar in the money stock is spent. There are two principal ways of calculating velocity. (1) *Income velocity* is the number of times the average dollar is spent on final products (that is, GNP ÷ M). (2) *Transactions velocity* is the number of times the average dollar is spent on *any* transaction (including those for intermediate goods and financial assets). That is, total spending ÷ M. (p. 251)

vertical merger. See *merger*.

workable competition. A compromise that limits monopoly power while allowing firms to become big enough to reap the economies of scale. A practical alternative to the often unattainable goal of perfect competition. (p. 502)

yellow-dog contract. Contract in which an employee agrees not to become a member of a union. (p. 603)

yield. Of a bond, the discount rate at which the present value of coupon payments plus the repayment of principal equals the current price of the bond. (p. 222) Of real capital, see *rate of return*.

zero-base budgeting. A budgeting technique that requires items to be justified anew beginning at a zero funding base, without regard to past expenditures. (p. 187)

Index

Page numbers in **boldface** indicate definitions and key concepts.

Open market operations:
  in interest rate stabilization, 316
  (*See also* Federal Reserve System, open
    market operations)
Open shop, **605**
Opportunity cost, 24, 422, **424**–425
  and comparative advantage, 544
  and definition of rent, 637
  of equity capital (normal profit), 630
  of labor, 594
    compared to transfer price, 594–595*n*.
Option demand, 536
Organization of Petroleum Exporting
    Countries (*see* OPEC)
Output:
  of the firm: in colluding oligopoly, 483
    in monopolistic competition, 493
    in monopoly, compared to perfect
      competition, 464
  gap, **170**, 328
  with kinked demand, 487–488
  restrictions on: by colluding oligopolists,
    483, 485
    by government, 473
    in various types of market, 535
Overcapacity in OPEC, 486

Pacific Southwest Airlines, 496
Page, Bruce, 115*n*.
Panic, 113, 199, 233–243
Par value, **355**
Paradox of thrift, 160
Paradox of value, 434–435
Pareto, Vilfredo, 441
Pareto-improvement, 441
Pareto-optimum, 441
Parity:
  in agricultural prices, 392
  in gold standard, 351
Parity price in agriculture, 392
Partnership, 97
Patents, 456
Payments:
  circular flow of, 36–37, 127, 157, 159
    with government sector added, 177
Peak of cycle, 299
Pechman, Joseph A., 89–90
Pegged bond prices, 317
Pegged exchange rates, 354–356
People's Republic of China, 47
Perfect competition, 49, 434–455
  compared to other market forms, 481, 535
  conditions for efficiency, 437–439
  demand facing individual firm, 459, 460
  indifference curve analysis of, 453–455
  reservations about, 444–448
  supply and demand in, 50–53
Permanent income hypothesis, 345*n*.
Perpetuity, 222
  (*See also* Bonds)
Personal income, 136
Personal saving, 135
Phelps, Edmund S., 279–286

Philippines, Republic of the, 76
Phillips, A.W., 266
Phillips curve, **266**, 269, 276, 333*n*.
  long-run, 279–286, **281**, 336
Picketing, 615
Planned investment, 152
Policy dilemma, 269
Political business cycle, 314
Pollution, 507–518
  air, 511
  control measures: physical limits on
    emissions, 513
    recycling, 514, 517–518
    subsidies for installing pollution-control
      equipment, 508, 514
    taxes on polluting goods, 510, 512–514,
      580–581
  costs of reducing, 508
  and economic growth, 508
  as external cost, 509
  impossible to eliminate completely,
    reasons why, 509
  as increasing problem over time, 516
  noise, 511
  recent reductions in, 507–508
Population growth:
  changes in response to resource scarcity,
    656
  and economic growth, 6
  and labor supply, 69
Positive economics, 29
Poverty, 15–16, 680–685, **681**
  causes versus symptoms of, 682–683
  clinical, 682
  and college graduates, 682*n*.
  government policies to reduce (*see*
    Antipoverty policies)
  historical reduction in, 685
  of nations (*see* Less-developed countries)
  people suffering from, 681–682
  and population growth, 656
  poverty line, 15, **681**
Pratt and Whitney, 479
Preferred stock, 102
Premature inflation, 270
Present value, **222**, 243*n*.
Price:
  of colluding oligopolists, 483
  focal point, 490
  government regulation of, 467
  with kinked demand, 487–488
  leadership, 489
  in monopolistic competition, 493
  of OPEC oil, 484
  in perfect competition, compared to
    monopoly, 464
Price ceiling, 62
Price competition:
  cutthroat, 496
  in international trade, 540–541
  in move to monopoly, 458, 484
  workable, 502
  (*See also* Nonprice competition)
Price discrimination, 468

Price descrimination:
  by private monopolist, 468–472, 583
  by public utility, 478
Price flexibility, 144–145
Price floor, 449
Price index, 126, 272
Price leadership, 489
Price maker (monopolist), 459, 481–482
Price searcher (oligopolist), 481–482
Price taker (perfect competitor), 459,
    481–482
Price-wage flexibility, 144
Prices:
  and aggregate demand, 268–269
  allocation function of, 57, 441–442
  consumer, 12
  in depression, 144–145
  fluctuations in, 445–448
  increase in, 11
  information function of, 14, 48, 60
  in stock market, 116
  and wage-price guideposts, 274
Prime rate of interest, **221**
Principal (face value), 102
Privately-owned natural resource, 648–649
Procyclical policy, 309
Producer surplus, 400–401, **425**, 429–430
Product differentiation, 492, 493
Production:
  assembly line, 34
  factors of, 22
  substitution in, 24–25
Production possibilities curve, 23
  in general equilibrium, 453–455
  and international trade, 545, 547
  as production frontier, 25
  reasons for curvature, 23–24
Profit:
  business, 105–106
  economics above normal, 424–**425**, 433
    versus accounting, 424
  as form of income, 630
  normal, 424–425, 433
  in Soviet Union, 701–702, 704
Profit and loss (P and L) statement, 105
Profit maximization:
  alternative objectives of firm, 475–476
  calculations of, 428–429
Progressive tax, 77
Proletariat in Marxist economics, 699
Propensity (*see* Marginal propensity)
Property tax, 80, 186*n*.
Proportional tax, 77
Proposition 13 (California, 1978), 186*n*.
Proprietors' income, 136*n*.
Proprietorship, 97
Prospectus, 115
Protection from imports:
  arguments for, 559–563
  compared to free trade, 563
  to diversify economy, 561
  and foreign retaliation, 563
  by government purchasing policy, 563
  by quotas, 564, 569–573